W9-BUK-183

central america
on a shoestring

Robert Reid, Jolyon Attwooll, Matthew D Firestone, Carolyn McCarthy, Andy Symington, Lucas Vidgen

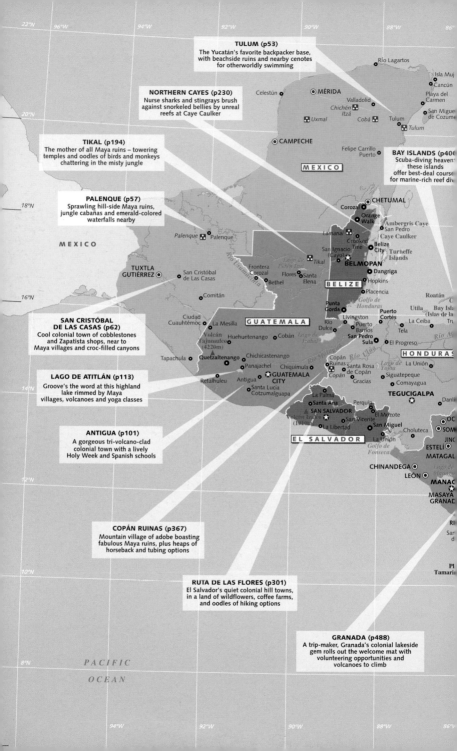

TULUM (p53)
The Yucatán's favorite backpacker base, with beachside ruins and nearby cenotes for otherworldly swimming

NORTHERN CAYES (p230)
Nurse sharks and stingrays brush against snorkeled bellies by unreal reefs at Caye Caulker

TIKAL (p194)
The mother of all Maya ruins – towering temples and oodles of birds and monkeys chattering in the misty jungle

BAY ISLANDS (p40∢)
Scuba-diving heaven∢ these islands offer best-deal course∢ for marine-rich reef div∢

PALENQUE (p57)
Sprawling hill-side Maya ruins, jungle cabañas and emerald-colored waterfalls nearby

SAN CRISTÓBAL DE LAS CASAS (p62)
Cool colonial town of cobblestones and Zapatista shops, near to Maya villages and croc-filled canyons

LAGO DE ATITLÁN (p113)
Groove's the word at this highland lake rimmed by Maya villages, volcanoes and yoga classes

ANTIGUA (p101)
A gorgeous tri-volcano-clad colonial town with a lively Holy Week and Spanish schools

COPÁN RUINAS (p367)
Mountain village of adobe boasting fabulous Maya ruins, plus heaps of horseback and tubing options

RUTA DE LAS FLORES (p301)
El Salvador's quiet colonial hill towns, in a land of wildflowers, coffee farms, and oodles of hiking options

GRANADA (p488)
A trip-maker, Granada's colonial lakeside gem rolls out the welcome mat with volunteering opportunities and volcanoes to climb

CARIBBEAN
SEA

0 ——— 150 km
0 ——— 90 miles

LA MOSKITIA (p429)
Wild, remote rain forest –
explore it in a dugout canoe or just
sit back in Garifuna villages

JAMAICA

✪ KINGSTON

Islas Santanilla
(Swan Islands, Honduras)

ISLA DE OMETEPE (p503)
A fantasy island formed by joined volcanoes,
with lovely villages, great beaches,
hiking and prehistoric rock art

CORN ISLANDS (p516)
One-time pirate hub, now a
(seriously) low-key Caribbean kick-backer
with fresh lobster and cheap dives

**PARQUE NACIONAL
TORTUGUERO (p571)**
Road-free 'mini Amazon' that is home
to jigsaw canals, turtle-watching sites
and Creole cuisine

**PUERTO VIEJO DE
TALAMANCA (p565)**
Costa Rica's party central,
with palm-backed beaches and
good breaks for expert surfers

BOCAS DEL TORO (p681)
Archipelago for island-hoppers
seeking surf spots, village bars
and a deserted beach or two

**BOQUETE & THE CHIRIQUÍ
HIGHLANDS (p674)**
Cool, coffee-scented hills where quetzal-lined
roads lead up Volcán Barú and rafting
junkies bounce through narrow canyons

Laguna de
Caratasca

La Moskitia

Río Patuca

Río Coco

Cayos Miskitos
(Nicaragua)

○ PUERTO
CABEZAS

NICARAGUA

Isla de Providencia
(Colombia)

○ BOACO

JUIGALPA
○

Laguna de
Perlas

Río Escondido

Rama
○

Isla de San Andrés
(Colombia)

BLUEFIELDS

Corn Islands
(Islas del Maíz,
Nicaragua)

Isla de
Ometepe

El Castillo
○

Bahía
Punta
Gorda

Los Chiles ○

○ LIBERIA

Volcán Arenal
(1633m)

El Coco ○

○ Tortuguero

Monteverde ○

COSTA RICA

PUERTO
LIMÓN
○

Península de
Nicoya

SAN JOSÉ ✪

PUNTARENAS ○

○ Jacó

CARTAGO ○

Turrialba ○

Cahuita ○

Golfo
de
Nicoya

Montezuma ○

Quepos ○

Puerto Viejo
de Talamanca
○

COLÓN ○

Archipiélago de San Blas

Chepo ○

San Isidro
de El General
○

Volcán
Barú
3475m
BOCAS DEL
TORO

PANAMA
CITY
✪

Bahía de
Panamá

San Vito ○

Parque Nacional
Corcovado ○

Boquete ○

○ DAVID

PANAMA

PENONOMÉ ○

LA PALMA ○

Golfo de los Mosquitos

SANTIAGO ○

Península
de Osa

Golfo de
Chiriquí

Chitré ○

Golfo de
Panamá

Archipiélago
de las Perlas

Yaviza ○

**PARQUE NACIONAL
CORCOVADO (p618)**
Remote national wonder of coastal
rain forest where macaws circle
above and whales dance offshore

Isla de
Coiba

Península
de Azuero

PANAMA CITY (p648)
Not all Central American capitals are
boring; enjoy the great colonial
district with Havana-esque faded
charm, plus canal trips

COLOMBIA

Responsible Travel

Central America overflows with those incredible 'What? Where? You did what?' places that can, well, change your life. But visitors can bring changes for the destinations too – some of which are not good. In the last 50 years, the region has seen the erosion of traditional customs, deforestation, and rising illicit drug use and prostitution. Sometimes tourism is a culprit. Ecotourism has caught on, particularly in Costa Rica, saving many hectares of forest from the saw. Still, ecotourism is an often-abused buzzword. Here are a few ways to help.

TIPS

- **Go overland** Take buses, not planes – if coming from the USA consider taking a bus across Mexico
- **Give right** Handouts to kids encourage begging; give directly to schools or clinics instead
- **Buy local** Try to eat and stay at family-owned places and use community-owned services
- **Cold showers** Avoid hot showers if water is heated by a wood fire
- **Never litter** Carry out all your trash when camping or hiking. Pick up trash when you can, or join in the annual Lago de Atitlán clean-up (p117)
- **Respect local traditions** Dress appropriately when visiting local churches or traditional communities (p21)
- **Be curious** Ask locals about ways to avoid mistakes some travelers make – let us know what you learn

INTERNET RESOURCES

www.eco-indextourism.org Many links on sustainable travel.
www.ecotourism.org Links to ecofriendly businesses.
www.planeta.com Includes a free 93-page e-book.
www.tourismconcern.org.uk UK-based organization dedicated to promoting ethical tourism.
www.transitionsabroad.com Focuses on responsible travel.

VOLUNTEER!

Volunteering is the new travel – some tips follow; see p733 for more.

- Preserve turtle-nesting sites – from poachers and reckless tourists – at Barca de Oro, Nicaragua (p486) or Costa Rica's Parque Nacional Tortuguero (p571)
- Ask around at volunteer hubs including Quetzaltenango (p141) and in Costa Rica (p631)
- Teach English: options include Cumaro (p315) and San Salvador (p284) in El Salvador

6

Contents

The Authors

ROBERT REID
Coordinating Author, Mexico's Yucatán & Chiapas

Raised in Oklahoma, Robert has considered Mexico his second home since he got a clay sun god at Teotihuacán when he was five. He's since returned 13 times, once vomiting in a sombrero in a Puerto Vallarta taxi, and other times pursuing the ever-elusive *español* while staying with inspiring families in Guanajuato, San Cristóbal de Las Casas and Mexico City. After five years at Lonely Planet, Robert now writes from his apartment in Brooklyn. See photos from his trips at www.robertreid.info.

JOLYON ATTWOOLL
Honduras

Jolyon went to all sorts of lengths to fund his first trip to Central America, including spending a wintry morning playing sponsored tiddlywinks up London's Parliament Hill. He made it, both up the hill and to the continent, where he volunteered in the beautiful Guatemalan highlands. First dipping into Honduras in 2002, he seized the chance to see the majestic Copán Ruinas and spot angel fish in West Bay. Jolyon has also contributed to Lonely Planet's *Chile, England* and *Sydney* guides.

MATTHEW D FIRESTONE
Panama

Matt is a biological anthropologist and epidemiologist, though he prefers moonlighting as a freelance travel writer. His first visit to Panama was in 2001 during a spring break from college. While his classmates were partying in Panama City, Florida, Matt was dining on *tapas* and dancing salsa in Panama City, Panama. Matt now knows how to cook a mean ceviche and his four-step ain't half bad. The secret to both is simple – spice things up with diced habanero chiles or a few rounds of rum and coke with lime.

CAROLYN MCCARTHY
Costa Rica & El Salvador

Carolyn was born and bred a gringa but has spent the last nine years traveling the Americas from Alaska to Tierra del Fuego. This trip introduced her to the ecstasy of surfing and the intrigue of traveling with an ex-guerilla guide. She contributes frequently to the column *Travels with Lonely Planet* and has coauthored *South America on a Shoestring* and *Ecuador & the Galapagos Islands*. She lives in Chile, where she guides treks and writes on pioneer Patagonia. Her blog is www.carolynswildblueyonder.blogspot.com.

LONELY PLANET AUTHORS

Why is our travel information the best in the world? It's simple: our authors are independent, dedicated travellers. They don't research using just the Internet or phone, and they don't take freebies in exchange for positive coverage. They travel widely, to all the popular spots and off the beaten track. They personally visit thousands of hotels, restaurants, cafés, bars, galleries, palaces, museums and more – and they take pride in getting all the details right, and telling it how it is. For more, see the authors section on www.lonelyplanet.com.

ANDY SYMINGTON   Nicaragua

Andy hails from Australia and got his first sniff of the sulphur of a Central American volcano a decade ago. From his base in northern Spain, he hops across the Atlantic whenever humanly possible for more brimstone and piping-hot *nacatamales* (bundles of cornmeal, pork, vegetables and herbs wrapped in banana leaf). Andy has authored many guidebooks, including several Lonely Planet titles.

LUCAS VIDGEN   Guatemala & Belize

Lucas has been traveling and working in Latin America for more than a decade. He lives in Quetzaltenango, Guatemala, where he is a director of the NGO EntreMundos and publishes the city's leading culture and nightlife magazine, *XelaWho*. Lucas contributed to the previous edition of *Central America on a Shoestring*, as well as *Guatemala, Belize & Yucatán*, *Argentina* and *South America on a Shoestring*. He is the sole author of the *Guatemala* country guide. His Spanish is OK, but he misses potato cakes and his mum.

CONTRIBUTING AUTHOR

Dr David Goldberg wrote the Health chapter. He completed his training in internal medicine and infectious disease at Columbia-Presbyterian Medical Center in New York City, where he also served as voluntary faculty. At present, he is an infectious-diseases specialist in Scarsdale, New York, and the editor-in-chief of www.mdtravel health.com.

Destination Central America

The Maya city of Palenque (p57) surrounded by verdant rain forest, Chiapas, Mexico

Easy to overlook on a map, this compact seven-country link between North and South America is a dynamo of culture, ancient ruins, wildlife and activities – a true backpackers' paradise. Nowhere else packs in as much in so slender a frame. For starters, try climbing trembling and lava-gurgling volcanoes – many perfect cones poke above the cloud line, like something out of a kindergarten drawing. Less-strenuous jungle walks lead past unforgettable, overgrown Maya pyramids or into the lairs of the puma, sloth, howler monkey and quetzal. Surfing towns are found up and down the Caribbean and Pacific shorelines, where waves slap at white- and gold-sand beaches. No excuses if you've never surfed; lessons are cheap. If you prefer getting under water, diving outfits can get you certified and bellying up with nurse sharks at coral reefs for some of the world's lowest prices. Don't fuss if you want to go somewhere other than a beach to relax. In lazy-day Spanish-colonial towns, haciendas transformed into language schools and hostels line cobbled streets where vendors in cowboy hats push squeaky-wheeled carts. Or you can arrange homestays in Maya or Moskito villages, where many traditions live on as if the 'Conquest' were a bad dream.

Many visitors reach the region overland: bus or boat connections from Mexico (and the USA) are a breeze; some continue on to South America. But, with so much on offer, more travelers are making Central America their sole destination. Already Mexico's Yucatán (included in this guide), Guatemala, Belize and Costa Rica are big-time destinations, and Nicaragua is now being billed as the next big thing. No worries if you haven't been here yet. Some of the world's most rewarding, yet to be 'discovered' destinations await you (such as El Salvador's Ruta de las Flores, or the ultra-raw jungle of Honduras' La Moskitia or near Panama's Darién Gap). If you want to know what the travel world will be bragging about tomorrow, go find it in Central America now.

HIGHLIGHTS

BEST BEACHES

Little Corn Island (Nicaragua) ▪ Totally chilled, still-unspoiled Caribbean island with US$5 snorkeling, US$10 beach huts and fresh fish cooked up at a slo-o-ow pace (p518)

Roatán, Bay Islands (Honduras) ▪ The region's hub for the best (and cheapest) scuba-diving courses; plus God-sent white-sand beaches at West Bay (p410)

Pavones (Costa Rica) ▪ End-of-the-road beach town attracts surfers and beach bums, with nights at a beachfront cabin from US$8 and US$20 for a yoga retreat (p622)

Bocas del Toro (Panama) ▪ A Caribbean six-island archipelago with laid-back locals, sea turtles, kayakers and surfers eyeing the Caribbean beaches (p681)

Tulum (Mexico) ▪ Mexico's backpacker hub is getting overexposed but sand-floor bungalows, surf-side Maya ruins and nearby sinkhole swimming holes still fill great lazy days (p53)

BEST ACTIVITIES

Volcano Climbs ▪ These conical beauties are mesmerizing to look at, and better to climb. Nicaragua's unreal volcano-formed Isla de Ometepe (p503) extends past the cloud line, while Central America's highest point at Guatemala's Tajumulco (p140) is for experienced hikers only

Surfing ▪ Board-toting surfers – or wannabes – are pouring into Central America for gnarly breaks in Nicaragua (p486), Hawaii-style (and some less intense) breaks off Bocas del Toro's islands, Panama (p681), beginners' breaks at Playa Tamarindo, Costa Rica (p593) and 'surfing villages' at El Salvador's La Costa del Bálsamo (p293)

Rafting & Boat Trips ▪ The white-water rafting buzz rings loudest at Honduras' La Ceiba (p392) and Costa Rica's Río Pacuare (p567), while DIY boat adventures are best in Costa Rica's canal maze near Tortuguero (p570)

Diving & Snorkeling ▪ Caribbean reefs rank high among the world's underwater highlights: notably Honduras' Bay Islands (p406), Belize's northern cayes (p230) and Mexico's Cozumel (p51)

Hiking ▪ El Salvador's Parque Nacional El Imposible (p304) tempts hikers with possible walks to Pacific views and swimming holes; if noises in the dark don't scare you, take a guided night hike in Nicaragua (p494) and Costa Rica (p577)

Crystal-clear water laps against a tranquil caye, Bocas del Toro (p681), Panama

Ready for the colorful procession to mark Semana Santa (p109), Antigua, Guatemala

BEST FESTIVALS & EVENTS

Carnaval (Panama) ■ The meaning of life answered: in costume, with dance (and drink) during the nation's raucous four days preceding Ash Wednesday; the best are in Panama City (p658) and at off-the-beaten-track Las Tablas (p695)

Semana Santa (Guatemala) ■ Hundreds of revelers in purple robes wander the cobbled streets of Antigua, which are covered in carpets of flower petals and colored sawdust (p101)

Palo de Mayo (Maypole; Nicaragua) ■ A month-long party for fertility – the non-stop dancing, loud music and outrageous floats of Bluefields are a far cry from the original British tradition (p513)

Chichicastenango Market (Guatemala) ■ Central America's most famous Maya market fills this mountain village's streets on Sunday and Thursday with open-air stalls selling masks, colorful clothes, produce and toys (p128)

Mérida Weekends (Mexico) ■ Who needs a beach when weekends mean partying like this? The cobbled center closes for a pedestrian-only unapologetic ode to joy, with salsa bands, dancing, taco stands – every Saturday and Sunday (p45)

BEST WILDLIFE

Darién Province (Panama) ■ Wilder than the Amazon, the Gap is ruled by its majority – wildlife: pumas, jaguars, tapirs, howler monkeys, bulldog-sized rodents and wild boars. Tours here are expensive but crucial for night hikes or dugout canoe rides to remote reserves (p703)

Barrier Reefs (Belize, Mexico) ■ Swarms of tropical fish – plus nurse sharks and stingrays – cuddle up to snorkelers and divers at reef sites in Belize's northern cayes (p230), while in remote Punta Allen, Mexico (p56) tours meet up with dolphins

Parque Nacional Tortuguero (Costa Rica) ■ Along 'mini-Amazon' river canals, caimans (and 400 species of bird) goof-off inches from your canoe, while sea turtles nest on the Caribbean coast (p570)

Parque Nacional Soberanía (Panama) ■ A birder's highlight just outside Panama City: about 500 species of tropical birds have been spotted on walks along the Pipeline Road (p666)

Lago de Yojoa (Honduras) ■ Over 400 bird species – including the ever-elusive quetzal – exercise their wing muscles around the mountainous lake (p359)

BEST HISTORIC SITES

Tikal (Guatemala) ▪ Steep Classic-period Maya pyramids and towering ceiba trees that house scores of howler monkeys, emerge from the jungle floor. Where else could have been the site for the rebel base camp in *Star Wars*? (p194)

Panama Canal (Panama) ▪ Sneaky US diplomacy and land-cutting miracles led to this early 20th-century, 80km link between oceans west and east. Going through by your own barge costs US$30,000 – or just US$5 to visit (p664)

Around Perquín (El Salvador) ▪ Somber ex-guerrilla headquarters from the nation's civil war – with abandoned bunkers, bomb craters and a massacre site – is a chilling testimony against war (p315)

Palenque (Mexico) ▪ The Maya world's finest setting: a sprawling city founded 2000 years ago where mountains, jungle, plains and hammock cabañas meet (p57)

León (Nicaragua) ▪ A Sandinista heartland remains linked with the past; Nicaragua's progressive rival to Granada is a richly colonial town, and you explore its original incarnation under the shadow of Volcán Momotombo (p480)

BEST OFF-THE-BEATEN-TRACK PLACES

Río Dulce Boat Trips (Guatemala) ▪ Outside Livingston, boats drift past jungle-frocked gorges and through a reserve where manatees hang out; the best bet is sticking around for DIY dugout canoe trips and visits to Q'eqchi' villages (p183)

Río San Juan (Nicaragua) ▪ Take a boat ride on the tree-lined Río San Juan past the pirate-fighting Spanish fortress (where everyone else turns around) and all the way to San Juan del Norte on the Caribbean coast (p511)

Mountain Towns (El Salvador) ▪ Out-of-the-way kick-back spots missed by most include quiet Alegría's flower-lined porches, crater lake and coffee plantations (p306), and Juayúa in the Ruta de Las Flores (p301)

Darién Gap (Panama) ▪ Rugged and difficult, the Darién Gap area awaits for *Heart of Darkness* trips into Central America's most untamed wilds – one option is a boat ride into jaguar turf at Río Sambú (p708)

La Moskitia (Honduras) ▪ This huge remote pocket of Honduras boasts canoe trips from Garífuna villages and frisky wildlife scenes, including sea turtles and hundreds of bird species (p429)

MARGIE POLITZER

Sunshine highlights the baroque façade of the 18th-century Iglesia de la Recolección (p482), León, Nicaragua

ITINERARIES

Central America's slim figure – with a curve here and there – gives just a little room for creative looping itineraries. The easiest way, time willing, is going from top to bottom (or bottom to top). That said, there are a couple of multicountry trips with one gateway that can be taken without much backtracking. To see it all (essentially a combination of everything that follows), give yourself at least three months. If you only have two or three weeks, though, you're best sticking with a country or two. Or just drop in and see where the wind directs you – hey, it's your trip.

See p737 for information on open-jaw air tickets to Central America, and p742 for the duration of some major bus trips.

NORTHERN LOOP
Guatemala, Mexico, Belize, Honduras & El Salvador
This route loops through much of the region's northern highlights, starting from **Guatemala City** (p89). Head straight to colonial **Antigua** (p101) for a few days, doing a volcano climb and perhaps a crash course in Spanish. Then get a chicken bus to other highland sites; at stunning **Lago de Atitlán** (p113) skip the gringoburg of Panajachel for a few days of hiking and swimming from an atmospheric base such as hippie-friendly **San Marcos La Laguna** (p126) before continuing on to **Chichicastenango** (p128) to see the famous Maya market. Add a couple

Mountains, jungle, beaches, ruins: this diverse route is the classic introductory trip to Central America, mixing plenty of culture, adventure and serious relaxation. Many visitors linger in one place longer than expected, and save a slice or three for the next trip.

of extra dollars a day to the budget and venture north to Mexico on a 'Chiapas loop' to witness modern Maya life at the mountain town of **San Cristóbal de Las Casas** (p62) and the Maya ruins amid the jungle at **Palenque** (p57). Visit the riverside ruins of **Yaxchilán** (p62) en route to the mother of Maya sites, back in Guatemala, **Tikal** (p194). Bus east to Belize, stopping for a Frisbee golf round at a jungle base outside hilly **San Ignacio** (p244) before splashing into the Caribbean's wonderful reefs at laid-back **Caye Caulker** (p230).

Caye-hop south, stopping at off-beat **Hopkins** (p252) or more mainstream **Placencia** (p253), before boating to Guatemala's **Lívingston** (p180) to take a serious jungle boat trip along the **Río Dulce** (p183).

Cross into Honduras and head for the cobblestone town of **Copán Ruinas** (p367), offering river tubing trips, horseback rides over mountains, and the namesake ruins. Bus to **Gracias** (p378), and thank the colonial town for its proximity to a quetzal-rich national park.

Southward in El Salvador, stop in the kitschy mountain town **La Palma** (p321) for hikes over high-up log bridges. Bypass San Salvador for the Pacific 'surf villages' of **La Costa del Bálsamo** (p293), where you can get US$10 lessons. Catch a Guatemala City bus from San Salvador.

SIDE TRIPS
If you're big on ruins, detour from Palenque to colonial **Mérida** (p45) stopping at **Uxmal** (p48), then visit **Chichén Itzá** (p44) and **Tulum** (p53). Bus to Belize, then go west to Tikal.

If you've 'done Mexico,' though, skip it. From Chichicastenango head to **Nebaj** (p133) for day hikes and a few days in **Quetzaltenango** (p136) to explore volcanoes and traditional villages. Then bounce on the bus for three days on an unreal 150km journey to **Cobán** (p162) and on to Tikal.

Need to have more water? Before seeing Copán, detour to the party-activities hub of **La Ceiba** (p392) and boat to the **Bay Islands** (p406) for some diving.

SOUTHERN LOOP
Costa Rica, Panama & Nicaragua
Nicaragua and Panama frame the more tourist-trodden Costa Rica. Starting in **San José** (p538), take the bus-and-boat trip to the English-speaking Caribbean coast and turtle country at **Tortuguero** (p570), then boat and bus back south to the party-surf town of **Puerto Viejo de Talamanca** (p565). Cross into Panama and boat along narrow, tree-lined canals to the Caribbean archipelago of **Bocas del Toro** (p681) for island-hopping and a surf day. Then head to Central America's nicest capital, **Panama City** (p648), with its Havana-like charm and a look at the **Panama Canal** (p664). Bus west, via David, to the cool coffee highlands around **Boquete** (p674) and look out over the Pacific *and* Caribbean from atop **Volcán Barú** (p678).

Bus back to Costa Rica, taking the ferry from Puntarenas for checking out the boho hangout of **Montezuma** (p599) on Península de Nicoya, near swimming holes, wilderness beaches and surfing in **Malpaís** (p601).Get back to Puntarenas to reach Nicaragua's double-volcano **Isla de Ometepe** (p503), after hammock swings and rum at fun, but gringofied, **San Juan del Sur** (p500), then visit colonial **Granada** (p488), with volcanoes and eerie night hiking. Bus, via Managua, to Rama for a boat to Bluefields and a boat out to **Little Corn Island** (p518) for serious snorkeling and kick-back time.

Retrace your steps to Managua for a direct bus back to San José.

HOW LONG?
Minimum: 5-8 weeks

WHEN TO GO?
Any time. Just before or after peak season (December to April) misses most crowds and tropical storms

BUDGET?
US$25-40 per day, US$10 more at beach towns and in Mexico

HOW LONG?
5-7 weeks

WHEN TO GO?
Any time. Just before or after peak season (December to April) misses most crowds and tropical storms

BUDGET?
US$20-40 per day, more at beach towns

Witness Central America's greatest wildlife scene in the more expensive (and popular) Costa Rica, before feeling that 'whoa now!' jolt of crossing into its much less-visited, cheaper neighbors. Both are in the running for the 'new Costa Rica,' with volcanoes and a rich coastline on either ocean side.

SIDE TRIPS

An alternate trip back to Costa Rica from Nicaragua is across the border at Los Chiles, after taking a boat ride along the **Río San Juan** (p511). In Costa Rica, bus via Ciudad Quesada, to **La Virgen** (p583), a rafting highlight.

If you have a splurge fund, consider an unreal (very) adventure near the **Darién Gap** (p703) in Panama, or take a flight to visit the Kuna at the fascinating San Blas islands at the **Comarca de Kuna Yala** (p700).

HOW LONG?

5-7 weeks

WHEN TO GO?

Generally dry season (December to April); note mountain hikes will get sloppy (and dangerous) in peak rainy season (September to October), while rains can dampen Bay Islands' trips November to February

BUDGET?

Guides for hikes or dives add to costs; count on US$40-50 per day

ACTION ALL THE WAY!

Into activities? The great outdoors is fun in an isthmus with volcanoes, mountains, rivers and waves to get your fix in. If you've never surfed or gone diving, no excuses! Central America is a great place to learn.

Starting in Guatemala's highlands, get into the regional swing with a guided bike ride around **Antigua** (p108). Chicken-bus it to wee **Nebaj** (p133) and arrange a three-day hike through the Cuchumatanes Mountains to **Todos Santos** (p150). From colonial Quetzaltenango, set aside two days to climb Central America's highest point, **Volcán Tajumulco** (p140).

Bus via Guatemala City to Honduras' **Copán Ruinas** (p367), a more touristy hub with great US$20 horseback rides and its famous ruins. Campers should make their way to **Parque Nacional Montaña de Celaque** (p381), near Gracias, and take butterfly-lined paths to campsites in the cloud forest. Bus to **La Ceiba** (p392), Honduras' activities and party center, with canopy tours and rafting tours of the Río Cangrejal. Boat out to the **Bay Islands** (p406), for snorkeling or great reef dives and US$25 certification courses.

Southwest in El Salvador, stop in artsy **Suchitoto** (p318) and go by horseback to former FLMN hideouts at Volcán Guazapa. Pass on the capital for **La Libertad** (p290), the nation's surf capital. Bus to Nicaragua,

stopping in colonial **León** (p480) for a climb up and slide down a nearby volcano. Give a couple days at least for **Isla de Ometepe** (p503), a volcano island in a sea-sized lake with hikes up to – and past – the clouds.

Costa Rica is flooded with options (and visitors). DIY canoe rides through the **Tortuguero** (p570), accessed via Río San Juan, remains a Central America highlight. In the south, **Parque Nacional Chirripó** (p616) has a well marked two-day trail to the country's highest mountain, with a US$10 bunkhouse way up.

In Panama detour from David to **Boquete** (p674), near Volcán Barú and rivers to raft. Brush up on your newly tested surf skills at one of the region's best waves, at **Santa Catalina** (p693). Before you end your trip, get some roller blades to traverse the causeway along the mouth of the Panama Canal near **Panama City** (p656). Or just see a flick.

'I ONLY HAVE TWO WEEKS!'

Laments such as this crop up all the time: 'I want to see Central America but only have a couple weeks; where should I go?' The best advice is sticking with some highlights in a country or two. Perhaps sample 'tomorrow's Central America' in El Salvador and Nicaragua; many first-timers often stick with Guatemala. An 'open jaw' ticket – flying into one place and out of another – helps you get the most out of your time.

Apart from choosing a sample from the earlier itineraries, here are a couple stabs at what you can accomplish in just 14 days.

The Box Ticker: Panama to Guatemala

All of Central America in 14 days? You nuts? OK. Here's a way to see most countries, traveling overland and mostly by day. Start with two

Central America is a paradise for the active – surfing, diving, hiking and boating options easily rank up with the region's top highlights. This trip – from Guatemala City to Panama City – assumes an open-jaw ticket.

With just two weeks up your sleeve, you can make a mad, crazy dash and try to see as much as you can, or you can just take it very, very easy soaking up the culture of a people who are not about hurrying.

nights in **Panama City** (p648) – see the canal and colonial Casco Viejo. Bus 15 hours to **San José** (p538), arriving at 3am on the Tica Bus. Taxi to one of the hostels with a pool; do a day trip to **Parque Nacional Braulio Carrillo** (p556) to climb a volcano. Get the morning bus for a 10-plus-hours trip to Nicaragua's colonial wonder **Granada** (p488) for a couple nights wandering past the plaza's mango trees and to take a canopy tour down a volcano. Wake *early* for a long day: get the Tegucigalpa bus (roughly 10 hours) and a Copán Ruinas bus (seven more), and allow yourself two full days' rest in **Copán Ruinas** (p367) – but not forgetting the nearby Maya ruins. Get a shuttle bus (six hours) to **Antigua** (p101) for the last couple of days in the volcano-studded highlands, hopefully squeezing in a day trip to the **Chichicastenango market** (p128). End the trip in Guatemala City.

Get Real: Belize to Honduras

Wherever you go, travel's ultimate highlight is the local people you meet. This trip – from Belize City to Tegucigalpa – gets local on Central America's arsenal, sticking with traditional villages where long-rooted traditions live large. Hang out with Garífuna in **Dangriga** (p250), best during the Garífuna Settlement Day festival (November 19), then sing songs with a Maya family at a homestay outside **Punta Gorda** (p257).

Ferry to Puerto Barrios, Guatemala and bus to **Cobán** (p162) to stay in the cloud forest for a couple days with a Q'eqchi' family.

Bus east into Honduras, where you can hang on the beach and try local coconut bread at low-key Garífuna villages such as **La Ensenada** (p391) then bus from **Santa Rosa de Copán** (p376) to see the Lenca market at cliff-hugging **Belén Gualcho** (p381). It's a seven-hour bus ride to Tegucigalpa.

Getting Started

Some travelers argue that the more you sit and think about a trip, and the more you build it up, the more disappointing it is when you get there. Bollocks. Half of the fun is reading up, planning, getting tickets, talking with just-back travelers and studying maps – even if all your planning gets tossed out the window once you arrive.

This chapter helps answer the first big questions for a trip, including when to go and what kind of cash you'll need. For more information, also see the Central America Directory (p719).

For climate charts of select cities in Central America, see p723; see also Climate in the Directory of each country chapter.

WHEN TO GO

When are you free? Any time of year will be pretty good (as long as a hurricane isn't on the same itinerary). Beaches are best for a dip around February; the hills remain refreshingly cool about August. However, the seasons here are less distinguished by temperature, and more by weather and tourist activity.

Peak tourist season coincides with the dry season – known as *verano* (summer), which is roughly between Christmas and Easter's Semana Santa celebrations (attractions in themselves). Though hotels fill up at this time – and raise their prices – you'll usually find a room even in big-time tourist destinations such as Antigua in Guatemala, or Cancún in Mexico. On either side of this period – mid-November or mid-April – can be the best time to visit.

WHAT TO TAKE

Almost everything can be found in towns of significant size in Central America. However, there are some items that can be hard to find or expensive to the point of offense.

- An alarm clock is necessary to make it on those early buses (and many do leave early).
- Take books if you're certain to read or be waiting for transport. However, new and used books in English are available at book exchanges in big cities and tourist hangouts.
- Camping gear if you plan to camp; bring it all (except fuel for the stove) as equipment isn't often available, and what is can be costly.
- Condoms and birth-control pills are available in larger towns, but it's convenient to bring your own.
- A flashlight is definitely needed for powerless beach huts and checking out ruins.
- Photocopies: copy your passport, airline ticket, any visas and traveler's check numbers; pack these separately from the originals.
- A peek at a snapshot or two of the family back home will be appreciated by your new Central American friends. Single women may want to bring a photo of a fictitious husband (and a ring).
- Rain gear: a thin waterproof jacket and a rainproof sack for your pack is a God send; you may be dry in the bus, but your pack on top can get soaked.
- Repellant: this must-have is not as readily available as in Central America, so you might as well get it now.
- A Spanish phrasebook as these guys are more expensive here than back home.
- A universal sink plug & clothesline for washing your laundry and hanging up wet clothes.
- A water filter bottle is great if you're camping or going into Honduras' La Moskitia. Aquamira has a good instant-purified water bottle for US$19..

Most days during the rainy or wet season, called *invierno* (winter) – roughly May through November or early December – are blessed with variable pockets of sunshine and cheaper airfares. Often a suddenly blackened sky will drop rain in the afternoon for an hour or two, and then clear up again. But flooding and days of rain can happen, particularly problematic for those mountain hikes. Hurricanes and tropical storms are an even more serious concern, as they can last for days (most often coming in September and October up and down the Caribbean coast) and affect the whole region.

COSTS & MONEY

Central America is not an expensive place to travel. Guatemala, Honduras and Nicaragua are the cheapest countries to visit, with El Salvador and Panama comprising the second tier. Travel costs in Belize, Costa Rica and Mexico are a jump up from other Central American countries (particularly those Mexican buses!), but even in these countries you can still usually find dorm beds for as low as US$8 or US$10, and a bed in a guesthouse for US$15.

How Much Do You Need?

In general, it's possible to get by on a daily budget of US$15 (in Nicaragua) to US$40 (in Mexico), depending on which country you're in. This range is a bare minimum per day, involving staying in a hostel with a free breakfast and internet access, having a simple lunch and dinner, seeing an attraction and riding a few hours to the next town. Bring more than you think you'll need and allow yourself the means for a splurge now and then for nice meals, drinks and hotels with air-con, as well as for a snorkel trip, a tour or a guide. Staying in a reasonable hotel room with air-con will cost you an extra US$15/20 for Nicaragua/Mexico. Sample costs are provided on the first page of each country chapter.

How to Carry Money

It's wise to store some spare US dollars in case of an emergency – at least a couple days' budget. ATMs are widely available in the region; though, if

---

HOW MUCH?

Bottle of beer US$0.70-2

Bus ride (3hr) US$1.60-14

Dorm bed US$3-15

Hotel double US$8-30

Internet access per hr US$1-2

Set lunch US$1-5

---

10 TIPS TO STAY ON A BUDGET

- Always ask the price before agreeing to any services.
- Eat set lunches in local markets, buy boiled corn from street vendors – cut back on those tempting Western brekkies (at US$3 or US$4 a pop).
- Walk around – from bus stations, to museums across town – to save using taxis.
- Team up with fellow travelers – solo travelers often pay the same as a couple pays, and a group of three or four sharing a hotel room can work out cheaper than staying in a hostel.
- Cut back on the *carves* (beer), partiers. A buck or two per bottle adds up.
- Avoid repeatedly buying small bottles of water; buy water in bulk, drink boiled water or bring a purifier.
- Go 2nd-class; cheaper buses – those stuffed ex-US school buses painted in bright colors – can be up to 50% cheaper.
- Slow down. Slower travel means less transport, more time to figure out the cheap deals.
- See fewer countries – fewer countries means fewer entry visas and less distance to travel.
- Skip Mexico, Costa Rica, Belize and Caribbean party towns – all are pricier.

DOS & DON'TS

- Do tip 10% at restaurants unless a service charge has been included.
- Do use the formal *usted* to address locals until they go to *tú* first.
- Do read up on recent history – many locals may be suffering from recent civil wars that your country may or may not have contributed to – it's worth knowing beforehand.
- Don't go into shops shirtless or in a bikini – though the beach may be nearby, some communities are offended by informal attire.
- Don't expect everything to rush at New York pace.
- Don't take photographs of religious ceremonies or people without asking.

your personal identification number (PIN) is more than four digits, ask your bank if it will be accepted before heading off. For general information on money for the region, see p729, as well as the Money sections in each country's Directory.

Foreigner Prices
Note that many museums and national parks throughout Central America charge higher admission fees for foreign tourists. It's sometimes about twice what locals pay, but still pretty cheap. Keep in mind what the locals earn before complaining. Some places may offer student discounts, otherwise don't haggle; they're set prices.

CONDUCT
There are a few things to keep in mind about 'being good' in Central America. Remember life here probably goes at a slower pace than yours back home. See also Responsible Travel (p4).

Introductions
A simple *buenos días* or *buenas tardes* (good morning or good afternoon to English speakers) should preface your conversation, including simple requests. When you enter a room, even a public place such as a restaurant or waiting room, it's polite to make a general greeting to everyone. It's also nice to say hello to your bus mate (and your bus mate's chicken).

Indigenous People
The term *indio* or *india* to refer to indigenous people is generally quite rude; the word *indígena* for indigenous men and women is widely used.

Dress
It's worth paying attention to your appearance here. Latin Americans on the whole are very conscious of appearance, grooming and dress; it's difficult for them to understand why a foreign traveler (assumed to be rich) would dress scruffily, when even impoverished Central Americans do their best to look neat. Your relations can be smoother if you're looking spick-and-span. This also applies for dealings with officialdom (ie immigration officials and police).

Casual dress is becoming more acceptable, though. You may see local women wearing miniskirts – an unthinkable occurrence in the not-so-distant past – but not everyone appreciates this attire, and some locals may find it offensive. As a foreigner, it's a good idea to steer toward the conservative, so as not to offend. A general rule is to notice what the people around you

PRE-TRIP INSPIRATION

Films

A bit of celluloid can whet the appetite for a sense of Central America before a trip. Several big-budget films have been set in various parts of Central America. It feels icky to say it, but Mel Gibson's *Apocalypto* offers a remarkably graphic version of Classic-era Maya life (though set in post-Classic period, but oh well, the two periods were only five or six centuries apart). For an idea of the jungle's scope, see *Jurassic Park* or *Congo*, both filmed in Costa Rica. Some scenes of the James Bond flick *Moonraker* were filmed in Guatemala. The best of this mainstream bunch, however, is *The Mosquito Coast* (starring Harrison Ford), which was set in Honduras and shot in Belize.

The more serious side of things are handled in a number of films. *Salvador* is Oliver Stone's take on El Salvador's civil war. The top of the must-sees includes Gregory Nava's memorable *El Norte*, which follows two Guatemalan refugees trying to reach the USA, and Barbara Trent's *The Panama Deception*, a pull-no-punches documentary on the US invasion of Panama.

Woody Allen's *Bananas* is a banana-republic spoof set on the fictional island of San Marcos; not real Central America, but it's funny.

Print

Travelers along the Ruta Maya (Maya Route) should read a bit about those ancient civilizations. Michael D Coe's *The Maya* or the fascinating *Breaking the Maya Code* are probably the best. For travelogues, Peter Moore's *The Full Montezuma* recounts a late '90s trip with a new lady friend from back in Australia. Paul Theroux's *The Old Patagonia Express: By Train Through the Americas* includes the region, and his *Mosquito Coast* prompted the film. Ronald Wright's *Time Among the Maya* is a classic travelogue of the Ruta Maya, though now in its third decade. *The Path Between the Seas*, by David McCullough, follows the efforts to make the Panama Canal. Published in 1992, Tina Rosenberg's still-engaging *Children of Cain* tackles political violence in Latin America. See p722, as well as many of the Books sections in each country's Directory for other recommended reading.

But for the best reading of all, see what other travelers are writing about Central America at Lonely Planet's discussion board, **Thorn Tree** (http://thorntree.lonelyplanet.com). See p728 for a list of useful online sources.

wear and dress accordingly (though that doesn't mean all the guys should wear black Metallica T-shirts though).

Shorts are usually worn by both sexes only at the beach and in coastal towns. You'll notice that many local women swim with T-shirts over their swimming suits, and you may want to do the same or be prepared to receive a lot of male attention. T-shirts are also a great way of avoiding sunburn. See p734 for more suggestions for women travelers.

Show particular reserve in how you're dressed when entering churches. Shorts, short skirts and tank tops are a definite no-no.

Another consideration about your appearance is safety. Even cheap imitation jewelry (much less a video camera dangling around your neck) spells 'r-i-c-h a-s h-e-l-l' to many would-be thieves, particularly in the capitals. See p724 for more on basic travel safety.

Snapshots

CURRENT EVENTS

Visitors sticking with beaches, colonial towns, Maya ruins and jungle walks may not notice that Central America is undergoing rampant urbanization. According to a UN estimate, the years since 1970 have seen all countries in the region except Guatemala move from a predominately rurally based society to a predominately urban one (most markedly in El Salvador). Villagers and farmers are running out of work options as more land is used for timber and cattle (largely to supply US hamburger chains). Meanwhile, rising real-estate prices – partly spurred on by the inflow of money sent from family members living abroad (and expat Americans and Europeans finding homes in Central America, particularly in Costa Rica and Mexico) – are hurting the chances of many to buy land. Increasingly, those without means – and some estimates suggest 60% to 70% of Central America lives below the poverty line – are simply heading for the city (if not to the USA via Mexico).

'If we cannot export goods, we will keep exporting people.'

OSCAR ARÍAS SÁNCHEZ, COSTA RICAN PRESIDENT AND WINNER OF THE 1987 NOBEL PEACE PRIZE

Joining the new arrivals to Central American capitals are convicted criminals, sent back home from the USA (as mandated by recent legislation) following any gang-related convictions. Unsurprisingly, the growing reports of gang activity in Central America and murder occur mostly in urban areas. In El Salvador, for example, about 10 people are murdered a day, while in the first 10 months of 2005 Guatemala reportedly saw 4300 killings (and very few convictions). Disturbingly, some of the murders are of street children.

The most infamous gang is the Mara Salvatrucha (or MS-13), a highly organized, multinational gang founded in Los Angeles and named after army ants – the total membership supposedly tops 100,000. (For more see p269.) Very few travelers witness such violence; see p724 for more information.

For insight into the multinational Mara Salvatrucha gang, download the 2006 report 'The World's Most Dangerous Gang' by *National Geographic's* 'Explorer' series on iTunes.

Killings aren't limited to the streets. In February 2007 three Salvadoran congressmen who had driven into Guatemala were stopped by Guatemalan police, searched (in vain) for drugs, then killed execution-style. Several officers were arrested, then killed in their jail cells. No one is sure what's afoot, but some observers believe the events hint at how far corruption may extend in Guatemala's police force and government, through which roughly two-thirds of the USA's cocaine supply travels en route from South America.

Politics, meanwhile, swing both left and right. In Chiapas the leftist Zapatista militia-army (see p63) has shown some signs of slowing down in recent years, though its leader Subcomandante Marcos made a highly publicized motorcycle tour across Mexico in 2006. Elsewhere many civil-war figures from the '80s are re-emerging in politics. In Nicaragua former president and Sandinista leader Daniel Ortega was voted back in office in 2007 (using pink as a campaign color!), while El Salvador has elected many

---

ARRRGHHH YOU INTO PIRATES?

Pirates loved (raiding) Central America. A few sites to see include the following:

Anti-pirate castles Guatemala's El Castillo de San Felipe (p176) and Nicaragua's El Castillo (p511) on the Río San Juan were built to keep pirates' looting at bay.

Trujillo, Honduras (p401) Henry Morgan plundered it in 1643; the town got revenge by executing 'modern-day pirate' William Walker two centuries later.

Panama City Panamá Viejo got itself plundered by Henry Morgan in 1671, who paid a kind of respect to the 'pirate priest' at the Iglesia de San José (p654).

ex-FMLN guerrillas to its congress. On the other hand, the civil-war–era, right-wing leader of Guatemala, Ríos Montt, sought a term in congress in 2007, while a survivor of one of Montt's ordered raids, Maya writer Rigoberta Menchú, ran for president.

A key political issue for discussion is the Central American Free Trade Agreement (Cafta), an arangement to open the local economies of Costa Rica, El Salvador, Guatemala, Honduras, Nicaragua and the Dominican Republic to US trade and investment. Cafta was set to go into effect by January 2007, but governments chose to drag their heels instead. Only El Salvador had changed local laws in line with the agreement in a timely manner, and Costa Rica (supposedly the USA's top ally in Central America) had yet to ratify the agreement, with protests erupting over the issue (signs at one San José rally proclaimed 'the north is invading us again').

A more welcome invasion is tourism. Despite the record-breaking damage of hurricanes to many popular destinations in 2005 (Stan killed 1620 people in Mexico, Guatemala and El Salvador, while Wilma amassed over US$20 billion in damages, mostly in the tourist zones of the Yucatán), the numbers of travelers pouring into Central America have increased by double-digit percentages in the 2000s. Belize, for example, is booming, from almost zero annual cruise-ship visitors not long ago to a figure over twice its population. Cargo-carrying ships, meanwhile, have traveled through the Panama Canal without a hitch since the US transferred control of the canal to Panama in 1999.

This has pleasantly surprised many, enough so that in 2006 the nation overwhelmingly endorsed an ambitious US$5 billion plan to expand canal operations.

Thomas E Skidmore's *Modern Latin America* has a 48-page summary of Central America's contemporary history. Costa Rican Hector Perez-Brignoli's *A Brief History of Central America* is a readable 222-page overview of the region.

HISTORY

Most believe the first Central Americans were peoples from Asia who migrated 20,000 or so years ago across the frozen Bering Strait from Russia to Alaska and down through the Americas. Others argue that seafaring Asians crossed to present-day California only about 11,000 years ago. Either way, things have gotten decidedly more tense in the last few thousand years. Ever cruel, Mother Nature has unleashed hurricanes, volcanic eruptions and mudslides, wrecking new settlements, while rival city-states battled each other. Then the Europeans showed up.

Europeans, Meet 'Americans'

By the time the first Europeans with shiny helmets arrived in Central America – Christopher Columbus (Cristóbal Colón to his Spanish crew) made it here in 1502 – the region's greatest civilizations had already dissipated into the jungle (see p31).

Most of the 'Indians' who did meet the Spanish lived in small tribes, as corn farmers or hunter-gatherers. Other than a few scattered highland towns, and larger ones at present-day Managua and Granada in Nicaragua, nothing here rivaled the power centers of the Aztecs or Incas of the time.

COLONIAL HISTORY – TIMELINE

1484	1698	1739	1823	1862
Portugal snubs hopeful explorer Christopher Columbus (aka 'the mistake of '84')		Panama joins Nueva Andalucía (later called Colombia)		Britain declares Belize a colony
	Scotland (!) tries and fails to colonize Darién, Panama		Short-lived Central American Federation forms	

TOP FIVE BASTARDS

Many outsiders, not to mention local dictators, have wreaked havoc on countless Central Americans. Here are five contenders for the hall of shame:

- **Pedro Arias de Ávila** Spanish founder of Panama City who literally roasted many indigenous locals alive or fed them to the dogs.

- **Pedro de Alvarado** Spaniard whose burning alive of captives in the 1520s, including many conquered Guatemalan Quiché leaders, disturbed even Cortés, himself no nice guy.

- **William Walker** American bully in the 1850s who aided León, then declared himself president and tried to take over Central America (p447); fate (and justice) caught up with him at a firing squad in Trujillo, Honduras (p402).

- **Allan W Dulles** The CIA director who, in 1954, masterminded the coup against the Guatemalan government to protect US interests (which included bananas); despite massacres and oppression instigated by the installed government, the coup became a template for future CIA campaigns.

- **Ronald Reagan** US president of the 1980s who broke records for outside interference – backing Guatemalan death squads, the Salvadoran military junta, and Contras launching attacks from Honduras against Nicaragua's Sandinistas (p333).

Conquest & Colonization

The Spanish conquistadors – mostly poor, illiterate criminals sniffing out get-rich schemes – moved in independent factions, sometimes warring against each other. The first Spanish settlement in Central America was established in Panama in 1509, but further conquests were put on snooze. Instead, Panama served as a base for Francisco Pizarro's takeover of the Inca empire in Peru. Meanwhile, in February 1519, Hernán Cortés landed at the isle of Cozumel and led his savage attacks on Mexico to the north.

Also in 1519 Pedro Arias de Ávila settled Panama City and began a bloody trip north, which involved displaying incredible cruelty to the indigenous population. In 1524 he established León and Granada in today's Nicaragua, while Cortés' brutal lieutenant Pedro de Alvarado based his own takeover of the Guatemala and El Salvador areas. With control over the region up for grabs, the two forces inevitably clashed in present-day Honduras.

Amid this, indigenous tribes fought each other, the Spanish (though some fought *with* the Spanish against rival clans) and smallpox (in present-day Mexico about 90% of the indigenous population died in the first 75 years of Spanish occupation). Many who weren't killed became slaves.

Eventually 'Guatemala' (Central America, including Chiapas but not Panama) was established as part of the viceroyalty of Mexico (then called Nueva España). The indigenous population was subjected to violent rule, tempered slightly after pleas to King Carlos V of Spain by Dominican friar Bartolemé de Las Casas in 1542. A colonial capital was established at Antigua in 1543. After a 1773 earthquake destroyed it, a new capital was created at Guatemala City.

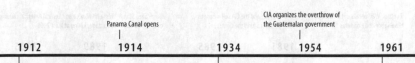

1912	1914	1934	1954	1961
US sends marines to set up national guard in Nicaragua	Panama Canal opens	Nicaraguan national guard assasinates anti-US politician Sandino, beginning the Somoza dynasty	CIA organizes the overthrow of the Guatemalan government	Guatemala's 36-year civil war begins

Independence

Colonial trade restrictions and governments run exclusively by Spanish-born Spaniards eroded the patience of many criollos (people born in Latin America of Spanish parentage). The first Central American revolt, following Mexico's the previous year, flared in San Salvador in 1811 (led by priest José Matías Delgado and Manuel José Arce), but was quickly suppressed. By 1821 Mexico's viceroy (Agustín de Iturbide) defected to the rebels and Guatemala's leaders reluctantly signed the first acts of independence. Spain finally let go for good on September 15, 1821. Guatemala was annexed by Iturbide's forces; conservatives welcomed the union. But Delgado and Arce staged a brief revolt in El Salvador (and they even wanted to join the USA!).

See p476 for our author's interview with a Nicaraguan mother who lost two sons in her country's revolution.

Iturbide's reign was soon overthrown, and Central American states declared independence from Mexico in 1823 (Chiapas stayed with Mexico). The federation of five states – Guatemala, Honduras, El Salvador, Nicaragua and Costa Rica – led a brief, shaky existence (though they did manage to abolish slavery decades before the USA did). Arce became the first president, but succumbed to dictator tendencies and was overthrown. In 1837 a largely indigenous mob marched on Guatemala City and the federation dissolved in 1838, with the republics setting out on their own. See the History sections in individual country chapters for details on how they panned out.

The USA & Central America

Starting in 1823 with the Monroe Doctrine (a 'civilizing' policy of 'America for the Americas'), the USA has butted in on many of Central America's affairs. William Walker notoriously tried to take over the region in the mid-19th century and spurred on the era of 'banana republics,' the unfortunate tag for some of the region's more bendable governments. As bananas started bringing in big money, the US-funded United Fruit Company took control in 1899. In 1954, when the Guatemalan government planned to break up large estates into small private plots, the CIA orchestrated an invasion from Honduras. Soon after, the Guatemala civil war broke out, leading to 200,000 deaths.

In the 1980s Ronald Reagan channeled US$500 million to back the Salvadoran military, and illegally sold weapons to Iran to fund the Contras fight against the Nicaraguan Sandinistas.

JOIN THE 'MOUSTACHE EXPERIMENT'

Stick around and you'll notice many Central American men sport *bigotes* (moustaches) resembling fuzzy caterpillars. This book's authors strove to find out which country had the highest per-capita moustache tally, making random counts of 100 men in big cities and small towns of Central America. Turns out Guatemala and Panama (both with 10% tallies of mustached men; tssk!) are the most bare-faced, while only Nicaragua (57.7%) has a majority letting it grow. Other respectable counts include Mexico (44.5%), Honduras (36%), Costa Rica (35.5%) and El Salvador (30.5%), while Belize (14.5%) fell below the regional average of 29.8%. The search for truth can't stop here – let us know your tabulations.

'Football War' breaks out between El Salvador and Honduras	Reagan and the CIA sell weapons to Iran to fund the Contras	Hurricanes Stan & Wilma hit Mexico and Central America, causing over US$20 billion in damage, killing at least 2000
1969	**1981** **1985**	**1989** **2005**
	Belize gets independence; Reagan becomes US president	US troops blare Van Halen's 'Panama' to irritate Noriega, hiding out at the Vatican Embassy

THE CULTURE
People

Along the northern Pacific slopes are heavy populations of indigenous groups (over half of Guatemala is Maya) and ladino or mestizo (person of mixed indigenous and Spanish ancestry). It changes gradually to the south, as European features become more noticeable. In Costa Rica criollos account for over 95% of the population. On the Caribbean, descendents of Africans dominate populations, while communities of Mennonites (in Belize) and Asians (throughout) add to the mix.

INDIGENOUS PEOPLES

Today all Central American countries have groups, larger or smaller, of *indígena* (indigenous people). The largest surviving groups are the Maya communities of Guatemala, Belize, and Mexico's Chiapas and Yucatán Peninsula. Communities in the Guatemalan highlands (Chichicastenango and Lago de Atitlán, among others) and San Cristóbal de Las Casas, Chiapas, are known for traditional costumes, such as goat-fur vests and multistriped blouses.

In Honduras and Nicaragua are many other indigenous groups, including the Tolupanes (Jicaque), Pech (Paya), Tawahka (Sumo), Lenca, Chorti and Miskito peoples. Nicaragua is also home to the Rama. El Salvador has small numbers of Izalco and Pancho, descended from the Pipil. Costa Rica has few native inhabitants, but they include Boruca, Cabecar, Guatuso and Terraba. In Panama there are significant groups of Guaymí, Kuna and Chocóes, which are broken into two groups the Emberá and Wounaan, who still live deep in the Darién Gap. Panama's Kuna are a particular success story, as they run their area as an autonomous zone of 400 islands on the Caribbean coast and control all revenue and tourism investment.

Throughout the past 500 years, many indigenous groups have given up traditional dress and language for the cell phone-toting urban, ladino society. Others live as independently as governments will allow and transform what's introduced to fit into their own customs.

PEOPLE OF AFRICAN DESCENT

Black people inhabit much of the Caribbean coast and many are descended from Africans brought to the West Indies (primarily Jamaica) as slaves. Black Creoles (of mixed British and African descent) account for most of Belize's population. The Spanish brought many slaves to the region, especially to Panama, but most came from the Caribbean during the 19th century as laborers (not slaves) to work on banana plantations.

Along the northern coast, the Garífuna are another group, descended from West African slaves and Carib Indians. They were transplanted to Honduras in 1797 from the Caribbean island of St Vincent, eventually establishing communities in Belize, Guatemala, Honduras and Nicaragua.

Arts
LITERATURE

Poetry's huge. Nicaraguan poet Rubén Darío (1867–1916) lived a debaucherous life (eg waking up hungover and married), but spoke for much of Latin America with his own *modernismo*, political style. His provocative 'To Roosevelt' criticized the US president (Theodore, not Franklin) following the US invasion of Panama in 1903. He wrote: 'Our America, trembling with hurricanes, trembling with Love: zero men with Saxon eyes and barbarous souls, our America lives…Be careful.' *Stories & Poems/Cuentos y Poesías* is a bilingual collection of his works.

And We Sold the Rain: Contemporary Fiction from Central America (1988; edited by Rosario Santos) is a great collection of 20th-century writings from regional authors, with indigenous people a major theme.

Say *indígena* (indigenous) in Central America and not *indio* (Indian), a term which is outright offensive to some (particularly in Costa Rica).

To learn how women have increasingly added to the Central American literary scene, see *Writing Women in Central America: Gender & Fictionalization of History* by Laura Barbas-Rhoden.

LOCAL LORE

Understanding the traditions and lore of any region is key to understanding the heart and spirit of its people. Here are our favorites from each country:

- **Belize – Why mosquitoes buzz around ears** A Belizean legend tells of 'Mosquito' and 'Wax' being friends until Wax borrowed US$5 and didn't pay it back. Wax avoided Mosquito for months, until one day Mosquito found him and Wax jumped into the nearest hole to hide – an ear. Ever since, Mosquito buzzes around ears trying to collect the debt.

- **Costa Rica – La Negrita** Costa Rica's mysterious 'Black Virgin' (now Costa Rica's patron saint) is a statuette of an indigenous Virgin Mary, first found in 1635. Per tradition, whenever it's taken it reappears at the spot it was originally, at the Basílica de Nuestra Señora de Los Ángeles, built in her honor in 1824.

- **El Salvador – The Siguanaba** This mythical hottie seduces men, then turns grotesque and whorish, causing her victims to drop dead or go batty. Siguanaba travels with her mischievous little boy Cipitío, who approaches women washing at rivers and hurls rocks at them.

- **Guatemala – La Llorana** This is the legend of a beautiful peasant woman who, jilted by her lover, drowned his children in the local river. Grief-stricken, she then drowned herself. Late at night, near water, you can sometimes hear the woman wailing, bemoaning the loss of the children.

- **Honduras – Little Virgin** She's just longer than your finger – but what a fuss she's caused! Found centuries ago in a cornfield, the 6cm-tall wooden statue of the Virgin of Suyapa (see p350), is thought to have healing powers. When thieves seized her, there was a nationwide hunt until she was found in the men's room of a Tegucigalpa restaurant (see p346).

- **Mexico – Chamula** Folks in the often-visited Maya village San Juan Chamula believe that foreigners – who they call 'Germans' – reach their village by 'following the lightning,' which 'leads to gold.' Visitors aren't likely to see a newborn, as they are carefully kept out of strangers' (including inhabitants of the next village) sight. If you should see one, the mother will ask you to kiss her baby *immediamente* to ensure no bad spirits are exchanged.

- **Nicaragua – La Carretanagua** This ghostly oxcart can be heard driving down pueblo streets at the darkest hours of the darkest nights. Driven by a skull-faced phantom, it makes a hideous racket and means someone in the village will die during the night. It is perhaps connected to folk memories of the depredations wrought by Spanish plunderers arriving with teams of oxen.

- **Panama – Teribe** According to the Teribe tribe, *indios conejos* (rabbit Indians) are nocturnal warriors who live deep in the jungle. They are pale white with stripes on their backs and dwarfish in size, like giant rabbits. Although they are nearly invincible under cover of night, they can easily be killed if ambushed while sleeping during the day.

El Salvador's Roque Dalton was also a radical poet and was eventually executed by fellow communists, who may have wrongly taken him for a CIA spy. *Miguel Marmol* is a collection of his works in English.

Guatemalan Miguel Ángel Asturias (1899–1974) won the Nobel Prize for literature (1967) for his vilification of Latin American dictators in *El Señor Presidente*.

A Quiché Maya writer from Guatemala, Rigoberta Menchú (b 1959), won the 1992 Nobel Peace Prize for her incredible recount of the Guatemalan civil war in *I, Rigoberta Menchú: An Indian Woman in Guatemala*. It later ignited a controversy when some elements of the book were claimed to be false (which she acknowledged). Menchú has received death threats for years, which kept her in exile, but she returned to make a bid for the presidency in late 2007.

MUSIC

Music is everywhere. Throughout much of the region everyone seems to love the xylophone-like marimba, proudly believed to be a Guatemalan invention. A Maya instrument, the *chirimía* (like an oboe) can still be heard in churches in the Guatemalan highlands. Salsa is huge everywhere, with big bands frequently playing outdoor shows for late-night plaza-packing crowds. A famous salsa singer is Panamanian Ruben Blades (now the country's minister of tourism), though perhaps better known for his acting in films such as *Once Upon a Time in Mexico*.

In recent years, reggae and other Afro-Caribbean sounds have increasingly spilled out from the Caribbean coastline to more stereos throughout the region. The Garífuna's drum-heavy traditional music, called *punta*, is made with conch shells, maracas and serious hip-shaking; it's based on West African traditions.

Good times to hear Garífuna's *punta* music and dance are at Honduras' festivals (p384) and Belize's Garífuna Settlement Day (November 19; p250).

Religion

Roman Catholicism, introduced by the Spaniards, has since been Central America's principal religion, while Protestant sects have been predominant in British-influenced Caribbean areas. Things are tipping more toward Protestantism in the past couple decades, however, as waves of translated Bible-toting missionaries representing various evangelical religions (as well as Jehovah's Witnesses, Mennonites, Mormons and Seventh-Day Adventists) are coming on humanitarian projects. The Church of Scientology even opened a location in Managua. Some missionaries go to simply build schools, clinics or help rebuild after a natural disaster; many programs, however, openly hope to convert an *evangelico* (as non-Catholic converts are called) or two. Some missionaries sermonize in plazas, criticize the 'unbelief' of 'ancestral worship' and keep tabs on millions of 'unreached people.'

Ethnic groups, however, continue to practice and preserve their traditional religions, sometimes fused with Catholicism. Maya beliefs and folk remedies, for example, have long been 'tolerated' by Catholic priests. Here, animist beliefs and chicken sacrifices freely merge with the (occasional moonshine-drinking) saints. The Garífuna of the region's Caribbean coastal areas continue to practice their traditional African-based religion, emphasizing the worship of ancestral spirits, in addition to Christianity.

ENVIRONMENT
The Land

Considering its diversity, Central America is remarkably wee, measuring just 523,780 sq km (about the size of France or Texas; about 2% of Latin America) with never more than 280km separating the Caribbean Sea and Pacific Ocean.

Borders are not always set in stone. A recent maritime-border dispute off the Caribbean coast between Nicaragua and Honduras went as far as a UN court in early 2007.

Created from four shifting tectonic plates over millions of years, Central America is the new kid on the block. As the world's major continental plates were slowly drifting into current positions from the Pangea land mass, this region surfaced from the sea and somersaulted snugly as a skinny, altruistic, 2400km land bridge between the two bigger Americas. Central America's two major plates (Cocos and Caribbean) still go at it, colliding at 10cm per year (geological light speed). Some day, far off, Central America may even split into two.

All that tectonic action helped create 300-or-so volcanoes. Central America's among the world's most active volcano zones; Guatemala's Volcán Fuego is one of the fieriest. Many volcanoes burp lava or ash on a regular basis, and bigger eruptions occur. Even 'extinct' ones sometimes erupt, as Costa Rica's Volcán Irazú did in 1963. El Salvador's Volcán Izalco emerged from ground level to its 1910m apex in the past 250 years. (Note to worried moms: none of Central America's volcanoes made the Top 20 list of death by natural disaster.)

Earthquakes rock the region as well. Over the years, San Salvador has been rebuilt nine times, and Antigua (Guatemala) has still not fully recovered from its 1773 quake.

Several cordilleras (mountain ranges) stretch for hundreds of kilometers down the Central American strip, broken by valleys and basins with fertile volcanic soil. Narrow, slightly sloping plains run along the coasts. When hurricanes or tidal waves hit, mudslides are common.

Wildlife

Central America's diverse and abundant animal and plant species owes much to the region's bridge position between North and South America. Hundreds of continental runaways and migrators, such as jaguars and oak trees, have spilled into Central America – and stuck around.

ANIMALS

If you see a turtle nesting site, do not startle the fragile newborn by flashing your camera in its face – even if operators say it's OK, it is *not*.

Central America has 7% of the world's species on just 0.5% of the world's land mass. Costa Rica and Belize, in particular, are known for their abundant wildlife.

Many mammals can be discovered in the jungle: monkeys (spider, howler, squirrel), cats (jaguars, pumas, ocelots), sloth, anteaters, bats and agoutis (simply fantastic creatures). Even more impressive are the number of birds that live or migrate here. Over 900 species have been recorded in Panama alone. The many birds of the region include toucans, macaws, parrots, harpy eagles and hummingbirds. Lucky visitors can spot a quetzal (ket-*sal*), the national bird (and inspiration for the name of the currency) of Guatemala and an important Maya symbol. These 35cm-long birds have bright green, red and white feathers; the March-to-June breeding season is the easiest time to spot one. (Louie Irby Davis' *A Field Guide to the Birds of Mexico and Central America* is a great birding guide.)

The areas in and around rivers, lakes and coastlines are home to many fish species. Amphibians and reptiles include sea, river and land turtles, crocodiles, frogs (watch out for the poisonous arrow frog) and iguanas.

Garrobo (www.garrobo .org) is a great site devoted to the Central American environment. Volcano freaks can access photos and updated details at www.rci .rutgers.edu/~carr.

Only a few of the many snake species are poisonous, notably the shy and tiny coral snake and large *barba amarilla* (or fer-de-lance). Some spiders such as the tarantula can be as big as a person's face.

Deforestation and hunting have left a mark on many species, such as the quetzal, with some species facing extinction.

PLANTS

There are five major types of vegetation zones in Central America, all influenced by differing altitudes, climates and soils.

On the Caribbean coast, up to 850m, tropical rain forest has canopies of tall trees and lush ground cover. The Pacific coastal strip (and northern Belize) is home to tropical dry forest, with trees and shrubs parched brown during the dry season.

Higher up, from 850m to 1650m, the cooler climate is home to a mixed upland forest of evergreens, pines and deciduous oaks. One of the loveliest terrains, just higher up again, is the cloud forest. The extreme humidity helps tall trees from drying out, which protect an herb- and moss-covered floor from direct sunlight.

A few areas above 3000m have alpine vegetation, with short grasses (such as the Chilean *páramo* in Costa Rica) and flowering herbs.

National Parks & Reserves

Central America has some 250 national parks, nature reserves and other protected areas. The most remote parks – such as Reserva de Biósfera Maya that comprises much of northern Guatemala – include vast areas with no infrastructure. Meanwhile, some of the most popular parks (such as Costa Rica's Parque Nacional Manuel Antonio) are touristed to the point of threatening the environment.

Environmental Issues

Central America's position between two oceans (and their hurricanes and tropical storms) makes its environment particularly vulnerable. Humans have an impact too. Deforestation of tropical rain forest – the 'lungs of the planet' – continues at a reckless pace. In 1950 about 60% of Central America was covered by tropical forest. About half that remains forested today. Some 95% of El Salvador's original forest is gone, while Guatemala reportedly clears 3% to 5% of its Reserva de Biósfera Maya (in El Petén) annually. Hamburgers are as much to blame as timber, as the expansion of livestock farms increases.

Scientists predict that millions of additional species remains undiscovered, with some plant species potentially important for pharmaceutical purposes. The forests are also still home to indigenous peoples, such as the Miskito in Honduras and Nicaragua, and the Choco of Panama. In addition, deforestation has led to soil erosion, which results in severe flooding and mudslides, as evidenced by Hurricane Stan in 2005.

Occasionally new problems are not our fault, such as in early 2007, when a waterborne fungal disease wiped out several amphibian groups in Panama, including the rockhopper frog.

Meanwhile ecotourism remains a buzz word heard by all of Central American governments. Organizations of national parks and reserves are devoted to help conserve and protect natural environments, but in some cases 'ecotourism' is going too far, developing to the point of harming what it is designed to protect.

However, Central America still has some wilderness areas where the forests are largely unexplored, such as the Darién region of Panama.

THE MAYA

It's not a contest, but of the New World's three biggest pre-Columbian civilizations (Aztec, Inca and Maya), Maya is usually considered the greatest. During its peak (around AD 750), possibly 10 million people thrived in stone cities of up to 200,000 inhabitants. The Maya's turf sprawled over much of present-day southern Mexico, Guatemala, Belize, El Salvador and Honduras (making up the Ruta Maya). The Maya elite used hieroglyphs to record battles, reigns, beliefs and precise planetary movements. Atop towering blood-red pyramids were vaulted temples adorned with bas-relief tributes to the gods. Many Maya from neighboring cities who saw these impressive pyramids were soon tortured and executed: the captured were not treated kindly.

Much remains unknown of the Maya, however. New theories are rolled out regularly, particularly about why, at the peak of power, the Maya world suddenly collapsed.

History

During the Maya pre-Classic period (2000 BC–AD 250), the first prototypes for the great art to come were drafted at cities such as the giant El Mirador (Guatemala). Two masterful calendars were developed: a 260-day year,

A few worthy books include *The Good Alternative Travel Guide*, Mark Mann's *The Community Tourism Guide* and Adrian Forsyth's entertaining *Tropical Nature: Life & Death in the Rain Forests of Central & South America*.

Put in a little time to help the environment by volunteering. Near Tikal, help with local wildlife projects (see p189). In Costa Rica, help sea turtle populations by monitoring nesting sites (p631). See p733 for more on volunteering.

'I blame two things for the recent decay of the local Mayan traditions: cell phones and missionaries.'

SAN CRISTÓBAL DE LAS CASAS, MEXICO, RESIDENT

DID *APOCALYPTO* GET IT RIGHT?

Of all people, Mel Gibson became the first Hollywood hotshot to put the Maya on the big screen. Watching *Apocalypto* (2006) – shot in Yucatec language in Veracruz, Mexico and also Costa Rica (neither Maya areas) – certainly affects how you'll see the ruins on your travels, with its images of elaborately pierced and tattooed villagers, and limestone-covered workers gathering materials to build pyramids.

But some viewers haven't been happy.

The Guatemalan 'commissioner of racism' called the film racist, for implying that the collapsing Maya 'deserved rescue' by the Spanish.

Others lamented Mel's extravagant use of sacrifice – which, to be fair, *was* (at some level) a part of Maya life (see Bonampak's blood-curdling murals; p62). More problematic for some purists is that the film set a Classic-era–looking city in the post-Classic time period, and that the flat Yucatán hardly resembles the mountainous settings from scenes that were filmed in Costa Rica.

For more on the making of the film, check out Luke Dittrich's funny piece for *Esquire* magazine (www.esquire.com).

and a 365-day *haab* ('vague' year), with five dreaded unlucky days at the end of 18 20-day months. The earliest known use of the calendar dates from 36 BC.

Maya cities as we know them best took shape during the Classic period (AD 250–900), when Palenque, Tikal, Cobá and Copán flourished. Pyramids skyrocketed, topped with ornate stone roof combs, not the thatched huts atop most central Mexican sites.

Then, in the late Classic period (800–900), came the collapse. Cities were abandoned, population numbers diminished; those who remained lived in small hut communities scattered about the region. Common theories for what happened include overpopulation, war between city-states, revolution and drought.

> According to the Maya calendar, time is cyclical and divided into 5200-year *kalpas* (eras) that end in destruction. The present era is set to end, by global annihilation, on December 23, 2012.

Most post-Classic (900–1500) activity occurred in the Yucatán (notably Chichén Itzá), based on a union of overtaken Maya and their new lords from the north, the Toltecs.

At the time of the Spanish conquest, Tulum was still occupied, but the heyday of Maya civilization was clearly past, with the giant cities lost in jungle. Still, the weakened Maya put up one of the toughest resistances to the Spanish in the Americas.

Beliefs & Rituals

According to the Popul Vuh (aka the 'Maya Bible'), which was written post-conquest by Quiché Maya, it took the great god K'ucumatz three tries to get humans right. The first two failures involved making people from mud then wood, before humans were successfully made with ground corn and water.

Corn, or maize, has always played a huge role for the Maya. Some even tattooed their faces to resemble kernels. A surprising crucifix-like shape

THE MAYA – TIMELINE

Beginning of the present era, per Maya astronomers	Start of Tikal settlement	London first settled by Romans	Palenque, in its prime, is conquered by Toniná	Chichén Itzá is conquered by Toltecs; its renaissance follows
3114 BC	1800	700	100	AD 43	400	730	900	987
	Fired-clay pottery is introduced in Mesoamerica	First settlements begin at Palenque	Copán founded in modern-day Honduras	Palenque is abandoned

on monuments actually symbolizes corn husks. Even now, some Catholic churches have altars to maize.

Another part of worship was sacrifice, which wasn't limited to slaves and captured foes; children, dogs and squirrels were also offerings for the many Maya gods. Some ceremonies involved painful rituals such as women slicing their tongues and threading them with thorn-studded rope, or men jabbing needles into their penises.

Other painful procedures where merely cosmetic, such as tying flat boards to infants in order to flatten foreheads. Some Maya skulls have been found with hundreds of small holes in them.

Modern Currents

Some visitors are surprised to learn that the Maya are very much alive in northern Central America and southern Mexico, rebounding from the disease and destruction the European colonists introduced 500 years ago. The guttural languages, such as Yucatec and Quiché, are still widely spoken, and populations are growing. Estimates suggest there are six million Maya today. Guatemala is said to be 60% Maya, and Mexico's biggest indigenous population is that of the Yucatec in the Yucatán Peninsula.

These population figures, however, don't mean the struggle for equality ended with independence from Spain in 1821. In 1847 the War of the Castes erupted in the Yucatán, with Maya rebels nearly driving out whites for good. More recently, the Guatemalan Civil War in the 1980s saw some 400 Maya villages wiped out by government troops and paramilitaries. In Chiapas in 1994, a guerrilla force of chiefly Tzotzil and Tzeltal Maya kicked off the Zapatista 'revolution' – seeking more say in how public land is used in the wake of Nafta (North American Free Trade Agreement).

Over the generations, many alien products and ideologies (coffee, Coca-Cola, Catholicism, marimba etc) have been absorbed into daily life, without completely replacing traditional ways and beliefs. For generations, the Chamula community outside San Cristóbal de Las Casas, Mexico, used *chicha* (in Mexico, a corn-based drink) to help them burp out evil spirits in holy places; after the Spanish introduced Catholicism, and the Americans Coca-Cola, the Chamula simply began using bottles of the fizzy soda in cathedrals where, on occasion, a chicken is sacrificed.

The so-called 'last unconquered tribe' of the Maya are the 700-or-so Lacandón who live in primitive communities in Chiapas' jungles in south Mexico. After so much resistance, many of these Maya, known for their long hair with bangs and white robes, are changing their religious beliefs, largely the result of missionaries.

READING UP ON MAYA HISTORY

The best introduction to Maya history is Mayanist Michael D Coe's enduring *The Maya*, while his surprisingly engaging *Breaking the Maya Code* reviews the wacky, bitchy world of Mayanists. Much of what we do know about the Maya comes from a Spaniard who destroyed hundreds of priceless Maya books and idols in the 16th century. Friar Diego de Landa, a Franciscan, was ordered by his superiors to write a detailed book on Maya customs and took a stab at a Maya alphabet. Much is described in his *Yucatán Before and After the Conquest*.

	Quiché king Tecun defeated by Alvarado, near Quetzaltenango		George Lucas uses Tikal as site of the rebel base in *Star Wars*		First Maya-language film *(Apocalypto)* released; Quiché writer Rigoberta Menchú runs for president of Guatemala
1224	**1524**	**1847**	**1977**	**1994**	**2007**
Chichén Itzá is abandoned		The War of the Castes in the Yucatán ends when the Maya rebels return home for corn harvest		Zapatistas take over San Cristóbal de Las Casas, Chiapas	

Mexico's Yucatán & Chiapas

HIGHLIGHTS

- **Maya ruins** Explore millennium-old ruins: Chichén Itzá (p44) is the best known, but Palenque (p57), Yaxchilán (p62) or Toniná (p62) offer more intimate encounters with hidden chambers (and monkeys)
- **Tulum** Long stretches of white-sand beaches, and its own namesake ruins, but no longer a quiet backpacker hub, it still has cheap sleeps and plenty of space (p53)
- **San Cristóbal de Las Casas** Pull on a sweater and sip fresh espresso in the cool, mountainous 'Zapatista capital,' one of the Americas' finest colonial-era towns (p62)
- **Mérida** Put your best salsa foot forward during the more-than-lively, street-spilling weekend fair in this Spanish-colonial wonder near to Maya ruins and flamingos (p45)
- **Off the Beaten Track** Untouched and out-of-the-way fishing village Punta Allen (p56) is within a protected reserve and offers snorkel trips to dolphin hangouts

FAST FACTS

- **Area** Quintana Roo (50,212 sq km); Yucatán state (38,212 sq km); Chiapas (74,211 sq km); 162,635 sq km in total
- **ATMs** Plentiful, using Cirrus and Plus systems
- **Budget** US$40-50 per day
- **Capital** Mexico City
- **Costs** Budget room US$15-30, 3hr bus ride US$14, set lunch US$4.50
- **Country Code** ☎ 52
- **Electricity** 110V AC, 60 Hz (same as the USA)
- **Famous for** Maya ruins, white sand and turquoise water, Zapatistas, tacos, hammocks
- **Head of State** Presidente Felipe Calderón
- **Languages** Spanish & two dozen Maya languages
- **Money** US$1 roughly = M$11 (pesos)
- **Phrases** ¿Mande? (come again?), chingadera (f***ed-up situation)
- **Population** 6.9 million (Yucatán, Quintana Roo & Chiapas states)
- **Time** GMT plus 6 hours; GMT minus 5 hours during daylight saving time
- **Traveler's Checks** Cashed at banks & casas de cambio (1-3% commission)
- **Visas** Not required for residents of USA, Canada, EU, Australia, New Zealand & some other countries

TRAVEL HINTS

Second-class buses save you 20% over 1st-class buses. If you don't like overnight buses, there's a lone day bus between Mérida and Palenque.

OVERLAND ROUTES

From Guatemala it's easy to loop into Mexico – from Quetzaltenango to San Cristóbal de Las Casas, then back to Tikal via Palenque, or into Belize from Chetumal, south of Tulum.

Mexico's southeast is made up of very different neighbors: the Yucatán Peninsula is home to a flat limestone shelf and beaches, Chiapas has mountains, forests and brisk temperatures. Both have fabulous Maya ruins. It makes for great travel. Despite the Yucatán's cruise-ship hubbub, it's more than tempting to work into your itinerary a few days of lazing on perfect beaches away from the tourist scene. The reefs off Cozumel provide among the world's finest dives, and cheap beachside hostels or cabañas can be found in Tulum, Playa del Carmen and Isla Mujeres. Inland, lively Mérida is the most *Mexican* town in the area, with scores of day-trip potential (including Maya ruins and Gulf of Mexico beaches and flamingos).

West of the Yucatán, Chiapas is worth the effort to see ruins mingling with hills and jungle and Maya communities living traditional lives in lofty places where you'll need a sweater in August. The ruins at Palenque are wonderful, but laid-back San Cristóbal de Las Casas is the best place to take in Chiapas. The town is a colonial marvel with indie-house movie theaters, fresh Chiapas coffee and four or five days' worth of day trips.

CURRENT EVENTS

In 2005 two hurricanes slammed into Mexico's south. Hurricane Wilma took its time passing the Yucatán's resort areas, bringing 150km/h gusts that bent trees, closed docks and wrecked businesses. Hurricane Stan was worse for Chiapas, where flimsy homes in mountain villages washed away as rivers rose. Since, much of the Yucatán has rebounded 100%, though Chiapas has had a harder time. One resident told us, 'All the funding went to Cancún and the resorts. We got nothing.'

Meanwhile, with corn (much of which comes from the USA) increasingly being used to create ethanol, corn flour prices – thus the all-important tortilla price – jumped by 400% in early 2007, and tens of thousands took to the streets in protest.

HISTORY

The Maya set up many city-states across the broad south of Mexico, though the population and activity had declined before the Spanish arrived. For more on Maya history, see p24. A couple of Spaniards – Diego de Mazariegos in present-day Chiapas, and Francisco de Montejo in the Yucatán – had the area under Spanish control by the mid 16th century. Mexico won independence from Spain in 1821, and pulled in Chiapas from the United Provinces of Central America in 1824.

Long oppressed by Spaniards and criollos (Latin Americans of Spanish lineage), the Maya rose in the War of the Castes in 1847, leading to destroyed churches and many massacres. The brimming sense of inequality didn't settle with peace in 1901. As Nafta (the North American Free Trade Agreement) kicked into effect in 1994, the mainly Maya Zapatistas stormed San Cristóbal de Las Casas; their struggle has quietened in recent years, now that they run seven autonomous zones (called *caricoles*, or snails) outside San Cristóbal. But it's not over.

TRANSPORTATION

GETTING THERE & AWAY

Air

Cancún's international airport is the major entry point to the region, with daily direct flights to many US cities as well as US$300 round-trip flights (including visa) to Cuba. Other than a direct flight to Flores (Guatemala), Cancún is less useful for flying into Central or South America, with many southward flights routed through Mexico City, Miami or Dallas. See p41 for details of flights and airlines in Cancún. Cozumel, Mérida and Chetumal have international airports with less frequent services.

Boat & Bus

Mexico borders Guatemala and Belize to the south, and there are an array of border crossings between them.

From the Yucatán, travelers can connect to buses to Belize (or on to Flores, Guatemala) via Chetumal (p56), just north of Corozal, Belize.

From Chiapas, there are three major border crossings to Guatemala. Southeast of Palenque,

---

DEPARTURE TAX

A departure tax equivalent to about US$23 is levied on international flights from Mexico. It's usually included in the price of your ticket, but if it isn't, you must pay in cash during airport check-in.

at Frontera Corozal, it's possible to boat over to Bethel and get a bus; tour packages ease the uncertainties of this journey (p61). South of San Cristóbal de Las Casas, the best way into Guatemala is at Ciudad Cuauhtémoc, near La Mesilla, Guatemala (p69). Another option is crossing into Guatemala from the Mexican border town of Tapachula, further southwest.

GETTING AROUND
Air
The most 'tempting' regional flight is Cancún–Tuxtla Gutiérrez (near San Cristóbal de Las Casas) for a whopping US$280 one way via Mexico City, which saves you the possibility of an overnight bus to Chiapas.

All domestic flights get two taxes tacked on: a 15% consumer tax and a US$8.50 airport tax.

Boat
Ferry services connect Cancún with Isla Mujeres and Playa del Carmen with Cozumel. Ferries also go to Isla Holbox from north of Cancún. Most visitors to Yaxchilán go by boat.

Bus
Mexico's bus system is luxurious, with frequent services, compared to much of Central America's; many buses have air-con, toilets, reserved seating and movies. And you pay for it – prices have gone up by 25% in the past few years, so brace yourself to pay US$50 to get from Cancún to Palenque.

Buses in the Yucatán rarely fill, but try to reserve ahead for night buses between the Yucatán and Chiapas. You can book some 1st-class buses through **Ticket Bus** (in Mexico ☎ 1800 702 8000; www.ticketbus.com.mx).

In some cases 2nd-class buses are 15% to 20% cheaper, and many are almost as nice as 1st-class. Price ranges in this chapter include 2nd-class buses, and 1st-class and 'deluxe' services such as UNO. There are many bus companies; shop around for the one that suits you.

Note: there have been occasional highway robberies on overnight buses over the years. You can store bags in the secure luggage hold.

Car & Motorcycle
To rent a car or scooter you'll need to show a valid driver's license (your country's license is OK) and a major credit card.

Colectivo
Many locals prefer piling into suburban vans or VW colectivos (shared taxis or minibuses), which travel on shorter routes. They cost about the same as a 2nd-class bus but colectivos go frequently.

THE YUCATÁN

Those who say there's no street cred or authenticity in the Yucatán haven't spent much time away from the Playa del Carmen and Cancún ped malls with 'one tequila, two tequila, three tequila…floor' T-shirt shops. Stretching like a giant, flat limestone thumb between the turquoise Caribbean and murky Gulf of Mexico, the broad Yucatán overflows with local culture.

Yucatán state has Mexico's highest concentration of indigenous people (about 60%). Inland and steamy Mérida is a lively colonial-era city built with stones from Maya pyramids; its weekend-long party is worth shifting your itinerary to experience. Maya ruins, such as Tulum and Chichén Itzá, get most visitors, while early-morning arrivals at Cobá or Dzibichaltún often get the pyramids to themselves. Beach-wise, you can find expanses of sand to yourself in Reserva de la Bíosfera Sian Ka'an, south of Tulum, which is still one of the area's most backpacker-oriented laid-back bases.

CANCÚN
☎ 998 / pop 700,000
Overdeveloped, inauthentic, expensive and (other than the beaches) rather ugly: it's easy to not like Cancún. Built for mass tourism – very successfully – in the 1970s, Cancún certainly doesn't lack for white-sand beachfront on the blissfully turquoise Caribbean. It's fine to stop here for a day – though Isla Mujeres offshore is a more relaxed base – plus its center has its moments.

Enduring Cancún means following the locals: stay and eat in town, take the local bus out with packed lunch to hop onto the resorts' beaches, and return for drinks in town.

Orientation
Cancún's Zona Hotelera, home to the resorts and beaches, is set along Blvd Kukulcán, which curves around a curved sandy spit (actually an island). Ciudad Cancún, just west,

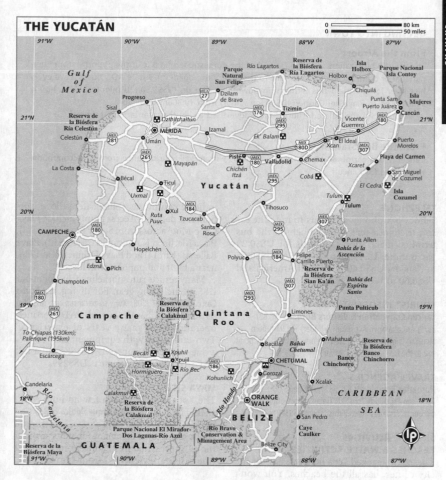

THE YUCATÁN

is home to *el centro* (downtown), on and around Av Tulum between the bus station and Av Cobá. The airport is 16km south of downtown. All sites are in downtown unless otherwise specified.

Information
EMERGENCY
Call ☎ 060.

IMMIGRATION
Immigration office (☎ 884 1655; Av Náder 1 at Av Uxmal; ☺ 9am-1pm Mon-Fri)

INTERNET ACCESS
Internet cafés downtown range from US$0.90 to $1.20 per hour.

La Taberna Ciberb@r (Av Yaxchilán 23; ☒) Restaurant-bar with internet area and wi-fi.

MEDICAL SERVICES
Centro de IMSS Hospital (☎ 884 1108; Av Cobá; ☺ 24hr)
Hospital Americano (☎ 884 6133; Viento 15 at Av Tulum; ☺ 24hr) English-speaking doctors, south of downtown.

MONEY
There are several banks with ATMs on Av Tulum, between Avs Cobá and Uxmal, as well as at the airport.

POST
Post Office (cnr Avs Xel-Há & Sunyaxchén) Located west of downtown.

GETTING INTO TOWN

From the Airport

The 'shuttle bus station' is at the far end of the domestic terminal (exit the airport – from international or domestic – and walk right to the end of the building), where ADO buses leave every half hour for the main bus terminal in downtown Cancún (US$3.50, 20 minutes). Also, hourly shuttles go to Playa del Carmen (US$8, one hour) from 10:30am to 8:45pm.

Don't fall for the inflated 'shuttle' rates advertised inside the international terminal.

From the Bus Station

Cancún's **bus terminal** (cnr Avs Uxmal & Tulum) is within walkable distance from all accommodations listed for Cancún.

TELEPHONE

Telmex pay phones are easily found. The *caseta teléfonica* (call station) behind the bus terminal makes domestic calls for US$0.20 per minute, US$0.15 to the USA, US$0.25 to Canada, US$0.40 to Central America and US$0.60 to Western Europe.

TOURIST INFORMATION

Cancún Convention & Visitors Bureau (☎ 887 3379; Av Cobá btwn Avs Tulum & Náder; 🕑 9am-6pm Mon-Fri) English-speaking staff are nice, but will only point you to the free glossy *Map @migo*.

TRAVEL AGENCIES

Nómadas Travel (☎ 892 2320; Av Cobá 5; 🕑 10am-7pm Mon-Fri, 10am-2pm Sat) Travel agency offers student discounts, arranges Cuba flights (about US$300 return).

Sights & Activities

BEACHES & WATER ACTIVITIES

The resort-packed **Zona Hotelera**, east of the city center, has all the beaches. You won't find any solitude, but the water is gorgeous. By Mexican law, you can plop yourself in front of any luxury hotel for the day (all nonmilitary beachfront is for public use). The only catch is getting to them. About a dozen blue-and-white *'Acesso a playa'* signs on the main road mark legal access points. Or you can discreetly walk through a hotel lobby to the beach.

From downtown, frequent buses head out along Blvd Kukulcán to the zone. Up to Km 9 you pass along shallower and calmer beaches facing north (and Isla Mujeres). The better ones begin at Playa Tortugas (Km 6) and Playa Caracol (Km 8.5), near Punta Cancún, where the boulevard curves southward for 13km. The undertow can be dangerous along this long east-facing stretch – watch for flags that indicate conditions (blue: safe; yellow: caution; red: danger). Access points include Playa Chac-Mool across from Señor Frog's (Km 9.8), Playa Marlín at Kukulcán Plaza (Km 12), Playa Ballenas (Km 14) and Playa Delfines (Km 17.5), near a bluff and popular with locals.

Many resorts run snorkeling trips for about US$30, including gear. For diving, try **Scuba Cancún** (☎ 849 7508; www.scubacancun.com.mx; Blvd Kukulcán Km 5), a family-owned, PADI-certified operation with many years of experience. Two-tank dives with equipment cost US$68, a one-day resort course is US$88, and a full PADI-certification course is US$299.

MAYA SITES

The Zona Hotelera has a few ho-hum Maya sites. The biggest, **Zona Arqueológica El Rey** (Blvd Kukulcán Km 18.5; admission US$3; 🕑 8am-5pm) is more about seeing the 500 iguanas that live around the 47 short structures dating from AD 1200 (the best lizard viewing is from 1pm to 2pm).

DOWNTOWN

That downtown's hidden-away central **Parque las Palapas**, west of Av Tulum via the pedestrian Tulipanes streets, is fading a little doesn't take away from its many cult fans or local adoration. Head over in the evening to see what events or bands are set up and grab tacos for cheap. Nearby Tulipanes has some nightlife too.

Several blocks west, **Mercado 28** is a bustling little market with cheap food, *artesanías* (handicrafts) and black-magic shops.

Courses

El Bosque del Caribe (☎ 884 1065; www.cancun-language.com.mx; Av Náder 52) offers Spanish-language courses in groups; a 15-hour week costs US$135.

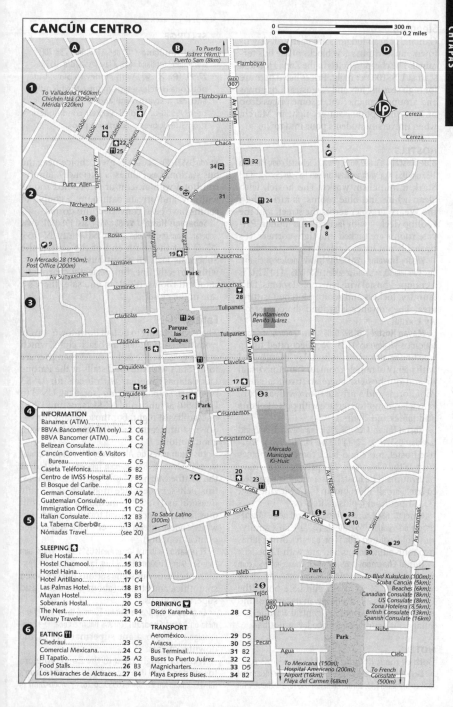

CANCÚN CENTRO

0 — 300 m
0 — 0.2 miles

To Puerto
Juárez (4km);
Puerto Sam (8km)

To Valladolid (160km);
Chichén Itzá (205km);
Mérida (320km)

Flamboyán
Flamboyán
Chaca
Chaca

Punta Allen
Nicchehabi
Rosas
Rosas

To Mercado 28 (150m);
Post Office (200m)

Av Sunyaxchén
Jazmines
Jazmines
Gladiolas
Gladiolas
Orquídeas
Orquídeas

Av Yaxchilán
Roble
Roble
Palmera
Palmera
Laurel
Laurel
Margaritas
Margaritas
Alcatraces
Alcatraces

Av Tulum
Pino
Lima

Av Uxmal
Azucenas
Azucenas
Tulipanes
Tulipanes
Claveles
Claveles
Crisantemos
Crisantemos

Park
Park
Park

Parque
las
Palapas

Ayuntamiento
Benito Juárez

Av Nader
Av Tulum

Mercado
Municipal
Ki-Huic

Av Cobá
Av Cobá

Av Xcaret
Av Tulum

Jaleb
Tejón
Tejón
Lluvia
Lluvia
Agua
Pecan

Brisa
Nube
Nube
Cielo
Sierra
Nube
Av Bonampak

Cereza
Cereza

To Blvd Kukulcán (100m);
Scuba Cancún (5km);
Beaches (6km);
Canadian Consulate (8km);
US Consulate (8km);
Zona Hotelera (8.5km);
British Consulate (13km);
Spanish Consulate (16km)

To Sabor Latino
(300m)

To Mexicana (150m);
Hospital Americano (200m);
Airport (16km);
Playa del Carmen (68km)

To French
Consulate
(500m)

MEX 307
MEX 307

INFORMATION
Banamex (ATM)	1	C3
BBVA Bancomer (ATM only)	2	C6
BBVA Bancomer (ATM)	3	C4
Belizean Consulate	4	C2
Cancún Convention & Visitors Bureau	5	C5
Caseta Telefónica	6	B2
Centro de IMSS Hospital	7	B5
El Bosque del Caribe	8	C2
German Consulate	9	A2
Guatemalan Consulate	10	D5
Immigration Office	11	C2
Italian Consulate	12	B3
La Taberna Ciberb@r	13	A2
Nómadas Travel	(see 20)	

SLEEPING
Blue Hostal	14	A1
Hostel Chacmool	15	B3
Hostel Haina	16	B4
Hotel Antillano	17	C4
Las Palmas Hotel	18	B1
Mayan Hostel	19	B3
Soberanis Hostal	20	C5
The Nest	21	B4
Weary Traveler	22	A2

EATING
Chedraui	23	C5
Comercial Mexicana	24	C2
El Tapatio	25	A2
Food Stalls	26	B3
Los Huaraches de Alctraces	27	B4

DRINKING
Disco Karamba	28	C3

TRANSPORT
Aeroméxico	29	D5
Aviacsa	30	D5
Bus Terminal	31	B2
Buses to Puerto Juárez	32	C2
Magncharters	33	D5
Playa Express Buses	34	B2

Sleeping

Cancún's cheap lodgings are nearly all downtown, most within a few blocks of the bus terminal. The cheapest hotels in the Zona Hotelera start at US$100 per night. Prices listed here are for high season (July and August, at Christmas and around Semana Santa); some prices drop off-season. Options can get tight in March, when university students pour into town.

HOSTELS

Blue Hostal (☎ 892 4673; www.bluehostal.com; Palmera 1-3; dm US$10, r with/without air con US$30/25; 🔀 💻) Stark minimalism works. The hostel, with clean white and blue rooms, is airier than the Weary Traveler across the street, and the rooftop deck – with Jacuzzi! – is louder. Private rooms are tucked into tight corners. It's probably not for early sleepers.

Weary Traveler (☎ 887 0191; www.mexicohostels.com.mx; Palmera 30; dm/r incl breakfast US$10/35; 💻) This is a cramped hostel with fan-cooled rooms, DIY laundry, lockers and rooftop kitchen–sitting area. The entrance is around the corner on Av Uxmal.

Mayan Hostel (☎ 892 0103; www.cancunhostel.com; Margaritas 17; dm/r US$11/35; 🔀) Decorated like a tree house, this pleasant hostel is friendly and with plenty of ramble room for Cancún's usual in-and-out hostels. There are two thatched-roof dorms and a private room with air-con, plus a large rooftop terrace with potted plants and tables and chairs.

Hostal Haina (☎ 898 2081; Orquideas 13; dm/r incl breakfast US$11/39; 🔀 💻) The Haina is an inn-like hostel, more laid-back than party places such as the Chacmool. The private rooms have bathrooms. The hostel has a nice little garden in back, small TV room up front with internet (US$1 per hour), plus a kitchen.

Nest (☎ 884 8967; www.hostalalcatraces.com; 49 Alcatraces; dm incl breakfast US$11.50-14; 🔀 💻) This family-run, gold-colored villa is on a leafy corner; it has two four-bunk dorms and one with 12 beds.

Hostal Chacmool (☎ 887 5873; www.chacmool.com.mx; Gladiolas 18; dm incl breakfast US$15, r with/without bathroom US$40/35; 🔀 💻) Boxy and bare-bone, the Chacmool has lots of energy on its terrace (and funk bands), overlooking central Parque Las Palapas. It's a little overpriced, but not bad.

HOTELS

Both of the following have dorm rooms too.

Las Palmas Hotel (☎ 884 2513; hotelpalmascancun@hotmail.com; Palmera 43; dm incl breakfast US$10, d without/with air-con US$25/30; 🔀 💻) A great choice near the bus station, Las Palmas is a friendly, family-run hotel with air-con or fan-cooled rooms with TV and private bathroom; a couple of rooms have been converted into dorms.

Soberanis Hostal (☎ 884 4564, 800 101 0101; www.soberanis.com.mx; Av Cobá 5; dm/d incl breakfast US$12/55; 🔀 💻) At the south end of the center, the Soberanis feels all about business at times, with perfectly fine, but perfectly charmless, standard rooms. It's clean and safe (there's a safe in the closet).

Eating

There's fun eating to be had downtown – away from the Zona Hotelara's beach clubs, which are more geared to sell T-shirts than prepare food. Start with the food stalls at the Parque Las Palapas, popular with locals for US$3 breakfasts, *comida corrida* (set meal; US$3 to US$3.50) at lunch and US$1 tacos and US$2 quesadillas at night. For those itching for sit-down stuff, nearby Av Yaxchilán is lined with good options.

Los Huaraches de Alcatraces (Alcatraces 31; huaraches US$2.80; 🕒 8:30am-6pm Tue-Sun) Located at the southeastern end of Parque Las Palapas, this self-service place makes ready-made quesadillas (US$2) – including mushroom ones, and *huaraches* (oval tortillas covered in white cheese, green-pepper sauce and choice of meat topping).

El Tapatío (Av Uxmal 30; set meals US$5.50; 🕒 8am-1am Mon-Sat, 9am-11:30pm Sun) This Jalisco-styled restaurant churns out some serious pitcher-sized smoothies and shakes (about US$2.50), and superb set meals.

Comercial Mexicana (cnr Avs Tulum & Uxmal; 🕒 7am-midnight) and **Chedraui** (cnr Avs Tulum & Cobá; 🕒 7am-midnight) are two giant supermarkets in the downtown area.

It can be tough to eat in the Zona Hotelera for under US$10. Places such as **Señor Frog's** (Blvd Kukulcán Km 9.8; dishes US$9.50-26; 🕒 noon-2am) is to Mexican cuisine what the Hard Rock Café is to Jimi Hendrix.

Drinking & Nightlife
DISCOS
Discos are generally mellower downtown. In addition to the following, Av Yaxchilán is a good place to find alcohol or mystic rhythms. Many clubs at the Zona Hotelera are loud, booze-oriented places where MCs urge women to display body parts and often charge around US$10 or US$15 for admission (including a drink). Most clubs don't open until 10pm and pep up around midnight. Some options include the following:

City Beach Club (☎ 883 2452; Blvd Kukulcán Km 9) Popular disco on the beach.

Dady'O (☎ 800 234 9797; Blvd Kukulcán Km 9) Five levels of dancing with a fake cave and laser beams.

Hostal Chacmool Terraza (cnr Alcatraces & Gladiolas) The downtown hostel's terrace hosts funk shows, and is a pretty good spot to sit and sip.

Sabor Latino (☎ 892 1916; cnr Avs Xcaret & Tankah; ✆ closed Sun-Tue in low season) Long live salsa, and other tropical styles, in this lively spot southwest of downtown.

GAY & LESBIAN VENUES
The sizable gay scene awakes only well after sunset. Lesbian couples often frequent clubs including the downtown **Disco Karamba** (☎ 884 0032; cnr Azucenas & Av Tulum), above Ristorante Casa Italiana. The Karamba has live music and cheap drinks.

Getting There & Away
AIR
Cancún's **international airport** (☎ 848 7200) is busy, with many direct international flights coming in daily. There's an ATM in the arrival hall.

Aviacsa flies via Mexico City to Tuxtla Gutierrez, near San Cristóbal de Las Casas in Chiapas, for about US$280 one way. Flights to Mexico City, on Aviacsa or Magnicharters, are about US$160 one way. Aviacsa also flies to Flores (US$199 one way) and on to Guatemala City.

Aerocaribe and Cubana have daily flights to Havana, Cuba (US$300 return).

US discount airline **Jet Blue** (www.jetblue.com) connects Cancún with New York City and Boston. One of several Mexican discount airlines is **VivaAerobus** (www.vivaaerobus.com) with cheap one-ways to Monterrey.

The following airlines are represented in Cancún:

Aeroméxico (☎ 886 0003; Av Cobá 80)
American Airlines (☎ 886 0163; Airport)
Aviacsa (☎ 887 4211; www.aviacsa.com; Av Cobá 37)
Continental (☎ 886 0040; Airport)
Copa (☎ 886 0652; Airport)
Cubana (☎ 886 0192; Airport)
Delta (☎ 800 123 4710, 886 0367; Airport)
Grupo Taca (☎ 887 4110; Airport)
Magnicharters (☎ 884 0600; Av Náder 94)
Mexicana (☎ 886 0068; Av Tulum 269) South of the center.
Northwest (☎ 886 0646; Airport)
United (☎ 800 003 0777; Airport)

BOAT
See p43 for information on ferries to Isla Mujeres.

BUS
Cancún's modern **bus terminal** (☎ 884 5542; cnr Avs Uxmal & Tulum) is within walking distance of all downtown hotels. You can leave small/big bags with an attendant upstairs for US$0.40/0.80 per hour.

Following are some of the major routes serviced daily:

Chetumal US$17-21; 6hr; many buses
Chichén Itzá US$14; 3hr; hourly (cheaper 2nd-class buses take 4½hr)
Chiquila (en route for Isla Holbox) US$7; 3½hr; at 7:50am, 12:40pm, 1:45pm daily
Mérida US$19-25; 4-6hr; many buses
Mexico City (TAPO or Terminal Norte) US$106-125; 22-24hr; 4 per day
Palenque US$49-57; 13hr; 5 per day 2:15-8:30pm
Playa del Carmen US$3.40-4.80; 1hr; buses every 10min; many Playa Express & Mayab buses. (For service from the airport, see p38.)
San Cristóbal de Las Casas US$72; 17-18hr; 4 per day
Tulum US$5.40; 2½hr; many buses
Valladolid US$7.80-11; 2-3hr; many buses

Across from the bus terminal, a few doors from Av Tulum, is the mini **Playa Express terminal** (Pino), where air-conditioned buses leave regularly for Playa del Carmen (US$3.20) from 4am to 10pm.

Getting Around
Shuttles to the Cancún airport leave from the bus terminal every 20 to 40 minutes from 4:30am to 11:30pm. To reach the Zona Hotelera from downtown, catch any bus marked

---

EXPLORE MORE AROUND CANCÚN

In the eternal hunt for paradise in the white sand, here are a couple other options, reached from Cancún:

- The water up on the Gulf of Mexico is murkier, but many swear by sticking off the radar. On **Isla Holbox** there are no hostels, but there are US$25 beach houses. Buses from Cancún go to the ferry at Chiquila three times daily.

- Just 33km south of Cancún is the laid-back fishing village of **Puerto Morelos** with midrange accommodations and far fewer tourists.

'R1,' 'R2,' 'Hoteles' or 'Zona Hotelera' as it travels along Av Tulum toward Av Cobá, then eastward on Av Cobá. The one-way fare is US$0.65.

See opposite for information on reaching Puerto Juárez for the ferry service to Isla Mujeres.

Cancún's taxis do not have meters. Fares are supposedly set (a ride to Blvd Kukulcán Km 4 is US$9, to Km 8 is US$11; around downtown is about US$2.50), but agree on a price before getting in.

If you're thinking of renting a car, check the big guys (Avis, Dollar, Hertz, Alamo) online; web reservations for the following day are often cheaper than what you'll find in an office. If you must rent locally, it's about US$15 per day cheaper at Playa del Carmen.

ISLA MUJERES
☎ 998 / pop 13,500

Cynics say Mujeres' sun has set, but the wee 12km-long island– a long-time backpacker base – is still the saving grace for Cancún's over-developed beachfronts and high-end resorts. True, many day-trippers pour off the 25-minute boats for a day of beach, two-for-one beer specials and a snorkel trip. Wait till dark – when they leave – and the north-end town comes more to life, with locals chatting in front of wooden Caribbean-style homes and pedestrian strip Hidalgo braces itself for an evening of drinks and music.

How the 'Island of Women' got its name is debated: some say pirates kept their ladies here, others link it to the conquistadors' discovery of clay figurines of Ixchel (the Maya goddess of moon and fertility), one of which was found at the small ruin on the island's south end.

In October 2005, Hurricane Wilma hit Isla Mujeres hard, but the island got back on its feet quickly. Said a local expat, 'We knew it was coming and got ready. The day after we were all up and cleaning the streets.' Most businesses have reopened.

Orientation & Information

All ferries arrive at the north end of Isla Mujeres in the heart of the compact town, which is made up of a simple grid system. It's easy to find what you need. Av Rueda Medina lies parallel to water and loops around the island. Parallel to and inland from Av Rueda Medina is Calles Juárez, then ped-strip Hidalgo and Guerrero just north.

Addresses on the island rarely use house numbers.

Beat (Guerrero btwn Morelos & Madero; per hr US$1.50) Internet access.

Cosmic Cosas (cnr Guerrero & Matamoros) Used books store in Mañanas restaurant.

HSBC (Av Rueda Medina) ATM across from the ferry dock.

Immigration office (☎ 877 0189; Av Rueda Medina btwn Morelos & Madero; ☺ closed Sun)

Medical Center (Guerrero btwn Morelos & Madero)

Tourist office (☎ 877 0703; www.isla-mujeres-mexico .com; Av Rueda Medina btwn Morelos & Madero; ☺ Mon-Fri) Grab the free island map.

Sights

If you want a break from the water, bus or bike to the **Isla Mujeres Tortugranja** (☎ 877 0595; Carr Sac Bajo Km 5; admission US$3.20; ☺ 9am-5pm), south of town. The turtle farm has pools and protected shores for turtles and their eggs. You'll see several hundred sea turtles ranging from palm-sized to 300kg giants. From the bus stop, follow the sign to the right.

The dramatic **Punta Sur** (admission US$5.40), at the southern tip of the island (8km from town), is lovely but has been tackified with cartoonish figures put alongside a severely worn Maya ruin.

Activities

BEACHES & SWIMMING

The best swimming on the island is conveniently located in town at **Playa Norte** (North Beach; northwest if you want to get technical). The water is clear, calm and shallow – you can walk out a long way without getting your sombrero wet. Several beach bar-restaurants let you sit in their chairs if you buy food or drink. 'Two-fer' beer specials are US$2.50.

About 7km south of town, skip the touristy nature park of **Playa Garrafón** and opt for its northerly neighbor **Hotel Garrafón de Castilla** (☎ 877 0107; admission US$4; ✆ 9am-5pm). It has a roped-off swimming area with clear water and colorful fish. Snorkel gear is US$7. Taxis from town cost US$4.40.

DIVING & SNORKELING

Good reef and shark-cave dives are near the island – the best just to the southwest. El Frío (or Ultrafreeze) is a popular nonreef dive to a sunken boat in unusually cool water. Snorkelers should make sure their trips get to Manchones reef (best in the morning), and not just the reefs near the ferry docks. Renting snorkel gear is about US$10.

The following dive shops are among the many:

Cruise Divers (☎ 877 1190; Av Rueda Medina btwn Abasolo & Matamoros) Snorkel trips to Manchones are US$20 per person, one-/two-tank dives are US$45/55.

Sea Hawk Divers (☎ 877 1233; abarran@prodigy.net.mx; Carlos Lazo, north of Guerrero btwn Matamoros & López Mateos) Snorkel tours US$25, one-/two-tank dives US$35/50, PADI-certification course US$320.

The **Fishermen's Cooperative Booth** (Av Rueda Medina at Madero), near the dock, offers three-hour snorkel tours. Some visitors love it, but we've received a couple of complaints from women about harassment from some guides.

Sleeping

Between mid-December and March, many places are booked by midday. If planning to linger longer, watch for 'rooms for rent' signs.

Poc-Na Hostel (☎ 877 0090; www.pocna.com, info@pocna.com; cnr Matamoros & Carlos Lazo; campsites per person US$6, dm US$9-10, r US$24-32; ✖ ▯) The Yucatán's best beach-side hostel (there are only a couple of candidates) occupies an almost Cubist-style complex on its own big beach – on a slightly rougher north coast – the sand-floor courtyard and central *palapa*-topped (palm–leafed

roof) restaurant is a great hangout area. Staff rent bikes and serve drinks and meals. There are coed and women's dorms, plus a camping area. Reserve by email only.

Urban Hostel (☎ 202 4367; cnr Hidalgo & Matamoros; dm/r US$10/20) The Urban, a back-up hostel on the ped crawl, is a bit of a fan-cooled sweatbox room-wise, but lovingly run and has a bonus roof deck. The owners are pondering a 'hammock hotel' up top.

Hotel Carmelina (☎ 877 0006; Guerrero btwn Madero & Abasolo; s/d US$27/37) Family run, it's a motor hotel–style spot with purple-and-white scheme and some knick-knacks on the walls of the 29 clean, fan-cooled rooms.

Hotel Marcianito (☎ 877 0111; Abasolo btwn Juárez & Hidalgo; r US$35) The Marcianito is a simple hotel with clean, but small, rooms half a block from the ped strip. Upstairs front rooms get cross ventilation.

Eating

The ped mall Hidalgo reigns as the eating ghetto of Mujeres, with many open-air (and loud-late) restaurants to choose from.

El Paisano (Juárez btwn Abasolo & Matamoros) Get local in the heart of town. Blue-painted floor and murals overlook the fresh *tortas* (US$2) and fish tacos (US$3.60 for three).

Mercado municipal (Guerrero btwn Matamoros & López Mateos; set breakfasts/meals US$2.50/4.50) Four covered stalls in this small market have nice sit-down tables for good value meals.

Mañana (cnr Matamoros & Guerrero; dishes US$3-8) A colorful, traveler-oriented place with sidewalk stools, and sunburst walls inside, it's a great setting to eat up veggie burgers with fries (US$7) or set breakfasts (from US$3).

Restaurant Velazquez (Av Rueda Medina at Matamoros; seafood US$5-10) A family-run shack restaurant on the sand by the fishing docks, Velazquez churns out tasty filets and ceviche. Fresh red snapper is US$5.

Nightlife

Many restaurants double as bars (and vice versa), particularly along the lively walkway Hidalgo. **La Peña** (Guerrero btwn Bravo & Morelos), overlooking the water from north of the town plaza, is a fun spot with live music.

Getting There & Away

The best way to reach Isla Mujeres is from Puerto Juárez, 4km north of central Cancún, with the most frequent, earliest and latest service to/from the island. Enclosed boats zoom half hourly to the island (US$3.50, 25 minutes) from 5am to 11:30pm, and return to Cancún from 5:30am to midnight.

It's also possible to ferry from Punta Sam, about 4km north of Puerto Juárez; service is less regular. More expensive ferries serve day-trippers from three points in the Zona Hotelera, such as the Embarcadero (Blvd Kukulcán Km 4). Boats go four times daily (one-way/return US$10/15).

From Cancún, you can reach Puerto Juárez (or Punta Sam) by any bus heading north on Av Tulum that displays those destinations or 'Ruta 13' (US$0.40). 'R1' buses marked 'Puerto Juárez' make the trip too (US$0.65). A taxi from the bus terminal to Punta Juárez is about US$3.

Getting Around

Most people get around by bike, moped or – hilariously – four-seat golf carts. Standardized prices at the many rental places are loosely adhered to; bargain. **Ppe's Moto Rent** (☎ 877 0019; Hidalgo btwn Abasolo & Matamoros) is typical, with US$25 mopeds and US$55 golf carts.

Poc-Na Hostel rents bikes for US$10 a day.

A local bus occasionally runs down half of the island – stopping near Tortugranja. Taxis linger at the dock.

VALLODOLID

☎ 985 / pop 38,000

Yucatán's oldest colonial-era city, Vallodolid is a refreshing nod to laid-back, friendly authenticity – plus cheap prices – for those coming from modern beach towns. One-story, hacienda-style Spanish homes and one or two 16th-century churches line cobbled streets that are fun to wander about. Its super hostel makes a good base to explore nearby Chichén Itzá.

Like all good Spanish copycats, it's built on a grid around the central Parque Central, where you'll find ATMs, internet and a tourist information office.

Contact **Linguistic Center Yucatán** (☎ 856 1798; www.playacarguide.com/lcy.htm; Calle 43, No 203A btwn Calles 44 & 42) if you're interested in studying Spanish.

Sights

Cenote Dzitnup (Xkekén; admission US$2; ⏰ 7am-6pm), 7km west, is one of the area's more attractive cenotes, with stalactites dangling over your dip. Taxi out or rent a bike; go west on Calle 39 to the Mérida highway, and watch for the sign. A **bike-rental shop** (Calle 44 btwn Calles 39 & 41; per hr US$0.70; ⏰ 9am-8pm Mon-Sat, 9am-1pm Sun) is a block west of Parque Central.

It's possible to take a colectivo (about US$25 return) or taxi (US$35) to **Ek-Balam** ruins, about 25km north, where you can rappel into a cenote for US$10.

Sleeping & Eating

La Candelaria (☎ 856 2267; candelaria_hostel@hotmail .com; Calle 35 No 201F, at Calle 44; dm with/without HI card US$8/8.80, r from US$18/19.50) Converted from an old nunnery, the wonderful Candelaria has a remarkable well-groomed garden with half-covered kitchen. From the bus station, walk east on Calle 39, then left on Calle 44.

Hotel Zaci (☎ 856 2167; www.hotelzaci.com; Calle 44, No 191; r from US$25; ❌ ❌) The Zaci is a friendly, colonial-style hotel, with a nice pool.

The cheap-and-tasty food at **Bazar Municipal** (Plaza Grande, cnr Calles 39 & 40; set meals US$2.50; ⏰ 7am-10pm) is made by neighboring stalls, all sharing nice tables overlooking the plaza.

Getting There & Away

The main **bus station** (cnr Calles 39 & 46) is two blocks west of the plaza. Frequent buses go to Cancún (US$7.40 to US$11, two hours), Mérida (US$7.40 to US$11, two hours) and Chichén Itzá (US$2 to US$3.60, 45 minutes).

Just outside the station, on Calle 46, are colectivos that regularly go to Pisté (US$2), near Chichén Itzá (sometimes continuing to the ruins).

CHICHÉN ITZÁ

If carvings of decapitated skulls and heart-eating eagles, or body-filled cenotes and nine-level pyramids, don't satisfy you, then come for the acoustics of a Pink Floyd show, as regular clapping echoes attest. Chichén Itzá is one of Mexico's most famed archaeological sights.

The temples were closed for climbing in 2006 (after a woman fell to her death).

The **site** (admission US$9.50, night show US$3; ⏰ 8am-5 or 6pm, night show 7pm winter, 8pm summer), 41km west of Valladolid, was a modest late-Classic town before war-torn Toltecs from Tula, in central Mexico, conquered it in AD 987. An unlikely harmony followed, with experienced Maya architects masterfully adhering to the imagery of the Toltec feathered-serpent cult of Quetzalcóatl (Kukulcán in Maya).

The city was abandoned around 1224.

YUCATÁN'S BEST MAYA SITES

For Architecture

- Chichén Itzá (opposite)
- Uxmal (p48)

For Views

- Toniná (p62)
- Cobá (p55)
- Chinkultic (p70)

For Overall 'Experience'

- Palenque (p57)
- Yaxchilán (p62)

Exploring the Site

About 100m beyond the gate, you'll enter the Great Plaza. In the middle, the imposing **El Castillo** (The Castle) pyramid is designed to represent the Maya calendar in stone and is famous for the moving serpent illusion on its staircase, visible during the spring and autumn equinoxes. Inside the pyramid is a pre-Toltec pyramid with a red jaguar throne, reached by a sweat-box chamber – now closed.

Just northeast (back to the left as you enter the plaza) is Gran Juego de Pelota, the biggest **ball court** in Mesoamerica. The acoustics are terrific: try chatting with a friend on opposite sides.

Across the plaza from El Castillo is a 300m path north to **Cenote Sagrado** (Sacred Cenote), where some 50 skeletons have been found.

Back in the plaza, on the eastern end, stands the impressive **Templo de los Guerreros**, with a *chacmool* (Maya sacrificial stone) looking over the warrior-carved columns. Behind is the shady **Grupo de las Mil Columnas** (Group of the Thousand Columns). Beyond, a path leads through the forest past the **Mercado**, with a sunken courtyard rimmed by columns and a lone palm out of step.

The path leads past a replica of a traditional home, then another goes a few hundred meters south to the unusual **Caracol** (Snail), once used as an observatory (and a rare building you can climb). Just beyond is the **Edificio de las Monjas** (Nunnery).

Your entrance fee allows you to return to see the nightly **light-and-sound show**.

Getting There & Away

Direct 'Chichén Itzá' buses stop at the ruins' parking lot (at the western entrance); the gift store sells tickets to Vallodolid (US$2 to US$3.60, frequent), Cancún (US$9.40 to US$14.20) Mérida (US$5.40 to US$8), Playa del Carmen (US$18, two afternoon buses) and Tulum (US$10.40, one afternoon bus). The site has a luggage-storage room if you're in transit. No buses leave here after 5pm. After this time, walk or taxi to the Piste town, 2.5km west, where later buses and colectivos stop and go.

MÉRIDA

☎ 999 / pop 793,000

Not on the beach and not caring, Mérida is the Yucatán's most Mexican town – with Conquest-era buildings made from Maya pyramids and a weekend fair of all-day dancing, music and open-air tacos that makes 'festive' a too-small word. It's a great place to make day trips – to superb Maya ruins (such as Uxmal), cenotes, flamingo reserves and, yes, beaches.

Founded by Francisco de Montejo the Younger in 1540, Mérida was built atop the Maya town of T'hó.

Orientation & Information

Mérida's sequentially numbered grid makes finding your away easy. Even-numbered streets run north-south; odd-numbered streets run east-west. The Plaza Grande – between Calles 60 and 62, and 63 and 61 – is a 10-minute walk north from the few bus stations.

Banks and ATMs are easy to find in the center. **Cibercafé Santa Lucía** (cnr Calles 55 & 62; per hr US$1.20; ☼ 8am-1am) can also help with calls to the USA/elsewhere (US$0.40/0.50 a minute).

You'll find several travel agencies along Calles 60 and 62, north of the plaza. Best is Nómadas Travel (at Nómadas Hostel), which offers student discounts, arranges cenote tours and has great handouts on DIY day trips.

There are a few information centers in town; drop by the **City Tourist Office** (☎ 924 0000 ext 80119; Calle 62, Palacio Municipal; ☼ 8am-8pm Mon-Sat, 8am-noon Sun) for its 9:30am walking tour (Monday to Saturday).

Sights

Try to be in Mérida for the all-day fair every Saturday and Sunday. For sights near to Mérida, see the boxed text, p48.

MEXICO'S YUCATÁN & CHIAPAS

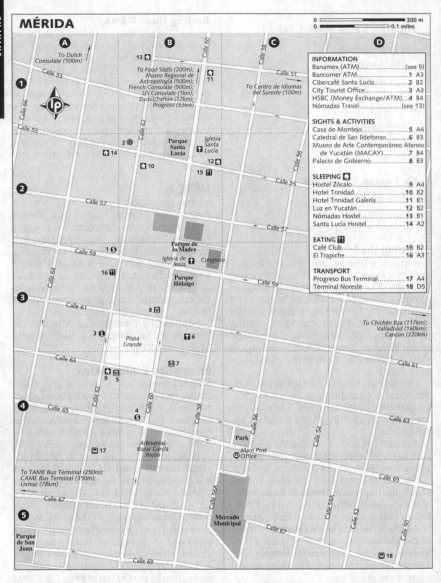

MÉRIDA

0 ————— 200 m
0 ————— 0.1 miles

INFORMATION
Banamex (ATM)..........................(see 5)
Bancomer ATM...............................1 A3
Cibercafé Santa Lucía....................2 B2
City Tourist Office..........................3 A3
HSBC (Money Exchange/ATM)......4 B4
Nómadas Travel........................(see 13)

SIGHTS & ACTIVITIES
Casa de Montejo.............................5 A4
Catedral de San Ildefonso...........6 B3
Museo de Arte Contemporáneo Ateneo
  de Yucatán (MACAY)..................7 B4
Palacio de Gobierno.....................8 B3

SLEEPING
Hostel Zócalo..................................9 A4
Hotel Trinidad...............................10 B2
Hotel Trinidad Galería.................11 B1
Luz en Yucatán..............................12 B2
Nómadas Hostel............................13 B1
Santa Lucía Hostel........................14 A2

EATING
Café Club.......................................15 B2
El Trapiche.....................................16 A3

TRANSPORT
Progreso Bus Terminal.................17 A4
Terminal Noreste...........................18 D5

To Dutch Consulate (100m)
Calle 53
To Food Stalls (200m);
Museo Regional de Antropología (500m);
French Consulate (900m);
US Consulate (1km);
Dzibilchaltún (17km);
Progreso (33km)
To Centro de Idiomas del Sureste (100m)
Calle 51
Calle 55
Parque Santa Lucía
Iglesia Santa Lucía
Calle 57
Calle 55
Calle 57
Parque de la Madre
Iglesia de Jesús
Congreso
Calle 59
Parque Hidalgo
Calle 59
Calle 61
Plaza Grande
Calle 61
Calle 63
Calle 65
Calle 63
Park
Main Post Office
Artesanías Bazar García Rejón
To TAME Bus Terminal (250m);
CAME Bus Terminal (350m);
Uxmal (78km)
Calle 67
Mercado Municipal
Parque de San Juan
Calle 69
Calle 67
Calle 65
To Chichén Itzá (117km);
Valladolid (160km);
Cancún (320km)

The **Plaza Grande** (or *zócalo*) is rimmed by Mérida's most historic buildings, most built from disassembled Maya pyramids. Most obvious are the 42m towers of the **Catedral de San Ildefonso** (Mesoamerica's oldest cathedral; 1598) – much of its interior was destroyed during the Mexican Revolution (1910–29). Next door is the worthwhile **Museo de Arte Contemporaneo**

Areneo de Yucatán (Macay; ☎ 928 3191; Calle 60; admission free; ☽ 10am-6pm Wed-Sun), with rooms highlighting local artist Fernando Castro Pacheco.

At the south of the square, you can walk into the courtyard of the home of the founding conquistadors at the **Casa de Montejo** (1549; Calle 63), now a Banamex bank. Also go past the armed guards at the **Palacio del Gobierno** (1892; Calle 61), facing the plaza's northeast corner, to see Pacheco's impressive wall-sized murals upstairs.

Nine blocks north of the plaza, on ritzy Paseo de Montejo, the great **Museo Regional de Antropologia** (cnr Montejo & Calle 43; admission US$3.70; 8am-8pm Tue-Sat, 8am-2pm Sun), in the ornate Palacio Canton, explains why the Maya deformed their children's skulls, and displays jewelry, carvings and artifacts (with English subtitles).

Several blocks south of the plaza, the sprawling **Mercado Municipal** (btwn Calles 56 & 56a, south of Calle 65) is a fascinating area to wander about.

Sleeping

Santa Lucia Hostal (928 9070; www.hostalstalucia .com; Calle 55 No 512; dm US$7.50, r with/without bathroom US$23/20;) The Santa Lucia is one of several nice hostel-in-a-historic building options, coming with a small courtyard, and hey, air-con.

Nómadas Hostel (924 5223; www.nomadastravel.com; Calle 62 No 433; hammock & dm US$8.50, r with/without bathroom US$23/18;) This is a very well-run hostel that keeps quiet after 11pm, with a lovely open courtyard, great travel tips, free salsa lessons and mixed and single-sex dorms. There's plenty of space for a tent or hammock in the back. You get a free toast-and-coffee breakfast.

Hostel Zócalo (930 9562; hostel_zocalo@yahoo .com.mx; Calle 63 No 508; dm/s/d US$9/13/21) Set in a museumlike building next to the Casa de Montejo, the grand 1st-floor hostel has high ceilings, kitchen and free breakfast. All rooms have shared bathrooms.

Hotel Trinidad (923 2033; www.hotelestrinidad .com; Calle 62 No 464; r US$22-45;) Lush courtyards and a sense of fun give this hotel a bump in quality over a hostel. Most rooms have private bathroom, there's a communal kitchen, and guests can use the pool in their nearby **Hotel Trinidad Galería** (923 2463; cnr Calles 51 & 60).

Eating

At Parque Santa Ana, **food stalls** (cnr Calles 60 & 47; 6am-2pm) serve cheap eggs and tacos.

El Trapiche (Calle 62 btwn Calles 59 & 61; sandwiches & mains US$1.80-$4.50) This colorful two-room eatery offers pastas and Yucatecan specialties.

Café Club (Calle 55 No 496; set breakfasts US$3-6; 7am-5pm Mon-Sat) It's a pleasant café that draws locals for coffee and set breakfast deals. A veggie sandwich costs US$1.80.

Getting There & Away

Mérida's bus stations, all south of the plaza, include the following:

> **SPLURGE**
>
> **Luz en Yucatán** (924 0035; www.luzenyuca tan.com; Calle 55 No 499; r US$35-80;   ) Made from a late 16th-century convent behind Santa Lucia Cathedral, the Luz is an inspired 10-room spot with many large, well-furnished colonial-era-meets-modern rooms and a pool in back.

CAME Bus Terminal (Calle 70 btwn Calles 69 & 70) Buses to Cancún (US$21-23.50, four hours, frequent), Chetumal (US$22, six hours, four daily), Mexico City (US$91-107, 22 hours, six daily), Palenque (US$32, nine hours, three or four daily), Playa del Carmen (US$25.40, 5½ hours, eight daily), San Cristóbal de Las Casas (US$41, 13 hours, one daily) and Tulum (US$16.30, four hours, three daily).

Progreso Bus Terminal (Calle 62 btwn Calles 65 & 67) Buses go regularly to Progreso (US$1.30, one hour) and Dzibilchaltún (US$0.70, 45 minutes).

TAME Bus Terminal (cnr Calle 69 & 68) Buses go to Uxmal (US$3.50, 1½ hours, eight daily) and on the Ruta Puuc (US$12 return) at 8am daily.

Terminal Noreste (Calle 67 btwn Calles 52 & 50) Buses to Chichén Itzá (US$5.20-7.20, two hours), Izamal (US$3, 90 minutes) and Valladolid (US$7.60-11.60, two to three hours).

PLAYA DEL CARMEN
 984 / pop 60,000

This long, beachside town is definitely booming. Just over a decade ago, it was a mere out-of-the-way fishing village seen only for its ferry service to Cozumel. Now it keeps a firm grip as the 'Riviera Maya' hub, with direct buses from Cancún airport (68km north) and a cruise-ship stop.

It's easy to enjoy and loathe the pet-iguana souvenir stands along Quinta Av, but the glimmer of nearby turquoise water, white sand and fine open-air restaurants makes it fun for a couple days.

And unlike Cancún, it's more thoughtfully developed – with zoning restrictions keeping new resorts from shooting up a dozen stories.

Orientation & Information

Most visitors arrive at the older (Centro) bus station at the southern end of Quinta Av; its northern reaches are sometimes called 'Little Italy' due to the number of Italians out there. See www.playamayanews.com or www .playainfo.com for information on the region.

Centro del Salud (☎ 873 0493; 15 Av near Av Juárez) Mérida's main hospital.

Cibernet (Calle 8; per hr US$1.50) Internet café near Quinta Av.

Dr Mario Abarca (☎ 804 3433; Av 10 btwn Av Juárez & Calle 2; ⊙ 10am-9pm Mon-Sat) Very nice English-speaking doctor receives calls 24 hours a day.

El Point (10 Av btwn Calles 2 & 4; per hr US$2; ⊙ 8am-2am) Internet access and international calls.

Emergency (☎ 066)

Lavandería Giracaribe (10 Av btwn Calles 12 & 14; ⊙ 8am-9pm Mon-Sat) Drop-off laundry service.

Left luggage (Terminal del Centro, cnr Av Juárez & Quinta Av) Lockers upstairs cost US$5 for 24 hours.

Tourist office (☎ 873 2804; cnr Av Juárez & 15 Av; ⊙ 9am-8pm Mon-Fri, 9am-5pm Sat & Sun) English-speaking staff and brochures, near the post office.

Tourist police kiosks (☎ 873 0291) Main Plaza (cnr Av Juárez & Quinta Av); Calle 14 (Quinta Av & Calle 14)

Sights & Activities
BEACHES

Miles of white-sand beaches stretch out from busy Playa, but finding a spot with elbow room is harder than it used to be. Locals flood the beach on Sunday, the only day the cruise ships aren't at port. Anything near the town center is pretty much packed – the area around the Cozumel ferry isn't crowded with hotels at least. Some like the beach clubs further north, such as **Mamitas** (north of Constituyentes, access via Calle 28), which can be busy, but it's not a bad spot actually, with a broader beach, a good restaurant, thatch umbrellas, lounge chairs (US$2 to use), and a pool. The similar **El Tukan** is next door. Five more minutes' walk north are undeveloped stretches (for the time being) backed by a wire fence.

Topless bathing is permitted. Note that run-and-grab thefts can happen, and there

---

EXPLORE MORE FROM MÉRIDA

Mérida may be inland, but it's near such juicy stuff you can easily spend a week in the area. See p47 for transport details. Ask at Nómadas Travel in Mérida (p45) about cenote tours. The day-long **Ruta Puuc bus** (book at TAME bus station; about US$34 incl entry fees) visits five sights, including Uxmal, the superb Labná, Xlapak, Sayil and Kabah. Stops at most are quick – about 30 minutes – but you get two hours at Uxmal. Avoid weekends when the bus may be packed.

■ The top day out is to **Uxmal** (admission US$9.50; ⊙ 8am-5pm), sprawling Maya ruins that flourished from AD 600–900. It's intricate, *puuc*-style architecture includes many fanciful carvings (such as the ever-present rain god *chac*), plus iguanas as big as bulldogs. There's a sound-and-light show included in the price (8pm summer, 7pm winter). Uxmal can be reached by bus from Mérida several times a day.

■ About 17km north of Mérida, the quieter Maya site of **Dzibilchaltún** (admission US$6.30; ⊙ 9am-5pm) features interesting structures at either end of a 1km-long *sacbé* (road), including 130m-long Estructura 44 facing a 16th-century Spanish chapel in ruins and the squat Templo de las Siete Muñecas (Temple of the Seven Dolls), which glows on the equinoxes. There's also an open-air cenote you can swim in. Ask the bus driver to drop you off by the ruins, where it's a 1km straight walk.

■ The lovely little 'yellow town' of **Izamal**, 90 minutes drive northeast of Mérida, is worth a lazy part of a day to see its (yellow) Convento de San Antonio de Padua (1562) and to climb the region's largest pyramid, the rather overgrown **Kinich-Kamó**, a few blocks north.

■ About 33km north of Mérida, **Progreso** is the go-to, quick-beach-fix for *meridanos*. There's a nice white-sand beach and a 7km wharf to see, but the water ain't the Caribbean and it gets windy in the afternoons. Add flamingos to a beach, and **Celestún** – set in a 591-sq-km nature reserve – makes a fun day trip March to September, when flamingos come in droves. It's tricky to arrange on your own, as a visit requires a US$120 boat ride. Travel agents in Mérida organize trips for about US$40 or US$45.

■ Break up the long Mérida–Palenque journey in the colonial-era city of **Campeche**, which has a nice waterfront, a Maya museum and is near bicycle trips, waterfalls and the Xpujil ruins. The **Monkey Hostel** (☎ 981-811 6500; www.hostalcampeche.com; cnr Calles 10 & 57; dm US$8.50) is good for central dorms.

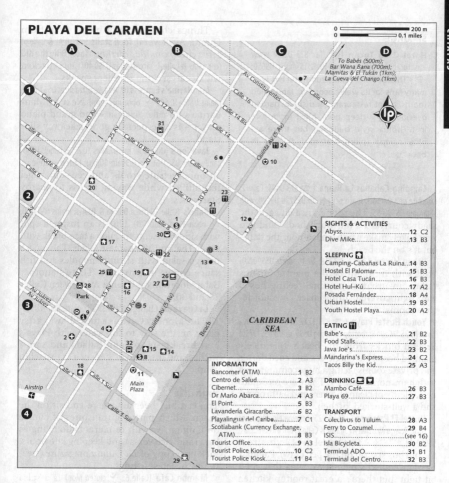

PLAYA DEL CARMEN

SIGHTS & ACTIVITIES
Abyss.....................................12 C2
Dive Mike..............................13 B3

SLEEPING
Camping-Cabañas La Ruina.....14 B3
Hostel El Palomar...................15 B3
Hotel Casa Tucán....................16 B3
Hotel Hul-Kú..........................17 A2
Posada Fernández...................18 A4
Urban Hostel..........................19 B3
Youth Hostel Playa.................20 A2

EATING
Babe's....................................21 B2
Food Stalls.............................22 B3
Java Joe's...............................23 B2
Mandarina's Express...............24 C2
Tacos Billy the Kid..................25 A3

DRINKING
Mambo Café...........................26 B3
Playa 69.................................27 B3

TRANSPORT
Colectivos to Tulum................28 A3
Ferry to Cozumel....................29 B4
ISIS.................................(see 16)
Isla Bicycleta..........................30 B2
Terminal ADO.........................31 B1
Terminal del Centro................32 B3

INFORMATION
Bancomer (ATM).......................1 B2
Centro de Salud........................2 A3
Cibernet...................................3 B2
Dr Mario Abarca.......................4 A3
El Point....................................5 B3
Lavandería Giracaribe...............6 B2
Playalingua del Caribe..............7 C1
Scotiabank (Currency Exchange,
   ATM)....................................8 B3
Tourist Office...........................9 A3
Tourist Police Kiosk.................10 C2
Tourist Police Kiosk.................11 B4

have been reports of sexual assault too. Increased numbers of strolling tourist police have helped cut back incidents.

DIVING & SNORKELING
Mexico's best diving is offshore between Playa and Cozumel. Most serious divers head to Cozumel, though one local diver claims, 'We have more fish' (not necessarily true).

There are several dozen dive operators in town, offering one-/two-tank dives for about US$40/60 and cenote dives from US$100. PADI-certification courses are about US$350.

Reef snorkel tours with snacks and gear run US$20 to US$35; cenote trips are about US$50.

A couple of good shops include **Abyss** (☎ 873 2164; www.abyssdiveshop.com; Calle 12), which has a 90-minute snorkel tour (US$20), and **Dive Mike** (☎ 803 1228; www.divemike.com; Calle 8).

Courses
Playa has a few Spanish-language schools. **Playalingua del Caribe** (☎ 873 3876; www.playalingua .com; Calle 20 btwn Avs 5 & 10) has great facilities (including a swimming pool!); five four-hour days in groups costs US$185.

Sleeping
Playa del Carmen has more than 200 places to stay. High-season rates (listed here) generally run from around mid-December through March.

SPLURGE

Hotel Casa Tucán (☎ /fax 873 0283; www .casatucan.de; Calle 4 btwn 10 & 15 Avs; r US$50; 🔊) This German-Texan–run hotel has won many fans for its well-decorated, fan-cooled rooms, great restaurant, and shady garden overlooking a deep pool. Most rooms are in a 'hotel' style building, but there are nice *palapa* (palm leaf–roofed) huts in back too.

Camping-Cabañas La Ruina (☎ 873 0405; Calle 2; campsite or hammock space per person US$7, d US$20, with bathroom US$30-55) The rooms are a bit aged, the shady courtyard a bit roughshod – and you won't likely make new friends among the staff – but it's on the beach.

Urban Hostel (☎ 803 3378; Av 10; dm/r US$10/20) 'Roll with it' might be the mantra for this rather un-urban communal-feeling hostel with tight covered sitting space and cubicle-style rooms.

Youth Hostel Playa (☎ 803 3277; www.hostelplaya .com; Av 25 & Calle 8; rooftop camping US$5, dm/d US$12/35) Several blocks from the beach, this nicely planned hostel has single-sex and coed dorms and private rooms facing a huge common area with hammocks and TV. There are mosquito nets, plenty of clean showers and bathrooms, and a well-stocked kitchen.

Hostel El Palomar (☎ 803 2606; www.elpalomarhos tel.com; Quinta Av btwn Av Juárez & Calle 2; dm incl breakfast US$12-13, d US$38) A fine hostel right across from the old bus station on the ped crawl, Palomar has fan-cooled single-sex dorms that get a bit tight, but there's a great rooftop kitchen overlooking the water, big lockers and the double rooms are nicely decorated. You can pay US$13 if you prefer to stay in the four-bed dorm.

Posada Fernández (☎ 873 0156; 10 Av near Calle 1; r with fan/air con US$30/40; 🔊) It offers simple, clean private rooms just south of the old bus station.

Hotel Hul-Kú (☎ 873 0021; 20 Av btwn Calles 4 & 6; r US$45; 🔊) Nice rooms and patio nooks overlook a small pool at this hotel.

Eating

Go see what grabs you on Quinta Av. There's a lot: US$2 pizza slices, US$4.50 set breakfasts, US$6 Mexican mains. Some Playa restaurants add a service charge to the bill.

Things change just a block away from Quinta Av. Several **food stalls** (cnr 10 Av & Calle 6) serve cheap *comidas corridas*. **Tacos Billy the Kid** (cnr 15 Av & Calle 4; tacos/tortas US$0.40/1.20) is packed with locals seeking excellent snacks.

Mandarina's Express (Quinta Av; pizza slices US$1.60-2, mains US$5-10.50; 🕐 6pm-midnight) Next to Mandarina's upscale pizzeria – and grand piano player – is an especially good takeaway slice stand.

Java Joe's (Quinta Av btwn Calles 10 & 12; bagels US$3, sandwiches US$4-6; 🕐 6:30am-10pm) Here you can sit on streetside stools and get your bagel fix fulfilled while waving across to nearby Starbuck's.

Babe's (Calle 10 btwn Quinta & 10 Avs; mains US$4-10; 🕐 noon-11pm Mon-Sat) This is an inspired spot with sidewalk seats to enjoy a taco break with super Thai and Vietnamese salads. The superb mango salad with shrimp, noodles and fish sauce comes in two sizes. There's another Babe's location on Quinta Av between Calles 28 and 30.

La Cueva del Chango (Calle 38 off Quinta; mains US$5-12) The 'Monkey Cave' is a tucked-away artsy place on the way to the water with Playa's best breakfasts, organic salads and sandwiches, and inspired dishes such as pistachio soup.

Nightlife

You can buy beer anywhere and sit on the beach. Much partying transpires of course on Quinta Av, with restaurants doubling as bars (and vice versa) and keeping late hours. Pick up a copy of *La Quinta* magazine (free) to see the latest listings.

Mambo Café (Calle 6; 🕐 closed Mon) is a salsa place with salsa classes at 9:30pm (US$8); you'll need the skills once the bands hit the stage.

GAY & LESBIAN VENUES

Playa is the Yucatán's gay hub. There are two clubs, **Playa 69** (Quinta Av btwn Calles 4 & 6; www.gay playadelcarmen.com; 🕐 closed Mon), with a pink-and-black dance floor and dark corners, and **Bar Wana Bana** (Quinta Av btwn Calles 30 & 32).

Getting There & Away

BOAT

Two ferries to Cozumel (US$11, 35 minutes) leave side by side on the hour between 5am and 10pm. EkonoKlass (US$4.50, one hour) makes four trips across in a smaller boat.

BUS

Playa has two bus terminals. The older one (and it looks new), **Terminal del Centro** (cnr Juárez & Quinta Avs), gets all the 2nd-class, Cancún and Tulum action. The newer one, **Terminal ADO** (☎ 803 0950; cnr Av 20 & Calle 12), a 10-minute walk away, connects Playa with Mexico City, Chetumal, Mérida and Chiapas.

Services run as follows:

Cancún US$3.40; 1hr; depart every 10 min

Cancún International Airport US$8; 1hr; hourly from 8am to 6pm

Chetumal US$12-20; 5hr; many buses

Chichén Itzá US$18; 3-4hr; bus at 8am

Mérida US$25; 5hr; 10 per day from ADO

Mexico City US$109; 24hr; 4 per day

Palenque US$45-53; 12-13hr; 4 per day

San Cristóbal de Las Casas US$57-68; 15-19hr; 4 per day

Tulum US$2.20-3.40; 1hr; many buses

Valladolid US$14; 3hr; 5 per day

COLECTIVO

Frequent shared vans head south to Tulum (US$2.50, 45 minutes) from Calle 2 near 20 Av from 5am to 10pm, stopping anywhere along the highway on the way (not bad for cenote-hopping).

Getting Around

ISIS (☎ 879 3111; Hotel Casa Tucán, Calle 4) rents cars from US$44 per day (including tax and insurance).

Isla Bicycleta (☎ 879 4992; www.playadelcarmenbikes .com; Calle 8; ☼ 9am-1pm, 3-6pm) rents good bikes for US$80/12 per half/full-day .

COZUMEL

☎ 987 / pop 90,000

Tear-shaped and a little sad, the 647-sq-km island of Cozumel receives 6.5 million tourists a year, but only one in 30 actually stays the night. Most visitors are docked for the day from cruise ships. Locals are used to these big spenders and touts wander around. But these hurdles can be broken at first plunge (with air tank or snorkel) at the world-famous reefs offshore – better than Playa's, no doubt.

Hurricane Wilma all but closed up Cozumel until the cruise-ship docks reopened in early 2007; the reefs were largely unaffected.

The Maya first settled here around AD 300. Many indigenous rebels fleeing the War of the Castes resettled here in the mid-1800s. After a chewing-gum boom (and bust), tourism became the island's savior, starting after Jacques Cousteau praised its underwater charms in 1961.

Orientation & Information

Ferries from Playa arrive at the Muelle Fiscal, the main dock right in San Miguel de Cozumel, the island's chief town, which sits more than midway up the island's west side. The airport is 2km northeast of town.

Bancomer (Av 5 Norte) Bank and ATM on east side of the plaza.

Cozumel International Clinic (☎ 872 1430; Calle 5 Sur 21-B) Hyperbaric chamber.

Crew Office (Av 5 btwn Calles Dr Adolfo Salas & 3 Sur; ☼ 10am-10pm) Internet access and telephone service.

Cruz Roja (Red Cross; cnr Av 20 Sur & Calle Dr Adolfo Salas)

Express Lavandería (Calle Dr Adolfo Salas btwn 5 & 10 Avs Sur) Drop-off laundry service.

Post office (Calle 7 Sur at Av Rafael Melgar; ☼ Mon-Fri)

Tourist office (☎ 869 0212; ☼ 9am-5pm Mon-Fri) Upstairs in the main plaza (Plaza del Sol). Friendly staff hand out maps and can answer some questions. There's also an info booth by the pier.

Sights & Activities

IN TOWN

If it's raining, you won't be disappointed with the well-presented, four-room **Museo de la Isla de Cozumel** (Av Rafael Melgar btwn Calles 4 & 6 Norte; admission US$3; ☼ 9am-5pm), with exhibits on coral, pirates and the old Cozumel basketball team (descriptions in English and Spanish).

The **Mini-Golf** (cnr Calle 1 Sur & Av 15 Sur; 18-hole game US$6; ☼ closes dusk) is a nice mini-golf course; you get walkie-talkies to buzz in beer orders.

DIVING

Great year-round visibility and more than 100 diving sites have made Cozumel one of the world's most popular diving destinations. Marine life is plentiful, including eagle rays, eels, barracudas, turtles and sharks. Popular dives (including some that can be snorkeled) include Santa Rosa Wall, Punta Sur Reef, Colombia Shallows and Palancar Reef (still great for snorkeling). Lonely Planet's *Diving & Snorkeling Cozumel* has more information.

Cozumel is also home to over 100 dive operations. Prices vary, but in general a two-tank dive runs US$70 (equipment is US$18 more), a one-day introductory course with a two-tank dive is US$90 and a four-day PADI-certification course costs about US$360.

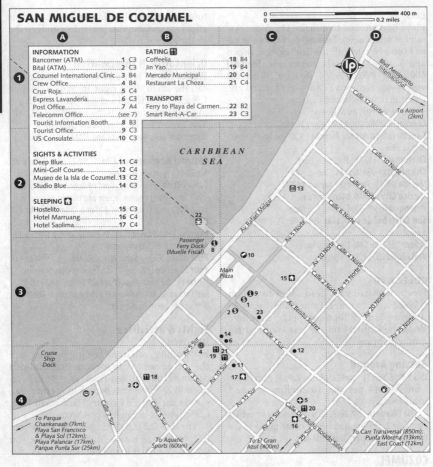

SAN MIGUEL DE COZUMEL

INFORMATION
Bancomer (ATM).....................1 C3
Bital (ATM)............................2 C3
Cozumel International Clinic...3 B4
Crew Office............................4 B4
Cruz Roja...............................5 C4
Express Lavandería..................6 C3
Post Office..............................7 A4
Telecomm Office................(see 7)
Tourist Information Booth.......8 B3
Tourist Office.........................9 C3
US Consulate.......................10 C3

SIGHTS & ACTIVITIES
Deep Blue............................11 C4
Mini-Golf Course..................12 C4
Museo de la Isla de Cozumel.13 C2
Studio Blue..........................14 C3

SLEEPING
Hostelito..............................15 C3
Hotel Marruang.....................16 C4
Hotel Saolima.......................17 C4

EATING
Coffeelia..............................18 B4
Jin Yao................................19 B4
Mercado Municipal...............20 C4
Restaurant La Choza.............21 C4

TRANSPORT
Ferry to Playa del Carmen.....22 B2
Smart Rent-A-Car..................23 C3

CARIBBEAN SEA

To Airport (2km)

Cruise Ship Dock

Main Plaza

Passenger Ferry Dock (Muelle Fiscal)

To Parque Chankanaab (7km);
Playa San Francisco
& Playa Sol (12km);
Playa Palancar (17km);
Parque Punta Sur (25km)

To Aquatic Sports (600m)

To El Gran Azul (400m)

To Carr Transversal (850m);
Punta Morena (13km);
East Coast (12km)

Plan at least a day ahead for 9am dives or snorkeling trips.

A few recommended dive shops:

Aquatic Sports (☎ 872 0640; www.scubacozumel.com; Av 15 Sur & Calle 21 Sur)

Deep Blue (☎ /fax 872 5653; www.deepbluecozumel .com; Av 10 Sur at Calle Dr Adolfo Salas)

Studio Blue (☎ 872 4414; Calle Dr Adolfo Salas 121) Gets good reports from readers.

SNORKELING

The best snorkeling sites are reached by boat. Touts on the dock will let you know about half-day trips for US$25, but they don't reach the best spots at the south of the island (such as Palancar Reef or Colombia Shallows). Snorkel trips with diving operators run to US$45 or so; another option is renting a motorbike and going to Playa Palancar (where you can arrange a 90-minute snorkeling trip for US$21).

EXPLORING THE ISLAND

Taxis are extortionately priced – try US$20 one way to Playa Palancar, 17km south – and there's no public transportation. Consider renting a moped or car. In a rewarding day, with a moped, it's possible to take the following counterclockwise loop around the island. From town, follow Av Rafael Melgar south (as it becomes Costera Sur) to reach the calm west-side beaches, or go east on Av Benito Juárez to connect with the Carr Transversal (Cross Island Road) and the rougher east coast.

Down the West Side

Parque Chankanaab (admission US$10), about 7km south of town, is a touristy snorkel spot that's not the island's best.

There are a few beach clubs about 5km further south at **Playa San Francisco** and **Playa Sol**. Nearby is the turnoff inland to **El Cedral**, a small town with a shack-sized Maya ruin.

It's worth stopping at **Playa Palancar**, about 17km south of town. There's free access to a calm beach, plus a restaurant, and snorkel trips to the reef run through most of the day. You can rent snorkel gear, kayaks and sailboats.

Sadly, the island's gorgeous southern tip is now only accessible by entering the overpriced **Parque Punta Sur** (admission US$10), where you can see crocs around Laguna de Colombia, ride a pontoon boat, and visit a lighthouse.

Up the East Side

Facing open ocean, the surf here is rough (often dangerous), and the shoreline wind-whipped and beautiful. Far fewer visitors make it over here. Surfing is possible, but be cautious of the undertow: drownings occur. Pricey, but good, seafood can be found at restaurants scattered along the road.

About 4km north from the Parque Punta Sur turnoff, **Playa Bonita** (to the south of Punta Chiqueros) usually has calmer swimming conditions than beaches to the north. Offshore rocks at **Playa Chen Río**, a few kilometers north, create a small protected area which is good for a dip. Further north, **Coconuts** (mains US$6-12) is a Tex-Mex restaurant on a cliff.

Punta Morena is the island's top surf spot. Shortly after is the turn back to town.

Sleeping

Hostelito (☎ 869 8157; www.hostelito.com; Av 10 Norte btwn Calles Juárez & 2 Norte; dm/r US$12/35; 🖳) Cozumel's only hostel is an inspired one with a giant ocean-blue dorm with 26 beds and bamboo décor – very clean. There are two private rooms, plans for a kitchen and wi-fi access.

Hotel Marruang (☎ 872 1678; Calle Dr Adolfo Salas 440; r US$22) The Marruang is a hot-pink budget hotel that offers clean, fan-cooled rooms across from the Mercado Municipal.

Hotel Saolima (☎ 872 0886; Calle Dr Adolfo Salas 260 btwn Avs 15 & 10 Sur; r with fan/air con US$25/30; 🍴) It has 20 simple pink-and-white rooms.

Eating

Cheapest of all eating places are the appealing market *loncherías* (food stalls) at the **Mercado Municipal** (Calle Dr Adolfo Salas btwn Avs 20 & 25 Sur), which serve seafood, egg breakfasts and Indonesian (!) meals for US$3 to US$4.

Jin Yao (Calle Dr Adolfo Salas 198; dishes from US$3.50) This take-out Chinese counter is particularly good if you need a noodle hit.

Coffeelia (Calle 5 Sur btwn Avs Rafael Melgar & 5 Sur; set breakfasts US$4-6, snacks US$2.50; 🕑 7:30am-11pm Mon-Fri, 1-11pm Sat) An old house turned arty hangout, it has fine food and good service, plus old *National Geographic* magazines to leaf through.

Restaurant La Choza (☎ 872 0958; cnr Calle Dr Adolfo Salas & Av 10 Sur; mains US$8-14; 🕑 7am-10:30pm) A popular *palapa*-style restaurant, away from the main touristy crawl, it specializes in (very big) Mexican meals. Mariachis lurk.

Getting There & Around

Most international flights are routed through the USA or Mexico City.

A couple of ferry companies connect Playa del Carmen with Cozumel (see p50).

Taxis are very expensive. **Smart Rent-A-Car** (☎ 877 5651; cnr Av 10 & Calle 1 Sur) rents VW bugs from US$38 per day, scooters for US$25.

TULUM

☎ 984 / pop 10,000

Playa is for the partiers, Tulum is for the beach bums. For over a decade, Tulum has been a big-time backpacker Yucatán HQ, with sand-floor huts on wide stretches of white sand near the fairly compact namesake Maya ruins. Big spenders, like they do, have followed the backpacker-pioneers in droves in recent years; already the first major hotel has plopped on the beach, and there's talk of another taking over cheapie hut spots in the future.

Orientation & Information

Spread-out Tulum has three parts: the rapidly developing town, where buses and colectivos pull in, the ruins (a couple kilometers north), and the 'zona hotelera' 3km east. The bus terminal is towards the south end of town. Toward the north along the main road is a useful landmark – a football field by the city hall in between two roundabouts.

Most services you'll need are in town. Half a block north and opposite the bus station is an English-speaking **doctor's office** (☎ 807 6666).

HSBC, another block up at city hall, has a 24-hour ATM and currency exchange. The Weary Traveler (see later) stores small/big bags for US$1.50/3 per 24 hours.

Dangers & Annoyances

Lonely Planet has received many reports of snag-and-sprint incidents, as well as bags getting nicked from locked huts. If staying in one of the cheapie sand-floor huts near the ruins consider storing your valuables in town.

Tulum Ruins

Seeing Mexico's most-visited Maya site atop surf-splashed Caribbean cliffs, it's not hard to imagine a post-Classic Maya or two begging for a transfer here. These days the location of the relatively small roped-off **ruins** (admission US$4.50; ☺ 8am-5pm) may be more impressive than the site itself. Many visitors charge through them as a dip on the beach awaits behind.

Tulum is believed to have been an important port town during its post-Classic heyday (AD 1200–1521). Named by the Spanish, Tulum is Maya for 'wall.' The site's original name was Zama, or 'Dawn' – watch the sunrise to realize why. Tulum was one of Mexico's last ancient cities to be abandoned, about 75 years after the Spanish conquest.

Colectivos (US$1.50) and taxis (US$4.50) go from town to the old entrance road at Crucero Ruinas, about 800m from the ticket booth. The ticket booth is also reached by foot or taxi from the beach road near the cabañas.

EXPLORING THE SITE

Past the ticket booth, you enter the compact rectangular site near its northwest corner. Heading east you pass the **Casa del Cenote** (House of the Cenote), named for the small pool at its southern base. Above, you can look over the site – set just south on a waterfront bluff is the **Templo del Dios del Viento** (Temple of the Wind God). Past it is the biggest site, **El Castillo** (The Castle), whose Toltec-style *kukulcanes* (plumed serpents) are evidence of the late post-Classic period. Just south are the steps down to the beach, and above are many cliffside vantage points for your camera.

West, roughly in the middle of the site, the interesting two-story **Templo de Las Pinturas** (Temple of the Paintings) features relief masks (and murals on its unapproachable inner wall).

Diving & Snorkeling

Cenote dives and snorkel trips are a bigger draw than Tulum's offshore reefs.

Cenote Dive Center (☎ 871 2232; www.cenotedive.com; Av Tulum) offers guided trips to Dos Ojos cenote (aka Hidden Worlds). It's US$45/110 to snorkel/dive, including wetsuit and equipment.

Beach accommodations offer trips as well. Zazil Kin cabañas in the zona hotelera offers one-/two-tank dives (US$40/60) and snorkeling trips (US$25).

Sleeping

IN TOWN

Hotel El Crucero (☎ 871 2610; www.el-crucero.com; Tulum Crucero; dm/r US$10/30; 🖳) This is a laid-back place off the highway at the entrance to ruins, with aged but fine rooms, about 1km walk from the beach.

Hostel Tulum (☎ 871 2089; Calle Jupiter 20; dm/r incl breakfast US$11/36; 🖳) Clinical but clean and big, the Tulum is across the highway, and just south, from the Weary Traveler.

Weary Traveler Hostel (☎ 871 2390; www.intulum .com; Av Tulum; dm US$12) This welcoming hostel is the best cheapie in town. There are several dorms, each fan-cooled and with private bathrooms; in low season some are available as private rooms. The central courtyard has food – including US$3 salad buffets.

Hotel Addy (☎ 871 2423; Calle Polar Ote 92; s/d US$28/33) On a side street a few hundred meters north of the bus station, the Addy has enormous rooms with TV and fan.

ZONA HOTELERA

A few kilometers from town, Tulum's beachfront can feel like a deserted island. The cheapies generally don't take reservations; show up by 11am and see if something turns up. The best place to start is the bare-bone four-pack immediately south of the ruins (US$4.50 by taxi); turn left a couple of kilometers from the access road. There are many more options – many midrange – extending 10km south from the access road.

Four choices near the ruins from south to north include:

Mar Caribe (cabañas from US$20, camping or hammocks per person US$5) Nice and simple, but on the beach access path; the higher-priced cabañas are on raised platforms.

Zazil Kin (cabanas_zazilkin@yahoo.com.mx; r US$37-47) Nicest and most popular of the four, with a dive center.

Santa Fe (camping or hammocks per person US$5, cabañas US$20) Primitive bungalow, barest of the four.

El Mirador (☎ 879 6019; savana@qroo1.telmex.net.mx; hammock/bed in cabañas from US$15/22) Grubbier but pleasant option.

Options heading south of the access road include:

Tribal Village (camping or hammocks US$10, cabañas US$25) Nice cement-floor cabañas in shady area facing rocky stretch of water.

Papaya Playa (www.papayaplaya.com; cabañas from US$40) Good cement-floor cabañas on fine beach, 1km south of access road.

Zahra Hotel (☎ 984-801 0092; cabañas with/without bathroom from US$45/35; 💻) Another 1km south, Zahra's cheapie Chan and Tunich cabañas are side by side with the upscale US$200 rooms, with a nicely tucked-away beach just behind.

Cabaña Los Arrecifes (☎ 879 7307; www.losarrecifes tulum.com; bungalows from US$40) About 4km south, Arrecifes has pricier hotel-style rooms and 10 sand-floor cabañas and an excellent beachfront.

Eating

All the beach places have restaurants – you'll find (often) more memorable and friendly service in town, and many of the best options (French, Italian, Argentine) are between the two roundabouts (100m north of the bus station).

Díaz Taquería (Av Tulum; three tacos US$2.40) With red plastic chairs and no alcohol, this local favorite focuses on good tacos. There's a mushroom *gringa* (big taco with cheese) for US$1.40.

San Francisco de Asís, at the beach turnoff, is the town's biggest supermarket.

Getting There & Around

The **bus terminal** (Av Tulum) won't sell tickets on long-distance buses to Cancún or Playa del Carmen until 30 minutes before departure. Buses leaving Tulum:

Cancún US$5.40-7.20; 2hr; many buses
Chetumal US$11.40-14.40; 3½-4hr; many buses
Chichén Itzá US$10.40; 3½hr; at 9am & 2:30pm daily
Cobá US$2.80; 30min; 4 per day 7am-6pm
Mérida US$12.20-18.60; 4hr; many buses
Palenque US$42.40; 15hr; 4.40pm & 6.10pm
Playa del Carmen US$2.20-3.40; 1hr; many buses
Valladolid US$5-6; 2hr; 7 per day

Shared vans leave for Playa del Carmen (US$2.50) every 30 minutes from 5am to 10pm from the Terminal de Servicio Foraneo, about 250m north of the bus station. A 2pm van goes to Punta Allen (US$15; two to three hours).

Taxi fares are fixed. There's a stand by the bus terminal with posted fares. It's US$4.50 to many cabañas. Many places rent bicycles.

AROUND TULUM

About 4km west of Tulum is **Grand Cenote**, a fine spot to cool off with a swim en route to Cobá. You'll need to organize your own transport to get here.

Cobá

A Classic-era Maya city set deep in tropical jungle, the fascinating Cobá **ruins** (admission US$3.70; ⏰ 7am-5pm), 48km northwest of Tulum, are more linked with distant Tikal than Tulum or Chichén Itzá. Be at the gates when they open and you may not see another person for two hours.

Cobá was home to 55,000 Maya at its peak (between AD 800 and 1100). Many amazing regional *sacbés* (stone-paved avenues) led here. The longest runs 100km to Yaxuna, near Chichén Itzá. The name – from the Maya word *koba* (believed to mean 'ruffled waters') – likely refers to the reedy, croc-filled lakes in the area.

A little Yucatec may help you with locals: try *¿bix a bel?* (literally: 'how is your road?,' used as 'what's up?').

El Bocadito (☎ 984 206 7070; r US$15-25) has slightly scruffy fan-cooled rooms if you miss the 6pm bus to Tulum.

EXPLORING THE SITE

Only a few of the estimated 6500 structures have been excavated. The four principal groups are spaced apart. You can rent bikes for US$3 after 8am. If you walk through the jungle trails, expect to stay a minimum of three hours at the site.

Approximately 100m along the main path is **Grupo Cobá**, with an enormous pyramid and corbelled-vault passages. After 500m, the road forks: the left leads to the Nohoch Mul pyramid, the right to Grupo Macanxoc. Either way passes the **Conjunto Pinturas** (Collection of Paintings), 100m further, which has a couple of stelae.

If conscious of time, skip **Grupo Macanxoc**, 500m away (which has a few eroded stelae depicting women from Tikal) and head northeast past the **Grupo Nohoch Mul** and continue to the right (east) to the semicircular Xaibé structure, the juncture of four *sacbés*. To the north, past a couple of structures, you'll see the 42m high **Nohoch Mul** (Big Mound), a half-excavated pyramid you can climb to look over the jungle canopy. It's a 1.5km, half-hour walk back to the entrance gate.

GETTING THERE & AWAY

Most buses serving Cobá stop at El Bocadito – a 10-minute walk (past the lake) from the ruins. Buses continue on to Valladolid and Chichén Itzá.

Reserva de la Biósfera Sian Ka'an

Beach resorts are inching closer to the 5000-sq-km Sian Ka'an Biosphere Reserve, a World Heritage site of protected jungle, marsh, mangrove and beachfront. It can be reached from the highway to Chetumal, south of Tulum, or better from the rough road south of Tulum's Zona Hotelera (the van to Punta Allen from Tulum goes through here, though most visitors go by their own wheels, usually 4WD vehicles). Only a portion of the biosphere can be visited – and very little if not on an organized tour. Tour companies in Tulum include the following:

CESiaK (☎ 987-71 2499; www.cesiak.org; Tulum Crucero) Offers full-day tours of the ecosystems, a look at Xlapak Maya ruins and a float down a fresh-water canal (US$68). Also has bird-watching tours (US$70) and kayak trips (US$45).

Tucan Kin (☎ 01-800 702 4111; Weary Traveler Hostel, Av Tulum) Leads mostly walking tours of the biosphere from the highway (US$40).

CESiaK runs 15 wonderful beachside **cabañas** (r with shared bathroom US$78-100) about 11km south of the Tulum Zona Hotelera access road. You could get here by the Punta Allen van and arrange tours here; there's a restaurant.

Punta Allen

A magical spot, buried at the end of a scarred road deep in the Sian Ka'an (56km from Tulum), Punta Allen is a sand-road fishing village of 70 families and a few kooky expats. The beach is largely untouched – meaning washed-up seagrass stays there. Snorkeling trips to offshore coral reefs, with turtles and dolphins, are remarkable (about US$120 per group).

A fun place to stay is **Posada Sirena** (☎ 984-877 8521; posadasirena@prodigy.net.mx; www.casasirena.com; cabañas US$30-50) with four colorful rooms run by the 'mermaid of Punta Allen,' a transplanted Californian.

A van goes to Punta Allen from Tulum at 2pm daily and returns to Tulum at 5am daily; it's also possible to go by bus and boat from Felipe Carrillo Puerto, 95km south of Tulum.

CHIAPAS

Mexico's southernmost (and poorest) state is a wonderland of ruins, jungle, waterfalls and mountains, an area once part of Spanish-controlled 'Guatemala' and which feels, in comparison with the Yucatán, far more 'Central America' than 'Mexico.' Those waking up on overnight buses from the Yucatán usually start with the magical Maya city of Palenque

---

GETTING TO COROZAL, BELIZE

Visitors heading south to Belize must change buses in **Chetumal**, the capital of Quintana Roo state. It's a hmm-and-go type of place other than the remarkable **Museo de la Cultura Maya** (☎ 983-832 6838; cnr Avs de los Héroes & Gandhi; admission US$5; 🕑 9am-7pm Tue-Thu & Sun, 9am-8pm Fri & Sat), simply the best museum on Maya culture. The comfortable **Hotel Ucum** (☎ 983-832 0711; Av Gandhi 167; d with fan/air-con US$20/25; P 🏊 🍴) is nearby.

Chetumal's notable bus terminals are several blocks apart, both 2km north of the town's center. The **main bus terminal** (near Avs Insurgentes & Belice) has frequent connections to Palenque and up the coast. From here regular direct buses leave for Corozal/Orange Walk/Belize City for US$2/3/6, and two buses go on to Flores, Guatemala (US$40), leaving at 6:20am and 2:30pm. The Nuevo Mercado Lázaro Cárdenas has 2nd-class buses to Belize.

Note that those arriving from Palenque get here around 1am or 3am. Afternoon/evening buses go to Palenque, frequent buses head north toward Cancún.

Be prepared to show evidence of the payment of your 'nonimmigrant fee' (p73) to leave Mexico. See p240 for information on crossing into Mexico from Belize.

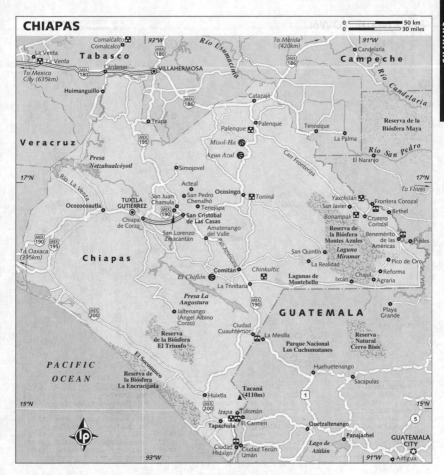

CHIAPAS

on the foothills of lush mountain jungle where you can sleep in hammocks and screened-in cabañas.

Further up, way up, is the lovely Spanish colonial town of San Cristóbal de Las Casas, the town masked Zapatista rebels put on the international map in the 1990s. Both serve as compelling bases for day trips to ruins rarely visited, waterfalls and fascinating Maya villages where a 'buenos dias' sometimes gets a confused shrug.

DANGERS & ANNOYANCES

There's been isolated incidents of robberies on buses along the route from Palenque to San Cristóbal, but we haven't heard of any recently. Some visitors have been robbed while walking on access roads to waterfalls outside Palenque.

PALENQUE
☎ 916 / pop 37,000

Ancient Palenque sits like a king on a throne of jungle where plains meet mountains. It ranks up with Tikal for the top Maya sites, and as far as personal exploration goes, that you can climb most temples (and swing in hammocks in the jungle overnight nearby) makes it incomparably more rewarding than Chichén Itzá.

A few kilometers east, the modern Palenque town is something like a fast-food town, made to get folks in and out, quickly and smoothly.

MEXICO'S YUCATÁN & CHIAPAS

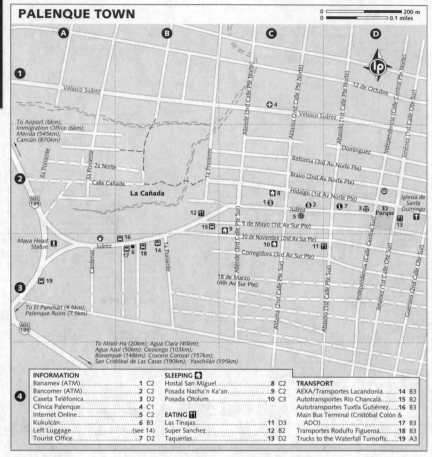

PALENQUE TOWN

INFORMATION		
Banamex (ATM)....................1	C2	
Bancomer (ATM)...................2	C2	
Caseta Telefónica.................3	D2	
Clínica Palenque................4	C1	
Internet Online...................5	C2	
Kukulcán............................6	B3	
Left Luggage.....................(see 14)		
Tourist Office.....................7	D2	

SLEEPING		
Hostal San Miguel...............8	C2	
Posada Nacha'n Ka'an.........9	C2	
Posada Otolum..................10	C3	

EATING		
Las Tinajas......................11	D3	
Super Sanchez.................12	B2	
Taquerías........................13	D2	

TRANSPORT		
AEXA/Transportes Lacandonia........14	B3	
Autotransportes Río Chancalá......15	B2	
Autotransportes Tuxtla Gutiérrez......16	B3	
Main Bus Terminal (Cristóbal Colón &		
ADO)...................................17	B3	
Transportes Rodulfo Figueroa........18	B3	
Trucks to the Waterfall Turnoffs......19	A3	

Orientation

Hwy 199 meets the town's active main street, Juárez, at the intersection with a statue of a big Maya head. From here Juárez heads east past the bus stations and 800m to the central square (El Parque).

Most town streets have two names, with a recently added numbering system that most businesses ignore (as do addresses that follow).

A little south of the big Maya head, the 7.5km road to the ruins and El Panchán turns off Hwy 199.

Information

IMMIGRATION

Immigration office (Hwy 199; 8am-2pm & 5-8pm) About 6km north of town; take a colectivo marked 'Playas.'

INTERNET ACCESS

Internet Online (Juárez; per hr US$0.80; 7:30am-11pm)

LEFT LUGGAGE

Left luggage (Juárez; per hr US$0.20; 7am-11pm) The café next to Transportes Lacandonia charges half the cost of the nearby ADO bus station.

MEDICAL SERVICES

Clínica Palenque (345 0273; Velasco Suárez 33; 8:30am-1:30pm & 5-8pm) Dr Alfonso Martínez speaks English.

MONEY

Bancomer (Juárez) It's about 1½ blocks west of El Parque.

TELEPHONE

Caseta teléfonica (Juárez) At Posada Yax-Ha, a block west of El Parque, it receives international calls for US$0.05 per minute. Calls to the USA/Europe/Australia cost US$0.30/0.40/0.50 per minute.

TOURIST INFORMATION

Tourist office (cnr Juárez & Abasolo; ☿ 9am-9pm Mon-Sat, 9am-1pm Sun) Small and not much help other than a few brochures and a town map.

TRAVEL AGENCIES

Palenque's abundant travel agencies can get you to the ruins or to Guatemala. You can also book tours at El Panchán.

Kukulcán (☎ 345 1506; www.kukulcantravel.com; Juárez; ☿ 6am-9pm) Next to the ADO bus station, it offers reliable service with friendly English-speaking staff (and Palenque beer mugs!).

Palenque Ruins

The ancient **ruins** (admission US$4.50; ☿ site 8am-4:45pm, museum 9am-4pm Tue-Sun) include some 500 excavated buildings (of 1453 found) spread over a sloping 15 sq km. From the turnoff on Hwy 199, just west of town, it's 6km to the museum.

There are entrances to the site from the museum (walking uphill as the everyday Maya would have done) and the main entrance, 1.5km further. Get here from Palenque by regular colectivo (marked 'Ruinas'; US$1 one way) or taxi.

Guides (who speak Spanish, English, French or Italian) are available at the main entrance. A two-hour tour for up to seven people is US$45.

Many tours combine a few hours at the ruins with visits to Agua Azul and other waterfalls in the mountains. Three hours is enough to whip through the ruins.

HISTORY

The Maya name of Palenque (Palisade in Spanish) is believed to have been Baak. It was first occupied around 100 BC and its prime time was around the 7th century AD (when the population was probably 8000), which was centered around the reign of K'inich Hanab Pakal (who died at the age of 80 in 683). Many of Palenque's plazas and buildings were built during the reigns of Pakal and his son and successor, Kan Balam (or Snake Jaguar). Most buildings were painted red, from dyes made from squashed insects.

Palenque didn't fare well in 8th-century combat with neighbor rival, Toniná (65km south). It was abandoned around 900 and sat hidden by jungle for centuries. In 1773, after hearing stories about stone palaces in the jungle from Maya hunters, a Spanish priest led a trip there. Others followed, excavations began. One occupant was Count de Waldeck who, in his 60s, lived atop a pyramid for two years (1831–33). A few years later, John L Stephens, an amateur archaeology enthusiast, wrote insightfully about the site. King Pakal's secret crypt was discovered in 1952 – one of the biggest finds in the Maya world.

LAS INSCRIPCIONES GROUP

Just after the main entrance, this group of four buildings stands side by side on your right. Last in line is the **Templo de las Inscripciones** (Temple of the Inscriptions; closed to entry), Palenque's tallest building – an eight-level temple with stairs rising 25m. The roof comb at the top is a reconstruction. Inside is Pakal's tomb. His skeleton and jade mask were moved to Mexico City (where the mask was stolen in 1985), but the giant sarcophagus lid remains. The remarkably carved slab has glyphs recounting Pakal's reign, though its full meaning is debated.

Behind the temple, a path leads through the jungle to **Templo del Bello Relieve** (Temple of the Beautiful Relief); you'll need a flashlight to see anything inside.

EL PALACIO

At the end of the lawn, diagonally opposite from the Templo de las Inscripciones, the **Palace** is a big, fun, complex structure with a maze of corridors and vaulted galleries set around four courtyards.

Rising from the southwestern courtyard, the tower (believed to be an observatory) was re-created in 1955. The u-shaped stones below are Maya toilets, guides claim. Within the southern halls, there are stone beds where royals slept. Along the eastside pillars, look for Spaniard vandals' names, carved in the 18th century.

LAS CRUCES GROUP

Just southeast of El Palacio, on a slight hill, stands this interesting group, all dedicated to Pakal's son, Kan Balam. Entering the plaza, the **Templo de la Cruz Foliada** (Temple of the Foliated Cross) is straight ahead, shrouded in jungle with an impressive mountain backdrop. To the left (north), the biggest of the three is **Templo de la Cruz** (Temple of the Cross); on the plaza's west side, the **Templo de la Sol** (Temple of the Sun) has Palenque's best-preserved roof comb – some argue (weakly) it shows an Asian influence.

Carvings atop each so Kan Balam (big guy) and Pakal (little one) on either side of a central object: corn, cross (for the ceiba tree, not Jesus) and the Jaguar God.

OTHER GROUPS

These groups see far fewer visitors.

On the south side of Las Cruces, a path leads into the jungle to the shaded **Acropolis Sur**, which was closed indefinitely at research time.

Back in the sun and north of El Palacio is **Grupo Norte's** strip of temples. On the western side, the **Templo del Conde** (Temple of the Count) is the place where the Count de Waldeck made his home for a couple of years.

Past the stream to the east, a fork to the right leads to the overgrown **Grupo C**. Heading to the exit, the path goes along the stream past more wildly overgrown ruins – some are very interesting to walk around. **Grupos 1 and 2** are slightly back up the hill past the bridge. Along the way is a waterfall and inviting pools of clear cool water (no swimming here though). The path ends on the road, near the **museum** (with English subtitles), which is well worth a look.

Sleeping

IN TOWN

Palenque town has plenty of 10- to 15-room jobbies. Juárez has many, but it's quieter on the backstreets.

Posada Nacha'n Ka'an (☎ 345 4737; 20 de Noviembre 25; dm/s/d US$7/15/18) It has well-kept but basic rooms run by a sweet family – dad speaks English and is prone to chatting. The big rooftop dorm has lots of space and a (needed) breeze. There's a communal closet to lock up bags. Rooms have bathroom, TV and fan. The family runs a small café with US$2.50 breakfasts.

Hostal San Miguel (☎ 345 0152; Hidalgo 43; r US$15) The San Miguel is cuter outside than in, but it has fine rooms with a fan and private bathroom.

Posada Otolum (☎ 916 101 7560; 20 de Noviembre No 77; s/d US$15/20) The Otolum is a colorful place with small but nice fan-cooled rooms with TVs.

EL PANCHÁN

Stay out here if you can. Set in dense jungle, 4.5km from town on the road to the ruins, El Panchán has five places offering basic cabañas, campsites or posts to tie a hammock. Many travelers who expect to stay a night leave a week later.

In high season, finding a vacant cabaña can be tough in the afternoon. Phones often don't work, and email addresses are rarely checked (seemingly). So stay in town if you arrive after dark. A 'Ruinas' colectivo gets you to El Panchán.

Rakshita's (camping & hammocks US$2, dm/s/d US$7/10/15) Shoddy new-age atmosphere with lots of space, murals on cabañas, and an eternally empty 'pool.' It's US$2 extra to rent hammocks.

Chato's Cabanas (☎ 348 0520; el_panchan@yahoo .com.mx; camping & hammocks US$3, s/d US$13/18) Handles reservations for a couple of cabaña outfits.

Jungle Palace (camping & hammocks US$3, s/d US$10/ 12, tr with bathroom US$25) Nice spot along a stream.

Margarita & Ed Cabanas (☎ 341 0963 rarely answered; r from US$17; 🖵) Less scenic, but definitely the nicest cabañas, all with fans. The 'hotel'-style rooms have air-con.

Eating

In town, tourist-oriented cafés are abundant along Juárez and around El Parque. The *taquerías*, on the east side of El Parque, are great spots to sit, eat and watch the scene.

Las Tinajas (cnr 20 de Noviembre & Abasolo; set breakfasts US$2.80-3.70, dishes US$6-7; 🕑 7am-11pm) A friendly and breezy spot on a side street, it attracts locals and travelers. The food is quite good, but the tasty *rabalo* fish is priced by size and staff will bring you the biggest one.

Don Mucho's (mains US$3.50-8, breakfast US$1.50-3.50; 🕑 7:30am-midnight) The main eating spot in El Panchàn is surprisingly good and amazingly not overpriced. There's live music at 8:30pm.

Super Sanchez (Juárez) This grocery store is located a couple blocks east of Palenque's bus terminals.

Getting There & Away

Buses serving Palenque sometimes get a bad rap for theft. Keep an eye on your gear.

Several bus terminals are on Juárez, a few blocks east of Hwy 199. The main **ADO bus terminal** (☎ 345 1344) has services to Cancún (US$49.60, 13 hours), Chetumal (US$28.60, 7½ hours, two night buses), Mérida (US$31.60, nine hours, two daily), Mexico City (US$67.20, 16 hours, three daily), San Cristóbal de Las Casas (US$12, 4½ hours) and Tulum (US$42.40, 11 hours, two night buses).

A far better deal, on fine buses, for San Cristóbal is via **AEXA/Transportes Lancandonia** (☎ 345 2630), which sends five or so daily buses (via Ocosingo) for US$7.50. Also, Ruta Maya has cheaper buses to Tulum (US$25) and Cancún (US$30).

Autotransportes Río Chancalá (☎ 341 3356; 5 de Mayo 120) sends frequent vans to Cruzero Corozal (US$5, 2½ hours), a 16km taxi ride from Frontera Corozal and boats to Guatemala. (Some colectivos go direct to Frontera Corozal; ask.)

See below for information on getting to Bonampak, Yaxchilán and the popular waterfalls west of town: Agua Azul and Miso-Ha.

Getting Around

Colectivos to El Panchán and the ruins (US$1 one-way) run every 15 minutes from 6am to 6pm. Catch one heading west on Juárez, across from the main bus terminal.

Taxis charge about US$4 to El Panchán, US$5 to the ruins.

AROUND PALENQUE

Often tours offered by travel agencies are as cheap as going on your own, and make getting to places much easier.

Waterfalls

There are a couple of dandies off the mountainous Hwy 199 heading south to San Cristóbal, each known for amazing colors (best in spring) and fine swimming areas. Most impressive is **Agua Azul** (60km south, 4.5km off highway), with a 1km walk up to the best swimming spots in the blue water. **Misol-Ha** (20km south of Palenque, 1.5km off the highway) has a big pool below a 35m drop, plus nearby cabins. The water gets chocolaty after rain.

Organized day trips with an hour at Misol-Ha and three at Agua Azul cost US$10, not including admission (US$1 each). Ocosingo-bound trucks stop at the Hwy 199 turnoffs to the falls (about US$3 one way, from 6am to 6pm), but there have been several reports of machete-armed thieves robbing tourists on the walk to the falls (particularly at Agua Clara, another falls in the area). Sometimes trucks are available to reach the falls for US$2 or so.

Maya Ruins

Southeast of Palenque – en route to Flores, Guatemala – are a couple of very big-deal Maya sites: Bonampak and Yaxchilán. An organized day trip to see both (including admission, transportation and lunch) is about US$50; a two-day trip combining a visit with an overnighter in a Lacandon village is US$80. It's also possible to see them en route to Tikal, Guatemala (see below).

Visiting them without a tour will cost more and may mean overnight stays, some waits and long walks on access roads; you can access both by the Crucero Corozal colectivo from Palenque.

GETTING TO FLORES, GUATEMALA

The trip between Palenque and Flores (near Tikal) is easiest on a full-transportation package (two buses and boat) from a Palenque travel agency. The eight-hour trip costs about US$35 per person, leaving typically at 6am. A worthwhile option that most agencies pawn includes visiting the remarkable Maya sites of Yaxchilán and Bonampak; the two-day trip (including a night in a Lacandon village) finishes in Flores, and costs about US$90.

If you do the trip on your own, be prepared for waits. From Palenque, take a colectivo to **Crucero Corozal**, 16km from **Frontera Corozal** (which you reach by taxi), where boats cross the Río Usumacinta to Bethel, Guatemala, where you can find chicken buses to Flores. The boat costs about US$80; we've heard some travelers weren't allowed to wait for fellow travelers to share the costs.

Another adventurous way to cross is busing from Palenque to **Tenosique, Guatemala**, then catching a van to El Ceibo (US$3, 1½ hours), where its possible to find a boat going to El Naranjo (US$30; about three hours). Then you catch a bus to Flores (at least six hours). Note: Mexico has no immigration at this border – handle this in Palenque before you set out.

See p202 for details on crossing this border from Guatemala.

BONAMPAK

A small site, 148km from Palenque, **Bonampak** (admission US$3; 🕑 8am-4pm) is famed for its brightly colored, narrative (and unfinished) murals set in three rooms midway up the tall acropolis. In the middle room, scenes of torture and sacrifice are shown; note the decapitated head and blood squirting from a captive's fingers just above and left of the door, behind you as you enter.

The gate site is 3km from the San Javier junction on the highway. At the gate you can catch a shuttle (about US$5) for the 9km trip to the ruins.

Nearby is an amazing Lacandon village, inhabited by the only unconquered group of Maya.

YAXCHILÁN

Set far from roads on the banks of the Río Usumacinta, **Yaxchilán** (admission US$3.80; 🕑 8am-4:45pm), 195km from Palenque (road and river), is reached by boat from Frontera Corozal. Many of its carvings now reside in the British Museum, but its jungle setting, ornate facades, roof combs and *loud* howler monkeys make for a memorable visit.

Heading west past the entrance, shortly after the Pequeña Acropolis turnoff, the path forks; go right for a dramatic entrance to the long Gran Plaza, lined with buildings and lintels. Up a steep stairway to the southwest is Edificio 33, the site's most impressive building. Behind a path leads further up to the southwest to the more remote Edificios 39, 40 and 41 – you'll need 30 minutes at least for this. You can return to the boats by the Pequeña Acropolis. Tour groups get just two hours here.

From Frontera Corozal, you can boat here for about US$60 for up to three people, US$120 for 10.

TONINÁ

Even the hardened sometimes start to feel queasy on the tortuous road twisting and turning its way up from Palenque to San Cristóbal. Although most travelers skip it, there's a superb halfway rest point near friendly **Ocosingo**, where you can take in the Maya site of **Toniná** (admission US$3.80; 🕑 9am-5pm) in about four hours, then continue your trip. The massive hillside temple complex is fun to walk around, with hidden chambers leading up to a 70m pyramid overlooking the lovely ranchland outside Ocosingo. The ride 16km east from town passes an army base outside a Zapatista territory, as marked with a handwritten sign.

To reach the site from the destination bus station, walk a couple of blocks west (uphill), then south (at the 'centro' sign) toward the market (about four blocks downhill). Combis run half-hourly (or so) from the west side of the market to the site (US$1 each way). There are also taxis around, but a ride is about US$10.

You can find a hotel and ATM on Ocaingo's plaza, half way down to the market.

SAN CRISTÓBAL DE LAS CASAS

☎ 967 / pop 130,000

Set in the cool broad Jovel valley, San Cristóbal is a Spanish-colonial wonder – with low-lying haciendas fit snug on tight sidewalks and cobbled streets – but everything else about the area is richly embedded in the world of the modern Maya. The town, made famous when Zapatistas took control (briefly) in 1994, is surrounded by Maya villages in the hills where traditions live full force. Day trips nearby, plus the town's excellent coffee, arthouse films and lively markets, make it hard to stay less than a week.

Founded as San Cristóbal in 1528, its extended name honors Bartolomé de Las Casas, who was appointed bishop of Chiapas in 1545 and became an outspoken defender of the indigenous. For more details of the the Zapatista rebellion staged here; see opposite.

At 2100m, it gets chilly here all year.

Orientation

Plaza 31 de Marzo (but everyone calls it *zócalo*) is the heart of the town, north of the bus terminals (where the Pan-Americana cuts through the southern reaches of town) on Insurgentes.

Extending east of the *zócalo*, Real de Guadalupe and Madero comprise something of a tourist zone, with many cafés and guesthouses. Along the *zócalo's* western side, 20 de Noviembre (to north) and Hidalgo (to south) have been transformed into a pedestrian mall, quite a hit with locals.

Information

BOOKSTORES

There are many places to find books along Real de Guadalupe.

La Pared (Hidalgo 2; 🕑 10am-2pm & 4-8pm Tue-Sat, 2-7pm Sun) The sweet Floridian owner offers a big selection of English-language novels and guidebooks.

ZAPATISTAS!

Cult heroes of Chiapas and the world, the left-wing peasant group of the Ejército Zapatista de Liberación Nacional (EZLN) fight for indigenous rights in one of Mexico's poorest states. More than one in four people in Chiapas are Maya, but hold few cards in how their land is used. The Zapatistas splashed onto international news on January 1, 1994, when they protested the first day by Nafta by storming and briefly occupying San Cristóbal de Las Casas. Most wore handmade uniforms and all wore masks – a people who had been invisible and muted by centuries, suddenly found their identity by hiding it.

The Zapatistas quickly made an impact: Benetton offered an ad deal (declined), Oliver Stone trolled for film fodder (never materialized), the USA poured over half a billion dollars in military aid (for the Mexican army) and an advisor to a US company called for the Zapatistas to be 'eliminated.'

The always-masked Zapatista founder – the pipe-smoking Subcomandante Marcos – has been a colorful and unusual leader. He apologized to startled tourists after occupying San Cristóbal ('we apologize…but this is a revolution'), wrote a children's book with gods preoccupied with sex and tobacco (*The Story of Colors*), and succeeded in what other socialist revolutionaries such as Che Guevara and Fidel Castro failed: integrating into the indigenous life. Rather than push Marxist and class doctrines, he shifted to focus on indigenous rights, and left room for religion. When the Zapatistas spoke to the Mexican Congress in 2001 – after president Vicente Fox boasted he could solve the problem in '15 minutes' – it was not Marcos who took the podium, but a Maya woman called Comandanta Esther.

Many find it surprising that the Zapatistas don't want to overthrow the government. As Marcos says, 'We are indigenous people and we are Mexicans. And we want to be both.' The chief crux of Zapatista demands has been to release Zapatista prisoners, close seven Mexican military bases in the area and to recognize the San Andrés Accords, which granted Chiapas more power in how indigenous land was used; the government approved the act in 1996, but it never came into effect. Meanwhile, Zapatista life continues, particularly in seven autonomous zones called *caricoles* (snails).

Critics of the Zapatistas often point out the many cases of Zapatistas seizing ranchland from the wealthy in the area around Ocosingo, including an instance of forcing out the US owners of a Zapatist-sympathetic ranch hotel.

In recent years, the government seems content to ignore the movement, and the tactic has been more effective than the paramilitary raids of the mid '90s that lead to the Acteal massacre (where 43 were killed). The movement has faded from international press and some locals in San Cristóbal even murmur how some Zapatista leaders have defected, taking grant money to build big homes. But Marcos has kept busy, after a nationwide 2006 motorcycle tour he published a thriller novel *The Uncomfortable Dead*, written with Mexican author Paco Ignacio Taibo II.

Reading Up

It's less fashionable to write about the Zapatistas these days, so the best books are a little dated. A couple of good ones are *The Zapatista Reader*, edited by Tom Hayden, and *Rebellion in Chiapas: An Historical Reader*, edited by John Womack. **Global Exchange** (www.globalexchange.com) has many articles and even 'reality tours' to Chiapas. Official Zapatista websites include zeztainternazional .org and enlacezapatista.ezln.org.mx.

IMMIGRATION

Immigration office (Instituto Nacional de Migración; ☎ 678 6594; Diagonal El Centenario 30; ☒ 9am-2pm Mon-Fri) This office is situated about 1.2km to the west of the main bus station along the Pan-Americana Hwy.

INTERNET ACCESS

Internet-café rates range from US$0.50 to US$1 per hour. There's wi-fi access at La Selva café (see later).

Los Faroles (Real de Guadalupe 33; per hr US$0.50; ☒ 9:30am-10pm)

SAN CRISTÓBAL DE LAS CASAS

LAUNDRY

Lavandaría (5B Belisario Domínguez; ⏲ 8am-8pm Mon-Sat) Same-day service, about US$3.

LEFT LUGGAGE

Across from the OCC bus station's left luggage (per hr US$0.40), **El Paso** (Insurgentes 79C; per 24hr US$2) is cheaper for long-term storage.

MEDICAL SERVICES

General Hospital (☎ 678 0770; Insurgentes)

MONEY

Banamex (⏲ 9am-4pm Mon-Fri, 10am-2pm Sat) On the *zócalo*; has ATM and currency exchange.

POST

Post Office (Madero)

TELEPHONE

El Locutorio (Belisario Domínguez, near Real de Guadalupe; 🕑 8am-10pm) Make calls to the USA or Canada (US$0.20 per minute), Europe (from US$0.30). There's another location at Cresencio Rosas at Cuauhtémoc.

TOURIST INFORMATION

Municipal tourist office (☎ 678 0665; turismo _municipalidad@yahoo.com.mx; 🕑 8am-8pm) English-speaking staff run two booths in the *zócalo*.
Sedetur (☎ 678 6570; Hidalgo 1B, 1st fl; 🕑 8am-8pm Mon-Sat, 9am-3pm Sun) Hidden-away office with plenty of brochures and maps.

TRAVEL AGENCIES

Most travel agencies in town are located along Real de Guadalupe, and offer similar services (including day trips, horseback riding, and useful ticket deals to Guatemala). Compare their prices. All are open roughly from 8am to 9 or 10pm daily. A few good ones are listed here:
Otisa (☎ 678 1933; otisa@otisatravel.com; Real de Guadalupe 3C)
Trotamundos (☎ 678 7021; trota_chis@hotmail.com; Real de Guadalupe 26C)
Viajes Chincultik (☎ 678 0957; Real de Guadalupe 34) At Posada Margarita.

Sights & Activities

MAYA MEDICINE DEVELOPMENT CENTER

Do visit the terrific **Centro de Desarrollo de la Medicina Maya** (☎ 678 5438; www.laneta.apc.org/omiech; Av Salomón González Blanco 10; admission US$2; 🕑 10am-6pm Tue-Fri, 10am-4pm Sat & Sun), one of the best museums of Maya culture anywhere. Its four thematic rooms illustrate how herbs, prayers, candles and skunk urine (!) have helped ease the ills of Maya for generations. A booklet (in English, French, German and Italian) explains the exhibits.

There's a graphic 12-minute video (in Spanish) on the unique way Maya women give birth. In the back building, various herbal medicines are for sale – a shampoo to fight balding is US$3.

To get there, walk 1km north of Santo Domingo. It's US$1.50 by taxi.

NA BOLOM

This gorgeous 19th-century colonial **museum** (☎ 678 1418; www.nabolom.org; Guerrero 33; admission US$3.25, with 2hr tour in English & Spanish at 11:30am & 4:30pm US$4.30; 🕑 10am-5pm) is the former hacienda of Swiss anthropologist-photographer Gertrude (Trudy) Duby-Blom, who died in 1993. Trudy and her Danish husband, Frans Blom, devoted much of their lives trying to preserve the cultures of the indigenous people in Chiapas, and their organization is still very active.

Tours are worth the extra US$1 for the guides' insight of regional groups (particularly the Lacandones). The house is also a hotel and restaurant (reserve ahead for the US$12 dinners).

TEMPLO DE SANTO DOMINGO & AROUND

San Cristóbal's prettiest church, **Templo de Santo Domingo** (20 de Noviembre), is open for a peek, but its finest asset is its ornate western facade. Surrounding it is the town's best souvenir **market** where many Maya vendors sell textiles, leather goods, and Zapatista dolls and T-shirts. Just north, the **Sna Jolobil showroom** (☉ 9am-2pm & 4-6pm Mon-Sat) is a cooperative of 800 weavers from around the region; detailed textiles are organized by pueblo, providing a good way to gauge the diversity in styles.

Don't miss having a looksee through the bustling **Mercado Municipal**, sprawling in the side streets to the northeast. You may only make it to San Juan Chamula, but villagers from all the Maya towns come in to hawk produce, wool and hairy piglets here.

OTHER SIGHTS

There are two hills with churches to check out. **Cerro de Guadalupe**, at the eastern end of Real de Guadalupe, offers the better views (and the squeakier floored church, Iglesia de Guadalupe). Southwest of the *zócalo*, and covered by forest, is the **Cerro de San Cristóbal**, with the Iglesia de San Cristóbal at the top.

Pleasant **Templo del Carmen** (Hidalgo; ☉ 10am-1pm Mon-Sat) is south of the *zócalo*.

The decrepit steps off Dr Navarro are begging for a name: perhaps the **Coleto Steps**? Take them up to Comitán to see nearby **Iglesia de Cerrollito** and walk downhill to Na Bolom.

Tours

It's possible to take tours to local sights and villages, including San Juan Chamula, or to go on cycling tours around the countryside. See p68 for more details.

Courses

San Cristóbal has a handful of good Spanish-language schools. The best:

Instituto Jovel (☎ /fax 678 4069; www.institutojovel .com; Madero 45) Private classes (three hours per day) plus homestay is US$235 per week, plus registration fee.

Sol Maya (☎ 674 6720; www.solmaya.org; Hermanos Domínguez 25A) Two ex-Jovel teachers set up this school off the steps up Cerro de San Cristóbal – probably the city's best views. Courses are US$120 per week. It offers coffee-farm tours on request.

Volunteering

Habitat Para La Humanidad (Habitat for Humanity; ☎ 678 9003; Real de Mexicanos 26A; ☉ 9am-noon & 4-7pm Mon-Fri, 9am-2pm Sat) takes volunteers to help build houses in a few area communities.

Xojobal Melel (☎ 678 1958; www.melelxojobal.org.mx) needs volunteers to help mostly Maya children with various educational activities.

Festivals

Feria de la Primavera y de la Paz (Spring and Peace Fair) is a week-long splash (with bullfights) after Easter Sunday; in late October is **Festival Cervantino Barroco**, with many cultural events. Also, follow the frequently heard fireworks that signal one of the 20-some neighborhoods' saint-based festivals.

Sleeping

Some hotels boost prices July to August, and around Christmas and Semana Santa, but generally not these lower-priced ones.

HOSTELS

Posada Doña Rosita (☎ 678 0923; Ejército Nacional 13; dm incl breakfast US$4, d with/without bathroom US$14/10) This posada has quite basic rooms in the homey setting of a friendly señora who practices natural medicine. There are a couple of other posadas on the block with more comfort.

Backpackers Hostel (☎ 674 0525; www.backpack ershostel.com.mx; Real de Mexicanos 16; dm US$5-6, s/d incl breakfast US$15/20; ☐) It's an excellent hacienda-style hostel with four- and 10-bunk dorms and five private rooms (each with bathroom) wrapped around a grassy courtyard. One dorm is for women only. There's free internet, plus table football and a nightly bonfire.

La Casa de José (☎ 674 7667; lacasadejose2004@yahoo .com.mx; Josefa Ortíz de Domínguez 32A; dm/s/d incl breakfast US$5/12/17; ☐) A bit closer to bus station, José keeps a well-kept hostel.

Hostal Los Camellos (☎ 967 116 0097; www.losca mellos.over-blog.com; Real de Guadalupe 110; dm US$6, s/d US$10/16, with bathroom US$13/20) The Kathmandu-let-it-be groove is on high at this friendly hostel with open patios and colorful rooms. Some dorms have private bathroom.

Posada Mexico (☎ 678 0014; posadamexico@hotmail .com; Josefa Ortíz de Domínguez 12; dm US$8, r with/without bathroom US$26/22) The most-popular hostel in San Cristóbal gets a 'wow' at first look, with an immaculate TV room (with bean-bag chairs, bar and pool table) and mountain views from the garden. The dorms are a bit tight (one is women-only), and the 11 (slightly overpriced) rooms fill quickly.

GUESTHOUSES

Posada Casa Real (☎ 678 1303; Real de Guadalupe 51; r per person US$7) A colorful but aged posada where all rooms have shared bathroom.

Posada San Agustín (☎ 678 1816; Ejército Nacional 7; s/d US$15/20) An inviting, family-run guesthouse, it has 15 nicely decorated rooms, plenty of hot water and a view up top.

Posada Los Morales (☎ 678 1472; Allende 17; d/tr US$17/22) Made-over recently, this 23-room guesthouse scales the side of the Cerro de San Cristóbal, with nice views and – sacre bleu! – fireplaces, perfect for those chilly nights.

Hotel Posada Jovel (☎ 678 1734; www.mundochiapas .com/hotelposadajovel; Paniagua 27; d from US$30; 🖳) This neat minisplurge is a two-part hotel-posada on either side of the street; higher-priced rooms surround a garden.

Posada Margarita (☎ 678 0957; Real de Guadalupe 34; s/d US$35/45) The Margarita, a recently renovated, longtime go-to, is pricey but nice with TVs and wood-beam ceilings.

Eating

EAST OF THE ZÓCALO

Real de Guadalupe is lined with options; Madero has some cheapie family spots.

La Pera (MA Flores 23; mains $2.50-8; 🕑 1-11pm Mon-Sat) This artsy place, with jovial students huddled around candle-lit tables on wooden floors, serves a mix of well-prepared Mexican and Italian food, plus sandwiches and salads.

TierrAdentro (Real de Guadalupe 24; set breakfasts US$2.80-3.80; 🕑 8am-11pm; 🖳) It has a sun-roofed-covered patio and comes with wi-fi access, good coffee and food all day.

El Gato Gordo (Real de Guadalupe 20; dishes US$3-4.50; 🕑 1-11pm Wed-Mon) Decorated like a bong shop, the popular Fat Cat is best known for its US$2.80 vegetarian deal.

La Casa del Pan (Dr Navarro 10; mains US$3-6; 🕑 closed Mon) This parent of the Real de Guadalupe outlet (following) is more inviting. The pizza, fajitas, chile rellenos and a US$7 set meal are all veggie, all organic. It makes packed lunches too.

La Casa del Pan Papalotl (Real de Guadalupe 55; buffet US$6; 🕑 9am-10pm) Come for the knockout vegetarian buffet (from 2pm to 5pm) – with desserts and fresh organic dishes.

Super Mas (Real de Guadalupe 22) A big grocery store.

SOUTH OF THE ZÓCALO

Food stalls (Insurgentes; dishes US$1.50-2.50) These open-air stalls, next to the Templo de San Francisco, serve comidas economicas (cheap set meals).

Madre Tierra (Insurgentes 19; set breakfasts US$2.20-5.80, mains $2.50-5) San Cristóbal's best breakfast place – and excellent for its pizza, spinach cannelloni and sandwiches too – the cozy Madre Tierra has inside tables and six tables in a courtyard. There's also a good bakery with fresh bread, brownies and pizza slices.

Drinking

Chiapas is coffee country – the Altura variety is the best; here are a couple of cafés that brew beans bought direct from the coffee farmers.

Café Museo Café (MA Flores 10; 🕑 9am-9:30pm) Café and small museum fun by cooperative of 15,000 farmers.

La Selva (Rosas 9; 🕑 9am-11:30pm; 🖳) Roomy, with wi-fi access.

Booze flows all over town – though most options are on and around Real de Guadalupe. Here are a few diverse standouts.

Bar Revolución (20 de Noviembre & 1 de Marzo; 🕑 noon-11:30pm Mon-Sat) A great corner bar with a jazz, rock or reggae band playing and Emiliano Zapata murals. The music starts at 9pm, and local hipsterfolk and travelers often fill the place.

Latino's (Madero 23; 🕑 8pm-3am Mon-Sat) This loud and bright dance spot draws Coleto salseros. Has a US$1.50 cover Thursday to Saturday.

Los Amigos (Honduras 4; 🕑 9am-8pm) It's a fun but unrowdy cantina that's popular with snacking families.

Entertainment

San Cristóbal is a movie town, with several places playing heaps of interesting arthouse films (including many Zapatista documentaries with English subtitles). Admission is US$2 per film.

Cineclub La Ventana (☎ 678 4297; Insurgentes 19)

El Puente (☎ 678 3723; Real de Guadalupe 55)

Kinoki (☎ 678 0495; 1 de Marzo 22) Best for indie films, with a laid-back lounge.

Shopping

Nemizapata (Real de Guadalupe 45; 🕑 9:30am-8:30pm Mon-Sat) is a colorful Zapatista-run store with Zapatista art, T-shirts and organic coffee.

Getting There & Away

Tuxtla Gutiérrez airport is 85km north. **Mexicana** (☎ 678 9309; Belisario Domínguez 2B) sells tickets for Mexico City and Cancún (US$280, via Mexico City).

Long-distance buses leave from several terminals on the Pan-Americana, near the corner of Insurgentes, where you'll find the **OCC Bus Terminal** (☎ 678 0291) for 1st-class buses (OCC is the cheapest). You can also buy tickets for these at **Ticket Bus** (☎ 678 8503; Real de Guadalupe 5; ☒ 7am-11pm Mon-Sat, 9am-5pm Sun) in the center.

Across the highway, **AEXA** (☎ 678 6178) has cheaper, perfectly good 2nd-class services to Palenque. Further west, Transportes Lacandonia (TL) has dodgier 2nd-class services.

Daily departures include:

Cancún US$61-72 (OCC); US$30 (TL); 18hr; 4 daily
Ciudad Cuauhtémoc US$10 (OCC); 3½hr; 4 daily
Comitán US$3 (OCC); 2hr; frequent buses
Mérida US$45 (OCC); 14hr; 1 night bus daily
Mexico City US$77-91 (OCC); US$30 (TL); 19hr; 10 daily
Palenque US$8.20-13 (OCC); US$7.50 (AEXA); 4½-5hr; frequent buses

Shared vans leave from various spots nearby to Tuxtla Gutiérrez (stopping at Chiapa de Corzo if you request) and to Comitán (US$2.50 to US$3.50, from 4am to 9pm or so).

For details on getting to Maya hill towns (such as San Juan Chamula), see opposite.

AROUND SAN CRISTÓBAL

Many travelers visit the following sights on a guided tour from San Cristóbal.

Maya Villages

It is hard to find more memorable experiences in this world than taking in (respectfully!) a glimpse of Tzotzil or Tzeltal life in the Maya villages in the hills outside San Cristóbal. The traditions of the past mingle exotically with the modern world – farmers in sheep-fur vests and women in multicolored tunics and thick black-wool skirts bringing Pepsi and chickens into Catholic churches that have pine-needle floors – but it has fostered a 'zoolike' mentality for some visitors.

Do *not* take photos inside any church or of any person without permission; it's believed to steal spirits. Be careful not to step on candles on the floor. And try not to stand and stare at those in worship. But feel free to say 'hello' outside churches – like anywhere, locals are happy to talk about their lives to those earnestly interested. In 2005 a tourist who photographed someone without permission, got punched out in Chamula.

TOURS

It's absolutely worth going with a knowledgeable guide who can describe the fascinating background. Respectful agencies around town book tours to visit the Tzotzil pueblo of San Juan Chamula, 10km north, and nearby San

---

LOCAL VOICES: CHAMULA CHAT

San Juan Chamula is the area's most visited Maya village, as many as 300 people come daily. We talked with 45-year-old Pedro, who checks tickets at the church.

■ **Does that sheep-fur tunic [an itchy black-haired chuj] you're wearing have any special significance?** Oh, no. It was just cold this morning so I put this on. People know where I'm from when I wear it – it's the common clothing of Chamula. So I like it.

■ **Why do you think there's so much interest in your village?** Tourists come to visit to see ceremonies they don't have – like drinking fizzy drinks and killing chickens in the church.

■ **Is tourism good or bad for the village?** The village gets some money for the church from the tickets, so it's good.

■ **Some visitors anger locals though, don't they?** Some, yes. The most important thing is not taking photographs in the church – we tell them, but still they do. Ah, many times! This steals the spirits of the saints. It's part of our beliefs.

■ **Have you traveled?** No, only to Cancún to work. It's beautiful, but the police wouldn't let me sell my *artesanías*.

■ **Any future travel plans?** I want to go to the USA, just to see it. Do you have space to take me?

As told to Robert Reid

GETTING TO THE GUATEMALA HIGHLANDS

There's two ways to reach Guatemala via the convenient **Ciudad Cuauhtémoc–La Mesilla** border: DIY bus rides or by a shuttle service offered daily. Several travel agencies in San Cristóbal offer the 'shuttle' service at 7:30am daily to either near Quetzaltenango (US$28, eight hours), Panajachel (US$28, eight hours) or Antigua (US$38, 11 hours). This saves a taxi/colectivo ride across the border and offers hotel pick-up. It goes on demand and is not direct; you'll catch a shuttle to the border, then another will be waiting for you on the other side of the border.

Going on your own, though, saves 50%. Catch a bus to Ciudad Cuauhtémoc and pass through Mexican immigration. Colectivos (about US$0.80) make the 4km trip to Guatemalan immigration; be sure to get your passport stamped at both. In La Mesilla, many 'chicken buses' leave throughout the day. Some travelers swear by the 'shuttle,' though.

For the reverse trip, see p152. There's also an alternate crossing via Tapachula, Mexico.

Lorenzo Zinacantán, plus some other towns, for US$13 to US$16. A terrific option are the 4½-hour trips (in English) with **Alex & Raul** (☎ 967 678 3741; US$13), who lead small groups that leave at 9:30am daily from the black cross on the west side of the San Cristóbal cathedral by the *zócalo*; just show up. They can arrange tours to Tenejapa on Thursday and Sunday ($15 per person, minimum four). **Los Pingüinos** (☎ 967 678 0202; Ecuador 8B; ♈ 10am-2:30pm, 3:30-7pm Mon-Sat) rents bicycles and leads good tours, including one to Chemula, from about US$25.

TOWNS

San Juan Chamula, by far the area's most popular destination, is a conservative and fiercely independent Tzotzil community where polygamy is active. Chamula has a big Sunday market and a colorful church (admission US$1.50 paid in the town hall nearby) with a pine needle–covered floor, hundreds of lit candles, and worshippers drinking soda to usurp evil spirits. Feel free to try out some Tzotzil: *k'usi aw otan* (hello) or *licalto* (so long). **San Lorenzo Zinacantán** is another Tzotzil village and is known for flowers, floral textiles, and a festival around August 10.

Other towns in the area see fewer visitors. **Tenejapa**, 25km northeast, has a small museum and many woven items for sale (Thursday is market day). **Amatenango del Valle**, 37km southeast (take a Comitán-bound van from the Pan-Americana) is famed for its *animalito* pottery.

Colectivos go direct to these towns (from 6am to 6pm) from San Cristóbal (see Map p64 for departure points).

Other Sights

Organized day trips take in many of these sites, but going on your own allows you to add on a couple of worthy and less-visited sites.

CANYONS & JAGUARS

A super day trip – and a break from the mountain chill – is a 'two-fer' to the grubby colonial town of Chiapa de Corzo (60km northwest), where 1½-hour **boat trips** (US$10; ♈ 9am-4.30pm) drift through stunning, kilometer-high **Cañón del Sumidero**, with lots of monkeys and crocodiles to spot. From San Cristóbal, get on a Tuxtla-bound colectivo to the Chiapa de Corzo turnoff (US$3.50, 45 minutes), then hop on a centro-bound combi (US$0.40); boats are two blocks south of the plaza.

Afterwards take a combi to Tuxtla Gutiérrez, Chiapas' modern capital, which is home to the remarkable **Zoomat** (☎ 961-614 4765; admission US$2; ♈ 8:30am-5pm Tue-Sun), a zoo with a jungle setting so real it can unnerve visitors and certain guidebook researchers. From Tuxtla's center (a couple of blocks northwest of the combi depot), take a marked colectivo. Get to Tuxtla (US$0.90, 25 minutes) from Chiapa de Corzo in a 'Chiapa-Tuxtla' combi; the vans back to San Cristóbal can be found at 2a Av Sur Oriente at 4a Calle Oriente Sur (a couple of blocks east of the combi depot).

San Cristóbal's travel agencies offer half-day tours of the canyon (only) for US$15.

COMITÁN & AROUND

Few visitors stop in Comitán (90km southeast of San Cristóbal) so they miss its darling little colonial center, where there are a couple of museums, a sculpture-filled plaza, promenade eating spots, and a helpful **tourist information center** (☎ 963 632 4047; ♈ 8.30-7pm Mon-Fri, 9am-2pm Sat), on the plaza. The center is 10 blocks north of the bus station (US$1.80 by taxi).

A nice sleeping spot is **Posada La Flores** (☎ 963 632 3334; 1a Av Pte Nte 17; s/d from US$8/13), northwest of the plaza.

There's plenty to do around Comitán. About 40km southwest, mighty **El Chiflón** is a 70m waterfall that splashes visitors after a 1.3km walk up. Vans go to the falls (US$2, 45 minutes) half-hourly from a block east of Comitán's OCC bus station on Blvd Domínguez Sur.

About 45km southeast of Comitán is the turnoff for the oft-overlooked **Chinkultic ruins** (admission US$3; ⊙ 10am-4pm), which requires a 2km walk. There's a steep walk up to the 'acropolis' overlooking a cenote. Often no-one is there.

The remarkably colored network of **Lagunas de Montebello** (8km from the Chinkultic turnoff) draw many visitors to 'ooh' at. The national park has two parts; the most popular is at Bosque Azul, where you can ride horses (about US$5), hike on a 2.5km loop, see lakes colored emerald and green, and hike to Grutas San Rafael del Arco (worth it – the river breaks through a wall of rock).

Combis go to Lagunas de Montebello (US$2.50, one hour) from 2a Av Pte Sur 23 (a few blocks south of Comitán's plaza).

San Cristóbal's agencies offer day trips of El Chiflón and Lagos de Montebello (missing Chinkultic or Comitán) for about US$23.

MEXICO DIRECTORY

ACCOMMODATIONS

If you're dorming it, a bunk is US$10 to US$12; if you go 'private,' Yucatán rates (around US$30 or US$40 for a double) are higher than in Chiapas (about US$15 or US$20). You'll need a towel and soap for many cheap stays; most hostels provide sheets, but many lack mosquito nets (but not mosquitoes). Some places on the beach and in Palenque charge US$5 to US$7 for a space for a tent or hammock.

Prices in this chapter are for high season, generally mid-December through February,

---

BOOK ACCOMMODATIONS ONLINE

For more accommodations reviews and recommendations by Lonely Planet authors, check out the online booking service at www.lonelyplanet.com. You'll find the true, insider lowdown on the best places to stay. Reviews are thorough and independent. Best of all, you can book online.

---

plus Semana Santa and, sometimes, summer (July and August).

ACTIVITIES

Diving the Yucatán is a big highlight, with super reefs off Cozumel (p51), but also near Isla Mujeres (p42) and Punta Allen (p56). Also fun is snorkeling or diving in cenotes between Playa del Carmen and Tulum. You can rappel into one at Ek-Balam (p44). There are kayak trips at the Reserva de la Biósfera Sian Ka'an (p56). In the highlands, you can arrange good bike trips from San Cristóbal de Las Casas (p62).

BOOKS

If you're venturing north to Oaxaca, Mexico City or further inland on the Yucatán Peninsula, pick up Lonely Planet's *Mexico* or *Yucatán*, or *Mexico City*.

BUSINESS HOURS

Most stores geared to locals (not tourists) are open from 9am to 7pm, with an hour or two off for lunch, Monday to Saturday. Tourist-related businesses usually don't take a break for siesta (this includes tourist offices).

CLIMATE

It's always hot in the Yucatán and around Palenque. Wet season, from May to October, makes the air sticky and hot. Hurricane season runs chiefly July to September. In the Chiapas highlands, temperatures cool considerably, hovering between 10°C and low 20°C all year.

CUSTOMS

The normal routine when you enter Mexico by air is to complete a customs declaration form (which lists duty-free allowances), then place it in a machine. If the machine shows a green light, you pass without inspection. If a red light shows, your baggage will be searched.

DANGERS & ANNOYANCES

Incidents of theft and sexual assault on Yucatán beaches aren't unknown. The beach towns of Cancún, Cozumel and Playa del Carmen have tourist police strolling on beaches to help deter would-be crimes. The political situation in Chiapas, meanwhile, has simmered in recent years, but remains uncertain. There are a few military checkpoints, particularly near the Guatemala border. Military bases are located near (the presently quiet) Zapatista-run autonomous zones in the hills north of San Cristóbal.

Always count your change carefully, as short-changing (and overcharging) occurs, particularly in the Yucatán.

DISCOUNT CARDS

The ISIC student card, the IYTC card for travelers under 26, and ITIC card for teachers can help you obtain reduced-price air tickets to or from Mexico at student- and youth-oriented travel agencies. Hostels affiliated with the Hostelling International (HI) saves about US$1 per night.

EMBASSIES & CONSULATES
Embassies & Consulates in Mexico

Many countries have a consulate in Cancún; exceptions include Australia, New Zealand and Central American countries other than Belize.

Australia (☎ 551-101 2265; www.mexico.embassy .gov.au; Rubén Darío 55, Polanco, Mexico City)

Belize (☎ 887 8417; Av Náder 34, 1st fl, Cancún) Enter via Lima.

Canada (☎ 998-883 3360; Plaza Caracol II No 330, Blvd Kukulcán Km 8.5, Zona Hotelera, Cancún)

France Cancún (☎ 998-267 9722; Calle Pirgo 24); Mérida (☎ 999-944 4215; Calle 33D No 528)

Germany (☎ 998-884 5333; Punta Conoco No 36, Cancún)

Guatemala Cancún (☎ 998-883 8296; Av Náder 148)

Italy (☎ 998-884 1261; Alcatraces No 39, Cancún)

Netherlands (☎ 998-886 0134; Mexicana Terminal 2, Cancún Airport, Cancún)

New Zealand (☎ 555-283 9460; kiwimexico@compu serve.com.mx; Balmes 8, Los Morales, Mexico City)

Spain (☎ 998-848 9900; Edificio Oásis, Blvd Kukulcán Km 16.5, Zona Hotelera, Cancún)

UK (☎ 998-881 0100; The Royal Sands, Blvd Kukulcán Km 13.5, Zona Hotelera, Cancún)

USA Cancún (☎ 998-883 0272; Plaza Caracol II, 2nd fl, No 320-323, Blvd Kukulcán Km 8.5, Zona Hotelera); Cozumel (☎ 987-872 4574; Villa Mar Mall, Main Plaza btwn Avs 5 & Melgar); Mérida (☎ 999-925 5011; Paseo de Montejo 453)

Mexican Embassies & Consulates Abroad

The following is a list of Mexican embassies and consulates outside Central America.

Australia (☎ 02-6273 3963; www.mexico.org.au; 14 Perth Ave, Yarralumla, Canberra, ACT 2600)

Canada (☎ 613-233-8988; www.embamexcan.com; 45 O'Connor St, Suite 1500, Ottawa, ON K1P 1A4)

France (☎ 01 53 70 27 70; www.sre.gob.mx/francia; 9 rue de Longchamp, 75116 Paris)

Germany (☎ 030-269 3230; www.embamex.de; Klingelhöferstraße 3, 10785 Berlin)

UK (☎ 020-7235 6393; www.sre.gob.mx/reinounido; 8 Halkin St, London SW1X 7DW)

USA embassy (☎ 202-728-1600; www.embassyofmexico .org; 1911 Pennsylvania Ave NW, Washington, DC 20006); consulate New York (☎ 212-217-6400; 27 E 39 St); consulate San Francisco (☎ 415-354-1700; 532 Folsom St)

FESTIVALS & EVENTS

During most festivals, banks and government offices close their doors to join the party. Big events include **Día de los Reyes Magos** (Three Kings' Day; January 6), **Carnaval** (late February or early March); **Semana Santa** (Easter Week), **Día de los Muertos** (Day of the Dead; November 2) and **Día de Nuestra Señora de Guadalupe** (Day of Our Lady of Guadalupe; December 12).

FOOD

Look out for *'comidas corridas'* or *'comidas economicas.'* These basic set meals, served for lunch (and into the afternoon), are widespread and cheap (US$3 to US$4.50). They usually come as soup, a meat dish with rice, a drink and dessert. Restaurants tend to keep long hours – often 7am to 10pm or midnight daily.

GAY & LESBIAN TRAVELERS

Cancún and Playa del Carmen are the biggest destinations. In May, the five-day Cancún International Gay Festival is parade-free but includes many events.

Here are a few websites with gay-friendly listings and other useful tips:

www.aquiestamos.com Contains Cancún listings.

www.gay.com In depth 'guides' to Cancún, Playa del Carmen and Mérida.

www.gaymexico.net Cancún link includes info on a gay parade.

HOLIDAYS

The chief holiday periods are Christmas to New Year, Semana Santa (the week leading up to Easter and up to a week afterwards) and mid-July to mid-August. Others include Día de la Constitución (Constitution Day; February 5), Día del Trabajo (Labor Day; May 1), Cinco de Mayo (May 5), Día de la Independencia (Independence Day; September 16) and Día de la Raza (Columbus Day; October 12).

INTERNET ACCESS

Internet cafés are easy to find anywhere in places listed in this chapter other than Punta Allen and the far-flung ruins. It costs about US$1.50 to US$2 per hour to get behind a machine.

LEGAL MATTERS

Mexican law presumes an accused person is guilty until proven innocent. If you're arrested, you have the right to notify your embassy or consulate. Also, the national tourism ministry **Sectur** (☎ 078, 800 987 8224) offers 24-hour phone advice.

Police or military checkpoints are normally looking for drugs, weapons or illegal migrants.

MAPS

Guía Roji publishes a useful map called *Mundo Maya* (US$6) that covers the Yucatán and Chiapas. Look for it in gas stations and convenience stores.

MONEY

The Mexican peso (M$) is divided into 100 centavos. Nearly all prices in this chapter are in US dollars (US$). At research time M$10.80 was equal to the US dollar.

The best way to get pesos in Mexico is from widely available ATMs *(cajeros automáticos)*, which use the Cirrus and Plus systems. You can cash money or traveler's checks at banks or at many *casas de cambio* (exchange houses). It's generally possible to change Canadian dollars, euros and British pounds.

Not many cheap accommodations or restaurants accept credit cards, but most travel agencies selling air tickets do.

Costs are higher in Yucatán than in Chiapas. At most restaurants, a 10% tip is expected; some resort towns expect US levels of 15%.

Exchange Rates

The table shows currency exchange rates at the time this book went to press.

Country	Unit	Pesos (M$)
Australia	A$1	9.20
Canada	C$1	10.10
euro zone	€1	14.60
Japan	¥100	8.80
New Zealand	NZ$1	8.30
UK	£1	21.70
USA	US$1	10.80

POST

Post offices are typically open Monday to Friday, and Saturday morning. Post offices will hold letters for you as *lista de correos* (up to 10 days) or poste restante (longer).

RESPONSIBLE TRAVEL

Tourists wreak havoc on coral reefs off the Yucatán shore. Some highly promoted Disneyfied beach parks, such as Xcaret (not included here), receive criticism for their dolphin shows and damage to the ecosystems.

Maya communities remain richly traditional. Be careful when visiting such communities; *never* photograph unless you have permission as it's deeply offensive, nor should you photograph objects such as saints in churches, which are regarded as sacred by the Maya.

Try to buy products – hammocks, handicrafts, coffee – directly from the source, or from shops that represent them. We've tried to flag some.

STUDYING

Spanish-language schools are more expensive in Mexico than in the rest of Central America. San Cristóbal de Las Casas (p66) has the most-developed language-school scene, but there are also schools available in Cancún (p38), Valladolid (p44) and also in Playa del Carmen (p49).

TELEPHONE

Local phone calls are cheap, but domestic long-distance and international calls can be expensive unless you call from a *caseta telefónica* (or *locutorio*), which offer international calls from US$0.30 or US$0.40 per minute.

Area codes are three digits, local numbers are seven digits. To make calls to/from Mexico:

Calling Mexico from abroad Dial your international access code, then ☎ 52 (Mexico's country code), followed by the area code and seven-digit number.
Calling abroad from Mexico Dial ☎ 00, followed by country code, area code and number.
Calling long-distance in Mexico Dial ☎ 01, followed by the three-digit area code and local number.

Collect calls are very costly. To make one, dial ☎ 090 for an international operator.

WARNING

We always hear from travelers paying dozens of dollars for short calls using a credit card. Simply don't use credit-card phones; many are scams, charging as much as US$30 for the first minute.

Cell Phones

The most widespread cellular phone system in Mexico is **Telcel** (www.telcel.com). Amigo cards, for recharging Telcel phones, are widely available.

Phonecards

To use a Telmex card phone, get the card called *tarjeta Ladatel* from convenience stores, sold in various denominations. It's US$0.10 per minute for local calls, US$0.40 for national calls and US$0.50 for the USA. Other international calls are much more expensive.

Some phone (or calling) cards from other countries can be used for making phone calls from Mexico by dialing special access numbers:

AT&T (☎ 01 800 288-2872, 01 800 462-4240)
Bell Canada (☎ 01 800 123-0200, 01 800 021-1994)
BT Chargecard (☎ 01 800 123-0244)
MCI (☎ 01 800 674-7000)
Sprint (☎ 01 800 877-8000)

TOILETS

These vary, but are generally never horrendous. And you pay for what you get (usually US$0.20 or US$0.30 a tinkle). Bus stations often keep quite clean ones.

TOURIST INFORMATION

'Tourist information' in many places means handing out brochures (and maybe plugging tours). Municipal and state-run tourist offices are set up in most towns; some have English-speaking staff, which vary in usefulness.

State-run websites include
Chiapas (www.turismochiapas.gob.mx)
Quintana Roo (sedetur.qroo.gob.mx in Spanish)
Yucatán (www.mayayucatan.com)

VISAS & DOCUMENTS

Citizens of many countries (including the USA, Canada, EU countries, Australia, New Zealand and Japan) are among those who do not presently require visas to enter Mexico as tourists. The list does change; check with a Mexican embassy or consulate.

When entering Mexico, all tourists must obtain a tourist card (Forma Migratoria

---

> **PAID YOUR 'NONIMMIGRANT FEE' YET?**
>
> All visitors to Mexico must pay a 'nonimmigrant fee' (*derecho para no immigrante*; DNI) of around US$20. It's automatically included with outbound air tickets, but if you go by land, you must pay the fee at a bank (see the list on the card). The bank will stamp your card 'paid,' and you'll need to give it to immigration upon exiting Mexico. Most borders have banks handy, but paying beforehand saves time – and possibly a trip back to a town bank.
>
> When leaving Mexico, if you're planning to return soon, tell immigration, who sometimes allow visitors to keep tourist cards for US$10.

para Turista; FMT) from Mexican immigration. Officers will write in the length of your stay; although the maximum is 180 days for most nationalities (Australians' max is 90), let the officer know how long you want to stay, as he/she sometimes puts in fewer than the maximum. If that happens, it can be extended – to the maximum – at an immigration office for free, or extended beyond the maximum for about US$20. If you lose the card you'll (supposedly) have to pay a fine of about US$45.

Travelers under 18 are sometimes required to show notarized consent forms from their parents! Officials are less likely to ask than airline staff when boarding. If you're under 18, check with a Mexican consulate before you go.

VOLUNTEERING

Habitat for Humanity or Na Bolom in San Cristóbal de Las Casas (p66) run projects in Chiapas.

Centro Ecológico Akumal (www.ceakumal.org) accepts volunteers in its efforts to preserve the environment in the heart of resort country in the Yucatán.

Also see p733 for organizations that arrange projects from outside the region.

Guatemala

HIGHLIGHTS

- **Río Dulce** Soak in a warm waterfall, go jungle hiking and take in Garífuna culture (p174)
- **Tikal** Ignore the tour groups – this is the country's number-one tourist attraction for good reason (p194)
- **Antigua, Quetzaltenango & Lago de Atitlán** Eat, drink and sleep well while studying Spanish and climbing volcanoes in Guatemala's most cosmopolitan and picturesque cities (p101 & p136) near a fabulous highland lake (p113)
- **Semuc Champey** Find out why people call this the most beautiful spot in the whole country (p167)
- **Best journey** Huehuetenango–Cobán: half-beautiful new road, half-hellish dirt track, with spectacular views from start to finish (p152)
- **Off the beaten track** Grab some time in the green room at the country's largely undiscovered surf capital, Sipacate (p157)

FAST FACTS

- **Area** 108,890 sq km (smaller than the US state of Louisiana, a bit bigger than England)
- **ATMs** Plentiful
- **Budget** US$15-30 per day
- **Capital** Guatemala City
- **Costs** Budget hotel in Guatemala City US$10, bottle of beer US$2, 3hr bus ride US$3, set lunch US$3
- **Country Code** ☎ 502
- **Electricity** 115V to 125V, 60Hz; US-type plugs
- **Famous for** Maya sites
- **Head of State** President Oscar Berger
- **Languages** Spanish, Maya
- **Money** US$1 = Q7.90 (quetzals); US dollars readily accepted
- **Phrases** De huevos (cool), papichulo (handsome man), Chapín (Guatemalan)
- **Population** 13.1 million
- **Time** GMT minus 6 hours, minus 5 hours in daylight savings
- **Traveler's Checks** Cashed at major banks (ATMs are easier)
- **Visas** North American and most EU citizens need only a valid passport

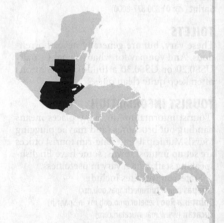

TRAVEL HINTS

Pack light, and you can put your backpack inside the bus. Everything is negotiable (almost).

OVERLAND ROUTES

From Mexico enter Guatemala at Tecún Umán–Ciudad Hidalgo or La Mesilla–Ciudad Cuauhtémoc. From El Salvador enter via Anguiatú; from Honduras via Agua Caliente; and from Belize via Benque Viejo del Carmen.

Guatemala is a magical place. If you're into the Maya, the mountains, the markets or any of a million other things, you're bound to be captivated. People come and they stay. Or they leave and return. There's almost too much going on here, and even the shortest trip down the road takes you to completely different places, with new challenges and surprises. Don't be surprised if you hear yourself saying, 'we'll have to come back and do that, *next time.*'

Wanna surf in the morning and learn Spanish in the afternoon? No problem. Descend a volcano, grab a shower and hit the sushi bar for dinner? You can do that. Check out a Maya temple and be swinging in a beachside hammock by sunset? Easy.

Guatemala's got its problems, but they mainly keep to themselves (although if you go looking for trouble, who knows what you'll find). Ten years after the official end to the civil war, this isn't the scary place that your mother fears it is. Travel here, once fraught with danger and discomfort, is now characterized by ease – you can do pretty much whatever you want, and your experience will only be limited by your imagination and time.

CURRENT EVENTS

It's hard to find the silver lining to the clouds that hang over Guatemala's political situation. Recently rated the worst democracy in Latin America (and *that's* some stiff competition right there), the country faces some seemingly insurmountable obstacles.

Most worrying is the continued presence of José Efraín Ríos Montt on the landscape. Responsible for the death of at least 15,000 indigenous people during his various reigns as dictator, this US-backed evangelical Christian is also wanted by Spanish authorities for his part in the burning of the Spanish embassy and subsequent deaths of 37 people. At the time of writing, Ríos Montt was running for Congress, and if elected will be immune from prosecution.

The legal system is slow to act, and when it does it tends to favor the rich. In villages, lynchings are a near-daily occurrence as the rural population loses patience waiting for an under-resourced police force to possibly investigate rapes, robberies and murders, and maybe send perpetrators to an overburdened court from where they may get sent for a short stay in an overcrowded prison. Crime is not just a rural problem – a recent study reported that private security guards now far outnumber members of the police force.

General despair and good reason have made many lose faith in the government's ability or will to ever solve any of these problems. The hundreds of NGOs operating in the cities and countryside are a testament to international concern and local initiative. Indigenous pride is making a comeback – the Maya and other indigenous groups are beginning to organize politically, both in voter turnout and more strident calls for self-determination. Rigoberta Menchú, Nobel Prize winner and indigenous

activist looks likely to run for president, a development which already has right-wing commentators slyly sinking in the boot in the national press.

Hurricane Stan hit the country's northwest in October 2005, causing massive devastation and loss of life. The country's infrastructure, never wonderful, was torn apart as roads and villages were buried under landslides, and bridges, electricity, power and phone lines went down. An optimistic government estimate said that it would take about five years to repair the damage.

Cafta (the Central America Free Trade Agreement, or *Tratado de Libre Comercio* – TLC in Spanish) seems to be an inevitable step in the country's economic future, even though, at the time of writing, Guatemala was dragging its feet in ratifying it. The Agreement has few supporters outside of government and big business, and most people see promises of resulting employment and economic development as hollow at best.

Mining is another hot topic. Multinational companies (using the same employment and development arguments) are moving in to exploit the country's mineral wealth in regions such as San Marcos and El Estor, despite massive protests from community and environmental groups. Police have responded to peaceful occupations with the use of violent evictions.

The country was left effectively bankrupt when, at the end of his term, ex-President Alfonso Portillo of the FRG looted the social security fund and fled to Mexico, where he is today, no doubt chuckling at unsuccessful extradition attempts.

The year 2006 was a bad one for money all around – two large banks went under amid a storm of accusations of dodgy deals and

GUATEMALA

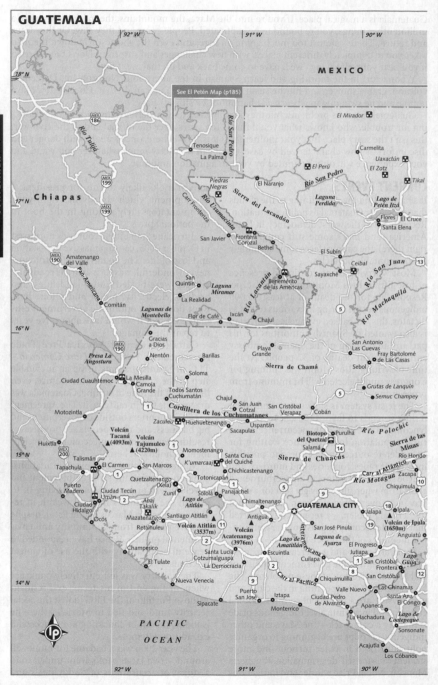

See El Petén Map (p185)

MEXICO

Chiapas

PACIFIC OCEAN

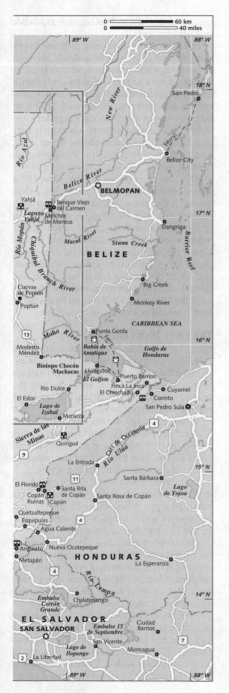

unsecured loans and then, just as the Christmas season was approaching, the Central Bank withdrew huge amounts of old Q100 bills from circulation, with the idea of replacing them. Problem was, the new bills hadn't even been printed yet. Banks were left literally without money, as were thousands of people who were unable to withdraw more than the equivalent of US$80 per day.

Current President Oscar Berger, of the Gran Alianza Nacional coalition, has managed to stay relatively untouched by political scandal since he took office in 2003 – critics say this is because he hasn't really done *anything*, let alone anything bad. The next elections are slated for late 2007. General dissatisfaction with the current administration (Berger's approval rating plummeted from 89% in 2004 to 52% at the start of 2006) has placed Álvaro Colom of the center-leftist Unidad Nacional de la Esperanza ahead in the opinion polls and a real possibility to take over as president.

HISTORY

Earliest estimates put humans in what is now Guatemala as far back as 11,000 BC. The prevailing theory is that they got here by walking across an ice bridge from Siberia (pretty compelling if you compare a Tibetan with a Bolivian).

Once their traditional food sources (mammoths, wild nuts and berries) began to dry up, these early inhabitants became farmers, domesticating corn, beans, tomatoes, chilies, turkeys and dogs for the dinner table. The improvement in the stability of the food supply led to population growth, an improvement in agricultural techniques, the development of early art forms and a language that is traceable to what many Maya speak today.

Maya astronomers count the present era as starting at 3114 BC. Archaeologists generally put the birth of the Maya civilization (the pre-Classic Period) at around 2000 BC.

Rise & Fall of the Maya

Further developments in agriculture and increases in population gave these early civilizations time and resources to develop artistic and architectural techniques.

Between 800 BC and AD 100 population centers such as El Mirador in the Petén and Kaminaljuyú (site of present-day Guatemala City) grew with trade and conquest and hundreds (if not thousands – many are yet to be uncovered) of temples and ceremonial centers were built. Guatemala's most famous Maya site, Tikal, came into its own around the start of the Classic Period – AD 250.

The history of these – and many other – city states was troubled at best, characterized by broken military alliances, food shortages and droughts. The best not-too-academic reading on this time is in Simon Martin and Nicholas Grube's *Chronicle of the Maya Kings and Queens* (2000).

By the time the Spanish arrived, Maya civilization was already in trouble. Some centers, such as El Mirador had already been abandoned and others such as Tikal and Quiriguá had shrunk to the size of minor towns. Theories suggest that many abandoned the Petén in favor of the highlands, setting up capitals in K'umarcaaj (see p132), Iximché (p122), Zaculeu (p148), and Mixco Viejo.

Relocation didn't bring peace, though – soon, Toltec tribes, having abandoned the Yucatán, moved in and began to take control. Infighting amongst tribes, overpopulation and the resulting strain on the food supply combined to make conditions very favorable to the Spanish when they arrived in 1523. For more information see p31.

Conquest & Colonization

The Spanish didn't just walk on in, as many think. Spirited resistance was met, most notably from the K'iche (in a famous battle led by Tecún Umán, near present-day Quetzaltenango). In yet another sad episode in Guatemalan history, the neighboring Kaqchiquel not only refused to join forces with the K'iche, they actually joined the Spanish and fought against them!

It didn't take long for the Spanish to shaft the Kaqchiquel, though, and pretty soon most of the Maya were under Spanish control, the exceptions being the Rabinal (who have largely maintained their culture) and the Itzáes, who, hidden out on the island of Flores in El Petén were unconquered until 1697.

The 19th Century

During the short existence of the United Provinces of Central America, liberal president Francisco Morazán (1830–39) instituted reforms aimed at correcting three persistent problems: the overwhelming power of the Church; the division of society into a Hispanic upper class and an *indígena* (of indigenous origin) lower class; and the region's impotence in world markets.

But unpopular economic policies, heavy taxes and an 1837 cholera epidemic led to an *indígena* uprising that brought conservative Rafael Carrera to power. Carrera ruled until 1865 and undid much of Morazán's achievements. His government allowed Britain to take control of Belize in exchange for construction of a road between Guatemala City and Belize City. The road was never built, and Guatemala's claims for compensation never resolved.

The liberals regained power in the 1870s under president Justo Rufino Barrios, a rich, young coffee *finca* (plantation) owner who ruled as a dictator. He embarked on a program of modernization – constructing roads, railways, schools and a modern banking system. Unsurprisingly, Barrios also did everything possible to encourage coffee production, including promoting forced relocation and labor. Succeeding governments generally pursued the same policies of control by a wealthy minority and repression of opposition.

The Early 20th Century

From 1898 to 1920, Manuel Estrada Cabrera ruled as a dictator. He fancied himself an enlightened despot, seeking to turn Guatemala into a 'tropical Athens,' while looting the treasury, ignoring education and spending millions on the military.

When Estrada Cabrera was overthrown, Guatemala entered a period of instability that ended in 1931 with the election of General Jorge Ubico, who modernized the country's health and social welfare infrastructure.

In the early 1940s Ubico dispossessed and exiled the German coffee *finca* owners. He assumed a pro-Allied stance during the war, but openly admired Spain's General Franco. In 1944 he was forced into exile.

Philosopher Juan José Arévalo came to power in 1945, establishing the nation's social security system, a bureau of *indígena* affairs, a modern public health system and liberal labor laws. His six years as president saw 25 coup attempts by conservative military forces.

Arévalo was succeeded in 1951 by Colonel Jacobo Arbenz Guzmán, who looked to break up estates and foster high productivity on small farms. But the US supported the interests of large companies such as United Fruit, and in 1954 (in one of the first documented covert

CIA operations) the US government orchestrated an invasion from Honduras led by two exiled Guatemalan military officers. Arbenz was forced to step down and land reform never took place. Violence, oppression and disenfranchisement ensued, fueling the formation of guerrilla groups and fomenting discord.

Civil War

During the 1960s and '70s, economic inequality, surging urban migration and the developing union movement forced oppression to new heights. Amnesty International estimates that 50,000 to 60,000 people were killed in Guatemala during the political violence of the 1970s. Furthermore, the 1976 earthquake killed about 22,000 people and left about a million homeless.

In 1982 General José Efraín Ríos Montt initiated a 'scorched earth' policy, which is believed to have resulted in the extermination of the populations of over 400 villages at the hands of the military. President Ríos Montt, an evangelical Christian, was acting in the name of anti-insurgency, stabilization and anticommunism. An estimated 15,000 people, mostly Maya men, were tortured and massacred; 100,000 refugees fled to Mexico. In response four guerrilla organizations united to form the URNG (Guatemalan National Revolutionary Unity).

In August 1983 Ríos Montt was deposed in a coup led by General Oscar Humberto Mejía Victores, but the human-rights abuses continued. It was estimated that more than 100 political assassinations and 40 abductions occurred every month under the new ruler. The USA suspended military aid to the government, leading to the 1985 election of civilian Christian Democrat Marco Vinicio Cerezo Arévalo – but not before the military secured immunity from prosecution and control of the countryside.

The 1990s

In 1990 Cerezo Arévalo was succeeded by Jorge Serrano Elías, who reopened dialogue with the URNG. But the talks collapsed, Serrano's popularity declined, and he came to depend more on the army for support. On May 25, 1993, Serrano carried out an *autogolpe* (auto coup), suspending the constitution and ruling by decree. Although supported by the military, the coup was unsuccessful and Serrano was forced into exile. Congress

elected Ramiro de León Carpio, the Solicitor for Human Rights and an outspoken critic of the army, to complete Serrano's term.

In March 1995 the USA announced another suspension of aid due to the government's failure to investigate the murder or disappearance of US citizens in Guatemala. These cases included the 1990 murder of Michael Devine and URNG leader Efraín Bámaca Velásquez, whose wife, US attorney Jennifer Harbury, had been conducting a protest (covered in the international media) since his disappearance in 1992. Eventually it was revealed that he had been murdered. Claims were made of CIA involvement in both of the murders, which the US government denied.

The Signing of Peace Accords

In 1996 Álvaro Enrique Arzú Irigoyen of the middle-right PAN (Partido de Avanzada Nacional) was elected. In December he and the URNG signed peace accords ending the 36-year civil war – a war in which an estimated 200,000 Guatemalans were killed, a million were left homeless and untold thousands 'disappeared.'

The accords called for accountability for the armed forces' human-rights violations and resettlement of one million refugees. They also addressed the identity and rights of indigenous peoples, health care, education and other basic social services, women's rights, the abolition of compulsory military service and the incorporation of the ex-guerrillas into civilian life.

It's been a rocky road since the war's end. Bishop Juan Gerardi, coordinator of the Guatemalan Archbishop's Human Rights Office (Odhag), was beaten to death outside his home in 1998, and in May 1999 a minuscule 18% of the population came out to vote down referenda that would have permitted constitutional reforms integral to the peace process. On an encouraging note, the country's Maya population has mobilized politically since the signing of the peace accords.

The greatest challenge to peace stems from inequities in the power structure. It's estimated that 70% of the country's arable land is owned by less than 3% of the population. According to a UN report, the top 20% of the population has an income 30 times greater than the bottom 20%. Or, as most Guatemalans will tell you, there are seven families who 'own' Guatemala.

Discrimination against indigenous people, deeply ingrained in society, results in poverty and misery for most of the population. How the need for economic and social reforms is met may be the most important factor in creating a true and lasting peace.

Guatemala Today

In November 1999 Guatemala held its first peacetime elections in nearly 40 years. In a runoff, conservative and confessed murderer Alfonso Portillo of the FRG (Frente Republicano Guatemalteco) defeated Oscar Berger of the incumbent PAN party. Portillo promised to be tough on criminals, citing his murders as proof of his ability to defend his people. For many human-rights observers, more disturbing than this muddy logic was that Ríos Montt also ran on the FRG ticket and advised Portillo. (Ríos Montt went on to become the leader of Congress.)

Portillo vowed to clean up the judicial system, crack down on crime, tax the rich and respect human rights. In March 2000 he invited UN observers to stay beyond their targeted December 2000 departure date. However, some moves, such as bolstering municipal police squads with national troops and sending most of his family to Canada in self-imposed exile, were particularly worrisome.

In 2002 the UN representative for indigenous peoples, after an 11-day Guatemalan tour, stated that 60% of Guatemalan Maya were still marginalized by discrimination and violence. Poverty, illiteracy, lack of education and poor medical facilities are all much more common in rural areas, where the Maya population is concentrated.

International organizations from the European Parliament to the Interamerican Human Rights Commission criticized the state of human rights in Guatemala. Human Rights workers were subjected to threats and killings by perpetrators acting with seeming impunity. President Portillo failed to carry out a promise to disband the presidential guard and he doubled the defense budget, taking it beyond the maximum level fixed in the Peace Accords.

Lawlessness and violent crime increased dramatically. The US 'decertified' Guatemala (meaning it no longer considered it an ally in the battle against the drugs trade) in 2002. The same year Amnesty International reported that criminals were colluding with sectors of the police, military and local affiliates of multinational corporations to flout human rights.

Most worryingly of all, Ríos Montt himself was named FRG candidate for the late-2003 presidential elections, and then, incredibly, was given the go-ahead by the country's constitutional court – despite a constitutional ban on presidents who had in the past taken power by coup (which Ríos Montt did in 1982). The FRG blatantly showed its colors in the run-up to the election by making sizeable 'compensation' payments to former members of the Civil Defense Patrols (PACs), who had carried out many atrocities during the civil war.

THE CULTURE
The National Psyche

You'll be amazed when you first reach Guatemala just how helpful, polite and unhurried Guatemalans are. Everyone has time to stop and chat and explain what you want to know. This is apparent even if you've just crossed the border from Mexico, where things aren't exactly rushed either. Most Guatemalans like to get to know other people without haste, feeling for common ground and things to agree on. Some observers explain this mild manner as a reaction to centuries of repression and violence by the ruling class, but whatever the truth of that, it makes most Guatemalans a pleasure to deal with.

What goes on behind this outward politeness is harder to encapsulate. Few Guatemalans exhibit the stress, worry and hurry of the 'developed' nations, but this obviously isn't because they don't have to worry about money or employment. They're a long-suffering people who don't expect wealth or good government but make the best of what comes their way – friendship, their family, a good meal, a bit of good company.

Outwardly, it appears that family ties are strong, but beneath the surface you may find that the real reason that three generations live together in one house has more to do with economics than affection.

Guatemalans are a religious bunch – agnostics and atheists are very thin on the ground. People will often ask what religion you are quite early in a conversation. Unless you really want to get into it, saying 'Christian' generally satisfies.

Orthodox Catholicism is gradually giving way to evangelical Protestantism amongst the ladinos, with the animist-Catholic syncretism of the traditional Maya always present. People's faiths give them hope, not only of better things in the afterlife but also of improvements in the here and now – whether through answered prayers or, in the evangelicals' case, of a more sober, more gainful and happier existence without alcohol, gambling or domestic violence.

The tales of violence – domestic, civil war, criminal – that one inevitably hears in Guatemala sit strangely with the mild-mannered approach you will encounter nearly everywhere. Whatever the explanation, it helps to show why a little caution is in order when strangers meet.

Some say that Guatemala has no middle class, just a ruling class and an exploited class. It's true that Guatemala has a small, rich, ladino ruling elite whose main goal seems to be to maintain wealth and power at almost any cost. It also has an indigenous Maya population, comprising more than half the people in the country, which tends to be poor, poorly educated and poorly provided for and has always been kept in a secondary role by the ruling elite.

The Maya villagers' strengths lie in their family and community ties and traditions. Those who do break out of the poverty cycle, through business or education, do not turn their backs on their communities. But as well as these two groups at the extremes, there is also a large group of poor and middle-class ladinos, typically Catholic and family-oriented but with aspirations influenced by education, TV, international popular music and North America (of which many Guatemalans have direct experience as migrant workers) – and maybe by liberal ideas of equality and social tolerance. This segment of society has its bohemian/student/artist circles whose overlap with educated, forward-looking Maya may hold the greatest hope for progress toward an equitable society.

Lifestyle

The majority of Guatemalans live in one-room houses of brick, concrete blocks or traditional *bajareque* (a construction of stones, wooden poles and mud), with roofs of tin, tiles or thatch. They have earth floors, a fireplace (but usually no chimney) and minimal possessions – often just a couple of bare beds and a few pots. These small homes are often grouped in compounds with several others, all housing members of one extended family. Thus live most of Guatemala's great Maya majority, in the countryside, in villages and in towns.

The few wealthier Maya and most ladino families have larger houses in towns and the bigger villages, but their homes may still not be much more than one or two bedrooms and a kitchen that also serves as a living area. Possessions, adornments and decorations may be sparse. Middle-class families in the wealthier suburbs of Guatemala City live in good-sized one- or two-story houses with gardens. Most such residences will have their gardens walled (and the walls topped with razor wire) for security. The elite few possess rural as well as urban properties – for example a coffee *finca* on the Pacific Slope with a comfortable farmhouse, or a seaside villa on the Pacific or Caribbean coast.

Despite modernizing influences, traditional family ties remain strong at all levels of society. Extended-family groups gather for weekend meals and holidays. Old-fashioned gender roles are strong too: many women have jobs to increase the family income but relatively few have positions of much responsibility. Homosexuality barely raises its head above the parapet: only in Guatemala City is there anything approaching an open gay scene, and that is pretty much for men only.

Traveling in Guatemala you will encounter a much wider cross-section of Guatemalans than many Guatemalans ever do, as they live their lives within relatively narrow worlds. The Guatemalans you'll meet on the road, though, will also tend to be among the most worldly and open-minded, as a result of their contact with tourists and travelers from around the globe. If you spend time studying Spanish or work on one of the many volunteer projects, you stand an even higher chance of meeting Guatemalans interested in learning – in other cultures, in human rights, in music and the arts, in improving the position of women, the indigenous and the poor. Guatemala has a broad web of people, often young, with these kinds of concerns.

By UN figures 6.4 million Guatemalans – more than half the population – live in poverty. The official national minimum wage is only US$130 a month in urban areas and US$120 in rural areas – and not everyone is entitled even to this. A typical teacher earns around US$180 a month. Poverty is most prevalent in rural, indigenous areas, especially the highlands. Wealth, industry and commerce are concentrated overwhelmingly in sprawling, polluted Guatemala City, the country's only large city and home to about 18% of its people.

Population

Of Guatemala's 13.1 million people, some 50% to 60% are indigenous – nearly all of this indigenous population is Maya, although there is a very small population of non-Maya indigenous people called the Chinka' (Xinca) in the southeastern corner of the country. The rest of Guatemala's population are nearly all ladinos – descended from both the Maya and from the European (mostly Spanish) settlers. There are also a few thousand Garífuna (descended from Caribbean islanders and shipwrecked African slaves) around the Caribbean town of Lívingston.

The Maya are spread throughout the country but are most densely concentrated in the Highlands, which are home to the four biggest Maya groups, the K'iche' (Quiché), Mam, Q'eqchi' (Kekchí) and Kaqchiquel. Maya languages are still the way most Maya communicate, with approximately 20 separate (and often mutually unintelligible) Maya languages spoken in different regions of the country. It's language that primarily defines which Maya people someone belongs to. Though many Maya speak some Spanish, it's always a second language – and there are many who don't speak any Spanish.

The overall population is densest in the highland strip from Guatemala City to Quetzaltenango, the country's two biggest cities. Many towns and large villages are dotted around this region. Some 40% of the population lives in towns and cities, and 44% are under 15 years of age.

ARTS
Literature

Guatemalan writer Miguel Ángel Asturias won the Nobel Prize in literature in 1967. Best known for his thinly veiled vilification of Latin American dictators in *El Señor Presidente*, Asturias also wrote poetry (collected in *Sien de Alondra*, published in English as *Temple of the Lark*). Other celebrated Guatemalan writers include poet Luis Cardoza y Aragón and short-story master Augusto Monterroso. Gaspar Pedro Gonzáles' *A Mayan Life*

is claimed to be the first novel written by a Maya author.

Music

Music is a very important part of Guatemalan society, and a source of pride is that the marimba may have been invented here. (Other possibilities are that this xylophone-type instrument might have been brought from Africa by slaves, or created/refined in the New World.) The Maya also play traditional instruments including the *chirimía* (of Arabic origin and related to the oboe) and reed flute.

Guatemalan tastes in pop music are greatly influenced by the products of other Latin American countries. Reggaeton is huge – current favorites being Daddy Yankee, Don Omar and Calle 13.

Guatemalan rock went through its golden age in the '80s and early '90s. Bands from this era such as Razones de Cambio, Bohemia Suburbana and Viernes Verde still have their diehard fans. The most famous Guatemalan-born musician is Ricardo Arjona, who has lived in Mexico since the '90s.

Architecture

Modern Guatemalan architecture, apart from flashy bank and office buildings along Guatemala City's Av La Reforma, is chiefly characterized by expanses of drab concrete with reinforcing rods poking out of the roof, waiting on funds to build the next story. Some humbler rural dwellings use a traditional wall construction known as *bajareque*, where a core of stones is held in place by poles of bamboo or other wood then covered with stucco or mud. Village houses are increasingly roofed with sheets of tin instead of tiles or thatch – less aesthetic but also less expensive.

The ancient Maya ruins and Spanish colonial structures in Antigua are impressive works of architecture. Interestingly, Maya embellishments can be found on many colonial buildings (such as the lotus flowers adorning Antigua's La Merced) – an enduring testament of the Maya laborers forced to carry out European architectural concepts.

Weaving

Guatemalans make many traditional *artesanías* (handicrafts), both for everyday use and to sell to tourists and collectors. Crafts include basketry, ceramics and wood carving, but the most prominent are weaving, embroidery and other textile arts practiced by Maya women. The beautiful traditional clothing *(traje)* made and worn by these women is one of the most awe-inspiring expressions of Maya culture.

The *huipil* (a long, sleeveless tunic) is one of several types of garment that have been in use since pre-Hispanic times. Other colorful types include: the *tocoyal,* a woven head-covering often decorated with bright tassels; the *corte,* a piece of material 7m or 10m long that is used as a wraparound skirt; and the *faja,* a long, woven waist sash that can be folded to hold what other people might put in pockets.

It's generally in the heavily Maya-populated highlands that colorful traditional dress is still predominant, but you'll see it in all parts of the country. The variety of techniques, materials, styles and designs is bewildering to the newcomer, but you'll see some of the most colorful, intricate, eye-catching and widely worn designs in Sololá and Santiago Atitlán, near the Lago de Atitlán, Nebaj in the Ixil triangle, Zunil near Quetzaltenango, and Todos Santos and San Mateo Ixtatán in the Cuchumatanes mountains.

SPORT

The sport that most ignites Guatemalans' passion and enthusiasm is football (soccer). Though Guatemalan teams always flop in international competition, the 10-club Liga Mayor (Major League) is keenly followed by reasonably large crowds. The two big clubs are Municipal and Communications, both from Guatemala City. The *Classico Gringo* is when teams from Quetzaltenango and Antigua (the two big tourist towns) play. The national press always has details on upcoming games. Admission to games runs from US$2 to US$3.50 for the cheapest areas and US$12 to US$20 for the best seats.

RELIGION

Roman Catholicism is the predominant religion in Guatemala, but it is not the only religion by any stretch of the imagination. Since the 1980s evangelical Protestant sects, around 75% of them Pentecostal, have surged in popularity and it is estimated that 30% to 40% of Guatemalans are now evangelical. These numbers continue to grow as evangelical churches compete hard for further souls.

Catholicism's fall can also be attributed in part to the civil war. Catholic priests were, on occasion, (and still are) outspoken defenders of human rights, and attracted persecution (or worse) from dictators at the time, especially from Ríos Montt. As a result, many Catholic churches in rural areas simply closed down during this time and evangelical ones moved in to fill the vacuum.

The number of new evangelical churches in some towns and villages, especially indigenous Maya villages, is astonishing. You will undoubtedly hear loud Guatemalan versions of gospel music pouring out of some of them as you walk around, and in some places loudspeakers broadcast the music and its accompanying preaching across entire towns. One reason for the evangelicals' success is their opposition to alcohol, gambling and domestic violence.

Catholicism in the Maya areas has never been exactly orthodox. The missionaries who brought Catholicism to the Maya in the 16th century wisely permitted aspects of the existing animistic, shamanistic Maya religion to continue alongside Christian rites and beliefs. Syncretism was aided by the identification of certain Maya deities with certain Christian saints and survives to this day. A bizarre example is the deity known as Maximón in Santiago Atitlán, San Simón in Zunil and Ry Laj Man in San Andrés Itzapa near Antigua, who seems to be a combination of Maya gods, the Spanish conquistador Pedro de Alvarado and Judas Iscariot (see the boxed text, p114).

The Maya still worship at a number of places sacred since ancient times, bringing offerings and sacrificing chickens to gods who predate the arrival of the Spanish. Each place has its own different set of gods – or at least different names for similar gods.

Visitors might also be able observe traditional Maya ceremonies in places such as the Pascual Abaj shrine at Chichicastenango, the altars on Laguna Chicabal outside Quetzaltenango, or El Baúl near Santa Lucía Cotzumalguapa, but a lot of traditional rites are off-limits to foreigners.

ENVIRONMENT
The Land

Consisting primarily of mountainous forest highlands and jungle plains, Guatemala covers an area of 109,000 sq km. The western highlands hold 30 volcanoes, reaching heights of 3800m in the Cuchumatanes range northwest of Huehuetenango. Here, land not cleared for Maya *milpas* (cornfields) is covered in pine forests, although these are dwindling rapidly.

The Pacific Slope holds rich coffee, cacao, fruit and sugar plantations. Down along the shore the volcanic slope meets the sea, yielding vast, sweltering beaches of black volcanic sand.

Guatemala City lies at an altitude of around 1500m. To the north, the Alta Verapaz highlands gradually give way to El Petén, whose climate and topography is similar to the Yucatán: hot and humid or hot and dry. Southeast of El Petén is the banana-rich valley of the Río Motagua, dry in some areas, moist in others.

Guatemala is at the confluence of three tectonic plates, resulting in earthquakes and volcanic eruptions. Major quakes struck in 1773, 1917 and 1976. Its dynamic geology includes a tremendous system of surface-level and subterranean caves. This type of terrain – known as karst – riddles the Verapaces region and has made Guatemala a popular spelunking destination. Surface-level caves have been used for Maya ceremonies since ancient times.

Wildlife
ANIMALS
The country's abundance of animals includes 250 species of mammal, 600 bird species, 200 species of reptile and amphibian, and numerous butterflies and other insects.

The national bird, the resplendent quetzal, is often used to symbolize Central America. Though small, the quetzal is exceptionally beautiful. The males sport a bright red breast, brilliant blue-green across the rest of the body and a spot of bright white on the underside of the long tail.

Other colorful birds include toucans, macaws and parrots. Boasting the ocellated turkey (or 'Petén turkey') – a large, impressive, multicolored bird reminiscent of a peacock, Tikal is a birding hot spot, with some 300 tropical and migratory species sighted to date. Several woodpecker species, nine types of hummingbirds and four trogon species are just the beginning of the list. Also in the area are large white herons, hawks, warblers, kingfishers, harpy eagles (rare) and many others.

Although Guatemala's forests host several mammal and reptile species, many remain difficult to observe. Still, visitors to Tikal can enjoy the antics of the omnipresent *pizotes* (coatis, a tropical mammal related to raccoons) and might spy howler and spider monkeys.

Other mammals deeper in the forest include jaguars, ocelots, pumas, peccaries, agoutis, opossums, tapirs, kinkajous (nocturnal arboreal mammals), *tepezcuintles* (pacas, white-spotted brownish rodents), white-tailed and red brocket deer, armadillos and very large rattlesnakes. Reptiles and amphibians in the rest of Guatemala include at least three species of sea turtle (leatherback, *tortuga negra* and olive ridley) and two species of crocodile (one found in El Petén, the other in the Río Dulce). Manatees also frequent the waters around Río Dulce.

PLANTS
Guatemala has over 8000 plant species in 19 different ecosystems, ranging from coastal mangrove forests to mountainous interior pine forests to high cloud forests. In addition, El Petén supports a variety of trees, including mahogany, cedar, ramón and sapodilla.

The national flower, the *monja blanca* (white nun orchid), is said to have been picked so much that it's now rare in the wild. Nevertheless, the country has around 600 species of orchid, a third of which are endemic.

Guatemala also has the perfect climate for *xate* (*sha*-tay), a low-growing palm that thrives in El Petén and is prized in the developed world as a flower-arrangement filler. *Xateros* (*xate* collectors) live in the jungle for months at a time, disrupting its fragile ecosystem. The same type of degradation is perpetuated by *chicleros*, men who harvest *chicle* for chewing gum.

National Parks & Reserves
Guatemala has 92 protected areas, including biosphere reserves, national parks, protected biotopes, wildlife refuges and private nature reserves. Even though some areas are contained within other, larger ones, they amount to 28% of the national territory.

Many of the protected areas are remote and hard to access by the independent traveler; the table (p86) shows those that are easiest to reach and/or most interesting to visitors (but excludes the volcanoes, nearly all of which are protected, and areas of mainly archaeological interest).

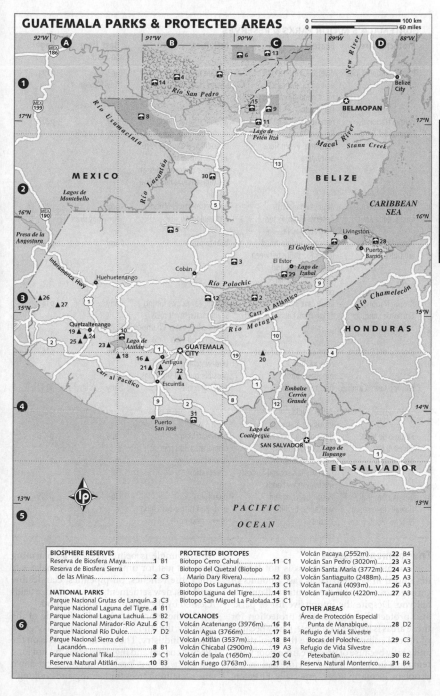

GUATEMALA PARKS & PROTECTED AREAS

GUATEMALA

BIOSPHERE RESERVES
Reserva de Biosfera Maya..............**1** B1
Reserva de Biosfera Sierra
de las Minas...............................**2** C3

NATIONAL PARKS
Parque Nacional Grutas de Lanquín..**3** C3
Parque Nacional Laguna del Tigre...**4** B1
Parque Nacional Laguna Lachuá....**5** B2
Parque Nacional Mirador-Río Azul..**6** C1
Parque Nacional Río Dulce...........**7** D2
Parque Nacional Sierra del
Lacandón....................................**8** B1
Parque Nacional Tikal.................**9** C1
Reserva Natural Atitlán..............**10** B3

PROTECTED BIOTOPES
Biotopo Cerro Cahuí.................**11** C1
Biotopo del Quetzal (Biotopo
Mario Dary Rivera)...............**12** B3
Biotopo Dos Lagunas................**13** C1
Biotopo Laguna del Tigre..........**14** B1
Biotopo San Miguel La Palotada..**15** C1

VOLCANOES
Volcán Acatenango (3976m)......**16** B4
Volcán Agua (3766m)................**17** B4
Volcán Atitlán (3537m)..............**18** B4
Volcán Chicabal (2900m)...........**19** A3
Volcán de Ipala (1650m)............**20** C4
Volcán Fuego (3763m)...............**21** B4

Volcán Pacaya (2552m)............**22** B4
Volcán San Pedro (3020m)........**23** A3
Volcán Santa María (3772m)......**24** A3
Volcán Santiaguito (2488m)......**25** A3
Volcán Tacaná (4093m)............**26** A3
Volcán Tajumulco (4220m).......**27** A3

OTHER AREAS
Área de Protección Especial
Punta de Manabique............**28** D2
Refugio de Vida Silvestre
Bocas del Polochic.................**29** C3
Refugio de Vida Silvestre
Petexbatún............................**30** B2
Reserva Natural Monterrico......**31** B4

GUATEMALA'S MAJOR PARKS & RESERVES

Protected Area	Features	Activities	Best Time to Visit	Page
Parque Nacional Tikal	diverse jungle wildlife among Guatemala's most magnificent Maya ruins	wildlife spotting, seeing Maya city	any, Nov-May drier	p194
Parque Nacional Laguna del Tigre	remote, large park within Reserva Maya; freshwater wetlands, Petén flora and fauna	wildlife spotting including scarlet macaws, monkeys, crocodiles, visiting El Perú archaeological site, volunteer opportunities at Las Guacamayas biological station	any, Nov-May drier	p203
Parque Nacional Mirador-Río Azul	national park with Reserva Maya; Petén flora and fauna	jungle treks to El Mirador archaeological site	any, Nov-May drier	p204
Parque Nacional Río Dulce	beautiful jungle-lined lower Río Dulce between Lago de Izabal and Caribbean; manatee refuge	boat trips	any	p183
Parque Nacional Grutas de Lanquín	large cave system 61km from Cobán	visiting caves, swimming, seeing bats; don't miss the nearby Semuc Champey lagoons and waterfalls	any	p167
Biotopo del Quetzal	easy-access cloud forest reserve; howler monkeys, birds	nature trails, bird-watching, possible quetzal sightings	any	p162
Biotopo Cerro Cahuí	forest reserve beside Lago de Petén Itzá; Petén wildlife including monkeys	walking trails	any	p194
Refugio de Vida Silvestre Bocas del Polochic	delta of Río Polochic at western end of Lago de Izabal; Guatemala's second-largest freshwater wetlands	bird-watching (more than 300 species), howler monkey observation	any	p176
Reserva Natural Hawaii (in Reserva Natural Monterrico)	Pacific beaches and wetlands; birdlife, turtles	boat tours, bird- and turtle-watching (turtle nesting)	Jun-Nov	p159

Environmental Issues

Environmental consciousness is not largely developed in Guatemala, as vast amounts of garbage strewn across the country will quickly tell you. Despite the impressive list of parks and protected areas, genuine protection for those areas is harder to achieve, partly because of official collusion to ignore the regulations and partly because of pressure from poor Guatemalans in need of land. Deforestation is a problem in many areas, especially El Petén, where jungle is being felled at an alarming rate not just for timber but also to make way for cattle ranches, oil pipelines, clandestine airstrips, new settlements and new maize fields cleared by the slash-and-burn method.

On the more populous Pacific side of the country, the land is mostly agricultural or given over to industry. The remaining forests on the Pacific coastal and highland areas are not long for this world, as local communities cut down the remaining trees for heating and cooking.

Nevertheless, a number of Guatemalan organizations are doing valiant work to protect their country's environment and biodiversity. The following are good resources for finding out more about Guatemala's natural parks and protected areas:

Alianza Verde (www.alianzaverde.org, in Spanish; Parque Central, Flores, Petén) Association of organizations, businesses and people involved in conservation and tourism in El Petén; provides information services such as *Destination Petén* magazine, and Cincap, the Centro de Información Sobre la Naturaleza, Cultura y Artesanía de Petén, in Flores.

Arcas (Asociación de Rescate y Conservación de Vida Silvestre; ☎ /fax 2478 4096; www.arcasguatemala.com; 4 Av 2-47, Sector B5, Zona 8 Mixco, San Cristóbal, Guatemala) NGO working with volunteers in sea-turtle conservation and rehabilitation of Petén wildlife.

Asociación Ak' Tenamit (in Guatemala City ☎ 2254 1560, in Río Dulce 7908 3392; www.aktenamit.org; 11a Av A 9-39, Zona 2, Guatemala City) Maya-run NGO working to reduce poverty and promote conservation and ecotourism in the rain forests of eastern Guatemala.

Cecon (Centro de Estudios Conservacionistas de la Universidad de San Carlos; ☎ 3361 6065; www.usac .edu.gt/cecon, in Spanish; Av La Reforma 0-63, Zona 10, Guatemala City) Manages six public *biótopos* and one *reserva natural*.

Conap (Consejo Nacional de Áreas Protegidas; ☎ 2238 0000; http://conap.online.fr; Edificio IPM, 5a Av 6-06, Zona 1, Guatemala City) The government arm in charge of protected areas.

Fundación Defensores de la Naturaleza (☎ 2440 8138; www.defensores.org.gt, in Spanish; 7a Av 7-09, Zona 13, Guatemala City) NGO that owns and administers several protected areas.

ProPetén (☎ 7926 1370; www.propeten.org; Calle Central, Flores, Petén) NGO that works in conservation and natural resources management in Parque Nacional Laguna del Tigre.

Proyecto Ecoquetzal (☎ /fax 7952 1047; www.eco quetzal.org; 2a Calle 14-36, Zona 1, Cobán, Alta Verapaz) Works in forest conservation and ecotourism.

TRANSPORTATION

GETTING THERE & AWAY
Air
Guatemala's two major international airports are in Guatemala City (Aeropuerto La Aurora; p99) and Flores, near Tikal (p192).

Destinations include Belize City, Cancún, Tapachula and Chetumal (Mexico), Havana, Houston, Los Angeles, Madrid, Managua,

---

> **DEPARTURE TAX**
>
> A US$30 departure tax (plus US$3 airport security tax) is charged on all international flights leaving Guatemala. All passengers on domestic flights are charged a US$1 departure tax, payable at the airport.

Mérida (Yucatán), Mexico City, Miami, New York, Palenque (Chiapas), Panama City, San Francisco, San José (Costa Rica), San Pedro Sula (Honduras), and San Salvador.

The following airlines are represented in Guatemala City with many having offices in Aeropuerto Internacional La Aurora:

American Airlines (www.aa.com) airport (☎ 2260 6550); city (☎ 2422 0000; Guatemala City Marriott Hotel, 7a Av 15-45, Zona 9)

Continental Airlines (www.continental.com) airport (☎ 331 2051/2); city (☎ 2385 9601; Edificio Unicentro, 18a Calle 5-56, Zona 10)

Copa Airlines (☎ 2385 5555; www.copaair.com; 1a Av 10-17, Zona 10, Guatemala City)

Cubana (☎ 2367 2288/89/90; www.cubana.cu; Local 29, Edificio Atlantis, 13a Calle 3-40, Zona 10, Guatemala City)

Delta Airlines airport (☎ 2260 6439); city (☎ 1 800 300 0005; Edificio Centro Ejecutivo, 15a Calle 3-20, Zona 10)

Grupo TACA (Aviateca, Inter, LACSA, Nica, TACA; www .taca.com) airport (☎ 2260 6497); city (☎ 2470 8222; Av Hincapié 12-22, Zona 13)

Iberia (www.iberia.com) airport (☎ 2260 6337); city (☎ 2332 0911, 2332 3913; Oficina 507, Edificio Galerías Reforma, Av La Reforma 8-00, Zona 9)

Mexicana (www.mexicana.com) airport (☎ 2260 6335); city (☎ 2333 6001; Local 104, Edificio Edyma Plaza, 13a Calle 8-44, Zona 10)

United Airlines (www.unitedguatemala.com) airport (☎ 2260 6481); city (☎ 2336 9900; Oficina 201, Edificio El Reformador, Av La Reforma 1-50, Zona 9)

Land
Guatemala is linked to Chiapas (Mexico) by two official highway routes and three road-and-river routes; to Belize by one road route and one sea route; and to Honduras and El Salvador by numerous overland routes.

The most popular and easily accessible entry points to Guatemala from Mexico are at Tecún Umán–Ciudad Hidalgo, and at La Mesilla–Ciudad Cuauhtémoc. More adventurous routes take you by country bus and riverboat from Yaxchilán in Chiapas via the Río Usumacinta or the Río de la Pasión to

GUATEMALA

El Petén. For information on these routes, see p202.

Most border crossings between Guatemala and neighboring countries are now well established, including the so-called jungle route from eastern Guatemala to Honduras and the road-and-river routes between El Petén and Chiapas.

Several international bus routes connect Guatemala with Mexico, Belize, El Salvador and Honduras. When traveling between Guatemala and neighboring countries, you will often have the choice of a direct, 1st-class bus or a series of 'chicken buses.' The latter option usually takes longer but is always cheaper and more interesting.

International bus destinations from Guatemala City include: Belize City, El Carmen–Talismán (Mexican border), El Florido–Copán (Honduras), La Mesilla–Ciudad Cuauhtémoc (Mexican border), Managua (Nicaragua), San Salvador (El Salvador), Tapachula (Mexico) and Tecún Umán–Ciudad Hidalgo (Mexican border).

Sea & River

On the Caribbean coast, boats leave Punta Gorda (Belize) for Puerto Barrios and Lívingston. Passage from Omoa (Honduras) to Lívingston is also possible, although it might be difficult to arrange in low season. Generally, sea passage is easiest to and from Puerto Barrios, as this is an active transit point. No car ferries are available.

Three river crossings connect Chiapas, Mexico, to El Petén, Guatemala. These are good alternatives for travelers visiting Palenque and Tikal in one trip. All involve a combination of bus and boat travel. See the boxed text, p202 for details.

GETTING AROUND
Air

In addition to the international airports in Guatemala City and Santa Elena–Flores, there are domestic airports in Coatepeque, Cobán, Huehuetenango, Playa Grande, Puerto Barrios, Quetzaltenango, Quiché, Retalhuleu and Río Dulce. However, the only *scheduled* domestic flights operating at the time of research are between Guatemala City and Flores.

Bicycle

Cycling is coming into its own in Guatemala. You can join biking tours or take to the hills independently. Bicycles can be rented in Antigua, Flores, Panajachel and Quetzaltenango. Remember that few drivers are accustomed to sharing the roads with bikes.

Boat

Speedy motorboats called *lanchas* are becoming the norm for transportation on Lago de Atitlán and between Puerto Barrios, Lívingston and Río Dulce, replacing bigger, cheaper ferries.

A few of Guatemala's natural reserves and archaeological sites are accessible only – or preferably – by water.

Bus

Buses go just about everywhere in Guatemala, and where they don't, you'll find minivans and trucks picking up the slack. Fares are generally cheap (around US$1 per hour), although comfort levels vary. If you can't bear another jaunt on a 'chicken bus,' ask if there is a Pullman service available. These larger, coach-style buses are way more comfortable, leave from major destinations and only cost slightly more than the 2nd-class buses.

If you're traveling light, keep your luggage with you inside the bus. Otherwise, heave it onto the roof or stuff it into the luggage compartment and keep your eye on it.

Long-distance buses rarely have toilets, but usually stop for 20-minute meal and bladder-relief breaks at appropriate times. If not, drivers will stop to let you fertilize the roadside.

Car & Motorcycle

Although few people do, it's possible to hire a car at the airport in Guatemala City, in Antigua and Quetzaltenango. You can hire motorcycles in Antigua, Quetzaltenango and Panajachel. For general information about driving around the region, see p743.

Hitchhiking

Hitching in the Western sense of the word is not practiced in Guatemala because it is not safe. However, where the bus service is sporadic or nonexistent, pickup trucks and other vehicles serve as public transportation. Stand by the side of the road, hold your arm out and someone will stop. You are expected to pay the driver as if it were a bus, and the fare will be similar. This is a safe and reliable system used by locals and travelers; get used to severe overcrowding.

Local Transportation

Local buses (available only in Guatemala City and Quetzaltenango) are crowded and cheap. Few Guatemalan taxis are metered, and fares can be exorbitant. If you don't like the price quoted, walk away. Then go back and bargain. Then walk away again. Repeat process until a reasonable price is established.

GUATEMALA CITY

pop 3.1 million

Depending on who you talk to, Guatemala's capital (known universally as 'Guate') is either big, dirty, dangerous and utterly forgettable or big, dirty, dangerous and fascinating. Either way, there's no doubt that there's an energy here unlike that found in the rest of Guatemala, and the extremes that categorize the whole country are in plain view.

It's a place where dilapidated buses belch fumes next to BMWs and Hummers, where skyscrapers drop shadows on shantytowns, and where immigrants from the countryside and the rest of Central America eke out a meager existence, barely noticed by the country's elite.

This is the real cultural capital of Guatemala – the writers, the thinkers, the artists mostly live and work here. All the best museum pieces go to the capital, and while nearly every city-dweller dreams of getting away to Antigua or Monterrico for the weekend, this is where they spend most of their time, a fact reflected in the growing sophistication of the restaurant and bar scene.

ORIENTATION

Guatemala City, like almost all Guatemalan towns, is laid out according to a logical grid system. Avenidas run north–south; calles run east–west. Streets are usually numbered from north and west (lowest) to south and east (highest); building numbers run in the same directions, with odd numbers on the left side and even on the right heading south or east. However, Guatemala City is divided into 15 *zonas*, each with its own version of the grid. Thus 14a Calle in Zona 10 is a completely different street several miles from 14a Calle in Zona 1, though major thoroughfares such as 6a Av and 7a Av cross several zones.

Addresses are given in this form: '9a Av 15-12, Zona 1,' which means '9th Av above

15th St, No 12, in Zona 1.' The building will be on 9th Av between 15th and 16th Sts, on the right side as you walk south. Beware of anomalies, such as diagonal *rutas* and vías and wandering *diagonales*.

Short streets may be suffixed 'A,' as in 14a Calle A, running between 14a Calle and 15a Calle.

Maps

Intelimapas' *Mapa Turístico Guatemala*, Inguat's *Mapa Vial Turístico* and Inter- national Travel Maps' *Guatemala* all contain useful maps of Guatemala City.

Sophos (☎ 2334 6797; Av La Reforma 13-89, Zona 10) One of the most reliable sources of maps.

Instituto Geográfico Nacional (IGN; ☎ 2332 2611; www.ign.gob.gt in Spanish; Av Las Américas 5-76, Zona 13; ✆ 9am-5pm Mon-Fri) Sells 1:50,000 and 1:250,000 topographical maps of all parts of Guatemala (US$6 each).

INFORMATION

Bookstores

Sophos (☎ 2334 6797; Av La Reforma 13-89, Zona 10) Relaxed place to have a coffee and read while in the Zona Viva. A good selection of books in English on Guatemala and the Maya, including guidebooks and maps.

Vista Hermosa Book Shop (☎ 2369 1003; 2a Calle 18-50, Zona 15) Ditto.

Emergency

Ambulance (☎ 123)
Fire Department (☎ 123)
Police (☎ 110 or 120)

Internet Access

Zona 1 is thronged with inexpensive internet cafés. Elsewhere, rates tend to be higher.

Café Internet Navigator (14a Calle east of 6a Av, Zona 1; per hr US$0.80; ✆ 8am-8pm)

Carambolo Café Internet (14a Calle east of 7a Av, Zona 1; per hr US$1.30; ✆ 8:30am-8:30pm)

Internet (Local 5, 6a Av 9-27, Zona 1; per hr US$0.65; ✆ 8am-7pm)

Web Station (2a Av 14-63, Zona 10; per hr US$2.60; ✆ 10am-midnight Mon-Sat, noon-midnight Sun) One of the cheapest in the Zona Viva.

Laundry

Lavandería El Siglo (12a Calle 3-42, Zona 1; ✆ 8am-6pm Mon-Sat) Charges US$4 for up to 12lb (5.5kg).

Medical Services

Guatemala City has many private hospitals and clinics. Public hospitals and clinics

GUATEMALA CITY

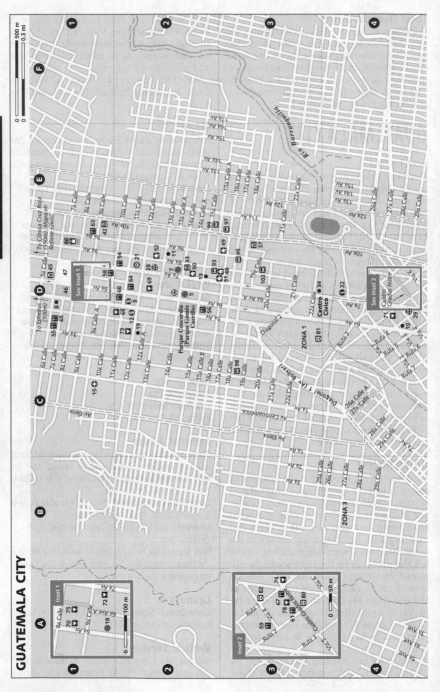

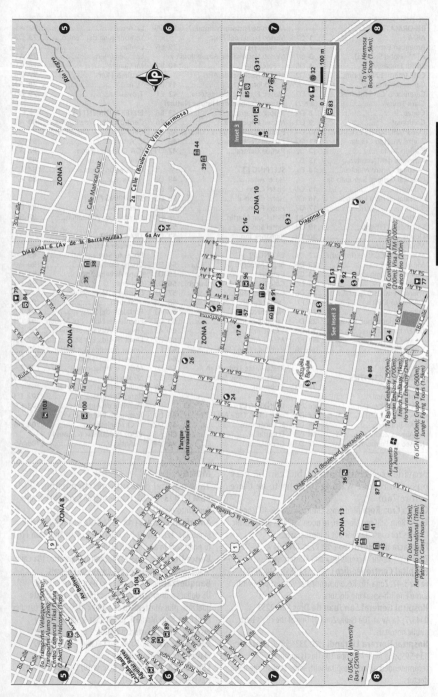

GUATEMALA

INFORMATION
ABM.......................................1 C7
American Express....................2 E7
ATM (Hotel Stofella)................3 D7
British Embassy.......................4 D8
Café Internet Navigator...........5 D2
Canadian Embassy...................6 E8
Carambolo Café Internet..........7 D2
Clark Tours...........................(see 2)
Conap....................................8 D1
Credomatic.............................9 D2
Departamento de Extranjería...10 D4
Digital Mundo Celular.............11 D2
Edificio Testa.........................12 D2
Farmacia del Ejecutivo............13 D2
Hospital Centro Médico...........14 E6
Hospital General San Juan de
   Dios..................................15 C1
Hospital Herrera Llerandi.........16 E7
Iberia....................................17 D7
Internet.................................18 A1
Lavandería El Siglo.................19 D2
Lloyds TSB.............................20 D8
Main Post Office.....................21 D2
Main Tourist Office (Inguat).....22 D4
Mexican Embassy....................23 D6
Salvadoran Embassy................24 C7
Sophos..................................25 E7
Spanish Embassy....................26 C6
Telefónica Office....................27 F7
Telgua...................................28 D2
Telgua Telephone Office.........29 D4
US Embassy............................30 D6
Visa ATM...............................31 F7
Visa ATM............................(see 8)
Web Station...........................32 F7

SIGHTS & ACTIVITIES
Casa MIMA.............................33 D2
Centro Cultural
   Metropolitano..................(see 21)
Civic Center...........................34 D3
Jardín Botánico......................35 D5
La Aurora Zoo........................36 B8
Museo de Ferrocarril...............37 D3

Museo de Historia Natural........38 D5
Museo Ixchel del Traje
   Indígena............................39 E6
Museo Nacional de Arqueología y
   Etnología............................40 B8
Museo Nacional de Arte
   Moderno.............................41 B8
Museo Nacional de Historia......42 E1
Museo Nacional de Historia Natural
   Jorge Ibarra.......................43 B8
Museo Popol Vuh....................44 E6
Palacio Nacional de la Cultura...45 D1
Parque Centenario...................46 D1
Parque Central........................47 D1

SLEEPING
Hotel Ajau.............................48 D3
Hotel Capri............................49 D3
Hotel Colonial........................50 D2
Hotel Fenix............................51 D2
Hotel San Martin.................(see 48)
Hotel Spring...........................52 D2
Xamanek Inn..........................53 D8

EATING
Bagel Factory.........................54 D2
Café de Imeri.........................55 D1
Café-Restaurante Hamburgo....56 D2
Cafetería Patsy.......................57 D7
Doner Kebab..........................58 D1
Flamenco...............................59 A3
La Chapinita...........................60 D7
L'Osteria................................61 A3
Marea Alta.............................62 D7
Parrillada Doña Sara................63 E1
Picadily.................................64 D2
Restaurante Long Wah.............65 D1
Restaurante Rey Sol................66 D2
Tarboosh................................67 A3

DRINKING
Blue Town Café Bar................68 D2
El Encuentro..........................69 D2
El Portal.................................70 A1
Genetic..................................71 D4

La Arcada..............................72 A1
La Bodeguita del Centro..........73 D2
La Playa.................................74 A3
Las Cien Puertas.....................75 A1
Mi Guajira..............................76 F7
Rattle & Hum.........................77 D8
Suae......................................78 A3
TrovaJazz...............................79 D5

ENTERTAINMENT
Centro Cultural de España........80 A3
Centro Cultural Miguel Ángel
   Asturias.............................81 D3
IGA Cultural Center.................82 A3
Kahlua...................................83 F8
La Estación Norte....................84 D5
Mr Jerry.................................85 F7

SHOPPING
Mercado Central.....................86 D1
Mercado de Artesanías............87 B8

TRANSPORT
American Airlines....................88 C8
Buses to Santiago Atitlán.........89 A6
Chatía Gomerana....................90 A6
Copa Airlines..........................91 D7
Cubana..................................92 D8
Escobar y Monja Blanca Bus
   Station...............................93 D2
Fortaleza del Sur.....................94 A6
Fuente del Norte Bus Station....95 D3
Hedman Alas Bus Station.........96 D7
Línea Dorada Bus Station.........97 E3
Líneas América Bus Station......98 C3
Litegua Bus Station.................99 E2
Melva Internacional...............100 C5
Mexicana...........................(see 6)
Pullmantur...........................101 F7
Rutas Orientales...................102 D3
Terminal de Autobuses..........103 C5
Transportes Rébuli & Veloz
   Quichelense......................104 A6
Veloz Poaquileña & Buses a
   Antigua............................105 A5

provide free consultations but can be very busy. To reduce waiting time, try to be there before 7am.

Clínica Cruz Roja (Red Cross Clinic; 3a Calle 8-40, Zona 1; 8am-5:30pm Mon-Fri, to noon Sat) This public clinic charges for consultations but is inexpensive.

Farmacia del Ejecutivo (2238 1447; 7a Av 15-01, Zona 1; 24hr) Accepts Visa and MasterCard.

Hospital Centro Médico (2332 3555, 334 2157; 6a Av 3-47, Zona 10) Recommended private hospital with some English-speaking doctors.

Hospital General San Juan de Dios (2253 0443/7; 1a Av at 10a Calle, Zona 1) One of the city's best public hospitals.

Hospital Herrera Llerandi (2334 5959, emergency 334 5955; 6a Av 8-71, Zona 10) This is another recommended private hospital with some English-speaking doctors.

Money
Take normal precautions when using ATMs.

ABM (2361 5602; Plazuela España, Zona 9) Changes euros into quetzals.

American Express (2331 7422; Centro Comercial Montufar, 12a Calle 0-93, Zona 9; 8am-5pm Mon-Fri, to noon Sat) In an office of Clark Tours.

Banco Uno (2366 2191; Edificio Unicentro, 18a Calle 5-56, Zona 10) Changes cash euros into quetzals.

Banquetzal airport arrivals (6am-9pm) Changes US dollars and American Express traveler's checks into quetzals, plus MasterCard and Amex ATM; airport departures (6am-8pm Mon-Fri, to 6pm Sat & Sun) Currency exchange and a MasterCard ATM.

Edificio Testa (cnr 5a Av & 11a Calle, Zona 1) Visa, MasterCard and Amex ATMs.

Lloyds TSB (14a Calle 3-51, Zona 10) Changes euro traveler's checks.

MasterCard ATM (Hotel Stofella, 2a Av 12-28, Zona 10)
Visa ATMs (cnr 5a Av & 6a Calle, Zona 1); (2a Av, Zona 10) South of 13a Calle.

Post
Main post office (7a Av 11-67, Zona 1; ☉ 8:30am-5pm Mon-Fri, to 1pm Sat) In the huge pink Palacio de Correos. There's also a small post office at the airport.

Telephone
Telgua street card phones are plentiful.
Telefónica office (2a Av btwn 13a & 14a Calles, Zona 10) Telefónica phone cards are fairly common too; cards can be bought at the Telefónica office.

Tourist Information
Inguat main tourist office (☎ 2331 1333, 2331 1347; informacion@inguat.gob.gt; 7a Av 1-17, Zona 4; ☉ 8am-4pm Mon-Fri) Located in the lobby of the Inguat (Guatemalan Tourism Institute) headquarters in the Centro Cívico. The office has limited handout material, but staff are extremely helpful; Aeropuerto La Aurora (☎ 2331 4256; arrivals hall; ☉ 6am-9pm)

DANGERS & ANNOYANCES
Street crime, including armed robbery, has increased in recent years. Use normal urban common sense: don't walk down the street with your wallet bulging out of your back pocket, and avoid walking downtown alone late at night. Work out your route before you start so you're not standing on corners looking lost or peering at a map; pop into a café if you need to find your bearings. It's safe to walk downtown in the early evening, as long as you stick to streets with plenty of lighting and people. Stay alert and leave your valuables in your hotel. Don't flaunt anything of value, and be aware that women and children swell the ranks of thieves here. The incidence of robbery increases around the 15th and the end of each month, when workers get paid.

The area around 18a Calle in Zona 1 has many bus stations and even more lowlifes and hustlers. Nearly half of Zona 1's robberies happen here, the worst black spots being the intersections with 4a, 6a and 9a Avs. This part of town (also a red-light district) is notoriously dangerous at night; if you are arriving by bus at night or must go someplace on 18a Calle at night, take a taxi.

The more affluent sections of the city – Zona 9 and Zona 10, for example – are safer, but don't let your guard down. Thieves have figured out that rich people hang out in fancy areas, and so sometimes work the area in

---

GETTING INTO TOWN
From the Airport
Aeropuerto La Aurora is in Zona 13, in the southern part of the city, about 10 to 15 minutes from Zona 1 by taxi, 30 minutes by bus.

For the city bus, cross the road outside the arrivals exit and climb the steps. At the top, with your back to the terminal building, walk to the left down the approach road (about 100m), then turn right to the bus stop. Bus 83 'Terminal' and No 83 'Bolívar' go to Parque Central in Zona 1, passing through Zonas 9 and 4 en route: you can get off at any corner along the way. Bus 83 'Terminal' goes up 7a Av through Zonas 9, 4 and 1; bus 83 'Bolívar' goes via Av Bolívar and then 5a Av. Both run about every 15 minutes, from 6am to 9pm, and cost US$0.15. Going from the city center to the airport, No 83 'Aeropuerto' goes south through Zona 1 on 10a Av, south through Zonas 4 and 9 on 6a Av, passes by the west end of La Aurora Zoo and the Zona 13 museums and stops outside the international terminal. It then continues southward passing close to all Zona 13 guesthouses.

Taxis wait outside the airport's arrivals exit. Official fares are posted on signs (US$8 to US$9 to Zona 9 or 10, US$10 to Zona 1, US$30 to Antigua) but in reality you may have to pay a bit more. Be sure to establish the destination and price before getting in. A tip is expected. Prices for taxis to the airport, hailed on the street, are likely to be lower – around US$6 from Zona 1. For **Antigua**, shuttle minibuses are more economical if there's only one or two of you (see p113).

From the Bus Terminal
Going by city bus, the best way into town from the Terminal de Autobuses in Zona 4 is to walk a few blocks east to 6a Av and catch any bus going north (such as bus 83 'Aeropuerto'). This saves you getting caught in the traffic snarls around the terminal itself. The same holds true in reverse if you want to get to the terminal by city bus.

groups of two or three. The Zona Viva, in Zona 10, has police patrols at night. But even here, going in pairs is better than going alone.

All buses are the turf of adroit pickpockets. Some armed robberies happen on buses too, although mainly in outlying zones.

Never (never!) try to resist if confronted by a robber.

SIGHTS
Zona 1
PARQUE CENTRAL
Most of the city's notable sights are in Zona 1 near Parque Central (officially the Plaza de la Constitución), which is bounded by 6a and 8a Calles and 6a and 7a Avs.

Every town in the New World had a plaza used for military exercises, reviews and ceremonies. On the plaza's northern side would be the *palacio de gobierno* (colonial government headquarters). On another side, preferably east, was a church (or cathedral). The other sides of the square could house additional civic buildings or imposing mansions. Parque Central is a good example of this classic town plan.

Visit on Sunday, when locals stroll, play in the fountains, gossip, neck and groove to salsa music. Otherwise, try for lunchtime or late afternoon. You'll be besieged by shoe-shine boys, Polaroid photographers and sellers of kitsch.

PALACIO NACIONAL
On Parque Central's north side is the magnificent **Palacio Nacional de la Cultura** (☎ 2253 0748; 6a Calle; ⊙ 9-11:45am & 2-4:45pm Mon-Fri, 9-10:45am & 2-3:45pm Sat & Sun), built at enormous cost by dictator/president Jorge Ubico (1931–44). It's the third palace to stand here. It often hosts revolving exhibitions featuring contemporary Guatemalan artists.

You can go wandering independently, or else free tours take you through a labyrinth of gleaming brass, polished wood, carved stone and frescoed arches (painted by Alberto Gálvez Suárez). Notable features include the 2000kg gold, bronze and Bohemian-crystal chandelier in the reception salon, and two Moorish-style courtyards.

CENTRO CULTURAL METROPOLITANO
On the 1st floor of the **Palacio de Correos** (12a Calle & 7 Av; ⊙ 9-5pm Mon-Fri) you'll find this surprisingly avant-garde cultural center,

hosting art exhibitions, book launches, handicraft workshops and film nights.

CASA MIMA
This wonderfully presented **museum and cultural center** (8a Av & 14a Calle; ⊙ 9am-12:30pm, 2-6pm Mon-Fri, 9am-5pm Sat) is set in a house dating from the late 19th century. The owners of the house were collectors with eclectic tastes ranging from French neorococo, Chinese, Art Deco to indigenous artifacts. The place is set up like a functioning house, filled with curios and furniture spanning the centuries.

MERCADO CENTRAL
Until it was destroyed by the earthquake of 1976, the **central market** (9a Av btwn 6a & 8a Calles; ⊙ 7am-6pm Mon-Sat, 6am-noon Sun), east of the cathedral, was where locals bought food and other necessities. Reconstructed in the late 1970s, the new market specializes in touristy items such as cloth, carved wood, worked leather and metal, basketry and other handicrafts. Except for the odd tour group, not that many tourists make it here – if you're a hard bargainer, you might get a good deal. Vegetables and other daily needs are on sale on the lower floor – check it out for a sensory overload. The city's true 'central' food market is in Zona 4.

MUSEO DE FERROCARRIL
The **Railway Museum** (18a Calle btwn 9a & 10a Avs; ⊙ 9am-4:30pm Tue-Fri, 10am-4:30pm Sat & Sun) is one of the cities more intriguing museums (and the only one with a Domino's Pizza attached). Documented here are the glory days of the troubled Guatemalan rail system, along with some quirky artifacts, like hand-drawn diagrams of derailments and a kitchen set up with items used in dining cars. You can go climbing around the passenger carriages, but not the locomotives.

MUSEO NACIONAL DE HISTORIA
The **National History Museum** (☎ 2253 6149; 9a Calle 9-70; admission US$4; ⊙ 8:30am-4pm Mon-Fri) is a jumble of historical relics with an emphasis on photography and portraits. Check the hairstyles of the 19th-century politicos.

Zona 2
Zona 2, north of Zona 1, is a mostly middle-class residential district, though its northern end holds the large Parque Minerva, which is

surrounded by golf courses, sports grounds and the buildings of the Universidad Mariano Gálvez.

PARQUE MINERVA

Minerva, the Roman goddess of wisdom, technical skill and invention, was a favorite of President Manuel Estrada Cabrera. Her park is a placid place, good for walking among the eucalyptus trees and sipping a cool drink. However, watch out for pickpockets and purse-snatchers.

The prime sight here is the **Mapa En Relieve** (Relief Map; admission US$4; ☉ 9am-5pm), a huge relief map of Guatemala. Constructed in 1904 under the direction of Francisco Vela, the map shows the country at a scale of 1:10,000, but the height of the mountainous terrain has been exaggerated to 1:2000 for dramatic effect. You may note that Belize features on the map – a hangover from the fact that most Guatemalans consider this to be Guatemalan territory. The Mapa En Relieve and Parque Minerva are 2km north of Parque Central along 6a Av, but that street is one-way heading south. To get there take bus V-21 northbound on 7a Av just north or south of Parque Central.

Civic Center Area

The Centro Cívico complex, constructed during the 1950s and '60s, lies around the junction of Zonas 1, 4 and 5. Here you'll find the Palace of Justice, the headquarters of the Guatemalan Institute of Social Security (IGSS), the Banco del Quetzal, the city hall and the Inguat headquarters. The Banco del Quetzal building bears high-relief murals by Dagoberto Vásquez depicting the history of his homeland. City Hall holds a huge mosaic by Carlos Mérida.

On a hilltop across the street from the Centro Cívico is the **Centro Cultural Miguel Ángel Asturias**, which holds the national theater, a chamber theater and an open-air theater, as well as a small museum of old armaments.

Other than the Centro Cívico, this area is known mostly for its markets and bus stations, all thrown together in the chaotic southwestern corner of Zona 4 near the railway.

Zona 10

East of Av La Reforma, the posh Zona 10 holds two of the city's most important museums, both in large new buildings at the Universidad Francisco Marroquín.

Museo Ixchel del Traje Indígena (☎ 2331 3634/8; 6a Calle Final; admission US$3; ☉ 9am-5pm Mon-Fri, to 1pm Sat) is named for Ixchel, wife of Maya sky god Itzamná and goddess of the moon, women, reproduction and textiles, among other things. Photographs and exhibits of indigenous costumes, textiles and other crafts show the incredible richness of traditional highland art. If you enjoy seeing Guatemalan textiles, you must make a visit to this museum.

Behind it is the **Museo Popol Vuh** (☎ 2361 2301; www.popolvuh.ufm.edu; adult/child US$3/1; ☉ 9am-5pm Mon-Fri, to 1pm Sat), where well-chosen polychrome pottery, figurines, incense burners, burial urns, carved-wood masks and traditional textiles fill several exhibit rooms. Other rooms hold colonial paintings and wood and silver objects. A faithful copy of the Dresden Codex, one of the precious 'painted books' of the Maya, is among the most interesting pieces. This is an important collection, especially given its precolonial emphasis.

The Universidad de San Carlos de Guatemala has a large, lush **Jardín Botánico** (Botanical Garden; Calle Mariscal Cruz 1-56; admission US$0.80; ☉ 8am-3:30pm Mon-Fri, to noon Sat) on the northern edge of Zona 10. The admission includes the university's **Museo de Historia Natural** (Natural History Museum) at the site.

Zona 13

The major attraction in the city's southern reaches is Parque Aurora, with its zoo, children's playground, fairgrounds and several museums. One of the museums, the Moorish-looking **Museo Nacional de Arqueología y Etnología** (☎ 2472 0489; Sala 5, Finca La Aurora; admission US$4; ☉ 9am-4pm Tue-Fri, 9am-noon & 1:30-4pm Sat & Sun), has a collection of Maya artifacts from all over Guatemala, including stone carvings, jade, ceramics, statues, stelae and a tomb. Models depict the ruins at Tikal and Zaculeu. Exhibits in the ethnology section highlight the various indigenous peoples and languages in Guatemala, with emphasis on traditional costumes, dances and implements of daily life.

Facing it is the **Museo Nacional de Arte Moderno** (☎ 2472 0467; Sala 6, Finca La Aurora; admission US$1.30; ☉ 9am-4pm Tue-Fri, 9am-noon & 2-4pm Sat & Sun), which holds a collection of 20th-century Guatemalan art, especially paintings and sculpture.

Nearby is the **Museo Nacional de Historia Natural Jorge Ibarra** (☎ 2472 0468; 6a Calle 7-30; admission US$1.30; ☉ 9am-4pm Tue-Fri, 9am-noon & 2-4pm Sat & Sun), whose claim to fame is its large collection of dissected

GUATEMALA

animals. Several hundred meters east of these museums is the city's official handicrafts market, the **Mercado de Artesanías** (Crafts Market; ☎ 2472 0208; cnr 5a Calle & 11a Av; ⏲ 9:30am-6pm), just off the access road to the airport. It's a sleepy place where shopkeepers display the same items available in hotel gift shops.

La Aurora Zoo (☎ 2472 0894; adult/child US$2.50/1; ⏲ 9am-5pm Tue-Sun) is not badly kept as zoos go, and the lovely, parklike grounds alone are worth the admission fee.

SLEEPING

Zona 1

Shoestringers tend to head straight for Zona 1. Prices in Guate are higher than in the rest of the country, but there are a few bargains. Many of the city's cheaper lodgings are 10 to 15 minutes' walk south from Parque Central.

Hotel San Martin (☎ 2238 0319; 16a Calle 7-65; r with/without bathroom US$9/7) If you're on a serious budget, the San Martin's the one to go for – nothing fancy, but good solid value and reasonably clean.

Hotel Fenix (☎ 2251 6625; 7a Av 15-81; r US$8, with bathroom & TV US$11) For Zona 1 budget digs, the Fenix does alright, with a fair bit of charm (most of it crumbling off the walls). The high ceilings, spacious rooms and old-time feel keep this a popular option.

Hotel Capri (☎ 2232 8191; 9a Av 15-63; s/d US$9/14, with bathroom US$14/21; P) This modern three-story number is in a decent location, and rooms are set back from the street so they're quiet. Big windows looking onto patios and light wells keep the place sunny and airy.

Hotel Ajau (☎ 2232 0488; hotelajau@hotmail.com; 8a Av 15-62; s/d US$10/14, with bathroom US$16/20; 🖳) If you're coming or going to Cobán, the Ajau's the obvious choice, being right next door to the Monja Blanca bus station. Otherwise, it's still a pretty good deal, with lovely polished floor tiles and cool, clean rooms.

Hotel Spring (☎ 2230 2858; hotelspring@hotmail.com; 8a Av 12-65; s/d/tr US$12/17/22, with bathroom US$17/22/26 or US$25/31/37; P 🖳) With a beautiful courtyard setting, the Spring has a lot more style than other Zona 1 joints. It's central but has quiet sunny patios. The 43 rooms vary greatly, but most are tall, spacious and clean. Have a look around if you can. All rooms have cable TV. It's worth booking ahead.

Hotel Colonial (☎ 2232 6722; www.hotelcolonial.net; 7a Av 14-19; s/d/tr US$17/22/27, with bathroom US$25/30/35; P) This is a large old house converted to

a hotel with spacious communal areas and heavy, dark, colonial decor. It's a very well-run establishment whose 42 rooms are clean, good-sized and adequately furnished. Nearly all have a bathroom and TV.

Zona 10 & Zona 13

Xamanek Inn (☎ 2360 8345; www.mayaworld.net; 13a Calle 3-57, Zona 10; dm US$14, r with bathroom US$35; 🖳) A welcome newcomer in the often-overpriced Zona Viva area is this comfy little hostel. Dorms are spacious and airy, separated into male and female. Rates include a light breakfast and free internet. There's a book exchange, kitchen use and skype calling for US$0.30 per minute.

Guesthouses are springing up all over the place in a middle-class residential area in Zona 13. They're very convenient for the airport, and staff will pick you up or drop you off there. There are no restaurants out here, but these places offer breakfast and have the complete lowdown on home-delivery fast food in the area.

Patricia's Guest House (☎ 2261 4251, in English 5402 3256; 19 Calle 10-65; r per person US$12) The most relaxed and comfortable option is in this family house with a sweet little backyard where guests can hang out. They also offer private transport around the city and shuttles to bus stations.

Dos Lunas (☎ /fax 2261 4248; www.xelapages.com /doslunas; 21a Calle 10-92; dm US$12, s/d US$15/30; P 🖳) An old faithful, the Dos Lunas has excellent common areas, a cramped dorm and a couple of very nice private rooms. Book through their website. Dos Lunas also offers onward-travel packages and Flores flights at good prices.

EATING

Cheap eats are easily found, as fast food and snack shops abound. To really save money, head for Parque Concordia, in Zona 1 bounded by 5a and 6a Avs and 14a and 15a Calles, whose west side is lined with stalls serving sandwiches and snacks at rock-bottom prices from early morning to late evening. Fine dining is concentrated in Zona 10.

Zona 1

Dozens of restaurants and fast-food shops are strung along and just off 6a Av between 8a and 15a Calles.

Doner Kebab (10 Calle 6-35; kebabs US$3; ⏲ breakfast, lunch & dinner) For a quick Turkish food fix in the center, it's hard to beat the authentic flavors in this place. Nothing fancy in the décor, but you *can* get six beers for US$7.

Café de Imeri (6a Calle 3-34; mains US$3-5; ☺ 8am-7pm Tue-Sat) Completely out of step with the majority of Zona 1 eateries, this place offers interesting breakfasts, soups and pastas. The list of sandwiches is impressive and there's a beautiful little courtyard area out back.

Parrillada Doña Sara (9a Calle & 9a Av; mains US$3.50-5; ☺ lunch & dinner) A lot of places call themselves Argentine steakhouses, but this one recreates the atmosphere almost exactly, with photo-covered walls, cheap wine and good (but not great) steaks.

Restaurante Rey Sol (11a Calle 5-51; meals around US$4; ☺ 8am-5pm Mon-Sat) Good, fresh ingredients and some innovative cooking keep this strictly vegetarian restaurant busy at lunchtimes.

Bagel Factory (cnr 7a Av & 10 Calle; bagels US$4; ☺ breakfast, lunch & dinner) Anywhere outside of NYC, bagels can be a dodgy proposition, but these guys do OK. Fresh ingredients, plenty of options, a superclean environment and a sunny courtyard make this place a winner.

Café-Restaurante Hamburgo (15a Calle 5-34; set lunch or dinner US$4-6; ☺ 7am-9:30pm) This bustling spot facing the south side of Parque Concordia serves good Guatemalan food, with chefs at work along one side and orange-aproned waitresses scurrying about. At weekends a marimba band adds atmosphere.

Restaurante Long Wah (6a Calle 3-70; dishes US$4-6; ☺ 11am-10pm) With friendly service and decorative red-painted arches, the Long Wah is a good choice from Zona 1's other concentration of Chinese eateries, in the blocks west of Parque Centenario.

Picadily (cnr 6 Av & 11a Calle; mains US$4-8; ☺ lunch & dinner) Right in the thick of the 6a Av action, this bustling restaurant does OK pizzas and pastas ands good steak dishes. The place is clean and street views out of the big front windows are mesmerizing.

Zona 4

Tarboosh (Vía 5, Cuatro Grados Norte; mains US$6-15; ☺ lunch & dinner Tue-Sun) Done out like a harem (but tastefully), this place offers authentic Middle Eastern fare such as falafel (US$6.50), *kibellah* and delicious mezzeh (appetizer) platters (US$20).

Flamenco (Vía 4, Cuatro Grados Norte; tapas US$6, mains US$10; ☺ lunch & dinner Tue-Sun) Catch a breeze and take a breather on the upstairs balcony at this tapas bar and Spanish restaurant.

L'Osteria (Vía 5 & Ruta 2, Cuatro Grados Norte; mains US$7-10; ☺ lunch & dinner Tue-Sun) Excellent Italian dishes – mostly pizzas and pastas – and a good wine list. The shady terrace out front earns top marks for people-watching.

Zona 10

A string of (mostly) nameless *comedores* opposite the Los Proceres mall serve up the cheapest eats in Zona 10. There's nothing fancy going on here – just good, filling eats at rock-bottom prices.

Cafetería Patsy (Av La Reforma 8-01; set lunch US$3.50; ☺ 7:30am-8pm) A bright, cheerful place popular with local office workers, it offers subs, sandwiches and good-value set lunches.

La Chapinita (1 Av 10-24; mains US$4-6; ☺ breakfast, lunch & dinner) Home-style Guatemalan food served in more or less formal surrounds can be hard to come by in Zona 10, but this place does it well at good prices. Tables out front on the shady terrace are cool and breezy.

Marea Alta (10a Calle 1-89; mains US$10-20; ☺ lunch & dinner) Specializing in imported seafood, this place has some good prices considering the location. The lunchtime buffet (Monday to Wednesday; US$13) is a winner, as is the surf and turf platter (US$10).

DRINKING & NIGHTLIFE
Zona 1

Staggering from bar to bar along the darkened streets of Zona 1 is not recommended, but fortunately there's a clutch of good drinking places all within half a block of each other just south of Parque Central.

Las Cien Puertas (Pasaje Aycinena 8-44, 9a Calle 6-45) This superhip (but not studiously so) little watering hole is a gathering place for all manner of local creative types and other colorful characters. It's in a shabby colonial arcade that is sometimes closed off for live bands.

La Arcada (7 Av 9-10) Drop into this friendly little neighborhood bar for a few drinks – they'll let you pick the music, or spin some of their own – anything from Guat Rock to ambient trance.

El Portal (Portal del Comercio, 6a Av; ☺ 10am-10pm Mon-Sat) This atmospheric old drinking den serves fine draft beer (around US$2 a mug) and free tapas. Ché Guevara was once a patron. Sit at the long wooden bar or one of the wooden tables. To find it, enter the Portal del Comercio arcade from 6a Av a few steps south of Parque Central.

GAY & LESBIAN VENUES

Don't get too excited about this heading: there are a couple of places worthy of mention for men, and nothing much for women.

Genetic (Ruta 3 No 3-08, Zona 4; ☾ 9pm-1am Fri & Sat, 8am-1pm Sun) This used to be called Pandora's Box and has been hosting Guatemala's gay crowd since the '70s, although it gets a mixed crowd and is one of the best places in town to go for trance/dance music. It has two dance floors, a rooftop patio and a relaxed atmosphere with a mainly under-thirty crowd.

Ephebus (4a Calle 5-30, Zona 1; ☾ 9pm-1am Thu-Sat) A well-established gay disco-bar in a former private house near the city center, often with strippers.

El Encuentro (Local 229, Centro Capitol, 6a Av 12-51, Zona 1; ☾ 5pm-midnight Mon-Sat) This quiet bar, in the back of a noisy downtown mall, is another gay meeting place.

Zona 4

Guate's restaurant-bar precinct, Cuatro Grados Norte, is taking over from Zona 10 as *the* place to go out. You can just have a drink at any of the restaurants along here, but there are a couple of good bars.

Suae (Vía 5, Cuatro Grados Norte) Hip, but not exclusive, this bar has a great, laid-back ambience in the day and heats up at night. Rotating art exhibitions, a funky clothes boutique and guest DJs all add to the appeal.

La Playa (Vía 5 & Ruata 1, Cuatro Grados Norte) With a heap of pool tables and cheap beer on tap, this upstairs bar is as good a place as any to start your night.

Zona 10

The best place to go bar-hopping is around the corner of 2a Av and 15a Calle – there's plenty of places to choose from – check and see who's got the crowd tonight.

Mi Guajira (2 Av 14-42) This happening little disco-bar has a pretty good atmosphere and goes fairly light on the snob factor. Music varies depending on the night, but be prepared for anything from salsa to reggaeton to trance.

Zona 12

For a seriously down to earth night out, you should go out partying with the students from USAC, Guatemala's public university. The strip of bars along 31a Calle at the corner of 11a Av, just near the main entrance to the university all offer cheap beer, loud music and bar junk food. Like student bars all over the world, they're busy any time of day, but nights and weekends are best. A taxi out here from the center should cost about US$6 if it's not too late, or you can catch any bus that says 'USAC' that doesn't go along Av Petapa.

El Tarro (31a Calle 13-08) The most formal of the bunch (in that it has menus, vaguely comfortable seats and draft beer), has a dance floor out back.

Liverpool (31a Calle 11-53) Plenty of pool tables and cheap drinks keep this place swinging.

Ice (31a Calle 13-39) This one heats up later into the night, when the dance floor fills up with students dancing salsa, merengue and reggaeton.

Live Music

La Bodeguita del Centro (12a Calle 3-55, Zona 1) There's a hopping, creative local scene in Guatemala City, and this large, bohemian hangout is one of the best places to connect with it. There's live music of some kind almost every night from Tuesday to Saturday, usually starting at 9pm, plus occasional poetry readings, films or forums. Entry is usually free, with a charge of US$2.50 to US$5 on Friday and Saturday nights.

Rattle & Hum (4a Av & 16 Calle, Zona 10) One of the last places in Zona 10 to still be hosting live music, this Australian-owned place has a warm and friendly atmosphere.

Blue Town Café Bar (11a Calle 4-51, Zona 1) If La Bodeguita doesn't really suit you, check out this nearby youthful spot that hosts live bands.

TrovaJazz (Vía 6 No 3-55, Zona 4) Jazz, blues and folk fans should look into what's happening here.

Discotecas

La Estación Norte (Ruta 4, 6-32, Zona 4) As far as mega discos go, this one around the corner from Cuatro Grados Norte is kind of interesting. It's done out in a train theme, with carriages for bars and platforms for dance floors. Dress well, but not over the top.

Zona 10 has a bunch of clubs attracting twenty-something local crowds along 13a Calle and adjacent streets such as 1a Av. The area's exclusivity means that door staff are well versed in the old 'members only' routine. If you want to try your luck, the universal rules apply: dress up, go before 11pm and make sure your group has more women than men in it. Check flyers around town for special nights. Here are a couple to get you started:

Kahlua (cnr 15a Calle & 1a Av, Zona 10) For electronica and bright young things.

Mr Jerry (13a Calle 1-26, Zona 10) For salsa and merengue.

ENTERTAINMENT

Two very good cultural centers in Cuatro Grados Norte host regular theatrical performances and other artistic events. It's always worth dropping in or checking their websites to see what's on.

IGA Cultural Center (www.iga.edu; Ruta 1, 4-05, Zona 4) The Instituto Guatemalteco Americano hosts art exhibitions and live theater.

Centro Cultural de España (www.centrocultural espana.com.gt; Via 5 1-23, Zona 4) The Spanish Cultural center hosts an excellent range of events, including live music, film nights and art exhibitions, mostly with free admission.

Centro Cultural Miguel Ángel Asturias (☎ 232 4042; 24a Calle 3-81, Zona 1) Cultural events are also held here.

Movie and some other listings can be found in the *Prensa Libre* newspaper. The English language magazine *Revue* (www.revuemag .com) has events details, although it focuses more on Antigua. Your hotel should have a copy, or know where to get one. Free events mags in Spanish come and go. At the time of writing *El Azar* (elazarcultural@yahoo.es) had the best info. Pick up a copy at any cultural center listed above.

SHOPPING

Mercado de Artesanías (Crafts Market; ☎ 472 0208; cnr 5a Calle & 11a Av, Zona 13; ◷ 9:30am-6pm) This sleepy official market near the museums and zoo sells similar goods in less crowded conditions.

For fashion boutiques, electronic goods and other first-world paraphernalia, head for the large shopping malls such as **Centro Comercial Tikal Futura** (Calz Roosevelt 22-43, Zona 11).

For a more everyday Guatemalan experience, take a walk along 6a Av between 8a and 16a Calles in Zona 1. This street is always choked with street stalls noisily hawking everything from cheap pirated DVDs and CDs to shoes, underwear and overalls.

GETTING THERE & AWAY
Air

Guatemala City's **Aeropuerto La Aurora** (code GUA; ☎ 2260 6415) is the country's major airport. All international flights to Guatemala City land and take off here. At the time of writing, the country's only *scheduled* domestic flights are between Guatemala City and Flores. The major carrier, Grupo TACA, makes two round-trip flights daily (one in the morning, one in the afternoon), plus an extra flight four mornings a week that continues from Flores to Cancún (Mexico) and flies back from in the afternoon. See p87 for contact details.

Tickets to Flores cost around US$127/204 one-way/round-trip with Grupo TACA, but some travel agents, especially in Antigua, offer large discounts on these prices.

Bus

Buses from here run all over Guatemala and into Mexico, Belize, Honduras, El Salvador and beyond. Most bus companies have their own terminals, some of which are in Zona 1. The Terminal de Autobuses, in Zona 4, is used only by some 2nd-class buses. The city council has been on a campaign to get long-distance bus companies out of the city center, so it may be wise to double check with Inguat or your hotel about the office location.

INTERNATIONAL

Belize City (Belize) Linea Dorada (☎ 2232 9658; 10a Av & 16 Calle, Zona 1) has 1st-class buses (US$40, 16 hours), with a few hours wait in Flores. Alternatively, take a bus to Flores/Santa Elena and an onward bus from there.

Chetumal (Mexico) Take a bus to Flores/Santa Elena, where daily buses leave for Chetumal (see p192).

Ciudad Pedro de Alvarado/La Hachadura (Salvadoran border) Buses to Taxisco depart from the Terminal de Autobuses (US$2, two hours, every 30 minutes 5am-4pm). Some continue to the border; otherwise change at Taxisco where buses leave for the border every 15 minutes until 5pm.

Ciudad Tecún Umán/Ciudad Hidalgo (Mexican border) Fortaleza del Sur (☎ 2230 3390; Calz Aguilar Batres 4-15, Zona 12) has buses (US$8, six hours, 250km, 20 daily 12:15am-6:30pm).

Copán (Honduras) Hedman Alas (☎ 2362 5072/5; 2a Av 8-73, Zona 10) has 1st-class buses (US$36, five hours, 238km, 5am daily), which continue to San Pedro Sula and La Ceiba. It's cheaper and slower to take a bus to Chiquimula, then another to the border at El Florido, then another to Copán.

El Carmen/Talismán (Mexican border) Fortaleza del Sur (☎ 2230 3390; Calz Aguilar Batres 4-15, Zona 12) has buses (US$6.50, seven hours, 290km, 20 daily 12:15am-6:30pm).

La Mesilla/Ciudad Cuauhtémoc (Mexican border) Transportes Velásquez (☎ 2440 3316; Calz Roosevelt 9-56, Zona 7) has buses (US$9, seven hours, 345km, every 30 minutes 8-11am). From Ciudad Cuauhtémoc there are fairly frequent buses and vans on to Comitán and San Cristóbal de Las Casas.

Melchor de Mencos (Belizean border) Fuente del Norte (☎ 2251 3817; 17a Calle 8-46, Zona 1) goes hourly (US$10.50, 11 hours, 600km), with a special Maya de Oro service (US$17) at 10:30pm.

San Salvador (El Salvador) Melva Internacional (☎ 2331 0874; 3a Av 1-38, Zona 9) runs buses via the border at Valle Nuevo (US$10, five to six hours, 240km, hourly 5:15am-4:15pm); Tica Bus (☎ 2366 4038; Blvd Los Proceres 26-55, Zona 10) departs daily (US$9.50, 12.30pm). From San Salvador, Tica Bus services all other Central American capitals except Belize City. King Quality & Confort Lines (☎ 2369 0404/56; 18a Av 1-96, Zona 15) runs luxury buses (US$20; 6:30am, 8am, 2pm & 3:30pm), with connections to Tegucigalpa & Managua; Pullmantur (☎ 2332 9785/6; Holiday Inn, 1a Av 13-22, Zona 10) has luxury buses (7am, 1pm and 3pm).

Tapachula (Mexico) Transportes Galgos (☎ 2253 9131; 7a Av 19-44, Zona 1) has buses (US$21.50, six to seven hours, 290km, 7:30am and 1:30pm); Línea Dorada (☎ 2232 9658; 16a Calle & 10a Av, Zona 1) departs twice daily (US$33, 7am and 4pm); Tica Bus (☎ 2366 4038; Blvd Los Proceres 26-55, Zona 10) departs daily (US$19, noon). From Tapachula buses run to many points in Mexico.

Tegucigalpa (Honduras) Hedman Alas (☎ 2362 5072/5; 2a Av 8-73, Zona 10) departs daily (US$54, 12 hours, 700km, 5am) with 1st-class buses.

DOMESTIC

Antigua (US$0.65; 1¼hr; 45km; every few minutes 5am-9pm) Buses depart from 1a Av between 3a and 4a Calle, Zona 7. See p113 for details on shuttle minibuses.

Biotopo del Quetzal Escobar y Monja Blanca (☎ 2238 1409; 8a Av 15-16, Zona 1) has buses (US$4, 3½hr, 156km, hourly 4am-5pm), via El Rancho & Purulhá.

Chichicastenango Veloz Quichelense (41 Calle btwn 6a & 7a Avs, Zona 8) has buses (US$1.55, 3hr, 145km, hourly 5am-8pm).

Chiquimula Rutas Orientales (☎ 2253 7282; 19 Calle 8-18, Zona 1) departs regularly (US$2.60, 3hr, 170km, every 30 minutes 4:30am-6pm).

Cobán Escobar y Monja Blanca (☎ 2238 1409; 8a Av 15-16, Zona 1) has buses (US$4.25, 4½hr, 213km, hourly 4am-5pm) stopping at El Rancho & the Biotopo del Quetzal.

Escuintla See La Democracia & Puerto San José (US$1.25, 1hr, 57km)

Esquipulas Rutas Orientales (☎ 2253 7282; 19 Calle 8-18, Zona 1) has buses (US$4, 4½hr, 222km, every 30 minutes 4:30am-6pm).

Flores/Santa Elena Fuente del Norte (☎ 2251 3817; 17a Calle 8-46, Zona 1) runs buses (US$9-17, eight to 10 hours, 500km, 18 daily); Línea Dorada (☎ 2232 9658; 16a Calle & 10 Av, Zona 1) also has buses (US$23; 9am, 9pm & 10pm).

Huehuetenango Los Halcones (☎ 2439 2780; Calz Roosevelt 37-47, Zona 11) departs thrice daily (US$6.50, five hours, 266km, 7am, 2pm and 5pm); Transportes Velásquez (☎ 2440 3316; Calz Roosevelt 9-56, Zona 7) buses also stop at Huehuetenango. All go by the Interamericana.

La Democracia Chatía Gomerana (cnr 4a Calle & 8a Av, Zona 12) has buses (US$1.50, two hours, 92km, every 30 minutes 6am-4:30pm), stopping at Escuintla.

Lívingston See Puerto Barrios and Río Dulce; from either place you can reach Lívingston by boat (see p179 & p175).

Monterrico Take one of the half-hourly buses from the Terminal de Autobuses to Taxisco (US$1.50, two hours, 5am-4pm) and change there for a bus to La Avellana (US$1, one hour, 12 daily 7am-6pm) and from there take a boat (see p160).

Nebaj Take a bus to Santa Cruz del Quiché and another from there.

Panajachel Transportes Rébuli (☎ 2230 2748; 41a Calle btwn 6a & 7a Calles, Zona 8) departs hourly (US$2, 3½ hours, 150km, 7am-4pm); also by Pullman bus (US$4.25, 9:30am).

Poptún Take a bus headed to Flores.

Puerto Barrios Litegua (☎ 2253 8169, 15a Calle 10-40, Zona 1) departs every half-hour (US$11/5.50 in 1st/standard class Pullman, five hours, 295km, 4:30am-6pm).

Puerto San José Various companies run about every 15 minutes (US$2, 2½hr, 90km, 5am-6pm) from 4a Calle between 7a & 8a Avs, Zona 12, via Escuintla.

Quetzaltenango Transportes Álamo (☎ 2251 4838; 12 Av A 0-65, Zona 7) has buses (US$6, five hours, 205km, six daily 8am-5:30pm); Líneas América (☎ 2232-1432; 2a Av 18-47, Zona 1) has seven buses between 5am and 7:30pm; Transportes Galgos (☎ 2253 4868; 7a Av 19-44, Zona 1) has seven buses between 5:30am-5pm. All are Pullman services.

Quiriguá Take a Puerto Barrios bus (see p173 for details on getting from the highway to Quiriguá ruins).

Retalhuleu Fortaleza del Sur (☎ 2230 3390; Calz Aguilar Batres 4-15, Zona 12) has buses (US$6, three hours, 196km, 20 daily 12:10am-7:10pm).

Río Dulce Litegua (☎ 2232 8169, 15a Calle 10-40, Zona 1) departs regularly (US$6, six hours, 280km; 6am, 9am, 11:30am & 1pm). Flores-bound buses stop at here.

Salamá Transportes Dulce María (☎ 2253 4618; 17a Calle 11-32, Zona 1) departs hourly (US$3, three hours, 150km, 5am-5pm).

Santa Cruz del Quiché Buses depart from the Terminal de Autobuses every 15 to 20 minutes (US$3.50, 3½ hours, 163km, 5am-5pm).

Santa Elena See Flores/Santa Elena.

Santa Lucía Cotzumalguapa Take a bus to Escuintla and another from there.

Santiago Atitlán Various companies depart from 4a Calle btwn 8a & 9a Avs, Zona 12 every half-hour (US$3.50, four hours, 165km, 4am-5pm).

Sayaxché Fuente del Norte (☎ 2251 3817; 17a Calle 8-46, Zona 1) departs at 4pm (US$12) & 7pm (US$15) via Río Dulce and Flores (11 hours, 560km) and at 5:30pm via Cobán (US$12, 10 hours, 420km).

Tecpán Veloz Poaquileña (1a Av btwn 3a & 4a Calles, Zona 7) departs every 15 minutes (US$1, two hours, 92km, 5:30am-7pm).

Tikal Take a bus to Flores/Santa Elena and onward transportation from there.

Shuttle Minibus

Door-to-door minibuses run from the airport to any address in Antigua (usually US$10 per person, one hour). Look for signs in the airport exit hall or people holding up 'Antigua Shuttle' signs. The first shuttle leaves for Antigua about 7am and the last around 8pm or 9pm. Shuttle services from Guatemala City to popular destinations such as Panajachel and Chichicastenango (both around US$25) are offered by travel agencies in Antigua such as Sin Fronteras – see p105.

GETTING AROUND
Bus

If you spend any time in Guatemala City, especially Zona 1, its buses will become a major feature of your existence as they roar along, belching great clouds of black smoke. Still, buses are cheap, frequent and, although very crowded in peak hour, useful. They are not, however, always safe. Theft and robbery are not unusual; there have even been murders on board, but most of this nastiness happens late at night or in outlying suburbs. Buses cost US$0.15 (Q1) per ride: have a coin ready – you pay the driver as you get on, but he won't hold the bus as you fumble around.

To get from Zona 1 to Zona 10, take bus 82 or 101 southbound on 10a Av between 8a and 13a Calles. These buses swing west to travel south down 6a Av for 1km or so before swinging southeast along Ruta 6 (Zona 4) then south along Av La Reforma. For the main Inguat tourist office, get off on 6a Av at 22a Calle (Zona 1) and walk east along 22a Calle, then south down the far (east) side of 7a Av.

Traveling north *to* Zona 1, buses 82 and 101 go along Av La Reforma then 7a Av, Zona 4 (passing right by Inguat) and 9a Av, Zona 1.

Taxi

Plenty of taxis cruise most parts of the city. Fares are negotiable: always establish your destination and fare before getting in. Zona 1 to Zona 10, or vice-versa, costs around US$5.50 to US$8. If you want to phone for a taxi, **Taxi Amarillo Express** (☎ 2232 1515) has metered cabs that often work out cheaper than others, although true *capitaleños* will tell you that taximeters are all rigged and you get a better deal bargaining.

ANTIGUA

pop 45,200

In all the long, boring discussions about where the 'real Guatemala' is, you can be sure the word Antigua has never come up. This is fantasyland – what the country would look like if the Scandinavians came in and took over for a couple of years. It's a place where power lines run underground, building codes are adhered to, rubbish is collected, traffic diverted and stray dogs 'disappear' mysteriously in the middle of the night.

But you'd be a fool to miss it. Antigua's setting is gorgeous, nestled between three volcanoes, and its streetscapes offer photo opportunities at every turn. The language-school scene is thriving, hindered only by the fact that nearly everybody speaks at least a little English. The hostels offer colonial-chic accommodations and the dining is some of the best in the country.

The most exciting time to visit Antigua is during Semana Santa – especially Good Friday. It takes planning (reserve hotels at least four months in advance), as this is the busiest week of the year. Other busy times are June through August and November to April.

Antigua is cold after sunset, especially between September and March, so bring warm clothes, a sleeping bag or a blanket. Antigua

GUATEMALA

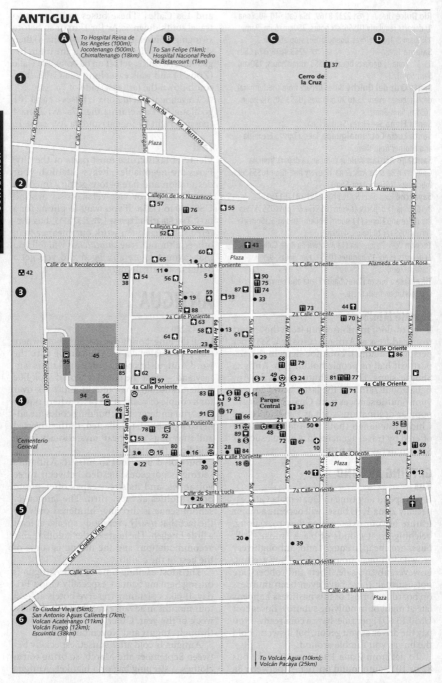

ANTIGUA

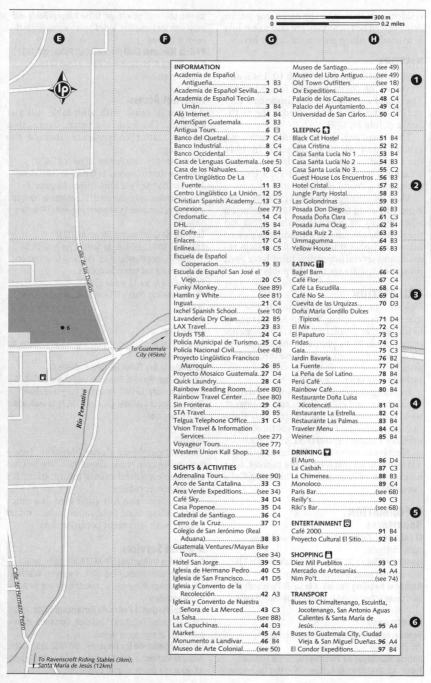

0 — 300 m
0 — 0.2 miles

GUATEMALA

INFORMATION
Academia de Español Antigueña...........................**1** B3
Academia de Español Sevilla...**2** D4
Academia de Español Tecún Umán...........................**3** B4
Aló Internet............................**4** B4
AmeriSpan Guatemala...........**5** B3
Antigua Tours.........................**6** E3
Banco del Quetzal...................**7** C4
Banco Industrial.....................**8** C4
Banco Occidental....................**9** C4
Casa de Lenguas Guatemala..(see 5)
Casa de los Nahuales.............**10** C4
Centro Lingüístico De La Fuente............................**11** B3
Centro Lingüístico La Unión...**12** D5
Christian Spanish Academy....**13** C3
Conexion...........................(see 77)
Credomatic.............................**14** C4
DHL..**15** B4
El Cofre..................................**16** B4
Enlaces...................................**17** C4
Enlínea...................................**18** C5
Escuela de Español Cooperacion.....................**19** B3
Escuela de Español San José el Viejo............................**20** C5
Funky Monkey....................(see 89)
Hamlin y White...................(see 81)
Inguat.....................................**21** C4
Ixchel Spanish School.........(see 10)
Lavandería Dry Clean............**22** B5
LAX Travel...............................**23** B3
Lloyds TSB..............................**24** C4
Policía Municipal de Turismo.**25** C4
Policía Nacional Civil............(see 48)
Proyecto Lingüístico Francisco Marroquín.....................**26** B5
Proyecto Mosaico Guatemala.**27** D4
Quick Laundry........................**28** C4
Rainbow Reading Room......(see 80)
Rainbow Travel Center........(see 80)
Sin Fronteras..........................**29** C4
STA Travel...............................**30** B5
Telgua Telephone Office.......**31** C4
Vision Travel & Information Services.........................(see 27)
Voyageur Tours...................(see 77)
Western Union Kall Shop......**32** B4

SIGHTS & ACTIVITIES
Adrenalina Tours.................(see 90)
Arco de Santa Catalina.........**33** C3
Area Verde Expeditions.......(see 34)
Café Sky.................................**34** D4
Casa Popenoe........................**35** D4
Catedral de Santiago.............**36** C4
Cerro de la Cruz....................**37** D1
Colegio de San Jerónimo (Real Aduana)........................**38** B3
Guatemala Ventures/Mayan Bike Tours...........................(see 34)
Hotel San Jorge.....................**39** C5
Iglesia de Hermano Pedro.....**40** C5
Iglesia de San Francisco........**41** D5
Iglesia y Convento de la Recolección.....................**42** A3
Iglesia y Convento de Nuestra Señora de La Merced.........**43** C3
La Salsa..............................(see 88)
Las Capuchinas......................**44** D3
Market....................................**45** A4
Monumento a Landívar..........**46** B4
Museo de Arte Colonial.......(see 50)

Museo de Santiago................(see 49)
Museo del Libro Antiguo......(see 49)
Old Town Outfitters............(see 18)
Ox Expeditions......................**47** D4
Palacio de los Capitanes.........**48** C4
Palacio del Ayuntamiento......**49** C4
Universidad de San Carlos......**50** C4

SLEEPING 🛏
Black Cat Hostel **51** B4
Casa Cristina..........................**52** B2
Casa Santa Lucía No 1 ....**53** B4
Casa Santa Lucía No 2 ....**54** B3
Casa Santa Lucía No 3............**55** C2
Guest House Los Encuentros ..**56** B3
Hotel Cristal...........................**57** B2
Jungle Party Hostal................**58** B3
Las Golondrinas.....................**59** B3
Posada Don Diego...................**60** B3
Posada Doña Clara **61** C3
Posada Juma Ocag.................**62** B4
Posada Ruiz 2.........................**63** B3
Ummagumma........................**64** B3
Yellow House..........................**65** B3

EATING 🍴
Bagel Barn.............................**66** C4
Café Flor................................**67** C4
Café La Escudilla....................**68** C4
Café No Sé.............................**69** D4
Cuevita de las Urquizas..........**70** D3
Doña María Gordillo Dulces Típicos.........................**71** D4
El Mix....................................**72** C4
El Papaturo............................**73** C3
Fridas.....................................**74** C3
Gaia.......................................**75** C3
Jardín Bavaria........................**76** B2
La Fuente...............................**77** C4
La Peña de Sol Latino.............**78** B4
Perú Café **79** C4
Rainbow Café.........................**80** B4
Restaurante Doña Luisa Xicotencatl......................**81** D4
Restaurante La Estrella...........**82** C4
Restaurante Las Palmas..........**83** B4
Traveler Menu **84** C4
Weiner...................................**85** B4

DRINKING 🍷
El Muro..................................**86** D4
La Casbah..............................**87** C3
La Chimenea..........................**88** B3
Monoloco..............................**89** C4
Paris Bar.............................(see 68)
Reilly's...................................**90** C3
Riki's Bar............................(see 68)

ENTERTAINMENT 🎭
Café 2000...............................**91** B4
Proyecto Cultural El Sitio.........**92** B4

SHOPPING 🛍
Diez Mil Pueblitos..................**93** C3
Mercado de Artesanías...........**94** A4
Nim Po't...............................(see 74)

TRANSPORT
Buses to Chimaltenango, Escuintla, Jocotenango, San Antonio Aguas Calientes & Santa María de Jesús............................**95** A4
Buses to Guatemala City, Ciudad Vieja & San Miguel Dueñas.**96** A4
El Condor Expeditions............**97** B4

Calle de los Duelos

To Guatemala City (45km)

Río Pensativo

Calle del Hermano Pedro

To Ravenscroft Riding Stables (3km);
Santa María de Jesús (12km)

residents are known by the nickname *panza verde* (green belly), as they are said to eat lots of avocados, which grow abundantly here.

HISTORY

Antigua was founded on March 10, 1543, and served as the colonial capital for 233 years. The capital was transferred to Guatemala City in 1776, after Antigua was razed in the earthquake of July 29, 1773.

The town was slowly rebuilt, retaining much of its traditional character. In 1944 the Legislative Assembly declared Antigua a national monument, and in 1979 Unesco declared it a World Heritage Site.

Most of Antigua's buildings were constructed during the 17th and 18th centuries, when the city was a rich Spanish outpost and the Catholic church was ascending to power. Many handsome, sturdy colonial buildings remain, and several impressive ruins have been preserved and are open to the public.

ORIENTATION

Volcán Agua is southeast of the city and visible from most points; Volcán Acatenango is to the west; and Volcán Fuego (Fire) – easily recognizable by its plume of smoke and red glow – is to the southwest. These three volcanoes (which appear on the city's coat of arms) provide easy reference points.

In Antigua compass points are added to the avenidas and calles. Calles run east–west, so 4a Calle west of Parque Central is 4a Calle Poniente; avenidas run north–south, so 3a Av north of Parque Central is 3a Av Norte.

Most buses arrive at the Terminal de Buses, a large open lot just west of the market, four blocks west of Parque Central along 4a Calle Poniente.

INFORMATION

Bookstores

El Cofre (6a Calle Poniente 26) Second-hand books, mainly in English.

Hamlin y White (☎ 7832 7075; 4a Calle Oriente 12A) New and used books in several languages.

Rainbow Reading Room (7a Av Sur 8) Thousands of used books in English and Spanish for sale, rent or trade.

Emergency

Bomberos Municipales (Municipal Firefighters; ☎ 7831 0049)

Policía Municipal de Turismo (Municipal Tourism Police; ☎ 7832 7290; 4a Av Norte; ⊙ 24hr) The helpful

tourism police will go with you to the National Police and assist with the formalities, including any translating that needs to be done.

Policía Nacional Civil (National Civil Police; ☎ 7832 0251; Palacio de los Capitanes, Parque Central) Lodge formal reports here.

Internet Access

Antigua is awash with affordable internet services. The best, for price, connection quality and/or convenience, include the following:

Aló Internet (5a Calle Ponient 28; per hr US$0.80)

Conexion (Centro Comercial La Fuente, 4a Calle Oriente 14; per hr US$0.80; ⊙ 8:30am-7:30pm) All-purpose communications center charges US$2 per hour to hook up your laptop, plus printing, photocopying and CD-burning services.

El Cofre (6a Calle Poniente 26; per hr US$1)

Enlaces (☎ 832 5555; 6a Av Norte 1; per hr US$0.80; ⊙ 8am-7:30pm Mon-Sat, 8am-1pm Sun) Good connections, smoking and nonsmoking areas.

Enlínea (5a Av Sur 12; per hr US$1)

Funky Monkey (Pasaje El Corregidor, 5a Av Sur 6; per hr US$1)

Laundry

Laundries are everywhere, especially along 6a Calle Poniente.

Lavandería Dry Clean (6a Calle Poniente 49; ⊙ 7am-7pm Mon-Sat, 9am-6pm Sun) Charges US$3.75.

Quick Laundry (6a Calle Poniente 14; ⊙ 8am-5pm Mon-Sat) Fast and reliable. Charges US$3.25 to wash and dry a 2.25kg load.

Media

The Antigua-based *Revue Magazine* (www .revuemag.com) runs about 90% ads, but has reasonable cultural events information. It's available everywhere.

La Cuadra, also Antigua-based, is a much more underground publication, which mixes politics with irreverent commentary.

Medical Services

Casa de los Nahuales (☎ 7832 0068; 3a Av Sur 6) Offers alternative medical and spiritual services, including Mayan horoscopes, massages, aromatherapy and Bach flower remedies.

Hospital Nacional Pedro de Betancourt (☎ 7832 2801) This public hospital in San Felipe, 2km north of the center, has an emergency service.

Hospital Reina de los Ángeles (☎ 7832 2258; Calle Ancha de los Herreros 59) If possible, you're probably best off going to a private hospital such as this.

Money

Banco del Quetzal (4a Calle; ◯ 8:30am-7pm Mon-Fri, 9am-1pm Sat & Sun) Often has the best exchange rates and has a MasterCard ATM outside. Also changes US dollars (cash and traveler's checks). It faces Parque Central.

Banco Industrial (5a Av Sur 4; ◯ 9am-7pm Mon-Fri, to 5pm Sat) Has Visa ATMs and changes US dollars (cash and traveler's checks).

Credomatic (Portal del Comercio; ◯ 9am-7pm Mon-Fri, to 1pm Sat) Gives Visa and MasterCard cash advances. Changes US dollars (cash and traveler's checks).

Lloyds TSB (cnr 4a Calle Oriente & 4a Av Norte; ◯ 9am-3:30pm Mon-Fri, 9:30am-12:30pm Sat) Gives Visa and MasterCard advances. Changes US dollars (cash and traveler's checks).

Post

DHL (☎ 832 0073; 6a Calle Poniente 34) Offers door-to-door service.

Post office (cnr 4a Calle Poniente & Calz de Santa Lucía) West of Parque Central, near the market.

Telephone

Many businesses, including several internet cafés, offer cut-rate international calls. Some of these are done through internet telephone – very cheap, however the line quality is quite unpredictable.

Funky Monkey (5a Av Sur 6, Pasaje El Corregidor) Offers internet calls anywhere in the world for between US$0.15 and US$0.40 per minute.

Guatemala Ventures (☎ /fax 832 3383; 1a Av Sur 15) Rents cell phones on which you can call the US for US$0.10 per minute or Europe for US$0.20, for US$10 per week (with a US$50 deposit).

Western Union Kall Shop (6a Av Sur 12; ◯ 8:30am-6pm Mon-Fri, to 4pm Sat) Pay US$0.30 per minute to call the USA or Canada, US$0.45 to Mexico, Central America or Europe, US$0.55 to South America and US$0.60 to anywhere else.

Tourist Information

Antigua Guatemala: The City and its Heritage, by long-time Antigua resident Elizabeth Bell, is well worth picking up at a bookstore: it describes all of the city's important buildings and museums, and neatly encapsulates Antigua's history and fiestas.

Inguat (☎ 7832 0763; Palacio de los Capitanes, Parque Central; ◯ 8am-12:30pm & 2:30-5pm Mon-Fri, 9am-12:30pm & 2:30-5pm Sat & Sun) Has free city maps, bus information and schedules of Semana Santa events; staff try to find the answers to any curly ones you might throw at them.

Travel Agencies

Everywhere you turn in Antigua, you'll see travel agencies offering tours to interesting sites around Antigua and elsewhere in Guatemala, international flights, shuttle minibuses and more. Reputable agencies include the following:

Adrenalina Tours (☎ 7832 1108; www.adrenalina tours.com; 5a Av Norte 31) Specialists in the Western Highlands, can arrange everything from tours and shuttles to domestic and international flights.

LAX Travel (☎ /fax 7832 1621; laxantigua@intelnet.net .gt; 3a Calle Poniente 12) International flight specialist.

Sin Fronteras (☎ 7832 1017; www.sinfront.com; 5a Av Norte 15A) Sells one-way international air tickets; issues student and youth cards for US$8; sells International Travel Maps; runs tours to Cuba among other destinations.

STA Travel (☎ 7832 4080; www.isyta.com; 6a Calle Poniente 21) Offers student and teacher airfares and a change-of-date and lost-ticket-replacement service for tickets issued by student/youth travel agencies; issues student, teacher and youth cards (US$8).

Vision Travel & Information Services (☎ 7832 3293; www.guatemalainfo.com; Casa de Mito, 3a Av Norte 3) Tours ranging from Tikal to local coffee *fincas* are offered here, as are shuttle services and many guidebooks (including Lonely Planet titles).

Voyageur Tours (☎ 7832 4237; www.travel.net.gt; Centro Comercial La Fuente, 4a Calle Oriente 14) Operates some good-value shuttle minibus services.

DANGERS & ANNOYANCES

Antigua isn't quite as mellow as it seems. Although you'll probably never have a problem, be wary at night. Armed robberies (and worse) have occurred on Cerro de la Cruz, on Volcán Pacaya and at the cemetery, both of which should be considered off-limits unless you're escorted by the Tourist Police. Crime against tourists has dropped dramatically since the formation of this agency (see opposite for contact details).

SIGHTS

Parque Central

The gathering place for locals and visitors alike, on most days the plaza is lined with villagers selling handicrafts to tourists; on Sunday it's mobbed and the streets on the east and west sides are closed to traffic. Things are cheapest late Sunday afternoon, when the peddling is winding down.

The plaza's famous fountain was built in 1738. At night, mariachi or marimba bands play in the park.

GUATEMALA

PALACIO DE LOS CAPITANES

Begun in 1558, the Captain-Generals' Palace was the governmental center of all Central America from Chiapas to Costa Rica until 1773. The stately double-arcaded façade, which marches proudly along the southern side of the Parque, was added in the early 1760s. Today the palace houses the Inguat tourist office, national police and office of the governor of Sacatepéquez department.

CATEDRAL DE SANTIAGO

On the park's east side, Catedral de Santiago was founded in 1542, damaged by earthquakes many times, badly ruined in 1773 and only partially rebuilt between 1780 and 1820. In the 16th and early 17th centuries, Antigua's churches had lavish baroque interiors, but most – including this one – lost this richness during post-earthquake rebuilding. Inside, a crypt contains the bones of Bernal Díaz del Castillo, historian of the Spanish conquest, who died in 1581. If the front entrance is closed, you can enter at the rear or on the south side.

PALACIO DEL AYUNTAMIENTO

The City Hall, on the north side of the park, dates mostly from 1743. In addition to town offices, it houses the **Museo de Santiago** (☎ 7832 2868; admission US$1.30; ⊙ 9am-4pm Tue-Fri, 9am-noon & 2-4pm Sat & Sun) in the former town jail, exhibiting furnishings, artifacts and weapons from colonial times. Next door is the **Museo del Libro Antiguo** (Old Book Museum; ☎ 7832 5511; admission US$1.30; ⊙ 9am-4pm Tue-Fri, 9am-noon & 2-4pm Sat & Sun), with exhibits of colonial printing and binding, including a replica of Guatemala's first printing press, which began work here in the 1660s.

UNIVERSIDAD DE SAN CARLOS

Now in Guatemala City, San Carlos University was founded in Antigua in 1676. What used to be its main building (built in 1763), half a block east of the park, houses the **Museo de Arte Colonial** (☎ 7832 0429; 5a Calle Oriente 5; admission US$3.25; ⊙ 9am-4pm Tue-Fri, 9am-noon & 2-4pm Sat & Sun), with some expressive sculptures of saints and paintings by leading Mexican artists of the era such as Miguel Cabrera and Juan de Correa.

Churches

Once glorious in their gilded baroque finery, Antigua's churches have suffered indignities from both nature and humankind. Rebuilding after earthquakes gave the churches thicker walls, lower towers and belfries, and bland interiors, and moving the capital to Guatemala City deprived Antigua of the population needed to maintain the churches in their traditional glory. Still, they are impressive. In addition to those noted here, you'll find many others scattered around town in various states of decay.

LA MERCED

At the north end of 5a Av is **Iglesia y Convento de Nuestra Señora de La Merced**, Antigua's most striking colonial church.

La Merced's construction began in 1548. Improvements continued until 1717, when the church was ruined by earthquakes. Reconstruction was completed in 1767, but in 1773 an earthquake struck again and the convent was destroyed. Repairs to the church were made from 1850 to 1855; its baroque facade dates from this period. Inside the **monastery ruins** (admission US$0.40; ⊙ 9am-6:30pm) is a fountain 27m in diameter – possibly the largest in Central America.

SAN FRANCISCO

The town's next most notable church is the Iglesia de San Francisco (east end of 8a Calle). It dates from the mid-16th century, but little of the original building remains. Rebuilding and restoration over the centuries have produced a handsome structure. All that remains of the original church is the resting place of Hermano Pedro de San José Betancourt, a Franciscan monk who founded a hospital for the poor and earned the gratitude of generations. He died here in 1667; his intercession is still sought by the ill, who pray here fervently.

LAS CAPUCHINAS

The Iglesia y Convento de Nuestra Señora del Pilar de Zaragoza, usually called **Las Capuchinas** (cnr 2a Av Norte & 2a Calle Oriente; nonstudent/student US$4/2; ⊙ 9am-5pm), was founded in 1736 by nuns from Madrid. Destroyed repeatedly by earthquakes, it is now a museum, with exhibits on religious life in colonial times. The building has an unusual structure of 18 concentric cells around a circular patio.

CHURCH RUINS

A massive ruin at the west end of 1a Calle Poniente, the **Iglesia y Convento de la Recolección**

(Av de la Recolección; US$4; 🕘 9am-5pm), is among Antigua's most impressive monuments. Built between 1701 and 1708, it was destroyed in the 1773 earthquake.

Near La Recolección, at Alameda de Santa Lucía and 1a Calle Poniente, **Colegio de San Jerónimo** (cnr Calz de Santa Lucía & 1a Calle Poniente; US$4; 🕘 9am-5pm), also called the Real Aduana, was built in 1757 by friars of the Merced order. Because it did not have royal authorization, it was taken over by Spain's Carlos III in 1761. In 1765 it was designated for use as the Royal Customhouse, but was destroyed in the 1773 earthquake.

Casa Popenoe

This beautiful **house** (☎ 7832 3087; 1a Av Sur 2; admission US$1.30; 🕘 2-4pm Mon-Sat) was built in 1636 by Don Luis de las Infantas Mendoza. After the 1773 earthquake, the house stood desolate for more than 150 years until it was bought in 1929 by agricultural scientist William Popenoe and his wife Dorothy. Their painstaking, authentic restoration yields a fascinating glimpse of how a royal official lived in 17th-century Antigua.

Monumento a Landívar

At the west end of 5a Calle Poniente is the Landívar Monument, a structure of five colonial-style arches set in a little park. The poetry of Rafael Landívar, an 18th-century Jesuit priest, is esteemed as the colonial period's best, even though he wrote much of it in Italy after the Jesuits' expulsion from Guatemala. Landívar's Antigua house was nearby on 5a Calle Poniente.

Market

At the west end of 4a Calle Poniente, across Calzada de Santa Lucía, sprawls the market – chaotic, colorful and always bustling. The frenzied mornings are the best time to come. Official market days are Monday, Thursday and Saturday.

Cerro de la Cruz

On the town's northeast side is the Hill of the Cross, offering fine views over Antigua and south toward Volcán Agua. Don't come here without a Tourist Police escort (see p104), as it's notorious for muggers. The Tourist Police was formed because of robberies here; reportedly no crime against tourists has taken place on the hill since.

ACTIVITIES

Two professional, established and friendly outfits offering a big range of activities are **Old Town Outfitters** (☎ /fax 7832 4171; www.bikeguatemala .com; 5a Av Sur 12C) and **Guatemala Ventures/Mayan Bike Tours** (☎ /fax 7832 3383; www.guatemalaventures .com; 1a Av Sur 15). Drop by either place to chat about possibilities.

Ox Expeditions (☎ 7832 0074; www.guatemalavolcano .com; 1 Av Sur 4B) are a new outfit offering rigorous climbing opportunities in the area. Part of their profits goes to local environmental projects.

Climbing the Volcanoes

Although foreigners climbing the volcanoes around Antigua were sometimes robbed, raped or murdered, recent tourist safety measures have reduced the problem dramatically.

VOLCÁN PACAYA

Because of its status as the only active volcano near Antigua, Volcán Pacaya (2552m) attracts the most tourists and the most bandits. The situation is improving, however, since each group is now accompanied by a security guard (little comfort when he turns out to be pre-pubescent). Guards or no, a hike up Pacaya still entails risks. Still, travelers now are more likely to be hurt by flaming rocks and sulfurous fog than criminals. Climbers have suffered serious, even fatal, injuries when the volcano erupted unexpectedly while they were near the summit.

Get reliable safety advice before you climb. Check with your embassy in Guatemala City or with the tourist office in Antigua. If you decide to go, make sure you're with reputable guides, arranged through an established agency.

Wear adequate footwear (volcanic rock can shred shoes), warm clothing and, in the rainy season, some sort of rain gear. Carry snacks, water and a flashlight.

OTHER VOLCANOES

The volcanoes nearer Antigua (Agua, Fuego and Acatenango) are inactive and attract fewer tourists. Still, they are impressive and offer magnificent views.

Volcán Agua (3766m) looms over Antigua, south of town. Various outfitters in Antigua can furnish details about the climb. To get to the mountain, follow 2a Av Sur or Calle de los Pasos south toward El Calvario (2km), then

GUATEMALA

continue via San Juan del Obispo (another 3km) to Santa María de Jesús, a tiny village in the shadow of the volcano. This is the jumping-off point for treks. The main plaza is also the bus terminal. Comedor & Hospedaje El Oasis, a tidy little pensión, offers meals and beds.

You could also climb the other two volcanoes near Antigua: **Volcán Acatenango** (3976m) and **Volcán Fuego** (3763m). All three companies listed above offer tours up these volcanoes.

Cycling

Old Town Outfitters (☎ /fax 7832 4171; www.bikegua temala.com; 5a Av Sur 12C) rents quality bikes with gloves, helmets and maps for US$8/12 per half/whole day. It also has a great range of mountain bike tours at all levels of difficulty, from the gentle Sip & Cycle Coffee Tour (US$25) or the exhilarating one-day Cielo Grande Ridge Ride (US$45) to the two-day Pedal & Paddle Tour (US$140 to US$175), which includes kayaking and hiking at the Lago de Atitlán.

Guatemala Ventures/Mayan Bike Tours (☎ /fax 832 3383; www.guatemalaventures.com; 1a Av Sur 15) also rents good mountain bikes for US$2 per hour, and offers some tasty bike tours from intermediate to expert levels. It does hike-and-bike tours to Volcán Acatenango (US$49 to US$109, one or two days) and bike-and-kayak trips to Lago de Atitlán and Monterrico (both two days, US$129).

Horseback Riding

Ravenscroft Riding Stables (☎ 7832 6229 afternoons; 2a Av Sur 3, San Juan del Obispo), 3km south of Antigua on the road to Santa María de Jesús, offers English-style riding, with scenic rides of three, four or five hours in the valleys and hills around Antigua, for US$15 per hour per person. Reservations and information are available through the **Hotel San Jorge** (☎ 7832 3132; 4a Av Sur 13). You can reach the stables on a bus bound for Santa María de Jesús.

Guatemala Ventures/Mayan Bike Tours offers full-day rides on trails around Volcán Agua for US$49, although, at the time of writing, these had been cancelled due to security concerns.

White-Water Rafting

Area Verde Expeditions (☎ /fax 7832 3383; mayan bike@guate.net; 1a Av Sur 15), in Café Sky, offers a variety of one- to five-day rafting tours year-round.

Sin Fronteras (☎ 7832 1017; 3a Calle Poniente 12), representing Maya Expeditions in Antigua, and it also leads a variety of day trips and multiday tours on several rivers.

COURSES
Dancing

You can learn to salsa at several places around town. **La Salsa** (☎ 5400 0315; www.lasalsadance.com; 7 Av Norte 11) comes highly recommended, both for teaching style and lack of 'sleaze factor.'

Spanish

Antigua is world-famous for its many Spanish-language schools. Prices, teacher quality and student satisfaction vary greatly, so shop around. Ask for references and talk to ex-students. The Inguat tourist office has a list of reputable schools, including the following:

Academia de Español Antigueña (☎ 7832 7241; www.spanishacademyantiguena.com; 1a Calle Poniente 10) A highly recommended school, only hiring experienced teachers. They can arrange volunteer work in the area too.

Academia de Español Sevilla (☎ /fax 7832 5101; www.sevillantigua.com; 1a Av Sur 8) This school has a good free activity program, and offers a shared student house as an accommodation option.

Academia de Español Tecún Umán (☎ /fax 7832 2792; www.escuelatecun.com; 6a Calle Poniente 34A) Also has a school on Lago de Atitlán.

Casa de Lenguas Guatemala (☎ 7832 4846; www .casadelenguas.com; 6a Av Norte 40) This school has group classes (US$65 per week) as well as individual classes (US$95 per week).

Centro Lingüístico De La Fuente (☎ 7832 2711; www.delafuenteschool.com; 1a Calle Poniente 27)

Centro Lingüístico La Unión (☎ /fax 7832 7337; www.launion.conexion.com; 1a Av Sur 21) Many classes take place in the school's pretty patio; discounts are given for good test results!

Christian Spanish Academy (☎ 7832 3922; www.learncsa.com; 6a Av Norte 15) Very professional outfit where students get to report on the teachers weekly.

Escuela de Español Cooperacion (☎ 7812 2482; www.geocities.com/escuela_coop; 7 Av Norte, No 15B) A highly recommended school run as a cooperative, ensuring teachers get paid fairly.

Escuela de Español San José el Viejo (☎ 7832 3028; www.sanjoseelviejo.com; 5a Av Sur 34) Professional, 30-teacher school with pool, superb gardens, tennis court and own tasteful accommodations.

Ixchel Spanish School (☎ /fax 7832 7137; www.ixchel school.com; 3a Av Sur 6) Comfortable, welcoming school with enjoyable group activities and lush garden.
Proyecto Lingüístico Francisco Marroquín (☎ /fax 7832 2886; www.plfm-antigua.org; 7a Calle Poniente 31) Antigua's oldest Spanish school, founded in 1971; it's run by a nonprofit foundation working to preserve Maya languages and culture; courses in some of these are also available.

Classes start Mondays at most schools, though you can usually be placed with a teacher any day of the week. The busiest seasons are January, and April to August – some schools request advance reservations for these times. Instruction is usually one-on-one and costs between US$65 to US$115 per week for four hours of classes daily, five days per week. You can enroll for up to 10 hours a day of instruction. Most schools offer room and board with local families, where you'll often have your own room, usually with shared bathrooms, for around US$55 per week (including three meals daily except Sunday). Homestays are supposed to promote the 'total immersion' concept of language learning, but often there are several foreigners staying with one family and separate mealtimes for students and the family. Make a point of inquiring about such details if you really want to be totally immersed.

Antigua is not for everyone who wants to study Spanish; there are so many foreigners about, it takes some real discipline to converse in Spanish rather than your native tongue. Many enjoy this social scene, but if you think it will bother you, consider studying in Xela, El Petén or elsewhere, where there are fewer foreign students and more opportunities to dive into Spanish.

VOLUNTEERING

AmeriSpan Guatemala (☎ 7832 0164; www.ameri span.com; 6a Av Norte 40A) Can hook you up with volunteer opportunities all over Guatemala. It charges a US$50 registration fee.
Proyecto Mosaico Guatemala (☎ /fax 7932 0955; Casa de Mito, 3a Av Norte 3; ☘ 2-4pm Mon-Fri) A nonprofit organization providing volunteers and resources to more than 60 projects in Guatemala. It's interested in people with medical experience but there's work for periods from one week to one year doing things as varied as carpentry, teaching, environmental protection, helping HIV-positive kids and organic farming. You should be over 18 and fit.

TOURS

Elizabeth Bell, author of books on Antigua, leads three-hour cultural walking tours of the town (in English and/or Spanish) at 9:30am Tuesday, Wednesday, Friday and Saturday. On Monday and Thursday tours start at 2pm. The cost is US$18 (US$15 for Spanish students and project volunteers). Reservations are suggested and can be made at **Antigua Tours** (☎ /fax 7832 5821; www.antiguatours.net; Portal de Santo Domingo, 3a Calle Oriente 28, in Casa Santo Domingo Hotel). Vision Travel and Sin Fronteras (p105) also offer daily city walking tours, visiting a variety of convents, ruins and museums. These firms also do interesting tours of villages and coffee or macadamia plantations for US$20 to US$30.

Cycling, horseback riding and white-water rafting tours are also available (see p108).

Many travel agencies offer tours to more distant places, including Tikal, Copán, Río Dulce, the Cobán area, Monterrico, Chichicastenango, Guatemala City and Panajachel (see p105). Two-day trips to Tikal, flying from Guatemala City to Flores and back, cost between US$150 and US$300, largely depending on where you stay. A hectic one-day Tikal round-trip costs US$150 to US$180. Two-day land tours to Copán (some also including Quiriguá and Río Dulce) are between US$115 and US$150.

On long-distance tours be sure of what you are paying for – some of the cheaper 'tours' simply amount to shuttling you to Guatemala City then popping you on a public bus.

FESTIVALS & EVENTS

Antigua really comes alive in **Semana Santa** (Holy Week), when hundreds of people dress in purple robes to accompany the most revered sculptural images from the city's churches in daily street processions remembering Christ's Crucifixion and the events surrounding it. Dense clouds of incense envelop the parades and the streets are covered in breathtakingly elaborate *alfombras* (carpets) of colored sawdust and flower petals.

The fervor and the crowds peak on Good Friday, when an early morning procession departs from La Merced church, and a late afternoon one leaves from the Escuela de Cristo church. There may also be an enactment of the Crucifixion in Parque Central. Have ironclad Antigua room reservations well in advance of Semana Santa, or plan to stay in Guatemala City or another town and commute to the festivities.

Processions, *velaciones* (vigils) and other events actually go on every weekend through Lent, the 40-day period prior to Holy Week. Antigua's tourist office has schedules of everything, and the booklet *Lent and Holy Week in Antigua*, written by Elizabeth Bell, gives explanations.

It seems that Guatemala City's entire population of pickpockets decamps to Antigua for Semana Santa; they target foreign tourists especially.

SLEEPING

When checking a budget establishment, look at several rooms, as some are much better than others.

Posada Ruiz 2 (2a Calle Poniente 25; s/d with shared bathroom US$3/6) The rough-hewn archway over the entrance is by far the most impressive aspect of this super cheapie, but it has a sociable patio area and the bathrooms are moderately clean.

Guest House Los Encuentros (☎ 7832 4232; 7a Av Norte 60; dm/s/d US$5/6/12; 🖳) Nothing fancy going on here – the rooms are basic, the bathrooms shared, but this family-run place has a great feel to it in this often-impersonal town. Kitchen access and breakfast is available.

Ummagumma (☎ 7832 4413; www.ummagumma hostel.blogspot.com; 7a Av Norte 15; dm/s/d US$5/7/12, s/d with bathroom US$10/20) Slightly tatty at the edges, the Ummagumma has some of the best atmosphere in town – it's a great place to relax, meet people and hang out on the leafy rooftop terrace. Kitchen access for guests.

Black Cat Hostel (☎ 7832 1229; www.blackcatantigua .com; 6a Av Norte 1A; dm US$6.50) The Black Cat is a near-inexplicably happening hostel right in the middle of the action. The dorms are cramped, you can't use the kitchen, but the place is hopping, both as a hostel and the bar out front for the nightly happy hour. Plenty of tours are on offer, plus free movies, good local advice and a huge breakfast included in the price.

Jungle Party Hostal (☎ 7832 0463; www.jungleparty hostal.com; 6a Av Norte 20; dm US$7) One of Antigua's hottest hostels keeps going from strength to strength, with a great hostel atmosphere, bar service, hammock hangouts and the famous all-you-can-eat Saturday barbecue.

Hotel Cristal (☎ 7832 4177; Av el Desengaño 25; s/d US$8/12, s/d with bathroom US$10/14) There's some good solid value on offer here, even if the place is a little out of the center. Rooms at the front can be noisy and the bathrooms aren't huge, but it's well priced by Antigua standards.

Casa Santa Lucía No 1 (☎ 7832 7418; Calz de Santa Lucía Sur 9; s or d US$13) Of all the Santa Lucías in town, this is probably the nicest and definitely the most central. Why is it the cheapest? Another mystery of Guatemala…

Posada Juma Ocag (☎ 7832 3109; Calz de Santa Lucía Norte 13; s/d US$12/14) Sun bursts through the patio at this cheerful little hotel – the budget prices belying the tranquil atmosphere. Grab a room upstairs for even more peace in this central location.

Yellow House (☎ 7832 6646; main@granjaguar.com; 1a Calle Poniente 24; s/d US$8/16; ☒ 🖳) Rooms here are simple but clean, with comfy beds, wooden furniture, pastel walls and big mosquito nets on the windows. Try to get one upstairs. The shared bathrooms are immaculate and use solar-heated water. Rates include use of the guest kitchen, unlimited internet and drinking water.

Posada Doña Clara (☎ 5432 6091; 5a Av Norte 16; s/d US$12/18) The maze of rooms set around leafy patios just keeps unwinding, but persevere and head for the rear upstairs, where they're most spacious and the balconies come with volcano views.

Casa Cristina (☎ 7832 0623; www.casa-cristina.com; Callejón Campo Seco 3A; s/d US$16/20) A near-overdose of quaint in this comfy little two-story hotel – they lay it on thick with the indigenous bedspreads and soft pastel paint job, but it's a quiet spot in a good area and a good deal for the price.

Las Golondrinas (☎ 7832 3343; drrios@intel.net .gt; 6a Av Norte 34 Apt 6; s/d US$12/24, with kitchen US$15/30) This is an excellent option for serious self-caterers; on offer here are apartment-like rooms with balconies (and views). Good weekly and monthly discounts are usually available.

If the above are full, don't despair, Antigua has many more hotels. Here are a few good ones:

Posada Don Diego (☎ 7832 1401; posadadon_diego@ hotmail.com; 6a Av Norte 52; s/d US$18/20) No-frill rooms set around a pretty patio.

Casa Santa Lucía No 3 (☎ 7832 1386; 6a Av Norte; s/d US$19) A stylish colonial-style hotel with plain rooms boasting blasting hot showers.

Casa Santa Lucía No 2 (☎ 7832 7418; Calz de Santa Lucía Norte 21; s or d US$19; 🅿) Spacious rooms with plenty of colonial charm.

EATING

The cheapest eating in town is the good, clean, tasty food served from street stalls a block west of Parque Central in the early evening. Small restaurants north of the bus station on Alameda de Santa Lucía do good value set lunches for around US$2.50. Note that most formal restaurants in Antigua whack on a 10% tip before presenting the bill. It should be itemized, but if in doubt, ask.

Guatemalan & Latin American

Doña María Gordillo Dulces Típicos (4a Calle Oriente 11) This shop opposite Hotel Aurora is filled with traditional Guatemalan sweets, and there's often a crowd of Antigüeños lined up to buy them.

Café La Escudilla (4a Av Norte 4; pasta US$2.50-3.25, meat US$3.50-5.50; 7am-midnight) Hugely popular with travelers and language students, La Escudilla is an inexpensive patio restaurant with tinkling fountain, lush foliage and some tables under the open sky. The food on offer is simple but well prepared and there are plenty of vegetarian options, as well as economical breakfasts and a one-course set lunch or dinner for under US$2.40. At the back you'll find Riki's Bar.

Restaurante Doña Luisa Xicotencatl (4a Calle Oriente 12; sandwiches & breakfast dishes US$3-4; 7am-9:30pm) Probably Antigua's best-known restaurant, this is a place to enjoy the colonial patio ambiance over breakfast or a light meal. The bakery here sells many kinds of breads, including whole grain. Check out the hot-from-the-oven banana bread at around 2pm daily.

La Peña de Sol Latino (5a Calle Poniente; mains US$3-8; lunch & dinner) With good, cheap and innovative food and free live music nightly, this little indoor/outdoor place is fast becoming one of the hottest bar-restaurants in town. Get there before 7pm for a good table.

Cuevita de las Urquizas (2 Calle Oriente 9D; mains US$4-5; lunch & dinner) Sumptuous *típico* (regional specialties) is the draw here – all kept warming in earthenware pots out front – a dirty trick as the smells wafting out are impossible to go past. Hugely popular with locals, it's worth getting here early to avoid waiting for a table.

Fridas (5a Av Norte 29; snacks US$2.50-4, mains US$6-8; lunch & dinner) Dedicated to Ms Kahlo, this bright bar-cum-restaurant serves tasty, if not cheap, Mexican fare and is always busy.

Perú Café (4a Av Norte 7; mains US$7-11; lunch & dinner Tue-Sun) Enjoy tasty Peruvian specialties at this pretty patio restaurant. The excellent *causas* are like burgers, with layers of mashed potato instead of bread; *ají de gallina* is chicken in yellow chili sauce with baked potatoes, parmesan and rice.

El Papaturo (2 Calle Oriente 4; mains US$8-11; lunch & dinner) If you've got a hankering for Salvadorian food, but you're not likely to make it that far, check this place out for some authentic dishes and good steak plates.

International Cuisine

Bagel Barn (5a Calle Poniente 2; bagels US$2-3.25; 6am-9pm) Just off Parque Central, this is popular for bagels with almost any filling, and breakfasts and coffee. They also offer decaf espresso, although we fail to see the point.

Restaurante La Estrella (4a Calle Poniente 3; mains US$2.50-4; lunch & dinner) An efficient, friendly, economical Chinese restaurant, the Estrella has several tofu options.

Jardín Bavaria (7a Av Norte 49; breakfast US$2.20, mains US$2.20-4.50; 7am-1am Mon-Sat, off-season 1pm-1am Mon-Sat, 9am-3pm Sun) This is a bar-restaurant with a verdant patio and spacious roof terrace, offering a mixed Guatemalan-German menu, including buffalo steak and suckling pig. There's a good range of beers and US$4.50 Sunday buffet lunches.

Café No Sé (1 Av Sur 11C; mains US$3-5; breakfast, lunch & dinner) Advertising uncomfortable seats, confused staff and battered books, this is a pleasantly down-beat option amongst all of Antigua's finery. There's a little bit of everything here – breakfast (including one option of a shot of mescal and two boiled eggs; US$2.50), burritos, fried chicken, sandwiches, movies, a tequila bar and live music.

Weiner (Calz Santa Lucía Norte 8; mains US$3-7) Possibly the biggest Wiener schnitzel you've ever seen, alongside some good value set lunches and the sort of beer list you'd expect from a German restaurant.

Traveler Menu (6a Calle Poniente 14; mains US$4-5; dinner Tue-Sun) Not nearly as unimaginative as the name would imply, this little bar and restaurant serves up big portions of food that you may have been craving (chow mein, curry etc) in an intimate candlelit environment.

Rainbow Café (7a Av Sur 8; mains US$4-6; 7am-midnight) Fill up from an eclectic range of all-day breakfasts, curries, stir-fries, Cajun chicken, guacamole and more, and enjoy the relaxed patio atmosphere. The Rainbow has a bookshop and travel agency on the premises.

GUATEMALA

Café Flor (4a Av Sur 1; mains US$4-8; ☻ 11am-11pm) The Flor makes a good stab at Thai, Indonesian and Chinese food. Dishes come in generous quantities and there's live music nightly.

Restaurante Las Palmas (6a Av Norte 14; mains US$6-8) Twinkling lights and gentle guitar music make this a popular romantic dinner spot. The staples are chicken, seafood, steaks and pasta; try the fettuccine with goat's cheese, shrimps, herbs and garlic.

Gaia (5a Av Norte 35; mains US$7-10; ☻ lunch & dinner) An almost painfully hip Middle Eastern flavored restaurant with an excellent menu, long wine and cocktail list and *nargilehs* (water pipes) for US$6.

Here are some other goodies:

El Mix (4 Calle Sur 2A; mains US$3-5; ☻ breakfast, lunch & dinner) Good breakfasts and a mind-boggling array of make-your-own sandwich options.

La Fuente (4a Calle Oriente 14; mains US$4; ☻ 7am-7pm) A pretty courtyard with lots of vegetarian options and good breakfasts.

DRINKING & NIGHTLIFE

Antigua's bar scene is jumping, except for the nationwide law that says that all bars must close at 1am. Many people roll in from Guatemala City for a spot of Antigua-style revelry on Friday and Saturday. Eateries La Peña de Sol Latino, Café No Sé and Rainbow Café are all good places to go for drinks.

Riki's Bar (4a Av Norte 4; ☻ until midnight) Behind Café La Escudilla this old favorite gets packed every evening with Antigua's young, international scene of locals, travelers and language students. For quieter moments, slip through to the low-key Paris Bar in the rear.

Monoloco (5a Av Sur 6, Pasaje El Corregidor) The 'Crazy Monkey' is the place that everybody goes until they get sick of it, so it has a real party atmosphere with plenty of newcomers. It's a two-level place (semi-open-air upstairs, with benches and long tables), with sports on TV and good-value food.

Reilly's (5a Av Norte 31; ☻ 1:30pm-1am) Guatemala's only Irish bar (so far), Reilly's is sociable and relaxed, with a young international clientele. Sadly, small bottles of Guinness are US$4.50 – more than double the cost of local beers!

El Muro (3a Calle Oriente 19D) A friendly little neighborhood pub with a good range of beers, it has some decent snacks and plenty of sofas to lounge on.

Discotecas

La Casbah (☎ 832 2640; 5a Av Norte 30; admission US$2.50-4 with 1 drink; ☻ 9pm-1am Mon-Sat) This two-level disco near the Santa Catalina arch has a warm atmosphere and is gay-friendly and quite a party most nights.

La Chimenea (cnr 7a Av Norte & 2a Calle Poniente) This is the latest hot spot for salsa and merengue dancers.

ENTERTAINMENT
Arts & Concerts

Proyecto Cultural El Sitio (☎ 7832 3037; www.elsitio cultural.org, in Spanish; 5a Calle Poniente 15) This arts center has lots going on, from music, dance and theater events (including plays in English) to exhibition openings most Saturdays. Stop by to check the schedule.

Cinema & TV

Several cinema houses show a wide range of Latin American, general-release and art-house movies, some in English, some in Spanish, usually for US$1.30 to US$2. Check the programs of the following:

Bagel Barn (5a Calle Poniente 2) Café with movies at 8pm.

Café 2000 (☎ 832 2981; 6a Av Norte 2) Café showing free movies on big screen.

Proyecto Cultural El Sitio Movies usually on Tuesday evening.

For North American and European sports on TV, check the programs posted at Café 2000 and Monoloco.

SHOPPING

Nim Po't (www.nimpot.com; 5a Av Norte 29) This shop boasts a huge collection of Maya dress, as well as hundreds of masks and other wood carvings. This sprawling space is packed with *huipiles*, *cortes* (wraparound skirts), *fajas* (waist saches) and more, all arranged according to region, so it makes for a fascinating visit whether you're in the market or not.

Diez Mil Pueblitos (6a Av Norte 21; diezmilpueblitos@yahoo.com) One of the country's few exclusively fair-trade stores (where the majority of profits go to producers), it sells an excellent selection of quality handmade products as well as crepes and coffee in the café out back.

Mercado de Artesanías (Handicrafts Market; 4a Calle Poniente; ☻ 8am-8pm) At the west end of town by the main market, this market sells masses of Guatemalan handicrafts – mostly not top quality but with plenty of colorful variety in masks, blankets, jewelry, purses and so on. Don't be afraid to bargain.

GETTING THERE & AROUND
Bus
Buses to Guatemala City, Ciudad Vieja and San Miguel Dueñas arrive and depart from a street just south of the market. Buses to Chimaltenango, Escuintla, San Antonio Aguas Calientes and Santa María de Jesús go from the street outside the west side of the market. If you're heading out to local villages, it's best to go early in the morning and return by mid-afternoon, as bus services drop off dramatically as evening approaches.

To reach highland towns such as Chichicastenango, Quetzaltenango, Huehuetenango or Panajachel (except for the one direct daily bus to Panajachel), take one of the frequent buses to Chimaltenango, on the Interamericana Hwy, and catch an onward bus from there. Making connections in Chimaltenango is easy, as many friendly folks will jump to your aid as you alight from one bus looking for another. Alternatively, you can take a bus from Antigua heading toward Guatemala City, get off at San Lucas Sacatepéquez and change buses there – this takes a little longer, but you'll be boarding closer to the capital so you're more likely to get a seat.

Chimaltenango (US$0.50, 30 minutes, 19km, every 15 minutes 5am-7pm)

Ciudad Vieja (US$0.30, 15 minutes, 7km) Take a San Miguel Dueñas bus.

Escuintla (US$0.80, one hour, 39km, 16 buses daily, 5:30am-5pm)

Guatemala City (US$1, 1¼ hours, 45km) Every few minutes between 6am-7pm.

Panajachel El Condor Expeditions (☎ 5498 9812; 4a Calle Poniente 34) One Pullman bus at 7am daily (US$5, 2½ hours, 146km).

San Antonio Aguas Calientes (US$0.30, 30 minutes, 9km, every 20 minutes 6:30am-7pm)

San Miguel Dueñas (US$0.25, 30 minutes, 10km) Buses every few minutes between 6am-7pm (placards just say 'Dueñas').

Santa María de Jesús (US$0.30, 30 minutes, 12km, buses every 45 minutes 6am-7:30pm)

Shuttle Minibus
Numerous travel agencies offer frequent and convenient shuttle services to places including Guatemala City, La Aurora International Airport, Panajachel and Chichi. They also go less frequently (usually on weekends) to places further afield such as Río Dulce, Copán Ruinas (Honduras) and Monterrico. These services cost a lot more than ordinary buses (for example, from US$7 to US$10 to Guatemala City, as opposed to US$1 on a chicken bus), but they are comfortable and convenient, with door-to-door service at both ends

Taxi & Tuk Tuk
Taxis and tuk tuks wait where the Guatemala City buses stop and on the east side of Parque Central. A ride in town costs around US$1.60. A taxi to or from Guatemala City usually costs US$30 (US$40 after midnight).

THE HIGHLANDS – LAGO DE ATITLÁN

Guatemala's most dramatic region – the highlands – stretch from Antigua to the Mexican border northwest of Huehuetenango. Here the verdant hills sport emerald green grass, cornfields and towering stands of pine, and every town and village has a story.

The traditional values and customs of Guatemala's indigenous peoples are strongest in the highlands. Maya dialects are the first language, Spanish a distant second. The age-old culture based on maize (from which the Maya believe that humans were created) is still alive; a sturdy cottage set in the midst of a thriving *milpa* (cornfield) is a common sight. And on every road you'll see men, women and children carrying burdens of *leña* (firewood), to be used for heating and cooking.

The poster child for Guatemala's natural beauty, the volcano-ringed Lago de Atitlán has been attracting tourists for decades. Surrounded by small villages, the lake deals with its popularity well. The only place that feels really played out is Panajachel – the other villages maintain a quiet air, while offering a reasonable degree of comfort. This area was particularly badly hit by Hurricane Stan – see (p125) for more information.

DANGERS & ANNOYANCES
Although most visitors never experience any trouble, there have been incidents of robbery, rape and murder in the highlands. The most frequent sites for robberies are unfortunately some of the most beautiful – the paths that

THAT'S ONE SMOKIN' GOD

The Spanish called him San Simón, the ladinos (persons of mixed indigenous and European race) named him Maximón and the Maya know him as Rilaj Maam (ree-lah-mahm). By any name, he's a deity revered throughout the Guatemalan Highlands. Assumed to be a combination of Maya gods, Pedro de Alvarado (the Spanish conquistador of Guatemala) and the biblical Judas, San Simón is an effigy to which Guatemalans of every stripe go to make offerings and ask for blessings. The effigy is usually housed by a member of a *cofradia* (Maya Catholic brotherhood), moving from one place to another from year to year, a custom anthropologists believe was established to maintain the local balance of power. The name, shape and ceremonies associated with this deity vary from town to town, but a visit will be memorable no matter where you encounter him. For a small fee, photography is usually permitted, and offerings of cigarettes, liquor or candles are always appreciated.

In Santiago Atitlán, Maximón is a wooden figure draped in colorful silk scarves and smoking a fat cigar. Locals guard and worship him, singing and managing the offerings made to him (including your US$0.25 entry fee). His favorite gifts are Payaso cigarettes and Venado rum, but he often has to settle for the cheaper firewater Quetzalteca Especial. Fruits and gaudy, flashing electric lights decorate his chamber; effigies of Jesus Christ and Christian saints lie or stand either side of Maximón and his guardians. Fires may be burning in the courtyard outside as offerings are made to him.

In Nahualá, between Los Encuentros and Quetzaltenango, the Maximón effigy is à la Picasso: a simple wooden box with a cigarette protruding from it. Still, the same offerings are made and the same sort of blessings asked for. In Zunil, near Quetzaltenango, the deity is called San Simón but is similar to Santiago's Maximón in custom and form.

San Jorge La Laguna on Lago Atitlán is a very spiritual place for the highland Maya; here they worship Rilaj Maam. It is possible that the first effigy was made near here, carved from the *palo de pito* tree that spoke to the ancient shamans and told them to preserve their culture, language and traditions by carving Rilaj Maam. (*Palo de pito* flowers can be smoked to induce hallucinations). The effigy in San Jorge looks like a joker, with an absurdly long tongue.

In San Andrés Itzapa near Antigua, Rilaj Maam has a permanent home, and is brought out on October 28 and paraded about in an unparalleled pagan festival. This is an all-night, hedonistic party where dancers grab the staff of Rilaj Maam to harness his power and receive magical visions. San Andrés is less than 10km south of Chimaltenango, so you can easily make the party from Antigua.

run around Lago de Atitlán. The security situation is forever changing here – some months it's OK to walk between certain villages, then that route suddenly becomes dangerous.

If you do plan to go walking, use common sense – don't take any more money than you need, or anything that you really don't want to lose. Walk in groups of at least six and (one piece of local advice), consider taking a machete along (for deterrent purposes only, naturally). If you do run into trouble, don't resist – chances are your life is worth more than your camera.

There are persistent rumors about a Japanese tourist who was lynched for taking a photo of a child in the highlands. This is slightly misleading. What he actually did was pick up a crying child in an effort to comfort it, which led the locals to think that a kidnapping was afoot. Fears of foreigners kidnapping children are common in the highlands, so use some restraint. And, of course, ask permission before taking photos of people.

GETTING THERE & AROUND
The Highlands

The curvy Interamericana Hwy, also known as Centroamérica 1 (CA-1), passes through the highlands on its way between Guatemala City and the Mexican border at La Mesilla. Driving the 266km between Guatemala City and Huehuetenango can take five hours, but the scenery is beautiful. The lower Carr al Pacífico (CA-2), via Escuintla and Retalhuleu, is straighter and faster; it's the better route if you're trying to reach Mexico as quickly as possible.

The Interamericana is thick with bus traffic. As most places you'll want to reach are off the Interamericana, you may find yourself waiting at junctions such as Los Encuentros and Cuatro Caminos to connect with a bus or pickup. Travel is easiest on market days and in the morning. By mid or late afternoon, buses may be scarce, and short-distance local traffic stops by dinnertime. On remote routes, you'll probably be relying more on pickups than buses for transportation.

Lago de Atitlán

Following the Interamericana 32km west from Chimaltenango, you'll reach the turnoff for the back road to Lago de Atitlán via Patzicía and Patzún. The area around these two towns

has been notable for high levels of guerrilla and bandit activity in the past, so stay on the Interamericana to Tecpán Guatemala, the starting point for a visit to the ruined Kaqchiquel capital of Iximché (*eesh*-im-chay).

Another 40km west along the Interamericana from Tecpán is the Los Encuentros junction. It's a new town serving people waiting to catch buses. The road to the right heads north to Chichicastenango and Santa Cruz del Quiché. From the Interamericana a road to the left descends 12km to Sololá and another 8km to Panajachel, on the shores of Lago de Atitlán.

If you are not on a direct bus, you can get off at Los Encuentros and catch another bus or minibus, or flag a pickup, from here down

GUATEMALA

LAGO DE ATITLÁN

0   10 km
0   6 miles

To Interamericana Hwy (1km)

To Interamericana Hwy (9km); La Cuchilla (9km); Los Encuentros (11km); Chichicastenango (28km)

Río Panacha

Sololá

1

Río Panajachel

Río Patcaj

Santa Lucía Utatlán

Santa Cruz La Laguna

San Jorge La Laguna

San Andrés Semetabaj

Jaibalito

Panajachel

Río Los Molinos

Tzununá

San Marcos La Laguna

1

Santa Catarina Palopó

Los Robles

Santa Clara La Laguna

Boats

Lago de Atitlán

Godínez

San Juan La Laguna

San Pedro La Laguna

San Antonio Palopó

To Patzún (16km); Patzicía (30km); Chimaltenango (47km)

Volcán ▲ San Pedro (3020m)

● Cerro de Oro

Agua Escondida

Chuitinamit 🏛

14

▲ Cerro de Oro (1892m)

11

● Santiago Atitlán

San Lucas Tolimán

Volcán ▲ Tolimán (3158m)

Río Madre Vieja

🏛 Mirador

Río Cutzán

Volcán ▲ Atitlán (3537m)

11

Río Santa Teresa

LP

To Chicacao (6km)

To Carr al Pacífico (20km); Cocales (20km); Santa Lucía Cotzumalguapa (43km)

Pochuta 10

to Panajachel or up to Chichicastenango; it's a half-hour ride to either place.

The road from Sololá descends through pine forests, losing more than 500m in elevation on its 8km course to Panajachel. Sit on the right for breathtaking views of the lake and volcanoes.

PANAJACHEL

pop 15,000

The busiest and most built-up lakeside settlement, Panajachel ('Pana' to pretty much the entire country) has developed haphazardly and, some say, in a less than beautiful way. Several different cultures mingle on Panajachel's dusty streets.

Ladinos and gringos control the tourist industry. The Kaqchiquel and Tz'utuhil Maya from surrounding villages come to sell their handicrafts to tourists. Tour groups descend on the town by bus for a few hours or overnight.

Its excellent transport connections and thumping nightlife make it a favorite for weekending Guatemalans. During the week, things quiet down, but the main street, Calle Santander, remains the same – internet café after handicrafts store after restaurant after travel agent, but you need only go down to the lakeshore to understand why Pana attracts so many visitors.

Information

BOOKSTORES

Bus Stop Books (Centro Comercial El Dorado, Calle Principal) A good selection of mainly used books to swap and buy and a small selection of guidebooks.

Gallery Bookstore (Comercial El Pueblito, Av Los Árboles) Sells and exchanges used books, and sells a few new ones, including some Lonely Planet guides.

Libros del Lago (Calle Santander) Has an excellent stock of books, including Latin American literature in English and other languages on Guatemala, the Maya and Mesoamerica, plus maps and guidebooks.

EMERGENCY

Policía de Turismo (Tourist Police; ☎ 7762 1120; Municipalidad, Calle Principal)

INTERNET ACCESS

As you'd expect, Pana has plenty of places to check your email and surf the web. The standard price is US$0.50 to US$1 per hour; typical opening hours are 9am to 10pm, perhaps slightly shorter on Sunday.

Jade Internet (Centro Comercial San Rafael, Calle Santander)

MayaNet (Calle Santander 3-62)

Planet Internet (Calle Santander) Has good connections.

LAUNDRY

Lavandería Viajero (Edificio Rincón Sai, Calle Santander; ☷ 8am-7pm) Reliable place; charges US$0.45 per pound (600g).

MEDICAL SERVICES

The nearest hospital is at Sololá.

Centro de Salud (Clinic; Calle Principal; ☷ 8am-6pm Mon-Fri, to 1pm Sat)

MONEY

Banco Agromercantil (cnr Calles Principal & Santander; ☷ 9am-6pm Mon-Fri, to 1pm Sat) Changes US-dollar cash and traveler's checks, and has a MasterCard ATM.

Banco Industrial (Comercial Los Pinos, Calle Santander) Has Visa ATM.

Credomatic (Centro Comercial San Rafael, Calle Santander) Does Visa and MasterCard cash advances and changes US-dollar cash.

POST

DHL (Edificio Rincón Sai, Calle Santander) Courier service.

Post office (cnr Calles Santander & 15 de Febrero) About 200m from the lake.

TELEPHONE

Some internet cafés and travel agencies on Calle Santander offer moderately cheap phone calls – around US$0.15 per minute to North or Central America, US$0.25 per minute to Europe. Try Jade Internet or Planet Internet. For local calls there's a line of card phones outside **Telgua** (Calle Santander).

TOURIST INFORMATION

Inguat (☎ 5874 9450; Centro Comercial San Rafael Local 11, Calle Santander; ☷ 9am-5pm) This tourist office is on the main street. There are a few brochures available and staff can answer straightforward questions.

Sights & Activities

The **Reserva Natural Atitlán** (☎ 7762 2565; www.atitlanreserva.com; admission US$5; ☷ 8am-5pm) is down the spur leading to Hotel Atitlán and makes a good day trip. The well-designed nature reserve has trails, an interpretive center, zip lines, camping, a butterfly farm, small shade coffee plantation, lots of monkeys and an aviary.

Lago de Atitlán offers phenomenal **hiking** and **cycling**. You can walk from Panajachel to

Santa Catarina in about an hour, continuing to San Antonio in about another hour; it takes only half as long by bicycle, on hilly roads. Or take a bike by boat to Santiago, San Pedro or another village to start a tour of the lake. Several places along Calle Santander rent bicycles; rates start around US$12 per day. Equipment varies, so check your bike first.

ATI Divers (☎ 7762 2621; www.laiguanaperdida.com; Plaza Los Patios, Calle Santander; ☿ 9:30am-1pm Mon-Sat), leads dive trips from Santa Cruz La Laguna (p127). A four-day PADI-certification course costs US$205. The best time to dive here is between May and October, when the water is clear.

ATI Divers organize the annual garbage cleanup of the lake, during which several tons of trash are collected. This event, typically held in September, is a great opportunity to give something back to the community and make new friends.

Visitors short on time should consider a **boat tour** around the lake. A typical tour lasts around seven hours and visits San Pedro, Santiago and San Antonio for US$8 per person. To arrange a tour, head to the pier at the foot of Calle del Balneario and start bargaining. Most travel agencies also arrange boat tours. **Kayaks** are also rented from here from US$4 per hour.

Courses
Panajachel has a niche in the language-school scene. Two well set-up schools are **Jardín de América** (☎ /fax 7762 2637; www.jardindeamerica.com; Calle 14 de Febrero, 3a Av Peatonal 4-44) and **Jabel Tinamit** (☎ 7762 0238; www.jabeltinamit.com; Calle Santander). Both have ample gardens and good atmospheres. Four hours of one-on-one study five days per week, including a homestay with a local family, will cost around US$120 per week at either place. Other schools include **Centro de Tutoría e Idiomas** (CTI; ☎ 7762 0259/1005; 2a Av Peatonal 1-84, Zona 2) and **Spanish School Maya** (☎ 7810 7196; Callejón Santa Elena), both of which teach some Maya languages as well as Spanish.

Festivals & Events
The festival of **San Francisco de Asís**, held on October 4, is celebrated with massive drinking and fireworks.

Sleeping
HOSPEDAJES & HOTELS
Budget travelers here will rejoice at the profusion of family-run *hospedajes* (guesthouses).

They're simple – perhaps two rough beds, a small table and a light bulb in a bare boarding room – but cheap. Most provide clean toilets and some have hot showers. More expensive hotels offer generous discounts for longer stays.

Casa Linda (☎ 7762 0386; Callejón El Capulin; s/d US$5/7, with bathroom US$9/12) Spotless little rooms down an alley off Calle Santander. Upstairs, they get a good breeze and the balconies are good for that afternoon siesta.

Villa Lupita (☎ 5511 0541; Callejón Don Tino; s/d US$6/7.50, with bathroom US$7/8.50) Family-run Lupita is great value if you feel like staying in the town center. The 18 clean, secure rooms have comfortable beds, reading lamps and colorful carpets, and they offer free coffee and drinking water. The shared hot-water bathrooms are clean and the roof terrace affords good views.

Rooms Santander (☎ 7762 1304; s/d US$5/8, with bathroom US$9/12) One of Panajachel's longest-running budget hostelries, the Santander is still going strong with clean rooms on two levels around a small patio full of trees. It's off Calle Santander.

Hospedaje García (☎ 7762 2787; Calle 14 de Febrero 2-24; s/d US$5/9, with bathroom US$15/20) The rooms with bathroom here are OK – clean enough, but the real winners are the cheaper ones – they're about twice the size and have balconies looking out onto the patio.

Mario's Rooms (☎ 7762 2370; Calle Santander; s/d US$6.50/9, with bathroom US$9/13) Offering some of the best budget rooms in town, Mario's smallish rooms face a cheery, plant filled courtyard and have blasting hot showers.

Casa Loma (☎ 7762 1447; Calle Rancho Grande; s/d US$5/10, with bathroom US$20/26) Excellent value, solid wooden rooms are on offer at this place. The huge grassy lawn out the back is a great place to hang out.

Hospedaje Tzutujil (☎ 7762 0102; s/d US$8/10, with bathroom & cable TV US$14/18) Down a little alley set among cornfields, the Tzutujil is one of the best budget deals in town with clean, modern rooms, balconies and firm beds. All upstairs rooms have fantastic mountain views. The alley way is located off Calle del Balneario.

Hotel Viñas del Lago (☎ 7762 0389; Playa Pública; s/d with bathroom US$10/13; Ⓟ) Don't let the garish paint job put you off – the big, airy rooms upstairs here have some of the best views in town.

Hospedaje Jere (☎ 7762 2781; jere_armando@yahoo.com; Calle Rancho Grande; s/d with bathroom US$10/13;

GUATEMALA

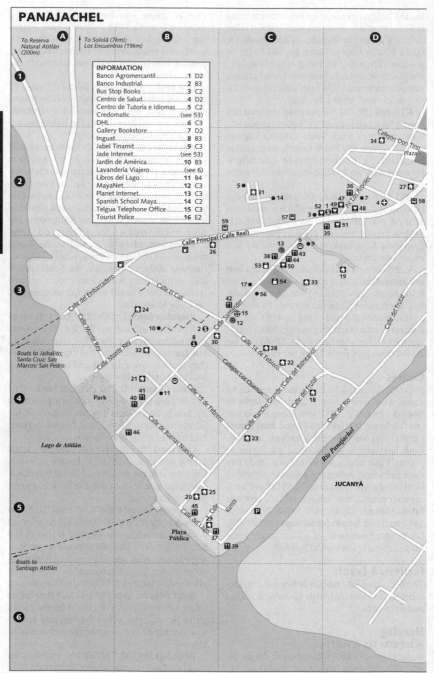

PANAJACHEL

To Reserva
Natural Atitlán
(200m)

To Sololá (7km);
Los Encuentros (19km)

To Reserva
Natural Atitlán
(200m)

Callejón Don Tino
Plaza

INFORMATION

Banco Agromercantil	1 D2
Banco Industrial	2 B3
Bus Stop Books	3 C2
Centro de Salud	4 D2
Centro de Tutoría e Idiomas	5 C2
Credomatic	(see 53)
DHL	6 C3
Gallery Bookstore	7 D2
Inguat	8 B3
Jabel Tinamit	9 C3
Jade Internet	(see 53)
Jardín de América	10 B3
Lavandería Viajero	(see 6)
Libros del Lago	11 B4
MayaNet	12 C3
Planet Internet	13 C3
Spanish School Maya	14 C2
Telgua Telephone Office	15 C3
Tourist Police	16 E2

Av Los Árboles

Calle Principal (Calle Real)

Calle El Cal

Calle del Embarcadero

Calle Monte Rey

Boats to Jaibalito;
Santa Cruz; San
Marcos; San Pedro

Calle Santander

Calle Monte Rey

Calle 14 de Febrero

Callejón Los Quenun

Calle Rancho Grande (Calle del Balneario)

Calle del Frutal

Calle del Frutal

Calle del Río

Park

Calle 15 de Febrero

Calle de Buenas Nuevas

Lago de Atitlán

Río Panajachel

JUCANYÁ

Calle del Lago

Calle Ramos

Playa
Pública

Boats to
Santiago Atitlán

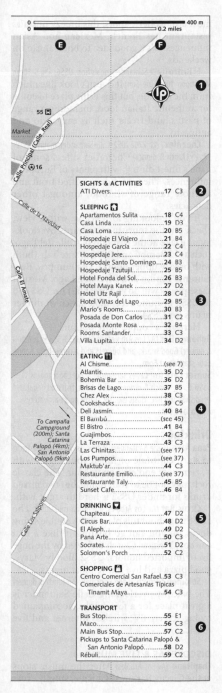

SIGHTS & ACTIVITIES
ATI Divers.....................17 C3

SLEEPING 🏠
Apartamentos Sulita 18 C4
Casa Linda 19 D3
Casa Loma 20 B5
Hospedaje El Viajero 21 B4
Hospedaje García 22 C4
Hospedaje Jere.....................23 C4
Hospedaje Santo Domingo...24 B3
Hospedaje Tzutujil................25 B5
Hotel Fonda del Sol..............26 B3
Hotel Maya Kanek 27 D2
Hotel Utz Rajil 28 C4
Hotel Viñas del Lago 29 B5
Mario's Rooms......................30 B3
Posada de Don Carlos 31 C2
Posada Monte Rosa..............32 B4
Rooms Santander..................33 C3
Villa Lupita...........................34 D2

EATING 🍴
Al Chisme............................(see 7)
Atlantis.................................35 D2
Bohemia Bar 36 D2
Brisas de Lago......................37 B5
Chez Alex 38 C3
Cookshacks...........................39 C5
Deli Jasmín...........................40 B4
El Bambú............................(see 45)
El Bistro 41 B4
Guajimbos.............................42 C3
La Terraza.............................43 C3
Las Chinitas........................(see 17)
Los Pumpos........................(see 37)
Maktub'ar.............................44 C3
Restaurante Emilio..............(see 37)
Restaurante Taly...................45 B5
Sunset Cafe..........................46 B4

DRINKING 🍸
Chapiteau.............................47 D2
Circus Bar.............................48 D2
El Aleph................................49 D2
Pana Arte.............................50 C3
Socrates................................51 D2
Solomon's Porch 52 C2

SHOPPING 🛍
Centro Comercial San Rafael.53 C3
Comerciales de Artesanías Típicas
   Tinamit Maya...................54 C3

TRANSPORT
Bus Stop...............................55 E1
Maco.....................................56 C3
Main Bus Stop......................57 C2
Pickups to Santa Catarina Palopó &
   San Antonio Palopó.........58 D2
Rébuli...................................59 C2

🅿 🖥) The Jere's big, tastefully decorated rooms are another class act in this part of town. The owners also operate shuttle services and have free internet for guests.

Hotel Fonda del Sol (☎ 7762 0407; h_fondadel sol@yahoo.com; Calle Principal; s/d US$7/14, with bathroom US$12/24; 🅿) The more expensive rooms here are heavy on stonework and light on other decoration. The cheaper ones are an excellent budget choice – large, wood-paneled rooms with comfy beds and random decorations. It's near the bus stop.

Hotel Utz Rajil (☎ 7762 0303; gguated@yahoo.com; Calle 14 de Febrero; s/d with bathroom US$13/19) The Utz Rajil is a modern, three-story hotel with bigger rooms than most. Try to snag a front one as their big balconies have good views.

Posada Monte Rosa (☎ 7762 0055; Calle Monte Rey; s/d with bathroom US$13/20) A short distance off Calle Santander, rooms here are sizable with colorful Mayan fabric curtains and fronted by patches of lawn. Unfortunately, they don't take phone reservations.

Posada de Don Carlos (☎ 7762 0658; Callejón Santa Elena 4-45; s/d with bathroom US$15/20) Huge upstairs rooms face a balcony overlooking a lush courtyard in this place, and the bathrooms with full-sized tubs are unbeaten in this price range.

Apartamentos Sulita (☎ 7762 2514; Calle del Frutal 3-42; cabin per week US$125) These cute little one- or two-person cabins are a great option if you're going to be hanging around for a while – they come fully equipped with kitchen, lounge, bathroom and one bedroom. Cable TV is available on request.

There are plenty more:

Hospedaje El Viajero (☎ 7762 0128; www.sleeprent buy.com/elviajero; s/d US$10/13) No frills, but nice and close to the lake.

Hospedaje Santo Domingo (☎ 7762 0236; Calle Monte Rey; s/d US$5/8, with bathroom US$10/13) Quiet rooms set around a relaxed central garden.

Hotel Maya Kanek (☎ 7762 1104; Calle Principal; s/d with bathroom US$14/18; 🅿) Has good value motel-style rooms around a cobbled courtyard in the town center.

CAMPING

Campaña Campground (☎ 7762 2479; Carr a Santa Catarina Palopó; per person US$4) This campground is located 1km out of town on the road to Santa Catarina Palopó. Amenities include a kitchen, book exchange, luggage storage and pickup from Pana.

Eating

The cheapest places to eat are by the beach at the mouth of the Río Panajachel. The cook shacks on the shore have rock-bottom prices, as do the food stalls around the parking lot. Across the street, you can fill up for US$4 at any of several little restaurants, all of which offer priceless lake views.

Deli Jasmín (Calle Santander; items US$3-5; ☺ breakfast, lunch Wed-Mon) This tranquil garden restaurant serves a great range of healthy foods and drinks to the strains of soft classical music. Breakfast is served all day, and you can buy whole wheat or pita bread, hummus or mango chutney to take away.

Al Chisme (Comercial El Pueblito, Av Los Árboles; mains US$3-5; ☺ breakfast, lunch & dinner) The Al Chisme offers Tex-Mex, vegetarian and pasta dishes, and more expensive meat and fish as well as home-style food such as biscuits and gravy (US$3). Its streetside patio is most popular in the evening, especially when there's live music.

Guajimbo's (Calle Santander; mains US$4-6) This Uruguayan grill is one of Pana's best eateries, serving up generous meat and chicken dishes with vegetables, salad, garlic bread and either rice or boiled potatoes. You won't leave hungry. Try the *chivita Hernandarias* (tenderloin cooked with bacon, mozzarella, peppers and olives). There are vegetarian dishes too, and good-value breakfasts, and bottomless cups of coffee for US$0.70.

Las Chinitas (Plaza Los Patios, Calle Santander; mains or set lunch US$4-6.50) Las Chinitas serves up unbelievably delicious, moderately priced food. Try the Malaysian curry with coconut milk or the satay, both with rice, tropical salad and your choice of tofu, tempeh, chicken, pork or prawns.

Atlantis (Calle Principal; mains US$4-9; ☺ breakfast, lunch & dinner) This café-bar serves up some excellent submarines (US$4) alongside more substantial meals. The beer garden out the back is the place to be on a balmy night.

Maktub'ar (Calle Santander 3-72; mains US$5-7; ☺ breakfast, lunch & dinner) The garden setting here is an excellent, relaxed place to hang out during the day. At night, once happy hour kicks in, things start to liven up. The menu runs from sandwiches and burgers to larger meals, but the real winner is the wood-fired thin-crust pizza.

La Terraza (☎ 7762 0041; Calle Santander; mains US$6-11; ☺ lunch & dinner) One of Calle Santander's most atmospheric spots, this breezy upstairs restaurant has French, Mexican and Asian influences. It's a good idea to book ahead on weekends.

El Bistro (Calle Santander; meals from US$6; ☺ 5-10pm Mon, noon-10pm Tue-Sun) It doesn't look like much from the outside, but this is the place to come for authentic Italian food, including a range of pastas, and treats such as carpaccio and antipasto.

Chez Alex (☎ 7762 2052; Calle Santander; mains US$10-17; ☺ lunch & dinner) Chez Alex offers some of Pana's finest dining, with plenty of European influences. There's fondue, stuffed trout and a whole range of seafood, amongst other delicacies.

If you're looking for cheapie with a view, check out the touristy restaurants overlooking the lake at the east end of Calle del Lago, such as El Bambú and Restaurante Taly (both with breezy upper floors), Los Pumpos, Restaurante Emilio and Brisas de Lago. Most of these places will do you breakfast for US$1.50 to US$2 or quite acceptable lunch or dinner mains for US$4.

Here are a couple more options:

Bohemia Bar (Av Los Árboles; mains US$3-5; ☺ lunch & dinner) Good snacks and burgers and a three-hour happy hour starting at 6pm.

Sunset Café (cnr Calles Santander & del Lago; mains US$6-8; ☺ lunch & dinner) Good meat, fish and vegetarian dishes and live music nightly at this open-air eatery with a lake vista.

Drinking

Pana Arte (Calle Santander) This is a good place to start, continue or finish your night, with a seemingly endless happy hour. The classic rock may not be to your liking, but two mixed drinks for under US$2 is hard to argue with.

Circus Bar (Av Los Árboles; ☺ noon-midnight) The best thing about this place is the double swing doors, so you can go busting in like a real cowboy. Yeehaw! Closely followed by the huge list of imported liquors, US$2 Bloody Marys, good pizza and live music most nights.

Solomon's Porch (Calle Principal; ☺ lunch & dinner) The balcony overlooking Calle Santander is a great place for a few drinks, accompanied by big screen TV, wireless internet and live music.

DISCOTECAS & LIVE MUSIC

Chapiteau (Av Los Árboles) After the music stops at the Circus Bar or Al Chisme, simply cross the street and come here, a disco-bar with billiards upstairs.

El Aleph (Av Los Árboles) Located a couple of doors down, this bar has occasional trance and hip-hop DJ sessions or live music.

Socrates (Calle Principal) Opposite the start of Av Los Árboles, Socrates is a large disco-bar playing thumping Latin pop, highly popular with the Guatemalan teens and twenty-somethings (and a smattering of gringos) who descend on Pana at weekends and holidays. The assorted folk pictured on the walls run the gamut from Albert Einstein to Jerry García of the Grateful Dead.

Al Chisme (Comercial El Pueblito; Av Los Árboles) Often serves up neat jazz or piano music on Friday or Saturday nights.

Sunset Café (cnr Calles Santander & del Lago; 🕒 11am-midnight) Head here for sunset (and later) drinks overlooking the lake. It's popular, with great views, food, a bar and live music nightly.

Shopping

Comerciales de Artesanías Típicas Tinamit Maya (🕒 7am-7pm) One of Guatemala's most extensive handicrafts markets, this market sells traditional clothing, jade, leather items, wood carvings and more. You can get good deals if you're patient and bargain.

Getting There & Away

BOAT

Passenger boats for Santiago Atitlán depart from the public beach at the foot of Calle del Balneario. All other departures leave from the dock at the foot of Calle del Embarcadero. The big, slow ferries are generally only used for the Santiago run, with fast, frequent *lanchas* (small motorboats) going elsewhere. Boats stop running around 4:30pm.

One-way passage anywhere on Lago de Atitlán costs US$1.30, but prepare to get done like a sucker. Generally, foreigners end up paying around US$2.50. You can hold out for the local fare, but you may have to let a few boats go by. One way to keep the cost down is to ignore all middlemen (or boys as the case may be) and negotiate the fare directly with the captain.

Another route goes counterclockwise around the lake, stopping in Santa Cruz La Laguna (15 minutes), Jaibalito, Tzununá, San Marcos La Laguna (30 minutes), San Juan La Laguna and San Pedro La Laguna (40 minutes). After departing Panajachel from the

Calle del Balneario dock, the boats stop at another dock at the foot of Calle del Embarcadero before heading out (or vice versa, when arriving at Panajachel).

BUS

The town's main bus stop is where Calles Santander and Real meet, across from the Banco Agrícola Mercantil. Rébuli buses depart from the Rébuli office on Calle Real.

International

Ciudad Tecún Umán (Mexican border) By the Pacific route (210km), take a bus to Cocales and change there; by the highland route (210km), bus to Quetzaltenango and change there.

La Mesilla (Mexican border) (six hours, 225km) See Huehuetenango following.

Domestic

Antigua (US$5, 2½ hours, 146km) A direct Pullman bus departs from the Rébuli office at 10:45am Monday to Saturday. Or take a Guatemala City bus and change at Chimaltenango.

Chichicastenango (US$1.50, 1½ hours, 37km) About eight buses between 7am-4pm. Or take any bus heading to Los Encuentros and change buses there.

Cocales (Carr al Pacífico) (US$1, 2½ hours, 70km, eight buses 6:30am-2:30pm)

Guatemala City Transportes Rébuli departs 10 times daily between 5am-2:30pm (US$2.50, 3½ hours, 150km). Or take a bus to Los Encuentros and change there.

Huehuetenango (3½hr, 140km) Bus to Los Encuentros and wait there for a bus bound for Iluehue or La Mesilla. Or catch a bus heading to Quetzaltenango, alight at Cuatro Caminos and change buses there. There are buses at least hourly from these junctions.

Los Encuentros (US$1, 35 minutes, 20km) Take any bus heading toward Guatemala City, Chichicastenango, Quetzaltenango or the Interamericana.

Quetzaltenango (US$2, 2½ hours, 90km, six buses 5am-4pm) Or bus to Los Encuentros and change there.

San Lucas Tolimán (US$1.20, 1½ hours, 28km, 4pm) Or take any bus heading for Cocales, get off at the San Lucas turnoff and walk about 1km into town.

Santa Catarina Palopó (US$0.80, 20 minutes, 4km) Daily buses; or get a pickup at the corner of Calles Real and El Amate.

Sololá (US$0.60, 20 minutes, 8km) Frequent direct local buses; or take any bus heading to Guatemala City, Chichicastenango, Quetzaltenango or Los Encuentros.

MOTORCYCLE

Maco (☎ 7762 0883; Calle Santander) rents motorbikes for around US$8/40 per hour/day.

GUATEMALA

SIDE TRIPS FROM PANA

Sololá

Sololá (population 9000) lies along trade routes between the *tierra caliente* (Pacific Slope 'hot lands') and *tierra fría* (the chilly highlands). All the traders meet here, and Sololá's Friday market – a local, rather than a tourist, affair – is one of the highlands' best. The plaza next to the cathedral comes ablaze with the colorful costumes of people from a dozen surrounding villages, and neatly arranged displays of meat, vegetables, fruit, housewares and clothing occupy every available space.

Every Sunday morning the *cofradías* (traditional religious brotherhoods) parade ceremoniously to the cathedral for their devotions. On other days, Sololá sleeps.

It's a pleasant walk from Sololá down to the lake, whether on the highway to Panajachel (9km) or on the path to Santa Cruz La Laguna (10km).

Iximché

Off the Interamericana near the small town of Tecpán lie the **ruins of Iximché** (admission US$4; 🕒 8am-4:30pm), capital of the Kaqchiquel Maya. Set on a flat promontory surrounded by cliffs, Iximché (*eesh*-im-chay; founded in the late 15th century) was easily defended against attack by the hostile Quiché Maya.

When the conquistadors arrived in 1524, the Kaqchiquel formed an alliance with them against the Quiché and the Tz'utuhils. The Spaniards set up headquarters next door to the Kaqchiquel capital at Tecpán Guatemala, but Spanish demands for gold and other loot soured the alliance; the Kaqchiquel were defeated in the ensuing battles.

Entering Tecpán, you'll see signs for the unpaved road leading less than 6km south to Iximché. You can walk, see the ruins and rest, then walk back to Tecpán in around three hours. Minibuses leave regularly from the center of town (US$0.20, 10 minutes) for the ruins. Go in the morning so you can return to the highway by early afternoon, before bus traffic dwindles.

The archaeological site has a small museum, four ceremonial plazas surrounded by grass-covered temple structures and ball courts. Some structures have been cleaned and maintained; on a few, the original plaster coating still exists, and traces of the original paint are visible. Tecpán has a couple of basic hotels and eateries. Veloz Poaquileña runs buses to Guatemala City (US$1, two hour, every 30 minutes, 5:30am to 7pm) from in front of the church.

SANTA CATARINA PALOPÓ & SAN ANTONIO PALOPÓ

Four winding kilometers east of Panajachel lies Santa Catarina Palopó. Here, narrow streets paved in stone blocks run past adobe houses with roofs of thatch or corrugated tin, and the gleaming white church commands your attention. Chickens cackle, dogs bark and the villagers go about their daily life dressed in beautiful clothing. It's interesting to imagine that this is what all the lakeside villages would once have been like.

Except for appreciating village life and enjoying stunning views, there's little to do. This is one of the best places to buy the luminescent indigo *huipiles* you see around Lago de Atitlán. Look for vendors on the path to the shore, or pop into one of the simple wooden storefronts. Several little *comedores* on the main plaza sell refreshments, and the open-air **Restaurante Laguna Azul** (mains US$4-6), on the lakeshore below the Villa Santa Catarina, does reasonably priced chicken, fish and meat dishes. **Posada Don Vitalino** (☎ 7762 2660; s/d US$7/14) offers basic, decent rooms with hot showers.

The road continues past Santa Catarina 5km to San Antonio Palopó, a larger but similar village where men and women in traditional clothing tend their terraced fields and clean mountains of scallions by the lakeshore.

See above for transportation details. From Panajachel, you can walk to Santa Catarina in about an hour, continuing to San Antonio in another. Bicycling is another option.

SANTIAGO ATITLÁN

South across the lake from Panajachel, on the shore of a lagoon squeezed between the volcanoes of Tolimán and San Pedro, lies Santiago

Atitlán, known to everybody as Santiago. It's the most workaday of the lake villages, home to Maximón (mah-shee-*mohn*; see p114), who is paraded around during Semana Santa – a good excuse to head this way during Easter. The rest of the year, Maximón resides with a caretaker, receiving offerings. He changes house every year, but he's easy enough to find by asking around. If that's too much work, local children will take you to see him for a small tip.

Although the most visited village outside Panajachel, Santiago clings to the traditional lifestyle and clothing of the Tz'utuhil Maya. The best days to visit are market days (Friday and Sunday, with a lesser market held on Tuesday).

Orientation & Information

The street straight ahead from the dock leads up to the town center. Every tourist walks up and down this street, so it's lined with craft shops and art galleries.

You'll find a lot of fascinating information about Santiago, in English, at www.santiagoatitlan.com.

Santiago has a post office, a Telgua telephone/fax office and a bank where you can change US dollars and traveler's checks. There's a MasterCard ATM located on the square.

Sights

At the top of the slope is the main square, flanked by the town office and a huge centuries-old **church**. Within are wooden statues of the saints, each of whom gets new handmade clothes every year.

On the carved pulpit, note the figures of corn (from which humans were formed, according to Maya religion), as well as a literate quetzal bird and Yum-Kax, the Maya god of corn. A similar carving is on the back of the priest's chair.

A memorial plaque at the back commemorates Father Stanley Francis Rother, a missionary priest from Oklahoma; beloved by the local people, he was murdered in the church by ultrarightist death squads in 1981.

There are many rewarding **day hikes** around Santiago. Unfortunately, owing to robberies and attacks on tourists in the Atitlán area, it's highly advisable to go with a guide (ask in your hotel for a reputable one) and tourist police escort. You can go with a guide and

two tourist police up any of the three **volcanoes** (US$80 per group), or to the **Mirador de Tepepul**, about 4km south of Santiago (US$30 for two), or to **Cerro de Oro**, some 8km northeast (US$28 for two).

Walking to San Pedro La Laguna is not recommended, unless the security situation improves, since this remote route has a robbery risk.

Sleeping & Eating

Hotel Tzanjuya (☎ 590 7980; s/d US$4/6, with bathroom US$6/8) Up the hill on the main street, this modern tiled hotel is reasonable value. You get a choice of lake or volcano views. Note that it is prohibited, as signs point out, to spit on the walls here.

Hotel Chi-Nim-Yá (☎ 7721 7131; s/d US$4/8, with bathroom US$6/11) This simple hotel is 30m to the left from the first crossroads as you walk up from the dock. The 22 rooms, around a central courtyard, are bare and clean, with concrete floors. The nicest is No 6 on the upper floor, which is large and airy, with lots of windows and lake views.

Hotel Lago de Atitlán (☎ 7721 7174; s/d with bathroom from US$10/12) Go four blocks uphill from the dock then turn left to this hotel, whose reception is in the hardware store next door. It's a modern five-story building (rather an anomaly in this little town). Rooms are bland but mostly bright, many having large windows with decent views. Go up on the rooftop for great sunsets.

El Pescador (set lunch US$4; ✪ breakfast, lunch & dinner) Two blocks up the street straight ahead from the dock, this is a good, clean restaurant with big windows, white-shirted waiters and neatly laid tables. A typical *menú del día* (set lunch) might bring you chicken, rice, salad, guacamole, tortillas and a drink.

There are plenty of cheap *comedores* above the market next to the plaza.

Getting There & Away

Boats to Santiago from Panajachel take about an hour; from San Pedro La Laguna 20 minutes. As you disembark, children greet you selling clay whistles and little embroidered strips of cloth.

They can act as guides, find you a taxi or lead you to a hotel, for a tip.

Buses to Guatemala City (US$3.50, three hours) leave from the main square regularly throughout the day.

GUATEMALA

SAN PEDRO LA LAGUNA
pop 10,000

It all comes down to what you're looking for – price wars between competing businesses keep San Pedro among the cheapest of the lakeside villages, and the beautiful setting attracts long-term visitors whose interests include (in no particular order): drinking, fire twirling, African drumming, Spanish classes, volcano hiking and hammock swinging.

Right alongside this whirling circus, San Pedro has a very conservative side – there's plenty of traditional dress and subsistence agriculture going on. You'll see coffee being picked and spread out to dry on wide platforms at the beginning of the dry season.

Orientation & Information

San Pedro has two docks. The one on the south side of town serves boats going to and from Santiago Atitlán. Another dock, around on the east side of town, serves boats going to and from Pana. At either, walk uphill to reach the center of town. Alternatively, from the Santiago dock, you can take your first right and follow the beaten path for about 15 minutes to the other side of town. Along this path is where a lot of the tourist-oriented businesses start up. To take this route coming from the Panajachel dock, take your first left and then a right into the little alley across from the Hospedaje Casa Elena; a sign painted on the wall says 'to El Balneario.'

You can exchange US dollars and traveler's checks at **Banrural** (8:30am-5pm Mon-Fri, 9am-1pm Sat) in the town center. It also has a MasterCard ATM. There's internet access at D'Noz, Casa Verde Internet and the Internet Café, just up the street from the Panajachel dock. The typical access rate is a little under US$1 per hour. You can make calls to North America/Europe for US$0.65/0.90 per minute at D'Noz.

Sights & Activities

Looming above the village, **Volcán San Pedro** (3020m) almost asks to be climbed by anyone with a bit of energy and adventurous spirit. The Volcano has recently been placed within an ecological park to minimize environmental damage caused by hikers and also improve the security situation, which wasn't great before. Guides can take you up here from San Pedro for US$13, including entrance fee. The ascent is through fields of maize, beans and squash,

followed by primary cloud forest. Take water, snacks, a hat and sunblock.

Once you've watched the sunset, one of the best places to be is soaking in these solar-heated tubs at **Thermal Waters** (admission per person US$3; 9am-9pm), down a small path next to the Buddha Bar. Book ahead so they have a pool nice and hot for you when you arrive.

Big Foot Adventures (7721 8203; sanpedro laguna@yahoo.com) offers treks to volcanoes, the Indio's Nose and Santa Cruz for US$10 to US$12. Horse treks cost US$2.50 per hour and they rent bikes for US$1.50/7 per hour/day.

Several **walks** between San Pedro and neighboring villages make terrific day trips, although armed muggings on the lonely roads between villages are not uncommon. See the warning at the start of this chapter. You can walk west to San Juan La Laguna (30 minutes), San Pablo La Laguna (1½ hours), San Marcos (three hours), Jaibalito (five hours) and finally, Santa Cruz (all day). From the last three you can easily hail a *lancha* back to San Pedro until around 3pm.

Kayaks are available for hire turning right from the Pana dock. Prices start at US$1.50 per hour.

Courses

The standard price for four hours of one-on-one Spanish classes, five days per week, is US$50 to US$55. Accommodations with a local family, with three meals daily (except Sunday), usually costs US$40. Schools can also organize other accommodation options. Schools include the following:

Cooperativa Spanish School (5398 6448; www .cooperativeschoolsanpedro.com) Run as a cooperative (therefore guaranteeing fair wages for teachers), this school comes highly recommended. A percentage of profits goes to needy families around the lake. After school activities include videos, conferences, salsa classes, volunteer work, kayaking and hiking. The office is halfway along the path between the two docks.

Escuela Mayab (5556 4785) Down a laneway coming off the street between the two docks, this well-organized school holds classes under shelters in artistically designed gardens. Activities include videos, kayaking and horse treks, although tuition is cheaper without these things. They are associated with a medical clinic in Nahuala and can organize volunteer work for doctors, nurses and assistants.

GUATEMALA

IN THE PATH OF STAN

In October 2005 Hurricane Stan slammed into the west coast of Guatemala, killing hundreds and leaving thousands homeless. Areas hardest hit were the coastal regions, San Marcos and Huehuetenango province, and the area around Lago de Atitlán.

Much of the devastation was caused by landslides, as mud from deforested hillsides slid down and buried villages below. This is what happened in Panabaj, a village behind Santiago Atitlán. The slide happened at night, causing many to be buried as they slept. Exact figures vary, but everybody agrees that there were at least 250 people buried underneath the mudslide.

A frantic, week-long rescue effort began, but had to be abandoned as the land was too unstable and the work became dangerous. President Berger announced that the area, the size of six football fields, would become a burial ground, as the risk of infection from unearthed corpses was too great.

Massive protests from victim's families fell on deaf ears, and the Forensic Anthropology Foundation NGO, more experienced at excavating civil war mass graves, moved in to help recover the bodies.

Government relief and reconstruction efforts have been characteristically slow, and more than a year after the tragedy displaced families were still living in makeshift refuges. To learn more about relief efforts, log on to www.puebloapueblo.org.

La Mysticoteca (☎ 5871 0506; www.freewebs.com /lamysticoteca) Turning right from the Pana dock and following the 'Yoga and Massage' signs brings you to this health and wellness center. There are courses in Shiatsu massage, reiki and meditation. You can also practice yoga (US$3.50) here or come for reiki (US$10), sound healing (US$17) or massages (from US$15).

Cielo Maya (☎ 5928 6189; ☽ 2-5:30pm) On the path between the docks, this Tz'utuhil women's collective sells fair-trade woven goods and offers weaving and beading classes from US$2 per hour, materials not included.

Sleeping
NEAR THE PANA DOCK

Hotel Xocomil (☎ 5598 4546; xocomil333@yahoo.com; s/d US$2/4) Up the lane to the right just after the Gran Sueño is this place – definitely in the basic backpacker category, with quiet rooms around a cement courtyard.

Hotel Mansión del Lago (7721 8124; 3a via & 4a Av, Zona 2; s/d US$4/8) Straight up from the Pana dock, you'll see this concrete monster. Rooms are good and big, with wide balconies and lake views. A room at the top costs another US$2.

Gran Sueño (☎ 7221 8110; 8a Calle 4-40, Zona 2; s/d US$5/10) On the street going left from the Mansión is the Gran Sueño. Rooms here are OK-sized, spotless with tiled floors, cable TV, and good hot showers. Get one upstairs for glimpses of the lake.

Hotel Nahual Maya (☎ 7721 8158; 6 Av 8 C-12; s/d US$5/10) This modern construction isn't the loveliest piece of architecture you're likely to see in Guatemala, but the rooms are big and homey and have little balconies with hammocks out front.

BETWEEN THE DOCKS

Hotel Mikaso (☎ 5173 3129; www.mikasohotel.com; 4a Callejon A 1-88; dm/r US$8/30) Fans of Antigua's colonial-hotel scene will find some comforting memories in this built-new-to-look-old construction. Really the only 'fine' hotel in San Pedro, rooms are big and well-furnished, and the rooftop bar and Spanish restaurant (p126) have lovely lake views. Dorms are spacious, spotless and a good deal for large groups.

Hostel Jarachik (☎ 5571 8720; 4a Calle 2-95, Zona 2; s/d US$8/10) This happening little hostel is a newcomer in town and rightly popular. Rooms are clean and bright. Get one on the top floor for light and ventilation.

Hotelito El Amanecer Sak'cari (☎ 812 1113, 721 8096; www.hotelsakcari.com; 7a Av 2-12, Zona 2; s/d US$8/12; P) On the left just after San Pedro Spanish School, the Sak'cari has clean, tangerine-colored rooms. They vary greatly in size and comfort, so have a look around. Right down the back, rooms have big balcony areas out front with excellent lake views and hammocks.

NEAR THE SANTIAGO DOCK

Hotel Peneleu (☎ 5925 0583; 5a Av 2-20, Zona 2; s/d US$3/6) It doesn't look like much from the outside, but once you get past the dirt yard, you'll find a clean, modern hotel with some of the best budget rooms in town. Try to get No 1 or 2, which are up top, with big windows overlooking the lake. To find it, go 80m up Calle Principal from Hotel Villasol, then along the street to the left.

Hotel Villa Sol (☎ 7721 8009; cnr 7a Av & Calle Principal; s/d US$3/4, with bathroom US$5/8; **P**) The 45 rooms here, just 200m up from the Santiago dock, are bare but clean; those with a bathroom look onto a grassy courtyard.

Eating

There are plenty of places to get your grub on around the Pana dock:

Alegre Pub (8a Calle 4-10; mains US$3-6; ☺ breakfast, lunch & dinner) Near the Pana dock, the Alegre is always, well, *alegre* (happy), with a real British pub feel – drinks specials, a Sunday roast and trivia nights. There are free movies twice a week in the way laid-back rooftop garden and loads of free, reliable tourist info. The big breakfast fry-up will make Brits weep with homesickness.

Fata Morgana (8a Calle 4-12; mains US$4-6; ☺ breakfast, lunch & dinner, closed Wed) Really good coffee has finally made it to San Pedro thanks to this little Italian restaurant-café-bakery. Also on offer are some good basic pastas and excellent homemade breads and pastries.

Chile's (4a Av 8-12; mains US$4-7; ☺ breakfast, lunch & dinner) Chile's deck overlooking the Pana dock and lake will always be a popular dining option. The party starts later here, too, with free salsa classes and dance music through the week.

D'Noz (4a Av 8-16; mains US$4-7; ☺ breakfast, lunch & dinner) This is upstairs above Nick's and is another popular hangout – it's about as close as San Pedro gets to a cultural center, with a global menu, free movies, a big bar, board games and a lending library.

The following restaurants are on the path between the two docks:

Buddha Bar (2a Av 2-24; mains US$6-8; ☺ lunch & dinner, closed Tue) The Buddha's an excellent place to hang out – downstairs there's a pool table, upstairs a restaurant doing convincing versions of Thai, Indian and other Asian dishes.

Mikaso (4a Callejón A 1-88; mains US$6-8; ☺ breakfast, lunch & dinner) With a real live Spanish chef, this is the place to come for Iberian delights. If you want the paella (US$8 per person) you'll have to give 24 hours notice.

Drinking & Nightlife

El Barrio (7a Av 2-07, Zona 2; ☺ 5pm-1am) This cozy little bar on the path between the two docks has one of the most happening happy hours in town, with food till midnight and drinks till 1am. There's a good cocktail and snacks list and a couple of chilled-out outside areas.

Alegre Lounge (8a Calle 4-10) It has a range of ridiculous drinks specials, such as US$0.30 Cuba Libres all through the week.

Freedom Bar (8a Calle 3-95, Zona 2; ☺ to 1am) The hardest-partying bar in town, the Freedom has good lounging areas, a pool table, a (relatively) huge dance floor and often hosts guest DJs on weekends. It's on the first street to your left coming up from the Pana dock.

Getting There & Away

Unless you want to bring a vehicle, it's easiest to reach San Pedro by passenger boats, which come here from Panajachel and from Santiago.

SAN MARCOS LA LAGUNA
pop 3000

Without doubt the prettiest of the lakeside villages, the flat shoreline here has paths snaking though banana, coffee and avocado trees. The town has become something of a magnet for hippies-with-a-purpose, who believe the place has a particular spiritual energy, and is an excellent place to learn or practice meditation, holistic therapies, massage, Reiki and other spiritually oriented activities.

Whatever you're into, it's definitely a great place to kick back and distance the everyday world for a spell. Lago de Atitlán is beautiful and clean here, with several little docks you can swim from.

Activities & Courses

Guy (☎ 5854 5365) at Restaurant Sol y Tul offers paragliding rides in the mornings from Santa Clara down to San Juan (US$60). It's an exhilarating experience, offering some great photo opportunities.

The town's greatest claim to fame is **Las Pirámides Meditation Center** (☎ 5205 7151; www .laspiramidesdelka.com), on the path heading inland from Posada Schumann. Every structure on the property is built in a pyramid shape and oriented to the four cardinal points. Among the many physical (eg yoga, massage) and metaphysical (eg Tarot readings, channeling) offerings is a one-month lunar meditation course that begins every full moon and covers the four elements of human development (physical, mental, emotional and spiritual). Most sessions are held in English. The last week of the course requires fasting and silence by participants. Nonguests can come for meditation or Hatha yoga sessions Monday to Saturday (US$4).

Accommodations in pyramid-shaped houses are available for US$15 per day and are only offered to people interested in joining the course. This includes the meditation course, use of the sauna and access to a fascinating multilingual library. A restaurant serves vegetarian fare. The best chance to get a space is just prior to the full moon. Las Pirámides has a private dock; all the *lancheros* know it and can drop you here.

Sleeping

Hotel El Unicornio (s/d US$5/9) A favorite with the budget-conscious, El Unicornio has eight rooms in small, thatched-roofed A-frame bungalows among verdant gardens, sharing hot-water showers, nice hangout areas, a sauna and an equipped kitchen. To get here turn left past Hotel La Paz, or walk along the lakeside path and turn right after Las Pirámides.

Hotel La Paz (☎ 7702 9168; r per person US$6) Along a side path off the track behind Posada Schumann, the mellow La Paz has rambling grounds holding two doubles and five dormitory-style rooms. All are in bungalows of traditional *bajareque* (a stone, bamboo and mud construction) with thatched roofs, and some have loft beds. Antiques, art works, the organic gardens and vegetarian restaurant, the traditional Maya sauna and the music and book room all contribute to making this a special place.

Aaculaax (☎ 5803 7243; www.aaculax.com; s/d from US$12/15) An artful, atmospheric hotel that looks like it grew out of the rock by itself, this place is constructed using recycled materials like old bottles. Each room is unique, and most have good lake views. There's a bar-chill-out area on the top floor with board games and comfy seating.

Posada del Bosque Encantado (☎ 5208 5334; gringamaya@yahoo.com; s/d US$13/21) Set in jungly grounds that could well be an enchanted forest, the rooms in this posada strike a good balance between rustic and stylish. Each room has a loft with a double bed and another bed downstairs. Walls are mud brick, beds are big

and firm, and there are hammocks strewn around the place.

Eating

A couple of *comedores* around the plaza sell tasty, good-value Guatemalan standards.

Il Giardino (mains US$2.75-5.25) This excellent vegetarian restaurant, owned by a Costa Rican–Italian couple, is set in a tranquil, spacious garden reached just before Hotel Paco Real. Main dishes include pizzas, spaghetti and fondues. The burritos with salsa and melted mozzarella are a treat.

Il Forno (mains US$6-10; ☽ lunch & dinner) Serves up delicious pizzas cooked in their wood-fired oven. To get there follow the signs from the main path to the dock.

Sol y Tul (mains US$6-10; ☽ breakfast, lunch & dinner) Out on the balcony at this French-influenced restaurant are some of the best lake views in town. Meals are huge and the service is friendly. To get there turn left from the main dock and follow the path for 20m.

Getting There & Away

You can drive to San Marcos from the Interamericana Hwy; the turnoff is at Km 148. The walk or drive between Santa Clara La Laguna and San Marcos is incredible.

See p121 for information on passenger boats.

JAIBALITO

Accessible only by boat or on foot, Jaibalito hosts Guatemala's most magical hotel. Perched on a secluded cliff facing volcanoes, **La Casa del Mundo Hotel & Café** (☎ 218 5332, 204 5558; www.lacasadelmundo.com; r US$27, with bathroom US$55; ✗) has gorgeous gardens, swimming holes and a hot tub overhanging the lake. All rooms have views and are impeccably outfitted with comfortable beds, *típico* (typical of the region) fabrics and fresh flowers. The aatached restaurant is fantastic. You can rent kayaks or bikes here. Reservations (by telephone) are advisable.

SANTA CRUZ LA LAGUNA
pop 5680

For all practical purposes this place consists of four hotels spread along the lakeside near the dock: it's the earthiest of the lake options, and also the home of the lake's scuba-diving outfit, ATI Divers. The main part of the village is uphill from the dock.

ATI Divers (☎ 7762 2621; www.laiguanaperdida.com) offers a four-day PADI open-water diving certification course (US$205), as well as a PADI high-altitude course and fun dives, including one in a volcano caldera. It's based at La Iguana Perdida hotel.

Good walks from Santa Cruz include the beautiful lakeside walking track between Santa Cruz and San Marcos, about four hours one way. You can stop for a beer and a meal at La Casa del Mundo en route (see p127). Or you can walk up the hill to Sololá, a 3½-hour walk one way.

Sleeping & Eating

La Iguana Perdida (☎ 5706 4117; www.laiguanaperdida .com; dm US$3, r US$8-10) Some might say they're going a bit overboard on the whole rustic thing, but this is still a good place to hang out, enjoy the lake views and meet other travelers. There's no electricity and the showers in the bathrooms (all shared) are lovely and cold! Meals are served family-style, with everyone eating together; a three-course dinner is US$5.50. You always have a vegetarian choice, and everything here is on the honor system: your tab is totaled up when you leave. Don't miss the Saturday night cross-dressing, fire and music barbecues!

Arca de Noé (☎ 5515 3712; arcasantacruz@yahoo .com; s/d US$8/12, with bathroom US$22/24) Spread out along the lakeside, the rooms and bungalows at this place are spacious with good views. It's just that the concrete bed bases are a bit of a let down.

Getting There & Away

See p121 for details on passenger boats. Not every boat stops here, but they will if you tell the captain as you get on.

THE HIGHLANDS – QUICHÉ

A largely forgotten little pocket of the country, most visitors to this region are on a quick in-and-out for the famous market at Chichicastenango, reached by a winding road north of the Interamericana. Further to the north is Santa Cruz del Quiché, the departmental capital; on its outskirts lie the ruins of K'umarcaaj (or Gumarcaah), also called Utatlán, the last capital city of the Quiché Maya.

More adventurous souls come for the excellent hiking around Nebaj, and the breathtaking backdoor route to Cobán.

For introductory information on the highlands, including a warning, see p113.

Getting There & Away

The road to Quiché leaves the Interamericana Hey at Los Encuentros, winding its way north through pine forests and cornfields, down into a steep valley and up the other side.

CHICHICASTENANGO

pop 49,000

Surrounded by valleys, with nearby mountains looming overhead, Chichicastenango seems isolated in time and space from the rest of Guatemala. When its narrow cobbled streets and red-tiled roofs are enveloped in mists, it's magical.

Chichi is a beautiful, interesting place with shamanistic and ceremonial undertones despite gaggles of camera-toting tour groups. *Masheños* (citizens of Chichicastenango) are famous for their adherence to pre-Christian religious beliefs and ceremonies. You can readily see versions of these old rites in and around the Iglesia de Santo Tomás and at the shrine of Pascual Abaj on the outskirts of town.

Chichi has always been an important trading town, and its Sunday and Thursday markets remain fabulous. If you have a choice of days, come on Sunday, when the *cofradías* often hold processions.

History

Once called Chaviar, this was an important Kaqchiquel trading town long before the Spanish conquest. Just prior to the arrival of the conquistadors, the Kaqchiquel and the Quiché (based at K'umarcaaj near present-day Santa Cruz del Quiché) went to war. The Kaqchiquel abandoned Chaviar and moved to Iximché, which was easier to defend. The conquistadors came and conquered K'umarcaaj, and many of its residents fled to Chaviar, which they renamed Chugüilá (Above the Nettles) and Tziguan Tinamit (Surrounded by Canyons).

These names are still used by the Quiché Maya, although everyone else calls the place Chichicastenango, a foreign name given by the conquistadors' Mexican allies.

GUATEMALA

CHICHICASTENANGO

INFORMATION
Acses Computación............(see 12)
Bancared ATM.....................1 C1
Banco Industrial..................2 C2
Banrural.............................3 C1
Hospital El Buen Samaritano...4 B1
Internet Digital...................5 C1

SIGHTS & ACTIVITIES
Iglesia de Santo Tomás.........6 C2
Mural.................................7 C2
Museo Regional...................8 B2
Shrine of Pascual Abaj...........9 A4

SLEEPING
Chalet House......................10 D1
Hospedaje Salvador..............11 B3
Hotel Girón........................12 C1
Hotel Mashito......................13 B2
Hotel Tuttos.......................14 B3
Mini-Hotel Chichicasteca......15 C1
Posada El Teléfono...............16 B1

EATING
Casa de San Juan.................17 B2
La Parrilla..........................18 C1
La Villa de los Cofrades.........19 C1
Los Cofrades.......................20 C1
Tu Café.............................21 C2
Tziguan Tinamit 22 C1

TRANSPORT
Buses to Guatemala City, Panajachel
 & Interamericana..............23 C1
Buses to Santa Cruz del
 Quiché & Nebaj.................24 C1

Information

Most banks change US dollars and traveler's checks, including **Banrural** (6a Calle east of 5a Av; 9am-5pm Sun-Fri, 9am-1pm Sat) and **Banco Industrial** (10am-2pm Mon, 10am-5pm Wed & Fri, 9am-5pm Thu & Sun, 10am-3pm Sat), almost next door. Banrural has a MasterCard ATM and there's a **Bancared ATM** (cnr 5a Av & 6a Calle) along the street that takes Visa.

Acses Computación (6a Calle), east of 5a Av and **Internet Digital** (5a Av 5-60) charge US$0.80 per hour for internet use. The **post office** (7a Av 8-47) is on the road into town.

Dangers & Annoyances

Like any small town, Chichi is fairly hassle-free to walk around. Be aware, though, that pickpockets love the jammed streets when the market's in full swing. The picturesque cemetery on Chichicastenango's western edge is a decidedly unsavory place to wander, even in groups. There have been several reports of tourists robbed at gunpoint.

Sights & Activities

Make sure you check out the fascinating mural that runs alongside the wall of the town hall on the east side of the plaza, which also serves as the market. The mural is dedicated to the victims of the civil war and tells the story of the war using symbology from the Popol Vuh.

MARKET

Maya traders from outlying villages come to Chichi on Wednesday and Saturday evenings in preparation for the indigenous market, one of Guatemala's largest. You'll see them carrying bundles of long poles up the narrow cobbled streets to the square, then laying down their loads and spreading out blankets to cook dinner and sleep in the arcades surrounding the square.

Just after dawn on Sunday and Thursday, the poles are erected into stalls, which are hung with cloth, furnished with tables and piled with goods.

In general, the tourist-oriented stalls sell carved-wood masks, lengths of embroidered cloth and garments; these stalls are around the market's outer edges in the most visible areas. Behind them, the center of the square is devoted to locals needs: vegetables and fruit, baked goods, macaroni, soap, clothing, spices, sewing notions and toys. Cheap cookshops provide lunch for buyers and sellers alike.

Most stalls are taken down by late afternoon. Prices are best just before the market breaks up, as traders would rather sell an item cheap than carry it back with them.

Arriving in town the day before the market to pin down a room is highly recommended. In this way, too, you'll be up early for the action. One traveler wrote to say it's worth being here on Saturday night to attend the Saturday night mass. Otherwise, you can always come by bus, or by shuttle bus; market day shuttle buses come from Antigua, Panajachel and Guatemala City, returning in early afternoon. The market starts winding down around 3pm or 4pm.

IGLESIA DE SANTO TOMÁS

Although dedicated to the Catholic rite, this simple **church** (cnr 5a Av & 8a Calle), dating from about 1540, is more often the scene of rituals that are only slightly Catholic and more distinctly Mayan. The front steps of the church serve much the same purpose as did the great flights of stairs leading up to Maya pyramids. For much of the day (especially on Sunday), the steps smolder with copal incense, while indigenous prayer leaders called *chuchkajaues* (mother-fathers) swing censers containing *estoraque* (balsam) incense and chant magic words in honor of the ancient Maya calendar and their ancestors.

It's customary for the front steps and door of the church to be used only by important church officials and by the *chuchkajaues,* so

you should go around to the right and enter by the side door.

Inside, the floor of the church may be spread with pine boughs and dotted with offerings of corn, flowers and bottles of liquor; candles are everywhere. The candles and offerings on the floor are in remembrance of the ancestors, many of whom are buried beneath the church floor just as Maya kings were buried beneath pyramids. Photography is not permitted in this church.

MUSEO REGIONAL

In the arcade facing the square's south side is the **Museo Regional** (5a Av 4-47; admission US$0.80; 8am-noon & 2-4pm Tue-Sat, to 2pm Sun), which holds exhibits of ancient clay pots and figurines, flint and obsidian (glass formed by the cooling of molten lava) arrowheads and spearheads, copper ax heads, metates and a jade collection.

SHRINE OF PASCUAL ABAJ

Before you have been in Chichi very long, some village lad will offer to guide you (for a tip) to a pine-clad hilltop on the town's outskirts to have a look at Pascual Abaj (Sacrifice Stone), the local shrine to Huyup Tak'ah, the Maya earth god. Said to be hundreds – perhaps thousands – of years old, the stone-faced idol has suffered numerous indignities at the hands of outsiders, but locals still revere it. *Chuchkajaues* come here regularly to offer incense, food, cigarettes, flowers, liquor and Coca-Cola to the earth god. They may even sacrifice a chicken – all to express their thanks and hope for the earth's continuing fertility. The site also offers nice views of the town and valley.

Tourists have been robbed walking to Pascual Abaj – the best plan is to go in a large group. To get there, walk down the hill on 5a Av from the Santo Tomás church, turn right onto 9a Calle and continue downhill along this unpaved road, which bends to the left. At the bottom of the hill, when the road turns sharply right, bear left and follow a path through the cornfields, keeping the stream on your left. Signs mark the way. Walk to the buildings just ahead, which include a farmhouse and a **mask-making workshop**. Greet the family here. If the children aren't in school, you may be invited to see them perform a local dance in full costume on your return from Pascual Abaj (a tip is expected).

MIXING IT UP

Much is made of the blend of Catholicism and Maya beliefs. And indeed, one survival technique for the Maya was to 'accept' Catholicism, and simply rename their objects of worship. This is most obvious in that Mary is associated with the moon and the stars whereas God or Jesus represents the sun.

But the Maya were using the cross long before the Spanish arrived – for them the four points represent the sun, the Earth, the moon and people. Four is an especially holy number for the Maya, as they believe that the world is supported at its four corners by gods.

One Maya creation story that obviously owes little to the bible is that of Old Jesus and Young Jesus. The story goes that one day the two Jesuses found a tree with wax at the top. The young one climbed the tree and started dropping the wax down to the old one, who made an army from it. But young Jesus dropped too much wax, angering the old one, who ordered his army to bite off the tree trunk, causing Young Jesus to fall to his death.

Old Jesus went to tell his mother, the Virgin Mary, what happened and she banished him to a mountaintop, where he found an umbilical cord, climbed to heaven and became the sun, at which point his mother became the moon.

Walk through the farm buildings to the hill behind, then follow the switchbacking path to the top and along the ridge. Soon you'll reach a clearing and see the idol in its rocky shrine. The idol looks like something from Easter Island. The squat stone crosses near it have many levels of significance for the Maya, only one of which pertains to Christ. The area of the shrine is littered with past offerings, and the bark of nearby pines has been stripped away in places to be used as fuel in the incense fires.

Festivals & Events

Quema del Diablo (Burning of the Devil; December 7) Residents burn their garbage in the streets to release the evil spirits within. Highlights include a marimba band and a daring fireworks display that has observers running for cover.

Feast of the Immaculate Conception (December 8) Don't miss the early-morning dance of the giant cartoon characters in the plaza.

Feast of Santo Tomás (December 13-21) When pairs of brave (or crazy) men fly about at high speeds suspended from a pole.

Sleeping

As Chichi has few accommodations, arrive early on Wednesday or Saturday if you want to secure a room before market day.

Posada El Teléfono (8a Calle A 1-64; s/d US$4/8) Not exactly luxury, but the rooms here are comfortable enough and good value for the price. The view of the town's technicolor cemetery from the rooftop is a draw in itself. There's a kitchen that guests can use.

Hospedaje Salvador (☎ 7756 1329; 5a Av 10-09; s/d US$5/7, with bathroom US$8/10) Huge and crumbling, the Salvador still scrapes together a bit of character, but it's mostly just budget digs for market days. Rooms get better as you go higher: Nos 49 to 52 on the top floor are light and airy, with good views. Try negotiating for a discount.

Mini-Hotel Chichicasteca (☎ 7756 2111; 5a Calle 4-42; s/d US$5/9) This hotel's adequately clean rooms with bare brick walls are a decent budget choice. It's conveniently located for both the bus stop and plaza.

Hotel Mashito (☎ 7756 1343; 8a Calle 1-72; s/d US$5.50/11, with bathroom US$7/14) Another cheapie-but-goodie, also on the road to the cemetery, is this place, offering plain but comfortable rooms in a big family house.

Hotel Tuttos (☎ 7756 1540; 12a Calle 6-29; s/d with bathroom US$10/12) Up on a hill away from the chaos of the market area, the Tuttos has good-sized, fairly clean rooms. The terrace and rooms out back have great views over the valley behind town.

Hotel Girón (☎ 7756 1156; 6a Calle 4-52; s/d with bathroom US$11/15; P) There's plenty of varnished pine going on here, but the paint job's cheery, rooms are big and spotless, and the proximity to the market can't be beat for the price. There are broad, sunny walkways in front of the rooms for catching a few rays.

Chalet House (☎ 7756 1360; www.chalethotelguatemala.com; 3a Calle C 7-44; s/d with bathroom US$15/22) The cozy Chalet House has good beds, homey touches and private hot-water bathrooms. Rooms get better the further upstairs you go, so ask to see a few.

Eating

On Sunday and Thursday, eating at the cookshops set up in the center of the market is the cheapest way to go. Don't be deterred by the fried-food stalls crowding the fringe – dive into the center for wholesome fare. On other days, look for the little *comedores* near the post office on the road into town.

Casa de San Juan (4a Av; dishes US$3-5; ☺ breakfast, lunch & dinner) The San Juan is one of the few eateries in town with style – art on the walls and the tables themselves, jugs of lilies, wrought-iron chairs – and its food is great too, ranging from burgers and tortillas to homemade cakes and more traditional dishes. There are balcony tables overlooking the market and live music some nights.

Tu Café (5a Av; mains US$3.50-5; ☺ lunch & dinner) The *plato vegetariano* here is soup, rice, beans, cheese, salad and tortillas, for a reasonable US$3.50. Add *lomito* (a pork fillet) and it becomes a *plato típico* (US$4.50).

Tziguan Tinamit (5a Av 5-67; mains US$3.50-6; ☺ lunch & dinner) For a more down-to-earth dining experience, check out this local eatery, with good pastas (US$4) and hit-and-miss pizzas (US$5).

La Villa de los Cofrades (6a Calle A, main plaza; dishes US$4-6; ☺ breakfast, lunch & dinner) You can't beat this location in the arcade on the north side of the plaza. This is a fine café for breakfast, crepes or larger meals, with an Italian influence and good strong coffee.

La Parrilla (6a Calle 5-37; mains US$5-6; ☺ lunch & dinner) A meat lover's dream, La Parrilla serves up every cut imaginable, chargrilled, in a quiet courtyard setting.

Los Cofrades (cnr 6a Calle & 5a Av; 2-course lunch or dinner US$6-7; ☺ breakfast, lunch & dinner) This bright upstairs restaurant (enter from 6a Calle) serves up some excellent set meals and has a decent drinks list. Go for a table out on the balcony – inside the atmosphere is very dining hall.

Getting There & Away

Buses heading south to Los Encuentros, Panajachel, Quetzaltenango, Guatemala City and all other points reached from the Interamericana normally arrive and depart from the corner of 5a Calle and 5a Av, one block uphill from the Arco Gucumatz arch. Buses heading north to Santa Cruz del Quiché stop half a block downhill on the same street. On market days, however, buses to or from the south may stop at the corner of 7a Av and 9a Calle, to avoid the congested central streets.

Antigua (3½ hours, 108km) Take any bus heading for Guatemala City and change at Chimaltenango.

Guatemala City (US$3, three hours, 145km, every 20 minutes 4am-5pm)

Los Encuentros (US$1.50, 30 minutes, 17km) Take any bus heading south for Guatemala City, Panajachel, Quetzaltenango and so on.

Nebaj (103km) Take a bus to Santa Cruz del Quiché and change there.

Panajachel (US$2.50, 1½ hours, 37km, about eight buses 5am-2pm) Or take any southbound bus and change at Los Encuentros.

Quetzaltenango (US$3, three hours, 94km, seven buses) Mostly in the morning; or take any southbound bus & change at Santa Cruz del Quiché.

Santa Cruz del Quiché (US$1.50, 30 minutes, 19km, every 20 minutes 5am-8pm)

On market days, shuttle buses arrive en masse mid-morning, bringing tourists from Panajachel, Antigua, Guatemala City and Quetzaltenango. They depart around 2pm. If you're looking to leave Chichi, you can usually catch a ride out on one of these.

SANTA CRUZ DEL QUICHÉ
pop 18,700

The capital of the department, Santa Cruz – which is usually called 'El Quiché' or simply 'Quiché' – is 19km north of Chichicastenango. This small, dusty town is quieter and more typical of the Guatemalan countryside than Chichi. Few tourists come here, but those who do come are treated well. Saturday is the main day for the **market**, making things slightly more interesting and way more crowded.

K'umarcaaj

\The **ruins** (admission US$2.50; ☺ 8am-5pm) of the ancient Quiché Maya capital are 3km west of El Quiché. Start out of town along 10a Calle and ask the way frequently. No signs mark the way and no buses ply the route. A taxi there and back from the bus station, including waiting time, costs around US$12. Consider yourself lucky if you succeed in hitching a ride with other travelers.

The kingdom of Quiché was established in late post-Classic times (about the 14th century) from a mixture of indigenous people and Mexican invaders. Around 1400 King Gucumatz founded his capital here at K'umarcaaj and conquered many neighboring cities.

Eventually, the kingdom of Quiché extended its borders to Huehuetenango, Sacapulas, Rabinal and Cobán, even coming to influence the peoples of the Soconusco region in Mexico.

Pedro de Alvarado led his Spanish conquistadors into Guatemala in 1524, and it was the Quiché, under their king, Tecún Umán, who organized the defense of the territory. In the decisive battle fought near Quetzaltenango on February 12, 1524, Alvarado and Tecún Umán locked in mortal combat. Alvarado won. The defeated Quiché invited the victorious Alvarado to visit their capital, where they secretly planned to kill him. Smelling a rat, Alvarado enlisted the aid of his Mexican auxiliaries and the anti-Quiché Kaqchiquel, and together they captured the Quiché leaders, burnt them alive and then destroyed K'umarcaaj.

The history is more interesting than the ruined city, of which little remains but a few grass-covered mounds. Still, the site – shaded by tall trees and surrounded by defensive ravines (which failed to save the city from the conquistadors) – is a beautiful place for a picnic. It's also used by locals as a religious ritual site; a long tunnel beneath the plaza is a favorite spot for prayers and chicken sacrifices.

Sleeping & Eating

Hotel San Pascual (☎ 7755 1107; 7a Calle 0-43, Zona 1; s/d US$5/8, with bathroom US$11/14; [P]) Between the bus station and plaza, this is a clean and friendly hotel with plants in its two courtyards. More expensive rooms have big clean bathrooms and cable TV.

Hotel Leo (☎ 7765 0776; 1 Av 9-02, Zona 5; s/d US$10/12) An excellent deal right around the corner from the bus terminal, with spacious, quiet rooms and good clean bathrooms.

San Miguel (cnr 2 Av & 5 Calle, Zona 1; snacks US$2-3; ☽ breakfast & lunch) It's a little bakery café that injects a bit of style into Santa Cruz's eating scene. The environment is friendly and tranquil with some excellent baked goods and sandwiches on offer.

Café La Torre (2a Av, Zona 1; mains US$3-5; ☽ breakfast, lunch & dinner) If you want to escape the hectic streets for a while, this little upstairs café is a good place to do it and catch some plaza views at the same time. Snacks include burgers and sandwiches, and good-value set lunches (US$3) are available.

Getting There & Away

Many buses from Guatemala City to Chichicastenango continue to El Quiché. The last bus from El Quiché headed south to Chichicastenango and Los Encuentros leaves mid-afternoon.

El Quiché is the jumping-off point for the somewhat remote reaches of northern Quiché, which extend all the way to the Mexican border. Departures from the bus station include the following:

Chichicastenango (US$1.50, 30 minutes, 19km) Take any bus heading for Guatemala City.

Guatemala City (US$4, 3½ hours, 163km, every 20 minutes, 3am-5pm)

Los Encuentros (US$2.50, one hour, 36km) Take any bus heading for Guatemala City.

Nebaj (US$3, 2½ hours, 75km, eight buses 8:30am-5pm)

Sacapulas (US$2, one hour, 45km, every 30 minutes 8:30am-5pm) Or take any bus heading for Nebaj or Uspantán.

Uspantán (US$3.50, three hour, 75km) Buses at roughly 9:30am, 10:30am, 1:30pm, 3pm and 3:30pm.

NEBAJ

pop 11,000 / elevation 1900m

Set deep in a bowl in the dramatic, largely untouched Cuchumatanes mountains, Nebaj's foreigner population consists of equal parts hardcore hikers and volunteers who work with the desperately poor communities in the surrounding countryside.

The locals, removed from modern influences, proudly preserve their ancient way of life. They make excellent handicrafts (mostly textiles) and the Nebaj women wear beautiful *huipiles*.

Nebaj's remote location has been a blessing and a curse. The Spaniards found it difficult to conquer (they laid waste to the inhabitants when they finally did). In more recent times, guerrilla forces made the area a base of operations, drawing strong measures from the army to dislodge them – particularly during the short, brutal reign of Ríos Montt. The few surviving inhabitants of these villages either fled across the border into Mexico or were herded into 'strategic hamlets.' Refugees are still making their way back home here.

Information

Banrural (2a Av 46; ☽ 9am-4pm Mon-Fri, to 1pm Sat), one block east from the northeast corner of the Parque, then half a block north, changes US dollars and traveler's checks and has a

Visa ATM. The **post office** (5a Av 4-37) is one block north of the Parque. **Centro de Internet Cámara de Comercio** (2a Av; ☺ 8am-9pm), in the same block as Banrural, charges US$0.50 per hour online.

There's a heap of fascinating and helpful information about Nebaj in Spanish at www .nebaj.org. If you can't understand Spanish, the maps and listings are still useful. The Guías Ixil website (www.nebaj.com) also has good information on hiking, volunteering and studying in the area.

Activities

Guias Ixil (☎ 5311 9100; www.nebaj.com; 3a Calle, Zona 1), in the El Descanso building, offers hikes with informative young local guides. Like all the other enterprises in this building, a portion of Trekking Ixil's profits goes to a community project. Short one-day hikes, costing US$6 for one person plus US$3 for each extra person, go to **Las Cataratas** (a series of waterfalls on the Río Las Cataratas north of town), or around town with visits to the **sacred sites** of the *costumbristas* (people who still practice pre-Christian Maya rites). They also arrange longer hikes, including overnighters to Todos Santos (three days, US$120 one person, US$40 for an additional person).

Las Cataratas is actually easy enough to reach on your own: walk 1.3km past Hotel Il-ebal Tenam along the Chajul road, to a bridge over a small river.

Immediately before the bridge, turn left (north) onto a gravel road and follow the river. Walking downriver for 45 minutes to an hour, you'll pass several small waterfalls before reaching a larger waterfall about 25m high.

Festivals & Events

Nebaj's **annual festival** (August 12-15) honors La Virgen de la Asunción.

Sleeping

Popi's Hostel (☎ 7756 0159; 5a Calle 6-74; dm US$3.50) An excellent choice for the truly budget conscious are the comfortable if plain rooms at this popular café-bakery. Choose your bed carefully – some sag dramatically.

Hotel Ixil (☎ 7756 0036; cnr 9 Calle & 2 Av, Zona 5; s/d US$9/12) A great little budget hotel, it has clean, bright rooms set around a plant-filled courtyard. Rooms have cable TV and good hot showers.

Eating

Popi's Restaurant (5a Calle 6-74; mains US$2-4) For all your baked goods needs, head straight to Popi's. You can also buy a mean selection of breads and pies here to take away, and some good comfort food, such as BBQ pork ribs (US$3.50).

El Descanso (3a Calle, Zona 1; mains US$3-5; ☺ breakfast, lunch & dinner) Probably the most comfortable café in the entire highlands, this two-story place has a bar and lounge areas, good music and board games, and serves everything from salads to sandwiches to *churrascos* (grilled steak). It was started as a Peace Corps project as a sustainable way for local youth to earn money and shares its building with Trekking Ixil and the Nebaj Language School. A portion of the profits from all these businesses goes to fund a lending library in town for children and young adults.

Getting There & Away

About eight daily buses run to and from Santa Cruz del Quiché (US$3, 2½ hours), via Sacapulas (US$1.50, 1½ hours). The best time to get one is between 5am and 8am, and the last departure may be no later than noon, but there are plenty of minibuses running this route, so you shouldn't get stuck. There's an 11pm bus all the way to Guatemala City via Chichicastenango.

Coming from Cobán (six hours), you must change buses several times, but it's nearly possible to make Nebaj in one day. It's easier to reach Nebaj from Huehuetenango or from El Quiché, going via Sacapulas, as buses are more frequent.

Buses leave Nebaj for Quiché via Sacapulas (US$3) at 6am, 11:30am and 2pm daily, and minibuses leave whenever full in daylight hours.

SACAPULAS TO COBÁN

Heading east out of Sacapulas, the road meanders up sadly deforested slopes before reaching the village of **Uspantán**. Rigoberta Menchú, the 1992 Nobel Peace Prize laureate, grew up a five-hour walk from Uspantán. Be aware that Menchú is not universally loved around here.

If you're headed to Cobán by bus, you may end up spending the night in Uspantán, as the last minibus leaves town at 4pm (US$3.50, four hours). It can get very cold here. **Pensión Galindo** (5a Calle 2-09; s/d US$3.50/7), about three

GUATEMALA

EXPLORE MORE OF QUICHÉ

Nebaj is the jumping-off point for many picturesque hikes around Quiché. Below are just a few options. If you want to do these without a guide, pick up a copy of *Trekking en la Región Ixil*, available from Guías Ixil (see opposite).

- **Cocop**, one of the worst-hit villages of the civil war, is an easy four hours from Nebaj

- Stay in community-run lodges on a three-day loop through Xeo, Cotzal and Ak'Txumbal

- Catch a bus or pickup to **Salquil Grande**, then take a gorgeous two-hour stroll past waterfalls to the village of **Parramos Grande**

---

blocks from the plaza, has a dozen tiny, clean rooms around a neat little patio open to the stars. **Hotel Doña Leonar** (☎ 7951 8041; 6a Calle 4-25; s/d from US$10/12) offers a lot more comfort. A Banrural bank on the plaza will change US dollars.

Along with the Huehue to Sacapulas leg of the same highway, the Uspantán–Cobán road (see East Toward Cobán, p150) is one of the most gorgeous rides in Guatemala. Sit on the right for views.

WESTERN HIGHLANDS

Dramatic scenery, traditional villages, excellent hiking and the traveler's oasis of Quetzaltenango are what really shine in this region. Roads and buses are some of the worst in the country, making travel tough but rewarding.

For introductory information on the highlands, including a warning, see p113

CUATRO CAMINOS

Heading westward from Los Encuentros, the Interamericana Hwy twists and turns ever higher into the mountains, bringing increasingly dramatic scenery and cooler temperatures. After 59km you come to the important highway junction known as Cuatro Caminos (Four Roads), where you can continue north (straight on) to Huehuetenango (77km), turn

east to Totonicapán (12km) or turn southwest to Quetzaltenango (13km).

Buses pass through Cuatro Caminos about every half-hour from 6am to 6pm on their way between Quetzaltenango and Totonicapán.

TOTONICAPÁN

pop 94,700 / elevation 2500m

San Miguel Totonicapán is a pretty Guatemalan highland town known for its artisans. Shoemakers, weavers, tinsmiths, potters and woodworkers all make and sell their goods here. Market days are Tuesday and Saturday; it's a locals' market, not a tourist affair, and it winds down by late morning.

Flanking Totonicapán's parque (as the plaza is called) are the requisite **colonial church** and a wonderful **municipal theater**, built in 1924 in the neoclassical style and restored in recent years. **Agua Caliente hot springs**, a popular local bathing place is 2km from the parque.

Sights & Activities

Casa de la Cultura Totonicapense (☎ 7766 1575; www .larutamayaonline.com/aventura.html; 8a Av 2-17), left of Hospedaje San Miguel, holds displays on indigenous culture and crafts. It also administers a wonderful 'Meet the Artisans' program that allows tourists to meet artisans and local families, observing how they live, work and play. The prices for four people, on a per person basis, range from US$49, but for 15 to 20 people the per person cost is US$24. An alternative program, for two/six/10 people, costs US$15/10/6 per person, and takes you on foot to nearby villages to visit community development projects, natural medicine projects, schools, artisans' workshops and Maya sacred sites. All tours are in Spanish.

Festivals & Events

Apparition of the Archangel Michael (May 8) Features fireworks and traditional dances.

Feria Titular de San Miguel Arcángel (Name-Day Festival of Archangel Saint Michael; September 24-30) Peaks on September 29.

Festival Tradicional de Danza (late October – dates vary) Totonicapán keeps traditional masked dances very much alive with this festival.

Sleeping & Eating

Casa de la Cultura clients can stay with local families for around US$18 per person, including dinner and breakfast.

Hospedaje Paco Centro (☎ 7766 2810; 3a Calle 8-22, Zona 2; s/d US$5.50/11, with bathroom US$8/16) A clean, tidy place with big bare rooms, it's a couple of blocks from the lower plaza. Rooms with bathroom have TV. Front rooms get a bit of street noise.

Restaurante Bonanza (4a Calle 8-16, Zona 2; meals US$4-6; ☺ breakfast, lunch & dinner) Toto's most formal restaurant won't blow your mind, but it will fill your stomach. Mostly meat, with a few seafood and veggie options.

Getting There & Away

Buses between Totonicapán and Quetzaltenango (passing through Cuatro Caminos) run frequently throughout the day. Signs in the bus window say 'Toto.' The ride from Cuatro Caminos is along a beautiful pine-studded valley. The last direct bus to Quetzaltenango (US$0.50, one hour) leaves Toto at 6:30pm.

QUETZALTENANGO (XELA)

pop 140,400 / elevation 2335m

Quetzaltenango, – which the locals kindly shorten to Xela (*shell*-ah), itself an abbreviation of the original Quiché Maya name, Xelajú – may well be the perfect Guatemalan town – not too big, not too small, enough foreigners to support a good range of hotels and restaurants, but not so many that it loses its national flavor. The Guatemalan 'layering' effect is at work in the city center here – once the Spanish moved out, the Germans moved in and their architecture gives the zone a somber, some would say Gothic, feel.

Xela attracts a more serious type of traveler – people who really want to learn Spanish, and then stay around and get involved in myriad volunteer projects on offer.

It also functions as a base for a range of spectacular hikes through the surrounding countryside – the constantly active Santiaguito and highest-point-in-Central-America Tajumulco volcanoes, and the picturesque, fascinating three-day trek to Lake Atitlán to name a few.

History

Quetzaltenango came under the sway of the Quiché Maya of K'umarcaaj in the 14th century. Before that it had been a Mam Maya town.

With the formation of the Federation of Central America in the mid-19th century,

Quetzaltenango initially decided on federation with Chiapas and Mexico, instead of with Central America. Later, the city switched alliances and joined the Central American Federation, becoming an integral part of Guatemala in 1840. The late-19th century coffee boom augmented Quetzaltenango's wealth. Plantation owners came to buy supplies, and coffee brokers opened warehouses. The city prospered until 1902, when a dual calamity – an earthquake and a volcanic eruption – brought mass destruction.

Still, Xela's position at the intersection of the roads to the Pacific Slope, Mexico and Guatemala City guaranteed it some degree of affluence. Today it's again busy with commerce.

Orientation

The heart of Xela is the Parque Centroamérica, shaded by old trees, graced with neoclassical monuments and surrounded by the city's important buildings.

The main bus station is Terminal Minerva, on 7a Calle, Zona 3, on the western outskirts and next to one of the city's main markets. First-class bus lines have their own terminals.

Minibuses run between Terminal Minerva and Parque Centroamérica – listen for helpers yelling 'parque' or 'terminal' respectively.

Information

BOOKSTORES

El Libro Abierto (Map p139; 15a Av A 1-56, Zona 1) Great selection of books in English and Spanish on Guatemala and the Maya, plus guidebooks, fiction, dictionaries, language textbooks and maps; will buy used books.

North & South (Map p137; 8 Calle & 15 Av, Zona 1) A wide range of books focusing on Latin America, politics, poetry and history. Also plenty of new and used guidebooks and Spanish student resources.

Vrisa Bookstore (Map p139; 15a Av 3-64, Zona 1) Excellent range of second-hand books in English and European languages. One of the best noticeboards in town.

EMERGENCY

Bomberos (Firefighters; ☎ 7761 2002)
Cruz Roja (Red Cross; ☎ 7761 2746)
Policía Municipal (☎ 7761 5805)
Policía Nacional (☎ 7765 4991/2)

INTERNET ACCESS

Email access here is some of the cheapest in Guatemala, at around US$0.25 to US$0.80 per hour. These are just some of the places available:

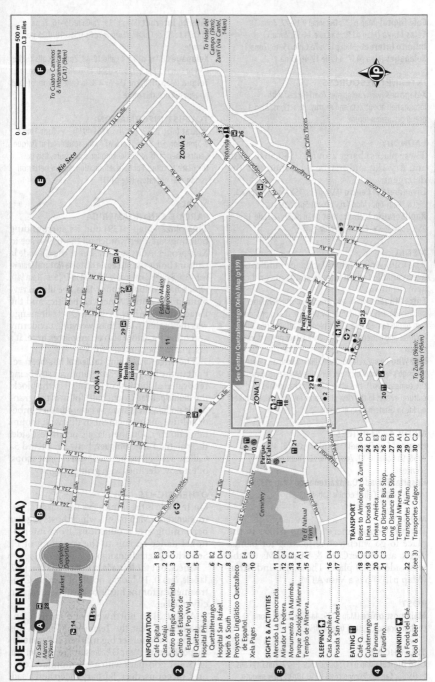

Café Digital (Map p137; Diagonal 9 19-77, Zona 1)
Celas Maya (Map p139; 6a Calle 14-55, Zona 1)
Infinito Internet (Map p139; 7a Calle 15-16, Zona 1)
Xelapages (Map p137; 4 Calle 19-48, Zona 1)

INTERNET RESOURCES
Xelapages (www.xelapages.com) Packed with information about Xela and nearby attractions. Also a useful discussion forum.

LAUNDRY
These places charge around US$0.50 to wash and dry 1kg and maybe a bit more for the detergent:
Lavandería El Centro (Map p139; 15a Av A 3-51, Zona 1; 8:30am-6pm Mon-Fri, 8:30am-5pm Sat)
Rapi-Servicio Laundromat (Map p139; 7a Calle 13-25A, Zona 1; 8am-6pm Mon-Sat)

MEDIA
The following English-language publications are available free in bars, restaurants and cafés around town:
Entre Mundos (www.entremundos.org) Newspaper published every two months by the Xela-based organization of the same name. It has plenty of information on political and current events, and volunteer projects in the region.
XelaWho (www.xelawho.com) Billing itself as 'Quetzaltenango's leading Culture & Nightlife Magazine' (where's the competition?), this little magazine has details of cultural events in the city, plus some fairly irreverent takes on life in Guatemala in general.

MEDICAL SERVICES
Hospital San Rafael (Map p137; 761 4414, 761 2956, 9a Calle 10-41, Zona 1) Has 24-hour emergency service.
Hospital Privado Quetzaltenango (Map p137; 761 4381, Calle Rodolfo Robles 23-51)

MONEY
Parque Centroamérica (Map p139) is the place to go when you're looking for banks. There are MasterCard & Visa ATMs on the west side of the plaza. The Banco Industrial (Map p139) has a Visa ATM.

POST
Main post office (Map p139; 4a Calle 15-07, Zona 1) Central location, east of Telgua office.

TELEPHONE
Café Digital (Map p137; Diagonal 9 19-77, Zona 1) Calls to USA or Canada/Europe costs US$0.10/0.15 per minute.

Infinito Internet (Map p139; 7a Calle 15-16, Zona 1) Calls to US or Canada/Europe costs US$0.10/0.15 per minute.
Xelapages (Map p137; 4 Calle 19-48, Zona 1) Calls to the USA or Canada/Europe costs US$0.15/0.20 per minute.
Telgua (Map p139; cnr 15a Av A & 4a Calle) Plenty of card phones outside this office.

TOURIST INFORMATION
Inguat (Map p139; /fax 7761 4931; 8am-1pm & 2-5pm Mon-Fri, 8am-1pm Sat) At the south end of Parque Centroamérica. If you're looking for a brochure, this is the place to come. For hard information, you're better off asking tour operators (see p141).

Sights
PARQUE CENTROAMÉRICA
This plaza (Map p139) and its surrounding buildings are pretty much all there is to see in Xela proper. At its southeast end, the Casa de la Cultura holds the **Museo de Historia Natural** (admission US$0.80; 8am-noon & 2-6pm Mon-Fri, 9am-1pm Sat), which has exhibits on the Maya, the liberal revolution in Central American politics and the Estado de Los Altos, of which Quetzaltenango was the capital. Marimbas, weaving, taxidermy and other local lore also claim places here. It's fascinating because it's funky.

The once-crumbling **cathedral** has been rebuilt in the last few decades and was still being renovated at the time of writing. Up the block, the **municipalidad** (town hall) follows the grandiose neoclassical style so favored as a symbol of culture and refinement in this wild mountain country. On the plaza's northwest side, the palatial **Pasaje Enríquez**, between 4a and 5a Calles, was built to be lined with elegant shops, but it now declines with grungy dignity.

OTHER SIGHTS
On 1a Calle is the impressive neoclassical **Teatro Municipal** (Map p139), which hosts regular performing arts productions, from international dance recitals to the crowning of La Señorita Quetzaltenango.

Check out the **Mercado La Democracia** (Map p137; 1a Calle, Zona 3), 10 blocks north of Parque Centroamérica, for the hustle of a real Guatemalan city market.

About 3km northwest of Parque Centroamérica, near the Terminal Minerva bus station and another big market, is **Parque Zoológico Minerva** (Map p137; admission free; 9am-5pm Tue-Sun), a zoo-park with a few monkeys, coyotes, raccoons, deer, Barbary sheep and a sad,

CENTRAL QUETZALTENANGO (XELA)

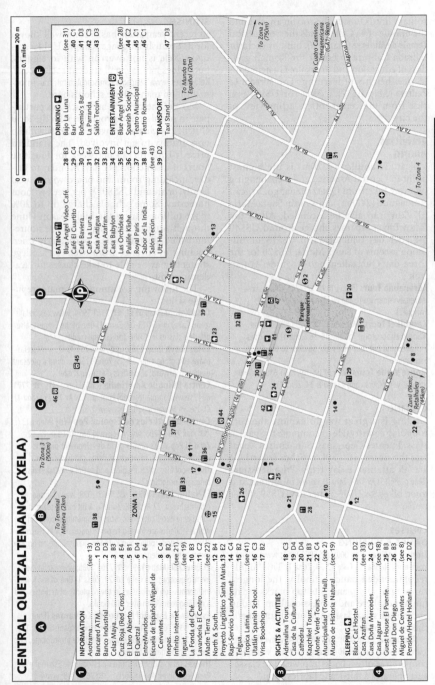

INFORMATION

Asotrama...................................(see 13)	
Bancared ATM..............................1 D3	
Banco Industrial...........................2 D3	
Celas Maya.................................3 B3	
Cruz Roja (Red Cross)......................4 E4	
El Libro Abierto............................5 B1	
El Quetzal..................................6 D4	
EntreMundos................................7 E4	
Escuela de Español Miguel de	
Cervantes..............................8 C4	
Inepas.....................................9 B2	
Infinito Internet.......................(see 19)	
Inguat....................................10 B3	
La Fonda del Ché..........................11 C2	
Lavandería El Centro......................(see 22)	
Madre Tierra..............................12 B4	
North & South.............................13 E2	
Proyecto Lingüístico Santa María..........14 C4	
Rapi-Servicio Laundromat..................15 B2	
Telgua....................................(see 41)	
Tropica Latina............................16 C3	
Utatlán Spanish School....................17 B2	
Vrisa Bookshop............................ B2	

SIGHTS & ACTIVITIES

Adrenalina Tours..........................18 C3	
Casa de la Cultura........................19 D4	
Cathedral.................................20 D4	
Kaachikel Tours...........................21 B3	
Monte Verde Tours.........................22 C4	
Municipalidad (Town Hall).................(see 2)	
Museo de Historia Natural.................(see 19)	

SLEEPING

Black Cat Hostel..........................23 D2	
Casa Azafran..............................(see 33)	
Casa Doña Mercedes........................24 C3	
Casa Jaguar...............................(see 18)	
Guest House El Puente.....................25 B3	
Hostal Don Diego..........................26 B3	
Miguel de Cervantes.......................(see 8)	
Pensión/Hotel Horiani.....................27 D2	

EATING

Blue Angel Video Café.....................28 B3	
Café El Cuartito..........................29 C4	
Café Baviera.............................30 C3	
Café La Luna.............................31 E4	
Casa Antigua.............................32 D3	
Casa Azafran.............................33 B2	
Casa Babylon.............................34 C3	
Las Orchideas...........................35 B2	
Palalife Klishe..........................36 C2	
Royal Paris..............................37 C2	
Sabor de la India........................38 B1	
Salón Tecún.............................(see 43)	
Utz Hua.................................39 D2	

DRINKING

Bajo La Luna.............................(see 31)	
Bari....................................40 C1	
Bohemio's Bar...........................41 D3	
La Parranda.............................42 C3	
Salón Tecún............................43 D3	

ENTERTAINMENT

Blue Angel Video Café....................(see 28)	
Spanish Society..........................44 C2	
Teatro Municipal.........................45 C1	
Teatro Roma.............................46 C1	

TRANSPORT

Taxi Stand..............................47 D3	

GUATEMALA

solitary lion. Outside the zoo on an island in the middle of 4a Calle stands the neoclassical **Templo de Minerva** (Map p137), built by dictator Estrada Cabrera to honor the Roman goddess of education and to inspire Guatemalans to new heights of learning. The **Mirador La Pedrera** (Map p137), a 3km (or US$4) taxi ride from the center, offers a fine view of the city.

Activities

HIKING

Volcán Tajumulco (4220m) is the highest point in Central America and a challenging two-day hike from Quetzaltenango. Volcán Santiaguito (2488m) and Volcán Santa María (3772m) can also be ascended. All of the following companies charge around US$40 for a two-day Tajumulco trip, US$15 for full-moon ascents of Santa María, US$70 for the three-day Quetzaltenango–Lago de Atitlán trek.

Adrenalina Tours (Map p139; ☎ 7761 4509; www .adrenalinatours.com; 13a Av, Zona 1, inside Pasaje Enríquez)

Kaqchikel Tours (Map p139; ☎ 5294 8828; www .kaqchikeltours.com; 7a Calle 15-36, Zona 1) Also does a challenging two-day hike right up close to the active Santiaguito.

Monte Verde Tours (Map p139; ☎ 7761 6105; www .monte-verdetours.com; 13a Av 8-34, Zona 1)

CYCLING

Cycling is a great way to explore the surrounding countryside or commute to Spanish class. Fuentes Georginas, San Andrés Xequl and the steam vents at Los Vahos (see p145) are all attainable day trips. **Vrisa Bookstore** (Map p139; 15a Av 3-64, Zona 1) rents mountain and town bikes for US$3.50 per day, US$9.50 per week.

Courses

DANCE & WEAVING

Tropica Latina (Map 000; ☎ 5892 8861; www.xelawho .com/tropicalatina; 5a Calle 12-24, Zona 1) This highly recommended dance school is the longest running in town, and gets top marks for its fun atmosphere and professionalism. Group and private salsa classes and private merengue classes are offered.

Asotrama (Map 000; ☎ 7765 8564; www.xelapages .com/asotrama; 3a Calle 10-56, Zona 1) This women's cooperative offers backstrap weaving classes and operates a fair-trade fabrics shop.

SPANISH

In recent years, Xela has become well known for its Spanish-language schools. Unlike Antigua, Xela is not overrun with foreigners, but it does have a small student social scene. **Xelapages** (www.xelapages.com/schools.htm), has information on many of the schools here.

Most of the city's Spanish schools participate in social-action programs with the local Quiché people and provide students with an opportunity to get involved. The standard price is US$110/125 per week for four/five hours of instruction per day, Monday to Friday, including room and board with a local family, or around US$80/95 per week without homestay. Some schools charge up to 20% more tuition during the high season (June through August), and many require nonrefundable registration fees, particularly when booking in advance from overseas. College students may be able to take classes for academic credit.

The following are among the many reputable schools:

Casa Xelajú (Map p137; ☎ 7761 5954; www.casaxelaju .com; Callejón 15 D13-02, Zona 1) One of the biggest, also offering classes in K'iche and college credits.

Celas Maya (Map p139; ☎ /fax 7761 4342; www.celas maya.edu.gt; 6a Calle 14-55, Zona 1) Set around a pleasant garden-courtyard; also offers classes in K'iche'.

Centro Bilingüe Amerindia (CBA; Map p137; ☎ 7771 8049; www.languageschool.com.gt; 12a Av 10-27, Zona 1) Classes in Mayan languages as well.

Centro de Estudios de Español Pop Wuj (Map p137; ☎ /fax 7761 8286; www.pop-wuj.org; 1a Calle 17-72, Zona 1) Pop Wuj's profits go to development projects in nearby villages, in which students can participate. The school also offers medical and social work specialist language programs.

El Nahual (Map p137; ☎ 7765 2098; www.languages elnahual.com; 27 Av 8-68, Zona 1) A bit out of town, but runs some excellent, grass roots community projects in which students are invited to participate, such as teaching classes for underprivileged kids and maintaining an organic community garden.

El Quetzal (Map p139; ☎ 7765 1085; www.xelawho .com/elquetzal; 10a Calle 10-29, Zona 1) One of the few indigenous-run businesses in town, plenty of activities and a reading room with over 300 books.

Escuela de Español Miguel de Cervantes (Map p139; ☎ 7765 5554; www.learn2speakspanish.com; 12a Av 8-31) Friendly female owner, intimate atmosphere, also has accommodation (p142).

Inepas (Map p139; Instituto de Estudios de Español y Participación en Ayuda Social; ☎ 765 1308; www

.inepas.org; 15a Av 4-59) Offers a range of cheap accommodations other than living with a family; also organizes worthy projects in which students are invited to participate.

Madre Tierra (Map p139; ☎ 7761 6105; www.madre -tierra.org; 13a Av 8-34, Zona 1) Plenty of activities; runs its own reforestation project; classes held in pretty courtyard in classic colonial house.

Mundo en Español (Map p139; ☎ 7761 3256; www .elmundoenespanol.org; 8a Av Calle B A-61, Zona 1) Over 17 years' experience, family atmosphere, gym, garden and accommodation on premises.

Proyecto Lingüístico Quetzalteco de Español (Map p137; ☎ /fax 763 1061; www.hermandad.com; 5a Calle 2-42, Zona 1) This very professional and politically minded school also runs the Escuela de la Montaña, a language school with a maximum enrollment of eight, on an organic coffee *finca* in the mountains near Xela; participation in local culture and volunteering are strongly encouraged.

Proyecto Lingüístico Santa Maria (Map p139; ☎ 7765 8136; 3a Calle 10-56, Zona 1) With a young staff and good atmosphere, it has had nonprofit status since 1984. Can organize volunteer work with Maya women's weaving cooperative. The director writes books on Spanish grammar and usage.

Utatlán Spanish School (Map p139; ☎ 7763 0446; www.xelapages.com/utatlan; Pasaje Enríquez, 12a Av 4-32, Zona 1) Young and energetic with plenty of parties and activities.

Volunteering

Xela has several organizations that need volunteers. The Asociación Hogar Nuevos Horizontes, La Escuela de la Calle and Red International are all organizations based in Quetzaltenango.

EntreMundos (Map p139; ☎ 7761 2179; www.entre mundos.org; El Espacio, 6a Calle 7-31, Zona 1) Apart from providing volunteer resources and matching volunteers with projects, this organization actively seeks volunteers for capacity building workshops for NGOs and to produce their bimonthly newspaper.

Tours

Adrenalina Tours (Map p139; ☎ 7761 4509; www.adrena linatours.com; Pasaje Enríquez, Zona 1) A professional, knowledgeable and amiable outfit providing a range of trips in the Xela area, including Zunil, Fuentes Georginas and little-visited parts of the department of Huehuetenango. Also offers shuttles around the country, international flights and personalized trips all over Central America.

Monte Verde Tours (Map p139; ☎ 7761 6105; www .monte-verdetours.com; 13a Av 8-34, Zona 1) Also offers tours in the Xela area, beach trips, ecotours and tours of local coffee farms, as well as shuttle buses and guided bike tours.

Festivals & Events

Xela Music Festival (late March or early April) Organized by the Alianza Francaise, this one- or two-day festival sees city streets blocked off, as local musicians play on five or six stages around the city center.

Feria de la Virgen del Rosario (Feria Centroamericana de Independencia; September 15-22) Xela's big annual party. Residents kick up their heels at a fairground on the city's perimeter, and there's plenty of entertainment at selected venues around town.

Juegos Florales Centroamericanos The prizes in this international Spanish-language literary competition hosted by the city are awarded at this time too.

Sleeping

All of the following are in Zona 1.

Casa Kaqchikel (Map p137; ☎ 7761 2628; 9a Calle 11-26; dm US$4, s/d US$5.50/10, with bathroom US$8/12) There's only a few rooms in this old wooden house, but they're all good value – big and comfortable. The superfriendly family who run the place can whip you up a Guatemalan meal, or you can use the kitchen.

Pensión/Hotel Horiani (Map p139; ☎ 7763 5228; 12a Av 2-23; s/d US$4/6) There's very little in the way of frills on offer here, but the small plain rooms upstairs set around a plant-filled patio have a certain charm to them. Enter from 2a Calle.

Posada San Andres (Map p137; 4 Calle D 12-41; www .guesthousesanandres.com; s/d US$4/7) Undergoing renovations at the time of writing, this old wooden house has spacious, bare rooms with shared bathrooms and kitchen access. A few sticks of furniture and some art on the walls make the place comfortable enough.

Hostal Don Diego (Map p139; ☎ 5511 3211; hostal dondiego@gmail.com; 6a Calle 15-12; dm US$4.50, s/d US$6/10) A beautiful little budget choice – rooms are OK, with parquetry floors and good firm beds. Kitchen access and a sunny courtyard are other bonuses. They offer reduced rates for weekly or monthly stays, with or without kitchen use.

Guest House El Puente (Map p139; ☎ 7765 4342; 15a Av 6-75; s/d US$5.50/8, with bathroom US$8/10) An intimate little place, it has five good-sized rooms, kitchen access and a grassy garden area. Discounts for longer stays keep the place filled with long-termers.

GUATEMALA

Casa Azafran (Map p139; ☎ 7763 0206; casababylon restauraneyhotel@yahoo.com; 15 Av A 3-33; s/d US$10/12, with bathroom US$14/20) A classic old house on a quiet street just out of the center. Each room is spacious, with two big firm beds, closets and cable TV. One has a fireplace.

Miguel de Cervantes (Map p139; ☎ 7765 5554; www .learn2speakspanish.com; 12a Av 8-31; s/d US$7/14) These basic but comfortable wood and concrete rooms are set around one of the cutest court-yards in Xela. When there's water pressure, the showers in the shared bathrooms rock.

Black Cat Hostel (Map p139; ☎ 5037 1871; black catxela@gmail.com; 13a Av 3-33; dm US$7; s/d US$11/17) Xela's newest hostel is a good deal and a great place if you're looking to meet up with other travelers. There's a sunny courtyard, a bar-restaurant and lounge-TV area. Rates include a big breakfast.

Casa Doña Mercedes (Map p139; ☎ 7765 4687; cnr 6a Calle & 14 Av; r US$20) Some of Xela's best looking budget rooms are on offer here at this newish little guest house in the heart of downtown. Rooms have shared bathrooms, but are oth-erwise extremely comfortable, with carpeted floors or wooden floorboards, cable TV and closets.

For long-term stays, an option is renting an apartment. Read all the fine print and know the terms for deposits, gas and electricity charges before plunking down cash.

Casa Jaguar (☎ 5446 3785; Pasaje Enríquez; r/apt per person per month US$131/266) Rents fully furnished apartments with cable TV and free gas for the first month. Also available are rooms with access to shared kitchen and bathroom facilities.

Eating

As with hotels, Quetzaltenango has a broad selection of places to eat. Cheapest are the food stalls around the small market to the east of the Casa de la Cultura, where snacks and substantial main-course plates are sold for US$1 or less. All of the following are in Zona 1.

GUATEMALAN & LATIN AMERICAN CUISINE
Blue Angel Video Café (Map p139; 7a Calle, Zona 1; snacks US$2-4; ☺ lunch & dinner) Economical café with excellent, healthy foods and an awesome tea selection – popular with language students.

Utz Hua (Map p139; cnr 12a Av & 3a Calle; meals US$3.50) Delicious, authentic Guatemalan and Quet-zalteco dishes for equally yummy prices. The restaurant is well (if slightly frantically) deco-rated, and it's worth stopping by to check out the indoor thatched roof, if nothing else.

Cubatenango (Map p137; 19a Av 2-06; mains US$4-6; ☺ breakfast, lunch & dinner Mon-Sat) Authentic Cuban food with a Miami twist is the go here – *ropa vieja* (shredded beef), *moros y cristianos* (black beans and rice) and *vaca frita* (fried beef). The *tostones* (fried, mashed, savory bananas) are worth the trip alone and they make a mean *mojito*.

INTERNATIONAL CUISINE
Café Q (Map p137; Diagonal 12 4-46; mains from US$3.50; ☺ 7-10pm Mon-Fri) The varied international flavors at Q's include interesting vegetarian options such as falafel, soy burgers and chick-pea soup.

Sabor de la India (Map p139; 2a Calle 15 A 2-34; mains US$4-6; ☺ lunch & dinner Tue-Sat, dinner Sun) Serves probably the most authentic Indian dishes in the country, whipped up by a friendly Indian-Guatemalan couple. Portions are huge and there are plenty of vegetarian options.

Las Orchideas (Map p139; 4a Calle 15-45; mains US$4-6; ☺ lunch & dinner Tue-Sat) Hanging out for some Thai food? This is the place. Green curry, *pad thai*, satay, oodles of noodles and sticky rice with papaya to round things out.

Salón Tecún (Map p139; Pasaje Enríquez; burgers, salads, sandwiches US$4-6; ☺ breakfast, lunch & dinner) On the west side of Parque Centroamérica, the Tecún, consistently Xela's busiest bar, serves good bar food including the best burgers in town.

Casa Antigua (Map p139; 12a Av 3-26; meals US$4-8; ☺ breakfast, lunch & dinner) An excellent, tranquil spot right in the middle of downtown. Sand-wiches are big, chunky affairs and there's plenty of steaks flame grilling out front.

Casa Babylon (Map p139; cnr 13a Av & 5a Calle; mains US$4-12; ☺ lunch & dinner Mon-Sat) With the widest menu in town, the Babylon is a travelers' fa-vorite. Dishes run from big, tasty sandwiches to Guatemalan classics such as *pepian* (stew) to more exotic fare such as fondue and Middle Eastern choices.

El Panorama (☎ 5319 3536; Map p137; 13a Av A; meals US$4-8; ☺ dinner Wed-Fri, lunch & dinner Sat & Sun) This Swiss owned restaurant (a 10-minute slog up the hill at the south end of town) does good set meals and raclette. The view is amazing and it's a romantic spot for that special night out.

Il Giardino (Map p137; 19a Callejón 8-07; mains US$5-9; ☺ lunch & dinner Wed-Mon) The best pizzas in town are made by the Italian-descended family that run this place. It's set around a big leafy indoor garden and offers pasta, steaks and good salads and sandwiches, too.

Royal Paris (☎ 7761 1942; Map p139; 14a Av A 3-06; meals from US$5; ⏰ lunch & dinner Tue-Sun) Xela's oldest French restaurant has some lovely cheesy steak dishes, cheap set lunches and live music on Friday and Saturday nights (reservations recommended).

Casa Azafran (Map p139; 15 Av A 3-33; mains from US$6) Serving up the most elaborate French food in town, this well-decorated, intimate restaurant is a romantic choice with some decadent options such as lobster tails on the menu.

CAFÉS
Coffee plays an important part in Xela's economy, and there are plenty of places where you can grab a cup.

Café La Luna (Map p139; 8a Av 4-11; snacks US$2; ⏰ 9:30am-9pm Mon-Fri, 4-9pm Sat & Sun) La Luna is a comfortable, relaxed place to hang out and eat a cake, salad or sandwich. The hot chocolate is the specialty – the coffee is so-so. Choose any of several rooms: décor is in similar vein to Café Baviera but the music is classical instead of jazz.

Café Baviera (Map p139; 5a Calle 13-14; dishes US$3-4; ⏰ 7am-8:30pm) This European-style café has good coffee, roasted on the premises, and is a decent place for breakfast or a snack (crepes, croissants, soups and salads). The wooden walls are hung with countless photos and clippings on Xela and international themes.

Café El Cuartito (Map p139; 13a Av 7-09; ⏰ 7am-midnight Wed-Mon) Xela's hippest café does a good range of snacks and juices, and coffee just about any way you want it. Weekends they often have DJs spinning laid-back tracks, and there's always art on the walls by local contemporary artists.

Drinking & Nightlife
The live music scene is particularly strong in Xela. For details on what's on, pick up a copy of *XelaWho* or check www.xelawho.com. All of the following are in Zona 1.

BARS & CLUBS
Salón Tecún (Map p139; Pasaje Enríquez; ⏰ 8am-1am) On the west side of Parque Centroamérica, and busy all day and night with a healthy crowd of Guatemalans and foreigners, the Tecún claims to be the country's longest-running bar (since 1935). Don't miss it.

Bajo La Luna (Map p139; 8a Av 4-11; ⏰ 8pm-1am Thu-Sat) An atmospheric wine and cheese bar set in a cellar with exposed beams. Liters of Chilean red go for US$6.

Pool & Beer (Map p137; 12a Av 10-21; ⏰ 5pm-midnight) An excellent place for some drinks and a few games of pool. At the time of writing, the tables hadn't been trashed and the cues were straight.

Bohemio's Bar (Map p139; 5a Calle 12-24; ⏰ 8pm-1am Tue-Sat, Zona 1) Some nights it's mellow, some nights it goes berserk, but this friendly little bar, a few steps away from the Central Park, is always worth a look in.

La Parranda (Map p139; cnr 6a Calle & 14a Av) This is the hottest place in town for dancing and drinking. On Wednesdays there are free salsa classes, other nights have guest DJs and drinks giveaways.

Bari (Map p139; 1a Calle 14-31; ⏰ 8pm-1am Thu-Sat) This little bar has live *trova*, pop and rock music Thursday to Saturday, and sells a good selection of wine and draft beers.

La Fonda del Ché (Map p137; 15a Av 7-43; ⏰ 7pm-1am Tue-Sat) *Trova* and other guitar music nightly.

Palalife Klishe (Map p139; 15a Av & 4 Calle; ⏰ 5pm-1am Tue-Sat) This 'open minded' disco-bar is always fun and attracts a mixed crowd, with good dance music, drinks specials and drag shows on Saturday nights.

Entertainment
Spanish Society (Map p139; cnr 4a Calle & 14a Av A, Zona 1) This cultural center hosts a women's theater group who stage monthly performances, and occasionally has events such as book launches and poetry readings.

Other recommendations:

Teatro Municipal (Map p139; 1a Calle) Cultural performances are presented at this beautiful venue.

Teatro Roma (Map p139; 14a Av A) Facing Teatro Municipal; sometimes screens interesting movies.

Blue Angel Video Café (www.xelawho.com/blueangel; Map p139; 7a Calle 15-79, Zona 1; US$1.30) Shows Hollywood videos nightly.

Getting There & Away
BUS
For 2nd-class buses, head out to the **Terminal Minerva** (Map p137; 7a Calle, Zona 3), a dusty, noisy, crowded yard in the west of town. Buses leave frequently for many highland destinations. Leaving or entering town, some buses make a stop east of the center at the *rotonda*, a traffic circle on Calz Independencia, marked by the

Monumento a la Marimba. Getting off here when you're coming into Xela saves the 10 or 15 minutes it will take your bus to cross town to Terminal Minerva.

First-class companies operating between Quetzaltenango and Guatemala City have their own terminals.

All the following buses depart from Terminal Minerva, unless otherwise indicated.

International
Ciudad Tecún Umán (Mexican border) (US$3.50, 3½ hours, 129km, hourly 5am-2pm)
El Carmen/Talismán (Mexican border) Take a bus to Coatepeque (US$2.50, two hours, every 30 minutes) and get a direct bus to El Carmen (US$2.50, two hours).
La Mesilla (Mexican border) (US$3, 3½ hours, 170km) Buses at 5am, 6am, 7am, 8am, 1pm & 4pm. Or bus to Huehuetenango and change there.

Domestic
Almolonga (for Los Vahos) (US$0.50, 15 minutes, 6km, every 15 minutes 5:30am-5pm) With a stop for additional passengers at the corner of 9a Av and 10a Calle.
Antigua (170km) Take any bus heading to Guatemala City via the Interamericana and change at Chimaltenango.
Chichicastenango (US$3, three hours, 94km) Buses at 5am, 6am, 9:30am, 10:45am, 11am, 1pm, 2pm and 3:30pm. If you don't get one of these, take a bus heading to Guatemala City by the Interamericana and change at Los Encuentros.
Cuatro Caminos (US$0.50, 30 minutes, 11km) Take any bus for Huehuetenango, Momostenango, Totonicapán, San Francisco El Alto etc.
Guatemala City Transportes Álamo (☎ 7763 5044; 14a Av 5-15, Zona 3) has seven Pullman buses (US$6, four to five hours, 205km) between 4:30am and 4:45pm; Líneas América (☎ 7761 4587; 7a Av 3-33, Zona 2) has six pullmans between 5:15am and 3:30pm; Transportes Galgos (☎ 7761 2248; Calle Rodolfo Robles 17-43, Zona 1) has five Pullmans between 3am and 3pm; Línea Dorada (☎ 7767 5198; cnr 12a Av & 5a Calle, Zona 1) has two 1st-class buses (US$8, 4am and 2:30pm). Each departs from their own terminals. Cheaper 2nd-class buses depart Terminal Minerva every 30 minutes between 3am and 4:30pm, but they make many stops and take longer.
Huehuetenango (US$2, two hours, 90km, every 30 minutes 5am-5:30pm)
Momostenango (US$1, 1¼ hours, 26km, every 30 minutes 6am-5pm)
Panajachel (US$2.50, 2½ hours, 90km) Buses at 5am, 6am, 8am, 10am, noon and 3pm. Or take any bus for Guatemala City via the Interamericana and change at Los Encuentros.

Retalhuleu (US$1.50, one hour, 46km, every 30 minutes 4:30am-6pm) Look for 'Reu' on the bus; 'Retalhuleu' won't be spelled out.
San Andrés Xecul (US$0.80, 40 minutes) Buses every hour or two, 6am to 3pm. Or take any bus to San Francisco El Alto or Totonicapán; get out at the Esso station at the Moreiria junction and flag a pickup.
San Francisco El Alto (US$0.60, one hour, 15km, roughly every 15 minutes 6am-6pm)
San Martín Sacatepéquez (San Martín Chile Verde) (US$0.80, 45 minutes, 22km) Various companies have buses that leave when full. Placards may say 'Colomba' or 'El Rincón.' Minibuses also serve this route.
Totonicapán (US$1, one hour, 22km, every 20 minutes 6am-5pm) Departing from the *rotonda* on Calz Independencia. Placards generally say 'Toto.'
Zunil (US$0.60, 20 minutes, 10km, every 30 minutes 7am-7pm) With an additional stop at the corner of 9a Av and 10a Calle, southeast of Parque Centroamérica.

SHUTTLE MINIBUS
Adrenalina Tours (p141) runs shuttle minibuses to many destinations including Guatemala City (US$30 per person), Antigua (US$25), Chichicastenango (US$15), Panajachel (US$15), and San Cristóbal Las Casas in Mexico (US$35). Monte Verde Tours (p141) offers the same runs for slightly cheaper prices.

Getting Around
Inguat has information on city bus routes. City buses charge US$0.15, doubling the fare after 7pm and on holidays. Taxis wait at the stand on the north end of Parque Centroamérica. Línea Dorada has a door-to-door shuttle service (US$3) for passengers getting their 4am departure. Cab fare between Terminal Minerva and the city center is around US$4.50.

AROUND QUETZALTENANGO (XELA)
The beautiful volcanic countryside around Quetzaltenango makes for exciting day trips. The natural steam baths at Los Vahos are primitive; the baths at Almolonga are basic, cheap and accessible; and the hot springs at Fuentes Georginas are idyllic.

Feast your eyes and soul on the wild church at San Andrés Xecul, hike to the shores of Laguna Chicabal from Xela or simply hop on a bus and explore the scores of traditional villages that pepper this region. Market days in surrounding towns include Sunday in Momostenango, Monday in Zunil, Tuesday and Saturday in Totonicapán and Friday in San Francisco El Alto.

Los Vahos

Hikers will enjoy a trip to the rough-and-ready sauna/steam baths at **Los Vahos** (The Vapors; admission US$3; 8am-6pm), about 3.5km from Parque Centroamérica. To get there take a bus headed for Almolonga and ask to get out at the road to Los Vahos, which is marked with a small sign: 'A Los Vahos.' From here it's a 2.3km uphill walk (around 1½ hours) to Los Vahos. The views are remarkable.

San Andrés Xecul

About 10km northwest of Xela is San Andrés Xecul, surrounded by fertile hills. This small town boasts perhaps the most bizarre **church** anywhere – technicolor saints, angels, flowers and climbing vines share space with whimsical tigers and monkeys on its shocking-yellow facade. The village has no visitor facilities.

The annual **festival** is held on November 29 and 30 – a good time to visit. The easiest way to get here is by taking any northbound bus from Xela and alighting at the Esso station at the Morería crossroads and hailing a pickup or walking the 3km uphill. Buses returning to Xela line up at the edge of the plaza and depart until about 5pm.

Zunil

pop 10,900 / elevation 2076m

Zunil is a pretty agricultural market town in a lush valley framed by steep hills and dominated by a towering volcano. As you approach from Quetzaltenango, you'll see it framed as if in a picture, with its white colonial church gleaming above the red-tiled and rusted-tin roofs of the low houses.

On the way to Zunil the road passes **Almolonga**, a vegetable-growing town 6km from Quetzaltenango. Just over 1km beyond Almolonga is **Los Baños**, an area with natural hot sulfur springs. Several little places along here have bathroom installations; most are decrepit, but if a cheap hot-water bathroom is your desire, you may want to stop. Tomblike enclosed concrete tubs rent for US$2 to US$3 per hour.

Zunil, founded in 1529 as Santa Catarina Zunil, is a typical Guatemalan highland town. The cultivated plots, divided by stone fences, are irrigated by canals; you'll see the indigenous farmers scooping water from the canals with a shovel-like instrument and throwing it over their plants. Women wash clothes near the river bridge, in pools of hot water that emerge from the rocks.

SIGHTS

Another attraction of Zunil is its particularly pretty **church**; the ornate facade, with eight pairs of serpentine columns, is echoed inside by a richly worked silver altar. On market day (Monday) the plaza in front of the church is bright with the predominantly red traditional garb of locals buying and selling goods.

Half a block downhill from the church plaza, the **Cooperativa Santa Ana** (7:30am-6pm) is a handicrafts cooperative in which over 500 local women participate. Handicrafts are displayed and sold here, and weaving lessons are offered.

While you're in Zunil, visit the image of **San Simón**, an effigy of a local Maya hero venerated as a (non-Catholic) saint. The effigy is moved each year to a different house; ask anyone where to find San Simón. You'll be charged a few quetzals to visit him and take pictures (see p114).

The **festival of San Simón** is held each year on October 28, after which the effigy is moved to a new house. The **festival of Santa Catarina Alejandrí**, official patron saint of Zunil, is celebrated on November 25. Almolonga celebrates its **annual fair** on June 27.

GETTING THERE & AWAY

From Zunil, which is 10km from Quetzaltenango, you can continue to Fuentes Georginas (8km), return to Quetzaltenango via the Cantel road (16km), or alternatively, take Hwy 9S down through lush countryside to El Zarco junction on the Carr al Pacífico. Buses depart Zunil for Xela from the main road beside the bridge.

Fuentes Georginas

This is the prettiest natural **spa** (admission US$2.50; 8am-5pm Mon-Sat, to 4pm Sun) in Guatemala. Here, pools of varying temperatures are fed by hot sulfur springs and framed by a high wall of tropical vegetation. Fans of Fuentes Georginas were dismayed when a massive landslide destroyed several structures (including the primary bathing pool) in 1998 and crushed the Greek goddess that previously gazed upon the pools. After restoration, spa regulars realized the landslide had opened a new vent.

As a result, the water is hotter than ever. Although the setting is intensely tropical, the mountain air keeps it deliciously cool all day.

GUATEMALA

The site has a restaurant and three sheltered picnic tables with cooking grills (bring your own fuel). Down the valley are seven rustic **cottages** (s/d/tr/q US$12/16/20/24), each with a shower, a barbecue area and a fireplace to ward off the mountain chill at night (wood and matches are provided; US$3.25 for extra wood). Included in the price of the cottages is access to the pools all day and night. Trails here lead to two nearby volcanoes: **Volcán Zunil** (three hours each way) and **Volcán Santo Tomás** (five hours each way). Going with a guide is essential. They're available (ask at the restaurant) for US$14 for either trip, whatever the number of people in the group.

GETTING THERE & AWAY

Take any bus to Zunil, where pickups wait to take you 8km up to the springs (30 minutes). Negotiate the price. They'll probably tell you it's US$4.50 round-trip, but when you arrive at the top they may say it's US$4.50 each way. If there are many people in the group, they may charge US$1 per person. Unless you want to walk back down the hill, arrange a time for the driver to return. Note that Monte Verde Tours and Adrenalina Tours (p141) in Quetzaltenango offer shuttle services directly here from Xela for US$5, including waiting time.

You can walk from Zunil to Fuentes Georginas in about two hours (8km uphill). Hitching is not good on the Fuentes Georginas access road. You might luck out on weekends.

If you're driving, walking or hitching, go uphill from Zunil's plaza to the Cantel road (about 60m), turn right and go downhill 100m to a road on the left marked 'Turicentro Fuentes Georginas, 8km.' This road (near the bus stop on the Quetzaltenango–Retalhuleu road – note that there are three different bus stops in Zunil) heads off into the mountains; the baths are 9km from Zunil's plaza.

San Francisco El Alto
pop 45,000 / elevation 2630m

High on a hilltop overlooking Quetzaltenango stands San Francisco El Alto, Guatemala's garment district. Every inch is jammed with vendors selling sweaters, socks, blankets, jeans and more. Bolts of cloth spill from overstuffed storefronts, and that is on the quiet days! On Friday the town explodes as the real market action kicks in. The large plaza, surrounded by the church and *municipalidad* and centered on a cupola-like *mirador* (lookout), is

covered in goods. Stalls crowd into neighboring streets, and the press of traffic is so great that a special system of one-way roads is established. Vehicles entering the town on market day must pay a small fee.

This is regarded as the country's biggest, most authentic market, but it's not nearly as heavy with handicrafts as are the markets in Chichicastenango and Antigua. Beware of pickpockets and stay alert.

Around mid-morning when the clouds roll away, panoramic views can be had throughout town, especially from the church roof. The caretaker will let you up.

Banco Reformador (2a Calle 2-64; ☉ 8:30am-7pm Mon-Fri, 9am-1pm Sat) changes US dollars and traveler's checks and has a Visa ATM.

San Francisco's big party is the **Fiesta de San Francisco de Asís**, celebrated around October 4 with traditional dances such as La Danza de Conquista and La Danza de los Monos.

Hotel Vista Hermosa (cnr 2a Calle & 3a Av; s/d with bathroom US$8/16) does indeed have beautiful views from its big, comfortable rooms.

For food, **El Manantial** (☎ 738 4373; 2a Calle 2-42; mains US$2.50-3), a couple of blocks below the plaza, is pleasant and clean, serving up steaks and a few *típica* dishes.

Buses to San Francisco leave Quetzaltenango (passing through Cuatro Caminos) frequently throughout the day (US$0.60, one hour). Because of San Francisco's one-way streets, you'll want to get off on 4a Av at the top of the hill (unless you like walking uphill) and walk towards the church. To go back, buses run downhill along 1a Av.

Momostenango
pop 28,000 / elevation 2200m

Beyond San Francisco El Alto, and 35km from Quetzaltenango, Momostenango is Guatemala's famous center for *chamarras* (thick, heavy woolen blankets). The villagers also make ponchos and other woolen garments. As you enter the plaza, you'll see signs inviting you to watch blankets being made and purchase the finished products. The best time to do this is market day, Sunday; haggle like mad. A basic good blanket costs around US$13, perhaps twice as much for an extra-heavy 'matrimonial.'

On market days, the streets will be thronged and so buses will often leave you on 3a Calle. It's about a five-minute walk to the plaza from here – follow the crowd or head towards the church spires.

Momostenango is also noted for its adherence to the ancient Maya calendar and traditional rites. Ceremonies coordinated with the important dates of the calendar take place in the hills about 2km west of the plaza. It's not easy to witness these rites, although try Takiliben May Wajshakib Batz (see below).

INFORMATION

Banrural (1a Calle, Zona 2; ☺ 9am-4pm Mon-Fri, to 1pm Sun), a block south of the plaza, changes US dollars and traveler's checks and has a Visa ATM.

The post office is across the park on the eastern corner. Medical services are available at the **hospital** (cnr 1a Calle & 3a Av) near the bus stop. The **Centro Cultural** (☺ 8am-6pm Mon-Fri, 8am-1pm & 2-5pm Sat) in the *municipalidad* building is good for tourist information.

SIGHTS & ACTIVITIES

Momostenango's **Los Riscos** (The Crags) are peculiar geological formations on the edge of town. The eroded pumice spires rise into the air like something from *Star Trek*. To get there, take the left heading downhill from the bus stop at the Artesanía Palecom; look for the sign that says 'Entrada.' At the first intersection, you'll see another sign hanging from a corner store reading 'A Los Riscos.' Cross the bridge and head uphill about 50m and take a right onto 2a Calle, continuing about 120m to the formations.

Takiliben May Wajshakib Batz (☎ 7736 5537; 3a Av A 6-85, Zona 3), just past the Texaco at the entrance to town, teaches classes in Maya ceremonies. Its director, Rigoberto Itzep Chanchavac, a Maya priest, does horoscopes (US$5) and private consultations and hosts ceremonial workshops. His **tuj** (traditional Maya sauna; per person US$10; ☺ 3-6pm Tue & Thu) requires advance bookings.

FESTIVALS & EVENTS

Picturesque **diablo (devil) dances** are held in the plaza a few times a year, notably on Christmas Eve and New Year's Eve. The homemade devil costumes can get quite campy and elaborate: all have masks and cardboard wings, and some go the whole hog with fake fur suits and heavily sequined outfits. Dance groups gather in the plaza with a five- to 13-piece band, drinking alcoholic refreshments during the breaks. For entertainment, they are at their best around 3pm, but the festivities go late into the night.

The annual fair, **Octava de Santiago**, is celebrated from July 28 to August 2.

SLEEPING & EATING

Accommodations are very basic.

Posada de Doña Pelagia (☎ 7736 5175; 2a Av A 2-88, Zona 1; s/d US$2/3) Very basic, door-bumps-bed type rooms set around a courtyard. They're good enough for a night.

Hospedaje y Comedor Paclom (cnr 2a Av & 1a Calle, Zona 2; d US$7) This serviceable *hospedaje*, a block uphill from the first plaza, has rooms facing a courtyard crammed with plants and birds.

Restaurante La Cascada (1a Calle 1-35, Zona 2; meals US$3; ☺ breakfast, lunch & dinner) A bright and clean upstairs eatery serving up good-value set meals. The food is simple and filling, and there are some good views of the church spires and surrounding hills.

GETTING THERE & AWAY

You can get buses to Momostenango from Quetzaltenango's Terminal Minerva (US$0.80, 1½ hours), or Cuatro Caminos, or San Francisco El Alto. Buses run about every half-hour, with the last one back to Quetzaltenango normally leaving Momos at 4:30pm.

Laguna Chicabal

This magical lake is nestled in a crater of the Volcán Chicabal (2900m). The 'Center of Maya-Mam Cosmovision,' it's an intensely sacred place and a hotbed for Maya ceremonies. Maya priests come from all over to make offerings here, especially around May 3. Visitors are definitely not welcome at this time. Do not visit Laguna Chicabal during the first week of May.

The lake is about a two-hour hike from **San Martín Chile Verde** (also known as San Martín Sacatepéquez), a friendly, interesting village about 25km from Xela and notable for the traditional dress worn by the village men. To get to the lake, head down from the highway toward town and look for the sign on your right (you can't miss it). Hike 45 minutes uphill through fields and past houses until you crest the hill. Continue hiking downhill for 15 minutes to the ranger station, where you pay a US$2.50 entrance fee. From here, it's another 30 minutes uphill to a *mirador* and then a whopping 615 steep steps down to the edge of the lake. Start early for the best visibility; clouds and mists envelop the volcano and crater by early afternoon.

GUATEMALA

The thick vegetation ringing the lake hides picnic tables and sublime campsites. Treat the lake with the utmost respect.

Xelajú buses leave Quetzaltenango every 30 minutes until 4pm for San Martín Chile Verde; hail a pickup to get back.

HUEHUETENANGO
pop 99,300 / elevation 1902m

Mostly a stopping-off point for more interesting places, Huehue (*way*-way) offers few charms of its own, but some people do love it for its true Guatemalan character. Either way, there are enough eating and sleeping options here to keep you happy, and the sight of the Cuchumatanes mountain range (highest in Central America) in the background makes for some striking scenery.

The lively *indígena* market is filled daily with traders who come down from surrounding villages. Surprisingly, the market area is about the only place you'll see traditional costumes in this town, as most of its citizens are ladinos wearing modern clothes. Coffee growing, mining, sheep raising, light manufacturing and agriculture are the region's main activities.

For travelers, Huehue is usually a leg on the journey to or from Mexico – the logical place to spend your first night in Guatemala. The town is also the perfect staging area for forays deeper into the Cuchumatanes or through the highlands on back roads.

Orientation & Information

The town center is 4km northeast of the Interamericana Hwy, and the bus station is off the road linking the two, about 2km from each. Almost every service of interest to tourists is in Zona 1, within a few blocks of Parque Central.

For city buses from the bus station to the town center, leave the east side of the bus station through the gap between the Díaz Álvarez and Transportes Fronterizos offices. During hours of darkness until 11pm and after 2am, 'Centro' buses (US$0.40) go intermittently from the street outside; in daylight hours, cross this street and walk through the covered market opposite to a second street, where 'Centro' buses (US$0.20) depart every few minutes. To return to the bus station from the center, catch the buses outside Barbería Wilson (6a Av 2-22). A taxi between the bus terminal and town center costs US$4.

Banrural (cnr 6a Av & 3a Calle; 9am-7pm Mon-Fri, to 1pm Sat) and **Corpobanco** (cnr 6a Av & 3a Calle; 8:30am-7pm Mon-Fri, to 12:30pm Sat) both change US dollars and traveler's checks. There are Visa ATMs at Bancafé and Banco Industrial, a block further north.

The **post office** (2a Calle 3-54; 8:30am-5:30pm Mon-Fri, 9am-1pm Sat) is half a block northeast of the parque.

Génesis Internet (2a Calle 6-37; 8:30am-1pm & 3-7pm Mon-Sat) and **Interhuehue** (3a Calle 6-65B; 9am-12:30pm & 2-6pm) charge US$0.60 per hour for internet access.

The **Mexican Consulate** (5a Av 4-11; 9am-noon & 3-5pm Mon-Fri) is in the same building as the Farmacia del Cid.

Sights & Activities
PARQUE CENTRAL
Huehuetenango's main plaza is shaded by old trees and surrounded by the town's imposing buildings: the *municipalidad* (with its band shell on the upper floor) and the huge colonial church. The plaza has its own little relief map of Huehuetenango Department.

ZACULEU
With ravines on three sides, Zaculeu ('White Earth' in the Mam language), a late post-Classic religious center, occupies a strategic defensive location that served its Mam Maya inhabitants well. It finally failed, however, in 1525 when Gonzalo de Alvarado and his conquistadors laid siege to the site for two months. It was starvation that ultimately defeated the Mam.

The parklike **Zaculeu archaeological zone** (admission US$4.50; 8am-6pm), about 200-sq-meters, is 4km west of Huehuetenango's main plaza. Cold soft drinks and snacks are available. A small museum at the site holds, among other things, skulls and items found in a tomb beneath Estructura 1, the tallest structure at the site.

Restoration by the United Fruit Company in the 1940s has left Zaculeu's pyramids, ball courts and ceremonial platforms covered by a thick coat of graying plaster. Many of the restoration methods were not authentic to the buildings, but the work goes further than others in making the site look as it might have done to the Mam priests and worshipers when it was still an active religious center. What is missing, however, is the painted decoration, which was applied to the wet plaster

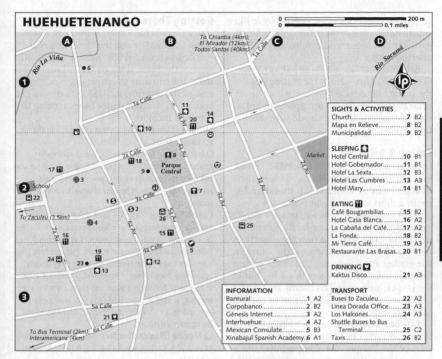

HUEHUETENANGO

0 ——————— 200 m
0 ——————— 0.1 miles

To Chiantla (4km);
El Mirador (12km);
Todos Santos (40km)

Rio La Viña

Rio Sacumá

SIGHTS & ACTIVITIES
Church.........................7 B2
Mapa en Relieve.........8 B2
Municipalidad.............9 B2

SLEEPING
Hotel Central.............10 B1
Hotel Gobernador......11 B1
Hotel La Sexta...........12 B3
Hotel Las Cumbres.....13 A3
Hotel Mary................14 B1

EATING
Café Bougambilias......15 B2
Hotel Casa Blanca......16 A2
La Cabaña del Café.....17 A2
La Fonda...................18 B2
Mi Tierra Café............19 A3
Restaurante Las Brasas....20 B1

DRINKING
Kaktus Disco..............21 A3

INFORMATION
Banrural.....................1 A2
Corpobanco................2 B2
Génesis Internet..........3 A2
Interhuehue................4 A2
Mexican Consulate.......5 B3
Xinabajul Spanish Academy.6 A1

TRANSPORT
Buses to Zaculeu........22 A2
Linea Dorada Office.....23 A3
Los Halcones..............24 A3
Shuttle Buses to Bus
    Terminal.................25 C2
Taxis.........................26 B2

Parque
Central

Market

School

To Zaculeu (3.5km)

To Bus Terminal (2km);
Interamericana (4km)

as in frescoes. The buildings show a great deal of Mexican influence, and were probably designed and built originally with little innovation.

Buses to Zaculeu (US$0.50, 20 minutes) leave about every 30 minutes, 7am to 6pm, from in front of the school at the corner of 2a Calle and 7a Av. A taxi from the town center costs US$8 one-way (US$10 from the bus station). One hour is plenty of time to look round the site and museum.

EL MIRADOR
This is a lookout point in the Cuchumatanes overlooking Huehuetenango, 12km from town (one hour by bus). On a sunny day it offers great views of the entire region and many volcanoes. A beautiful poem, *A Los Cuchumatanes*, is mounted on plaques here. Any bus from Huehue heading for Todos Santos, Soloma or Barillas comes past here.

Courses
Xinabajul Spanish Academy (☎ /fax 7764 1518; 6a Av 0-69) Offers one-to-one Spanish courses and homestays with local families.

Festivals & Events
Fiestas Julias (July 13-20) This special event honors La Virgen del Carmen, Huehue's patron saint.
Fiestas de Concepción (December 5-6) Honoring the Virgen de Concepción.

Sleeping
Hotel Central (☎ 7764 1202; 5a Av 1-33; s/d US$4/8) This rough-and-ready little number might be to your liking. Rooms are simple, large and plain. Bathrooms are downstairs. The pillared wooden interior balcony gives the place a sliver of charm and it sure is central.

Hotel Gobernador (☎ /fax 7764 1197; 4a Av 1-45; s/d US$5/7, with bathroom US$7/10) A little maze of rooms (don't get lost!), some much better than others – check your bed for spongability factor and your window for openability and you should be happy.

Hotel Las Cumbres (☎ 7764 1189; 4a Calle 6-83; s/d US$6/8, with bathroom US$8/12) You're definitely getting what you pay for here – concrete boxes with a weird smell. Front rooms get plenty of street noise.

Hotel La Sexta (☎ 7764 1488; 6a Av 4-29; s/d with bathroom US$14/17; P) Judging by the parking-

GUATEMALA

garage exterior, this place doesn't look like much, but it's one of the better deals in town, even if the bathrooms do look like improvized afterthoughts.

Hotel Mary (☎ 7764 1618; 2a Calle 3-52; s/d with bathroom US$14/17) This is really the cutting edge of the budget hotel payoff – you can have clean, central, spacious or well equipped, but not all four. Grungy rooms and an odd smell are the only problems here.

Eating & Drinking

La Cabaña del Café (2a Calle 6-50; dishes US$2-3; ☺ 8am-9pm) Huehue's best coffee (and donuts, incidentally) can be found in this imitation log cabin a short walk from the plaza.

Hotel Casa Blanca (7a Av 3-41; set lunch US$2.50; ☺ breakfast, lunch & dinner) For lovely surroundings, you can't beat the two restaurants at this classy hotel, one indoors, the other in the garden. Breakfasts cost US$3 to US$5 (on Sunday, from 8am to 11am, it's a big buffet for US$4), burgers and croissants are around US$3, and steaks (try filet mignon or cordon bleu) are around US$6.

Café Bougambilias (5a Av; breakfast US$3) One of three *comedores* in a line along the southern part of the Parque, the Bougambilias has a team of busy cooks preparing food on the ground floor, while the two upper floors have tables with views over the park and plenty of fresh air. It's good for all meals, with large serves of straightforward food.

Mi Tierra Café (4a Calle 6-46; mains US$3-5; ☺ breakfast, lunch & dinner; ☒) This is an informal café-restaurant serving good home-made soups and burgers. The cooks also take a good crack at some international dishes, muffins and a range of other goodies. Good, cheap and filling set lunches are available.

La Fonda (2a Calle 5-35; mains US$3-5; ☺ breakfast, lunch & dinner) A few steps from Parque Central, this clean, reliable place serves varied Guatemalan and international fare including good-value pizzas.

Restaurante Las Brasas (4a Av 1-36; mains US$5-8; ☺ breakfast, lunch & dinner) Half a block from Parque Central, this is one of Huehue's best restaurants. With a good combination of steaks and Chinese on the menu, it should be pushing multiple buttons.

Kaktus Disco (6a Calle 6-38; ☺ 9pm-late Fri & Sat) There's not a whole lot going on in the Center, nightlife-wise. This little disco is about your best bet afterhours.

Getting There & Away

Línea Dorada has a central **office** (☎ 7764 1617; 4a Calle 6-62, Zona 1) inside the Hotel Imperial.

The bus terminal is in Zona 4, 2km southwest of the plaza along 6a Calle. Local buses make the trip from the street one block to the east of the terminal for US$0.40, or you can take a taxi. Long-distance buses serving this terminal include:

Antigua (230km) Take a Guatemala City bus and change at Chimaltenango.

Cobán (142km) No direct service; take a minibus to Aguacatán, change there for Sacapulas, there for Uspantán and there for Cobán. The road is paved up to Uspantán and the entire trip could be done in seven hours with good connections.

Cuatro Caminos (US$2, 1½ hours, 77km) Take any bus heading for Guatemala City or Quetzaltenango.

Guatemala City (five hours, 266km) Los Halcones Pullman buses (US$8) leave at 4:30am, 7am and 2pm from their town-center terminal on 7a Av; Línea Dorada buses leave from in front of the Hotel California opposite the terminal (US$10) at 2:30pm and 11pm. From the main terminal, around 20 buses (US$4 to US$6) leave between 2am and 4pm by Transportes El Condor, Díaz Álvarez and Transportes Velásquez.

La Mesilla (Mexican border) (US$2, two hours, 84km) At least 20 buses between 5:45am and 6:30pm, by various companies.

Nebaj (68km) Take a bus to Sacapulas, or a bus to Aguacatán and a pickup on Sacapulas, then another bus from Sacapulas to Nebaj.

Panajachel (159km) Take a Guatemala City bus and change at Los Encuentros.

Quetzaltenango (US$2, two hours, 90km) At least 14 buses between 6am and 2:30pm, by various companies.

Sacapulas (US$2, 2½ hours, 42km) Buses at 11:30am (Rutas García) and 12:45pm (Transportes Rivas).

Soloma (US$3, three hours, 70km) About 16 buses daily between 2am and 10pm by Transportes Josué and Autobuses del Norte.

Todos Santos Cuchumatán (US$3, three hours, 40km) Buses at around 3:45am, 5:30am, 11:30am, 12:45pm, 1:30pm, 1:45pm, 2pm, 2:45pm and 3:45pm by the Flor de María, Mendoza, Pérez, Todosanterita, Concepcionerita and Chicoyera companies; some buses do not run Saturday.

AROUND HUEHUETENANGO
Todos Santos Cuchumatán
pop 3500 / elevation 2450m

Way up in the highlands, Todos Santos is as raw as Guatemalan village life gets – dramatic mountain scenery, mud streets, beans and tortillas and everything shut by 9pm. There are a couple of language schools operating here and this is the end point for the spectacular hike from Nebaj. Hiking is also good in the local hills. Saturday is market day, with a smaller market on Wednesday.

The post office and **Banrural** (⊗ 8:30am-5pm Mon-Fri, 8am-noon Sat) are on the central plaza. The bank changes US dollars and traveler's checks.

Todos Santos Internet (⊗ 9am-9pm), 30m off the main street, 400m back toward Huehue from the church, charges US$1.60 per hour for internet access.

If you're coming to Todos Santos in winter, bring warm clothes.

COURSES
Todos Santos' two language schools are controlled by villagers and make major contributions to community projects – funding a library, medicines, school materials, and scholarships for village kids to go to high school in Huehue.

Academia Hispano Maya (www.hispanomaya.org/)
Opposite Hotelito Todos Santos.

Nuevo Amanecer (escuela_linguistica@yahoo.com)
Down the main street 150m, opposite the church.

The standard weekly price for 25 hours' one-on-one Spanish tuition, with lodging and meals in a village home, is US$115. Included are guided walks, movies, seminars on local life and issues, and saunas. All three schools also offer classes in Mam and in Maya weaving (weaving costs around US$1 per hour or US$35 for a week's course). Individual language classes cost US$4 per hour. The schools can put you in touch with volunteer work in reforestation and English teaching.

FESTIVALS & EVENTS
Todos Santos is famous for the annual horse races held on **El Día de Todos los Santos** (November 1), the culmination of a week of festivities and an all-night male dancing and *aguardiente* (sugarcane liquor) drinking spree on the eve of the races. Traditional foods are served throughout the day, and there are mask dances.

SLEEPING & EATING
Hotel Casa Familiar (☎ 7783 0656; s/d US$4/8) The simple wooden rooms here are far from luxurious, but the place is run by a friendly family and there are plenty of extra blankets on hand. The rooms here are clean with windows re-

vealing fine views. The hotel also has a sauna and a restaurant where chicken dishes cost around US$3, or *mosh* (porridge), granola and banana costs US$2.

Hotelito Todos Santos (☎ 7783 0603; s/d with bathroom US$8/12) Along a side street that goes off to the left a few meters up the hill beside the plaza, this has Todos Santos' most comfortable rooms – bare but clean with tile floors and firm beds. Three of the four rooms with a bathroom open onto the street, separate from the main part of the hotel upstairs. The hotel has a casual café, sinks for washing clothes, and hot water.

You can arrange **rooms with local families** (per person US$2-2.50, with three meals US$4.50) through the language schools irrespective of whether you're studying. You'll get your own bedroom, and share the bathroom and meals with the family. A week's full board should cost US$25.

Comedor Martita (meals around US$2.25) This simple family-run *comedor*, opposite Hotel Mam, serves the best food in town, prepared with fresh ingredients by friendly hosts. You walk through the kitchen to get to the eating area, which has a nice view over the town and valley. A typical meal might be boiled chicken, rice, vegetables, beans, a *refresco* (soft drink) and coffee.

Restaurante Cuchumatlan (meals US$2-8) Todos Santos' most formal restaurant is nothing flash, but they take a good stab at pizzas, stir-fries and curries. It's also the only place in town you'd really want to have a beer, and there's a good selection of used books on sale.

ENTERTAINMENT
All the language schools show movies on Guatemalan, Maya and Latin American themes in the evening, with a small charge (usually about US$0.80) for nonstudents. The English-language documentaries *Todos Santos* and *Todos Santos: The Survivors*, made in the 1980s by Olivia Carrescia, are particularly fascinating to see here on the spot. They focus on the traditional life of Todos Santos and of the devastation and terror of the civil war, when, by some accounts, 2000 people were killed in the area.

GETTING THERE & AWAY
Half a dozen buses leave for Huehuetenango (US$3, three hours) between 4:45am and 6:30am, then usually three others between

GUATEMALA

GUATEMALA

LA MESILLA & THE MEXICAN BORDER

Four kilometers separate the Mexican and Guatemalan immigration posts at La Mesilla and Ciudad Cuauhtémoc, and you'll have to drive, walk, hitch or take a collective taxi (US$0.80) between them. The strip in La Mesilla leading to the border post has a variety of services, including a police station, post office and a Banrural.

Money changers at the border give a good rate if you're exchanging your dollars for their pesos or quetzals, a terrible one if you want dollars for your pesos or quetzals.

If you get marooned in La Mesilla, try **Hotel Mily's** (d US$15), which has rooms with fan, cable TV and private hot-water bathroom; bargaining may be in order. Further down the hill is the superbasic **Hotel El Pobre Simón** (r per person US$2).

Good onward connections are available from the border post east to Huehuetenango and northwest to Comitán.

See p69 for information on crossing the border from Mexico.

---

noon and 1pm. Daily buses head northwest to Concepción Huista, San Antonio Huista and Jacaltenango. Times are erratic, but the 5am departure is fairly reliable.

East Toward Cobán

Always inspiring, the road from Huehuetenango to Cobán is rarely traveled and often rugged. Starting early and with several transfers, you can make the 150km trip in one day. It's well worth it for the views of highland life along the way. Adventurous types craving more can continue the odyssey via the Cobán to Poptún route.

Starting high in the Cuchumatanes mountains, you climb out of Huehuetenango en route to **Aguacatán**, from where you'll have panoramic views of pine-covered slopes and fertile valleys below. The road then snakes down through the Río Blanco valley to **Sacapulas**, along the Río Negro. This makes a good stopover, but if you left early you can certainly make it to Cobán in one day. For more on the eastward continuation of this route, see Sacapulas to Cobán (p134).

THE PACIFIC SLOPE

Divided from the highlands by a chain of volcanoes, the flatlands that run down to the Pacific are known universally as La Costa. It's a sultry region – hot and wet or hot and dry, depending on the time of year, with rich volcanic soil good for growing coffee at higher elevations, and palm oil seeds and sugarcane lower down.

Archaeologically, the big draws here are Abaj Takalik and the sculptures left by

pre-Olmec civilizations around Santa Lucía Cotzumalguapa

The culture is overwhelmingly ladino, and even the biggest towns are humble affairs, with low-rise wooden or concrete houses and the occasional palm-thatched roof.

Guatemalan beach tourism is seriously underdeveloped. Monterrico is the only real contender in this field, helped along by a nature reserve protecting mangroves and their inhabitants. Almost every town on the beach has places to stay, although more often than not they're very basic affairs. Sipacate gets the best waves and is slowly developing as a surf resort, although serious surfers find much more joy in Mexico or El Salvador.

RETALHULEU

pop 42,000 / elevation 240m

Arriving at the bus station in Retalhuleu or Reu (ray-oo) as it's known to most Guatemalans, you're pretty much guaranteed to be underwhelmed. The neighborhood's a tawdry affair, packed out with dilapidated wooden cantinas and street vendors.

The town center, just five blocks away, is like another world – a majestic, palm-filled plaza, surrounded by some fine old buildings. Even the city police get in on the act, hanging plants outside their headquarters.

On the outskirts are the homes of wealthy plantation owners, impressive weekend getaways and the gated communities that are springing up all over the country.

The real reason most people visit the town is for access to the Abaj Takalik site, but if you're up for some serious down-time, a couple of world-class fun parks are just down the road.

Orientation & Information

The town center is 4km southwest of the Carr al Pacífico, along Calz las Palmas, a grand boulevard lined with towering palms. The **bus terminal** (10a Calle btwn 7a & 8a Avs) is northeast of the plaza. To find the plaza, look for the twin church towers and walk toward them.

There is no official tourist office, but people in the *municipalidad*, on 6a Av facing the east side of the church, do their best to help.

Banco Industrial (cnr 6a Calle & 5a Av; ☺ 9am-7pm Mon-Fri, 10am-2pm Sat) and **Banco Occidente** (cnr 6a Calle & 6a Av) change US dollars and traveler's checks, and give cash advances on Visa cards. Banco Industrial has a Visa ATM. **Banco Agromercantil** (5a Av), on the plaza, changes US dollars and traveler's checks and has a MasterCard ATM.

Internet (cnr 5a Calle & 6a Av; per hr US$0.80) provides internet access.

Sights & Activities

The **Museo de Arqueología y Etnología** (6a Av 5-68; admission US$1.30; ☺ 8am-5:30pm Tue-Sat) is a small museum with archaeological relics. Upstairs are historical photos and a mural showing the locations of 33 archaeological sites around Retalhuleu.

You can **swim** (admission US$1.30) at Siboney Hotel (out on the Carr al Pacífico) even if you're not staying there.

Sleeping

Hotel América (☎ 7771 1154; 8a Av 9-32, Zona 1; s/d with bathroom US$11/15) A trusty budget option just down the street from the bus terminal, the América has spotless rooms with fan and TV.

Hotel Genesis (☎ 7771 2855; 6a Calle 6-27, Zona 1; s/d with bathroom US$15/28; 🖳) A good-value hotel sporting plenty of homely features (but not so many windows) and an excellent, central location.

Posada Don José (☎ 7771 0180; posadadonjose@hotmail.com; 5a Calle 3-67, Zona 1; s/d US$20/26; 🅿 🖳 🖳) A beautiful colonial-style hotel built around a huge swimming pool. Swan dives from the top balcony are tempting, but unwise. Rooms are spacious and comfortable, if a bit dated.

Eating & Drinking

Reu seems to be slightly obsessed by pizza – 5a Av north of the plaza is almost wall-to-wall pizzerias.

Cafetería La Luna (5a Calle 4-97; lunch with drink US$2.90; ☺ breakfast, lunch & dinner) Opposite the west corner of the plaza, this is a town favorite for simple but filling meals in a low-key environment.

Lo de Chaz (5a Calle 4-65; mains US$3-4; ☺ breakfast, lunch & dinner) A simple place, right off the plaza, serving up good breakfasts, icy beer, soups, snacks and seafood.

CROSSING INTO MEXICO

Getting to Ciudad Hidalgo (Mexico) via Ciudad Tecún Umán (Guatemala)

This is the better and busier of the two Pacific Slope border crossings; a bridge links Ciudad Tecún Umán with Ciudad Hidalgo. The border is open 24 hours, and banks change US dollars and traveler's checks. Several basic hotels and restaurants are available, but there's no real point in lingering here.

Minibuses and buses depart until about 6pm along the Carr al Pacífico to **Coatepeque, Retalhuleu, Mazatenango, Escuintla** and **Guatemala City**. Direct buses to **Quetzaltenango** (US$3.50, 3½ hours) leave until about 2pm. If you don't find a bus to your destination, take one to Coatepeque or, better, Retalhuleu, and change buses there. On the Mexican side, buses run from Ciudad Hidalgo to the city of **Tapachula** (US$1.50, 45 minutes, every 20 minutes from 7am to 7:30pm).

Getting to Talismán (Mexico) via El Carmen (Guatemala)

A bridge across the Río Suchiate connects El Carmen with Talismán. The border is open 24 hours. It's generally easier and more convenient to cross at Tecún Umán. There are few services at El Carmen, and those are very basic. Most buses between here and the rest of Guatemala go via **Ciudad Tecún Umán**, 39km south, then along the Carr al Pacífico through **Coatepeque, Retalhuleu** and **Escuintla**. On the way to Ciudad Tecún Umán most stop at **Malacatán** on the road to San Marcos and Quetzaltenango, so you could try looking for a bus to **Quetzaltenango** there, but it's more dependable to change at **Coatepeque** (US$2, two hours from El Carmen) or Retalhuleu.

On the Mexican side, minibuses run frequently between Talismán and **Tapachula** (US$1, 30 minutes) up till about 10pm.

Bar La Carreta (5a Calle 4-50) For cocktails, check out this bar, next to Hotel Astor.

Flamingo Disco (4a Av & 5a Calle A; ☺ Wed-Sat 10pm-1am) Reu's biggest disco really gets going on Friday, but Saturday is a good bet too.

Getting There & Away

Most buses traveling along the Carr al Pacífico detour into Reu. Departures include the following:

Champerico (US$0.60, one hour, 38km) Buses every few minutes 6am-7pm.

Ciudad Tecún Umán (US$2, 1½ hours, 78km, buses every 20 minutes 5am-10pm)

Guatemala City (US$6, three hour, 196km, buses every 15 minutes 2am-8:30pm)

Quetzaltenango (US$1.50, one hour, 46km, buses every 30 minutes 4am-6pm)

Santa Lucía Cotzumalguapa (US$2.50, two hours, 97km) Some Escuintla or Guatemala City-bound buses might drop you at Santa Lucía; otherwise get a bus to Mazatenango ('Mazate') and change there.

Local buses go to El Asintal (for getting to Abaj Takalik).

ABAJ TAKALIK

The active archaeological dig at Abaj Takalik (ah-*bah*-tah-kah-*leek*, Quiché for 'standing stone') is 30km west of Retalhuleu. Large 'Olmecoid' stone heads discovered here date the site as one of the earliest in the Maya realm. The site has yet to be restored and prettified, so don't expect a Chichén Itzá or Tikal. But if you want to see archaeology as it's done, pay a visit. This site is believed to be one of the few places where the Olmec and Maya lived together.

To reach Abaj Takalik by public transportation, catch a bus from Retalhuleu to El Asintal (US$0.25, 30 minutes), which is 12km northwest of Reu and 5km north of the Carr al Pacífico (Hwy CA-2). The buses leave from a bus station on 5a Av A, 800m southwest of Reu plaza, about every half-hour between 6am to 6pm. Pickups at El Asintal provide transportation on to Abaj Takalik, 4km further by paved road. You'll be shown around by a volunteer guide, whom you will probably want to tip. You can also visit Abaj Takalik on tours from Quetzaltenango (p141).

CHAMPERICO

The most accessible beach from Xela, Champerico isn't a bad place for a quick dip, although the rubbish-strewn sand and heavy undertow are definite turn offs. It's a good place to avoid on weekends when the place packs out, but midweek is much mellower. A string of beachfront *comedores* serve up good-value seafood dishes.

Beware of strong waves and an undertow if you go in the ocean, and stay in the main, central part of the beach. If you stray too far in either direction you put yourself at risk from impoverished, potentially desperate shack dwellers who live toward the ends of the beach. Tourists have been victims of violent armed robberies here. Most beachgoers come on day trips, but there are several cheap hotels and restaurants: **Hotel Neptuno** (☎ 7773 7206; s/d US$6/8), on the beachfront, is the best bet. The last bus back to Retalhuleu goes about 6:30pm.

SANTA LUCÍA COTZUMALGUAPA

pop 26,500 / elevation 356m

A very ordinary coastal town, Santa Lucía stretches haphazardly over a couple of hills. The pace is sleepy and there's no real reason to be here, except to check out the remarkable archaeological sites outside of town, where huge, severe stone heads sit nestled among sugar plantations.

The local people are descended from the Pipil, an indigenous culture known to have historic, linguistic and cultural links with the Náhuatl-speaking peoples of central Mexico. During early Classic times, the Pipil grew cacao, the currency of the time. They were obsessed with the Maya-Aztec ball game, and with the rites and mysteries of death. Pipil art, unlike the flowery, almost romantic Maya style, is cold and severe, but it's finely done. Just how these 'Mexicans' ended up in the midst of Maya territory remains unexplained.

Orientation & Information

Santa Lucía Cotzumalguapa is northwest of the Carr al Pacífico. In its main square, several blocks from the highway, are copies of some of the region's famous carved stones. The town has a few basic hotels and restaurants.

The main archaeological sites to visit are Bilbao, a *finca* right on the outskirts of town; Finca El Baúl, a large plantation further from town, at which there are two sites (an interesting hilltop site and the *finca* headquarters); and Finca Las Ilusiones, which has collected most of its findings into a museum near the *finca* headquarters.

Taxi drivers in Santa Lucía's main square will take you round all three sites for about US$25 without too much haggling, although you could do better. In this hot and muggy climate, riding at least part of the way is a very good idea. If you do it all on foot and by bus, pack a lunch; the hilltop site at El Baúl is perfect for a picnic.

Banco Industrial (cnr 4a Av & 4a Calle), a block north of the park, changes US dollars and traveler's checks and has a Visa ATM.

Sights & Activities
BILBAO
This ceremonial center flourished about AD 600. Plows have unearthed (and damaged) hundreds of carved stones during the last few centuries; thieves have carted off many others. In 1880 many of the best stones were removed to museums abroad, including nine to the Dahlia Museum in Berlin.

Known locally as simply *Las Piedras* (The Stones), this site actually consists of several sites deep within a sugarcane *finca*. To get there you leave town northward on the road passing Iglesia El Calvario. From the intersection past the church, go 2.7km to a fork in the road just beyond a bridge; the fork is marked by a sign saying 'Los Tarros.' Take the right-hand fork, passing a settlement called Colonia Maya on your right. After you have gone 1.5km from the Los Tarros sign, a dirt track crosses the road: turn right here, between two concrete posts. Ahead now is a low mound topped by three large trees: this is the **hilltop site**. After about 250m fork right between two more identical concrete posts, and follow this track round in front of the mound to its end after some 150m, and take the path up on to the mound, which is actually a great ruined temple platform that has not been restored.

Although some stones are badly worn, others bear Mexican-style circular date glyphs and more mysterious patterns that resemble those used by people along the Gulf Coast of Mexico near Villahermosa.

To continue to El Baúl, backtrack to where you turned right just beyond El Calvario church. Buses to El Baúl pass this point every few hours; you can also hitch. If driving, you'll have to return to the town center along 4a Av and come back out on 3a Av, as these roads are one-way.

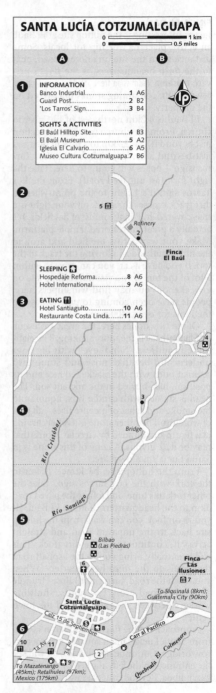

SANTA LUCÍA COTZUMALGUAPA

0 —————— 1 km
0 —————— 0.5 miles

INFORMATION
Banco Industrial..........................1 A6
Guard Post..................................2 B2
'Los Tarros' Sign........................3 B4

SIGHTS & ACTIVITIES
El Baúl Hilltop Site.....................4 B3
El Baúl Museum...........................5 A2
Iglesia El Calvario.......................6 A5
Museo Cultura Cotzumalguapa.7 B6

SLEEPING
Hospedaje Reforma.....................8 A6
Hotel International.......................9 A6

EATING
Hotel Santiaguito......................10 A6
Restaurante Costa Linda........11 A6

GUATEMALA

FINCA EL BAÚL

Just as interesting is the hilltop site at El Baúl, an active place of worship for locals. Some distance from the site on another road, next to the *finca* headquarters, is the *finca's* private **museum** (admission free; ☑ 8am-4pm Mon-Fri, 8am-noon Sat), containing stones uncovered on the property.

El Baúl is 4.2km northwest of El Calvario church. From the church (or the intersection just beyond it), go 2.7km to a fork in the road just beyond a bridge; look for the 'Los Tarros' sign – buses will go up to here. Take the right fork (an unpaved road). From the Los Tarros sign it's 1.5km to the point where a dirt track crosses the road; on your right is a tree-covered 'hill' in the midst of flat fields. It's actually a great, unrestored temple platform. Make your way across the field and around the hill's south side, following the track to the top. If you have a car, you can drive to within 50m of the top. If you visit this hilltop site on a weekend, you may find worshipers here; people have been coming to pay homage to the idols for over 1400 years.

Of the two stones here, the great grotesque **half-buried head** is the more striking. The elaborate headdress, 'blind' eyes with big bags underneath, beaklike nose and smug grin seem at odds with the blackened face and its position, half-buried in the ancient soil. The head is stained with candle wax, liquor, and the smoke and ashes of incense fires – all part of worship. The other stone is a relief carving of a figure surrounded by circular motifs that may be date glyphs. A copy of this stone is in Santa Lucía's main square.

From the hilltop site, backtrack 1.5km to the fork with the Los Tarros sign. Take the other fork this time, and follow the paved road 3km to the headquarters of Finca El Baúl. (If you're on foot, you can walk from the hilltop site back to the unpaved road and straight across it, continuing on the dirt track. This will eventually bring you to the asphalt road that leads to the *finca* headquarters. When you reach the road, turn right.) Buses trundle along this road every few hours, shuttling workers between the refinery and the town center.

Approaching the *finca* headquarters (6km from Santa Lucía's main square), cross a narrow bridge. Continue uphill and you will see the entrance on the left, marked by a machine-gun pillbox. Beyond, you pass workers' houses and a sugar refinery on the right, and finally come to the headquarters, guarded by several men with rifles. Ask permission to visit the museum and a guard will unlock the gate.

Within the gates, sheltered by a *palapa* (a thatched palm leaf-roofed shelter with open sides), are numerous sculpted figures and reliefs found on the plantation, some of which are very fine. Unfortunately, nothing is labeled.

MUSEO CULTURA COTZUMALGUAPA

This indoor **museum** (admission US$1.30; ☑ 8am-4pm Mon-Fri, to noon Sat) is very close to Bilbao – set in the *finca* that controls the Bilbao cane fields – but, paradoxically, access is more difficult. Your reward is the chance to view hundreds of objects that have been collected from the fields over the centuries.

Leave the town center heading east along Calz 15 de Septiembre, which joins the highway at an Esso station. Go northeast for a short distance, then take an unpaved road on the left (just before another Esso station); this road leads 1km to Finca Las Ilusiones and its museum. If the key-keeper isn't around you're limited to the many stones collected around the outside of the museum.

Sleeping & Eating

Hospedaje Reforma (4a Av 4-71; s/d US$4/7) This hotel has exactly three things going for it: it's cheap, central and the patio is decorated with stuffed boars' heads. And if you like sleeping in dark, airless little concrete cells, make that four.

Hotel Internacional (☎ 7882 5504; Callejón los Mormones; s/d US$10/12.50; P ⛒) Down a short lane (signposted) off Carr al Pacífico is the best budget hotel in town. It has clean, good-sized rooms with a fan, cold showers and a TV. Air conditioning costs US$10 extra.

Restaurante Costa Linda, on the highway about 150m east of Hotel el Camino, is a friendly and clean place serving tasty meat and seafood at reasonable prices. The restaurant at the **Hotel Santiaguito** (mains US$10-12), 100m *west* of Hotel El Camino is a good option and a swimming pool that nonguests can use for US$2.50 per day.

Getting There & Away

As the CA-2 now bypasses Santa Lucía, lots of buses don't come into town. Coming to Santa Lucía from the east, you'll almost certainly need to change buses at Escuintla (US$0.80,

30 minutes). From the west you'll probably have to change at Mazatenango (US$1.50, 1¼ hours). At Cocales, 23km west of Santa Lucía, a road down from Lago de Atitlán meets the CA-2, providing a route to or from the highlands. Eight buses daily run from Cocales to Panajachel (US$2, 2½ hours, 70km), between about 6am and 2pm.

LA DEMOCRACIA
pop 5800 / elevation 165m
A sleepy little village on the way to the beach, La Democracia makes it on the map for further investigation into the mysterious, ancient culture that carved the heads found around Santa Lucía. More of these can be seen in the main square here, and the local museum has a surprisingly good collection of artifacts, considering its location.

At the **Monte Alto archaeological site**, on the outskirts of La Democracia, huge basalt heads have been found. Although cruder, the heads resemble those carved by the Olmec near Veracruz several thousand years ago.

Today these heads are arranged around La Democracia's main plaza. As you come into town from the highway, follow signs to the *museo*, which will lead you left, then left again, and left yet again.

Facing the plaza, along with the church and the modest Palacio Municipal, is the small, modern **Museo Regional de Arqueología** (admission US$3; ⏱ 9am 4pm Tue-Sat), which houses some fascinating archaeological finds. The star of the show is an exquisite jade mask. Smaller figures, 'yokes' used in the ball game, relief carvings and other objects make up the rest of this small but important collection.

Sleeping & Eating
Guest House Paxil de Cayala (☎ 7880 3129; s/d with bathroom US$7/10) Half a block from the plaza, La Democracia's only place to stay is OK for the night, with big, mosquito-proofed rooms.

The flour tortillas stuffed with meat from the little roadside stands around the plaza are delicious, and a bargain at US$2.50.

Burger Chops (mains US$3-5; ⏱ breakfast, lunch & dinner) Also just off the square, this is as close as the town gets to a restaurant.

Getting There & Away
The Chatía Gomerana company runs buses every half-hour from 6am to 4:30pm, from Guatemala City to La Democracia (US$2.50,

two hours) via Escuintla. From Santa Lucía Cotzumalguapa, catch a bus 8km east to Siquinalá and change there.

SIPACATE
An hour and a half down the road from Santa Lucía is Guatemala's surf capital. Waves here average 6ft (2m), the best time being between December and April. The town is separated from the beach by the canal de Chiquimulilla. Oddly unexploited, there are only a couple of hotels on the beach here, the most accessible being **Rancho Carrillo** (☎ 5517 1069; cabin from US$40; 🏊), a short boat ride (US$2.80 return) from town, where the only trouble you will have sleeping is from the noise of crashing waves. Call ahead and you'll probably be able to get a better price. Surfboards are available for rent here.

There are a couple of cheaper, basic **hospedajes** (s/d US$4/7) in town, but remember you'll be paying for that boat ride every day. Buses from Guatemala City (US$4, 3½ hours) pass through La Democracia en route to Sipacate every two hours.

ESCUINTLA
Hot, noisy and crowded, Escuintla has good bus connections and very little else for the average traveler. **Banco Reformador** (cnr 4a Av & 12a Calle; ⏱ 9am-6pm Mon-Fri, to 1pm Sat), two blocks north of the bus station, changes US dollars and traveler's checks and has a Visa ATM. Escuintla has some marginal hotels and restaurants. If stranded, try the **Hotel Costa Sur** (☎ 5295 9528, 12a Calle 4-13; s/d with bathroom US$12/16; 🏊), a couple of doors from Banco Reformador, which has decent, cool rooms with TV and fan. Air con costs an extra US$3.

All buses from the terminal pass along 1a Av, but if you really want a seat, head to the main bus station in the southern part of town, just off 4a Av. Its entrance is marked by a Scott 77 fuel station. Buses go to Antigua (US$1.20, one hour) about every half-hour from 5:30am to 4:30pm. Buses for Guatemala City (US$2.30, 1½ hours) go about every 20 minutes from the street outside from 5am to 6pm. Buses to Puerto San José (US$1, 45 minutes), some continuing to Iztapa, have similar frequency. Buses coming along the Carr al Pacífico may drop you in the north of town, meaning a sweaty walk through the hectic town center if you want to get to the main terminal.

GUATEMALA

PUERTO SAN JOSÉ, LIKÍN & IZTAPA

Guatemala's most important seaside resort, **Puerto San José** leaves much to be desired. If you're eager to get into the Pacific surf, head south from Escuintla 50km to Puerto San José and neighboring settlements.

Puerto San José (population 14,000) was Guatemala's most important Pacific port in the latter half of the 19th century and well into the 20th. Now superseded by Puerto Quetzal to the east, the city languishes. Its beach, inconveniently located across the Canal de Chiquimulilla, is reached by boat. You'd do better to head west along the coast 5km to **Balneario Chula mar**, which has a nicer beach and a suitable hotel or two.

About 5km east of Puerto San José is **Balneario Likén**, Guatemala's only upmarket Pacific resort, beloved by the well-to-do Zona 10 set from Guatemala City.

Another 12km east of Puerto San José is **Iztapa**, Guatemala's first Pacific port, used by prolific conquistador Pedro de Alvarado in the 16th century. When Puerto San José was built in 1853, Iztapa's reign as the port of the capital city came to an end, and the city relaxed into a tropical torpor from which it has never really emerged.

Iztapa has gained notoriety as a premier **deep-sea fishing** spot. World records have been set here and enthusiasts can fish for marlin, sharks and yellow-fin tuna, among others. November through June is the best time to angle for sailfish. Aside from fishing, lounging is the prime pastime. The town has a post office but no bank.

Should you want to stay, the **Sol y Playa Tropical** (☎ 7881 4365/6; 1a Calle 5-48; s/d with bathroom US$10/20; ⊠) has tolerable rooms, with fan, on two floors around a swimming pool. On the beach, **Rancho Maraca Ibo** (s/d US$7/14) offers probably the worst accommodation deal in Guatemala, with very basic cabañas, sporting a bed with a reed mat instead of a mattress.

The bonus about Iztapa is that you can catch a bus from Guatemala City all the way here (US$3, three hours). They leave about every half-hour between 5am to 6pm, traveling via Escuintla and Puerto San José. The last bus heading back from Iztapa goes around 5pm. You can reach Monterrico by paved road from Iztapa: follow the street 1km east from Club Cervecero bar, where the buses terminate, and get a boat across the river to Pueblo Viejo (US$0.80 per person in passenger *lanchas;* US$4 per vehicle, including passengers, on the vehicle ferry). From the far side buses leave for the pretty ride to Monterrico (US$1.50, one hour) at 8am, 11:30am, 2pm, 4pm and 6pm.

MONTERRICO

A favorite for weekending Guatemalans (and Antigua-based language students), Monterrico is a relatively pretty town that is slowly developing into a coastal resort.

Many hotels are humble operations – although a few big boys are moving in – as is much of the town. On the outskirts, particularly to the south, are some very opulent weekend houses owned by Guatemala City fat cats. Seeing these monsters next to simple thatched roof huts is a stark reminder of the polarity of Guatemalan economic reality.

Swimming is good here, and there's occasionally a wave worth surfing. Take care, though – a vicious undertow claims victims every year.

Weekends can be hectic. Come on a weekday and you'll find a much mellower scene (with lower hotel prices). The village has a post office (on Calle Principal) but no bank. Internet access is available from **Walfer** (per hr US$1.80) on the main street.

Proyecto Lingüístico Monterrico (☎ 5558 9039) is a recommended Spanish school based in central Monterrico, offering 20 hours of individual classes for US$75. It can arrange homestays with local families for US$50 per week, including meals on six days.

Behind the beach, on the other side of town, is a large network of mangrove swamps and canals, part of the 190km Canal de Chiquimulilla. Also in the area is a large wildlife reserve and a center for the hatching and release of sea turtles and caimans (crocodilians similar to alligators).

Sights

A big attraction is the **Biotopo Monterrico-Hawaii**, a 20km-long nature reserve of coastal mangrove swamps filled with bird and aquatic life. The reserve is a breeding area for endangered leatherback and ridley turtles, who lay their eggs on the beach in many places along the coast.

Canals lace the swamps, connecting 25 lagoons hidden among the mangroves. Boat tours, passing through the mangrove swamps and visiting several lagoons, take around 1½ to two hours and cost US$10 for one person, US$6.50 for additional people. Sunrise is the best time for wildlife. If you have binoculars, bring them for bird-watching which is best in January and February. Locals will approach you on the street (some with very impressive-looking ID cards), offering tours, but if you want to support the Tortugario (who, incidentally, have the most environmentally knowledgeable guides), arrange a tour directly through the Cecon-run Tortugario Monterrico.

Tortugario Monterrico visitors center (admission US$1.20; ✆ 8am-noon & 2-5pm) is just a short walk east down the beach and back a block from the Monterrico hotels (left, if you're facing the sea). Several endangered species of animals are raised here, including leatherback, olive ridley and green sea turtles, caimans and iguanas. There's an interesting interpretative trail and a little museum with pickled displays in bottles.

The Arcas-run **Reserva Natural Hawaii** (✆ 2478 4096 in Guatemala City; www.arcasguatemala.com) comprises a sea-turtle hatchery with some caimans 8km east along the beach from Monterrico. It is separate from and rivals Cecon's work in the same field. Volunteers are welcome year-round, but the real sea turtle-nesting season is from June to November, with August and September being the peak months. Volunteers are charged US$50 a week for a room, with meals extra and homestay options with local families. A bus (US$0.50, 30 minutes) leaves the Monterrico jetty at 6am, 11am, 1:30pm and 3:30pm (and 6:30pm except Saturday) for the bumpy ride to the reserve. Pickups also operate on this route charging US$3.25 per person. Check out the website for more information.

Sleeping & Eating

All hotels listed here are on the beach, unless otherwise stated. To save a difficult, hot walk along the beach, take the last road to the left before you hit the sand. All these hotels either front or back onto it. The majority have restaurants serving whatever is fresh from the sea that day. Many accommodations offer discounts for stays of three nights or more. Reserve for weekends if you want to avoid a long hot walk while you cruise around asking for vacancies. Weekend prices are given here. Midweek, you'll have plenty more bargaining power.

Johnny's (✆ 7762 0015; johnnys@backpackamericas .com; dm US$6, s & d US$23; 4-person bungalows US$43; P 🖳 🌊) A lot of people are unimpressed by Johnny's – it's the first place you come to turning left on the beach, and one of the biggest operations here. It's got a decent atmosphere though, and attracts a good mix of backpackers and family groups.

Brisas del Mar (✆ 5517 1142; s/d US$7/14; P 🌊) Behind Johnny's, one block back from the beach, this popular newcomer offers good-sized rooms and a second-floor dining hall with excellent sea views.

El Kaiman (✆ 5517 9285; r per person US$7; P 🌊) Further along the beach, you'll find this other cheapie, which is much worn around the edges. Rooms are in a two-story concrete block set back from the beach. The beachfront area is much more appealing, with hammocks and a decent restaurant.

El Mangle (✆ 5514 6517; r with fan/air-con US$26/50; P 🌊) Eclectic decorations fill the grounds of this friendly little place 100m further along the beach. Rooms are decent sized, with hammocks strung on individual porches. The restaurant here pumps out some very tasty wood-fired pizza.

Dulce y Salado (✆ 5817 9046; cabin per person with breakfast & lunch US$27; P 🌊) The furthest from town, about 2km east of the center. Neat little thatched roof cabins set around a good-sized swimming pool. The place is Italian owned, so the restaurant out front does good pastas (US$6) and excellent coffee. Midweek, prices halve, but don't include meals.

Taberna El Pelicano (mains US$7-10; ✆ lunch & dinner Wed-Sat) By far the best place to eat in town, with the widest menu and most interesting food, such as seafood risotto (US$8), beef carpaccio (US$6) and a range of jumbo shrimp dishes (US$14).

There are many simple seafood restaurants on Calle Principal. For the best cheap eats, hit either of the two nameless *comedores* on the last road to the right before the beach, where you can pick up an excellent plate of garlic shrimp, rice tortillas, fries and salad for US$4.

Drinking & Nightlife

El Animal Desconicido (✆ 8pm-late Thu-Sat) Really the only bar in town, this gets very happening on weekends, with happy hours, cocktails and excellent music. Comfy seating fills up early out front, and the rest of the place starts

160 COBÁN & CENTRAL GUATEMALA •• Salamá

rocking around 11pm. To find it, go down the main street 'til you hit the beach, then walk 200m to your right.

Getting There & Away

There are two ways to get to Monterrico. You can take a bus to Iztapa (four hours from Guatemala City), catch a *lancha* across the canal to Pueblo Viejo and hop on another bus to Monterrico (US$1, one hour). This is the longer alternative, but it's a pretty journey, revealing local life at a sane pace.

The other option is to head to La Avellana, where *lanchas* and car ferries depart for Monterrico. The Cubanita company runs a handful of direct buses to and from Guatemala City (US$4, four hours, 124km). Alternatively you reach La Avellana by changing buses at Taxisco on Hwy CA-2. Buses operate half-hourly from 5am to 4pm between Guatemala City and Taxisco (US$3, 3½ hours), and roughly hourly from 7am to 6pm between Taxisco and La Avellana (US$1, 40 minutes), although taxi drivers will tell you that you've missed the last bus, regardless of what time you arrive. A taxi between Taxisco and La Avellana costs around US$6.50.

Shuttle buses also serve La Avellana. You can take a round-trip from Antigua, coming on one day and returning the next (US$9 one-way, 2½ hours). Voyageur Tours (p105) comes to La Avellana three or four times weekly in the low season, daily in peak periods, with a minimum of three passengers. On Saturday and Sunday, they pick up in Monterrico (not La Avellana) from outside Proyecto Lingüístico Monterrico at 3pm for the round-trip. They charge US$6.50 from Monterrico to Antigua, so it's best not to buy a round-trip ticket in Antigua; they'll take you on to Guatemala City (US$11 total) if you wish. Other shuttle services also make the Antigua–Monterrico trip.

From La Avellana, catch a *lancha* or car ferry to Monterrico. The collective *lanchas* charge US$0.60 per passenger for the half-hour trip along the Canal de Chiquimulilla, a long mangrove canal. They start at 4:30am and run more or less every half-hour or hour until late afternoon. From Monterrico they leave at 3:30am, 5:30am, 7am, 8am, 9am, 10:30am, noon, 1pm, 2:30pm and 4pm. You can always pay more and charter your own boat. The car ferry costs US$13 per vehicle.

COBÁN & CENTRAL GUATEMALA

This region holds some of the best, most rewarding opportunities for getting off the beaten track. While the tour buses are all whizzing between the capital and Tikal, independent travelers are finding a wealth of undiscovered gems.

Semuc Champey and Lanquín are on everybody's list if you're in Guatemala, but there are literally hundreds more caves, waterfalls and other natural attractions to check out, mostly scattered around the well-established travelers' hub of Cobán. Check www.asociasionasiqmuc.guate.ws for a little inspiration.

SALAMÁ

pop 24,200 / elevation 940m

A wonderful introduction to Baja Verapaz's not-too-hot, not-too-cold climate, Salamá is a town with a couple of attractions. Excellent information on the area is available at www.laverapaz.com.

Hwy 17, also marked as CA-14 on maps, leaves the Carr al Atlántico at El Rancho, 84km from Guatemala City. It heads west through dry, desert-like lowlands, then turns north and ascends into the forested hills. The turnoff for Salamá is 47km from Guatemala City.

Banrural (🕑 9am-5pm Mon-Fri, to 1pm Sat) on the south side of the plaza (opposite the church) changes cash and traveler's checks, and has a Visa and MasterCard ATM. Internet access (US$0.80 per hour) is available at Telgua, just east of the plaza. A police station is one block west of the plaza.

Sights

Attractive Salamá has some reminders of colonial rule. The main plaza boasts an ornate **colonial church** with gold encrusted altars and a carved pulpit (look for it to the left before the altar). Be sure to check out Jesus lying in a glass coffin with cotton bunting in his stigmata and droplets of blood seeping from his hairline. Thick mascara and the silver lamé pillow on which he rests his head complete the scene. The Salamá **market** is impressive for its colorful, local bustle, particularly on Sunday.

GUATEMALA

Tours

EcoVerapaz (☎ 7940 0146; ecoverapaz@hotmail.com; 8a Av 7-12, Zona 1) has local, trained naturalists offering interesting tours throughout Baja Verapaz, including caving, birding, hiking, horseback riding and orchid trips. The company also goes to Rabinal to check out its museum and crafts, and arranges trips to see the famous rodeos of Baja Verapaz. Guides speak some English. One-day tours are US$40 per person and group discounts are offered.

Sleeping

Turicentro Las Orquídeas (☎ 7940 1622; Carr a Salamá Km 147; per tent US$4.50) Travelers with camping gear may want to check out this place. Here, a few kilometers east of Salamá out on Hwy 17, the Turicentro has a grassy area for camping plus a café, pool and open spaces hung with hammocks. You can use the pool (US$2 per person per day) even if you're not camping here.

Hotel Rosa de Sharon (☎ 5774 8650; 5a Calle 6-39; s/d with bathroom US$7.50/12; **P**) The neat, bright rooms here loom over the busy market area, but they're set back from the road, so remain peaceful. They're big and clean with whacky decorations such as wrought iron hat stands made to look like trees.

Posada de Don Maco (☎ 7940 0083; 3a Calle 8-26; s/d with bathroom US$8/14; **P**) This clean, family-run place has simple but spacious rooms with fan and good bathrooms. The courtyard boasts a collection of caged squirrels.

Eating

Café Deli-Donas (15a Calle 6-61; cakes US$1.30, sandwiches US$2, licuados US$0.90) This exceedingly pleasant little café (where even the bathrooms smell good) is like an oasis in Salamá's busy market zone. Excellent coffee, homemade cakes and light meals are the go here.

Antojitos Zacapanecos (cnr 6a Calle & 8a Av; mains US$2-3) For something a little different in the fast-food vein, check out the huge flour tortillas filled with pork, chicken or beef from this place. Better yet, grab one to go and have a picnic in the plaza.

Restaurante El Balcón de los Recuerdos (8a Av 6-28; mains US$5-7; ☯ breakfast, lunch & dinner Mon-Sat) This restaurant, a half-block west of the plaza on the road to La Cumbre, is spacious, fan-cooled, and has a central fountain. Here you can choose from a typical list of grilled meats, fish, prawns and seafood soup.

Getting There & Away

Buses going to Guatemala City (US$3 to US$4.50, three hours, 151km) depart hourly between 3am and 8pm from the northeast corner of the park. There is a Pullman at 4am. Arrive early for a seat. Buses coming from Guatemala City continue west from Salamá to Rabinal (US$1.50, 40 minutes, 19km) and then 15km further along to Cubulco.

Buses for San Jerónimo leave from in front of the *municipalidad* (east side of the plaza) every half-hour from 6am to 5:30pm (US$0.40, 25 minutes). Buses for La Cumbre (US$0.60, 25 minutes) and Cobán (US$2.50; 1½ to two hours) leave just downhill from the corner of 15 Calle and 6a Av about every 30 minutes from early morning to 4pm.

AROUND SALAMÁ

Ten kilometers along the road to Salamá from the Cobán Hwy you come to the turnoff for **San Jerónimo**. Behind the town's beautiful **church**, a former sugar mill is now a **museum** (admission free; ☯ 8am-4pm Mon-Fri, 10am-noon & 1-4pm Sat & Sun) with a decent collection of unlabeled artifacts and photographs. On the town plaza are some large stones that were carved in ancient times.

Nine kilometers west of Salamá along Hwy 5 is **San Miguel Chicaj**, known for its traditional **fiesta** (September 25–29) and weaving.

Continue along the same road another 10km to reach the colonial town of **Rabinal**, founded in 1537 by Fray Bartolomé de Las Casas as a base for proselytizing. Rabinal has gained fame as a center for pottery-making (look for the hand-painted chocolate cups) and citrus-growing. Rabinal is also known for its adherence to pre-Columbian traditions. Try to make the annual **fiesta of Saint Peter** (January 19-25; things reach a fever pitch on January 21), or **Corpus Cristi**. Market day is Sunday. Two small hotels, **Posada San Pablo** and **Hospedaje Caballeros**, can put you up if you wish to stay.

It's possible to continue from Rabinal another 15km west to **Cubulco** or about 100km south to Guatemala City. Hwy 5 to Guatemala City passes through several small villages en route. It's best to tackle this road with a 4WD vehicle. Buses ply this remote route very slowly. Along the way you can stop to visit the **ruins of Mixco Viejo** (admission US$4), near San Juan Sacatepéquez, about 25km from Guatemala City.

BIOTOPO DEL QUETZAL

Along the main highway (CA-14) 34km north of the turnoff for Salamá is the Biotopo Mario Dary Rivera reserve, commonly called the **Biotopo del Quetzal** (admission US$2.50; ⏲ 7am-4pm); it's at Km 161, near the village of Purulhá (no services). The ride along here is sobering: entire hillsides are deforested and covered in huge sheets of black plastic meant to optimize growing conditions for *xate,* a green palm exported for use in floral arrangements.

If you intend on seeing a quetzal, Guatemala's national bird, you'll likely be disappointed – the birds are rare and elusive, and their habitat is almost destroyed. The best time to see them is between February and September. However, it's still worth a visit to explore their lush, high-altitude cloud forest habitat.

Two well-maintained trails wind through the reserve past several waterfalls, most of which cascade into swimmable pools. Deep in the forest is **Xiu Ua Li Che** (Grandfather Tree), some 450 years old, which was alive when the conquistadors fought the Rabinals in these mountains.

Trail maps in English and Spanish are sold at the visitors center for US$0.70. They contain a checklist of 87 birds commonly seen here. Other animals include spider monkeys and *tigrillos,* similar to ocelots. Good luck.

The reserve has a visitors center, a little shop for drinks and snacks, and a camping and barbecue area. The ruling on camping changes often. Check by contacting **Cecon** (☎ 3361 6065; www.usac.edu.gt/cecon, in Spanish; Av La Reforma 0-63, Zona 1, Guatemala City), which administers this and other *biotopos.* Services in the area include the following.

Hotel y Comedor Ranchito del Quetzal (☎ 5368 6397; s/d US$5/10, with bathroom US$7.50/15; Ⓟ), carved out of the jungle on a hillside 200m away from the Biotopo entrance, has good-sized, simple rooms with cold showers in the older wooden building and hot showers in the newer concrete one. Reasonably priced, simple meals (mains US$3.50) are served, and there are vegetarian options.

Getting There & Away

Any bus to/from Guatemala City will set you down at the park entrance. Heading in the other direction, it's best to flag down a bus or microbus to El Rancho and change there for your next destination. The road between the Biotopo and Cobán is good – smooth and fast (although curvy). As you ascend into the evergreen forests, you'll still see tropical flowers here and there.

COBÁN

pop 57,600 / elevation 1320m

Not so much an attraction in itself, but an excellent jumping-off point for the natural wonders of Alta Verapaz, Cobán is a prosperous city with an upbeat air. Return visitors will marvel at how much (and how tastefully) the town has developed since their last visit.

This was once a stronghold of the Rabinal Maya. In the 19th century, German immigrants moved in, founding vast coffee and cardamom *fincas* and giving Cobán the look and feel of a German mountain town. The era of German cultural and economic domination ended during WWII, when the US prevailed upon the Guatemalan government to deport the powerful *finca* owners, many of whom supported the Nazis.

Guatemala's most impressive indigenous festival, the folkloric festival of **Rabin Ajau**, takes place in late July or early August.

Orientation & Information

Most services of interest to travelers are within a few blocks of the plaza. Most buses will drop you out of town at the terminal north of town. It's a 15-minute walk or US$1 taxi ride to the plaza from there. The heart of Cobán is built on a rise, so unless what you're looking for is in the dead center, you'll be trudging uphill and down.

There's a **tourist office** (⏲ 10am-5pm Mon-Sat) on the plaza, but unless your question is very basic, they'll probably send you to the tourism people in the **municipalidad** (town hall; ☎ 952 1305, 951 1148), where some switched-on young staff work in an office behind the police office. Casa D'Acuña (p165) can also give you loads of information.

The post office is a block southeast of the plaza on the corner of 2a Av and 3a Calle. There are plenty of card phones outside Telgua on the plaza.

At least four places offer internet service. The going rate is US$0.80 per hour. **Access Computación** (1a Calle 3-13; ⏲ 9am-7pm Mon-Fri, 8am-6pm Sat) is in the same complex as Café El Tirol. **Cybercobán** (3a Av 1-11, Zona 4; ⏲ 8:30am-7pm Mon-Sat) is 200m east of the plaza. **Mayan Internet** (6a Av 2-28; ⏲ 8:30am-8pm Mon-Sat, 2:30-9pm Sun), with fast connections, is 500m west of the plaza.

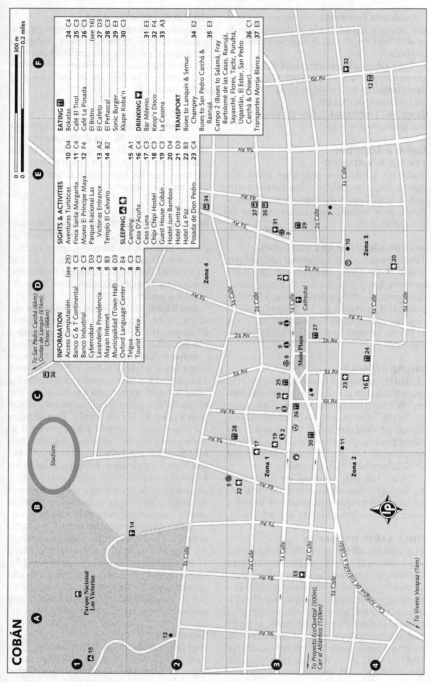

COBÁN

INFORMATION
Access Computación	(see 25)	
Banco G & T Continental	1	C3
Banco Industrial	2	C3
Cybercobán	3	D3
Lavandería Providencia	4	C3
Mayan Internet	5	B3
Municipalidad (Town Hall)	6	D3
Oxford Language Center	7	E4
Telgua	8	C3
Tourist Office	9	C3

SIGHTS & ACTIVITIES
Aventuras Turísticas	10	D4
Finca Santa Margarita	11	C4
Museo El Príncipe Maya	12	F4
Parque Nacional Las Victorias Entrance	13	A2
Templo El Calvario	14	B2

SLEEPING 🛏 🏠
Camping	15	A1
Casa D'Acuña	16	C4
Casa Luna	17	C3
Chipi Chipi Hostel	18	C3
Guest House Cobán	19	C3
Hostel Jam Bamboo	20	D4
Hotel Central	21	D3
Hotel La Paz	22	B3
Posada de Don Pedro	23	C4

EATING 🍴
Bokatas	24	C4
Café El Tirol	25	C3
Café La Posada	26	C3
El Bistro	(see 16)	
El Cafeto	27	D3
El Peñascal	28	C3
Sonic Burger	29	E3
Xkape Koba'n	30	C3

DRINKING 🍸
Bar Milenio	31	E3
Keop's Disco	32	F4
La Casona	33	A3

TRANSPORT
Buses to Lanquín & Semuc Champey	34	E2
Buses to San Pedro Carchá & Raxruhá	35	E3
Campo 2 (Buses to Salamá, Fray Bartolomé de las Casas, Raxrujá, Sayaxché, Flores, Tactic, Purulhá, Uspantán, El Estor, San Pedro Carchá & Chisec)	36	C1
Transportes Monja Blanca	37	E3

To San Pedro Carchá (6km); Grutas de Lanquín (61km); Chisec (66km)

To Proyecto EcoQuetzal (300m); Carr al Atlántico (120km)

Carr Antigua de Entrada a Cobán

To Vivero Verapaz (1km)

Parque Nacional Las Victorias

Stadium

Main Plaza

Cathedral

Zona 4
Zona 1
Zona 3
Zona 2

300 m
0.2 miles

Lavandería Providencia (☾ 8am-noon & 2-5pm Mon-Sat), on the south side of the plaza, will wash 3.2kg for US$1.50; drying costs US$2.50 per hour.

The following banks are good for changing US dollars and traveler's checks:

Banco Industrial (1a Calle 4-36 cnr 1a Calle & 7a Av) The 7a Av branch has a Visa ATM.

Banco G & T Continental (1a Calle) Has a MasterCard ATM. Opposite Hotel La Posada.

Sights & Activities

TEMPLO EL CALVARIO

You'll get a fine view over town from this church atop a long flight of stairs at the north end of 7a Av Zona 1. Indigenous people leave offerings at shrines and crosses in front of the church.

PARQUE NACIONAL LAS VICTORIAS

This forested 0.82-sq-km **national park** (admission US$0.80; ☾ 8am-4:30pm, walking trails 9am-3pm), right in town, has ponds, barbecue, picnic areas, campgrounds, children's play areas, a lookout point and extensive trails. The entrance is near the corner of 3a Calle and 9a Av, Zona 1. It's an isolated spot – consider hiking in a group.

VIVERO VERAPAZ

Orchid lovers mustn't miss a chance to see the many thousands of species at this famous **nursery** (☎ 7952 1133; Carr Antigua de Entrada a Cobán; admission US$1.80; ☾ 9am-noon & 2-4pm). The rare *monja blanca*, or white nun orchid (Guatemala's national flower), grows here, as do hundreds of miniature orchid species. The national orchid show is held here each December.

Vivero Verapaz is on the Carr Antigua de Entrada a Cobán, about 2km from the town center – a 40-minute walk southwest from the plaza. You can hire a taxi for around US$4.

FINCA SANTA MARGARITA

This working **coffee farm** (☎ 7952 1586; 3a Calle 4-12, Zona 2; admission US$2.50; ☾ guided tours 8am-12:30pm & 1:30-5pm Mon-Fri, 8am-noon Sat) offers guided tours of their operation. From propagation and planting to roasting and exporting, the 45-minute tour will tell you all you ever wanted to know about these powerful beans. At tour's end, you're treated to a cup of coffee and can purchase beans straight from the roaster for US$3 to US$7 per 0.5kg. The talented guide speaks English and Spanish.

MUSEO EL PRÍNCIPE MAYA

This private **museum** (☎ 7952 1541; 6a Av 4-26, Zona 3; admission US$1.30, ☾ 9am-6pm Mon-Sat) features a collection of pre-Columbian artifacts, with an emphasis on jewelry, other body adornments and pottery. The displays are well designed and maintained.

Courses

The **Oxford Language Center** (☎ 5892 7718; www .olcenglish.com; 4a Av 2-16, Zona 3) charges around US$170 for 20 hours of Spanish lessons, with discounts for groups. Their rational for charging more than the competition is that they pay their teachers better.

Tours

Aventuras Turísticas (☎ /fax 7951 4213; www.aven turasturisticas.com; 3a Calle 2-38, Zona 3), in Hostal de Doña Victoria, leads tours to Laguna Lachuá, the caves of Lanquín, Semuc Champey, Tikal and Ceibal, and will customize itineraries. It employs French-, English- and Spanish-speaking guides.

Casa D'Acuña (☎ 7951 0484; casadacuna@yahoo.com; 4a Calle 3-11, Zona 2) offers its own tours to Semuc Champey, the Grutas de Lanquín and other places further afield. Its guides are excellent.

Proyecto EcoQuetzal (☎ /fax 7952 1047; www .ecoquetzal.org; 2a Calle 14-36, Zona 1; ☾ 8:30am-1pm & 2-5:30pm Mon-Fri) is an innovative project offering 'ethnotourism' trips in which participants hike to nearby villages in the cloud forest and stay with a Q'eqchi' Mayan family. To maximize the experience, travelers are encouraged to learn some Q'eqchi' words and stay with their host family for at least two days. For US$42 you'll get a guide for three days, lodging for two nights and six meals. Your guide will take you on hikes to interesting spots. The men of the family are the guides, providing them an alternative, sustainable way to make a living.

Reservations are required at least one day in advance. The Proyecto also rents boots, sleeping bags and binoculars at reasonable prices, so you needn't worry if you're unprepared for such a rugged experience. Participants should speak at least a little Spanish. With a month's notice, this outfit also offers quetzal-viewing platforms; contact the office for details.

Sleeping

Chipi Chipi Hostel (☎ 5226 0235; 1a Calle 3-25, Zona 1; dm US$3.50) This new hostel is a total winner in terms of location, and offers decent shared rooms, sleeping four in two bunks. The patio has hammocks and the young staff are full of info and tips.

Hotel La Paz (☎ 952 1358; 6a Av 2-19, Zona 1; s US$4, s/d with bathroom US$6/10; P) This cheerful, clean hotel, 1½ blocks north and two blocks west of the plaza, is an excellent deal. It has many flowers, and a good cafeteria next door. They claim to have hot water.

Casa Luna (☎ 7951 3528; 5a Av 2-28, Zona 1; dm US$6; r per person US$7.50) Modern rooms set around a pretty, grassy courtyard. Dorms have lockers and private rooms are well decorated. The shared bathrooms are spotless.

Guest House Cobán (cnr 5a Av & 2a Calle, Zona 1; s/d US$6/12, with bathroom US$7.50/15) A basic but comfortable little guest house in a good location. The beds are firm and the family who runs it is superfriendly. Rates include breakfast.

Hostel Jam Bamboo (2a Av 4-33, Zona 2; dm US$6) Definitely party central in Cobán's hostel scene – this one isn't for your retiring types. But if you're looking to meet people and listen to live music (Tuesday to Sunday), this is your place. Rooms are spacious, with three beds per room and a bathroom in each.

Posada de Don Pedro (☎ 7951 0562; 3a Calle 3-12 Zona 2; s/d US$6/12) This family-run place has spacious rooms with terracotta tiled floors around a happy little courtyard. There are good sitting areas to while the day away.

Casa D'Acuña (☎ 7951 0482; casadacuna@yahoo .com; 4a Calle 3-11, Zona 2; dm/d US$6.50/13) This clean and very comfortable European-style hostel has four dorms (each with four beds) and two private doubles, all with shared bathroom with good hot-water showers. Also here is a fabulous restaurant called El Bistro, a gift shop, laundry service and reasonably priced local tours.

Hotel Central (☎ 7952 1442; 1a Calle 1-79, Zona 1; s/d with bathroom & TV US$16/20) Reasonable sized rooms with just a touch of mold on the walls and lovely outdoor sitting areas make this a decent choice.

Camping (per person US$3) is available at Parque Nacional Las Victorias, right in town. Facilities include water and toilets, but no showers.

Eating

Most of Cobán's hotels have their own restaurants.

Xkape Koba'n (2a Calle 5-13, Zona 2; snacks US$2) The perfect place to take a breather or while away a whole afternoon is this beautiful, artsy little café with a lush garden out back. The cakes are homemade, the coffee delectable and there are some interesting handicrafts on sale.

Café El Tirol (Oficinas Profesionales Fray Bartolomé de las Casas, 1a Calle 3-13; breakfast US$2-4; ☽ Mon-Sat) Another good central café, the Tirol claims to have Cobán's best coffee (we disagree) and offers several types of hot chocolate. It's a cozy little place in which to enjoy breakfasts, pastries and coffee or light meals, with a pleasant terrace away from the traffic.

El Cafeto (2a Calle 1-36 B, Zona 2; mains US$3-4; ☽ breakfast, lunch & dinner) This cute little café right on the square does good, light set lunches (US$3), has a half-decent wine selection and serves delicious coffee.

Sonic Burger (1a Calle 3-50, Zona 3; burgers from US$3, set meals US$3-5) The best burgers in town are served in a young, almost-hip environment. The food is cheap, the drinks expensive – go figure.

Café La Posada (1a Calle 4-12, Zona 2; ☽ 1-9pm; snacks under US$4) This café has tables on a veranda overlooking the square, and a comfortable sitting room inside with couches, coffee tables and a fireplace. All the usual café fare is served. Snacks comprise nachos, tortillas, sandwiches, burgers, tacos, tostadas, fruit salad etc.

Bokatas (4a Calle 2-34, Zona 2; mains US$4-10; ☽ dinner) This large outdoor eatery pumps out equal portions of big juicy steaks and loud disco music. Also on offer is a decent paella for two or three people (US$24), and a range of seafood and Mediterranean options.

El Peñascal (5a Av 2-61; mains US$8-10; ☽ lunch & dinner) Probably Cobán's finest dining option, this one has plenty of regional specialties, Guatemalan classics, mixed meat platters, seafood and snacks in a relaxed, upmarket setting.

El Bistro (4a Calle 3-11; fish, steak & chicken mains US$8.50-13; ☽ from 7am) Casa D'Acuña's restaurant offers authentic Italian as well as other European-style dishes served in an attractive oasis of tranquility to background classical music. In addition to protein-oriented mains, there is a range of pastas (US$4 to US$5.30), salads, home-made breads, cakes and outstanding desserts.

In the evening, food trucks (kitchens on wheels) park around the plaza and offer some of the cheapest dining in town. As always, the one to go for has the largest crowd of locals hanging around chomping down.

GUATEMALA

Drinking & Nightlife

Cobán has several places where you can get down and boogie.

Bar Milenio (3a Av 1-11, Zona 4) Has a bar, food, a pool table and mixed-music disco.

La Casona (cnr 8a Av & 2 Calle, Zona 2; admission US$2-3; ☻ Thu-Sat) A mega-disco with balcony seating and bow-tied waiters.

Keops Disco (3a Calle 4-71, Zona 3; admission US$4) A popular disco; wear your best gear.

Getting There & Away

BUS

The CA-14/Carr al Atlántico route is the most traveled circuit between Cobán and the outside world, but buses also serve other off-the-beaten-track routes. Consider taking the phenomenal route between Cobán and Huehuetenango (see p152). Or head from Cobán to El Estor, on Lago de Izabal, or to Poptún in El Petén on the backdoor route via Fray Bartolomé de Las Casas.

Many buses leave from Cobán's new bus terminal, east of the stadium. Buses to Guatemala City, Salamá, Lanquín and many other destinations depart from completely different stations. The bus stops are shown on the map. From Cobán, buses include the following destinations:

Biotopo del Quetzal (US$1, 1¼ hours, 58km) Any bus heading from Monja Blanca for Guatemala City will drop you at the entrance to the Biotopo.

Chisec (US$1.95, two hours, 66km) 10 buses from Campo 2 between 6am and 5pm.

Flores (five to six hours, 224km) Go to Sayaxché and take an onward bus or minibus from there.

Fray Bartolomé de Las Casas via Chisec (US$4, three hours, 121km); via San Pedro Carchá (US$4.50, four hours, 101km) Several buses and minibuses depart from Campo 2 between 5am and 3:30pm. Buses might just say 'Las Casas.'

Guatemala City (US$4 to US$6, four to five hours, 213km) Transportes Monja Blanca (☎ 7951 3571; 2a Calle 3-77, Zona 4) has buses leaving for Guatemala City every 30 minutes between 2am and 6am, then hourly till 5pm.

Lanquín (US$2 to US$3, 2½ to three hours, 61km) Minibuses depart from the corner of 3a Calle and 3a Av, Zona 4, from 7am to 4pm. Check times as they seem to be fluid.

Playa Grande (for Laguna Lachuá) (US$6.50, four hours, 141km) Frequent buses and minibuses from Campo 2. Playa Grande is sometimes called Cantabal.

Puerto Barrios (6½ hours, 335km) Take any bus headed to Guatemala City and change at El Rancho junction.

Río Dulce (6½ hours, 318km) Take any bus headed to Guatemala City and change at El Rancho junction. You may have to transfer again at La Ruidosa junction, 169km past El Rancho, but there is plenty of transportation going through to Río Dulce and on to Flores.

Salamá (US$3, 1½ hours, 57km) Frequent minivans leave from Campo 2, or take any bus to Guatemala City and change at La Cumbre.

Sayaxché (US$7, four hours, 184km) Buses at 6am and noon, and *microbuses* from early until 1pm, from Campo 2.

Uspantán (US$4.50, 4½ hours, 94km) Microbuses go from Campo 2 with a stop at Oficinas Fray Bartolomé de Las Casas.

AROUND COBÁN

Cobán (indeed all of Alta Verapaz) is becoming a hot destination for adventure travel. Not only does the area hold scores of villages where you can find traditional Maya culture in some of its purest extant form, it also harbors caves, waterfalls, pristine lagoons and many other natural wonders.

San Juan Chamelco

About 16km southeast of Cobán is the village of San Juan Chamelco, with swimming at **Balneario Chio**. The **church** here, which dates back to the colonial period and may have been the first church in Alta Verapaz, sits atop a small rise and has awesome views of the villages below. Mass is still held here in Spanish (5pm Sunday) and Q'eqchi' (7am and 9:30am Sunday).

In Aldea Chajaneb, 12km from Cobán, **Don Jerónimo's** (☎ 2308 2255; www.dearbrutus.com/donjeronimo; s/d US$25/45) rents comfortable, simple bungalows. The price includes three ample, delicious vegetarian meals fresh from the garden. He also offers many activities, including tours to caves and the mountains, and inner tubing on the Río Sotzil. The **Rey Marcos Cave** is near here.

The caves go for more than 1km into the earth, although chances are you won't get taken that far. A river runs through the cave (you have to wade through it at one point) and there are some impressive stalactites and stalagmites.

Buses to San Juan Chamelco leave from 4a Calle, Zona 3, in Cobán. To reach Don Jerónimo's, take a bus or pickup from San Juan Chamelco toward Chamil and ask the driver to let you off at Don Jerónimo's. When you get off, take the footpath to the left for 300m, cross the bridge and it's the first house on the right. Alternatively, hire a taxi from Cobán (US$6.50).

Grutas de Lanquín

The best excursion from Cobán is to the caves near Lanquín, a pretty village 61km east. If you get this far, be sure to visit Semuc Champey (right) as well.

The **Grutas de Lanquín** (admission US$3; ✆ 8am-4pm) are a short distance northwest of the town and extend several kilometers into the earth. You must first stop at the police station in the *municipalidad* (town hall) in Lanquín, pay the admission and ask them to open the caves; there is no attendant at the caves. The caves have lights, but bring a powerful flashlight anyway. You'll also need shoes with good traction, as it's slippery inside.

Although the first few hundred meters of cavern has been equipped with a walkway and electric lights, most of this subterranean system is untouched. If you're a neophyte spelunker, think twice about wandering too far – the entire extent of this cave has yet to be explored, let alone mapped. Aside from funky stalactites and stalagmites, these caves are crammed with bats; at sunset, they fly out of the mouth of the cave in dense, sky-obscuring formations. The river here gushes from the cave in clean, cool and delicious torrents; search out the hot pockets near the shore.

The sublimely located **El Retiro** (✆ 7983 0009; hammock/dm US$3/4, s/d US$6/12) is about 500m along the road beyond Rabin Itzam. Be warned – it's the sort of place you could lose yourself for months (and it looks like some have). *Palapas* look down over green fields to a beautiful wide river, the same one that flows out from the Lanquín caves. It's safe to swim, even inner tube if you're a confident swimmer. Attention to detail in every respect makes this a backpackers' paradise. Excellent vegetarian food (three-course dinners US$4.50) is available in the hammock-lined restaurant.

In Lanquín **Rabin Itzam** (s/d US$3.50/7, with bathroom US$13/16) has big rooms with balconies and good views. The wooden doors are carved with Maya symbols. This place is quiet and private. **El Recreo** (✆ 7983 0057; hotel_el_recreo@hotmail.com; s/d US$10/20; P ☒), between the town and the caves, is more attractive and more expensive. It has large gardens, two swimming pools and a restaurant.

La Estancia de Alfaro (mains US$3-5; ✆ breakfast, lunch & dinner) This large outdoor eatery halfway between town and El Retiro serves up good-sized plates of steak, eggs and rice, and gets rowdy and beerish at night.

Buses operate several times daily between Cobán and Lanquín, continuing to Cahabón. Buses leave Lanquín to return to Cobán at 3am, 4am, 5:30am and 1pm, and there are assorted microbuses with no fixed timetable. Since the last reliable return bus departs so early, it's best to stay the night.

Semuc Champey

Nine kilometers south of Lanquín, along a rough, bumpy, slow road, is **Semuc Champey** (admission US$4), famed for its great natural limestone bridge 300m long, on top of which is a stepped series of pools of cool, flowing river water that's good for **swimming**.

The water is from the Río Cahabón, and much more of it passes underground, beneath the bridge. Although this bit of paradise is difficult to reach, the beauty of its setting and the perfection of the pools, which range from turquoise to emerald green, make it all worthwhile.

If you're visiting on a tour, some guides will take you down a rope ladder from the lowest pool to the river, which gushes out from the rocks below.

It's possible to camp at Semuc Champey, but be sure to pitch a tent only in the upper areas, as flash floods are common. It's risky to leave anything unattended, as it might get stolen.

The place now has 24-hour security which may reassure potential campers, but you need to bring everything with you.

Las Marías (✆ 7861 2209; www.posadalasmarias.com; dm US$3, s/d US$6/9.50, with bathroom US$9.50/14) is a rustic, laid-back place by the road 1km short of Semuc Champey. There are a couple of dorm rooms and three private rooms, all in wooden buildings in a verdant setting. Cool drinks and vegetarian food are available (full dinner US$2.60) from the restaurant where you can see the Río Cahabón flowing past. They offer cave tours (US$4/5.50 for guests/nonguests), tubing, walking tours and shuttles to Cobán for US$4.

You can camp here for US$1.50 and rent a hammock for US$2.

Pickups run from the plaza in Lanquín to Semuc Champey – your chances of catching one are better in the early morning and on market days, Sunday, Monday and Thursday. If there are a lot of local people traveling, expect to pay US$0.65; otherwise, it's US$1.95. The walk is long and hot.

GUATEMALA

BACKDOOR PETÉN ROUTES

The Cobán to Poptún route via Fray Bartolomé de Las Casas used to be a desolate dirt road. Nowadays, plenty of buses and pickups ply the decent roads. This route is a great opportunity for you to get off the Gringo Trail and into the heart of Guatemala.

The hospitable town of **Fray Bartolomé de Las Casas**, often referred to as 'Fray' (pronounced fry), is sizable for the middle of nowhere. You can't make it from Cobán to Poptún in one shot, so you'll be spending the night here. Banrural, just off the plaza, changes US dollars and traveler's checks. The post office and police station are nearby. The *municipalidad* (town hall) is on the plaza.

The friendly **Hotel La Cabaña** (☎ 7952 0352; 2a Calle 1-92 Zona 3; s/d US$3.50/7, with bathroom US$8/16) has the best accommodations in town. Eating options are limited here – you could try in the restaurant of Hotel Bartolo, behind the plaza. Otherwise grab a steak (with tortillas and beans; US$1.50) at the informal BBQ shacks that open up along the main street at night.

One daily bus departs from the plaza at 3am for Poptún (US$5, five to six hours, 100km). Buses for Cobán leave hourly between 4am and 4pm. Some go via Chisec (3½ hours, US$4). Others take the slower route via San Pedro Carchá.

Another backdoor trip you could take goes from Cobán to Sayaxché and El Ceibal (see p166). You can also go via Raxrujá (many services), west of Fray Bartolomé de Las Casas. One bus daily leaves Fray for Sayaxché at 10am (4½ hours, 117km).

ZACAPA & CHIQUIMULA

In the steamy, hill studded flatlands that run down to the southern border, cowboy culture lives on. Packing a pistol is not uncommon here – indeed, it goes well with the big hat and boots. Most travelers use the area as a gateway to El Salvador and Honduras, but others come for the religious pilgrimage to Esquipulas or to check out the dinosaur museum at Estanzuela.

ESTANZUELA

pop 10,000

En route to Chiquimula, you turn off the Carr al Atlántico onto the CA-10 and into the Río Motagua valley, a hot, 'dry tropic' area that once supported a great number and variety of dinosaurs. Three kilometers south of the Carr al Atlántico you'll see a small monument on the right (west) side of the road commemorating the terrible earthquake of February 4, 1976.

Less than 2km south of the monument is the small town of Estanzuela, with its **Museo de Paleontología, Arqueología y Geología Ingeniero Roberto Woolfolk Sarvia** (☎ 7941 4981; admission free; ☺ 9am-5pm). This interesting museum holds bones of dinosaurs, a giant ground sloth some 30,000 years old and a prehistoric whale. Also on display are early Maya artifacts. To get here, go 1km west from the highway directly through town, following the small *museo* signs.

CHIQUIMULA

pop 44,200 / elevation 370m

Capital of its namesake department, Chiquimula lies in a mining and tobacco-growing region on CA-10, 32km south of the Carr al Atlántico. Although small, it's a major market town for eastern Guatemala. It's also a transportation point and overnight stop for those en route to Copán in Honduras (the reason most travelers stop here). Among other things, Chiquimula is known for its sweltering climate, decent budget hotels and the flower-packed central plaza, wired for sound and pumping out nonstop powerschmaltz.

Orientation & Information

Chiquimula is easy to get around on foot.

The **post office** (10a Av btwn 1a & 2a Calles) is in an alley around the side of the building opposite the bus station. **Telgua** (3a Calle) is a few doors downhill from Parque Ismael Cerna. Check email at **Biblioteca El Centro** (cnr 4a Calle & 8a Av; per hr US$0.80; ☺ 8am-7pm Mon-Fri, 8am-6pm Sat & Sun). The busy **market** is right by Telgua.

Many banks will change US dollars and traveler's checks. **Banco G&T** (7a Av 4-75, Zona 1; ☺ 9am-8pm Mon-Fri, 10am-2pm Sat), half a block south of the plaza, changes both and also gives cash advances on Visa and MasterCard. **Banrural** (cnr 2a Calle & 10a Av, Zona 1) has a Visa ATM.

Viajes Tivoli (☎ 7942 4915; 8a Av 4-71, Zona 1) can help you with travel arrangements.

Sleeping

Hotel Dario (☎ 7942 0192; 8a Av 4-40, Zona 1; s/d US$4/6, with bathroom US$9/12) Big, plain rooms around a leafy courtyard. Upstairs rooms share a breezy sitting area, but have shared bathrooms.

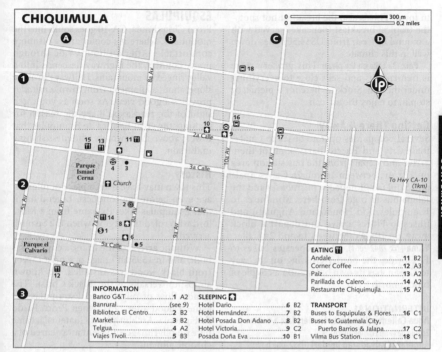

CHIQUIMULA

INFORMATION		
Banco G&T.....................1 A2		
Banrural.....................(see 9)		
Biblioteca El Centro......2 B2		
Market......................3 B2		
Telgua.......................4 A2		
Viajes Tivoli...............5 B3		

SLEEPING		
Hotel Dario..................6 B2		
Hotel Hernández...........7 B2		
Hotel Posada Don Adano 8 B2		
Hotel Victoria..............9 C2		
Posada Doña Eva 10 B1		

EATING		
Andale.......................11 B2		
Corner Coffee 12 A3		
Paíz...........................13 A2		
Parillada de Calero........14 A2		
Restaurante Chiquimujla....15 A2		

TRANSPORT		
Buses to Esquipulas & Flores.......16 C1		
Buses to Guatemala City,		
Puerto Barrios & Jalapa..17 C2		
Vilma Bus Station..........18 C1		

Hotel Hernández (☎ 7942 0708; 3a Calle 7-41, Zona 1; s/d US$5.50/8, s/d with bathroom US$11/13; P ☒ ☒) It's hard to beat the Hernández – it's been a favorite for years and keeps going strong, with its central position, spacious, simple rooms and good-sized swimming pool. Be sure to check out the carp pond in the *pila* (laundry trough).

Posada Doña Eva (☎ 7942 4956; 2a Calle 9-61, Zona 1; s/d US$8/12) Set way back from the busy streets, the cool, clean rooms here offer a minimalist approach to comfort, with bathrooms, TV and fans.

Hotel Victoria (☎ 7942 2732; cnr 2a Calle & 10a Av; s/d with bathroom US$9/12) If you're just looking for somewhere to crash close to the bus terminal, these rooms are a pretty good bet. Clean and not too cramped, with TV and a decent *comedor* downstairs. Get one at the back – the street noise can be insane.

Hotel Posada Don Adano (☎ 7942 3924; 8a Av 4-30, Zona 1; s/d with bathroom US$13/20; P ☒) The Don offers the best deal in this price range – neat, complete rooms with TV, fan, air-con, a couple of sticks of furniture and good, firm beds.

Eating

There's a string of cheap *comedores* an 8a Av behind the market. At night snack vendors and taco carts set up along 7a Av opposite the plaza, selling the cheapest eats in town.

Andale (8a Av 2-34, Zona 1; mains US$3-5; ☾ lunch & dinner) For that late-night (until 11pm) Tex-Mex munchout, this is the place to be – big burritos, tacos (three for US$1.50) and cheap beer in a relaxed, clean environment.

Restaurante Chiquimujla (3a Calle 6-51; breakfast US$2-3.25, mains US$4-7) In Hotel Chiquimulja, this is an impressive palm-roofed building on two levels. Relax with a lovely long drink and choose from the list of pasta dishes, prawns and grilled meats. The *parillada* platter for two is a real heart-stopper, in more ways than one.

The Corner Coffee (6a Calle 6-70, Zona 1; mains US$4-8; ☾ lunch & dinner) You could argue with the syntax, but this air-con haven right on the lovely Parque el Calvario serves up the best range of steaks, pasta, burgers and bagels in town.

Parillada de Calero (7a Av 4-83; mains US$5-8; ☾ breakfast, lunch & dinner) This is an open-air steakhouse, serving the juiciest flame-grilled cuts in town. This is also the breakfast hot spot – the tropical breakfast (pancakes served with a mound of fresh fruit; US$4.50) goes down well in this climate.

Paíz (3a Calle on the plaza) This grocery store is tremendous and sells close to everything under the sun. Stock up here for a picnic, or stop in to enjoy the air-con.

Getting There & Away

Several companies operate buses to Guatemala City and Puerto Barrios; all of them arrive and depart from the bus station area on 11a Av, between 1a and 2a Calles. Ipala and San Lúis Jilotepeque *microbuses* and the Jalapa bus also go from here. Minibuses to Esquipulas, Río Hondo and Anguiatú and buses to Flores arrive and depart a block away, on 10a Av, between 1a and 2a Calles. **Vilma** (☎ 7942 2064), which operates buses to El Florido, the border crossing on the way to Copán, has its own bus station a couple of blocks north.

INTERNATIONAL

Agua Caliente (Honduran border) Take a minibus to Esquipulas and change there.

Anguiatú (Salvadoran border) (US$2, one hour, 54km) Hourly minibuses between 5am and 5:30pm.

El Florido for Copán (Honduran border) (US$2, 1½ hours, 58km) Minibuses depart from the Vilma bus station every 30 minutes from 5:30am to 4:30pm.

DOMESTIC

Esquipulas (US$2, 45 minutes, 52km) Minibuses run every 10 minutes, 4am to 8pm. Sit on the left for the best views of the basilica.

Flores (US$10, seven to eight hours, 385km) Transportes María Elena (☎ 7942 3420) goes at 6am, 10am and 3pm.

Guatemala City (US$5, three hours, 169km) Rutas Orientales and other companies depart at least hourly, from 3am to 3:30pm. The 3am bus leaves from the plaza, the rest from the bus station.

Puerto Barrios (US$5, 4½ hours, 192km, every 30 minutes 4am-6pm)

Quiriguá (US$4, two hours, 103km) Take a Puerto Barrios bus.

Río Dulce (US$4.50, three hours, 144km) Take a Flores bus, or a Puerto Barrios bus to La Ruidosa junction and change there.

Río Hondo (US$2, 35 minutes, 32km) There are minibuses every 30 minutes from 5am to 6pm. Or take any bus heading for Guatemala City, Flores or Puerto Barrios. On Sunday Guatemala City buses won't let you on for Río Hondo – take a minibus.

ESQUIPULAS

From Chiquimula, CA-10 goes south into the mountains, where it's cooler and a bit more comfortable. After an hour's ride through pretty country, the highway descends into a valley ringed by mountains. Halfway down the slope, about a kilometer from town, a *mirador* provides a good view. As soon as you catch sight of the place, you'll see the reason for coming: the great Basílica de Esquipulas that towers above the town, its whiteness shining in the sun.

History

This town may have been a place of pilgrimage even before the conquest. Legend has it that Esquipulas takes its name from a Maya lord who ruled this region when the Spanish arrived.

With the arrival of the friars, a church was built, and in 1595 an image of Christ carved from black wood was installed. It's known almost universally as the 'Black Christ.' The steady flow of pilgrims to Esquipulas became a flood after 1737, when Pedro Pardo de Figueroa, Archbishop of Guatemala, came here on pilgrimage and went away cured of a chronic ailment.

Delighted with this development, the prelate commissioned a huge new church to be built on the site. It was finished in 1758, and the pilgrimage trade has been the town's livelihood ever since.

Esquipulas is assured a place in modern history, too. Beginning here in 1986, President Vinicio Cerezo Arévalo brokered agreements with the other Central American leaders on economic cooperation and conflict resolution. These became the seeds of the Guatemalan Peace Accords, which were finally signed in 1996.

Orientation & Information

The basilica is the center of everything. Most of the good cheap hotels are within a block or two, as are numerous small restaurants. The highway does not enter town; 11a Calle, also sometimes called Doble Vía Quirio Cataño, comes in from the highway and is the town's 'main drag.'

The **post office** (6a Av 2-15) is about 10 blocks north of the center. **Telgua** (cnr 5a Av & 9a Calle) has plenty of card phones. Check your email at **Global.com** (3a Av opposite Banco Internacional; per hr US$0.80).

A number of banks change US dollars and traveler's checks. **Banco Internacional** (3a Av 8-87, Zona 1) changes both, gives cash advances on Visa and MasterCard, is the town's American Express agent and has a Visa ATM.

January 15 is the annual **Cristo de Esquipulas festival**, with mobs of devout pilgrims coming from all over the region to worship at the altar of the Black Christ.

Sights & Activities

BASILICA

A massive pile of stone that has resisted earthquakes for almost 250 years, the basilica is approached through a pretty park and up a flight of steps. The impressive facade and towers are floodlit at night.

Inside, the devout approach **El Cristo Negro** with extreme reverence, many on their knees. Incense, the murmur of prayers and the scuffle of sandaled feet fill the air. When throngs of pilgrims are here, you must enter the church from the side to get a close view of the famous Black Christ. Shuffling along quickly, you may get a good glimpse before being shoved onward by the press of the crowd. On Sunday, religious holidays and (especially) during the festival, the press of devotees is intense. Otherwise, you may have the place to yourself.

CUEVA DE LAS MINAS

The **Centro Turístico Cueva de las Minas** (admission US$1.50; 6:30am-4pm) has a 50m-deep cave (bring your own light), grassy picnic areas, and the Río El Milagro, where people come for a miraculous dip. The cave and river are half a kilometer from the entrance gate, which is behind the basilica's cemetery, 300m south of the turnoff into town on the road heading off toward Honduras. Refreshments are available.

Sleeping

Esquipulas has an abundance of accommodations. On holidays and during the annual festival, every hotel in town is filled, whatever the price; weekends are busy as well, with prices substantially higher. On nonfestival weekdays, ask for a *descuento* (discount). For cheap rooms, look in the streets immediately north of the towering basilica.

Pensión Santa Rosa (7943 2908; cnr 10a Calle & 1a Av, Zona 1; s/d US$5/8, with bathroom US$14/17) Some splashes of color make this a cheerier-than-usual budget choice. Rooms with shared bathroom are plainer; those with bathroom have a bit of furniture and cable TV. The Hotel San Carlos II next door is similar, as is the Pensión La Favorita, and there are several others on this street.

Hotel Monte Cristo (7943 1453; www.hotelmonte cristo.i8.com; 3a Av 9-12, Zona 1; s/d US$10/12, s/d with bathroom US$15/18; P) Good-sized rooms with a bit of furniture and superhot showers. A policy of not letting the upstairs rooms till the downstairs ones are full might see you on the ground floor.

GETTING TO EL SALVADOR

See p298 for information on crossing the border from El Salvador.

To Santa Ana via Anguiatú

Thirty-five kilometers from Chiquimula and 14km from Esquipulas, Padre Miguel junction is the turnoff for **Anguiatú**, the border of El Salvador, which is 19km (one hour) away. Minibuses pass frequently, coming from Chiquimula, Quezaltepeque and Esquipulas.

The border at Anguiatú is open from 6am to 7pm. Plenty of trucks cross here. Across the border there are hourly buses to **San Salvador**, passing through **Metapán** and **Santa Ana**.

To Santa Ana via San Cristóbal

Hourly buses (US$3.50, one hour) connect El Progresso on the Guatemalan side with the border crossing at **San Cristóbal**.

To Las Chiminas

Frequent minibuses connect Guatemala City, Cuilapa and Valle Nuevo (the border crossing for **Las Chinamas** in El Salvador). Note that there's nowhere to stay between Cuilapa and the border.

Hotel Posada Santiago (☎ 7943 2023; s/d US$10/14, with bathroom & cable TV US$20; P) With some interesting (but don't get excited) architecture, these rustic/chic rooms are some of the most attractive in town. They're spacious and clean, with good showers and cable TV.

Hotel El Peregrino (☎ 7943 1054; 2a Av 11-94, Zona 1; s/d US$10/15, with bathroom US$15/20; 🛋) It has hotel-style rooms looking out onto plant-filled balconies. The rooftop pool is what makes this place.

Eating

Esquipulas' budget restaurants are clustered around the north end of the park, where hungry pilgrims can find them readily. Most eateries are open from 6:30am until 9pm or 10pm.

The street running north opposite the church – 3a Av – has several eateries.

Restaurante Calle Real (breakfast US$2-4, mains US$4-6; ☯ breakfast, lunch & dinner) Typical of many restaurants here, this big eating barn turns out cheap meals for the pilgrims. There's a wide menu, strip lighting and loud TV.

Restaurant El Angel (☎ 7943 1372; cnr 11a Calle & 2 Av; mains US$4-8; ☯ lunch & dinner) This main-street Chinese eatery does all the standard dishes, plus steaks and a good range of *licuados* (fresh fruit drink, blended with milk or water). Home delivery is available.

Restaurante La Frontera (breakfast US$3-5, mains US$5-11) Opposite the park and attached to Hotel Las Cúpulas, this is a spacious, clean place serving up a good variety of rice, chicken, meat, fish and seafood dishes for good prices.

La Hacienda (cnr 2a Av & 10a Calle, Zona 1; mains from US$6; ☯ breakfast, lunch & dinner) The best steakhouse in town also serves up some decent seafood and pasta dishes. There's a café-bakery attached and the breakfasts (US$5.50) are a good (but slightly pricey) bet.

Getting There & Away

Buses to Guatemala City arrive and depart from the **Rutas Orientales bus station** (☎ 7943 1366; cnr 11a Calle & 1a Av), near the entrance to town. Minibuses to Agua Caliente arrive and depart across the street; taxis also wait here, charging the same as the minibuses, once they have five passengers.

Minibuses to Chiquimula and to Anguiatú depart from the east end of 11a Calle; you'll probably see them hawking for passengers along the main street.

INTERNATIONAL

Agua Caliente (Honduran border) (US$1.80, 30 minutes, 10km) Minibuses every 30 minutes from 6am to 5pm.
Anguiatú (Salvadoran border) (US$1.50, one hour, 33km) Minibuses every 30 minutes from 6am to 6pm.

DOMESTIC

Chiquimula (US$1.50, 45 minutes, 52km) Minibuses every 15 minutes from 5am to 6pm.
Flores (US$12, eight to 10 hours, 437km) Transportes María Elena (☎ 7943 0448) has buses at 4am, 8am and 1pm from east of the basilica, amid the market.
Guatemala City (US$7, four hours, 222km) Rutas Orientales *servicio especial* buses depart at 6:30am, 7:30am, 1:30pm and 3pm; ordinary buses depart every 30 minutes from 4:30am to 6pm.

IZABAL

This lush little corner of the country really packs in the attractions. The Río Dulce–Lago de Izabal area is gorgeous and largely untouched. The Garífuna enclave of Lívingston shows a whole other side to Guatemala and the little-visited ruins at Quiriguá have some of the finest carvings in the country.

QUIRIGUÁ

Quiriguá's archaeological zone is famed for its intricately carved stelae – gigantic sandstone monoliths up to 10.5m tall – that rise like ancient sentinels in a quiet tropical park. Visiting the ruins is easy if you have your own transportation, more difficult if you're traveling by bus. From the Río Hondo junction it's 67km along the Carr al Atlántico to **Los Amates**, which has a couple of hotels, a restaurant and a bank. The village of Quiriguá is 1.5km east of Los Amates. See opposite for details of how to get to the archaeological site from here.

History

Quiriguá's history parallels that of Copán, of which it was a dependency during much of the Classic period. The location lent itself to the carving of giant stelae. Beds of brown sandstone in the nearby Río Motagua had cleavage planes suitable for cutting large pieces. Although soft when first cut, the sandstone dried hard. With Copán's expert artisans nearby for guidance, Quiriguá's stone carvers were ready for greatness. All they needed was a leader to inspire them – and pay for the carving.

That leader was Cauac Sky (AD 725–84), who sought Quiriguá's independence from Copán. In a war with his former suzerain, Cauac Sky took Copán's King 18 Rabbit prisoner in 737 and beheaded him soon after. Independent at last, Cauac Sky called up the stonecutters and for the next 38 years they turned out giant stelae and zoomorphs dedicated to his glory.

In the early 20th century the United Fruit Company bought all the land around Quiriguá and turned it into banana groves. The company is gone, but the bananas and Quiriguá remain. In 1981, Unesco declared Quiriguá a World Heritage Site.

Ruins

It's hot and there are mosquitoes everywhere, but the park-like **archaeological zone** (admission US$4; ◷ 7:30am-5pm) is unforgettable. The giant stelae on the Great Plaza are awe-inspiring despite their worn condition.

Stelae A, C, D, E, F, H and J, were built during the reign of Cauac Sky and carved with his image. **Stela E** is the largest Maya stela known, standing 8m above ground, with about another 3m buried in the earth. It weighs almost 60,000kg. Note the elaborate head-dresses; the beards on some figures (an oddity in Mayan art and life); the staffs of office held in the kings' hands; and the glyphs on the stelae's sides.

At the far end of the plaza is the **Acropolis**. At its base are several zoomorphs, blocks of stone carved to resemble real and mythic creatures. Frogs, tortoises, jaguars and serpents were favorite subjects. The low zoomorphs can't compete with the towering stelae in impressiveness, but are superb as works of art, imagination and mythic significance.

A small *tienda* (shop) near the entrance sells cold drinks and snacks, but you'd be better off bringing a picnic.

Sleeping & Eating

Both of the hotels listed below have restaurants. There seems to be a bit of a price war going on in Quiriguá – just mention that you're going to have a look at the other place and listen to the prices plummet. To get to them both, walk down the main street, veering right at the first fork and then follow the road around to the left at the bend.

Hotel El Paraíso (s/d US$5.50/8, with bathroom US$8/11) The better of the two hotels in town,

the rooms with shared bathrooms here are fine, plus you get to use the shower with the awesome mountain views.

Hotel y Restaurante Royal (☎ 7947 3639; s/d US$5.50/8, with bathroom US$8/11) The first hotel you come to, this one has small but adequate rooms – those with bathrooms are a lot nicer. The restaurant serves both meat and vegetarian meals.

Getting There & Away

Buses running along the routes Guatemala City–Puerto Barrios, Guatemala City–Flores, Esquipulas–Flores or Chiquimula–Flores will drop you off or pick you up at the turnoff to Quiriguá town. Better yet, drivers will drop you at the turnoff to the archaeological site if you ask.

The transportation center in this area is Morales, about 40km northeast of Quiriguá. It's not pretty, but it's where the bus for Río Dulce originates. If a seat isn't important, skip Morales and wait at the La Ruidosa junction for the Río Dulce bus.

Getting Around

From the turnoff on the highway (1.5km from Quiriguá town) it's 3.4km to the archaeological site. Buses and pickups provide transportation between the turnoff and the site for US$0.80 each way. If you don't see one, don't fret; it's a nice walk on a dirt road through banana plantations to get there.

If you're staying in Quiriguá and walking to and from the archaeological site, take the shortcut along the railway line from the village through the banana fields, crossing the access road near the site entrance.

LAGO DE IZABAL

Guatemala's largest lake is starting to register on travelers' radars. Most visitors stay at Río Dulce village, north of the bridge where Hwy CA-13, the road leading north to Flores and Tikal, crosses the lake's east end. East of this bridge is the beautiful Río Dulce, which opens into El Golfete lake before flowing into the Caribbean at Lívingston; a river trip is one of the highlights of a visit to eastern Guatemala.

Other lake highlights include El Castillo de San Felipe (an old Spanish fortress) and the Bocas del Polochic river delta. Many quiet and secluded spots in this area await your exploration.

GUATEMALA

Río Dulce

At the east end of the Lago de Izabal where it empties into the Río Dulce, this town still gets referred to as Fronteras. It's a hangover from the days when the only way across the river was by ferry, and this was the last piece of civilization before embarking on the long, difficult journey into the Petén.

Times have changed. A huge bridge now spans the water and the Petén roads are some of the best in the country. The town sees most tourist traffic from yachties – the US coast guard says this is the safest place on the western Caribbean for boats during hurricane season. The rest of the foreigners here are either coming or going on the spectacular river trip down to Livingston (see p183).

ORIENTATION & INFORMATION

The places listed here – except for Hotel Backpacker's and Casa Guatemala – are on the north side of the bridge. Get off near Río Bravo Restaurant. Otherwise you'll be walking the length of what is purported to be Central America's longest bridge – a steamy 30-minute walk.

Many businesses in the area use radio to communicate. You can make calls at Cap't Nemo's.

Tijax Express, in the little lane between the river and the Fuente del Norte office, is Río Dulce's unofficial tourist information center. Bus, *lancha*, hotel and other important travel details are available here. It's open every day and English is spoken. There are two similar places near Tijax, Otitours and Atitrans. You can book *lanchas*, tours, sailing trips and shuttles with all three.

If you need to change cash or traveler's checks, hit one of the four banks in town, all on the main road. **Banco Industrial** (9am-5pm) has a Visa ATM. Banrural has Visa and MasterCard ATMs. Banco Agromercantil will give cash advances on credit cards if there is a problem with the ATMs.

Cap't Nemo's Communications (7am-8pm Mon-Sat, 9am-2pm Sun), beside Bruno's on the river, offers email (US$2 per hour) and international phone and radiophone calls. The website www.mayaparadise.com has loads of information about Río Dulce.

TOURS

Aventuras Vacacionales (/fax 7832 5938; www.sailing-diving-guatemala.com; Centro Comercial María, 4a Calle Poniente 17, Antigua) runs fun sailing trips on the sailboat *Las Sirenas* from Río Dulce to the Belize reefs and islands (US$400, seven days) and Lago Izabal (US$180, four days). Their office is in Antigua but you can hook up with them in Río Dulce. They make the Belize and lake trips in alternate weeks.

SLEEPING

By the Water

The following three places are out of town on the water, which is the best place to be. You can call or radio them from Tijax Express and they'll come and pick you up.

Casa Perico (7930 5666, VHF channel 68; dm US$5.50, s/d US$6/7, with bathroom US$20/27) One of the more low-key options in the area, this is set on a little inlet about 200m from the main river. Cabins are well built and connected by boardwalks. The Swiss guys who run it offer tours all up and down the river, and put on an excellent buffet dinner (US$6), or you can choose from the menu (mains US$3 to US$4). The place has a good book exchange and a young, fun atmosphere.

Hacienda Tijax (7930 5505/7, VHF channel 09; www.tijax.com; camping per person US$3, s/d from US$8/13 to US$34/39;) This 500-acre hacienda, a two-minute boat ride across the cove from Bruno's, is a special place to stay. Activities include horseback riding, hiking, birding, sailboat trips and tours around the rubber plantation. Accommodation is in lovely little cabins connected by a boardwalk. Most cabins face the water and there's a very relaxing pool/bar area. Access is by boat or by a road that turns off the highway about 1km north of the village. The folks here speak Spanish, English, Dutch, French and Italian, and they'll pick you up from across the river; ask at the Tijax Express office.

Hotel Backpacker's (7930 5169; casaguatemal@guate.net; dm US$4, s/d US$8/16, with bathroom US$10/20) Across the bridge, this is a business run by Casa Guatemala and the orphans it serves. It's an old (with the emphasis on old) backpacker favorite, set in a rickety building with very basic rooms. Volunteer work is available here, either working in the hotel or the nearby children's refuge. The bar kicks on here at night. If you're coming by *lancha* or bus, ask the driver to let you off here to spare yourself the walk across the bridge.

El Tortugal (5306 6432; www.tortugal.com; bungalows US$20) The best looking bungalows on the river are located here, five minutes *lan-*

cha ride east from town. There are plenty of hammocks, the showers are seriously hot and kayaks are free for guest use.

In Town
Bruno's (☎ 7930 5721; www.mayaparadise.com/bru noe.htm; dm US$5, s/d US$6/12, with bathroom US$23/33; **P** ⚹ ⚹) A path leads down from the north-west end of the bridge to this riverside hang-out for yachties needing to get some land under their feet. The cheapest rooms here are barely worth looking at, but the dorms are clean and spacious and the new building offers some of the most comfortable rooms in town, with air-con and balconies overlooking the river. They're well set up for families and sleep up to six, charging US$10 per additional person over the doubles rate.

Las Brisas Hotel (☎ 7930 5124; s/d with bathroom US$10/13; ⚹) This hotel is opposite Tijax Express. All rooms are clean enough and have three beds and fans. Three rooms upstairs have bathroom and air-con (US$40). It's central and good enough for a night, but there are much better places around.

EATING
Restaurante La Carreta, (breakfast US$2, mains US$5-8) While most of the waterside joints are serving up pricey food with romantic views, this *palapa*-style restaurant off the highway on the road toward San Felipe (with charming views of the neighbor's backyard) is keeping it real for the locals, with big serves at low prices. The surf and turf (US$9.50) comes highly recommended.

Restaurant Los Pinchos (breakfast US$3, mains US$6-10; ☺ breakfast, lunch & dinner) With an open-air deck over the lake, this place has some good eats and a very local flavor. They don't get too fancy, but there is a good range of steaks, seafood and Chinese dishes on offer in a relaxed environment.

Bruno's (breakfast US$2.60-4, mains US$10) Another open-air place right beside the water, Bruno's is a restaurant-sports bar with satellite TV and video; its floating dock makes it popular with yachties.

GETTING THERE & AWAY
Beginning at 7am, 14 Fuente del Norte buses a day head north along to Poptún (US$4, two hours, 99km) and Flores (US$6.50, four hours, 208km). The 12:30pm, 7:30pm, 9:30pm and 11:30pm buses continue all the way to

Melchor de Mencos (US$12) on the Belizean border. With good connections you can get to Tikal (279km) in a snappy six hours. In the other direction, at least 17 buses daily go to Guatemala City (US$6.50, six hours, 280km) with Fuente del Norte and Litegua. Línea Dorada/Fuente del Norte has 1st-class buses departing at 1:30pm for Guatemala City and 2:30pm for Flores (both US$18). This shaves up to an hour off the journey times.

Minibuses for Puerto Barrios (US$2.50, two hours) leave when full from the roadside opposite Tijax Express.

Atitrans' shuttle minibus operates from their office on the highway. Shuttles to Antigua cost US$37, to Copán Ruinas US$30 and Guatemala City US$30 with a minimum of four passengers in each case. Otitours and Tijax Express offer much the same.

Fuente del Norte buses leave for El Estor (US$1.30, 1½ hours, 43km) from the San Felipe and El Estor turnoff in the middle of town, hourly from 7am to 4pm.

Colectivo lanchas go down the Río Dulce (from the new dock) to Lívingston, usually requiring eight to 10 people, charging US$12 per person. The trip is beautiful and there are often several tourlike halts along the way (see p183). If everyone wants to get there as fast as possible, it takes one hour without stops. Boats usually leave from 9am to about 2pm.

The Road to Flores
North across the bridge is the road into El Petén, Guatemala's vast jungle province. It's 208km to Santa Elena and Flores, and another 71km to Tikal.

The entire stretch of road from the Carr al Atlántico to Santa Elena has been paved, so it's a smooth ride all the way from Río Dulce to the Tikal ruins.

The forest here is disappearing at an alarming rate, falling to the machetes of subsistence farmers. Sections are felled and burned off, crops are grown for a few seasons until the fragile jungle soil is exhausted, then the farmer moves deeper into the forest to slash and burn anew. Cattle ranchers have contributed to the damage, as has the migration of Guatemalans from the cities to El Petén.

Mariscos
Mariscos is the principal town on the lake's south side. Ferries from here used to be the main access to El Estor and the north side of

the lake, but since a road was built from Río Dulce to El Estor, Mariscos has taken a back seat. As a result, **Denny's Beach** (☎ 2337 4946; VHF channel 63; www.dennysbeach.com; campsite US$4, hammock US$2, cabaña per person US$5-10), 10 minutes by boat from Mariscos, is a good place to get away from it all.

It offers tours, hiking and swimming, and host full-moon parties. When you arrive in Mariscos, radio them to pick you up. Otherwise, hitch a ride with a *cayuco* (dugout canoe) at the market for US$1.30 or go to Shop-n-Go and hire a speedboat for US$13, fine if you're a group. Karlinda's is another place to stay in Mariscos; it has a restaurant and offers lake tours.

El Castillo de San Felipe

The fortress and **castle** (admission US$2.80; ☉ 8am-5pm) of San Felipe de Lara, about 3km west of the bridge, was built in 1652 to keep pirates from looting the villages and commercial caravans of Izabal. Although it deterred the buccaneers a bit, a pirate force captured and burned the fortress in 1686. By the end of the next century, pirates had disappeared from the Caribbean and the fort's sturdy walls served as a prison. Eventually, the fortress was abandoned and became a ruin. The present fort was reconstructed in 1956.

Today, the castle is protected as a park and is one of the lake's principal tourist attractions. In addition to the fort, the site has a large park, with barbecue/picnic areas, and you can swim in the lake.

Near the Castillo, **Hotel Don Humberto** (☎ /fax 7930 5051; s/d US$8/11; P) has basic rooms with big beds and good mosquito netting. It's nothing fancy, but more than adequate for a cheap sleep.

San Felipe is on the lakeshore, 3km west of Río Dulce. It's a beautiful 45-minute walk between the two, or colectivo pickups provide transportation for US$0.50, running about every half-hour. In Río Dulce pickups stop at the corner of the highway and the road to El Estor; in San Felipe they stop in front of Hotel Don Humberto, at the entrance to El Castillo.

Boats coming from Lívingston will drop you in San Felipe if you ask them. The Río Dulce boat trips usually cruise by El Castillo. Some will let you get out and visit the castle. Or you can come over from Río Dulce by private launch for US$8.

Finca El Paraíso

On the lake's north side, between San Felipe and El Estor, the **Finca El Paraíso** (☎ 7949 7122; admission US$1.30) is a popular day trip from Río Dulce and other places around the lake. At the *finca,* which is a working ranch, you can walk to an incredibly beautiful spot in the jungle where a wide, hot waterfall drops about 12m into a clear, deep pool. You can bathe in the hot water, swim in the cool pool or duck under an overhanging promontory and enjoy a jungle-style sauna. Also on the *finca* are several interesting caves and good hiking. You can rent bungalows for US$25 per double.

The *finca* is on the Río Dulce–El Estor bus route, about one hour (US$0.90) from Río Dulce and 30 minutes (US$0.60) from El Estor. The last bus in either direction passes around 4:30pm to 5pm.

El Estor

Gorgeously sited and rarely visited, this small town looks over the Lago de Izabal to the Sierra de las Minas. It's most often used as a staging point for visits to the **Bocas del Polochic**, a highly biodiverse wildlife reserve at the west end of the lake, but is also a gateway for the difficult but possible back route to Lanquín and Cobán.

ORIENTATION & INFORMATION

El Estor is an easily negotiable town. Buses from Río Dulce terminate at Parque Central, on whose east side is **Café Portal** (☉ 6:30am-10pm), which provides excellent information, tours and transportation. **Banrural** (cnr 3a Calle & 6a Av; ☉ 8:30am-5pm Mon-Fri, 9am-1pm Sat) changes US dollars and American Express traveler's checks. The **municipal police** (cnr 1a Calle & 5a Av) are near the lakeshore.

The Asociación Feminina Q'eqchi' sells clothes, blankets and accessories made from traditional cloth woven by the association's members. To find it go two blocks north along 5a Av from Parque Central, then two blocks west. All profits benefit the women involved in the program.

SLEEPING & EATING

Hotel Central (☎ 949 7497; 5a Av; s/d with bathroom US$7/10; P) This hotel provides rooms with fan at the northeast corner of Parque Central.

Restaurante Típico Chaabil (☎ 7949 7272; west end 3a Calle; r with bathroom per person US$10; P) Although they go a bit heavy on the log-cabin feel, these rooms are the best deal in town. Get one upstairs for plenty of light and good views. The restaurant here, on a lovely lakeside terrace, cooks up delicious food, such as *tapado* (the Garífuna seafood and coconut stew; US$8). The water here is crystal clear and you can swim right off the hotel's dock.

Hotel Vista al Lago (☎ 7949 7205; 6a Av 1-13; s/d with bathroom US$10/20) Set in a classic, historic building down on the waterfront, this place has plenty of style, although the rooms themselves are fairly ordinary. Views from the upstairs balcony are superb.

Café Portal (Parque Central; mains US$3-5) Serves a broad range of fare with some vegetarian options.

GETTING THERE & AWAY

For information on buses from Río Dulce, see p175. The schedule from El Estor to Río Dulce is hourly, 6am to 4pm.

The road west from El Estor to Panzós and Tucurú to Tactic, south of Cobán, has a bad reputation for highway holdups and robberies, especially around Tucurú. We do not recommend it, but a bus leaves El Estor's Parque Central at 1am heading for Cobán (US$7, six hours) where there are many buses to Lanquín. A safer, slower way of getting to Lanquín is by taking the truck that leaves El Estor's Parque Central at 9am for Cahabón (US$2, four to five hours), and then a bus or pickup straight on from Cahabón to Lanquín the same day. This route is not recommended in the reverse direction because the truck leaves Cahabón about 4am, meaning you have to spend the preceding night in impoverished Cahabón, where things can get dodgy after dark.

There are no public boat services between El Estor and other lake destinations. Private *lanchas* can be contracted, although this can be pricey. Ask at your hotel.

PUERTO BARRIOS

pop 62,700

The country becomes even more lush, tropical and humid heading east from La Ruidosa junction toward Puerto Barrios. Port towns have always had a reputation for being slightly dodgy, and those acting as international borders doubly so. Perhaps the town council wants to pay homage to that here. Or perhaps the edgy, slightly sleazy feel is authentic. Either way, for foreign visitors, Puerto Barrios

is mainly a jumping-off point for boats to Punta Gorda (Belize) or Lívingston, and you probably won't be hanging around.

The powerful United Fruit Company owned vast plantations in the Río Motagua valley. It built railways (whose tracks still run through the middle of town) to ship produce to the coast. Puerto Barrios was built early in the 20th century to put that produce onto ships sailing for New Orleans and New York. Laid out as a company town, Puerto Barrios has long, wide streets arranged neatly on a grid. Many of its Caribbean-style wood-frame houses are on stilts.

Orientation & Information

Its spacious layout means you must walk or ride further in Puerto Barrios to get from place to place. It's 800m from the bus terminals in the town center to the Muelle Municipal (Municipal Boat Dock) at the end of 12a Calle, from which passenger boats depart.

Banco Industrial (7a Av btwn 7a & 8a Calles; ⊗ 9am-5pm Mon-Fri, to 1pm Sat) changes US dollars and traveler's checks and has a Visa ATM. **Banco Reformador** (8a Av btwn 9a & 10a Calles; ⊗ 8:30am-5pm Mon-Fri, 9am-1pm Sat) changes US dollars only and has a MasterCard ATM.

The **immigration office** (cnr 12a Calle & 3a Av; ⊗ 24hr) is a block from the Muelle Municipal. Come here for your entry or exit stamp if you're arriving from or leaving for Belize. If you're heading to Honduras, you get your exit stamp at another immigration office on the road to the border.

Go online at **Cybernet del Atlántico** (7a Calle; per hr US$0.80), west of 2a Av.

El Muñecón, at the intersection of 8a Av, 14a Calle and the Calz Justo Rufino Barrios, is a statue of a dock worker; it's a favorite landmark and monument in the town.

Sleeping

Hotel Xelajú (☎ 7948 0482; 8a Av btwn 9a & 10a Calles; s/d US$5/8, with bathroom US$8/12) The Xelajú is right in the town center, facing the market, but it's secure: no rooms are let after 10pm and 'señoritas de clubes nocturnos' are not allowed. It has clean fan-cooled rooms and its own generator for when the electricity fails.

Hotel Lee (☎ 7948 0685; 5a Av btwn 9a & 10a Calles; s/d US$5/9, with bathroom US$8/14) This is a friendly, family-owned place close to the bus terminals. The rooms are a bit cramped but clean, and have fans, TV, drinking water and Chinese art.

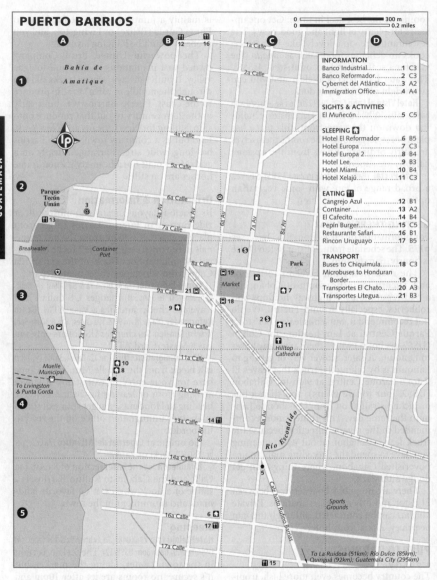

PUERTO BARRIOS

Bahía de Amatique

Parque Tecún Umán

Breakwater

Container Port

Muelle Municipal

To Livingston & Punta Gorda

Market

Park

Hilltop Cathedral

Río Escondido

Sports Grounds

Cra Justo Rufino Barrios

To La Ruidosa (51km); Río Dulce (85km); Quiriguá (92km); Guatemala City (295km)

0 — 300 m
0 — 0.2 miles

INFORMATION
Banco Industrial...................**1** C3
Banco Reformador.................**2** C3
Cybernet del Atlántico.........**3** A2
Immigration Office...............**4** A4

SIGHTS & ACTIVITIES
El Muñecón........................**5** C5

SLEEPING
Hotel El Reformador **6** B5
Hotel Europa **7** C3
Hotel Europa 2...................**8** B4
Hotel Lee...........................**9** B3
Hotel Miami.......................**10** B4
Hotel Xelajú......................**11** C3

EATING
Cangrejo Azul **12** B1
Container...........................**13** A2
El Cafecito **14** B4
Pepín Burger......................**15** C5
Restaurante Safari.............**16** B1
Rincon Uruguayo **17** B5

TRANSPORT
Buses to Chiquimula..........**18** C3
Microbuses to Honduran
  Border.............................**19** C3
Transportes El Chato.........**20** A3
Transportes Litegua...........**21** B3

Hotel Miami (☎ 7948 0537; 3a Av btwn 11a & 12a Calles; s/d US$5.50/8, with air-con US$12/24; P ❋) Not bad if you want to save your pennies to spend on other things…otherwise a bit grim.

Hotel Europa (☎ 7948 0127; 8a Av btwn 8a & 9a Calles; s/d US$7/12; P) Not quite up to the standards of the Europa 2, the Europa scrapes in thanks to their quiet rooms and firm beds.

Hotel Europa 2 (☎ 7948 1292; 3a Av btwn 11a & 12a Calles; s/d US$8/10; P) The best of the budget options in the port area, this hotel just 1½ blocks from the Muelle Municipal is run by a friendly family and has clean rooms (with fan and TV), arranged around a parking courtyard.

Hotel El Reformador (☎ 7948 0533; reformador@ intelnet.net.gt; cnr 7a Av & 16a Calle; s/d US$13/18.50, with air-con US$22/28; (P) ⛰) Like a little haven away from the hot busy streets outside, the Reformador offers big, cool rooms set around leafy patios. The rooms with air-con lead onto wide interior balconies. There is a restaurant here.

Eating

Pepín Burger (17a Calle btwn 8a & 9a Avs; snacks from US$2; ☉ closed Tue) Come here for an almost mind-boggling array of snacks, fajitas, good-value burgers and more serious meals on an open-air upstairs terrace.

El Cafecito (13a Calle 6-22; mains US$4-10; ☉ breakfast, lunch & dinner) This sweet little air-conditioned spot whips up some of the most interesting food in town – Portuguese dishes such as *fei-joda* (stewed beans, pork, beef, chicken and other stuff; US$6) and a good range of seafood and sandwiches.

Rincon Uruguayo (cnr 7a Av & 16a Calle; mains US$4-12; ☉ lunch & dinner) Being that the concepts of 'big' and 'juicy' are so rarely applied to Guatemalan steak, this outdoor eatery comes as a relief. Chorizo, BBQ chicken and *chivitos* (steak sandwiches) are also available.

Container (7a Calle; snacks US$3; ☉ lunch & dinner) The oddest café in town – made from two shipping containers, with fine bay views, thatched huts out over the water and plenty of cold, cold beer. It's at the western end of the street.

Restaurante Safari (☎ 7948 0563; cnr 5a Av & 1a Calle; seafood US$6.50-10; ☉ 10am-9pm) The town's most enjoyable restaurant is on a thatch-roofed, open-air platform right over the water about 1km north of the town center. Locals and visitors alike love to eat and catch the sea breezes here. It serves excellent seafood of all kinds including the specialty *tapado* (that great Garífuna casserole); chicken and meat dishes are less expensive (US$3 to US$6). There's live music most nights. If it's full, the Cangrejo

Azul next door offers pretty much the same deal, in a more relaxed environment.

Getting There & Away
BOAT
Boats depart from the Muelle Municipal at the end of 12a Calle.

A ferry departs for Lívingston every day at 10am and 5pm; the trip takes 1½ hours and costs US$2. From Lívingston, it leaves for Puerto Barrios at 5am and 2pm. Get to the dock from 30 to 45 minutes early to make sure you get a seat.

Smaller, faster *lanchas* depart from both sides whenever there are a dozen passengers; they take 30 minutes and cost US$4.50.

Most of the movement from Lívingston to Puerto Barrios is in the morning, returning in the afternoon. From Lívingston, your last chance may be the 2pm ferry, especially during the low season when fewer travelers are shuttling back and forth.

BUS & MINIBUS
Transportes Litegua (☎ 7948 1172; cnr 6a Av & 9a Calle) leaves for Guatemala City (US$7, five to six hours, 295km), via Quiriguá and Río Hondo, 15 times between 1am and noon, and at 4pm. *Directo* services avoid a half-hour detour into Morales.

Buses to Chiquimula (US$4, 4½ hours), also via Quiriguá, leave every half-hour, 4am to 4pm, from the east side of the 6a Av and 9a Calle corner.

For Río Dulce, take a Chiquimula bus to La Ruidosa junction (US$1, 50 minutes) and change to a bus or minibus (US$1, 35 minutes) there.

TAXI
Most cabs charge around US$3 for ridiculously short rides around town.

GETTING TO HONDURAS

Minibuses leave Puerto Barrios for the Honduras frontier (US$1.30, 1¼ hours) every 20 minutes from 5:30am to 6pm, from 6a Av outside the market. The paved road to the border turns off the CA-9 at **Entre Ríos**, 13km south of Puerto Barrios. Buses and minibuses going in all directions wait for passengers at Entre Ríos, making the trip from the border fairly easily, whichever direction you are traveling in. Minibuses from Puerto Barrios stop en route to the border at Guatemalan immigration, where you might have to pay US$1.30 for an exit stamp. Think of it as one last tip to Guatemalan officialdom. Honduran entry formalities may leave you US$1 to US$3 lighter.

See p386 for information on crossing the border from Honduras.

For information on crossing via Copán, Honduras, see p170.

PUNTA DE MANABIQUE

This promontory to the north of Puerto Barrios is being slowly and carefully developed for ecotourism by the conservation group, **Fundary** (☎ 7948 0435; www.guate.net/fundarymanabique; 17a Calle, Puerto Barrios). As well as sporting Guatemala's best Caribbean beaches, the area offers endless bird-watching, hiking, sport fishing and other nature-based activities. **El Saraguate** (per person US$9), a simple lodge, has been constructed and serves simple, good meals. You can arrange tours of the area from here. For transport information and to make reservations, contact Fundary.

LÍVINGSTON

pop 17,000

Quite unlike anywhere else in Guatemala, this largely Garífuna town is fascinating in itself, but also an attraction for a couple of good beaches, and its location at the end of the river journey from Río Dulce.

Unconnected by road from the rest of the country (the town is called 'Buga' – mouth – in Garífuna, for its position at the river mouth), boat transport is (logically) quite good here, and you can get to Belize, the cayes, Honduras and Puerto Barrios with a minimum of fuss.

The Garífuna (Garinagu, or Black Carib) people of Lívingston and southern Belize are the descendants of Africans brought to the New World as slaves. They trace their roots to the Honduran island of Roatán, where they were forcibly settled by the British after the Garífuna revolt on the Caribbean island of St Vincent in 1795. From Roatán, the Garífuna people spread out along the Caribbean Coast, from Belize to Nicaragua. Intermarrying with Carib Indians, as well as with Maya and shipwrecked sailors of other races, they've developed a distinct culture and language incorporating African, *indígena* and European elements.

Town beaches are largely disappointing, as the jungle comes to the water's edge. Those beaches that do exist are often clogged with vegetation and unsafe for swimming, thanks to contaminated water. Safe swimming is possible at Los Siete Altares (p184) and Playa Blanca.

Orientation & Information

After half an hour you'll know where everything is. The **immigration office** (Calle Principal; ☯ 6am-7pm) issues entry and exit stamps for travelers ar-

riving direct from or going direct to Belize or Honduras. Outside their normal hours, you can knock at any time. Leaving Guatemala by boat, travelers pay US$10 exit tax.

Email services (US$3 per hour) are offered by **Labug@net** (Calle Principal) and at the **Happy Fish** (Calle Principal), a restaurant.

Banrural (Calle Principal; ☯ 9am-5pm Mon-Fri, to 1pm Sat) changes US dollars and traveler's checks. Several private businesses do, too.

Laundry service is available at Hotel Casa Rosada.

Sights

The **Museo Multicultural de Lívingston** (☯ 9am-6pm Tue-Sun; admission US$2), upstairs on the municipal park in front of the public dock, has some excellent displays on the history and culture of the area, focusing on the ethnic diversity, with Garífuna, Q'eqchi, Hindu and ladino cultures represented. While you're here check out the open-air alligator enclosure in the park.

The best beach in the area is **Playa Blanca** (admission US$2), around 12km from Lívingston. This is privately owned and you need a boat to get there (see below).

Use mosquito repellent and other precautions, especially in the jungle; mosquitoes near the coast carry malaria and dengue fever.

Dangers & Annoyances

Lívingston has its edgy aspects and a few hustlers operate here, trying to sweet-talk tourists into 'lending' money, paying up-front for tours that don't happen. Take care with anyone who strikes up a conversation for no obvious reason on the street or elsewhere.

Like many coastal places in Guatemala, Lívingston is a *puente* (bridge) for northbound drug traffic. There's little in the way of turf wars – the industry is fairly stable – but there are some big-time players around and a lot of money at stake. Keep your wits about you.

The beach between Lívingston and the Río Quehueche, and Siete Altares had a bad reputation for some years, but locals 'took care' of the troublemakers (we don't really want to know details). It now makes a fine walk, with some great swimming at the end of it. You can go independently or as part of a tour.

Tours

Exotic Travel (☎ 7947 0048; www.bluecaribbeanbay.com; Restaurante Bahía Azul, Calle Principal) A well-organized operation with several good trips. Its popular

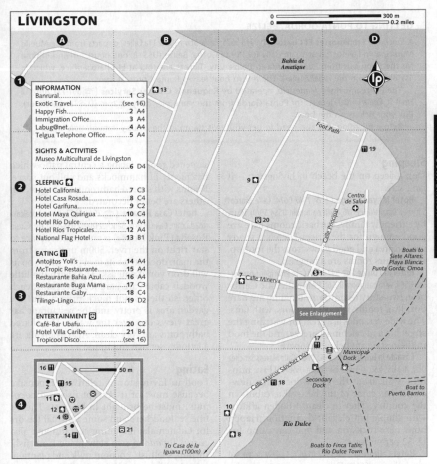

LÍVINGSTON

INFORMATION	
Banrural	1 C3
Exotic Travel	(see 16)
Happy Fish	2 A4
Immigration Office	3 A4
Labug@net	4 A4
Telgua Telephone Office	5 A4

SIGHTS & ACTIVITIES	
Museo Multicultural de Lívingston	
	6 D4

SLEEPING	
Hotel California	7 C3
Hotel Casa Rosada	8 C4
Hotel Garífuna	9 C2
Hotel Maya Quirigua	10 C4
Hotel Río Dulce	11 A4
Hotel Ríos Tropicales	12 A4
National Flag Hotel	13 B1

EATING	
Antojitos Yoli's	14 A4
McTropic Restaurante	15 A4
Restaurante Bahía Azul	16 A4
Restaurante Buga Mama	17 C3
Restaurante Gaby	18 C4
Tilingo-Lingo	19 D2

ENTERTAINMENT	
Café-Bar Ubafu	20 C2
Hotel Villa Caribe	21 B4
Tropicool Disco	(see 16)

Ecological Tour/Jungle Trip takes you for a walk through town, out west up to a lookout and on to the Río Quehueche, where you take a half-hour canoe trip down to Playa Quehueche. Then you walk through the jungle to Los Siete Altares (The Seven Altars; see p184), a series of freshwater falls and pools about 5km northwest of Lívingston. Hang out there for a while then walk down to the beach and back along it to Lívingston. The trip costs US$10 including a box lunch. This is a great way to see the area, and the friendly local guides also give you a good introduction to the Garífuna people who live here.

Another tour goes by boat first to the Seven Altars, then on to the Río Cocolí where you can swim, and then on to Playa Blanca for two or three hours. This trip goes with a minimum of six people and costs US$13.

They also offer day trips to the **Cayos Sapodillas** (or Zapotillas), well off the coast of southern Belize, where there is great snorkeling (US$40 plus US$10 to enter the cays plus US$10 exit tax) and to Punta de Manabique for US$16 per person. A minimum of six people is needed for each of these trips.

Festivals & Events

Semana Santa (Easter week) Packs Lívingston with merrymakers.

Garífuna national day (November 26) Celebrated with a variety of cultural events.

Virgin of Guadalupe (December 12) Celebrations dedicated to Mexico's patron saint.

GETTING TO PUNTA GORDA, BELIZE

A *lancha* of **Transportes El Chato** (☎ 9948 5525; 1a Av btwn 10a & 11a Calles) departs from the Muelle Municipal in Lívingston at 10am daily for Punta Gorda, Belize (US$18, one hour), arriving in time for the noon bus from Punta Gorda to Belize City. Tickets are sold at El Chato's office, which is 1½ blocks from the *muelle* (pier). The return boat leaves Punta Gorda at 4pm.

The Belizean-owned *Mariestela*, operated by **Requena's Charter Services** (☎ 501-722 2070; 12 Front St, Punta Gorda) departs for Punta Gorda from the same pier daily at 2pm (US$18, one hour). Buy your tickets on the boat.

Before boarding you also need to get your exit stamp at the nearby immigration office.

Sleeping

Don't sleep on the beach in Lívingston – it isn't safe.

Hotel Maya Quirigua (☎ 7947 0674; Calle Marcos Sánchez Díaz; s/d US$3/6, with bathroom US$4.50/9) Run by a friendly family, the basic rooms here are good enough for the price. There's a shady garden area and good views from the rooftop. Downstairs rooms are a bit grim.

Hotel Río Dulce (☎ 947 0764; Calle Principal; r per person US$4, with bathroom US$6) This authentic Caribbean two-story wood-frame building has bare but clean rooms, in various colors, with fans. The wide verandas are great for watching the street life and catching a breeze, and the food in the restaurant below is superb.

Casa de la Iguana (☎ 7947 0064; Calle Marcos Sánchez Díaz; dm US$4.50, s/d with bathroom US$8/13) Five minutes' walk from the main dock, this newcomer has some of the best-value cabins in the country. They're clean, wooden affairs, with simple but elegant decoration. Happy hour here rocks on and you can camp for US$2 per person.

Hotel California (☎ 7947 0178/6; Calle Minerva; s/d with bathroom US$6/8) Down a quiet street, the California offers good, basic rooms on the 2nd floor (ones on the first floor are a little stuffy). There's an OK restaurant and some shady places to hang out.

National Flag Hotel (☎ 7947 0247; Barrio San José; s or d with bathroom US$8) The big tiled rooms here are an excellent deal, even if the location is a bit remote. There are good views from the shady rooftop terrace.

Hotel Garifuna (☎ 7947 0183; Barrio San José; s/d with bathroom US$7/10) About a five-minute walk from the main street, the big breezy rooms are a solid budget choice. Beds are good, bathrooms are spotless and the folks are friendly.

Hotel Ríos Tropicales (☎ 7947 0158; www.mctropic .com; Calle Principal; s/d US$7/14, with bathroom US$13/25) The Ríos Tropicales has a variety of big, well-screened rooms facing a central patio which has plenty of hammocks and chillout space. Rooms with shared bathroom are bigger, but others are better decorated.

Hotel Casa Rosada (☎ 7947 0303; www.hotelcasa rosada.com; Calle Marcos Sánchez Díaz; r US$20) The Casa Rosada (Pink House) is an attractive place to stay right on the river, 500m upstream from the main dock; it has its own pier where boats will drop you if you ask. The charming little wooden cabins are jammed up against each other, so there's not much privacy, but the garden area is pretty and the restaurant has great views out over the water. The shared bathrooms are very clean. Also available are a laundry service and tours.

Eating

Food in Lívingston is relatively expensive because most of it (except fish and coconuts) must be brought in by boat. There's fine seafood here and some unusual flavors for Guatemala, including coconut and also curry. *Tapado*, a rich stew made from fish, shrimp, shellfish, coconut milk and plantain, spiced with coriander, is the delicious local specialty. A potent potable is made by slicing off the top of a green coconut and mixing in a healthy dose of rum. These *coco locos* hit the spot.

Antojitos Yoli's (Calle Principal; items US$0.50-2) This is the place to come for baked goods. Especially recommended is the coconut bread and pineapple pie.

Restaurante Gaby (Calle Marcos Sánchez Díaz; mains US$3-5; breakfast, lunch & dinner) For a good honest feed in underwhelming surrounds, you can't go past Gaby's. She serves up the good stuff – lobster, *tapado*, rice and beans and good breakfasts at good prices. The *telenovelas* (TV soap operas) come free.

McTropic Restaurante (Calle Principal; mains US$4-10; breakfast, lunch & dinner) Some of the best value seafood dishes in town are on offer at this laid-back little place. Grab a table streetside for people watching and sample some of their good Thai cooking.

Tilingo-Lingo (Calle Principal; mains US$5-10; ☼ breakfast, lunch & dinner) An intimate little place down near the beach. They advertise food from 10 countries and make a pretty good job of it, with the Italian and East Indian dishes being the standouts.

Restaurante Bahía Azul (Calle Principal; mains US$6-12; ☼ breakfast, lunch & dinner) The Bahía's central location, happy décor and good fresh food keep it popular. The menu's wide, with a good mix of Caribbean, Guatemalan and Asian influences. They open early for breakfast.

Restaurante Buga Mama (Calle Marcos Sánchez Díaz; mains US$8-11; ☼ breakfast, lunch & dinner) Enjoying the best location of any restaurant in town, profits go to the Asociación Ak Tenemit. There's a wide range of seafood and other dishes on the menu, including a very good *tapado* (US$9). Most of the waiters here are trainees in a community sustainable-tourism development scheme, so service can be sketchy, but forgivable.

Drinking

Adventurous drinkers should try *guifiti*, a local concoction made from coconut rum, often infused with herbs. It's said to have medicinal as well as recreational properties.

A handful of bars down on the beach to the left of the end of Calle Principal pull in travelers and locals at night (after about 10pm or 11pm). It's very dark down here, so take care. The bars are within five minutes' walk from each other, so you should go for a wander and see what's happening. Music ranges from *punta* to salsa, merengue and electronica. On Fridays things warm up but Saturday is party night – often going till 5am or 6am.

Happy hour is pretty much an institution along the main street, with every restaurant getting in on the act. One of the best is at Casa de la Iguana.

Entertainment

A traditional Garífuna band is composed of three large drums, a turtle shell, some maracas and a big conch shell, producing throbbing, haunting rhythms and melodies. The chanted words are like a litany, with responses often taken up by the audience. *Punta* is the Garífuna dance; it's got a lot of gyrating hip movements.

Quite often a roaming band will play a few songs for diners along the Calle Principal around dinnertime. If you like the music, make sure to sling them a few bucks. Several places around town have live Garífuna music, although schedules are unpredictable:

Café-Bar Ubafu Probably the most dependable. Supposedly has music and dancing nightly, but liveliest on weekends.

Hotel Villa Caribe Diners can enjoy a Garífuna show each evening at 7pm.

Tropicool Disco Next door to Restaurante Bahía Azul, this is a small mainstream disco, which sometimes pulls a crowd.

Getting There & Away

Frequent boats come downriver from Río Dulce and across the bay from Puerto Barrios; see those sections, earlier in this chapter, for details. There are also international boats from Honduras and Belize and also a boat that goes direct to Punta Gorda on Tuesdays and Fridays at 7am (US$20, one hour), leaving from the public dock. In Punta Gorda the boat connects with a bus to Placencia and on to Belize City. The boat waits for this bus to arrive from Placencia before it sets off back for Lívingston from Punta Gorda at about 10:30am.

Exotic Travel (p180) operates combined boat and bus shuttles to La Ceiba (the cheapest gateway to Honduras' Bay Islands) for US$45 per person, with a minimum of six people. Leaving Lívingston at 7:30am or earlier will get you to La Ceiba in time for the boat to the islands, making it a one-day trip if you want to (which is nearly impossible to do independently).

If you are taking one of these early international departures, get your exit stamp from immigration in Lívingston (see p180) the day before.

AROUND LÍVINGSTON
Río Dulce Cruises

Lívingston is the starting point for boat rides along the Río Dulce. Passengers enjoy the jungle scenery, swim, picnic and explore the **Biotopo Chocón Machacas**, 12km west along the river.

Almost anyone in Lívingston can tell you who's organizing trips upriver. Exotic Travel makes trips daily, as do La Casa Rosada hotel and the Happy Fish restaurant. Many travelers use these tours as one-way transportation to

Río Dulce, paying around US$11. If you want to return to Lívingston the cost is US$20. It's a beautiful ride through lush scenery, with several places to stop on the way.

Or you can simply walk to the dock and arrange a trip, thereby supporting the many local boat captains. *Generally* speaking, there are two scheduled departures from the public dock, at 9:30am and 1:30pm. The morning trip is often more tourlike, taking up to 2½ hours and the afternoon one is an express service, taking one hour. This is not set in stone, and both cost US$13.

Shortly after you leave Lívingston headed upriver, you'll enter a steep-walled gorge called **Cueva de la Vaca**, its walls hung with great tangles of jungle foliage and bromeliads. Tropical birdcalls fill the air. Just beyond is **La Pintada**, a graffiti-covered rock escarpment. Further on, a thermal spring forces sulfurous water out at the base of the cliff, providing a delightful place for a swim.

Emerging from the gorge, the river eventually widens into **El Golfete**, a lakelike body of water that presages the even vaster Lago de Izabal.

On the north shore of El Golfete is the **Biotopo Chocón Machacas**, a 7600-hectare reserve established to protect the river, mangrove swamps and the manatees that inhabit the waters. A network of 'water trails' provides ways to see the reserve's flora and fauna. A nature trail begins at the visitors center (US$2.50), winding its way through forests of mahogany, palms and rich tropical foliage. Jaguars and tapirs live in the reserve, although seeing one is unlikely. The walruslike manatees are even more elusive. These huge mammals can weigh up to a ton, yet glide effortlessly beneath the river.

From El Golfete, the boats continue upriver, passing increasing numbers of expensive villas and boathouses, to the village of Río Dulce, where the road into El Petén crosses the river, and to the Castillo de San Felipe on Lago de Izabal (p176).

Los Siete Altares

The Seven Altars is a series of freshwater falls and pools about 5km (1½-hours' walk) northwest of Lívingston along the shore of Bahía de Amatique. It's a pleasant goal for a beach walk and a good place for a picnic and swim. Follow the shore northward to the river mouth and walk along the beach until it meets the

path into the woods (about 30 minutes). Follow this path all the way to the falls.

Boat trips go to the Seven Altars, but locals say it's better to walk there to experience the natural beauty and the Garífuna people along the way. About halfway along, next to the rope bridge is **Gaviottas Restaurant** (mains US$5-7; ☽ lunch & dinner), serving decent food and ice-cold beers and soft drinks.

Finca Tatin

This wonderful, rustic B&B is at the confluence of Ríos Dulce and Tatin, about 10km from Lívingston. **Finca Tatin** (☎ 5902 0831; www .fincatatin.centroamerica.com; dm US$5, s/d US$8/13, with bathroom US$15/20) is a great place for experiencing the forest. Four-hour guided walks and kayak trips, some visiting local Q'eqchi' villages, are offered. Accommodation is in individually decorated wood-and-thatched cabins scattered through the jungle. There are trails, waterfalls and endless river tributaries that you can explore with one of the *cayucos* (dugout canoes) available for guest use (US$10 per day). Guided night walks through the jungle offer views of elusive nightlife, and cave tours are good for swimming and soaking in a natural sauna. You can walk to Lívingston from here in about four hours, or take a kayak and they'll come pick you up (US$13).

Lanchas traveling between Río Dulce and Lívingston (or vice-versa) will drop you here. It costs around US$4 from Lívingston, 20 minutes away. Or the *finca* may be able to send its own *lancha* to pick you up at Lívingston (per person US$4, minimum two people).

EL PETÉN

Once synonymous with bad roads and impassible jungle, this region has been tamed over the years. Ever since the Maya exodus in the 9th century AD, this has been Guatemala's least-populated region, but continued government efforts to populate it have been hugely successful. In 1950 barely 15,000 people lived here. Now the number is more like 500,000. It's no surprise that most people you meet were born elsewhere.

The regional superstar is, of course, Tikal, but many visitors are far more blown away by 'lesser' ruins such as Yaxhá and the massive, largely unexcavated sites at El Mirador and Nakbé.

In 1990 the Guatemalan government established the one-million-hectare Maya Biosphere Reserve, which includes most of northern El Petén. The Guatemalan reserve adjoins the vast Calakmul Bioshere Reserve in Mexico and the Río Bravo Conservation Area in Belize, forming a reserve of over two million hectares.

Many visitors linger in Poptún, a small town 113km southeast of Santa Elena that has been a popular backpacker layover for years.

GETTING THERE & AROUND

The roads leading into El Petén have now all been paved, so travel is fast and smooth. Unfortunately, improved access has encouraged the migration of farmers and ranchers from other areas, increasing the pressure on resources and leading to even more deforestation in a region whose forests were already disappearing at an alarming rate.

The Guatemalan government has developed the adjoining towns of Flores, Santa Elena and San Benito, on the shores of Lago de Petén Itzá, into the region's tourism base. Here you'll find an airport, hotels and other services. A few small hotels and restaurants are at Tikal, but other services there are limited.

POPTÚN

pop 19,500 / elevation 540m

Poptún is about halfway between Río Dulce and Flores, and makes a good stopover en route to Tikal, especially if you're coming via Fray Bartolomé de Las Casas.

Most buses and minibuses stop on the main road through town: Fuente del Norte buses stop by the Shell station; minibuses to San Luís, 16km south, go from the next corner south, and minibuses to Flores start half a block further along. **Banco Industrial** (5a Calle 7-98; 🕙 9am-5pm Mon-Fri, 9am-1pm Sat) has a Visa ATM and changes US dollars and Visa and American Express traveler's checks. One block along 5a Calle, **Banrural** (🕙 8:30am-5pm Mon-Fri, 9am-1pm Sat) has a MasterCard ATM and changes US dollars and American Express traveler's checks.

Sleeping & Eating

Finca Ixobel (☎ 5892 3188; www.fincaixobel.com; camping per person US$3, dm US$4, tree houses & bungalows s US$10-17, d US$13-30; **P** ⬜ ⬛) This friendly, relaxed 400-acre spot offers tent sites, *palapas* for hanging hammocks, beds and good home-made meals with veggie options galore. Swimming, horseback riding, camping trips, inner tubing on the river and a famous, thrilling cave trip (which even includes bodysurfing rapids) are all organized on a daily basis, for a reasonable charge.

Meals here are excellent, including the all-you-can-eat buffet dinner for US$7. After 9pm many people move on to the pool bar, where reasonably priced cocktails and other drinks are served. Volunteer opportunities exist for bilingual English-Spanish speakers; volunteers get free room and board.

The turnoff for the *finca* is marked on Hwy 13. In the daytime, you can ask the bus or minibus driver to let you off there; it's a 15-minute walk to the *finca*. At night, or if you don't feel like making the walk, get off the bus in Poptún and take a taxi for US$4. It's not advisable to walk to the *finca* at night – it's an isolated spot. When you leave Finca Ixobel, most buses will stop on the highway to pick you up, but not after dark. The *finca* offers shuttles to Flores for US$5.50. Shuttles coming from Flores should drop you at the gate, but check first.

Hotel Izalco (☎ 7927 7372; 4a Calle 7-11; s/d US$5.50/11, with bathroom US$7/14) Small but clean rooms with TV and good mosquito netting. Some of those with bathroom don't have a fan. And you want a fan.

Hotel Posada de los Castellanos (☎ 7927 7222; cnr 4a Calle & 7a Av; s/d with bathroom US$7/14) In Poptún town, this hotel has average rooms with TV, arranged around a shady courtyard.

Getting There & Away

Bus departures from Poptún include the following:

Flores/Santa Elena (two hours, 113km) Fuente del Norte buses (US$3) go every hour or two almost around the clock; minibuses (US$3.50) leave about every 30 minutes from 6am to 6pm.

Fray Bartolomé de Las Casas (US$6, five hours, 100km) One bus departs at 10am from the market area. If you want to push on from Las Casas to Lanquín the same day, try getting a Guatemala City-bound bus as far as Modesto Méndez (also called Cadenas), 60km south on Hwy 13, and changing there to a westbound bus or minibus to Las Casas.

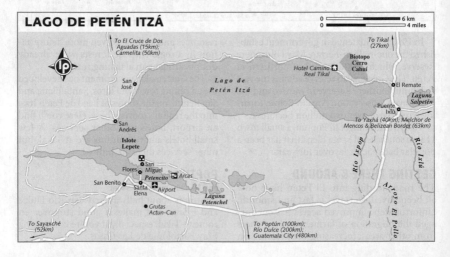

LAGO DE PETÉN ITZÁ

0 ─────── 6 km
0 ─────── 4 miles

To El Cruce de Dos Aguadas (15km); Carmelita (50km)

To Tikal (27km)

San José

Lago de Petén Itzá

Hotel Camino Real Tikal

Biotopo Cerro Cahuí

El Remate

Laguna Salpetén

San Andrés

Puente Ixlú

To Yaxhá (40km); Melchor de Mencos & Belizean Border (63km)

Islote Lepete

Río Ixpop

Río Ixlú

Flores · San Miguel

San Benito · *Petencito* · Arcas

Santa Elena · Airport

· *Grutas Actun-Can*

Laguna Petenchel

Arroyo El Pollo

To Sayaxché (52km)

To Poptún (100km); Río Dulce (200km); Guatemala City (480km)

Guatemala City (US$7 to US$10.50, six to seven hours, 387km) Fuente del Norte buses go about every 30 minutes from 5:30am to midnight.

Río Dulce (US$3.25 to US$4, two hours, 99km) Fuente del Norte buses run about every 30 minutes from 5:30am to midnight.

FLORES & SANTA ELENA

pop Flores 23,700, Santa Elena 29,000 / elevation 110m

Flores is spectacularly located on an island in Lago de Petén Itzá. Small hotels and restaurants line the lakeside streets, meaning you don't have to shell out the big bucks to get a room with some awesome views. It does have a slightly twee, built-up edge to it, though, and many Tikal-bound shoestringers opt for the natural surrounds and tranquility of El Remate (p193), just down the road.

A 500m causeway connects Flores to the lakeshore town of Santa Elena, where you'll find banks, supermarkets and buses. Adjoining Santa Elena to the west is San Benito (population 22,000). There's not really much for the average traveler here, unless you're up for a night of slumming it in one of the town's numerous cantinas. The three towns form one large settlement that is usually referred to simply as 'Flores.'

History

Flores was founded on a *petén* (island) by the Itzáes after their expulsion from Chichén Itzá. They named the place Tayasal. Hernán Cortés peaceably dropped in on King Canek of Tayasal in 1524 on his way to Honduras. Only in March 1697 did the Spaniards finally bring Tayasal's Maya forcibly under their control.

At the time of conquest, Flores was perhaps the last major functioning Maya ceremonial center; it was covered in pyramids and temples, with idols everywhere. The God-fearing Spanish soldiers destroyed these buildings, and no trace remains.

Tayasal's Maya fled into the jungle and may have started anew, giving rise to stories of a 'lost' Maya city; some believe this is El Mirador, near the Guatemala–Mexico border.

Orientation

The airport is on the eastern outskirts of Santa Elena, 2km from the causeway connecting Santa Elena and Flores. Most buses arrive and depart from the new bus terminal 1km south of the causeway.

Information

EMERGENCY

Hospital San Benito (☎ 7926 1459)
Policía Nacional (☎ 7926 1365)

INTERNET ACCESS

Flores.Net (Map p188; Av Barrios, Flores; per hr US$1.30)
Internet Petén (Map p188; Calle Centroamérica, Flores; per hr US$1.60; ☾ 8am-10pm)
Naomi's Café (Map p188; Calle Centroamérica, Flores; per hr US$1.80)

LAUNDRY

Mayan Princess Travel Agency (Map p188; Calle 30 de Junio, Flores; ☾ 8am-8pm) US$3.30 to wash and dry a load.

MONEY

Banquetzal (☾ 7am-noon & 2-5pm) Located at the airport; changes US dollars and traveler's checks.
Banrural (Map p188) Just off Parque Central in Flores; changes US dollars and traveler's checks.

Other banks are on 4a Calle in Santa Elena. Banks that change US dollars and American Express US-dollar traveler's checks include:
Banco Agromercantil (Map p191; ☾ 9am-6pm Mon-Fri, 9am-1pm Sat) Has a MasterCard ATM.
Banco Industrial (Map p191; ☾ 9am-7pm Mon-Fri, 10am-2pm Sat) Has a Visa ATM.

Many travel agencies and places to stay will change US dollars, and sometimes traveler's checks, at poor rates.
San Juan Travel (Map p188; ☎ 926 0041/2, 926 2146; Playa Sur, Flores) Also changes Belizean dollars and Mexican pesos, and give Visa, MasterCard, Diner's Club and American Express cash advances. Also at 2a Calle, Santa Elena.

POST

Post office Flores (Map p188; Av Barrios, Flores); Santa Elena (Map p191; 4a Calle east of 7a Av)

TELEPHONE

Martsam Travel (Map p188; ☎ /fax 926 3225; Calle 30 de Junio, Flores) Offers phone and fax services.

TOURIST INFORMATION

Asociación Alianza Verde (☎ /fax 7926 0718; www.alianzaverde.org) This association, dedicated to sustainable, responsible, low-impact tourism in the Maya Biosphere Reserve runs Cincap. It also publishes *Destination Petén*.
Cincap (Map p188; Centro de Información Sobre la Naturaleza, Cultura y Artesanía de Petén; Petén Nature, Culture & Handicrafts Information Center; ☎ 926 0718;

GUATEMALA

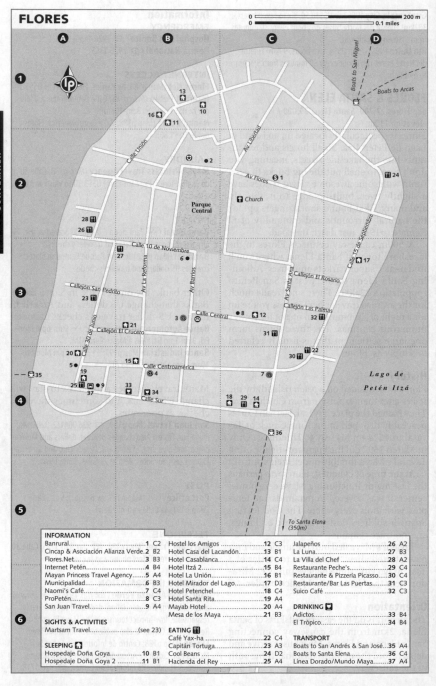

FLERES

mercadeo@peten.net; Parque Central, Flores; 🕙 9am-noon & 2-9pm) Has interesting displays on archaeological sites, conservation areas and the culture of El Petén. It also sells local handicrafts and has an information desk, where you can ask about visits to some of the region's remoter natural and archaeological sites.

Inguat (☎ 7926 0533; 🕙 7am-noon & 3-5pm) At the airport.

TRAVEL AGENCIES
Several agencies offer trips to archaeological sites, shuttle minibuses and other services.

Martsam Travel (Map p188; ☎ /fax 7926 3225; www .martsam.com; Calle 30 de Junio, Flores) This is a well-established, well-organized agency with a particularly wide range of services.

San Juan Travel (Map p188; Calle 30 de Junio; ☎ 7926 0041; sanjuant@internetdetelgua.com.gt; 2a Calle, Santa Elena & Playa Sur, Flores) Runs various shuttles and tours, and has the most regular service to Tikal and Palenque.

Sights & Activities
The limestone caves of **Grutas Actun-Can** (admission US$2; 🕙 8am-5pm), also called La Cueva de la Serpiente (Cave of the Serpent), holds no serpents, but the cavekeeper may give you the rundown on the cave formations, which suggest animals, humans and various scenes. Bring a flashlight and adequate shoes – it can be slippery. Explorations take 30 to 45 minutes. At the cave entrance is a shady picnic area.

Actun-Can is a good goal for a long walk from Santa Elena. Head south on 6a Av past the Telgua office. About 1km from the center of Santa Elena, turn left, go 300m and turn right at the electricity generating plant. Go another 1km to the site. A taxi costs US$3.

Volunteering
The **Estación Biológica Las Guacamayas** (p203), in the Parque Nacional Laguna del Tigre, and the rehabilitation center at **Arcas** (Asociación de Rescate y Conservación de Vida Silvestre; ☎ /fax 5476 6001; www.arcasguatemala.com), about 12km east of Santa Elena, both offer the chance of volunteer work with wildlife. At Las Guacamayas you pay US$9 per day for the first two weeks, US$8 per day the third week and US$7 per day the fourth week, and provide your own food. If you're interested contact **ProPetén** (Map p188; Proyecto Petenero para un Bosque Sostenible; ☎ 7926 1370; www.propeten.org; Calle Central, Flores; 🕙 9am-5pm Mon-Fri), the Guatemalan NGO that owns the station. At Arcas you pay US$110 per week including food.

Sleeping
FLORES
Hostel los Amigos (Map p188; ☎ 5584 8795; www.amigo shostel.com; Calle Central; dm US$3.50; 🖳) Flores' one true hostel, with eight-bed dorms and hammocks on offer, this could be a disaster, but the place has such a cool atmosphere that it all hangs together. Nightly bonfires, happy hours, good food – you know the deal…

Hospedaje Doña Goya (Map p188; ☎ 7926 3538; hospedajedonagoay@yahoo.com; Calle Unión; dm US$3.50, s/d US$8/11, with bathroom US$11/13) This family-room guesthouse is one of the best budget choices in town and often full as a result. The beds are comfortable, the water's hot and there's a roof terrace with a palm-thatched shelter and plenty of hammocks from which to enjoy lake views. The eight-person dorms are spacious and clean.

Hospedaje Doña Goya 2 (Map p188; ☎ 7926 3538; hospedajedonagoay@yahoo.com; Calle Unión; dm/s/d US$3.50/8/11, with bathroom US$11/13) Doña Goya's second effort is even better than her first – there's a definite jungle theme running through this one, with banisters made to look like climbing vines. Rooms are good-sized and spotless, most of them with some sort of view.

Hotel Mirador del Lago (Map p188; ☎ 7926 3276; s/d with bathroom US$6/8) Compared to what else is on offer for these prices on the island, this is a good deal. Rooms are bare but functional, and upstairs they catch good afternoon breezes.

Hotel Casablanca (Map p188; ☎ 5699 1371; Playa Sur; s/d with bathroom US$7.50/13) The first hotel you reach coming off the causeway is also one of the best in the budget game – simple, spacious rooms and a great terrace for lake-gazing.

Hotel Petenchel (Map p188; ☎ 7926 3359; s/d with bathroom US$7.50/13) Eight rooms set around a lush little courtyard just off the causeway. The rooms are spacious, with firm beds. In the event that El Petén ever experiences a chilly night, have no fear – showers here are superhot.

Hotel Casa del Lacandon (Map p188; ☎ 7926 4359; Calle Unión; s/d US$8/13) If you can get one of the upstairs rooms at the back, this is one of the best budget deals in town. Rooms have a couple of beds, a clothes rack (!) and windows with sweeping views of the lake.

Mayab Hotel (Map p188; ☎ 7926 4094; mcestra@gmail .com; Calle 30 de Junio; s/d US$12/16; 🖳) Decent-sized rooms with cable TV and hot showers. The real bonus here is the upstairs balcony that overlooks the lake and the back gate, leading directly to the shoreline.

Mesa de los Maya (Map p188; ☎/fax 7926 1240; mesamayas@hotmail.com; s/d US$15/20, with air-con US$5 extra; 🖾) The Mesa's one of the stalwarts in the Flores hotel scene – it's been around (nearly) forever and they know what they're doing. Rooms are smallish but well decorated, with good touches like reading lamps and pleasant paint jobs.

Three more budget hotels with respectable, fan-cooled rooms:

Hotel Itzá 2 (Map p188; ☎ 7926 3654; Av La Reforma; s/d with cold-water bathroom US$6/8)

Hotel Santa Rita (Map p188; ☎ 7926 3224; Calle 30 de Junio; s/d with bathroom US$7/12) Smallish rooms with shared balconies and a couple of good hangout areas.

Hotel La Unión (Map p188; ☎ 7926 3584; Calle Unión; s/d US$8/13, with view US$16)

SANTA ELENA

Hotel Continental (Map p191; ☎ 7926 0095; 6a Av; s/d US$5/9, with fan, bathroom & TV US$9/12; P 🖾) A 51-room hotel south of Calz Viriglio Rodríguez Macal, with friendly reception staff, the Continental has a range of rooms on three floors along a courtyard painted in vaguely refreshing shades of blue and green. Bathrooms are good and clean, but there's no hot water.

Hotel San Juan (Map p191 ☎ 7926 2146; 2a Calle; s/d from US$6/8, with bathroom US$9/11) Another cheap Santa Elena hotel, but less attractive.

Hotel Posada Santander (Map p191 ☎ 7926 0574; 4a Calle; s/d with bathroom US$6/9.50) A simple, spotless and friendly family-run hostelry in a convenient but loud location. The rooms are definitely secure (there are bars on the windows *and* the TVs) and have cold-water bathrooms. The attached *comedor* serves good basic meals for US$2.

Hotel Sac-Nicté (Map p191 ☎ 7926 0092, 926 1731; 1a Calle; s/d from US$9/11) The rooms here are tolerably clean and will do in a pinch. They all have bathroom and fan, and those upstairs have small balconies from which you might just glimpse the lake. Staff will pick you up free from the airport, where the hotel has a desk.

Eating

On the menu at many places is a variety of local game, including *tepezcuintle* (paca, a rabbit-sized jungle rodent), *venado* (venison), armadillo, *pavo silvestre* (wild turkey) and *pescado blanco* (white fish). You may want to avoid dishes that might soon jump from the menu to the endangered species list.

FLORES

Cool Beans (Map p188; Calle 15 de Septiembre; mains US$3-6; 🕙 lunch & dinner Wed-Mon) An earthy sort of place with a thatched roof and hammocks. Good coffee, decent breakfasts and tasty snacks are what's on offer here. You can just make out the lake by peering through the lush garden down the back. Be warned – the kitchen closes at 9:01pm sharp.

La Villa del Chef (Map p188; Calle Unión; mains US$3-6; 🕙 breakfast, lunch & dinner) Go out the back (keep going) to reach the rustic little deck built out over the water in this newish place with a varied menu. You can choose from a good selection of Arabic, seafood, Guatemalan and international dishes. Don't miss the 6pm happy hour.

Capitán Tortuga (Map p188; Calle 30 de Junio; mains US$3.50-7; 🕙 breakfast, lunch & dinner) A long, barn-like place stretching down to a small lakeside terrace, 'Captain Turtle' serves large plates of a wide variety of tasty food – pizzas, steaks, chicken, pasta, salads, sandwiches, tacos – at medium prices. Big tour groups turn up here from time to time.

Café Yax-ha (Map p188; Calle 15 de Septiembre; mains US$4-5; 🕙 breakfast, lunch & dinner Wed-Mon) Literally wallpapered with photos and articles relating to archaeology and Maya sites, this café-restaurant serves up the standard range of dishes. What's really special here is the prehispanic menu items and Itzá dishes – the spicy chicken with yuca (US$4) comes recommended.

Restaurante & Pizzería Picasso (Map p188; Calle 15 de Septiembre; pizza US$4-6; 🕙 lunch & dinner Tue-Sun) Still going strong after all these years, this Italian-owned pizzeria does the best pizzas in town, with artwork on the walls courtesy of you-know-who and a cool little courtyard area.

Jalapeños (Map p188; Calle 30 de Junio; mains US$4-10; 🕙 breakfast, lunch & dinner) Maybe you don't need any more Mexican food, but if you do, this is the place – airy and breezy, serving all your (Tex) Mex faves with a couple of international dishes thrown in. The zucchini chicken in creamy sauce with black olives (US$7) is one good example.

La Luna (Map p188; cnr Calle 30 de Junio & Calle 10 de Noviembre; mains US$7-11; 🕙 lunch & dinner Mon-Sat) In a class by itself, this very popular restaurant cultivates a classic tropical ambience, with potted palms to catch the breeze from the whirling overhead fans. The food is continental and

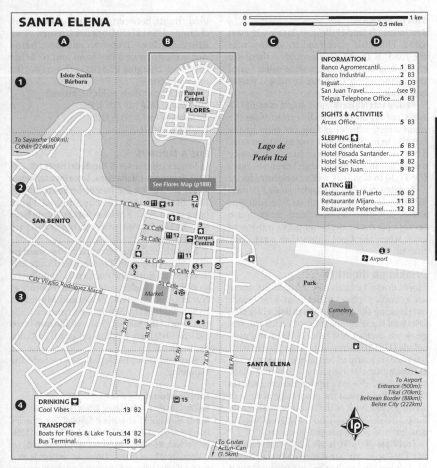

delectable, with innovative chicken, fish and beef dishes the likes of which you'll be hard-pressed to find anywhere else in Guatemala. There are also good pasta and vegetarian options, such as falafel, salad and rice, for US$4 to US$5.

Restaurante/Bar Las Puertas (Map p188; ☎ cnr Calle Central & Av Santa Ana; mains US$8-9; ⏱ 8am-late Mon-Sat) This popular restaurant and bar serves good, if pricey, food. There's live music some nights (mainly on weekends). The *camarones a la oriental* (prawns served with vegetables and rice) are a treat. For something cheaper the Las Puertas has 10 ways of doing spaghetti and nine types of salad. Round it off with a crepe (US$2). Breakfasts (US$3 to US$4) are good here, too.

Hacienda del Rey (Map p188; Calle 30 de Junio; mains US$8-15; ⏱ breakfast, lunch & dinner) One of the more atmospheric restaurants on the island (except for their terrible radio selection), this place does Argentinean-style steaks. There's also a range of tacos and snacks (US$2 to US$3) in case you're just here for the US$1 beer deal.

More cheap eats in Flores? No problem.

Food stalls (Parque Central; tacos & burritos US$1) A good place to dine cheap on *antojitos* (snacks).

Restaurante Peche's (Map p188; Playa Sur; mains US$3.50-4.50; ⏱ 4am-10pm) Inexpensive plates of meat, rice, tortillas and salad.

Suico Café (Map p188; Calle 15 de Septiembre; mains US$4-6; ⏱ lunch & dinner) Japanese food in El Petén? The Japanese owners take a fair stab at your faves (miso soup, tempura, sushi).

SANTA ELENA

Restaurante Petenchel (Map p191; 2a Calle 4-20; mains US$3-7) This little place (and its sister across the road) is trying hard enough – there are checked tablecloths and a wide selection of dishes including Chinese, ceviches, pastas and steak.

Restaurante Mijaro (Map p191; 4a Calle; mains US$3.50-4.25) Cool off at this friendly *comedor* on the main street, which has fans not only inside but also in its little thatch-roofed garden area. They do good long *limonadas* (lime-juice drink) and snacks like sandwiches and burgers (US$1.30 to US$2) as well as weightier food.

Restaurante El Puerto (Map p191; 1a Calle 2-15; mains US$5-8; ☑ lunch & dinner) With its lakefront position, this open-air beer barn–steak house serves up a mean steak and packs out weekends when the Cool Vibes club next door fires up.

Drinking & Nightlife

Flores doesn't exactly jive at night but there are a couple of places to hang out. The terrace overlooking the lake at **Hotel La Unión** (Map p188; Calle Unión) is a magnificent spot watch the sun go down over a Cuba Libre (US$1) or a piña colada (US$2). Flores' little *Zona Viva* (nightlife zone) is a strip of bars along the Playa Sur. **El Trópico** (Map p188; Playa Sur) is a popular place to start, and if you're up for dancing **Adictos** (Map p188; Playa Sur) was the place to be at time of writing. Nearly all of the lakeside restaurants have afternoon happy hours, a great way to unwind and watch the sun go down.

Cool Vibes (Map p191; 1a Calle 2-25; ☑ 7pm-1am Thu-Sat) This open-air bar-dance club was Santa Elena's hot spot at the time of writing. And it *is* kind of fun to be out shaking your thing in the fresh air, lakeside.

Entertainment

Movies are shown at **Las Puertas** (US$1.50) every night. There are occasional archaeological/cultural lectures at Café Yax-ha.

Locals gather in the cool of the evening for long drinks, snacks and relaxation in Parque Central, where a marimba ensemble plays some nights.

Getting There & Away

AIR

The airport at Santa Elena is usually called Flores airport and sometimes Tikal airport. TACA is the only airline with regularly sched-

uled flights between here and the capital, charging US$127/204 one way/return. Two Belizean airlines, Tropic Air and Maya Island Air, each fly twice a day from and to Belize City, both charging US$103 each way for the one-hour trip.

Contact numbers at Flores airport:

Inter/Grupo TACA (☎ 7926 1238)
Maya Island Air (☎ 7926 3386)
Tropic Air (☎ 926 0348)

BUS & MINIBUS

In Santa Elena, buses of **Fuente del Norte** (☎ 7926 0517), **Transportes María Elena**, **Línea Dorada/Mundo Maya** (☎ 7926 1788) and **Transportes Rosita** (☎ 7926 1245) all stop at the main bus terminal. Flores has a second office of **Línea Dorada/Mundo Maya** (☎ 7926 3649; Playa Sur), where its buses also pick up passengers.

Santa Elena's bus terminal is also used by the chicken buses of Transportes Pinita and Transportes Rosío and *microbuses* (minibuses) to El Remate, Melchor de Mencos, Poptún, El Naranjo and Sayaxché. Buses and Minibuses to San Andrés and San José go from 5a Calle just west of the market. Buses of **San Juan Travel** (☎ 7926 0041) leave from its office on 2a Calle, Santa Elena.

Bus and minibus departures include the following.

International

Belize City (Four to five hours, 220km) Línea Dorada/Mundo Maya (US$15.50) leaves at 5am and 7am, returning from Belize City at 2pm and 5pm. San Juan Travel (US$20) goes at 5am, returning from Belize City at 9:30am and 4:30pm. These buses to Belize City all connect with boats to Cayo (Caye) Caulker and Ambergris Caye. It's cheaper but slower from Flores to take local buses to the border and on from it (see details for Melchor de Mencos below).

Bethel (Mexican border) (US$4, four hours, 127km) Fuente del Norte departs at 5am; Pinita goes at 5am, 8am, noon and 1pm. Returning, Fuente del Norte leaves Bethel at 4pm and Pinita at 5am, noon and 2pm.

Chetumal (Mexico) (seven to eight hours, 350km) Via Belize City Línea Dorada/Mundo Maya (US$23) leaves at 6am, returning from Chetumal at 2pm. San Juan Travel (US$25) goes at 5am, with departures for Flores from Chetumal at 9:30am and 4:30pm. Check Belizean visa regulations before you set off.

La Técnica (Mexican border) (US$6, five hours, 140km) Pinita leaves at 5am and 1pm, and starts back from La Técnica at 4am and 11am.

Melchor de Mencos (Belizean border) (two hours, 100km) Minibuses (US$3.50) go about every hour from

5am to 6pm; Transportes Rosita buses (US$2.50) go at 5am, 11am, 2pm, 4pm and 6pm; a Pinita bus (US$3) goes at 8am. See p201 for more information on crossing the border here.

Palenque (Mexico) See Shuttle Minibus, below.

Domestic

Cobán (US$6.50, six hours, 245km) Transportes Rosío leaves the market bus stop at 10:30am. Or take a bus or minibus to Sayaxché, from where a bus leaves for Cobán at 10am. (See also the Shuttle Minibus section, below.)

El Naranjo (Río San Pedro) (US$4, four hours, 151km) Minibuses go about every hour from 5am to 6pm.

El Remate (US$2, 40 minutes, 29km) Minibuses go about hourly from 6am to 1pm, and a few times between 1pm and 6pm. Buses and minibuses to/from Melchor de Mencos will drop you at Puente Ixlú junction, 2km south of El Remate.

Esquipulas (US$11, 10 hours, 440km) Transportes María Elena goes at 6am, 10am and 2pm via Chiquimula (US$9, nine hours).

Fray Bartolomé de Las Casas (US$5.50, five hours, 178km) Transportes Rosío departs the market at 10:30am.

Guatemala City (eight to 10 hours, 500km) Fuente del Norte has 29 departures from 3:30am to 11pm, costing US$10 to US$12 except for the 10am and 9pm buses (US$19) and the 2pm, 8pm and 10pm departures (US$15); Línea Dorada/Mundo Maya has deluxe buses at 10am and 9pm (US$30) and an *económico* (US$16) at 10pm; Transportes Rosita goes at 7pm (US$8) and 8pm (US$11).

Poptún (two hours, 113km) Take a Guatemala City-bound Fuente del Norte bus (US$3) or a minibus (US$3.60) leaving about every 30 minutes from 5am to 6pm.

Puerto Barrios Take a Guatemala City-bound Fuente del Norte bus and change at La Ruidosa junction, south of Río Dulce.

Río Dulce (4½ hours, 212km) Take a Guatemala City-bound bus with Fuente del Norte (US$8) or Línea Dorada (US$11.50/22 *económico*/deluxe).

San Andrés (US$1, 30 minutes, 20km) Buses and minibuses about hourly from 5am to 5pm.

San José (US$1, 45 minutes, 25km) Buses and minibuses about hourly from 5am to 5pm.

Sayaxché (US$2, 1½ hours, 60km) Minibuses about every 30 minutes from 5am to 6pm; Pinita buses go at 11am, 2pm and 2:30pm.

Tikal See Shuttle Minibus, following.

SHUTTLE MINIBUS

San Juan Travel (☎ 7926 0041; sanjuant@internetdetelgua.com.gt); Flores (Map p188; Playa Sur) Santa Elena (Map p191; Hotel San Juan, 2a Calle) operates shuttle minibuses to Tikal (US$4/6 one-way/round-trip, 1¼ hours each way). They leave hourly from 5am to 10am and usually at 2pm. Most hotels and travel agencies can book these shuttles for you and the vehicles will pick you up where you're staying. Returns leave Tikal at 12:30pm, 2pm, 3pm, 4pm, 5pm and 6pm. If you know which round-trip you plan to be on, ask your driver to hold a seat for you or arrange a seat in a colleague's minibus. If you stay overnight in Tikal and want to return to Flores by minibus, it's a good idea to reserve a seat with one of the drivers when they arrive in the morning. Outside the normal timetable, you can rent a whole minibus for US$35.

San Juan also does shuttles to Cobán (US$20), Palenque (Mexico; US$30) and Corozal (the border crossing for Bonampak, Mexico; US$25).

Getting Around

A taxi from the airport to Santa Elena or Flores costs US$2. Tuk tuks will take you anywhere between or within Flores and Santa Elena for US$0.80. La Villa del Chef (p190) rents mountain bikes for US$6 for up to four hours and US$8 for four to 12 hours.

Lanchas making tours around Lago de Petén Itzá depart from the Santa Elena end of the causeway. Colectivo boats to San Andrés and San José, villages across the lake, depart from San Benito, on the west side of Santa Elena and alongside Hotel Santana in Flores (US$0.40 if the boat leaves full, US$8 for one passenger). You can also contract the *lancheros* for lake tours; bargain hard.

EL REMATE

The closest decent accommodation to Tikal can be found in this enchanting village on the shores of Lago de Petén Itzá. It's a mellow little place – two roads, basically – much more relaxed and less built up than Flores. Most hotels here are set up for swimming in – and watching the sun set over – the lake.

El Remate is known for its wood carving. Several handicrafts shops on the lakeshore opposite La Mansión del Pájaro Serpiente sell local handicrafts and rent canoes, rafts and kayaks.

From El Remate an unpaved road snakes around the lake's northeast shore to the Biotopo Cerro Cahuí, the luxury Hotel Camino Real Tikal and on to the villages of San José and San Andrés, on the northwest side of the lake. It's possible to go all the way around the lake by road.

With their newfound prosperity, Remate-cos have built a *balneario municipal* (municipal beach) just off the highway; several cheap pensions and small hotels have opened here as well.

Sights & Activities

At the northeast end of Lago de Petén Itzá, about 43km from Santa Elena and 3km from the Flores–Tikal road, the **Biotopo Cerro Cahuí** (admission US$2.50; 6:30am-dusk) covers 651 hectares of subtropical forest. Within are mahogany, cedar, ramón, broom, sapodilla and cohune palm trees, as well as many species of lianas and epiphytes, these last including bromeliads, ferns and orchids. The hard wood of the sapodilla was used in Mayan temple door lintels, some of which have survived from the Classic period to our own time. Chicle is still sapped from the trees' innards.

Among the many animals within the reserve are spider and howler monkeys, ocelots, white-tailed deer, raccoons, armadillos, numerous species of fish, turtle and snake, and *Crocodylus moreletti* – the Petén crocodile. Depending upon the season and migration patterns, you might see kingfishers, ducks, herons, hawks, parrots, toucans, woodpeckers and the beautiful ocellated (Petén) turkey, which resembles a peacock.

A network of loop trails starts at the road and goes uphill, affording a view of the lake and Lagunas Salpetén and Petenchel. A trail map is at the entrance.

The admission fee includes the right to camp or sling your hammock under small thatched shelters inside the entrance. There are toilets and showers, but El Remate is the closest place to get supplies.

Sleeping & Eating

Hotel Sak-Luk (5494 5925; main road; dm/hammock/bungalow per person US$2/3/4) This little slice of hippy heaven offers huts, dorms and hammocks in adobe constructions scattered around a lush hillside. There's a good restaurant offering Italian and vegetarian dishes and they can organize jungle treks and trips to the Biotopo Cerro Cahuí.

Mon Ami (7928 8413; www.hotelmonami.com; North road; dm US$5 d with bathroom US$15-25) Along the north shore road (1200m from the main Tikal road), this place has a good balance of wild jungle and French sophistication. The restaurant (mains US$3.25 to US$4.25, crepes

US$2) serves good French and Guatemalan food in a peaceful palm-thatched, open-walled area. Try the *carne al vino* (meat cooked in wine) with rice and tomato salad, or the big *ensalada francesa* (French salad).

Hostal Hermano Pedro (s/d with bathroom US$7/14) Set in a great two-story wood and stone house 20m off to the right from the main road. The basic, spacious rooms here are how budget hotels should be – clean, simple and comfortable, with just a couple of frills.

Casa Mobega (7909 6999; dm US$7.50) Fairly bursting with character, this secluded little spot has a collection of two-story open-walled thatched houses spread out over a hillside. Bathrooms are shared and beds have mosquito nets.

Restaurante Cahuí (mains US$4-6; breakfast, lunch & dinner) While most people eat in their hotels here, this is a popular option. People come for the big, wholesome meals and stay for the lake views from the big wooden deck overlooking the water and the extensive wine and beer list.

Getting There & Around

El Remate is linked to Flores by a public minibus service (see p192).

A minibus leaves El Remate at 5:30am for Tikal, starting back from Tikal at 2pm (US$4 round-trip). Any El Remate accommodations can make reservations. Or you can catch one of the shuttles or regular minibuses passing through from Flores to get to Tikal. They normally charge US$2.50 per person. For Melchor de Mencos on the Belizean border, get a minibus or bus from Puente Ixlú, 2km south of El Remate.

For taxis, ask at Hotel Sun Breeze or Hotel Don Juan. A one-way ride to Tikal or Flores costs about US$18.

TIKAL

Towering pyramids poke above the jungle's green canopy to catch the sun. Howler monkeys swing noisily through the branches of ancient trees as brightly colored parrots and toucans dart from perch to perch in a cacophony of squawks. When the complex warbling song of some mysterious jungle bird tapers off, the buzz of tree frogs fills the background and it will dawn on you that this is, indeed, hallowed ground.

Certainly the most striking feature of **Tikal** (2361 1399; admission US$7; 6am-6pm) is its steep-sided temples, rising to heights of more than 61m. But Tikal is different from Copán, Chichén Itzá, Uxmal and most other great Maya sites because it is deep in the jungle. Its many plazas have been cleared of trees and vines, its temples uncovered and partially restored, but as you walk from one building to another you pass beneath the dense rainforest canopy. Rich, loamy smells of earth and vegetation, a peaceful air and animal noises all contribute to an experience not offered by other Maya sites.

You can, if you wish, visit Tikal in a day trip from Flores or El Remate. You can even make a (literally) flying visit from Guatemala City in one day, using the daily flights between there and Flores airport. But you'll get more out of Tikal if you spend a night here, enabling you to visit the ruins twice and to be here in the late afternoon and early morning, when other tourists are rare and wildlife more active.

History

Tikal is set on a low hill above the surrounding swampy ground – which might be why the Maya settled here around 700 BC. Another reason was the abundance of flint, used to make clubs, spearheads, arrowheads and knives. Flint could also be exported in exchange for other goods. Within 200 years, the Maya of Tikal had begun to build stone ceremonial structures, and by 200 BC a complex of buildings stood on the site of the North Acropolis.

CLASSIC PERIOD

The Great Plaza was beginning to assume its present shape and extent two thousand years ago. By the dawn of the early Classic period, about AD 250, Tikal had become an important, heavily populated religious, cultural and commercial city. King Yax Moch Xoc, whose reign began around AD 230, founded the ruling dynasty.

Under King Great Jaguar Paw (who ruled in the mid-4th century), Tikal adopted a new, brutal method of warfare used by the rulers of Teotihuacán in central Mexico. Rather than meeting their adversaries in hand-to-hand combat, the army of Tikal encircled their enemy and killed them by throwing spears. This first use of 'air power' among the Maya of Petén enabled Tikal to conquer Uaxactún and become the dominant kingdom in the region.

By the middle of the Classic period, during the mid-6th century, Tikal sprawled over 30 sq km and had a population of perhaps 100,000. In 553 Lord Water ascended to the throne of Caracol (in southwestern Belize), and by 562, using the same warfare methods learned from Tikal, conquered and sacrificed Tikal's king. Tikal and other Petén kingdoms suffered under Caracol's rule until the late 7th century.

TIKAL'S RENAISSANCE

Around 700 a powerful king named Moon Double Comb (682–734), also called Ah Cacau (Lord Chocolate), 26th successor of Yax Moch Xoc, ascended Tikal's throne. He restored not only its military strength, but also its primacy as the Maya world's most resplendent city. He and his successors were responsible for building most of the surviving temples around the Great Plaza. He was buried beneath the staggering height of Temple I.

Tikal's greatness waned around 900, part of the mysterious general collapse of lowland Maya civilization.

No doubt the Itzáes, who occupied Tayasal (now Flores), knew of Tikal in the late post-Classic period (1200–1530). Perhaps they even came to worship at the shrines of their old gods. Spanish missionary friars left brief references to these jungle-covered structures, but these writings moldered in libraries for centuries.

REDISCOVERY

It wasn't until 1848 that the Guatemalan government sent an expedition, under Modesto Méndez and Ambrosio Tut, to visit the site. In 1877 Dr Gustav Bernoulli of Switzerland visited Tikal and removed lintels from Temples I and IV to Basel, where they are still on view in the Museum für Völkerkunde.

Scientific exploration at Tikal began with the arrival of English archaeologist Alfred P Maudslay in 1881; others who continued his work include Teobert Maler, Alfred M Tozzer and RE Merwin. Tozzer worked at Tikal from the beginning of the century until his death in 1954. Tikal's inscriptions were studied and deciphered by Sylvanus G Morley.

Since 1956 archaeological research and restoration has been carried out by the University of Pennsylvania and the Guatemalan Instituto de Antropología e Historia. In the mid-1950s an airstrip was built to make access

GUATEMALA

TIKAL

Complejo P

Grupo H

Complejo M

Calz
Maler

Calz
Maudslay

Complejo Q

Complejo R

Complejo O

Aguada
Calz

Grupo F

Acrópolis
del Norte

Templo IV

Baño de
Vapor

Calz Tozzer

Plaza
Oeste

Templo II

Plaza
Este

Gran
Plaza

Complejo N

Templo III

Templo I

Palacio las
Ventanas

Templo 38

Aguada
Templo

Acrópolis
Central

Templo del
Talud-Tablero

Embalse
del Palacio

Aguada
Escondida

Pyramid

Templo V

El Mundo Perdido

Plaza
de
los
Siete
Templos

Acrópolis
del Sur

Grupo G

Templo de
las Calaveras

easier. In the early 1980s the road between Tikal and Flores was paved, and direct flights abandoned. Tikal National Park was declared a Unesco World Heritage Site in 1979.

Orientation & Information

The 550-sq-km Parque Nacional Tikal contains thousands of separate ruined structures.

The central area of the city occupied about 16 sq km, with more than 4000 structures.

The road from Flores enters the national park 17km south of the ruins. The gate opens at 6am. Here you pay the entrance fee; if you enter after about 3pm, your ticket should be stamped with the following day's date, making it valid for that next day, too. Multilingual guides are

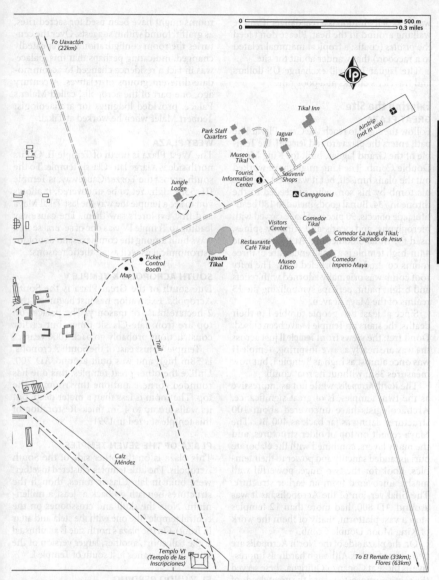

0 — 500 m
0 — 0.3 miles

To Uaxactún
(22km)

Tikal Inn

Airstrip
(not in use)

Park Staff
Quarters

Jaguar
Inn

Museo
Tikal

Tourist
Information
Center

Souvenir
Shops

Jungle
Lodge

Campground

Comedor
Tikal

Comedor La Jungla Tikal;
Comedor Sagrado de Jesus

Visitors
Center

Restaurante
Café Tikal

Comedor
Imperio Maya

Ticket
Control
Booth

Aguada
Tikal

Museo
Lítico

Map

Trail

Calz
Méndez

Templo VI
(Templo de las
Inscripciones)

To El Remate (33km);
Flores (63km)

GUATEMALA

available at the visitors center (US$50 for a half-day tour for up to five people). These guides always display their accreditation carnet, listing the languages they speak.

Near the visitors center are Tikal's three hotels, a camping area, a **tourist information center** (🕐 8am-4pm), a few small *comedores*, a post office, a police post and two museums. From the visitors center it's a 1.5km walk (20 to 30 minutes) southwest to the Gran Plaza. To visit all the major building complexes, you must walk at least 10km, so wear comfortable shoes.

It's a good idea to wear shoes with good rubber treads that grip well. The ruins here can be very slick from rain and organic material, especially during the wet season. Bring plenty of water, as dehydration is a real danger if you're walking around in the heat. Please don't feed the *pisotes* (coatis; a tropical mammal related to a raccoon) that wander about the site.

The Jaguar Inn will exchange US dollars and traveler's checks at a poor rate.

Exloring the Site

GREAT PLAZA

Follow the signs to reach the Great Plaza. The path enters the plaza around **Temple I**, the Temple of the Grand Jaguar, built for King Moon Double Comb. The king might have worked out the plans himself, but it was erected above his tomb by his son, who succeeded to the throne in 734. Burial goods included 180 beautiful jade objects, 90 pieces of bone carved with hieroglyphs, and pearls and stingray spines, used for ritual bloodletting. At the top of the 44m-high temple is a small enclosure of three rooms covered by a corbeled arch. The lofty roof comb was originally adorned with reliefs and bright paint, perhaps symbolizing the 13 realms of the Maya heaven.

Since at least two people tumbled to their deaths, the stairs up Temple I have been closed. Don't fret: the views from **Temple II** just across the way are nearly as awe-inspiring. Temple II was once almost as high as Temple I, but now measures 38m without its roof comb.

The **North Acropolis**, while not as impressive as the twin temples, is of great significance. Archaeologists have uncovered about 100 structures dating as far back as 400 BC. The Maya rebuilt on top of older structures, and the many layers, combined with the elaborate burials, added sanctity and power to their temples. Look for the two huge, powerful wall masks, uncovered from an earlier structure. The final version of the Acropolis, as it was around AD 800, had more than 12 temples atop a vast platform, many of them the work of King Moon Double Comb.

On the plaza side of the North Acropolis are two rows of stelae. Although hardly as impressive as those at Copán or Quiriguá, these served the same purpose: to record the great deeds of the kings of Tikal, to sanctify their memory and to add 'power' to the surrounding structures.

CENTRAL ACROPOLIS

On the south side of the Great Plaza, this maze of courtyards, little rooms and small temples is thought by some to have been a residential palace for Tikal's nobility. Others believe the tiny rooms might have been used for sacred rites, as graffiti found within suggests. Over the centuries the room configuration was repeatedly changed, indicating perhaps that this 'palace' was in fact a residence changed to accommodate different groups of relatives. A century ago, one part of the acropolis, called Maler's Palace, provided lodgings for archaeologist Teobert Maler when he worked at Tikal.

WEST PLAZA

The West Plaza is north of Temple II. On its north side is a large late-Classic temple. To the south, across the Tozzer Causeway, is Temple III, 55m high. Yet to be uncovered, it allows you to see a temple the way the last Tikal Maya and first explorers saw them. The causeway leading to Temple IV was one of several sacred ways built among the complexes, no doubt for astronomical as well as aesthetic reasons.

SOUTH ACROPOLIS & TEMPLE V

Due south of the Great Plaza is the South Acropolis. Excavation has just begun on this 2-hectare mass of masonry. The palaces on top are from late-Classic times, but earlier constructions probably go back 1000 years.

Temple V, just east of the South Acropolis, is 58m high and was built around AD 700. Unlike the other great temples, this one has rounded corners and one tiny room at the top. The room is less than a meter deep, but its walls are up to 4.5m thick. Restoration of this temple started in 1991.

PLAZA OF THE SEVEN TEMPLES

This plaza is on the other side of the South Acropolis. The little temples, clustered together, were built in late-Classic times, though the structures beneath go back at least a millennium. Note the skull and crossbones on the central temple (the one with the stela and altar in front). On the plaza's north side is an unusual triple ball court; another, larger version of the same design stands just south of Temple I.

EL MUNDO PERDIDO

About 400m southwest of the Great Plaza is El Mundo Perdido (The Lost World), a complex of 38 structures surrounding a huge pyramid. Unlike the rest of Tikal, where late-Classic construction overlays earlier work, El Mundo Perdido holds buildings of many different periods. The large pyramid is thought to be pre-Classic with some later repairs and renovations, the

Talud-Tablero Temple (or Temple of the Three Rooms) is an early Classic structure, and the Temple of the Skulls is late-Classic.

The pyramid, 32m high and 80m along its base, had huge masks flanking each stairway but no temple structure at the top. Each side displays a slightly different architectural style. Tunnels dug by archaeologists reveal four similar pyramids beneath the outer face; the earliest (Structure 5C–54 Sub 2B) dates from 700 BC, making the pyramid the oldest Maya structure in Tikal.

TEMPLE IV & COMPLEX N

Complex N, near Temple IV, is an example of the 'twin-temple' complexes popular during the late-Classic period. These complexes are thought to have commemorated the completion of a *katun*, or 20-year cycle in the Maya calendar. This one was built in 711 by King Moon Double Comb to mark the 14th *katun* of *baktun* 9. (A *baktun* is about 394 years.) The king is portrayed on Stela 16, one of Tikal's finest.

Temple IV, at 64m, is Tikal's highest building. It was completed about 741, in the reign of King Moon Double Comb's son. A series of steep wooden steps and ladders take you to the top.

TEMPLE OF THE INSCRIPTIONS (TEMPLE VI)

Compared to Copán or Quiriguá, Tikal sports relatively few inscriptions. The exception is this temple, 1.2km southeast of the Great Plaza. On the rear of the 12m-high roof comb is a long inscription; the sides and cornice of the roof comb bear glyphs as well. The inscriptions give us the date AD 766. Stela 21 and Altar 9, standing before the temple, date from 736. Badly damaged, the stela has now been repaired.

NORTHERN COMPLEXES

About 1km north of the Great Plaza is **Complex P**. Like Complex N, it's a late-Classic twin-temple complex that probably commemorated the end of a *katun*. **Complex M**, next to it, was partially torn down by late-Classic Maya to provide material for the causeway – now named after Alfred Maudslay, who is most widely known for his photographs of Central American ruins – that runs southwest to Temple IV.

Complexes Q and R, about 300m due north of the Great Plaza, are late-Classic twin-pyramid complexes. Complex Q is perhaps the best example of the twin-temple type, as it has been mostly restored. Stela 22 and Altar 10 are excellent examples of late-Classic Tikal relief carving, dated 771.

Complex O, due west of these complexes on the west side of the Maler Causeway, has an uncarved stela and altar in its north enclosure. The point of stelae was to record happenings – why did this one remain uncarved?

MUSEUMS

Tikal has two museums. The **Museo Lítico** (Museum of Stone; admission US$1.30; 🕙 9am-5pm Mon-Fri, to 4pm Sat & Sun), the larger of the two, is in the visitors center. It houses a number of stelae and carved stones from the ruins. Outside is a large model showing how Tikal looked around AD 800. The photographs taken by Alfred P Maudslay and Teobert Maler of the jungle-covered temples in various stages of discovery in the late 19th century are particularly striking.

The **Museo Tikal** or **Museo Cerámico** (Museum of Ceramics; admission US$1.30; 🕙 9am-5pm Mon-Fri, to 4pm Sat & Sun) is near the Jaguar Inn. It has some fascinating exhibits, including the burial goods of King Moon Double Comb, carved jade, inscribed bones, shells, stelae, ceramics and other items recovered from the excavations.

Bird-Watching

Around 300 bird species (migratory and endemic) have been recorded at Tikal. Early morning is the best time to go; even amateurs will have their share of sightings. Ask at the visitors center about early-morning and late-afternoon tours. Bring binoculars, tread quietly and be patient and you'll probably see some of the following birds:

- tody motmots, four trogon species and royal flycatchers around the Temple of the Inscriptions
- two oriole species, collared aracaris, and keel-billed toucans in El Mundo Perdido
- great curassows, three species of woodpecker, crested guans, plain chachalacas and three species of tanager around Complex P
- three kingfisher species, jacanas, blue herons, two sandpiper species and great kiskadees at the Tikal Reservoir near the entrance; tiger herons in the huge ceiba tree along the entrance path
- red-capped and white-collared manakins near Complex Q; emerald toucanets near Complex R

GUATEMALA

> **WARNING**
>
> The Temple of the Inscriptions is remote, and there have been incidents of robbery and rape of single travelers and couples in the past. Though safety has been greatly improved at Tikal, ask a guard before you make the trek out here, or come in a group.

Hiking

The Sendero Benilj'a'a, a 3km trail with three sections, begins in front of the Jungle Lodge. Ruta Monte Medio and Ruta Monte Medio Alto (both one hour) are accessible year-round. Ruta Monte Bajo (35 minutes) is accessible only in summer. A short interpretive trail called El Misterio de la Vida Maya (The Mystery of Maya Life) leads to the Great Plaza.

Tours

All the hotels can arrange guided tours of the ruins, as well as tours to other places in the region. Day tours from Flores/Santa Elena (US$45 to US$65 per person) can be arranged through Martsam Travel (p189).

Sleeping

The days of bribing a guard and sleeping on top of Temple IV are gone – if you are caught in the ruins after hours, you'll be escorted out, for security reasons. Nowadays, the best way to catch solitude and get an early glimpse of the wildlife is to camp at the entrance.

Other than camping, there are a few places to stay at Tikal. Most are booked in advance by tour groups. It may be best to stay in Flores or El Remate and visit Tikal on day trips.

On the other hand, staying at Tikal enables you to relax and savor the dawn and dusk, when most of the jungle fauna can be observed.

There's no need to make reservations if you want to stay at Tikal's **campground** (per person US$4) opposite the visitors center. This is a large, grassy area with a clean bathroom block, plenty of space for tents and *palapa* shelters for hanging hammocks.

Jaguar Inn (☎ 7926 0002; www.jaguartikal.com; camping per person US$3.25, hammocks per person US$5; s/d US$33/53; P 🍴 🖵) Although the little duplex bungalows here are kinda jammed together, it still makes a decent and (relatively) cheap

sleep in the park. Hammocks on the little porches are a bonus, but nobody's likely to get excited about paying US$6 for an hour of internet. If you don't have a tent, you can rent one for US$6.50 per person. The electricity goes off at 9pm.

Jungle Lodge (☎ 7861 0446; www.junglelodge.guate .com; s/d US$35/40, with bathroom US$69/86; P 🍴) By far the sweetest of the accommodation options in the park, these mostly self-contained bungalows are well spaced throughout the jungly grounds. There's a swimming pool, large garden grounds, and a restaurant-bar with breakfast for US$5 and lunch or dinner for US$10.

As you arrive in Tikal, look on the right-hand side of the road to find the little *comedores:* **Comedor Imperio Maya**, **Comedor La Jungla Tikal**, **Comedor Tikal**, and **Comedor Sagrado de Jesús** (all 🕒 5am-9pm). Comedor Tikal seems to be the most popular. These *comedores* offer rustic and agreeable surroundings and are run by local people serving huge plates of fairly tasty food at low prices. Chicken or meat dishes cost around US$4.50, pasta and burgers a little less.

Picnic tables beneath shelters are located just off Tikal's Gran Plaza, with soft-drink and water peddlers standing by, but no food is sold. If you want to spend all day at the ruins without having to make the 20- to 30-minute walk back to the *comedores,* carry food and water with you.

Getting There & Away

For details of transportation to and from Flores and Santa Elena, see p192. Coming from Belize, you could consider taking a taxi from the border to Tikal for around US$50. Otherwise, get a bus to Puente Ixlú, sometimes called El Cruce, and switch to a northbound minibus or bus for the remaining 36km to Tikal. Note that there is little northbound traffic after lunch. Heading from Tikal to Belize, start early in the morning and get off at Puente Ixlú to catch a bus or minibus eastward. Be wary of shuttles to Belize advertised at Tikal – these have been known to detour to Flores to pick up passengers!

UAXACTÚN

Uaxactún (wah-shahk-*toon*), 23km north of Tikal along a poor, unpaved road through the jungle, was Tikal's political and military rival in late pre-Classic times. It was eventually conquered by Tikal's King Great Jaguar Paw in the mid-4th century, and was subservient to its great southern sister for centuries thereafter.

When you arrive, sign your name at the guard's hut (at the edge of the derelict airstrip). About halfway down the airstrip, roads go off to the left and to the right to the ruins.

Villagers in Uaxactún live in houses lined up along the airstrip. They make a living by collecting chicle, *pimienta* (allspice) and *xate* (*sha*-tay; a frond exported for floral arrangements) from the surrounding forest.

Ruins

The pyramids at Uaxactún were uncovered and stabilized to prevent further deterioration; they were not restored. White mortar is the mark of the repair crews, who patched cracks to keep out water and roots. Much of the work on the famous **Temple E-VII-Sub** was done by Earthwatch volunteers in 1974.

Turn right from the airstrip to reach Groups E and H, a 15-minute walk. Perhaps the most significant temple here is E-VII-Sub, among the earliest intact temples excavated, with foundations going back perhaps to 2000 BC. It lay beneath much larger structures, which have been stripped away. On its flat top are sockets for poles that would have supported a wood-and-thatch temple.

About 20 minutes-walk to the northwest of the runway you'll find Groups A and B. At **Group A** early excavators sponsored by Andrew Carnegie cut into the temple sides indiscriminately, looking for graves, occasionally using dynamite. This process destroyed many temples, which are now being reconstructed.

If you are visiting Uaxactún from Tikal, no fee is charged. But if you are going to Uax-

actún without stopping to visit Tikal, you still have to pass through the Parque Nacional Tikal and will have to pay a US$3 Uaxactún-only fee at the park entrance.

Tours to Uaxactún can be arranged at hotels in Tikal. The Jungle Lodge (opposite) has a trip departing at 8am daily and returning at 1pm, costing US$60 for one to four people.

Sleeping & Eating

Aldana's Lodge (camping per person US$2.50, r per person US$4) To the right off the street leading to Grupos B and A, Aldana's has alternative, cheaper accommodations, but has erratic water supplies. It offers tours to other sites. Camping using their equipment costs US$3 per person.

Campamento, Hotel & Restaurante El Chiclero (☎ /fax 7926 1095; camping US$5, s/d US$14/17) On the north side of the airstrip, this place has 10 small and very basic rooms with good mattresses and mosquito-netted ceilings and windows. It does the best food in town (US$6 for soup and a main course with rice). Accommodation prices are very negotiable. Also here is a small museum with shelves full of Maya pottery from Uaxactún and around. Staff can organize trips to more remote sites such as El Mirador, Xultún, Río Azul, Nakbé and La Muralla.

A few basic *comedores* also provide food: Comedor Uaxactún is the most popular.

Getting There & Away

A Pinita bus supposedly leaves Santa Elena for Uaxactún (US$3) at 1pm, passing through Tikal about 3pm to 3:30pm, and starting back for Santa Elena from Uaxactún at 6pm. But its schedule is rubbery and it can arrive in Tikal any time up to about 5pm and in Uaxactún up to about 6:30pm. During the rainy season (from May to October, sometimes extending

---

GETTING TO SAN IGNACIO, BELIZE

It's 100km from Flores to **Melchor de Mencos**, the Guatemalan town on the border with Belize. See p192 for information on bus services to the border and also on more expensive services going right through to **Belize City** and **Chetumal, Mexico**.

The road to the border diverges from the Flores–Tikal road at **Puente Ixlú** (also called El Cruce), 27km from Flores. It continues paved until about 25km short of the border. The stretch between Puente Ixlú and the border has been the scene of a few highway robberies.

There should be no fees at the border for entering or leaving Guatemala, and none for entering Belize. There are money changers at the border with whom you can change sufficient funds for immediate needs.

See p249 for information on crossing the border from Belize.

into November), the road from Tikal to Uaxactún can become pretty muddy: locals say it is always passable but a 4WD vehicle might be needed during the wet.

If you're driving, the last chance to fill your fuel tank as you come from the south is at Puente Ixlú, just south of El Remate. A taxi from El Remate to Uaxactún and back, including waiting time, should cost about US$60; bargain hard.

From Uaxactún, unpaved roads lead to other ruins at El Zotz (about 30km southwest), Xultún (35km northeast) and Río Azul (100km northeast).

SAYAXCHÉ & CEIBAL

Sayaxché, on the south bank of the Río de la Pasión, 61km southwest of Flores, is the closest town to nine or 10 scattered Maya archaeological sites, including Ceibal, Aguateca, Dos Pilas, Tamarindito and Altar de Sacrificios. Otherwise, for travelers it's little more than a transportation halt between Flores and Cobán.

Minibuses and buses from Santa Elena stop on the north bank of the Río de la Pasión. Frequent ferries (US$0.15 for pedestrians, US$2 for cars) carry you across to the town.

Banoro (9am-4pm Mon-Fri, 10am-1pm Sat), just up the main street from Hotel Guayacán, changes US dollars and traveler's checks.

Hotel Yaxkin (7928 6429; s/d with bathroom US$7.50/15) has surprisingly big rooms in a brick and concrete wonderland 50m up from the boat landing. Try to get one away from the front as the street noise is formidable.

Café del Río (mains US$3-5; breakfast, lunch & dinner) is the most atmospheric place to eat in town and is actually across the river on the big wooden dock built out over the water. Forget about the US$0.50 return trip and enjoy the wholesome food, sweet breezes and icy beer.

GETTING TO CHIAPAS (MEXICO)

The only route with regular transportation connections is via **Bethel** or **La Técnica** on the eastern (Guatemalan) bank of the Río Usumacinta and **Frontera Corozal** on the Mexican bank. See p192 for details of bus services to and from Bethel and La Técnica and shuttle minibus services all the way through to **Palenque**. Guatemalan immigration is in Bethel: bus drivers to La Técnica will normally stop and wait for you to do the formalities in Bethel.

It's cheaper and quicker from La Técnica than from Bethel, but crossing at La Técnica means a longer bus journey on the Guatemalan side. Minibuses (US$5, three hours) leave Frontera Corozal for Palenque at about 5am, 10am, noon and 3pm.

If you want to stay in the Usumacinta area, perhaps to visit the Maya ruins at **Yaxchilán** on the Mexican side of the river, the riverside **Posada Maya** (7861 1799; s/d/tr US$9/18/28), 1km outside Bethel, has a great location and comfortable thatched bungalows, plus tent and hammock shelters. Boats from Bethel to Yaxchilán cost between US$15 and US$25 per person for four to 12 people, round-trip.

See p249 for information on crossing the border from Mexico.

Other Routes

You can also cross into Mexico by boat down the Río de la Pasión from **Sayaxché** to **Benemérito de las Américas** or down the Río San Pedro from **El Naranjo** to **La Palma**. But there are no regular passenger services on either river and you will probably have to rent a boat privately for around US$80 on the Río San Pedro or US$100-plus on the Río de la Pasión. Both trips take around four hours. La Palma has transportation connections with Tenosique, Tabasco, from where minibuses leave for **Palenque** up to 5:30pm. Benemérito has good bus and minibus connections with Palenque. Both Sayaxché and El Naranjo have bus and minibus connections with **Flores** (see p192).

A possible alternative on the Río San Pedro route is to get a boat from El Naranjo only as far as **El Ceibo**, on the border, for around US$30. From El Ceibo there are a few buses on to Tenosique (US$3, 1½ hours), the last one leaving about 5:30pm. Mexico has no immigration facilities at Benemérito or El Ceibo: you have to get your passport stamped at Frontera Corozal or Tenosique or, failing that, in Palenque.

El Naranjo, Tenosique and Benemérito all have a few basic accommodations.

Restaurant Yaxkin, a couple of doors from Hotel Mayapán, is typical of the few other eateries in town: basic, family-run and inexpensive.

Ceibal

Unimportant during the Classic period, Ceibal grew rapidly thereafter, attaining a population of perhaps 10,000 by AD 900. Much of the growth might have been due to immigration from what is now Chiapas, in Mexico, because the art and culture of Ceibal seems to have changed markedly during this period. The post-Classic period saw the decline of Ceibal, after which its low ruined temples were quickly covered by thick jungle.

Ceibal is not one of the most impressive Maya sites, but the journey to Ceibal is among the most memorable. A two-hour voyage on the jungle-bound Río de la Pasión brings you to a primitive dock. After landing you clamber up a rocky path beneath gigantic trees and vines to reach the archaeological zone.

Smallish temples, many still (or again) covered with jungle, surround two principal plazas. In front of a few temples, and standing seemingly alone on jungle paths, are magnificent, intact stelae. Exploring the site takes about two hours.

See p189 for travel agents who offer tours to Ceibal. Otherwise, talk to any of the boatmen in Sayaxché. They charge around US$46 per boatload, round-trip including waiting time. You should hire a guide to see the site, as some of the finest stelae are off the plazas in the jungle. Most *lancheros,* conveniently, also serve as guides.

If you wish, you can get to Ceibal cheaper by land: get any bus, minibus or pickup heading south from Sayaxché on Hwy 5 (toward Raxrujá and Chisec) and get off after 9km at Paraíso (US$0.80), from which a dirt track leads 8km east to Ceibal. You might have to walk the last 8km. In the rainy season this stretch may not be passable.

GETTING THERE & AWAY

See p192 for details of minibuses and buses from Flores. The round-trip schedule is similar.

Southbound from Sayaxché, buses and minibuses leave at 5am, 6am, 10am and 3pm for Cobán (US$7, five hours). Most, if not all of these go via Raxrujá and Sebol, not via Chisec. Other minibuses and buses go just to Raxrujá (US$3.50), about hourly from 7am to 3pm. For Chisec, you can change in Raxrujá or at San Antonio Las Cuevas. Vehicles may start from the southern riverbank or they may start from the Texaco station opposite Hotel Guayacán.

For river transportation, talk to any of the boatmen on the riverbank, or to **La Gaviota Tours** (☎ 7928 6461), with an office 200m to the left of where boats dock. A trip all the way down the Río de la Pasión to Benemérito de las Américas (Mexico), with stops at the ruins of Altar de Sacrificios and Guatemalan immigration at Pipiles, should cost between US$130 and US$180.

REMOTE MAYA SITES

Several sites of interest to archaeology buffs and adventurous travelers are open for limited tourism. Few can be visited without a guide, but many businesses in Flores and Santa Elena offer trips to sites deep in the jungle. Few of these tours offer anything approaching comfort, and you should be prepared for buggy, basic conditions.

The ceremonial site of **Yaxhá**, on the lake of the same name, is about 48km east of El Remate. Scholars believe it may have been a vacation spot for Maya nobility during the Classic period. The ruins here include a large plaza and two temples. A ruined observatory sits on Topoxté island in the middle of the lake.

El Zotz is about 25km west of Tikal. Zotz means 'bat,' and you'll encounter plenty on a trek here. Among the many unexcavated mounds and ruins is Devil's Pyramid, which is so tall that you can see the temples of Tikal from its summit. Trips to El Zotz can be extended to include a trek to Tikal.

El Perú, 62km northwest from Flores in the Parque Nacional Laguna del Tigre, lies along the Scarlet Macaw Trail. The trek starts in Paso Caballos and continues by boat along the Río San Pedro. Several important structures here have been dated to between AD 300 and 900. Archaeologists believe El Perú was an important commercial center.

Another destination in Parque Nacional Laguna del Tigre that is sometimes combined with El Perú trips is the **Estación Biológica Las Guacamayas** (Scarlet Macaw Biological Station) on the Río San Juan. This is a scientific station surrounded by rain forest, where among other things scarlet macaws and white tortoises are observed.

GUATEMALA

GUATEMALA

LOCAL VOICES – NORA LÓPEZ, LABORATORY DIRECTOR, THE MIRADOR PROJECT

One of the major archaeological excavations being undertaken in Guatemala is at El Mirador, a remote Maya site in El Petén (see below). Buried in jungle for centuries, the importance of this megacity is only just starting to be understood. We caught up with Nora López to find out how the dig's going.

■ **What's special about El Mirador?** For one thing, it's huge. We're still mapping, but it looks like El Mirador occupied 23 sq km. Around the city were others such as Nakbé and Florida, connected by stone 'highways' that are up to 23km long. Altogether, we're looking at an area of around 2000 sq km. Another is that, because there wasn't much water near the site, hydraulic irrigation systems were used to grow crops needed to feed so many workers.

■ **What's the most exciting thing you've found?** Plenty of little things. Small things contribute to the big picture. I'm interested in bones, so I like finding burials, even though it implies more work. Once a body is uncovered we have to work around the clock or else it can get damaged by weather or stolen by thieves.

■ **How do you see the relation between tourism and archaeology?** It can be excellent, but it has to be managed. What you see at more popular sites is a lot of damage – crowds trampling things and not understanding what they're looking at. If you keep the groups small, visitors can be informed and educated. Mass tourism doesn't really do anything but provide photo opportunities.

As told to Lucas Vidgen

El Mirador is buried within the furthest reaches of the Petén jungle, just 7km from the Mexican border. A trip here involves an arduous 60km trek in primitive conditions. The metropolis at El Mirador flourished between 150 BC and AD 150, when it was abandoned for mysterious reasons. The site holds the tallest pyramid ever built in the Maya world: El Tigre is over 60m high, and its base covers 18,000 sq meters. Its twin, La Danta (Tapir), although technically smaller, soars higher because it's built on a rise. There are hundreds of buildings at El Mirador, but almost everything is still hidden beneath the jungle.

This trip is not for the faint of heart. For more on this incredible site, see the September, 1987 *National Geographic* article 'An Early Maya Metropolis Uncovered: El Mirador.' This is the most thorough mainstream investigative report ever written about the site.

GUATEMALA DIRECTORY

ACCOMMODATIONS

This chapter's accommodations coverage includes places where a typical double (room for two people) costs US$20 or less. Doubles under about US$10 are generally small, dark and not particularly clean. A typical US$20 double should be clean, sizable and airy, with a bathroom, TV and, in hot parts of the country, a fan.

Unless otherwise specified, the bathroom facilities offered at accommodations are shared.

Room rates often go up in touristy places during Semana Santa (Easter week), Christmas to New Year's and July to August. Semana Santa is the major Guatemalan holiday week of the year, and prices can rise by anything from 30% to 100% on the coast, in the countryside – anywhere Guatemalans go to relax – as well as in such international-tourism destinations as Antigua. At this time advance reservations are a must.

Room rates are subject to two large taxes – 12% IVA (value-added tax) and a 10% tax to pay for the activities of the Guatemalan Tourism Institute (Inguat). All prices in this book include both taxes.

BOOK ACCOMMODATIONS ONLINE

For more accommodations reviews and recommendations by Lonely Planet authors, check out the online booking service at www.lonelyplanet.com. You'll find the true, insider lowdown on the best places to stay. Reviews are thorough and independent. Best of all, you can book online.

Camping can be a hit-or-miss affair, as there are few designated campgrounds and safety is rarely guaranteed. Where campsites are available, expect to pay from US$3 to US$5 per night.

Travelers attending Spanish school have the option of living with a Guatemalan family. This is usually a pretty good bargain – expect to pay between US$35 and US$60 per week for your own room, shared bathroom, and three meals daily except Sunday. It's important to find a homestay that gels with your goals. Some families host several students at a time, creating more of an international hostel atmosphere than a family environment.

ACTIVITIES
Caving
Guatemala attracts cavers from all over the world. The limestone area around Cobán is particularly riddled with cave systems whose true extents are far from known. The caves of Lanquín (p167) are open for tourist visits. There are also exciting caves to visit from Finca Ixobel (p186), near Poptún.

Climbing & Hiking
Guatemala's volcanoes are irresistible challenges, and many of them can be climbed in one day from Antigua or Quetzaltenango. There's further great hill country in the Ixil Triangle and the Cuchumatanes mountains north of Huehuetenango, especially around Todos Santos.

The Lago de Atitlán is surrounded by spectacular trails (p116), although robberies here have made some routes inadvisable. Hikes of several days are perfectly feasible, and agencies in Antigua, Quetzaltenango and Nebaj can guide you. In the Petén jungles, hikes to remote archaeological sites such as El Mirador and El Perú (opposite) offer an exciting challenge.

Cycling
There's probably no better way to experience the highlands than by bicycle. Panajachel, Quetzaltenango and Antigua, in particular, are the best launch points, with agencies offering trips and/or equipment.

Horseback Riding
Opportunities for a gallop, trot or even a horse trek are on the rise. Antigua, Santiago Atitlán, and El Remate all have stables.

Water Sports
You can dive inside a volcanic caldera at Lago de Atitlán (p128), raft the white-water of the Río Cahabón near Lanquín, sail from the yachtie haven of Río Dulce, and canoe or kayak the waterways of Monterrico, Livingston, or the Bocas del Polochic or Punta de Manabique.

Wildlife & Bird-Watching
Few national parks and reserves have many tourist facilities, but they do have lots of wildlife- and bird-watching.

Fine bird-watching locales in the Petén jungles include Tikal (p194), El Mirador (opposite), Cerro Cahuí (p194), Laguna Petexbatún and (for scarlet macaws) Las Guacamayas biological station (p203).

Elsewhere, the wetlands of Bocas del Polochic, Punta de Manabique and Monterrico, the Río Dulce and Laguna Lachuá national parks and the Biotopo del Quetzal (p162) also provide lots of avian variety.

Mammals are more elusive but you should see several species at Tikal. Monkey fans will also be happy at the Reserva Natural Atitlán (Panajachel; p116), the Bocas del Polochic (p176) and Cerro Cahuí (p194).

BOOKS
For more in-depth information, grab a copy of Lonely Planet's *Guatemala* guide.

Guatemalan Journey, by Stephen Benz, is another one to enjoy while you're in Guatemala. It casts an honest and funny modern traveler's eye on the country. So does Anthony Daniels' *Sweet Waist of America,* also published as *South of the Border: Guatemalan Days,* where the medic author pinpoints some of the country's quirky contradictions.

In *Sacred Monkey River,* Christopher Shaw explores by canoe the jungle-clad basin of the Río Usumacinta, a cradle of ancient Maya civilization along the Mexico–Guatemala border – a great read.

Bird of Life, Bird of Death, by Jonathan Evan Maslow, subtitled 'A naturalist's journey through a land of political turmoil,' tells of the author's searches for the resplendent quetzal ('bird of life') – which he found increasingly endangered, while the zopilote (vulture; 'bird of death') flourished.

See p33 for suggested books on the Maya and p723 for travel literature selections that cover Guatemala and surrounding countries.

GUATEMALA

BUSINESS HOURS

Guatemalan shops and businesses are generally open from 8am to noon and 2pm to 6pm, Monday to Saturday, but there are many variations.

Banks typically open 9am to 5pm Monday to Friday (again with variations), and 9am to 1pm Saturday. Government offices usually open 8am to 4pm, Monday to Friday. Official business is always best conducted in the morning.

CLIMATE

Although Guatemala is officially the 'Land of Eternal Spring,' temperatures can be freezing at night in the highlands. In the dry season – from late October to May – the highlands are warm and delightful, but even then, nights are never hot.

Guatemala's coasts are tropical, rainy, hot and humid. Temperatures often reach 32°C to 38°C (90°F to 100°F), and the humidity abates only slightly in the dry season. On the Caribbean side, rain is possible any time. Cobán has about one month of dry weather (April), though you can catch some less-than-soggy spells between November and March.

The vast jungle lowland of El Petén has a tropical climate that is seasonally hot and humid or hot and dry. December and January are the coolest months, while March and April are like hell on earth.

For climate charts see p723.

DANGERS & ANNOYANCES

Drunk, alone, lost, late at night and loaded with cash is the stupidest way to walk around Guatemala. And pretty well most combinations of the above items are kind of stupid. A lot of people come here and do stuff that they would never do back home. Sometimes they get away with it. Sometimes it backfires. Use your intuition and chances are you'll stay out of trouble.

That said, no-one could pretend that Guatemala is a very safe country. The daily papers are full of gory stuff that Guatemalans do to each other every day. Thankfully for travelers, a lot of it is gang violence and they keep it to themselves.

Rapes and murders of tourists do happen occasionally. The two most frequently reported types of nasty incident involving tourists are highway robberies (when a vehicle is stopped and its occupants relieved of their

> **LOSIN' IT**
>
> For such a poor country, it's surprising how few scams there actually are in operation in Guatemala. Really the only ones you have to worry about are the old classics (eg someone sprays ketchup or some other sticky liquid on your clothes, then an accomplice appears to help you clean up the mess who robs you in the process). Other methods of distraction, such as dropping a purse or coins, or someone appearing to faint, are also used by pickpockets and bag snatchers.
>
> Markets are good hunting grounds for pickpockets all across the country, and you should be on your guard in all crowds, particularly when you're weighed down with baggage and distracted.

belongings) and robberies on walking trails. For a scary litany of recent incidents, visit the website of Guatemala City's **US embassy** (http://usembassy.state.gov/guatemala) and click on 'Recent Crime Incidents Involving Foreigners.' Further, marginally less alarming, information is on the website of the **US Department of State** (www.ds-osac.org) and the website of the **UK Foreign and Commonwealth Office** (www.fco.gov.uk).

Vehicles carrying tourists, such as shuttle minibuses and buses along heavily traveled routes, seem to be a prime target for highway robbery. On this basis, some people argue that chicken buses are the most risk-free way to travel, but chicken buses are certainly not exempt from holdups.

Robberies against tourists on walking trails tend to occur in isolated spots on well-known walks. Some trails around the Lago de Atitlán and on Volcán Agua outside Antigua are particularly notorious (see p113).

The Tikal archaeological site, Volcán Pacaya and Cerro de la Cruz (Antigua), all the scenes of several incidents not so long ago, have become, for now, safer because of increased police and ranger presence designed to protect tourism.

A third danger category is pickpocketing, bag-snatching, bag-slitting and the like in crowded bus stations, buses, streets and markets, but also in empty, dark city streets.

Hiking on active volcanoes obviously has an element of risk. Get the latest story before you head out. In the wet season, go up volcanoes in the morning before rain and possible thunderstorms set in. A Canadian tourist was killed by lightning on Volcán Pacaya in 2002.

There have been a few bizarre incidents in which foreign visitors have been unjustly suspected of malicious designs on Guatemalan children. In 2000 a Japanese tourist comforting a crying child, and his driver, were killed in Todos Santos by crowds inflamed by rumors of satanists at large in the area. A woman taking photographs of children in a town near Cobán was nearly murdered by a hysterical crowd apparently afraid that she wanted children's organs for transplant operations.

Be careful not to put yourself in any situation that might be misinterpreted. Any crowd can be volatile, especially when drunk or at times of political tension.

For more information on dangers and annoyances, see p724.

Reporting a Robbery or Theft

After a theft you may need a statement from the police for your insurance company. Tell them: *'Yo quisiera poner una acta de un robo'* (I'd like to report a robbery). This should make it clear that you merely want a piece of paper and aren't going to ask the police to do anything active.

DISABLED TRAVELERS

Guatemala is not the easiest country to negotiate with a disability. Although many sidewalks in Antigua have ramps and cute little inlaid tiles depicting a wheelchair, the streets are cobblestone, so the ramps are anything but smooth and the streets worse!

Many hotels in Guatemala are old converted houses with rooms around a courtyard that is wheelchair accessible. The most expensive hotels have facilities such as ramps, elevators and accessible toilets. Transportation is the biggest hurdle for disabled travelers: travelers in a wheelchair might consider renting a car and driver, as buses will prove especially challenging, due to lack of space.

Mobility International USA (www.miusa.org) advises disabled travelers on mobility issues, runs exchange programs (including in Guatemala) and publishes some useful books. Also worth consulting are **Access-Able Travel Source** (www.access-able.com) and **Accessible Journeys** (www.disabilitytravel.com).

Transitions (☎ 7832 4261; transitions@guate.net; Colonia Candelaria 80, Antigua) is an organization aiming to increase awareness and access for disabled persons in Guatemala.

EMBASSIES & CONSULATES
Embassies & Consulates in Guatemala

All of the following are embassies in Guatemala City:

Belize (☎ 2367 3883; embelguate@yahoo.com; 5a Av 5-55, Zona 14, Europlaza 2, Office 1502)

Canada (☎ 2363 4348; gtmla@international.gc.ca; 8th fl, Edificio Edyma Plaza, 13a Calle 8-44, Zona 10)

El Salvador (☎ 2360 7660; emsalva@intel.net.gt; Av Las Américas 16-46, Zona 13)

Germany (☎ 2364 6700; embalemana@intelnet.net.gt; Edificio Plaza Marítima, 20a Calle 6-20, Zona 10)

Honduras (☎ 2366 5640; embhond@intelnet.net.gt; 19a Av 'A' 20-19, Zona 10)

Mexico (☎ 2420 3400; 2a Av 7-57, Zona 10)

Spain (☎ 2379 3530; embaespa@terra.com.gt.es; 6a Calle 6-48, Zona 9)

UK (☎ 2367 5425/6/7/8/9; embassy@intelnett.com; 11th fl, Torre Internacional, 16a Calle 00-55, Zona 10)

USA (☎ 2326 4000; www.usembassy.state.gov/guatemala; Av La Reforma 7-01, Zona 10)

Guatemalan Embassies & Consulates Abroad

You'll find a full list of Guatemala's embassies and consulates at www.minex.gob.gt /sistemaprotocolo/protocolos/cmisiones .asp. The following listings are embassies, unless otherwise noted:

Australia Consulate (☎ 02-9327 7348; 5 Weldodon Lane, Woolahra, Sydney 2025)

Canada (☎ 613-233 7237; embguate@ottawa.net; 130 Albert St, Suite 1010, Ottawa, Ontario K1P 5G4)

France (☎ 01 42 27 78 63; embguafr@easynet.fr; 73 rue de Courcelles, Paris 75008)

Germany (☎ 228-358 609; embaguate_bonn@ compuserve.com; Zietenstrasse, 16, 5300 Bonn 2)

Japan (☎ 03-34001830; fax 03-3400 1820; 38 Kowa Bldg, Rm 905, 4-12-24 Nishi-Azabu, 106-0031, Tokyo)

Mexico Mexico City (☎ 55-5540 7520; meroldan@iserve .net.mx; Av Explanada 1025, Lomas de Chapultepec, 11000); consulate in Chetumal (☎ 983 832 30 45; Av Independencia 326); consulate in Ciudad Hidalgo, Chiapas (☎ 962 628 01 84; 5a Calle Oriente s/n entre 1a & 3a Norte); consulate in Comitán, Chiapas (☎ 963 632 04 91; fax 963 632 26 69; 1a Calle Sur Poniente 26); consulate in Tapachula, Chiapas (☎ 962 625 63 80; 3a Av Norte 85); also consulates in Puebla and Tijuana.

Netherlands (☎ 355 7421; PO Box 10224, 7301 GE, Appeldoorn)

GUATEMALA

Spain (☎ 913 44 14 17; embespaña@minex.gob.gt; Calle Rafael Salgado 3, 100 derecha, 28036, Madrid)
UK (☎ 020-7351 3042; embgranbretana@minex.gob.gt; 13 Fawcett St, London SW10 9HN)
USA (☎ 202-745 4952/53/54; www.guatemala-embassy.org; 2220 R St NW, 20008, Washington DC) Consulates in Chicago, Houston, Los Angeles (www.guatemala-consulate.org), Miami, New York and San Francisco (www.sfconsulguate.org).

FESTIVALS & EVENTS

Events of national significance include the following:

El Cristo de Esquipulas (January 15) This superdevout festival in Esquipulas brings pilgrims from all over Central America to catch a glimpse of the Black Christ housed in the Basilica.

Semana Santa (March/April; Holy Week, the week leading up to Easter Sunday) Statues of Jesus and Mary are carried round the streets of towns all round the country, followed by devout, sometimes fervent, crowds, to mark Christ's crucifixion. The processions walk over and destroy *alfombras* (elaborate carpets of colored sawdust and flower petals). The week peaks on Good Friday.

Fiesta de la Virgen de la Asunción (August) Peaking on August 15, this is celebrated with folk dances and parades in Tactic, Sololá, Guatemala City and Jocotenango.

Día de Todos los Santos (All Saints' Day; November 1) Sees giant kite festivals in Santiago Sacatepéquez and Sumpango, near Antigua, and the renowned horse races in Todos Santos.

Quema del Diablo (The Burning of the Devil; December 7) Starts at around 6pm throughout the country when everyone takes to the streets with their old garbage, physical and psychic, to stoke huge bonfires of trash. This is followed by impressive fireworks displays.

FOOD & DRINK
Food

Desayuno chapín, or Guatemalan breakfast (*chapín* is a local term for Guatemalans), is a large affair involving (at the least) eggs, beans, fried plantains, tortillas and coffee. Anywhere tourists go, you'll also find a range of other breakfasts on offer, from light continental-style affairs to US-style bacon, eggs, *panqueques* (pancakes), cereals, fruit juice and coffee. Breakfast is usually eaten between 6am and 10am.

Travelers attempting an Atkins diet may have to put it on hold for the duration. Guatemala is carbohydrate heaven – don't be surprised if your plate has rice, potatoes and corn and is served up with a healthy stack of tortillas.

Lunch is the biggest meal of the day and is eaten between about noon and 2pm. Eateries usually offer a fixed-price meal of several courses called an *almuerzo* or *menú del día*, which might include from one to four courses and is usually great value. A simple *almuerzo* might consist of soup and a main course featuring meat with rice or potatoes and a little salad or vegetables, or just a *plato típico*: meat or chicken, rice, beans, cheese, salad and tortillas.

La cena (dinner) is, for Guatemalans, a lighter version of lunch, usually eaten between about 7pm and 9pm. Even in cities, few restaurants will serve you much after 10pm. In rural areas, sit down no later than 8pm to avoid disappointment. In local and village eateries, supper might be the same as breakfast: eggs, beans and plantains. In restaurants catering to tourists, dinner might be anything from pepper steak to vegetarian Thai curry.

On the coast, seafood is the go. In Lívingston make sure you try the delicious coconut and seafood stew called *tapado*. Elsewhere, your fish or shrimp is generally fried, but you can always specify it be cooked differently – *con ajo* (with garlic). These plates generally come with salad, fries and tortillas. Also good is *caldo de mariscos*, a seafood stew that generally contains fish, shrimp and mussels.

Alcoholic Drinks

Breweries were established in Guatemala by German immigrants in the late 19th century, but they didn't bring a heap of flavor with them. The two nationally distributed beers are Gallo (*gah*-yoh, rooster) and Cabro (goat). The distribution prize goes to Gallo – you'll find it everywhere – but Cabro is darker and more flavorful. Moza is the darkest local beer, but its distribution is limited. Brahva, the Guatemalan-produced version of the Brazilian Brahma beer, is preferred by many foreigners (and some locals) and is becoming more widely available.

Ron (rum) is one of Guatemala's favorite strong drinks, and though most is cheap in price and taste, some local products are exceptionally fine. Zacapa Centenario is a smooth, aged Guatemalan rum made in Zacapa. It should be sipped slowly, like fine cognac. Ron Botrán Añejo, another dark rum, is also good. Cheaper rums such as Venado are often mixed with soft drinks to make potent but cooling drinks such as the Cuba Libre of rum and

Coke. On the coast you'll find *cocos locos*, green coconuts with the top sliced off and rum mixed with the coconut water.

Aguardiente is a sugarcane firewater that flows in cantinas and on the streets, and gets you drunk hard and fast. Look for the signs advertising Quetzalteca Especial. This is the *aguardiente* of choice.

Ponche is a potent potable made from pineapple or coconut juice and rum, served hot.

Nonalcoholic Drinks

Although Guatemala grows some of the world's richest coffee, a good cup is only generally available in top-end restaurants and some tourist restaurants and cafés, because most of the quality beans are exported. If you're really picky, ask if it's *de la maquina* (from the machine). *Té negro* (black tea), most often made from bags, is usually drinkable. Herbal teas are much better. *Té de manzanilla* (chamomile tea), common on restaurant and café menus, is a specific remedy for queasy gut.

Jugos (fresh fruit and vegetable juices), *licuados* (milkshakes) and *aguas de frutas* (long, cool, fruit-flavored water drinks) are wildly popular and with good reason: they rock. Many cafés and eateries offer them, and almost every village market and bus terminal has a stand with a battalion of blenders. The basic *licuado* is a blend of fruit or juice with water and sugar. A *licuado con leche* uses milk instead of water.

Limonada is a delicious thirst-quencher made with lime juice, water and sugar. Try a *limonada con soda*, which adds a fizzy dimension, and you may have a new drink of choice. *Naranjada* is the same thing made with orange juice.

On the coast, the most refreshing nonalcoholic option is a green coconut – you'll see them piled up roadside. The vendor simply slices the top off with a machete and sticks a straw in. If you've never drunk green coconut juice, you have to give it a go – it's delicious!

Agua pura (purified water) is widely available in hotels, shops and restaurants. Salvavida is a universally trusted brand. You can order safe-to-drink carbonated water by saying 'soda.'

Soft drinks as a whole are known as *aguas* (waters). If you want straight, unflavored water, say '*agua pura*,' or *you* may be asked '¿*Qué sabor?*' ('What flavor?').

GAY & LESBIAN TRAVELERS

Few places in Latin America are outwardly gay-friendly, and Guatemala is no different. Technically, homosexuality is legal for persons 18 years and older, but the reality can be another story, with harassment and violence against gays too often poisoning the plot. Guatemala City and Quetzaltenango have a small community of transvestite streetwalkers who are often the victims of violent assault. Don't even consider testing the tolerance for homosexual public displays of affection here.

Although Antigua has a palatable – if subdued – scene, affection and action are still kept behind closed doors; there are mixed reports on how public displays go down. In Guatemala City, Genetic and Ephebus (both p98) are the current faves. Quetzaltenango's Palalife Klishe (p143) is surprisingly liberal, with a good, mixed scene and weekly drag shows. In large part, though, gays traveling in Guatemala will find themselves keeping it low-key and pushing the twin beds together.

The websites the **Gully** (www.thegully.com) and **Gay.com** (www.gay.com) have some articles and information relevant to Guatemala.

HOLIDAYS

The main Guatemalan holiday periods are Semana Santa (Easter Week), Christmas-New Year's and July and August. During Semana Santa room prices rise in many places and it's advisable to book accommodations and transportation in advance.

Guatemalan public holidays:

New Year's Day January 1
Easter (Holy Thursday to Easter Sunday inclusive) March/April
Labor Day May 1
Army Day June 30
Assumption Day (Día de la Asunción) August 15
Independence Day September 15
Revolution Day October 20
All Saints' Day November 1
Christmas Eve afternoon December 24
Christmas Day December 25
New Year's Eve afternoon December 31

INTERNET ACCESS

Most medium-sized towns have cybercafés, with fairly reliable connections. Internet cafés typically charge less than US$1 per hour.

If you're traveling with a notebook or handheld computer, be aware that your modem may not work once you leave your home country. The safest option is to buy a reputable 'global' modem before you leave home, or buy a local PC-card modem if you're spending an extended time in any one country. A second issue is the plug: Guatemala uses 110V, two-pronged, flat plugs like those found in the USA. Third, unless you're sporting a completely wireless system, you'll have to hunt down a hotel room with a phone jack to plug into – or find a jack you can use somewhere else.

If you really want to travel with a laptop, consider using a local ISP, unless you use an international server with access numbers in Guatemala such as AOL or CompuServe.

INTERNET RESOURCES

Gringo's Guide (www.thegringosguide.com) Useful info on the country's main travel destinations.

Guatemala (www.visitguatemala.com) Moderately interesting official site of Inguat, the national tourism institute.

Lanic Guatemala (http://lanic.utexas.edu/la/ca/guatemala) The University of Texas' magnificent set of Guatemala links.

La Ruta Maya Online (www.larutamayaonline.com) Reasonably useful mixed bag.

LEGAL MATTERS

Police officers in Guatemala are sometimes part of the problem rather than the solution. The less you have to do with the law, the better.

Whatever you do, don't get involved in any way with illegal drugs: don't buy or sell, use or carry, or associate with people who do – even if the locals seem to do so freely. As a foreigner you are at a distinct disadvantage, and you may be set up by others. Drug laws in Guatemala are strict and, although enforcement may be uneven, penalties are severe. If you do get caught buying, selling, holding or using drugs, your best first defense might be to suggest you and the officer 'work things out.' Tricky.

MAPS

The best overall country map for travelers is International Travel Maps' *Guatemala* (1:500,000), costing around US$10 in Guatemala. The cheaper *Mapa Turístico Guatemala,* produced locally by Intelimapas, tends to be the most up-to-date on the state of Guatemala's roads, many of which have been newly paved in recent years. It also includes plans of many cities. Inguat's *Mapa Vial*

Turístico is another worthwhile map. Guatemala City, Antigua, Panajachel and Quetzaltenango all have bookstores selling some of these maps: see city sections. For 1:50,000 and 1:250,000 topographical sheets of all parts of Guatemala, head to the Instituto Geográfico Nacional (p89).

MEDIA

Among Guatemala's many Spanish language newspapers are **La Prensa Libre** (www.prensalibre.com), **El Siglo Veintiuno** (www.sigloxxi.com) and **La Hora** (www.lahora.com.gt). El Quetzalteco is Quetzaltenango's thrice-weekly newspaper.

USA Today, the *Miami Herald* and the *Los Angeles Times* are sold in luxury hotels and some city and airport bookstores in the region. *Newsweek* and *Time* are also sometimes available.

MONEY

Guatemala's currency, the quetzal (Q; pronounced ket-*sahl*), has been fairly stable in the region of Q8=US$1 for several years. The quetzal is divided into 100 centavos.

You'll find ATMs (cash machines, *cajeros automáticos*) for Visa/Plus System cards in all but the smallest towns, and there are MasterCard/Cirrus ATMs in many places too, so one of these cards is the best basis for your supplies of cash in Guatemala. In addition, many banks give cash advances on Visa cards, and some on MasterCard. You can pay for many purchases with these cards and with American Express cards.

If you don't have one of these cards, a combination of American Express US-dollar traveler's checks and a limited amount of US cash is the way to go. Take some of these as a backup even if you do have a card. Banks all over the country change US-dollar cash, and many of them change US-dollar traveler's checks too. American Express is easily the most recognized traveler's check brand.

In many places you can make payments with US dollars, and a few places will accept traveler's checks. Currencies other than the US dollar are virtually useless in any form, although a small handful of places will now change cash euros.

Banks generally give the best exchange rates on both cash and traveler's checks. If you can't find an open bank, you can often change cash (and occasionally checks) in travel agencies, hotels or shops.

Some towns suffer from change shortages: always try to carry a stash of small bills.

A 10% tip is expected at restaurants. In small *comedores* tipping is optional, but follow the local practice of leaving some spare change. Tour guides are generally tipped around 10%, especially on longer trips.

Exchange Rates

The table shows currency exchange rates at the time this book went to press.

Country	Unit	Quetzals (Q)
Australia	A$1	6.70
Canada	C$1	7.40
euro zone	€1	10.70
Japan	¥100	6.40
New Zealand	NZ$1	6.10
UK	UK£1	15.80
USA	US$1	7.90

PHOTOGRAPHY

Photography is a sensitive subject in Guatemala. Always ask permission before taking portraits, especially of Maya women and children. Don't be surprised if your request is denied. Indigenous children make a habit of requesting payment (usually one quetzal) in return for posing. In certain places, such as the church of Santo Tomás in Chichicastenango, photography is forbidden. Maya ceremonies (should you be so lucky to witness one) are off-limits for photography unless you are given explicit permission. If local people make any sign of being offended, you should put your camera away and apologize immediately, both out of respect and for your own safety. Never take photos of army installations, men with guns or other sensitive military subjects.

POST

The Guatemalan postal service was privatized in 1999. Generally, letters take eight to 10 days to travel to the US and Canada and 10 to 12 days to reach Europe. Almost all cities and towns (but not villages) have a post office where you can buy stamps and send mail. A letter sent to North America costs around US$0.40 and to anywhere else around US$0.50.

The Guatemalan mail system no longer holds poste restante or general delivery mail. The easiest and most reliable way to receive mail is through a private address. American Express offices will hold mail for card members and people using their traveler's checks. It is important to address mail clearly: the last lines should read 'Guatemala, Centro América.'

RESPONSIBLE TRAVEL

By spending money in small, local businesses, staying for extended periods, volunteering and interacting with 'everyday' people, you have the potential to have a positive effect on Guatemala.

Readers should be aware that, while Guatemala certainly uses its Maya heritage to decorate hotel rooms and as eye candy on tourism posters, there is a history of serious neglect of indigenous people. A recent study showed that government spending per capita is lowest in the departments which have the highest indigenous population.

You can do your bit by buying handicrafts directly from the makers or at cooperatives. Many language schools claim to help the local population. Unfortunately, this has become something of a marketing gimmick, and there are some operators who do no such thing – make some independent inquiries before swallowing what they tell you wholesale.

There are many worthwhile NGOs working to improve the situation. You'll find contact details, p213.

Drugs are everywhere in Guatemala, and ridiculously cheap when compared to the prices back home. Be aware that many younger Guatemalans see travelers as role models, and don't understand that the wild behavior that they see is (sometimes) just vacation madness. The other side of it is that, sadly, selling drugs to tourists is much more profitable than just about any other profession, so by being a customer you may be contributing to somebody's decision to drop out of school and become a full-time dealer.

STUDYING

Guatemala is celebrated for its many language schools. A spot of study here is a great way not only to learn Spanish but also to meet locals and get an inside angle on the culture. Many travelers heading down through Central America to South America make Guatemala an early stop so that they can pick up the Spanish skills they need for their trip.

Guatemalan language schools are a lot cheaper than those in Mexico, but few people go away disappointed. There are so many schools to choose from that it's essential to check out a few of them before choosing. It's not hard to see whether a school is professional and well organized, or whether its teachers are qualified and experienced.

Antigua is the most popular place to study, with about 75 schools. Quetzaltenango, the second-most popular, attracts a more serious type of student; Antigua has a livelier students' and travelers' social scene. San Pedro La Laguna and Panajachel on the Lago de Atitlán both have a handful of language schools, and if you'd like to learn Spanish while hanging out in a remote mountain town, there are schools in Todos Santos and Nebaj. On average, schools charge US$110 to US$120 for four hours of one-on-one classes five days per week plus accommodations with a local family.

You can start any day at many schools, any week at all of them, and study for as long as you like. Decent schools offer a variety of elective activities from salsa classes to movies to volcano hikes. Many schools offer classes in Mayan languages as well as Spanish.

TELEPHONE

Guatemala has no area or city codes. Calling from other countries, dial the international access code, ☎ 00 in most countries, then the Guatemala country code, ☎ 502, then the eight-digit local number. The international access code from Guatemala is ☎ 00.

Many towns and cities frequented by tourists have privately run call offices where you can make local and international calls for reasonable rates. If the telephone connection is by internet, the rates can be very cheap (US$0.15 per minute to the USA, US$0.25 to Europe), but line quality is unpredictable. Calling from a hotel is the most expensive way of telephoning.

A number of companies provide public phone services. The most common street phones, found all over Guatemala, are those of Telgua, for which you need to buy a Telgua phone card (tarjeta telefónica de Telgua) from shops and kiosks. Card sales points may advertise the fact with red signs saying 'Ladatel De Venta Aquí.' The cards come in denominations of 20, 30 and 50 quetzals: you slot them into a Telgua phone, dial your number, and the display will tell you how much time you have left.

Unless it's an emergency, don't use the black phones placed strategically in tourist towns that say 'Press 2 to call the United States free!' This is a bait and switch scam; you put the call on your credit card and return home to find you have paid between US$8 and US$20 per minute.

Telgua street phones bear instructions to dial ☎ 147 110 for domestic collect calls and ☎ 147 120 for international collect calls. The latter number is usually successful for the USA and Canada, less so for the rest of the world.

Cell phones are widely used. If you want to rent one in Guatemala, try **Guatemala Ventures** (☎ /fax 7832 3383; 1a Av Sur 15) in Antigua, **Xelapages** (☎ 7761 4395; 4a Calle 19-48) in Quetzaltenango or **Digital Mundo Celular** (☎ 5614 2731; 13a Calle 8-16, Zona 1) in Guatemala City.

Prepaid cell phones are cheap – you can pick up a basic model for around US$20 (often with your first US$15 worth of calls free), then buy cards pretty much everywhere to stock it up. Buying a local chip and using your own phone is an option, but compatibility issues (plus the risk of loss/theft) prevent most people from doing so.

Public fax service is available in most sizable towns: look for 'Fax' signs outside shops and offices.

TOURIST INFORMATION

Guatemala's national tourism institute, **Inguat** (www.visitguatemala.com), has information offices in Guatemala City, Antigua, Panajachel, Quetzaltenango and Flores; a few other towns have departmental, municipal or private-enterprise tourist information offices. See city sections for details. Inguat operates a free 24-hour tourist information and assistance line; call ☎ 1-801 464 8281.

The Guatemalan embassies in the USA, Germany, France, Italy, Spain and the UK can provide some tourist information.

VISAS & DOCUMENTS

Citizens of the USA, Canada, EU countries, Norway, Switzerland, Australia, New Zealand, Israel and Japan are among those who do not need visas for tourist visits to Guatemala. On entry into Guatemala you will normally be given a 90-day stay (the number 90 will be written in the stamp in your passport). This can normally be extended for a further 90 days at the **Departamento de Extranjería** (Foreigners' Office; ☎ 2411 2411; 6a Av 3-11, Zona 4, Guatemala City; ⏱ 8am-

2:30pm Mon-Fri), on the second floor of the Inguat headquarters. For an extension take with you *one* of the following:

- a credit card with a photocopy of both of its sides
- an air ticket out of Guatemala with a photocopy
- US$500 worth of traveler's checks

The extension will normally be issued in the afternoon of the working day after the day you apply.

Citizens of Iceland, South Africa and eastern European countries are among those who do need visas to visit Guatemala. Inquire at a Guatemalan embassy well in advance of travel.

Visa regulations are subject to change and it's always worth checking them with a Guatemalan embassy before you go.

In 2006 Guatemala joined the CA-4, a Central American trade agreement, designed to facilitate the movement of people and goods between Guatemala, El Salvador, Nicaragua and Honduras. The bad news for travelers is that on entering the CA-4 region, you now get 90 days for the entire region, meaning that after the original 90 days and one extension, you have to leave (officially for 72 hours). From Guatemala the logical exits are Mexico and Belize. For more information on the CA-4, see p733.

VOLUNTEERING
If you really want to get to the heart of Guatemalan matters and you've altruistic leanings, consider volunteer work. Volunteering is rewarding and exposes foreigners to the rich and varied local culture typically out of reach for the average traveler. Opportunities abound, from caring for abandoned animals and kids to tending fields. Travelers with specific skills such as nurses, doctors or teachers are particularly encouraged to investigate volunteering in Guatemala.

Most volunteer posts require basic or better Spanish skills and a minimum time commitment. Depending on the position and the organization, you might have to pay for room and board for the duration of your stay. Before making a commitment, you might want to talk to past volunteers and read the fine print associated with the position.

Some excellent sources of information on volunteer opportunities are Proyecto Mosaico Guatemala and AmeriSpan Guatemala, both in Antigua (see p109), and EntreMundos, based in Quetzaltenango (see p141). Many language schools have close links to volunteer projects and can introduce you to the world of volunteering.

WOMEN TRAVELERS
Women should encounter no special problems traveling in Guatemala. In fact, solo women will be pleasantly surprised by how gracious and helpful most locals are. The primary thing you can do to make it easy for yourself while traveling here is to dress modestly. Modesty in dress is highly regarded, and if you practice it you will usually be treated with respect.

Specifically, shorts should be worn only at the beach, not in town, and especially not in

---

VOLUNTEERING: OUR TOP PICKS

There are a wealth of volunteering opportunities available in Guatemala. A lot of them center on education and environmental issues. Here are a few off-beat ones that may appeal to many travelers:

AIDG (www.aidg.org) Works with Guatemalan engineers to provide renewable energy solutions for rural villages, and offers volunteer installation projects.

Ak' Tenamit (www.aktenamit.org) Grass-roots organization working to promote ecotourism around the Río Dulce area.

Arcas (www.arcasguatemala.com) Works to protect the endangered sea turtle population on the southern coast. Also has projects in El Petén.

EntreMundos (www.entremundos.org) Produces a bimonthly newspaper and acts as a bridge between volunteers and NGOs.

Ix Canaan (www.ixcanaan.org) A community library and literacy project in El Remate in El Petén.

Proyecto Payaso (www.proyectopayaso.org) A traveling clown troupe specializing in community AIDS awareness and education.

the highlands. Skirts should be at or below the knee. Wear a bra, as going braless is considered provocative. Many local women swim with T-shirts over their swimsuits; in places where they do this, you might want to follow suit to avoid stares (and sunburn).

Women traveling alone can expect plenty of attempts by men to talk to them. Often they are just curious and not out for a foreign conquest. It's up to you how to respond, but there's no need to be intimidated. Consider the situation and circumstances (on a bus is one thing, on a barstool another) and stay confident. Try to sit next to women or children on the bus if that makes you more comfortable. Local women rarely initiate conversations, but usually have lots of interesting things to say once the ball is rolling.

Nasty rumors about Western women kidnapping Guatemalan children for a variety of sordid ends have all but died down. Still, women travelers should be cautious around children, especially indigenous kids.

Although there's no need to be paranoid, the possibility of rape and assault does exist. Use your normal traveler's caution – avoid walking alone in isolated places or through city streets late at night, and don't hitchhike.

WORKING
Some travelers find work in bars, restaurants and places to stay in Antigua, Panajachel or Quetzaltenango, but the wages are just survival pay. Río Dulce is the place to go if you're looking to crew on a boat around the Caribbean or north to the States.

If you are considering working here, bear in mind that the job you take could probably go to a Guatemalan, and the argument that 'they come to my country and take our jobs' is a particularly relevant one.

Belize

HIGHLIGHTS
- **Northern cayes** The second-biggest reef in the world has plenty of places to strap on your flippers (p230)
- **Lamanai** Spot crocs, birds and turtles on the boat ride to impressive Maya ruins (p238)
- **Hopkins** It may be a one-street beach town with very little to do, but that's why we love it (p252)
- **Best journey** Fishing, snorkeling and camping your way south on an island-hopping sailing tour from Caye Caulker to Placencia (p232)
- **Off the beaten track** The Barton Creek Outpost is a little slice of Eden that won't stay undiscovered for too long (p248)

FAST FACTS
- **Area** 22,966 sq km (slightly larger than Wales or the US state of Massachusetts)
- **ATMs** Foreign cards accepted at Belize Bank ATMs in major towns and cities
- **Budget** US$40-60 per day
- **Capital** Belmopan
- **Costs** Budget hotel in Belize City US$20, bottle of beer US$2, 3hr bus ride US$5, set lunch US$5
- **Country Code** ☎ 501
- **Electricity** 110V AC, 60 Hz (same as the USA)
- **Famous for** Reef diving, that Madonna song (*La Isla Bonita*)
- **Head of State** Prime Minister Said Wilbert Musa
- **Languages** English, Spanish, Creole, Garífuna
- **Money** US$1 = BZ$2 (Belize dollars); US dollars accepted everywhere
- **Phrases** *Arright?* (an all-purpose hello/how's it going type greeting), *ackin' up* (misbehaving), *fer real* (seriously)
- **Population** 312,200
- **Time** GMT minus 6 hours
- **Traveler's Checks** Cashed at major banks, some restaurants and hotels, and some exchange houses
- **Visas** Not required for citizens of North America, Australia, New Zealand and most EU countries

TRAVEL HINTS
Keep a Belizean dollar in a separate pocket – somebody might ask you for it. And stop walking so fast.

OVERLAND ROUTES
The Mexican border town of Chetumal has good connections into Belize. The other popular entry point is Benque Viejo del Carmen on the Guatemalan border on the road from Tikal.

BELIZE

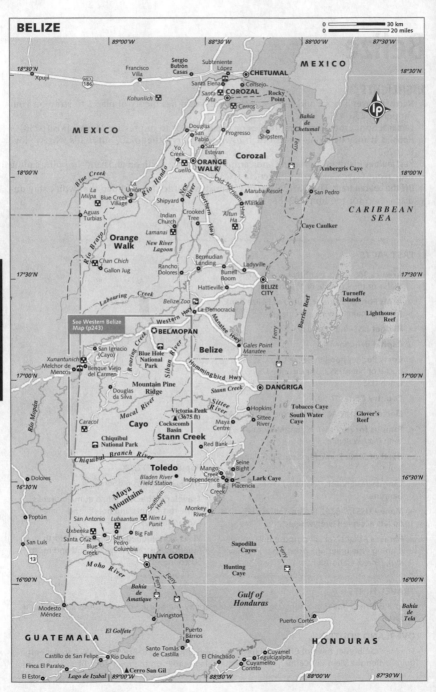

BELIZE

0   30 km
0   20 miles

MEXICO

Xpujil
Francisco Villa
Sergio Butrón Casas
Subteniente López
CHETUMAL
Santa Elena
Consejo
Kohunlich
Santa Rita
COROZAL
Rocky Point
Cerros
Bahía de Chetumal

MEXICO

Douglas
San Pablo
Progresso
Shipstern
Yo Creek
San Estevan
Corozal
Ambergris Caye
Blue Creek
La Unión
La Milpa
Blue Creek Village
ORANGE WALK
Cuello
Old Northern Hwy
Aguas Turbias
Shipyard
Indian Church
Crooked Tree
Maruba Resort
Maskall
San Pedro
C A R I B B E A N
S E A
Lamanai
Altun Ha
Caye Caulker

Orange Walk
Rio Bravo
New River Lagoon
Chan Chich
Rancho Dolores
Bermudian Landing
Ladyville
Gallon Jug
Burrell Boom
Hattieville
BELIZE CITY
Turneffe Islands

Labouring Creek
Belize Zoo
La Democracia
Lighthouse Reef

See Western Belize Map (p243)
Western Hwy
BELMOPAN
Belize
Gales Point Manatee
Barrier Reef

Xunantunich
San Ignacio (Cayo)
Blue Hole National Park
Benque Viejo del Carmen
Melchor de Mencos
Mountain Pine Ridge
Douglas da Silva
DANGRIGA

Caracol
Cayo
Victoria Peak (3675 ft)
Cockscomb Basin
Stann Creek
Hopkins
Sittee River
Maya Centre
Tobacco Caye
South Water Caye
Glover's Reef

Chiquibul National Park
Branch River
Red Bank
Mango Creek
Seine Bight

Toledo
Bladen River Field Station
Independence
Big Creek
Placencia
Lark Caye

Dolores
Maya Mountains
Monkey River
Poptún
San Antonio
Lubaantun
Nim Li Punit
Southern Hwy
Sapodilla Cayes
San Luís
Uxbenka
Santa Cruz
Blue Creek
San Pedro Columbia
Big Fall
Hunting Caye

PUNTA GORDA
Moho River
Bahía de Amatique

Modesto Méndez
Livingston
GUATEMALA
El Golfete
Puerto Barrios
Puerto Cortés
HONDURAS
Bahía de Tela

Castillo de San Felipe
Río Dulce
Santo Tomás de Castilla
El Chinchado
Cuyamel
Tegucigalpita
Finca El Paraíso
Cerro San Gil
El Estor
Lago de Izabal
Cuyamelito
Corinto

Gulf of Honduras

Belize bumps and grinds to a whole different groove from the rest of Central America. Creole culture is dominant here and everybody knows the words to even the most obscure Bob Marley songs. Ever wanted to hear a policeman tell you that every little thing was going to be all right? Come to Belize.

Then there are the Garífuna. Master percussionists, proud 'cause they were never slaves, still eating and speaking how they did when they got here 200 years ago.

And there's the Maya, mestizos and Latinos. Some have 'always' been here, some came more recently, fleeing nasty situations in their homelands. Nearly everybody speaks English, but Spanish speakers outnumber the rest. In some of the Maya villages down south, there are people who only speak Mopan or Kekchí.

Throw in some caves to tube, the second-biggest reef in the world to dive, white sands and turquoise waters out on the cayes, some good eatin', a barefoot, beer-drinking, hammock-swinging lifestyle and much, much more trouble to get in, and you can see why you're coming to Belize.

CURRENT EVENTS

The privatization debate in Belize continues (the main topic of debate being what can we sell off now?). In one of the worst examples, when the water company was sold off, the legislation gave the new owners the right to *all* the water in Belize – including rainwater and rivers, meaning that people could theoretically be charged for rainwater collected in private tanks and water pumped from rivers. We're waiting on a test case to go through the courts.

Belize is a major transshipment point for the northbound drug trade, and gang violence is on the rise. A contributing factor is a recent US law which sees foreign-born nationals convicted of gang-related crimes deported to their country of origin. They come back, hook up with other members of the old gang and it's business as usual.

The government's much-lauded re-issue of bonds to finance the external debt will indeed free the country from burdensome interest payments until about 2012. Once they have to start repaying the new debt, though, interest repayments will be even higher. So the books aren't going to be balanced anytime soon.

The Chalillo Dam on the Macal River, a hydroelectric project that flooded wildlife habitat and Maya sites, sold to the populace as an easy way for cheaper electricity has turned out to be a massive disappointment at the very best. Electricity prices have actually gone up since the dam went into operation!

Possibly the biggest strain on the country's infrastructure comes from tour boat visitors. To give you an idea of the way things are heading, 14,183 people arrived by cruise ship in 1998. By 2005 that number had grown to 800,331. Compare this with the 236,573 people who arrived by other means in the same year and you will see that it's big business and big crowds that the country's main attractions have to deal with.

HISTORY

Belize certainly earns its place on the Ruta Maya – ruins are everywhere and the Maya population is still thriving, particularly in the southwest.

Pre-Columbian Belize

The Maya have been in Belize since the first human habitation. One of the earliest settlements in the Maya world, Cuello, was near present day Orange Walk. Maya trade routes ran all through the country, and the New River, Rio Hondo and Belize River all played an important role in early trade and commerce. The earliest known site in the Belize River Valley is Cahal Pech, near San Ignacio. It was settled between 1500 and 1000 BC. Lamanai (p238) surged in importance around 200 to 100 BC.

During the end of the pre-Classic period (from around AD 250 to 550), Belizean settlements waned in importance as political power shifted to Guatemalan cities such as Tikal. All this changed in AD 562 when Caracol in western Belize conquered Tikal. By 650 Caracol was at its peak, with a population of 150,000, over twice the size of modern-day Belize City. The city retained its regional importance even after defeat by Naranjo (from Guatemala) in 680.

The decline of the Maya around 750 has always been somewhat mysterious, but most theories center around droughts. Increased sacrificial activity (remains of which are to be seen in the Cayo District's caves) around this time bears witness to these theories, as sacrifices were probably made to appease the rain god, Chac. For more on Maya history, see p31.

Pirate's Paradise

In the opinion of its 16th-century Spanish conquerors, Belize was a backwater, good only for its harvestable logwood, which was used to make dye. Far from being profitable, Belize was dangerous, because the barrier reef tended to tear the keels from ships attempting to approach the shore.

The lack of effective government and the onshore safety afforded by the barrier reef attracted English and Scottish pirates to Belizean waters during the 17th century. They operated freely, capturing booty-laden Spanish galleons. In 1670, however, Spain convinced the British government to clamp down on the pirates' activities. Most of the unemployed pirates went into the logwood business.

During the 1780s the British actively protected the loggers' interests, at the same time assuring Spain that Belize was indeed a Spanish possession. But this was a fiction. By this time, Belize was already British by tradition and sympathy, and it was with relief and jubilation that Belizeans received the news, on September 10, 1798, that a British force had defeated the Spanish armada off St George's Caye.

Into the 19th Century

Being British did not bring prosperity. Belize was still essentially one big logging camp. When the invention of synthetic dyes killed the logwood trade, the colony's economy crashed. It was revived by the trade in mahogany during the early 19th century, but this too collapsed when African sources of the wood brought fierce price competition.

Belize's next trade boom was in arms, ammunition and other supplies sold to the Maya rebels in the Yucatán who fought the War of the Castes during the mid-19th century. The war also brought a flood of refugees from both sides to Belize. The Maya brought farming skills that were of great value in expanding the horizons and economic viability of Belizean society.

Guatemala has never really accepted the idea of Belize – they've been claiming the land ever since the Spanish left. In 1859 Britain and Guatemala signed a treaty that gave Britain

rights to the land provided that the British built a road from Guatemala to the Caribbean coast. The treaty still stands, but the road has never been built, and many Guatemalan-made maps show Guatemala extending all the way through Belize to the coast.

20th Century & Modern Times

The Belizean economy worsened after the WWII, leading to agitation for independence from the UK. The country's first general election was held in 1954, and the People's United Party (PUP) won handsomely on leader George Price's pro-independence platform. On September 21, 1981, the colony of British Honduras officially became the independent nation of Belize.

Many educated (and especially older) Belizeans will tell you that the widespread corruption and nepotism in Belize today are a result of the country becoming independent too early, before democratic institutions had a chance to take hold. It's an argument that's likely to ruffle a few feathers if you decide to take it for a spin.

Since independence, the political landscape has been one of one-term governments (the United Democratic Party, or UDP, being the other player there), corruption scandals, power struggles and broken electoral promises. In 2003 PUP won an unprecedented second term, but stability was not at hand. In 2005 citizens threw off their normally easygoing demeanor and rioted in the streets of Belmopan over inflation, taxes and a wage freeze for public servants.

THE CULTURE
The National Psyche

Rule number one in Belize: give respect and you'll get respect. Belizeans are friendly and curious by nature, but often wait to see what you're like before deciding how they're going to be. Treat them well, they're bound to do the same for you. Walk around with a scowl and you aren't going to be making any friends.

Belize's long association with the UK has left some odd legacies. Perhaps because of this (and the language thing), the country is more closely aligned with the USA than with other Central American countries. US consumer imports are hugely popular (accounting for nearly half of the country's total imports) and much of the popular culture is imported directly from the States. You'll

SQUEEZE YOUR BELIZE

Everyone's always bitching about how expensive Belize is. Here's the bad news: it's true. Things cost more here, especially some essentials such as accommodation and beer. Here's the good news: it's not as bad as people make out, and there are some pain-free ways not to bust your budget. A few of our faves:

Do the legwork Most towns are small – pack light and you'll never need a taxi.

Cool it with the air-con Take a shower, then crank the fan – you'll be freeeezing.

Camp it up There are good, cheap camping spots in San Ignacio, Caye Caulker, Bullet Tree Falls, Barton Creek, Monkey Bay, Hopkins, Glover's Reef, Altun Ha and Crooked Tree.

Buddy up Single room rates (if they exist) can be 90% of the price of a double. Get a triple with others and you're laughing.

Chicken, beans and rice Even some expensive restaurants keep it real by having this classic on the menu, often at a fraction of the price of other items. Learn to love this dish.

Get it to go Take-away food and groceries are available everywhere, as are good picnic spots.

Thirsty? Juices are expensive, and often disappointing. Green coconuts, on the other hand, are delicious, cheap and refreshing. Invest in a machete and serve yourself.

Buy in bulk They say you can drink the tap water. If you are buying purified, buy gallons (or more) depending on how long you're staying in town.

Get the party started right Hardly anybody goes out 'til 11 or midnight, and every corner store sells beer. You do the math.

Get picked up If you're going off the track, call the hotel you're planning to stay at – maybe they can arrange cheap/free transport.

Thumb it We haven't heard a Belizean hitching horror story in years. Use your common sense, particularly if you're female.

see a lot more Tupac T-shirts than you will Bellanova ones.

Widespread corruption in the middle and upper levels of government has left most Belizeans with a healthy cynicism when it comes to politicians. The woeful state of the economy and huge gap between rich and poor doesn't make them think much better of the private sector.

Lifestyle

With compulsory education and a relatively stable democracy, you would expect Belize to be doing alright by its citizens. Unfortunately, this isn't the case. The country has never been rich, and a reliance on agriculture, fishing and, lately, the tourism industry hasn't done much to change that. As a result, many Belizeans live in very basic circumstances. New houses are often made from cinder-block boxes; old ones from warped and rotting wood that has seen much better days. It is estimated that one-third of the population live below the poverty line. This should be grim, but it ain't that bad. Above all, the folk here know how to have a good time – check out any karaoke bar on a Friday night and you'll see enough Belikin beer consumption and smiling faces

to know that, for some at least, things either aren't as bad as they look on paper or the people get on with life regardless.

People

For such a tiny country, Belize enjoys a fabulous, improbable ethnic diversity. Creoles – descendants of the African slaves and British pirates who first settled here to exploit the country's forest riches – make up the country's largest ethnic group. Racially mixed and proud of it, Creoles speak a fascinating, unique dialect of English that, though it sounds familiar at first, is not easily intelligible to a speaker of standard English.

One-third of Belize's people are mestizos (persons of mixed European and Central American indigenous ancestry), some of whose ancestors immigrated from the Yucatán during the 19th century.

The Maya people of Belize make up about 10% of the population and are divided into three linguistic groups. The Yucatec live in the north near the Yucatán border, the Mopan live in western Belize around the border town of Benque Viejo del Carmen, and the Kekchí inhabit far southern Belize in and around Punta Gorda. In recent years,

BELIZE

political refugees coming in from Guatemala and El Salvador have added to Belize's Maya population.

Southern Belize is the home of the Garífuna (or Garinagus, also called Black Caribs), who account for less than 10% of the population. The Garífuna are of South American indigenous and African descent. They look more African, but they speak a language that's much more indigenous and their unique culture combines aspects of both peoples.

Other ethnic groups in Belize include small populations of Europeans, North Americans, Chinese and people from east India.

ARTS
Cinema
Belize has been the location for many film shoots over the years, most notably *Mosquito Coast* (1986) starring Harrison Ford and River Phoenix, based on the novel by Paul Theroux; *Heart of Darkness* (1984) starring John Malkovich, from the novel by Joseph Conrad; and *Dogs of War* (1980) with Christopher Walken.

Music
Music is by far the most popular art form in Belize, from the ubiquitous karaoke bars to the reggae-soaked cayes and the ribcage-rattling tunes pumped out on every bus in the country. Styles are much more Caribbean than Latin – after a few weeks you'll be an expert on calypso, soca, steel drums and, quite possibly, reggae.

Punta rock is the official musical style of Belize. Its origins are from the music of the Garífuna – drum heavy with plenty of call and response. This music is designed to get your hips moving. Probably the most famous *punta* rockers are Pen Cayetano (who has collaborated with various artists) and the Punta Rebels.

The blending of Garífuna rhythms with reggae dancehall and soca has produced a new generation of *punta* rockers who often rely on electronic accompaniment as opposed to live musicians. If you want to catch one of these lively shows, keep an eye out for Super G and the Griga Boyz.

The Parranda style, which owes its roots to more traditional Garífuna arrangements with acoustic guitar, drums and shakers is most widely associated with artists such as Andy Palacio and Paul Nabor.

Brukdown, another Belizean style, was developed by Creoles working in logging camps during the 18th and 19th centuries. It involves an accordion, banjo, harmonica and a percussion instrument – traditionally a pig's jawbone is used, the teeth rattled with a stick. Wilfred Peters' Boom and Chime band is perhaps the best-known of the brukdown artists.

The Maya of Belize are off on their own tangent when it comes to music. Most notable here is the flute music of Pablo Collado and the traditional marimba (played with large wooden xylophones, double bass and drum kit) of Alma Beliceña.

SPORT
Like any Central American country worth its stripes, Belize is a soccer-playing nation, but you'll find that the sport of choice for many kids is basketball. If you're up for it, you can easily jump in on a game – it's a great way to meet locals and keep warm on those chilly Caribbean afternoons.

Like all good Commonwealthers, Belizeans enjoy a spot of cricket. The best place to catch a match is at the MCC grounds in Belize City.

RELIGION
Belize's mixture of religions follows its ethnic composition. Roman Catholics and Protestants (mainly Anglicans and Methodists, but also Mennonites, Seventh Day Adventists and Jehovah's Witnesses) prevail, but Belize's tradition of tolerance has welcomed Buddhists, Hindus and Muslims. Maya communities continue to practice traditional Maya rites, usually blended with Catholicism.

ENVIRONMENT
The Land
Belize is mostly tropical lowland, typically hot and humid for most of the year. Rainfall is lightest in the north, heaviest in the south. The southern rain forests receive almost 4m of precipitation annually, making the south the country's most humid region.

An exception to Belize's low-lying topography and hot, sticky climate can be found in the Maya Mountains, which traverse western and southern Belize at elevations approaching 1000m. The mountains enjoy a more pleasant climate than the lowlands – comfortably warm during the day, cooling off a bit at night.

ctatedllze ful.

Victoria Peak, in Cockscomb Basin Wildlife Sanctuary, and Doyle's Delight, in Toledo near Belize's southern border, vie for highest peak status – both are around 3680ft (1104m). Doyle's Delight is said to be about 13ft (3.9m) taller, but Victoria Peak is more visible and the popular favorite for tallest mountain status.

The country's coastline and northern coastal plain are largely covered in mangrove swamp, which indistinctly defines the line between land and sea. Offshore, the limestone bedrock extends eastward into the Caribbean for several kilometers at a depth of about 16.5ft (5m). At the eastern extent of this shelf is the second-longest barrier reef in the world (behind Australia's Great Barrier Reef).

Wildlife

The lush tropical forests contain huge ceiba trees as well as mahogany, guanacaste and cohune palms, all festooned with orchids, bromeliads and other epiphytes and liana vines. Much of the shorelines of both the mainland and the islands are cloaked in dense mangrove.

Baird's tapir is Belize's national animal. The *gibnut* or paca *(tepezcuintle),* a rabbit-size burrowing rodent, is abundant. Other tropical animals include the jaguar, ocelot, howler monkey, spider monkey, peccary, vulture, stork and anteater.

There are 60 species of snake in the forests and waters of Belize, but only a handful are dangerous: the boa constrictor, the fer-de-lance, the coral snake and the tropical rattlesnake.

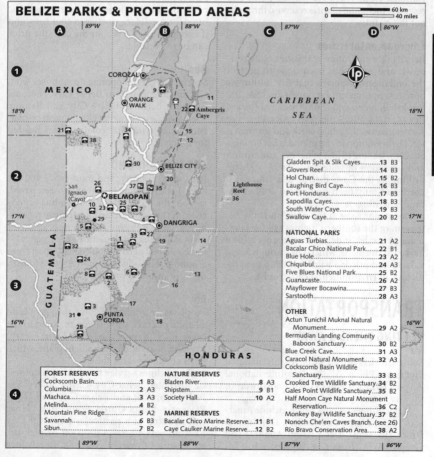

Two types of crocodile call Belize home – the American crocodile, which lives in fresh- and saltwater, and Morelet's croc, which only lives in freshwater and doesn't eat people.

Belize's birdlife is varied and abundant, with hummingbirds, keel-billed toucans, woodpeckers and many kinds of parrots and macaws.

In the seas there are turtles, lobsters, manatees and a great variety of fish.

National Parks & Protected Areas

Nearly 40% of land in Belize is protected, either by national organizations or private trusts. Much of the Maya Mountain forest south of San Ignacio is protected as the Mountain Pine Ridge Forest Reserve and Chiquibul National Park. There are smaller parks and reserves, including marine reserves, throughout the country.

Environmental Issues

Belize takes environmental issues quite seriously, and much has been done to protect the endangered species that live within its borders. Species under threat include the hawksbill, green and leatherback sea turtles, the Morlet's and American crocodiles, the scarlet macaw, the jabiru stork and the manatee. Deforestation for farmland is becoming a concern, leading to loss of habitat, soil erosion and salination of waterways. Small scale oil drilling in the Cayo district is a concern – there had only been one minor spill at the time of writing.

One major issue at the moment is the extension of the southern highway to the Guatemalan border. Independent engineers have looked at the plans, which cut through Maya villages and pristine wilderness and are predicting an environmental catastrophe.

TRANSPORTATION

GETTING THERE & AWAY
Air

Belize City has two airports. All international flights use Philip SW Goldson International Airport (BZE), 9 miles (16km) northwest of the city center.

Major airlines serving Belize include American (from Miami and Dallas), Continental (from Houston), Delta (from Atlanta) and Grupo TACA (from Los Angeles). Most in-

ternational air routes to Belize City go via these gateways.

Grupo TACA also offers direct flights between Belize City and Guatemala City (Guatemala), San Salvador (El Salvador), and San Pedro Sula (Honduras), as well as connecting flights from Nicaragua, Costa Rica and Panama.

Boat

The *Gulf Cruza* runs between Puerto Cortés and Placencia, with stops in Big Creek (see p255), every Friday, returning on Monday morning.

Scheduled boats and occasional small passenger boats ply the waters between Punta Gorda in southern Belize and Lívingston and Puerto Barrios in eastern Guatemala. Refer to p257 for details. These boats can usually be hired for special trips between countries, and if enough passengers split the cost, the price can be reasonable.

Bus

Several companies operate direct buses from Chetumal (Mexico) to Belize City. National Bus runs between Belize City and Benque Viejo del Carmen on the Guatemalan border, connecting with Guatemalan buses headed for Flores.

GETTING AROUND

It's a small country, and most roads you are likely to be traveling on have now been paved, so even the most hellish chicken-bus experience isn't likely to last too long (patience, grasshopper). Bus is the mode of transportation for most Belizeans, so departures are frequent – there's no real need to book ahead, apart from around public holidays, but it *is* wise to turn up early and snag yourself a seat.

Air

People *do* fly within Belize, but then people do all sorts of crazy stuff. If you're going to the cayes, it's a lot more fun (and a lot less scary) to grab a boat rather than a light plane, which takes about the same time.

Two airlines service two principal domestic air routes: Belize City–Caye Caulker–San Pedro–Corozal; and Belize City–Dangriga–Placencia–Punta Gorda. Sometimes planes will not stop at a particular airport if they have no passengers to drop off or pick up, so be sure to reserve your seat in advance

DEPARTURE TAX

Departure taxes and airport fees of US$30 are levied on non-Belizean travelers departing Goldson International Airport in Belize City for foreign destinations. There is no departure tax if you are leaving by boat. The exit tax at Belizean land border crossing points is US$15.

Regardless of how you leave the country, you'll be required to pay an additional US$3.75, which is the PACT (Protected Areas Conservation Tax). Funds from this tax help to maintain Belize's impressive tracts of protected natural areas. For more information, see www.pactbelize.org.

whenever possible. Tickets for both airlines can be booked through most of the hotels and tour agencies within the country. See p229 for details.

Boat

Fast motor launches zoom between Belize City, Caye Caulker and Ambergris Caye frequently every day. Even faster boats run between Corozal and Ambergris Caye, and a handy ferry service runs between Placencia and Mango Creek.

Be sure to bring sunscreen, a hat and clothing to protect you from the sun and the spray. If you sit in the bow, there's less spray, but you bang down harder when the boat goes over a wave. Sitting in the stern will give you a smoother ride, but you may get soaked.

Bus

Most Belizean buses are used US school buses, although a few 1st-class (don't get excited) services are available. The larger companies operate frequent buses along the country's three major roads. Smaller village lines tend to be run along local work and school schedules: buses run from a smaller town to a larger town in the morning, and then they return in the afternoon. Fares average about US$1.50/2.50 per hour's ride on a local/express bus.

Each major bus company has its own terminal. Outside Belize City, bus drivers will pick up and drop off passengers at undesignated stops – either tell the driver's helper where you want to get off or flag them down on the roadside to get on.

Pilferage of luggage has been a problem, particularly on the Punta Gorda route. Give your luggage only to the bus driver or conductor, and watch as it is stored. Be there when the bus is unloaded and retrieve your luggage at once.

Car & Motorcycle

If you plan to drive in Belize, you'll need to bring a valid driver's license from your home country. Hiring cars can be expensive, and you must be 25 years or older and pay with credit card. Depending on the season, rental rates can hit US$80 per day, and hammering out a deal with a taxi driver can get you a much better deal.

Taxi

Except for in Belize City, you're never really going to need a taxi (unless you are incredibly drunk, or lazy, or both). The towns just aren't that big. In Belize City, the fixed fare is US$3 in the daytime, within the city. At night, the price gets a bit more flexible (in an upwards direction). Offer what you think is fair, based on the day rates, and don't get too het up over a dollar's difference.

BELIZE CITY

pop 66,100

While it's no longer the capital, Belize City retains its importance. It's got the shops the schools and the population and there's a buzz on the streets unlike anywhere else in the country.

Sitting right on the coast and straddling the Haulover Creek, the city should be a picturesque place. It has its moments, but many of the old wooden houses have fallen victim to hurricanes or fire and the modern construction is of the fairly bland concrete-block style.

Still. There's no better place to see Belize in action. The bars and discos pack out almost nightly, Albert St comes alive during the day and the northern neighborhoods around Fort George and Newton Barracks boast kilometers of seaside parks, which fill up in the afternoons with locals catching a breeze.

ORIENTATION

Haulover Creek, a branch of the Belize River, runs through the middle of the city, separating the commercial center (bounded

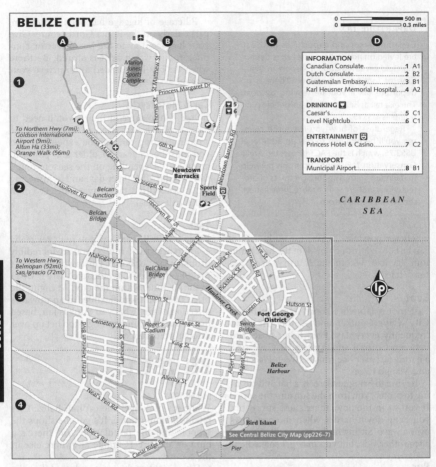

BELIZE CITY

0 ⊢——————⊣ 500 m
0 ⊢——————⊣ 0.3 miles

INFORMATION	
Canadian Consulate.......................1 A1	
Dutch Consulate.........................2 B2	
Guatemalan Embassy....................3 B1	
Karl Heusner Memorial Hospital....4 A2	

DRINKING 🍸	
Caesar's.................................5 C1	
Level Nightclub........................6 C1	

ENTERTAINMENT 🎭	
Princess Hotel & Casino...............7 C2	

TRANSPORT	
Municipal Airport.......................8 B1	

CARIBBEAN SEA

To Northern Hwy (7mi);
Goldson International
Airport (9mi);
Altun Ha (33mi);
Orange Walk (56mi)

To Western Hwy;
Belmopan (52mi);
San Ignacio (72mi)

See Central Belize City Map (pp226–7)

by Albert, Regent, King and Orange Sts) from the slightly more genteel residential and hotel district of Fort George to the northeast.

Just south of the Swing Bridge and Haulover Creek is the old part of town, which can be slightly seedy, especially at night, and Belizeans (especially those from the northern suburbs) use the term 'southside' to refer to all things ghetto.

The Swing Bridge joins Albert St with Queen St, which runs through the Fort George district and its pleasant King's Park neighborhood. The bridge, a product of Liverpool's ironworks, was built in 1923 and is the only known working bridge of its type in the world. Its operators manually rotate

the bridge open at 5:30am and 5:30pm daily, just long enough to let tall boats pass and to bring most of the traffic in the city center to a halt.

At the bridge's northern end is the Belize Marine Terminal (Map pp226–7), which is used by motor launches traveling to Caye Caulker and Ambergris Caye.

INFORMATION
Bookstores
Image Factory Art foundation (Map pp226-7; 91 N Front St; www.imagefactory.bz) The best selection of books by Belizean writers, plus many art-oriented titles.
Thrift & Book Town (Map pp226-7; 4 Church St, upstairs) An incredible jumble of new and used books on most subjects.

Emergency

Ambulance ☎ 90
Fire Department ☎ 90
General Emergency/Police ☎ 911
Tourist Police ☎ 227 6082

Internet Access

KGs Cyber Café (Map pp226-7; 60 King St; per hr US$3; ⏰ 9am-6pm) Unreliable connections, but not bad for the price.
Turton Library (Map pp226-7; 156 N Front St; per hr US$2; ⏰ 9am-5pm Mon-Fri, 9am-noon Sat; 😵) Cheapest access in town, fast connections and air-con.

Laundry

G's Laundry (Map pp226-7; 22 Dean St) Charges US$5 per load. Most hotels can arrange laundry service for you at similar prices.

Medical Services

Karl Heusner Memorial Hospital (Map p224; ☎ 223 1548; Princess Margaret Dr) In the northern part of town.

Money

Banks are mostly on Albert St, just south of the Swing Bridge. The following have ATMs that accept foreign cards.
First Caribbean International Bank (Map pp226-7; 21 Albert St; ⏰ 8:30am-2:30pm Mon-Thu, 8am-4:30pm Fri)
Belize Bank (Map pp226-7; 60 Market Sq; ⏰ 8:30am-4pm Mon-Fri)

Post

Post office (Map pp226-7; N Front St; ⏰ 8am-noon & 1-5pm Mon-Sat) Facing the Marine Terminal building.

Telephone

BTL (Map pp226-7; cnr Albert & Church Sts; ⏰ Mon-Sat; 😵) Sells phonecards and has private cabins with air-con where you can make local and international calls.

Tourist Information

Belize Tourism Board (BTB; ☎ 223 1910; www .belizetourism.org; ⏰ 8am-noon & 1-5pm Mon-Fri); Tourist Village (☎ 223 5623); international airport (☎ 225 3412) At the time of writing, the main office was way out on the Northern Hwy, but a new central office should be running at the corner of Regent and South Sts by the time you get here. Ask for a copy of *Destination Belize* (free) for a run-down on many tourist services in the country.
Belize Audubon Society (Map pp226-7; ☎ 223 5004; www.belizeaudubon.org; 12 Fort St) Offers information on national parks and wildlife reserves throughout the country.

DANGERS & ANNOYANCES

Yes, there is petty crime in Belize City, but it's not as bad as some doomsayers will tell you. Take the same commonsense precautions that you would in any major city. Don't flash wads of cash, expensive camera equipment or other signs of wealth. Don't leave valuables in your hotel room. Don't use or deal in illicit drugs. Don't walk alone at night, and avoid deserted streets, even in daylight.

It's always better to walk in pairs or groups and to stick to major streets in the city center, Fort George and King's Park. Especially avoid walking along Front St south and east of the Swing Bridge; this is a favorite area for muggers.

Report any incidents or hassles to the BTB or the Tourist Police so staff will be aware of trouble spots and patterns.

SIGHTS & ACTIVITIES

In just a few hours it's possible to take in many of the city's major sights and sounds by foot, which are all in central Belize City (Map pp226-7).

BELIZE

GETTING INTO TOWN

From the Airport
The taxi fare to or from the international airport is US$20. It's a half hour (3km) walk from the air terminal out along the access road to the Northern Hwy, where it's easy to catch a bus going either north or south.

From the Bus Station
The National bus station (Map p224) is on the west bank of the Collet canal, about five-minutes' walk from the Swing Bridge. As you exit the terminal, turn left, then take the first right along Orange St. This is a dodgy area – if you arrive at night, it's worth paying the US$3 for a taxi to your hotel.

CENTRAL BELIZE CITY

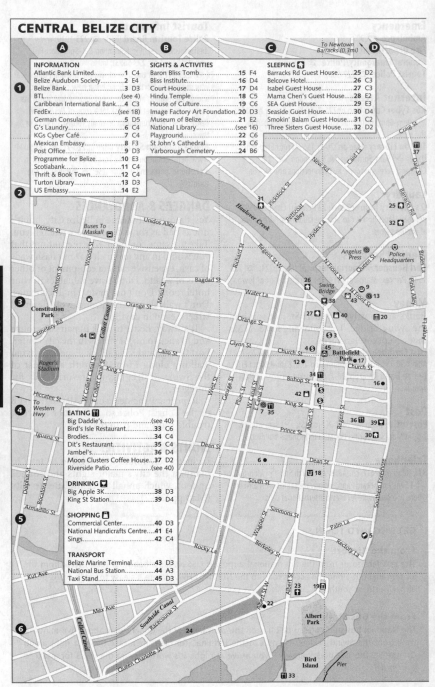

INFORMATION
Atlantic Bank Limited..............1 C4
Belize Audubon Society...........2 E4
Belize Bank...........................3 D3
BTL......................................(see 4)
Caribbean International Bank....4 C3
FedEx.................................(see 18)
German Consulate...................5 D5
G's Laundry...........................6 C4
KGs Cyber Café.....................7 C4
Mexican Embassy....................8 F3
Post Office.............................9 D3
Programme for Belize.............10 E3
Scotiabank...........................11 C4
Thrift & Book Town................12 C4
Turton Library.......................13 D3
US Embassy..........................14 E2

SIGHTS & ACTIVITIES
Baron Bliss Tomb...................15 F4
Bliss Institute.........................16 D4
Court House..........................17 D4
Hindu Temple.........................18 C5
House of Culture.....................19 C6
Image Factory Art Foundation..20 D3
Museum of Belize...................21 E2
National Library...................(see 16)
Playground...........................22 C6
St John's Cathedral................23 C6
Yarborough Cemetery............24 B6

SLEEPING
Barracks Rd Guest House........25 D2
Belcove Hotel.......................26 C3
Isabel Guest House................27 C3
Mama Chen's Guest House.....28 E2
SEA Guest House...................29 E3
Seaside Guest House..............30 D4
Smokin' Balam Guest House....31 C2
Three Sisters Guest House......32 D2

EATING
Big Daddie's........................(see 40)
Bird's Isle Restaurant.............33 C6
Brodies...............................34 C4
Dit's Restaurant....................35 C4
Jambel's..............................36 D4
Moon Clusters Coffee House...37 D2
Riverside Patio....................(see 40)

DRINKING
Big Apple 3K........................38 D3
King St Station......................39 D4

SHOPPING
Commercial Center................40 D3
National Handicrafts Centre....41 E4
Sings..................................42 C4

TRANSPORT
Belize Marine Terminal...........43 D3
National Bus Station..............44 A3
Taxi Stand...........................45 D3

BELIZE

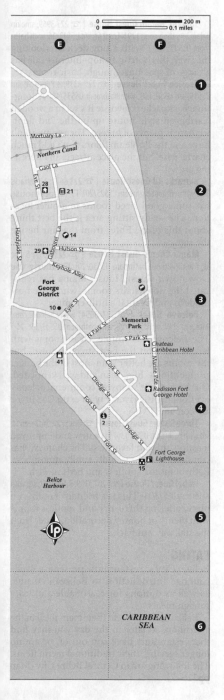

BELIZE

Central Belize City

Starting from the Swing Bridge, walk south along Regent St, one block inland from the shore. The large, modern **Commercial Center** to the left, just off the Swing Bridge, replaced a ramshackle market dating from 1820. The ground floor holds a food market; offices and shops are above.

As you continue down Regent St, you can't miss the prominent **Court House**, built in 1926 as the headquarters for Belize's colonial administrators. It still serves administrative and judicial functions.

Battlefield Park is on the right across from the Court House. Always busy with vendors, loungers, con artists and other slice-of-life segments of Belize City society, the park offers welcome shade in the midday heat.

Turn left just past the Court House and walk one block to the waterfront street, called Southern Foreshore, to find the **Bliss Institute**. Belize City's prime cultural institution, it's home to the National Institute for Culture and History, which stages periodic exhibits, concerts and theatrical works. Baron Bliss was an Englishman with a happy name and a Portuguese title who came here on his yacht to fish. When he died – without ever actually setting foot on the mainland – he left the bulk of his wealth in trust to the people of Belize. Income from the trust has paid for roads, market buildings, schools, cultural centers and many other worthwhile projects over the years.

Continue walking south to the end of Southern Foreshore, then south on Regent St to the **House of Culture** (☎ 227 3050; admission US$5; 🕑 8:30am-4:30pm Mon-Fri), built in 1814. Formerly called Government House, this was the residence of the governor-general until Belize attained independence in 1981. Today it holds the tableware once used at the residence, along with exhibits of historic photographs and occasional special exhibits. The admission price is a bit steep to look at old crockery, but you can stroll around the pleasant grounds for free.

Down beyond the House of Culture you'll come to **Albert Park**, which gets nice sea breezes and has a well-maintained playground, and **Bird Island**, a recreation area with a basketball court and an open-air restaurant that serves snacks and cool drinks.

Inland from the House of Culture, at the corner of Albert and Regent Sts, is **St John's Cathedral**, the oldest Anglican church in Central America, dating from 1847.

A block southwest of the cathedral is **Yarborough Cemetery**, whose gravestones outline the turbulent history of Belize going back to 1781.

Walk back to the Swing Bridge northward along Albert St, the city's main commercial thoroughfare. Note the unlikely little **Hindu temple** between South and Dean Sts.

Northeastern Neighborhoods

Heading straight along Queen St from the Swing Bridge, you'll soon come to the city's quaint wooden central police headquarters. At the end of Queen St, look left to see the old Belize prison, now the **Museum of Belize** (admission US$5; ✆ 9am-5pm Mon-Fri, 9am-1pm Sat). The top floor of the museum features rotating exhibitions on Maya life while the ground floor focuses on the history of different towns in Belize.

Turning right down Gabourel you'll pass the US embassy, set among some pretty Victorian houses. Continue on Gabourel La and take a left at Hutson St to get to the sea, where if you head south (a right turn) on Marine Pde you'll pass **Memorial Park**, the Chateau Caribbean Hotel and the Radisson Fort George Hotel. At the southern tip of the peninsula you'll reach the **Baron Bliss Tomb**, next to the Fort George lighthouse. A small park here offers good views of the water and the city.

Walk back to the Swing Bridge along Fort St (which eventually turns into Front St). The **Image Factory Art Foundation** (81 N Front St; ✆ 9am-noon & 2:30-6pm Mon-Fri, 9am-noon Sat), near the Marine Terminal, displays work by Belizean artists.

SLEEPING

Budget accommodations are mainly clustered around the Marine Terminal, and the area a little to the north. A 9% lodging tax will be added to the cost of your room. In addition, some hotels will tack on a service charge, often around 10%. Prices listed here (and throughout this chapter) include tax and service charge. In low season, you may be able to bargain your way out of paying either or both of these.

The following are in Central Belize City (Map pp226-7).

SEA Guest House (✆ 223 6798; 18 Gabourel La; r from US$15) One of the old backpacker standbys, the SEA keeps it real with foam mattresses in breezy upstairs rooms.

Smokin' Balam Guest House (✆ 223 3969; smokinbalam2@yahoo.com; 129 N Front St; s/d US$13/16, with bathroom US$23; 🖵) With a tiny deck overlooking the river, this hotel-giftshop–internet café has a range of spacious-enough, basic rooms.

Seaside Guest House (✆ 227 8339; 3 Prince St; dm US$15, s/d US$25/38, with bathroom US$35/48) A long-time backpackers favorite it's set in a wooden Caribbean style house up on the 2nd floor, so there is plenty of breeze. The rooms aren't huge and the linoleum floors don't add much charm-wise, but the place attracts an interesting crowd.

Barracks Rd Guest House (✆ 223 6671; 12 Barracks Rd; r with/without bathroom US$25/20) This guesthouse has some good-sized rooms in a quiet location. The shady sitting area is the best thing about this place. Enter from the lane beside the sign.

Mama Chen's Guest House (✆ 223 2057; 5 Eve St; r with/without bathroom US$30/20) Formerly the Downtown Guest House, Mama has renovated the downstairs rooms, which are now modern and fresh, if a little cramped.

Belcove Hotel (✆ 227 3054; www.belcove.com; 9 Regent St W; s/d US$21/28, with bathroom US$32/36; 🐾) The Belcove has simple, clean rooms with fan. It's not on the best street in town, but the rooms are better than most of the budget competition – big, clean and well ventilated. Out back, there's a lovely communal balcony overlooking the river. Pay an extra US$10 for air-con and TV.

Three Sisters Guest House (✆ 203 5729; 36 Queen St; s/d with bathroom US$27/30) In a new and improved location, this old favorite still has homey, spacious rooms and a friendly family atmosphere. Bathrooms are spotless and beds newish.

Isabel Guest House (✆ 207 3139; 3 Albert St; s/d with bathroom US$28/33) This is a friendly, family-run place, offering three airy and spotless rooms with plenty of homey decoration. Enter from the stairway out back.

EATING

Belize City's restaurants present a well-rounded introduction to Belizean cuisine, as well as options for reasonable and tasty foreign meals.

Belizeans usually eat their main meal in the afternoon, so later in the day you may find that restaurants have run out of, or are no longer serving, their traditional menu items. The following are in Central Belize City (Map pp226-7).

Big Daddie's (2nd fl, Commercial Center; breakfast from US$3.50, lunch US$3-5) It's good for hearty meals at low prices. Lunch is served cafeteria-style from 11am and lasts until the food is gone. Breakfasts of fry jacks (fried tortilla dough), eggs, beans and bacon are US$3.50, burgers about US$2. Head upstairs for river views.

Dit's Restaurant (50 King St; mains US$5, burgers US$2; ☺ breakfast, lunch & dinner) A homey place with a loyal local clientele, Dit's offers huge portions at low prices and serves up the stew chicken you'll be dreaming about long after you've returned home. Homemade cakes and pies make a good dessert at US$1 per slice.

Bird's Isle Restaurant (Bird's Isle; mains US$8-12; ☺ lunch & dinner Mon-Sat) Down at the south end of town, this place serves up good burgers and reasonably priced meals in a shady, open-air location.

Jambel's (2B King St; mains from US$10; ☺ lunch & dinner) Jambel's specializes in Jamaican-Belizean food (Jam Bel, get it?). The leafy courtyard is a favorite with travelers, and the menu features plenty of funky seafood dishes, soups and salads. Draft beer is available.

Moon Clusters Coffee House (25 Daly St; ☺ 9am-6pm) The coolest café in town, serving up six types of espresso, frappuccino and donuts and pastries. The Attitude Adjuster (five shots of espresso) is not recommended for those with heart conditions.

Brodie's (Map pp226-7; 2 Albert St; ☺ 8:30am-7pm Mon-Fri, 8:30am-5pm Sat, 8:30am-1pm Sun) This department store has the best downtown grocery supplies for picnics and long bus trips.

DRINKING & NIGHTLIFE

Weekends are your best bet to party in Belize City. There are a few places to have a beer in the center, but the real action takes place 1.2 miles (2km) north, about a US$3 taxi ride.

Big Apple 3K (Map pp226-7; Regent St W) This is the best bar in the center, with a breezy deck out back and live music Friday through Sunday.

King St Station (Map pp226-7; King St) Poolside out back of Bellevue Hotel is a good place to grab a few beers. Friday nights you can get your karaoke on.

Caesar's (Map p224; Newtown Barracks Rd) A good place to start your night, Caesar's caters to a mostly Latino crowd – the music and the action on the small dance floor testify to this. The crowd starts turning up at about 10:30pm.

Level Nightclub (Map p224; 190 Newtown Barracks Rd; admission US$5) Just south of Caesar's, the Level

is a bigger place playing classic pop remixes and other commercial dance tracks. It's fairly empty until about 11:30pm.

ENTERTAINMENT

Princess Hotel & Casino (Map p224; Newtown Barracks Rd) This is the only cinema in Belize City; check daily papers for what's showing. Also here are a bowling alley–video arcade, a couple of upmarket bars and, of course, the casino.

The **Bliss Institute** (Map pp226-7; ☎ 227 2458; Southern Foreshore) Belize's fanciest entertainment venue hosts occasional concerts and plays. Stop by for their monthly program.

SHOPPING

Sings (Map pp226-7; Albert St; ☺ 9am-6pm Mon-Sat) This is the first place to check for inexpensive souvenirs and presents, including a full range of Belikin paraphernalia.

National Handicrafts Centre (Map pp226-7; 3 Fort St; ☺ 8am-4pm Mon-Sat) This has an excellent selection of Belizean crafts, from wood carvings to artwork, Maya textiles to tourist tat. Despite being on just about every bus tour's itinerary, prices are reasonable.

GETTING THERE & AWAY

Air

For information on international travel to Belize City, see p222. Belize City's Municipal Airport (TZA; Map p224) is 1.5 miles (2.5km) north of the city center, on the shore. You can take domestic flights from the international terminal, but it's always cheaper (sometimes way cheaper) to depart from the Municipal Airport.

Local Belizean airlines include the following two:

Maya Island Air (☎ 223 1140; www.mayaairways.com)
Tropic Air (☎ 223 5671; www.tropicair.com)

There are two main domestic air routes: Belize City–Caye Caulker–San Pedro–Corozal; and Belize City–Dangriga–Placencia–Punta Gorda. Fares and duration are similar on both airlines, and there are hourly departures on most routes during daylight hours.

Caye Caulker US$26; 20min
Corozal US$61; 45min flying time, but you have to connect with another flight in San Pedro
Dangriga US$30; 15min
Placencia US$59; 35min
Punta Gorda US$76; 1hr
San Pedro US$26; 20min

BELIZE

Boat

Fast motor launches zoom between Belize City, Caye Caulker and Ambergris Caye frequently every day.

The **Belize Marine Terminal** (Map pp226-7; ☎ 223 5752; www.cayecaulkerwatertaxi.com; N Front St) at the north end of the Swing Bridge, is the main dock for boats to the northern cayes.

The efficient Caye Caulker Water Taxi Association operates fast, frequent launches between Belize City and Caye Caulker (US$7.50) and San Pedro (US$10) on Ambergris Caye, with stops on request at Caye Chapel (US$7.50) and St George's Caye (US$12.50). Boats leave roughly every hour from 8am to 5pm. Against the wind, the trip to Caulker takes 30 to 45 minutes. The San Pedro ride takes 45 minutes to an hour.

Bus

National Transportation (Map pp226-7; ☎ 227 2255; West Collet Canal) has a near monopoly on the Belizean bus scene, with **James Transportation** (☎ in Punta Gorda 702 2049) also running some of the routes heading south. National has their own terminal, while James buses leave from the street outside it. For information on getting to the terminal, see p225. Below is a list of popular destinations. Note that while local buses are marginally cheaper, express buses are generally much comfier and faster.

Belmopan local/express US$2/3.50; 1hr; half-hourly departures

Benque Viejo del Carmen local/express US$4/6; 3hr; half-hourly departures

Chetumal (Mexico) local/express US$5/7; 4hr

Corozal local/express US$4.50/6; 3hr; hourly departures

Dangriga local/express US$5/7; 3-4hr; regular departures

Orange Walk local/express US$2.50/3.50; 2hr; hourly departures

Placencia local/express US$10/13; 4hr; regular departures

Punta Gorda local/express US$11/13; 8-10hr; regular departures

San Ignacio local/express US$3.50/5.50; 3hr; half-hourly departures

GETTING AROUND
Taxi

Trips by taxi within Belize City (including to/ from Municipal Airport) cost US$3 for one or two people and, oddly, US$8 for three or four. If you phone for a cab instead of hailing one on the street, the price may go up. Secure the price in advance and perhaps check first with hotel staff about what's reasonable.

THE NORTHERN CAYES

Belize's go-to place for water-based fun are two tiny cayes to the northeast of Belize City. Diving, snorkeling, windsurfing, sailing – it's all here. Protected sea grass along the shoreline doesn't really encourage swimmers, and most people swim off docks that jut into deeper water. If you just want to laze around on the beach, southern towns such as Hopkins (p252) or Placencia (p253) might be a better bet.

Caye Caulker is commonly thought of as the low-budget island, where hotels and restaurants are less expensive than on the resort-conscious Ambergris Caye, though with Caulker's booming popularity its residents are fighting to keep the distinction.

See p252 for details on the cayes further south.

CAYE CAULKER
pop 1300

A short hop from Belize City, Caye Caulker remains a backpacker favorite. Prices here are reasonable by comparison and there's none of the exclusive air found on the other cayes.

For all practical purposes, Caulker's a tiny place. You could make a tour of it in less than two hours.

The village is located on the southern portion of the island. Actually, Caulker is two islands, since Hurricane Hattie split the island just north of the village. The split is called, simply, the Split (or the Cut). It has a tiny beach, with swift currents running through it. North of the Split is mostly undeveloped land, and part of it has been declared a nature reserve.

The water's good for swimming here, but sea grass is the problem. Jump off a dock, or head north to the Split.

Orientation & Information

The village has two principal streets: Front St to the east and Back St to the west. The distance from the Split in the north to the village's southern edge is little more than a half mile (0.8km).

South of the village is the **Belize Tourism Industry Association** (☎ 226 2251), on the site of the **Caye Caulker Mini Reserve**. Here you can get information on what to see and do on the island, then stroll an interpretive trail identifying the

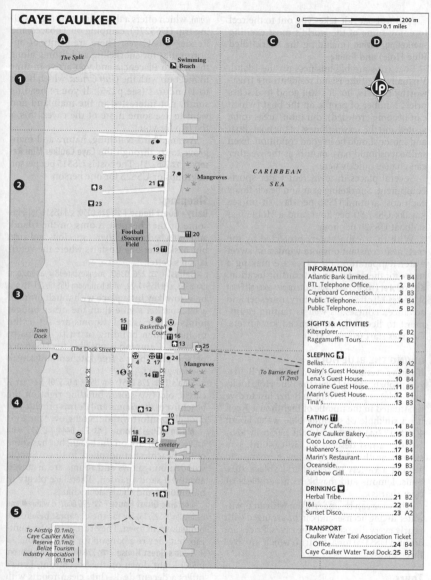

CAYE CAULKER

0 —————— 200 m
0 —————— 0.1 miles

The Split

Swimming Beach

Mangroves

CARIBBEAN SEA

Football (Soccer) Field

Town Dock

Basketball Court

(The Dock Street)

Mangroves

To Barrier Reef (1.2mi)

Back St

Middle St

Front St

Cemetery

To Airstrip (0.1mi);
Caye Caulker Mini
Reserve (0.1mi);
Belize Tourism
Industry Association
(0.1mi)

BELIZE

INFORMATION	
Atlantic Bank Limited	1 B4
BTL Telephone Office	2 B4
Cayeboard Connection	3 B3
Public Telephone	4 B4
Public Telephone	5 B2

SIGHTS & ACTIVITIES	
Kitexplorer	6 B2
Raggamuffin Tours	7 B2

SLEEPING	
Bellas	8 A2
Daisy's Guest House	9 B4
Lena's Guest House	10 B4
Lorraine Guest House	11 B5
Marin's Guest House	12 B4
Tina's	13 B3

EATING	
Amor y Cafe	14 B4
Caye Caulker Bakery	15 B3
Coco Loco Cafe	16 B3
Habanero's	17 B4
Marin's Restaurant	18 B4
Oceanside	19 B3
Rainbow Grill	20 B2

DRINKING	
Herbal Tribe	21 B2
I&I	22 B4
Sunset Disco	23 A2

TRANSPORT	
Caulker Water Taxi Association Ticket Office	24 B4
Caye Caulker Water Taxi Dock	25 B3

island's flora and fauna. Call first, as hours are irregular. Caye Caulker has its own website (www.gocayecaulker.com).

Atlantic Bank Limited (Middle St; 8am-2pm Mon-Fri, 8:30am-noon Sat) does cash advances on Visa card and has a Visa/MasterCard ATM.

Cayeboard Connection (Front St; per hr US$6) provides internet access.

Activities

The surf breaks on the barrier reef, easily visible from the eastern shore of Caye Caulker. However, don't attempt to swim out to it – the local boaters speed their powerful craft through these waters and are completely heedless of swimmers. Swim only in protected areas.

A short boat ride takes you out to the reef to enjoy some of the world's most exciting **snorkeling**, **diving** (including the shark-filled Blue Hole) and **fishing**.

Boat trips are big business on the island. Virtually all of the island residents are trustworthy boaters, but it's still good to discuss price, number of people on the boat (which can become crowded), duration, areas to be visited and the seaworthiness of the boat. Boat and motor should be in good condition. Even sailboats should have motors as the weather can change quickly here.

Several places in town rent water-sports equipment. Snorkeling gear and beach floats each cost around US$5 per day, sit-on sea kayaks US$7.50 per hour, and a Hobie Cat sailboat US$20 per hour.

With their calm waters protected by the reef, near constant onshore winds and sweet water temperature, the cayes are making a name for themselves as a kitesurfing location. **Kitexplorer** (☎ 623 8403; www.kitexplorer.com; off Front St; ☹ Nov-Jul) offers introductory, refresher and advanced courses, as well as renting equipment to licensed, experienced kitesurfers. Courses start from US$130.

DIVING THE BLUE HOLE

If you've ever seen a tourism poster for Belize, you probably know what the Blue Hole looks like – a lot of people come to Belize just to dive it. Situated in the middle of Lighthouse Reef, it's a sinkhole of startling blue water about 400ft (122m) deep and 1000ft (305m) wide.

After a fast descent to 130ft (40m), you swim beneath a stalactite-laden overhang and among a variety of reef sharks (black tips, bulls, lemons and maybe hammerheads or tiger sharks).

The dive can be undertaken with an open-water diving license, and can be arranged with nearly every dive shop on the cayes. Prices are around US$190 for a day trip (which involves three dives).

Tours

A variety of inland trips can be arranged from the cayes. The most popular is the Altun Ha river trip, which stops at Maruba Resort (about 20km north of Altun Ha) for lunch, swimming and horseback riding. The cost is US$80.

One tour gaining in popularity is with **Raggamuffin Tours** (☎ 226 0348; www.raggamuffintours

.com), which offers a three-day, two-night sailing trip (US$275), camping on Tobacco and Rendezvous Cayes. There are plenty of opportunities for snorkeling and fishing along the way to Placencia and you arrive in time to meet up with the *Gulf Cruza*, which heads to Honduras (see p255). If you're heading south, not interested in the mainland and want to see some more of the cayes, this is the trip for you.

Arrange bird-watching, nature and mangrove tours through the **Caye Caulker Mini Reserve** (☎ 226 2251). The cost is US$15 per person in groups or US$25 for one person.

Sleeping

Daisy's Guest House (☎ 226 0150; s/d US$11/18) Has some of the cheapest rooms on the island, and not a bad deal, either – spacious and airy, but basic. Get one upstairs where the ventilation's better.

Bellas (☎ 226 0360; monkeybite38@yahoo.com; dm US$8, s/d US$11/22, with bathroom US$19/22) It's a new, low-key little place with much more of a backpacker's vibe than the other budget joints on the island. Rooms are set in the main wooden building or rustic cabins in the yard. Camping is possible for US$6 per person and there's free kitchen and kayak use for guests.

Tina's (☎ 226 0351; dm US$9, r US$20) Set in a classic old two-storey building right on the beachfront, the rooms and dorms provide just enough comfort without going over the top.

Marin's Guest House (☎ 226 0444; r US$15, with bathroom US$20) Not on the beach, but has some of the beachiest atmosphere in town. Simple wooden bungalows and rooms are arranged around a sandy garden. There are plenty of hammocks and shady deck chairs.

Lorraine Guest House (☎ 226 0002; d with/without bathroom US$25/15) By far the cheapest beachside bungalows in town. They're in need of a paint-job, but they're a bargain for the location.

Lena's Guest House (☎ 226 0106; r with bathroom US$30) Right down on the beachfront, Lena's offers a decent deal – big, clean rooms with newish beds and overhead fans. The wide communal balconies have excellent views.

Eating

You'll find prices higher here than on the mainland, though not as high as the restaurants in San Pedro. The seafood is good, but don't forget your old friend, stew chicken.

Do your part to avoid illegal fishing: don't order lobster outside its mid-June to mid-February season or conch outside of October to July.

Caye Caulker Bakery (Middle St) The place to pick up fresh bread, rolls and similar goodies.

Amor y Cafe (breakfast about US$5; 6-11:30am) If it's breakfast you're after, this is one of the hot spots. There are only a few tables, but homemade bread, fresh fruit and excellent coffee hit the spot.

Marin's Restaurant (meals around US$9; lunch & dinner) Up on the 2nd floor among the treetops, this place serves up hearty Belizean fare and seafood dishes.

Coco Loco Cafe (sandwiches US$5; 7am-9pm Mon-Sat) The best range of sandwiches, bagels and cakes come out of this friendly little café out the back of a gift shop–art gallery. There's good coffee, too.

Oceanside (meals US$8-12; dinner) This place has the liveliest beach barbecue on the island. Staff put tables out across the street at night and serve good-value seafood such as blackened snapper fillets (US$8). It's also a great place for live music.

Habanero's (mains US$12-20; dinner) By far the most atmospheric place to eat in town. Dine by the light of a hurricane lamp and enjoy the seafood kebabs in coconut sauce (US$20) while gazing through the extensive cocktail list.

Rainbow Grill (mains US$10-25; lunch & dinner) Set out on a deck over the water, this is one of the more popular eating-drinking places in town. Prices are reasonable and daily specials (such as two big lobster tails for US$23) are an excellent deal.

Drinking & Nightlife

Herbal Tribe (Front St) Of the multitude of happy hours, this bar has the best atmosphere. It's a breezy place with mellow grooves and two rum drinks for US$2.50 from 6pm to 8pm.

Sunset Disco (US$5; from midnight) On the west side of the island, this disco has weekend dances and a rooftop bar with snacks.

I&I is the happening reggae bar; the **Oceanside** (Front St) often hosts live bands.

Getting There & Away

Maya Island Air (226 0012; www.mayaairways.com) and **Tropic Air** (226 0040; www.tropicair.com) offer regular flights between Caye Caulker, Ambergris Caye (US$26) and the Belize City air-

ports (international terminal US$47, domestic US$26).

The **Caye Caulker Water Taxi Association** (226 0992; www.cayecaulkerwatertaxi.com) runs boats to Belize City (US$7.50) and Ambergris Caye (US$7.50). The schedule is posted outside their office near the boat dock. Water taxis also run to St George's Caye and Caye Chapel.

Getting Around

Caulker is so small that most people walk. If need be, you can rent a bicycle (US$10 per day) or golf cart (US$50 per day) or use the golf-cart taxi service, which costs US$5 for a one-way trip anywhere on the island.

AMBERGRIS CAYE & SAN PEDRO
pop 10,500

By far the most developed of the cayes, Ambergris is still fairly laid-back. San Pedro is a true town – more impressive in a lot of ways than the nation's capital, but there are enough sandy streets and beachside bars to maintain the impression of a tropical paradise.

Outside of town, mostly to the south, large resorts and gated retirement villages are springing up with frightening regularity. Even so, there are still a surprising amount of budget-friendly establishments in the downtown area.

Most of the island's population lives in the town of San Pedro, near the southern tip. The barrier reef is only a half mile (800m) east of San Pedro.

San Pedro started life as a fishing town but is now Belize's prime tourist destination. More than half of the tourists who visit Belize fly straight to San Pedro and use it as their base for excursions elsewhere.

Orientation

San Pedro has three main north–south streets, which used to be called Front St (to the east), Middle St and Back St (to the west). Now these streets have tourist names – Barrier Reef Dr, Pescador Dr and Angel Coral Dr – but some islanders still use the old names.

The river at the end of Pescador Dr is as far as you can go by car. From there, you can cross the river on a toll bridge (US$5 return) to reach a bike and golf-cart trail that runs north for at least 13km. Most travelers take the road only as far as Sweet Basil for lunch, or the Palapa Bar for drinks, before heading back to San Pedro.

BELIZE

Information

BOOKSTORES

Barefoot Books (Pescador Dr; 10am-4pm Mon-Sat) A good range of new and used books, including guidebooks, birding and marine-life texts.

INTERNET ACCESS

Caribbean Connection (Barrier Reef Dr; per hr US$4)

LAUNDRY

Several laundromats lie at the southern end of Pescador Dr, among them **Nellie's Laundromat** (per pound US$1).

MEDICAL SERVICES

Lion's Club Medical Clinic (226 2851; Lion St) Across the street from the Maya Island Air terminal at the airport.
San Carlos Medical Clinic (226 2918; Pescador Dr) Just south of Caribeña St, it treats ailments and does blood tests. There's also a pharmacy and pathology lab on site.

MONEY

You can change money easily in San Pedro, and US dollars and traveler's checks are accepted in most establishments. Major banks are:
Atlantic Bank Limited (Barrier Reef Dr; 8am-noon & 1-3pm Mon, Tue, Thu; 8am-1pm Wed, 8am-1pm & 3-6pm Fri, 8:30am-noon Sat)
Belize Bank (Barrier Reef Dr; 8am-3pm Mon-Thu, 8am-1pm & 3-6pm Fri, 8:30am-noon Sat) Has a Visa/MasterCard ATM.

POST

Post office (Buccaneer St; 8am-noon Mon-Fri, 1-5pm Mon-Thu, 1-4:30pm Fri) Off Barrier Reef Dr.

TOURIST INFORMATION

Various private roadside **tourist kiosks** (10am-9pm) are scattered around town – they're tour consolidators and make commissions by gathering groups together for tours. Otherwise they can be reasonably helpful with general enquiries. Tourist information is also available on the caye's own website (www.ambergris caye.com).

Activities

Ambergris is good for all water sports: scuba diving, snorkeling, sailboarding, boating, swimming, deep-sea fishing and sunbathing. Many island hotels have their own dive shops, which rent equipment, provide instruction and organize diving excursions.

In fact, just about any local can put you in touch with someone organizing water-sports trips.

Snorkeling and picnicking excursions cost from US$30. The going rental rate for a snorkel, mask and fins is US$8. Manatee-watching off Goff's Caye can be added to a snorkeling trip (US$105).

Sailsports Belize (226 4488; www.sailsportsbelize .com) rents windsurfers for US$22 per hour and sailboats for US$22 to US$48 per hour; lessons are available. Kitesurfing courses are available from US$165.

All beaches are public, and most waterside hotels and resorts are generous with their lounge chairs on slow days. While sandy beaches are plentiful, protected sea grass at the waterline makes entry from the shore not terribly pleasant, so you'll be swimming from piers. Swimming is best off the pier at Ramon's Village, south of town.

Tours

The *Winnie Estelle*, a 66-ft (21m) island trader moored at the Paradise Resort Hotel pier, at the north end of Barrier Reef Dr, goes out on daily snorkeling trips to Caye Caulker (US$30 to US$75).

The *Reef Runner* glass-bottom boat, also found on Barrier Reef Dr, makes daily reef trips for US$25 per person. The aptly named *Rum Punch II*, a wooden sailboat, runs sunset cocktail cruises for US$25 (book at tour agents in town).

Tours are available to the Maya ruins at Altun Ha (US$80) and Lamanai (US$135) or beyond to the Belize Zoo, Xunantunich, Crooked Tree Bird Sanctuary, the Community Baboon Sanctuary, Mountain Pine Ridge and Tikal (Guatemala). Any hotel, travel agency or dive shop can fill you in on tours, or contact **Seaduced by Belize** (226 2254) or **Bottom Time Dive Shop** (226 2348).

Sleeping

Competition for guests on San Pedro is fierce, and taxi drivers are often rewarded commissions for bringing guests to hotels. Often this commission is tacked on to the cost of your room, so try to make reservations in advance or show up unescorted.

Pedro's Inn (226 3825; Coconut Dr; s/d US$12.50/23, r with bathroom US$50) Out on the residential side of the island, this has by far the cheapest single rooms in town. It's a simple place, lacking

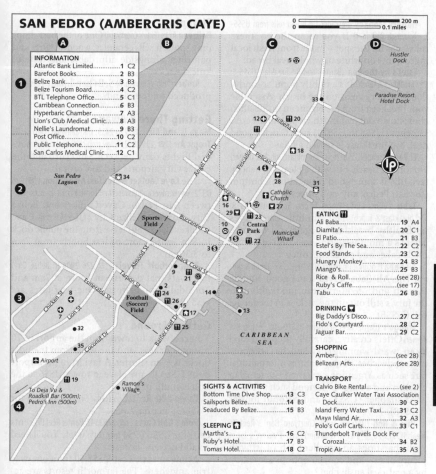

SAN PEDRO (AMBERGRIS CAYE)

0 ━━━━━━━━ 200 m
0 ━━━━━━━━ 0.1 miles

INFORMATION
Atlantic Bank Limited...............1 C2
Barefoot Books......................2 B3
Belize Bank........................3 B3
Belize Tourism Board..............4 C2
BTL Telephone Office..............5 C1
Carribbean Connection.............6 B3
Hyperbaric Chamber...............7 A3
Lion's Club Medical Clinic........8 A3
Nellie's Laundromat...............9 B3
Post Office.......................10 C2
Public Telephone.................11 C2
San Carlos Medical Clinic.......12 C1

San Pedro Lagoon

Hustler Dock

Paradise Resort Hotel Dock

Sports Field

Central Park

Football (Soccer) Field

Municipal Wharf

CARIBBEAN SEA

Airport

To Deja Vu &
Roadkill Bar (500m);
Pedro's Inn (500m)

Ramon's Village

EATING
Ali Baba.........................19 A4
Diamita's........................20 C1
El Patio..........................21 B3
Estel's By The Sea..............22 C2
Food Stands.....................23 C2
Hungry Monkey..................24 B3
Mango's..........................25 B3
Rice & Roll...............(see 28)
Ruby's Caffe................(see 17)
Tabu.............................26 B3

DRINKING
Big Daddy's Disco..............27 C2
Fido's Courtyard...............28 C2
Jaguar Bar......................29 C2

SHOPPING
Amber...........................(see 28)
Belizean Arts..................(see 28)

TRANSPORT
Calvio Bike Rental............(see 2)
Caye Caulker Water Taxi Association
   Dock...........................30 C3
Island Ferry Water Taxi........31 C2
Maya Island Air................32 A3
Polo's Golf Carts................33 C1
Thunderbolt Travels Dock For
   Corozal.........................34 B2
Tropic Air.........................35 A3

SIGHTS & ACTIVITIES
Bottom Time Dive Shop........13 C3
Sailsports Belize................14 B3
Seaduced By Belize............15 B3

SLEEPING
Martha's..........................16 C2
Ruby's Hotel.....................17 B3
Tomas Hotel.....................18 C2

BELIZE

---

in nearly every conceivable comfort, but the friendly vibe more than makes up for that.

Martha's (☎ 226 2778; miguelperez@btl.net; Pescador Dr; s/d with bathroom US$20/25) An excellent budget deal; it's not on the beach, but has spacious, well-appointed rooms. Don't get one at the back – you'll be listening to the party at Jaguar's Temple disco all night.

Tomas Hotel (☎ 226 2061; Barrier Reef Dr; r with bathroom US$35) Anywhere else, these plain, functional rooms would be overpriced, but in the middle of San Pedro, big clean rooms like these tend to go for a whole lot more.

Ruby's Hotel (☎ 226 2063; Barrier Reef Dr; s/d with bathroom US$20/40) Set in a classic wooden beachfront building, Ruby's has long been a backpacker favorite. Times have changed

since this was a hippy hangout, but the hotel hasn't much.

Eating

Several small cafés in the center of town serve cheap, simple meals. The best places for low-budget feasting are the stands in front of Central Park, where you can pick up a plate of stewed chicken with beans and rice, barbecue and other delicacies for about US$2.

Ruby's Caffe (Barrier Reef Dr; snacks from US$3) Next to Ruby's Hotel, this is a tiny place with good cakes and pastries but it opens at unpredictable hours.

Diamita's (meals US$3.50; ☿ breakfast & lunch) Has a simple menu of well-priced items. Beware the large coffee – it's truly large.

Hungry Monkey (Pescador Dr; bread rolls from US$5-7; ☺ lunch & dinner) If you're on the go, these rolls/subs hit the spot – made from fresh local ingredients on white or wholemeal bread.

Estel's by the Sea (Barrier Reef Dr; breakfast US$6-8; ☺ breakfast & lunch) It's a rightly popular sandy-floored eatery right on the beach. Assemble your breakfast from the big menu inside, then chow down out front with views and breezes. Lunches (US$8 to US$20) aren't such a good deal, but breakfast is served all day.

El Patio (mains US$6-20; ☺ breakfast, lunch & dinner) Not on the beach, but with a pleasant, beachy feel, this is some good eatin' at rock bottom (for San Pedro, anyway) prices.

Tabu (Vilma Linda Plaza, Tarpon St; burgers US$8; ☺ breakfast & lunch) This hip little café serves up healthy breakfasts, bagels and burgers. There's a mouthwatering selection of home-made cakes and excellent coffee.

Ali Baba (Coconut Dr; mains US$10-15; ☺ lunch & dinner) The Ali Baba serves some good Middle Eastern and Mediterranean food, although the jury's still out on the pickles in the falafel roll (US$5).

Mango's (Barrier Reef Dr; mains US$10-20; ☺ lunch & dinner) Offers creative, carefully prepared food by an award-winning chef. Lunches are gourmet sandwiches, dinner features international fare such as Argentine steaks and Guatemalan chicken and a range of seafood such as blackened snapper (US$15) and coconut lobster (US$18).

Rice & Roll (Upstairs, Fido's Courtyard, Barrier Reef Dr; meals US$15-20; ☺ lunch & dinner) San Pedro's best sushi bar does an excellent job of it, with plenty of raw and cooked options served up by a real-deal sushi chef.

Drinking & Nightlife

Fido's Courtyard (Barrier Reef Dr) This bar, near Pelican St, is the landlubbers' favorite, with live music most nights.

Big Daddy's Disco (Barrier Reef Dr) Right next to San Pedro's church, this is a hot nightspot, often featuring live reggae, especially during winter.

Jaguar Bar (Barrier Reef Dr) Near Big Daddy's, this jungle-themed bar is often closed off-season, but it rocks in winter.

Deja Vu (Coconut Dr) A big air-conditioned disco south of town. Friday's the night to be here.

Roadkill Bar (Coconut Dr) Out front of the Deja Vu, this laid-back open-air bar often has live music.

Shopping

Belizean Arts (Fido's Courtyard) One of the best shopping spots, it sells ceramics, woodcarvings and paintings alongside affordable and tasteful knickknacks.

Amber (Fido's Courtyard) Sells handmade jewelry produced on the island.

Getting There & Away

Maya Island Air (☎ 226 2435; mayaairways.com) and **Tropic Air** (☎ 226 2012; www.tropicair.com) offer several flights daily between San Pedro and the Belize City airports and to Corozal.

The **Caye Caulker Water Taxi Association** (☎ 226 0992; www.cayecaulkerwatertaxi.com) runs boats between San Pedro, Caye Caulker and Belize City. Boats to Belize City (US$10) via Caye Caulker (US$7.50) leave from the public dock in San Pedro more or less hourly from 7am to 3:30pm.

Thunderbolt Travels (☎ 226 2904 in Belize City) has boats that depart San Pedro at 7am and 3pm daily for Corozal. One-way fares are US$22.50.

Getting Around

You can walk to town from the airport in 10 minutes or less, and the walk from the boat docks is even shorter. A taxi from the airport costs US$3 to any place in town, US$6 to the hotels south of town.

Calvio Bike Rental (Pescador Dr) rents bikes for US$8/38 per day/week.

Polo's Golf Carts (☎ 226 3542; Barrier Reef Dr) rents carts for US$65/250 per day/week. You'll need a valid drivers' license.

Minivan taxis cost US$2.50 for a one-way trip anywhere. The far north resorts are accessed by water taxi.

NORTHERN BELIZE

Much more Latino than the rest of the country, you'll find whatever Spanish you have useful here. The landscape is flat and lush, mostly given over to farming, although there are a couple of interesting and easily accessible wildlife reserves.

Some important Maya sites can be found here, too. The most popular, Lamanai, is reached by a riverboat ride which is a joy in itself, but the national favorite must be Altun Ha, whose image has been immortalized on banknotes and beer bottle labels.

BERMUDIAN LANDING COMMUNITY BABOON SANCTUARY

In 1985 local farmers organized to help preserve the endangered black howler monkey and its habitat. Care is taken to maintain the forests along the banks of the Belize River, where the black howler, found only in Belize, feeds, sleeps and – at dawn and dusk – howls (loudly and unmistakably).

At the **Community Baboon Sanctuary** (☎ 220 2181; www.howlermonkeys.org; admission US$5; ☽ 8am-5pm), in the village of Bermudian Landing, you can learn all about the black howler and the 200 other species of wildlife found in the reserve. A one-hour guided nature walk is included with your admission, arranged at the visitors center. Horseback riding is available for US$25, as are three-hour canoe trips (US$25) and 1½-hour night hikes (US$10).

Sleeping & Eating

Rustic accommodations are available at the reserve but are best arranged in advance. There is a good basic restaurant in the visitors center. **Village homestays** (d with 2 meals US$25) can be arranged here, too.

Nature Resort (☎ 223 3668; naturer@btl.net; d with/without bathroom US$42/28) Adjacent to the visitors center, it rents well-maintained cabañas.

Howler Monkey Resort (☎ 220 2158; www.howlermonkeylodge.com; cabañas per person US$15) Set on a bend in the river, this place has a curiously uncared-for air, but it has a beautiful setting and accommodations are clean and good value.

Getting There & Away

The Community Baboon Sanctuary is in Bermudian Landing, 26 miles (42km) west of Belize City – an easy day trip from Belize City or the cayes.

If you're driving, turn west off the Northern Hwy at the Burrell Boom turnoff (Mile 13). From there it's another 12 miles (20km) of dirt road to the sanctuary.

National operates buses to Bermudian Landing (US$2, one hour). Some travelers catch one of the frequent Northern Hwy buses heading to the Mexican border, get off at Burrell Boom and hitch the 13 miles (8km) to the sanctuary. If you hitch, take the usual precautions.

ALTUN HA

Northern Belize's most famous Maya ruin is **Altun Ha** (admission US$5; ☽ 9am-5pm), 34 miles (55km) north of Belize City along the Old Northern Hwy. The site is near Rockstone Pond village, south of Maskall.

Altun Ha (Maya for 'Rockstone Pond') was undoubtedly a small but rich and important Maya trading town, with agriculture also playing an essential role in its economy. Altun Ha had formed as a community by at least 600 BC, perhaps several centuries earlier, and the town flourished until the mysterious collapse of classic Maya civilization around AD 900.

Of the grass-covered temples arranged around the two plazas here, the largest and most important is the **Temple of the Masonry Altars** (Structure B-4), in Plaza B. The restored structure you see dates from the first half of the 7th century and takes its name from altars on which copal was burned and beautifully carved jade pieces were smashed in sacrifice.

In Plaza A, Structure A-1 is sometimes called the **Temple of the Green Tomb**. Deep within it was discovered the tomb of a priest-king dating from around AD 600. Tropical humidity had destroyed the king's garments and the paper of the 'painted book' of the Maya that was buried with him, but many riches were intact: shell necklaces, pottery, pearls, stingray spines used in bloodletting rites, jade beads and pendants, and ceremonial flints.

Modern toilets and a drinks shop are on site.

Sleeping & Eating

Camping, though not strictly legal, is sometimes permitted; ask at the site.

Mayan Wells Restaurant (☎ 220 6039; cabin US$30, camping per person US$5, meals US$6; ☽ restaurant breakfast & lunch; Ⓟ ▣) About 2km before reaching Altun Ha, this is a popular stop for lunch or refreshments. The one cabin is simple but adequate and camping is allowed on the premises; bathroom and shower facilities are available.

Getting There & Away

The easiest way to visit Altun Ha is on one of the many tours running daily from Belize City (US$40 half day including admission); most travel agents in town can line you up with one. You can also tour from San Pedro on Ambergris Caye (see p234).

To get here by public transportation, catch an afternoon bus departing the National Bus Terminal (Map pp226–7) for the town of Maskall, north of Altun Ha. Get off at Lucky Strike, from where it's a 3.5km walk/hitch (on a very lightly trafficked road) to Altun Ha.

BELIZE

CROOKED TREE WILDLIFE SANCTUARY

Midway between Belize City and Orange Walk, 3.5 miles (5.5km) west of the Northern Hwy, lies the fishing and farming village of Crooked Tree. In 1984 the Belize Audubon Society succeeded in having 5 sq miles (12 sq km) around the village declared a **wildlife sanctuary** (admission US$4; ☺ 8am-4pm) principally because of the area's wealth of birdlife. The best time of year for wildlife watching is in May, when the water in the lagoon drops to its lowest level and the animals must come further out into the open to reach their food.

Day trips to Crooked Tree are possible, but it's best to stay the night so you can be here at dawn, when the birds are most active. Trails weave through the villages and you can spot plenty of species on your own, but you'll get further and see more on a guided tour. In fact, for those interested in viewing birds and other wildlife, a guided nature tour of this sanctuary is among the most rewarding experiences in Belize.

Tours cost US$70 to US$80 for groups of four (less per person for larger groups) and usually include a boat trip through the lagoon, a walk along the elevated boardwalk and viewing time atop the observation towers. Arrangements can be made through the visitors center or your hotel. More information can be obtained from the **Belize Audubon Society** (Map pp226-7; ☎ 223 5004; www.belizeaudubon.org; 12 Fort St, Belize City).

Sleeping & Eating

Rhaburn's Rooms (☎ 225 7035; s/d US$10/15) On the other side of the cricket field from the visitor center, these are four neat wooden rooms in a friendly family house. The shared bathroom has hot water and there's a comfy balcony out front.

More **rooms** (s/d US$10/15) are available in private houses around town. The visitor center has a map – ask which ones are currently operating.

You can camp at **Bird's Eye View Lodge** (☎ 205 7027; per person US$6) and **Paradise Inn** (☎ 225 7044; per tent US$10), which also rents good-value cabins with lagoon views from US$40 for two people. Both of these places have good restaurants serving reasonably priced meals.

Getting There & Away

The road to Crooked Tree village is 30 miles (48km) up the Northern Hwy from Belize City, 25 miles (40km) south of Orange Walk. The village is 3.5 miles (5km) west of the highway via a causeway over Crooked Tree Lagoon.

If you want to take a bus round-trip to Crooked Tree, you'll have to spend the night there. Jex Bus offers daily services departing Belize City's National bus station for Crooked Tree village at 4:30pm and 5:30pm daily; return trips leave Crooked Tree at 5am, 6:30am and 7am.

If you start early from Belize City or Corozal, you can bus to Crooked Tree Junction and walk or hitch the 3.5 miles (5.5km) to the village.

RÍO BRAVO CONSERVATION AREA

Protecting 240,000 acres (97,000 hectares) of tropical forest and its inhabitants, the Río Bravo Conservation Area is the flagship project of the Programme for Belize (PFB).

In addition to the wealth of plant and animal life here (including all five of Belize's cats – jaguar, puma, ocelot, jaguarundi and margay, 200 tree species and over 390 bird species), more than 60 Maya sites have been discovered on the land. The preeminent site is **La Milpa**, the third-largest Maya site in Belize, believed to have been founded in the late pre-Classic period. Its 5-acre Great Plaza (one of the largest discovered in the Maya world) is surrounded by four 27m-high pyramids.

La Milpa Field Station is near Gallon Jug on the road to Chan Chich Lodge. Visiting and transportation arrangements must be made in advance through **Programme for Belize** (PFB; Map pp226-7; ☎ 227 5616; www.pfbelize.org; 1 Eyre St, Belize City). The cost of a dorm/cabaña is US$44/55 per person. La Milpa is a little tricky to get to, but there are a variety of methods – contact the PFB for details.

LAMANAI

By far the most impressive site in this part of the country is Lamanai, in its own archaeological reserve on the New River Lagoon near the settlement of Indian Church. Though much of the site remains unexcavated and unrestored, the trip to Lamanai, by motorboat up the New River, is an adventure in itself.

Take along a sun hat, sunblock, insect repellent, shoes (rather than sandals), lunch and water.

As with most sites in northern Belize, Lamanai ('Submerged Crocodile,' the original

Maya name) was occupied as early as 1500 BC, with the first stone buildings appearing between 800 and 600 BC. Lamanai flourished in late pre-Classic times, growing into a major ceremonial center with immense temples long before most other Mayan sites.

Unlike at many other sites, the Maya lived here until the coming of the Spanish in the 16th century. British interests later built a sugar mill, now in ruins, at Indian Church. The archaeological site was excavated by Canadian David Pendergast in the 1970s and 1980s.

New River Voyage

Most visitors opt to reach Lamanai by taking a spectacular boat ride up the New River from the Tower Hill toll bridge south of Orange Walk. On this trip, you motor 1½ hours up-river, between riverbanks that are crowded with dense jungle vegetation. En route, your skipper-guide points out the many local birds and will almost certainly spot a crocodile or two. You will also pass the Mennonite community at **Shipyard**. Finally you come to New River Lagoon – a long, broad expanse of water that can be choppy during the frequent rain showers – and the boat dock at Lamanai.

Exploring the Site

A tour of the **ruins** (admission US$5; ☼ 9am-5pm) takes 90 minutes minimum, more comfortably two or three hours. Of the 60 significant structures identified here, the grandest is **Structure N10-43**, a huge, late pre-Classic building rising more than 111ft (34m) above the jungle canopy. It's been partially uncovered and restored. Not far from N10-43 is Lamanai's ball court, a smallish one, partially uncovered.

To the north along a jungle path is **Structure P9-56**, built several centuries later, with a huge stylized mask of a man in a crocodile-mouth headdress 13ft (4m) high emblazoned on its southwest face.

Near this structure are a small **temple** and a ruined **stela** that once stood on the temple's front face. Apparently some worshipers built a fire at the base of the limestone stela and later doused the fire with water. The hot stone stela, cooled too quickly, fractured and toppled. The stela's bas-relief carving of a majestic figure is extremely fine.

A small **museum** near the boat landing exhibits some interesting figurative pottery and large flint tools.

Getting There & Away

The operators will tell you different, but most tours are roughly the same. One reliable outfit is **Jungle River Tours** (☎ 302 2293; lamanaimayatour@btl .net; 20 Lovers' Lane, Orange Walk). River trips to Lamanai generally run at around US$45 per person for a tour including lunch, guide, fruit and admission fees.

If you're really keen, you may be able to get a good deal for the boat trip only by going down to the boat landing at the toll bridge and negotiating with the fishermen there.

Though the river voyage is much more convenient and enjoyable, Lamanai can be reached by road (36 miles/58km) from Orange Walk via Yo Creek and San Felipe. A bus service from Orange Walk is available but limited, making a day trip impossible.

ORANGE WALK
pop 15,900

Nestled on a bend in the New River (the old one seems to have gone missing), Orange Walk is a small, fairly unremarkable town surrounded by citrus, papaya and sugarcane plantations. The country's biggest rum distillery is here, but most tourists are in town for the fascinating boat trip to the ruins at Lamanai (see opposite).

The Northern Hwy, called Queen Victoria Ave in town, serves as the main road. The center of town is shady Central Park, on the east side of Queen Victoria Ave. The town hospital is in the northern outskirts, readily visible on the west side of Northern Hwy.

Sleeping

Akihito Hotel (☎ 302 0185; 22 Queen Victoria Ave; r US$15-35; ⌘) Offering the best budget deals in town, the Akihito's cheaper rooms are serviceable concrete boxes with spotless shared bathrooms (and scorching hot water). The more expensive rooms have air-con, private bathrooms and cable TV.

Lamanai Riverside Retreat (☎ 302 3955; Lamanai Alley; r US$30) It offers good-value cabins in a lovely setting down by the river, a five-minute walk south of town. The restaurant here is deservedly popular. The boats to Lamanai will pick you up here.

Orchid Palm Inn (☎ 322 0719; www.orchidpalminn .com; Queen Victoria Ave; r with fan/air-con US$40/45; ⌘) This is a reasonably classy new hotel right across from the bus stop. Beds are big and some of the furnishings surprisingly hip.

BELIZE

Eating

Mercy's Place (52 Queen Victoria Ave; burritos US$2) This is a hole-in-the-wall taco and burrito joint that's hugely popular with the locals. It could be a bit dodgy for those with unaccustomed stomachs, however.

Happy Valley (32 Main St; meals US$3-6) The happy Valley is popular for drinks (it can't be the loud pop music…surely) and its standard range of Chinese meals. It also serves good-value breakfasts from 7:30am.

Juanita's (8 Santa Ana St; meals from US$4; ⊙ breakfast, lunch & dinner) Opposite the Shell fuel station, this is a simple place with tasty local fare at low prices.

Lamanai Riverside Retreat (Lamanai Alley; meals US$6-15; ⊙ breakfast, lunch & dinner) Hugely popular with locals for its laid-back, breezy location and excellent prices, this riverside restaurant gives the feeling of calm and isolation, even though it's only a short walk from town.

Getting There & Away

Buses run hourly for Belize City (US$2.50, two hours) and Corozal (US$2, one hour), and points in between, with additional southbound runs in the early morning and northbound runs in the late afternoon to accommodate work and school schedules. All services use the bus stop on the corner of Queen Victoria Ave and St Peter St.

COROZAL

pop 9000

This gateway to Mexico (and the northern cayes) is far enough from the border to have the best of both worlds – that fascinating mix of cultures that border towns have, without the associated sleaze and hassle.

Corozal is a pretty place, with many parks and seaside promenades. South of town, retirees from the USA are moving in fast, attracted by the climate and easy-going lifestyle.

Though Maya have been living around Corozal since 1500 BC, modern Corozal dates from only 1849. In that year, refugees from the War of the Castes in Yucatán fled across the border to this safe haven. They founded a town and named it after the cohune palm, a symbol of fertility. For years it had the look of a typical Caribbean town, until Hurricane Janet roared through in 1955 and blew away many of the old wooden buildings on stilts. Much of Corozal's cinderblock architecture dates from the late 1950s.

Orientation & Information

Corozal is arranged around a town square in the Mexican style. You can walk easily to any place in town.

The main road is 7th Ave, which briefly skirts the sea before veering inland through town. The old town market and custom house has recently been converted to house the **BTB office** (⊙ 9am-4:30pm Mon-Fri, 9am-noon Sat) and the **Corozal museum** (admission free; ⊙ 9am-4:30pm Mon-Fri, 9am-noon Sat).

The **Belize Bank** (⊙ 8am-1pm Mon-Fri, 3-6pm Fri) on the north side of the plaza has a Visa/MasterCard ATM and offers currency exchange, as do various *casas de cambio* (currency exchange offices) around town.

Internet services are provided at **Cyber Zone** (Park St N).

Cerros Archaeological Site

Cerros (also called Cerro Maya; admission US$5; ⊙ 8am-5pm) flourished as a coastal trading center in late pre-Classic times. Unlike at other Maya sites, little subsequent construction from the Classic and post-Classic periods covers the original structures here because, at around AD 150, Cerros reverted rapidly to a small, unimportant village. Thus the site has given archaeologists important insights into Maya pre-Classic architecture.

Climb **Structure 4**, a temple more than 65ft (20m) high, for stunning panoramic views. Though the site is still mostly a mass of grass-covered mounds, the center has been cleared and consolidated and it's easy to see how the plaza structures were designed to fit together. Also notable are the **canals** that ring the site,

---

GETTING TO CHETUMAL, MEXICO

Corozal is 8 miles (13km) south of the border crossing at Santa Elena–Subteniente López. Most of the frequent buses that travel between Chetumal (Mexico) and Belize City stop at Corozal. Otherwise, hitch a ride or hire a taxi (expensive at US$12) to get to **Santa Elena**. Buses running between Corozal and Chetumal will wait for you to complete border formalities. You'll have to pay a tourist fee of around US$19 to leave Belize.

See p56 for information on crossing the border from Mexico.

COROZAL

0 ————— 300 m
0 ————— 0.2 miles

To Mexican
Border (8mi)

Fort Barlee

Plaza

School

Corozal
Bay

To Airstrip;
Belize City (96mi)

To Cerros (10mi)

INFORMATION
Belize Bank.............................1 D1
BTB Office..........................(see 7)
BTL Telephone Office............2 C2
Cyber Zone............................3 D1
Public Phone..........................4 C3
Public Phone..........................5 C2
Public Phone..........................6 C1

SIGHTS & ACTIVITIES
Corozal Museum....................7 C2

SLEEPING 🏠
Corozal Guest House...............8 C2
Hotel Maya.............................9 A4
Las Palmas............................10 C2
Maya World Guest House.....11 D1

EATING 🍴
Cactus Plaza.........................12 B3
Chon Saan Palace.................13 C2
Marcelo's Pizza......................14 D1
Patty's Bistro.........................15 D1

DRINKING 🍷
Purple Toucan.......................16 D1

TRANSPORT
Boats to Cerros Archaeological
   Site....................................17 A4
Taxi Stand.............................18 C2
Taxi Stand.............................19 C2
Thunderbolt Travels Dock.....20 D2

BELIZE

which have remained mysteriously clear of vegetation through the ages.

This small site is located on a peninsula 3.5 miles south of Corozal across the bay. Most people catch a boat to the site, but you can drive there on a rough dirt road. Tours (approximately US$25 per person including guide) can be arranged through your hotel. You can also charter a boat (US$50) or arrange for a fisherman to take you over to the site to explore independently. The boat trip takes about 15 minutes; then you walk 10 minutes to the site.

Sleeping

Corozal Guest House (☎ 402 0634; 22 6th Ave; r US$22) There's a lot to be said for not staying in the

cheapest place in town, and this place says it all.

Maya World Guest House (☎ 624 4979; simple88 elegance@yahoo.ca; 16 2nd St N; s/d with bathroom US$22/28) The big, simple rooms here are by far the best budget deal in town. Upstairs, there's a breeze and good sitting areas. Downstairs the rooms have bathrooms. All go for the same price.

Hotel Maya (☎ 422 2082; www.hotelmaya.net; 7th Ave; r with bathroom US$32) On the main road between 9th and 10th Sts S, this is the long-time budget favorite. Breakfast is available and bikes rent for US$10 per day.

Las Palmas (☎ 422 0196; www.hotellaspalmas.com; 123 5th Ave S; r with bathroom from US$45) The old Nestor's, this place has been chintzed beyond recognition – floral bedspreads, big bathrooms etc. The ground-floor rooms can get a little airless.

Eating

Marcelo's Pizza (25 4th Ave; mains US$5-8; ☺ breakfast, lunch & dinner; ☒) Marcello's sells very cheesy pizzas (to match the décor, perhaps?), burgers (US$2.50) and Belizean dishes in sweet air-con luxury.

Cactus Plaza (6 6th St S; mains US$6-12; ☺ dinner Wed-Sun) This place serves some excellent, authentic Mexican dishes, such as tacos, *salbutes* (stuffed tortilla) and *panuchos* (fried tortilla spread with black bean paste and toppings) in a bright, clean environment.

Chon Saan Palace (5th Av; mains US$6-15; ☺ lunch & dinner) It's the best Chinese restaurant in town, with a long menu and some pleasant decorations.

Patty's Bistro (13 4th Ave N; meals US$8-12; ☺ lunch & dinner) Serves up some of the best home cooking in town, with walls covered in graffiti from satisfied diners.

Drinking & Nightlife

Cactus Plaza (6 6th St S) A lively spot for drinks. Most of the action happens on the sidewalk out front, but the disco inside gets pumping on weekends.

Purple Toucan (52 4th Ave) In the running for the title of seediest joint in town, this is midway between bar, disco and pool hall. The beer garden out the back is good for a drink or two.

Getting There & Away

Corozal has its own airstrip, about 1 mile (1.6km) south of the town center, reached by taxi (US$5). It's only an airstrip, with no shelter or services. Taxis meet all incoming flights.

Maya Island Air (☎ 422 2333; mayaairways.com) and **Tropic Air** (☎ 422 0356; www.tropicair.com) each have three flights daily between Corozal and San Pedro on Ambergris Caye (US$39 one-way, 20 minutes). From San Pedro you connect with flights to Belize City and beyond.

Boats operated by **Thunderbolt Travels** (☎ 422 0026) departs Corozal at 7am and 3pm daily for San Pedro. One-way fares are US$22.50.

Buses leave Corozal and head south via Orange Walk (US$2.50, one hour) to Belize City (US$6, three hours) at least every hour from 4am to 7:30pm, with extra buses in the morning.

WESTERN BELIZE

This region doesn't really jibe with your classic image of Belize. Out here, the largely unspoilt landscape is dotted with caves, mountain peaks rising to over 3000ft (900m), waterfalls and Maya sites. There are plenty of opportunities for exploration.

STARTING WEST ON THE WESTERN HIGHWAY

Heading west from Belize City along Cemetery Rd, you'll pass right through Lords Ridge Cemetery and soon find yourself on the Western Hwy. In 15 miles (25km) you'll pass Hattieville, founded in 1961 after Hurricane Hattie wreaked destruction on Belize City, and in another 13 miles (21km) you'll come to the Belize Zoo.

Belize Zoo & Tropical Education Centre

In natural surroundings on 29 acres (12 hectares), the **Belize Zoo & Tropical Education Centre** (☎ 220 8004; www.belizezoo.org; Mile 29, Western Hwy; adult/child US$8/4; ☺ 8:30am-5pm except major holidays) displays native wildlife. On a self-guided tour (45 to 60 minutes) you'll see over 125 native animals, including jaguars, ocelots, howler monkeys, peccaries, vultures, storks, crocodiles, tapirs and *gibnuts*. The zoo is on the north side of the highway (a sign marks the turnoff).

Competing for customers just west of the zoo on the Western Hwy are **Cheers** (Km 50 Western Hwy) and **Amigo's** (Km 52 Western Hwy). Each serves Belizean, Mexican and American dishes accompanied by ice-cold Belikins, all at moderate prices.

Guanacaste National Park

Further west down the highway, at the junction with Hummingbird Hwy, is **Guanacaste National Park** (admission US$2.50; ☺ 8am-4:30pm), a small 52-acre (21-hectare) nature reserve at the confluence of Roaring Creek and the Belize River.

A hike along the park's 2 miles (3km) of trails will introduce you to the abundant and colorful local birdlife. After your hike, you can head down to the Belize River for a dip in the park's good, deep swimming hole.

Getting Around

Buses run at least hourly along the Western Hwy and upon request will drop you at the zoo,

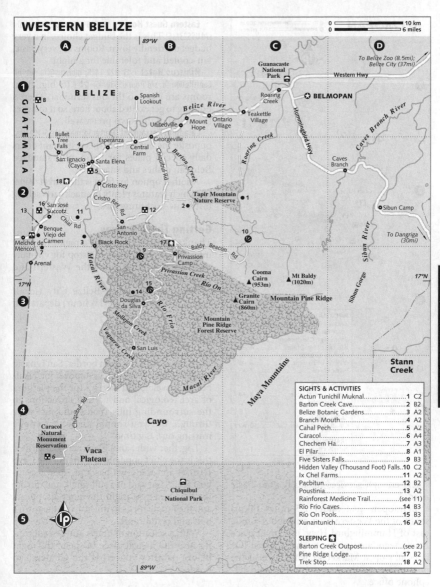

WESTERN BELIZE

SIGHTS & ACTIVITIES
Actun Tunichil Muknal	1 C2
Barton Creek Cave	2 B2
Belize Botanic Gardens	3 A2
Branch Mouth	4 A2
Cahal Pech	5 A2
Caracol	6 A4
Chechem Ha	7 A3
El Pilar	8 A1
Five Sisters Falls	9 B3
Hidden Valley (Thousand Foot) Falls	10 C2
Ix Chel Farms	11 A2
Pacbitun	12 B2
Poustinia	13 A2
Rainforest Medicine Trail	(see 11)
Río Frio Caves	14 B3
Río On Pools	15 B3
Xunantunich	16 A2

SLEEPING
Barton Creek Outpost	(see 2)
Pine Ridge Lodge	17 B2
Trek Stop	18 A2

by Guanacaste National Park, or anywhere else along the highway, and at Belmopan.

BELMOPAN
pop 15,900

Travelers arriving in Belize's capital are faced with that most basic of all existential questions: What am I doing here? Thankfully,

the town provides a ready answer: changing buses.

Founded in 1961 after Hurricane Hattie wiped out much of Belize City, the idea (hey – let's all pack up and move to the middle of nowhere with a bunch of public servants) hasn't really caught on yet. There are embassies, government buildings and, if you do get

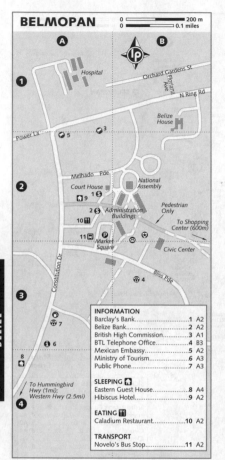

BELIZE

stuck, enough services to satisfy your basic needs.

Belmopan, just under 2.5 miles (4km) south of the Western Hwy and about a mile east of Hummingbird Hwy, is a small place easily negotiated on foot. The regional bus lines all stop at Market Sq, which is near the post office, police station, market and telephone office.

Belize Bank (Constitution Dr) Has an ATM that accepts international cards.

Internet Café (☼ 8am-8pm; per hr US$2.50) In the bus station, it's as good a place as any to while away your time.

Sleeping & Eating

Belmopan is a town for bureaucrats and diplomats, not one for budget travelers.

Eastern Guest House (☎ 623 6066; Constitution Dr; s/d US$23/35) This is the budget choice, in a very budget unfriendly town. Rooms are very basic, fan-cooled and tolerable for a night.

Hibiscus Hotel (☎ 822 1418; hibiscus@btl.net; off Constitution Dr; s/d from US$30/45; ✷) Its big, clean rooms are close to the bus terminal. There's nothing to get excited about here, so it matches the mood of the town pretty well.

Caladium Restaurant (Market Sq; mains US$5-10) Just opposite the bus station, this restaurant offers daily special plates for US$4, plus standard Belizean dishes and snacks.

Another option for food is the **market** (Market Sq), which features plenty of snack carts selling tasty, low-cost munchies.

Getting There & Away

Thanks to its location near a major highway intersection, Belmopan is a stop for virtually all buses operating along the Western and Hummingbird Hwys.

Buses to and from Belize City (local/express US$3/4.50, one/1¼ hour) depart half hourly.

SAN IGNACIO (CAYO)
pop 18,300

Way out near the western border, San Ignacio would be little more than a stopover for Tikal-bound travelers if it weren't for the plethora of archaeological and natural attractions in the surrounding hills. You could just whiz through, but you should know that you're missing out. Big time.

Together with Santa Elena across the river, this is the chief population center of the Cayo District and the town has a prosperous, up-beat feel. That said, it's still small, and during the day, quiet. At night the quiet disappears and the jungle rocks to music from the town's bars and restaurants.

With a selection of hotels and restaurants, it's also the logical place to spend the night before or after you cross the Guatemalan border.

Orientation

San Ignacio is west of the river; Santa Elena is to the east. Two bridges join the towns and are usually both one-way – the newer, northern-most bridge leads traffic into San Ignacio, and Hawkesworth Bridge, San Ignacio's landmark suspension bridge, leads traffic out of town. During the rainy season, however, the new bridge often floods, and traffic is diverted to Hawkesworth Bridge. Burns Ave is the town's main street. Almost everything in town is accessible on foot.

Information

There is a small BTB office with irregular hours in the market square.

Belize Bank (Burns Ave; 8am-1pm Mon-Thu, 8am-1pm & 3-6pm Fri) has a Visa and MasterCard ATM and changes traveler's checks, as do restaurants and hotels. Atlantic Bank is also on Burns Ave.

The **post office** (8am-noon & 1-5pm Mon-Fri, 8am-1pm Sat) is on the upper floor of Government House, near the bridge.

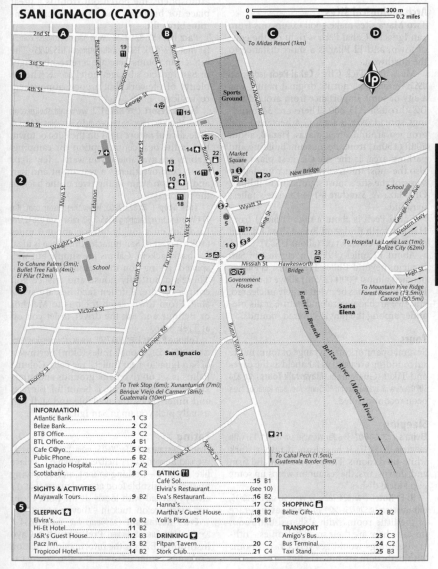

SAN IGNACIO (CAYO)

0   300 m
0   0.2 miles

To Midas Resort (1km)
Sports Ground
Market Square
New Bridge
School
To Hospital La Loma Luz (1mi); Belize City (62mi)
Hawkesworth Bridge
Government House
Missiah St
To Mountain Pine Ridge Forest Reserve (13.5mi); Caracol (50.5mi)
Santa Elena
Eastern Branch
Belize River (Macal River)
San Ignacio
To Cohune Palms (3mi); Bullet Tree Falls (4mi); El Pilar (12mi)
To Trek Stop (6mi); Xunantunich (7mi); Benque Viejo del Carmen (8mi); Guatemala (10mi)
To Cahal Pech (1.5mi); Guatemala Border (9mi)

BELIZE

INFORMATION	
Atlantic Bank	1 C3
Belize Bank	2 C2
BTB Office	3 C2
BTL Office	4 B1
Cafe C@yo	5 C2
Public Phone	6 B2
San Ignacio Hospital	7 A2
Scotiabank	8 C3

SIGHTS & ACTIVITIES	
Mayawalk Tours	9 B2

SLEEPING	
Elvira's	10 B2
Hi-Et Hotel	11 B2
J&R's Guest House	12 B3
Pacz Inn	13 B2
Tropicool Hotel	14 B2

EATING	
Café Sol	15 B1
Elvira's Restaurant	(see 10)
Eva's Restaurant	16 B2
Hanna's	17 C2
Martha's Guest House	18 B2
Yoli's Pizza	19 B1

DRINKING	
Pitpan Tavern	20 C2
Stork Club	21 C4

SHOPPING	
Belize Gifts	22 B2

TRANSPORT	
Amigo's Bus	23 C3
Bus Terminal	24 C2
Taxi Stand	25 B3

Cafe C@yo (4 Burns Ave; per hr US$3) offers internet access, shows movies on Monday nights and serves up some yummy sandwiches and Italian food.

The basic San Ignacio Hospital is up the hill off Waight's Ave, west of the center. Across the river in Santa Elena is Hospital La Loma Luz.

Archaeological Sites

Two Maya sites make good excursions from San Ignacio. Cahal Pech is right on the edge of town, and El Pilar is a short distance to the northwest.

Maya for 'Tick City,' **Cahal Pech** (admission US$5; ☼ 6am-6pm), not its original name, was a city of some importance from around 900 BC through AD 800. There are 34 buildings spread over 6 acres (2.4 hectares) and grouped around seven plazas. **Plaza B**, about 500ft (150m) from the museum building and parking area, is the site's largest plaza and also the most impressive. It's surrounded by some of the site's most significant buildings. Off Plaza A, **Structure A-1** is the site's tallest pyramid.

Cahal Pech is about a mile (1.6km) from Hawkesworth Bridge off Buena Vista Rd. You can walk or catch a taxi (about US$3).

About 12 miles (19km) northwest of San Ignacio, beyond Bullet Tree Falls, **El Pilar** is perched almost 900ft (275m) above the Belize River. El Pilar has been left largely uncleared, and five archaeological and nature trails meander among the jungle-covered mounds.

Tours

Several operators offer a range of tours in the surrounding area and as far afield as the cayes and Tikal, Guatemala. **Mayawalk Tours** (☎ 824 3070; www.mayawalk.com; 19 Burns Ave, San Ignacio) has been recommended.

Sleeping

Elvira's (☎ 804 0243; 6 Far West St; s/d US$11/13, with bathroom US$14/17) It has clean, if rather stark white-tiled rooms. The beds are new and firm and, downstairs, the restaurant whips up some good local dishes.

Hi-Et Hotel (☎ 824 2828; 12 West St; s/d US$10/15, with bathroom US$20/25; ✗) The one saving grace of the little rooms with a shared bathroom upstairs here are their small balconies – otherwise things would get very close. Rooms with bathroom are much better.

Tropicool Hotel (☎ 824 3052; 30A Burns Ave; s/d US$12/15, cabins US$30) The rooms in the main building are nothing special – clean enough, with good beds (and, for some reason, dart board), but the wooden cabins out back are a good deal.

J&R's Guest House (☎ 824 2502; 20 Far West St; s/d US$12.50/20) A modern home with a family atmosphere, the porch out front is a great place for breakfast and to watch the hummingbirds flit.

Pacz Inn (☎ 824 4538; www.paczguesthouse.com; 4 Far West St; s/d US$15/20, with bathroom US$20/25) The big, clean rooms here are a refreshing sight in San Ignacio's budget-hotel scene. There's plenty of tilework, but a good atmosphere regardless.

Midas Resort (☎ 824 3172; www.midasbelize.com; Branch Mouth Rd; camping per person US$4, cabins US$43) A little slice of nature right on the edge of town, this is the best central option for camping. Cabins are available if you want a few steps up in comfort; there's a restaurant and bar, and you can swim in the river at the back of the property.

Trek Stop (☎ 823 2265; www.thetrekstop.com; Km 114 Western Hwy; camping US$5/7.50, cabins s/d US$12/20) Laid out on a jungly hillside about 6 miles (10km) west of San Ignacio, this place is ideal for backpackers. Cabins are simple but well spaced, giving you the feeling of seclusion. There's a butterfly house and frisbee golf course on site. Kitchen facilities are available. From town, catch the bus to Melchor or Benque and ask the driver to let you off at Trek Stop.

Cohune Palms (☎ 600 7508; www.cohunepalms.com; cabins US$35-55) About 3 miles (5km) northwest of San Ignacio, near Bullet Tree Falls, Cohune Palms is set on riverbank grounds and offers kitchen access. The site is beautiful. Bicycles and inner tubes are available and staff can usually pick you up in San Ignacio.

Eating

Elvira's Restaurant (6 Far West St; mains US$4-6; ☼ breakfast, lunch & dinner) Every Belizean town has a place like Elvira's – nothing to look at, but serving up such irresistible food at good prices that it's always packed with locals. If the pork chops and mash are on, tuck in – they're a treat.

Eva's Restaurant (22 Burns Ave; mains US$4-7; ☼ breakfast, lunch & dinner) Pretty much a Cayo institution, Eva's is the informal information exchange center in town. It's also where expats gather to bitch about Belize, their own country and lots of other things.

Hanna's (5 Burns Ave; meals US$4-7; ☾ lunch, dinner) Hanna's menu just keeps on growing, and cooks serve consistently good food at reasonable prices. Most of your Belizean faves are here, plus a good range of Asian and vegetarian dishes.

Café Sol (West St; meals from US$5; ☾ breakfast, lunch & dinner) The Sol has the most imaginative menu in town, with plenty of vegetarian options and excellent coffee. Grab a table on the balcony out front and watch the world go by.

Yoli's Pizza (Simpson St; pizzas US$10-15, slices US$1.50-2; ☾ lunch & dinner) With a mellow little courtyard eating area out front, this neighborhood pizzeria gets the thumbs up from expats as the best pizza in town.

Drinking & Nightlife

Pitpan Tavern (10 Savannah St) The name may have changed, but the deal remains the same – a happy hour from 5 to 7pm, reggae bands, drunk locals and drunker foreigners.

Stork Club (18 Buena Vista St; admission US$2.50-7.50; ☾ Thu-Sat) Inside the supersnazzy San Ignacio Resort Hotel, this disco consistently comes to life when the bars empty out. Wear something nice – but not too nice.

Getting There & Away

Buses from San Ignacio's Market Sq run to and from Belize City (local/express US$5/7, two/three hours) and Belmopan (local/express US$2/3, 1½ hours/45 mins) nearly every half hour.

See the boxed text (p249) for travel to Benque Viejo del Carmen and onwards to Guatemala.

Amigo's Bus (☎ 622 0283; 1 Western Hwy, Santa Elena) has 1st-class buses running to Chetumal, Mexico (US$20, four hours), Belize City (US$10, two hours) and Flores, Guatemala (US$15, three hours). Staff can also book 1st-class bus tickets from Flores to Guatemala City.

The taxi stand is located on the traffic circle opposite Government House. Rates can be surprisingly high for short trips (a trip of a few miles can easily cost US$5 to US$10).

MOUNTAIN PINE RIDGE AREA

South of the Western Hwy, between Belmopan and the Guatemalan border, the land begins to climb toward the heights of the Maya Mountains, which separate the Cayo District

from the Stann Creek District to the east and the Toledo District to the south.

In the heart of this highland area – a land of macaws, mahogany, mangoes and jaguars – over 300 sq miles (777 sq km) of tropical pine forest has been set aside as the **Mountain Pine Ridge Forest Reserve**. The reserve and its surrounding area are full of rivers, pools, waterfalls and caves to explore.

Rainforest Medicine Trail

This herbal-cure research center is at **Ix Chel Farms** (admission US$5; ☾ 8am-noon & 1-5pm), 8 miles (13km) southwest of San Ignacio up Chial Rd.

Dr Eligio Pantí, who died in 1996 at age 103, was a healer in San Antonio village who used traditional Maya herb cures. Dr Rosita Arvigo, an American, studied medicinal plants with Dr Pantí, then began several projects to spread the wisdom of traditional healing methods and to preserve the rain-forest habitats, which harbor an incredible 4000 plant species.

One of her projects was the establishment of the **Rainforest Medicine Trail**, a self-guiding path among the jungle's natural cures.

Caves

If you want to visit any of the following caves you'll have to join a tour. Ask at your hotel or **Mayawalk Tours** (opposite).

The **Río Frio Caves** are the region's most-visited and famous caverns, but gaining in popularity is **Barton Creek Cave** (tours around US$35 per person). One of the more popular day trips offered out of San Ignacio, the cave holds spooky skulls and bones, and pottery shards from the ancient Maya. To see them you'll have to negotiate some very narrow passages.

Attracting the most raving recommendations is **Actun Tunichil Muknal** (around US$80 per person). In an effort to prevent looting of the Maya bones and artifacts within, and to keep general wear and tear to a minimum, only a couple of tour operators are allowed to run tours here at this point.

Pools & Waterfalls

At **Río On Pools**, small waterfalls connect a series of pools that the river has carved out of granite boulders. Some of the falls double as water slides. The pools at tranquil **Five Sisters Falls**, accessible by an outdoor-elevator ride (small charge, usually US$2) at Five Sisters Lodge,

BELIZE

are connected by five falls cascading over a short drop-off.

The region's aquatic highlight is **Hidden Valley (or Thousand Foot) Falls**, southeast of San Antonio. Hiking trails surround the falls and a viewing platform at the top of the cascade is a great spot for catching a Mountain Pine Ridge vista. The falls actually are around 1500ft (450m) high, but they aren't spectacular in the dry season.

Archaeological Sites

The highlands here hold two Maya ruins of interest, one small and one huge.

Pacbitun, a small site, 12 miles (20km) south of San Ignacio via Cristo Rey Rd, near San Antonio, seems to have been occupied continuously through most of Maya history, from 900 BC to AD 900. Today only lofty **Plaza A** has been uncovered and partially consolidated. **Structures 1 and 2**, on the east and west sides of the plaza, respectively, are worth a look. Within them, archaeologists discovered the graves of noble Maya women buried with a variety of musical instruments, perhaps played at their funerals.

Some 53 miles (86km) south of San Ignacio via Chiquibul Rd lies **Caracol** (admission US$8; 8am-5pm) a vast Maya city hidden in the jungle. The site encompasses some 35 sq miles (88 sq km), with 36,000 structures marked so far.

Caracol was occupied in the post-Classic period from around 300 BC until AD 1150. At its height, between AD 650 and 700, Caracol is thought to have had a population of 150,000 –

not much less than the entire population of Belize today.

Highlights of the site include **Caana** (Sky-Palace) in Plaza B, Caracol's tallest structure at 138ft (42m; reportedly still Belize's tallest building); the **Temple of the Wooden Lintel**, dating from AD 50, in Plaza A; the **ball court** with a marker commemorating Caracol's defeat of rivals Tikal in AD 562 and Naranjo in AD 631; and the central acropolis, containing a royal **tomb**.

Sleeping

The forests and mountains of the greater Mountain Pine Ridge area are dotted with small inns, lodges and ranches offering accommodations, meals, hiking, horseback trips, caving, swimming, bird-watching and similar outdoor activities.

Barton Creek Outpost (662 4797; www.bartoncreek outpost.com; per person US$5, camping free) In a country full of gorgeous places, this one shines. Nestled in a riverbend about 200m from the Barton Creek Cave (see p247), it's the sort of place you come for a day and stay for a week. Accommodation is basic – a mattress on the floor or a hammock, but a little discomfort is definitely worthwhile. Good simple meals are available. For transport here, get in touch with Cafe C@yo in San Ignacio (p245).

There's very little else on offer for the budget traveler; if you've got a group together, **Pine Ridge Lodge** (600 4557; www.pineridgelodge .com; 4-person cottages US$104) is about your best bet. The cottages have no electricity, but have hot-water bathrooms, screened porches and romantic, kerosene lamp lighting.

To get to this area, either join a tour or get the hotel you are staying at to pick you up. Otherwise, you'll need to organize your own transport.

WEST TO GUATEMALA

From San Ignacio it's another 10 miles (16km) southwest down Western Hwy to the Guatemalan border.

Xunantunich

Belize's most accessible Maya site of significance, **Xunantunich** (admission US$5; 7:30am-4pm), pronounced soo-*nahn*-too-neech, is reached via a free ferry crossing at San José Succotz, about 7 miles (12km) west of San Ignacio. From the ferry it's a 1-mile walk (2km) uphill to the ruins.

EXPLORE MORE OF WESTERN BELIZE

Western Belize has plenty of opportunities for getting off the beaten track. Here's just a few:

- **Branch Mouth** is a local swimming spot 20 minutes walk from San Ignacio where the Macal and Mopan Rivers meet
- Take a mellow canoe ride from San Ignacio to the **Belize Botanic Gardens**, a sanctuary, boasting 400 tree species and over 160 types of orchid
- The outdoor sculpture park of **Poustinia** has works by international and local artists

---

GETTING TO TIKAL, GUATEMALA

Buses run from San Ignacio to **Benque Viejo del Carmen**, the border town for crossing into Guatemala, nearly every half hour. From the bus station, it's another 3km to the border. A taxi will cost US$5.

Cross early in the morning to have the best chance of catching buses onward. Get your passport (and, if applicable, your car papers) stamped at the Belizean station, then cross into Guatemala. The border station is supposedly open 24 hours a day, but try to cross during daylight hours. If you need a Guatemalan visa or tourist card (see p212), obtain it before you reach the border.

A bank at either side of the border changes money, but the itinerant moneychangers often give you a better deal – for US cash. The rates for exchanging Belizean dollars to Guatemalan quetzals and vice versa are sometimes poor.

Both Transportes Pinita and Transportes Rosalita buses westward to **Santa Elena–Flores (Guatemala)** depart town the Guatemalan side early in the morning. Sometimes available are more comfortable – and more expensive – minibuses (US$6 per person); many travelers feel this is money well spent.

To go on to **Tikal**, get off the bus at El Cruce (Puente Ixlú), 22 miles (36km) east of Flores, and wait for another bus, minibus or obliging car or truck to take you the final 21 miles (35km) north to Tikal.

See p201 for information on crossing the border from Guatemala.

The site's dominant structure, **El Castillo** (Structure A-6), rises 130ft (40m) above the jungle floor. The stairway on its northern side – the side you approach from the courtyard – goes only as far as the temple building. To climb to the **roof comb** you must go around to the southern side and use a separate set of steps. On the temple's east side, a few of the masks that once surrounded the structure have been restored. Structure A-11 and Plaza A-3, formed a residential 'palace' area for the ruling family.

Guides can be hired for a one-hour tour for US$13, but the site can easily be navigated independently.

Buses on their way between San Ignacio and Benque Viejo del Carmen will drop you at the ferry. Ferry hours are 8am to noon and 1pm to 5pm; crossing is on demand and free for both foot passengers and cars.

Benque Viejo del Carmen

A sleepy town 2 miles (3km) east of the Guatemalan border, Benque Viejo del Carmen has few services for travelers, and you're better off staying in San Ignacio (p244). The town stirs from its normal tropical somnolence in mid-July, when the **Benque Viejo Festival** brings three days of revelry. Buses run to and from Belize City nearly every 30 minutes (local/express US$4/6, 2½/three hours).

Chechem Ha

This **Maya cave** (☎ 820 4063; US$20 per person; ☼ tours 9:30am & 1:30pm) comes complete with ancient cer-

emonial pots. Members of the Morales family, who discovered the cave, act as guides, leading you up the steep slope to the cave mouth, then down inside to see what the Maya left. Call ahead to reserve a space and enquire about getting a ride here from San Ignacio. Bring strong shoes, take water and a flashlight.

You can camp at Chechem Ha or sleep in one of the simple **bunks** (per person incl meals US$40).

SOUTHERN BELIZE

Often overlooked by travelers, the south has its fair share of charms. Well worth a look are the Garífuna towns of Dangriga and Hopkins, as are the remote but budget-friendly cayes at Tobacco Caye and Glover's Reef, which is great for diving and snorkeling.

Down south, Placencia draws the crowds, but remains low-key in all but absolute peak season. Punta Gorda is the jumping off point for the little visited Toledo district, home of unrestored ruins, natural wonders and traditional villages.

HUMMINGBIRD HIGHWAY

Heading southeast from Belmopan, the Hummingbird Hwy stretches 49 miles (79km) to the junction of the Southern Hwy and the turnoff to Dangriga. It is almost entirely paved, but be prepared to slow for roadwork or sudden transitions to dirt road.

BELIZE

BELIZE

LOCAL VOICES – AUSTIN RODRIGUEZ, GARÍFUNA DRUM MAKER

The drum is at the center of Garífuna music and music is at the center of their culture. Who better, then, to give us the lowdown on the Garífuna than the man who makes the drums?

■ **When did you start making drums?** I've been doing this for 35 years. Nobody taught me. I just started looking at drums, seeing how they were made. Then I started making them.

■ **Garífuna music seems to be growing...** Out in the world, yes. We've always had our music, our musicians, but yes, internationally it's becoming more known. Punta Rock is well known now, and that's a modern expression of our rhythms, even though other Central Americans are taking credit for it.

■ **Garífuna culture was in trouble for a while. Is it making a comeback?** It never went anywhere. Some parts of the culture have always been strong – the music, the food. When we came from St Vincent's we brought the seeds. Whenever we moved, we took seeds so we could eat our food. What we *are* losing is the language. For a long time the Creoles banned kids from speaking Garífuna in school, so the only way to learn was to speak it at home. Now it's not so open, but that attitude's still there. The Creoles want us to disappear, or assimilate.

■ **Traditional cultures sometimes have trouble adapting to modern times...** The Garífuna were always fishers and farmers, but that's changing. When everybody produced, everybody traded. It produced a caring attitude. When somebody died, the whole village grieved. When somebody needed help on their farm, everybody helped. When a child was misbehaving, the village took care of it. There was a culture of respect. Now it's different – we're all individuals. Nobody has time for each other, and we're losing the unity.

■ **If you could say one thing to your people?** I'd say to stay strong. Keep singing the songs and keep the language alive. If we lose that we lose everything.

As told to Lucas Vidgen

Blue Hole National Park

The **Blue Hole** – focus of the like-named **national park** (admission US$4; ☷ 8am-4pm) – is a cenote (*se-noh-tay*; water-filled limestone sinkhole) some 328ft (100m) in diameter and 108ft (33m) deep. Fed by underground tributaries of the Sibun River, it's deliciously cool on the hottest days and makes an excellent swimming hole.

The park visitors center is about 11 miles (18km) south of Belmopan on Hummingbird Hwy. At the center is the trailhead to **St Herman's Cave**, a large cavern once used by the Maya during the Classic period. This is one of the few caves in Belize you can visit independently, although a guide is required if you wish to venture in further than 150 yards. Also here are a series of nature trails and an observation tower.

The trail to the Blue Hole itself starts at a parking area about a mile further down the highway. (Car break-ins have been reported here, so be careful with your belongings.) You don't have to stop at the visitors center if you're just going for a swim; an attendant is posted at the trail to the Blue Hole to collect your money.

DANGRIGA

pop 11,500

Dangriga is the largest town in southern Belize. Much smaller than Belize City, it's friendlier and quieter and a great place to get amid the Garífuna culture. The best time to do this is November 19, which is **Garífuna Settlement Day**, a frenzy of dancing, drinking and celebration of the Garífuna's heritage. For the rest of the year you'll find the folks here a bit more laid-back, but equally welcoming. As the sun goes down and the Belikins come out, the air fills with the sounds of Garífuna drumming and the lilting tones of the Garífuna language.

Orientation & Information

Stann Creek empties into the Gulf of Honduras at the center of town. Dangriga's main street is called St Vincent St south of the creek and Commerce St to the north. The bus station is at the southern end of Havana St just north of the Shell fuel station. The airstrip is a mile (2km) north of the center, near the Pelican Beach Resort. The Riverside Café serves as the unofficial water-taxi terminal where you can arrange trips out to the southern cayes with local fishermen or tradespeople. It's best to stop in by 10am to find out when boats will be leaving.

Belize Bank (24 St Vincent St; 8am-1pm Mon-Thu, 8am-4:30pm Fri) has a Visa and MasterCard ATM.

You can get your clothes washed and check your email at the same time at **Val's Laundry** (1 Sharp St). A load costs US$1 per pound, an hour on the internet costs US$2.

Sights

Eight miles (13km) northwest of town on Melinda Rd is **Marie Sharp's Factory** (520 2087; 7am-noon & 1-4pm), the source of Belize's beloved hot sauce. Casual tours, often led by

Marie herself, are offered during business hours.

The **Gulisi Garífuna Museum** (Stann Creek Valley Rd; admission US$5; noon-7pm Tue-Fri, 8am-2pm Sat) provides an excellent overview of the vibrant Garífuna culture in photographs, film and music. Workshops and language courses are held here. It's about 1.2 miles inland from the bus station – any bus leaving town can drop you here.

Sleeping & Eating

Val's (623 1949; valsbelize@yahoo.com; 1 Sharp St; dm US$7.50, apt US$25;) Val had fans from all over the world back when she just had a laundry. Then she put in internet access. Then dorm rooms. Then a mini-apartment. Go Val. The

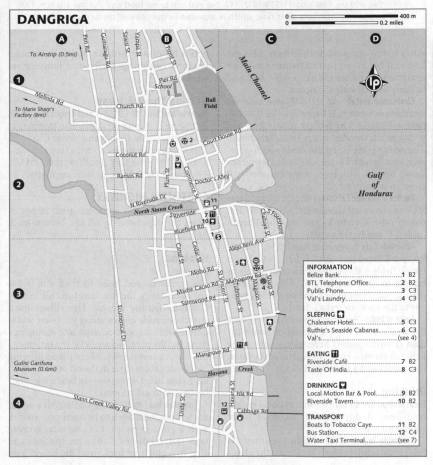

DANGRIGA

0 — 400 m
0 — 0.2 miles

To Airstrip (0.5mi)

To Marie Sharp's Factory (8mi)

Pier Rd School

Ball Field

Main Channel

Gulf of Honduras

North Stann Creek

Gulisi Garífuna Museum (0.6mi)

Havana Creek

INFORMATION	
Belize Bank.....................................1	B2
BTL Telephone Office....................2	B2
Public Phone..................................3	C3
Val's Laundry.................................4	C3

SLEEPING	
Chaleanor Hotel............................5	C3
Ruthie's Seaside Cabanas.............6	C3
Val's..(see 4)	

EATING	
Riverside Café...............................7	B2
Taste Of India...............................8	C3

DRINKING	
Local Motion Bar & Pool..............9	B2
Riverside Tavern.........................10	B2

TRANSPORT	
Boats to Tobacco Caye................11	B2
Bus Station..................................12	C4
Water Taxi Terminal................(see 7)	

BELIZE

TOBACCO CAYE, SOUTH WATER CAYE & GLOVER'S REEF

Tobacco Caye, South Water Caye and the resorts of Glover's Reef are all accessed by boat from Dangriga. Their distance from Belize City has kept casual visitors away, protecting the reef from much human impact. Dolphins, manta rays and manatees are commonly sighted, and the quantity and variety of coral that is on display is incredible. Good snorkeling and diving can be had right off the shore from the cayes.

Tobacco Caye is a 5-acre (2-hectare) island catering to travelers on a low-to-moderate budget. Diving, fishing, snorkeling and hammocking are the favorite pastimes here. Lodging possibilities include **Lana's** (☎ 520 5036; d with shared bathroom incl 3 meals per person US$30), which has 10 spartan rooms; and **Gaviota's** (☎ 509 5032) with rooms for about the same price.

Passage to Tobacco Caye can be arranged along the river near the Riverside Café in Dangriga. The cost is around US$18 one-way.

Glover's Atoll Resort (☎ 520 5016; www.glovers.com.bz; camping/dm/cabins per week US$106/160/213), on Glover's Reef's Northeast Caye, offers budget accommodations on a 9-acre (3.6-hectare) atoll about 20 miles (32km) from the mainland. Facilities at the resort are rustic, but the 360-degree Caribbean view can't be beat. It's a good deal for budget travelers, but extras – water, food, equipment – can add up. Meals cost US$9 to US$12, but you can bring food and use the kitchen. Call ahead or email to arrange a boat ride, which is included in the price of the accommodation.

---

dorm rooms are good, with lockers, fans galore and big clean shared bathrooms. The apartment has a sofa, sink, double bed and balcony overlooking the ocean.

Chaleanor Hotel (☎ 522 2587; www.toucantrail .com/chaleanor-hotel.html; 35 Magoon St; s/d US$11/18, with bathroom US$30/50) The budget rooms here are pretty much wooden boxes (with window!). The saving grace being the shady rooftop terrace, strung with hammocks and offering sea views. Rooms with bathrooms are about 10 steps up in comfort.

Ruthie's Seaside Cabanas (☎ 522 3184; cnr Magoon St & Yemeri Rd; s/d with bathroom US$23/28) Clean and comfy cabins, right by the seaside. There's cable TV and hot showers.

Riverside Café (S Riverside Dr; mains US$5-8; ☼ breakfast, lunch & dinner) Just east of the North Stann Creek Bridge, this café serves tasty meals at budget to moderate prices. This is a good place to ask about fishing and snorkeling trips out to the cayes or treks inland.

Taste of India (28 St Vincent St; mains US$5-10; ☼ lunch & dinner Mon-Sat) A huge selection of South Indian favorites awaits here, along with some Belizean classics. Heaps of vegetarian options, tasty lassis and a reasonable chai.

Drinking

Local Motion Bar & Pool (Commerce St) Loud music, cold beer, dodgy characters…what more could you want?

Riverside Tavern (St Vincent St) Just south of the bridge, this club (known locally as 'the club')

gets a bit of a crowd for midweek karaoke sessions, but things really start jumping on weekends.

Getting There & Away

Maya Island Air (☎ 522 2659) and **Tropic Air** (☎ 226 2012) serve Dangriga on flights also stopping at Placencia, Punta Gorda and Belize City.

Boats service the local cayes (see above).

Buses to Belize City (local/express US$5/7, 4½ hours) via Belmopan leave regularly.

SOUTHERN HIGHWAY

South of Dangriga are some great opportunities for experiencing off-the-beaten-track Belize.

Hopkins
pop 1800

The words 'hi' and 'hello' fly thick and fast as you walk along the one street of this mainly Garífuna fishing village. The village itself stretches a mile or two along the coast and is dotted with accommodation and eating options, but the pace is leisurely (in the extreme) – this is not a resort town. Many places offering beachside cabins close in the off season. If you have your heart set on staying beachside, your best bet is to ask around.

Yagudah Inn (☎ 503 7089; s/d US$10/15) It's one of the few places in town to be open year-round, with a good restaurant at the side, serving tasty seafood dishes. Rooms are spacious and airy, in a block set back from the beach. You can set up your tent on the beachfront for US$7.50 a person.

Ransom's (www.members.tripod.com/~cabanabelize; s/d US$15/30) Oozing with charm and bursting with plant life, this little beachfront place has a few well-decorated rooms and a fully equipped cabin out back.

Windschief (☎ 523 7249; www.windschief.com; big/small cabin US$25/45) It has big, wooden cabin-style rooms with sea views. There's a cocktail bar, hammocks, discount for long stays, windsurfers for rent and Hopkins' only (so far) full-moon parties.

Most restaurants serve good, inexpensive seafood and Belizean dishes, including *gibnut* (small rodent similar to a guinea pig) from around US$5. Try Iris's, the Watering Hole or Innie's.

King Kassava at the north end of town is the place to go for beer, play pool and reggae music.

Buses pass four times a day in either direction to Placencia (US$3, two hours) and Dangriga (US$3, one hour).

Sittee River

Another small coastal village where you can get away from it all is Sittee River. **Glover's Atoll Bunkhouse** (☎ 509 7099; dm US$10, d with bathroom US$30) is where the boat to Glover's Reef picks up passengers. Next door is the more gracious, good-value **Toucan Sittee** (☎ 523 7039; www.toucan sittee.info; d/r US$13/24), offering riverside rooms as well as two apartments. A couple of buses a day that travel the Dangriga–Hopkins–Placencia route stop at Sittee River.

Cockscomb Basin Wildlife Sanctuary

Almost halfway between Dangriga and Independence is the village of Maya Centre, where a track goes 6 miles (10km) west to the **Cockscomb Basin Wildlife Sanctuary** (admission US$5; ⏲ 7:30am-4:30pm). Sometimes called the Jaguar Reserve, this is a prime place for wildlife-watching. The varied topography and lush tropical forest within the 98,000-acre (39,000-hectare) sanctuary make it an ideal habitat for a wide variety of native Belizean fauna.

Visitor facilities at the reserve include a campsite (US$2.50 per person), several dorm-style rental cabins with solar electricity (US$18 per person, kitchen use US$1 per person), a visitors center and numerous hiking trails. The walk through the lush forest is a pretty one, and though you cannot be

assured of seeing a jaguar, you will certainly enjoy seeing many of the hundreds of other species of birds, plants and animals in this rich environment. No public transportation to the reserve is available. A taxi from Maya Centre will cost about US$12.

For information, or to book a cabin, contact the **Belize Audubon Society** (Map pp226-7; ☎ 223 5004; www.belizeaudubon.org; 12 Fort St, Belize City).

PLACENCIA
pop 900

Perched at the southern tip of a long, narrow, sandy peninsula, Placencia is 'the caye you can drive to.' Not too long ago, the only practical way to get here was by boat from the mainland. Now a road runs all the way down the peninsula and an airstrip lies just north of town. But Placencia still has the wonderful laid-back ambience of the cayes, along with varied accommodations and friendly locals. The palm-lined beaches on its east side attract an international crowd looking for sun and sand, and they make low-key pastimes such as swimming, sunbathing and lazing about the preferred 'activities' for many visitors.

Orientation & Information

The village's main north–south 'street' is actually a narrow concrete footpath that threads its way among simple wood-frame houses (some on stilts) and beachfront lodges. An unpaved road skirts the town to the west, ending at the peninsula's southern tip, which is the bus stop.

An easy walk takes you anywhere in town. The airstrip is about half a mile (0.8km) from the start of the village.

At the south end of town you'll find the wharf, fuel station, bus stop and icehouse. Nearby, Atlantic Bank Limited has an ATM, which often snatches cards, and a slightly more reliable one 2km north. Check your email at **De Thatch Café** (see p255; per hr US$5; ⏲ 7am-midnight).

The tourist information center, opposite the main bus stop, keeps irregular hours, but staff are helpful and have plenty of printed material on hand. Laundry service is available from most of the hotels and guesthouses on the peninsula for US$5 a load.

Tours

Vying to sign up customers for tours of the region are **Ocean Motion Guide Service**

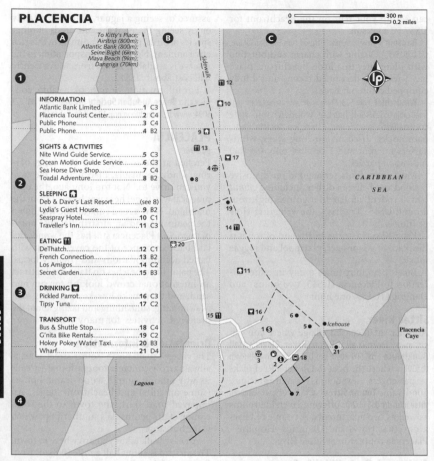

PLACENCIA

To Kitty's Place;
Airstrip (800m);
Atlantic Bank (800m);
Seine Bight (6km);
Maya Beach (9km);
Dangriga (70km)

CARIBBEAN
SEA

Icehouse

Placencia
Caye

Lagoon

INFORMATION
Atlantic Bank Limited.............1 C3
Placencia Tourist Center.........2 C4
Public Phone..........................3 C4
Public Phone..........................4 B2

SIGHTS & ACTIVITIES
Nite Wind Guide Service.........5 C3
Ocean Motion Guide Service....6 C3
Sea Horse Dive Shop...............7 C4
Toadal Adventure...................8 B2

SLEEPING
Deb & Dave's Last Resort......(see 8)
Lydia's Guest House................9 B2
Seaspray Hotel....................10 C1
Traveller's Inn.....................11 C3

EATING
DeThatch.............................12 C1
French Connection................13 B2
Los Amigos..........................14 C2
Secret Garden.......................15 B3

DRINKING
Pickled Parrot......................16 C3
Tipsy Tuna...........................17 C2

TRANSPORT
Bus & Shuttle Stop................18 C4
G'nita Bike Rentals................19 C2
Hokey Pokey Water Taxi........20 B3
Wharf.................................21 D4

BELIZE

(☎ 523 3162) and **Nite Wind Guide Service** (☎ 523 3487), both operating out of small offices near the wharf.

On a pier in the main part of the village is **Sea Horse Dive Shop** (☎ 523 3166; www.belizescuba .com), doing certification courses and dives for certified divers.

For inland tours, including kayaking and canoeing expeditions, check what's on offer with **Toadal Adventure** (☎ 523 3207; www.toadalad venture.com), which operates out of Deb and Dave's Last Resort.

Sleeping

Placencia has lodgings in all price ranges. Budget and midrange accommodations are in the village.

Traveler's Inn (☎ 523 3190; s/d US$10/12.50, with bathroom US$15/17) A classic beachside no-frills joint, the Inn keeps it real with linoleum floors, mostly mosquito-proof windows and creaky fans.

Lydia's Guest House (☎ 523 3117; lydias@btl.net; s/d US$15/20) Lydia's has spacious, clean rooms in a quiet part of the village. Views from the upstairs balcony are worth the price alone and there's kitchen access.

Deb & Dave's Last Resort (☎ 523 3207; www.toad aladventure.com; r US$22) Basic wooden rooms are set around a leafy garden and there are good screened sitting areas. It's in a quiet but central location.

Seaspray Hotel (☎ 523 3148; www.seasprayhotel .com; r US$27-64) The 'economy' rooms are fairly ordinary, but they have bathroom, fan and fridge. The more expensive rooms are larger and have porches and sea views.

Eating

Los Amigos (mains US$6-12; ☺ breakfast, lunch & dinner) The Amigos' policy of undercutting the competition's price and serving delicious food in an open walled thatch hut keeps staff busy every night.

De Thatch (mains US$9-13; ☺ breakfast, lunch & dinner; ▣) Food here is pricey for this part of town, but the setting – in a wood floored *palapa* (palm–leafed shelter) right on the beach – and the mounds of fresh seafood on the menu make it worthwhile. Burritos, burgers and other snacks are more reasonably priced.

Secret Garden (breakfast US$4.50, mains US$10-15; ☺ breakfast, lunch & dinner) Tucked away in a lush little corner of the village, there's no sea view here, but plenty of fresh and imaginative seafood and Creole dishes. Excellent coffee, too.

French Connection (☎ 523 3656; mains from US$15; ☺ dinner Wed-Sat, lunch Sun) This is the place for a romantic splurge. Modern French cuisine and Belize fusion is the go here, with a big emphasis on seafood. Reservations are recommended.

Drinking

Most bars and many restaurants have sundown happy hours, usually featuring rum and juice for US$1. The Pickled Parrot always has a good crowd and the Tipsy Tuna, a towering 'sports bar' with occasional live music and the happening little beachfront bar is usually more hit than miss.

Getting There & Around

Maya Island Air (☎ 523 3475; www.mayaairways.com) and **Tropic Air** (☎ 523 3410; www.tropicair.com) offer daily flights linking Placencia with Belize City and Dangriga to the north and Punta Gorda to the south. Taxis meet most flights.

There are regular buses from Belize City to Placencia (local/express US$10/13, four hours) via Dangriga.

Being that most buses *leave* Placencia ridiculously early (5am or 6am), the quickest (and most enjoyable) way out of town is on the **Hokey Pokey Water Taxi** (US$5), which departs Placencia five times between at 10am and 6pm for **Mango Creek**. It's a 15-minute zip

through the mangroves. At Mango Creek, walk five minutes up the main street, turn left at the gas station and wait in front of Sherl's Restaurant. Buses to Punta Gorda (US$4.50, two hours) and Belize City (US$9, 4½ hours) roll in every hour or so. Many boats will do a charter run to and from Mango Creek for US$20 for up to six people.

The **Gulf Cruza** (☎ 523 4045) makes a Placencia–Big Creek–Puerto Cortés (Honduras) run on Friday, leaving Placencia at 9:30am, arriving at Puerto Cortés at 2pm. Cost to Puerto Cortés is US$50. The boat takes passengers only, no vehicles.

G'nita bike rentals rents bicycles for US$2.50/12.50 per hour/day.

NIM LI PUNIT

About 24 miles (38km) northwest of Punta Gorda, just west of the Southern Hwy, stand the ruins of **Nim Li Punit** (Big Hat; admission US$5; ☺ 9am-5pm). Named after the headgear worn by the richly clad figure on Stela 14, Nim Li Punit may have been a tributary city to the larger, more powerful Lubaantun (see p257).

The **South Group** of structures was the city's ceremonial center and is of the most interest. Although the plaza has been cleared, the structures surrounding it are largely unrestored. Have a look at the stelae, especially **Stela 14**, at 33ft (10m) the longest Maya stela yet discovered, and **Stela 15**, which dates from AD 721 and is the oldest work recovered here so far.

PUNTA GORDA
pop 5300

'Sleepy' is an understatement for this southern seafront town. People here are so laid-back they can't even be bothered calling the town by its full name – all over Belize it's known simply as PG.

Rainfall and humidity are at their highest, and the jungle at its lushest, here in Toledo District. Prepare yourself for at least a short downpour almost daily and some sultry weather in-between.

PG was founded for the Garífuna who emigrated from Honduras in 1832. Though it's still predominantly Garífuna, it's also home to the usual bewildering variety of Belizean citizenry: Creoles, Kekchí Maya, expat Americans, Brits, Canadians, Chinese and people from eastern India.

BELIZE

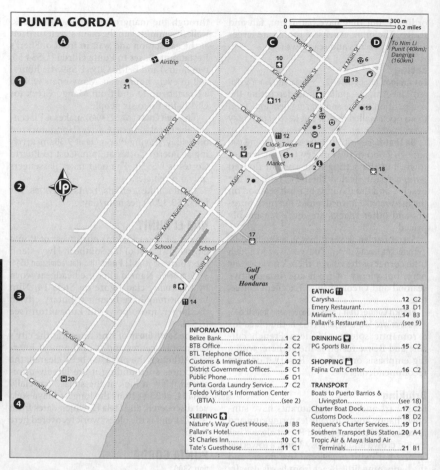

PUNTA GORDA

INFORMATION
Belize Bank...............................1 C2
BTB Office................................2 C2
BTL Telephone Office..................3 C1
Customs & Immigration...............4 D2
District Government Offices.........5 C1
Public Phone.............................6 D1
Punta Gorda Laundry Service......7 C2
Toledo Visitor's Information Center
(BTIA)...............................(see 2)

SLEEPING
Nature's Way Guest House........8 B3
Pallavi's Hotel..........................9 C1
St Charles Inn.........................10 C1
Tate's Guesthouse...................11 C1

EATING
Carysha.................................12 C2
Emery Restaurant....................13 D1
Miriam's.................................14 B3
Pallavi's Restaurant..............(see 9)

DRINKING
PG Sports Bar.........................15 C2

SHOPPING
Fajina Craft Center..................16 C2

TRANSPORT
Boats to Puerto Barrios &
Livingston.........................(see 18)
Charter Boat Dock...................17 C2
Customs Dock.........................18 D2
Requena's Charter Services.......19 D1
Southern Transport Bus Station..20 A4
Tropic Air & Maya Island Air
Terminals...........................21 B1

Orientation & Information

The town center is a triangular park with a bandstand and a distinctive blue-and-white clock tower. Saturday is market day, when area villagers come to town to buy, sell and barbecue. It's a fascinating and colorful mix-up.

The **BTB office** and **Toledo Visitors' Information Center** (☎ 722 2531; 8am-noon & 1-5pm Tue-Fri, 8am-noon Sat) share office space. There's usually somebody around.

Belize Bank (cnr Main & Queen Sts; 8am-1pm Mon-Thu, 8am-4:30pm Fri) is across from the town square. It has both a MasterCard and Visa ATM.

The **Punta Gorda Laundry Service** (2 Prince St) charges US$1 per pound.

Carysha (Queen St; per hr US$2.50; 8am-5pm Mon-Sat) provides internet access.

Sleeping

Nature's Way Guest House (☎ 722 2119; 65 Front St; s/d US$10/15) One of the better budget hotels in Belize. There's a shady courtyard with plenty of hammock action and excellent breakfasts (tofu available) for US$3.50.

St Charles Inn (☎ 722 2149; 23 King St; s/d with bathroom US$15/22) One of the spiffiest budget deals in town, the rooms may be a bit heavy on the brown for some, but they're spacious, come with cable TV and have some good balcony areas for hanging out.

Tate's Guesthouse (☎ 722 0007; 34 Jose Maria Nunez St; s/d US$15/22;   ) Tate's has tidy little rooms in a family-run guesthouse. Coffee is free, internet is US$2.50 per hour and there's a microwave for guest use.

Pallavi's Hotel (☎ 722 2414; 19 Main St; s/d with bathroom US$16/21) Has reasonable rooms with a recommended restaurant downstairs.

Eating & Drinking

Carysha (Queen St; snacks US$2-3; 🖳) Offers excellent, locally grown coffee, good snacks, a two-for-one book exchange and internet access, all on the central square.

Pallavi's Restaurant (19 Main St; meals from US$4) Has standard Belizean family cooking and good breakfasts.

Emery Restaurant (Main St; meals US$6-8) Serves fresh-fish specials daily, good Mexican food and quite possibly the best fried chicken to be had in all of Belize.

Miriam's (Front St; 🕑 breakfast, lunch & dinner; mains US$7-10) An excellent blend of east Indian and Caribbean flavors awaits at this seaside place with breathtaking views over the bay.

PG Sports Bar (cnr Main & Prince Sts) A good bet for live music on weekends. It's a good-sized, fairly standard bar, incongruously enhanced by a staggering collection of US sports photos and posters.

Getting There & Away

Punta Gorda is served daily by **Maya Island Air** (☎ 722 2856; www.mayaairways.com) and **Tropic Air** (☎ 722 2008; www.tropicair.com). Ticket offices are located at the airport.

Requena's Charter Services (☎ 722 2070; 12 Front St) operates the *Mariestela*, with boats departing Punta Gorda at 9am daily for Puerto Barrios (Guatemala). Tickets cost US$18 one-way. Guatemalan-operated **Transportes El Chato** (☎ 502-9948 5525; 1a Av btwn 10a & 11a Calle, Puerto Barrios) has one departure daily at 4pm (US$18, one hour). Buy your tickets on the boat.

One boat goes to Lívingston, Guatemala (US$15) at 10am daily.

Buses depart regularly for Belize City (local/express US$11/13, seven/six hours).

AROUND PUNTA GORDA
Local Villages

The **Toledo Ecotourism Association** (TEA; ☎ 722 2096; www.plenty.org/mayan-ecotours; Front St, Punta Gorda), at the Punta Gorda BTB, runs a Village Guesthouse and Ecotrail Program that takes participants to any of 13 traditional Mopan Maya, Kekchí Maya, Creole and Garífuna villages.

Accommodation is offered in specially built, rustic but comfortable guesthouses and costs US$9 per person per night. A one-off US$5 fee is also charged per visit. Meals in family homes cost US$5 and activities on offer such as nature tours, music, dancing and storytelling cost around US$4 per hour. The tours don't include transportation; check with the TEA for village bus schedules. Local buses run between the villages and Punta Gorda most days for US$5; special charter trips are very expensive – around US$80 – so plan accordingly, although hitching in this part of the world isn't very difficult or dangerous.

More than 85% of the tour fee stays in the village with the villagers, helping them achieve a sustainable, ecofriendly economy as an alternative to traditional slash-and-burn agriculture.

Lubaantun

The Maya ruins at **Lubaantun** (Fallen Stones; admission US$5; 🕑 8am-5pm), 1 mile (1.6km) northwest of the village of San Pedro Columbia, have been excavated to some extent but not restored. The many temples are still mostly covered with jungle, so you will have to use your imagination to envisage the great city that once thrived here.

Archaeologists have found evidence that Lubaantun flourished until the late 8th century AD, after which little was built. The site covers a square mile (3 sq km) and holds the only ruins in Belize with curved stone corners. Of its 18 plazas, only the three most important

---

EXPLORE MORE OF SOUTHERN BELIZE

Southern Belize is off the beaten track, but if you'd like to go even further, there are plenty of good options.

■ Spot manatees, turtles or birds, or grab some Creole drumming classes at **Gale's Point Manatee**

■ Hike along jungle trails past caves and waterfalls in the home of the largest concentration of scarlet macaws in Central America at **Red bank**

■ **Bladen River Field Station**, set on 1100 acres of private reserve, has 50km of trails to hike and jaguars, tapirs, howler monkeys and crocodiles to spot

---

BELIZE

(Plazas III through V) have been cleared. **Plaza IV**, the most important of all, is built along a ridge of hills and surrounded by the site's most impressive buildings: Structures 10, 12 and 33. A visitors center on the site exhibits Maya pottery and other artifacts.

San Antonio & Blue Creek

The Mopan Maya of San Antonio are descended from former inhabitants of the Guatemalan village of San Luis, Petén, just across the border. The San Antonians fled oppression in their home country to find freedom in Belize. They brought their ancient customs with them, however, and you can observe a traditional lowland Mayan village on a short visit here.

About 4 miles (6km) west of San Antonio, near the village of Santa Cruz, is the archaeological site of **Uxbenka**, which has numerous carved stelae.

About 12 miles (20km) south of San Antonio lies the village of Blue Creek, and beyond it the **nature reserve** (admission US$1) of Blue Creek Cave. Hike into the site along the marked trail (less than 1.6km) and enjoy the rain forest around you and the pools, channels, caves and refreshingly cool waters of the creek system.

Guided nature walks – which include a canopy walk and a climb to an observation deck accessed by rope ladder (you must wear helmet and harness for your protection) – are available from the site for about US$15 per hour.

BELIZE DIRECTORY

ACCOMMODATIONS

Lodgings in Belize are generally more expensive and of lower comfort than in neighboring countries. Some have great charm and are well worth the cost; most are just places to stay.

BOOK ACCOMMODATIONS ONLINE

For more accommodations reviews and recommendations by Lonely Planet authors, check out the online booking service at www.lonelyplanet.com. You'll find the true, insider lowdown on the best places to stay. Reviews are thorough and independent. Best of all, you can book online.

On the coast there are plenty of cabins to choose from, although they are nearly always more expensive than staying in hotels. Many hotels offer single rooms (from US$15), but a lot charge simply for the room (starting at US$20), so if you really want to save money it's a good idea to hook up with other travelers.

The HI (Hosteling International) is nonexistent in Belize, but there are a few places around offering dorm-style accommodations costing from around US$10. This is a good way to save money and meet people.

During the peak seasons (mid-December to April, and June through August) prices can be higher and lodging harder to find.

ACTIVITIES

Snorkeling and diving are best on the cayes. Boats depart Ambergris (p233) and Caulker (p230) cayes on day and overnight voyages to the best spots. Lonely Planet's *Diving & Snorkeling Belize* provides detailed descriptions of dive sites and extensive photos of underwater wildlife.

Horseback riding, canoeing and kayaking, hiking, bird-watching and archaeology are all possibilities in the Cayo District of western Belize (p248 and p242).

BOOKS

Belizean historian Assad Shoman's *13 Chapters in the History of Belize* is a detailed account of the history of the country and tends not to glamorize the colonial past as some other studies do.

Warlords and Maize Men: A Guide to the Maya Sites of Belize, by Byron Foster, is recommended for its descriptions of the lives of the Maya.

Snapshots of Belize: An Anthology of Short Fiction, published in Belize by Cubola Productions, features short stories of past and present Belize.

BUSINESS HOURS

Banking hours vary, but most banks are open 8am to 1:30pm Monday to Thursday and 8am to 4:30pm Friday. Most banks and many businesses and shops close on Wednesday afternoon. Shops are usually open 8am to noon Monday to Saturday and 1pm to 4pm Monday, Tuesday, Thursday and Friday. Some shops have evening hours from 7pm to 9pm on those days as well.

Most businesses, offices and city restaurants close on Sunday. Note that in smaller towns, the popular Belizean restaurants usually close before 6pm.

CLIMATE

The busy winter season runs from mid-December to April, and a second peak occurs June through August. The dry season (November to May) is the best time to travel (although prices can be higher and lodging can be harder to find). If you do visit in summer (July to November), be aware that this is hurricane season. Belize City was badly damaged by hurricanes, with heavy loss of life, in 1931, 1961 and 1978.

For climate charts, see p723.

DANGERS & ANNOYANCES

Petty theft is the greatest danger (and annoyance) to travelers in Belize. Take care not to show obvious signs of wealth. Keep a close eye on camera equipment, don't leave valuables in plain view in cars and try to watch your bags when you're on a bus. Belize City has a bad reputation, mostly a hangover from the past, but you should still exercise normal precautions.

If you're driving, be extra careful – Belize is renowned for road accidents. Wear your seat belt, and be aware of what's going on in front and behind you.

DISABLED TRAVELERS

Unfortunately, Belize's infrastructure for travelers with a disability is virtually non-existent. See p726 for general advice about traveling in the region.

EMBASSIES & CONSULATES
Embassies & Consulates in Belize

Canada (Map p224; ☎ 223 1060; cdncon.bze@btl.net; 80 Princess Margaret Dr, Belize City)
Germany (Map pp226-7; ☎ 222 4369; seni@cisco .com.bz; 57 Southern Foreshore, Belize City)
Guatemala (Map p224; ☎ 223 3150; 8 A St, Belize City)
Honduras (☎ 224 5889; 114 Bella Vista, Belize City)
Mexico (Map pp226-7; ☎ 223 0193/0194; 18 North Park St, Belize City) embassy (☎ 822 0497; Embassy Sq, Belmopan)
Netherlands (Map p224; ☎ 223 2953; mchulseca@btl .net; cnr Baymen Av & Calle Al Mar, Belize City)
UK (☎ 822 2146; Embassy Sq, Belmopan)
USA (Map pp226-7; ☎ 227 7161; Gabourel La & Hutson St, Belize City)

Belizean Embassies & Consulates Abroad

Belize's overseas diplomatic affairs are generally handled by British embassies and consulates. Belize has embassies in the following countries. For Belizean embassies in other Central American cities please refer to the relevant country chapter in this book.
Canada consulate (☎ 604-687 6459; Suite 1120, 595 Howe St, Vancouver, BC, Canada V6C 2T5)
Mexico embassy (☎ 525-520 1274; embelize@prodigy .net.mx; 215 Calle Bernardo de Galvez, Col Lomas de Chapultepec, Mexico DF 11000)
UK high commission (☎ 44 20-7723 3603; bzhc-lon@ btconnect.com; 3rd fl, 45 Crawford Pl, London, W1H 4LP)
USA embassy (☎ 202-332 9636; www.embassyofbelize .org; 2535 Massachusetts Ave NW, Washington, DC 20008)

FESTIVALS & EVENTS

On major holidays, banks, offices and other services are closed. National holidays are denoted with an asterisk.

The following list describes the major holidays and festivals; they may well be celebrated for several days around the actual date:
New Year's Day* (January 1)
Fiesta de Carnival (February; Sunday to Tuesday before the beginning of Lent) Celebrated in northern Belize.
Baron Bliss Day* (March 9) Honors the memory of one of the great benefactors of Belize.
Holy Week (April; held in the week leading up to Easter Sunday) Various services and processions.
Labor Day* (May 1)
Commonwealth Day* (May 25)
Feast of San Pedro (June; date varies) San Pedro, Ambergris Caye.
Lobster Season opens (successive weekends in June and early July, after the season officially opens, usually early June) Placencia, Caye Caulker and San Pedro.
Costa Maya Festival (August; dates vary) San Pedro, Ambergris Caye – a celebration of Maya coastal culture with participants from Belize and the Yucatán.
National Day* (St George's Caye Day; September 10)
Independence Day* (September 21)
Pan American Day* (Columbus Day; October 12)
Garífuna Settlement Day* (November 19) Hopkins and particularly in Dangriga (p250).
Christmas Day* (December 25)
Boxing Day* (December 26)

FOOD & DRINK
Food

Belize has never developed an elaborate native cuisine. Recipes are mostly borrowed – from the UK, the Caribbean, Mexico and the USA.

BELIZE

Each community has its own local favorites, but Garífuna and Maya dishes and traditional favorites such as boil-up rarely appear on restaurant menus. Even so, there is some good food to be had, especially the fresh fish options near the sea.

Rice and beans prevail on Belizean menus and plates. They're usually served with other ingredients – chicken, pork, beef, fish, vegetables, even lobster – plus some spices and condiments such as coconut milk. 'Stew beans with rice' is stewed beans on one side of the plate, boiled rice on the other side and chicken, beef or pork on top.

Meals are not usually spicy, but the popular Marie Sharp's hot sauces are on virtually every table to liven things up if you need it.

Garífuna dishes sometimes appear on restaurant menus, but there are very few Garífuna restaurants in the country. If you have a chance to try a Garífuna meal you shouldn't pass it up. The dish you may see on some menus is 'boil-up,' a stew made of root vegetables and beef or chicken. Less common is *alabundinga,* a dish of grated green bananas, coconut cream, spices, boiled potato and peppers served with fried fish fillet (often snapper) and rice.

Some restaurants serve wild game such as armadillo, venison and the guinea pig–like *gibnut* (also called 'paca'). Conservationists frown on this practice. Lobsters are in season from mid-June to mid-February (to discourage poaching, don't order them the rest of the year), and conch season begins when lobster season ends.

Alcoholic Drinks

Local beer is good and inexpensive. Belikin is about the only brand you're ever likely to see (except in fancy bars), so get used to it. It comes in regular, light, stout and premium. Ask for a beer, you'll get a regular. Penny-pinchers should note that, while the stout is stronger, it costs the same.

You'll see plenty of rum drinking going on. One Barrel has won a few prizes for best rum in the Caribbean (quite an honor). Coconut rum is also popular, often with pineapple juice, in the drink known as the 'panty-ripper.'

Nonalcoholic Drinks

Bottled drinks are cheap, and all the usual soft drinks are available. Juices are available everywhere, but often made from concen-trate. Specify if you want a fresh juice – staff may be able to help you out. Opinion is divided on whether tap water is safe to drink – bottled water is cheap and readily available, anyway. Coffee is widely available but often disappointing. Instant is the most common. Espresso is available in better restaurants and cafés.

GAY & LESBIAN TRAVELERS

Unfortunately, the rules for gay and lesbian travelers in Belize seem to be the same as those in most Central American countries – keep it low key, and look but don't touch. While it's an incredibly tolerant society, underlying Latino machismo and traditional religious beliefs combine to make public displays of same-sex affection a pretty bad idea. **Maya Travel Services** (www.mayatravelservices.com) has more Belize-specific information.

See p727 for general information about traveling in the region.

INTERNET ACCESS

All but the smallest of towns have cybercafés. The smaller the town, however, the higher the rates (up to about US$8 per hour out on the cayes) and the slower the service.

INTERNET RESOURCES

Belize by Naturalight (www.belizenet.com) Covers just about everything visitors might want to know.

Belize First Magazine (www.belizefirst.com) Information of interest to travelers and expats. Especially helpful are reader recommendations on lodgings, restaurants and tours.

Belize Forums (www.belizeforum.com/cgi-bin /ultimatebb.cgi) An excellent bulletin board with mostly reliable information.

Belize Tourism Board (www.travelbelize.org) Has comprehensive tourist information.

LANGUAGE

Belize is officially English-speaking, and most of its citizens, with the exception of new arrivals from Guatemala, Honduras and Mexico, read and speak English fluently. Creole people speak their own colorful dialect (arguably a language) as well as standard English, flavored with the Caribbean's musical lilt. You'll hear Garífuna in the south. Spanish is the first language in the north and in some towns in the west. Other languages in the mix are Maya, Chinese, Mennonite German and Hindi.

MAPS

If you're driving, pick up a copy of Emory King's annual *Driver's Guide to Beautiful Belize,* sold in bookstores and gift shops in Belize City. The guide has basic maps and detailed route descriptions – which is helpful since road markers in Belize are few and far between.

For more detail, the 1:350,000 *Belize,* published by International Travel Maps and Books of Vancouver is widely available throughout the country.

MEDIA
Newspapers & Magazines

Most Belizean newspapers are supported by one political party or another, and as a consequence, much space is devoted to political diatribe. The left-leaning *Amandala* (www .amandala.com.bz) has the largest circulation in the country. The *Belize Times* (www.belizetimes .bz) represents the PUP perspective, while the *Guardian* (www.guardian.bz) goes in to bat for the UDP. The *Reporter* (www.reporter.bz) appears to present the most neutral coverage.

Belize News (www.belizenews.com) has links to most of the country's media.

Radio

LOVE-FM (spreading the love etc) is the most widely broadcast radio station in Belize, with spots at 95.1 and 98.1 on the dial. It's a beguiling mix of local news, public-service announcements ('Belizeans! Be kind to tourists!') and the world's best (and worst) love songs. KREM at 96.5 plays a more modern selection of music.

MONEY

The Belizean dollar (BZ$) is divided into 100 cents. Coins come in denominations of one, five, 10, 25 and 50 cents, and one dollar; bills (notes) are all of the same size but differ in color and come in denominations of two, five, 10, 20, 50 and 100 dollars. Be sure to carry small denominations if you're heading off the tourist trail.

Prices in the country are generally quoted in Belizean dollars, written as '$30 BZE,' though you will also occasionally see '$15 US.' To avoid surprises, be sure to confirm with service providers whether they are quoting prices in US or Belizean dollars.

For general information on costs and money in Central America see p20.

ATMs

ATMs are the easiest way of getting cash. Belize Bank seems to have the least temperamental machines. There are ATMs in all major towns and some small ones.

Credit Cards

Credit cards are useful, particularly when buying cash from a bank. Visa and MasterCard are the most widely accepted. Some tour operators and higher-end hotels and restaurants accept cards (sometimes charging 5% for the service), but it's always best to have a good supply of the folding stuff on hand.

Exchange Rates

The value of the Belizean dollar has been pegged to the US dollar at a rate of 2:1 for some years now. The table shows currency exchange rates at the time this book went to press.

Country	Unit	Belize Dollar (BZ$)
Australia	A$1	1.70
Canada	C$1	1.90
euro zone	€1	2.80
Japan	¥100	1.64
New Zealand	NZ$1	1.60
UK	UK£1	4.10
USA	US$1	2

Exchanging Money

Most businesses accept US currency in cash without question. They usually give change in Belizean dollars, though they may return US change if you ask for it. Many also accept US-dollar traveler's checks.

Canadian dollars and UK pounds sterling are exchangeable at any bank, although non-US-dollar traveler's checks are not consistently accepted by Belizean banks. It is difficult if not impossible to exchange other foreign currencies in Belize.

Moneychangers at border-crossing points will change your US cash for Belizean dollars legally at the standard rate of US$1=BZ$2. If you change money or traveler's checks at a bank, you may get only US$1=BZ$1.97; they may also charge a fee of BZ$5 (US$2.50) to change a traveler's check.

International Transfers

The fastest way to have money transferred from abroad is with Western Union. It has offices all over the country and charges US$85 for a US$1000 transfer.

POST

A postcard sent by airmail to Canada or the USA costs US$0.15; a letter US$0.30. To Europe it's US$0.20 for a postcard and US$0.40 for a letter. Address poste restante (general delivery) mail to: (name), c/o General Delivery, (town), (district), Belize, Central America. To claim poste restante mail, present a passport or other identification; there's no charge.

RESPONSIBLE TRAVEL

Many people come to Belize to appreciate the natural beauty of the country. Belizeans are quite conscientious about maintaining their environment, and visitors should show the same respect.

Don't remove coral or shells from the sea, and mind your fins when snorkeling or diving; coral is fragile and endangered. Avoid buying items made from turtle shell or coral. Don't swim with manatees or attempt to piggyback a sea turtle. You may like it, but they find it very stressful.

Don't take or buy Maya artifacts – it's illegal, and some say you'll be hexed!

Use air-con sparingly. It's expensive and places an enormous strain on local energy reserves. Instead, move more slowly than normal and use fans (or hang out in the lobby of fancy hotels); you'll find that you adjust to the heat after a few days.

When in the jungle, stay on trails to avoid trampling plants. Appreciate wildlife from a distance. Never feed wild animals, including those in the sea.

STUDYING

Educational opportunities are scarce in Belize – a shame, because there is no language barrier to deal with. You can, however, learn Creole drumming at the **Maroon Creole Drum School** (methos_drums@hotmail.com; US$8 per hr) in Gale's Point Manatee, a charming little village 1½ hours south of Belize City.

Archaeology students may be able to pick up some field work credits by working on one of the many digs around the country (see right).

TELEPHONE

The country's telephone system is operated by **Belize Telecommunications Ltd** (BTL; www.btl.net), with offices in major cities. Telephones are generally very reliable (and inexpensive) when calling within the country. International calls are sometimes a different story. BTL has an online directory.

Local calls cost BZ$0.25 (US$0.13). Telephone debit cards are sold in denominations of BZ$10, BZ$20 and BZ$50. In some stores you can choose your amount and they just print out a docket with your pin number on it.

TOURIST INFORMATION

The government-run **BTB** (www.travelbelize.org) maintains tourist offices in Belize City, Punta Gorda and Corozal. They're generally underfunded, but staffed by friendly folks who usually do what they can to answer your questions.

TOURS

Organized tourism isn't all that big in Belize yet, but you will find yourself on tour if you're heading out on dive trips on the cayes (p230) or Placencia (p253) or exploring around the Cayo district (p247).

VISAS & DOCUMENTS

Citizens of the EU and many countries (among them Australia, Canada, Mexico, New Zealand, the USA and many Caribbean nations) do not need to obtain a Belizean visa in advance, provided you have a valid passport and an onward or round-trip airline ticket (with a departure from Belize, or any other country in the region). A visitor's permit valid for 30 days will be stamped in your passport at a border crossing or at the airport. One month extensions are easily obtainable from any immigration office for US$12.50. Details on visa requirements for other visitors are available from any Belizean embassy (see p259) or ask your travel agent.

VOLUNTEERING

Belize is full of volunteer opportunities; not surprisingly, many of them are environmentally based. Most programs expect volunteers to pay, and costs can vary wildly.

Help for Progress (progress@btl.net) Belizean NGO that works with grass-roots organizations in fields such as education, gender issues, citizen participation and environment.

Teachers for a Better Belize (www.tfabb.org) US-based organization that sends volunteers to schools in the Toledo district to train local teachers.

Plenty International (www.plenty.org) Has opportunities to work with community groups and cooperatives in the Toledo district.

There are a number of organizations that run volunteer expeditions in Belize. Among them are **Explorations in Travel** (www.volunteertravel.com) and **Trekforce Expeditions** (www.trekforceworldwide .com). The other big opportunity that exists is helping out at the various archaeological sites around the country. These positions can be expensive, though, and you'll definitely be doing more digging and wheel barrowing than brushing dust off crystal skulls, but they can be rewarding and fascinating, if that's what you're into. Check www.famsi.org, www .mesoweb.com or www.archaeology.org for more details.

WOMEN TRAVELERS

Men in Belize can be forward and at times aggressive with comments about women's appearance. This can be uncomfortable and embarrassing, but shouldn't be considered threatening (although commonsense rules for women should be followed). Do as your mother told you in elementary school: ignore them, and they'll go away. And (you may have heard this from mom, too), the more modestly you're dressed, the less attention you'll receive.

WORKING

Officially you need a resident's visa to get a job in Belize. You might, however, pick up some work on the cayes or in Placencia working in bars, but the pay won't be anything to get excited about.

El Salvador

HIGHLIGHTS

- **Ruta de las Flores** Charge the western highlands: hiking *cafétales*, stepping in hot springs and chowing at the weekend food fairs (p301)
- **Playa El Tunco** Ride four great breaks, string a hammock under the palms and soak up the lax atmosphere (p293)
- **Parque Nacional Imposible** Steal stunning ridge-top views and splash in river pools hiking from the park's remote backdoor (p300)
- **Alegría** Immerse yourself in the idyllic tiny-town life of El Salvador's mountain-top flower capital (p306)
- **Punta Roca** Nail the longest break in Central America, or at least buy a real surfer a beer to hear about it (p290)
- **Off the beaten track** Put your trust in an ex-guerrilla guide while exploring the rugged territory of the former FMLN stronghold of Perquín (p315)

FAST FACTS

- **Area** 21,040 sq km (smallest in Central America)
- **ATMs** Plentiful, using Cirrus & Plus systems
- **Budget** US$25-30 per day
- **Capital** San Salvador
- **Costs** Budget hotel US$10, bottle of beer US$1.50, 3-hr bus ride US$1.60, bean & cheese *pupusa* US$0.35, surfboard rental US$10 per day
- **Country Code** ☎ 503
- **Electricity** 110V AC at 60 Hz (same as USA)
- **Famous for** Guns, ex-guerrillas, surf spots
- **Head of State** President Antonio Elías Saca
- **Languages** Spanish, Náhua
- **Money** US dollar
- **Phrases** *Que chivo* (how cool); *un cachete* (a favor); *guaro* (alcohol)
- **Population** 6.7 million (most populated in Central America)
- **Time** GMT minus 6 hours, no daylight savings time
- **Traveler's Checks** Cashed at banks; show passport and original receipts
- **Visas** Tourist cards at border or airport US$10

TRAVEL HINTS

If you want to blend in with locals, travel with a duffel bag and wear neat clothes and long pants. A simple, '*Buenos días/buenas tardes*' and '*¿Como va?*' (Good morning/afternoon. How's it going?) launches any encounter (in the market, a hotel or elsewhere) the right way. It might open doors.

OVERLAND ROUTES

From Guatemala, enter through Anguiatú, San Cristóbal or La Hachadura. From Honduras, El Poy or El Amatillo are best; you can exit El Salvador via Perquín, but you cannot enter there.

EL SALVADOR

Resilient, real and sometimes raw, El Salvador is caffeine for the senses. It's hard to digest it all: the frank talk of war survivors next to whimsical folk art; and the rickety Rhode Island school buses recast as psychedelic chariots, tossing passengers to the pavement without hitting one full stop.

For a traveler El Salvador is something of a puzzle. It needs time for you to absorb and unravel. You have to be careful. But there is no reconciling the homicide statistics and the not-so-distant war with such, well, friendliness. It is too tempting to invent some explanation. Here, like in most industrialized countries, you won't find abundant wildlife or primary forest. Yet, tromping a landscape of countless volcanoes, mountains, swimming holes and a wild Pacific coast offers real off-the-brochure adventure.

El Salvador emerged from a decade-long civil war and various natural disasters doggedly pursuing stability. Many residents found it abroad – where nearly a third of El Salvador's nationals now live and work, sending home monthly contributions known as *remesas*. Other *Guanacos* (as they call themselves) stood their ground. One local said, 'We have the war. We keep going. We have Hurricane Mitch. We have Hurricane Stan. Then we have some earthquakes, but Salvadorans, we keep on going.'

Resilience. It should be the mantra of every traveler.

CURRENT EVENTS

Remittances from abroad are soaring, creating a boom in everything from commerce to construction. The new thing is custom resorts for *hermanos lejanos* (distant brothers and sisters) sweating it out for Uncle Sam, who prefer homecoming to include a chaise lounge and air-con. It shows confidence that the Hilton has set up shop in Zona Rosa, San Salvador's swankest barrio.

Yet violence continues to permeate El Salvador. The crime tally rose for 2006, including an increase in murders (3596) and extortion. The dialogue on how to fight crime is heating up. Clergy and activists aren't so sure that President Antonio Saca's aggressive Super Mano Dura (Super Hard Hand) plan is effective against prolific *maras* or gangs. Law enforcement has gotten so desperate that the police will pick up suspects wearing baggy hip-hop styles solely on their fashion election. Gangs tend to hang out in the tough neighborhoods and police control most of the tourist areas, so it's unlikely that visitors will encounter gang members.

HISTORY
Traders & Raiders

Paleo-Indian peoples populated El Salvador as early as 10,000 years ago, literally leaving their mark with cave paintings in modern Morazán. Around 2000 BC the Olmecs followed, leaving as their legacy the Olmec Boulder, a giant head sculpture similar to those from Mexico, found near Casa Blanca.

El Salvador was once a key regional trading center. Archaeological remains reveal diverse influences, from Pipil, Teotihuacan and Maya in the west to Lenca, Chorti and Pok'omama in the east. The step pyramid ruins at Tazumal, San Andrés and Casa Blanca show 3000 years of nearly constant pre-Hispanic habitation.

When Spanish conquistador Pedro de Alvarado arrived in 1524, he saw a country dominated by Pipils, descendants of Toltecs and Aztecs. These northern peoples (from modern-day Mexico) dubbed their home Cuscatlán, 'Land of Jewels.' Their maize-based farming economy flourished enough to support several cities and a sophisticated culture with pursuits that included hieroglyphics, astronomy and mathematics. Their dialect is related to modern Náhua.

From Indigo to Independence

Spanish rule started with a year-long struggle against the Pipil. The Spaniards prevailed and laid claim to the land, transforming it into plantations of cotton, balsam and indigo. Agriculture boomed throughout the 1700s, with indigo the number one export. A small group of Europeans, known as the 'fourteen families,' controlled virtually all of the colony's wealth and agriculture, enslaving indigenous peoples and Africans to work the land.

Conflict simmered under this gross imbalance of power. A revolt against Spain in 1811 was led by Padre (Father) José Delgado. While it failed, it had planted a seed of discontent. Independence was gained 10 years later, on September 15, 1821, when El Salvador became part of the Central American Federation.

Though governments came and went, the wealthy held tight to their fortunes and

EL SALVADOR

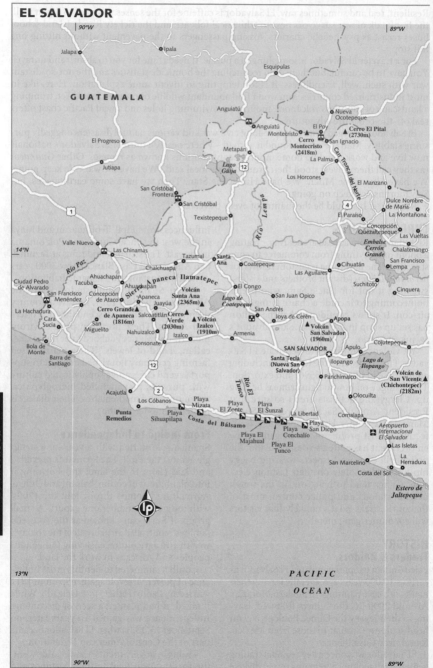

EL SALVADOR

GUATEMALA

PACIFIC

OCEAN

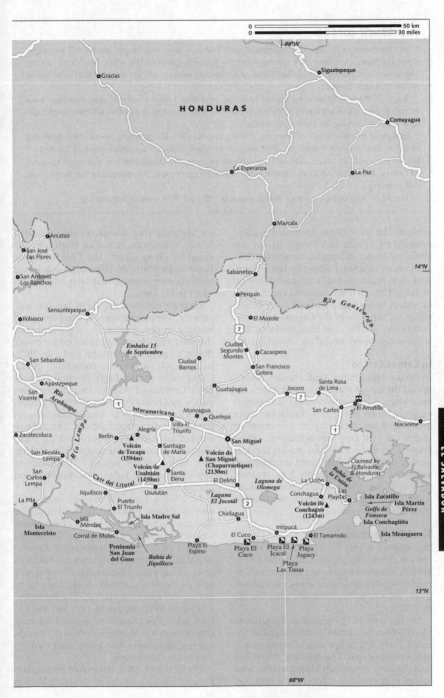

EL SALVADOR

THE SEARCH GOES ON

When government forces razed villages during the civil war, they didn't always kill everyone. Some children, taken from their mothers' arms or found helpless on the killing field, were spared. Those survivors were either divvied up as prizes among military officers or exported for adoption in the USA and Europe.

Many of these children grew up not knowing who their families were or even that they were adopted. Even surviving family members were at first reluctant to request an official search right after the war, fearing for their own safety.

In light of governmental indifference, the organization Pro-Búsqueda formed to find displaced children and reconnect them to their original families. Through a combination of DNA tests, family accounts, adoption files and newspaper reports, Pro-Búsqueda has managed to solve 317 cases. An estimated 5000 children were displaced by the war, Pro-Búsqueda has many cases still pending.

For more information, contact **Pro-Búsqueda** (☎ 2235 1039; www.probusqueda.org).

control. The same clique continued to comprise the ruling elite and, though slavery was abolished, many indigenous became landless and poverty-stricken. Pushing for land reform, Anastasio Aquino led an indigenous rebellion in 1883. Though it was subdued and Aquino executed, he became a national hero. El Salvador withdrew from the Central American Federation in 1841, but Independence Day continues to be celebrated on September 15.

In Comes Coffee

In the late 19th century, synthetic dyes undermined the indigo market and coffee took the main stage. A handful of wealthy landowners expanded their properties, displacing more indigenous people. Coffee became the most important cash crop and *cafétaleros* (coffee growers) earned purses full of money that was neither taxed nor redistributed at reasonable wages to the workers. By the 20th century, 95% of El Salvador's income derived from coffee exports, but only 2% of Salvadorans controlled that wealth.

The 20th Century

Intermittent efforts by the poor majority to redress El Salvador's social and economic injustices were met with severe repression. The vindictive government vigorously eradicated union activity in the coffee industry during the 1920s.

In January 1932, Augustín Farabundo Martí, a founder of the Central American Socialist Party, led an uprising of peasants and indigenous people. The military responded brutally by systematically killing anyone who looked indigenous or supported the uprising.

La Matanza (the Massacre) exterminated 30,000 individuals, including Martí who was killed by firing squad. The FMLN (Frente Farabundo Martí de Liberación Nacional) revolutionary army would later take up his name in his honor.

Over the course of the 1970s, landlessness, poverty, unemployment and overpopulation became serious problems. In government, the polarized left and right tangled for power through coups and electoral fraud. In 1972, José Napoleon Duarte, cofounder of the Christian Democrat Party (Partido Democrático Cristiano; PDC), ran for president supported by a broad coalition of reform groups. When his victory was denied amid allegations of fraud, protests followed. The military averted an attempted coup, and the right responded to increasing guerrilla activity by creating 'death squads.' Thousands of Salvadorans were kidnapped, tortured and murdered.

In 1979 a junta of military and civilians overthrew President Carlos Humberto Romero and promised reforms. When promises were not met, opposition parties banded together as the Frente Democrático Revolucionario (FDR) and allied with the FMLN, a revolutionary army composed of five guerrilla groups for whom armed struggle appeared as the only means of change. The successful revolution in Nicaragua in 1979 had encouraged many Salvadorans to demand reforms. One of them was Monsignor Oscar A Romero, a formerly conservative priest who took up the cause of the people.

On March 24, 1980, outspoken Archbishop Romero was assassinated while saying Mass in the chapel of the San Salvador Divine Providence Cancer Hospital. His murder ignited an armed insurrection that same year that was to turn into a civil war.

Civil War

El Salvador became enmeshed in violence. The rape and murder in late 1980 of four US nuns performing relief work in El Salvador prompted the Carter administration to suspend military aid. But in 1981, the newly elected Reagan administration, bristling from the threat of Nicaragua's socialist revolution, pumped huge sums into the moribund Salvadoran military (over US$500 million in 1985 alone). Uncle Sam's support would effectively prolong the conflict. When guerrillas gained control of areas in the north and east, the military retaliated by decimating villages. In 1981, the US-trained elite Atlacatl Battalion exterminated 757 men, women and children in El Mozote

(p317), Morazán. As many as 300,000 citizens fled the country.

In 1982, Major Roberto D'Aubisson, founder of the extreme-right Arena party, became president of the legislative assembly and enacted a law granting the legislative body power over the president. D'Aubisson created death squads targeting trade unionists and agrarian reform supporters. In response, the FMLN offensive blew up bridges, cut power lines and destroyed coffee plantations and livestock – anything to stifle the economy. When the government ignored an FMLN peace proposal, the rebels refused to participate in the 1984 presidential elections, in which Duarte won over D'Aubisson. For the next few years the PDC and FMLN engaged in peace talks unsuccessfully. Death squads continued pillaging, and the guerrillas continued to undermine the military powers and jeopardize municipal elections.

MARA SALVATRUCHA

The front-page of El Salvador's dailies is plastered with gang busts or grisly reports of the newly fallen. Usually the credit is given to Mara Salvatrucha, considered one of the most dangerous criminal gangs in the Americas. Known for gruesome beheadings, machete murders and tattooed members, the group actually has its roots in the USA.

In the 1980s, Salvadoran refugees new on the block in the slums of Los Angeles were getting regularly beaten up and victimized by Mexican gangs. In response they formed Mara Salvatrucha. *Mara* is slang for gang, *salva* for Salvadoreño and *trucha* means the clever trout. The gang is also known as MS-13. The opposing 18th street gang eventually became known as Mara 18 or M-18. Today these gangs have an estimated 100,000 members between them, mostly in El Salvador, Honduras, Guatemala, Nicaragua, Mexico and the USA.

Maras started by dabbling in petty crime and theft. Between 2000 and 2004, the US government attempted to eliminate the gang problem by exporting some 20,000 illegal immigrants, felons and known gang members to Central America. Without family, education, jobs or even Spanish, it didn't take long for *maras* to return to gangs and upping the stakes. Over time they have expanded into the Colombian and Mexican drug cartels, the sex trade and the traffic of illegal immigrants.

In Central America, gangs had a reputation for warring between opposing groups, with little consequence to the public. The Salvadoran government's first plan Mano Dura ('operation hard hand') sought to curb gang activities by giving police broad powers. On Christmas Eve 2004, Mara Salvatrucha responded with the brutal murder of 28 passengers in a Honduras bus assault, leaving a note that slammed antimara laws.

The current president Antonio Saca campaigned and won on plan Super Mano Dura ('operation Super Hard Hand'), which expanded already broad police powers. Now having tattoos and looking homey is reason enough for arrest. Yet, with an average of 10 murders per day, El Salvador remains one of the most violent countries in the world.

What gives? While the public continues to clamor for crackdowns, a lack of funding for forensics training and a lack of willingness of neighbors to testify means that even a slew of zealot arrests won't add up to convictions. Judges are reluctant to hold suspects with no evidence beyond the tattoos on their arms and face. The same gang members are captured hundreds of times and let out hundreds of times, in what has become a way of life.

The Price of Peace

Hope for peace neared in 1989, when the FMLN offered to participate in elections if the government agreed to a postponement to ensure democratic polls. Their calls were ignored and Alfredo Cristiani, a wealthy Arena businessman, was elected president. The FMLN's response was a major attack on the capital. In retaliation, the military killed an estimated 4000 'leftist sympathizers.' Among these enemies of the state were six Jesuit priests, their housekeeper and her daughter, shot to death at the Universidad Centroamericana on November 16.

UN-mediated negotiations began between the government and FMLN in April 1990. Among the first agreements was a human-rights accord signed by both parties. Yet, violent deaths actually increased in 1991 when a UN mission arrived to monitor human rights.

On January 16, 1992, a compromise was finally signed. The FMLN became an opposition party, and the government agreed to various reforms, including dismantling paramilitary groups and death squads, replacing them with a national civil police force. Land was to be distributed to citizens and human-rights violations to be investigated. But instead, the government gave amnesty to human-rights abusers.

During the course of the 12-year war, an estimated 75,000 people were killed, and the US government gave a staggering US$6 billion to the Salvadoran government's war effort.

Modern Currents

The FMLN has mostly proven to be a model example of a former guerrilla organization transitioning to mainstream politics. The left-wing party scored large victories in the 2000 and 2003 congressional elections, although it didn't gain a majority. On the presidential level, Salvadorans continue to prefer conservatives, electing Antonio Elías Saca in 2004.

This may have something to do with the current national obsession: gangs and crime. Saca's campaign hinged on the anti-gang plan 'Super Mano Dura' (a tougher follow-up to the last administration's blockbuster, 'Mano Dura'). While cracking down has impacted murder rates, some deplore the human-rights violations of aggressive arrests and detainments.

Natural disasters continue to plague El Salvador. In 2005, Hurricane Stan left thousands homeless and killed 69, only days after Volcán Santa Ana erupted, triggering landslides and ruining coffee and other crops. Much of the damage from these disasters remains, even as occasional tremors persist.

Slow economic growth has had its impacts. Many wonder if the remittances sent back from Salvadorans living abroad may be changing the famous Salvadoran work ethic. Temporary foreign workers (about 10,000 Nicaraguans and Hondurans) work the coffee and sugarcane harvests for low wages that can't compare to family contributions pouring in from abroad.

THE CULTURE
The National Psyche

Most travelers who have been to El Salvador rate its people as the best part. Straight-talking, strong-minded and hard-working, Salvadorans are also extremely helpful and almost universally friendly (even gangbangers can rustle up charm when interviewed). Salvadorans have a powerful sense of justice and freely express their opinion. The civil war still looms large in the national psyche, as it must – not only are the memories too searing to forget, but many wartime leaders (and their disciples) remain in positions of power. At the same time, Salvadorans are genuinely dismayed to learn that many foreigners know little about El Salvador beyond the war. They will eagerly volunteer information and assistance.

Lifestyle

With a strong work ethic, Salvadorans have quickly raised their country from the wreckage of civil war to nearly the top of Central America's economic ladder. Remittances sent home from Salvadorans living abroad, which annually total three billion dollars (16% of national GDP), provide a significant boost and are changing the way Salvadorans live and work. Poverty and unemployment persist, with 30% of the population below the poverty line, mostly in rural areas. That said, El Salvador enjoys the highest minimum wage in Central America (about US$150 per week) and is notably more prosperous than neighboring countries.

People

Salvadorans show more European physical traits than other Central Americans, due largely to the brutal repression of indigenous

BEHIND THE SCENES OF NAÏVE ART

Holy scenes, strange birds, unabashed rainbow colors: the childlike images of Fernando Llort Choussy have come to symbolize hope in a war-torn Central America. Compared to Miro and Picasso, Llort differs with earnest iconography and flat tropical hues in a style dubbed as primitive modern.

Ironically, this strong Latin American identity was forged when he went to France to study architecture and then theology. Religious symbols are recurring motifs in his artwork. He prefers the rough and everyday to the exalted, saying, 'The hands in developed societies are not worth anything anymore.'

When Llort returned to El Salvador in the early 1970s, he arrived to the tensions and violence leading up to the civil war. Llort moved to La Palma, a distant mountain town in the north, to take refuge. The apparent simplicity of a life in harmony with nature further informed his style. He started La Semilla de Dios (God's seed), a workshop to teach others his craft and professionalize local artisans.

Llort has since lived in San Salvador and abroad, but the workshop is still going strong in his former studio. You can find his work on the face of the Metropolitan Cathedral in San Salvador as well as in the White House, MoMA and the Vatican.

people and minor Afro-Caribbean influence. Roughly 94% of the population is *mestizo* (a mixture of Spanish and indigenous) but fair features are not uncommon. Indigenous people are descended from the Pipils, with Toltec and Aztec roots. Government brutality against them has taken its toll, and they now represent only 1% to 5% of the population. Few speak Náhua or wear traditional dress.

ARTS

While less prolific or varied as the crafts in neighboring Guatemala or Honduras, El Salvador's artisan products can be innovative and high quality. Fernando Llort's Naïve Art inspired an industry of brightly painted crafts in childlike motifs in the community of La Palma. Guatajiagua in Morazán produces unique black pottery with a Lenca influence and Ilobasco is known for its *sorpresas,* intricate miniatures hidden in ceramic shells (see p307). Regional museums and galleries can point the way for those wishing to visit artists' workshops.

Poetry is beloved in El Salvador. Iconoclast poet Roque Dalton was exiled for radical politics. He eventually returned home to aid the guerrilla cause but was executed by his own side under suspicion that he was a CIA operative. Notable works include *Taberna y Otros Lugares* (1969), a political vision in verse, and *Miguel Marmol.* Progressive poet Claudia Lars wrote spare, bold erotic poetry and is considered one of the country's foremost writers.

Using the pen name Salarrué, lauded writer Salvador Efraín Salazar Arrué's *Cuentos de Barro* (Tales of Mud), published in 1933, marks the beginning of Central America's modern short-story genre. For further information about these and other modern writers, see **Concultura** (www.dpi.gob.sv), the country's official arts and culture board, which has a bibliography of Salvadoran authors.

Films *Romero,* produced by Ellwood Kieser in 1988, and *Salvador,* directed by Oliver Stone, offer Hollywood versions of the civil war.

RELIGION

El Salvador, like the rest of Latin America, is experiencing an explosive growth of evangelical churches. Their fiery services seem to have brought fresh energy to faith. Town square services with booming speakers are becoming an all-too-typical way of spreading 'the word.' Yet, the country remains over 80% Catholic, and has a long tradition of liberation theology. Before and during the war, priests and missionaries were often outspoken critics of government repression – many, such as Archbishop Óscar Romero, were killed for their stands.

ENVIRONMENT
The Land

The Land of Volcanoes, El Salvador has two volcanic ranges spanning east to west, spicing the views, as well as daily life, with a little drama. Much of the land is deforested but mountains in the far north are blanketed in pine and oak, jagged rock formations and cloud forests. The Río Lempa bisects the country with a fertile swath of land. While El Salvador is the only Central American country not to have a Caribbean coast, there is over 300km of Pacific coastline bordering mangroves, estuaries and tropical dry forest. Lakes and freshwater lagoons provide drinking water and recreation.

Wildlife

El Salvador was drastically deforested over the 20th century, as a result, many species of plants and animals ceased to exist in the country. However, national parks and protected lands still maintain good biodiversity.

The country has over 800 animal species. Almost half are butterflies, with bird species second in number, with about 330 resident species (and 170 migratory) including quetzals, toucans, herons, kingfishers, brown pelicans, egrets, parakeets and sandpipers. The remaining mammal species number around 200 and can be seen mostly in reserves. They include opossums, anteaters, porcupines, agoutis, ocelots, spider monkeys and white-tailed deers. In all, about 90 species are in danger of extinction, including marine turtles, armadillos and over 15 types of hummingbird.

With so much of the land cultivated, few original plants still exist. Small stands of balsam trees survive along the western Pacific coast (dubbed the Costa del Bálsamo) and mangroves line many estuaries. Bosque Montecristo and El Imposible offer the widest variety of indigenous plants, and Parque Nacional los Volcanes offers good vegetation. Plants in these areas include mountain pines, oaks, figs, magueys, ferns and orchids.

National Parks & Reserves

El Salvador has only four official national parks, but there are a number of locally or privately administered reserves.

Barra de Santiago A remote bar of mangrove-fringed estuaries and beaches on the Pacific Coast. (See p304.)

Cerro El Pital El Salvador's highest peak. *Torogoz* (blue-crowned motmots) and quetzals can be observed on its piney slopes. (See p321.)

La Laguna de Alegría An emerald-green lake fed by hot springs, in the crater of dormant Volcán de Tecapa. Ocelots and coatis are among wildlife inhabiting primary growth forest surrounding the lake. (See p307.)

Laguna El Jocotal This freshwater lagoon east of Usulután is an important sanctuary for migratory birds from October to March. (See p307.)

Parque Nacional El Imposible Near El Salvador's western limit; one of the last remnants of original tropical forest with waterfalls, views and numerous endangered plant and animal species. (See p304.)

Parque Nacional los Volcanes (Cerro Verde) A volcano crater forest with amazing views of nearby Izalco and Santa Ana volcanoes. Highlights include emerald toucanets, motmots and hummingbirds. (See p294.)

Parque Nacional Montecristo-El Trifinio A mountainous cloud forest reserve at the borders of El Salvador, Honduras and Guatemala. Wildlife includes pumas, spider monkeys and agoutis. Giant ferns, orchids and bromeliads are abundant. (See p298.)

Parque Nacional Walter T Deininger This dry tropical forest on the Pacific Coast is the habitat for 87 bird species, deer, pacas and motmots. (See p291.)

Environmental Issues

Overpopulation and the exploitation of the land for export crops (such as coffee, sugar and cotton) continue to propel El Salvador's massive deforestation. High population density remains the principal obstacle to the

---

SHAKE, RATTLE & ROLL

In 2001 a massive earthquake centered off the Salvadoran coast rocked Central America. Measuring 7.6 on the Richter scale, it killed 800 Salvadorans and leveled entire towns and many historical buildings. In the upmarket suburb of Santa Tecla in San Salvador, the quakes triggered a landslide which crushed homes and trapped all in its path. Its deforestation had made the hillside unstable. In all, more than 100,000 were left homeless.

Though much of the damage has been repaired, travelers will notice lingering effects. Churches remain in rubble and walls sport tell-tale cracks. During the research of this edition, tremors near Ahuachapán toppled over 200 meager dwellings, leaving inhabitants homeless. Residents dragged their mattresses out on the street so they could sleep soundly (while others didn't sleep at all!). In all this excitement, you have to remember that El Salvador is the land of volcanoes, with shifting plate tectonics. Though it's hard to detect bitterness among stalwart Salvadorans, these rumbles and shiftings can still worry a traveler.

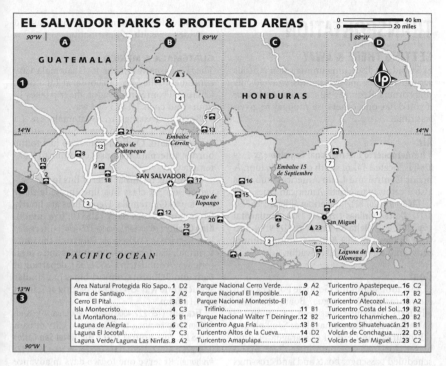

EL SALVADOR PARKS & PROTECTED AREAS

Area Natural Protegida Río Sapo..**1** D2	Parque Nacional Cerro Verde............**9** A2
Barra de Santiago......................**2** A2	Parque Nacional El Imposible..........**10** A2
Cerro El Pital.............................**3** B1	Parque Nacional Montecristo-El
Isla Montecristo........................**4** C3	Trifinio..................................**11** B1
La Montañona............................**5** B1	Parque Nacional Walter T Deininger..**12** B2
Laguna de Alegría......................**6** C2	Turicentro Agua Fría...................**13** B1
Laguna El Jocotal.......................**7** C3	Turicentro Altos de la Cueva..........**14** D2
Laguna Verde/Laguna Las Ninfas..**8** A2	Turicentro Amapulapa...................**15** C2

Turicentro Apastepeque..**16** C2
Turicentro Apulo..............**17** B2
Turicentro Atecozol.........**18** A2
Turicentro Costa del Sol...**19** B2
Turicentro Ichanmichen..**20** B2
Turicentro Sihuatehuacán.**21** B1
Volcán de Conchagua......**22** D3
Volcán de San Miguel.....**23** C2

regeneration of ecosystems. Today, 17% of the country is forested, with only 2% to 5% of that primary forest. As a result, many native species have become endangered or extinct.

Deforestation and unplanned urban sprawl intensify the effects of natural disasters. In recent years El Salvador has been repeatedly pummeled by Mother Nature, producing a laundry list of disasters. In 1998, floods caused by Hurricane Mitch produced 200 fatalities and 70,000 homeless, acutely damaging the lower Río Lempa. Earthquakes in 2001 brought on landslides and destroyed buildings, killing 1159 people and destroying or damaging almost 300,000 homes.

Before the earthquakes, environmental groups had issued increasingly dire warnings about those very issues for a house-filled hillside in the wealthy neighborhood of Santa Tecla. When the earthquake hit, the slope collapsed, burying dozens of houses and untold numbers of people in a suffocating wall of mud.

Most recently, the eruption of Santa Ana volcano in October, 2005, coupled with Hurricane Stan's torrential rains, unleashed scores of landslides, with the largest loss of life in poor areas built on steep slopes or riverbeds.

Río Lempa, a crucial watershed, suffers from pollution, as do many other rivers and lakes. Meanwhile, uncontrolled vehicle emissions challenge urbanites' respiratory functions in any metropolitan area. In 2006, the government vowed to take on the most visible problem – trash. The lack of proper disposal sites means gangs of vultures circling roadside dumps are a common sight.

Turicentros

The Instituto Salvadoreño de Turismo (ISTU) created turicentros (recreational complexes) between the late 1950s and 1970s, most near lakes and natural springs or in forests. Most have swimming pools, restaurants and no-frills cabins. As most are close to a main town, they attract crowds on weekends. The price is the same for all: US$0.80 admission, US$0.70 parking and US$4 cabin rental (day use only). All are open 8am to 4pm. Contact the Ministerio de Trabajo in San Salvador (see p279) for reservations.

TRANSPORTATION

GETTING THERE & AWAY

El Salvador's discerning immigration officials scrutinize entry and exit stamps, so avoid cutting corners. Request a 90-day visa in advance if you'd like one, otherwise you may be given less time.

Air

The **Aeropuerto Internacional Comalpa** (☎ 2339 8264) is located 44km south of San Salvador. A major Central and Latin American hub, it is also a gateway to North American cities.

TACA (☎ 2267 8222), **American Airlines** (☎ 2298 0777), **United Airlines** (☎ 2279 3900), **Continental** (☎ 2207 2040), **Delta Air Lines** (☎ 2275 9292) and **Copa Airlines** (☎ 2209 2672) are among others providing services to El Salvador.

Boat

El Salvador shares the Golfo de Fonseca with Honduras and Nicaragua. Boats occasionally ferry passengers between La Unión (El Salvador), Coyolito, Amapala or San Lorenzo (Honduras), and Potosí (Nicaragua). Going by sea does not save time since there are no scheduled passenger boats and land crossings are relatively close.

Bus

In San Salvador most international buses leave from **Terminal Puerto Bus** (Map p281; Alameda Juan Pablo II at 19a Av Norte). Take city bus 29, 101D, 7C or 52 to get there. Other departure points are indicated below. Santa Ana and San Miguel also have international bus services.

For private transfers, contact **Suchitoto Tours** (☎ 2513 1667; suchitoto.tours@gmail.com). The owner Miguel takes travelers direct to destinations

---

ENTRY & DEPARTURE TAXES

US citizens and some other nationalities may be required to pay for a US$10 tourist card upon arrival at El Salvador's airport. There's a US$32 departure tax to fly out of the airport, often already included in the cost of your plane ticket. The new Central America-4 agreement allows for travel between the borders of Guatemala, Honduras, El Salvador and Nicaragua with one entry fee, for details see p327.

---

in El Salvador, Guatemala and Honduras and provides a wealth of information.

GUATEMALA & MEXICO

The Tica Bus that runs to Guatemala City continues to the Mexican border at Tapachula, Chiapas. From San Salvador, the trip takes 12 hours and costs US$23 one way.

Border crossings to Guatemala are La Hachadura, Las Chinamas, San Cristóbal and Anguiatú. Ordinary buses go just to the border, international buses continue to Guatemala City.

From the Terminal Puerto Bus in San Salvador second-class bus lines provide daily service to Guatemala. Departures are hourly from 4am to 3pm daily (US$10, five hours). **King Quality** (☎ in San Salvador 2271 1361) offers deluxe service to Guatemala City from the same terminal, featuring air-con, movies and a meal (one way/round-trip US$26/33), departing at 6am and 3:30pm; Comfort Lines has similar service (one way US$22), departing at 7:30am and 1:30pm.

Tica Bus (☎ 222 4808; www.ticabus.com; ☻ 8am-4:30pm) has service to Guatemala City at 6am (US$11, five hours) from the **Hotel San Carlos** (Map p281; ☎ 2222 8975; Calle Concepción btwn 10a & 12a Avs Norte). Reserve one to two days in advance and arrive at the San Carlos a half-hour early. Tica Bus is inside the hotel.

Pullmantur (Map p278; ☎ 2243 1300; www.pullmantur.com in Spanish; Hotel Sheraton Presidente; Av La Revolución, Zona Rosa) also serves Guatemala City. Departures are Monday through Saturday at 7am and 3pm, and Sunday at 7am and 3pm (US$26/41 for executive/1st class, 4½ hours). Purchase tickets at the Pullmantur office in the hotel.

Ordinary buses to the borders leave San Salvador from the Terminal de Occidente, usually connecting through Sonsonate, Santa Ana, Ahuachapán or Metapán.

For La Hachadura, take bus 205 to Sonsonate (US$0.70, 1½ hours) and transfer to bus 259 (US$0.80, 1½ hours) to the border.

For Las Chinamas, take bus 202 to Ahuachapán (from Santa Ana, use bus 210) and transfer to bus 263.

For San Cristóbal, bus 498 leaves from the Terminal del Occidente five times daily. Alternatively, take bus 201 to Santa Ana, where bus 236 leaves every half-hour for the border. Either way, the trip takes about three hours and costs US$2.50.

To Anguiatú, take bus 201 to Santa Ana and transfer to bus 235 via Metapán.

HONDURAS
Border crossings to Honduras include El Poy, El Amatillo and Sabanetas/Perquín. Note that there is no Salvadoran immigration post at Sabanetas/Perquín. It is OK to leave the country here only if you don't plan on returning.

International buses to Honduras leave from Terminal Puerto Bus in San Salvador. (International buses can also be picked up in Santa Ana and San Miguel; see p297 and p311.) Air-conditioned King Quality buses leave every day for Tegucigalpa at 6am and 1:30pm (US$28, six hours) and San Pedro Sula at 5am and 12:30pm (one way/round-trip US$28/41, six hours).

Ordinary buses to the border leave from the Terminal de Oriente. For El Poy, bus 119 leaves the Terminal de Oriente via La Palma (US$1.60, three hours), departing every half-hour from the terminal. At the border, you can pick up a bus or colectivo (shared taxi) to Nueva Ocotepeque and continue by bus from there.

For El Amatillo take bus 306 or 346 from San Salvador via San Miguel (US$3, four hours; express service also available). After crossing the border, you can catch a bus to Tegucigalpa or Choluteca. Microbuses also go from El Amatillo to the Nicaraguan border at Guasaule (US$5, two hours).

NICARAGUA, COSTA RICA & PANAMA
Tica Bus leaves the Hotel San Carlos at 5am and arrives in Managua, Nicaragua, between 5pm and 6pm (US$25 one way). If continuing on, spend the night and leave the following morning at 5am. The bus arrives in San José, Costa Rica, between 3pm and 4pm (US$42 one way from San Salvador). It then leaves at 10pm for Panama (US$61 one way from San Salvador), where you arrive between 3pm and 4pm the following day, making for a grand total of three days of bus travel.

King Quality has daily services to San José, Costa Rica (US$48, 18 hours) leaving at 3:30am from the Terminal Puerto Bus.

Car & Motorcycle
If you drive into El Salvador, you must show a driver's license (an international driving permit is accepted) and proof that you own the vehicle. You must also fill out extensive forms. Car insurance is available and advisable but not required. Vehicles may remain in El Salvador for 30 days. If you wish to stay longer, it's best to leave the country and drive back in rather than attempt to deal with the Transport Ministry.

GETTING AROUND
Boat
You'll need to use a boat to get around the Bahía de Jiquilisco in eastern El Salvador for any trips in the Golfo de Fonseca, near La Unión. Otherwise, water transportation is rare.

Bus
Intercity buses are retired American school buses, scrubbed and painted wild colors. Most bus terminals are as chaotic and dirty as the area around them. Information is rarely posted, but other passengers can point you in the right direction. It can be hard to determine which bus on a given route is leaving first – engine revving and false starts play for passengers. Try following the crowd. There are no ticket offices; purchase your ticket on the bus once you're seated.

Buses run frequently to points throughout the country and are very cheap (US$0.40 to US$4). Some weekend fares increase up to 25%. Routes to some eastern destinations have different categories: *ordinario, especial* and *super especial*. The latter two options cost more, but they are faster and more comfortable. Most intercity bus services begin between 4am and 5am and end between 6pm and 7pm.

Car & Motorcycle
Most roads in El Salvador are paved and a pleasure to drive. By driving around the country you can see more in less time. The downside is searching for unmarked roads and turnoffs. Gas is not cheap either. A gallon of regular unleaded is about US$3.30.

Get in the habit of lightly honking, especially when passing or before turning a curve. Also watch for signals from other cars, usually a hand waving for you to pass them or for them to cut you off. Police set up checkpoints, especially on roads to border crossings. Carjacking is a problem, as is getting parts stolen off your parked car. Don't drive alone in areas of ill repute and park in safe places. Car insurance is a good idea, but not required.

Rental cars are available in San Salvador and San Miguel. In San Salvador they include:

Alamo Uno Rent a Car (Map p278; ☎ 2211 2111; Blvd del Hipódromo 426)

Avis (Map p278; ☎ 2261 1212, airport 2339 9268; www .avis.com.sv in Spanish; 43a Av Sur 127)

Budget (Map p278; ☎ 2260 4333; www.budget.com.sv in Spanish; 1a Calle Poniente 2765; US$35 daily)

Quick Rent a Car (☎ 2229 6959; www.quickrentacar .com.sv in Spanish) Offers hotel or airport pick up/drop off.

Hitchhiking

Buses or collective pick-ups go just about anywhere you could want to go, so hitching isn't usually necessary. If you do get a ride somewhere, it's customary to give (or at least offer) a small payment. Both men or women usually hop in the back of pickup trucks, but women might think twice before climbing into a car of only men.

SAN SALVADOR

pop 1.8 million (metropolitan area)

The cosmopolitan center of El Salvador is a city cranking with energy. Witness the buses stuffed with limbs akimbo, bountiful bars and downtown, where vendors overtake the pavement, allowing traffic a cool inch on each side. Commerce, from street to swanky mall, thrives. It is partly about consumption, partly about curiosity – San Salvador's appetite for the new is voracious.

It's easy for the first impression of the city to be daunting. Crime, after all, looms large. Travelers may see headlines of gang violence, meet survivors of the war or bump into the rifleman guarding the neighborhood ice-cream parlor. As San Salvador may be a city of impressions, however, it's also one of encounters. People are unusually eager to greet visitors and offer a hand. This confident, lefty metropolis has great music and museums on offer, as well as hipster bars and coffee shops. There's enough going on here to extend a trip a day or two, or even a week, in order to explore.

Travelers should visit the parks and *centro* during daytime only, and take taxis after dark. The gang area of Soyopango (east of town) should be avoided. If you're at all intimidated, exploring the city on a Sunday offers a slow start.

HISTORY

San Salvador was founded in 1525 by the Spanish conqueror Pedro de Alvarado, about 30km northeast of where it now stands, near Suchitoto. It was moved to its present site three years later, and declared a city in 1546. It was here in San Salvador in 1811 that Father José Matías Delgado first called for Central American independence. Once this was achieved, San Salvador became the capital of the united Provinces of Central America from 1834 to 1839 when El Salvador gained its own independence. It has since been the capital of El Salvador.

Natural disasters have beleaguered the city, including more than a dozen major earthquakes (and hundreds of smaller ones). San Salvador was destroyed by tremors in 1854 and 1873, by the eruption of Volcán San Salvador in 1917 and yet again by floods in 1934. The earthquake of October 10, 1986 caused considerable damage, and the most recent on January 13, 2001, contributed its share.

From assassinations to student protests, San Salvador served as a flashpoint in El Salvador's long civil war. In November 1989, the FMLN's 'final offensive' brought bitter fighting into the city streets. To quell the attack, government forces bombed neighborhoods thought to harbor guerrillas and their supporters. Hundreds of civilians and soldiers on both sides died. The attack and counterattack left parts of the city in shambles, and proved that neither the government nor the guerrillas would win the war militarily. After a 26-month stalemate, peace accords were signed in 1992.

The declining economy during the war sparked an internal migration from the countryside to the city of mostly poor families and laborers; today over a quarter of the population of El Salvador inhabits the metropolitan area of the capital. Though San Salvador produces nearly 65% of the national GDP, unemployment is high and people do whatever they can to get by – vendors of all ages ply the streets and major intersections, selling everything from candy to cell phone chargers. On buses, vitamins and other supplements are marketed with vigor and creativity.

ORIENTATION

San Salvador follows the same grid pattern as most Central American cities. Unfortunately, signage is sparse in the central area (check for names on the street curbs). From the zero point at the cathedral, Av España goes north and Av Cuscatlán south; Calle Arce runs to the west and Calle Delgado to the east.

Avenidas (avenues) run north–south, and change from 'Sur' (South) to 'Norte' (North) when they cross the major east–west artery (Calles Arce and Delgado). Likewise, avenues are odd- or even-numbered depending on whether they are east or west of the north–south artery (Avs Cuscatlán and España). So, 5a Av Sur is south of Calle Arce and west of Av Cuscatlán (because it's odd-numbered). Calles (streets) are similarly ordered, only using 'Oriente' (East; abbreviated 'Ote') and 'Poniente' (West; abbreviated 'Pun' or 'Pte'). It's confusing to the visitor at first, but you'll quickly learn the orderliness of it. The odd-even thing can be tricky, ie 25a Av is one block from 27a Av, but it is more than 25 blocks from 26a Av!

Av España leads up to 29a Calle Poniente, which heads west to the Universidad Nacional de El Salvador at the intersection of Blvd de los Héroes and Calle San Antonio Abad. Av Cuscatlán crosses Blvd Venezuela, which links the east and west bus terminals, and continues south to Parque Balboa and Puerta del Diablo, crossing the airport highway along the way.

From the city center, 1a Calle Poniente and Calle Rubén Darío, to the north and south of Arce respectively, are the main roads to the wealthier west.

INFORMATION
Bookstores
Bookmarks (Map p278; www.bookmarks.com.sv; Centro Comercial Basilea, Col San Benito) A good source for English magazines, paperback bestsellers in English, and travel books (including Lonely Planet).
Centro de Intercambio y Solidaridad (CIS; Map p278; Colonia Libertad, Av Bolivar No 103) This center for peace and social justice has a good library for students and volunteers.
La Ceiba Libros (Map p283; Metrocentro, 1st fl, Blvd de los Héroes) Stock up on Salvadoran history and literature in Spanish here.

Emergency
Police (Map p283; ☎ 2261 0630; Calle Berlin; ⏲ 24hr)

Immigration
Immigration Office (Direccíon General de Migracíon y Extranjería; Paseo General Escalón Map p281; ☎ 2202 9650, 2221 2111; ⏲ 9am– 5pm Mon-Fri, 9am-1pm Sat) For visa renewal and other immigration matters.

Internet Access
Internet cafés are plentiful along Calle Arce, near the Universidad Tecnológica. Around Blvd de los Héroes check out the following:
Cybercafé Genus (Map p283; Av Izalco 102-A; per hr US$1; ⏲ 9am-11pm Mon-Fri, 10am-8pm Sat & Sun)
PC Station (MetroSur, Blvd de los Héroes; per hr US$1; ⏲ 7am-10pm Mon-Sat, 9am-7pm Sun) Offers web-based international calling.

EL SALVADOR

GETTING INTO TOWN FROM THE AIRPORT

Shuttles operated by **Taxis Acacya** (Map p281; airport ☎ 2339 9282, in town ☎ 2271 4937; cnr 19a Av Norte & 3a Calle Poniente) offer the best way to/from the airport. The trip costs US$4 and takes 45 minutes. In **San Salvador**, shuttles leave from Taxis Acacya behind the Puerto Bus Terminal, at 6am, 7am, 10am and 2pm. From the airport, they depart at 9am, 1pm and 5:30pm.

Microbus 138 (US$0.60, 45 to 60 minutes, every 10 minutes) passes the airport traveling to and from the city center. Pick it up just south of Plaza Barrios in town. The bus doesn't enter the terminal area and the stop is easy to miss. Politely pester the driver and his assistant to stop at the airport. If heading into town, cut through the parking lot to reach the highway (a 75m walk) and a bus shelter. Once downtown, a taxi costs US$4 to US$7. Bus 30 goes to Metrocentro and Blvd de los Héroes (from Plaza Barrios walk two blocks north, turn right one block to Parque Libertad).

You can also go directly from the airport to **La Libertad** – it's about the same distance as San Salvador. Take bus 133 to the *puente a Comalapa* (Comalapa overpass) a few minutes away. A path leads up onto the intersecting road; from there it's 100m to the town of Comalapa, where bus 187 or 495 goes every 20 minutes to La Libertad (US$0.35).

A taxi between San Salvador or La Libertad and the airport costs US$20 – don't bother trying to bargain.

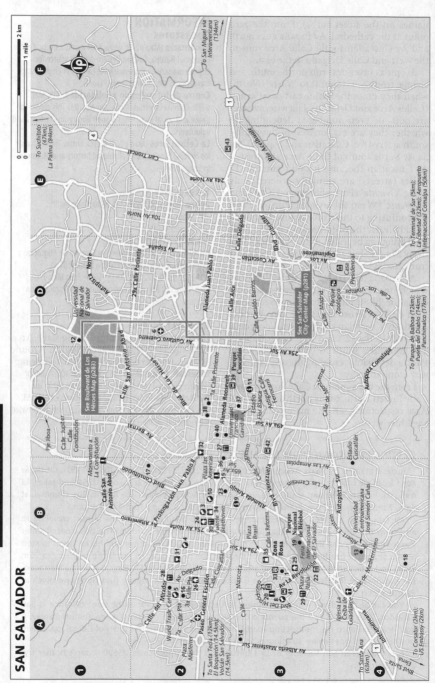

SAN SALVADOR

EL SALVADOR

0 ─── 2 km
0 ─── 1 mile

To Suchitoto (47km); La Palma (84km)

To San Miguel via Interamericana (134km)

Carr Troncal

Río Acelhuate

24a AV Norte

10a AV Norte

Universidad Nacional de El Salvador

29a Calle Poniente

Autopista a Norte

AV España

Calle Poniente

Alameda Juan Pablo II

Calle Arce

Calle Delgado

Blvd Olivdato

AV Cuscatlán

See San Salvador City Center Map (p281)

Calle Gerardo Barrios

Calle Madrid

Parque Zoológico

Casa Presidencial

AV Los Diplomáticos

Calle Los Viráfitos

AV Irazú

To Terminal de Sur (5km); La Libertad (32km); Aeropuerto Internacional Comalpa (50km)

AV Gustavo Guerero

25a AV Sur

See Boulevard de Los Héroes Map (p283)

Calle San Antonio Abad

Blvd de Los Héroes

7a Calle Poniente

Parque Cuscatlán

Alameda Roosevelt

Universidad Francisco Gavidia

Estadio Flor Blanca

Antigua Calle Ferrocarril

49a AV Sur

AV Independencia

AV de la Revolución

Calle de Mediterráneo

Pje Jiboa

Calle Júpiter Calle Constitución

Monumento a La Constitución

Calle San Antonio Abad

Blvd Constitución

AV Bernal

AV Altamirano

Prolongación Juan Pablo II

Plaza las Américas

25a Calle Sur

Blvd Juan Pablo II

Alameda Araujo

AV de la Revolución

Blvd Venezuela

Calle Progreso

AV Las Amapolas

Estadio Cuscatlán

Autopista Sur

Universidad Centroamericana José Simeón Cañas

74a AV Norte

Faente 34

Beethoven

Plaza Brasil

79a AV Sur

Zona Rosa

Parque Nacional de Béisbol

Feria Internacional

Calle la Reforma

Feria de El Salvador

AV Albert Einstein

AV Calle del Mirador

World Trade Center

Paseo General Escalón

Plaza Masferrer

Calle Mirador

Calle Delgado

7a Calle Pte

3a Calle Pte

Calle Cuscatlán

Calle La Mascota

Av Albert Einstein

Rodrigo

Blvd Del Hipódromo

AV La Reforma

Plaza Italia

Calle de Guadalupe

Iglesia La Ceiba de Guadalupe

Interamericana

AV Alberto Masferrer Sur

To Santa Tecla (12km); El Boquerón (14.5km); Volcán San Salvador (14.5km)

To Parque de Balboa (12km); Puerta del Diablo (14km); Panchimalco (17km)

To Santa Ana (63km)

To Consatir (2km); US Embassy (2km)

Blvd Santa Elena

Near the center:

Ciber Snack (Map p281; cnr 2a Av Sur & 4a Calle Ote; per hr US$1; ☯ 7:30am-6:30pm Mon-Sat)

Infocentros (Map p281; 19a Av Norte; per hr US$1; ☯ 7am-8:30pm Mon-Fri, 7am-6pm Sat) International calls available.

Laundry
Lavapronto (Map p283; Calle Los Sisimiles 2949; ☯ 7am-6pm Mon-Fri, 7am-5pm Sat) Charges US$4 per load. Many hotels do laundry as well.

Medical Services
Hospital Bloom (Map p283; ☎ 2225 4114; Blvd de los Héroes at Av Gustavo Guerrero/25a Av Norte) Public hospital with long lines. Specializes in children's treatment.

Hospital de Diagnóstico (Map p278; ☎ 2226 8878; Calle 21 Pte at 2a Diagonal) Considered one of the country's best hospitals, relatively inexpensive.

Hospital Diagnóstico Escalón Map p278; ☎ 2264 4422; 3a Calle Pte) Recommended by the US embassy.

Money
Banks and 24-hour ATMs are found throughout the capital, issuing US dollars.

Banco Credomatic (Map p283 & p281) Branches located in the *centro* and next to the Super Selectos supermarket, in the Centro Comercial San Luis, off Calle San Antonio Abad. Changes traveler's checks or gives cash advances on MasterCard.

Banco Cuscatlán (Map p283 & p281) ATMs that accept all cards are located in Metrocentro Mall and Galerías Mall, where you may be charged a fee. Branches change

traveler's checks and can give cash advances on Visa cards.

Casas de Cambio (Map p281) Changes foreign currency.

Dispensa de Don Juan (Map p281) Near Plaza Barrios, has several ATMs and is probably the most secure place to withdraw money in the *centro*.

Post
Correos Central (Map p281; Centro Gobierno; ☯ 7:30am-5pm Mon-Fri, 8am-noon Sat) A smaller branch is in Metrocentro by the Blvd de los Héroes entrance (Map p283).

Tourist Information
Corsatur (☎ 2243 7835; corsatur@salnet.net; ☯ 8am-12:30pm, 1:30-5:30pm) Inconveniently located outside the city; offers maps, brochures and a sometimes-handy magazine. Its airport branch is usually unmanned.

ISTU (Map p281; ☎ 2222 8000; istu@mh.gob.sv; Calle Rubén Darío 619; ☯ 8:30am-noon, 1-4pm Mon-Sat) General information about El Salvador's national parks and *turicentros*.

Ministerio de Trabajo's Auxiliary Office (Map p278; ☎ 2298 8739; Calle Nueva Dos 19; ☯ 8am-12:30pm, 1:30-4pm Mon-Fri) Issues permits to stay at the four government-run workers' vacation centers in Lago de Coatepeque, El Tamarindo, La Palma and La Libertad. Apply here in person with your passport and the number of people in your group. Plan your stay between Wednesday and Saturday (the centers are closed other days), and workers get weekend preference. Calling ahead may help expedite paperwork, or it may take a few days. Centers don't provide linen.

Peace Corps (☎ 2207 6000; www.peacecorps.gov) These days this US volunteer organization is dedicating

EL SALVADOR

PEOPLE PACKING HEAT

Enter El Salvador and you'll wonder if you've stumbled onto an NRA convention. Banks, hotels and even bikini boutiques are patrolled by clean-shaven guards packing M16s and 9mm pistols. While the war is long over, this security-obsessed country employs over 18,000 security guards. In addition, there are countless private citizens accessorizing with arms, easily purchased in gun shops at the mall among the boutiques.

Yet the tide might be turning. In an effort to curb violence, the legislature passed a series of measures banning guns in public areas in December, 2006. Will it affect availability? Maybe not. Of the estimated 500,000 firearms in El Salvador, 60% are illegal. A 10-month period in 2006 saw 3000 murders in the country. The stricter measures of President Anthony Saca's Super Mano Dura (Super Hard Hand) policy create more arrests but few convictions. To combat violence, law enforcement will have to somehow quell that old culture of combat and the conditions that lead to crime.

more efforts to creating sustainable tourism in rural areas. If you want to get off the beaten track, they may be a good resource, although the office is not equipped for public visits. Volunteers are certainly receptive to visitors to tourism projects. At the time of research the office was being moved so call for further information.

SalvaNatura (Map p278; ☎ 2279 1515; www.salva natura.org in Spanish; 33 Av Sur 640; ☽ 8am-12:30pm, 2-5:30pm Mon-Fri) Friendly and helpful staff manage Parque Nacional El Imposible and Parque Nacional los Volcanes. Call before visiting either park.

DANGERS & ANNOYANCES

Travelers may not experience it first-hand, but crime is a serious problem in San Salvador. Pick-pocketing occurs in broad daylight. Travel light, skip flashy jewelry and watches, and stay aware of your belongings, especially on buses, in market areas and street crowds. If you are robbed, just hand over the goods. Locals recommend taking taxis after 8pm. The center is off-limits for walking around at night, along with Parque Cuscatlán. Ample nightlife lines Calle San Antonio Abad and Blvd de los Héroes, but take a cab to get to your hotel. Don't use the shortcut from Blvd de los Héroes to Ximena's Guest House and La Estancia at night.

Pollution is a consistent pest, rankled in place by the surrounding mountains. Thick vehicle exhaust, especially from buses, can leave you with runny eyes and a sore throat. Prevent the inevitable cold by eating right and being careful about germs.

Accidents between cars and pedestrians are frequent and frightening. Be extra-careful crossing the street. Pedestrians don't have the right of way and no car will chivalrously cede it to you.

SIGHTS
City Center

El centro overloads the senses with blaring beats, sputtering traffic and crowds squeezing through the artery of busy markets. It is far more interesting than the sterile suburbs, and long-term makeovers are finally starting to bear fruit. The main plaza is **Plaza Barrios**, where local protests usually begin or end. Two blocks east is **Parque Libertad**, where a winged statue of Liberty holds court.

CATEDRAL METROPOLITANA

Fernando Llort painted the colorful *campesino* motif façade of this beige stucco building (Map p281). Its blue and yellow checked dome faces Plaza Barrios and marks the center of the city's street grid. Completed in 1999 after years of renovation, the cathedral stands on the site of an earlier version that burned in 1956. Archbishop Oscar A Romero's tomb is underneath, visited by Pope John Paul II in March 1993.

IGLESIA EL ROSARIO

In spite of appearances, which show a dilapidated hangar, this austere construction (Map p281) is one of the more interesting churches in the country. A soaring arched roof with stained-glass panels covers a unique interior adorned with scrap-metal figures. More stone and metal statues stand on the side across from the entrance. The father of Central American independence, Padre Delgado, is buried here.

OTHER HISTORICAL BUILDINGS

Government headquarters before the devastating 1986 earthquake, the ornate **Palacio Nacional** (Map p281) occupies the west side of the plaza. Built in the early 20th century of Italian marble, the palace displays the classical style fashionable at the time. The imposing **Biblioteca Nacional** (Map p281) is on the plaza's south end. The **Teatro Nacional** (Map p281) east from the cathedral along Delgado, was erected in 1917 and functioned as a movie house for 50-odd years before an opulent renovation added ornate gilt boxes, sensuous ceiling mural and red velvet galore. West down 6a Calle Poniente, you'll see the Gothic towers of the decaying **Iglesia El Calvario** (Map p281).

West of the Center

Calle Rubén Darío heads west from the center, changing names a couple of times along the way. Bus 52 rumbles down the entire length of this road. When the street is Alameda Roosevelt, it passes pleasant **Parque Cuscatlán** (Map p278), where women sell *pupusas* and kids kick soccer balls. Further along, it passes **Estadio Flor Blanca** (Map p278), the national stadium, where soccer matches and the occasional rock concert are held. At 65a Av, you come to **Plaza las Américas** (Map p278), with the statue **El Salvador del Mundo** (Map p278). Symbolic of the country, it depicts Jesus on top of the world. Continuing west the road becomes Paseo Gral Escalón, going through the fashionable Colonia Escalón. Further west you hit Plaza Masferrer.

MUSEO NACIONAL DE ANTROPOLOGÍA DAVID J GUZMÁN

This outstanding anthropology **museum** (Map p278; Av La Revolución; admission US$1.50; ⊙ 9am-5pm Tue-Sun) has two floors of well-presented exhibits

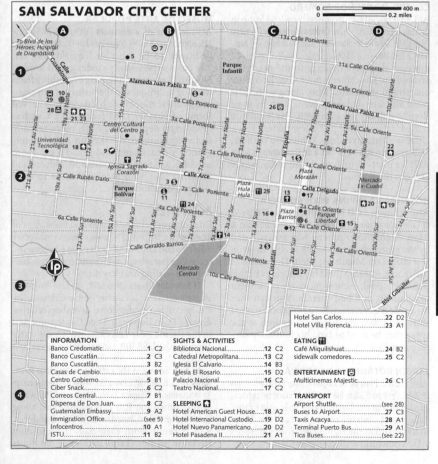

SAN SALVADOR CITY CENTER

0 ——————— 400 m
0 ——————— 0.2 miles

INFORMATION	
Banco Credomatic	1 C2
Banco Cuscatlán	2 C3
Banco Cuscatlán	3 B2
Casas de Cambio	4 B1
Centro Gobierno	5 B1
Ciber Snack	6 C2
Correos Central	7 B1
Dispensa de Don Juan	8 C2
Guatemalan Embassy	9 A2
Immigration Office	(see 5)
Infocentros	10 A1
ISTU	11 B2

SIGHTS & ACTIVITIES	
Biblioteca Nacional	12 C2
Catedral Metropolitana	13 C2
Iglesia El Calvario	14 B3
Iglesia El Rosario	15 D2
Palacio Nacional	16 C2
Teatro Nacional	17 C2

SLEEPING	
Hotel American Guest House	18 A2
Hotel Internacional Custodio	19 D2
Hotel Nuevo Panamericano	20 D2
Hotel Pasadena II	21 A1
Hotel San Carlos	22 D2
Hotel Villa Florencia	23 A1

EATING	
Café Miquilishuat	24 B2
sidewalk comedores	25 C2

ENTERTAINMENT	
Multicinemas Majestic	26 C1

TRANSPORT	
Airport Shuttle	(see 28)
Buses to Airport	27 C3
Taxis Acacya	28 A1
Terminal Puerto Bus	29 A1
Tica Buses	(see 22)

EL SALVADOR

on the Maya, Salvadoran history, arts, religion and economy. Prehistoric rock carvings occupy an adjacent garden. All explanations are in Spanish; so it's well worth bringing a dictionary.

MUSEO DE ARTE DE EL SALVADOR (MARTE)

The modern-art **museum** (Map p278; adult/student US$1.50/0.50; 🕙 10am-6pm Tue-Sun) opened in May 2003, and houses a permanent collection of top Salvadoran painters. Rotating exhibits are topical and highly politicized, featuring mostly Latin American artists. Getting here is an uphill walk from the anthropology museum, just behind the large Monumento a la Revolución.

CENTRO MONSEÑOR ROMERO

At Universidad Centroamericana José Simeón Cañas ('La UCA'), the **Centro Monseñor Romero** (Map p278; Calle de Mediterraneo; admission free; 🕙 8am-noon, 2-6pm Mon-Fri, 8-11:30am Sat) is a well-organized museum that pays homage to the martyred archbishop. The center is housed in the former quarters of six Jesuits, who, along with their maid and her daughter, were slain in their sleep by military forces in 1989. The Jesuits are buried in the chapel just a few meters away. UCA students give tours. While you're there, walk over to **Iglesia la Ceiba de Guadalupe** (Map p278), a pretty church on the highway, where you can catch a bus.

HOSPITAL LA DIVINA PROVEDENCIA

Also known as **El Hospitalito** (Map p278; Av 'B' at Calle Toluca; admission free; 🕙 usually 8am-noon & 2-5pm) Monseñor Romero was assassinated by government agents while giving mass in this chapel on March 24, 1980. The chapel is still in use. Romero lived his last years in this public hospital, eschewing more prominent assignments and bodyguards. You can tour his modest quarters, where his blood soaked shirt and robes are displayed, as well as the typewriter he used to type his famously stirring homilies.

JARDÍN BOTÁNICO LA LAGUNA

Also called **Plan de la Laguna** (Map p278; admission US$0.50; 🕙 9am-5:30pm Tue-Sun), this cool botanical garden sits at the bottom of a volcanic crater. Take bus 44 from the center, and ask the driver to let you off at the right spot, from where it's a 1km downhill walk to the garden.

Boulevard de los Héroes

MUSEO DE LA PALABRA Y LA IMAGEN

Formed 'against the chaos of amnesia,' the **Museum of the Word & Image** (Map p283; 27 Av Norte 1140; www.museo.com.sv; admission US$2; 🕙 8am-noon & 2-5pm Mon-Fri, 8am-noon Sat) documents El Salvador's culture and history. Exhibits are incredible if searing, including modern-art installations and black-and-white war photos. Content includes the revolutionary movement of the 1970s and '80s and portraits of indigenous groups and women in history. Director Carlos Henríquez Consalvi, a Venezuelan-born journalist, was the founder and front voice for Radio Venceremos, a radio station crucial to the pro-guerrilla cause. There's a reconstructed radio station and an interesting library with DVDs in English.

MUSEO DE ARTE POPULAR

A little gem of a **museum** (Map p283; Av San José 125; admission US$1; 🕙 10am-5pm Tue-Fri, 10am-6pm Sat) dedicated to El Salvador's quirky folk art. The curator personally guides guests around four small rooms, explaining everything from weaving techniques to the history of *sorpresas*, miniature scenes of life hidden under carved forms of eggs or fruit (see p307). *Cuadros* (paintings) depict village life, more recently including humorous takes on illegal immigration or marriage and sex. To get more up close, ask for the names and addresses of known artists who receive visitors to their village workshops.

ACTIVITIES

Friendly and bilingual Julio and Gabi Vega of **Akwaterra** (☎ 2263 2211; www.akwaterra.com) offer tailor-made land- and water-based ecotours, including horseback riding and mountain biking, and surfing and kayaking.

El Salvador Divers (Map p278; ☎ 2264 0961; www .elsalvadordivers.com; 3A Calle Pte; 🕙 9am-6:30pm Mon-Fri, 9am-1pm Sat) is a professional dive shop offering dives in Lago Ilopango, Lago Coatepeque and in the Pacific near Los Cóbanos. Open-water courses cost US$300, two-tank fun dives cost US$65.

El Salvador's only rafting outfit **Ríos Aventuras** (Map p278; ☎ 2298 0335; www.riosaventuras.com .sv in Spanish; Av Olímpica 3597) offers white-water rafting down the Río Lempa, Río Paz, along the Guatemalan border and Río Banderas. Rapids range from easy class II-III to class III-IV in winter. Trips include three hours

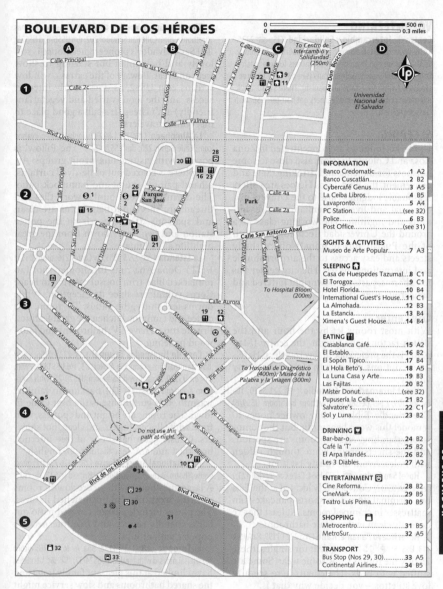

BOULEVARD DE LOS HÉROES

0   500 m
0   0.3 miles

INFORMATION
Banco Credomatic.................1 A2
Banco Cuscatlán....................2 B2
Cybercafé Genus...................3 A5
La Ceiba Libros......................4 B5
Lavapronto............................5 A4
PC Station.........................(see 32)
Police....................................6 B3
Post Office.......................(see 31)

SIGHTS & ACTIVITIES
Museo de Arte Popular..........7 A3

SLEEPING
Casa de Huespedes Tazumal....8 C1
El Torogoz..............................9 C1
Hotel Florida.........................10 B4
International Guest's House....11 C1
La Almohada.........................12 B3
La Estancia...........................13 B4
Ximena's Guest House...........14 B4

EATING
Casablanca Café....................15 A2
El Establo.............................16 B2
El Sopón Típico.....................17 B4
La Hola Beto's.......................18 A5
La Luna Casa y Arte...............19 B3
Las Fajitas............................20 B2
Mister Donut.....................(see 32)
Pupusería la Ceiba.................21 B2
Salvatore's............................22 C1
Sol y Luna............................23 B2

DRINKING
Bar-bar-o..............................24 B2
Café la 'T'.............................25 B2
El Arpa Irlandés....................26 B2
Les 3 Diables........................27 A2

ENTERTAINMENT
Cine Reforma.........................28 B2
CineMark..............................29 B5
Teatro Luis Poma...................30 B5

SHOPPING
Metrocentro..........................31 B5
MetroSur..............................32 A5

TRANSPORT
Bus Stop (Nos 29, 30)............33 A5
Continental Airlines...............34 B5

EL SALVADOR

of rafting, plus breakfast, lunch, snacks and transportation from San Salvador. Cost per person US$60.

COURSES

Mélida Anaya Montes Spanish Language School
(CIS; Map p278; ☎ 2235 1330; www.cis-elsalvador.org; Colonia Libertad, Av Bolivar 103) Named after a promi-

nent educator who became an FMLN commander amid growing government repression, this language school incorporates social and political themes. Language classes meet for four hours daily and cost US$100 per week, plus a one-time US$25 application fee and a weekly US$12.50 administration fee. Homestays for US$70 a week, including two meals per day, are available.

VOLUNTEERING

Centro de Intercambio y Solidaridad (CIS; ☎ 2235 1330; www.cis-elsalvador.org; Colonia Libertad, Av Bolivar 103) There are opportunities for volunteers to help teach English to low-income Salvadorians (see p327) or observe elections (with conversational Spanish). There's a 10-week minimum commitment and teachers get half-price Spanish classes in return.

SLEEPING

Upmarket lodgings are concentrated in Zona Rosa and Colonia Escalón, also close to some hotspots for dancing and drinking. Safe and convenient, the Blvd de los Héroes area offers reasonable lodgings close to the Universidad Nacional and lively bohemian bars, restaurants and nightlife. The working-class area around the Universidad Tecnológica (south of the Puerto Bus terminal) offers shady streets and easy access to the airport shuttle and international buses. The city center has few charms, parts are downright tattered and dangerous after dark.

City Center

With most rooms let by the hour and the sketch-factor high at night, the *centro* (Map p281) is the preference of few travelers. Here's a few options if you can't resist its gritty vitality.

Hotel Internacional Custodio (☎ 221 5810; 10a Av Sur 109; r per person with/without bathroom US$9/6) The friendly Bible-reading owner hopes to remodel this worn behemoth, but the rumor is longstanding. At least rooms are spacious and the sheets bright white though ridden with holes. Avoid the musty 1st floor.

Hotel San Carlos (☎ 2222 1664; Calle Concepción 121; r per person US$12) Conveniently located at the Tica bus terminal, this dive sports pancake-thin mattresses in cramped rooms. At least they're decently clean with private bathroom.

Hotel Nuevo Panamericano (☎ 2221 1199; 8a Av Sur 113; US$15; P ✲) Not a deal for singles, these 26 tidy tile rooms show some wear. Some are stuffed with beds. The clients here seem to love stilettos – you decide why that is.

Boulevard de los Héroes

You can easily walk to bars and restaurants on Calle San Antonio Abad or Blvd Universitario, or down to Metrocentro mall. Buses to the bus terminals, Zona Rosa and the center (and from there, the airport) all pass here. All are on Map p283.

Ximena's Guest House (☎ 260 2481; www.ximenas guesthouse.com; Calle San Salvador 202; dm US$6-8, d US$25; 💻) San Salvador's pioneer guesthouse is still lovely and bohemian but starting to show wear and tear. Beware of the extras – window screens cost US$2, as does hourly internet access, and the food (varied and vegetarian-friendly) ain't cheap. It's still a good place to meet other travelers.

La Almohada (☎ 2211 8021; almohadajosep@yahoo .com; Calle Berlín 220; dm US$7; 💻) 'The Pillow' is popular with visiting non-profit groups. Atmosphere is coaxed out of tie-dyed curtains, a hand-painted mural and hammock patio. The dorm has metal bunks, worn tiles and threadbare sheets but bathrooms are clean and spacious. It's across from the police station and two doors down from the great nightlife at La Luna.

La Estancia (☎ 2275 3381; Av Cortés 216, dm/d US$7/ 17; 💻) Doña Ana runs this homey spot (an unmarked lilac-trim house) catering to Peace Corps volunteers since its inception. While dorms feel stuffy, the patios, TV room, free coffee and common kitchen are great features. Private rooms have TV, bathrooms and faux-wood paneling.

Casa de Huespedes Tazumal (☎ 2235 0156; www .hoteltazumalhouse.com; 35a Av Norte 3, s/d US$18/25, with air-con US$20/28; s/d with bathroom US$20/25, with bathroom & air-con US$25/35; 💻) Basking in familial warmth, this guesthouse is the best value in town. The rooms are bright and spotless, with fresh white linens, towels and clean, hot showers. Guests get a half-hour of free internet, breakfast and ample assistance in English.

International Guest's House (☎ 2226 7343; i_guest house@hotmail.com; 35a Av Norte 9 Bis; s/d US$18/35; 💻) A large guesthouse with secure, low-lit rooms showing worn tile and mismatched fixtures. The pluses include a large, covered patio out back, friendly service and free internet. It's popular with groups.

El Torogoz (☎ 2235 4172; 35a Av Norte 7B; eltoro goz@telsal.net; s/d with breakfast US$24/37; 💻 📺) Prices have climbed at this pleasant family hotel and the shared bathrooms and slow service might make you wonder why. But nice features include a brick courtyard with plants, cable TV and a small swimming pool.

Hotel Florida (☎ 2260 2540; www.hotelflorida sofia.com; Pasaje los Almendros 115; s/d with fan US$24/30, s/d with air-con US$35/60; ✲) Modern and sunny, this friendly hotel might not be the bargain it once was, but it is still reliable and clean.

EL SALVADOR

The best features are the bouncy mattresses and rooftop terrace with views. Showers are solar-powered. There's no sign but you'll find it behind El Soplón Típico.

Near Universidad Tecnológica

This area west of *el centro* (Map p278) is safer and more relaxed than downtown. It's near the Universidad Tecnológica, where there's a bunch of cheap eats and internet cafés. It's convenient to the Terminal Puerto Bus for international buses. Take taxis at night.

Hotel American Guest House (☎ 271 0224; 17 Av Norte 119; s/d US$12/14, with bathroom US$15/20) An old-fashioned home where large, dark rooms have hardwood furniture and bubbling wallpaper. It's entertaining to browse the mix of tacky and truly compelling antiques. There's an onsite *cafetería*.

Hotel Pasadena II (☎ 2221 4786; 3a Calle Poniente 1037; s/d with fan US$12/17) Good value with attentive staff, but not as charming as the Villa Florencia next door. Bathrooms lack shower curtains and the décor is plain. Rooms in the back are quieter.

Hotel Villa Florencia (☎ 2221 1706; www.hotel villaflorencia.com in Spanish; 3a Calle Poniente 1023; s/d/t US$13/19/21) A lovely colonial place in top shape, with remodeled rooms with terracotta tiles and fresh linens. Enjoy the sunny fern-lined courtyard and new upstairs rooms with great light. It's next to a quiet funeral home.

Zona Rosa & Colonia Escalón

Casa Australia (Map p278; ☎ 223 7905; Blvd Venezuela 3093; s US$15, s/d with air-con US$25/30; P ▢) This relaxing, bright home is run by the energetic María Lidia. Singles are small but cheery and immaculately kept, doubles are average size. In a convenient, safe and quiet location. Breakfast is US$2 extra.

Hotel Villa Florencia Zona Rosa (Map p278; ☎ 2257 0236; www.hotelvillaflorencia.com in Spanish; Av La Revolución; s/d/t US$41/53/73; ▢ ▢ P) Ritzy and reasonably priced, this small hotel offers impeccable service and luxuriant touches (think gold tones and chandeliers). Loaner computers with wi-fi are available. There's a lovely stone courtyard and sleek café serving breakfast.

La Posada del Rey I (Map p278; ☎ 2264 5245; www |.posadadelreyprimero.com in Spanish; Pasaje Dordelly, Colonia Escalón; s/tw US$44/70; ▢ ▨) On the swanky side of town you'll find this fortress-like hotel with a placid atmosphere and top service. Carved colonial furniture and bucolic paintings of the countryside set the scene for a real retreat. Rooms are well-appointed and sunny and there's free wireless and an upmarket onsite restaurant. Prices may be negotiable at slow times.

EATING
City Center & Around

The center has plenty of eateries but few standouts. For a quick bite check out the **sidewalk comedores** (mains US$1-3) a block west of Plaza Barrios dishing up *panes de pollo* (big chicken sandwiches) and *bistec encebollada* (onion grilled beef).

Le Croissant (Map p278; 1a Calle Pte 3883; Colonia Escalón; pastries US$1-3; ☒ 7:30am-6:30pm) Crusty, fresh baguettes and a gorgeous selection of pastries will tempt even the not-hungry traveler. There's no seating, so grab it to go.

Cafetería Arco Iris (Map p278; 59a Av Sur; mains US$2-3; ☒ breakfast & lunch Mon-Sat) Come early for a wide selection of *comida a la vista* (meal served buffet-style), which includes vegetables and rice as well as a few meat choices.

Café Maquilishuat (Map p281; Simáu Centro, 1st fl; mains US$2-6; ☒ 7:30am-7pm) Upmarket for a *cafetería* (with hand-painted ceramics and flatscreen TV), this super-sparkling eatery offers a welcome escape from the hubbub. Grab a pastry or dine on *típica*, usually meat, crepes or rice, washing it down with *atole* (cinnamon rice milk).

La Ventana (Map p278; ☎ 2264 4885; 83 Av Norte 510 at 9a Calle Poniente; mains US$4-9; ☒ 8-1am Tue-Sat, 10-12:30am Sun) A hip and hot eatery where the food falls second to atmosphere. Enjoy the deck seating and bohemian backdrop. The menu offers German sausages, pastas, pizzas and Mexican fare. Service can be pitifully slow and indifferent.

Las Cofradias (Map p278; ☎ 2264 6148; Calle de Mirador, Colonia Escalón; buffet US$7; ☒ dinner) A lesson in everything Salvadoran. Bring your hunger (it's all you can eat) and stack a hand-made pottery plate with *tamales de elote* (corn tamales), *riguras* (tortillas in a corn husk), *gallina* (hen) and *nuegados* (plantains and yucca with honey and cinnamon).

Las Vacas Gordas (Map p278; ☎ 2243 3939; Blvd Hipódromo, Zona Rosa; mains US$8-22; ☒ noon-midnight Mon-Sat, noon-6pm Sun) Feast on quality meats ranging from filet mignon to rib-eye at this upmarket eatery. Check out regular two-for-one specials. Seating in the shady courtyard is especially posh.

EL SALVADOR

Boulevard de los Héroes

Calle San Antonio Abad has the best dining options but the many spots in and around the Metrocentro mall are clean and convenient. All are on Map p283.

Pupusería la Ceiba (Calle San Antonio Abad; mains US$1-3; ☿ closed Sun) Whether you're grabbing a dollar breakfast of tamales, coffee and eggs or downing a few hot *pupusas*, this corner café is a bargain.

Casablanca Café (Calle San Antonio Abad; mains US$2-3; ☿ 7:30am-5pm Mon-Sat) What this cement cafeteria lacks in ambience it makes up for with tasty *comida a la vista* ranging from coconut chicken to beef mains and salads.

Mister Donut (MetroSur; mains US$2-4; ☿ 6am-8pm) There's a surprising retro appeal to this updated donut shop in the mall, upgraded to serve sandwiches and tamales in leatherette booths.

Sol y Luna (cnr Blvd Universitario & Av C; mains US$2-4; ☿ 8am-5:30pm) Enjoy rare vegetarian fare served in hearty cafeteria-style. Loaves of cashew-almond bread, salads and fruit shakes round out the options.

La Luna Casa y Arte (☎ 2260 2921; www.lalunacasay arte.com; Calle Berlín 228; mains US$2-7; ☿ noon-2am Mon-Fri, 4:30pm-2am Sat) It's an arts venue (right) that happens to have outstanding grilled sandwiches, home-made soups and salads. The coffee bar and desserts prove worthy too.

Las Fajitas (Blvd Universitario; mains US$3-6; ☿ lunch & dinner) Tex-Mex goes festive with paper cutouts and wooden benches. The *pinchos* (beef-kebabs) are juicy and gigantic, and the tacos come with a range of salsas to sample.

Salvatore's (35a Av Norte; mains US$3-6; ☿ lunch & dinner) Come to this convenient neighborhood joint for cheap personal pizzas or whopping plates of pasta.

El Sopón Típico (Pasajes las Palmeras & los Almendros; mains US$5; ☿ 10:30am-9pm) Whet your appetite for roasted chicken, fresh corn tortillas and home-made *curtido* (spicy pickled cabbage). The adventurous can go for rabbit, rooster or roasted goat. Fresh and tart *arrayan* juice complements nicely. There's open-air ambience with heaps of wooden tables and benches, and friendly staff manning the crackling grill.

La Hola Beto's (Calle Lamatepec; mains US$5-12; ☿ noon-10:30pm) Great service and seafood are Beto's forte, but the Zona Real offers a wide selection of restaurant-bars.

El Establo (☎ 2226 9754; Blvd Universitario; mains US$6-10; ☿ lunch & dinner) Locals pack 'the stable'

for hefty portions of grilled meat, Argentine chorizo sausage and chicken, served alongside refried beans and *tostones* (fried plantains).

DRINKING
Bars & Clubs

La Luna Casa y Arte (Map p283; ☎ 2260 2921; www .lalunacasayarte.com; Calle Berlín 228; ☿ noon-2am Mon-Fri, 4:30pm-2am Sat) Hands-down El Salvador's best nightlife, with a mantra, '*No importa como llegues, la onda es llegar*' (who cares how you get here, the vibe is to arrive). Check out the website for the weekly rotation of live jazz, rock and salsa (usually Friday), as well as free films and live poetry. The food (see left) is good too.

Les 3 Diables (Map p283; Calle San Antonio Abad at Av Izalco; ☿ 7pm-2am Mon-Sat) Weekday drink specials and rowdy crowds keep this spot spinning. Who cares if there's no dancefloor? The aisles fill with young professionals, Peace Corps volunteers and students grooving to alt rock and pop.

Bar-bar-o (Map p283; www.bar-bar-o.com; ☿ 6pm-2:30am) A sleek spot with cheap eats, DJ (world and African rhythms) and free live music on weekends. Check out the website for listings.

Café la 'T' (Map p283; Calle San Antonio Abad 2233; ☿ 10am-9:30pm Mon-Wed, 10am-11pm Thu-Sat) This is a little lefty café with live music (jazz or folk) on some Fridays (US$2) and free films on Wednesday and Thursday at 7:30pm. There's light food, beer and wine but the coffee is mighty fine.

El Arpa Irlandés (Map p283; Av A across from Parque San José; ☿ 3pm-2am, closed Sun) With Guinness on tap and a pot of stew on the stovetop, this pub is a friendly spot to grab a pint or shoot some pool.

La Ventana (Map p278; ☎ 2264 4885; 83 Av Norte 510 at 9a Calle Poniente; mains US$4-9; ☿ 8-1am Tue-Sat, 10-12:30am Sun) Lively and upmarket, this social hive continues to be a perennial local favorite with cheap Belgian ales and German beers.

Jala la Jarra (Map p278; Av las Magnolias 206; ☿ 9:30pm-2am Wed-Sat; cover US$5) This is a groovy bar and disco. Dress well to fit in with the rich, young somebodies. This is one of a row of popular clubs and pubs in the swishy Zona Rosa neighborhood on Av Las Magnolias.

Gay & Lesbian Venues

Yascuas & Milenio (Map p278; Condominios Juan Pablo II on Prolongación Juan Pablo II; ☿ 9:30pm-1am Thu-Sat) Two gay bar-discos in the same building.

ENTERTAINMENT

Look for *Diario de Hoy*'s Thursday pullout section *Planeta Alternativa* for weekly concert and event listings.

Cinemas

Hollywood films with Spanish subtitles dominate the theater while some bars listed earlier have alternative movie nights. Major newspapers have schedules. Wednesday is half price.

Cine Reforma (Map p283; ☎ 2225 9588; Blvd Universitario) Discounts on random Tuesdays.

CineMark (Map p283; ☎ 2261 2001; Metrocentro, 3rd fl, Blvd de los Héroes; admission US$3)

Cinépolis (Map p278; Galerías Escalóon) A new 11-screen megaplex.

La Luna Casa y Arte (Map p283; ☎ 2260 2921; www .lalunacasayarte.com in Spanish; Calle Berlín 228; admission free) Screenings at 8pm Wednesday.

Multicinemas Majestic (Map p281; ☎ 2222 5965; Av España; admission US$1.75)

Theater

Teatro Luis Poma (Map p283; ☎ 2261 1029; Metrocentro; admission US$5) A modern playhouse with great offerings, strangely set at the mall.

SHOPPING

The gallery of La Palma artist Fernando Llort is four long blocks south of Plaza Masferrer.

El Arbol de Dios (Map p278; Calle la Mascota; admission free; 🕓 9am-9:30pm Mon-Sat) houses an extensive

collection of his work, including sophisticated pieces unlike his simpler and better-known wood paintings.

A garden array of Che and Romero T-shirts, cheap shoes and *artesanía* can be found in this army barracks turned public market **Mercado Ex-Cuartel** (Map p281; Calle Delgado; 🕓 7:30am-6pm Mon-Sat, 7:30am-2pm Sun). Swag includes hammocks on hooks and brightly embroidered cotton. Scrutinize crafts since quality varies widely.

New boards and accessories, as well as unlimited beta on surf breaks, are available at **Pacific Surf & Sport** (Map p278; ☎ 2245 1584; Blvd El Hipodromo 14, Zona Rosa; 11am-8pm Mon-Sat).

GETTING THERE & AWAY

Air

Aeropuerto Internacional Comalpa, 50km southeast of San Salvador, is a major Central American hub. Airline offices in San Salvador include:

American Airlines (Map p278; ☎ 2298 0777; Edificio La Centroamericana, Alameda Roosevelt)

Continental (Map p283; ☎ 2207 2040; Metrocentro Mall, 2nd fl)

Copa Airlines (Map p278; ☎ 2209 2672; World Trade Center I, cnr 89a Av Norte & Calle del Mirador)

Delta Air Lines (Map p278; ☎ 2275 9292; World Trade Center I, cnr 89a Av Norte & Calle del Mirador)

TACA (Map p278; ☎ 2267 8222; Galerías Escalón, street level)

United Airlines (Map p278; ☎ 2279 3900; Galerías Escalón, street level)

Bus

San Salvador has three main terminals for national long-distance buses. Buses serving all points east and a few northern destinations arrive and depart from the **Terminal de Oriente** (Map p278; Alameda Juan Pablo II), on the eastern side of the city. Buses serving all points west, including the Guatemalan border, arrive and depart from the **Terminal de Occidente** (Map p278; Blvd Venezuela near 49a Av Sur). In the south of the city **Terminal de Sur** (Map p278; Autopista a Comalapa), also called Terminal San Marcos, serves destinations to the south and southeast.

See p274 for information on international buses leaving from the hotels and Terminal Puerto Bus.

TERMINAL DE ORIENTE
To get to the terminal, take bus 9, 29 or 34 from the city center; bus 29 or 52 from Blvd de los Héroes; bus 7C or 34 from Terminal

Occidente; or bus 21 from Terminal de Sur. Frequent departures include:

Chalatenango Bus 125 (US$0.90; 2hr)

El Poy (Honduran border) Bus 119 (US$1.60; 3hr)

Ilobasco Bus 111 (US$0.70; 1½hr)

La Palma Bus 119 (US$1.50; 2¾hr)

La Unión Bus 304 (US$3; 4hr) faster *especial* service available

San Miguel Bus 301 (US$1.15-2.40; 3hr) faster *especial* service available

San Sebastián Bus 110 (US$0.70, 1½hr)

San Vicente Bus 116 (US$0.85; 1½hr)

Suchitoto Bus 129 (US$0.80; 1½hr)

Usulután Bus 302 (US$1.50; 2¾hr) departs at 7am & 8am only, or use Terminal de Sur

TERMINAL DE OCCIDENTE

To get here, take bus 34 from the city center; bus 44 from Blvd de los Héroes (get off at Blvd Venezuela and walk a few blocks west to the terminal); or bus 7C or 34 from Terminal Oriente. Frequent departures include:

Ahuachapán Bus 202 (US$1; 2¼hr)

Cerro Verde Santa Ana Bus to El Congo (US$0.80; 40min), then Bus 248

Joya de Cerén Bus 108 to San Juan Opico (US$0.55; 1¾hr)

La Hachadura Bus 205 to Sonsonate (US$1.45; 3½hr), then Bus 259

La Libertad Bus 102 (US$0.55; 1hr), catch it at its terminal near Parque Cuscatlán or in front of (not inside) Terminal Oriente

Lago de Coatepeque Santa Ana bus to El Congo (US$0.80; 40min), then Bus 248

Las Chinamas Bus 202 to Ahuachapán (US$1.50; 2½hr), then Bus 263

Los Cóbanos Bus 205 to Sonsonate (US$1.30; 2½hr), then Bus 257

Metapán Bus 201A (US$2.50; 1¾hr)

Ruinas de San Andrés Bus 201 (US$0.80; 40min) Santa Ana Bus to the turnoff to ruins.

San Cristóbal Bus 498 (US$1.25; 3hr)

Santa Ana Bus 201 (US$0.80; 1¼hr)

Sonsonate Bus 205 (US$0.70 *directo*, US$1 *especial*; 1¼hr)

TERMINAL DE SUR (TERMINAL SAN MARCOS)

To get here take bus 26 or microbus 11B from the city center; or bus 21 from Terminal Oriente. Departures:

Costa del Sol Bus 495 (US$1.10; 2½hr)

Puerto El Triunfo Bus 185 (US$1.50; 2hr)

Usulután Bus 302 (US$1.50; 2½hr) Faster *especial* service available.

Zacatecoluca Bus 133 (US$0.70; 1½hr)

GETTING AROUND

Bus

San Salvador's extensive bus network, from large smoke-spewing monsters to zippy microbuses, can get you just about anywhere. Fares are US$0.17 to US$0.23.

Buses run frequently from 5am to 7:30pm daily; fewer buses run on Sunday. Services stop between 7:30pm and 8:30pm; microbuses run later, until around 9pm. After 9pm you'll have to take a taxi.

In the center, it is fastest to walk a few blocks away from Plaza Barrios to catch your bus, as the traffic is hopelessly snarled most of the time. But if you have bags, it's safer and easier to get on a bus as soon as possible. Key routes include:

Bus 9 Goes down 29a Av Norte alongside the Universidad de El Salvador. Then it turns east toward the city center, heading past the cathedral and up Independencia past Terminal de Oriente.

Bus 26 Passes Plaza Barrios and Parque Zoológico on its way to Terminal del Sur.

Bus 29 Goes to Terminal de Oriente via the center. Buses stop between Metrocentro and MetroSur.

Bus 30 Heads downtown and is the best way to get to and from bus 138 to the airport. Pick it up on behind Metrocentro or at Parque Libertad in the center.

Bus 30B A very useful route, especially from Blvd de los Héroes. The bus goes east on Blvd Universitario, by Universidad Nacional, then southwest down Blvd de los Héroes to Metrocentro. From there, it goes west along Alameda Roosevelt, past the El Salvador del Mundo monument and continues west along Paseo Gral Escalón past Galerías mall. It then turns south at 79a Av and continues along Blvd del Hipódromo to Av Revolución, passing through the Zona Rosa and near the art and anthropology museums, then returns on Alameda Araujo, Roosevelt, and 49a Av Sur back to Metrocentro.

Bus 34 Runs from Terminal de Oriente to Metrocentro then down to the Zona Rosa, turning around right in front of Marte art museum. Passes Terminal de Occidente on return.

Bus 42 Takes you to the anthropology museum and La Ceiba de Guadalupe. The bus goes west along Calle Arce from the cathedral and continues along Alameda Roosevelt. At El Salvador del Mundo, it heads southwest along Alameda Araujo, passing the Mercado de Artesanías and Museo Nacional de Antropología David J Guzmán, and continues down the Carr Interamericana, passing La Ceiba de Guadalupe.

Bus 44 The bus to take to the Terminal de Occidente and UCA. The route heads southwest down Blvd de los Héroes past Metrocentro and down 49a Av. For the Terminal de Occidente get off at Av Venezuela and walk a few blocks west. The bus passes lower and upper entrances to UCA, and La Ceiba de Guadalupe, heading up Alameda Araujo, past Metrocentro to downtown.

Bus 101 Goes from Plaza Barrios in the center, past MetroSur, past the anthropology museum, past La Ceiba de Guadalupe and on to Santa Tecla.

Car & Motorcycle

Avoid driving through the city center. The traffic gets snarled in daytime and the area is unsafe at night. It's quickest to take major thoroughfares. One-way streets have an arrow painted on the pavement or signage. For details on car hire, see p275.

Taxi

Taxis are plentiful but unmetered so negotiate a price in advance. A ride in town should cost about US$4 to US$6 during daytime. Rates go up a few dollars late at night. License plates beginning with 'A' indicate a registered taxi, in theory they can be held accountable for problems. If you don't spot a passing taxi, call **Taxis Acacya** (Map p281; ☎ 2271 4937) or **Acontaxis** (☎ 2270 1176).

AROUND SAN SALVADOR

On San Salvador's outskirts, old melds with new in the oddest of ways. If you could climb the pyramids, the panorama would be obstructed by live wires and Pollo Campero. Ruins stride up to the highway (or vice-versa), as if no one ever considered separating the sacred from the here and now.

The roughneck port of La Libertad acts as the gateway to dozens of fast, powerful and fun surf breaks that incite wide grins. With some of the world's best waves, the Western Pacific coast is perhaps the only region with a consistent stream of foreign visitors, mostly surfers. The rural coast is often knocked hard by storms and other natural disasters as the steep coastal bluffs can be unstable.

CIHUATÁN

The modest ruins of **Cihuatán** (admission US$3; ☽ 9am-4pm Tue-Sun) were once an immense urban area alongside the Río Guazapa, possibly the largest pre-Columbian city between Guatemala and Peru. The city thrived for 100 years before being sacked and burned by unknown invaders in the 10th century AD. It was likely occupied by Maya, Lenca

and other groups joined together for commerce during an unstable period. A partial excavation shows evidence of two separate ceremonial centers and hundreds of buildings, a pair of ball courts and a large mound where a pyramid once stood, all surrounded by a low defensive wall.

From the Terminal de Oriente, take bus 119 toward Chalatenango and get off about 4km beyond Las Aguilares; ask the driver to let you off at Las Ruinas. It's a 900m walk to the site.

EL BOQUERÓN

Quezaltepeque (Volcán San Salvador) has two peaks. The higher peak, at 1960m, is called Picacho. The other, Boquerón (Big Mouth), is 1893m high and has a second cone within its crater – 45m high and perfectly symmetrical – formed in 1917. A paved road to the top affords an easy climb with unbelievable views as your reward. Bring a bag to pick up litter if you're so inspired.

Get an early start as busing from San Salvador takes a couple of hours. From Parque Cuscatlán, take bus 101A or B to Santa Tecla. From there, bus 103 departs from 6a Av Sur to the village of Boquerón. The bus comes sporadically, but pick-ups depart from the same place. The summit is 1km beyond the village.

RUINAS DE SAN ANDRÉS

In 1977 a step pyramid and a large courtyard with a subterranean section were unearthed in this **site** (admission US$3; ☽ 9am-5pm Tue-Sun), inhabited by Maya between AD 600–900. Experts believe that up to 12,000 people lived here. The city once dominated the Valle de Zapotitán and possibly the neighboring Valle de las Hamacas where San Salvador is now situated.

The ruins are interesting and peaceful, if not terribly impressive. Recently, cement walls protecting the original structures were restored back to the original stone and mortar. The main pyramid is called the Campana San Andrés for its bell shape. A trench in front of Estructura 3 shows how the platform was built with hundreds of thousands of adobe bricks. Another 15 mounds are yet to be unearthed.

The ruins are 300m north of the highway and 33km west of San Salvador in the Valle Zapotitán. Take the Santa Ana bus 201 from San Salvador's Terminal de Occidente and

EL SALVADOR

get off at km 33, at a small black sign for the ruins. If combining this with a visit to Joya de Cerén, visit Joya de Cerén first, then catch any bus on the highway for the short distance to San Andrés.

JOYA DE CERÉN

Called the Pompeii of America, UN World Heritage Site **Joya de Cerén** (www.cihuatan.org; admission US$3; ☺ 9am-5pm Tue-Sun) was a small Maya settlement buried under volcanic ash when the Laguna Caldera Volcano erupted in AD 595. Fleeing residents left behind a wealth of everyday items that provide clues into ancient planting, homebuilding and food storage.

The main compound consists of five small structures – for the layperson it's somewhat underwhelming. The remodeled museum offers a good collection of artifacts and models of the villages. One compelling piece is a small dish showing fingerprints smeared in the remains of an interrupted meal.

The site is 36km west of San Salvador – take bus 108 from Terminal de Occidente and get off after crossing the bridge over the Río Sucio.

LOS PLANES DE RENDEROS

Within this district you will find the popular **Parque Balboa** (admission US$0.80), a 28-hectare park preserved for family fun. There are trails for short walks, a skating rink, playgrounds and pre-Columbian-style sculptures. It is 12km from the city center.

Two kilometers past Parque Balboa is **Puerta del Diablo** (Devil's Door). Two towering boulders, reputedly once a single stone split in two, form a lookout with fantastic views, minus those of garbage strewn about. During the war this place was an execution point, the cliffs offering easy disposal of the bodies.

Take bus 12 'Mil Cumbres' from the east side of the Mercado Central, at 12a Calle Poniente. If you're driving, head down Av Cuscatlán until you see the signs.

Panchimalco

Toltec immigrants founded this tranquil town in a lush valley. The baroque church, completed in 1725 by indigenous craftsmen, features interesting woodwork; check out the indigenous Christ. Local cultural pride is evident in two cultural centers along 1a Av displaying ceramics and dance costumes. Both host cultural events open to the public.

Panchimalco is renowned for its religious festivals, particularly Palm Sunday, when residents march through the streets bearing decorated palm fronds. Early May's **Fería de Cultura de las Flores y las Palmas** features palm artistry, folk dancing and fireworks.

Bus 17 departs for Panchimalco from Av 29 de Agosto on the south side of the Mercado Central in San Salvador.

LA LIBERTAD

pop 20,100

This run-down port cranks to life early, with hardcore surfers toting their boards, lone fishermen casting at the rocky shore and women working market stalls. This is La Libertad at its most compelling. If you don't surf and aren't terribly interested in learning how, you may not find much of interest here. Though El Salvador is promoting it heavily as a tourist destination, this grit-worn city cries out for an extreme makeover, and why not, the surfing's world class. Shiny additions of a well-lit skate park in the center, new pick-ups emblazoned with 'Bendición de Díos' (God's blessing) and a new, ahem, mall at the east end of town at least show some effort.

Information

Banco Agrícola (Barrios east of the market or El Faro mall) Changes traveler's checks; there's a new 24-hour ATM at El Faro mall.

Cyber Fenix (2a Calle Pte; per hr US$1; ☺ 8am-8pm) Below the Surf Club Inn.

Post office (2a Calle Oriente) Near 2a Av Norte.

Dangers & Annoyances

La Libertad has become increasingly unsafe thanks to gang activity and a long-standing drug trade. Pick-pocketing and assaults are on the rise. Avoid the area southeast of the plaza at night (there's better nightlife at the restaurants east of the Lighthouse mall). A local surfer warns about frequent assaults and aggressive dogs on the walk by the cemetery on the walk to the point at Punta Roca. Surfers should go accompanied and not bring valuables. Dogs can be deterred by throwing rocks (near them, not at them).

Strong rip currents proliferate throughout the coast. Lifeguards only work weekends in La Libertad and Playa San Diego. Black clams raised in the estuary hold a high concentration of toxins; avoid eating them if you want to keep catching waves.

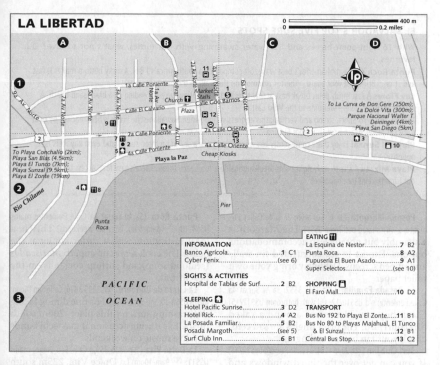

LA LIBERTAD

PACIFIC OCEAN

To Playa Conchalio (2km);
Playa San Blas (4.5km);
Playa El Tunco (7km);
Playa Sunzal (9.5km);
Playa El Zonte (19km)

Río Chilama

Punta Roca

Pier

Playa la Paz

Cheap Kiosks

To La Curva de Don Gere (250m);
La Dolce Vita (300m);
Parque Nacional Walter T
Deininger (4km);
Playa San Diego (5km)

INFORMATION		
Banco Agrícola	1	C1
Cyber Fenix	(see 6)	

SIGHTS & ACTIVITIES		
Hospital de Tablas de Surf	2	B2

SLEEPING		
Hotel Pacific Sunrise	3	D2
Hotel Rick	4	A2
La Posada Familiar	5	B2
Posada Margoth	(see 5)	
Surf Club Inn	6	B1

EATING		
La Esquina de Nestor	7	B2
Punta Roca	8	A2
Pupusería El Buen Asado	9	A1
Super Selectos	(see 10)	

SHOPPING		
El Faro Mall	10	D2

TRANSPORT		
Bus No 192 to Playa El Zonte	11	B1
Bus No 80 to Playas Majahual, El Tunco		
& El Sunzal	12	B1
Central Bus Stop	13	C2

Activities

BEACHES

The closest beach to the capital, La Libertad fills up with city dwellers on weekends. In the rainy season (March to October), the beach is rocky, covered with large black boulders, and the riptide, along with sewage, makes the water uninviting. In the dry season, the rocks get covered in sand, but the boulders are still whipped by the waves. If you just want to frolic in waves, hit the Costa del Bálsamo or go 4km east to sandy Playa San Diego.

SURFING

You'll find world-class surfing at Punta Roca, a lively right-hand break smack in front of town. Beginners launch at Playa La Paz (November to February), El Zonte or El Sunzal. Top surf spots with accommodations are found on the Costa Bálsamo (p293). For surfboard rental and repair, try:

Hospital de Tablas de Surf (☎ 2335 3214; 3a Av Norte 28-7) Not for broken femurs, Saul's hospital repairs, buys and sells boards, in addition to offering surfing lessons. Just knock if it appears closed.

HIKING

About 4km east of La Libertad along the Comalapa road, **Parque Nacional Walter T Deininger** (admission US$0.80, guide US$12; ☽ 7am-noon-1pm & 1-5pm) is named for the German settler who donated the land. It includes two types of forest: *caducifolio,* which sheds its leaves in summer, and *galería,* which retains its foliage year-round. A well-maintained 18km trail skirts the park; you must be accompanied by a ranger. Signs mark trails to Río Amayo, 'the Mystery Cave' and a lookout showing the forest cascading to the sea. Deer, raccoon and the endangered *tepezcuintle* (paca) can be spotted, in addition to many bird species, including the *torogoz* (blue-crowned motmot), El Salvador's national bird.

To visit Parque Deininger, you supposedly must obtain a permit from **ISTU** (☎ 2222 8000) in San Salvador (p279) five days prior to arrival. You might just try showing up and talking with the guard. It's a 15-minute ride from La Libertad – catch bus 187.

Sleeping

Since strolling around at night is inadvisable, choose your lodgings carefully.

EL SALVADOR

EL SALVADOR'S TOP FIVE SURF SPOTS

With 16 right-point breaks and 82° water swarming with sea turtles, what's not to love? Our favorites:

Punta Roca Yes, Central America's best wave, oft compared to South Africa's J Bay. A rocky bottom makes it fast and strong. Bring just your board – theft is common on the walk to the point (see p291)

Las Flores A fast sandy point break best at low tide. Picture a hollow take-off ending on a black sand beach. A 300m ride is possible – welcome to the Wild East.

Punta Mango Short, strong and vertical, this aggressive Indo-men Hawaiian-style break is best reached by boat from Las Flores beach or via bus from El Cuco.

Playa El Sunzal Enjoy these consistently big waves alongside a sea of brethren surfers and even kayakers (see opposite)

Playa Mizata A sharp, reefy right point break alongside a fun beach break. There's easy road access but check it out from the cliff (see opposite)

Posada Margoth (3a Av Sur btwn 2a & 4a Calles Poniente; s with shared bathroom US$5) The Margoth is a shambly but not unclean accommodations options. Expect to see corrugated tin walls and ripped screens. Definitely bring your own toilet paper.

La Posada Familiar (☎ 2335 3552; 3a Av Sur at 4a Calle Poniente; s/d US$10/12, s/d with bathroom US$12/15) Clean but cave-like rooms around a raked dirt courtyard. The plain singles are sad cells, check your fan before settling in.

Surf Club Inn (☎ 2346 1104; 2a Calle Pte; s/d US$12/15) If you can get over the tinted windows and mismatched velveteen furniture, these large cement rooms with sturdy mattresses are good value. Use the air-con to combat slight smells of mildew. It's inside a commercial plaza with a handy laundromat downstairs.

Hotel Rick (☎ 2335 3542; 5a Av Sur; d US$25; 🖳) These basic lodgings are kept in tip-top shape, though the bathrooms are just open stalls. The 2nd floor is brighter and airier.

Hotel Pacific Sunrise (☎ 2346 2000; www.hotelelsalvador.com; Calle El Obispo at Carr Litoral; s/d US$45/57) It sure feels like the Best Western but it's the finest digs in town, with spotless rooms and a pool overlooking the parking lot.

Eating

Pupusería El Buen Asado (3a Av Norte btwn El Calvario & 2a Calle Pte; mains US$3-4; 🕙 7am-9:30pm) If pupuserías could be fashionable, this place, serving big bean breakfasts, quick tacos and pupusas, would fit the bill.

La Esquina de Nestor (cnr 2a Calle Pte & 3a Av Norte; mains US$3-4; 🕙 10am-10pm) This tiny taquería (taco café) dishes up authentic Mexican tacos stuffed with shrimp or beef or al pastor (with roasted pork).

Punta Roca (5a Av Sur at 4a Calle Poniente; mains US$4-10; 🕙 8am-8pm, later on weekends) This is a local institution, with a surfer-family at the helm. The cook serves up superb mariscadas (seafood soup) and shrimp cocktails on the beachfront.

La Curva de Don Jere (☎ 2335 3436; Calle San Diego; mains US$8-10; 🕙 9am-10pm) For fine dining facing the crashing surf, try this place, 200m south of Shell, featuring occasional maríachi bands and live music on weekends.

La Dolce Vita (☎ 2335 3592; Calle San Diego; mains US$11; 🕙 9am-10pm) La Dolce Vita, 225m south of Shell, also has a great beachfront location where Chef Carmine serves up enormous seafood platters and pasta plates.

Super Selectos (Mall El Faro; 🕙 7:30am-8pm) For self-caterers.

Getting There & Away

There is no bus terminal. Bus 102 goes to and from San Salvador (US$0.55, one hour). In San Salvador, catch it at its terminal near Parque Cuscatlán or in front of – not inside – Terminal Oriente. In La Libertad, buses leave from the corner of 4a Av Norte and Calle Gerardo Barros.

See p277 for details of how to get to La Libertad from the airport.

To Sonsonate, take bus 287 (US$1.25, 2½ hours, 1:45pm only) from the bus stop at 2a Calle Poniente or bus 192 to Playa Mizata (see following) and change.

Getting Around

Surfers can take boards on all buses. Bus 80 goes west from La Libertad to Playa El Tunco and Playa El Sunzal (US$0.25; every 15 minutes from 4:30am to 6pm) or east to Playa

EL SALVADOR

San Diego (US$0.30, every 15 minutes from 5:40am to 6pm). Buses leave from 4a Av Norte at 2a Calle Oriente.

For Playa El Zonte or Playa Mizata take bus 192 (US$0.50, every 30 minutes from 7am to 5:30pm).

LA COSTA DEL BÁLSAMO

The Balsam Coast stretches from La Libertad westward to Sihuapilapa. Once there was a whole industry here surrounding the valuable aromatic oil extracted by burning the bark of live balsams. Today only a handful of trees remain and cotton has become the main cash crop.

From La Libertad, the road west twists around rocky headlands, giving glimpses of sheltered coves and sandy beaches (mostly private). Weekend hordes head for Playas Conchalío and El Majahual, the latter a wide swath of black sand bordered by endless seafood shacks and parking lots. Wait and you will find better options further on, a whole 50km of uninterrupted beaches.

Bus 80 goes as far as Playa El Sunzal. Beyond that, take the less frequent bus 192.

Sleeping & Eating
PLAYA COCHALÍO
Centro Obrero Dr Humberto Romero Alvergue (Ruta 2; free with permit) This worker's center has plain rooms and flimsy cots, fronting a rocky beach. Shacks by the beach gate serve food. Guests must obtain prior written permission from the Ministerio de Trabajo in San Salvador (p279).

PLAYA EL TUNCO
With a broad beach, narrow sandy streets and colorful matchbox homes, cool little El Tunco offers guests the most dining and lodging options of all the surf villages.

La Sombra (☎ 7729 5628; www.surflibre.com; dm/d US$5/10; dm/d/tr with bathroom US$7/14/21) Surfer José has crafted a great budget option with this new narrow two-story featuring wooden decks and cathedral ceiling rooms. The extras alone – cheap surf lessons/rentals (US$10), weekday kitchen use and free Zona Rosa bus pick-up in San Salvador – make it worthwhile.

Papaya's Lodge (☎ 2389 6231; www.papayasurfing .com; s/d US$8/14) A chill guesthouse run by local surf legend Jaime Delgado, aka Papaya. Small, clean rooms with shared bathroom have cement block walls and step out onto a shady

river deck backed by mangroves. The surf shop offers repairs and lessons.

Tortuga Surf Lodge (☎ 2389 6125; www.tortuga surflodge.net; campsites US$6, d with/without bathroom US$27/22) Steps from the surf, Tortuga's red-tile rooms are spacious and spotless. Bamboo railings, hand-carved furniture and cold beers (US$1.25) are nice touches.

Tekuani Kal (☎ 2389 6388; www.tekuanikal.com; s/d incl breakfast US$50/65; 🍴 🖥) Stone garden pathways traipse through manicured tropical gardens with rock fountains to six ultraprivate rooms. Each has an appealing earthy décor of Latin textiles and masks, but the grabber is the bamboo deck facing the surf. The restaurant offers a cool ambience and reasonably priced grilled chicken or pasta (US$6).

La Guitarra (🕒 3pm-3am Thu-Sun) Live shows (reggae, rock, jazz and funk) spice up this local bar, and there's a pool table. It's open sporadically.

Side-by-side seafood restaurants La Bocana and Erica's vie for customers. La Bocana's beachfront claim means it's slightly pricier.

PLAYA EL SUNZAL
Surfer's Inn (☎ 2389 6266; Carr Litoral Km 44; camp sites US$3, s/d US$5/8, with bathroom US$8/12) This is a basic family-run lodging with concrete rooms that are passably clean, set in a sandy yard with chickens. Guests can cook here (but not the chickens!)

San Patricio (☎ 2389 6107; Carr Litoral Km 44; s/d US$7/10, s/d with bathroom US$10/12 🍴) Run by a sweet family, this more modern hotel offers a shady cement porch and runty pool, but the rooms could stand a real good scrubbing.

PLAYA EL ZONTE & BEYOND
El Zonte is less developed than El Tunco but more ambient than Playa Sunzal. Show patience and courtesy – sometimes the surf gets a little crowded here.

Esencia Nativa (☎ 2302 6258; esencianativa@yahoo .com; s/d with fan US$10/15/20, r with bathroom & air-con US$30; 🅿 🍴 🖥) A cheerful boho atmosphere with ample (though sandy) lounge spaces. Big rooms have snug single beds and extras include a ping-pong table, surf classes and open-air café serving burgers and seafood.

Horizonte Surf Resort (☎ 2323 0099; saburo surfcamp@hotmail.com; s/d/t with air-con US$30/35/45; 🍴 🖥 🅿) No longer a budget paradise, the Horizonte still offers a clean, kick-back retreat. Perks include the manicured pool area,

EL SALVADOR

outdoor bar/common area, cheap surf lessons and board rentals (US$10 per day).

Playa Mizata sits 35km beyond El Zonte, home to some lovely and lesser-known right and left breaks (see p292). There are a few food shacks but no accommodations. The next spot of interest is Los Cóbanos, a series of small coves with El Salvador's best beaches and diving. To get here take the half-hourly bus 257 from Sonsonate (US$0.50, 40 minutes).

WESTERN EL SALVADOR

Western El Salvador is a stunning must for travelers. Start with Santa Ana – the country's seat of old money is a colonial city with dusty, sprawling markets and a dapper gentleman's air. Coffee plantations surround the region where some of the country's poorest live and work. On these twisty back roads bent *campesinos* haul bursting sacks, sorting ripe red berries. The Ruta de las Flores travels the sunny climes of flower farms, where cobblestone villages offer the pleasant illusion of time stopped. But adventures do await; volcano ascents, waterfall descents, hot springs and crater lakes make this the destination for active travelers.

PARQUE NACIONAL LOS VOLCANES

This **park** (admission US$1; ⊙ 8am-5pm) is a natural treasure, encompassing three major volcanoes (Cerro Verde, Volcán Santa Ana and Volcán Izalco) and thousands of hectares. It's a major bird sanctuary, with many migratory species passing through, including emerald toucanets, jays, woodpeckers, motmots and 17 species of hummingbird.

Active Volcán Izalco is the youngest in the group. Its cone began forming in 1770 from a belching hole of sulfuric smoke and today stands 1910m high. Izalco erupted throughout the 20th century, spewing smoke, boulders and flames and earning its reputation as 'the lighthouse of the Pacific.' Today, this bare, perfect cone stands devoid of life in an otherwise fertile land.

Without Izalco's stark drama but 400m higher, Santa Ana (also known as Ilamatepec) is El Salvador's third highest point. Its eruption in October, 2005 triggered landslides that killed two coffee pickers and forced the evacuation of thousands. The barren and windy summit affords spectacular views of a steep drop into the crater on one side and Lago Coatepeque on the other.

Assaults used to be a major problem, but the park service has instituted a mandatory guide service. Tourist police are posted along the trails and at the summits. Crime has dropped dramatically, but you should not hike solo.

Four-hour guided hikes to either volcano (Izalco US$1; Santa Ana US$1.80) begin at 11am *only* so don't arrive late! This also means you can't do both in one day. Wear sturdy shoes. A short alternative is a 40-minute nature trail which offers views of the lake and Volcán Santa Ana. It starts in the parking lot.

Sleeping & Eating

San Blas has two camping complexes in the shadow of Volcán Santa Ana. **Campo Bello** (☎ 2271 0853) offers round cement dwellings that sleep four. **Casa de Cristal** (☎ 2483 4713) has rustic cabañas. Call ahead for prices, camping possibilities and availability.

A local cooperative manages a rustic **campground** (☎ 2483 4713/4679, 2 adults US$35), 13km from San Blas heading towards Los Andes. Los Andes has a ranger who can also guide Santa Ana hikes. For information, contact **Salvanatura** (☎ 2279 1515; www.salvanatura.org, in Spanish) in San Salvador (see p279). More useful park information is at www.complejolosvolcanes.com.

Getting There & Away

Arrive by 11am since the guided hikes leave just once a day. The easiest, surest route is to come from Santa Ana, where bus 248 goes all the way to the entrance (see p297). The last bus leaves the park at 5pm but verify times with the driver who drops you off.

Leave early from San Salvador to make connections. Take any bus to Santa Ana and disembark at El Congo on the Carr Panamericana; walk uphill to the overpass and catch bus 248. Ask to be sure you're in the right place.

If you're driving, Parque Nacional Los Volcanes is 67km from San Salvador via Sonsonate or 77km by the more scenic route toward Santa Ana.

LAGO DE COATEPEQUE

Coatepeque is a sparkling blue crater lake under the looming peaks of Cerro Verde, Izalco and Santa Ana. It's 6km wide and 120m deep, surrounded by green slopes. The lake is a popular weekend retreat for San Salvador's

OOH OOH WITCHY WOMAN

The Siguanaba is a mythical hottie who seduces men, then upon further inspection, turns out to be grotesque and whorish. But the revelation comes too late to warn her man-victims – they directly drop dead or go batty. Siguanaba travels with her mischievous little boy Cipitío, who approaches women washing at rivers to hurl rocks at them. He never grows up, but here too appearances deceive. Those who've spied Cipitío up close report he's actually a tiny man.

The Siguanaba story comes from the era of coffee plantations when landowners threw luxuriant parties that spanned days. To keep the nosy neighboring *campesinos* (farmers) away the landowners invented terrific tales. And who knows? Perhaps they helped explain away the lovely ladies traveling to and from the fete.

These days, you'll hear *'Te has jugado la Siguanaba'* (Has the Siguanaba played with you?) if you're totally dazed or distracted.

elite. But there are a few cheap hotels here, and during the week it is peaceful. The bus enters the northeast side of the lake to an area with hotels and public access. For around US$4 or the price of a meal, you can relax and enjoy lake access at one of the hotels listed here.

Sleeping & Eating

Centro de Obreros Constitución (free with permit; ☺ Wed-Sun) This large government workers' complex offers 53 basic bungalows, each with three cots and a bathroom. Rooms are musty and the grounds are unkempt, but it's free. Bring linens and a mosquito net. (For a permit, visit the Ministerio de Trabajo in San Salvador; p279.)

Amacuilco Guest House (☎ 2441 6239; tent bed US$7, tr US$25) A backpacker haunt gone haunted. Rooms are wretched and ramshackle, the tent (out of a 1940s circus) is strange and not secure. Travelers have complained about thefts here, to boot you're charged US$2 to walk in the door.

Hotel Torremolinos (☎ 2441 6037; hoteltorremolinos@gmail.com; r per person US$7-10; mains US$4-20; ☺ 7am-9pm) Nothing beats the rustic setting of the lake pier for a leisurely lunch. There's live music on Sunday afternoon. While the hotel boasts the area's finest dining, the rooms are just small and standard, the cheaper ones in the adjacent annex have mildewed bathrooms.

Nantal Hostal (☎ 7888 0223; Carr al Cerro Verde Km 53.5) This charming garden house perched high above the lake was closed for remodeling at the last update. Check for new rates. There are four rooms with bathrooms (some with lake view). To get here take the Parque Nacional de los Volcanes bus from Santa Ana.

Comedor Patricar (mains US$2-5; ☺ 7:30am-8pm) Enjoy the no-frills *típica* and seafood. It's around the curve past Hotel Torremolinos with no lake view.

Getting There & Away

Buses 220 and 242 depart Santa Ana for the lake every half-hour. They pass El Congo and descend to shoreline, passing the Centro de Obreros, Amacuilco and Hotel Torremolinos in that order. The last return bus to Santa Ana leaves at 6pm.

SANTA ANA

pop 178,600

The colonial seat of old money in El Salvador, Santa Ana maintains its social conservativism and gentleman ways. The country's second-largest city has moved from coffee plantations to bustling commerce. Travelers will likely enjoy the leafy plaza and the lively food and bar scene. Its proximity to natural attractions and frequent buses make a worthwhile base for exploring the western reaches of the country.

Information

Ciberworld (Av Independencia Sur btwn 9a & 11a Calle Poniente; per hr US$1; ☺ 8am-7:30pm Mon-Sat, 9am-6pm Sun) Friendly service.

Banco Cuscatlán (Independencia Sur & 3a Calle Oriente) Has an ATM.

Red Cross (☎ 441 2645, 447 7213; cnr 1a Av Sur & 3a Calle Oriente; ☺ 24hr)

Virtu@l Center (3a Av Sur & 7a Calle Oriente; per hr US$0.60; ☺ 8am-7pm Mon-Fri, 8:30am-6pm Sat, 9am-1pm Sun)

Sights & Activities

Santa Ana's biggest attraction is its large neo-Gothic **cathedral**. Ornate moldings cover the front, and interior archways and pillars are painted slate and pink stripes (consider it preppy-neo-Gothic). The city's patron saint is feted in late July with parades and live music.

EL SALVADOR

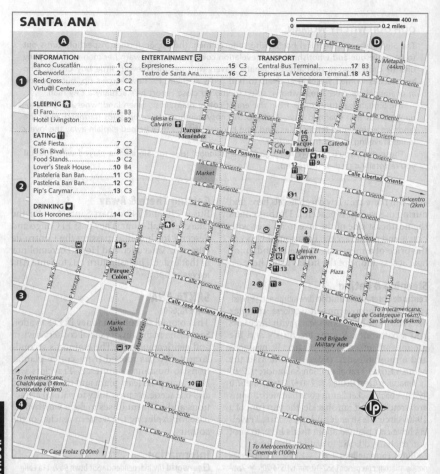

SANTA ANA

INFORMATION		ENTERTAINMENT		TRANSPORT	
Banco Cuscatlán	1 C2	Expresiones	15 C3	Central Bus Terminal	17 B3
Ciberworld	2 C3	Teatro de Santa Ana	16 C2	Espresas La Vencedora Terminal	18 A3
Red Cross	3 C2				
Virtu@l Center	4 C2				
SLEEPING					
El Faro	5 B3				
Hotel Livingston	6 B2				
EATING					
Café Fiesta	7 C2				
El Sin Rival	8 C3				
Food Stands	9 C2				
Lover's Steak House	10 B4				
Pastelería Ban Ban	11 C3				
Pastelería Ban Ban	12 C2				
Pip's Carymar	13 C3				
DRINKING					
Los Horcones	14 C2				

Sleeping

Casa Frolaz (☎ 2440 5302; www.casafrolaz.com; 29 Calle Pte; dm US$7) The best bet for travelers is this elegant home with a sunlit kitchen, cozy living area and garden. Spacious rooms have sturdy single beds, spotless bathrooms and laundry access. The hospitable owner Javier takes guests on day trips and provides transportation downtown.

El Faro (☎ 2447 7787; 14a Av Sur; s with/without bathroom US$11/8) El Faro has small, clean rooms centered around a tile courtyard filled with plants. Attractive landscape murals cover the

On the square west of the cathedral is the **Teatro de Santa Ana**, with an impressive, ornate interior. Other fine buildings ring Parque Libertad.

walls. The only downside is the seedy neighborhood – those ladies parked outside aren't selling *pupusas*.

Hotel Livingston (☎ 2441 1801; 10a Av Sur; d without/with cable TV US$10/15; 🅿) A cement block complex off the street, Livingston offers well-kept if cavernous rooms. Beds have mirrored headboards and the hodge-podge of sofas and chairs pass for décor. A good choice for quick access to the bus terminals.

Eating

Hit the row of **food stands** (1a Av Norte; US$1-2) on the plaza for enormous chicken sandwiches in soft bread, burgers and greasy fries. Everybody eats dribbling sandwiches on park benches while watching the world go by.

El Sin Rival (Calle Libertad Ote; cones US$0.50-1; 🕑 9am-9pm) Makles homemade natural sorbets so good it's outrageous. Try the tart *arrayán* or *mora* (blackberry).

Pastelería Ban Ban (Av Independencia Sur; pastries US$0.50-2.50; 🕑 8am-7pm) One of Santa Ana's charms is that the whole population breaks for coffee and cake mid-afternoon. It's likely that you'll find them here enjoying simple sandwiches and pastries in an air conditioned setting.

Café Fiesta (1a Calle Ote; mains US$1.50-3; 🕑 closed Sun) The Fiesta is an enormous cafeteria festooned with Pope memorabilia and a disco ball. Come here for no-nonsense Salvadoran fare from *pupusas* to *carne asada* (grilled steak).

Pip's Carymar (Av Independencia at 9a Calle Oriente; mains US$2-10; 🕑 8am-9:30pm) Locals seem to love this *cafetería*-style diner serving everything from pizza to pasta to sandwiches. Indoor and outdoor seating.

Lover's Steak House (☎ 2484 7511; 4a Av Sur at 17 Calle Pte; mains US$8-20; 🕑 lunch & dinner) When you can't consume one more *pupusa*, treat yourself to a generous dinner here. Options include a range of *bocadillos* (appetizers), whole roast rabbit or ample rice and seafood salads. The tiki-torch ambience might egg you on to romance.

Drinking & Entertainment

Los Horcones (☎ 2484 7511; 1a Av Norte; 🕑 10am-2am) For the perfect place to tipple a beer, consider this offbeat open-air spot overlooking the cathedral. Tree trunk pillars and hand-hewn benches provide a rustic setting. Ask about the curious display of old phones and abused typewriters.

Teatro de Santa Ana (☎ 2447 6268; 2a Calle Pte) Stop by for the current program of concerts, plays and dance performances.

Cinemark (Av Independencia at 35a Av Pte; admission US$3) For Hollywood action flicks and the occasional tear-jerker.

Getting There & Away

Santa Ana's bus terminal abuts the market on 10a Av Sur. Buses take at least 15 minutes to leave the terminal since they crawl through market stalls. Destinations include:

Ahuachapán Bus 210 (US$0.45; 1¼hr)

Lago de Coatepeque Buses 220, 242 (US$0.40; 1¼hr)

Las Chinamas (Guatemalan border) Take any Ahuachapán bus and transfer.

San Cristóbal (Guatemalan border) Bus 236 (US$0.50; 1hr)

San Salvador Bus 201 (*directo* US$0.80, 1½hr; *especial* US$1.25, 1¼hr) All buses also stop at Metrocentro in San Salvador.

Sonsonate Buses 209, 216 (US$0.55; 1½hr; 40km) Bus 216 departs from La Vencedora terminal (one block west of Parque Colón).

Tazumal, Chalchuapa Bus 218 (US$0.25; 30mins)

Buses departing from other locations in town include:

Anguiatú (Guatemalan border) Bus 235 (US$1.10) to Metapán and transfer.

Parque Nacional Los Volcanes (Cerro Verde) Bus 248 (US$0.85; 1¾hr, departs from La Vencedora Terminal one block west of Parque Colón at 7am, 8am, 10:15am, 11:20am, 12:20pm, 1:40pm, and 3:30pm. Last bus returns at 5pm. Confirm departure times.

Metapán Bus 235 (US$0.85; 1½hr) Departs from the corner of Av F Moraga Sur and 13a Calle Pte.

METAPÁN

pop 18,500

This medium-sized mountain town near the Guatemalan border is the nearest access to Parque Nacional Montecristo-El Trifinio, one of the country's most inaccessible (but beautiful) parks. It is closed from May to November to let the wildlife breed in peace. When it is open you need a 4WD vehicle to get there. Grubby around the edges, Metapán might not merit a visit if you're not headed for hiking.

Information

Fusión Ciber Café (2 Av Sur at 15 de Septiembre; per hr US$0.60)

Scotiabank (Av Igancio Gómez) Exchanges traveler's checks and has a 24 hour ATM.

Lago de Güija

On the El Salvador–Guatemala border, undeveloped and little-known **Lago de Güija** is stunning. Take advantage of the peace and swim and picnic. In dry season you can hike to archaeological sites and find rock carvings along the shore. It's several kilometers south of Metapán and 30km north of Santa Ana along CA12. To get there, take a Santa Ana-bound bus and get dropped off at the junction to the lake. It is a 2km walk from there.

Sleeping & Eating

Hotel California (☎ 2442 0561; s/d US$8/10) Convenient if you're headed to Guatemala, this hotel

GETTING TO GUATEMALA

To El Progreso

The **San Cristóbal–El Progreso** border is open 24 hours but cross during daylight hours. From Santa Ana, take bus 236 to San Cristóbal (US$0.50, one hour, every 20 minutes from 5:30am to 9pm). Buses on the other side of the border go to El Progreso. The last bus back from San Cristóbal is at 6pm.

To Guatemala City via Las Chinamas

Agencia Puerto Bus (☎ 2440 1608; 25a Calle Pte) offers ordinary and *especial* service to Guatemala City via **Las Chinamas–Valle Nuevo**. Ordinary buses (US$9, four hours) leave hourly from 5am to 4pm, except 7am. *Especial* buses (a well-spent US$11.50, 3½ hours) leave at 7am and 5:30pm. Another option is to catch a 1st-class bus at Las Chinamas.

To Chiquimula

From Metapán, microbuses run every half-hour to the **Anguiatú–Chiquimula** border (open 24 hours but more reliably from 6am to 7pm). On the Guatemalan side, buses run frequently to Chiquimula (one hour, last bus at 5:30pm) and onward to Guatemala City (three hours, last bus from Chiquimula at 3:30pm). This is the quickest route to Nuevo Ocotopeque or Copán Ruínas, Honduras. In El Salvador, the last bus from the border to Metapán is at 6:30pm.

See p171 for information on crossing the border from Guatemala.

on the roadside has plain, decent-sized rooms, some with views of El Trifinio. It's a five-minute walk out of town, 500m north of the terminal. Nearby eating options are scant.

Hotel Christina (☎ 2442 0044; 4a Av Sur btwn Calle 15 de Septiembre & 2a Calle; s/d US$12/15, with air-con US$18/23; 🅿️) Convenient to the bus terminal, shops and the internet café, this modern hotel offers clean but somewhat airless rooms. Those upstairs share a wide terrace with tables and hammocks overlooking a bustling street. It's three blocks downhill from the terminal.

Pollo Sheriff (Carr a la Frontera; mains US$1.50-5; 🕕 6am-10pm) A law-abiding fried chicken restaurant located in front of the bus terminal. Ask about the daily specials.

Getting There & Away

The bus terminal sits on the highway facing the entrance to town. For Santa Ana, take bus 235 (US$0.85, 1½ hours) or a *directo* (US$2.50, one hour). San Salvador bus 201A (US$2.50, 1¾ hours) departs seven times daily. Bus 235 and microbuses go to the Guatemalan border of Anguiatú (US$0.50, 30 minutes); the last leaves at 6:30pm. Bus 463 departs 5:30am and noon daily for the gorgeous and also hair-raising haul over the mountains to Citalá (US$2, three hours), close to the Honduran border crossing at El Poy.

PARQUE NACIONAL MONTECRISTO-EL TRIFINIO

Isolated and pristine, this borderland park boasts thick cloud forest canopy, exotic orchids and abundant wildlife. The borders of El Salvador, Honduras and Guatemala converge at the highest point (2418m), referred to as El Trifinio. Oak and laurel trees grow to 30m, and leaves intertwine to form a canopy impenetrable to sunlight. The forest floor provides a habitat for abundant exotic plant life including mushrooms, lichens and mosses, and tree ferns up to 8m tall. The temperature averages between 10°C and 15°C. This is the most humid region in the country, with 2000mm annual precipitation and 100% average relative humidity.

Animals seen (albeit rarely) include spider monkeys, two-fingered anteaters, porcupines, spotted and hooded skunks, pumas, red and gray squirrels, wild pigs, opossums, coyotes and agoutis. The forest is also home to at least 87 bird species, including quetzals, green toucans, woodpeckers, hummingbirds, nightingales, white-faced quail and striped owls.

There is no place to stay here – you must camp. Ask trail directions from the owner of the small shop here. You have a few options but none of the trails is well marked. Several hiking trails begin from Los Planes (about 1900m), a grassy clearing and in a bowl at the foot of Cerro Montecristo. Two trails lead about 1km each to wooden observation towers with views of the park and surrounding area. The trail you are probably looking for is the one to the top. The park highlight, it is a tough 7km climb through dense, misty cloud forest. At the summit a plaque marks the borders of the three countries. The views and the photo opportunities are outstanding.

Information

The area above Los Planes is closed from May to November, the breeding season of the local fauna. The remainder of the park is open the rest of the year, but you can only venture a few kilometers up the road.

To take full advantage of the park, you'll need to spend the night. Camping is free at Los Planes – bring all your own equipment, food and water. Get advance permission from the National Parks and Wildlife Service at the **Ministerio de Medio Ambiente** (☎ 2267 6259/6276; www .marn.gov.sv in Spanish; Alameda Araujo/Carr a Santa Tecla Km 5.5; 🕙 7:30am-4:30pm Mon-Fri) in San Salvador. Admission is US$6 per day for foreigners plus US$1.15 per vehicle, required for taxis as well.

Getting There & Away

Unfortunately, getting to Los Planes is a challenge, and not a cheap one. If you have a 4WD, you can drive there (22km from Metapán). **Francisco Monterrosa** (☎ 2402 2805) charges US$45 for day trips or US$85 to drop you off and return a day or two later. If he isn't available, look for other drivers in Metapán near the park turnoff.

If you wait at the road in early morning, you may be able to catch a ride with the rangers or residents of a small village in the park; but there are no guarantees and the trip back remains unresolved. You can walk to the gate (5km), but you can't walk beyond that without a private vehicle – that's the rule.

RUINAS DE TAZUMAL

The Maya ruins of **Tazumal** (admission US$3; 🕙 9am-5pm Tue-Sun), the most important and impressive in El Salvador, are in **Chalchuapa**, 13km west of Santa Ana on the way to Ahuachapán. In the Quiché language Tazumal means 'pyramid where the victims were burned.'

Archaeologists estimate that the area was first settled around 5000 BC. Part of a 10-sq-km zone, much is still buried under Chalchuapa. The excavated ruins span a period of

over 1000 years. While these ruins are very important for El Salvador, they pale in comparison to those in neighboring countries. A previous restoration that 'protected' the pyramids by covering them in concrete was severely damaged by Hurricane Stan. The new restoration, inaugurated in December 2006, restored the original stone-and-mortar construction in much of the ruins. Don't expect to get too close – a chain-link enclosure prevents visitors walking on the pyramids.

The **museum** displays artifacts showing active trade as far away as Panama and Mexico, with explanations in detailed English. Other finds, including the Estela de Tazumal, a 2.65m-high basalt monolith inscribed with hieroglyphics, are at the Museo Nacional David J Guzmán in San Salvador (see p281).

Bus 218 comes from Santa Ana, 14km (45 minutes) away. A sign on the main road through Chalchuapa points toward the ruins, about a five-minute walk from the highway. If driving from Santa Ana, stay right at the fork in the road, continuing toward Ahuachapán, then turn left at the Texaco station in Chalchuapa. The ruins are at the end of the road.

AHUACHAPÁN
pop 38,630

Ahuachapán is a pleasant colonial city in the highland hills, just 16km from Guatemala. Its bubbly mud pits and secret hot springs are the product of active geothermals that also drive the city power plant which supplies over 15% of the country's electrical power. It's also the start or endpoint of Ruta de las Flores, a series of beautiful villages strung through the coffee-rich mountains to the south.

The hubs of Plaza Concordia and Parque Menéndez are five blocks apart, connected by the busy commercial street Av Menéndez, which runs north–south.

Information

Most services and restaurants are nearer Plaza Concordia.

Ciber Café Cetcomp (2a Av Sur at 1a Calle Pte; per hr US$.60; 🕙 9am-8pm Mon-Fri, 9:30am-8:30pm Sat, 10am-9pm Sun)

Scotiabank (Av Menendez at 4 Calle Pte) Changes Amex and Visa traveler's checks.

Tours & Aventuras (☎ 2442 0016; www.elsalvador vacations.com.sv; 2 Av Norte 2-4; 🕙 8am-6pm Mon-Fri, 2-5pm Sat & Sun) Travel agency offering friendly tours of the area's sights.

EL SALVADOR

Sights & Activities

Green gardens and palms make **Plaza Concordia** an agreeable stop to catch a breeze. The kiosk occasionally holds concerts and free events. East of the plaza is Nuestra Señora de Asuncíon, with pretty *azuelo* floors and a stained-glass Virgin.

Ahuachapán bubbles with geothermic activity, evidenced by the steaming mud pits found about. To visit **Los Ausoles**, aka *los infernillos* (the little hells), contact Tours & Aventuras or guide **Carlos Alvarado Martínez** (☎ 2413 3360).

Sleeping, Eating & Drinking

Hotel San José (☎ 2413 0033; 6a Calle Ote 1; r per person US$8; ☷) Clean but cheerless, the hotel has ample cement rooms with high ceilings and private bathroom. Located right on Parque Menéndez and near the buses.

Hotel Casa Blanca (☎ 2443 1505; 2a Av Norte & Calle Barrios; s/d with fan US$20/30, with air-con US$35/59; P ☷ ▯ ▮) An elegant colonial home with all the creature comforts, so much so that it's a popular spot for gents and their lady friends. The spotless and spacious rooms all have TV and private hot-water bathrooms.

Restaurant Mixta 'S' (2a Av Sur at 1a Calle Pte; mains US$2-3; ☖ 8am-9pm) Friendly, fast and popular, the house specialty are *mixtas* – pitas stuffed with pickled veggies, salsa and meat or cheese, but it whips up a mean fruit shake too.

La Estancia (1a Av Sur btwn Calle Barrios & 1a Calle Oriente; mains US$2-4; ☖ 7am-6pm Mon-Sat) This airy mansion-turned-restaurant is ideal for breakfast or lunch, serving buffet-style *típica*.

Brisas de Santa Monica (☎ 2443 1471; Carr a las Chinamas km 101; cover US$4; ☖ 9pm-3am Fri & Sat) Cosmopolitan for Ahuachapán, this club on the Laguna del Lago offers free transportation for patrons, and employees speak English. Simply call for a hotel pick-up.

Getting There & Away

Buses line the market-choked Av Menéndez at 10a Calle Ote, one block north of the parque central. Microbuses to Apaneca leave from the highway turnoff, but the regular buses tend to be faster and more frequent. Buses for the Guatemalan border at Las Chinamas leave from 8a Calle Poniente, at the northwest corner of Parque Menéndez. The following buses travel to and from Ahuachapán:

Las Chinamas Bus 263 or Ruta 11 (US$0.50; 40min, 5am-7:30pm)

San Salvador Bus 202 (US$1; 2¼hr; *especial* US$2; 1¼hr)

GETTING TO GUATEMALA CITY

The **Las Chinamas–Valle Nuevo** border is open 24 hours but it's best to cross in daylight. Buses leave Ahuachapán from Parque Menéndez every 15 minutes (US$0.50, 5am to 7:30pm) for the Guatemala border. Cross the border 300m to the bus stop for service to Guatemala City via Cuilapa. Tica bus (US$3) passes every half-hour and is safer than 2nd-class service. The last bus from the border to Ahuachapán is at 5:45pm.

Santa Ana Bus 210 (US$0.45; 1hr) Alternatively, take the faster San Salvador bus, get off at Metrocentro and catch a local bus into town.

Sonsonate (via Apaneca & Juayúa) Bus 249 (US$0.85; 2hr)

Tacuba Bus 264 or Ruta 15 (US$0.60; 40min; 5:30am-7pm)

TACUBA

A mountain nook flanked by coffee crops and lush forests, Tacuba is one of the poorest regions in the country but a rewarding outdoor destination. It's on the north side of Parque Nacional El Imposible along Guatemala's rolling hills and a fast 14km to Ahuachapán on a newly paved road. While travelers' options are still few, watch as Tacuba's promising potential for ecotourism gets tapped.

Activities

Tropical mountain forest **Parque Nacional El Imposible** (p304) offers primary forest thick with rivers and vegetation. The area conserves a boggling array of plant and animal life, including pumas and black-crested eagles. Hiking can be strenuous but trekkers are rewarded by grand vistas of misty peaks and the gleaming Pacific Ocean.

The park is run by **Salvanatura** (☎ 2279 1515; www.salvanatura.org in Spanish; admission US$6). In theory you need to visit the San Salvador office to pay the entry fee and arrange for guide service (the guide service has no fee but a US$5 tip is customary). If you call, the park will radio a guide to collect your fee. Those just showing up will have better luck on weekends when there is more activity.

An excellent trip is a moderately strenuous downhill transect of the park. Enter from the north, cross dense forest with some spectacular vistas, skirt Cerro Leon and end at the main visitors center.

Should you have a mountain bike, a great ride is the 40km road between the park and Tacuba – mostly downhill from the Tacuba side. **Imposible Tours** (☎ 2417 4268; www.imposible tours.com; Hostal de Mamá y Papá; tours US$15), run by the energetic, amiable and borderline kooky Manolo González, offers a range of guided activities. His established hikes are popular but the canyoning might involve some risk. It is definitely not for those with acrophobia or without insurance. His new trips to the private **Termas Santa Teresa** (US$10), with seven hot and hotter pools, offers a welcome respite from all that sweaty activity.

Sleeping & Eating

Hostal Mamá and Papá (☎ 2417 4268; www.imposible tours.com; dm/d US$6/12, meals extra US$3) There's fantastic hospitality at this family home and surely nothing beats Mama's cooking. The rooms are rustic but well-kept brick and cement, each with an adjoining bathroom with a hot shower. Enjoy the rooftop views. For directions call ahead.

Sol de Media Noche (mains US$1.50-4; ⏰ 6:30am-5pm Mon-Sat) Run by a Salvadoran Hindu sect, this vegetarian café offers tasty carrot *tortas* and brown rice. It's two blocks past the plaza.

Getting There & Away

Bus 264 and Ruta 15 (US$0.60, 40 minutes, 5:30am to 7pm) go to Ahuachapán from the main plaza.

RUTA DE LAS FLORES

A winding ride through the heart of coffee country, this 36km stretch linking Sonsonate and Ahuachapán is named for the explosion of wildflowers found between October and February. Wander the colonial-style villages where chatty locals are quick to smile and coo over the novelty of blue eyes and backpackers. While locals consider the region perfect for lazy Sunday excursions, the adventure-minded can discover great hiking, horseback riding and mountain biking.

Bus 249 runs frequently between Sonsonate and Ahuachapán, stopping in all the towns along the way, including Juayúa, Apaneca and Ataco.

Juayúa

pop 10,100

Relaxed, colonial Juayúa is a hip-yet-quaint village flanked by coffee farms and volcanoes.

Travelers soak up its sunny, sleepy vibe, occasionally stirring to find the nearby waterfalls and hot springs. Religious pilgrims seek out the 'Cristo Negro,' carved by Quirio Cataño in the late 16th century, housed in the church, on the plaza which serves as the town's buzzing nucleus.

Weekends hum with festivity, thanks to a wildly popular **fería gastronómica** (food fair) where hordes of *capitalinos* and international visitors sample the region's best cuisine on the plaza with live bands. If you've never tried grilled frog or marinated rabbit, here's your chance (there's also sweet tarts and marzipan).

Juayúa has had a tumultuous past. Indigenous uprisings in the region ignited the revolutionary movement of 1932. Backed by the coffee elite, government forces brutally quelled the ill-organized insurrection. Today's indigenous people eschew traditional clothing and language for fear of standing out.

ORIENTATION & INFORMATION

Ideal for wandering, Juayúa is small and its streets follow a standard grid. The church is on the west side of the plaza and behind it the market.

Cyber & Equipment (1a Av Norte; per hr US$0.75; ⏰ 8:30am-9pm)

Juayútur (⏰ 9am-5pm Sat & Sun) Juayúa's tourist agency dispenses information about the town and area excursions at its kiosk on the east side of the plaza.

Scotiabank (Calle Monseñor Óscar Romero) Exchanges traveler's checks, gives Visa advances and is adding an ATM.

ACTIVITIES

A recommended hike and swim is to **Los Chorros de Calera**, a series of falls spewing from fractured cliffs to form large, cold pools. The **Ruta de las Seite Cascadas** follows the Río Bebedero over seven scenic drops. Consult Juayútur or Hotel Anáhuac for directions. Occasional thefts mean that certain activities are better undertaken with guides. Other guided excursions include lake visits, coffee tours and waterfall rappels.

SLEEPING & EATING

Hotel Anáhuac (☎ 2469 2401; www.tikal.dk/elsalvador; dm/s/d US$7/12.50/25; 🖳) Young owners César and Jenne have worked hard to make their home a backpacker haven, and it doesn't disappoint. The red-tile colonial building offers large, airy rooms and a grassy courtyard. Guests enjoy cooking and internet privileges.

César's hikes to hot springs and horseback riding tours are well worthwhile, and could stretch your stay a lot. Both Danish and English are spoken.

Hotel El Mirador (☎ 2452 2432; www.elmiradorjuayua .org; 4a Calle Poniente 4-4; s/d/tr US$15/25/40) Behind the church, this serene colonial hotel has cool tiles and a myriad dark, uncluttered rooms. Hot water is US$2 extra. Sneak up to the rooftop room for a panorama of town and volcanoes.

Casa de Huespedes Doña Mercedes (☎ 2452 2287; 2a Av Sur & 6a Calle Oriente; d with/without bathroom US$25/23) A quiet home with large, quality rooms featuring firm beds and spanking-clean shared bathrooms. It's two blocks east and one block south of the plaza.

Laura's Comida a la Vista (Calle Merceditas Cáceres; mains US$2-4; 7am-8pm Mon-Sat, 7am-3pm Sun) Enjoy the everyman atmosphere with options like veggie fritters, salads, meat, rice and salsa. It's four blocks from the park.

Taquería la Guadalupana (2a Calle Ote; mains US$2-5; lunch & dinner Tue-Sun) Irresistible Mexican – evidenced by the chicken in *mole poblano* and *nopal* (cactus) salads, served at cozy benches or in a shaded courtyard.

Tienda San José (main plaza; mains US$2-8; 8:30am-11pm) A mini-mart hides a surprisingly hip dining area, great for the late-night munchies.

RR (Calle Mercedes Caceres 1-4 Pte; mains US$6-16; lunch & dinner Tue-Sun) Where travelers repeat eat, you know you've found a hit. The friendly chef Carlos cooks El Salvadoran fare with international influence from stints in North America and Australia. Fresh salads and garlic stir-fry veggies set the scene, but meat's the star, including herbed sausages and steaks with tortillas and melted cheese.

GETTING THERE & AWAY
Bus 249 has services northwest to Apaneca (US$0.35, 20 minutes), Ataco (US$0.45, 30 minutes) and Ahuachapán (US$0.70, one hour) as also south to Sonsonate (US$0.50, 45 minutes) during daylight. Buses leave every 15 minutes from the park, or from four blocks west on weekends. For Santa Ana, bus 238 (US$0.50, 40 minutes) goes direct, leaving a few blocks west of parque central six times daily.

Apaneca
pop 8600
High in the Sierra Apaneca Ilamatepec, cool, cobblestone Apaneca (1450m) is the town that time forgot. Strolling is a major pastime here,

and while doing so you'll encounter some easy hikes and friendly locals. Other attractions include locally produced furniture made from cypress and coffee wood, and visiting the myriad flower and plant nurseries. The beautiful Iglesia San Andres was one of the oldest churches in the country until the January 2001 earthquake reduced it to rubble.

ORIENTATION & INFORMATION
The market is west of the park and the church is to the south. Buses drop off and pick up on the main street, right in front of the market. A tourist information booth operates on the plaza on weekends.

You can check email at **Cybercafé Apaneca** (3a Av Sur; per hr US$0.75; 8am-11pm), behind the former church. There are no banks.

SIGHTS & ACTIVITIES
The crater lakes **Laguna de las Ninfas** and **Laguna Verde**, north and northeast of town, are within hiking distance. The former is swampy, reedy and rife with lily pads; the latter is deep and cold. You can camp at **Chichicastepeque** (aka Cerro Grande), which at 1816m affords outstanding views of the region, although the antennae make it look a lot less wild. For directions or a guide stop by the tourist kiosk.

Vivero (nursery) tours make for a relaxed afternoon. **Vivero Alejandra** (7am-4pm Wed-Sun) is a short walk from the center (toward Juayúa). Come for the flowers and rare plants, but stay for the great little café, serving coffee, *quesadillas* and strawberries and cream. Other *viveros* include **Vivero Santa Clara**, across from Alejandra, and **Las Flores de Eloisa** (☎ 2433 0415), a small café 2km toward Ahuachapán.

Finca Santa Leticia, a hotel, restaurant and coffee farm just south of Apaneca, has a small **archaeological park** (admission US$5) in a coffee field. The highlight is two pot-bellied figures carved from huge basalt boulders, weighing between 6350kg and 11,000kg. Experts speculate that these 2000-year-old chubbies were created by early Maya in deference to their rulers. Catch any bus headed toward Juayúa and Sonsonate and ask for the Finca Santa Leticia.

SLEEPING & EATING
The best restaurants only open weekends when San Salvadorans come day-tripping.

Hostal Rural las Orquídeas (☎ 2433 0061; 4a Calle Poniente; s/d US$10/17) A cute red-roofed colonial place with décor by Granny. Rooms are smallish but clean, behind a courtyard with hammocks and rockers. To get here follow the signs two blocks north of the park and turn left.

Hostal la Magaña (☎ 2433 0268; Av Central btwn 4 & 6 Calles Sur; s/d US$10/20) Quiet and hospitable, this home has two large rooms steeped in burgundy and varnish, as well impeccable bathrooms. Guests can cook, or relax on the billowy living-room sofas.

Mercado Saludable (mains US$1.50-3; ☺ 6:30am-8pm) Cheap eats deluxe, this market facing the park offers good little eateries serving ham, eggs and beans, and *atole* as well as afternoon meals and *pupusas*.

La Cocina de Mi Abuela (☎ 2433 0100; cnr 1a Av Norte & 4a Calle Ote; mains US$7-11; ☺ 11am-7pm Sat & Sun) Considered one of El Salvador's best restaurants, serving high-quality meats and national fare. The desserts are magnificent.

For more options, check out resort lodges near Apaneca on the highway. Their upmarket restaurants offer the inevitable *buena vista* and a relaxed atmosphere to dally in.

GETTING THERE & AWAY
Bus 249 plies the route between Ahuachapán and Sonsonate, stopping in Apaneca every half-hour. The last bus runs between 7pm and 8pm. Ask a local to be sure.

Ataco
In this part of El Salvador, each town seems to be more picturesque and pleasing than the last. Ataco offers more cobblestone streets and melon-and-sky-colored homes. Fairly isolated from all three of El Salvador's largest cities, it remains off the map for most. This partly indigenous village can be reticent toward strangers, but a fledgling guide service and information kiosk have thrown out the welcome mat. Still, be extra courteous to locals, who are not used to tourism à la Antigua.

The **Tourist Information Kiosk** (☺ 7am-7pm Sat & Sun) is located at the entrance to town. You can pick up a handy street map here. Ask about guide services (US$3 to US$7 per person). Options to explore include **Salto de Chacala**, a 50m waterfall on the Río Matala, and **Chorros del Limo**, a spring which forms a broad pool ideal for a dip.

Lodgers can stay at **El Mesón de San Fernando** (☎ 2413 0169; 1a Calle Pte; r per person US$10, with bathroom US$25) with low, clean, cinder block rooms. Its redeemers include the garden and good restaurant serving a classic version of *gallo en chicha* (rooster in corn liquor).

The squat rooms at **Casa de Bambú** (☎ 2450 5175; 8a Av Sur at 2a Calle Ote; r without bathroom US$15; 💻) sit above the Salvadoran-Mexican restaurant – a meal of your choice is included in the rate.

For a quick cappuccino and pastry, stop by **Diconte-Axul** (2a Av Sur at Calle Central; ☺ 8am-6pm) for a treat in the lush garden. The shop also sells homemade textiles, tie-dyes and hand-painted objects. The rambling **market** (2a Av Sur) makes for a fascinating walkabout.

Bus 249 stops on the corner of 2a Calle Ote and 4a Av Sur. One heads north to Ahuachapán (US$0.35, 15 minutes), and south to Apaneca (US$0.25, 10 minutes), Juayúa (US$0.45, 30 minutes) and Sonsonate (US$0.70, one hour). Frequency is every 15 minutes.

SONSONATE
pop 65,100

Hot and menacing, Sonsonate offers little for the traveler other than the way to Ruta de las Flores, El Imposible or the Guatemalan border. Gang problems mar city life, yet the city's vivid **Semana Santa** celebration is a highlight.

The surrounding area does warrant exploration. The village of **Izalco**, 8km northeast at the foot of Volcán Izalco, was the site of a major indigenous revolt in 1932. Nearby is

---

EXPLORE MORE OF WESTERN EL SALVADOR

If you've a sense of adventure and an interest in how indigenous forms have transformed through time, check out the following:

■ View local artisans crafting basketry and furniture in **Nahuizalco**, but the real trip is to the night market, with indigenous treats such as grilled *garrobo* (lizard) and snake. There's no lodging – day-trip it from Sonsonate. Take bus 249 from Juayúa (to the highway turnoff, 500m away) or bus 53D from Sonsonate.

■ The ancient Nahual community of **Izalco** has famed religious wood carvings parading in both Catholic and indigenous rites. Access via Sonsonate bus 53A.

Atecozol, a *turicentro* with swimming holes, kiosks and gardens. The grounds feature stone sculptures by Agustín Estrada – one commemorates Atonatl, a feisty indigenous warrior who pegged conquistador Pedro de Alvarado with an arrow in 1524.

You can access the coastal points of **Los Cóbanos,** a prime diving destination, and **Barra de Santiago,** a protected mangrove forest reserve, from here. At Barra de Santiago you can rent canoes for estuary tours.

Orientation & Information

You'll find a lovely new bus terminal 2km east of the city center. The main north–south street is Av Morazán/Av Rafael Campos. To orient yourself in town, the church is on the east side of the parque central.

Banco Cuscatlán (Calle Marroquín at 4a Av Norte) Has a 24-hour ATM.

Infocentros (3 Calle Pte at Av Morazán; per hr US$1; 🕑 8am-6pm Mon-Sat; 🌐)

Post Office (1a Av Norte btwn 1 & 3 Calles Pte)

Sleeping & Eating

Dirt-cheap hotels are in the rough area by the old bus terminal – 'dirt' being the operative word here. Better options are in town.

Hotel Orbe (☎ 2451 1517; 4a Calle Ote at 2a Av Flavian Muchi; s/d with bathroom US$12/16, s/d with air-con US$16/20; 🌐) Well-worn after 35 years of business, the upshot of this place is it's well-scrubbed, friendly and convenient. You might get a cheaper rate if you can forfeit TV.

Hotel Plaza (☎ 2451 6626; 9a Calle Ote at 8a Av Norte; s/d US$35/45; 🅿 🌐 🏊) So what if it's stuck in the '80s? The Plaza's rooms are Alaska-cool with firm beds and cable TV. You can rest your traveling bones by the pool and the restaurant is worth trying too.

La Casona (3 Calle Pte btwn 1 & 3 Av Norte; mains US$1.50-4; 🕑 breakfast & lunch, closed Sun) *Comida a la vista* is dished up fresh and *pupusas* sizzle and steam in the city's best bargain restaurant, located in an antiquated building.

Jugos, Licuados y Más (1a Av Norte btwn 1 & 3 Calles Pte; 🕑 7am-6pm Mon-Sat) A blender bar with delectable fresh squeezed juices and *licuados.*

For junk-food feasting, try the **food stands** (7a Calle Ote at 10a Av Norte; 🕑 5-10pm) where you can grab burgers, sandwiches, fries and *pupusas.*

Getting There & Away

Take a taxi or bus 53C from the central park to the bus station. Destinations include:

GETTING TO GUATEMALA CITY

The **La Hachadura–Ciudad Pedro de Alvarado** border is open 24 hours, but it's best to cross in daylight. Bus 259 from Sonsonate drops you right at the border; Salvadoran and Guatemalan immigration posts are at the far side of the complex. In Guatemala, the bus stop is 1km away. Bicycle taxis cost US$0.50. Buses for Guatemala City (US$5, four hours) leave every half-hour via Chiquimulilla and Escuintla. The last bus from La Hachadura to Sonsonate is at 6pm.

Ahuachapán (via Juayúa, Apaneca & Ataco) Bus 249 (US$0.95; 2hr)

Barra de Santiago Bus 285 (US$1; 1¼hr; 10:30am & 4:30pm); or take bus 259 to turnoff and catch a pick-up.

La Hachadura Bus 259 (US$0.85; 1¾hr)

La Libertad Bus 287 (US$1.25; 2½hr)

La Perla Bus 261 (US$0.80; 1½hr)

Los Cóbanos Bus 257 (US$0.50; 40min)

Parque Nacional El Imposible Any La Hachadura bus to Puente Ahuachapío or Cara Sucia (US$0.45; 30min)

San Salvador Bus 205 (*directo* US$0.70; 1½ hr; *especial* US$1-1.25; 1½hr)

Santa Ana Bus 216 (US$0.65; 1¼hr)

The terminal also serves Izalco (bus 53A), Nahuizalco (bus 53D) and Acajutla (bus 252).

PARQUE NACIONAL EL IMPOSIBLE

Tropical mountain forest Parque Nacional El Imposible was named for the perilous gorge which used to claimed the lives of farmers and pack mules transporting coffee to the Pacific port. Decreed a national park in 1989, it sits in the Apaneca Ilamatepec mountain range between 300m and 1450m above sea level, and includes eight rivers which feed the watershed for Barra de Santiago and the mangrove forests along the coast.

This original forest – the remains of a threatened ecosystem – is still home to an extraordinary variety of plant and animal life, including pumas, tigrillos, wild boars, king hawks and black-crested eagles. Hiking can get muddy and steep but offers grand vistas of misty peaks and the gleaming Pacific Ocean.

Information

The main San Benito entrance is on the southeast side, beyond the hamlet of San Miguelito.

The park is run by **Salvanatura** (☎ 2279 1515; www .salvanatura.org in Spanish; entry US$6); in theory you need to visit the San Salvador office to pay the entry fee and arrange for guide service (there is no guide fee but a US$5 tip is customary). If instead you call the park, they can radio a guide to collect your fee. If you are just showing up you'll have better luck on weekends when there is more activity. The best time to visit is October to February, as the rainy season hinders travel.

The solar-powered visitors center has a modest museum and lookout tower with ocean views.

Major hikes:

Los Enganches An ideal picnic spot, this big swimming hole is reached by a trail (3.5km one way), which passes Mirador El Mulo and descends steeply. Along the way you'll pass Mirador Madre Cacao, with views of the southeastern part of the park. Look for agoutis and coatis.

Piedra Sellada A 4km trail to a swimming spot and a stone etched with Maya writings. Experts believe it dates to the Post Classic period, around AD 1500. To get here you'll take the Los Enganches trail; just before the end another trail cuts upriver 1km to Piedra Sellada.

Cerro El Leon A tough 8km circuit topping out on one of the park's highest peaks (1113m), starting in a lush, humid gorge and climbing through dense forest. This trail offers terrific panoramic views. From the visitors center the trail descends steeply 1km to the Río Ixcanal. Crossing the river you climb the other side, known as Montaña de los Águilares, to the summit. Return by a different route, along the narrow ridge between the Ixcanal and Guyapa river valleys. Allow several hours and bring plenty of water.

Sleeping & Eating

Hostal El Imposible (☎ 2411 5484; d midweek/weekend US$34/46, extra person US$6; 🏊) This is a cluster of ecofriendly A-frame cabins with composting and solar power. Cabins have two bunks, a double bed, bathroom, patio and free drinking water. The restaurant takes a stab at originality by serving gazpacho and rabbit.

Three large camping areas with toilets and grills are within walking distance of the visitors center; the furthest one (20-minute walk) is the least crowded. Camp free with your entrance fee, the visitors center rents gear (tents US$5 to US$7, bring bedding). Small fires are allowed and potable water is available.

Getting There & Away

From Sonsonate catch bus 259 toward La Hachadura and get off at Cara Sucia. From there, a bus leaves at 11am and a pick-up at

2pm (both US$2, one hour) for the main entrance. The trucks return to Cara Sucia every morning at 5:30am and 7:30am. If you think you might miss the pick-ups in Cara Sucia, you may be able to cut them off at Puente Ahuachapío (bridge), a few kilometers short of Cara Sucia. If the pick-ups have already passed, you may be able to hitch a ride (13.5km).

You can also visit the park from the northern side via Tacuba (p300).

EASTERN EL SALVADOR

El Salvador's east and northeast were poor areas populated by subsistence farmers before the war. The guerrillas' call for land reforms resonated strongly and the area became a wartime rebel stronghold. Much of the combat and atrocities took place here. Even communities that had remained neutral suffered terrible persecution and destruction.

Refugees who whiled away the war in Honduras have returned. The infrastructure destroyed during the war – bombed-out bridges and defunct ports – has largely been rebuilt. It's impossible not to notice the huge impact from the remittances sent from relatives working abroad (see p314). Boxy new gringo-style homes and booming commerce give a somewhat false impression of prosperity. But as eastern El Salvador 'comes back,' travelers will find that, among the forgotten beaches and quiet hill towns, there is a lot worth exploring.

There are two ways to travel east – along the Carr Interamericana or along the Carr del Litoral (CA2); the latter accesses the beaches, and the former the northern reaches.

EAST ALONG THE INTERAMERICANA

The Carr Interamericana goes east from San Salvador to San Miguel, on to La Unión and up again to the El Salvador–Honduras border at El Amatillo.

A few towns of interest lie between San Salvador and San Vicente on the Interamericana. **Cojutepeque**, 32km east of San Salvador, is a small town best known for the Cerro las Pavas (Hill of the Turkeys), featuring an outdoor shrine to the Virgen de Fátima, brought here from Portugal in 1949. Religious pilgrims come on Sunday and on May 13, **El Día de la Virgen**. In San Salvador, catch bus 113 from the Reloj de Flores, just west of the Terminal de Oriente; it's about a 45-minute ride.

EL SALVADOR

Further along the highway (54km from San Salvador or 22km from Cojutepeque) is the turnoff to **Ilobasco**, a town known for ceramics known as *sorpresas* (see the boxed text, opposite). Upon entering the town a string of *artesanía* shops line Av Carlo Bonilla. The annual **crafts fair** runs September 24 to 29. Take bus 111 or 142 from the Terminal de Oriente or from Cojutepeque.

Another 8.5km heading east along the Interamericana is the road to **San Sebastián**, known for woven hammocks and textiles, and unique as most of the weavers are male. The fair takes place at the end of January. Take bus 111 or catch a bus in Cojutepeque.

SAN VICENTE

pop 34,600

Set under the horn-topped Volcán Chichontepec in the Jiboa Valley, San Vicente is a relaxed little city worth a peek. Lots of musicians live here and it has a reputation for being gay-friendly. Approaching town you'll see the landmark clock tower – a cartoonish Eiffel Tower – sprouting up from green hills and farmland. The tower is closed from damage by the January 2001 earthquake. It also damaged El Pilar, a beautiful colonial church built in the 1760s. With any luck, both will reopen soon.

Orientation & Information

The cathedral sits on the east side of the park. A large army barracks takes up the entire block southwest of the park. The main drag, 1a Av, runs north–south, passing a block west of the park.

Banco Cuscatlán (2a Av Sur) Cashes traveler's checks and has a 24-hour ATM.

Fast Line Ciber Café (2a Calle Ote; per hr US$0.85; 9am-9pm)

Police (2303 7300; 1a Av Norte at 3a Calle Pte) Can arrange for an escort up the volcano.

Activities

The double-peaked **Chichontepec** (also known as Volcán San Vicente) offers a moderate climb through coffee plantations. Views are fantastic, though somewhat marred by the summit's helicopter pad and communications antenna. This eight-hour round-trip is relatively safe but it's best to go in a group or get a **police escort** (/fax 2396 3353) from Nuevo Tepetitán or San Vicente. Wear sturdy boots and bring a sweatshirt, lots of water and food for

you and your escorts. Take bus 191 (US$0.25, 20 minutes) to Nuevo Tepetitán, where the trail begins. Buses leave from the corner of Calle Alvaro Quiñonez de Osorio and 9a Av every half-hour from 6:30am; last return bus is at 7:15pm.

Sleeping & Eating

Hotel Central Park (2393 0383; s with fan/air-con US$10/15;) Location is everything, so enjoy the 2nd-floor terrace and small gay-friendly bar, since the actual accommodations are mediocre. Cement rooms smell slightly of mildew but the sheets are fresh and beds firm. The restaurant (open 6:30am to 10pm) below the hotel serves decent *típica*.

Casa de Huespedes El Turista (2393 0323; 4a Calle Pte 15 at 1 Av Sur; d US$10-15) San Vicente's best bargain offers ultratidy rooms (early arrivals pay more) which are a bit dated and small. Enjoy the hammock, leafy courtyard and roof with a view.

Comedor Rivolí (1 Av Sur; mains US$2-4; 7am-8:30pm) The most popular place in town, and justly so – check out the baked chicken, salads and roasted veggies, all fresh and homemade. This *comida a la vista* is served in a spotless dining room alongside rose gardens. Don't miss the delicious dollar *licuados*.

Getting There & Away

All buses pass by the parque central after leaving the bus terminal up the hill on 6a Calle and 15 Av. Beat the crowds at the park without hoofing it to the terminal by catching buses at 6a Calle and 2a Av. Departures include:

Alegría Catch an eastward bus from the Carr Interamericana and transfer at Villa El Triunfo.

Ilobasco Bus 530 (US$0.60; 1hr) Departures at 6:50am, 11am and 4pm.

San Miguel Bus 301 from the turnoff at the highway (US$1.50; 1½hr). Last bus at 6pm.

San Salvador Bus 116 (US$0.85; 1½hr) Last bus at 6pm.

Zacatecoluca Bus 177 (US$0.60; 50min)

ALEGRÍA

High in the mountains, Alegría is an unsung gem and one of El Salvador's most picturesque towns. At 1593m above sea level it's El Salvador's highest town. Young artists and new businesses are infusing energy into the quaint village of philosopher Alberto Masferrer. That's not to say it's bohemian – on certain nights rousing fire-and-brimstone sermons rock the plaza. Once coffee country, Alegría

---

TÍPICA OR PÍCARA?

Sorpresas (surprises) are little scenes and figures hidden in egg-sized shells, pioneered by folk artist Dominga Herrera of Ilobasco. Underneath a bulbous papaya or white chapel you'll find a charming microsized scene of village life – usually. One local artist got sassy and sculpted a couple in the giddy throes of sex. The illicit art was condemned by the town priest and briefly removed from stores. But prosperity may have beat out piety. *'Pícara'* (sinful) *sorpresas*, now available as matchbox copulation scenes, continue selling strong. Expect yours to come discreetly wrapped.

---

is now the nation's flower-growing capital, evidenced by some 230 *viveros* which fill porches, fields and backyards, leaving sweet smells in the air.

The friendly **tourist agency** (☎ 2628 1087; 1a Av Norte at 1a Calle Pte) can offer information about sights, nurseries and accommodations. Look for the kiosk or ask in the municipal office, both on the parque central. It also offers some worthy guided hikes (US$10 to US$15 per half-day) to coffee plantations, geothermal plants and sites related to philosopher and native-Alegrían Alberto Masferrer. The scenic crater lake **La Laguna de Alegría** (admission US$0.25) is a 2km downhill walk from town. Its icy waters are said to be medicinal. Don't miss the beautiful view from the **Mirador de las Cien Grados** – a vista point at the top of one hundred steps. Take the road toward Berlín to the steps.

Sleeping & Eating

Casa Alegre (☎ 7201 8641; www.lacasaalegre.zoomblog .com; Av Camilo Campos; d/tw US$10/20) Artists Memo and Paola have created a great shared space – just a few clean rooms with a shared mosaic-tile bath, but with relaxed warmth and style. The 1st floor is a gallery with modern works and recycled art. The couple offers free art classes to local kids. Volunteers are welcome to help.

Casa de Huéspedes la Palma (☎ 2628 1131; 1a Av Norte near Calle Alberto Masferrer; dm US$10; 🖳) Big rickety rooms with worn tiles and firm beds characterize this family guesthouse which also has a curious clutter of photos, carvings and religious dioramas. A plus is the onsite internet café serving coffee on the plaza.

Merendero Mi Puelito (mains US$1-5; ⏰ 7am-7pm) Alegría's best meal value is this worn café where beans simmer in cast-iron pots over an open flame and the whole family chips in. It's south of the park.

Getting There & Away

Alegría sits between the Interamericana and Litoral highways and is accessible from either side. From Carr Interamericana, catch a minibus from Villa El Triunfo to Santiago de María (US$0.30, 15 minutes), where buses leaves hourly for Alegría (US$0.60, 45 minutes). See Usulután (p308) for transportation from the Carr del Litoral side.

CARR DEL LITORAL

The Carr del Litoral (Hwy CA2) runs from San Salvador southeast through Zacatecoluca and Usulután, eventually coming to a crossroads with routes heading north to San Miguel and south to the Pacific coast.

The first town of any size southeast of San Salvador is **Zacatecoluca** (57km), near *turicentro* Ichanmichen. From there, the Litoral is a well-marked four-lane highway with shoulders, until you get to the Río Lempa. Beyond the bridge, the road narrows but maintains decent shape. Another 27km to the east is the departmental capital of Usulután.

The highway then skirts a rugged range to the south. The turnoff for what is arguably El Salvador's best beach, **Playa El Espino**, is just past El Tránsito, 10km east of Usulután. You'll need a 4WD to navigate the bumpy, windy road. It takes close to two hours to get there, but you are rewarded with your very own beach. Further east, **Laguna El Jocotál** is an important migratory bird sanctuary, sadly littered with trash. Your best bet is to tour the lagoon via canoe with a local.

The road then winds up into lava hills until the roundabout at El Delirio. From there, it's a straight shot north to San Miguel or south to Playa El Cuco and the eastern beaches.

ISLA MONTECRISTO

A steamy, pristine sanctuary for hundreds of pelicans and egrets, this island and estuary sit where the Río Lempa meets the Pacific Ocean. During the war, the island and its cashew plantation were abandoned and taken over by the FMLN. After 1992, it was resettled by local farmers taking advantage of the postwar land transfer program. In 1998 Hurricane

EL SALVADOR

Mitch caused the evacuation of the island and flooded the lower Lempa. These days there are about 25 families growing organic cashews as an export crop.

Guests can stay at **Hostal Lempa Mar** (☎ 2310 9901; www.gbajolempa.net; La Pita; r US$15; ☾ Wed-Sun), operated by a local development group. Simple cabins offer basic rooms with shared bathrooms and a comfortable terrace, and there are meals available in the restaurant. **Boat tours** travel through narrow corridors in the mangroves; some visit the cashew plantations as well. A fishing cooperative in Estero Jaltepeque can arrange **fishing trips** or the rental of traditional **canoes**.

La Pita and Montecristo are at the end of a 22km road which connects the Carr Litoral to the coast. The road can be rough in rainy season. Take bus 155 (US$0.70, 40 minutes) or a pick-up from the Texaco in San Nicolas Lempa, with departures between 6am and 5:30pm.

From La Pita, *lanchas* (small motorboats; US$14 round-trip) or canoes (US$2.50 one way) can take you out to the island.

USULUTÁN

pop 45,300

Tented market stands choke the streets of this chaotic departmental capital at the foot of 1450m Volcán de Usulután. Middle Eastern immigrants exert a strong influence over the town's commerce. But for travelers Usulután will probably serve as a way-station to Bahía de Jiquilisco and the lovely Playa El Espino. You can also reach the mountain hamlet of Alegría from here (p306).

Information

Banco Cuscatlán (2a Calle Ote near Av Dr Guandiquil) On the parque central, it cashes traveler's checks and has a 24-hour ATM.

Cyber Planet (4a Calle Ote btwn 2a & 4a Avs Norte; per hr US$0.50; ☾ 8:30am-6pm Mon-Sat, 8:30am-noon Sun; ☒)

Sleeping & Eating

Hotel Florida (☎ 662 0540; 4a Calle Oriente 26; s/d with bathroom US$9/14, with air-con US$12/24; ☒) With worn cement rooms and ratty bedspreads, this dated hotel by the market begs for remodeling. Still, guests will enjoy the shady balcony and meals from the kitchen.

Pastelería Trigo Puro (Calle Dr Penado; mains US$2-3; ☾ 7am-5pm Mon-Sat) Fat cinnamon rolls, donuts and coconut cookies beckon from the glass case

of this popular bakery, also serving *cafeteria*-style *típico*. It's one block west of the park.

Tortas Lito's (Calle Dr Federíco Penado at 1a Av Norte; mains US$2-3; ☾ 10am-8pm) Feast on tacos, enchiladas and *tortas* in this popular Mexican restaurant filled with picnic benches and the blaring sounds of salsa.

Adventurous eaters should follow the sniffing dogs to the **Mercado Central** (4a Av Norte btwn 2a & 4a), where a whole village of women are cooking up grilled chicken, pork stew and beans.

Getting There & Away

Usulután's main bus terminal is 1.5km east of the parque central (taxi US$2). The San Miguel terminal is west of town, but passengers can board along 1a Calle Ote, a block south of the parque central. Buses to Alegría, Puerto Triunfo and San Salvador all take 4a Calle west through town. Since most buses pass through town you don't have to go to the terminal (unless you want a seat).

Alegría; Bus 348 to Berlín (US$1; 1hr)

Playa El Cuco Bus 373 to El Delirio (US$0.70; 2hr)

Playa El Espino Buses 351, 358 (US$1.10; 1½hr) Catch them from a small lot 100m west of main terminal, across from a supermarket.

Puerto El Triunfo Bus 363 (US$0.50; 1hr) Leaves from a lot along the highway.

San Miguel Bus 373 (US$0.70; 1½hr) Take this bus to connect to La Unión.

San Salvador Bus 302 (*directo* US$1.50; 2½hr; *especial* US$2; 1½hr)

Zacatecoluca Bus 302 (US$0.70; 1½hr)

BAHÍA DE JIQUILISCO

With kilometer after kilometer of white sand pounded by surf, and inland mangroves facing the volcanoes, the Península San Juan del Gozo beckons with promise. The inland sector is a habitat for gray egrets, pelicans and other water birds. Fishing towns include **Corral de Mulas** and **Isla Méndez**. Other less-accessible beaches are at **Punta San Juan** on the peninsula's east end and **Isla Madre Sal**. Also called Isla Jobal, **Isla Espíritu Santo** has endless coconut groves and a coconut-oil processing plant, but the beaches are no big deal. The Pacific side has strong and powerful surf, so be careful.

The gateway to Bahía de Jiquilisco, seedy Puerto El Triunfo is best sped through. Redefining grim, the only lodging, Hotel El Jardín, has doubles for US$12 or charges hourly (at least the sheets are clean). The pier eateries overlooking the bay offer fresh fish, *pupusas* and *licuados*.

Corral de Mulas & Isla Mendez

Passenger boats to **Corral de Mulas** (US$2) leave in the early morning from the dock at the end of the main road. Be sure to ask for *El Icaco*, which is a better option to *Corral II*. Once there, cut through town on sandy – sometimes flooded – roads to the beach (30 minutes). The last boat back is at 4pm; if you miss it, ask for a lodging recommendation at the *alcaldía*.

Isla Méndez offers a bay beach with calm, shallow waters and a palm-frocked ocean beach with crashing surf. Due to bus schedules, travelers are obliged to stay the night. It could be interesting, however. Local community development group **Adesco** (☎ 7727 3453) can arrange US$10 overnight family homestays. It also arranges boat trips around the bay (US$35 per group) that travel through mangroves and Palacio de las Aves, home to hundreds of waterfowl. Bus 368 (US$1, 1¼ hours) goes to Isla Méndez from San Marcos Lempa (30km away on the Carr Litoral) at 1pm and 2pm, returning at 5:30am and 6:30am. From San Marcos Lempa buses go to Puerto El Triunfo (11km) frequently.

See Usulután (opposite) for bus information; the last bus to Puerto El Triunfo is at 4:40pm, the last one back to Usulután is at 5:30pm. From the highway turnoff, take bus 377 to San Miguel (US$1.35, 2½ hours, last bus 2:50pm) or bus 185 to San Salvador (US$1.55, two hours, every 30 minutes, last bus 2:50pm).

SAN MIGUEL

pop 183,200

Stewing in smog and heat with a brash-but-sentimental reputation, San Miguel feels more tropical and vigorous than the capital. Just witness its hectic market spilling out in all directions. One of El Salvador's largest cities, it's also the main hub for the eastern half of the country. Yet this city, founded in 1530, has faced its share of problems. Gangs have been a plague, battled by vigilante groups, and now strong-armed by Super Mano Dura. Sky-high unemployment makes effectively cleaning up the city a true challenge. It's the remittances sent from family members living abroad that keep the commerce moving. The energy of this place means that more urban-oriented travelers can have an interesting time in the thick of it.

Orientation

Parque David J Guzmán is parque central, with the cathedral to the east. The area is choked with traffic by day and dodgy by night, but it's unavoidable since the bus terminal and hotels are nearby. The area west of central park is quieter and more secure. Av Roosevelt (Carr Interamericana) skirts the southwestern edge of town, where you'll find the majority of nightclubs and a large Metrocentro mall.

Information

Banco Cuscatlán (4a Calle Oriente & Av Barrios) Exchanges traveler's checks and foreign currency and has a 24-hour ATM.

Banco Salvadoreño (Av Barrios & 6a Calle Pte) Cashes traveler's checks, does Visa cash advances and has a 24-hour ATM.

Immigration Office (Migración; ☎ 2660 0957; cnr 15a Calle Ote & 8a Av Sur; ☼ 8am-4pm Mon-Fri)

Infocentros (6a Calle Pte; per hr US$1; ☼ 7am-6pm Mon-Sat, 8am-noon Sun)

Post Office (4a Av Sur at 3a Calle Ote)

Dangers & Annoyances

Although gang violence has quieted with new security measures, the city center is still the wrong place to be once the sun sets. Make sure your hotel feels safe and secure at check in.

Sights & Activities

CENTRO

Facing Parque David J Guzmán, San Miguel's cathedral, **Catedral Nuestra Señora de la Paz**, dates from the 18th century. Around the corner, on 2a Calle Oriente, is the **Antiguo Teatro Nacional**, a neoclassical gem which functioned as a cinema during the silent-film era and later as the Telecom headquarters and a public hospital. The **Museo Regional del Oriente** is in the same building on the 2nd floor. The collection of pottery and photos is meager but it's free.

AROUND TOWN

Archaeology buffs will appreciate the **Ruinas de Quelepa**, grassy mounds covering 40 terraced ceremonial platforms, largely unexcavated. Lenca inhabited the site between the 2nd and 7th centuries AD, trading with Copán in Honduras as well as Mexico. Stone sculptures uncovered here are on display in the Museo Regional del Oriente. The ruins are 8km west of San Miguel off the Interamericana. From the cathedral, bus 90 to Moncagua (US$35, 30 minutes) passes them.

EL SALVADOR

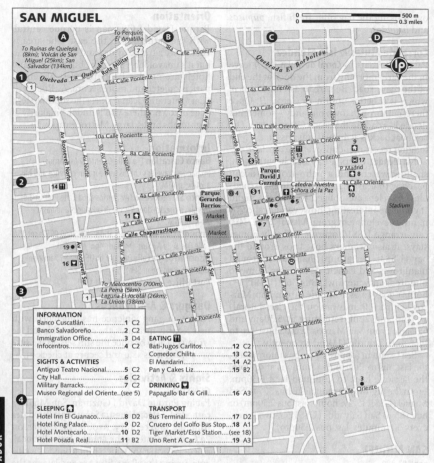

If you're game for a steep nine-hour slog, consider climbing 2130m **Volcano Chaparrastique**, aka Volcán de San Miguel, a towering cone southwest of San Miguel. Arrange police escorts through the **Chinameca Police Station** (☎ 2665 0074; fax 2665 1014). Request with two weeks' notice, if possible. The top affords gaping views of the coast and a patchwork of rolling farmland. The crater is hundreds of meters deep, with a jumble of boulders and virgins at the bottom. Weather can be windy; bring a sweatshirt and sunglasses as well as lots of water and food. Keep in mind you'll be providing lunch for your armed escorts (*pupusas?*). Get there with a rental car or take the Placitas bus from San Miguel at the corner of Calle Chaparrastique and 7a Av Sur and then arrange a taxi.

Festivals

Every November San Miguel honors the Virgen de la Paz with **Fiestas Patronales**, marking the occasion with holy processions and enormous, colorful sawdust carpets. Save yourself for its blowout finale, **Carnaval**, a citywide party held the last Saturday of November.

Sleeping

The cheapest places to stay are by the bus terminal, a gritty area unsafe after dark. If you stay out late take a cab.

Hotel Montecarlo (☎ 661 4113; 6a Calle Oriente; s/d with bathroom US$8/12, d with fan/air-con US$8/15; P 🐶) Like in the real Monte Carlo, you'll find high security (a surveillance camera) and gold trimmings (well, spray-on) spicing up this cheap motel. The best of the cheapies, it offers good beds and cable TV. Don't even think about swiping the remote control – it's bolted down.

Hotel Inn El Guanaco (☎ 2261 5029; 8a Av Norte at Pasaje Madrid; s/d US$20/30; ✷) Small and welcoming, El Guanaco has enormous spotless rooms with hot-water bathrooms and cable TV. For something quiet and removed, choose the 3rd floor. There's a pool table and promising smells wafting up from its ground-level restaurant.

Hotel King Palace (☎ 2661 1086; www.hotelking palace.com in Spanish; 6a Calle Ote 609; s US$22-28, deluxe d US$28-35; ✷ 🖳 🕸) Right across from the bus station, this business hotel's greatest asset is the helpful and professional staff. Spacious renovated rooms have flat-screen TVs; the cheapies are small but fine. All have blissful air-con. Take advantage of the little-used courtyard – it has a tiny pool that's, unfortunately, in view of the street vendors.

Hotel Posada Real (☎ 2261 7174; 7a Av & 2a Calle Poniente; s/d US$23/30; ✷) In the safer and subdued neighborhood west of the market, this well-kept pink two-story hotel offers bland but amenable rooms, with good beds, air-con and TV. Take an upstairs room; those downstairs smell of mildew.

Eating

The best value is *comida a la vista* for breakfast and lunch at a *comedor*; show up early when the trays are full and the food is fresh.

Pan y Cakes Liz (2a Calle Pte; mains US$1-3) Stack your tray with eggs, tamales, plantains, beans and coffee on the cheap at this friendly spot by the market.

Bati-Jugos Carlitos (1a Av Norte; mains US$1-5; ☽ breakfast & lunch Mon-Sat) The country's best *batidos* might be these fishbowl-sized tropical blends. While you're at it, grab a burger or a heaping plate of roast chicken and watch the soaps.

Comedor Chilita (8a Calle Oriente & 6a Av Norte Bis; mains US$2-3; ☽ 7am-10pm) This buzzing *cafeteria* spoons up a happy, huge variety that includes steamed veggies, spaghetti and roasted pepper chicken. After 4pm, it's all *pupusas* – use the side entrance on 8a Calle Oriente.

El Mandarin (Av Roosevelt Norte 407; mains US$4-10; ☽ 10am-9pm) Curb your craving for shrimp chow mien with the heaping portions (one serves two) at this Chinese restaurant with the Arctic air-con.

La Pema (mains US$5-12; ☽ 10:30am-4:30pm) It's blasphemy to come to this San Miguel institution and not order its famed *mariscada* (creamy seafood soup), served up with a mallet and thick cheese tortillas. Getting there is a trek (5km on the road to Playa El Cuco), but worth it.

Drinking

Locals love a party and you're likely to find it at *el triángulo*, the cluster of clubs at the triangle intersection of Av Roosevelt and the highway. Nightlife thrives between 10pm and 2am. Always ask the bartender to call a taxi – robberies have been committed by men posing as taxi drivers outside nightspots.

The upmarket **Papagallo Bar & Grill** (Plaza Chaparratisque, Av Roosevelt Sur; cover US$5) is where Latin and mainstream pop rule the rowdy dance floor and there's also the occasional live concert.

Getting There & Away
BUS

San Miguel's bus terminal has clearly marked bus lanes but there's no-one but fellow travelers or kiosk workers to advise on schedule changes and departure lanes. The surrounding area is rough-edged, so take a taxi to your hotel if you arrive at night. Destinations include the following:

El Amatillo (Honduran border) Bus 330 (US$1.75; 1½hr) At 10 minute intervals from 4am to 6pm.
El Cuco Bus 320 (US$1; 1½hr)
El Tamarindo Bus 385 (US$0.60; 2¼hr)
La Unión Bus 324 (US$1; 1¼hr)
Marcala, Honduras Bus 426 (US$3.50; 5½hr) Departs 4:40am and 11:40am.
Perquín Bus 332 (US$1.25; 3hr) Leaves at 6:20am, 9:50am, 10:20am, 12:40pm and 3:20pm. Alternately, take 328 to San Francisco Gotera and transfer to a pick-up.
Puerto El Triunfo Bus 377 (US$1.50; 2hr)
San Salvador Bus 301 (US$2.10; 3hr; *especial* US$3; 2 hr)
Usulután Bus 373 (US$1; 1½hr)

CAR

Hire a car through **Uno Rent A Car** (☎ 2661 0344; Av Roosevelt Norte)

LA UNIÓN
pop 23,600

The best thing about La Unión might be the way out. Like other ports the world over, it's seedy, drab and chaotic, but it also happens to be punishingly hot. Your shadow will simply wilt on the sidewalk. Hammocks hung from

EL SALVADOR

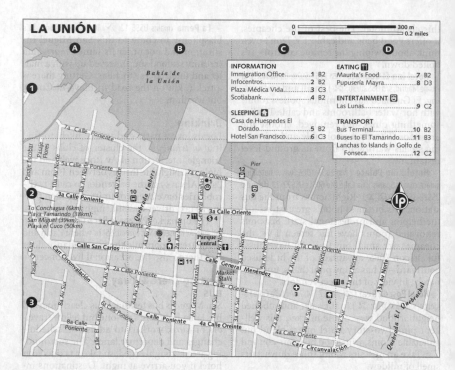

LA UNIÓN

INFORMATION
Immigration Office..............1 B2
Infocentros..........................2 B2
Plaza Médica Vida.............3 C3
Scotiabank..........................4 B2

SLEEPING
Casa de Huespedes El
   Dorado.............................5 B2
Hotel San Francisco...........6 C3

EATING
Maurita's Food....................7 B2
Pupusería Mayra................8 D3

ENTERTAINMENT
Las Lunas............................9 C2

TRANSPORT
Bus Terminal.......................10 B2
Buses to El Tamarindo.......11 B3
Lanchas to Islands in Golfo de
   Fonseca...........................12 C2

*Bahía de
la Unión*

To Conchagua (6km);
Playa Tamarindo (38km);
San Miguel (39km);
Playa el Cuco (50km)

crumbling colonial porches give some flavor of the past, and a new deep-sea port just outside town will receive cruise ships. In the meantime, the dock on the mudflats bustles with business.

Travelers come here to embark for the remote islands in the Golfo de Fonseca (opposite). Playa las Tunas and Playa Jaguey are the only good beaches on the coast west of La Unión, notwithstanding local enthusiasm for Playa El Cuco and El Tamarindo.

For some respite from the heat, and views of the gulf, head to **Conchagua**, at the base of the imposing volcano of the same name.

Information

Immigration Office (☎ 2604 4375; Av General Cabañas at 7a Calle Pte; ⏰ 6am-10pm) Next door to the post office, the sign says *Control Migración*. You must stop by here if you're arriving or departing by boat from Nicaragua or Honduras.

Infocentros (1a Calle Pte btwn 2a & 4a Avs; per hr US$1; ⏰ 8am-5:30pm Mon-Sat, 8am-noon Sun)

Plaza Médica Vida (☎ 2604 2065; Calle Gral Menéndez btwn 7a & 9a Avs Sur; ⏰ 24hr) A decent hospital near the center.

Scotiabank (2a Calle Ote btwn 1a Calle Sur & Av General Cabañas) Changes traveler's checks and has a 24-hour ATM.

Sleeping & Eating

Casa de Huespedes El Dorado (☎ 2604 4724; Calle San Carlos & 2a Av Norte; d US$8) An old-fashioned guesthouse plunk in the middle of the market madness. Its best feature is the quiet courtyard with gardenias and mangos. Rooms are somewhat dated and damaged but the elderly owners are cool.

Hotel San Francisco (☎ 2604 4159; Calle Gral Menéndez btwn 9a & 11a Avs Sur; s/d with air-con US$32/40; ❄) In a better area than the competition, this hotel sports a wide colonial porch and leafy courtyards. Rooms are spotless though dated, featuring hammocks and beds with pink sateen ruffles. Don't be put off if there are guests paying by the hour.

Pupusería Mayra (Calle Gral Menéndez; mains US$1-2; ⏰ 5-10pm) Superclean and kitschy (spot *The Last Supper* alongside the mounted elk), this is the spot for *panes de pollo* (chicken sandwiches) and fresh *pupusas*.

Maurita's Food (cnr Av Gral Cabañas & 3a Calle Poniente; meals US$2-6; ⏰ breakfast & lunch) A local mainstay once known as Cafetín El Marinero, friendly Maurita serves up well-prepared seafood, ceviche and *típica*. In a charmed pink colonial building with a wrap-around porch.

For fine seafood dining check out the waterfront east of the center. Nearby **Las Lunas** (3a Av Norte, Playa Los Coquitos; ☻ 2pm-2am) offers nightlife in the form of karaoke and occasional Saturday concerts under a thatched bar.

Getting There & Away
The bus terminal is on 3a Calle Poniente between 4a and 6a Avs Norte. Service include the following:

Conchagua Bus 382A (US$0.25; 15min)
El Amatillo (Honduran border) Santa Rosa de Lima bus 342 (US$0.90; 1hr) to San Carlos, transfer to bus 330 at the turnoff.
El Tamarindo Bus 383 (US$0.90; 1¾hr)
Las Playitas Bus 418 (US$0.80; 1hr)
San Miguel Bus 324 (US$0.85; 1¼hr; *especial* US$1; 1hr)
San Salvador Bus 304 (US$3; 4 hr; *especial* US$5; 3 hr)
Santa Rosa de Lima Bus 342 (US$0.90; 1½hr)

BEACHES NEAR LA UNIÓN
El Salvador has some great beaches but these are not among them. Extremely popular among Salvadorans from San Miguel and La Unión, they will probably impress backpackers as drab and crowded. Neither El Cuco, the most popular, nor El Tamarindo, the closest, are worth a stop. Be aware of potential jellyfish and manta rays – shuffle while walking out.

Broad and sandy **Playa Jaguey** is the best beach between El Tamarindo and El Cuco, with moderate surf. At Jaguey, a local road descends from the highway to an access road just east of a grassy parking area that leads to the beach. Private homes front the beach but you can still use it. There are no facilities.

Playa las Tunas is also pleasant enough, with a wide, flat beach reaching 100m to an estuary. The cluster of seaside restaurants serving fresh lobster, fish and oysters is packed on weekends. Among them is the lively **Rancho Las Tunas** (mains US$4-10; ☻ 7am-7pm), where live horn trios mingle among the relaxed crowd glugging *baldes cerveceros* (beer buckets on ice) and oysters by the dozen. The budget lodgings here are a disappointing lot – it's best left as a day trip.

From La Unión, bus 383 takes a circular route to El Tamarindo; it passes Las Tunas and Jaguey on the way. For a breezy shortcut, take the same bus only as far as Buenavista and catch a *lancha* across the inlet to El Tamarindo (US$0.25) and hop on bus 383 returning to La Unión via Jaguey and Las Tunas.

ISLANDS IN GOLFO DE FONSECA
Pillaged by 17th-century pirates and abandoned, only to be repopulated in the 20th century, these lush volcanic islands remain oblivious to tourism. Visitors might have romantic notions of this gorgeous inlet, but it's more a revelation of how isolated communities really live. There are fishing villages with

---

CROSSING THE BORDER

Getting to Tegucigalpa, Honduras
For Tegucigalpa (US$27, five hours), 1st-class **King Quality** (in San Salvador ☎ 2271 1361) buses stop at San Miguel's **Esso gas station** (Av Roosevelt at Ruta Militar) at around 8am and 3:30pm daily – be early just in case. Buy tickets at the gas station one day in advance.

Otherwise, bus 330 drops you 50m from El Amatillo on the Salvadoran border where a bridge crosses into Honduras. Honduran buses then go to **Choluteca** (US$1.50, 2¼ hours) and on to **Tegucigalpa** (US$2, 3½ hours); the last bus for both leaves at 5:30pm. The last bus from El Amatillo to San Miguel goes at 6:30pm.

See p435 for information on crossing the border from Honduras.

Getting to Nicaragua & Costa Rica
King Quality operates to **Managua** (US$27, nine hours), continuing on to **San José, Costa Rica** (US$47, 19 hours). It stops at San Miguel's Esso gas station at aabout 7:30am and 1:30pm.

From El Amatillo microbuses run from 5:30am to 5pm across the southern tip of Honduras to the Nicaraguan border town of **Guasaule** (US$5, two hours), where connections reach **León** and **Managua**.

EL SALVADOR

SPREADING THE WEALTH

War and economics have scattered 2.9 million Salvadorans from Mexico City to Melbourne. These hard-working *Guanacos* go where the jobs are, mostly to the USA, where many wash dishes or work in construction crews to sustain families and communities back home. *Remesas* (remittances) are not just petty cash but make up a whopping US$3 billion a year for the El Salvadoran economy.

Cinderella stories tell of remittances pooled by expat clubs to finance hometown improvements. The small community of El Piche in La Unión Department has had wells drilled, schools extended and clinics improved, all thanks to the town's Los Angeles cousins.

Yet the reality of remittances is that they are rarely saved and largely spent. The Inter-American Development Bank estimates that 85% of wired funds go to consumer spending – that means money for grocery bills, cell phones or designer track shoes. Consumerism in El Salvador has grown exponentially, evidenced by upmarket new malls and Kentucky Fried Chicken outlets. Banks act largely as money transfer agents, content to take a cut on transfers instead of promoting accounts, a disservice that perpetuates the perception that the poor don't save. Those who aren't saving grow increasingly dependent on that next check from abroad.

But what would happen if the USA tightened its reins on illegal workers? El Salvador's infrastructure is built for spending, not generating revenue. Farming would be out. The war scattered rural families and among returnees are a generation raised in urban refugee camps. It's little wonder that all but grandma and grandpa have turned their back on the family farm and resettled in urban areas, closer to the Western Union.

few services and black-sand beaches which are either trash-strewn or hard to get to. Take along food and water. In general, the more distant islands are more pristine.

The nearest island, **Isla Zacatillo**, has the largest community. Numerous coves with sandy beaches can be explored, but it's no tropical dreamscape. The principal village has a few stores and lodgings in a wooden shack over the bay. For solitary beaches, head for **Isla Martín Pérez**, just south of Zacatillo. More mountainous, **Isla Conchagüita** offers hiking. Fishing boats are neatly lined up under *enramadas* (arbors or protective awnings, typically made of wood or branches) along the beachfront of the main village. Locals say there are prehistoric rock carvings on the way out to Playa Brava, a black-sand beach an hour's walk from the village.

Isla Meanguera, the southernmost isle, was long the subject of territorial disputes with Honduras and Nicaragua, until an international court declared it part of El Salvador in 1992. It's the only island in the gulf with decent lodging – ask for directions at the ferry landing.

Hotel Paraíso de Meanguera (☎ 2648 0145; s/d US$12/15) has decent hammock-strewn rooms with cable TV and bathroom. Meals are available upon request, with seafood just US$3.

Perched over a peaceful cove, **Hotel El Mirador** (☎ 2648 0072) is a recommended hotel

and restaurant under renovation at the time of research; call before arriving. One of the island's best beaches, **Playa Majahual**, is a 45-minute walk; shuttles (US$1) depend on availability.

La Unión has services to Zacatillo (US$2, 20 minutes) and Meanguera (US$2.50, 1½ hours) from the pier. Departure times vary, but are generally from 10am to 10:30am, returning at 5am the next day. Day-trippers have to arrange a private pick-up.

A private 'express' *lancha* costs US$60 round-trip to Meanguera. Don't expect any bargains. Agree on a price before the journey starts, and pay only half up front to ensure your return trip. Ferries for the islands also depart from Las Playitas further down the coast.

Boat service from La Unión to Coyolitos, Honduras, and the port of Potosí, Nicaragua, is very infrequent. Ask a navy officer or a boatman. You could also try calling Hotel El Mirador on Isla Meanguera to see if it has a trip planned. Prices vary widely – we were quoted from US$10 to US$60. The wait may last days or weeks. The land route may not be too exciting, but neither is hanging out in La Unión.

There is a navy post at the pier – look for a little desk with a sailor behind it. He can be helpful.

MORAZÁN

North of San Miguel, Morazán Department was a guerrilla stronghold during the civil war. This impoverished agricultural area experienced some of the heaviest fighting. It is a fascinating place to visit, with the opportunity to speak with many whose firsthand experience of the war shaped their lives. The war museum in Perquín and a memorial in El Mozote are sobering reminders of the atrocities that befell fighters and families alike. Mountainous and cool, Morazán boasts the country's cleanest river, the Río Sapo, and plenty of hikes to waterfalls and war hideouts.

Indigenous traditions survive in villages around San Francisco Gotera, the department capital. The village of **Cacaopera** (bus 337 from San Francisco Gotera) has a small ethnographic **museum** (admission US$1; ☺ 9am-noon & 2-5pm Mon-Fri) with photo exhibits and artifacts from the local Kakawira indigenous community. Miguel Ayala of the museum is a good contact. Through the museum you can also arrange guided hikes in the dry season (December to April) to pre-Colombian petroglyphs (US$10 per group). The museum maintains a rustic **hostel** (☎ 2651 0251; dm US$5), without electricity or running water. You can bathe in the nearby Río Torola and cook on the wood-burning stove. Sure, it's roughing it, but the experience is undoubtedly unique.

The community at **Guatajiagua** produces quality black pottery in the Lenca tradition. Visit **Cedart** (Calle Principal; ☺ 8am-5pm Mon-Fri, 8am-noon Sat) crafts shop or ask the clerk to point you in the direction of local artist workshops.

Perquín

pop 5500

Perquín, at 1117m, was the FMLN headquarters during the war – its leftover bunkers and bomb craters are evidence of the former guerrilla presence. The opposition enjoyed broad popular support here and the rugged landscape thick with trees provided cover from military patrols. The town itself isn't beautiful but the cool mountain climate and strong historical significance make a trip here the highlight of El Salvador for most visitors.

SU CASA EN CUMARO

Community-based tourism provides travelers with an opportunity that's so grass roots it's part adventure. But, hey, that's why you're here, right? The upper Río Sapo watershed offers a glimpse of rural life as well as gorgeous waterfalls, swimming holes and hiking. Peace Corps volunteer Jason Seagle, who spent two years here, suggests the following:

- Explore the upper Río Sapo watershed where you'll find beautiful and friendly communities. Ask around for Don Santos, a guide for the Río Sapo Protected Area.
- Ask any kid to show you *la pileta*, the town swimming hole, and you'll likely be joined by an additional 20 kids.
- There's a small community library in Cumaro. Talk to Don Santos for the key and for help organizing a group of kids for reading hour. They're really into it.
- Talk with a local farmer to go out and spend the day working in their corn/coffee or sugar-cane field (depending on season).
- See Don Juan, Cumaro's school director, if you want to give volunteer classes. The school is always excited to work with international visitors.
- Talk with Marcos Hernandez to get involved in beekeeping. (Tip accordingly.)

For lodging in a beautiful log cabin on the property of a wonderful Salvadoran family, contact **Cabaña las Veraneras** (☎ 7733 4493; Caserío Cumaro; campsites/r per person US$2/6; meals US$1.50). Guests of Niña Nilda become one more member of the family. You can also contact the Prodetur office in Perquín for reservations.

To arrive from Perquín, take any pick-up (US$0.15) to the Arambala turnoff and take bus 332C (US$0.50) toward Joateca. Buses pass at 8am, 1:10pm, 3:10pm and 5pm. At the Caserío Cumaro turnoff start the 20-minute walk in to Las Veraneras (follow the signs for the pool). Happy adventures!

INFORMATION

Cyberspace (per hr US$1; ☺ 8am-9pm Sat-Thu, 8am-6pm Fri)

Prodetur (☎ 2680 4086; parque central; ☺ 8am-5pm Mon-Fri, 8am-2pm Sat) Perquín's helpful tour office organizes guided tours and hikes (US$15) with a few days' notice. Early August commemorates the signing of the peace accords with various guided trips available.

SIGHTS

A few blocks north of the park, the **Museo de la Revolución Salvadoreña** (Calle Los Héroes; admission US$1.50; ☺ 8:30am-4:30pm Tue-Sun) charts the causes and progress of the armed struggle with photos, posters, weapons and some histories of those who died in action. Weapons range from high-tech hardware to home-made bombs and mines. It can be a bit overwhelming.

Behind the main building is a bomb crater and the remains of the downed helicopter that carried Lieutenant Colonel Domingo Monterrosa, head of the notorious Atlacatl Battalion, to his death. You'll see the stu-

dios of the FMLN's clandestine station *Radio Venceremos* (We Will Win Radio), part of an elaborate hoax that used a radio transmitter rigged with explosives to bring Monterrosa's helicopter down. The exhibits are somewhat rundown and in Spanish only; tours of the museum by former guerrillas are available in Spanish.

The museum is also the contact point for ex-guerrilla guides who can take visitors on fascinating **guided trips** (groups US$15) throughout the war zone. The most popular destination is El Mozote (see opposite).

ACTIVITIES

Mountainous Perquín offers excellent hiking and river swimming. An abundance of orchids and butterflies make it a prime birding zone – 12 varieties of oriole have been spotted along with the rare chestnut-headed oropendola. The **Río Sapo** is one of three rivers cutting through the forest – you can swim or camp here after visiting El Mozote. **Quebrada de Perquín** is a smaller, craggier creek, also

---

LOCAL VOICES: THE GUERRILLA TURNED TOUR GUIDE

Efraín Pérez is a guide in Perquín's war museum. He was 11 when the Salvadoran army murdered his parents and two siblings in Jocoaitique. He joined rebel FMLN (Frente Farabundo Martí de Liberación Nacional) forces two years later and spent eight years traveling on foot and training with the guerrillas. He is now 35, utterly frank and serene. The war left him lame; he walks dragging one leg. We meet at the Museo de la Revolución Salvadoreña, taking a bench alongside a bomb crater.

■ **What do you like about being a guide?** The most important thing is to transmit a story to those who don't know it and to the country's younger generation who should know their own history. It is important that people know that in those years we were living the consequences of a government.

■ **How does your firsthand experience come in?** People come to the museum and say, 'I want to hear the history from someone who has lived it.' Because it's not the same to hear an explanation from someone who has, in theory, studied the war.

■ **Are the memories difficult to confront?** Ex-guerrilla commanders have come and said, 'Look, Efrain, tell us the story of these people'…Many ex-guerrillas can't recount stories about the war. Why? Because for that one needs preparation, one needs serenity and to be able to captivate [an audience].

■ **Are there moments when visitors surprise you?** Last year an American student apologized after learning about the US role in the war. 'Don't feel bad,' I said, 'These are things governments do to governments.'

■ **Do you enjoy your job?** Well, yes. But if I could do another job…since I am handicapped… this is my option (he laughs).

■ **But I think very few people could do this job.** Yes, very few.

As told to Carolyn McCarthy

good for swimming. **Cerro de Perquín** is a 10-minute hike from town, while **Cerro el Pericón** is a longer haul. Both offer gorgeous views. For guides consult Prodetur or the museum. For nearby community tourism opportunities, see p315.

SLEEPING & EATING

Eco Albergue Río Sapo (☎ 2680 4086/4087; campsites/dm per person US$3.50/6) Access to a swimming hole and a dozen hikes is the best reason for staying at these rustic dorm-style cabins at Area Natural Protegida Río Sapo. There's no electricity and limited water; bring your own food and flashlights. You can rent a tent (US$3) or sleeping bag (US$1) if you don't have your own. It's operated by Prodetur.

Hostal Perquín Real (☎ 2680 4158; r per person US$6) Large tile rooms with lumpy beds are relatively comfy, if not very private; the doors open right into the restaurant. The shared bathroom boils down to a bucket wash. Dining is convenient, with the restaurant serving fresh typical fare in an open-air setting.

La Posada de Don Manuel (☎ 2680 4037; s/d US$6/18) In this gigantic lumber mill-gone-guesthouse you'll find a dark *comedor* and small, bright cement rooms, with sturdy mattresses and fans. The common bathrooms could be cleaner. It's 500m before town.

Hotel Perkin Lenca (☎ /fax 2680 4046; www.perkinlenca.com; r per person incl breakfast US$15, 1-4 person cabin incl breakfast US$40-77) Perquín's finest accommodation option is this relaxed mountain lodge, with sunny oak and pine cabins that offer superb views of pine-forested slopes. The new doubles are excellent value. All accommodations have hot-water showers. Handicap access, area tours and a book exchange are in the works. The American owner, Ronald Brenneman, did relief work during the 1980s, building low-income refugee housing.

La Cocina de Ma'Anita (Hotel Perkin Lenca; mains US$3-11) This large country kitchen prepares hearty breakfasts with fresh juice, eggs and home-made wheat bread. A good dinner choice is grilled steak with roasted veggies and warm tortillas. Blue-sky days warrant outdoor seating on the stone patio.

GETTING THERE & AWAY

The CA7 north of San Miguel to the Honduran border is in good shape. Bus 332 runs from San Miguel to Perquín (US$1.50, 2½ hours) at 6am, 7am, 9:50am and 12:40pm.

> **GETTING TO MARCALA, HONDURAS**
>
> Bus 426 goes from Perquín to Marcala, Honduras (US$2.50, three hours) daily at 6:30am and 11:40am. It stops at Honduran immigration, where a 30-day tourist card is US$2. Due to a border dispute, there is no Salvadoran immigration or customs post at **Sabanetas–Marcala**; no problem for those leaving, but travelers entering El Salvador here could be turned back or fined later for entering without being stamped.

Alternatively, there's the more frequent bus 328 to San Francisco Gotera (US$0.70, 1½ hours) from which pick-ups go on to Perquín (US$0.50, one hour). The last bus back to San Miguel is at 4pm; the last pick-up to Gotera leaves at 5:40pm, but you have to catch the 5pm to make the last Gotera–San Miguel bus.

El Mozote

On December 11, 1981, government soldiers terrorized and executed the residents of this northern hill village. It's estimated that 757 people died: of the 143 victims uncovered, 131 were children. El Mozote is now a destination for those paying homage to the massacre. A tribute includes bright murals painted on the church, depicting the town as it was back then and as its children hope it to be someday. There is also a plaque with the names of those who had died and a rose garden planted over the collective grave of the massacred children. This modest village has no lodgings and few services.

A visit to El Mozote is a searing and heart-wrenching experience, one that could re-order your sense of the world. A local guide might talk about how her whole family, parents and siblings, were exterminated, while touring the village to point out the bomb scars and bullet holes. For some it might seem macabre, but the tour's impetus of '*Nunca Más*' (never again) aims to end senseless violence through this horrific example.

It's important to remain sensitive to the seriousness of the site. Locals are accustomed to an international presence; they've even set up snack bars and children tag behind visitors asking for handouts. As tempting as it is to give, it's best, however, if you donate directly to the box inside the tour office.

EL SALVADOR

From Perquín walk or take a pick-up 3km south to a fork in the highway, El Mozote is 10km from the paved road; Jateca-bound buses pass here at 8am. On the way you'll pass Arambala, once decimated by air raids. The same bus returns from El Mozote at 12:45pm and can drop you at the turnoff. Combine this trip with a visit to Río Sapo, a 30-minute walk from El Mozote.

Prodetur and the Museo de la Revolución Salvadoreña in Perquín (p316) can do trips here, but show respect by using local El Mozote guides once in the village.

NORTHERN EL SALVADOR

While whitewashed Suchitoto wins the hearts of local and international travelers searching for enchantment, the north has much more to offer. Here, little side trips turn into big adventures. The artisan town of Palma, with its crayon-color homes, dedicated workshops and lush mountain backdrop offers a cool borderland retreat. Bumpy bus rides run up craggy hills and pass through pine forests to take you (albeit slowly) where few outsiders venture.

Now boasting one of the country's lowest crime rates, the Chalatenango district was the scene of intense fighting between the government army and the FMLN guerrillas. Villages bore the brunt of the military's *tierra arrasada* (scorched land) tactics, which burned fields and killed livestock as a form of combat. The carnage precipitated an exodus, and it is not uncommon to run into locals who spent a dozen years in New York or Melbourne.

The main provider of water and hydroelectric power for El Salvador, Chalatenango Department faces a serious deforestation problem.

SUCHITOTO

Sure enough, tell San Salvadorans that you're Suchitoto bound and they give a nostalgic sigh. And rightly so, as this little town 47km north of the capital is everything El Salvador once was before the civil war and various natural disasters. In a setting of whitewashed colonials and cobblestone streets, it's gossipy, leftist-leaning and beaming with civic pride. A cultural capital during the indigo trade's heyday, it now has a burgeoning arts scene. A February arts-and-culture festival brings

in world-class performers and concerts, and performances or art exhibits are held almost weekly.

Suchitoto overlooks the Embalse Cerrón Grande, also known as Lago Suchitlán, a reservoir visitors can enjoy by boat. It is also a bird migration zone with over 200 species. Thousands of hawks and falcons fill the skies as the seasons change, and birds of all sorts nest in the relative safety of the islands.

It is presumed that Yaquis and Pipils settled in the area some 1000 years ago. El Salvador's capital was established near here in the early 16th century. More recently, some of the earliest fighting of the civil war began in Suchitoto, accompanied by much destruction and emigration. Today the town has rebounded to become the highland seat of national tourism.

Orientation & Information

La Iglesia Santa Lucía stands on the east side of the Parque Centenario, the town center. Signs to the lake lead you a block east of the park, left onto 3a Av Sur, then down steeply to the water (about 1km). You can also follow the street that forms the park's western edge (Av 15 de Septiembre); it merges with 3a Av Sur several blocks down. Parque San Martin is two blocks west and two blocks north of the town center.

Bring plenty of cash since there is nowhere to withdraw or change money in Suchitoto. Internet cafés abound; try **Infocentros** (Calle Francisco Morazán at Av 5 de Noviembre; per hr US$1; ☺ 8am-5pm) at the park. A great local resource, **El Gringo** (☎ 2335 1770; 8a Av Norte 9; free wi-fi with your own computer; ▢), aka Californian Robert Brozmorán, can download photos and give guidance on what the area has to offer (maybe patronize his small convenience store for the favor).

Suchitoto's **Tourism Office** (☎ 2335 1782; www .suchitoto-elsalvador.com; Calle Francisco Morazán at 2a Av Norte; ☺ 8am-4pm Wed-Sun) rents bikes (per hour US$1) and informs about hikes, activities and cultural events.

Sights & Activities

Geologic oddity **Cascada los Tercios** tumbles over a cliff of tightly packed hexagonal stone spires. The waterfall underwhelms when water is low (often), but the rock formation and the trip there are interesting enough. Take the road in front of the church south. It curves left, down and up again before intersecting with a soccer field. Turn left onto the main road and continue for about 1.5km. After a smoking garbage dump there's a gate on your left. Enter or continue to the next house, where one of the kids can guide you (it's family property). Upon request, boat tours can stop at the trail for the *cascadas* (waterfalls); walk up to the road, turn right and walk another four to five minutes.

It's a 1½-hour hike to **Salto El Cubo**, a 15m waterfall cascading into a pair of pools. You can climb from the lower one to the upper, hemmed in by rocks with the water crashing down from above. To get there, take Calle Francisco Morazán west out of town to a rocky trailhead, a narrow path descending steeply to the falls. A local Peace Corps volunteer working in conjunction with the tourist office put up signs.

Southwest of town, the former FMLN hideout of Volcán Guazapa is a popular **horseback riding** (6hr trip US$18) destination operated by an independent cooperative. Visitors can check out *tatús*, clever dugout hideouts, as well as craters and bomb shells. The tours are operated by an independent local cooperative and the quality may depend greatly on who is in charge (in general fewer riders means a better pick of healthy horses). Book trips through the tourism office or La Casona, preferably a day or two in advance.

The regional tourism office arranges city tours that include some 30 historical buildings. Also, browsing the **art galleries** can make an agreeable afternoon. Check out **Casa del Escultor** (☎ 2335 1836; www.miguelmartino.com; 2a Av Sur; ☾ Sat & Sun), the studio of acclaimed Argentine sculptor Miguel Martino.

For listings of local festivals see p325.

Sleeping & Eating

More lodging options are poised to spring up; ask locally for the newest budget options.

Casa de Rubia (☎ 2335 1833; Av 5 de Noviembre 29; r per person US$6; ☐) Great for those eking out a tight budget, this welcoming family home has basic rooms and a leafy backyard. The shared bathroom with old fixtures is somewhat rustic but clean. Breakfast available on request.

La Casona (☎ 2335 1969; www.lacasonasuchitoto.com; 4ta Calle Ote No 9; r US$12) Part of Jerry's alternative tourism is this leftist-run lodging with large cement rooms with bathrooms. Some travelers might not love bunking in what's essentially a bar but the large spaces make it fairly quiet.

La Villa Balanza (☎ 2335 1408; Parque San Martín; s/d US$15/20) The best value for travelers are these small bright rooms in a lovely stone courtyard. The only bummer is that the bathrooms are shared by the restaurant. Two annexes offer rooms of greatly varying quality, from spartan to somewhat swanky, most with good lake views. The restaurant serves good *típica* (mains US$2 to US$9) amidst art-crafted discarded bomb shells. Some come here just to check out the war memorabilia. It faces Parque San Martín.

Pupusería Niña Melita (6a Calle Ote btwn Calle al Lago & 3a Av Norte; pupusas US$0.25) How's this for hometown flavor? Melita hits the sidewalk nightly, frying up bean, zucchini or meat-filled *pupusas*, while her 96-year-old mother (nostalgic for mud ovens) decries the modernized recipe to passersby. Don't listen – they're delicious.

La Fonda del Mirador (☎ 2335 1126; 2a Av Sur 26A; mains US$4-10; ☾ 11am-6pm) Stunning views of the lake and river estuary make this the sunset spot in town. To boot, the food is great. The chicken sandwich with fries is an edifying value meal; for a treat try the snapper in tamarind sauce or seafood salad.

Casa del Escultor (☎ 2335 1836; www.miguelmartino .com; 2a Av Sur 26A; mains US$8-13; ☾ Sun) It's well worth splurging at this tiny reservations-only Argentine grill. Sausages, salad and wood-fire grilled meats are served with Argentine wines in a candlelit garden amid organic wood forms.

On weekends food vendors fill the plaza selling *riguas* (sweet buttery corn tortillas wrapped in a corn husk) and *fogonazo* (sugarcane juice), spiked with the strong stuff on request.

Drinking

After dinner grab a beer at **El Necio** (4a Calle Ote No 9; ☾ 6pm-1am), a classic watering hole fitted with Che posters and lefty memorabilia, owned by Jerry, an amiable ex-guerrilla. Patrons can get a little too friendly with single *señoritas* – they might be best to befriend the bartender.

The town's go-to nightspot is **Harlequín** (☾ 7pm-1am Fri-Sun), with eclectic tunes playing in a trellised garden with twinkling lights.

Getting There & Away

From San Salvador's Terminal de Oriente take bus 129. To return, the same bus departs from the corner of 1a Calle Pte and 4a Av Sur, a

EL SALVADOR

block west of Parque Centenario. By car, go toward Cojutepeque on the Interamericana. When you get to San Martín, turn left at the Texaco sign.

If you're headed north, catch Bus 163 to Las Aguilares (US$0.70, one hour), where buses pass for Chalatenango, Las Palmas and the El Salvador–Honduras border. A slower but more scenic option is to take a boat (per person US$5, 20 minutes) or car ferry (per person US$1, per car US$4) across Lago de Suchitlán to San Francisco Lempa and from there catch a bus to Chalatenango.

CHALATENANGO

pop 16,200

In the morning's first hours the market cackles to life, blocking traffic with piles of mandarins and pineapples stacked among bolts of fabric and cheap miniskirts. The north's largest city, 'Chalate' has taken a distinctly commercial route, as opposed to its sleepy neighbors. You dig it or you don't. The large military garrison on the plaza was built during wartime to rein in revolutionary activity in this FMLN stronghold. These days the only thing 'revolutionary' is the brisk business at the pay-per-hour hotels.

Orientation & Information

The parque central is divided by 3a Av, with the church on the east (uphill) side and the main park on the west (downhill) side. The market extends up the main east–west street, Calle San Martín-Calle Morazán. A huge army barracks stands north of the main park; most buses pick up and drop off on 3a Av, south of the park. One exception are the buses to Arcatao and Las Vueltas, which leave at the top of Calle Morazán, near the turnoff to the *turicentro*.

There's a 24-hour ATM at **Banco Cuscatlán** (4a Calle Pte near 6a Av Sur), and it also changes traveler's checks. Try **Cibercafé @halate Online** (1a Calle Ote at 5a Av Norte; per hr US$0.80; 8am-9:30pm Mon-Sat, 9am-1pm Sun) for internet access.

Sights

The **Iglesia de Chalatenango**, with its squat bell tower and bright chalky facade, sits on the east side of the parque central, a stone's throw from the military garrison.

A 20-minute walk from the parque central, **Turicentro Agua Fría** (admission US$0.80; 8am-5pm) has a lush park with picnic tables, but the

main draw are pools set with an artificial rock island topped by a waterslide. Dry season means water shortages – expect an overdose of chlorine. A cafeteria serves beer and meals. To get here, go up Calle Morazán (east) about 400m, and turn left at the big sign.

For panoramic views of the Cerrón Grande reservoir, climb **Cerro La Peña**, a 1½-hour hike starting at a trailhead before the *turicentro*. A number of roads and paths reach the top; as passersby for directions.

Sleeping & Eating

Hotel la Ceiba (☎ 2301 1080; d US$12) The only cheap hotel which doesn't seem to be an all-out bordello (we understand the residents of Chalate have their needs) is this two-story place behind the military garrison. It offers dark rooms, sturdy mattresses and fairly new installations.

La Posada del Jefe (☎ 2335 2450; Calle el Instituto, Barrio El Calvario; s/d US$15/20;) By far, the best bet in town is this family-run hotel, which has 12 impeccable cement rooms, all painted toothpaste-white and with rusted metal shelving. It's 10 blocks east of center, straight uphill. To get here take a little red mototaxi (US$0.70). It's kind of fun.

Comedor Carmary (3a Av; mains US$2-3; 7am-2pm Mon-Sat) This tidy cafeteria packed with bus-stop patrons serves tasty *comida a la vista*, which might include stewed chicken in tomatoes, plantains and the ubiquitous beans and rice, alongside tall glasses of fresh juice.

The open-air **market** (5am-1pm) offers a visual feast of veggies, fruits and grains, as well as stock to replenish your toiletries. It's just east of Av Fajardo.

Getting There & Away

Bus 125 runs regularly from San Salvador (US$0.90, two hours) and terminates on 3a Av Sur, a few blocks south of the church. To La Palma and El Poy, take bus 125 toward El Amayo (the highway intersection) and transfer to bus 119 (1½ hours) heading north.

See opposite for details on taking buses to local villages.

AROUND CHALATENANGO

The countryside around Chalate climbs into dry forest studded with toothy peaks and rugged tawny hills. The small villages in this remote area have stunning landscapes and interesting histories.

Beyond the Río Sumpul, **Arcatao** is a beautiful village in the mountains bordering Honduras. Ask in the municipal office about tours of the *tatus* (cave hideouts), which attest to Arcatao's former role as an FMLN stronghold. The local **Jesuit order** (☎ 2354 8009; bartolome2408@yahoo.com) receives guests and can set up guided tours of the area. Call ahead.

Northwest of Chalate, **Concepción Quezaltepeque** is a hammock-making center. You'll see women threading them along the side of the road. Prices range from US$30 to US$120, depending on size, length, thickness and material. Shops line the main street; browse a few first to compare quality.

La Montañona is a pine forest reserve at 1600m with prime views and pre-Columbian rock carvings. The civil war left several *tatus,* including one used by clandestine guerrilla radio station, Radio Farabundo, as well as an underground guerrilla hospital. You can stay in the small village: a rustic cabin has beds and shared bathroom (US$5 per night). Teresa Avilar cooks up basic meals. Call **Cesar Alas** (☎ 7723 6283) before going; he oversees the lodging and acts as a guide to the area.

A strenuous climb passing Dulce Nombre de María travels cobbled roads through pastel villages. Enjoy views of flat valleys sprung with volcanoes and the mountainous Honduran border beyond. North is **El Manzano**, a cooperative of ex-FMLN combatants. Its trails cross forest and coffee farms, and destinations include historic war sites and waterfalls. The top of El Pilón offers more incredible views. The *tienda* in the middle of town has information on lodging, meals and guides.

Getting There & Around

The following bus departures originate in Chalatenango:

Aracatao Bus 508 (US$1.15; 2hr) Departs hourly from 7am to 5:30pm from the top of Calle Morazán.

Concepción Quezaltepeque Bus 300B (US$0.35; 20min) At 3a Av Sur terminal in Chalate.

El Manzano No direct service. Take 125 to the *desvío* (turnoff) for Dulce Nombre de María to pick up bus 124 from San Salvador to Dulce Nombre de María. Take a pick-up to El Manzano.

La Montañona Buses 295 or 542 (US$1; 2hr) pass by the turnoff to Montañona, departing at 11:15am and 12:15am from 3a Av Sur between 1a and 3a Calles Pte. From the turnoff it's a steep 6km climb to the village – pick-ups often make the trip.

LA PALMA

At first glance, La Palma, at 1200m, resembles a coloring-book page zealously attended to by a seven-year-old. Its narrow streets are populated with tiny, tiled homes in garish tones of plum, mint and tangerine, some covered in fanciful murals or drawings. This artist village 84km north of San Salvador might border kitsch as well as Honduras, but it does make a cool visit. Lovers of the outdoors can enjoy the fresh air, verdant mountain views and some of the country's best hiking.

Painter Fernando Llort moved here in 1972, founding Naïve Art, a trend that still represents El Salvador around the world (p271). These bright, primitive images of mountain villages, *campesinos* or Christ images are painted on anything from seeds to church walls. He taught local residents how to create the same images and started a successful cooperative. Today 75% of the village makes a living by mass-producing these bright motifs.

Hikers often prefer lodging in the neighboring village of **San Ignacio** as it's closer to the trails.

Information

Banco Cuscatlán (Calle Barrios at 1a Calle Pte) Has a 24-hour ATM.

Ciber Pinto (Calle de Espina 83; per hr US$1; 🕒 8am-8pm)

Sights

Take some time to peruse the colorful streets of La Palma. Visitors are welcome to peek into workshops to see families painting away. Local cooperative **La Semilla de Dios** (3a Calle Pte at 5a Av Norte) crafts quality products in workshops behind the store. If you ask permission you can wander through the workshops and watch the painters and woodworkers at work.

Activities

Cerro El Pital (2730m) is the highest peak in El Salvador, but thanks to an access road, it is also one of the easiest to hike. From nearby San Ignacio, bus 509 to Las Pilas leaves you at Río Chiquito near the trail. It's about 1½ hours to the top, where spectacular views await. You will know you reached the summit when you find the cement block marking it. It is private property, so bring US$2 to cover admission.

Once there, ask for directions to **Piedra Rajada**, a huge cloven rock a half-hour walk from

---

GETTING TO SAN PEDRO SULA OR COPÁN RUINAS, HONDURAS

The bus from La Palma drops you about 100m from the El Salvador–Honduras border (open 6am to 6pm), where you pay US$2 to enter Honduras. From **El Poy**, you can take a bus or *colectivo* taxi to Nueva Ocotepeque, Honduras. From there buses leave hourly for San Pedro Sula. For Copán Ruinas, transfer at La Entrada.

The last bus to El Poy from La Palma (bus 119, US$0.50, 30 minutes) leaves at 7pm. The last bus south from El Poy to San Salvador leaves around 4:15pm.

See p383 for information on crossing the border from Honduras.

---

the summit, accessed by a nerve-wracking log bridge spanning a 25m drop. Don't try this one in wet weather.

Get more awe-inspiring vistas at **Miramundo**, a small, aptly named community perched on a steep hillside. Back at Río Chiquito, follow the right-hand fork for about an hour to Miramundo. Right on the trail, the ridge-top **Hostal Miramundo** (☎ 2230 0437; www.hostalmiramundo.com; per 6 people US$45) may have the best view of any lodging in El Salvador.

Great hikes around San Ignacio abound. For a guide, contact José Samuel Hernández, the owner of **Comedor y Artesanías El Manzana** (☎ 2305 8379; Carr La Palma-El Poy km 85), outside La Palma, or **Humberto Regalado** (☎ 2352 9138), who owns and maintains the trail to Peña Cayaguanca.

Buses to Las Pilas, passing through Río Chiquito, leave San Ignacio at 7am, 9:30am, 12:30pm, 2:30pm and 4:30pm and return at the same times.

Sleeping & Eating

Five kilometers south of town, Centro Obrero Dr Mario Zamora Rivas offers 15 remodeled cabins and a couple of pools, and is free with permission from the Ministerio de Trabajo in San Salvador (p279). Trails crisscross the forested grounds.

El Pital (☎ 2335 9344; r per person with bathroom US$10; 🏿) Well-kept but dowdy, these huge tile rooms have weary sofas and patched fixtures. The features include cable TV, minifridge and a fast-food eatery. It's popular with families.

Hotel La Palma (☎ 2305 9344; www.hotellapalma.com; r per person US$13) A quiet mountain getaway bordered by the Río La Palma, its expansion makes it feel more commercial than rustic. Accommodations are mostly comfortable, with a few drafty cabin rooms. Still, there's hammocks on the shady grounds, a pool (under renovation) and restaurant.

Quechelá Bed & Breakfast (☎ 2305 9328; quechela@navegante.com.sv; s/d with shared bathroom US$26/39) Worth the splurge, this mountain home offers wonderful hospitality. Rooms are spare but comfortable with ceramic tiles, and crisp linens on the beds. The living spaces show an artsy bent and impeccable taste. Breakfast is included. To get here take a mototaxi (US$0.50) from town.

Restaurante del Pueblo (mains US$1-5; 🕑 7am-9pm) If a dollar buys you a sandwich in thick bread, going all out means a good *plato típico* with grilled meat, bananas, beans, cheese and cream. It's down the road from the Hotel La Palma.

La Estancia (Calle Barrios 35; mains US$2-7; 🕑 7am-8pm) With a narrow balcony highly conducive to people-watching, this established restaurant mostly serves chicken or steak dinners. For snacking, US$2 tacos heaped with fresh tomatoes and *chirimol* hit the spot.

The village of San Ignacio has additional sleeping and eating options.

Getting There & Away

Bus 119 runs every half-hour from San Salvador's Terminal de Oriente to the El Salvador–Honduras border at El Poy, stopping at La Palma (US$1.50, three hours). Some enter San Ignacio, 3km to the north, others drop you off at the entrance.

From San Ignacio you can catch the bus to El Pital and its environs.

EL SALVADOR DIRECTORY

ACCOMMODATIONS

El Salvador has a decent selection of hotels but lacks the backpacker infrastructure that neighboring countries have. Consequently, hostels are few and those on very tight budgets must plan accordingly. As usual, couples get better deals than solo travelers. The cheapest places are often in seedy areas near bus terminals; paying a bit more is worthwhile for personal security. In many areas prostitution outranks tourism and travelers might find their only options are room-per-hour lodgings. This book attempts to include the safest and most secure options for travelers.

Camping and *eco-albergues* (eco-hostels; basic shared cabins, some with modest kitchen facilities) are appearing around popular outdoor destinations. Bring your own camping equipment, as the selection here is scant.

You can stay for free at *centros de obreros* (government workers' centers), which are huge compounds designed to give workers and their families a place to relax on the weekend. The main locations are Lago de Coatepeque, El Tamarindo, La Palma and outside La Libertad. You must reserve them advance at the appropriate office in San Salvador, see p279 for details.

Room rates are stable season to season, except during the summer holiday (first week of August), when hotels in popular towns fill up fast.

ACTIVITIES
Diving
Diving in El Salvador is more expensive and admittedly inferior to nearby Honduras or Belize. That said, it does offer one of the few coral reefs on the American side of the Pacific, as well as a chance to dive in crater lakes. The best time for diving is from October to February, especially December and January. One 5-star operator is **El Salvador Divers** (Map p278; ☎ 2264 0961; www.elsalvadordivers.com; 3a Calle Pte 5020, Col Escalon, El Salvador), offering open-water and advanced certification courses for around US$300.

Hiking
El Salvador has some excellent hiking, in spite of serious deforestation. Parque Nacional El Imposible (p304), near the border with Guatemala, offers the best combination of easy access and rewarding primary-forest hikes. The Ruta de las Flores offers waterfall and hot springs hikes; find guides for hire in Juayúa (p301). Further north, the pristinely beautiful Parque Nacional Montecristo-El Trifinio (p298) is renowned for wildlife. Access is difficult and it's closed during the May–November mating season. Parque Nacional los Volcanes (p294), with two climbable volcanoes, is a beautiful, if sometimes crowded, destina-

tion. Hikes from the northwestern towns of La Palma and San Ignacio offer stunning vistas. You can access El Salvador's highest peak (El Pital, 2730m; p321) from here. The northeastern state of Morazán, in particular Perquín, has a cool climate and fine hiking. As a longtime stronghold of the FMLN, it also has interesting and sobering sites related to the civil war.

Surfing
El Salvador is a steadily growing surf destination, with kilometer after kilometer of world-class breaks and virtually no one on them. Punta Roca, the country's finest wave, is at the scruffy port of La Libertad (p290), which is readily accessible from the capital. Several beaches west of La Libertad have excellent waves and better atmosphere, as well as all-service surf lodges. Your best bets for lessons are the Punta Roca resort or surfer Torsten Rode (he is found on Sunday in front of the Club Salvadoreño) in Playa Sunzal. Peak season is March to December.

BOOKS
Major Salvadoran authors (see p271) are available in translation. Joan Didion's *Salvador* is a moving account of the early days of the war. Nonfiction about the civil war includes *Massacre at El Mozote*, by Mark Danner, *Witness to War: An American Doctor in El Salvador*, by Charles Clements MD, and *Rebel Radio*, a fascinating, firsthand account of clandestine radio stations operated by FMLN guerrillas.

Óscar Romero: Memories in Mosaic, by María López Vigil, is a recommended account of the clergyman's life and political conversion told by those who knew him. *When the Dogs Ate Candles*, by Bill Hutchinson, is an anecdotal history of the conflict based on interviews with refugees. Archaeology buffs can read about Central America's Pompeii in *Before the Volcano Erupted: The Ancient Ceréen Village in Central America* by Payton Sheets.

BUSINESS HOURS
Businesses generally operate 9am to 6pm weekdays, while government offices are open 8am to 4pm. Some offices and stores close at lunchtime, between noon and 2pm, but this practice is fading. Banks are open 8am to 4pm or 5pm weekdays, and most open Saturday morning as well. Restaurants serve dinner early, and 4pm is *pupusa* hour.

CLIMATE

The *invierno* (wet season) is from May to October, and the *verano* (dry season) is from November to April. During the rainy season, it usually only rains at night.

In San Salvador, the maximum temperature varies from 27°C in November to 30°C in March and April; the minimum temperatures range from 16°C in January and February to 20°C in March. The coastal lowlands are the hottest region. For climate charts see p723.

CUSTOMS

Salvadoran border officials are among the most scrutinizing in the region. They check for previous entry and exit stamps. If you're entering on an international bus, your bags may well be searched. Carry your passport with you in all border regions, regardless of whether you're leaving the country, since there are a lot of police checkpoints (mostly searching for drugs).

DANGERS & ANNOYANCES

Crime shouldn't deter travelers from El Salvador any more than it does from the rest of Central America. Despite the country's reputation for violence, attacks on tourists are rare.

Be aware of pickpockets on buses and crowded streets. Take common-sense precautions: carry as little as possible on day trips, and avoid toting expensive backpacks, cameras, watches and jewelry. The more your clothing and travel gear blend in with the locals, the less you will be targeted. Before traveling, make copies of your credit cards and important documents; carry a copy with you and leave one with someone at home who could fax you them in a pinch. After dark it's best to take a taxi, even if the rates can be a little steep. This is particularly important in San Salvador, San Miguel, Sonsonate, La Unión and La Libertad.

Most volcano climbs are best done with a police escort, partly for your safety and partly so you won't get lost on unmarked and intersecting trails. The service is free, but you must request it by phone or in person a day in advance (and preferably more). Officers are friendly and trustworthy.

Of course, violence does occur. El Salvador has a high murder rate: about 10 violent deaths occur daily. The vast majority of perpetrators and victims are gang-affiliated. Two major *maras* (gangs) operate in the country (see p269). Travelers are unlikely to have encounters with a gang member as groups concentrate in neighborhoods with no outside appeal, and also because the police control most tourist areas. Still, visitors should avoid traveling at night. Weapons are widespread, so never resist a robbery – it's not worth it.

DISABLED TRAVELERS

There are many disabled people in El Salvador – most victims of war-related violence – but few services or amenities to make their lives easier. There are few well-maintained ramps and handrails or services for the visually and hearing impaired. However, disabled travelers (and all travelers) will find Salvadorans extremely friendly and eager to help.

EMBASSIES & CONSULATES
Embassies & Consulates in El Salvador

Australia, New Zealand and the UK do not have consular representation in El Salvador. Australians can get assistance at the Canadian embassy. Except for the US embassy, the following are in San Salvador.

Canada (☎ 2279 4655; Alameda Roosevelt at 63a Av Sur Torre A)

France (Map p278; ☎ 2279 4016; www.embafrancia.com .sv; 1a Calle Poniente 3718)

Germany (Map p278; ☎ 2247 0000; www.san-salvador .diplo.de; 7a Calle 3972)

Guatemala (Map p281; ☎ 2271 2225; 15a Av Norte btwn Calles Arce & 1a Calle Norte, Col Escalón)

Honduras (Map p278; ☎ 2263 2808; 89a Av Norte btwn 7a &9a Calle Pte, Col Escalón)

México (Map p278; ☎ 2243 0445; Calle Circunvalación & Pasaje 12, Col San Benito)

Nicaragua (Map p278; ☎ 2263 8789; Calle El Mirador btwn 93a & 95a Av Norte, Col Escalón)

USA (☎ 2278 4444 ext 2628; www.sansalvador.usem bassy.gov; Blvd Santa Elena Final, Antiguo Cuscatlán, La Libertad)

Salvadoran Embassies & Consulates Abroad

For a complete list, refer to www.rree.gob .sv/website/embajadas.html.

France (☎ 03314 720 4220; 12 Rue Galilée 75116, Paris)

Germany (☎ 49 30 206 4660; Joachim-Karnatz-Allee 47, 10557 Berlin)

Mexico (☎ 5281 5725; Temístocles 88, Col Polanco 11560, México DF)

UK (☎ 044 207 436 8282; Mayfair house, 3rd fl, 39 Great Portland St, London W1W7JZ)

USA (☎ 202 387 6511; 2308 California St, NW, Washington, DC 20008)

FESTIVALS & EVENTS

Fería Gastronómica A wonderful food fair held every weekend in Juayúa.

Festival de El Salvador (August 1-6) Celebrates El Salvador's patron saint; all cities have festivities with San Salvador's the biggest.

Festival del Invierno (August) Perquín's art and music festival popular with the boho crowd and college students.

Festival de Maíz (August) Suchitoto's corn harvest festival with religious processions and street parties.

Bolas de Fuego (August 31) To commemorate an eruption of Volcán San Salvador that destroyed the original town, Nejapa residents spar by throwing balls of fire then dance till dawn around street bonfires.

Festival de Hamacas (mid-November) Hammocks fill the streets of Concepción Quezaltepeque (p320) during this street fair.

FOOD & DRINK

A typical breakfast includes eggs, beans or *casamiento* (rice and beans mixed together), fried plantains, cheese, tortillas and coffee or juice. *Panaderías* usually offer a selection of morning cakes and coffee. Drinkable yogurt is also sold in most grocery stores. *Almuerzo* (lunch) is the largest meal of the day and often the most expensive.

El Salvador street food is all about *pupusas*, round cornmeal dough stuffed with a combination of cheese, refried beans, *chicharrón* (pork rinds), or *revuelta* (all three), and grilled. *Curtido*, a mixture of pickled cabbage and vegetables, provides the final topping. Most *pupuserías* open at around 4pm and some work the same sidewalk space for years. Also popular in the evening are *panes*, French breads sliced open and stuffed with chicken, salsa, salad and pickled vegetables.

Licuados (fruit drinks made with water or milk), *gaseosas* (soft drinks) and coffee are easily had in El Salvador. Note that *refresco*, which means soft drink in many countries, here means lemonade, *horchata* and other water-based drinks. A *refresco de ensalada* is not coleslaw puree, but a mixed fruit juice served with a spoon for the fruit salad floating on top, sangria style. Water can be bought in either bottles or half-liter bags.

Local beers include Pilsener [sic], the most popular, and Suprema, a lighter brew.

GAY & LESBIAN TRAVELERS

Gays receive little tolerance. Some hotels refuse to rent a room with one bed to two men; women will encounter less scrutiny.

Still, it's best to avoid public displays of affection. In San Salvador, the area around Blvd de los Héroes has cultural centers and clubs that, being more bohemian, are also more gay-friendly. Gay organization **Entre Amigos** (☎ 2225 4213; entreamigos@salnet.net; Av Santa Victoria No 50, near Blvd de los Héroes) is the most established in the country, dedicated mostly to HIV/AIDS outreach.

INTERNET ACCESS

The Salvadoran government sponsors dozens of internet cafés called Infocentros, from the capital to the tiny mountain towns. Most have air-con and fast connections. Privately run internet cafés offer similar services.

INTERNET RESOURCES

www.elsalvadorturismo.gob.sv Corsatur's official website is mildly better than reading a brochure.

www.lanic.utexas.edu/la/ca/salvador An excellent resource of Salvadoran websites, arranged by topic.

www.laprensa.com.sv Spanish-language website for one of El Salvador's major daily newspapers.

www.puntamango.com Website of Mango's Lounge surf shop in La Libertad; it tells you where to find the best waves in El Salvador.

www.salvanatura.org For reservations or information on Parque Nacional El Imposible and Parque Nacional Los Volcanes.

www.surfer.com.sv Shows off the west Pacific surf scene; links in English.

www.search-beat.com/elsalvador.htm Topic-based lists of Salvadoran websites.

LANGUAGE

Spanish is the national language. In a few indigenous villages a handful of people still speak the Nahua language of the Pipil, but there is academic interest in preserving it. Many Salvadorans pick up some English working in the USA, Australia and elsewhere, and English speakers pop up in the unlikeliest places.

LEGAL MATTERS

Law enforcement is strict and effective, from beat cops to border officials. Police are entitled to stop buses and search people and bags, and do so with some frequency, often helped by army soldiers. Bribes are generally not expected or accepted. If arrested cooperate and call your embassy, although if you have committed a crime there's little your embassy can do. Even minor offences require jail time.

EL SALVADOR

MAPS

Corsatur (see p279) and the Ministry of Tourism offer glossy maps of El Salvador and the capital, available at some hotels and tour offices. Map addicts should hit the **Centro Nacional de Registros** (IGN; Map p278; www.cnr.gob; 1a Calle Pte, San Salvador, 2nd fl; 🕑 8am-12:30pm & 2-5pm Mon-Fri), behind MetroSur, for high-quality city and country maps. Simple maps of hiking trails are sometimes available at respective visitors centers, but trails are usually well marked.

MEDIA

San Salvador's main newspapers are *La Prensa Gráfica* and the conservative *El Diario de Hoy*; check them for domestic and international news, plus entertainment listings. *El Mundo* and *El Latino* are thinner afternoon papers.

MONEY

In January 2001, El Salvador adopted the US dollar as official currency. The previous currency (the colón) technically still exists, but you'll probably never see one.

ATMs

ATMs are found in most cities and towns, with the exception of Suchitoto and Perquín. Banco Cuscatlán, Scotiabank and Banco Atlántida have the largest network of ATMs. It used to be that cash machines only accepted cards with the Plus/Visa symbol, but Cirrus/MasterCard cards now generally work as well. If the machine doesn't take your card you may get assistance inside the bank (this is also a sneaky way to avoid an ATM transaction fee – for a 'tarjeta de crédito' only).

Look for safer locking cabins to withdraw money and avoid taking out cash at night.

Bargaining & Tipping

Bargaining is less common here than in other Central American countries. A little back-and-forth is common with taxi drivers and market shopkeepers, but hard bargaining can seem a bit rude. Tip 10% in restaurants; it is not customary to tip taxi drivers, though rounding up the amount is appreciated.

Cash

Bring US dollars, preferably in US$20 bills and smaller. There is no need to buy, carry or use the old currency as ATMs have dollars. Only Banco Cuscatlán exchanges non-US currency. The border crossings have moneychangers.

Credit Cards

Credit cards are accepted in modern malls, high-end hotels and upmarket stores. Smaller establishments add a 6% to 12% surcharge. Visa cards encounter the least resistance. MasterCard is becoming more widely accepted while American Express is less common.

Exchange Rates

The table shows currency exchange rates at the time this book went to press.

Country	Unit	US Dollars (US$)
Australia	A$1	0.85
Canada	C$1	0.95
Euro Zone	€1	1.40
Japan	¥100	0.80
New Zealand	NZ$1	0.80
UK	UK£1	2.05

Traveler's Checks

Most Banco Cuscatlán, Scotiabank and Banco Atlántida branches change traveler's checks (passport and purchase receipt required). American Express checks are best. There are also Western Union offices in most towns.

POST

There are two rates for sending international mail: airmail and express mail. Letters sent by airmail to the USA should arrive in 10 days (US$0.50), to Europe and Asia up to 15 days (US$0.65). Letters sent express to the USA should take five days (US$1), to Europe and Australia 10 days (US$1.20). FedEx and DHL have offices in large cities.

RESPONSIBLE TRAVEL

Many travelers come to El Salvador with a notion of which 'side' they supported in the civil war (usually the FMLN). In fact, both sides committed terrible atrocities and in 12 years of war, neither came to fully represent (or betray) the ideals of the majority of Salvadorans. Visitors should not be hesitant to discuss the war, but should honor the personal experiences of everyday Salvadorans.

The country is fairly new to tourism and Salvadorans remain relatively unjaded toward backpackers. Hard bargaining, whether in taxis or in markets, is rare. Though prices are somewhat higher here than elsewhere, try not to be the ugly tourist haggling endlessly over what amounts to a few cents or dollars. It may be too late to reverse the unpleasant wheeling and dealing of Guatemala and elsewhere, but in El Salvador, an honest price and a friendly transaction are still the norm.

STUDYING
Options are few but some English institutes offer Spanish classes. The best is the **Centro de Intercambio y Solidaridad** (CIS; Map p278; ☎ 2226 2623; www.cis-elsalvador.org), which offers Spanish classes with progressive sensibilities. Homestays are available.

TELEPHONE
The country code when calling El Salvador from abroad is ☎ 503. Phone numbers usually have eight digits; there are no internal area codes. Telecom and Telefónica payphones accept their respective phonecards. Buy prepaid phonecards (in US$3, US$5 and US$10 denominations) at pharmacies and corner stores. Phone booths post local and international dialing instructions in English and Spanish. Some internet cafés offer web-based calling.

TOURIST INFORMATION
El Salvador has few tourist information offices and even fewer that provide more than fluff. Offices with friendly and informed staff include those in Perquín and Suchitoto. Juayúa and Apaneca have information kiosks open on weekends. Friendly hotel owners can be very helpful resources. In the capital you'll find the office of **Corporación Salvadoreña de Turismo** (Corsatur; ☎ 2243 7835; corsatur@salnet.net; Blvd Santa Elena, San Salvador; ☺ 8am-12:30pm, & 1:30-5:30pm), offering brochures and fliers. The **Instituto Salvadoreño de Turismo** (ISTU; Map p281; ☎ 222 8000; istu@mh.gob.sv; 719 Calle Rubén Darío btwn 9a & 11a Avs Sur, San Salvador; ☺ 8:30am-12:30pm & 1:30-4pm Mon-Sat) has very general information about El Salvador's national parks and *turicentros*.

VISAS & DOCUMENTS
Citizens of the USA, Canada, Australia, New Zealand, South Africa, Switzerland, Norway, Japan, Taiwan, Brazil, Argentina, Mexico, other Central American countries, Israel, and EU member countries do not need a visa, but must purchase a single-entry tourist card for US$10 when entering the country. For those who do need a prearranged visa, the cost is US$30. The standard length of stay is 30 days, but you can request up to 90 days – do so quickly before the official stamps your passport! If you leave and return within the allotted time, you can use the same tourist card.

The new Central America-4 agreement allows for travel between the borders of Guatemala, Honduras, El Salvador and Nicaragua with one entry fee and one passport stamp (in this case, be sure you ask for the 90-day option). If you are traveling overland, please note the change; it's possible you will have to 'remind' some border guards about the agreement.

No vaccinations are required unless you are coming from an area infected by yellow fever (some are recommended, however; see p744).

VOLUNTEERING
In San Salvador's Blvd de los Héroes area, **Centro de Intercambio y Solidaridad** (☎ 2235 1330; www .cis-elsalvador.org; Colonia Libertad, Av Bolivar 103) offers Spanish classes to tourists and English classes to low-income and activist Salvadorans, always with a strong emphasis on progressive politics. A friendly place to visit, the CIS has positions for volunteer English teachers (10-week minimum), and information about NGOs working on various issues, including community development, gang intervention, the environment and more. CIS cannot arrange an actual volunteer position, but can point you in the right direction. During national elections, you can volunteer with CIS's well-respected international election observer mission. CIS can also arrange 'solidarity partnerships' for groups interested in meeting with people and organizations related to a particular issue (eg labor, the civil war).

WOMEN TRAVELERS
Foreign women spark interest, there is no doubt. Men will hiss or catcall but for many it's harmless hormonal babble, as much about male bonding as the female passerby. Nearly all the men you actually meet are extremely courteous and polite. Solo women are unlikely to encounter dangerous situations if they take ordinary precautions. A good way to reduce unwanted attention is to ignore it, not make eye contact and wear clothing appropriate to the area (save shorts for the beach, the lycra leopard-skin hotpants for the club). On long bus rides, sitting next to a woman or kids avoids painful, 'Do you have a boyfriend?' conversations. At least, enjoy Latin culture's chivalric aspects while you're here.

EL SALVADOR

Honduras

HIGHLIGHTS

- **Bay Islands** Plunge into a magnificent underwater world, with marine life from seahorses to whale sharks (p406)
- **Copán Ruinas** Marvel at remarkable stone carvings and a fine museum, which bring to life an extraordinary Maya civilization (p367)
- **Gracias** Former capital of Central America, now a sleepy colonial town below stunning cloud forests (p378)
- **Lago de Yojoa** Binoculars at the ready: birdlife flourishes in this accessible beauty spot near the Pulhapanzak waterfalls (p359).
- **Best journey** Steel yourself for a bone-rattling ride along La Ruta Lenca, a series of little-visited highland communities with a proud indigenous heart (p357)
- **Off the beaten track** Discover one of Central America's last untamed wildernesses, the Reserva de la Biósfera del Río Plátano (p430)

FAST FACTS

- **Area** 112,090 sq km (about the size of England)
- **ATMs** Most accept debits cards using Plus systems; Unibanc machines accept all cards
- **Budget** US$25 per day, more on the Bay Islands
- **Capital** Tegucigalpa
- **Costs** Budget hotel room US$6-10, meal US$2-7, open-water diving course on Utila or Roatán US$250
- **Country Code** ☎ 504
- **Electricity** 110V AC, 60 Hz (same as the USA)
- **Famous for** Diving, Copán Ruinas
- **Head of State** President José Manuel Zelaya
- **Languages** Spanish on the mainland; Spanish and English on Bay Islands
- **Money** US$1 = L18.80 (lempiras); US dollars accepted on Bay Islands
- **Phrases:** *Baleadas* (large flour tortillas)
- **Population** 7.3 million
- **Time** GMT plus 8 hours
- **Traveler's Checks** Accepted in larger towns; you must show passport and receipt
- **Visas** Residents of the USA, the EU, Australia, Canada, Japan and New Zealand receive a 90-day tourist card on entry

TRAVEL HINTS

Antimalarial medication is highly recommended if traveling on the north coast or Bay Islands. Chloroquine – sold as 'Aralen' in most pharmacies – is the drug of choice. See p747 for dosage.

OVERLAND ROUTES

Border crossings include Corintos and El Florido (Guatemala), El Amatillo and El Poy (El Salvador), and Guasaule (Nicaragua). There are twice-weekly ferries to Belize, and occasional hitchhiker possibilities to Nicaragua and Jamaica.

Ever since Columbus cast his eyes starboard and spotted the lush tropical shores near Trujillo, travelers have been awed by Honduras' natural charms. Visitors now fall under the country's spell in a dizzying number of ways. Many travel the well-worn path from Copán Ruinas to the Bay Islands – and no wonder. The Maya crafted stone sculptures, built awe-inspiring temples, created myths, understood space and time – and few places tell their story better than Copán Ruinas. A bus-hop and a ferry-skip away lies another glorious kingdom, the brilliant underwater world of the Bay Islands. White-sand beaches, a laid-back Caribbean vibe and pulsing nightlife are other fine reasons to go.

Away from these tried-and-tested destinations, there is a different Honduras. The roads get bumpier but the rewards are rich – and the warm *catracho* (Honduran) welcome becomes more extravagant the further away you wander. This is a country where you can glide down jungle rivers and surprise tapirs drinking on the banks, trek in cloud forests and glimpse quetzals in the canopy, and wander the forgotten colonial capitals of Gracias and Comayagua. And – here's the real winner – travelers often skip through Honduras, so chances are you'll have a lot to yourself.

CURRENT EVENTS

Honduras is a beautiful country with many natural riches; it also struggles with some of the biggest social inequalities in the western hemisphere (the country recently slipped to 117th in the world development rankings).

The man currently charged with moving the country forward is José Manuel Zelaya, the cowboy-hat-wearing Olancho native who came into the Honduran presidency in January 2006. His honeymoon period quickly ground to a halt with accusations of cronyism and incompetence. Zelaya, a member of the Liberal Party, also stands accused of taking too many trips abroad and not concentrating enough on problems at home.

Those problems include endemic corruption and a high level of violent crime that has marred Honduras for decades. Prisons are more crowded in Honduras than in any other Central American country, and gangs remain a major problem that no policy seems to cure.

Meanwhile, foreign investors have also had a few jitters lately. The current administration opened the country's petroleum industry to a bidding process, angering US diplomats, while police raids on private telecommunications companies in La Ceiba at the beginning of 2007 did very little to inspire overseas confidence.

HISTORY
Pre-Columbian History

More than 3000 years ago, pre-Columbian settlers made their homes and farms in the fertile Copán, Sula and Comayagua valleys – although humans are thought to have roamed these lands from about 10,000 BC. Recovered pottery fragments suggest separate settlements and groups traded with each other.

At around the same time as the European Dark Ages, Copán Ruinas, the southeasterly outpost of the great Maya city-states, was basking in a golden era. Sculptors carved stone stelae unequalled in the Maya world and military men plotted successful campaigns, while mathematicians and astronomers calculated uncannily accurate calendars and planetary movements. For hundreds of years, a good slice of the Maya Classic Period (AD 250–900), the city dominated the region culturally, until its decline in the 9th century AD.

While the Maya came from the north, migrants from rain forest regions of South America, especially present-day Colombia, are also thought to have settled in the area. They are probably ancestors of indigenous peoples such as the Pech, Tawahka and Lenca who are still present in Honduras today.

Spanish Colonization

Columbus, on his fourth and final voyage, landed on the tropical shores near present-day Trujillo, Honduras. The day was August 14, 1502, and he named the place Honduras ('depths' in Spanish) for the deep waters off the north coast.

The town of Trujillo, founded in 1525 near where Columbus landed, was the first capital of the Spanish colony of Honduras, but the gleam of silver from the interior soon caught the conquistadors' eye. In 1537 Comayagua, in the center of Honduras, replaced Trujillo as the capital. It remained the political and religious center of Honduras until the capital was transferred to Tegucigalpa in 1880, where it remains today.

HONDURAS

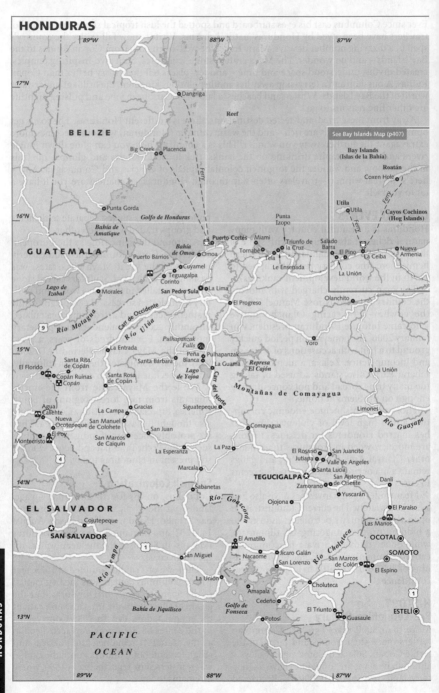

89°W   88°W   87°W

17°N

BELIZE

Dangriga

Reef

Big Creek • Placencia

Punta Gorda

16°N   *Golfo de Honduras*

GUATEMALA

Bahía de Amatique

Puerto Barrios

Cuyamel
Teguagalpa
Corinto

Lago de Izabal

Morales

San Pedro Sula • La Lima

El Progreso

Puerto Cortés
Bahía de Omoa Omoa
Miami
Tornabé
Tela
Le Ensenada
Triunfo de la Cruz
Punta Izopo

See Bay Islands Map (p407)

Bay Islands
(Islas de la Bahía)
Roatán
Coxen Hole

Utila
Utila

Cayos Cochinos
(Hog Islands)

Salado Barra
El Pino
La Ceiba
Nueva Armenia

La Unión

Olanchito

15°N

9

Río Motagua

Carr de Occidente

Río Ulúa

La Entrada

El Florido

Santa Rita de Copán
Copán Ruinas
Copán

Santa Bárbara
Pulhapanzak Falls
Peña Blanca • Pulhapanzak
La Guama

Lago de Yojoa

Represa El Cajón

Yoro

La Unión

Santa Rosa de Copán

Agua Caliente
Nueva Ocotepeque
El Poy
Montecristo

4

La Campa • Gracias

San Manuel de Colohete
San Marcos de Caiquín

San Juan

La Esperanza

Carr del Norte

Siguatepeque

Montañas de Comayagua

Comayagua

Limones

Río Guayape

14°N

EL SALVADOR

Cojutepeque

SAN SALVADOR

1

Marcala

La Paz

San Miguel

La Unión

La Esperanza

Sabanetas

Río Goascorán

El Amatillo
Nacaome

Jícaro Galán
San Lorenzo

Amapala
Cedeño

Golfo de Fonseca

Bahía de Jiquilisco

Potosí

Ojojona

El Rosario • San Juancito
Jutiapa • Valle de Angeles
Santa Lucía
San Antonio
TEGUCIGALPA de Oriente
Zamorano
Yuscarán

Danlí

El Paraíso

Las Manos

OCOTAL

SOMOTO

Río Choluteca

San Marcos de Colón
El Espino

Choluteca

El Triunto
Guasaule

ESTELÍ

1

13°N

PACIFIC OCEAN

89°W   88°W   87°W

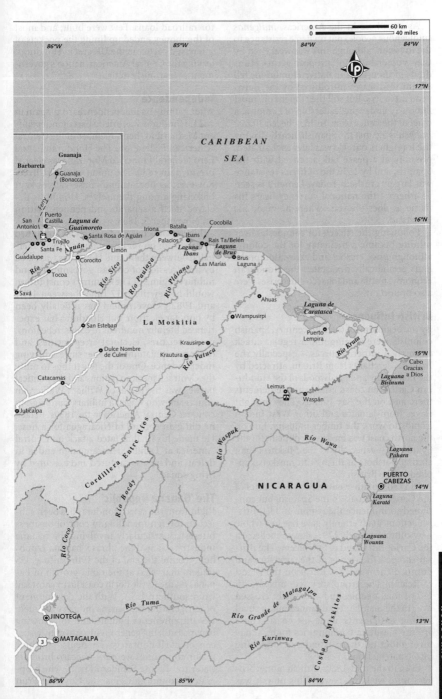

As elsewhere in the Americas, *indígenas* (indigenous people) put up fierce resistance to the invasion, although this was weakened by their vulnerability to European germs. Hundreds of thousands of native Hondurans fell victim to diseases introduced by the European intruders. But still they fought on, most famously under the leadership of Lempira, a chief of the Lenca tribe. In 1537 he led 30,000 *indígenas* against the Spanish, nearly driving the foreigners out. He was later assassinated, possibly at a peace talk arranged with the Spanish, and by 1539 the *indígena* resistance was largely crushed. Today, Lempira is seen as a hero – the national currency bears his name as does the state where he made his last stand.

Following the successful conquest, silver mining became a mainstay for the colony, although price crashes and excavation problems periodically devastated the Honduran economy. Cattle and tobacco enterprises were also important.

British Influence

By the beginning of the 17th century, Spanish colonists were coming under regular attack from rival imperial forces – especially the British. Merchants from Britain, attracted by the mahogany and hardwoods of the Honduran Caribbean coast, established settlements there and on the Bay Islands. They brought slaves from Jamaica and other West Indian islands to work the timber industry. Life on the north coast was made very difficult for the Spaniards – especially as the Miskito began aiming potshots at them with muskets supplied by the British.

In 1786 Britain eventually ceded control of the Caribbean coast to the Spanish, but continued to influence the region. In fact, British actions inadvertently gave rise to a whole new culture. In early 1797, slaves rebelled on the Caribbean island of St Vincent. The British shipped thousands of the survivors and dumped them at Port Royal on the island of Roatán. The group survived, mixed with indigenous people, and eventually crossed over to the mainland and fanned out in small fishing settlements along the coast. These are the Garífuna communities found today throughout northern Honduras, stretching into Guatemala and Belize.

Even in the mid-1860s, British moneybrokers were wielding power. This time it was for railroad loans. Few were built, and most of the money ended up lining the pockets of interested parties in the UK and in Honduras, leaving the Central American nation's government precariously in debt.

Independence

After gaining its independence from Spain in 1821, Honduras was briefly part of independent Mexico and then a member of the Central American Federation. The Honduran liberal hero General Francisco Morazán was elected president in 1830. The union was short-lived, however, as liberals and conservatives kept bickering among themselves. Honduras declared itself a separate independent nation on November 5, 1838.

Liberal and conservative factions continued to wrestle for power in Honduras. Power alternated between them, and Honduras was ruled by a succession of civilian governments and military regimes. (The country's constitution would be rewritten 17 times between 1821 and 1982.) Government has officially been by popular election, but Honduras has experienced literally hundreds of coups, rebellions, power seizures, electoral 'irregularities' and other manipulations of power since achieving independence. One of the few things to unify the Central American nations and the political parties was the threat of William Walker, an American, who waged a military campaign to conquer Central America in the 1850s. In fact, he did gain control of Nicaragua for a time. He made his final ill-fated attack on Central America at Trujillo. His campaign ended in defeat, and he was captured and executed by firing squad.

The 'Banana Republic'

Right from the start, Honduras has been subject to foreign meddling to control business interests, particularly involving the banana industry – hence the phrase 'banana republic.' Around the end of the 19th century, US traders marveled at the rapid growth of bananas on the fertile north coast just a short sail from southern USA. With the development of refrigeration the banana industry boomed. US entrepreneurs bought land for growing bananas utilzing generous incentives by a succession of Honduran governments. The three major companies were the Vaccaro brothers (later to become Standard Fruit), which operated around La Ceiba; the Cuyamel Fruit

Company near the Río Cuyamel and Tela; and after 1912, United Fruit, to the east, which by 1929 had swallowed up Cuyamel. The three companies owned a large part of northern Honduras, and by 1918, 75% of all Honduran banana lands were held by US companies.

Bananas provided 11% of Honduras' exports in 1892, 42% in 1903 and 66% in 1913. The success of the industry made the banana companies extremely powerful within Honduras, with policy and politicians controlled by their interests. Cuyamel Fruit Company allied itself with the Liberal Party, United Fruit with the National Party, and the rivalries between banana companies shaped Honduran politics.

20th-Century Politics

The USA increasingly came to influence Honduran affairs. In 1911 and 1912, when it appeared that banana interests were threatened by Honduran political developments, US president William Howard Taft sent the US Marines into Honduras to 'protect US investments.'

During the worldwide economic depression of the 1930s, in the midst of civil unrest, General Tiburcio Carías Andino was elected president, establishing a virtual dictatorship that lasted from 1932 until 1949, when US pressure forced him to cede power.

A two-month strike in 1954 – which became known as 'the Banana Strike' in which as many as 25,000 banana workers and sympathizers participated – remains a seminal moment in Honduran labor history. Unions were recognized, and workers gained rights that were unheard of in neighboring Central American countries.

A military coup in 1956 marked an important shift in Honduran politics. Although civilian rule returned in 1957, a new constitution put the military officially out of the control of civilian government. The military now had a much more important role in the country's politics, the legacy of which continues to this day.

In 1963 Colonel Osvaldo López Arellano led another military coup and ruled as president until 1975, apart from a brief return to democracy in 1971–2. He was forced to resign because of a scandal involving a US$1.25 million bribe from a US company, United Brands. He was replaced in a military coup by Colonel Juan Alberto Melgar Castro, who slowed

agrarian reform. He in turn was ousted by yet another military coup in 1978. This was led by General Policarpo Paz García, who eventually instigated democratic presidential elections in 1981. Military rule was finally over.

The 1980s

During the 1980s Honduras was surrounded by revolutions and conflict. In July 1979 the revolutionary Sandinista movement in Nicaragua overthrew the Somoza dictatorship, and Somoza's national guardsmen fled into Honduras. Civil war broke out in El Salvador in 1980 and internal conflict worsened in Guatemala.

Although Honduras experienced some unrest, its politics were far more conservative. An overpowering US influence directed the course of Honduran politics and created a strong Honduran military. Honduran government land and labor reforms between 1962 and 1980 also helped blunt populist uprisings.

With revolutions erupting on every side, and especially with the success of the Nicaraguan revolution in 1979, Honduras became the focus of US policy and strategic operations in the region. After the USA pressured the government to hold elections, a civilian, Dr Roberto Suazo Córdova, was elected president. Real power arguably rested with the commander-in-chief of the armed forces, General Gustavo Álvarez, who supported an increasing US military presence in Central America. US military involvement in Central America had increased dramatically following Ronald Reagan's election as US president. The USA funneled huge sums of money and thousands of US troops into Honduras as it conducted provocative maneuvers clearly designed to threaten Nicaragua. Refugee camps of Nicaraguans in Honduras were used as bases for a US-sponsored covert war against the Nicaraguan Sandinista government, known as the Contra war. At the same time the USA was training the Salvadoran military at Salvadoran refugee camps inside Honduras.

General Gustavo Álvarez was also responsible for the formation of the notorious Battalion 3-16, which targeted and 'disappeared' hundreds of political enemies. Although the repression was small-scale when compared with El Salvador and Guatemala, public alarm grew. Local opposition to the US militarization of Honduras also increased, creating problems for the Honduran government. In March 1984 General Álvarez was exiled by fellow officers, and General Walter López Reyes was appointed his successor. The Honduran government promptly announced it would reexamine US military presence in the country and in August suspended US training of the Salvadoran military within its borders.

The 1985 presidential election, beset by serious irregularities, was won by the Liberal Party candidate José Simeón Azcona del Hoyo, who had obtained only 27% of the votes. Rafael Leonardo Callejas Romero of the National Party, who had obtained 42% of the votes, lost.

In Washington, the Reagan administration was rocked by revelations it had illegally used money from arms sales to Iran to support anti-Sandinista Contras in Honduras. Large demonstrations followed in Tegucigalpa, and in November 1988 the Honduran government refused to sign a new military agreement with the USA. President Azcona Hoyo said the Contras would have to leave. With the election of Violeta Chamorro as president of Nicaragua in 1990, the Contra war ended and the Contras were finally out of Honduras.

Modern Currents

Elections in 1989 ushered in Rafael Leonardo Callejas Romero of the National Party (the loser of the 1985 election) as president; he won 51% of the votes and assumed office in January 1990. Early that year the new administration instituted a severe economic austerity program, which provoked widespread alarm and protest.

Callejas had promised to keep the lempira stable. Instead, during his four years in office, the lempira's value went from about two lempiras to the US dollar to eight. Prices in lempiras rose dramatically but salaries lagged behind. The average Honduran grew poorer and poorer, a trend that continues today.

In the elections of November 1993, Callejas was convincingly beaten by Carlos Roberto Reina Idiaquez of the center-right Liberal Party. Reina campaigned on a platform of moral reform, promising to attack government corruption and reform state institutions, including the judicial system and the military.

When Reina became president in January 1994, he assumed control of an economically suffering country and the lempira continued to devalue. By 1996 it had slid past 12 lempiras

to the US dollar and was heading for 13 (a dollar was worth around 19 lempiras at the time of research.)

On January 27, 1998, the Liberal Party's Carlos Roberto Flores Facusse took office as Honduras' fifth successive democratically elected president. He instigated a program of reform and modernization of the economy. These seemed to be moving in the right direction, but were tragically compromised by the devastating Hurricane Mitch in November 1998. The storms caused damage estimated at US$3 billion. According to some analysts, it set the country's economic development back by decades.

Much of the infrastructure was rapidly rebuilt after massive loans flooded into the country, but the tourism crash following September 11, 2001 did little to help.

In 2001, Ricardo Maduro from the National Party was elected president, largely on the back of his promises to reduce crime. Maduro was no doubt committed to the cause – his son was kidnapped and murdered in 1997. Despite pouring huge resources into the problem, crime continued largely unabated. In January 2006 José Manuel Zelaya became president (see p329).

THE CULTURE
The National Psyche

Generalizations don't – and shouldn't – come easily for a country with such wide-ranging cultures. The Ladino businessman will have a different outlook to the Garífuna fisherman, who may not have much in common with a Lencan subsistence farmer. However, Hondurans are less likely to reach a collective flashpoint than their neighbors, at least historically. While Guatemala, El Salvador and Nicaragua all fought fierce civil wars in the 1980s, Honduras remained relatively conflict-free; US intervention certainly played a role, but so, perhaps, did the go-with-the-flow nature of the people. Most visitors find Hondurans intensely proud of their country and will be taken aback by their friendliness and hospitality – although some feel that masks a reserve that makes many Hondurans difficult to get to know.

Lifestyle

Lifestyles in Honduras vary as widely as the country's shockingly unequal social spectrum. The fortunate economic elite often lead an Americanized lifestyle, driving SUVs and shopping at the latest air-conditioned malls. Far more commonly, Hondurans are forced to scratch a living. Poverty is perhaps at its most shocking in urban areas, where poor conditions are accompanied by the constant threat of violence.

In rural and coastal areas, the pressures are different but still intense. Many are being forced to give up their traditional lifestyles, and move to the city or look for seasonal work – on coffee plantations for example. Lack of opportunities at home have also forced many Hondurans to seek jobs in the USA. An estimated one million Hondurans are living and working in that country, at least half of them illegally.

Hondurans are hugely family-oriented, as is common in Central America. They often have a wider family network than many Europeans or North Americans are used to – aunts, uncles, grandparents, cousins and even more distant relatives often play a significant role in family life.

Another attitude in Honduran society is machismo. Women are often still treated as second-class citizens. Wages are much lower (women can expect to earn a third of the average male wage, according to a UN Development Program report) and reported levels of domestic abuse are disturbing. Stories of men who do a runner when their partner becomes pregnant are commonplace. There is some evidence of change. A powerful government campaign against domestic violence was running at the time of research, and organized women's groups and cooperatives are on the increase – but there is a way to go.

The same macho tendencies mean that gay culture is very much in the closet.

People

Honduras is experiencing the most rapid urbanization in Central America: the urban population was 44% in 1990, but the percentage of the population in cities is expected to hit 59% in 2010. Up to 90% of Hondurans are mestizo, a mixture of Spanish and *indígena*.

The Tolupanes (also called Jicaque or Xicaque) live in small villages dotting the departments of Yoro and Francisco Morazán. They are thought to be one of the oldest indigenous communities in Honduras.

The Maya-Chortí people live near the Guatemalan border, in the department of Copán, while the Lenca live in southwestern Honduras. They are notable for their colorful traditional clothing and headscarves.

Arguably the most ethnically diverse region of Honduras is La Moskitia. It is home to the Miskito people and the Pech (who are generally less outgoing than the Miskitos). The Pech also live along the highway from San Esteban to Tocao. In the interior of La Moskitia, the Tawahka inhabit the area around the Río Patuca – now designated as the Tawahka Asangni Biosphere Reserve. Numbering less than a thousand, they still have their own language. The Garífuna live on Honduras' north

THE FOOTBALL WAR

Legendary football manager Bill Shankly once said: 'Some people believe football is a matter of life and death...it is much more important than that.' Even Mr Shankly might have balked at Honduras' and El Salvador's sporting rivalry, which spilled off the pitch and onto the battlefield in the 1969 Guerra de Fútbol – the notorious Football (Soccer) War.

Tensions did not suddenly break out on the stadium terraces. In the 1950s and 1960s, a flagging economy forced 300,000 Salvadorans to seek better conditions in Honduras. However, the Honduran economy was itself ailing, and Salvadorans began to be targeted as scapegoats. In June 1969, Honduran authorities started throwing Salvadoran immigrants out of the country. A stream of Salvadoran refugees followed, alleging Honduran brutality.

In the same month, the two countries were playing World Cup qualifying matches against each other. At the San Salvador game, Salvadorans attacked Honduran fans, defiling the Honduran flag and mocking the anthem. Over the border, angry Hondurans then turned on Salvadoran immigrants. Tempers frayed further and the El Salvador army invaded Honduran territory on July 14, capturing Nueva Ocotopeque. Honduras retaliated with air strikes. A ceasefire was called after only six days, but around 2000 Hondurans lost their lives, while thousands of Salvadorans fled home.

For the record, El Salvador reached the Mexico World Cup finals, where it lost all three of its matches.

coast, from La Moskitia all the way across to Belize. Other people with African ancestry – descended from Caribbean immigrants who came to work on the banana plantations – live on the north coast and Bay Islands.

ARTS

Although not as well known for its art as Guatemala, Honduras does have some notable *artesanía*. Lenca pottery, with its black-and-white designs and glossy finish, can be of high quality and there are some skilful replica Maya carvings and glyphs in Copán Ruinas.

Honduras has a thriving visual arts scene. The 'primitivist' movement – often depicting scenes of mountain villages – is famous. José Antonio Velásquez (1906–83) is its most renowned exponent.

Musically, Honduran airwaves are usually filled with imported rhythms, but the country does have home-grown talent, including Guillermo Anderson, who combines folk with salsa, *punta* and rock. Karla Lara is another singer-songwriter whose folksy strumming is winning fans.

On the literary scene, Lucila Gamero de Medina (1873–1964), was one of the first Central American female writers. Rafael Heliodoro del Valle (1891–1959) was a respected journalist whose ideas had a lot of clout regionally. Ramón Amaya-Amador (1916–66), was a political writer who published *Prisión Verde* (1945) about life on a banana plantation. Juan Ramón Molina (1875–1908) is perhaps the country's best-loved poet while Roberto Quesada is one of Honduras' top living authors.

Dance is another popular art form – the Garífuna people of the north coast are known for their distinctive *punta* music and dance. If you get a chance to see a performance by the Ballet Folklórico Garífuna, don't miss it.

RELIGION

Honduras is nominally a Roman Catholic country, but that has changed rapidly in the last couple of decades with the rise of the evangelical movement. Just how many Roman Catholics have converted to evangelical Christianity is difficult to tell – figures are unreliable. The CIA World Factbook, at the start of 2007, claimed that 97% of Hondurans are Roman Catholic, yet Roman Catholic analysis concedes that at least 17% of Hondurans are now Protestant. Anecdotal evidence and polls suggest that many more Hondurans have been swayed to evangelical religion than CIA sources realize – perhaps around a quarter of the population.

Unlike neighboring Guatemala, few indigenous customs or beliefs have been integrated into Christian worship. However, a belief in witchcraft and superstition is common in some parts of Hondurans.

ENVIRONMENT

Honduras is a country of breathtaking natural beauty, with a huge range of bird, mammal, reptile and plant species. However, illegal logging, underresourced authorities and crass development projects are putting this under threat. While the environment has plenty of defenders, they face a tough struggle against developers, corruption and plain ignorance.

The Land

Countries don't come that big in Central America but, on the isthmus, Honduras weighs in as the second-largest (after Nicaragua), with an area of 112,090 sq km. It has coast on the Caribbean Sea (644km), and on the Pacific along the Golfo de Fonseca (124km). Guatemala is to the west, on the southwest is El Salvador and the Golfo de Fonseca, and to the southeast lies Nicaragua. The fertile north is by far the most developed – its banana plantations have long been a mainstay of the economy. Honduras' many islands include the Bay Islands and Hog Islands in the Caribbean and several in the Golfo de Fonseca.

Much of the Honduran interior is mountainous with peaks from 300m to 2849m high. There are many fertile highland valleys, but, unlike in Guatemala, there are no active volcanoes. Lowlands exist along both coasts and in several river valleys.

Wildlife

There is a dazzling array of flora and fauna in Honduras. Jaguars, tapirs, crocodiles and the mighty Ceiba tree are found in tropical zones; in the cloud forests are quetzals, rare butterflies, orchids and magnificent pine trees; while whale sharks, coral and seahorses thrive in the country's turquoise Caribbean waters. It is the sheer variety of habitats that allows so many different species to thrive. Honduras has mangrove swamps, freshwater lakes, oceans, lagoons, cloud forests, pine forests and tropical rain forests (considerably more than

Costa Rica, which somehow manages to hog the ecotourism limelight).

Much of the habitat is under threat from deforestation. Endangered species include the scarlet macaw (the national bird), Utilan iguana, manatee, quetzal, jaguar, whale shark and tapir. Their future depends on just how much protection Honduras' so-called protected areas can really offer.

National Parks & Protected Areas

Honduras has many ecologically protected areas, including *parques nacionales* (national parks), *refugios de vida* (wildlife refuges), biological reserves and biosphere reserves. More than one-fifth of Honduras qualifies as an existing or proposed protected area, but the effect of that is debatable. All too often the government lacks the resources – or the political will – to stop development and deforestation.

These are some of the more important protected areas, including marine reserves:

Lancetilla Botanical Gardens It has more than 700 plant species and 365 species of bird. See p390.

Parque Nacional Cusuco A cloud forest, with a large population of quetzals. See p366.

Parque Nacional Jeannette Kawas (Punta Sal) Habitats include mangrove swamps, a small tropical forest, offshore reefs, several coves and a rocky point. The park has a large number of migratory and coastal birds. See p391.

Parque Nacional La Tigra Near Tegucigalpa, this protects a beautiful cloud forest set in former mining country. See p351.

Parque Nacional Maritimo Cayos Cochinos The Cayos Cochinos (Hog Islands) are a protected reserve and proposed national marine park. Thirteen cays, two of them large, with beautiful coral reefs, well-preserved forests and fishing villages make up the reserve. See p399.

Parque Nacional Montaña de Celaque An elevated plateau, with four peaks more than 2800m above sea level, including Honduras' highest peak. See p381.

Parque Nacional Pico Bonito The park has high biodiversity and many waterfalls. Pico Bonito is the highest peak here, at 2436m. See p400.

Refugio de Vida Laguna de Guaimoreto Has mangrove forest and a great variety of wildlife, including birds, manatees and dolphins. See p405.

Refugio de Vida Punta Izopo Made up of tropical wet forest, mangrove forest and wetlands. It has many migratory birds, a beautiful rocky point and white-sand beaches. See p391.

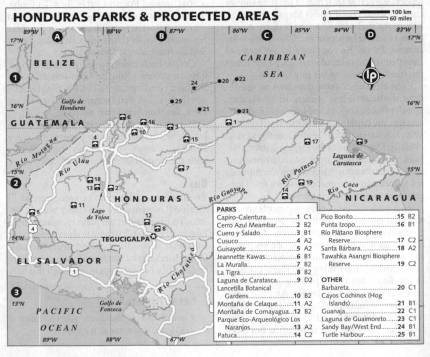

HONDURAS PARKS & PROTECTED AREAS

PARKS		
Capiro-Calentura	1	C1
Cerro Azul Meambar	2	B2
Cuero y Salado	3	B1
Cusuco	4	A2
Guisayote	5	A2
Jeannette Kawas	6	B1
La Muralla	7	B2
La Tigra	8	B2
Laguna de Caratasca	9	D2
Lancetilla Botanical Gardens	10	B2
Montaña de Celaque	11	A2
Montaña de Comayagua	12	B2
Parque Eco-Arqueológico Los Naranjos	13	A2
Patuca	14	C2

Pico Bonito	15	B2
Punta Izopo	16	B1
Río Plátano Biosphere Reserve	17	C2
Santa Bárbara	18	A2
Tawahka Asangni Biosphere Reserve	19	C2

OTHER		
Barbareta	20	C1
Cayos Cochinos (Hog Islands)	21	B1
Guanaja	22	C1
Laguna de Guaimoreto	23	C1
Sandy Bay/West End	24	B1
Turtle Harbour	25	B1

Refugio de Vida Silvestre Cuero y Salado The largest manatee reserve in Central America (although that's no guarantee of seeing one). Monkeys and birdlife also abound. See p400.

Río Plátano Biosphere Reserve A World Heritage site and the first biosphere reserve in Central America, the Río Plátano is 5251 sq km of lowland tropical rain forest with remarkable natural, archaeological and cultural resources. See p430.

Sandy Bay/West End Marine Reserve On the northwestern end of Roatán in the Bay Islands, this marine reserve has some of the most colorful coral reefs around. See p417.

Tawahka Asangni Biosphere Reserve A tropical rain forest on the ancestral lands of the Tawahka people, a very threatened indigenous groups. Access is by plane to Ahuas or Wampusirpi then by boat upstream to Krausirpe and Krautara, or by a multiday rafting trip down the Río Patuca from Juticalpa.

Turtle Harbor On the northwestern side of Utila in the Bay Islands, Turtle Harbor is another marine reserve and proposed national marine park visited frequently by divers.

Environmental Issues

Deforestation is the most pressing environmental issue facing Honduras today. Reliable reports suggest at least half of the pine timber coming from Honduras is illegal, and up to 80% of the mahogany harvest is illicit (sometimes reaching buyers in the US). Every year, around 2% of the country's forest cover is chopped to the ground – roughly four times the combined area of the Bay Islands.

Even Honduras' most treasured nature reserve, the Reserva de la Biósfera del Río Plátano, is under threat. Loggers and livestock landowners clear the land there with little resistance; in 1996, Unesco escalated the area into the 'at risk' category. Opposition to the logging is strong but faces huge challenges, from an underresourced national-parks agency to endemic corruption, not to mention the threat of violence from loggers keen to protect their interests.

Ill-considered tourist developments are another danger. A huge luxury complex near Tela is likely to put that area under strain. And a debate is raging about the wisdom of a proposed airport near the Copán archaeological site.

Meanwhile, overfishing (and illegal catches) in the Bay Islands are putting its magnificent reef ecosystem in danger. And the 1999 discovery of billions of tons of untapped oil reserves is likely to add to the concerns of those defending Honduras' beautiful but fragile natural resources.

TRANSPORTATION

GETTING THERE & AWAY
Air

Frequent direct flights connect Honduras with other Central American capitals and many destinations in North America, the Caribbean, South America and Europe. Most international flights arrive and depart from the airports at San Pedro Sula and Tegucigalpa. By far the busiest and largest airport is at San Pedro Sula. There are also direct flights between the USA and Roatán, coming from Houston, Miami, and most recently from Newark in New Jersey state during high season.

Boat

The only regularly scheduled passenger boat service between Honduras and another country is the small boat that runs twice weekly from Puerto Cortés to Dangriga, Belize. Otherwise, it might be possible to arrange passage with cargo or fishing vessels if you pay your way. On the Caribbean coast, you can try to find a boat around Puerto Cortés, Tela, La Ceiba, Trujillo, Palacios or the Bay Islands. The most common international destinations for these boats are Puerto Barrios (Guatemala), Belize and Puerto Cabezas (Nicaragua).

On the Pacific side, you might be able to get a ride on boats sailing between countries. But the land crossings are so close it might not be worth the effort. San Lorenzo and Coyolito are the main Honduran port towns in the gulf.

If you arrive or depart from Honduras by sea, be sure to clear your paperwork (entry and exit stamps, if necessary) immediately with the nearest immigration office.

Bus

To Guatemala, the main crossings are at El Florido (Guatemala), Agua Caliente and Corinto. To El Salvador, the main crossings are El Poy and El Amatillo; there is also a crossing at Sabanetas, across the highlands from Marcala. Only Honduras has an immigration post here because of a border dispute, although this may

---

DEPARTURE TAX

If you fly out of Honduras, you must pay US$35 departure tax at the airport.

change. The crossings to Nicaragua are at Las Manos (Honduras), El Espino and Guasaule (Nicaragua).

Frequent buses serve all of these border crossings. Most buses do not cross the border. You cross on foot and pick up another bus on the other side. The exceptions are international buses; the following provide services to San Salvador, Guatemala City, Antigua (Guatemala), Managua (Nicaragua), San José (Costa Rica) and Panama City:

El Rey Express (www.reyexpress.net)
Hedman Alas (www.hedmanalas.com)
King Quality (www.kingqualityca.com)
Tica Bus (www.ticabus.com)

GETTING AROUND
Air
Domestic air routes have proliferated in Honduras recently; it's now easy to fly to any of the Bay Islands from La Ceiba, Tegucigalpa and San Pedro Sula, and to fly between these three major cities. (Flights to the Bay Islands from Tegucigalpa and San Pedro Sula connect through La Ceiba.) Air routes into the Moskitia are also making that remote area more accessible.

Airlines include the following:

Aerolineas Sosa (☎ in San Pedro Sula 550 6545, in Tegucigalpa 233 5107, in La Ceiba 443 1894, in Roatán 445 1658; www.laceibaonline.net/aerososa/sosaingl.htm) Based in La Ceiba.

Atlantic Airlines (☎ in San Pedro Sula 557 8088, in Tegucigalpa 237 8597, in La Ceiba 440 2343, in Roatán 445 1179; www.atlanticairlines.com.ni) Based in Tegucigalpa.

SAMI (☎ Brus Laguna 433 8031, in La Ceiba 442 2565, in Puerto Lempira 433 6016)

TACA/Isleña (☎ in San Pedro Sula 516 1061, in Tegucigalpa 236 8222, in La Ceiba 441 3191, in Roatán 445 1088; www.taca.com)

Boat
Two passenger ferries, the luxury catamaran *Galaxy Wave* and the *Utila Princess II,* operate between La Ceiba and the Bay Islands. The *Galaxy Wave* goes to Roatán (1¾ hours), while the smaller, less fancy *Utila Princess II* goes to Utila. There is no service between the two islands – you have to go via La Ceiba. One (unreliable) scheduled service, the *Island Tour,* goes to and from Guanaja, leaving from Trujillo.

Cargo and fishing boats operate frequently between the coast and the Bay Islands. Boats leave Trujillo and La Ceiba for the Moskitia

every couple of days or so; you can also find cargo and fishing boats at the docks in Puerto Cortés, La Ceiba and Tela, as well as on all the Bay Islands.

In the Moskitia, almost all transportation is along the waterways. There are also watertaxis on Roatán from West End to West Bay, and from Coyolito on the Golfo de Fonseca over to the Isla del Tigre.

Bus
Buses are a cheap and easy way to get around in Honduras. The first buses of the day often start very early in the morning; the last bus usually departs in the late afternoon. Buses between Tegucigalpa and San Pedro Sula run until later.

On major bus routes, you'll often have a choice between taking a *directo* (direct) or *ordinario* (ordinary), which is also known as *parando* or *servicio a escala*. The *directo* is much faster and almost always worth the extra money, even on short trips.

Deluxe buses offer faster service between Tegucigalpa, San Pedro Sula, Copán Ruinas, Tela and also La Ceiba, using modern air-conditioned buses (sometimes including movies and soft drinks). *Ejecutivo* (executive) or *servicio de lujo* (luxury service) buses are much more expensive than *directo* buses, often double the prices. They can be a worthwhile splurge for long trips.

Microbuses or *rapiditos* are smaller minivanlike buses that cover some routes, and tend to go faster and leave more frequently than regular buses.

Chicken buses operate between major towns and their satellite villages.

Car & Motorcycle
The main highways are paved roads, mostly in reasonable condition. Away from the highways, roads tend to be unpaved. Conditions can vary wildly according to rainfall and the time of year, ranging from acceptable to unpassable.

Rental cars are available in Tegucigalpa, San Pedro Sula, La Ceiba and on Roatán. Prices start at around US$35 a day for an economy car and US$50 for a midsize one.

Taxi
Taxis are everywhere in Honduran towns. They don't have meters but most towns have a fixed about-town fare, starting at US$0.60 in

smaller places and going up to US$1. Taxis in San Pedro Sula and Tegucigalpa are more expensive. Expect to pay US$1.50 and US$2.20 respectively for a ride about town. Taxi fares increase at night. Expect longer journeys in a major city to cost around US$4. In the major cities, colectivos (shared taxis) ply a number of prescribed routes, costing around US$0.60 per passenger. Always confirm the fare before you leave. If it seems a rip-off, negotiate or wait for another.

Three-wheeled mototaxis have flooded into Honduras in the past few years. They are usually cheaper than taxis.

TEGUCIGALPA

pop 894,000

In many ways Tegucigalpa is a typical, sprawling Central American metropolis. The streets are often snarled with fume-belching traffic, while the crowds are thick and the pace is frenetic. However, the setting is spectacular – the city is nestled in a valley surrounded by a ring of mountains, and has a certain chaotic charm.

You may even feel a bit of affection for it when you glimpse a 16th-century church or the view across the precipitous city landscape, or perhaps after a fine meal at a restaurant. Expect this feeling to last until around the time you get stuck in the next traffic jam (not long).

At an altitude of 975m, Tegucigalpa has a fresher and milder climate than the country's coasts – although long-term residents report a steady temperature rise, as in many other areas of the world. The city is also struggling to cope with huge migration to its bright lights – you will see shantytowns clinging to the mountainsides in the upper reaches of the urban sprawl.

The name Tegucigalpa (Teh-goos-ee-*gal*-pa) is a bit of a mouthful; Hondurans often call the city Tegus (*teh*-goos) for short. The name, meaning 'silver hill' in the original local Nahuatl dialect, was given when the Spanish founded the city as a silver and gold mining center in 1578, on the slopes of Picacho. Tegucigalpa became the capital of Honduras in 1880, when the government seat was moved from Comayagua, 82km to the northwest. In 1938 Comayagüela, on the opposite side of the river from Tegucigalpa, became part of the city.

ORIENTATION

The city is divided by the Río Choluteca. On the east side of the river is Tegucigalpa, including downtown and more affluent districts such as Colonia Palmira. Plaza Morazán, often still called Parque Central, with the city's cathedral, is in the heart of the city. West of this, Av Miguel Paz Barahona is a pedestrian shopping street, extending four blocks from the plaza to Calle El Telégrafo; this section has been renamed Calle Peatonal, and it's a busy thoroughfare with many shops, restaurants and banks.

Across the river from Tegucigalpa is Comayagüela, which is poorer and dirtier, with a sprawling market, long-distance bus stations, budget hotels and *comedores* (cheap eating places). The two areas are connected by several bridges.

Maps

Instituto Geográfico Nacional (3 Av Barrio La Bolsa; ⏰ 7:30am-noon & 12:30-3:30pm Mon-Fri) sells detailed Honduran road and topographical maps.

GETTING INTO TOWN FROM THE AIRPORT

Toncontín International Airport is 6.5 traffic-snarled kilometers south of the center of Tegucigalpa. To get into town, walk out the main doors and catch a 'Loarque' bus (US$0.20, about 30 minutes) headed into town. The bus goes north on 4a Av; if you are planning to stay in **Comayagüela**, get off at the appropriate cross street and walk up. If you're staying in Tegucigalpa, stay on until the terminal at the end of the line (3a Av and 3a Calle in Comayagüela), where a cab to your hotel will cost a few dollars.

To get to the airport from Comayagüela, catch the Loarque bus (it will say 'Río Grande') at the terminal or anywhere on 2a Av north of 14a Calle (where it turns to cross the river). The airport, on your left, is hard to recognize – get off in front of a big Burger King and cross the street. A good option from the center is the colectivo (US$0.60), a van which leaves when full from their stop on Calle Morelos, five blocks west of Parque Central.

A private taxi to the airport costs about US$8.

INFORMATION
Bookstores
Metromedia Av San Carlos (☎ 221 0770; Av San Carlos;
☺ 10am-8pm Mon-Sat, noon-6pm Sun); Multiplaza Mall
(☎ 231 2410; Blvd Juan Pablo II; ☺ 8am-8pm) Sells
English-language books, magazines and more, including
day-old *New York Times*.

Emergency
Ambulance (☎ 195; ☺ 24hr) Red Cross.
Honduras Medical Center (☎ 216 1201; Av Juan
Lindo; ☺ 24hr) One of the best hospitals in the country.
Police (☎ 199, 222 8736; 5a Av; ☺ 24hr)

Immigration
Immigration office (☎ 220 6827; Av La Paz btwn
3a & 4a Avs; ☺ 7:30am-3:30pm Mon-Fri) For a fee of
US$20.50, you can arrange a month-long extension here.
Come early for same-day service.

Internet Access
Hondutel (☎ 222 1120; cnr Av Cristóbal Colón & Calle El
Telégrafo; per hr US$0.80; ☺ 7:30am-9pm Mon-Sat) Has
air-con and flatscreen Dells.
Multinet (Blvd Morazán; per hr US$1.10; ☺ 8am-
7:30pm Mon-Sat, 9:30am-7pm Sun) Reliable chain internet
café.
Mundo Virtual (☎ 238 0043; Calle Salvador Mendieta; per hr US$0.90; ☺ 7am-10pm Mon-Sat, 11am-8pm
Sun) Professional staff, lots of flat screens; downloads and
printing allowed.

Laundry
Dry Cleaning Lavandería Maya (☎ 232 3649; per 10lb
US$4; ☺ 8am-6pm Mon-Fri, 8am-4pm Sat)
Su-perc Jet (☎ 237 4154; Av Máximo Jérez/Juan
Gutemberg, Barrio Guanacaste; per 1lb US$0.30;
☺ 8am-6pm Mon-Sat) Laundry washed, dried and
folded. Drop it off in the morning, and it will be ready that
afternoon.

Money
Unibanc ATMs are dotted about the city, in-
cluding the airport, on the northeast corner
of Parque Central, in the Hedman Alas bus
terminal and in the shopping malls.
Banco Atlántida (Parque Central; ☺ 9am-4pm Mon-
Fri, 8:30-11:30am Sat) Changes traveler's checks and has
a 24-hour ATM.
BAC Credomatic (Blvd Morazán; ☺ 9:30am-5:30pm
Mon-Fri) Has an ATM.
Mundirama Travel (☎ 232 3909; cnr Avs República
de Panamá & República de Chile; ☺ 8am-5pm Mon-
Fri, 8am-noon Sat) Represents American Express; issues
traveler's checks and holds mail for cardholders.

Post
There's a DHL office near Mailboxes, Etc.
Comayagüela post office (6a Av btwn 7a & 8a Calles;
☺ 7:30am-5pm Mon-Fri, 8am-1pm Sat) In the same
building as the Hondutel office.
Downtown post office (cnr Av Miguel Paz Barahona &
Calle El Telégrafo; ☺ 7am-6pm Mon-Fri, 8am-1pm Sat)
Mailboxes, Etc (☎ 232 3184; Blvd Morazán; ☺ 8am-
6pm Mon-Fri, 9am-1pm Sat) Has Federal Express for
international deliveries and Viana for domestic.

Telephone
Most internet cafés have much cheaper rates
for international calls than Hondutel.
Hondutel (☎ 222 1120; cnr Av Cristóbal Colón & Calle
El Telégrafo; ☺ 7:30am-9pm Mon-Sat) Pricey state-run
call center.

Tourist Information
Amitigra (☎ 238 6269; Edificio Italia, 4th fl, office No 6,
Colonia Palmira; ☺ 8am-5pm Mon-Fri) Manages, and has
information on, Parque Nacional La Tigra.
Corporación Hondureña de Desarrollo Forestal
(Cohdefor; ☎ 223 4346; Colonia El Carrizal; ☺ 8am-4pm
Mon-Fri) The national office; you can get information
on Honduras' national parks, wildlife refuges and other
protected areas.
Instituto Hondureño de Turismo (☎ 222 2124, ext
510; www.letsgohonduras.com; 2nd fl, Edificio Europa,
cnr Av Ramon Ernesto Cruz & Calle República de México;
☺ 7:30am-3:30pm Mon-Fri) Has some information on
national parks and wildlife refuges. Not well-geared to
handle walk-in travelers.

Travel Agencies
Several reliable travel agencies are clustered
in front of and nearby Hotel Honduras Maya.
There are others on Calle Peatonal, near
Parque Central. Be aware that some agencies
charge just for the *cotización* (pricing out an
itinerary).
Mundirama Travel (☎ 232 3909; fax 232 0072;
Edificio Ciicsa, Avs República de Panamá & República de
Chile; ☺ 8am-5pm Mon-Fri, 8am-noon Sat) Can help with
travel planning, and is the local American Express rep.

DANGERS & ANNOYANCES
If you believe the papers, thieves will watch
your every step as soon as you step foot in
Tegucigalpa. No doubt, the capital can be
a dangerous place, like most developing-
world cities. However, with common sense,
you should be able to enjoy the city without
putting yourself at undue risk. During the day,
downtown Tegucigalpa and Colonia Palmira

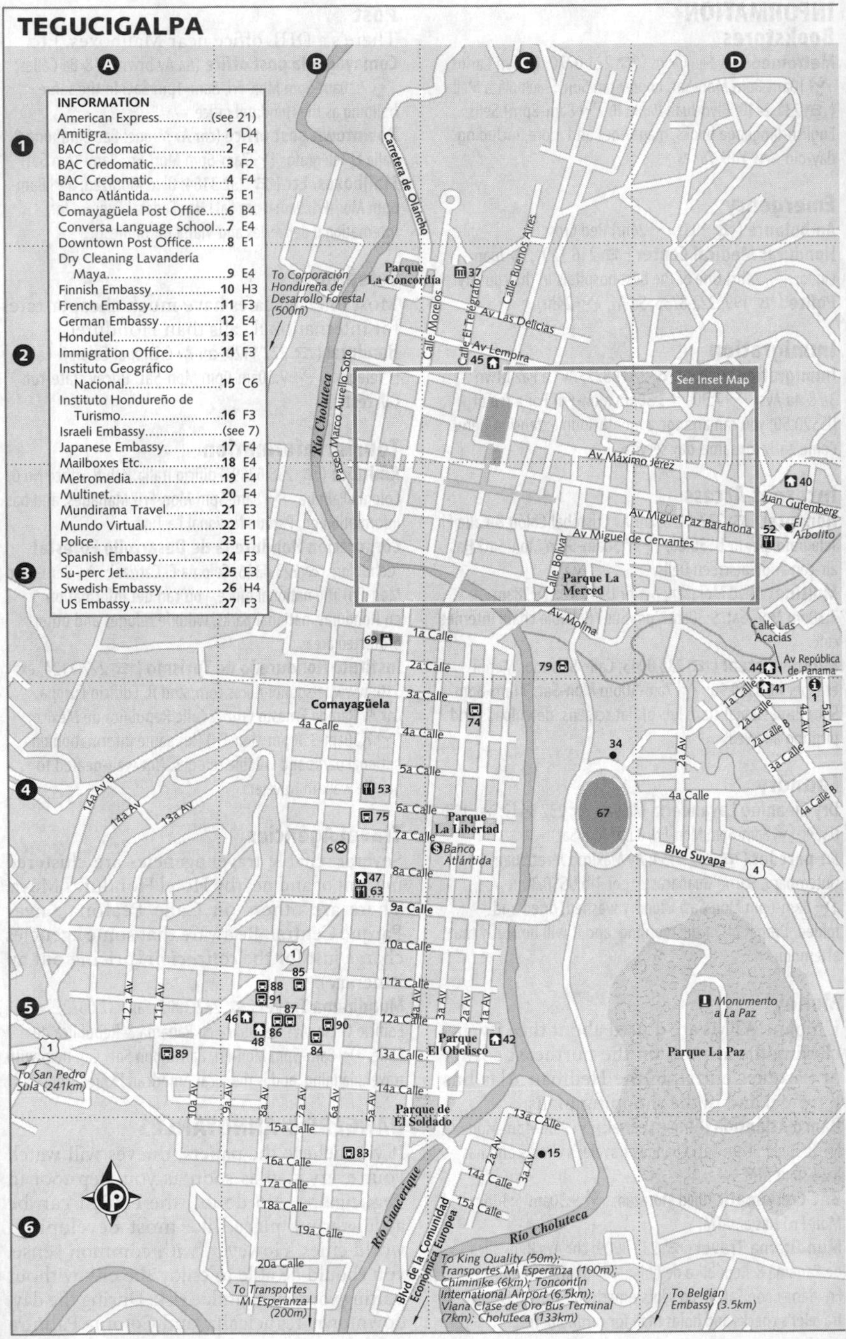

TEGUCIGALPA
A
B
C
D
1
2
3
4
5
6
INFORMATION
American Express..............(see 21)
Amitigra..............1 D4
BAC Credomatic..............2 F4
BAC Credomatic..............3 F2
BAC Credomatic..............4 F4
Banco Atlántida..............5 E1
Comayagüela Post Office......6 B4
Conversa Language School...7 E4
Downtown Post Office..........8 E1
Dry Cleaning Lavandería Maya..............9 E4
Finnish Embassy..............10 H3
French Embassy..............11 F3
German Embassy..............12 E4
Hondutel..............13 E1
Immigration Office..............14 F3
Instituto Geográfico Nacional..............15 C6
Instituto Hondureño de Turismo..............16 F3
Israeli Embassy..............(see 7)
Japanese Embassy..............17 F4
Mailboxes Etc..............18 E4
Metromedia..............19 F4
Multinet..............20 F4
Mundirama Travel..............21 E3
Mundo Virtual..............22 F1
Police..............23 E1
Spanish Embassy..............24 F3
Su-perc Jet..............25 E3
Swedish Embassy..............26 H4
US Embassy..............27 F3
To Corporación Hondureña de Desarrollo Forestal (500m)
Carretera de Olancho
Parque La Concordía
37
Calle Buenos Aires
Calle Morelos
Calle El Telégrafo
Av Las Delicias
Av Lempira
45
See Inset Map
Río Choluteca
Paseo Marco Aurelio Soto
Av Máximo Jerez
40
Juan Gutemberg
Av Miguel Paz Barahona
52
El Arbolito
Av Miguel de Cervantes
Calle Bolívar
Parque La Merced
Av Molina
Calle Las Acacias
Av República de Panamá
44
41
1
1a Calle
2a Calle
2a Calle B
3a Calle
4a Av
5a Av
2a Av
4a Calle
4a Calle B
69
1a Calle
2a Calle
3a Calle
79
Comayagüela
74
4a Calle
4a Calle
34
5a Calle
53
67
14a Av B
14a Av
13a Av
6a Calle
75
Parque La Libertad
7a Calle
Banco Atlántida
6
Blvd Suyapa
4
47
63
8a Calle
9a Calle
10a Calle
1
85
11a Calle
88
91
87
46
48
86
90
84
12 a Av
11a Av
3a Av
2a Av
1a Av
4a Av
12a Calle
Parque El Obelisco
42
Monumento a La Paz
Parque La Paz
89
13a Calle
To San Pedro Sula (241km)
14a Calle
10a Av
9a Av
8a Av
7a Av
6a Av
5a Av
Parque de El Soldado
15a Calle
13a Calle
83
16a Calle
2a Av
3a Av
15
17a Calle
14a Calle
18a Calle
15a Calle
19a Calle
Río Guacerique
Blvd de la Comunidad Económica Europea
Río Choluteca
20a Calle
To Transportes Mi Esperanza (200m)
To King Quality (50m); Transportes Mi Esperanza (100m); Chiminike (6km); Toncontín International Airport (6.5km); Viana Clase de Oro Bus Terminal (7km); Choluteca (133km)
To Belgian Embassy (3.5km)

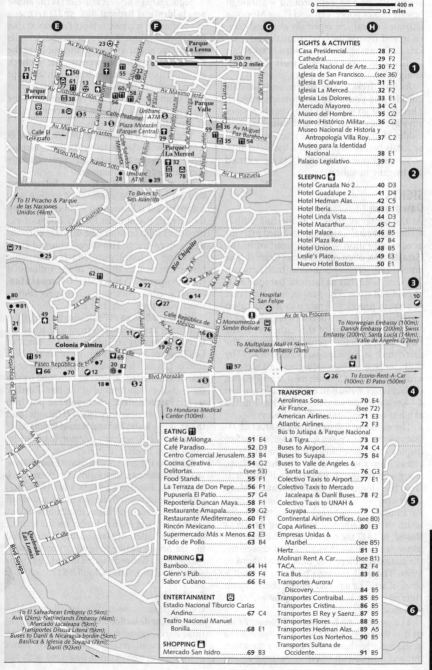

SIGHTS & ACTIVITIES		
Casa Presidencial	28	F2
Cathedral	29	F2
Galería Nacional de Arte	30	F2
Iglesia de San Francisco	(see 36)	
Iglesia El Calvario	31	E1
Iglesia La Merced	32	F2
Iglesia Los Dolores	33	E1
Mercado Mayoreo	34	C4
Museo del Hombre	35	G2
Museo Histórico Militar	36	G2
Museo Nacional de Historia y Antropología Villa Roy	37	C2
Museo para la Identidad Nacional	38	E1
Palacio Legislativo	39	F2

SLEEPING		
Hotel Granada No 2	40	D3
Hotel Guadalupe 2	41	D4
Hotel Hedman Alas	42	C5
Hotel Iberia	43	E1
Hotel Linda Vista	44	D3
Hotel Macarthur	45	C2
Hotel Palace	46	B5
Hotel Plaza Real	47	B4
Hotel Union	48	B5
Leslie's Place	49	E3
Nuevo Hotel Boston	50	E1

EATING		
Café la Milonga	51	E4
Café Paradiso	52	D3
Centro Comercial Jerusalem	53	B4
Cocina Creativa	54	G2
Delitortas	(see 53)	
Food Stands	55	F1
La Terraza de Don Pepe	56	F1
Pupusería El Patio	57	G4
Repostería Duncan Maya	58	F1
Restaurante Amapala	59	G2
Restaurante Mediterraneo	60	F1
Rincón Mexicano	61	E1
Supermercado Más x Menos	62	E3
Todo de Pollo	63	B4

DRINKING		
Bamboo	64	H4
Glenn's Pub	65	F1
Sabor Cubano	66	E4

ENTERTAINMENT		
Estadio Nacional Tiburcio Carías Andino	67	C4
Teatro Nacional Manuel Bonilla	68	E1

SHOPPING		
Mercado San Isidro	69	B3

TRANSPORT		
Aerolineas Sosa	70	E4
Air France	(see 72)	
American Airlines	71	E3
Atlantic Airlines	72	F3
Bus to Jutiapa & Parque Nacional La Tigra	73	E3
Buses to Airport	74	C4
Buses to Suyapa	75	B4
Buses to Valle de Angeles & Santa Lucía	76	G3
Colectivo Taxis to Airport	77	E1
Colectivo Taxis to Mercado Jacaleapa & Danli Buses	78	F2
Colectivo Taxis to UNAH & Suyapa	79	C3
Continental Airlines Offices	(see 80)	
Copa Airlines	80	E3
Empresas Unidas & Maribel	(see 85)	
Hertz	81	E3
Molinari Rent A Car	(see 81)	
TACA	82	F4
Tica Bus	83	B6
Transportes Aurora/ Discovery	84	B5
Transportes Contraibal	85	B5
Transportes Cristina	86	B5
Transportes El Rey y Saenz	87	B5
Transportes Flores	88	B5
Transportes Hedman Alas	89	A5
Transportes Los Norteños	90	B5
Transportes Sultana de Occidente	91	B5

HONDURAS

are usually fine to walk around – although beware of pickpockets around Plaza Morazán (Parque Central). Be especially alert and careful in and around the bus terminals and markets of Comayagüela. San Isidro Market is a particular hot spot for petty theft. Take taxis at night.

As for dress code: shorts and sandals quickly give you away as a foreign traveler. This should go without saying, but here goes anyway: keep your cash and valuables well hidden. Finally, seek advice from your hotel or locals before hopping on a local city bus. Some are prone to theft and 'taxing' carried out by gang members.

SIGHTS
Downtown
At the center of the city is the fine whitewashed **cathedral** – although its faded exterior needs restoration – and, in front of it, the **Plaza Morazán**, often called Parque Central. The domed 18th-century cathedral (built between 1765 and 1782) has an intricate baroque altar of gold and silver. The *parque*, with its statue of former president Francisco Morazán on horseback, is the hub of the city.

Three blocks east of the cathedral is the **Parque Valle**, with the **Iglesia de San Francisco**, the first church in Tegucigalpa, founded in 1592 by the Franciscans. The building beside it was first a convent, then the Spanish mint; it now houses the lackluster **Museo Histórico Militar** (☼ 8am-noon & 1-4pm Mon-Fri, 8am-noon Sat), which has limited exhibits on Honduras' military history.

The excellent **Galería Nacional de Arte** (☎ 237 9884; admission US$1; ☼ 9am-4pm Mon-Sat, 9am-1pm Sun) displays the work of Honduras' finest visual artists from the colonial era to the modern, along with some well-preserved religious artifacts. Just alongside is the 18th-century **Iglesia La Merced**. Both are housed in the Antiguo Paraninfo Universitario building, two blocks south of the cathedral and facing **Parque La Merced**. In 1847 the convent of La Merced was converted to house Honduras' first university; the national gallery was established there in 1996. The well-restored building is itself a work of art. The unusual modern building on stilts next door is the **Palacio Legislativo**, where Congress meets.

The nearby **Casa Presidencial** (Presidential Palace; cnr Paseo Marco Aurelio Soto & Calle Salvador Mendieta) is a grand building that used to serve as a museum, but was boarded up when we passed by.

Tegucigalpa's newest museum is the **Museo para la Identidad Nacional** (MIN; ☎ 222 2299; www .min-honduras.org in Spanish; Av Miguel Paz Barahona btwn Calles Morelos & El Telégrafo). After several delays, its doors were about to open to the public at the time of research but we were unable to check it out. It is reportedly a high-tech attempt to encapsulate the whole of Honduran history, from pre-Colombian civilization to the present. The museum is in the former Palace of Ministries, built in 1880.

The **Museo del Hombre** (☎ 220 1678; Av Miguel de Cervantes btwn Calles Salvador Corleto & Las Damas; admission free; ☼ 8:30am-noon & 2-5pm Mon-Fri) displays mostly contemporary Honduran art.

The **Museo Nacional de Historia y Antropología Villa Roy** (☎ 222 3470; admission US$1.50; ☼ 8:30am-3:30pm Wed-Sat) is housed on a hill overlooking the city, in the opulent former home of ex-president Julio Lozano. The displays chronologically re-create Honduras' colorful past, including archaeological and pre-Hispanic history, as well as the rise of the influential fruit companies. A block west is **Parque La Concordia**, a sedate park with carving reproductions from the Copán ruins.

Iglesia Los Dolores (1732), northwest of the cathedral, has a plaza out front and some attractive religious art inside. On the front of Los Dolores are figures representing the Passion of Christ – his unseamed cloak, the cock that crowed three times – all crowned by the more indigenous symbol of the sun. Further west is **Parque Herrera**, where you can pop into a peaceful 18th-century **Iglesia El Calvario**, and the striking **Teatro Nacional Manuel Bonilla**, dating from 1912, with an interior inspired by the Athens Theatre of Paris.

Chiminike (☎ 291 0339; www.chiminike.com; Blvd Fuerzas Armadas de Honduras; admission US$2.75; ☼ 9am-noon & 2-5pm Tue-Fri, 10am-1pm & 2-5pm Sat & Sun) is Tegucigalpa's popular new children's museum. About 7km south of central Tegus, its exhibits (Spanish only), range from a display on the human body to an outline of Maya history. Kids should like the *casa de equilibrio* (equilibrium house) – a small tilted house designed to highlight your sense of balance (admission US$1).

El Picacho
On this peak on the north side of Tegucigalpa is the **Parque de las Naciones Unidas** (United Nations Park), established to commemorate the UN's 40th anniversary. It has excellent views of the city, as well as a run-down **zoo** (adult/child

US$0.25/0.10; 9am-4:30pm Wed-Sun). On Sundays buses leaving from behind Iglesia Los Dolores go all the way to the park gates. Otherwise, take an El Hatillo bus (US$0.35, every 25 minutes from 5am to 10pm, 20 minutes) from Av Juan Gutemberg or Parque Herrera and get off at the junction; the last return bus is at 9pm. A taxi from the center costs US$5.

COURSES

Conversa Language School (☎ 231 1874; aerohond@ cablecolor.hn; Paseo República de Argentina 257; 8am-5pm Mon-Fri, 8:30am-12:30pm Sat) offers intensive courses (120 hours US$930). Homestays can also be arranged (per month, including two meals per day US$350).

SLEEPING

Downtown Tegucigalpa is safe during the day, although not at night. Comayagüela is a dodgy part of town but closer to the bus terminals. If you stay in Comayagüela, get taxis at night. Colonia Palmira is away from downtown, in a good neighborhood. Accommodations there are noticeably pricier.

Downtown

Hotel Iberia (☎ 237 9267; Calle Los Dolores, s with shared bathroom US$5.40/8.10, d with/without bathroom US$10.80/8.10) Easily the best cheapie downtown. Run by a nice family, it is an oasis of calm away from the hurly-burly of the street outside. Rooms are clean and the shared bathroom is fine (although hot water only runs from 6am to 8am). There is an upstairs common room with a TV – also good for an afternoon card game.

Nuevo Hotel Boston (☎ 237 9411, 238 0510; fax 237 0186; Av Máximo Jérez 321; s/tw US$12.20/19.50) A very good budget downtown hotel, if you can get past the rules and regulations (shirt and shoes at all times, no alcohol in the communal rooms). There is good news for giants – spick-and-span rooms, all set around a leafy courtyard, have large doorways and high ceilings. Another perk is the free coffee and cookies. Rooms facing the street are large, but noisy and not worth the extra charge for a small balcony.

Hotel Granada No 2 (☎ 237 4004; fax 237 4438; Subida Casamata 1326; s/d US$14.60/24.30; P 🅿 🖳) Comfortable bed: check. Secure: check. Clean: check. Free purified water and coffee: check. Just forget about any flourishes in this concrete block of a building. Rooms

have televisions and guests have 10 minutes' free internet.

Hotel MacArthur (☎ 237 9839; homacart@datum.hn; Av Lempira 454; s/d/tr with fan US$35/40/50, with air-con US$45/50/60; P 🅿 🖳) Rooms vary somewhat here: some are sparsely decorated and lack charm; others are cozy with views over nearby Iglesia Los Dolores. All are comfortable and good value. Rooms at the front have more character but are noisier. There is an inexpensive cafeteria serving breakfast and dinner, as well as an attractive pool that nobody seems to use.

Colonia Palmira

Hotel Guadalupe 2 (☎ 238 5009; 1a Calle; s/d US$17.30/20.55; P) Safe and comfortable, this has just one drawback: its Stalinist-style boxrooms let in little light and can make you feel you're trapped in a Cold War spy movie. Many volunteers stay here for the security and the good neighborhood.

Hotel Linda Vista (☎ 238 2099; www.lindavistahotel .com; Calle Las Acacias 1438; s/d US$40.60/58; 🖳) This very well-run small hotel has six rooms with mahogany furnishings, big closets and spacious bathrooms. The front garden is well tended and pretty, while the rear garden has a truly lovely view of the Tegucigalpa sprawl. Continental breakfast is included.

Leslie's Place (☎ 220 5325, www.dormir.com; Calzada San Martin 452; s/d with fan US$69/85; P 🖳) Small and intimate enough to almost call itself a boutique hotel, this is not your average backpackers. But if you fancy treating yourself, you won't find much better value than this charming hotel with Guillermo Yuscarán landscape paintings on the walls, and tasteful, authentic Honduran décor.

Comayagüela

Hotel Plaza Real (☎ 237 0084; 6a Av btwn 8a & 9a Calles; s/d with shared bathroom US$10.80/12.50, r with bathroom US$13.50) Set back from the street, this hotel is defined by a lush green courtyard area, with palms and a gazebo. Rooms are not bad, although overdue for a paint job. Hot water is on tap, as is purified water and coffee. Scuzzy jeans beware – there's a laundry station (hand-wash).

Hotel Hedman Alas (☎ 237 9333; 4a Av btwn 8a & 9a Calles; s/d US$15/17.30) So there's almost no natural light, but this is a good secure option in bus stations–ville. Neat rooms include brass-based lampshades and Impressionist prints. But the

HONDURAS

reams of fake flowers in the central *comedor* (dining room) are a little disturbing. Breakfast (US$2.20) is served between 7am and 9am.

Hotel Union (☎ 237 4213; fax 206 2477; 8a Av btwn 12a & 13a Calles; d/tr US$19/20.25) Rooms here have beds and very little space for anything else. New in 2005, the place looks older now. But the service is friendly and it's fine if all you want is just to crash out before a morning bus.

Hotel Palace (☎ 237 6660; 12a Calle btwn 8a & 9a Avs; s with fan & bathroom US$22.75; d with air-con US$42; P 🕭) A hefty grille door marks the inner entrance to the rooms here – enter the Fort Knox of Tegucigalpa hotels. Rooms are surprisingly pricey for what you get – a prison cell ambience right up to the barred windows, and curtains branded with the hotel name. But you do get cable TV and the beds are firm. There is also parking and a whole bunch of conveniently close bus stations.

EATING

Tegucigalpa's eating options range from street food to sophisticated candlelit restaurants serving refined global cuisine.

Downtown

La Terraza de Don Pepe (☎ 237 1084; Av Cristóbal Colón 2062; dishes US$2-4; 🕭 8am-10pm) Down-at-heel charm abounds in this famous, good-value central restaurant. Its daily specials are a steal and sometimes there is live music in the evenings. What really makes this place unique is an upstairs alcove formerly known as the men's restroom. In 1986 a statue of the Virgin of Suyapa was stolen from the Basílica de Suyapa. After a nationwide hunt, it turned up here. Now the former gentlemen's bathroom area is a little shrine, complete with aging newspaper clippings and photos of the event. Only in Latin America!

Restaurante Amapala (☎ 238 4417; Av Miguel Paz Barahona at Calle Salvador Corleto; dishes US$2-4; 🕭 11am-8pm) It is a bit rough-and-ready but this is a good place to stretch your lempira. Seafood is the specialty, closely followed by chicken platters which you get for a song. It looks onto tranquil Parque Valle. As in most Honduras restaurants, veg options are limited.

Cocina Creativa (☎ 222 4735; Av Miguel Paz Barahona; 🕭 8am-4pm Mon-Fri, 9am-2pm Sat) Cozy and low-key, this little place has hard-backed wooden chairs, paneled walls, an easy jazzy soundtrack and a friendly owner. *Licuados* (fruit milkshake drinks) and sandwiches are

great, while *platos del día* (dishes of the day) go for US$2.75.

Café Paradiso (☎ 237 0337; Av Miguel Paz Barahona 1351; mains US$3-6; 🕭 10am-10pm Mon, Wed, Fri & Sat, until 9:30pm Tue & Thu) Bohemians gather here, arguably Tegus' most cultured hangout, where European and Latin American dishes are served on cute round tables draped in yellow tablecloths. The service can be a bit chaotic – on the night we were there, the waitress was also the chef. There are often temporary art exhibitions decorating the walls. English-language movies are shown at 7pm Tuesday; poetry readings at 7pm Thursday. It is near El Arbolito.

Pupusería El Patio (☎ 235 9384; Blvd Morazán; mains US$4-7; 🕭 11am-1:30am) One of the most raucous, lively places in the city at the weekend, this beer-hall of a place heaves with people. Tables fill with bottles, and the karaoke gets more full-blooded as the night goes on. Dads, mums and kids join in the fun. Tacos and typical Honduran dishes are the main items on the menu.

Repostería Duncan Maya (☎ 237 2672; Av Cristóbal Colón; mains US$5-8; 🕭 8am-10pm Mon-Sat, 8am-9:30pm Sun) Head here if you want bustle and a buzzing atmosphere – this cavernous downtown restaurant and bar usually brims with people, running the sky-blue-clad waitresses off their feet (you may need to wait a while to get served). Don't expect a quiet evening, especially if the karaoke machine has been fired up.

Restaurante Mediterraneo (☎ 237 9618; Calle Salvador Mendieta; mains US$4-8; 🕭 10:30am-8pm) Not quite the bastion of sophisticated Mediterranean cooking that the name would have you believe, this bright restaurant caters mostly to suits and retail workers. You won't be dazzled by the cuisine – the brown vinyl seats have more luster than the carbonara – but it is tasty enough and the service is friendly. Vegetarians have some options, including Greek salad and moussaka.

El Patio (☎ 221 4141; Blvd Morazán; mains US$8-12; 🕭 10am-11pm Mon-Thu, 10am-1am Fri-Sun) The posh-restaurant branch of the city's two famous El Patio venues: waitresses dash between tables in traditional Honduran dress, while a mariachi band serenades diners in the vast open dining space. The meals are not cheap but the portions are enormous. The well-prepared meat is cooked on a large grill at one end of the dining area.

Some other options:

Rincón Mexicano (☎ 222 8368; cnr Av Cristóbal Colón & Calle El Telégrafo; mains US$3-5; 8am-9pm Mon-Thu, to 11pm Fri & Sat) Surprisingly cool and quiet little oasis, away from the noisy street. There are a few salads and the burritos are a good value at US$3.25.

Supermercado Más x Menos (cnr Avs La Paz & 4a; 7:30am-9pm Mon-Sat, 8am-8:30pm Sun) Large supermarket; good for day-trip supplies.

Food stands (mains US$0.50-1.50) At the side of Iglesia Los Dolores, these stands offer a variety of tempting lunchtime street-food dishes from *pupusas* (cornmeal mass stuffed with cheese or refried beans) and *baleadas* (flour tortillas) to beef and chicken grills.

Colonia Palmira

Café la Milonga (☎ 232 2654; Paseo República de Argentina 1802, mains US$5.50-8; noon-8:30pm Mon-Thu, to 9pm Fri, to 7pm Sat) Not your average stack-'em-high, sell-'em-cheap joint. In the well-heeled Colonia Palmira district, this is so good and excellent value. Unpretentious Argentine steaks are the choice dish in this low-key but sophisticated venue. Watch out for the events – including tango evenings and music recitals (including big names such as folk legend Guillermo Anderson).

Comayagüela

Centro Comercial Jerusalem (6a Av btwn 5a & 6a Calles; 8am-6pm Mon-Sat, to noon Sun) There are a cluster of cheap, clean *comedores*, with typical Honduran dishes, sandwiches and snacks. **Delitortas** (mains US$1-2), on the 3rd floor, has good daily specials (burger, fries and a soda for US$1.50).

Todo de Pollo (6a Av near 8a Calle, Comayagüela; mains US$2-3.50; breakfast, lunch & dinner) The name means 'everything of chicken' – can you guess what's on the menu? It's located next to Hotel Plaza Real.

DRINKING & NIGHTLIFE

Colonia Palmira hogs the best of Tegucigalpa's nightlife. There are also several bars and nightclubs along Blvd Morazán. Note that you won't be able to party 'til dawn in this city. Ricardo Alvarez, who became mayor of Tegucigalpa in 2006, controversially imposed a 2am curfew on the city's clubs and bars in a bid to clamp down on the night-time violence.

Glenn's Pub (6pm-2am Mon-Sat) During the day you would not even know it was here,

but this small hole-in-the-wall bar has a young crowd spilling out onto the sidewalk on weekend nights. Cheap beers flow, as do the tunes: a funky mix of Britpop, Bob Marley and other classics.

Sabor Cubano (☎ 235 9947; Paseo República de Argentina 1933; 11am-2pm & 6-11pm Tue-Thu, 11am-2pm & 6pm-2am Fri & Sat) Head here if your hips don't lie – this is Tegucigalpa's dance hotspot. There's no cover charge. It's just a pleasant, relaxed atmosphere with couples, some more elegant than others, moving the night away to the *una-dos-tres* of a salsa beat. It doubles as a restaurant.

Bamboo (☎ 236 5391; Blvd Morazán; cover US$6-8; 9pm-2am Wed-Sat) This is Tegucigalpa's most exclusive nightclub. Partygoers are mainly young twenty-somethings. Dress code: to the nines.

ENTERTAINMENT

Café Paradiso (Av Miguel Paz Barahona 1351; 9am-8pm Mon-Sat, to 9:30pm Tue & Thu) Shows English-language movies every Tuesday night at 7pm and has poetry readings on Thursday at 7pm.

Teatro Nacional Manuel Bonilla (☎ 222 4366; Av Miguel Paz Barahona) This characterful place hosts a variety of performing arts.

Cinemark (☎ 231 2044; www.cinemarkca.com; Multiplaza Mall, Blvd Juan Pablo II; tickets US$3) A modern multiscreen cineplex showing recent Hollywood fare.

Estadio Nacional Tiburcio Carías Andino (9a Calle at Blvd Suyapa) Across the river from Comayagüela, this stadium mainly holds soccer matches – things are never dull when soccer-mad fans take their seats on match day.

SHOPPING

Honduran handicrafts are sold at many places around town.

Mercado Mayoreo (8am-5pm Fri, 6am-3pm Sat) Every Friday and Saturday, this colorful cheap market sets up shop near the Estadio Nacional. There's a dazzling array of produce and stalls, hawking everything from birdcages to vegetables. It's an experience just to wander around, even if you don't want to buy anything. There are some great little *pupusa* cafés too – check out Pupusería Emanuel if you can – *que rico*!

Mercado San Isidro (about 7am-5pm) Located in Comayagüela, you can find just about anything for sale in this sprawling market, from vegetables to secondhand clothing to some excellent leatherwork and other crafts. Be aware that this is a favorite hunting ground of pickpockets.

Multiplaza Mall (Blvd Juan Pablo II; ⏰ 8am-10pm) New malls frequently crop up in Tegucigalpa, but this one is probably the most convenient for travelers. It's southwest of Colonia Palmira, with ATMs, bookstores, internet and a cinema.

GETTING THERE & AWAY
Air
The airport is 6.5km south of Tegucigalpa. See p340 for information on getting into town. Note that Honduras' main airport is in San Pedro Sula, not Tegucigalpa. Travelers looking for international flights should consider flying from there.

Aerolineas Sosa (☎ 233 5107, airport 234 0137; www.aerolineas.com; Blvd Morazán; ⏰ 8am-noon & 1-4pm Mon-Fri, 8am-noon Sat)

American Airlines (Edif Palmira; ☎ 800 220 1414 toll free, in Honduras 220 7585; ⏰ 8am-6pm Mon-Fri, 8am-noon Sat) Across from Hotel Honduras Maya.

Atlantic Airlines (☎ 237 8597, airport 234 9701; www.atlanticairlines.com.ni; cnr Avs La Paz & Juan Lindo; ⏰ 8am-5pm Mon-Fri, 8am-noon Sat)

Air France (☎ 236 0029; www.airfrance.com; cnr Avs La Paz & Juan Lindo; ⏰ 8am-5pm Mon-Fri, 8am-noon Sat)

Continental Airlines (☎ 220 0999, airport 233 3676; www.continental.com; Av República de Chile; ⏰ 8am-5pm Mon-Fri, 8am-2pm Sat)

Copa Airlines (☎ 235 5610, airport 291 0099; Av República de Chile; ⏰ 8am-6pm Mon-Fri, 8am-2pm Sun) In Hotel Clarion.

TACA (☎ 236 8222; www.taca.com; Blvd Morazán; ⏰ 8am-5pm Mon-Fri, 9am-5pm Sat, 9am-2pm Sun)

Destination	Fare
La Ceiba	US$80
Roatán (via La Ceiba)	US$120
San Pedro Sula	US$70
Utila (via La Ceiba)	US$120

Bus
Excellent bus services connect Tegucigalpa with other parts of Honduras; unfortunately, each bus line has its own station. Most are clustered in Comayagüela. See Map pp342–3 for locations. Keep a wary eye on your belongings in this part of town.

The free magazine *Honduras Tips* has a very useful bus routes section.

INTERNATIONAL & LONG-DISTANCE BUSES
Both **Tica Bus** (☎ 220 0579, www.ticabus.com; 16a Calle btwn 5a & 6a Avs, Comayagüela) and **King Quality** (www.kingqualityca.com; ☎ 225 5415; fax 225 2600; Blvd Commanded Economical European near 6a Av, Comayagüela) go to El Salvador, Guatemala, Nicaragua and the Mexican border, and have connections to Costa Rica and Panama. King Quality has two classes: 'Quality' is 1st class and 'King' is even more deluxe. Make sure you arrive 45 minutes before taking any international departures.

For more information, see opposite.

GETTING AROUND
Bus
City buses are cheap (US$0.20), loud, dirty and can be dangerous. Theft is common and buses are sometimes targeted by gangs. Unless you are confident about the areas you are going through, stick to the colectivos or taxis.

For getting to the airport, see p340.

Car & Motorcycle
Before hiring a vehicle be sure to ask about the deductible (the amount you pay before insurance kicks in) – it can be as high as US$1600. Hire rates average around US$50 per day.

Rental companies:

Avis (☎ 239 5712, airport 232 0088; www.avis.com; Blvd Suyapa, Edif Marina; ⏰ 8am-6pm)

Budget (☎ 235 9528, 265 8000; www.budget.com)

Econo Rent-a-Car (☎ 235 8582, airport 291 0107; Blvd Morazán; ⏰ 8am-6pm)

Hertz (☎ 238 3772, airport 234 3784; hertz@multivisionhn.net; Centro Comercio Villa Real; ⏰ 8am-6pm Mon-Sat)

Taxi
Taxis cruise all over town and honk to advertise when they are available. A ride in town costs around US$2.20.

A private taxi to the airport costs about US$8.

There are a couple of useful downtown taxi colectivo stops, particularly helpful for the airport, and Mercado Jacaleapa terminal (where buses depart for El Paraíso and Danlí). They charge US$0.60.

You will have to wait for them to fill up. Colectivos to the airport also leave from the stop on Calle Morelos, five blocks west of Parque Central.

BUSES FROM TEGUCIGALPA

International Buses

Destination	Bus line	Fare (one way)	Departures	Duration
Guatemala City (Guatemala)	Tica Bus	US$26	12:30pm	22hr (with overnight in San Salvador)
	Transportes King Quality	US$58/79 quality/king	6am	14hr (with 2hr layover in San Salvador)
Managua (Nicaragua)	Tica Bus	US$20	9am	8hr (via Danlí)
	King Quality	US$25/37 quality/king	6am & 2pm	7-8hr
Managua (Nicaragua)	Tica Bus	US$20	9am	8hr (via Danlí)
	King Quality	US$25/37 quality/king	6am & 2pm	7-8hr
San Salvador (El Salvador)	Tica Bus	US$15	12:30pm	6½hr
	King Quality	US$31/44 quality/king	6am & 2pm	6-7hr
Tapachula (Mexico)	Tica Bus	US$41	1pm	40hr (overnight in San Salvador, transfer in Guatemala City

Long-Distance Buses

Destination	Bus line	Phone	Fare	Type	Duration
Agua Caliente	Transportes Sultana de Occidente	237 8101	US$11.10	direct	9hr
Catacamas	Transportes Discovery	237 4883	US$4.60	direct	3¾hr
Choluteca	Transportes Mi Esperanza	225 1502	US$2.50	direct	3hr
Comayagua	Transportes El Rey	237 1462	US$2.30	normal	2hr
Copán Ruínas	Transportes Hedman Alas	237 7143	US$22	ejecutivo	7hr
El Paraíso	Transportes Discua Litena	230 0470	US$2.80	direct	2hr
Juticalpa	Transportes Aurora	237 3647	US$2.50	direct	3hr
La Ceiba	Transportes Hedman Alas	237 7143	US$22	ejecutivo	7½hr
	Transportes Cristina	220 0117	US$9.40	direct	7½hr
La Entrada	Transportes Sultana de Occidente	237 8101	US$8.10	normal	6hr
La Paz	Transportes Flores	237 3032	US$1.50	normal	2hr
Las Manos*	Transportes Discua Litena	230 0470	US$3.25	normal	3hr
San Pedro Sula	Transportes Hedman Alas	237 7143	US$15	ejecutivo	4hr
	Transportes El Rey	233 8561	US$6	direct	4hr
Santa Rosa de Copán	Transportes Sultana de Occidente	237 8101	US$6.10	normal	7hr
Siguatepeque	Transportes Empresas Unidas & Maribel	222 2071	US$2.20	normal	2½hr
Tela	Transportes Cristina	220 0117	US$9.40	normal	6hr
Trujillo	Transportes Contraibal	237 1666	US$11	normal	8hr

*Nicaraguan border; last bus from border to Ocotal (Nicaragua) at 4pm

AROUND TEGUCIGALPA

SUYAPA

The huge gothic **Basílica de Suyapa**, the most important church in Honduras, dominates the landscape on the Suyapa hillside, about 7km south of the center of Tegucigalpa.

The basilica is just up the hill from the **Universidad Nacional Autónoma de Honduras** (UNAH). The construction of the basilica, which is famous for its large, brilliant stained-glass windows, was begun in 1954, and finishing touches are still being added.

La Virgen de Suyapa is the patron saint of Honduras; in 1982 a papal decree made her the patron saint of all Central America. She is represented by a tiny painted wooden statue, only 6cm tall. Many believe she has performed hundreds of miracles. The statue is brought to the large basilica on holidays, especially for the annual **Feria de Suyapa** beginning on the saint's day (February 3), and continuing for a week; the celebrations attract pilgrims from all over Central America. Most of the time, however, the little statue is kept on the altar of the very simple old **Iglesia de Suyapa**, built in the late 18th and early 19th centuries. It's on the plaza a few hundred meters behind the newer basilica.

Buses for Suyapa (US$0.20, 20 minutes) leave from the gas station at 6a Av and 7 Calle in Comayagüela; see Map pp342–3. Get off at the university and walk the short distance from there.

SANTA LUCÍA

pop 2300

Perched among pine-covered hills, Santa Lucía is a charming old colonial mining town with a spectacular vista over the Tegucigalpa sprawl in the valley below. It is less obviously touristy than nearby Valle de Ángeles, which is part of its appeal.

Within its enchanting 18th-century *iglesia* are old Spanish paintings and a **statue of Christ of Las Mercedes**, donated to Santa Lucía by King Philip II in 1572. If the high arched wooden doors of the church are closed, walk around to the office at the rear and ask to have them opened for you. Apart from a few hikes, and one or two restaurants, there is very little to do in the town, apart from meandering along its tranquil streets and getting a feel for a Honduras that time forgot.

Sleeping & Eating

La Posada de Doña Estefana (☎ 779 0441; Barrio El Centro; d/tr US$25.75/31) This is a beautifully tranquil setting, with a fine panorama of the church. Its three rooms are pretty good too, done out in a colonial style with stained glass windows. When you consider the location, it is a bargain. Santa Lucía is such a low-key little place you may have to knock on the door or the garden gate a few times before anyone answers the door.

Restaurante & Bar Santa Lucía Colonial (☿ noon-midnight Fri & Sat, 10am-8pm Sun) Cute as a button from the outside, this start-up bar and restaurant is right on the main street (or as main as you get in this town), where the buses arrive and leave. Tacos and *típica* (regional specalties) dominate the menu. If this is closed there are a few other *comedores* dotted nearby.

Getting There & Away

Santa Lucía is 14km east of Tegucigalpa, 2km uphill from the road leading to Valle de Ángeles and San Juancito. Buses leave every 45 to 60 minutes from an Esso station off Av la Paz, near Hospital San Felipe (see Map pp342–3). Buses leave Tegus every 45 to 60 minutes from 7:30am to 8pm (US$0.40, 30 minutes). Return buses leave Santa Lucía from 7:30am to 8pm.

Another option is to take the Valle de Angeles bus from the same Hospital San Felipe stop, get off at the crossroads and walk the 2.5km into town.

VALLE DE ÁNGELES

pop 4600

Eight kilometers past Santa Lucía, Valle de Ángeles is another beautiful, former colonial mining town. An official tourist zone, the town has been restored to its original 16th-century appearance in parts, especially around the attractive parque central, where there is a handsome old church. The annual **fair** takes place on October 4.

Artisan souvenir shops line the streets, selling Honduran *artesanías,* including wood carvings, basketry, ceramics, leatherwork, paintings, dolls, wicker and wood furniture. Prices are usually less than in Tegucigalpa. One of the most distinctive artists' displays is one block south of the parque central in a flamboyantly pink building. **Galeria Sixtina** (☎ 766 2375; ☿ 10am-6pm) is the brainchild of a classically trained artist who has gathered

HONDURAS

artworks and contributed personally to this richly colorful collection. Angels, appropriately enough, are the central theme.

Valle de Ángeles is an easy day trip from Tegucigalpa, but it is also a quiet, relaxing place to stay. It gets busy on weekends and holidays; otherwise, the town is usually quiet.

Sleeping & Eating

Villas del Valle (☎ 766 2534; www.villasdelvalle.com; Carr a San Juancito; s/d US$13.50/19; ☒) These simple, neat brick-built cabins a short walk from the center are your best bet for lodging in Valle de Ángeles. The on-site restaurant is open until 6pm, and stays open later as a bar when the place is busier.

Posada del Ángel (☎ 766 2233; s/d US$20/28; P ☒ ☒ ☒) This has a higher opinion of itself than it should. Rooms wrap around a large area, with a pool as the centerpiece. While rooms are perfectly acceptable, service is not particularly warm; you'd expect better for the price. It is two blocks north of the *iglesia*.

Restaurante Turístico (☎ 766 2148; Carr a San Juancito; US$4-8; ☺ 9am-6pm) The most memorable eating option in town is a short walk above the main turnoff to Valle de Angeles. It is a classic colonial-style restaurant with an attractive terrace and an even better view over the town and valley below. Walk past the Posada del Ángel and keep walking uphill for a kilometer. It may extend its hours for groups in the evening.

On the central park:

Restaurante Jalapeño (mains US$3-6; ☺ lunch & dinner Tue-Sun) Has good veggie options.

El Anafre (☎ 766 2942; mains US$5.50-12; ☺ lunch & dinner) Serves up reasonable Italian fare.

Getting There & Away

Colectivo minibuses for Valle de Ángeles (US$0.75, 30 minutes, 6:45am to 7pm, every 45 minutes) depart from the Esso gas station stop near the Hospital San Felipe in Tegucigalpa. There are also cheaper, slower buses from the same spot (US$0.55, one hour, hourly). The last return minibus leaves from Valle de Ángeles at 5:45pm.

PARQUE NACIONAL LA TIGRA

A beautiful national park just a short hop from the capital city, **La Tigra** (adult/child US$10/5; ☺ 8am-4pm Tue-Sun, last entrance 2pm) is a lush cloud forest in former mining country belonging to the American-owned Rosario Mining Company.

The mining scars can still be seen. In 1980 this became Honduras' first national park – it is an essential water supply for the city. It has a great abundance of (elusive) wildlife, from pumas to peccaries, and is a botanist's delight, with lush trees, vines, lichens and large ferns, colorful mushrooms, bromeliads and orchids.

The climate at La Tigra is fresh and brisk; in fact it's often quite cold – bring plenty of warm clothes with you. Long pants and long sleeves are best, as the forest has many mosquitoes.

Information

Amitigra (☎ 238 6269; Edificio Italia, 4th fl, office No 6, Colonia Palmira, Tegucigalpa; ☺ 8am-5pm Mon-Fri) has information and manages overnight visits to the park. You can pay park/lodging fees here or at the park entrances. La Tigra has two entrances, Jutiapa and El Rosario. There are visitors centers at both entrances, where rangers are always on duty.

Hiking

There are eight trails, all well maintained and easy to follow. It is a rugged, mountainous area – people have been lost for days in the dense forest after they wandered off the trails. Both the Amitigra office and the visitors center have maps of the trails.

The **Sendero Principal** is the busiest and most direct route through the park. It is actually the old disused road leading from Tegucigalpa to the mines and runs 6km from Jutiapa to El Rosario. From Jutiapa, you descend past abandoned mines, small rivers and views over the San Juancito valley before reaching El Rosario. A more appealing trail is to **Sendero La Cascada**, which leads to a 40m waterfall. Coming from Jutiapa, follow the Sendero Principal over 1km to the Sendero La Cascada cut-off, located at a sharp bend in the trail. Descend the steep stone steps and continue another 2km past smaller falls and abandoned mines to a T-intersection: go straight to reach the falls (10 to 20 minutes), or left to reach El Rosario via Sendero La Mina. From El Rosario, **Sendero La Mina** leads you past abandoned mining buildings. Later, there is also a left turnoff to the falls (10 to 20 minutes).

Guides (not really needed) are available to take you along the trails. They are used especially for large groups (per group US$5 to US$20).

Sleeping & Eating

Cabaña Mirador El Rosario (☎ 987 5835; s/d US$15.50/ 24.50) This has great views, lovely rooms and easy access to the national park. The catch: there are only two rooms, so call ahead. Breakfast and dinner are available (US$2.25 to US$3.75).

Eco-Albergue El Rosario (r per adult/child US$15/10) This visitors center has nine simple rooms with fresh sheets. It is at the park entrance.

Cabañas & Eco-Albergue Jutiapa (per adult/child US$15/10) This new Jutiapa visitors center was about to open at the time of research. There should be six basic rooms, with a queen-size bed and a twin. Hot water is due to be available.

Both visitors centers have basic **comedores** (mains US$2.75-3.50; ☒ Jutiapa 7am-6pm Thu-Sun, El Rosario 7am-8pm daily).

Getting There & Away

The western entrance to the park, above Jutiapa, is the closest to Tegucigalpa, 22km away. In Tegus, take a bus (US$0.70, direct at 9am and 2pm) from the Dippsa gas station on Av Máximo Jérez at Av la Plazuela, across from a Banco Atlántida branch. Other buses (every 45 minutes, from 6am) toward El Hatillo from the same place can usually drop you at Los Planes, a soccer field 2km before the visitors center. On the return trip, a few buses leave from the visitors center, but most leave from Los Planes; the first is at 6am, the last around 3pm. After that you'll need to walk 4km to the next town (Los Limones), where buses run later. A taxi to this entrance from Tegus costs about US$20.

The eastern park entrance is at El Rosario, overlooking San Juancito, an atmospheric former mining town. From Tegucigalpa, buses to San Juancito (US$0.75, 1½ hours) leave from Mercado San Pablo (3pm Monday to Friday; 8am, 12:40pm and 3pm Saturday; 8am and 12:40pm Sunday), Valle de Ángeles bus stop, opposite Hospital San Felipe (5pm Monday to Friday), and Supermercado Más x Menos (4:30pm Saturday). From San Juancito, waiting pickup trucks will ferry you the last 4km to the park entrance (US$8.75, up to 10 people). Or you could walk, but it's very steep.

Buses to Tegus from San Juancito leave from the kiosk on the main road (6am and 6:50am Monday to Friday; 6am, 6:40am, 12:30pm and 2:30pm Saturday; 6:20am Sunday).

WESTERN HONDURAS

People have lived here for millennia, making their marks on the landscape in spectacular ways – most strikingly at the captivating Copán archaeological ruins. Travelers usually whizz from the ruins to the coast via San Pedro Sula, the underappreciated dynamo of the Honduran economy. Yet those who stay rarely regret it. The Montaña de Celaque cloud forests, dazzling Lago Yojoa birdlife, colonial charms of Comayagua and Gracias, and the slow-changing, colorful Ruta de Lenca communities, from Santa Rosa de Copán to Marcala, are all excellent reasons to linger.

The road between San Pedro Sula and Tegucigalpa is probably the most traveled in Honduras; it's 241km along Honduras' Carretera del Norte (Hwy 1), about a four-hour bus trip. The route passes Comayagua, Siguatepeque, the Lago de Yojoa and the beautiful Pulhapanzak waterfall (about 45 minutes west of the highway by bus).

This region, called the Valle de Comayagua, was well settled in pre-Columbian times, and agriculture has been practiced here for at least 3000 years. Fourteen archaeological sites have been identified in the department of Comayagua, and ancient pottery, jewelry and stone carvings have all been unearthed.

COMAYAGUA

pop 61,500

The former religious and political capital of Honduras, Comayagua spent years in the doldrums, harking back to the days when it used to be boss. That's different now – the powers-that-be are finally making the most of the city's many colonial charms. When power shifted southeast to Tegucigalpa in 1880, a legacy of ornate churches, pretty plazas and a grand cathedral remained. Recent makeovers and restorations have breathed new life into these architectural and historical attractions while two good museums provide more reasons to visit.

The city was founded as the capital of Honduras in 1537 by Spanish Captain Alonso de Cáceres, fulfilling the orders of the Spanish governor of Honduras to establish a new settlement in the geographic center of the territory. The town was initially called Villa de

COMAYAGUA

0 -------- 400 m
0 -------- 0.2 miles

To Ecosimco (500m)

Río Chiquito

7a Calle NO

6a Calle NO

5a Calle NO

4a Calle NO

3a Calle NO

2a Calle NO

1a Calle NO

El Blvd

Parque Central

Market

Parque La Merced

Calle Manuel Bonilla/ Calle Barrio Torón Dón

1a Calle SO

Hospital

To San Pedro Sula (157km)

Carr del Norte

To Soto Cano (15km); Tegucigalpa (84km)

INFORMATION	
Banco Atlántida (ATM).........1	A2
Banco de Occidente..............2	B2
Hondutel...........................3	B2
L@ Red.............................4	B2
Neon Macro net 5	A3
Police...............................6	B2
Post Office.........................7	B2
Tourist Office......................8	B2

SIGHTS & ACTIVITIES	
Cathedral............................9	B2
Iglesia La Merced...............10	B3
Iglesia San Francisco...........11	B2
Iglesia San Sebastián..........12	C4
Museo Colonial de Arte Religioso.........................13	B2
Museo Regional de Arqueología....................14	B2
Nuestra Señora de la Caridad.........................15	A1

SLEEPING	
Hotel America Inc................16	B3
Hotel Honduras..................17	B3
Hotel Maru.......................18	B3
Hotel Norimax...................19	B3

EATING	
La Gota de Limón...............20	B2
Repostéria y Cafetería La Economica......................21	B3
Restaurante Mang Ying.......22	A1
Villa Real.........................23	B2

TRANSPORT	
Buses to San Pedro Sula......24	B3
Buses to Tegucigalpa...........25	B3
Main Bus Stop...................26	B4

Santa María de Comayagua; in 1543 the name was changed to Villa de la Nueva Valladolid de Comayagua.

Comayagua was declared a city in 1557, and in 1561 the seat of the diocese of Honduras was moved from Trujillo to Comayagua because of its more favorable conditions, central position and closer proximity to the silver- and gold-mining regions. The religious history means it is an excellent place to witness **Semana Santa** celebrations. On the morning of Good Friday, religious images are carried in a street procession, over intricate carpets of colored sawdust.

An important source of income for the town is Soto Cano, an air base used by the US military. Better known as La Palmerola,

it formed a base for 2000 US soldiers during the 1980s when the Contra war was raging in Nicaragua. Since then, it's been converted to a Honduran base – or that's the official line – with about 550 American military personnel stationed there holding the Central American fort.

The base's strategic importance received a boost in 1999 when US bases were closed in Panama.

Orientation

Like most Honduran towns, life centers around the parque central, which has been tastefully refurbished with gardens, benches and piped-in music. Comayagua is walkable, though the area between the parque central

HONDURAS

and the hotels can feel lonely after dark. Solo travelers should consider taking a cab home if it's late.

Streets are also defined according to the compass: ie: NO for *noroeste* (northwest), NE for *noreste* (northeast), SO for *suroeste* (southwest), SE for *sureste* (southeast).

Information

EMERGENCY

Police (☎ 772 0080)
Red Cross (☎ 195, 772 0290)

INTERNET ACCESS

L@ Red (☎ 772 5041; Parque Central; ☼ 8am-10pm) Convenient internet access for US$1.15 per hour. Also has calls to the US for US$0.11 per minute.
Neon Macro.net (☎ 772 2418; 1a Calle NO; per hr US$1; ☼ 8am-10pm Mon-Sat, 8am-9pm Sun) Has slick flatscreens. Also does cheap phone calls (per minute to the USA US$0.10).

MONEY

Most banks and other services are clustered around the parque central.
Banco Atlántida (Parque Central) Has a Visa/Plus ATM machine.
Banco de Occidente (Parque Central) Changes Visa and Amex traveler's checks.

POST & TELEPHONE

These are together behind the cathedral:
Hondutel (1a Av NE btwn 4a & 5a Calles NO; ☼ 7am-9pm)
Post office (1a Av NE btwn 4a & 5a Calles NO; ☼ 8am-4pm Mon-Fri, to 11am Sat)

TOURIST INFORMATION

Ecosimco (Ecosistema Montaña de Comayagua; ☎ 772 4681; ecosimco@hondutel.hn; Camara de Comercio; ☼ 9am-noon & 1-5pm Mon-Fri) Manages the Montaña de Comayagua National Park (opposite); 500m north of town. Look for the big green gates.
Tourist office (☎ 772 2028; www.comayagua.hn; Parque Central; ☼ 8am-noon & 2-5pm Tue-Sat, 8am-noon Sun) Sporadically helpful; information on local attractions.

Sights

The **cathedral** (Parque Central; ☼ 7am-8pm) in the center of town is the largest colonial-era place of worship in Honduras. It was built from 1685 to 1715 and is adorned with intricate wooden carvings and gold-plated altars. The main altar is similar to that of the Teguci-

galpa cathedral; both were made by the same (unknown) artist. The clock in the cathedral tower is the oldest in the Americas and one of the oldest in the world. The Moors built it over 800 years ago for the palace of Alhambra in Granada. In 1620 it was donated to the town by King Phillip III of Spain. Look out for the older Roman-style IIII rather than IV on the clockface.

Other fine *iglesias* include **San Francisco** (founded 1560); **San Sebastián** (1580), on the south end of town; and the much remodeled **Nuestra Señora de la Caridad** (7a Calle NO at 3a Av NO; ☼ 7am-8pm), built at the end of the 16th century and used as a place of worship for the local indigenous community. Comayagua's first *iglesia* was **La Merced**. Building started in 1550 and it was consecrated as a cathedral in 1561; the plaza in front is very pretty. Another colonial *iglesia*, San Juan de Dios (1590), was destroyed by an earthquake in 1750, but samples of its artwork are on display in the Museo Colonial. If you read Spanish, look for a small book entitled *Las Iglesias Coloniales de la Ciudad de Comayagua*, which contains an interesting history of Comayagua and its churches. It's available at both museums.

Opened in 1962 the **Museo Colonial de Arte Religioso** (cnr Av 2a de Julio & 4a Calle NE; admission incl guide US$1.85; ☼ 9am-noon & 2-5pm Tue-Sun) was once the site of the first university in Central America, founded in 1632, and in operation for almost 200 years. Priests have occupied the building even longer, since 1558. Totally renovated in 2005, the museum contains artwork and religious paraphernalia from all five churches of Comayagua, spanning the 16th to the 18th centuries.

A block north of the cathedral, the **Museo Regional de Arqueología** (☎ 772 0386; admission US$1; ☼ 8:30am-4pm) displays some fine ancient Lenca artifacts, including pottery, *metates* (stone on which grain is ground), stone carvings and petroglyphs. Descriptions are in English and Spanish. It is housed in a former presidential palace.

Sleeping

Hotel Maru (☎ 772 1311; cnr Calle Manuel Bonilla & 1a Av NO; r with/without bathroom US$6.60/5.30) The rooms are very neat and face out onto a long courtyard here. Shared bathrooms are not pretty – shell out an extra dollar for a private one, but don't expect anything apart from a open pipe for your shower. Bring your own toilet paper.

Red-brick rooms provide some protection from the heat.

Hotel America Inc (☎ 772 0530; fax 772 0009; cnr 1a Av NO & 1a Calle NO; s/d US$8.25/11.50, with air-con US$12.25/18.25; ⊠ ⊠ ▢ ☒) This hotel has delusions of grandeur, but the good-sized rooms are comfortable enough despite some unnecessary flourishes. They come equipped with cable TV; there's also a swimming pool and reasonable restaurant on site.

Hotel Honduras (☎ 772 1877; cnr 2a Av NO & 1a Calle NO; s/d with fan US$10.80/12) Painted green and arranged along a narrow passageway, the rooms lack natural light, but the beds and the private bathrooms are clean enough.

Hotel Norimax (☎ 772 1210; cnr Calle Manuel Bonilla & El Blvd; s/d with fan US$10.75/12.50, with air-con US$13.50/16.30; ℗ ☒) Three floors of characterful, spotless rooms, with varnished doors and wooden bedsteads, are a very reasonable deal, though the bathrooms are cramped. All rooms have cable TV, and purified water is free.

Eating

La Gota de Limón (☎ 715 0627; tacos US$2, fajitas US$7; ☷ 11am-2am Mon-Sun) Fajitas and tacos are served on ruby tablecloths, there is colonial-style slate tiling, and a breezy outdoor patio above a mango tree – this Mexican restaurant has plenty of charm. It is just around the corner from the parque central. It doubles as a lively bar in the evening.

Villa Real (☎ 715 0101; 1a Av NE btwn 4a & 3a Calles NO; ☷ lunch & dinner Tue-Sun) This was closed when we passed through so we couldn't check it out. However, the restaurant has a handsome old colonial setting and a reputation for dishing up some of the finest Honduran cuisine around.

Repostería y Cafétería La Economica (☎ 772 2331; 1a Av NE, Parque la Merced; dishes US$3-5; ☷ 7am-8pm Mon-Sat) Cakes and lovely slushes (cappuccino US$0.60) are the order of the day at this café in an old colonial building. It's in a prize location overlooking the charming Plaza Merced.

Restaurante Mang Ying (☎ 772 0567; cnr 7a Calle NO & El Blvd; dishes US$4-8; ☷ 9:30am-10:30pm) Popular among locals, this continues the Central American Chinese-restaurant tradition of serving way more than you could ever eat. If you haven't eaten for about two days, order the Chop Suey Mang Ying, a mound of noodles, veggies, chicken, beef and shrimp.

Getting There & Away

Comayagua is about 1km east of the highway. To and from Tegucigalpa, Transportes El Rey (US$1.75, 1½ hours) stops at the Texaco gas

---

EXPLORE MORE AROUND COMAYAGUA

Visitors to Comayagua need not look far for cloud-forest escapes or ancient ruins.

- **Parque Nacional Montaña de Comayagua** (30,000 hectares) has two main trails leading through the cloud forest, from near the small village of Río Negro, 42km north of Comayagua, to waterfalls (no bathing). The park is managed by Ecosimco (opposite). Simple bunk-bed **accommodation** (☎ 990 0802) is available at the house of Don Avilio Velásquez in Río Negro. You can hire a guide (recommended) in Río Negro. Pickup trucks to Río Negro (US$1.75, four hours) leave from the south side of the Comayagua market at 11am, noon and 1pm.

- **Yarumela**, on the Río Humuya, between Comayagua and La Paz, consists of two major, mostly unexcavated, archaeological mounds. There is one significant reconstruction revealing a step pyramid with several platforms. Lencans are believed to have lived here around 2000 years ago. To get there, take a bus to La Paz, off the Tegucigalpa–San Pedro Sula highway. Taxis from La Paz cost about US$11 round-trip. If you have a vehicle, take the turnoff from the main CA-5 highway toward La Paz and go over the Río Humuya. Just before you come to a roundabout, follow a dirt road off to the right until you arrive at the site, a large mound on the right side of the road.

- **Tenampua**, constructed much later than Yarumela, around AD 1000 to 1100 at a time of war, is prime lookout territory, and a good defense stronghold. Its features include a ball court (possibly a sign of Maya influence), walls and more unexcavated mounds. The site is about 20km south of Comayagua. From there, take a Tegucigalpa-bound bus and ask the driver to let you off at the *sendero* (trail) for Tenampua; it's on the east side of the highway, just north of Restaurant Aquarios. The climb is steep and takes 1½ hours.

station at the highway turnoff, roughly 12 blocks from the *centro*. Transportes Catrachos (US$1.60, two hours, every 30 minutes) has a downtown terminal, although its station in Tegucigalpa is away from the center in a sketchy area. Transportes Rivera runs to San Pedro Sula (US$3.10, three hours, hourly 5am to 4pm). Buses to Marcala (US$2, three hours) leave just outside the Rivera terminal, departing at 6am, 8am, 10am, noon and 2pm.

Any Tegucigalpa–San Pedro bus will pick you up or drop you off at the turnoff, although you may have to pay the full fare. Check beforehand.

SIGUATEPEQUE

pop 45,260

Siguatepeque is an unremarkable town about halfway between Tegucigalpa (117km) and San Pedro Sula (124km), roughly two hours from both. It is known for its pleasant climate. You may want to stop at Siguatepeque to break your journey, although Comayagua is more interesting.

Orientation & Information

There are two squares in town. From the main highway 2km away, the first one you get to is dusty Plaza San Pablo, with basketball courts and the market. Three blocks east is the much more attractive parque central.

Banco Atlántida (Plaza San Pablo) Changes American Express traveler's checks.

Banco del Occidente (Plaza San Pablo) Near the plaza's southeast corner and now has an ATM.

Plaz@net (Plaza San Pablo; per hr US$0.80; 🕑 8am-9pm Mon-Sat, noon-7pm Sun) You can also make international calls.

Police (☎ 773 0042)

Sleeping

Hotel Boarding House Central (☎ 773 0108; Parque Central; s/d/tr with TV US$11/13.50/16.25) It does not look much from the outside, but the rooms are nicely kept and the management is friendly. It is well located on the parque central and has an airy central area.

Hotel Gómez (☎ 773 0868; Calle 21 de Junio; s/d fan & TV US$8.10/12.10; [P]) Simple rooms have wooden bed-frames with attractive headboards while the bathrooms boast real shower heads and hot water. There is also cable TV.

Hotel Sand River (☎ 773 3378; Parque Central; s/d US$7.30/14.50) Its walls could do with a white-wash and the bathrooms are cramped, but the 2nd-floor rooms have a pretty location overlooking the attractive parque central. Rooms include cable TV.

Eating

Several cheap *comedores* are between the plaza and the central park.

Pollos Kike No 1 (☎ 773 1281; Calle 21 de Junio; mains US$3; 🕑 9am-9pm) Next door to Pizzería Venezia, this place serves simpler fare (you can choose between chicken and chips, and, er, chicken and chips). Plates are stacked high and the setting is pleasant.

Chicken's Friends (☎ 773 1122; Parque Central; dishes US$3; 🕑 9am-9:30pm) Chicken could use some

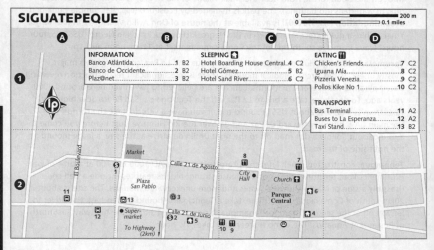

SIGUATEPEQUE

INFORMATION		SLEEPING 🛏		EATING 🍴	
Banco Atlántida	1 B2	Hotel Boarding House Central	4 C2	Chicken's Friends	7 C2
Banco de Occidente	2 B2	Hotel Gómez	5 B2	Iguana Mía	8 C2
Plaz@net	3 B2	Hotel Sand River	6 C2	Pizzería Venezia	9 C2
				Pollos Kike No 1	10 C2

TRANSPORT	
Bus Terminal	11 A2
Buses to La Esperanza	12 A2
Taxi Stand	13 B2

0   200 m
0   0.1 miles

El Boulevard

Market

Calle 21 de Agosto

Plaza San Pablo

Super-market

Calle 21 de Junio

To Highway (2km)

City Hall

Church

Parque Central

new friends here – chopped up, fried and served for three bucks a plate.

Iguana Mía (☎ 773 4955; Calle 21 de Agosto; dishes US$2-6; ☉ 7am-8:30pm) Popular with expats and volunteers, this vibrant Mexican restaurant has an eclectic menu with large portions.

Pizzería Venezia (☎ 773 2999; Calle 21 de Junio; dishes US$3.50-5.50; ☉ 9am-9pm) As well as excellent authentic pizzas, this venue dishes up good sandwiches with all the trimmings. It has outdoor seating and a simple interior with classic red-check tablecloths.

Getting There & Away

Most buses going between Tegucigalpa and San Pedro Sula will drop you on the main highway. A taxi into town costs US$1.90 or you can walk the 2km to the center.

Buses depart from an open lot a block west of Plaza San Pablo. Frequent departures run to San Pedro Sula from 4:35am to 4pm (US$2.50), while direct buses leave for Tegucigalpa every hour or even more often, from 4am to 5pm (US$2.20, 2½ hours, 117km).

There are also buses to La Esperanza (US$2) at 5:10am, 6:15am and 7am, which leave half a block west of the plaza in front of the Hospedaje Central (the owners operate the service).

LA ESPERANZA

pop 5480

Up in the highlands, slow-paced La Esperanza is known for its markets. The Lenca influence is strong here – you will see many women wearing the distinctive, colorful Lenca head dress. Don't forget your woolies – this is the highest town in Honduras and the cold can bite. In fact, the climate here allows a huge variety of fruits and vegetables to be grown, from strawberries to peaches and apples. La Esperanza is the capital of the Intibucá department, one of the poorest in Honduras, and attracts a large number of foreign volunteers, from Christian groups building latrines to general practitioners helping out in area clinics.

Orientation & Information

West is uphill in this town. There are few street names or numbers, but just about everything is on the main street or on the parallel street. The bus terminals are on the main road near the bottom of the hill, the parque central at the top. An old, slightly dilapidated church is on the east side. Check your email at Brassa-

vola.Net (Parque Central; per hr US$0.85; ☉ 9am-8pm) on the south side of the parque central. Hondutel and the post office are on the west of the same block, side by side like an old married couple. On the hill at the far western end of town is **La Gruta**, a small cave now converted into a chapel. For more on the tourist possibilities in the area, ask for Margoth López at the Restaurant La Hacienda.

Sleeping & Eating

Hotel Mejia Batres (☎ 783 7086; s/d with fold-up bed & shared bathroom US$4.30/7.60, tr with bathroom & TV US$16.20) Very convenient (just one block west of the parque central), this hotel has simple, clean rooms, especially the triples. Think twice about sharing a bathroom – flip-flops may not be enough.

Casa Mia Hostal (☎ 783 3778; s/d/tr US$9.75/18.40/22.70) Brand-new rooms without a hint of wear and tear also boast hot-water showers, enough space to swing a couple of cats (if you are so inclined) and a sweet little downstairs *comedor* (called Delis House) for those peckish moments. It is on the road that runs east to west, a block north of the parque central.

Restaurant La Hacienda (☎ 783 0244; mains US$3-6; ☉ 9am-10pm) A block west of the square, this is the most atmospheric place in town. The tables indoors are in a cute little dining room, liberally decorated with Lenca ceramics and tapestries, while the outdoor seating area is just as sweet. La Esperanza is not a hotspot for inventive cuisine and this is no different – choose from standard grills and tortilla fare.

Opalaca's (☎ 783 0503; dishes US$3-7; ☉ 10:30am-9:30pm) This place specializes in grills, which arrive sizzling in front of you. The colonial setting is handsome, although we wished they would turn some heating on and the terrible elevator-style piped music off. It is just west of the parque central.

Getting There & Away

Terminals are scattered in three different places, in the Honduran manner beloved of travelers and guidebook writers. For Tegucigalpa and San Pedro Sula, head to the **Transportes Carolina** (☎ 783 0521) terminal at the eastern end of town beyond the bridge. Buses to Marcala, Gracias and San Juan leave from a dirt lot by the *estadio* (stadium). Other local buses leave from the *mercado quemado* (burned market), a couple of blocks down

---

DISCOVER LENCA TRADITIONS

La Ruta Lenca, a series of villages stretching from Santa Rosa de Copán to Marcala and into El Salvador with a colorful indigenous presence, offers visitors the chance to learn about an array of deities, spirits and animals. These figure in the traditional Lenca *cosmovisión*, which offers the culture's explanation of the universe.

Shamans and healers play important roles in Lenca communities, each performing specific rituals and ceremonies. Animal sacrifice is sometimes practiced. Many modern Lenca communities have municipal governments, as well as an Alcaldía Auxiliar de la Vara Alta – who acts as a liaison between Lencans and the 'official' city government.

Animals often represent different qualities. Some communities still sprinkle ash around the house where a child is born; the animal that leaves its prints there will be the child's *nahual* (companion and protector) for life.

A few Lenca towns still practice the *guancasco*, a fascinating annual ceremony that confirms peace and friendship between neighbors. *Guancascos* take many forms, but typically include traditional costumes, processions and an elaborate exchange of greetings, statues of saints and other symbolic rites, including some introduced from Catholicism. The towns of **Yamaranguila** and **La Campa**, both on the **Ruta Lenca**, host *guancascos*.

---

from the central park. A ride around town to the terminals costs US$0.70.

Some destinations: Gracias (US$3.30, four hours, departs at noon, but arrive early as the minibus leaves when full); Marcala (US$1.75, 1½ hours, at 6:15am, 11:15am and 1pm); San Juan (US$1.70, two hours, at 11:30am, 2:15pm and 4:30pm); San Pedro Sula (US$4.35, 3½ hours, six departures between 4:30am and 1:30pm); take any San Pedro or Tegucigalpa bus to Siguatepeque (US$2.25, 1½ hours); and Tegucigalpa (US$4.40, 3½ hours, nine departures between 4:15am and 2pm).

Pickups to San Juan and Gracias are also an option.

MARCALA

pop 10,700

Marcala is a highland town with a strong indigenous heritage – it lies at the southern end of Honduras' Ruta Lenca. Although it looks unremarkable, the town is in prime coffee country – and there are several opportunities to see the world's favorite bean being harvested and prepared. Several hikes in the surrounding area take in picturesque waterfalls and caves.

Orientation & Information

There are no street names in Marcala. Orient yourself at the central park. The town hall is on the west side, while there is a small church to the north. One block northeast of the park are the post office and Hondutel. Just along from them is BanhCafé bank, which changes

small amounts of American cash. Several internet cafés are around town.

Cooperativa RAOS (☎ 764 5181) At this place, Miriam Elizabeth Pérez (Betty) is a mine of information on local sights.

Glob@l online (per hr US$1.10; ☺ 9am-8pm) Internet access, near the buses to La Esperanza (one block east and two north of the parque central).

Police (☎ 764 5715)

Tourist office (☺ 8am-noon & 1-5pm Thu-Tue) With a slate-tiled roof, this office stands in the southeast corner of the parque central.

Activities

La Estanzuela is one of several hikes in the area, going to a pretty waterfall and a cavern, **La Cueva del Gigante**, which has prehistoric paintings. It is on the way to La Esperanza. Ask how to get there at the tourist office.

Cooperativa RAOS (☎ 764 5181; tours per person US$5-13.50; ☺ 8am-noon & 1-4pm Mon-Fri, 8am-noon Sat), half a block north of the parque central, is Honduras' first organic farming cooperative. It sells its produce (excellent, as this author can personally vouch) and can arrange plantation tours.

Sleeping & Eating

Hotel San Miguel (☎ 764 5793; r US$8.10; **P**) A friendly, family-run guesthouse with bare rooms, electric showers and a cheap little *comedor* that uses a wood-fired oven for cooking. It also serves strong regional coffee. It's two blocks north then 2½ blocks east of the parque central, just beyond a whitewashed church.

Hotel Jerusalén Medina (☎ 764 5909; s/d US$13.65/17; P) Less personal but more upscale, this hotel has three floors facing a concrete car park. The rooms are well kept, with thick bedspreads and private bathrooms. It is one block north and two blocks east of the central park.

Casa Gloria (☎ 764 5869; dishes US$2.50-4; �---9am-9pm) At the southwestern corner of the park, this stately terracotta-colored spot offers buffet meals and service with a smile, in an old colonial-style house decorated with some fine Lenca ceramics.

Getting There & Away

Buses bound for San Miguel, El Salvador (US$3.50, 5½ hours), via Perquín (US$2.50, three hours), leave from a block west of the park at 5am and noon. There should be no fee to leave or enter Honduras, although other border posts do charge. The Honduran immigration office was closed when we crossed so it was free, but it might be different when open. There is no Salvadoran immigration post.

To get to Tegucigalpa, Transportes Lila, 1½ blocks east of the park, has departures at 8:45am, 10:30am and 2pm (US$2.90, four hours). The 8:45am service is *ejecutivo* (luxury class) and costs US$3.50. For San Pedro Sula, the same company has one service at 5:15am (US$4, five hours).

Buses to La Esperanza (US$1.60) leave at 6:45am, 11:15pm and 3pm from the basketball court across from BanhCafé, although this bus can be unreliable. Pickups from the Texaco gas station on the main highway turnoff outside of town are the alternative, and charge the same. Buses to Comayagua (US$1.80, 2½ hours) leave from two blocks east and one block south of the park at 6:30am, 8am, 11am, 1pm and 3pm, or you can connect in La Paz.

CUEVAS DE TAULABÉ

On the highway about 25km north of Siguatepeque and 20km south of the Lago de Yojoa is the entrance to the **Cuevas de Taulabé** (CA-5 Hwy, Km 140; adult/child US$2/0.55; �---8am-5pm), a network of underground caves with unusual stalactite and stalagmite formations. The entrance fee includes a guide. A tip may get you to some of the less visited areas. So far, the caves have been explored to a depth of 12km with no end in sight.

The first section of the caves have lights and a cement pathway; the pathway can be slippery, so wear appropriate shoes.

LAGO DE YOJOA

This picturesque lake lies 157km north of Tegucigalpa and 84km south of San Pedro Sula. It is a popular beauty spot with abundant birdlife. There are some spectacular wildlife-spotting opportunities, especially on the less developed west side, where there is also an excellent place to stay with its own microbrewery. More than 400 different bird species – over half the total in Honduras – have been spotted around the lake. One birder counted 37 different species in a single tree while sitting on his hotel terrace in the morning. Quetzals are also regularly sighted around here.

Fishing on the lake is good, especially black bass. Bring your own tackle, as it might not be available locally. Hotels around the lake can arrange boat trips.

The **Asociación de Municipios del Lago de Yojoa y su Área de Influencia** (Amuprolago; www.lagodeyojoa .info; ☎ 963 7335, 988 2300; �---8am-4pm Mon-Fri) may be a mouthful, but it is useful, with detailed current information about the lake and surrounding areas. It is just south of the town of Monte Verde.

Sleeping & Eating

D&D Bed & Breakfast and Micro Brewery (☎ 396 1279, 994 9719; www.dd-brewery.com; s/d US$8.70/11.90; camping per person US$2.20, cabins from US$21.60; ☒ ☒) Oregonian brewmaster Robert Dale set up this highly original and attractive place to stay, 2km from Peña Blanca, where accommodations vary from camping to an upscale cabin with Jacuzzi. The lush gardens have 73 different orchid species, while the on-site microbrewery produces some of Honduras' best beers. The good outdoor restaurant has homemade coffee and sodas. Oh, and you don't have to close your mouth when you shower – the running water is purified here, a legacy of the brewing process. Bird-spotting tours (US$20 to US$25) – either to the lake or spectacular Parque Nacional Montaña Santa Bárbara – can also be organized. The Mochito bus from the main San Pedro Sula terminal drops you at the entrance.

Hotel Agua Azul (☎ 991 7244; hotelaquaazul@emv .hn; r with fan/air-con US$20/29; P ☒) There is a fine restaurant and a pool with a lake panorama to go with the simple, clean wooden cabins at the Agua Azul. It's on the north side of the lake, 3km from the main highway.

El Cortijo del Lago (☎ 608 5527; johnachater@yahoo .com; dm US$5.50, cabañas US$11-16, r US$22-27) In a

---

EXPLORE MORE AROUND LAGO DE YOJOA

Pulhapanzak is a short (17.5km) hop from Lago de Yojoa. With a little more effort, you can get to more remote but rewarding ruins and mountainous wildlife refuges.

■ **Pulhapanzak**, a magnificent 43m waterfall on the Río Lindo, is an easy day trip from San Pedro (60km away), surrounded by some lush, well-preserved forest. It's a popular spot for swimming and can be crowded on weekends and holidays. You can camp here if you have your own gear. Entry to the area costs US$1.65. From San Pedro, take a bus to Mochito (US$1.65, one hour) and ask the driver to let you off at San Buenaventura. From there it is a well-marked 15-minute walk. The last bus back passes through San Buenaventura around 4pm.

■ **Parque Eco-Arqueológico Los Naranjos** (☎ 650 0004; admission US$5.40), northwest of the lake, was first occupied around 600 or 700 BC, and is thought to be the largest Lencan archaeological site. Excavation is still in its initial stages. The park includes trails for viewing semiexcavated ruins and to observe plants and wildlife, particularly birds. The D&D Bed & Breakfast (p359) is close to the park and can arrange guided tours.

■ East of the lake (and across the highway), **Parque Nacional Cerro Azul Meambar** (☎ 608 5510, in Tegucigalpa 773 2027; www.paghonduras.org/pancam.html; admission US$2) is a well-equipped and underexplored park with kilometers of trails leading to waterfalls, caves with ancient artifacts and untouched cloud forest. There is also a visitors center with dorm lodging, and camping gear is available for rent. The park entrance is down a turnoff from La Guama on the main CA-5 highway. Frequent pickups head to Santa Elena. From there, walking to the park's Los Pinos Lodge takes about one hour.

■ West of the lake, isolated **Parque Nacional Santa Bárbara** contains Honduras' second-highest peak, **Montaña de Santa Bárbara** (2744m). You will need a guide to visit the park, which is only minimally developed. To visit head to the town of San Luis Planes; a bus to San Luis Planes leaves Peña Blanca at 10:30am daily. Once there, ask for **Adán Teruel** (☎ 674 3304), who is known as the best guide in the area (US$8 to US$10 per day). He can sort out lodging too. You can also arrange tours at D&D Bed & Breakfast (see p359).

---

lovely setting right on the lake, this new option has a restaurant with good vegetarian options, as well as canoes and sailboats for rent. The dorms are unflashy, but tidy and well kept. Make sure you check out the sunroom upstairs. El Cortijo is 2km from the La Guama turnoff.

Getting There & Away

The easiest access to the lake is from San Pedro Sula. Get a bus to El Mochito from the main terminal (US$1.60, 1½ hours, every 45 minutes) to San Buenaventura (where the Pulhapanzak Falls are located; see above) and Los Naranjos.

The last bus back to San Pedro Sula leaves about 4pm. For the north side of the lake, change in Peña Blanca. From Tegucigalpa, get a San Pedro Sula–bound bus to La Guama. From there, take a bus or pickup from the left-hand turnoff toward Peña Blanca (US$0.50, every 25 minutes) where you can make your connection.

SANTA BÁRBARA
pop 15,800

About 53km west of Lago de Yojoa, Santa Bárbara, capital of the department of the same name, is a medium-sized colonial-era town with a striking cathedral. The large **Boarding House Moderno** (☎ 643 2203; s/d with fan US$8/12, with air-con US$13.50/19) has spacious but slightly dated rooms. All have cable TV.

You will have your most memorable meal at **Mesón Casa Blanca** (☎ 643 2839; mains US$2.50-3.50; ⏱ 7am-8:30pm). It is like eating in a family home in a time warp, with stuffed deer heads and old photos on the wall. Typical Honduran dishes are served.

Roads connect Santa Bárbara with the Tegucigalpa-San Pedro Sula and the San Pedro Sula-Nueva Ocotepeque highways. You can get a bus directly to Tegucigalpa from Santa Bárbara (202km) with Los Junqueños bus company, which has its own terminal 1½ blocks north of the parque central. From the main terminal, one block west of the parque central, buses run every half hour to San Pedro Sula until 5pm (US$2.50, 1½ to two hours, 94km).

SAN PEDRO SULA
pop 516,700

San Pedro Sula might play second fiddle to Tegucigalpa in terms of population and political matters, but when it comes to business and industry, it calls the shots. Often simply called San Pedro, the city is Honduras' economic engine-room, generating almost two-thirds of the country's GDP. Its airport is the country's most modern. Its restaurants and nightlife arguably outstrip those of the capital. Unfortunately, its gangland crime is also on a par.

Part of San Pedro's economic success is geographical: Exports are handled easily with the port of Puerto Cortés under an hour away. San Pedro originally made its wealth from bananas or *oro verde* (green gold) as locals call it. However, in 1998 flooding caused by Hurricane Mitch wiped out many of the plantations. Currently San Pedro makes its readies from the *maquila* (clothes-weaving) factories. The industry is not without controversy – high-profile cases in the US have highlighted some dubious sweatshop practices. There is little doubt, however, that the business is a vital source of income for many *sanpedranos* (residents of San Pedro).

San Pedro is extremely hot and humid from around April to September. The rainy season runs from May to November.

Orientation

Downtown San Pedro is circled by a highway bypass, the Circunvalación, which is lined with shopping malls, restaurants and banks. Within that circle, central San Pedro is flat with *avenidas* (avenues) running north-south and *calles* running east-west. The numbering begins where Primera (1a) Av crosses 1a Calle. From there the numbered *avenidas* and *calles* extend out in every direction: northeast (noreste, or NE), northwest (noroeste, or NO), southeast (sureste, or SE) or southwest (suroeste, or SO).

Every address has a numbered *calle* or *avenida* and is further specified by its quadrant. As ever, the bustling parque central marks the hub of the city.

The spectacular Merendón mountain chain looms to the west.

> ### GETTING INTO TOWN FROM THE AIRPORT
>
> San Pedro's Villeda Morales Airport, the largest and most modern in the country, is about 15km east of town. Coming from the airport, there is no direct bus but you can get a taxi just to the airport turnoff (US$3) and catch a bus into town. Otherwise, taxis cost about US$8 from the airport to town (but US$7 going the other way).

Information
BOOKSTORES

The **Pipas y Puros** (Parque Central) tobacco shop in the Gran Hotel Sula has a small selection of expensive magazines in English, and sometimes has day-old US newspapers.

EMERGENCY

Tourist police (☎ 550 3472; cnr 12a Av NO & 1a Calle O; ☽ 24hr)

INTERNET ACCESS

Internet y Más (5a Calle SO btwn 7a & 8a Avs SO; per hr US$0.80; ☽ 8:30am-7pm Mon-Sat)

Servicio Multiple (cnr 3a Calle SO & 5a Av SO; per hr US$0.55; ☽ 8am-8pm Mon-Sat) Cheapest internet in town is up a narrow staircase.

MONEY

The city's malls have banks with ATMs, and there's one at the Hedman Alas bus station.

BAC/Credomatic (5a Av NO btwn 1a & 2a Calles NO; ☽ 8am-7pm Mon-Fri, 8am-2pm Sat) Exchanges traveler's checks and has a Unibanc ATM. Also has a branch with ATM at the airport.

Banco Atlántida (Parque Central) This bank changes traveler's checks and has an ATM.

LAUNDRY

Lavandería Lavamatic (8a Av NO btwn 2a & 3a Calles NO; per lb US$0.40; ☽ 9am-6pm Mon-Sat)

POST

Post office (9a Calle & 3a Av SO; ☽ 8am-6pm Mon-Fri, 8am-noon Sat)

TELEPHONE

Hondutel (4a Av SO & 4a Calle SO; ☽ 7am-8:30pm) Expensive local and international phone service.

Servicio Multiple (cnr 3a Calle SO & 5a Av SO; ☽ 8am-8pm Mon-Sat) Good-value internet-based phone calls (to Europe US$0.20).

SAN PEDRO SULA

To Tamarindo Hostal (200m); Deriva (200m); Baleadas Express (600m)

To Confetti's (550m)

0 ——— 200 m
0 ——— 0.1 miles

To Pecos Bill (800m); Comisariato Los Andes (800m)

To Hostal E & N (300m)

INFORMATION
American Express..................(see 6)
BAC/Credomatic.......................1 C2
Banco Atlántida (ATM)..........2 C3
Fundación Ecologista..........(see 13)
Hondutel.................................3 C3
Internet y Más.........................4 B4
Lavandería Lavamatic............5 B2
Mundirama.............................6 C3
Pipas y Puros......................(see 18)
Post Office.............................7 C5
Servicio Multiple....................8 C3
Tourist Police.........................9 A2

SIGHTS & ACTIVITIES
Cathedral...............................10 C3
Mercado de Artesanías
  Guamilito.........................(see 11)
Mercado Guamilito...............11 B1
Museo de Antropología e Historia
  de San Pedro Sula..............12 C2
Museo de la Naturaleza........13 A2

SLEEPING 🛏
Hotel Real..............................14 B4
Hotel San José.......................15 B4
Hotel San Juan......................16 B4
Hotel Terraza.........................17 B3

Stadium

To Puerto Cortés (64km);

To Mango Steen (400m); Taca/Isleña (800m); Mesoamerica Travel (1km); Coca Cola sign (2.5km); Parque Nacional Cusuco (20km); Puerto Cortés (64km)

Parque Central

Train Station

To Avis (200m); Villeda Morales Airport (15km); Tela (87km); La Ceiba (190km)

To American Airlines (200m)

To Continental Airlines (200m)

To Multicines (200m); Cinemark (1km)

To Terminal Metropolitana Autobuses (Metropolitan Bus Terminal (5km)

EATING 🍴
Café Skandia...........................18 C3
Cafetería Pamplona................19 C3
El Fogoncito............................20 A2
La Dolce Vita..........................21 A2
Pizzería Italia..........................22 B2

DRINKING 🍷
Klein Bohemia........................23 B4

ENTERTAINMENT 🎬
Multicines Plaza Sula.............24 A2

TRANSPORT
Aerolíneas Sosa......................25 B3
Atlantic Airlines.....................26 A2
Buses to Cofradía...................27 B5
Buses to Progreso & Airport
  Turnoff...............................28 D3
Diana Express/ El Rey Express.29 A5
Transportes Casasola.............30 B4
Transportes Citul....................31 B4

Transportes Congolón............32 A5
Transportes Cotuc/Cotrailbal..33 D4
Transportes Hedman Alas......34 B2
Transportes Impala................35 D4
Transportes King Quality......36 A3
Transportes Sultana...........(see 38)
Transportes Tela Express........37 D3
Transportes Torito &
  Copanecos........................38 B5

HONDURAS

TOURIST INFORMATION
Fundación Ecologista (☎ 557 6598; 12a Av NO at 1a Calle NO; ☺ 8am-noon & 1-5pm Mon-Sat) Best place to go for information on Parque Nacional Cusuco.

TRAVEL AGENCIES
Mesoamerica Travel (☎ 557 8447; www .mesoamerica-travel.com; 8a Calle & 32a Avenida NO) Helpful, professional and knowledgeable; does interesting upscale tours, including a trip to a banana plantation.
Mundirama (☎ 552 3400; Edificio Martinez Valenzuela, 2a Calle SE) Located south of the cathedral, this is a travel agency and American Express agent; will hold mail for six months for Amex card and check users.

Dangers & Annoyances
San Pedro Sula is a very dynamic city with a lot going for it. It also has a serious crime and gang problem. Mostly it is gang member on gang member and travelers rarely get caught up. However, do be cautious. Avoid being flashy with your belongings (save the iPod for the long-distance bus journey) and dress with restraint (save the shorts for the beach). Taxis are a good idea, especially after dark. Downtown is dodgy after nightfall, as is the area east and south of it (where many of the budget hotels are). If you are confronted by muggers, the safest thing to do is cooperate.

San Pedro also bears the unfortunate label of the AIDS capital of Central America. Practicing safe sex is always important, and nowhere more so than here.

Sights & Activities
San Pedro's **cathedral**, which overlooks the parque central, is quite an ugly, blocky building, built in 1949, with scuffed yellow paint within. It is unkempt but a haven of peace away from the street noise. The fine **Museo de Antropología e Historia de San Pedro Sula** (☎ 557 1874; cnr 3a Av NO & 4a Calle NO; admission US$2; ☺ 9am-4pm Mon & Wed-Sat, 9am-3pm Sun) walks visitors through the history of the Valle de Sula from its pre-Columbine days to the modern era. It exhibits hundreds of archaeological artifacts in excellent condition, from the surrounding valley. Signage is in English and Spanish. Its entrance is 'guarded' by two large obsolete cannons.

The **Museo de la Naturaleza** (☎ 557 6598; 1a Calle 0 near 12a Av NO; admission US$1.10; ☺ 8am-4pm Mon-Fri, to noon Sat) has academic Spanish-language exhibits covering everything from paleontology to ecology.

Look west in San Pedro Sula, and your eyes will inevitably be drawn to the giant **Coca-Cola sign** up in the hills. Walking up there is a fine trek (three hours there and back at a leisurely pace). There is an excellent panorama of San Pedro and its green streets as a reward. To get there, simply follow 1a Calle west until it turns to the right and crosses a bridge. After the bridge, turn left at 2a Calle, go past an entrance barrier and carry on climbing. Your surroundings swiftly change from city to jungle. Amusingly, the *pulpería* (corner store) just beyond the giant letters only sells one type of cola drink: Pepsi.

In the last week of June, San Pedro celebrates a large **festival** in honor of its founding and the day of San Pedro.

Sleeping
San Pedro's budget options are mostly in a downtown area that gets dodgy after dark. There is now also an excellent hostel in a good part of town.

Hostal Tamarindo (☎ 557 0123; www.tamarindohostel.com; 9a Calle A btwn 10a & 11a Avs NO; dm US$8; r with air-con US$25; P ☒ ☐) A very welcome addition to the San Pedro accommodation scene, this friendly, colorful, safe hostel is a bit of a trek from the center but is in one of the best neighborhoods. It has a fresh, funky feel with bright murals, draped international flags and wood carvings. There is a 2nd-floor deck with hammocks, a large common room and a well-equipped kitchen. Rooms come with clean linen and cable TV. The owners are a lively, fun and helpful Honduran couple, who play in an up-and-coming band. English, German and Spanish are spoken.

Hotel San Juan (☎ 553 1488; 6a Calle SO 35-A btwn 5a & 6a Avs SO; d with/without bathroom US$9.80/5.10) A rabbit warren of a building in the packed, noisy core of town, this is an option if other, better places are full. Mattresses sag, but the basic rooms are kept reasonably clean. Some are windowless, others open onto a terrace.

Hotel San José (☎ 557 1208; 6a Av SO btwn 5a & 6a Calles SO; s/d US$7.60/10.30) Spartan, charmless medium-sized rooms branch off a long wide corridor. There's not a trimming in sight – it's a bed for the night and nothing more.

Hotel Real (☎ 550 7929; 6a Av btwn 6a & 7a Calle SO; d US$15.20, with air-con US$21.60; ☒) Easily the best value, most comfortable and secure of the central options, this hotel has clean rooms with slightly faded décor, all with cable TV.

They look out onto an attractive covered courtyard complete with a thatched bar. Cold water only.

Hotel Terraza (☎ 550 3108; 6a Av SO btwn 4a & 5a Calles SO; s/d US$13/21.75, r with air-con US$30; 🖳) Its rooms are airy, although the bright green décor might not be to everyone's taste. Private bathrooms have hot water. There is also a highly recommended, lempira-friendly restaurant that does a mean seafood soup and an excellent breakfast. This is a good central option.

Hostal E & N (☎ 552 5731; www.hostaleyn.com; cnr 5a Calle & 15a Av NO; s/d/tr with breakfast US$30/32/34; 🅿 🖳 🖳) This is a reasonable option if Hostal Tamarindo is full – it is a little further west in the same good part of town. Rooms can feel a bit small (they pack the beds in) but it includes air-con and hot water. It is a lot better value if you are in a group.

Eating

San Pedro Sula has a wide range of eating places catering to all budgets and a surprisingly broad range of cuisines. Many more upmarket places, as well as US fast-food franchises, are on Circunvalación. There is a whole bunch of cheap and cheerful *comedores* at Mercado Guimilito.

Baleadas Express (☎ 553 6208; 13a Calle NO btwn 11a & 12a Avs NO; meals US$1-2.50; 🕑 7am-1pm & 4-10:30pm Mon-Sat, 7am-noon Sun) Addictive and exceptionally good-value Honduran fast-food joint – there are no beef burger staples here, just giant *baleadas* with the filling of your choice. And there is plenty to choose from, including good vegetarian options.

Cafetería Pamplona (☎ 550 2639; Parque Central; dishes US$2-5; 🕑 7am-8pm Mon-Sat, 8am-8pm Sun) A bit of a San Pedro institution, this is a diner with a Honduran twist. It is good value although service can be offhand. Serves tasty, generously portioned *típica*.

Café Skandia (☎ 552 9999; Gran Hotel Sula, Parque Central; dishes US$3-5; 🕑 24hr) There are several good reasons to come to this café. It is cheap, bright and central, service is fast and pleasant, and you can have a waffle by an outdoor pool lined with palm trees. And, as a café that never sleeps, you get all sorts of characters passing through, from tourists and businessmen to diplomats and sugar daddies with their 'companions.' It's a slice of life to go with your sandwich.

Pecos Bill (☎ 557 5744; 6a-7a Calles NO & 14 Av NO; mains US$6-9; 🕑 11am-midnight Tue-Sun, 11am-3pm Mon) This is a strange, very Honduran combination –

a car wash alongside a massive open-air restaurant and bar. It does nothing by halves: from the huge trees that grow through the middle to the big grills that sizzle in front of you. It is run by an ex-professional soccer player and well worth a trek out – although beware the terrible karaoke.

Deriva (☎ 516 1012; 9a Calle btwn 10a & 11a Avs NO; mains US$5-12; 🕑 noon-9:30pm Mon-Sat) One of the classiest restaurants in Honduras, all soft background music and candlelight, this is the place to come for a blow-out if you are flying home tomorrow. With a specialist wine shop next door, grape is definitely the way to wash down the excellent Peruvian cuisine, although there are (expensive) imported beers on offer too.

Also check out:

La Dolce Vita (☎ 516 1547; 12a Av btwn 2a & 3a Calles NO; cones US$0.80; 🕑 1-9pm Tue-Sun) Craving proper ice-cream? This supercute little ice-cream parlor is the genuine article, run by a friendly Italian couple. The *gelateria* with myriad flavors is the best way to combat the tropical heat. There are also snacks and delicatessen.

Pizzería Italia (☎ 550 7094; 1a Calle O & 7a Av NO; dishes US$4.50-7.30; 🕑 10am-10pm) A garlic waft tempts you as soon as you pass between the two security guards into a cool air-con interior. Pizzas are a luxury in Honduras – these are reasonable, but not particularly cheap.

El Fogoncito (☎ 553 3000; 1a Calle O at 11a Av NO; mains US$5-10; 🕑 lunch & dinner) Reliable Tex-Mex is dished up at this popular Mexican restaurant. Its cantina style includes all the usual suspects from tacos to fajitas, as well as some more adventurous options. The bar makes it a good drinking option too.

Comisariato Los Andes (Av Circunvalación; 6a Calle NO; 🕑 8am-8:30pm) A supermarket good for cheap supplies.

Drinking & Nightlife

Klein Bohemia (☎ 552 3172; www.kleinbohemia.com; 7a Calle SO at 8a Av SO; 🕑 4:30pm-midnight Wed-Sat) Set up by Swiss expats who have since moved on, this central boho oasis is still going strong. Its bleak downtown setting is not promising, but appearances are deceptive. Venture to the upstairs bar, and you will find a cultured, young crowd. There are regular live bands and showings of independent films.

Mango Steen (22a Av btwn 1a & 2a Calle NO; 🕑 lunch, 6pm-midnight Mon-Sat) Modern lounge bar meets tropical garden here in this sleek nightspot that doubles as a Thai food restaurant. It attracts an international crowd. It is just beyond the Circunvalación – look for the sign on 1a Calle.

Confetti's (Av Circunvalación, near 7a Av NO; cover US$2-5; 🕑 9pm-3am Tue-Thu, to 5am Fri-Sun) This is one of the most enduring nightclubs in San Pedro Sula. House and techno keep the dance floor shaking.

Entertainment

There are many places around town, including Klein Bohemia (opposite), that show films. **Multicines Plaza Sula** (10a Av NO btwn 3a & 4a Calles NO) shows fairly recent Hollywood flicks for US$2.20.

Mall theaters include **Cinemark** (City Mall) and **Multicines** (Multiplaza Mall) with tickets for US$2 to US$3.

Shopping

Mercado Guamilito (8a & 9a Avs & 6a & 7a Calles NO; ☼ 7am-5pm Mon-Sat, 7am-noon Sun) is a huge market that runs the gamut of stalls from fruits and vegetables to household goods, tailors, and shoe-repairers. At the front, it also houses the **Mercado de Artesanías Guamilito**, with a wide selection of arts, handicrafts and gifts from all over Honduras, Guatemala and El Salvador.

Getting There & Away

AIR

Aeropuerto Internacional Ramón Villeda Morales is 15km east of San Pedro Sula (about a US$12 taxi ride). It is a larger, busier airport than the one serving Tegucigalpa. It is served by daily direct flights to all major cities in Central America; and several to US cities. Domestically it has flights to Tegucigalpa, La Ceiba and the Bay Islands.

International airlines:

American Airlines (☎ 553 3508, at airport 668 3244; Edificio Banco Ficohsa, Av Circunvalación at 5a Calle SO)

Continental (☎ 557 4141, airport 668 3208; Edificio Versailles, Av Circunvalación btwn 7a & 7a A Calles SO)

TACA (☎ 550 8222, airport 668 3292; fax 668 3333; Av Circunvalación 13 at 13a Av NO)

Domestic airlines:

Atlantic Airlines (☎ 557 7270, airport 668 7310; Plaza Monaco, 10a Av NO)

Aerolineas Sosa (☎ /fax 550 6545 & 550 6548; 1a Calle O btwn 7a & 8a Av SO; ☼ 8am-noon & 1-5pm Mon-Fri, 8am-noon Sat)

Isleña (☎ 516 1061, airport 668 3333; Av Circunvalación 13 at 13a Av NO)

BUS

San Pedro is a major land transportation hub; see p366 for details of major bus services. As in many Honduran cities, many bus companies operate from their own station –

although there is now a larger terminal, Terminal Metropolitana de Autobuses (Metropolitan Bus Terminal), 5km south of the center, built to gather all the companies together and relieve city congestion. Not all bus companies were operating from there at the time of research, although the number is growing. Of those, most still have services from their downtown terminals, but some companies do operate just from the terminal (most importantly those going to Pulhapanzak Falls). If you do need to get to the terminal, take any bus down 2a Av SE (US$0.20) or take a taxi for around US$2.50.

In San Pedro Sula, the terminals are clustered south of the parque central. Most are within walking distance of each other. The luxury lines, Transportes King Quality and Hedman Alas, have terminals west of the park; see the map for locations. The free magazine *Honduras Tips* has a useful bus routes section.

International Buses

International bus lines **Transportes Hedman Alas** (☎ 557 3477; 3a Calle NO btwn 7a & 8a Avs NO) is an expensive luxury line with services to Guatemala City and Antigua. **Transportes King Quality** (☎ 553 4547; cnr 2a Calle SO & 9a Av SO) has good service that is less harsh on the wallet. It departs to San Salvador at 1pm (US$28, seven hours) with a connection to Guatemala City. **Transportes La Sultana** (☎ 553 4930) goes to San Salvador (US$17.20, six hours, 6:15am); it's less expensive but less comfortable.

Getting Around

BUS

The fare on local buses is US$0.20, although limit your use where possible. They are subject to frequent robberies. There is no direct bus to the airport, but you can get on any El Progreso bus and ask the driver to let you off at the airport turnoff. From there, it's a long walk (25 minutes) with no shade; if you have bags, consider a taxi.

CAR & MOTORCYCLE

Car-rental agencies in San Pedro Sula:

Avis (☎ 553 0888, airport 668 3164; fax 668 3167; 1a Calle btwn 6a & 7a Av NE)

Budget (☼ airport 509 8000)

Econo rent a car (☼ airport 668 1881)

Hertz (☼ airport 668 3155)

Molinari Rent A Car (☎ 553 2639; Parque Central) At the Gran Hotel Sula.

HONDURAS

BUS SERVICES FROM SAN PEDRO SULA

Destination	Bus Line	Phone	Fare	Type	Duration
Agua Caliente	Transportes Congolón	553 1174	US$7.15	normal	5hr
*Comayagua	Transportes Diaz	no phone	US$2.70	direct	2hr
Copán Ruinas	Transportes Casasola	558 1659	US$5.50	direct	3hr
La Ceiba	Transportes Diana Express	550 8952	US$4.30	direct	3hr
	Transportes Hedman Alas	553 1631	US$8.30	ejecutivo	2½hr
Puerto Cortés	Transportes Impala	553 3111	US$1.60	direct	1hr
*Pulhapanzak & Lago de Yojoa	Transportes La Tiga	no phone	US$1.75	direct	1½hr
Santa Rosa de Copán	Transportes Torito	553 4930	US$4.20	direct	3hr
*Siguatepeque	Transportes Etul	520 7177	US$2.20	direct	3hr
Tegucigalpa	Transportes El Rey Express	550 8355	US$6	direct	4hr
	Transportes Hedman Alas	553 1361	US$8	ejecutivo	3½hr
Tela	Transportes Tela Express	551 8140	US$3	direct	1½hr
Trujillo	Transportes Cotuc/ Contraibal	557 8470	US$7.15	direct	5-6hr

*leaves from Terminal Metropolitana de Autobuses

TAXI

Average fares in town are around US$2. Taxis cost about US$7 to the airport.

PARQUE NACIONAL CUSUCO

Parque Nacional Cusuco (admission US$15; ☪ 8am-4:30pm), 45km west of San Pedro Sula in the impressive Merendón mountain range, is a cloud forest park. Its highest peak is **Cerro Jilinco** (2242m). Bird-watchers have spotted toucans and parrots, and quetzals are sometimes seen, mostly from April to June. There are also monkeys, reptiles and amphibians (a new species of toad was discovered here in 1981).

Five different trails are marked. The trails marked Quetzal and Las Minas lead up to **waterfalls** and **swimming holes**.

The **Fundación Ecologista** (☎ 557 6598; 12a Av NO at 1a Calle NO, San Pedro Sula; ☪ 8am-noon & 1-5pm Mon-Sat) is the best place to go for information on the park. You can also go there to book overnight accommodation in simple cabins, which are just before the park entrance. You'll need to book in advance.

Getting there by public transportation is a challenge, but it can be done. In San Pedro, catch a bus to Cofradía at the corner of 5a Av SO and 9a Calle SO (US$0.60, one hour, every 20 minutes); from Cofradía, pickups go up to the village of Buenos Aires (US$1.50, one hour), a few kilometers short of the park entrance and visitors center. The pickup times are irregular but they are most frequent in the morning. Making an early start is strongly recommended.

The park can be reached all year with 4WD vehicle; it is about two to three hours' drive from San Pedro Sula.

CARRETERA DE OCCIDENTE

From San Pedro Sula, the Carr de Occidente runs southwest to La Entrada, 124km away, where the road forks. One heads west to Copán Ruinas and the Guatemalan border, the other south to Santa Rosa de Copán, Nueva Ocotepeque and the two borders of Agua Caliente (Guatemala) and El Poy (El Salvador).

LA ENTRADA

La Entrada is an unattractive crossroads town with a reputation for narcotrafficking. Lots of buses and traffic pass through on the way northeast to San Pedro Sula, south to Santa Rosa de Copán and Nueva Ocotepeque, and southwest to Copán Ruinas.

Something must have gone wrong for you to be stuck in La Entrada, so treat yourself at **Hotel y Restaurant El San Carlos** (☎ 661 2228; r with air-con US$24; P ☒ ☒). There's an inviting pool here, and all rooms have private hot-water bathroom, cable TV and phone. It also has the best restaurant in town. The hotel is at the turnoff to Copán Ruinas (Hwy CA-11).

Buses pass through La Entrada frequently in all directions, stopping at the crossroads and/or in front of the bus terminal.

Some destinations: Copán Ruinas (US$2, two hours, 61km, hourly from 5am to 4:30pm), Nueva Ocotepeque (US$2.20, 3½ hours, 123km, every 20 minutes from 6am to 4pm), San Pedro Sula (*ordinario* US$1.80, 2½ hours, 124km, every 30 minutes; *directo* US$2.20, 1½ hours, express buses at 8:10am, 10:10am and 3:10pm), Santa Rosa de Copán (US$1.35, 1¼ hours, 44km, every 30 minutes from 6am to 6pm).

King Quality buses leave for San Salvador in El Salvador (at 8am daily); buses leave from Hotel y Restaurant El San Carlos.

COPÁN RUINAS

pop 6600

The beautiful, tranquil little town of Copán Ruinas, often simply called Copán, is about 1km from the famous Maya ruins of the same name. Sloping cobblestone streets, white adobe buildings with red-tile roofs and an attractive colonial church give it an aura of timeless peace. Although most travelers stop in Copán just for the ruins, the lovely surrounding countryside, good restaurants and nightlife are excellent reasons to stay longer.

Orientation

The renovated parque central, with the church on one side, is at the heart of town. The ruins are 1km outside of town, a pleasant 15-minute stroll along a footpath to one side of the highway to La Entrada. Las Sepulturas archaeological site is 2km further along.

Information

Banco Atlántida (8:30am-4pm Mon-Fri, 8:30am-11:30 Sat) On the parque central, changes US dollars and traveler's checks. It also has an ATM.

Banco BAC Credomatic (Parque Central) Has a Unibanc ATM that accepts Visa and MasterCard.

Hondutel (7am-9pm) Half a block south of the park.

La Casa de Todo (651 4185; 7:30am-9pm) Food, internet (per hour US$1) and laundry services (wash, dry and fold US$0.50 per lb) are all provided at this aptly named place.

Maya Connections (per hr US$1.40; 7:30am-6pm)

Post office (8am-noon & 2-4pm Mon-Fri, 8am-noon Sat) Half a block west of the park.

Dangers & Annoyances

The trail to Santa Rita Waterfalls used to be a no-go zone after several attacks in the area. It has been much safer of late, although it is still best to go in an organized group.

Sights

The fascinating Copán archaeological site, 1km outside of town, is the area's big draw. It and other fine places to visit in the area are covered on p371.

Museo de Arqueología Maya (651 4437; admission US$3; 8am-5pm Mon-Sun), on parque central, is a little dated but still worth a visit. The exhibits include excavated ceramics, fragments from the altars and the supports of the Maya ruins, an insight into the Maya's sophisticated use of calendars and a recreation of a female shaman's tomb. Some descriptions have English translations.

Enchanted Wings Butterfly House (651 4133; www.birdsofhonduras.com; adult/child US$5.50/2; 8am-4:30pm) is the brainchild of Robert Gallardo, a former Peace Corps volunteer and a renowned nature expert. The butterfly house is in a beautiful setting. There's something hypnotic about the butterflies and the spectacular tropical flora with around 200 species of orchids (which bloom from February to June). It is on the outskirts of town, walkable in about 20 minutes – or a short hop on mototaxi. You can also organize bird-watching tours from here.

Casa K'inich (651 4105; admission free; 8am-noon & 1-5pm Mon-Sun) includes an interactive recreation of the ancient football game practiced by the Copán residents more than a millennia ago. Displays are in three languages – English, Spanish and Chortí. Kids might get a kick out of the stela with a cutout hole to poke their heads through. There is a library and book exchange next door.

Mirador El Cuartel is a lookout, from the atmospheric ruins of an old jail, with a fine view of the town and surrounding countryside. Worth the climb.

The **Copán Ruinas fair** is celebrated from March 15 to 20.

Activities

Tour companies will also organize activities for you; see p369.

HORSERIDING

There is some fine horse-riding country around Copán Ruinas. It should be obvious, but don't hire a horse from a random kid on the street.

Horror stories abound of sickly horses, and lost or drunk guides trotting along the highway (whoopee!).

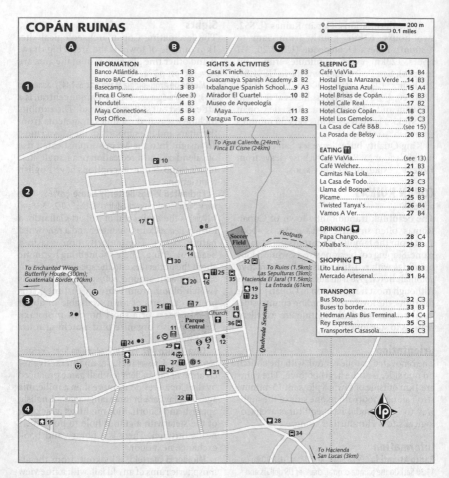

COPÁN RUINAS

INFORMATION			SLEEPING		
Banco Atlántida	1	B3	Café ViaVia	13	B4
Banco BAC Credomatic	2	B3	Hostal En la Manzana Verde	14	B3
Basecamp	3	B3	Hostel Iguana Azul	15	A4
Finca El Cisne	(see 3)		Hotel Brisas de Copán	16	B3
Hondutel	4	B3	Hotel Calle Real	17	B2
Maya Connections	5	B4	Hotel Clasico Copán	18	C3
Post Office	6	B3	Hotel Los Gemelos	19	C3
			La Casa de Café B&B	(see 15)	
SIGHTS & ACTIVITIES			La Posada de Belssy	20	B3
Casa K'inich	7	B3			
Guacamaya Spanish Academy	8	B2	EATING		
Ixbalanque Spanish School	9	A3	Café ViaVia	(see 13)	
Mirador El Cuartel	10	B2	Café Welchez	21	B3
Museo de Arqueología			Carnitas Nia Lola	22	B4
Maya	11	B3	La Casa de Todo	23	C3
Yaragua Tours	12	B3	Llama del Bosque	24	B3
			Picame	25	B3
			Twisted Tanya's	26	B4
			Vamos A Ver	27	B4
			DRINKING		
			Papa Chango	28	C4
			Xibalba's	29	B3
			SHOPPING		
			Lito Lara	30	B3
			Mercado Artesenal	31	B4
			TRANSPORT		
			Bus Stop	32	C3
			Buses to border	33	B3
			Hedman Alas Bus Terminal	34	C4
			Rey Express	35	C3
			Transportes Casasola	36	C3

0   200 m
0   0.1 miles

To Agua Caliente (24km);
Finca El Cisne (24km)

Soccer Field

Footpath

To Enchanted Wings
Butterfly House (300m);
Guatemala Border (10km)

To Ruins (1.5km);
Las Sepulturas (3km);
Hacienda El Jaral (11.5km);
La Entrada (61km)

Quebrada Sesesmil

Church

Parque Central

To Hacienda
San Lucas (3km)

Hacienda San Lucas (☎ 651 4495; www.haciendasan lucas.com) arranges excellent, hassle-free horse riding; see p372 for more on the hacienda. Your view from the saddle could take in Los Sapos, a local archaeological site. Three-hour rides cost around US$20.

Scenic, professional horseback tours, usually part of a day-long or overnight trip (see p371) are run by **Finca El Cisne** (☎ 651 4695; www .fincaelcisne.com). See also Tours, opposite.

BIRD-WATCHING

Rugged countryside around town means plenty of chances to spot hundreds of species of birds. Former Peace Corps volunteer Robert Gallardo, at Enchanted Wings Butterfly House, is one of the country's foremost experts on

wildlife, and has personally added 13 species to the list of birds found in Honduras. He organizes tours locally (per person per day US$25) and further afield. Also, see Tours, opposite.

Courses

Both the Spanish schools in Copán get very positive feedback. Prices listed here include a tour such as horseback riding or a trip to the Agua Caliente hot springs.

Guacamaya Spanish Academy (☎ 651 4360; www .guacamaya.com) Offers a package of 20 hours of one-on-one tuition for US$130. For US$70 more you can have full board and lodging with a local family. Its location is slightly more central than Ixbalanque's.

Ixbalanque Spanish School (☎ 651 4432; www .ixbalanque.com) In a swanky new location with terrific views, at the west end of town. It offers 20 hours of one-on-one instruction in Spanish for US$210 per week, including a homestay with a local family that provides three meals a day. Instruction only, for 20 hours per week, costs US$125.

Tours

A huge number of tours can be organized from Copán Ruinas. You can cave, tube a river, visit a Maya village, make tortillas or manufacture ceramics, plunge into hot springs, visit a coffee plantation or head off into the wilds.

Basecamp (☎ 651 4695; copan.honduras@viaviacafe .com; ☯ 8am-6pm) Run by the sparky people from Café ViaVia and the office is just opposite the restaurant. It offers nature hikes, horseback rides and an engaging alternative hike that lifts the lid on what life is really like for local residents. Some of the profits go toward a local education project. The only place to offer motorbike tours around the neighboring mountains. You can hire pickups here for US$30 a day. Shares an office with Finca El Cisne (p371), another excellent tour option.

Xukpi Tours (☎ 651 4435, 651 4503) Operated by the ebullient and extremely knowledgeable Jorge Barraza, who runs several ecological tours locally and further afield. His ruins and bird-watching tours are justly famous, and he'll do trips to all parts of Honduras and to Quiriguá (Guatemala).

Yaragua Tours (☎ 651 4147; www.yaragua.com) Half a block east of the park, leads tubing trips, hikes, horseback-riding trips, excursions to Lago de Yojoa and even some outings to nearby caves. Ask for Samuel, a well-respected and trusted local guide.

Sleeping

Hostal En la Manzana Verde (☎ 651 4652; dm US$4) This lovely 18-bed hostel is run by the same people at Café ViaVia. It's cheap as chips and a great place to meet people on the road. Neat, personalized kitchen shelves mean there's no need to argue about who raided whose supply – and there's even less reason to quibble with outdoor hammocks and beers for under a dollar. The hostel's rules are a riot. You can also wash your clothes in a *pila* (basin) out the back.

Hotel Los Gemelos (☎ 651 4077; fax 651 4185; r per person with shared bathroom US$4; [P]) This longtime backpacker favorite is still a hit with the budget brigade. The management is friendly and the compact, clean rooms surround a well-tended courtyard flowerbed. No need for your flip-flops in the shared shower – and there's even hot water in both the girls' and the boys' bathrooms. There's an 11pm curfew although it is not always strictly enforced.

Hostel Iguana Azul (☎ 651 4620; fax 651 4623; www .iguanaazulcopan.com; dm/s/d US$4/8/11) This characterful place keeps its standards just as high as when it set up a decade ago, with little flourishes even in the impeccably clean, tiled bathroom. It has two dormitories and three private rooms in a colonial-style ranch home. There's a small tropical garden, and the common area has books, magazines, travel guides and lots of handy travel tips.

Café ViaVia (☎ 651 4652; www.viaviacafe.com; s/d/tr US$12/14/19) Run by a group of very smart, friendly Belgians, this hotel has spotless rooms with private bathroom, tiled floors and comfy beds. There are only five rooms – best to email a booking if you can. The covered patio, great bar – often with live DJ – and restaurant make this the best travelers' meeting point in town. English, French, German, Dutch and, of course, Spanish are spoken.

Hotel Clásico Copán (☎ 651 4040/4411; s & d with TV US$15, d & tr with 2 double beds US$20; [P]) Good-sized rooms are on two levels around a patio with gently waving palm trees. If your budget will stretch, go for the more expensive top-floor rooms at the front, which have a small terrace and a great view of the mountains. All have a private hot-water bathroom and some have cable TV and fans.

La Posada de Belssy (☎ 651 4680; s/d/tr US$12/17/18) You get an excellent deal at this very friendly family-run place with a heap more character than average. Bedrooms are spick-and-span, but it is all about the upstairs terrace here. It has super views around Copán, hammocks and quaint wooden tables – perfect for whiling away a few lazy hours. The mom will whip up breakfasts and dinners on request (both US$2.75) and you can use the kitchen if you ask nicely. Free drinking water is also available.

Hotel Calle Real (☎ 651 4230; s/d/tr US$11/16/24; [P]) The target guest here is more middle-class Honduran than backpacker, although quite a few of the latter bed down at this spotless but unexciting hotel three blocks up the hill. The half-thatched, half-corrugated roof terrace has some hammocks and reasonable views. The price includes hot-water bathroom.

Hotel Brisas de Copán (☎ 651 4118; r US$16; [P] [X]) Readers enthusiastically recommend this family-run place with spotless rooms. All the rooms have TVs and en suites with hot water. The terrace has spectacular views of the town's valley setting and is a great place to sip a beer.

HONDURAS

La Casa de Café B&B (☎ 651 4620; fax 651 4623; www
.casadecafecopan.com, www.casajaguarcopan.com; s/d with
breakfast US$35/45) This impeccably decorated
B&B has rooms with carved wooden doors and
Guatemalan sculptures. It is four blocks from
the parque central. The setting is stunning –
the view over breakfast is of morning mists
rising around the Guatemalan mountains. The
American-Honduran owners also have an upscale house and apartment available (US$60 to
US$80 a night, negotiable for longer stays).

Eating

Llama del Bosque (☎ 651 4431; breakfast US$2-3.75,
mains US$3.25-5.50; ☺ 7am-9:30pm) This Copán in-
stitution is older than most of the backpackers coming through town. The chefs are well
practiced at whipping up excellent Honduran
specialties, soups, sandwiches and pastas, all
served in an airy venue, which includes an
attractive outdoor area.

Picame (☎ 651 3953; mains US$2.50-4; ☺ 7am-
9pm) There are only four little tables in this
great-value hole-in-the-wall with the hardest working chefs in town (a Dutch-Belize
partnership). Get there early to bag a seat or
be prepared to have takeaway. The burgers
are freshly prepared, and the *baleadas* are big
and filling.

Café ViaVia (breakfast US$1.50-2.50, mains US$3-5, daily
specials US$5; ☺ 7am-9:30pm) This inventive res-
taurant specializes in fine, vegetarian-slanted
global cuisine. The adjoining bar keeps the
atmosphere lively, friendly and fun. Or, if you
fancy a slower pace, take a seat on the outdoor
terrace and watch Copán amble by. Try the
excellent coffee or the homemade bread.

Carnitas Nia Lola (☎ 651 4196; main dishes US$3.50-
6.50; ☺ 7am-9pm) It's a bit of a theme bar, all
saloon doors, *faux* antique clutter and paraphernalia, but this remains a bustling, open-
air meeting and eating place two blocks south
of the plaza. There's a fine view from the top
floor, and waitresses show some impressive
platter-balancing skills – on their heads. There
are a couple of veggie options, but the staple
here is grilled meat. The bar is open until
10pm.

Twisted Tanya's (☎ 651 4182; mains US$6-10; ☺ 3-
10pm) A fine addition to the Copán culinary
scene, this upscale restaurant, specializing
in seafood pastas and filet mignon, is regularly packed out. The owner, larger-than-life
British expat Tanya, used to run the Twisted
Toucan in Roatán and is a good source of info

on the Bay Islands. And she hasn't forgotten
her traveler days – there's a backpacker special
from 4pm to 6pm for US$6, including soup,
pasta and a desert. Two-for-one cocktails run
at the same time.

Café Welchez (☎ 651 4070; cake US$1.60; ☺ 6am-
10pm) Part of the Hotel Marina Copán complex, but its prices are still reasonable. And
its varnished chairs prove a fine perch for
a caffeine fix – the café has a rare cappuccino machine. It also has slices of cake, in
ample portions to ward off hunger. You can
get breakfast here too, fairly cheaply.

Vamos A Ver (☎ 651 4627; sandwiches US$2-3.50,
fruit salad US$3; mains US$3.50-6; ☺ 7am-10pm) This
vegetarian-friendly option close to the parque
central has an attractive outdoor patio and
a menu with the international traveler in
mind. It includes homemade breads, Dutch
cheeses, tasty soups, a range of salads, rich
coffee, *licuados* (fresh-fruit drinks) and a wide
variety of teas.

Tunkul Bar (mains US$3-7; ☺ 7am-midnight) Not
quite the buzzing watering hole it once was,
this still offers generous portions of food (it's
famed for its nachos) and music. Happy hour
is in fact a happy two hours, running from
7pm to 9pm each night with two cocktails
for the price of one. Two blocks east of the
plaza.

La Casa de Todo (mains US$3.50-5, salads US$2-3;
☺ 7am-9pm) Homemade bread, yoghurt and
organic coffee are dished up in this café's verdant garden; veggie options, including salads,
are good. The service can be slow. Mainly light
meals and snacks are served.

Drinking & Nightlife

Xibalba's (☎ 651 4182; ☺ 6am-11pm) The name is
a Maya dialect word meaning underworld –
but if this is hell, we'll take it. It's cozy, has
swings, a spicy chicken curry (US$6), a 'Full
Monty' breakfast special (US$5 for 'bacon,
eggs, the works'), and happy hour from 3pm
to 5pm each day with two-for-one cocktails.
It's also known for its fine *mojitos*. Ah, for a
little time in purgatory.

Nights out in Copán followed a definite
pattern when we passed through. Of course,
trends change fast, but cocktails at Xibalba's
were the first stop, followed by a Port Royal
or two at Café ViaVia and then a trip to **Papa
Chango nightclub** (☺ 9pm-3am Wed-Sat), where a
reggaeton beat keeps the night going. See also
the eating listings (left) for more options.

GETTING TO ANTIGUA, GUATEMALA

Basecamp (☎ 651 4695; copan.honduras@viaviacafe.com; ☻ 8am-6pm) in Copán Ruinas runs a shuttle between these two towns (US$16, minimum four passengers, six hours) at noon. Scheduled shuttles leave Copán (US$16, minimum four passengers, six hours) and can drop you in Guatemala City (five hours) en route.

Moneychangers will approach you on both sides of the border anxious to change Guatemalan quetzals for Honduran lempiras, or either for US dollars. Usually they're offering a decent rate because there's a Guatemalan bank right there and the current exchange rate is posted in the Honduran immigration office – look for it. There's no bank on the Honduran side of the border. US dollars may be accepted at some establishments in Copán Ruinas, but it's best to change some money into lempiras.

Shopping

Items to look out for are leatherwear, woven baskets, textiles from Guatemala and tobacco. Check out La Casa de Todo east of the park, and the Mercado Artesenal, a block south of the park. Perhaps the most enticing souvenirs are replica Maya carvings made by a local man called **Lito Lara** (☎ 651 4138). He operates an informal shop out of his house – look for a plaque above his door. He'll be happy to show you his genuinely high-quality Maya carvings.

Getting There & Away

BUS & MINIBUS

Minibuses and pickups to and from Copán Ruinas to the Guatemalan border depart every 30 minutes (or when full), 6am to 6pm, and charge around US$1.10 – check the price beforehand. On the Guatemala side, buses to Esquipulas and Chiquimula leave the border regularly until about 4:30pm (see above).

Transportes Casasola (☎ 651 4078) is probably the best bet for getting to San Pedro Sula (US$5.50, three hours, departs 6am, 7am and 2pm). Its luxury coaches run at a fraction of the Hedman Alas prices – although they do pack in the passengers. The office is next door to the Hotel Clásico Copán, east of the parque central. It has connections onto Tela and La Ceiba.

Rey Express (☎ 651 4021) is slightly cheaper (and slightly less reliable) with departures to San Pedro Sula (US$4.50, three hours, 6am, 7am and 2pm).

Hedman Alas (☎ 651 4037) has its terminal just outside of town. It offers a luxury (and much more expensive) service to San Pedro Sula (US$14, three hours), Tegucigalpa (US$22, seven hours) and La Ceiba (US$22, seven hours); departures at 5:15am, 10:30am and

2:30pm daily. It also goes to Antigua, Guatemala (US$41, six hours) at 1:20pm each day.

If you want to leave at another time, you can easily take a bus to La Entrada (US$2, 2¼ hours, 61km) and transfer there to San Pedro Sula, or to Santa Rosa de Copán. Buses to La Entrada depart every 40 minutes from 4am to 5pm.

Getting Around

TAXI

Little three-wheeled mototaxis whizz around the cobbled streets. The going rate for a ride around town is $0.25 for locals. Most charge US$0.50 for foreign tourists. You don't have to pay gringo rates – it just depends on negotiation skills (in Spanish) and persistence. For a trip to the ruins, expect to pay around US$0.70.

AROUND COPÁN RUINAS

Macaw Mountain (☎ 651 4245, www.macawmountain .com; adult/child US$10/5; ☻ 9am-5pm) is a beautifully landscaped bird sanctuary about 2.5km outside of the town center. It is the brainchild of a former Roatán resident whose flock of rescued abandoned and endangered birds just kept on growing. The birds, which include macaws, parrots, toucans and some raptors, are treated with real care. Some are allowed out of their cages at feeding time, squawking and interacting with visitors. The entrance fee is high, but valid for three days – and you may well be tempted to return and relax in the tranquil forest setting. A restaurant and café are on-site. A mototaxi costs around US$1.10 each.

Visiting the **Finca El Cisne** (☎ 651 4695, www.finca elcisne.com; r per person incl 3 meals, horseback tour & admission to thermal baths US$65) highlands coffee and cardamom plantation, 24km from Copán

HONDURAS

Ruinas, is more a privileged invitation into a traditional hacienda family home than a tour. Founded in the 1920s and still operating, the *finca* (plantation) raises cattle and grows coffee and cardamom, but also produces corn, avocado, breadfruit, plantain, beans, oranges, star fruit and even some wood trees. Day tours include guided horseback riding through the forests and pastures (sometimes with a stop to swim in the nearby Rió Blanco) and tours of the coffee and cardamom fields and processing facilities. If you come during February or October, you can help out with the harvest. Carlos Castejón, a friendly, English-speaking, US-trained agronomist whose family owns the *finca,* leads most tours. Lodging is in a homey cabin; meals (cooked in a traditional wood-fired stove) and a visit to nearby hot springs are included. There's an office in Copán Ruinas, shared with Basecamp tours.

Day tours (per person US$50, minimum two people) include transportation to and from Copán Ruinas and lunch. The two-day-one-night packages (per person US$65) also includes transport and three meals; three-day-two-night stays (per person US$112) include five meals – at which point you might never want to leave.

Hacienda San Lucas (☎ 651 4495; www.haciendasanlucas.com; s/d with breakfast US$80/100) is a beautifully restored traditional hacienda on the tranquil outskirts of Copán. You have to dig deep to stay here...but there are other ways to get the flavor of the place. There is a terrifically atmospheric typical restaurant, with skillfully prepared traditional Honduran dishes. Horseback riding (US$20) and hiking (entrance US$2.75) are popular here too, for the beautiful views of town. The grounds include *Los Sapos* (the Toads), a Maya archaeological site believed to be related to fertility rites.

The **Agua Caliente** (admission US$1.10) hot springs 24km north of town are about an hour's drive along a beautiful mountain dirt road through lush, fertile mountains lined with coffee plantations. There are some dark and dingy changing rooms there, and a swing bridge across to a luxury spa that was in development when we visited.

There's no real need to go there though. Just head to the rocks arranged in the river, which mix the steaming hot springs with the cool river – and relax. Bring warm clothes if you come in the evening.

COPÁN ARCHAEOLOGICAL SITE

One of the most important of all Maya civilizations lived, prospered then mysteriously crumbled around the **Copán archaeological site** (www.copanhonduras.org; general admission US$15, museum US$7, tunnels US$15; ⏰ 8am-5pm, museum closes 4pm), now a Unesco World Heritage site. During the Classic period (AD 250–900), the city at Copán Ruinas culturally dominated the region for centuries. The architecture is not as grand as Tikal's but the city produced remarkable sculptures and hieroglyphics. Its culture was so developed, it is often labeled the 'Paris of the Maya world.' For a fuller understanding, be sure to visit the excellent Museum of Sculpture at the site.

The ruins are a pleasant 1km stroll outside of Copán (or a US$0.80 mototaxi). A visitors center, the museum and a café-gift shop are at the main entrance. A larger gift shop and a good cheap *comedor* are nearby. Hiring a guide, though expensive (around US$25 just for the ruins), is recommended, and many speak reasonable English. If you are alone, ask to share the costs with others. Las Sepulturas, a surprisingly undervisited site where you get a real sense of everyday life in the Classic Maya era, is just over 1km further out.

The booklet *History Carved in Stone: A Guide to the Archaeological Park of the Ruins of Copán,* by William L Fash and Ricardo Agurcia Fasquelle, is usually available for US$2 from the visitors center. For further reading see *Copán: The History of an Ancient Kingdom,* by William L Fash and E Wyllys Andrews (2005), the most authoritative account.

History
PRE-COLUMBIAN HISTORY

From dating ceramics discovered in the area, scientists believe people have lived in the Copán valley for more than three millennia – since at least 1200 BC. Craft and trade seemed to thrive early on – excavated artifacts show influences from as far afield as Mexico.

Around AD 426, one royal family came to rule Copán, led by a mysterious king named Mah K'ina Yax K'uk' Mo' (Great Sun Lord Quetzal Macaw). He ruled from 426 to 435. Archaeological evidence indicates that he was a great shaman; later kings revered him as the semidivine founder of the city. His dynasty ruled throughout Copán's golden age.

The early kings (from 435–628) remain shrouded in mystery – only a few names have

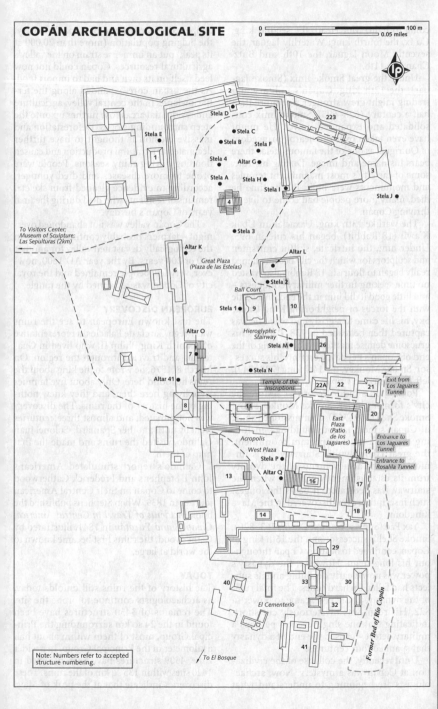

COPÁN ARCHAEOLOGICAL SITE

0 ————————— 100 m
0 ————————— 0.05 miles

Stela D
Stela E
1
Stela C
Stela B
Stela F
Stela 4
Altar G
Stela A
Stela H
Stela I
4
Stela J
3
223
2

To Visitors Center;
Museum of Sculpture;
Las Sepulturas (2km)

Stela 3

Altar K

Great Plaza
(Plaza de las Estelas)

Altar L

6

Stela 2

Ball Court

Stela 1   9   10

Altar O

Hieroglyphic
Stairway

7   Stela M   26

Stela N

Altar 41

Temple of the
Inscriptions   22A   22   21

11   20

8   Exit from
                                          Los Jaguares
                                          Tunnel

East
Plaza
(Patio
de los
Jaguares)   Entrance to
                   Los Jaguares
                   Tunnel

Acropolis   19
West Plaza
Stela P   Entrance to
Altar Q   Rosalila Tunnel

13   16   17

14   18

29

40   33   30

El Cementerio   32

41

Former Bed of Río Copán

To El Bosque

Note: Numbers refer to accepted
structure numbering.

HONDURAS

come to light: Mat Head, the second king; Cu Ix, the fourth king; Waterlily Jaguar, the seventh; Moon Jaguar, the 10th; and Butz' Chan, the 11th.

Under the great Smoke Imix (Smoke Jaguar), the 12th king, Copán's military and trading might grew stronger. For more than half a century (628–695), Smoke Imix consolidated and expanded power. He might have even taken over the nearby princedom of Quiriguá, as one of the famous stelae there bears his name and image. During his rule, some of the city's most magnificent temples and monuments were built. By the time he died, many more people had come to live in thriving Copán.

The warlike 13th king, Uaxaclahun Ubak K'awil (18 Rabbit), began his rule in 695. Under him, the intricate, skilful craftsmen and sculptors for which the city became famed really began to flourish. 18 Rabbit also wasted no time seeking further military conquests – and little good it did him in the end. In a battle with the forces of neighboring King Cauac Sky, his life came to a grisly end when he was captured then beheaded in 738. Perhaps his gruesome demise marked the beginning of the end of Copán's heyday. Certainly, his successor, Smoke Monkey, the 14th king (738–749), left little mark on Copán.

Possibly in a bid to record or restore the city's former glories, Smoke Monkey's son, Smoke Shell (749–763), commissioned some of Copán's most famous buildings, including the city's most important monument, the great Hieroglyphic Stairway. This immortalizes the achievements of the dynasty from its establishment until 755, when the stairway was dedicated. It bears the longest such inscription ever discovered in the Maya kingdom.

Yax Pac (Sunrise or First Dawn, 763–820), Smoke Shell's successor and the 16th king of Copán, continued to beautify Copán throughout his long reign. However, the dynasty's power was now clearly declining and its subjects had fallen on hard times. The final ruler of the dynasty, U Cit Tok', came to power in 822. His reign was mysteriously cut short, indicating that one single event – perhaps a military defeat – caused the end of a dynasty that spanned four centuries.

Until recently, the collapse of the civilization at Copán was a mystery. Now, archaeologists are beginning to understand what happened. Near the end of Copán's heyday, the bulging population (more than 20,000 at its peak) put an immense strain on the valley's agricultural resources. Copán could not now feed itself on its own and had to import food. As the urban core expanded along the fertile lowlands in the central valley, agriculture and residential areas rose further up onto the steep surrounding slopes. Deforestation and massive erosion is thought to have further decimated agricultural production and caused flooding during rainy seasons. People were prone to more diseases and died younger, according to evidence gleaned from skeletal remains of residents who died during the final years of Copán's heyday.

The Copán valley was not abandoned overnight – farmers probably continued to live in the ecologically devastated valley for another 100 or 200 years. By the year AD 1200, however, very few people remained and the royal city of Copán was reclaimed by the jungle.

EUROPEAN DISCOVERY
The first known European to see the ruins was Diego García de Palacios, a representative of Spanish King Philip II, who lived in Guatemala and traveled through the region. On March 8, 1576, he wrote to the king about the ruins he found here. Only about five families were living here then, and they knew nothing of the history of the ruins. The discovery was not pursued, and almost three centuries went by until another Spaniard, Colonel Juan Galindo, visited the ruins and made the first map of them.

Galindo's report stimulated Americans John L Stephens and Frederick Catherwood to come to Copán on their Central American journey in 1839. When Stephens published the book *Incidents of Travel in Central America, Chiapas, and Yucatán* in 1841, illustrated by Catherwood, the ruins first became known to the world at large.

TODAY
The history of the ruins still unfolds today, as archaeologists continue to probe the site. The remains of 3450 structures have been found in the 24 sq km surrounding the Principal Group, most of them within about half a kilometer of the Principal Group. In a wider zone, 4509 structures have been detected in 1420 sites within 135 sq km of the ruins. These discoveries indicate that at the peak of Maya

civilization here, around the end of the 8th century, the valley of Copán had over 20,000 inhabitants – a population not reached again until the 1980s.

In addition to examining the area around the Principal Group, archaeologists are continuing to explore and make new discoveries at the Principal Group itself. Five separate phases of building on this site have been identified; the final phase, dating from AD 650 to 820, is what we see today. But buried underneath the visible ruins are layers of other ruins, which archaeologists are exploring by means of underground tunnels. This is how the Rosalila temple was found, a replica of which is now in the Museum of Sculpture; below Rosalila is yet another, earlier temple, Margarita.

Occasionally the ruins are a stage for more controversial, political actions. In September 2005, 1500 indigenous Maya Chortí, descendants of the original builders of Copán, occupied the ruins and barred visitors. Their five-day occupation of the site was in protest at stalled government land reforms, aimed at giving indigenous communities a way of lifting themselves out of poverty. Several Maya Chortí leaders have been killed over the last few decades. While the protests have quietened recently, the stark social conditions for many of the 8000 Maya Chortí in the area remains a major, unresolved issue.

Museum of Sculpture

While Tikal is celebrated for its tall temple pyramids and Palenque is renowned for its limestone relief panels, Copán is unique in the Maya world for its sculpture. Some of the finest examples are on display at this impressive museum, opened in August 1996. Entering the museum is an experience by itself: You go through the mouth of a serpent and wind through the entrails of the beast before suddenly emerging into a fantastic world of sculpture and light.

The highlight of the museum is a true-scale replica of the Rosalila temple, which was discovered in nearly perfect condition by archaeologists in 1989 by means of a tunnel dug into Structure 16, the central building of the Acropolis. Rosalila, dedicated in AD 571 by Copán's 10th ruler, Moon Jaguar, was apparently so sacred that when Structure 16 was built over it, Rosalila was not destroyed but was left completely intact.

The original Rosalila temple is still in the core of Structure 16. Under it is a still earlier temple, Margarita, built 150 years before, as well as other platforms and tombs.

The Principal Group

The Principal Group is a group of ruins about 400m beyond the visitors center, across well-kept lawns, through a gate in a strong fence and down shady avenues of trees.

STELAE OF THE GREAT PLAZA

The path leads to the Great Plaza and the huge, intricately carved stelae portraying the rulers of Copán. Most of Copán's best stelae date from AD 613 to 738, especially from the reigns of Smoke Imix (628–95) and 18 Rabbit (AD 695–738). All seem to have originally been painted; a few traces of red paint survive on Stela C. Many stelae had vaults beneath or beside them in which sacrifices and offerings could be placed.

Many of the stelae on the Great Plaza portray King 18 Rabbit, including Stelae A, B, C, D, F, H and 4. Perhaps the most beautiful stela in the Great Plaza is Stela A (731); the original has been moved inside the Museum of Sculpture, and the one outdoors is a reproduction. Nearby, and almost equal in beauty, are Stela 4 (731); Stela B (731), depicting 18 Rabbit upon his accession to the throne; and Stela C (AD 782), with a turtle-shaped altar in front. This last stela has figures on both sides. Stela E (614), erected on top of Structure 1 on the west side of the Great Plaza, is among the oldest stelae.

At the northern end of the Great Plaza, at the base of Structure 2, Stela D (736) also portrays King 18 Rabbit. On its back are two columns of hieroglyphs; at its base is an altar with fearsome representations of Chac, the rain god. In front of the altar is the burial place of Dr John Owen, an archaeologist with an expedition from Harvard's Peabody Museum, who died during work in 1893.

On the east side of the plaza is Stela F (721), arguably the most beautiful of 18 Rabbit's sculptures. It has a more lyrical design, with the robes of the main figure flowing around to the other side of the stone, where there are glyphs. Altar G (800), showing twin serpent heads, is among the last monuments carved at Copán. Stela H (730) might depict a queen or princess rather than a king. Stela 1 (692), on the structure that runs along the east side of

HONDURAS

the plaza, is of a person wearing a mask. Stela J, further off to the east, resembles the stelae of Quiriguá in that it is covered in glyphs, not human figures.

BALL COURT & HIEROGLYPHIC STAIRWAY

South of the Great Plaza, across what is known as the Central Plaza, is the ball court (Juego de Pelota; AD 731), the second-largest in Central America. It is not exactly clear how this game was played, although participants probably kept a hard rubber ball in the air without using their hands; Casa K'inich (p367) has a video reconstruction. The one you see is the third ball-court built on this site; the other two smaller ones were buried by this construction. Note the macaw heads carved at the top of the sloping walls. The central marker in the court was the work of King 18 Rabbit.

South of the ball court is Copán's most famous monument, the Hieroglyphic Stairway, the work of King Smoke Shell. Today it's protected from the elements by a roof. This lessens the impact of its beauty, but you can still get an idea of how it looked. The flight of 63 steps bears a history – in several thousand glyphs – of the royal house of Copán; the steps are bordered by ramps inscribed with more reliefs and glyphs. The story inscribed on the steps is still not completely understood, because the stairway was partially ruined and the stones jumbled.

At the base of the Hieroglyphic Stairway is Stela M (AD 756), bearing a figure (probably King Smoke Shell) in a feathered cloak; glyphs tell of the solar eclipse in that year. The altar in front shows a plumed serpent with a human head emerging from its jaws.

Beside the stairway, a tunnel leads to the tomb of a nobleman, a royal scribe who might have been the son of King Smoke Imix. The tomb, discovered in 1989, held a treasure trove of painted pottery and beautiful carved jade objects that are now in Honduran museums.

ACROPOLIS

The lofty flight of steps to the south of the Hieroglyphic Stairway is called the **Temple of the Inscriptions**. On top of the stairway, the walls are carved with groups of hieroglyphs. On the south side of the Temple of the Inscriptions are the **East Plaza** and West Plaza. In the **West Plaza**, be sure to see Altar Q (AD 776), among the most famous sculptures here; the original is inside the Museum of Sculpture. Around its

sides, carved in superb relief, are the 16 great kings of Copán, ending with the altar's creator, Yax Pac. Behind the altar was a sacrificial vault in which archaeologists discovered the bones of 15 jaguars and several macaws that were probably sacrificed to the glory of Yax Pac and his ancestors.

TUNNELS

In 1999, archaeologists opened up to the public two tunnels that allow visitors to get a glimpse of pre-existing structures below the visible structures. The first, **Rosalila tunnel**, is very short and takes only a few visitors at a time. The famous temple is only barely exposed, and behind thick glass. The other tunnel, **Los Jaguares**, was originally 700m in length, but a large section has been closed, reducing it to about 80m, running along the foundations of Temple 22. This tunnel exits on the outside of the main site, so you must walk around the main site to get back in again. While interesting, it's hard to justify the US$15 extra you pay to get in.

Las Sepulturas

Often overlooked by visitors, Las Sepulturas is a tranquil escape from the crowds on the main ruins site. Although not as striking, the excavations here have shed light on the daily life of the Maya of Copán during its golden age.

Las Sepulturas, once connected to the Great Plaza by a causeway, was possibly the residential area of rich, powerful nobles. One huge, luxurious compound seems to have housed some 250 people in 40 or 50 buildings arranged around 11 courtyards. The principal structure, called the House of the Bacabs (officials), had outer walls carved with full-size figures of 10 males in fancy feathered headdresses; inside was a huge hieroglyphic bench.

To get to the site, you have to go back to the main road, turn right, then right again at the sign.

SANTA ROSA DE COPÁN

pop 28,700

Santa Rosa de Copán is a cool mountain town with cobbled streets and some lovely, restored colonial buildings. It doesn't have any world-class sights like Copán Ruinas, a few hours away. Consequently, it doesn't have as many tourists, which is part of its charm. It's just a quiet, beautiful little town with a fresh climate and friendly people. The annual **festival day** is

August 30. The town is also renowned for its colorful **Semana Santa** celebrations.

The town is up on a hill, 1.5km from the bus terminal on the highway. Most hotels are a short walk from the parque central, which has the police station to the north side, a lovely cathedral to the east and Hondutel to the west.

Information

EMERGENCY
Police (☎ 662 0091)

IMMIGRATION
The Immigration office is one block from the parque central.

INTERNET ACCESS
Tourist office (per hour US$0.80; ☺ 8am-noon & 1:30am-6pm Mon-Fri, 9am-noon & 1:30pm-6pm Sat) Good fast internet connection with new computers.
Zeus Cyber Café (per hr US$0.55; ☺ 8am-10pm Mon-Fri, 9am-9pm Sat-Sun) Also has international phone service for US$0.25 per minute.

MONEY
Banco Atlántida (Parque Central) Changes traveler's checks and gives cash advances on Visa cards. The ATM accepts Visa/Plus cards.
Banco del Occidente (Parque Central) In the same building as Western Union, it changes travelers' checks and gives cash advances on Visa cards.
Unibanc ATM (1a Calle) Just down from Banco del Occidente, takes Visa, Cirrus, MasterCard and American Express.

POST & TELEPHONE
These two are side by side on the west side of the parque central. Calling abroad is cheaper at Zeus Cyber Café.
Post office (☺ 8am-noon & 2-4pm Mon-Fri, 8am-noon Sat)
Hondutel (☺ 7am-9pm)

TOURIST INFORMATION
Tourist office (☎ 662 2234; ☺ 8am-noon & 1:30pm-6pm Mon-Fri, 9am-noon & 1:30pm-6pm Sat) In a kiosk in the central park, it has plenty of suggestions for places to eat and stay within Santa Rosa, as well as details on the town's cultural significance and historical buildings.

Sights
La Flor de Copán Cigar Factory (☎ 662 0185; tours US$3; ☺ 7am-noon & 1-5pm Mon-Fri, 7am-noon Sat), 2km out of town, shows visitors the craft behind making hand-rolled cigars. A taxi from town costs US$0.80. Tours are available in English.

Those who love a good cup of joe can see how their favorite bean is prepared at **Beneficio Maya** (☎ 662 1665; www.cafecopan.com; Colonia San Martín; ☺ 7am-noon & 2-5pm Mon-Fri, 7am-noon Sat), a coffee-processing plant. Tours to nearby *fincas* run during the coffee harvest season (November to February).

Tours
Lenca Land Trails (☎ 662 1375/1374; max@Lenca-Honduras.com; Calle Real Centenario near 3a Av NO) is run by Max Elvir, a well-known local guide, who operates out of Hotel Elvir and offers highly recommended tours to nearby indigenous Lenca villages and Parque Nacional Montaña de Celaque. Max speaks English.

Sleeping
Hotel El Rosario (☎ 662 0211; 3a Av NE btwn 1a & 2a Calles; s/d US$5.40/10.80, with bathroom US$8.10/16.20) Two blocks east of the park, next door to a dodgy by-the-hour place, this hotel is impeccably kept (mops were out in full force when we were here) with rooms off a long corridor. Beds are a bit soft but skylights add some natural brightness. It is managed by the señora who runs the pharmacy next door.

Hotel Alondra's (☎ 662 1194; 3a Av SO between 1a & 2a Calles SE; s/d US$13.50/21.60) One of the new options in town, this is a wholesome, family-run place, kept scrupulously tidy. The one drawback is the slightly gloomy rooms, but the private bathrooms all have hot water.

Hotel Santa Eduvigues (☎ 662 0380; 1a Calle NO, btwn 4a & 5a Av; s/d with cold-water bathroom US$10.80/13.50, with hot water US$13.50/19) Lanterns mark the front of this hotel. The darkened lobby may put some off, but the rooms have recently been refurbished and are clean and comfortable.

Hotel VIP Copán (☎ 662 0265; 1a Calle NE & 3a Av NE; s/d with fan US$17.25/31.35, s/d with air-con US$28.90/37.60; P ☺ ☐ ☒) This posh, central option has very comfortable rooms with uncreased bedspreads and shiny-tiled bathrooms. Some do not let much natural light in. Its adjoining Restaurante Mundo Maya (mains US$3.25 to US$5) has a good reputation locally and is open for all meals.

Eating
Pizza Pizza (☎ 662 1104; Calle Real Centenario near 6a Av NE; mains US$2-5; ☺ 11:30am-2pm & 5-9pm Thu-Tue) This appealing pizzeria, run by an American-Honduran family, concentrates on delivering the finest brick-oven pizza in town as well

as hunger-killing doorstopper sandwiches. Warren Post, the friendly owner, has lived in Santa Rosa for many years and is a good person to talk to about the area's attractions. There's also an English-language book exchange here.

Comedor Villa los Llanos (☎ 662 1256; 2a Av nr 1a Calle; dishes US$2-3; ⏰ 7am-8pm Mon-Sat) A good, honest, no-nonsense little *comedor*, this serves up hearty portions of staple Honduran dishes, from beans, scrambled eggs and plantains for breakfast to *carne* (meat, usually beef) and fried chicken platters for lunch and dinner.

Restaurante Las Haciendas (☎ 662 3518; 1a Calle SE btwn 2a & 3a Avs; dishes US$2-5; ⏰ 10am-10pm) Big wagon wheels guard the entrance to this grill specialist that has a pleasant, shady outdoor eating area. Vegetarians will not find much choice.

Restaurante & Bar Zotz (☎ 662 0829; Calle Real Centenario btwn 2a & 3a Av; mains US$3-4.50; ⏰ noon-3am Wed-Sat, noon-11pm Sun-Tue) The bar is what counts here – it is the sort of place where you can order your burgers and platters when the munchies strike midbeers. Americana rules – walls are cluttered with US number plates and other paraphernalia. It is popular with middle-class twenty-something Hondurans.

Drinking & Entertainment

Hotel Elvir (☎ 662 1374; cnr 3a Av NE & 1a Calle SE; ⏰ 3-10:30pm) Although the hotel is out of budget range, its rooftop bar is one of Santa Rosa's best spots for a drink. Sip your tipple of choice by a pool with fine views right over town.

Luna Jaguar Disco (3a Av SE near Calle Centenario; cover US$5.50; ⏰ 9pm-4am Wed-Sat) If you want to do a little dancing, this is virtually the only place in town to get down tonight. It is favored by the late-teen, early twenty-something crowd.

Cinema Don Quijote (☎ 662 2625; Plaza Saavedra; 1a Calle NE at 3a Av NE; US$1.90) Shows late-release Hollywood films.

Getting There & Away

Most Santa Rosa de Copán buses come and go from the Terminal de Transporte on the main highway, 1.5km from town. A colectivo into town costs US$0.75, the local bus costs US$0.25.

Sultana de Occidente (☎ 662 0940) buses to Tegucigalpa, San Salvador and Agua Caliente (Guatemala) depart from a separate terminal next door. **Congolón** (☎ 662 3834) has a terminal further up the highway nearer town and is a good option for San Pedro Sula, Nueva Ocotepeque and Tegucigalpa buses.

If you're going to San Pedro Sula, best catch a direct bus, which stops only once (at La Entrada). The regular buses are more frequent but slower.

Destinations from Santa Rosa:

Copán Ruinas (US$2, four hours, 107km, 11:30am, 12:30pm & 2pm) Very slow service; best to go direct to La Entrada and transfer.

Gracias (US$1.65, 1½ hours, 47km, every 45 minutes)

La Entrada (US$1.35, 1¼ hours, 44km) Same buses as to San Pedro Sula.

Nueva Ocotepeque Congolón buses (US$3, 2½ hours, 95km, five buses daily, first/last bus 8:30am/4:30pm)

San Pedro Sula Congolón (US$3.50, 2½ hours, 152km, six buses daily from 7:30am-6pm); regular buses (US$2.70, four hours, every 30 minutes until 5pm); express buses from the Terminal de Transporte (US$4.30, 2½ hours, 8am, 9:30am & 2pm)

San Salvador Sultana buses via El Poy (US$10, six hours, 8:30am)

Tegucigalpa Congolón (US$8.10, 7½ hours, 393km, 8am)

GRACIAS

pop 8600

Gracias is a small, tranquil cobblestone town 47km southeast of Santa Rosa de Copán. For a brief time in the 16th century, it was the capital of all Spanish-conquered Central America. Traces of its former grandeur remain in its centuries-old buildings and various colonial churches. The pace of life along its cobblestone streets rarely moves much faster than walking.

Gracias was founded in 1526 by Spanish Captain Juan de Chavez; its original name was Gracias a Dios (Thanks to God). The Audiencia de los Confines, the governing council for Central America, was established here on April 16, 1544; the buildings that the council occupied are still here. Eventually the town's importance was eclipsed by Antigua (Guatemala) and Comayagua.

The area around Gracias is mountainous and beautiful. Much of it is forested. The town makes a good base for exploring Parque Nacional Celaque. While you're here, don't miss a trip to the hot springs.

Orientation & Information

Gracias is a small town and everything is within walking distance. The post office and Hondutel are side by side, a block south of the parque central.

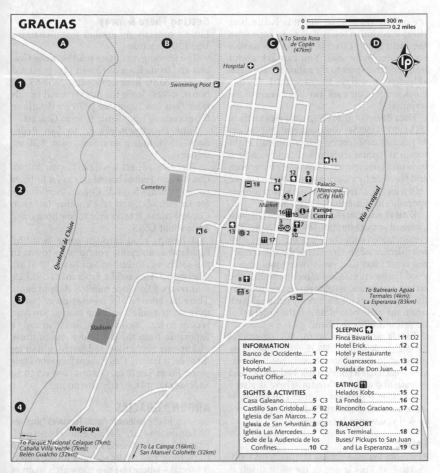

GRACIAS

To Santa Rosa
de Copán
(47km)

Hospital
Swimming Pool
Cemetery
Market
Palacio
Municipal
(City Hall)
Parque
Central
Río Arcagual
Stadium

To Balneario Aguas
Termales (4km);
La Esperanza (83km)

Mejicapa

To Parque Nacional Celaque (7km);
Cabaña Villa Verde (7km);
Belén Gualcho (32km)

To La Campa (16km);
San Manuel Colohete (32km)

INFORMATION
Banco de Occidente......1 C2
Ecolem..................2 C2
Hondutel................3 C2
Tourist Office..........4 C2

SIGHTS & ACTIVITIES
Casa Galeano............5 C3
Castillo San Cristóbal...6 B2
Iglesia de San Marcos...7 C2
Iglesia de San Sebastián..8 C3
Iglesia Las Mercedes....9 C2
Sede de la Audiencia de los
    Confines............10 C2

SLEEPING
Finca Bavaria...........11 D2
Hotel Erick.............12 C2
Hotel y Restaurante
    Guancascos..........13 C2
Posada de Don Juan......14 C2

EATING
Helados Kobs............15 C2
La Fonda................16 C2
Rinconcito Graciano....17 C2

TRANSPORT
Bus Terminal............18 C2
Buses/ Pickups to San Juan
    and La Esperanza....19 C3

Banco de Occidente (Parque Central) Exchanges traveler's checks and US dollars.

Ecolem (7:30am-9pm) Check email at this spot, near Guancascos.

Tourist office (Parque Central kiosk; 8am-noon & 1:30-4:30pm Mon-Fri) Has some useful information binders. You'll need to speak Spanish.

Sights & Activities

High on a hill west of the parque central, **Castillo San Cristóbal** (7am-5pm) is worth the walk for its excellent views of the town. Gracias has several colonial *iglesias*: **San Marcos**, **Las Mercedes** and **San Sebastián**. Next door to the Iglesia de San Marcos, the **Sede de la Audiencia de los Confines**, important in the town's history, is now the *casa parroquial*, the residence for the parish priest.

Casa Galeano (admission US$1.60; 9am-6pm) is in a beautiful restored colonial house with extensive gardens; this new museum does not fulfill its potential. There is an interesting local history and summary of the Lenca culture but signage is in Spanish only. In the gardens most of the signs with details of a whole range of trees have been broken.

Most of the area's other attractions, including fine hot springs and the Parque Nacional Montaña de Celaque, are a few kilometers out of town (see p380).

Sleeping

Hotel Erick (656 1066; s/d US$5.40/7; P) A perennial favorite among the budget traveler crowd, this is a clean, family-run hotel. Beds

HONDURAS

are on the saggy side, but this is the best cheapie option in town, if you can cope with the lurid green exterior. All rooms have a cold-water bathroom. You can ask about tours and transport to the national park here, although you will need some Spanish. It's one block north of the park, two blocks east of the terminal.

Finca Bavaria (☎ 656 1372; s/d/tr with bathroom US$5.40/9.75/13.50) Set on a peaceful 35,000-sq-m *finca de café* (coffee plantation), all eight rooms at Bavaria are large and basic with firm beds on a concrete base, hot-water bathroom and fan. Run by a German-Honduran couple (often away), there's also a bar, which is open sporadically. Camping is available too.

Hotel y Restaurante Guancascos (☎ 656 1219; www .guancascos.com; s/d/tw/tr US$12/14.50/20/21.50; P) The comfortable rooms here are the most tastefully decorated in Gracias, while the terrace restaurant has fine views over town and is good for meeting fellow travelers. Shame the service is slow and hotel management unhelpful. Tour guides for the nearby national park drum up trade here although the hotel takes no responsibility for them.

Posada de Don Juan (☎ 656 1020; s/d with fan US$15/21, with air-con US$20/25; P ☒ ☐) The motel-style rooms have recently been remodeled – each has a comfortable bed, fridge and private hot-water bathroom. There is also a good-value restaurant on site. This caters to a business clientele but is definitely worth a look if you want a bit of comfort.

Eating

Rinconcito Graciano (☎ 656 1171; mains US$1.50-3; ☽ 7am-9pm) This is one of the most original and authentic restaurants we found in all Honduras. It serves traditional Lencan dishes, prepared with organic ingredients, on lovely wooden tables in a bohemian setting. The place is run by a Gracias personality who is a big believer in slow foods and natural cooking. The menu is extremely good value. There are also some local ceramics and paintings for sale.

La Fonda (☎ 656 1244; Parque Central; mains US$3.50-5; ☽ 10am-10pm) This inexpensive restaurant has polite old-school señors in red shirts serving up well-made typical dishes. It is good for hamburger and chips-style snacks too.

Helados Kobs (Parque Central; ☽ 9am-9pm) An ice-cream stop serving myriad flavors, perfect for strolling round on a sunny afternoon.

Getting There & Away

Little mototaxis zip around town, charging US$0.70 for a ride.

The winding mountain road between Gracias and Santa Rosa de Copán is very scenic. Buses to Santa Rosa de Copán (US$1.65, 1½ hours, 47km) leave the bus terminal hourly from 5am to 4:30pm. See p378 for details on buses coming from Santa Rosa to Gracias.

Four direct services go to San Pedro Sula (US$4, four hours, 5am, 6am, 8:30am, 9:50am).

There is no direct service to Copán Ruinas. Catch a San Pedro–bound bus to La Entrada (or go to Santa Rosa de Copán, then change for La Entrada), and take another bus onto Copán Ruinas. It takes four to five hours, and costs about US$5.

A bumpy road through some beautiful highland countryside connects to towns in the southeast, including San Juan (US$1.60, one hour, 37km) and La Esperanza (US$3.25, four hours, 83km, one minibus daily at 5am). There has been talk for a long time of paving the road, but only the stretch around San Juan is done so far. Catch buses to San Juan and La Esperanza from the last bridge out of town. Pickups are also a tried-and-tested option for these destinations. Catch them from the same place. From San Juan, pickups connect to La Esperanza until the early afternoon.

AROUND GRACIAS

Bathing in the **Balneario Aguas Termales** (admission US$1.60; ☽ 6am-11:30pm) is a memorable experience. It is a rough-shod tourist attraction but the setting, practically within a forest, makes it special – where else can you watch wisps of steam rise from natural springs, as lush foliage sways above you? Four kilometers east of town, the hot springs have several pools at various temperatures. Go to the baths higher up where the water is warmer. There is a restaurant, bar and grubby changing rooms on site. You can walk it in about 90 minutes by road toward La Esperanza, or an hour if you take a shortcut off to the right after the last bridge out of town. A lot of people hitch rides there and back.

Several small towns near Gracias are also worth a visit. The Lenca people in this area produce some distinctive handicrafts. **La Campa**, a scenic little town 16km south of Gracias, is particularly known for its excellent pottery.

DETOUR TO BELÉN GUALCHO

Belén Gualcho is a picturesque colonial town clinging to the side of a mountain at 1600m above sea level, on the other side of Parque Nacional Montaña de Celaque. It is closer to Gracias, but road access is from Santa Rosa de Copán. Attractions include an interesting *iglesia* and a Lenca market on Sunday. There's an entrance to Parque Nacional Celaque here, but no checkpoint, no services, and only one trail, leading to San Manuel Colohete. Do not leave the trail, as even locals have become lost in this area.

A few buses go between here and Santa Rosa each day. There are a couple of basic places to stay and to eat, and there's even an internet café.

It has two hotels and workshops where you can see craftsmen and women shaping their art. **San Manuel Colohete**, 16km further, past La Campa, is another attractive little mountain town with a beautiful, recently restored, colonial church, famous for its 400-year-old fresco paintings. There is one hotel in town.

A once-daily bus leaves Gracias to San Manuel Colohete (US$1, one hour) at approximately 11:30am. It passes La Campa (US$0.75) at around 1pm. It departs San Manuel back to Gracias about 6am. Travel times can be considerably longer in the rainy season. Hitching is also possible around here.

PARQUE NACIONAL MONTAÑA DE CELAQUE

Celaque (which means, oddly, 'box of water' in the local Lenca dialect) is one of Honduras' most impressive national parks. It boasts **El Cerro de las Minas**, the country's highest peak at 2849m above sea level. Its slopes are covered by lush forest, which evolves in fascinating steps the higher you climb. The park contains the headwaters of several rivers, a majestic waterfall visible from the entire valley, and very steep slopes, including some vertical cliffs, totally inaccessible because of the dense forest.

The park is rich in plant and animal life. Pumas, ocelots and quetzals live here, but they are rarely seen. More common are beautiful butterflies, monkeys, black squirrels and reptiles, but you have to be very quiet and up very early to see much wildlife.

Information

The entrance fee (US$2.65) is payable at a small house about a kilometer from the beginning of the trails. You will be issued with a ticket here. Information on hiking in the park is available from Hotel Guancascos or the tourist office in Gracias' central park.

A visitors center at 1400m above sea level marks the entrance to the park.

Hiking & Camping

At the visitors center, there are basic, rustic bunks for 18 people, as well as a kitchen, water, a shower and latrines. Bring your own bedding if you can. It costs US$3 per person to stay overnight, whether camping or at the visitors center. Near the visitors center is a river, which is mighty tempting after a long grueling hike; however, the river provides drinking water, and so swimming here is strictly prohibited.

The next cabin, Campamento Don Tomás, is 2060m above sea level, and a four-hour uphill walk along a well-marked forest trail. You'll pass several small streams where you can collect water. Bring purification tablets or a filter. The camp has a tiny, dirty two-bunk shack. You'll be glad you carried a tent. There's a small latrine and no running water.

A second campground, El Narajo, is only a few kilometers away, but the trail is very steep (one to two hours). It's a pretty camp – just inside the cloud forest – but consider leaving your tent and bags at Don Tomás and climbing the summit as a day trip. From the second camp, it's another two or three hours on a beautiful rolling trail through the cloud forest to the summit. Because of clouds and tree cover, you might not see anything from the top, but there's a sign there all the same.

Many people misjudge the time they need for the climb. Some do the whole thing in a single day, but it's a very long haul. Even spreading it over two or three days, you should start hiking early. The trail is somewhat unclear in places – look for the colored ribbons. Do *not* wander off the trail; the forest is so dense it can be hard, or impossible, to find the trail again. A Dutch hiker disappeared here in 1998 and was never found; a Honduran hiker got lost and died in 2003.

Bring some warm clothes and adequate hiking boots – temperatures in the park are much chillier than in Gracias. It is also often damp and rainy.

HONDURAS

For a guide, your cheapest option is to go to the visitors center and ask the guardian, Don Miguel, to guide you. He charges US$16.50 per group, regardless of size. You will need some Spanish.

Another option is to organize a tour through the **Asociación de Guías** (☎ 656 0627).

Getting There & Away

The main entrance to the park is about 7km uphill from Gracias. Another entrance is at Belén Gualcho (p381), on the western side, but access is better from the Gracias side, which has more facilities and more pristine forest.

You can go on foot from Gracias to the park entrance – it takes about two hours. Look for the well-marked shortcut for those *a pie* (on foot). From the house where you pay your fees, it's about another half hour uphill to the park visitors center. However, we recommend saving your energy for hiking in the park. A bumpy mototaxi ride will take you there for about US$4.30 per person.

Alternatively, you could cab it (US$13.50) or arrange a lift through Hotel Erick or Hotel Guancascos in Gracias.

SAN JUAN

A slowly improving highway and the dogged efforts of Peace Corps volunteers have put this tiny, traditional mountain town on the tourist map. It is well worth a stop if you are looking for an opportunity to meet locals and learn about the lifestyle of this remote, undervisited part of the country.

Local guides and accommodation can be arranged through the local tourism cooperative. Ask for Gladys Nolasco, the president of the cooperative, whose house also doubles as the town's **visitors centre** (☎ 754 7150). Excursions include a trek to **la Cascada de los Duendes**, which goes through cloud forest and a series of waterfalls, ending with a coffee *finca* tour; and **el Cañon Encantado**, a tour of local beauty spots with the guide telling legends of the ghosts who inhabit it (Spanish only). Horseback riding, visits to traditional artisans, and coffee roasting and tasting tours can also be arranged.

Homestays cost around US$4 per person and meals in participating *comedores* cost around US$2. All buses and pickups going between Gracias (see p380) and La Esperanza (see p357) stop here.

NUEVA OCOTEPEQUE
pop 8900

In the southwest corner of Honduras, Nueva Ocotepeque is a crossroads town, with a lot of traffic to and from the nearby borders at Agua Caliente (Guatemala) and El Poy (El Salvador). There's not much to the town, but it's a surprisingly quiet place to stay overnight before or after crossing the border. To check emails, head to **Online World** (per hr US$0.80; ☯ 8am-8pm) next to Hotel Maya Chortí.

The **Reserva del Guisayote** is a biological reserve that is the easiest to access of any cloud forest in Honduras. It is 16km north of Nueva Ocotepeque via a paved road.

Sleeping & Eating

All the places to stay and eat in Nueva Ocotepeque are on or near or near Calle Intermedio, which runs through town.

Hotel Turista (☎ 653 3639; Av General Francisco Morazán; s/d US$3.25/5, with bathroom US$4.30/6.60) A bunch of cheap accommodations are near the bus stops and this is the best of them. It's very basic, but there are signs of regular cleaning. It is near the Toritos & Copaneca bus stop.

Hotel Maya Chortí (☎ 653 3377; Av General Francisco Morazán; s/d with fan US$11/19, with air-con US$14/24, incl breakfast; [P] [X]) Border town hotels are not normally known for their accommodating staff, but this is a welcome exception. Rooms have hot-water bathrooms and cable TV and there is a restaurant on-site.

Servi Pollo (dishes US$3-4; ☯ 9am-7pm) Well, you weren't expecting to get haute cuisine here, were you? This fast-food joint has fried and roast chicken, as well as hot dogs and hamburgers. From the bus stop go south, left at the Banco Occidente, then take the second right.

Getting There & Away

Two long-distance bus companies serve Nueva Ocotepeque: **Congolón** (☎ 653 3064) is half a block south of the parque central while **Toritos & Copaneca** (☎ 653 3405) is two blocks north of the park. Destinations:

Agua Caliente (US$0.90, 30 minutes, 22km) Buses leave every half-hour from the Transporte San José terminal two blocks north of the park.

El Poy/Salvadoran border (US$0.50, 15 minutes, 7km) Buses leave every 20 minutes from 6:30am to 7pm, departing from the same place as the Agua Caliente buses. Colectivo taxis also go to El Poy for US$0.75.

CROSSING THE BORDER

Getting to Esquipulas, Guatemala

The Honduras–Guatemala border at **Agua Caliente** is open from 4am to 7pm; go through Honduran immigration first, then catch a ride (US$0.80, 2km) up the hill to the Guatemalan post. From there buses go frequently to **Esquipulas** (10km, 30 minutes), where you can connect to **Guatemala City** or **Flores**. There are no accommodations in Agua Caliente; the last bus from Agua Caliente to Nueva Ocotepeque is at 6pm.

Getting to La Palma, El Salvador

The Honduras–El Salvador border at **El Poy** is open from 6am to 6pm. On both sides, the bus drops you about 100m from the border, where you can walk across and catch a bus onward.

There should be no fee to leave Honduras or to enter El Salvador, but Honduran immigration authorities may charge a small fee. Likewise, there should be no fee to leave El Salvador. On the Salvadoran side, buses leave frequently for **San Salvador** and **La Palma** The last one to San Salvador leaves El Poy around 4:15pm. On the Honduran side, the last bus from El Poy to Nueva Ocotepeque leaves at 7pm.

For information on crossing the border from El Salvador see p322.

La Entrada (US$4, 2½ hours, 123km) Take any San Pedro Sula bus.

San Pedro Sula (US$6, 4½ hours, 247km) Toritos & Copaneca has regular departures from 3am to 5:30pm, while Congolón has eight departures daily: first at midnight, last at 3:30pm.

Santa Rosa de Copán (US$2.40, 1½ hours, 95km) Take any San Pedro Sula bus.

Tegucigalpa (US$11, nine to 10 hours) Take the San Pedro Sula bus and transfer. One Toritos & Copaneca direct bus leaves at 11pm (US$13).

NORTHERN HONDURAS

The lush, tropical northern region of Honduras has seduced visitors for centuries – its natural wonders and easy Caribbean vibe make it difficult to resist.

Tangled among the beaches are mangrove swamps and tropical vegetation; beyond them lie virgin jungle, slopes and rivers that just scream out to adventure travelers. Whether it is the howler monkeys of Parque Nacional Jeannette Kawas, or the manatees of the wildlife refuge at Cuero y Salado, nature stands strong in this part of the country. All this despite the huge agricultural development on the fertile, narrow coastal plains, which have yielded enough bananas to float an entire economy.

La Ceiba is the region's party town, and a jumping-off point for the Bay Islands. Its *zona viva* (party zone) has kept many a good-time gringo under its spell for longer than

planned. Beyond its urban core are 1001 outdoor adventures: rafting down the Río Cangrejal, hiking in Pico Bonito or whizzing on a canopy tour in the coastal jungle. Stretching right along the coast are Garífuna villages, bastions of a culture rich with African and Carib heritage. The Garífuna are descendants of slaves abandoned by the British on Roatán at the end of the 18th century.

Most people (rightly) quickly skip through port town of Puerto Cortés, but the two other main towns, Tela and Trujillo, both have their charms – beaches, plentiful seafood and laidback people to name but a few.

The coast fills up with tourists during **Semana Santa** (Easter) when Hondurans enjoy a week of holidaying and making merry. Book in advance at this time and beware the prices – they can double. Most places are quiet the rest of the time.

DANGERS & ANNOYANCES

Travelers have been accosted and robbed on lonely stretches of beach outside La Ceiba, Tela and Trujillo, mostly by groups of youths. Some people have had belongings swiped from the beach while they were in the water. This was more of a concern a few years back and tourist police have helped address the problem.

However, do be vigilant. Do not walk along these beaches without company, and never after dark.

The north coast has a very high rate of HIV infection: plan accordingly.

HONDURAS

DIG THAT BEAT: INSIDE GARÍFUNA DANCING

Shaking to live Garífuna music is a highlight of the north coast. Musicians create a throbbing pared-down sound using large drums, a turtle shell, maracas and a big conch shell. Words are chanted, the audience responds and dancers begin to move their hips in physics-defying loops to the *punta*, a traditional Garífuna dance.

During mid July every year, the **national Garífuna dance festival** takes place in the small town of Baja Mar, near Puerto Cortés. All towns and villages have annual fiestas, and cultural events and gatherings of one kind or another happen throughout the year. **Garífuna Day** (April 12), a big holiday for all the Garífuna communities, commemorates the day in 1797 when the Garífunas arrived in Honduras. Often you can arrange for dances if you ask around at Garífuna villages.

Near Trujillo, the towns of Santa Fe and Santa Rosa de Aguán have their festivals on July 15 to 30 and August 22 to 29, respectively. The last three days are usually the most frenetic.

The National Ballet Folklórico Garífuna, based in Tegucigalpa, is a first-rate dance troupe that has performed around the world; if you get a chance to attend a performance, don't miss it.

PUERTO CORTÉS

pop 50,100

Puerto Cortés, 64km north of San Pedro Sula, is the westernmost of Honduras' major Caribbean towns. It is one of Honduras' principal deepwater ports, and over half of the country's export shipping trade, mostly bananas, pineapples and other produce, passes through here. However, there's not a lot of interest to travelers.

Information

BAC Credomatic (Parque Central) This bank has a Unibanc ATM.

Banco de Occidente (2a Av at 4a Calle; ☽ 8:30am-4:30pm Mon-Fri, 8:30am-noon Sat) On the corner of parque central; changes traveler's checks and gives cash advances on Visa cards.

Multinet Internet Café (Parque Central; per hr US$0.65; ☽ 8:15am-8pm Mon-Sat, 9:15am-7:15pm Sun) The most convenient internet café in town. International calls to the USA cost US$0.05 per minute.

Sights

Playa de Cieneguita, a few kilometers toward Omoa, is the most pleasant beach in the area and has a couple of beachside restaurants and upscale hotels. Other beaches at Travesía and Baja Mar (opposite) are accessible by local bus. The proximity to San Pedro Sula means the beaches here can get crowded on weekends and holidays.

Puerto Cortés' **annual fair** is held on August 15.

The main reason for coming to Puerto Cortés is its twice-weekly boat service to Belize, the only regularly scheduled boat transportation between the two countries.

Sleeping & Eating

There are plenty of places to stay in Puerto Cortés, although few nice ones. Below are two of the more acceptable options.

Hotel El Centro (☎ 665 1160; 3a Av btwn 2a & 3a Calles Este; s/d with fan US$13.30/18.75, with air-con US$18.15/23.50; P ⚒) Cramped but secure rooms are well kept and have clean bedding – there should be a small fashion warning: the walls are very orange. It is convenient to the bus stations.

Hotel Internacional Mr Ggeerr (☎ 665 4333; 9a Calle btwn 1a & 2a Avs; s/d/tr US$21/21/27; ⚒) Despite a pretty unpromising, seedy-looking facade, this is not too bad within. Rooms are a bit dingy, but linen is well starched and all rooms are air-conditioned, a definite plus in this sweltering port town. Turn right a block further east after Sport Boy's.

Sport Boy's (☎ 665 1141; 2a Av btwn 8a & 9a Calles; dishes US$2.50-5.75; ☽ 10am-10pm) Simple no-frills café serving filling, meat-heavy dishes, including hamburgers. There are a couple of basic salad options, and you can also choose from the 'sand wish' combos.

Getting There & Away

BOAT

Two different companies run crossings to Belize. The crossings are not always on time, and the schedule has changed several times recently. The **Express** (☎ 9848 4198) leaves Barra la Laguna, 3km southeast of Puerto Cortés, at 11:30am Monday to Big Creek and Placencia (three hours). Another company, **Water Taxi Nesymein Neydy** (☎ 3396 1380), goes to Belize at noon on Monday and Tuesday, again calling at Big Creek and Placencia. Tickets to each destination cost US$50, whichever boat you take. You need to be there by 9am to sign up, with your passport, on the day of travel. To get to the ferries, take any San Pedro–Omoa bus and get off at La Laguna. The office is in the fish market, under a bridge about 200m from the highway. You can also change lempiras to Belizean dollars at the dock.

Note that it may be cheaper and easier for you to get to Belize via the Guatemalan port of Puerto Barrios (see p179).

BUS
The two bus companies that service San Pedro Sula have terminals side by side on 4a Av between 3a and 4a Calles, one block north and half a block west of the parque central. **Citul** (☎ 665 0466) has express minibuses that leave every 15 minutes from 4am to 6pm (US$1.30) while **Impala** (☎ 665 0606) also runs every 15 minutes from 4am to 9pm (US$1.60). Make sure you get on a smaller, faster *directo* minibus unless you're seriously watching the lempira, in which case get one of the slower buses (US$1.10, every 10 minutes between both companies).

With its terminal half a block north, **Transportes Citral Costeños** (☎ 655 0888; 3a Calle Este) has buses to the Corinto border with Guatemala every 20 minutes (US$2, two hours). The last bus leaves at 4pm.

See the Travesía & Baja Mar (right) and Omoa (right) sections for information on buses to those areas.

TRAIN
A passenger train that used to operate between Puerto Cortés and Tela has now stopped permanently.

TRAVESÍA & BAJA MAR
Just to the east of Puerto Cortés, Travesía and Baja Mar are two seaside Garífuna villages. The beach at Travesía is cleaner than the one at Baja Mar. The road from Puerto Cortés runs along the sea, first through Travesía and on to Baja Mar; the two villages form a continuous row of wooden houses beside the sea, with small fishing boats lining the shore.

There are one or two restaurants in each village. Baja Mar is best known as the home of the Garífuna national dance festival (see opposite), held here every year between July 9 and 24. Members of all three dozen or so Garífuna communities in Honduras attend, sometimes dancing right through the night.

Sleeping & Eating
Hotel Frontera del Caribe (☎ /fax 665 5001; r US$13.25; P) Right on the beach in Travesía, this is the most pleasant place to stay near Puerto Cortés if you're on a budget. Seven upstairs rooms (sleeping up to three people), all with private bathroom and ceiling fan, are simple, clean and often have a pleasant sea breeze. Downstairs is an inexpensive beachside restaurant which serves breakfast, lunch and dinner.

The bus coming from Puerto Cortés stops just outside the door.

Getting There & Away
The bus to Travesía and Baja Mar departs from near the Citul terminal in Puerto Cortés at 7am, 10am, noon, 2pm, 3pm and 5pm; the last bus back leaves Baja Mar around 3:45pm, passing Travesía round 4pm. The bus runs less frequently on Sunday.

A taxi will take you between Puerto Cortés and Travesía in about 10 minutes for US$4.

OMOA
pop 5300
The small, snail-paced village of Omoa lies 18km west of Puerto Cortés on a broad, curving bay that makes for great sunsets. A longtime weekend getaway for San Pedro Sula residents, Omoa used to attract a steady stream of backpackers, most heading to or coming from nearby Guatemala. Now the highway to the border is paved, not so many stop. Controversial liquid-gas spheres haven't helped improve the town's appeal. That said, it's still not a bad place to break up a journey, with one good hostel and a clutch of seafood restaurants along the seafront. Omoa's **annual festival** is held on May 30.

Information
Buses to and from Omoa leave from the beach. If you're in a hurry, walk the 1km to the highway for more regular buses. Banco de Occidente changes traveler's checks. There are a few small *pulperías* on the highway and some fruit stands on the road to the beach. Check your email at Saonet Internet on the main road near the highway.

Sights
Omoa's claim to historical fame is its Spanish fortress (now with a museum), the **Fortaleza de San Fernando de Omoa** (admission US$2; ⏰ 8am-4pm Mon-Fri, 9am-5pm Sat & Sun). Built between 1759 and

HONDURAS

CROSSING THE BORDER

Getting to Puerto Barrios, Guatemala

The Guatemalan border is 3km past the town of **Corinto**. For now, you take a bus from Omoa to Corinto (US$2, every hour), where you go through Honduras immigration (exit stamp US$2) and then catch a pickup to the border. The road is now paved and Honduras immigration – and the bus stop – should have moved to the actual border by the time you read this. From there, Guatemalan buses connect to **Puerto Barrios**. The whole trip takes around four hours and costs about US$3.

There is no regular passenger boat service from Honduras to Guatemala.

See p179 for information on crossing the border from Guatemala.

Getting to Placencia, Belize

Boats to Belize leave from **Barra La Laguna** near Puerto Cortés every Monday and Tuesday to Dangriga and Placencia. Tickets (US$50) need to be purchased several hours or, ideally, a day in advance. See p384.

1777 under orders from King Fernando VII of Spain to protect the coast from rampant piracy, in 1779 the fortress was captured by the British after only a four-day battle. Still in good shape, the fort is maintained by the Instituto Hondureño de Antropología e Historia.

There are a couple of cool waterfalls and swimming holes in the area. They are a 45- and 60-minute walk respectively from Omoa; for safety, do not go alone.

Sleeping & Eating

Roli's Place (☎ 658 9082; rg@yaxpactours.com; campsite per person US$2.70, hammock US$2.70, dm US$3.80, r with shared bathroom US$8.60, r with bathroom & air-con US$16.20; ⊠) A well-equipped hostel, this has a communal kitchen and free use of kayaks and bicycles. There are now two well-furnished double rooms, for a bit more luxury, alongside dormitories, double rooms with shared showers, a terrace for hammocks and a tent area. There is purified water on tap. Watch out for the (numerous) hostel rules, including an 11pm curfew – the Swiss owner has little patience with rule-breakers. He operates a shuttle to La Ceiba and Puerto Barrios (see right).

Hotel Fisherman (☎ 658 9224; r per person US$8.10) About the only other half-decent budget option in town. Make sure you have a nose around before you take a room – some of the bathrooms are so tiny, you had better be ready to breathe in. The owners have a restaurant just opposite.

La Casa Romántica (dishes US$2-6; ⊙ 9am-9pm) The quirky German-speaking owner whips up some lovely seafood dishes, including red snapper and barracuda and some excellent

salads. The hours are unreliable, however, and there was talk of selling the restaurant when we visited. Turn left at the pier and walk about 100m down to see if it is still there.

Comedor Doña Rafa (dishes US$1-2; ⊙ 7am-8pm) A short walk up the main road from Roli's Place, this simple eatery is run by a chatty, friendly señora. It serves well prepared *típica* including eggs, beans, beef soup and more. A good breakfast option.

Getting There & Away

BUS

Buses direct to Omoa depart from Puerto Cortés every 20 minutes from 6am to 7:20pm (US$0.70, one hour). They depart just behind the Citul and the Impala terminals in Puerto Cortés. Most will take the turnoff on the highway, and drop passengers off on the beach. From Omoa to Puerto Cortés, buses depart every half hour from 4:30am to 6:30pm. From Puerto Cortés, buses leave frequently for San Pedro Sula, a transport hub.

Roli's Place runs shuttles to La Ceiba (US$20, minimum six people) or to Puerto Barrios in Guatemala (US$15).

TELA

pop 30,000

There is something about Tela. On the surface it's not much to look at. It is hot and humid, and the center is just another Honduran town – maybe moving at a slower pace. But after a day or so checking out its beaches, chatting to the locals and sampling the seafood, many find themselves falling for its languid, laid-back vibe.

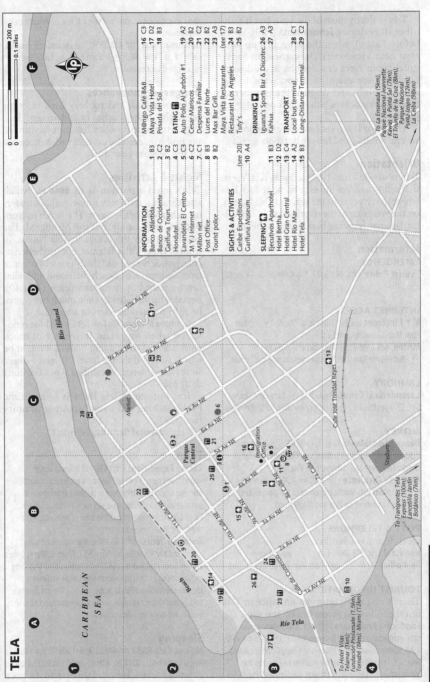

TELA

INFORMATION
Banco Atlántida..................................	1 B3
Banco de Occidente...........................	2 C2
Garífuna Tours...................................	3 B2
Hondutel..	4 C3
Lavandería El Centro..........................	5 C3
M Y J Internet....................................	6 C2
Milton net..	7 C1
Post Office...	8 B3
Tourist police....................................	9 B2

SIGHTS & ACTIVITIES
Caribe Expeditions.............................	(see 20)
Garifuna Museum...............................	10 A4

SLEEPING
Ejecutivos Aparthotel..........................	11 B3
Hotel Bertha......................................	12 D2
Hotel Gran Central.............................	13 C4
Hotel Rio Mar....................................	14 A2
Hotel Tela...	15 B3

EATING
Auto Pollo Al Carbón #1.....................	19 A2
César Mariscos...................................	20 B2
Despensa Familiar..............................	21 C2
Luces del Norte..................................	22 B2
Max Bar Grill.....................................	23 A3
Maya Vista Restaurante....................	(see 17)
Restaurant Los Ángeles......................	24 B3
Tuty's..	25 B2

M@ngo Café B&B............................	16 C3
Maya Vista Hotel.............................	17 D2
Posada del Sol.................................	18 B3

DRINKING
Iguana's Sports Bar & Discotec........	26 A3
Kahlua..	27 A3

TRANSPORT
Local bus terminal............................	28 C1
Long-Distance Terminal....................	29 C2

To La Ensenada (5km);
Parque Nacional Jeannette
Kawas & Punta Sal (7km);
El Triunfo de la Cruz (8km);
Parque Nacional
Punta Izopo (12km);
La Ceiba (98km)

Rio Hiland

Market

Parque
Central

Immigration
Office

Calle José Trinidad Reyes

Stadium

CARIBBEAN
SEA

Beach

Rio Tela

To Hotel Vilas
Telamar (1km);
Fundación Prolansate (1.5km);
Tornabé (8km); Miami (12km)

To Transportes Tela
Express (100m);
Lancetilla Jardín
Botánico (7km)

HONDURAS

Tela is sleepy most of the year, but it's another story during **Semana Santa** (Holy Week before Easter), when the town fills up with Honduran vacationers. During Semana Santa, hotel room rates can double, and advance bookings are essential if you want to get a bed. In July and August, the number of travelers skyrockets, although room rates are unchanged.

The town is a good base for excursions to several wildlife and beauty hotspots nearby.

Orientation

Tela is divided into two sections: Tela Vieja, the 'old town', on the east bank of Río Tela where the river meets the sea, and Tela Nueva, on the west side of the river, where Hotel Villas Telamar hugs the best stretch of beach.

Information

EMERGENCY
Tourist Police (☎ 448 2079; 11a Calle NE at 4a Av NE; ☺ 24hr)

INTERNET ACCESS
M Y J Internet (6a Av NE; per hr US$0.65; ☺ 7:30am-8pm Mon-Sat, 8am-2pm Sun)
Milton.net (☎ 415 3040; 10a Calle at 9a Ave NE; ☺ 8am-9pm) Ramshackle little internet and call center.

LAUNDRY
Lavandería El Centro (4a Av NE; ☺ 7am-6pm Mon-Sat) Charges US$3.50 to wash, dry and fold 10lb of clothes.

MONEY
Banco Atlántida (4a Av at 9a Calle NE; ☺ 8:30am-4:30pm Mon-Fri, 8:30-11:30am Sat) Changes traveler's checks and gives cash advances on Visa cards.
Banco de Occidente (☺ 8:30am-4:30pm Mon-Fri, 8:30-11:30am Sat) Northeast corner of the parque central. Does cash advances on Visa and MasterCard.

POST & TELEPHONE
Next door to each other:
Hondutel (☎ 448 2004; 4a Av; ☺ 7am-8:45pm)
Post office (4a Av; ☺ 8am-4pm Mon-Fri, 8am-noon Sat)

TOURIST INFORMATION
There's no tourist information office in Tela but the following places can fill the gaps.
Fundación Prolansate (☎ 448 2042; www.prolan sate-ecoturismo.com; Bo Independencia; ☺ 7am-noon & 1:30-5:30pm Mon-Sat, 8:30am-noon Sun) Opposite Villas Telamar. Promotes sustainable tourism in Tela and has information on Lancetilla Botanical Gardens and Punta Sal

and can organize educational visits. It is a 20-minute trek from town.
Garífuna Tours (☎ 448 2904; tours@hondutel.com; 9a Calle NE at 5a Ave NE; ☺ 7:30am-6:30pm) Local, well-established tour operation.

Dangers & Annoyances

Cases of assault and robbery used to occur regularly on the beaches in and around Tela. While the tourist police has mostly stopped the problem, exercise caution and do not walk on the beaches after dusk.

Sights & Activities

Tela's main attraction is its **beaches**, which stretch around the bay for several kilometers on either side of the town. The beach in front of the town is sandy, but can be littered. The beach just over the bridge in Tela Nueva, in front of Hotel Villas Telamar, is much better; its pale, powdery sand and shady grove of coconut trees are kept clean. Beach chairs and umbrellas can be rented by nonguests (each US$1.40). Beaches further afield, while much better, can be risky for solo travelers or after dusk.

Garífuna Museum (8a Calle NE) Closed for renovation when we passed through. Not much work seemed to be going on, but it might be worth seeing if things have changed – there were some interesting exhibits about Garífuna daily life.

Just outside of Tela there is some prime bird-watching and nature-spotting territory (see p390).

Tela's annual **fiesta day** is June 13.

Tours

Caribe Expeditions (☎ 448 9393; www.caribe expeditions.com; 3a Av NE) Seems a professional outfit, offering reasonable trips and excursions (minimum six people) to local wildlife reserves such as Punta Sal and Lancetilla. It was moving at the time of research. Ask at the Cesar Mariscos restaurant.
Garífuna Tours (☎ 448 2904; www.garifunatours .com; 9a Calle NE at 5a Ave NE; ☺ 7:30am-6:30pm) Offers all-day boat excursions (US$27), as well as bird-watching excursions to Los Micos Lagoon and kayak excursions to the Parque Nacional Punta Izopo. Bilingual tours (English and Spanish) are available. Some travelers report that the guides are not very informative.

Sleeping

M@ngo Café B&B (☎ 448 0388; 8a Calle NE btwn 4a & 5a Avs; s/d with fan US$8/11.70, with air-con US$16.50/21.25; ☒) A lot of backpackers end up here so it's not a bad place to meet people. It is fairly ordinary – you get basic, clean rooms with hot water. It is operated by Garífuna Tours. You can also rent bikes here (half a day US$4.10).

Posada del Sol (☎ 448 1895; 8a Calle NE btwn 3a & 4a Avs NE; s/d US$8.10/13.50) This easy-come, easy-go little family-run *posada* (pension) has well-scrubbed basic rooms with private bathroom (cold water only) and a bible. The family, who lives on-site, is relaxed and friendly and will chat to you as you lounge in the communal courtyard.

Hotel Tela (☎ 448 2150; 9a Calle NE btwn 3a & 4a Avs NE; s/d US$11/16.25; P) This matriarch of the Tela hotel scene offers one of the best deals in town, especially if there is more than one of you. It has not changed much over the years – the lino and varnish on the wooden floorboards have faded a little but its light, airy rooms remain elegantly simple. Only one room had a hot-water shower (number 11) when we were here. There's a large rooftop terrace and a restaurant.

Hotel Río Mar (☎ 448 1065; cnr 11a Calle NE & 2a Ave NE; r with fan US$15.75, with air-con US$31.50; ✖) Clean, unflashy rooms with cable TV and cold-water bathrooms. Rooms branch off a long, dark corridor. The beach is just a stone's throw away.

Hotel Bertha (☎ 448 3020; 8a Calle NE btwn 8a & 9a Avs NE; s/d US$11/22) This is not a bad deal, especially for a solo traveler. Although it is a little out of the way (it is close to the main Tela bus terminal), it is very well-kept, with floors you could eat off. Rooms have cable TV but no hot water.

Maya Vista Hotel y Restaurante (☎ 448 1497; www .mayavista.com, r with fan US$25, with air-con US$40-50; P ✖ 💻) Still one of the town's big traveler gathering spots and with good reason, even though it is pricier than most places. Most rooms have tasteful indigenous-inspired décor and a superb panorama of the bay. The stack-em-high design means you should have a floor (and therefore the view) to yourself. There is also a good restaurant on site.

Ejecutivos Aparthotel (☎ 448 1076; cnr 8a Calle NE & 4a Av NE; d/tr apt US$27/30; P ✖) Very clean and well kept, this is a possible long-term option, especially if you are in a group. The spacious, tiled apartments – dotted with crosses and religious decorations – have a well-equipped kitchen, two double beds, cable TV and hot-water bathroom.

Hotel Gran Central (☎ 448 1099; www.hotelgrancen tral.com; s/d US$40/50; ✖) If you fancy splashing

out, this is the place to do it. The renovated colonial building has been beautifully decorated by the well traveled, engaging French owners. The high-ceilinged rooms are painted in earth colors. There is a small bar, and breakfast is available. Note that the hotel is a little way from the center – but Tela is not hard to get around.

Eating

Seafood is plentiful, delicious and cheap in Tela. Seafood soups are a particular delicacy of the town; fish, shrimp, lobster and *caracol* (conch) are found in many restaurants. Another specialty of the town is *pan de coco* (coconut bread); you'll see Garífuna women or their children walking around town selling it. Try it – it's delicious.

Tuty's (☎ 448 0013; 9a Calle NE at 5a Av NE; dishes US$2-4; ☟ 7:30am-7pm Mon-Sat, 7:30am-3pm Sun) You'll find simple Formica tables, a bustling kitchen and friendly service (although you may have to wait for it) at this place just off parque central. There are omelet breakfasts if you are bored of *baleadas*, as well as pastries, juices and ice cream. Lunchtime options are particularly good value (sandwich and french fries US$2.50). It is next door to a good bakery.

Auto Pollo Al Carbón #1 (11a Calle NE at 2a Av NE; dishes US$2-4; ☟ 8am-11pm) Not a frill to be seen here: just simple roast-chicken platters served under a corrugated iron roof in an open-air shack, a wishbone's throw away from the Caribbean Sea.

Max Bar Grill (dishes US$2-4; ☟ 8am-3pm & 5-9pm Mon-Wed, 8am-3pm & 7pm-2am Thu-Sat, weekends only in low season) The friendly owners here are so laid-back they are almost horizontal. This is the kind of place that closes up when it has run out of food, and will have a day off when business is slow. If you do find the doors open, there are good-value chicken and pork lunch specials for around US$2.

Luces del Norte (☎ 448 1044; 11a Calle NE at 5a Av NE; dishes US$3.50-9; ☟ 7am-10pm) With its rustic, wooden setting and sea-salt faded paint, this remains as popular as ever among both backpackers and locals – it has some real devotees. Excellent seafood is dished up among the tropical plants that sway throughout the restaurant. Pick your own seafood style – the menu runs the gamut from pasta to paella.

Cesar Mariscos (☎ 448 2083; 3a Av NE; dishes US$5.50-9; ☟ 11am-10pm) A great open location by the beach boardwalk means you can spend your meal next to the ocean while enjoying its bounty. Seafood, of course, is the specialty here, prepared in soups, pastas or on the grill.

Maya Vista Restaurante (☎ 448 1497; off 9a Calle btwn 7a & 8a Avs; dishes US$3-11; ⏱ 7am-9pm) The view over Tela's bay is spectacular from this well-established traveler's favorite – it is quite something to eat your spaghetti and *camarones* (prawns) with the waves crashing below. Afternoon coffee and cake is also a good option.

Restaurant Los Angeles (☎ 448 2389; Calle del Comercio; ⏱ 10am-2pm & 5-9pm) This Chinese restaurant is just about the only Tela option where surf does not dominate the entire menu. Portions are enormous, even for the monstrous rations typical of Central America's Chinese restaurants. For about US$3, you can feast for the 5000.

Despensa Familiar (Parque Central; ⏱ 7am-7pm Mon-Sat, 7am-6pm Sun) Self-caterers should head to this central supermarket.

Drinking

The outdoor bar at the Maya Vista restaurant, with its fine ocean views, is about as good as it gets for an evening beer or frozen margarita; Max Bar Grill also gets lively on weekend nights.

The Iguana's Sports Bar & Discotec, in town, and Kahlua, just across the 11a Calle bridge, are both open Thursday to Sunday nights and are the most popular clubs with travelers.

Getting There & Away

BUS

Slower normal buses leave Tela every 20 minutes for La Ceiba (US$1.30, 2½ hours, 4am to 6pm) from the long-distance terminal at the corner of 9a Calle NE and 9a Av NE, three blocks northeast of the square. For quicker direct buses, you can take a taxi to the Dippsa gas station on the highway, where buses headed to La Ceiba from San Pedro Sula pass regularly.

Eight direct buses a day go to San Pedro Sula (US$3, two hours, 6am to 5pm) from the **Transportes Tela Express terminal** (2a Av NE) beyond the train tracks.

Local buses to the Garífuna villages near Tela depart from a dirt lot on the corner of 11a Calle and 8a Av (see p392 for times and schedules).

TRAIN

A train used to run between Puerto Cortés and Tela but is no longer in operation.

Getting Around

Tela has many taxis; a ride in town costs US$0.55. A taxi to Lancetilla or San Juan is about US$5; to Triunfo de la Cruz, La Ensenada or Tornabé the fare is around US$6. Mountain bikes can be rented at the **M@ngo Café B&B** (☎ 448 2856; 8a Calle NE & 5a Av NE) for US$7 for a full day.

AROUND TELA
Lancetilla Jardín Botánico

The second largest tropical garden in the world, the **Lancetilla Botanical Garden & Research Center** (www.lancetilla.org; admission US$6; ⏱ 7:30am-5pm, no entry after 4pm) was founded by the United Fruit Company in 1926 to experiment with the cultivation of various tropical plants in Central America. Although it is still an active research center, the public can now wander through this tropical wonderland of plant species from all corners of the globe. It has the largest collection of Asiatic fruit trees in the western hemisphere.

Admission includes an introductory tour, then you are free to roam the well-marked trails through the arboretum and main garden area. The bottom of the garden leads to a swimming hole.

Birdlife also thrives at Lancetilla – hundreds of species have been spotted, and this is a popular and accessible spot for birders. Each year on December 14 and 15 the Audubon Society conducts a 24-hour bird count; you can participate if you're here at that time. Migratory species are present from November to February. Bird-watching is best in the early morning or late afternoon.

There's a **visitor information office** (☎ 448 1740; ⏱ 7am-4pm Mon-Fri, 8am-noon Sat) where the park begins, and an explanatory map is available. You can arrange bird-watching tours (US$16) in advance by calling the information office ahead of time. Expect a very early morning start. Some information is also available from **Fundación Prolansate** (☎ 448 2042; www.prolansate -ecoturismo.com; Bo Independencia, Tela; ⏱ 7am-noon & 1:30-5:30pm Mon-Sat, 8:30am-noon Sun).

Accommodation is available, including **cabins** (US$20; ⏱) with three individual beds and private bathrooms. You need to call the visitor information office to book in advance.

HONDURAS

GETTING THERE AND AWAY

Lancetilla is 7km southwest of the center of Tela. A good way to get here is by bike, which you can rent in Tela. Five kilometers from town there is a turnoff from the highway that leads to the main gardens. You pay at a ticket office here. Alternatively, a taxi will take you there for around US$5. Buses do run directly there, carrying workers to the gardens. Call the information office for times.

Parque Nacional Jeannette Kawas

Standing on the beach at Tela, you can look out and see a long arc of land curving out to the west to a point almost in front of you. This point, **Punta Sal**, is part of the Parque Nacional Jeannette Kawas.

The park has several white-sand beaches, including the pretty **Playa Cocalito**. Offshore coral reefs make for fine **snorkeling**, and howler monkeys live in the forest. The park used to be known as Parque Nacional Marino Punta Sal. It was renamed for Jeannette Kawas, an environmental campaigner and former director of Prolansate, who was murdered in 1995 following her tireless work to protect the park from developers. There is a US$3 fee to enter.

On the park's east side is the **Laguna de los Micos** (Lagoon of the Monkeys) with mangrove forests, which harbors hundreds of bird species (especially from November to February, when migratory species flock here).

You can arrange day trips which include hiking, snorkeling and hanging out on Playa Cocalito. Both Garífuna Tours and Caribe Expeditions run here (see p388).

GETTING THERE & AWAY

Aside from day trips with the Tela tour companies, you can negotiate a trip with one of the boatmen who tie up under the bridge between old and new Tela. You can also make the trip from the town of Miami. From there you can do a day trip by boat or even walk to Punta Sal and camp there – although, we have received reports of assaults on this deserted stretch of beach.

Refugio de Vida Punta Izopo

Standing on the beach at Tela and looking to the east, you can see another point: **Punta Izopo**, part of the Punta Izopo Wildlife Refuge. Rivers entering the wildlife refuge spread out into a network of canals that channel through the tangle of mangrove forest. Monkeys, turtles and even crocodiles live here as well as many species of birds, including toucans and parrots.

You can arrange kayak trips through the Tela tour agencies (see p388). Gliding silently through the mangrove canals in a kayak, you can get close to the wildlife without disturbing it. It's 16km by road from Tela to Triunfo de la Cruz (below), a one-hour walk on the beach or a one-hour canoe ride.

Garífuna Villages

Several Garífuna villages are within easy reach of Tela. All of them are on the coast, with rustic houses right on the beach, fishing canoes resting on the sand and tiny restaurants serving delicious Garífuna food; the specialties are seafood soups and fish cooked in coconut. Although you can, in theory, quite easily walk to all these villages along the beaches, it is not always safe. They are mostly tranquil little places, although thefts and the occasional assault have been reported. Instead you could bus it or take a guided tour or a taxi along the access roads.

All villages have places to stay and at least a couple of restaurants beside the beach specializing in seafood (of course).

The closest village is attractive little **La Ensenada**, 3km east along the arc of the beach from Tela, just before you reach the point, Punta Triunfo, crowned by the Cerro El Triunfo de la Cruz. **Hotel Leoduvis** (☎ 935 3507; r with fan/air con US$14/19; P ✄) is well-maintained, with clean rooms. Cold-water showers only, but that is no big deal in this heat. There is a good beach just in front. There are seafood restaurants in La Ensenada (although most are only open on the weekend) and places to drink along the beach.

The larger village of **El Triunfo de la Cruz** can be reached by regular buses from Tela, departing from the corner on the east side of the market. It is the largest, most developed of the Garífuna villages, and doesn't have the same peaceful feeling of the other villages. There are a couple of reasonable places to stay. **Cabañas y Restaurante Colón** (☎ 986 5622; tw US$11-16, r with air-con US$24; P ✄) is in the center, with a bunch of cabañas a few footsteps away from the sand. There is a seafood restaurant (mains US$3.25 to US$10.75) on-site, open for all meals. The upmarket choice here is the **Caribbean Coral Inn** (☎ 994 9806; www.caribbeancoralinn.com;

GUIFITI: MOONSHINE SECRETS

The local moonshine on the north coast of Honduras is a mysterious concoction known as Guifiti (sometimes spelt Gifiti or Güfiti). Legend has it that it is a natural aphrodisiac, and aficionados claim all sorts of medicinal qualities, from helping diabetes to cleaning arteries. The exact recipe varies from brewer to brewer, although most versions will contain a base of *aguadiente* (a potent local gut-rot), as well as a blend of herbs and spices. In fact, there are rumors that in some versions not all of the ingredients are entirely legal. Perhaps this is why you cannot pick up a bottle from supermarket shelves. However, make a few discreet enquiries in most north-coast towns and villages, and it won't be long before you track down a dram – even in surprisingly upmarket locations. It's pretty powerful stuff so don't throw too many glasses down your throat too quickly. If you are keen to spread the love and take some home, you can buy a legal version of it in the Mercado Guamilito in San Pedro Sula (p365).

---

s/d incl breakfast US$51/62) with expensively rustic beachside cabins.

On the other side of Tela, to the west, is **Tornabé**, another Garífuna village, 8km away. It is a largish village. **Hotel the Last Resort** (☎ 995 2695; tw/tr US$27/43; P ✕) is not as bad as it sounds – but not as upscale as the price tag merits.

Past Tornabé, the beach road becomes rougher and can only be negotiated by 4WD. It continues for several more kilometers to **Miami**, a beautiful but basic village on a narrow sandbar between the Caribbean Sea and the Laguna de los Micos. This area may well change beyond recognition. The Inter-American Development Bank has approved a controversial 'soft' loan for a giant hotel complex and golf club to be built in the area – hardly a big step towards ecologically and culturally sensitive tourism. The ground was being prepared by builders at the time of research.

GETTING THERE & AWAY
Although you can walk along the beach from Tela to any of the villages, the walk is not always safe and should not be done alone or at night.

Buses to the Garífuna villages depart from the local bus terminal in Tela. There are two routes: one heading west to Tornabé, another heading east to Triunfo de la Cruz. Buses on both routes depart hourly from around 6am to 5pm; the fare is about US$0.50, and it takes about 30 to 45 minutes to reach the villages.

If you're driving or cycling, you can get to Tornabé by the beach road heading west from Tela. Be careful where you cross the sandbar at the Laguna de los Micos between San Juan and Tornabé; vehicles regularly get stuck in the sand here. You may need a 4WD vehicle to get past Tornabé to Miami. You can also get to

Tornabé from the highway; the turnoff, 5km west of Tela, is marked by a sign to 'The Last Resort.' To drive to La Ensenada or Triunfo de la Cruz, take the highway to the turnoff for Triunfo de la Cruz, 5km east of Tela. After 1km the road forks. Go left to La Ensenada, right to Triunfo de la Cruz.

LA CEIBA
pop 138,800
It is known as Honduras' party town – Tegucigalpa thinks, San Pedro Sula works and La Ceiba has fun, the saying goes. There is certainly a full and vibrant nightlife, which makes this port city, set beneath the magnificent Pico Bonito mountain, more than just a jumping-off point to the Bay Islands or La Moskitia. Certainly, *Ceibeños*, as the locals are known, are proud of their city, Honduras' third largest. It is not a particularly attractive place at first glance. The beaches are average at best, and the buildings are not much to write home about either. But with some fine bars and restaurants, and excellent adventure tourism just a short hop away, it is small wonder that many visitors linger longer than planned.

La Ceiba got its name from a very large ceiba tree that used to stand on the coast near where the pier is now.

Orientation
The heart of La Ceiba is its attractive, shady parque central. Av San Isidro, running from the east side of the plaza to the sea, is La Ceiba's main drag. A block or two over, Av 14 de Julio is another major commercial street. Av La República, running to the sea from the opposite side of the plaza, has train tracks down its center that used to transport Standard Fruit Company cargo to the pier.

LA CEIBA

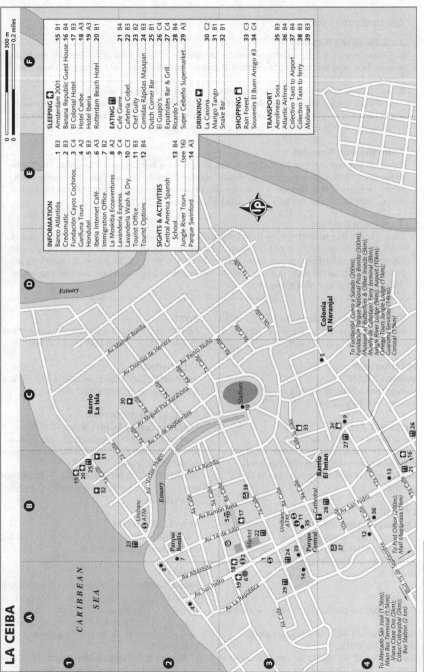

INFORMATION

Banco Atlántida	1	B3
Credomatic	2	B3
Fundación Cayos Cochinos	3	C4
Garífuna Tours	4	A2
Hondutel	5	B3
Iberia Internet Café	6	A3
Immigration Office	7	B2
La Moskitia Ecoaventuras	8	A2
Lavandería Express	9	C4
Lavandería Wash & Dry	10	C3
Tourist Office	11	B3
Tourist Options	12	B4

SIGHTS & ACTIVITIES

Central America Spanish School	13	B4
Jungle River Tours	(see 16)	
Parque Swinford	14	A3

SLEEPING

Amsterdam 2001	15	B1
Banana Republic Guest House	16	B4
El Colonial Hotel	17	B3
Hotel Caribe	18	A3
Hotel Iberia	19	A3
Rotterdam Beach Hotel	20	B1

EATING

Cafe Giarre	21	B4
Cafetería Cobel	22	B3
Chef Guity	23	B2
Comidas Rápidas Masapan	24	B3
Dutch Corner Bar	25	B1
El Guapo's	26	C4
Expatriates Bar & Grill	27	C4
Ricardo's	28	B4
Super Ceibeño Supermarket	29	A3

DRINKING

La Casona	30	C2
Mango Tango	31	B1
Snake Bar	32	B1

SHOPPING

Rain Forest	33	C3
Souvenirs El Buen Amigo #3	34	C4

TRANSPORT

Aerolíneas Sosa	35	B3
Atlantic Airlines	36	B4
Colectivo Taxis to Airport	37	B4
Colectivo Taxis to ferry	38	B3
Molinari	39	B3

CARIBBEAN SEA

Estuary

Barrio La Isla

Stadium

Colonia El Naranjal

Barrio El Iman

Parque Bonilla

Parque Central

Market

Av Manuel Bonilla
Av Dionisio de Herrera
Av Pedro Nuño
Av Miguel Paz Barahona
Av 15 de Septiembre
Av Victor Hugo
Av La Bastilla
Av Ramón Rosa
Av 14 de Julio
Av Atlántida
Av San Isidro
Av La República

To Fundación Cuero y Salado (200m);
Parque National Pico Bonito (300m);
Museum of Butterflies & Other Insects (3km);
Muelle de Cabotaje; Ferry terminal (8km);
Jungle River Lodge (9km); Airport (10km);
Omega Tours Jungle Lodge (11km);
Guaruma Servicios (14km);
Corozal (15km)

To Post Office (200m);
Mall Megaplaza (1km)

To Mercado San José (1.5km);
Main Bus Terminal (1.5km);
Viana Clase Oro (1.5km);
Cotuc/Cotraipbal (2km);
Bus Station (2 km)

GETTING INTO TOWN

To & From the Airport

La Ceiba's airport, the Aeropuerto Internacional Golosón, is 10km west of La Ceiba on the highway to Tela. Any bus heading west from the main bus terminal could drop you there. Taxis from Colectivo Taxensa leave from the southwest corner of parque central and pass the airport (US$0.70); you have to wait for the taxi to fill up. A normal taxi costs about US$3.

Coming from the airport, don't take one of the taxis right at the airport door, which charge about US$5 per person for the ride into town; walk out to the main road and flag down a colectivo which will take you into town for around US$0.70 per person.

From the Bus Terminal

The main bus terminal is at Mercado San José, about 1.5km west of central La Ceiba. The **Viana Clase Oro** (☎ 441 2330) express bus terminal is another 500m further west along the same street, at the Servicentro Esso Miramar. A local bus runs between the main bus terminal and the central plaza (US$0.17), or you can take a taxi (US$1.10; colectivo US$0.70).

To & From the Pier

Ferries to the **Bay Islands** operate from the Muelle de Cabotaje, about 8km (20 minutes) east of town. From the bus terminal or from town, taxis should take you there for US$5.50 per carload (up to four people); from the pier back to either location is US$1.70 per person. A colectivo goes from the town center from 7a Calle, a good lempira-saving option if you are traveling alone. There is no colectivo on the way back.

Over the estuary is Barrio La Isla, the city's *zona viva*, or party zone. There's a large Garífuna community on this side.

Information

IMMIGRATION

Immigration office (☎ 442 0638; 1a Calle near Av 14 de Julio; ⏰ 7:30am-3:30pm)

INTERNET ACCESS

Iberia Internet Café (Av San Isidro; per hr US$0.80; ⏰ 7am-9pm Mon-Fri, 8am-9pm Sat, 10am-8pm Sun) Next to Hotel Iberia. Reliable high-speed connections; good-quality international calls for US$0.17 per minute.

LAUNDRY

Lavandería Express (per 10lb US$3; ⏰ 7:30am-noon & 1-5:30pm) Near Expatriates Bar & Grill.
Lavandería Wash & Dry (per 10lb US$2.65; ⏰ 8am-noon & 1-5pm Mon-Sat) West of the stadium.

MONEY

All the banks in the Mall Megaplaza have ATMs.
Banco Atlántida (Av San Isidro) Changes traveler's checks and has an ATM.
Credomatic (☎ 443 0668; Av San Isidro) Opposite Hotel Iberia; use Visa and MasterCard here.

POST

Post office (Av Morazán at 14a Calle; ⏰ 8am-4pm Mon-Fri, 8am- noon Sat) A bit of a trek from the center.

TELEPHONE

Hondutel (Av Ramón Rosa btwn Calles 5a & 6a; ⏰ 7am-8:30pm) Domestic and international phone calls.

TOURIST INFORMATION

Fundación Cuero y Salado (☎ /fax 443 0329; www .cueroysalado.org; Av Ramón Rosa at 15a Calle; ⏰ 8am-noon & 1-5pm Mon-Fri, 8-11am Sat) Manages the Cuero y Salado Wildlife Reserve.
Tourist Office (☎ 440 3044; 8a Calle; ⏰ 8am-4:30pm Mon-Fri, 9am-1pm Sat) Helpful local tourist office located just off the park.

TRAVEL AGENCIES

Tour companies (opposite) are your best bet for booking travel services.

Sights

Parque Swinford (Av La República btwn 7a & 8a Calles) is a lush, tropical botanical oasis in the heart of La Ceiba, complete with a restored railway carriage from the area's track heyday. You will probably have to share it with a few smooching couples.

Museum of Butterflies & Other Insects (☎ 442 2874; www.hondurasbutterfly.com; Calle Escuela Internacional G-12,

Colonia El Sauce; adult/child US$3/1.50; 🕑 8am-5pm Mon-Sat) is a remarkable collection of over 12,000 butterflies, moths and other insects. Most of them were collected in Honduras by schoolteacher Robert Lehman, and all are displayed in cases covering the walls. Highlights include the largest moth in the world, with a 30cm (1ft) wingspan, and a gigantic quarter-pound beetle, the heaviest in the world. There's a self-guided tour and an interesting 25-minute video about butterflies and moths.

The city reaches its good-time peak at **Carnaval**, when it gets very busy. It's celebrated here during the third week in May; Saturday is the biggest day, with parades, costumes, music and celebrations in the streets.

Activities

La Ceiba is, quite rightly, the adventure and ecotourism capital of Honduras. See (right) for details of tour operators offering the following activities.

WHITE-WATER RAFTING & CANOEING

The **Río Cangrejal** offers some of the best white-water rafting in Central America. Both Jungle River Tours and Omega Tours offer trips. You will likely have fun on both. Omega Tours cost more, but its trips are better received. Canoe or kayak trips in nearby, less-visited lagoons such as **Cacao Lagoon** often turn up more monkey and bird sightings than trips to Cuero y Salado. Find out how long you'll be on the water and if lunch or excursions (like short hikes into Parque Nacional Pico Bonito) are included.

HIKING

Independent travelers can visit Cuero y Salado wildlife refuge and hike in the Pico Bonito National Park without joining an expensive tour group (see p400 for more on how to go it alone). Some of the more complicated trips are better done with a guide, including trips to area waterfalls and Garífuna villages. Guaruma Servicios is a good option for the Río Cangrejal side of Pico Bonito, while on the El Pino side, get in touch with the tourism committee at **Vivero Natural View** (☎ 368 8343, 371 9631).

CANOPY TOURS

Jungle River Tours operates an eight-cable circuit that lasts two hours and includes a 200m slide across the river (per person US$35,

reservation required). Like all Jungle River tours, a free night at the river lodge is included. There is now an even longer canopy tour about 500m past Sambo Creek, east of La Ceiba (see p399).

Festivals & Events

Visitors from far and wide descend on La Ceiba for its annual **Carnaval**, held during the week of May 15, which is the day of San Isidro, the town's patron saint. People dress up in costumes and masks and dance themselves silly; it's a great time.

Courses

The **Central America Spanish School** (☎ 440 1061; www.ca-spanish.com; Av San Isidro btwn 12a & 13a Calles) offers intensive language classes. A week's homestay and tuition costs US$190.

Tours

Garífuna Tours (☎ 448 2904; Av San Isidro at 1a Calle; www.garifunatours.com) Organizes rafting trips and tours of Pico Bonito and Cuero y Salado.

Guaruma Servicios (☎ 442 2673; www.guaruma .org) A worthwhile operation dedicated to boosting opportunities for the local community through sustainable tourism. It's based at the small village of Las Mangas in Río Cangrejal.

Jungle River Tours (☎ 440 1282/1268; www.jungle riverlodge.com) At Banana Republic Guest House, organizes white-water rafting trips (from US$35), canopy tours and hiking; rappelling and bouldering also available. Trips can include a free night at the jungle lodge.

La Moskitia Ecoaventuras (☎ 442 2124; www.hon duras.com/moskitia; Av 14 de Julio) Offers white-water rafting, tours of Pico Bonito and Cuero y Salado, and multi-day trips into La Moskitia. Based at Hotel Plaza Caracol.

Omega Tours (☎ 440 0334; www.omegatours.hn; Omega Tours Jungle Lodge, road to Yaruca Km 9) Set up by a former international kayaker, it offers white-water rafting (from US$44), and swimming, kayak and canoe trips, horseback riding, and jungle- and river-hiking tours. All trips include a free night at its jungle lodge. Slightly pricier but slicker than rival Jungle River Tours.

Tourist Options (☎ 440 0265; www.hondurastourist options.com; Blvd 15 de Septiembre) Friendly agency, arranging trips to Garífuna villages, Pico Bonito, Cuero y Salado and Cayos Cochinos, among others. In the Viajes Atlántida travel agency.

Sleeping

Accommodations are fairly uninspired in La Ceiba. Staying in the center is convenient, although it is eerily quiet at night. Barrio La

Isla is nearer the nightlife. There is now one decent hostel, which has improved things. More interesting accommodation is outside the city amid the tropical jungle by the Río Cangrejal.

DOWNTOWN

Banana Republic Guest House (☎ 441 9404, 440 1268; Av La República, www.jungleriverlodge.com; dm US$5, d with shared bathroom US$10; d/tr with bathroom US$13/19; P ▣) This is a welcome addition to La Ceiba's accommodation scene, which was short on good hostels. It is run by the same people who manage Jungle River Lodge. We trust this new site will be the same as the last – basic, clean, secure and a good place to bump into fellow travelers. A bus to the ferry terminal runs right outside.

Hotel San Carlos (☎ 443 0330; Av San Isidro btwn 5a & 6a Calle; s/d with bathroom US$6.50/8.10) Upstairs rooms are bare but efficiently scrubbed and with clean linen. It has the same owner as the midrange Hotel Iberia next door. In room 21 you can just squeeze a view of Pico Bonito through the mosquito net and glass slats. You do not have to go far for bread – it is set behind a bakery.

Hotel Caribe (☎ 443 1857; 5a Calle btwn Avs San Isidro & Atlántida; s/d US$6/10, with TV US$8/11, r with air-con & TV US$14; ✷) Large upstairs rooms with fans are a passable deal, although get flip-flops at the ready for the shared bathrooms. Linen is not always clean.

El Colonial Hotel (☎ 443 1953; fax 443 1955; Av 14 de Julio btwn 6a & 7a Calle; s with fan US$11, s/d with air-con US$14.50/18.50; ✷) Formerly one of the more upmarket places in town, this fell on hard times and has reinvented itself as one of the better downtown budget places. Spotless rooms have cold-water private bathrooms. The entrance is hard to find – look out for the doorway up some stairs in the central shopping district.

Hotel Iberia (☎ 443 0401; www.hoteliberia.com; Av San Isidro btwn 5a & 6a Calles; r US$25; P ✷) Not an amazing deal for what you pay (the rooms are past their overhaul date) but the service is friendly and the hotel is secure. The central location – just a few paces away from internet cafés and banks – is also a plus. Rooms have private hot-water bathrooms.

BARRIO LA ISLA

These two options are a good 15-minute walk from downtown, but a mere stumble away from the nightlife.

Amsterdam 2001 (☎ 443 2311; off 1a Calle; dm/d/tr US$5/9/13) On the same street as Rotterdam Beach. Run by a Dutch former sailor, this was the town's original backpackers' hangout. The rooms were clean when we visited but many other travelers have been unimpressed.

Rotterdam Beach Hotel (☎ 440 0321; off 1a Calle; d/tr US$10/15) Near the *zona viva* area. Rooms front onto an attractive, tropical garden with a wood-cabin reception. Rooms are clean and a good value. It is run by a Dutch-Honduran family.

RÍO CANGREJAL

Guaruma Community Lodge (☎ 443 0618, 442 2673; www.guaruma.org; s/d US$8/15) Set high in the mountainside community of Las Mangas, beyond the two jungle lodges, these hillside cabins were built by a local workforce. They are comfortable, basic and clean, and include hot water. Profits are channeled back into the community. There's a restaurant with good-value meals (US$3.30) for guests. You can organize walks with local guides through the surrounding jungle, including to the lovely El Bejuco waterfall. The one downer is that there is not much in the way of organized transfers. You'll have to make your own way by bus to Yaruca (see p399) or flag a pickup.

Jungle River Lodge (☎ 440 1268; www.jungleriver lodge.com; road to Yaruca Km 7; dm/d US$9/23) The rooms and dorms are rustic but the setting is a winner. On a hillside, the lodge overlooks the roaring Río Cangrejal. Sitting in the outdoor restaurant will be one of your more memorable Honduran experiences. Canopy tours start here; swimming, hiking and white-water rafting options are nearby. To get here, take a Yaruca bus from the main terminal and look for a sign on your right, or call and organize it with Banana Republic Guest House. You stay in the dorm room for free if you take an organized trip.

Omega Tours Jungle Lodge (☎ 440 0334, 965 5815; www.omegatours.hn; Road to Yaruca Km 9; s/d with shared bathroom US$10/14, cabins US$25-75) Set in the mountainside a little up from the river, Omega Lodge is a study in tasteful development. A trip with Omega Tours includes a clean, basic room at the bottom of the complex. A lot more pricey but very memorable are the cabins at the top – beautifully done out in a style best described as modernist German meets tropical tree cabin, and with superb views. The simpler Creek Cabin is elevated over running water. Outdoor showers are solar heated and no chemicals are used in the swimming pool. Among the tropical gardens is a bar and restaurant serving good dishes with a German twist. Take the Yaruca bus from the main terminal and look for a sign on your left, just beyond the Jungle River Lodge; or contact Omega to arrange a transfer.

Eating

DOWNTOWN

Cafetería Cobel (☎ 442 2192; 7a Calle at Av Atlántida; dishes US$2-3.50; ⦿ 6:30am-6pm Mon-Sat) Cheap little eatery where you can get your *comida típica* (typical lunch) for two bucks, including grilled meat or chicken with rice. The bustle means you may take a while to attract the attention of the neatly uniformed waitresses. There is air-con in the back room – or you can order a *licuado* (US$0.70) to cool down.

    Comidas Rápidas Masapan (☎ 442 0627; cnr 7a Calle & Av La República; dishes US$2.50-5.50; ⦿ 6am-8pm) Its cafeteria style may take you back to lunchtime in the fourth grade, but there's a good spread of cheap, filling and tasty dishes, whichever meal you slide your tray down the rails for. Dishes are mostly Honduran, but there are some pastas and Caribbean meals thrown into the mix. A very good budget option.

    El Guapo's (☎ 440 1302; 14a Calle with Av 14 de Julio; mains US$5.50-7; ⦿ lunch & dinner) This is run by a larger-than-life American and his Honduran partner. Grill dishes are heaped high and are surprisingly good value. The shaded outdoor tables are very pleasant despite the proximity of the main road. It hosts regular events at the restaurant, from literary evenings to live music.

    Café Giarre (cnr Av San Isidro & 13a Calle; dishes US$5.50-7.50; ⦿ 11:30am-10pm Wed-Mon, closed Sun morning) Take your pick from the outside terrace shaded by arching palm leaves or the cute little inside dining area at this elegant European-style café. Coffee-lovers are in for a treat – good espresso and cappuccinos are served here, as well as pasta, Italian cakes and tropical cocktails.

    Expatriates Bar & Grill (☎ 442 0938; 12a Calle, Barrio El Imán; dishes US$7-11; ⦿ 2:30pm-midnight) This is a slice of Americana under a thatched roof in the tropics. Big games are often screened here; the barbecued chicken wings are rightfully famous and vegetarian options are reasonable too. You may find yourself whiling away an evening drink speculating about the various expat characters that gather here. There is also a cocktail bar with a selection of fine cigars.

Ricardo's (☎ 443 0468; cnr Av 14 de Julio & 10a Calle; dishes US$11-15; ⦿ 11am-1:30pm & 5:30-10pm Mon-Sat) One of the finest restaurants in Honduras, Ricardo's is for the moneyed traveler or for a blow-out. Seafood dishes fetch almost North American prices, but with service this attentive, few complain. Hanging baskets dot the attractive garden patio; inside is the main dining room with air-con. There is an extensive wine list, including fine Chilean reds.

    Super Ceibeño Supermarket (7a Calle; ⦿ 7am-8pm Mon-Sat, 7am-7pm Sun) You can stock up on adventure rations.

BARRIO LA ISLA

Chef Guity (off 1a Calle; mains US$2.50-5; ⦿ 11am-10pm Tue-Sun) This is a simple open-air Garífuna restaurant. The service is friendly but as laid-back as a Sunday morning – don't go if your time is tight. However, the excellent *tapado* (a fish stew in coconut sauce) is definitely worth hanging around for. The restaurant is tucked away down a little unpaved side street.

    Dutch Corner Bar (1a Calle; dishes US$3-5; ⦿ 7am-10pm) Next to Rotterdam Beach Hotel and Amsterdam 2001 – and run by the same family – this serves simple, good-value dishes such as fried chicken and spaghetti.

Drinking & Nightlife

Most of La Ceiba's nightlife centers in and around 1a Calle in Barrio La Isla, known as the *zona viva*.

    La Casona (☎ 440 3471; admission US$3.25-5.50; ⦿ 9pm-2am Wed-Sat) It's the happening disco of the moment. Attracting a young, early-20s crowd, the venue is off a dirt road four blocks inland. The reggaeton tunes pump and the dance floor jumps, especially on weekend nights.

    Mango Tango (☎ 440 2091; ⦿ 5:30-11pm Wed-Mon) On the main strip, often packed with diners and drinkers enjoying the open-air ambience. It does cocktails (Tom Collins, Sex on the Beach) for about US$2.60.

    Snake Bar (⦿ 8am-3am) Has its doors open at most times of the day and night, although the party only really gets going well after dark.

    The Expatriates Bar & Grill (left) attracts a mix of foreigners and locals.

Entertainment

Cines Millenium (Mall Megaplaza; US$2.20; ⦿ screenings 7pm & 9pm) Two-screen-theater with recent Hollywood fare.

HONDURAS

Shopping

Mall Megaplaza (22a Calle at Av Morazán; ☉ 10am-9pm) A modern American-style mall with a cinema, food court, internet cafés, banks and ATMs as well as an airline office.

Souvenirs El Buen Amigo #3 (☎ 442 0716; 12a Calle, Barrio El Iman; ☉ 8am-6:30pm Mon-Sat) Has a good choice of Honduran *artesanía*, although it is a bit out of the way. It includes everything from Lencan pottery, to Maya replicas, and coffee – and its fair share of tack too.

Rain Forest (☎ 443 2917; Calle la Julia; ☉ 9am-noon & 2-5:30pm Mon-Fri, 9am-noon Sat) Has good-quality, but pricey, wooden artifacts, pottery, paintings and jewelry, and an English-language book selection.

Cigar buffs can get a wide range of local and imported cigars at the Expatriates Bar & Grill (p397).

Getting There & Away

La Ceiba's Aeropuerto Golosón is 10km west of downtown. Flights leave frequently for San Pedro Sula, Tegucigalpa, the Bay Islands and La Moskitia.

AIR

Aerolineas Sosa (☎ 443 1399, airport at airport 440 0692; Av San Isidro btwn 8a & 9a Calles)

Atlantic Airlines (☎ 440 2343, airport 440 1220; 11a Calle at Av República)

TACA/Isleña (☎ 441 3190, airport 443 2683, 441 2521; Mall Megaplaza, 1st fl, 22a Calle at Av Morazán)

Destination	Fare
Guanaja	US$87 (return US$105)
Puerto Lempira (Atlantic Airlines)	US$105 (return US$191)
Roatán (Atlantic Airlines)	US$48 (return US$88)
San Pedro Sula	US$66
Tegucigalpa	US$81

BOAT

Ferries to the Bay Islands operate from the Muelle de Cabotaje, about 8km east of town. Taxis will take you there for US$5.75 per carload (up to four people); coming back from the pier, it's US$1.45 per person. Be at the pier at least half an hour before departure to buy your ticket.

Two boats ply the waters between La Ceiba and the Bay Islands. The **Galaxy Wave** (☎ in La Ceiba 443 4633, in Coxen Hole 445 1795) sails twice daily to Roatán; the smaller **Utila Princess II** (☎ La Ceiba pier 408 5163) goes between La Ceiba and Utila,

also twice daily. Departures for Roatán are at 9:30am and 2pm (one way US$21.60, 1¾ hours). From Roatán, the boats leave Terminal Nueva, Dixon's Cove (between Coxen Hole and French Harbor) at 7am and 4:30pm.

For Utila (one way US$16.20, one hour), there are departures at 9:30am and 4pm, returning from the island at 6:20am and 2pm. Note that these times are particularly prone to change. Check before you depart.

You could ask around the Muelle de Cabotaje about boats to other destinations. Captains of cargo and fishing boats might be persuaded to take along a passenger, but the practice is officially discouraged so don't count on it.

BUS

Most bus traffic goes through the bus terminal at Mercado San José, about 1.5km west of the center of La Ceiba – but there are some important exceptions. A local bus runs between the bus terminal and the central plaza (US$0.20), or you can take a taxi (US$0.80). **Diana Express** (☎ 441 6460), **Catisa-Tupsa** (☎ 441 2539) and **Kamaldy** (☎ 441 2028) all have offices there. The **Viana Clase Oro** (☎ 441 2251) express bus terminal is another 500m further west along the same road, at the Esso gas station. **Cotuc** (☎ 441 2199), for Trujillo, shares its terminal with Cotraibal further down the main highway, while luxury bus company **Hedman Alas** (☎ 441 5347; www.hedmanalas.com) has its terminal on the main highway just east of the center.

Buses go from La Ceiba to the following locations:

Copán Ruinas (US$9.15) Take an early Diana Express service to San Pedro for the 1:30pm connection to the ruins.

El Porvenir (US$0.55, 45 minutes, 15km)

La Unión-Cuero y Salado (US$0.65, one hour, 20km, buses every 45 minutes 7am to 6pm (5pm Sunday) The last bus back to La Ceiba leaves La Unión at 4pm.

La Unión, Olancho (via Olanchito) (US$2.70, five to six hours, 6am, 6:30am and hourly from 7:45am to 4:45pm) Take bus from the terminal to Olanchito and transfer to a La Unión bus (US$3.50, three to four hours, noon only). Catch an early Olanchito bus to make the La Unión connection.

Nueva Armenia (US$1.35, 2½ hours, 40km) Buses leave La Ceiba at 9am, 11:20am, 12:30pm, 2pm, 3:30pm and 4:30pm.

Sambo Creek (US$0.50, one hour, 21km, every 40 minutes) First bus leaves La Ceiba at 6:10am, last leaves at 5pm. Last return bus leaves at 4:30pm.

HONDURAS

San Pedro Sula Diana Express and Catisa-Tupsa (US$4, 3½ hours, 202km, 5:45am to 5pm, every 45 minutes); Hedman-Alas (luxury service, US$13, three hours, 5:15am, 10am, 2pm, and 5:45pm); Viana Clase Oro (luxury service, US$10, 6:30am and 3pm)

Tegucigalpa Kamaldy (US$9.50, seven hours, 397km, 5:15am, 9am and 2:15pm); Viana Clase Oro (luxury service, 6½ hours, US$20, 6:30am, 10:30am, 2pm and 3pm); Hedman Alas (luxury service, US$21.50, 6½ hours, 5:15am, 10am and 2pm)

Tela (US$1.60, two hours, 103km, leaves main terminal every 30 minutes from 4:30am to 6pm) A quicker option is to take a San Pedro Sula bus (US$3, 1½ hours). Tell the driver you want to get off at Tela and the bus will stop on the highway above town.

Trujillo Cotuc and Cotraipal (US$4.30, three hours, every 45 minutes from 7:30am to 5pm) From main terminal: normal service (US$3.50, 4½ hours, nine buses daily, first at 4am, last at 3:20pm); direct service (US$4.65, 3½ hours, 6:10am).

Yaruca (US$0.70, at 9am, 10:30am, 11:30am, 12:30pm and 1:30pm)

Getting Around

CAR

There are plenty of rental agencies in La Ceiba:

Advance Rent A Car (☎ 441 1105; www.advancerent acar.com; Carretera a Tela; ☉ 8am-6pm Mon-Fri)

Molinari (☎ 443 0055; 8a Calle at Av República) At the Gran Hotel Paris, facing the parque central.

TAXI

Taxis in La Ceiba are easy to find – they will normally find you – and a ride anywhere in town costs US$0.80, going up to US$1.10 after 8pm.

AROUND LA CEIBA

Cayos Cochinos

Cayos Cochinos (the Hog Islands), 29km from La Ceiba and just 17km from the shore, can be visited as a day trip or camping trip from La Ceiba. Access is by motorized canoe from the town of Nueva Armenia or Sambo Creek, east of La Ceiba.

The Hog Islands and the waters and reefs around them are a designated biological marine reserve – it is illegal to anchor on the reef, and commercial fishing is prohibited. Consequently, the reefs are pristine and fish abundant. Diving and snorkeling are excellent around the islands, with black coral reefs, wall diving, cave diving, seamounts and a plane wreck. The islands are also known for their unique pink boas.

It is possible to go independently to the cays, although you will not save much money, and local boatmen are unlikely to have a radio or life-jackets. Day trips start at around US$35 per person. Several tour operators do them; see p395. It is worth contacting the foundation that campaigned for the marine park, **Fundación Cayos Cochinos** (☎ 442 2670; www.cayos cochinos.org; 13a Calle, Barrio El Iman, La Ceiba), for more information.

Rustic accommodations are available on some of the cays.

Garífuna Villages

Two seaside fishing villages are easy to reach from La Ceiba; **Corozal**, 15km east of La Ceiba, and **Sambo Creek**, 6km further east. Both places have thriving Garífuna communities, and you will see women in the striking traditional attire and headdresses. However, poverty here is tangible. There are also some good-value restaurants. You can arrange to see local musical groups in both villages. The beach at Sambo Creek is more attractive than Corozal's.

The **annual fair** at Corozal, held from January 6 to 18, attracts people from far and wide, especially on the weekends of the fair, when you'll find dancing, partying, games and competitions. The annual fair at Sambo Creek is held in June.

If you are out this way, don't miss the **Sambo Creek Spa & Canopy Tour** (☎ 990 3743, 960 8318; US$36), which whizzes you through the tree tops for more than an hour, and includes as long as you want in the hillside thermal springs. The turnoff to the canopy is to the left, about 500m further along from the Sambo Creek turnoff on the main highway to Trujillo.

At Sambo Creek, **Hotel El Centro** (s/d with shared bathroom US$8/16) is basic but well-kept, with cheerfully bright décor. It is on the main street.

Just out of town, at the bottom of a dirt track turnoff 200m past the main Sambo Creek entrance (walkable along the beach from Sambo Creek in the dry season), is **Helen's Hotel & Restaurant** (☎ 441 2017; s/d US$24, 1-bed cabin US$19; P 🍴 🖳 🏊). It has options to suit most budgets (although those on a serious shoestring have to sleep several to a bed). There are some nice touches – dried flowers in the bathrooms, carved doors – although some room interiors look a bit 19th century. The outdoor restaurant is also appealing. Lush gardens, two swimming pools, a terrapin pool and the adjoining black-sand beach are other pluses.

Right next door is **Hotel Canadien** (☎ 440 2099; s/d/tr US$41/41/51; P ⊠ ⊑ ⊒), a big white-washed building with pristine, tastefully decorated but expensive rooms. The restaurant has some spectacular views of the Caribbean Sea, which laps just outside the hotel. Evangelical church groups often stay here. You can also arrange trips to Cayos Cochinos from here.

Motorboat rides (per person approx US$25) can be arranged to Cayos Cochinos from here. However, going on organized trips is generally not much more expensive and you have a bit more security of mind (onboard radios for example).

At Corozal, **Brisas del Mar** (s/d US$5.50/11, with TV US$8.10/16.20) has stark blue barracks-style rooms, some with cable TV. It is toward the east of the village, almost on the beach. It has a Garífuna restaurant and bar right next door. A few short steps along the beach but a big step up in comfort is the new **Ocean View** (☎ 429 1025; s/d with TV US$55/75). It has four very well-appointed flats, including kitchen, hot water and dining room. Cheaper deals are on offer during the week and off season. Carpenters were carving the distinctive adjoining restaurant's chairs when we passed through. Local buses connect both villages with La Ceiba.

Finca El Eden

About 32 km west of La Ceiba at Km 158 on the highway, **Finca El Eden** (bertiharlos@yahoo.de; Carr a Tela, Km 158) has received good reviews for its pretty setting near a gorge, good camping, cabins and options for hiking and horseback riding. It is run by a German-Honduran couple.

REFUGIO DE VIDA SILVESTRE CUERO Y SALADO

On the coast about 30km west of La Ceiba, the Cuero y Salado Wildlife Refuge takes its name from two rivers, the Cuero and Salado, that meet at the coast in a large estuary. This estuary, now a reserve, protects varied and abundant wildlife; manatees are the most famous (and the hardest to see), but there are also howler and white-faced monkeys, sloths, agoutis (rabbit-sized rodents), iguanas, caimans and hundreds of bird species. Migratory birds are here from around August/September to April/May.

The small town of **La Unión** is the gateway to the reserve. From there, you catch a train to its entrance. At the end of the railroad track is a new **visitors center** (☎ 440 1990; park fee adult/child US$10/5) in Salado Barra, with a small but informative exhibition on the refuge. You can organize tours from here. For further information on the refuge, contact La Ceiba–based **Fundación Cuero y Salado** (☎ /fax 443 0329; www .cueroysalado.org; 19 Av at Av 14 de Julio, La Ceiba; ☺ 8am-noon & 1-5pm Mon-Fri, 8-11am Sat).

By far the best way to get around and see the reserve is by water. Canoe tours (US$8 for two people) can be arranged at the visitors center.

A well-maintained **dorm** (per person US$7) is a short walk away, and simple meals are available at the visitors center café. **Camping** (per person US$3) is also permitted.

Getting There & Away

To get to the reserve, take a bus to La Unión from La Ceiba's main terminal (US$0.50, 1½ hours, every 45 minutes from 6am to 4pm). From La Unión, jump on the *trencito* (a railcar) for the 9.5km ride on the old banana railroad to the visitors center in Salado Barra (one person US$10.50, two or more people US$5 each, 45 minutes, 7am to 2pm, every 1½ hours). Between trains, you can take a *burra*, a railcar basket pushed gondola-style by a couple of men with poles (per person US$5.30, one hour). Tell the *trencito* or *burra* drivers when you'd like to return; the last bus from La Unión to La Ceiba is at 4pm. If you walk along the railway tracks, it takes 1½ hours to reach the visitors center at a brisk pace (it's about 9.5km). When you reach the reserve, hire a boat and guide (US$17.60, up to seven people) for a two-hour trip through the reserve.

PARQUE NACIONAL PICO BONITO

Pico Bonito is the lush, forested area that climbs steeply behind La Ceiba. It is one of Honduras' best-known national parks, with an unexplored core area of 500 sq km. It has magnificent, varied forests at different elevations as well as rivers, waterfalls and abundant wildlife, including jaguars, armadillos, monkeys and toucans.

Pico Bonito itself is one of the highest peaks in Honduras at 2436m (and very difficult to climb). The main entrance to the park is at El Pino; from La Ceiba it is on the way to Tela. In El Pino, you can arrange tours, book accommodations in advance or arrange accommodations at the **Vivero Natural View tourist office** (☎ 368 8343, 371 9631).

The other entrance is at Río Cangrejal, up in the hills on the other side of La Ceiba. Almost every tour agency in La Ceiba offers Pico Bonito tours, mostly to the El Pino side.

For additional information about the park, contact the **Fundación Parque Nacional Pico Bonito** (Funapib; ☎ 442 0618; www.picobonito.org; Av 14 de Julio at 15a Calle, La Ceiba; ☺ 7:30am-5pm Mon-Fri, 8-11am Sat).

You can also see the park on horseback; several tour operators offer trips, see p395.

Entrance to Pico Bonito National Park is US$6.

Hiking

The park's first trail is still a favorite. It is a moderately difficult three-hour hike to **Cascada Zacate** (per person incl guide, transport & park entrance fee US$11). You'll hear the falls before you see them – in fact, they are also known as Cascada Ruidoso (noisy falls). You can organize this hike at the Vivero Natural View.

On the Río Cangrejal side, there is a lovely trail threading through some lush mountainside jungle to **El Bejuco** waterfall. Contact Guaruma Servicios (p395) to arrange a guide. Several of the lodges have their own trails, which are worth investigating.

Sleeping

For lodging on the Río Cangrejal side, see p396.

Centro Ecoturístico Natural View (☎ 368 8343, 371 9631; r US$11) A couple of simple rooms sleep two here. It is a few kilometers north of the highway. Camping is possible on the large grassy plot. This is also a good place to eat and relax après-hiking, with *palapa*-covered tables and shady hammocks.

Getting There & Away

Any bus headed toward Tela or San Pedro Sula can drop you at El Pino. To get to **Vivero Natural View** (☎ 368 8343, 371 9631) look for the purple tourist information sign on your right.

To get to the Río Cangrejal side of the park, take a Yaruca-bound bus from the main terminal in La Ceiba; see p398 for times.

TRUJILLO

pop 10,230

Sleepy, tropical Trujillo sits above the wide arc of the Bahía de Trujillo, an expanse of water that has seen the sails of Columbus and many a famous buccaneer. Things move at their own pace here. Whether you sample some of the excellent seafood or take in the town's nightlife, don't plan to do it in a rush. The town took a hammering at the hands of Hurricane Mitch in 1998 but now shows signs of its old self –

tourism is on the up, and language schools are reopening. Shrimp and the nearby port of Puerto Castilla plays an important role in the local economy. Trujillo is the capital of the department of Colón.

History

For a small town, Trujillo has had an important part in the history of Central America. It was near Trujillo, on August 14, 1502, that Columbus first set foot on the American mainland, having sailed from Jamaica on his fourth (and final) voyage. The first Catholic Mass on American mainland soil was said on the spot where he and his crew landed.

Founded on May 18, 1525, Trujillo was one of the earliest Spanish settlements in Central America. The first Spanish town in the colonial province of Honduras, it was the provincial capital until the seat was shifted to Comayagua in 1537. The Catholic bishop's seat remained in Trujillo until 1561, when it too was moved to Comayagua.

The Spanish used the port at Trujillo to ship out gold and silver from the interior of Honduras – and inevitably pirates soon came sniffing around. The Bahía de Trujillo was the scene of several great battles when the town was attacked by pirates, including Henry Morgan.

The Spanish built several fortresses, the ruins of which are still visible; the ruins of the fort of Santa Bárbara lie near the plaza in town. Despite the fortifications, the buccaneers prevailed, and after a sacking by Dutch pirates in 1643, the town lay in ruins for over a century until it was resettled in 1787. Trujillo was also the stage for William Walker's bid to take over Central America. It was doomed to failure – he was captured and executed by firing squad. His grave is now in the town center.

Information

EMERGENCY
Police (☎ 434 4038)

IMMIGRATION
Immigration office (☺ 8-11am & 2-4pm Mon-Fri) Long-term visitors seeking to extend their stay should visit here.

INTERNET ACCESS
Eco Tours Internet (per hr US$1; ☺ 7am-10pm Mon-Sat, 9am-10pm Sun) It's a bit of a scam – one hour here only actually includes 55 minutes and no downloads are allowed – but it is about the most reliable in town.

HONDURAS

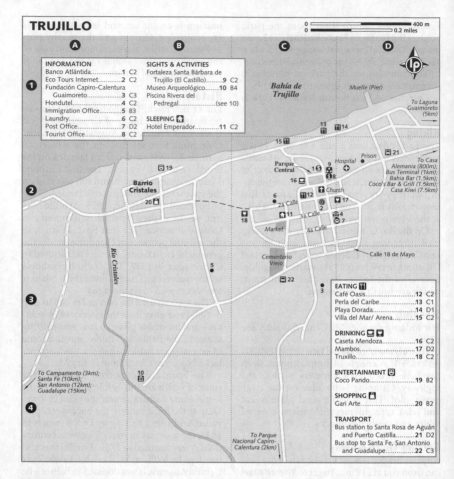

TRUJILLO

INFORMATION
Banco Atlántida...............1 C2
Eco Tours Internet............2 C2
Fundación Capiro-Calentura
    Guaimoreto.................3 C3
Hondutel........................4 C2
Immigration Office.............5 B3
Laundry..........................6 C2
Post Office......................7 D2
Tourist Office...................8 C2

SIGHTS & ACTIVITIES
Fortaleza Santa Bárbara de
    Trujillo (El Castillo).........9 C2
Museo Arqueológico.......10 B4
Piscina Rivera del
    Pedregal...................(see 10)

SLEEPING 🏠
Hotel Emperador.............11 C2

Bahía de Trujillo

Muelle (Pier)

To Laguna Guaimoreto (5km)

Barrio Cristales

Parque Central

Prison

Hospital

Church

To Casa Alemania (800m); Bus Terminal (1km); Bahía Bar (1.5km); Coco's Bar & Grill (1.5km); Casa Kiwi (7.5km)

Market

Calle 18 de Mayo

Cementerio Viejo

Río Cristales

To Campamento (3km); Santa Fe (10km); San Antonio (12km); Guadalupe (15km)

To Parque Nacional Capiro-Calentura (2km)

EATING 🍴
Café Oasis.....................12 C2
Perla del Caribe..............13 C1
Playa Dorada..................14 D1
Villa del Mar/ Arena.........15 C2

DRINKING 🍷 🍹
Caseta Mendoza..............16 C2
Mambos........................17 D2
Truxillo.........................18 C2

ENTERTAINMENT 🎭
Coco Pando....................19 B2

SHOPPING 🛍
Gari Arte.......................20 B2

TRANSPORT
Bus station to Santa Rosa de Aguán
    and Puerto Castilla........21 D2
Bus stop to Santa Fe, San Antonio
    and Guadalupe.............22 C3

LAUNDRY
Lavandería Colón (2a Calle; per 10lb US$2.80; 🕑 closed Sun)

MONEY
There are no MasterCard-friendly services in Trujillo.
Banco Atlántida (Parque Central) Changes cash, traveler's checks and has a Visa-card ATM.

POST & TELEPHONE
Eco Tours Internet (🕑 7am-10pm Mon-Sat, 9am-10pm Sun) Cheaper international phone service.
Hondutel (🕑 8am-4pm Mon-Fri) Next to the post office.
Post office (🕑 8am-noon & 2-4pm Mon-Fri, 8-11am Sat) Three blocks inland from the plaza.

TOURIST INFORMATION
The hostel Casa Kiwi has a folder full of local information and bus timetables. There is also a Fundación Capiro-Calentura Guaimoreto (Fucagua) office, although staff offer limited help.
Tourist office (☎ 434 4535; Parque Central, Barrio Buenos Aires; 🕑 8am-5pm) New municipal office run by a friendly fellow called Nelson. It is by the fort.

Sights
The ruins of a 17th-century Spanish fortress, the **Fortaleza Santa Bárbara de Trujillo** (☎ 434 4535; adult/child US$3/0.50; 🕑 9am-5pm), are in the center of town near the plaza, overlooking the sea. The fort has recently undergone a makeover and now includes a small museum. It houses

several old cannons and other historical relics. A plaque marks the place where North American adventurer/would-be conqueror William Walker was executed and there's an excellent view along the coast. The museum also has colonial and Garífuna artifacts on display, and it has occasional temporary displays.

There are several **beaches** in and around Trujillo, including one at the front edge of town. Ask if it is safe to swim. The water is not always the cleanest, especially in rainy season. There are also beachside open-air thatched-roof restaurant-bars near the airstrip, a 20-minute walk east along the beach from town. Casa Kiwi has a good stretch of beach away from any town pollution.

Near the Río Cristales, the **Museo y Piscinas Naturales Riveras del Pedegral** (adult/child US$1.90/US$1.10; ☺ 7am-5pm, hours vary) is a fascinating, eclectic and disorganized collection of exhibits. You'll find jade jewelry arranged higgledy-piggledy alongside ancient pre-Columbian archaeological relics as well Pech and Miskito artifacts. There are also a whole bunch of other random objects – check out the piece of a plane that crashed in the bay in 1985 for example. The museum admission includes entry to the gardens at the rear of the museum, with a couple of open-air swimming pools, and picnic- and children's play–areas.

Just west of town, where the Río Cristales flows into the sea, there is the largely Garífuna district of Barrio Cristales. You can see the **grave of William Walker** (see p447), who was buried in the town's cemetery following an ill-fated bid to conquer Central America. Other good places to visit (including Parque Nacional Capiro-Calentura) are a short distance from town.

Visitors descend upon Trujillo for the **Semana Santa** celebrations and it also gets busy for the **annual fair** of the town's patron saint, San Juan Bautista, in the last week of June (the exact day is June 24, but the festival goes on for a week).

Sleeping

Trujillo has a number of good places to stay. Most of the good ones are out of town. You should book ahead during Semana Santa.

Casa Kiwi (☎ dm/s/d US$4/6.50/8.10, cabins with air-con US$27; ℗ ⌗ ▣) This beachside hostel has justifiably become a magnet for backpackers. It's 7.5km out of town but that's no bad thing – most guests find everything they need at the restaurant and bar, not to mention its isolated stretch of beach. It is the kind of place where travelers find one- or two-night stays gently slipping into one or two weeks. For those heading to La Moskitia, this is an ideal place for picking up information and hooking up with other travelers going the overland route. Smart new cabins with pristine, blue-tiled bathrooms have broadened the appeal beyond the budget crew. A taxi from town should cost US$4.30.

Cabañas y Restaurante Campamento (☎ 991 3391; camping US$6, cabins with fan/air con US$35/37; ℗ ⌗ ▣) These comfortable beachfront bungalows 3km west of Trujillo each have a hot-water bathroom, and an ocean-facing porch. You can also camp under palm trees. A thatch-roofed restaurant (mains US$4 to US$15) is open for all meals and overlooks an inviting pool.

Hotel Emperador (☎ 434 4442; s & d US$8) This family-run place is the best of the downtown budget options. Its compact rooms face out onto a narrow courtyard – the mom runs a tight ship and won't let any dust settle. The family also runs a little adjoining cafeteria.

Casa Alemania (☎ 434 4466; camping US$5.50, d/tr US$25/27) With its distinctive, steep European-style sloping roof and impeccably decorated modern rooms, Casa Alemania is a notch above the in-town accommodations options. It is near the beach, a few minutes' walk from the main bus terminal. The on-site restaurant does all-you-can-eat breakfasts for US$6.

Eating

There are several good inexpensive restaurants in town.

Playa Dorada (☎ 434 3121; mains US$5-7; ☺ 8am-10pm) Touted as the most reliable seafood restaurant in town. A simple set-up where the ocean breezes drift off the beach into the dining area, it concentrates on the fundamentals – it's less fancy than some of its neighbors. The dishes, however, are delicious. We had a succulent *cangrejo* (king crab) soup.

Mambos (☎ 434 4013; 2a Calle; mains US$5.50-9; ☺ 9am-10pm Wed-Mon) This relaxed, airy venue is behind tinted doors. Photos of famous Latino songstrels are strewn around the walls. You can feel a bit surrounded by TVs (there are four of them). There's a dance floor for livelier weekend nights and an outdoor *champa* (thatch) area was being built at the time of research. The menu is identical to Oasis, which has the same owners.

HONDURAS

Restaurant Oasis Colonial (☎ 434 4828; 2a Calle; mains US$5.50-9; ☯ 9:30am-10:30pm Tue-Sun) Meals are set upon ruby tablecloths in this poky little dining room. It's quite a sweet, wannabe-bohemian type of place with reasonable food, where you can graffiti your name on the wall if you need to quell inner urges for wanton vandalism. It also sells cigars.

Caseta Mendoza (dishes US$3-7; ☯ 7am-8pm) This simple little patio café with a corrugated-iron roof and red wooden benches overlooks the parque central. You may have to shout for service, but when it comes you'll get decent coffee for next to nothing (US$0.30). It also does basic *típica* food dishes. It's a favorite hangout for local soldiers.

Drinking & Nightlife

In town, Truxillo is a popular nightspot with drinking and dancing, usually on the weekends. Beware of the special gringo rate.

Bahia Bar (mains US$4.50-7; ☯ 7am-10pm Mon-Thu, 7am-1am Fri & Sat) By the old airport runway, it has a bunch of sun lounges, and the beach party goes on well into the night at weekends.

Coco's Bar & Grill (dishes US$5-7.40; ☯ 10am-8pm Mon-Thu, 8am-10pm Fri-Sun) Near Bahia Bar, on the same beach, this is the Christopher Columbus resort's bid to grab a slice of the backpacker buck. It should work – it's a cheap little *champa* restaurant that has wallet-friendly plates such as fried fish and spaghetti, and beers for US$1.35.

Coco Pando (Barrio Cristales) In the mainly Garífuna neighborhood, discos are held Thursday to Sunday nights (cover US$1). The air fills with reggaeton and reggae beats on lively weekend nights – though the atmosphere can be intimidating. The nightclub is above a restaurant with exceptionally good-value Garífuna dishes.

At latest report, Villa del Mar was the nightlife hotspot with the Arena disco on the beach below the plaza, mainly for the early-20s crowd. Note that this is just a free-access party on the beach. There's no security. The playlist goes from merengue, *bachata* to reggae.

Shopping

Gari Arte (☎ 434 4365; Barrio Cristales) Offers a selection of Garífuna handicrafts, music and souvenirs.

Getting There & Away

AIR

Trujillo has an airport but, at the time of writing, it had been closed for years.

BOAT

The *Island Tour* passenger boat departs from the *muelle* (pier) at Trujillo for Guanaja in the Bay Islands twice a week (one way US$27, Thursday and Sunday, 3pm, 2½ hours) – but note that the service is regularly canceled or delayed. You could also try your luck hitching a ride to the Moskitia region, and the Nicaraguan coast – although none of these is a scheduled departure. Ask around among the fishing or cargo boats at the pier. Some say it's safe, others say they'd never set foot in these boats – you'll have to judge for yourself.

BUS

The two main bus companies, Cotraibal and Cotuc, operate from the large main bus terminal a kilometer from town, with direct and ordinary services. Be sure to get the direct – the ordinary ones tend to stop if a gecko blinks on the roadside, and can take hours longer.

There is another smaller terminal closer to town, where the local chicken buses and the services through Olancho depart.

Buses to La Ceiba (US$4.30, three hours) and onto San Pedro Sula (US$7.10, five to six hours) depart from the main terminal once or twice an hour from 1am to 1:45pm.

Two direct buses go to Tegucigalpa at 1am and 4:45am daily from the main terminal (US$11, 10 hours), going via La Ceiba and El Progreso. A Tegucigalpa-bound bus (12 hours) also goes along a dirt road via Juticalpa in Olancho (nine hours, US$7) leaving Trujillo at 5am from the gas station terminal closer to town. You can also get this bus if you arrive early at the Corocito turnoff. Or you can go via La Unión (change at Tocoa). Both services are on unpaved roads, and are not easy journeys.

Local buses go from Trujillo to the Garífuna villages of Santa Fe, San Antonio and Guadalupe to the west leaving from in front of the old cemetery. Buses to Puerto Castilla across the bay (going past Casa Kiwi) leave from the gas station terminal at 7:15am, 9:30am, 10:30am, 12:30pm, 2pm, 4pm and 6pm Monday to Saturday; Sunday departures are at 8am, 1pm and 5pm only. There are six return buses from Puerto Castilla (three on Sunday).

Getting Around

Taxis abound in the center of Trujillo. Fares around town are US$0.80. The taxi fare out of town is usually US$3 to US$4.30, although you will usually be quoted more.

AROUND TRUJILLO

Santa Rosa de Aguán

Paul Theroux's novel *The Mosquito Coast*, which was later made into a movie starring Harrison Ford, featured this small tropical town. Just 40km from Trujillo, Santa Rosa de Aguán is a good place to get a taste of the Moskitia if you don't have the time or the money to go all the way out there. The town was severely damaged during Hurricane Mitch – 44 people drowned – and it hasn't fully recovered. Still, it has an engaging, frontier-like atmosphere, and you can hire boats to take you up the Río Aguán, where you might catch sight of 3m alligators. Two very basic hotels charge US$3.50, and there's an annual **Garífuna festival** here from August 22 to 29. Five buses to Santa Rosa de Aguán leave Trujillo from the gas station terminal each day at 6:30am, 10am, 1pm, 3pm and 4:30pm. There is a reduced service on Sunday.

Parque Nacional Capiro-Calentura

The mountain behind Trujillo, called **Cerro Calentura**, 1235m above sea level at the summit, is part of the Capiro-Calentura National Park. You can get there simply by heading straight up the hill from town. The unpaved road goes right up to the summit, which is 10km from town. It is badly eroded in places and a 4WD is essential. You could also walk it in about 3½ hours. For a guided tour, ask Nelson in the **tourist office** (☎ 434 4535; Parque Central; ☼ 8am-5pm) in Trujillo.

On the way up the hill, you pass through a couple of distinct vegetation zones. At around 600m to 700m the vegetation changes from tropical rain forest to subtropical lowmountain rain forest, and you find yourself in a zone of giant tree ferns, with lush forest, large trees, vines and flowering plants. There's plenty of wildlife in the park, too, including many species of tropical birds and butterflies, reptiles and monkeys.

About a third of the way up, a couple of trails take off from the road to the left, leading to a waterfall and a tiny reservoir; they're not marked, but you can see them distinctly from the road. It can be sunny, clear and warm in Trujillo, and cloudy and much cooler at the top of the hill. If you're lucky, you can get a superb view from the top over the beautiful Valle de Aguán, along the coast as far as Limón, and across the bay. There is a radar station at the summit.

Information about the park is from the tourist office, or from the **Fundación Capiro-Calentura Guaimoreto** (Fucagua; ☎ 434 4294; ☼ 7:30am-noon & 1:30-5pm) – its office is about half way to the park entrance – although info can be quite vague. Entry to the park is US$2.15 but there isn't always someone around to collect it.

You're best off doing this in a group or with a guide. Although it is generally a safe walk, occasional attacks have been reported.

Laguna de Guaimoreto

Five kilometers east of Trujillo, past the airstrip and the Río Negro, is Laguna de Guaimoreto, a large lagoon with a natural passageway onto the bay. About 6km by 9km, the lagoon is a protected wildlife refuge; its complex system of canals and mangrove forests provide shelter to abundant animal, bird and plant life, including thousands of migratory birds between November and February, and the elusive manatee. There have even been reported panther sightings.

You can also hire **rowing boats** or **canoes** (and even someone to paddle for you) if you turn left down the road marked by the sign 'Refugio de Vida Laguna Guaimoreto' and call out when you get to the old bridge between Trujillo and Puerto Castilla. If your bargaining skills are up to it, you can rent canoes for around US$5.50.

Shipwreck

Just off the coast 2km east of Casa Kiwi on the road to Puerto Castillo is the wreck of a sunken ship that is good for **snorkeling**. It is close to the shore, and is easily accessible from the beach. Ask at Casa Kiwi for more details.

Garífuna Villages

West of Trujillo are three Garífuna villages, all with houses stretching along the beach. **Santa Fe**, the largest village, is about 10km west of Trujillo. Santa Fe has two *hospedajes*: **Mar Atlántico** (☎ 429 0593; r/tw US$8/11) and **Hotel Las Tres Orquidias** (☎ 429 9297; tw US$13.30), which just shades it as it is right on the beach. Both have simple rooms with fan, fresh sheets and private bathroom with cold water. **Comedor Caballero** (mains US$2-11; ☼ 8am-6pm), aka 'Pete's Place,' is renowned as the best restaurant in town. It's all about the seafood – go for the house special with huge dishes starting at US$7.

HONDURAS

A couple of kilometers further along from Santa Fe are the smaller, seldom-visited Garífuna villages of **San Antonio** and then **Guadalupe**. San Antonio has several seafood restaurants but no accommodations. In Guadalupe, the only sleeping option is **Hotel Franklin** (☎ 429 9046; s/d US$5.50/8) at the eastern end of the main street. Don't expect much. Let's just say, make sure you have flip-flops – and not just for the bathroom.

From Santa Fe, you can organize boat trips out to snorkel on an unspoiled reef called **Cayos Blanco**, out in front of town. It will set you back about US$35. The town's **annual fair** is July 15 to 30. The last three days are the most frenetic.

GETTING THERE & AWAY
Buses to Guadalupe leave from the old cemetery in Trujillo at 9:30am, 10:30am, noon, 1pm, 3pm and 5pm (Monday to Saturday), passing Santa Fe (US$0.75, 45 minutes) and continuing to San Antonio and Guadalupe (US$0.80, 1¼ hours).

Buses return from Guadalupe at 6:30am, 7am, 8am, 10am, noon and 2pm, passing Santa Fe 30 minutes later. On Sunday, just one bus leaves Guadalupe (at 7am) and returns from Trujillo at noon.

BAY ISLANDS

Spectacular diving and snorkeling draws visitors from around the world to the three Bay Islands (Islas de la Bahía) – Roatán, Utila and Guanaja – about 50km off the north coast of Honduras. Their reefs are part of the second-largest barrier reef in the world after Australia's Great Barrier Reef, and teem with fish, coral, sponges, rays, sea turtles and even whale sharks. Divers come year round, although the rainy season (November to February) puts a dampener on things – it makes diving trickier and some dive sites difficult to access. Diving here is very affordable.

Lodging and food (more expensive than on the mainland on all three islands) are easily cheapest on Utila, so the majority of backpackers go there. On the other hand, Roatán has better beaches and more nondiving things to do. Both islands have many aficionados. Diving is also good on Guanaja, though the prices on this island are prohibitive to most backpackers.

The island economy is based mostly on tourism and fishing, and shrimp and lobster catching.

HISTORY
Ruins on all three Bay Islands indicate that they were inhabited well before the Europeans arrived. Apparently human habitation began around AD 600, although the evidence is slim until after around AD 1000. The early settlers might have been Maya; there are also caves that perhaps provided shelter for groups of Pech (Paya), and Nahuatl-speaking people seem to have been here (Nahuatl was the language of the Aztecs in Mexico).

Christopher Columbus, on his fourth and final voyage to the New World, landed on the island of Guanaja on July 30, 1502. He encountered a fairly large population of *indígena*, whom he believed to be cannibals. The Spanish enslaved many islanders and sent them to work in the plantations of Cuba and in the gold and silver mines of Mexico.

English, French and Dutch pirates turned their attention to the islands, establishing settlements and raiding the gold-laden Spanish cargo vessels. The English buccaneer Henry Morgan established his base at Port Royal on Roatán in the mid-17th century; at that time, as many as 5000 pirates were ensconced on the island.

In March 1782, after many vain attempts, the Spanish waged a successful land attack against Port Royal, either killing or selling the pirates off as slaves.

One of the most influential events occurred on April 12, 1797. Thousands of Black Caribs were dumped by the British on Roatán, following a rebellion on the Caribbean island of St Vincent. This group settled at Punta Gorda, survived and mixed with the natives. Migrant groups reached the mainland, setting up small fishing and agricultural villages along the coast from Belize to Nicaragua. And the Garífuna were born.

The Bay Islands, along with the Moskitia in northeastern Honduras, remained in the hands of the British until 1859, when Great Britain signed a treaty ceding the Bay Islands and the Moskitia to Honduras. Only in the last few decades, however, when Honduran education officials decided that Spanish must be spoken in all the country's schools, did the islanders begin to speak Spanish. English, spoken with a broad Caribbean accent, remains

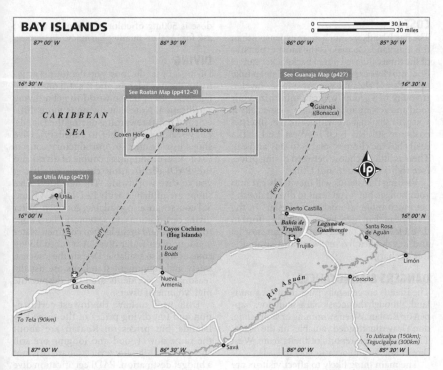

BAY ISLANDS

the preferred language of the most islanders, although more and more migrants from the mainland are shifting the balance.

The orientation of the islands is still, in many ways, more toward the UK and the USA than toward the Honduran mainland just 50km away; many islanders are more likely to have visited the US than their own capital, Tegucigalpa, and many have relatives in the US. The government focuses much of its tourism development efforts on the islands. Recently the Bay Islands were declared a Free Trade Zone, which means that businesses are exempt from the sales taxes applied on the mainland.

PEOPLE

The population of the Bay Islands is very diverse. Isleñas have heritage that includes African and Carib, European and other ancestry. English is the dominant spoken language, and Spanish is a second language. On Roatán there is a Garífuna settlement at Punta Gorda.

There are still some white descendants of early British settlers, especially on Utila. You might meet people who look like they just got off the boat from England, Scotland or Ireland, though actually their ancestors came here over a century ago.

Many islanders are strongly religious (you will quickly spot the number of churches). Be mindful of this in the way you dress – men going into shops without a shirt on can be taken as a sign of disrespect.

Recently, many Ladinos have come from the mainland, especially to Roatán, where taxi drivers and security guards are in high demand. The migration is changing the island's language; you hear much more Spanish here than just a few years ago.

There is also a significant population of foreigners, working for dive shops and other tourist-oriented businesses; in dive shops you often hear a variety of languages, including English, Spanish, German, Italian, French and Hebrew.

CLIMATE

The rainy season on the islands runs roughly from October or November to February. March and August are the hottest months; at other times the sea breezes temper the heat. Tropical storms are possible in September.

HONDURAS

COSTS

The Bay Islands are much more expensive than the mainland. Guanaja is the most expensive of the three, and well out of backpacker range. Roatán is less expensive, but still a steep hike up – it's not cheap if you are a lone traveler. If you're in a group, you can minimize your food and accommodation costs – especially if you get a shared place with a kitchen. Internet costs are still sky high in West End. Utila easily has the cheapest places to stay and eat. There is little to choose between diving prices (see right) on Roatán and Utila.

Visiting the islands will inevitably eat into your budget, but if you want to dive, it doesn't get much more affordable (or better) in the Caribbean than here. If you can only afford to dive a few times, or not at all, you can snorkel and kayak cheaply, or swim and sunbathe free of charge.

DANGERS & ANNOYANCES

The islands are generally safer than the mainland, although the occasional assault does happen on Roatán. When swimming or snorkeling, don't leave unattended valuables on the beach. There have been reports of thefts from West Bay in Roatán and occasionally in Utila.

The main thing likely to affect visitors are the mosquitoes and sand flies, which are voracious, especially during the rainy season. You'll need plenty of repellent, which you can bring along or buy on the islands. It's very important that you take antimalarial medication – five different strains of the disease have been identified on Roatán alone. Mosquitoes also carry dengue fever. The recommended dose is 500mg of chloroquine once a week; ask for 'Aralen' in any pharmacy.

DIVING

Diving is by far the most popular tourist activity on the Bay Islands, and it's still one of the cheapest places in the world to get a diving certification. Note that diving is more difficult and not as rewarding during the Islands' rainy season (November to February). Dive shops usually offer an introductory courses (basic instruction plus a couple of dives) and full PADI-certification courses qualifying you to dive worldwide. Though most dive shops are affiliated with PADI, NAWI and SSI courses are also available. An open-water diving certification course typically lasts three to four days and includes two confined-water and four open-water dives. Advanced diving courses are also available. Despite the low cost, safety and equipment standards are usually reasonable – accidents are rare, despite the high volume of divers.

Utila used to have the lowest certification and fun diving prices of the three Bay Islands, but prices on Roatán are about the same now. (Food and lodging are still cheaper on Utila, however.) Guanaja is not a budget destination. PADI certification dive packages on Utila and Roatán work out to at around US$230 to US$260. Fun dives are around US$25 to US$30 each, although you can often negotiate a discount if you are doing more than five days.

Don't make the mistake of selecting a diving course purely on the basis of price – you'll find the differences are small, anyway. In-

---

LOCAL VOICES: GARÍFUNA DIVEMASTER DAVID VALERIO

- **Have the Bay Islands changed much?** When I arrived, this island was just fishing boats – even just 10 years ago. Now this is a tourist place.

- **Have you always lived on the Bay Islands?** No. I used to work on a shrimp and shark fishing boat from La Ceiba, then I came to Roatán for work. I am now 40, and have been living here for 19 years – this is where I learned English.

- **How did you become a divemaster?** My first job here, I called 'no sleep' – I was watchman at the dive resort where I work. Then I started to drive the dive boat, and after that I began diving.

- **What do you like about working here?** The south side, where I work, has a very beautiful reef, with lots of soft corals. You have many fish including eagle rays, seahorses and my favorites, yellow tail snappers. Nobody goes fishing here, so you can get very close to the fish.

- **Describe your relationship to the sea.** I am from the Garífuna culture – we have always lived near the beach and made our living from the ocean. I am doing so now, just in a different way.

As told to Jolyon Attwooll

HONDURAS

SAFE DIVING IN THE BAY ISLANDS

Diving safety must be taken very seriously. Because Utila and Roatán are known as affordable places in the world to be certified as a diver, they attract many visitors looking for a bargain. Price-fixing is now helping dive outfits turn over enough money to ensure safety standards and environmental aims are upheld.

Generally the Bay Islands have an excellent safety record. The single biggest concern for a student diver on the Bay Islands should be quality of instruction and supervision. You should like and trust your instructor. Ask other divers for recommendations, not just for shops but for specific instructors and divemasters. It's perfectly OK to ask instructors how long they have been teaching and how long they have been on the island. If you're uncomfortable with a particular instructor, ask to move to a different course or simply go to a different shop.

Quality of equipment is also important. While it takes training to truly assess equipment, you can and should check certain things, like the O-ring on your tank isn't broken or frayed and whether your regulator hisses when you turn on the air. Arrive early to check your gear; if you're uncomfortable with something – even if the instructor assures you it's OK – ask for a replacement. Being comfortable and confident in the water is a crucial part of safe, enjoyable diving. Shops should also have their air analyzed three to four times per year, and have a certificate prominently displayed to prove it. If you don't see one, ask about it.

There are certain boat safety guidelines that shops should follow as well. All boats should have a captain who stays onboard (that is, who's not also your divemaster). All boats should have oxygen, usually carried in a green first aid kit, and a VHF radio – cell phone service is not reliable. Don't be afraid to ask about each of these things, and to have the instructor actually show you the items onboard – if enough divers did so, more shops would follow the rules; in the rare case of an emergency, they can make the difference between life and death.

Finally, no matter where you sign up, do not rely on your instructor or divemaster to anticipate every problem. Check your own equipment, assess your own comfort level and be vocal about your concerns. Actively monitor your own safety using the following guidelines:

- Accept responsibility for your own safety on every dive. Always dive within the limits of your ability and training.
- Use and respect the buddy system. It saves lives.
- Do not surface if you hear a boat motor, unless you are pulling yourself slowly up by the dive-boat mooring line. The Bay Islands have a lot of boat traffic, and accidents have occurred when boats collided with divers who were on the surface or just under it.
- Do not go into caves. Go through tunnels and 'swim-throughs' only with qualified guides.
- Don't drink or use drugs and then dive – it's stupid and can kill or injure you or the people around you.
- If you haven't dived for a while, consider taking a refresher course before you jump into deep water. It takes about an hour and only costs around US$15. It's much better to discover that you remember all your diving skills in 1.2m of water than to realize you don't in 12m of water.

stead, find a shop that has a good record and where you feel comfortable (for safe diving see above).

Qualified divers also have plenty of options, including fun dives, 10-dive packages, night dives, deep dives, wreck diving, customized dive charters and dives to coral walls and caves. There is a great variety of fish and marine life present, and the visibility is great. The waters between Roatán and Utila are among the best places in the world to view whale sharks, usually from May to September.

TRANSPORTATION
Getting There & Away
AIR

Several companies operate flights from the mainland of Honduras (La Ceiba) to the Bay Islands. Some flights originate at San Pedro Sula. Airlines include **Isleña/TACA** (☎ 445 1088, reservations 443 0179; www.flyislena.com), **Sosa** (☎ 445 1658; www.aerolineassosa.com) and **Atlantic Airlines** (☎ 445 1179; www.atlanticairlines.com.ni).

Delta and Continental both have flights to Roatán (see p418).

HONDURAS

FERRY

There are regular boat services from La Ceiba to Roatán and Utila and air services going to each of the Bay Islands. A less-reliable boat service runs from Trujillo to Guanaja. See each island for relevant times. Make sure you check the times as they are prone to change. Ferry companies still do not offer direct services between these islands – you have to go via La Ceiba. More private boat owners are now making the trip.

Ask around, you will quickly find out what is going on.

There are occasional ad hoc yachts from Utila to Belize, or Lívingston in Guatemala, but these are subject to the whims of yacht owners. Normally yacht owners advise a dive shop in Utila beforehand if they are planning a visit.

Getting Around

BOAT

Water taxis are used on Roatán between West End and the beach at West Bay, as well as at the community of Oak Ridge, where many of the houses are on stilts above the water. Water taxis are also common on Guanaja, where you'll need a boat to go between the main village, which is on a small cay, and the main island.

CAR & MOTORCYCLE

You can rent cars on Roatán and motorcycles on all three islands. However, renting vehicles here is not cheap (about US$50 a day), especially if fuel isn't included.

TAXI

Taxis ferry people all around Roatán, and to a lesser degree on Utila. Colectivo fares are reasonable (US$1 to US$2), but private rates are high (more than US$10).

ROATÁN

pop 65,000

Roatán is the largest and best known of the Bay Islands. It is about 50km off the coast of Honduras from La Ceiba. Long and thin (50km in length by 2km to 4km wide), the island is a real diving and snorkeling mecca, surrounded by over 100km of living reef. Its beaches are picture-postcard idyllic especially stretches along West End and West Bay, with clear turquoise water, colorful tropical fish, powdery white sand and coconut palms.

Dangers & Annoyances

Occasional assaults have occurred on the beach between West End and West Bay, although not for some time; this attractive beachside walk is fine during the day, but best avoided after sunset. Coxen Hole can get sketchy after nightfall and you should avoid hitching or waiting for taxis on the main roads outside of the towns after dark – robberies are not uncommon.

Roatán is sometimes used as a drugs thoroughfare. Be aware of that if you stumble across any particularly desolated coves.

West End

Curled around two small turquoise bays and laced with coconut palms, West End is a busy but pleasant village on the west end of the island. This is where virtually all backpackers and divers come, and the town's one sandy road is packed with restaurants, hotels and dive shops. Most accommodations are mid-range to expensive, but a few cheaper options exist, and more are being built.

ORIENTATION

It's impossible to get lost in West End, though some hotels and shops can be hard to find. The road from Coxen Hole intersects with the town's main sandy road at the eastern side of Half Moon Bay, the first of West End's two small bays. Buses and taxis to Coxen Hole wait at this intersection. Immediately to the right (north) are a few hotels, restaurants, bars and dive shops; further down are three more lodging options and also an internet café.

Left (south) from the intersection, the road curls around Half Moon Bay, passes a Baptist church and turns into 'the strip,' where you'll find most of West End's restaurants, bars and dive shops. You can walk end to end in five to 10 minutes. Water taxis to West Bay leave from a pier halfway down the strip.

INFORMATION

There are now two ATMs in West End. One is right at the entrance by the Coconut Tree supermarket. It gives Visa and MasterCard advances. The other Unibanc option is within the Hotel Dolphin lobby and accepts most cards. Internet connection on Roatán can be frustratingly sporadic and frequently drops out. Prices are just as painful.

Bamboo Hut Laundry (⊙ 10am-4pm Mon-Sat) On the main road, beyond most of the main restaurants and shops, this will wash, dry and fold up to 5lb of dirty clothes for US$4.

Barefoot Charlie's (⊙ 9am-9pm; per hr US$7) Weekly internet rates and a two-for-one book exchange are also available.

Paradise Computers (Half Moon Bay; per hr US$12.75; ⊙ 8am-10pm) Prepaid internet accounts available (one hour/nine hours US$10/60).

Police (Coxen Hole; ☎ 445 3438)

Roatán Online (www.roatanonline.com) A charmless but comprehensive guide to all things Roatán.

ACTIVITIES
Diving
The entire coastline of Roatán, especially the western tip, is dotted with dozens of dive sites, many just meters off the shore. With names such as Hole in the Wall, Sponge Emporium, Black Rock and Texas, Roatán is truly a diver's paradise, with endless variety and near-perfect diving conditions. Diving in Roatán used to cost more than on Utila, but the difference is now negligible. Roatán tends to have smaller classes than on Utila, and the reef is in slightly better shape. Most sites are nearby, so shops typically offer three to four one-tank dives per day, as opposed to two two-tank dives common on Utila. Prices are pretty standard among the shops: a four-day PADI open-water diving certification course costs around US$250 including instruction book and Marine Park fee; an advanced course is about the same; fun dives run from US$25 to US$30 per dive, less for more than five days.

Make sure you sign up with a diving outfit that belongs to the **West End & Sandy Bay Marine**

DON'T TOUCH THE CORAL!

Coral comes in many shapes, sizes and colors. Some coral, such as fan coral, resembles a plant. On the other hand, brain coral looks more like a rock. In fact coral is neither plant nor rock. It's an animal – and a delicate one at that. The coral in the Bay Islands (and throughout the region's entire barrier reef) is under pressure from pollution produced by humans and pumped into the water. In fact, a recent World Resources Institute report estimates that over 80% of the sediment and over half of all nutrients that damage the reefs come from Honduras, where large rivers drain agricultural run-off (one of the main causes of reef deterioration) into the Caribbean. Only with careful management will the wonderful underwater reef that skirts the coast of Central America be preserved.

All divers and snorkelers can help the conservation campaign. 'Don't touch the coral' is a refrain you will often hear in the Bay Islands, where thousands of inexperienced divers and snorkelers come every year to explore the magnificent reefs just a few yards offshore.

Coral is fascinating and beautiful, and many beginning (and experienced) divers are tempted to touch it. Even if you resist that temptation, it's easy to accidentally brush the coral with your fin or tank, either as you swim past or if you are still learning to maintain neutral buoyancy.

Avoiding such contact is extremely important. Coral has an invisible covering of slime that protects it, much like skin on other animals. Touching the coral can damage this protective covering, exposing the coral to infection and disease. Large segments of coral can be killed by a single brush of a diver's fin.

If you hit it hard enough, you can even break the coral; some places underwater are littered with coral fragments, broken by divers or heavy surf. Under ideal conditions, most coral grows about 1cm (less than half an inch) per year; even the fastest-growing sponges grow only an inch per year. The coral and sponge formations you see in the Bay Islands are the result of centuries of growth.

Coral could also sting you, most famously fire coral. Even coral that doesn't sting can be surprisingly sharp, and cuts from coral are slow to heal. (If you are stung by coral, vinegar helps stop the stinging and antibacterial cream helps it heal; no such luck for the coral, though.)

For the most part, the reefs around the Bay Islands remain healthy and pristine, thanks to the historically low number of divers. But those numbers have risen dramatically in recent years, especially among beginners, and the coral is already beginning to show signs of damage. With even more divers expected to come (not to mention legions of snorkeler-toting cruise ships), it is crucial for everyone to help preserve the reef.

HONDURAS

ROATÁN

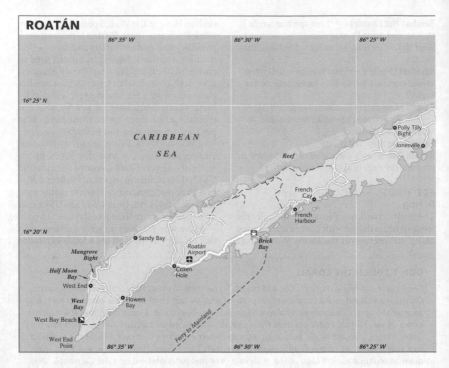

Park (www.roatanmarinepark.com). The reef is under enormous pressure, both from the building works and the amount of visitors, and this organization is campaigning strongly to conserve its beauty.

Prices for courses are now supposed to be standard among most of the dive outfits on the island, although not all adhere. But remember that price isn't everything (see boxed text, p409).

At the safety-first **Coconut Tree Divers** (☎ 445 4081, 403 8782; www.coconuttreedivers.com), very professional, experienced instructors head all the dives. There are also regular beers and BBQs on the deck overlooking Half Moon Bay after the day's diving is done, drawing a younger crowd. Fun dives cost US$20 apiece. There are cheap cabin beds (US$5) available just for divers.

Run by Alvin Jackson, a local instructor with almost three decades of experience, **Native Sons** (☎ 445 1214; www.nativesonsroatan.com) has a good reputation. All dives are led by instructors, not divemasters. Native Sons has fast, well-maintained boats which easily go to the more distant dive sites.

Owned and operated by the same British couple for more than a decade, **Ocean Connections** (☎ 327 0935; www.ocean-connections.com) has small classes and a friendly, noncompetitive atmosphere, catering to a slightly older crowd. It also has a dive shop. Packages are available with Sea Breeze Inn.

Pura Vida (☎ 445 4110, 403 8798; www.puravidaresort.com) is an Italian-run resort with a good reputation. Its instructors usually have five years' teaching experience, with at least three years' teaching on the islands. The instructors are multilingual and organize fun dives according to high or low season. If doing a dive course, there are a few dorm beds available for US$10 a night – you'll need to book ahead. There is also a fine Italian restaurant next door.

Capably managed by a young British couple, **Reef Gliders** (☎ 403 8243; www.reefgliders.com; next to Purple Turtle) has two modern Panga boats; it is very safety and conservation conscious. It also offers a Dive Master internship for an insight into running a dive business.

Sueño del Mar (☎ 445 4343; www.suenodelmar.com) is an upscale option with a well-equipped retail shop and beautifully kept accommodations –

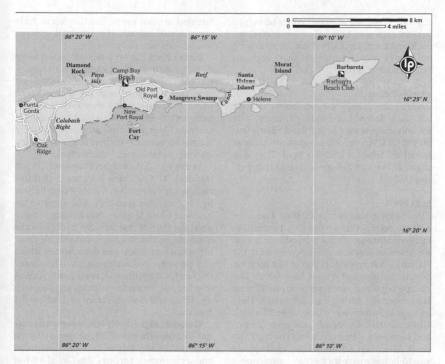

some include a balcony with sea view. It is geared toward the luxury end of the market (four-day open-water course with lodging US$403).

A relaxed, friendly dive shop on the main drag is **Tyll's Dive** (☎ 455 5322; www.tyllsdive.com).

West End Divers (☎ 368 0616; www.westenddivers .com), a small dive shop opposite the water-taxi pier, caters to a younger crowd.

Deep-Sea Diving
One of Roatán's most unusual activities is offered by Karl Stanley, the man behind the grandly named **Roatán Institute of Deep Sea Exploration** (www.stanleysubmarines.com; per dive US$500). A highly inventive, driven history major, Stanley became obsessed with submarines when he was nine years old. Now he has turned his passion into a commercially viable reality, having designed and built his own submergible. He takes passengers in the small yellow submarine, named *Idabel* after the Oklohoma location in which it was constructed, to a depth of up to 2000ft. Light doesn't penetrate to those depths and those who do dare to take the ride come face to face with some extraordinary marine life that very few ever get to see, including the elusive six-gilled sharks. Stanley freely admits you take the plunge at your own risk, and takes passengers' money after they dive.

Beaches & Snorkeling
Half Moon Bay has a small, nice beach and decent snorkeling, although there is some sea grass to wade through. Hire your snorkel equipment from the Marine Park Reserve office that overlooks the beach (US$5) – the money goes to help protect the reef. The beach at **West Bay**, about 4km southwest of West End village, is the most beautiful beach on Roatán – although more and more high-end resorts are lining the beach; you can rent beach chairs (per person US$5, or try just 'tipping' the guard) or bring a blanket and set up under the palms at the far end. There's fantastic snorkeling at the western end, and buoys to ward off the boats. You can easily rent snorkel equipment. Try Las Rocas at the beginning of the beach (per day US$6).

You can walk to West Bay from West End – just keep heading west along the beach – but the walk is not safe at night. Water taxis (per person each way US$2.15, 10 minutes) go back and forth regularly. Plan on returning by 5pm or so. A normal taxi there costs an extortionate US$10.

Horse-Riding

Roatán's surprisingly lush, undulating interior has some decent horse-riding country. The friendly, helpful people at **El Rancho Barrio Dorcas** (☎ 403 8754; www.barriodorcasranch.com) arrange horseback trips for US$30 a head. They also organize rides on full-moon nights (per person US$40).

SLEEPING

The cheapest way to stay in West End is in a dorm room with access to a communal kitchen. More are on the way (after research we heard of a new hostel opening near the Fu Bar) – ask around. If you're not keen on dorms, couples and groups have better and cheaper options. Accommodations fills up fast, especially during the high season (July to August, November to January and Easter). Unfortunately, few hotels take reservations, and then only with a credit card or bank deposit. Many taxi drivers will try to shepherd you to hotels where they get a commission – not all hotels play that game, so insist on stopping at your choice.

The people at Coconut Tree Divers are happy to hold your backpacks while you sort out your accommodations.

Georphi's Tropical Hideaway (☎ 445 4205; www .georphi.com; d with outside bathroom US$10, with bathroom & kitchen US$35, q with kitchen US$50; 🔀) Perhaps the best-value backpacker accommodations on the island, especially if you're with others. This is a sprawling collection of hexagonal cabins in lush, sloping grounds. All the cabins are sturdy-but-basic pine structures, some have a kitchen, and all have a private patio with hammocks. Rooms with air-con cost more. From the intersection, turn left and walk along the beach toward the end of the sandy road. It is on the same site as Rudy's eatery.

Chillies (☎ 445 4003; www.nativesonsroatan.com/chil lies.htm; r with shared bathroom US$18, cabins with shared bathroom & kitchen US$22, with bathroom US$27) This place is an ever-popular budget-traveler choice and it's with good reason. The shared bathrooms are unusually pleasant, while the landscaped gardens are lush. Cabins are a good option if you are in a couple. Shared kitchens are not great, but they serve their purpose well enough. It is affiliated with the Native Sons dive shop.

Burke's Place (☎ 445 4146; r with/without air-con US$30/20, studios US$25; 🅿 🔀) A traditional family-run place, with wooden accommodations set around a large yard with tall mango trees. Check the cabins first – they vary from perfectly kept to somewhat less pristine. Rooms in the main block are simple and clean and there is a good communal kitchen. It is five minutes' walk right off the main intersection.

Valerie's (dm US$5, r with shared bathroom US$15, with bathroom & TV US$25) There is a chance that this backpacker's institution will no longer be here by the time you read this. The eponymous Valerie, a Chicago native, was looking to move on at the time of research. Set back from the main street, this is a mad, ramshackle tumble of wooden rooms and dormitories, which charms some and repels others. The shared kitchen for the bottom dorm is nothing short of grim, but the upstairs dorms are a big step up. There is also a restaurant and bar on the premises.

Mariposa Lodge (☎ 445 4450; www.mariposa-lodge .com; d with shared bathroom US$25, extra person US$10, apt US$35) A short way behind the main sandy road and set in tropical gardens, this Canadian-run place is one of Roatán's most attractive lodgings. The apartments – fully kitted out with gas cookers and fridges – are a great place to kick back after a day's diving. Each has a deck with hammocks, some with fine sea views. A new cottage at the front of the lodge has three impeccably tidy new rooms, sharing a kitchen and bathroom.

Half Moon Resort (☎ 445 4008; s/d with fan US$30/40, with air-con US$38/50; 🔀) This is down at the bottom of a shaded cul-de-sac. Its location is a winner. The pine-constructed rooms are nothing fancy (you might expect fancier for the price), but when you tumble out of bed to the sun lounges right by the reef (prime snorkeling territory), you won't care. The on-site restaurant is good and the staff is friendly.

Sea Breeze Inn (☎ 445 4026; www.seabreezeroatan .com; r with air-con US$30, studio with/without air-con US$50/45, ste with/without air-con US$65/55; 🔀) This is a good option for families or groups. Rooms are neat, with plenty of character but not much space. The suites, however, are spacious, and are great places to chill out. Each has a fridge and microwave, and hammocks draped on the porch in front. Ask for the ocean-view suites up top if you can. It is a three-story wood building behind the Cannibal Café (to the south of the main intersection).

Posada Arco Iris (☎ 445 4264; www.roatanposada.com; s/d US$35/41, 4-bed apt US$55; 🍴 💻) Guatemalan tapestries and carvings, impeccably varnished floors, and an extended leafy, shady setting are some of the stylish touches that make this classy midscale choice stand out. Rooms and apartments are available – for groups it can work out reasonably cheaply. You do get free internet, use of a full kitchen (with the apartment), as well as beach chair and kayak use.

Posada Las Orquideas (☎ 445 4387; www.posadalas orquideas.com; s/d without kitchen US$35/40; s/d with kitchen US$40/46) Run by the same people who manage Posada Arco Iris, with similar amenities and tasteful décor. This is more secluded and has a jetty that is just for guests, jutting out over the pretty Gibson Bay. Go past Arco Iris and follow the signs.

Keifitos Plantation Retreat (www.keifitos.com; s/d US$30/60; 🍴) This is a cluster of cabins clinging to the hillside about 10 minutes' walk beyond the edge of town toward West Bay. The 14 cabins have superb views, if you can get a glimpse through the garden's mango trees. Cabins were being renovated at the time of research. Most have queen beds, all have hot water. There's a steep climb up a wooden stairwell steps to reach the cabins. The downside is you have to walk in the dark along the beach to get back if you go out in West End.

Casa del Sol (☎ 403 8887; d US$30, studio with kitchen US$60) A new set-up, this is right by the entrance to West End where the road forks off to West Bay. Billed as Mexican Riviera meets tropical island, it is a very good-value midrange option. Rooms have a Mexican-style colorwash, there are big ceramic floor-tiles and the bathroom sinks are hand-painted porcelain from El Salvador. The studios sleep four and have a kitchen and big bathtubs.

Other good options:

Milka's Rooms (☎ 445 4241; dm US$8, r US$25) This is a good cheapie, with four rudimentary but functioning kitchens. The three new cabins with hot water are the best deal, but all the rooms are adequate, if a little tight on space. To get there, follow the sign saying 'cheep price,' just behind Pura Vida.

Sue's Cabin (☎ 445 4488; r US$20) Set back from the main street, this is a freshly built cabin on a local family's land. It's quiet, simple and good value, with a kitchen and sporadically working hot water. Ask for Sue at Velva's Place restaurant.

Hotel Dolphin (☎ 445 4499; s/d US$25/30; 🍴) If a bunch of you don't mind sharing, try to bag the top floor here. There's nothing special about the room, but the view over Half Moon Bay is lovely. Other rooms are simple but nicer than the careworn concrete stairwell leading to them would have you expect. You pay more for the bay view.

EATING

Food in West End is pricey. A few basic places have reasonable prices. Staying in a place with a kitchen will cut costs, especially if you are in a group. Supermarket prices are lower in Coxen Hole, but it can be a pain to go there and back. If practical, shop in La Ceiba before getting on the ferry.

International Rotisserie Chicken (🕑 4:30-11pm, mains US$3-8; closed Sun) Easily the biggest bang for your buck this side of the mainland, this classic open-air budget option dishes up some genuinely tasty fare. Its few tables are often full to overflowing as tourists and locals queue for the roast chicken dishes, with healthily portioned sides of rice, beans, potato salad or coleslaw. Get there early.

Le Bistro (☎ 357 8599; mains US$5-9; 🕑 11am-10pm, shorter hours in low season) Another busy little venue, this new kid on the culinary block is excellent value for expensive Roatán. And get this for global cuisine – there's a French manager preparing Thai and Vietnamese dishes in the Caribbean. You could easily walk by here without noticing – it is wedged between shops. The *blau blau* (Vietnamese hotpot; two people US$19) is a treat.

Rudy's (☎ 445 4104; mains US$3.50-5; 🕑 6am-5pm Sun-Fri) The banana pancakes (US$3.50) are renowned at this pleasant open-air café. Service can drag a bit, but it just gives you more time to watch the waves washing in across the sandy main road. It also has reasonably priced lunch dishes, including spaghetti dishes, and good mugs of coffee go for US$1. Next door to International Rotisserie Chicken.

Cannibal Café (☎ 445 0020; 🕑 7am-10pm Mon-Sat) Seriously large tacos are a specialty here at this relaxed Mexican-food eatery. And are you big enough for the burritos challenge? Eat three and you get them free – but check out their size before you begin.

Lighthouse Restaurant (breakfast US$3.50-5, dinner US$7-10; 🕑 7:30am-10pm) Simple waterside restaurant serves good seafood in the evening – including grilled fish, shrimp salad and lobster. There are different, cheaper menus for breakfast and lunch.

Argentinian Grill (☎ 445 4264; mains US$3.50-13; ☯ 3-10pm Tue-Tue) Carnivores should head here for a splurge. As you would expect, steaks are the order of the day – and the wine (mainly from Chile and Argentina) washes it down rather nicely. Service can be snooty but magnificent sunsets compensate. It's just east (right) of the intersection, in front of Posada Arco Iris.

Velva's Place (☎ 445 4488; ☯ 7:30am-10pm Mon-Sat) Unpretentious home-cooking at this simple outdoor restaurant fuels a day's diving and/or snorkeling, or lazing at the beach. 'Island breakfast' – eggs, bacon, beans and toast – costs US$4, burgers are about the same, and fish and shrimp dishes go for US$7 to US$9. It is away from the hubbub of West End's main strip, about two minutes' walk east of the intersection.

There are four supermarkets in West End, with roughly the same high prices. Woody's (closed Saturday) is 100m north of the intersection, **Coconut Tree Market** (☯ 7am-8pm) is at the intersection, and there are two more between the Baptist church and Ocean Connections (one closed Saturday, the other closed Sunday). Watch out too for the pickup trucks that pass through, laden with cheap fresh fruits. As with all produce in Honduras, wash it before you eat – crops here are usually sprayed with DDT.

DRINKING & ENTERTAINMENT
Foster's is a well established bar on a long jetty, with hip-hop on weekend nights, attracting a mainly local crowd. Fu Bar (formerly the Black Pearl, though this venue has more name changes than P Diddy) is the *in* after-hours place of the moment. Live music and DJs keep the island party vibe alive deep into the night. Ask about the full-moon parties, which the resident DJs often organize. It is right out at the south end of the beach toward West Bay, just before Luna Beach Resort.

Sundowners (☯ 3-10pm) Across from Native Sons and Posada Arco Iris, this is a beachside bar, at its liveliest in the early evening when off-duty divers gather to watch the horizon turn brilliant shades of red. There is also the occasional beach-side grill and barbecue. Happy hour is 5pm to 7pm.

Purple Turtle (☎ 445 4483; 7am-midnight Mon-Sat) From Sundowners, revelers usually move onto this small, hole-in-the-wall bar with a lively, upbeat crowd, often showing live sports during the day.

Brick Oven (admission free; ☯ 5-10pm Wed-Mon) Recent big-budget movies are shown on video at this place (shows at 5pm and 7pm); you can't miss the flyers plastered all over West End. It cooks up some good thin-crust pizzas – but they ain't cheap (around US$11).

Blue Channel (pizzas & pastas US$7.50-9; ☯ 7am-1pm & 4.30-10pm, closed Fri) Opposite Ocean Connections, this has a big screen and shows more alternative movies (US$2.75, free if you are eating at the restaurant; shows at 8pm).

Coxen Hole
Coxen Hole is the largest town on Roatán, and home to government offices, banks, the post office and Hondutel. The airport is just outside town. People come here on business errands or to stock up at the supermarket, HB Warren (cheaper than the West End). Groceries are still cheaper in La Ceiba though; shop ahead if possible. Coxen Hole is not particularly attractive – it's hot, humid and there are no good beaches. Avoid walking around at night, as discos and bars can get rowdy.

ORIENTATION
The commercial section of Coxen Hole is a few short blocks. The HB Warren supermarket, with the tiny city park beside it, is at the center of town; everything of interest is nearby or on the road leading into town. Buses and taxis arrive and depart from in front of the city park. The airport is a five-minute drive east. The main through road in town is one way (west to east) – be careful if you are driving a rented car, as there are no signs telling you this.

INFORMATION
Emergency
Police (☎ 445 3438)

Internet Access
Hotel Juarez (☯ 7:30am-5pm Mon-Sat) Opposite HB Warren. The 2nd floor has internet access for US$0.80 for 15 minutes, much less extortionate than the West End set-ups.

Money
As well as the options following, BAC Credomatic has an ATM.
Banco Atlántida (Front St; ☯ 9am-4pm Mon-Fri, 8:30-11:30am Sat) Has an ATM; gives advances on Visa cards and changes traveler's checks. Queues are often long.
BGA (Front St; ☯ 8:30am-3:30pm Mon-Fri, 8:30-11:30am Sat) Changes American Express traveler's checks and gives cash advances on Visa cards. Also has an ATM. Located across from HB Warren.

Post

Post office (⏰ 8am-noon & 2-5pm Mon-Fri, 8am-noon Sat) Just opposite the BGA bank on the same side of the street as the HB Warren supermarket.

Telephone

Hondutel (⏰ 7am-8:30pm) Also on the main street.

SLEEPING & EATING

You probably won't want or need to stay in Coxen Hole, especially since the ferry terminal moved.

Hotel Juarez (☎ 445 1565; tr US$27) On the 3rd floor in the building opposite the HB Warren supermarket, this is not a bad option. Simple rooms with uneven wooden floorboards and cable TV are tidily kept. There's no hot water.

Restaurante Caribe Sol (☎ 445 0134; mains US$6-7; ⏰ 7:30am-5pm) In the same building as the Hotel Juarez, this has a basic *comedor*, with big chicken and pork dishes. It also has a huge Caribbean-style grill for four (US$37.80).

¿Qué Tal? Café (☎ 445 1007; mains US$6-8; ⏰ 8am-4pm) Located at the west entrance to town, at the intersection of the highway to West End. Reasonable salads and sandwiches, and a bright and breezy atmosphere. It also has a pulp fiction collection and one computer with internet access (per minute US$0.15).

HB Warren supermarket (☎ 445 1208; ⏰ 7am-7pm Mon-Sat) Stock up on groceries here.

SHOPPING

Yaba Ding Ding (☎ 445 1683; ⏰ 9am-5pm Mon-Sat) A well-stocked and surprisingly tasteful souvenir and postcard store. It's off the main street down a precinct toward the water.

French Harbour

French Harbour is the second-largest town on Roatán. An important port, it's home to a large fishing, shrimp and lobster fleet. With no decent budget hotels and restaurants, the area's main attraction for backpackers is the impressive **Arch's Iguana Farm** (☎ 975 7442; admission US$5; ⏰ 8am-3:30pm) in French Cay, just outside of town. It is a worthwhile stop. Less a farm than the house of a serious iguanaphile, everywhere you look you see iguanas – on the driveway, in the trees, under bushes, everywhere. In all around 3000 iguanas live here, some as long as 5ft (1.5m). Midday is feeding time, and the best time to visit. At the pier (at the Iguana Farm) an enclosed pool has a school of huge fish, several small sea turtles, and dozens of conches.

Oak Ridge

Oak Ridge is another port town on Roatán's eastern side, a somewhat more appealing town than French Harbour or Coxen Hole. It's known officially as José Santos Guardiola, but almost no one calls it by its Spanish name. The tiny town hugs a protected harbor, with wooden houses on stilts all along the shore and colorful boats plying the waters. More homes and shops are on a small cay just a two-minute motorboat ride from shore. Water taxis take passengers around the harbor and across to the cay for US$1.20; they dock in front of the bus stop.

Water taxis can also take you on a pleasant tour through mangrove canals to Jonesville, a small town on a nearby bight. A 45- to 60-minute boat tour costs US$20 for up to eight people. For another US$5, you can stop and eat at the locally famous Hole in the Wall restaurant. A shorter, cheaper trip (US$15, 30 minutes) goes to another part of the mangrove forest and isn't as good.

SLEEPING & EATING

The Hole in the Wall is a popular place with a sunny terrace, and all you-can-eat fresh shrimp for around US$10 on Friday and Sunday. West of Jonesville, you have to take a water taxi from Oak Ridge to get here, or combine it with a tour of the mangrove forest (up to eight people around US$20).

Reef House Resort (☎ 435 1482; www.reefhouseresort.com; 7-night package s/d per person US$900/799) This is an excellent, relaxed resort, favored by those who want to concentrate on diving. There is an unspoiled reef just in front, and divemasters instinctively know how to spot the wildlife. The resort is like being at a large family gathering – you talk about your latest underwater adventure over a hearty lunch and dinner in a central dining hall. Rooms are unshowy but very comfortable. You need to get here by water taxi from the pier in Oak Ridge.

Sandy Bay

About 4km before you reach West End is Sandy Bay, a quiet little community strung out along the seashore. It's not as developed as West End – although it is getting there – and it doesn't have a village center as such – it's just a long settlement along several kilometers of beach.

Anthony's Key Resort, long one of Roatán's best dive resorts, is not for budget travelers, but it is definitely worth a visit. It has the

Institute for Marine Sciences, a research and educational facility working with dolphins. There is a **dolphin show** (US$4 for nonguests; 🕑 4pm daily). You can also come face-to-face with a resident dolphin with the **Dolphin Beach Encounter** (per person US$50) or go on a **Dolphin Dive** (per person US$112). Some people initially feel uneasy about swimming with captive dolphins, but that usually fades when they see the happy, well-cared-for animals. The resort also houses the small but interesting **Roatán Museum** (☎ 445 3003; admission free; 🕑 8am-5pm), with reasonable displays on the island's archaeology, history, geology and wildlife. It includes what locals call *yaba ding ding* (pre-Columbian artifacts).

Across the road from Anthony's Key Resort, the lush **Carambola Botanical Gardens** (☎ 445 3117; admission US$5; 🕑 7am-5pm Mon-Sat, 7am-1pm Sun) covers 40 acres of protected hillside, with several nature trails filled with orchids, spice plants and an 'iguana wall.' It won't be long before you spot a wandering *agouti* (rodent-like animal). A lookout has views to Utila and, at the right time, into the dolphin show at Anthony's Key Resort. There is also the **Wind & Fun Windsurf School** (☎ 445 3292; jm_carvajal@yahoo .com; 🕑 9am-5pm Tue-Sun), which offers individual lessons for US$20 (one to two hours, including equipment); west of Blue Bahía Resort.

It's a stiff climb to **Rick's American Café** (☎ 445 3123; dishes US$8-15; 🕑 5-9:30pm Thu-Tue) but worth it for a fine panorama over the bay, good steaks and hamburgers, and an international menu. With satellite sports showing this is also a good option if there's a ball game you just can't miss. It has a large sign on the main road, west of Anthony's Key Resort.

Getting There & Away
AIR
Roatán's **Aeropuerto Juan Ramón Galvez** (☎ 445 1880) is a short distance east of Coxen Hole.

Isleña/TACA (☎ 445 1088, reservations 443 0179; www.flyislena.com), **Sosa** (☎ 445 1658; www.aerolineas sosa.com) and **Atlantic Airlines** (☎ 445 1179; www .atlanticairlines.com.ni) all have offices in Roatán's airport; they offer daily flights between Roatán and La Ceiba (all charge around US$42 each way), with domestic and international connections. At the time of research, **Continental** (☎ 445 0224; www.continental.com) operated nonstop flights from Houston to Roatán on Saturday and Sunday, and from Newark (high season only); **Delta** (☎ 550 1616; www.delta.com) had flights from Atlanta on Saturday only.

BOAT
The **Galaxy Wave** (☎ 445 1795) is a sleek, comfortable catamaran ferry service that zips between the island and the mainland in about 1½ hours. The boat leaves Roatán from a new terminal in Dixon's Cove (between Coxen Hole and French Harbour) at 7am and 2pm, and leaves from La Ceiba at 9:30am and 4:30pm. It costs US$21.50 each way. The swells can be bumpy – ask for the anti–sea sickness tablets if your tummy is sensitive. There is no direct service from Roatán to Utila – you have to go to La Ceiba first.

Getting Around
BICYCLE
Captain Van's (☎ 445 4076; 🕑 8am-4pm), across from the church in West End, rents bicycles for US$10 per day.

BOAT
Many towns – Oak Ridge, West End, West Bay – have regular water-taxi services. Anywhere else, you can fairly easily hire someone to take you wherever you want to go. In West End, colectivo boats to West Bay (per person US$2.10, last one from either end around 5pm) leave from the pier near Bamboo Hut Laundry. You have to wait until they fill up.

BUS
Roatán has two bus routes, both originating in Coxen Hole.

Bus 2 (ruta 2) is the one you're most likely to use – it goes west from Coxen Hole past Sandy Bay and on to West End and West Bay. Minibuses depart both ends every 15 minutes from 6am to 6pm. The cost is US$0.80 to go to West End; it's a 25-minute ride on a good road.

Bus 1 goes east from Coxen Hole past the airport to French Harbour, past Polly Tilly Bight, through Punta Gorda and on to Oak Ridge. Minibuses depart every half hour from 6am to 5:30pm and cost US$0.70 to US$1.20 depending on your destination, but can be deadly slow and full to the gills. The trip takes about 10 minutes from Coxen Hole to the airport, another 20 minutes to French Harbour, and an hour more to Oak Ridge.

In Coxen Hole, the bus stop is in front of the small park beside the HB Warren supermarket in the center of town. In West End, wait for the bus at the main intersection, where all the taxis are parked. If the minibus is empty, be sure it's a colectivo so you don't get charged the taxi rate. Minibuses don't run on Sunday.

CAR & MOTORCYCLE
Car rental agencies on Roatán:

Best Car Rental (☎ 445 1494; www.roatanbestcarrent al.com; airport; ☺ 7am-5pm)

Captain Van's (☎ 445 4076; ☺ 8am-4pm) Across from the church in West End, this rents motorcycles (US$50 per day) and scooters (US$45 per day), as well as push bikes (US$10). It has the best reputation for safety and maintenance.

Caribbean Rent a Car (☎ 455 6950, airport 455 1430; www.caribbeanroatan.com; ☺ 8am-6pm) Outside the airport.

Roatán Island Rental (☎ 455 6759; www.roatan islandrental.com; French Harbour; ☺ 8am-5pm)

Sandy Bay Rent a Car (☎ 445 1710; Sandy Bay; ☺ 7am-5pm)

HITCHHIKING
Although Lonely Planet cannot recommend hitching, it is easy on Roatán in the daytime, and usually safe. It's much more difficult – and risky – to get a ride at night.

TAXI
Taxis operate around the island. Many are colectivos during the day and don't charge much more than buses; from West End to Coxen Hole, a colectivo is US$1.40 per person. From Coxen Hole to French Harbour it is US$1.10. Again, if you are the first passenger, let the driver know you want to go colectivo. As everywhere in Honduras, always clarify the price of the ride before you start.

UTILA
pop 6000

Utila has a slow, welcoming place, where the locals and visitors interact much more frequently than on Roatán, mainly because everyone is in the same town. Dive courses and fun dives cost about the same here as on Roatán – maybe slightly less – but food and lodging is noticeably cheaper – although more expensive than on the mainland. Utila's shops focus on certification courses, and classes can be larger than on Roatán. Utila does not have the beaches that Roatán does, and the snorkeling isn't as good, but the strong local presence and culture make for a unique, refreshing island experience. The party scene is stronger here, which appeals to younger backpackers.

Utila is a small island, about 13km long and 5km wide, with tiny cays dotted on the south side. It is the closest island to the mainland, just 29km away. Utila is mostly flat, with only one small hill. The population lives almost entirely in one settlement on a curving bay; another small settlement is on a cay about a 20-minute boat ride away.

Orientation
Utila is very easy to find your way around. East Harbour (known as Utila Town) is the only town on the island, with one main road and a smaller one, known generally as Cola de Mico road, that intersects with the road in front of the pier. At the east end of the main road is the old airport, just a few hundred meters from the main intersection and a good place for snorkeling. At the western end of the road is Chepes beach, also good for snorkeling.

The public jetty, where the ferries arrive and depart, is at the intersection of the town's two main roads. There, you can turn left, right or go straight; several dive shops send people to meet the boat and hand out maps with the location of competing shops mysteriously absent. There used to be a notion that shops and restaurants were better or worse depending on the direction you turned from the pier, but that is completely irrelevant now – you'll find good (and not so good) places in all directions. Besides, the town is so small, you can check out literally every shop and hotel in less than an hour. Captain Morgan's Dive Center, right at the intersection, will watch your backpack while you go to look for a place to stay.

Supermarkets, the post office, Hondutel and a Spanish school are on the main road.

Information
BOOKSTORES
Bundu Café (☎ 425 3557) On main road east of the intersection; has a decent selection of books in English and other languages, including a range of preloved Lonely Planet titles.

EMERGENCY
Police (☎ 425 3145)

IMMIGRATION
There's an immigration office on the first floor of the Palacio de Municipio building next to the public jetty.

> **GETTING INTO TOWN**
>
> **From the Airport**
>
> Cabs try to charge US$15 (at night US$20) although prices are usually negotiable. It's worth making a little more effort: walk out the airport gates, cross the road and taxis are a third of the price or less (agree on a fare before getting in). Even cheaper, take a colectivo taxi to Coxen Hole (US$1.10) then a minibus (US$0.80) or another colectivo (US$1.40) to West End.
>
> **From the Pier**
>
> Taxis are the quick, easy and expensive way to get to West End. Drivers have a price sharking system in operation from the pier – the going rate is quoted at US$15 a ride. You can usually barter it down to a more reasonable US$10. If you haven't got much stuff, walk 150m to the main road (wait on the far side) and flag a colectivo (US$1.10 to Coxen Hole, then US$1.40 from Coxen Hole to West End) or a minibus (US$0.80). Minibuses don't run on Sunday.

INTERNET ACCESS & TELEPHONE

Utila has numerous internet centers, and some dive shops also offer internet access to students. The cheapest at last check:

Caye Caulker Cyber Café (East Main St; per hr US$1.85; 9am-8pm) Right next to the Central American Spanish School, this has a low-cost connection, as well as cheap international calls.

INTERNET RESOURCES

The website www.aboututila.com has general info and news about Utila.

LAUNDRY

Next to Central American Spanish School, this laundry with no name will wash, dry and fold clothes for US$0.40 for pants or shirts, and US$0.11 per underwear. It is open from 7am to 4pm.

MONEY

Most dive shops and many hotels accept lempira, US dollars, traveler's checks and credit cards (usually with service fee).

Banco BGA (8am-3:30pm Mon-Fri, 8:30-11:30am Sat) Changes traveler's checks and give cash advances on Visa cards. It now has the only ATM in town. Plan your finances in advance as the machine does run out of notes.

POST

The post office is right by the public dock.

Sights & Activities

WILDLIFE-WATCHING

The **Iguana Research & Breeding Station** (☎ 425 3946; www.utila-iguana.de; admission US$2.15; 2-5pm Mon, Wed & Fri), east of Mamey Lane, studies and protects the endangered Utila iguana. The island's rapid development and a lack of environmental planning have seriously threatened this endemic species, which survives in a small section of mangrove forest. Visitors get to see plenty of these fascinating, spiny tailed critters on a tour of the research station. Station workers can also arrange other wildlife-spotting tours to the far side of the island. There are some volunteer opportunities too.

DIVING

Utila's south shore has warm crystal-clear waters filled with tropical fish, corals, sponges and other marine life. On the north side, a plunging wall makes for great drift and deep diving. Animal life is richer in Roatán overall, but Utila is famous for the magnificent whale sharks that gather here from March to April and September to October.

Most dive shops start a course almost every day, and many offer instruction in various languages. As on Roatán, there is a lot more to consider than simply price (although most have a price agreement so there should not be the variety there once was).

Firstly, safety: see the boxed text, p409, for questions you should be asking. Secondly, and just as crucially, the environment: does the dive school you are looking at have a responsible, sustainable attitude toward the reefs? A group of dive shops have started up the **Utila Dive and Safety Environmental Council** (www .udsec.com) – it is worth checking that your dive school is signed up to that. PADI open-water dive courses take three to four days and cost around US$240, including a US$3-per-day reef fee, which goes toward the upkeep of the buoys and coral. Dive schools often have

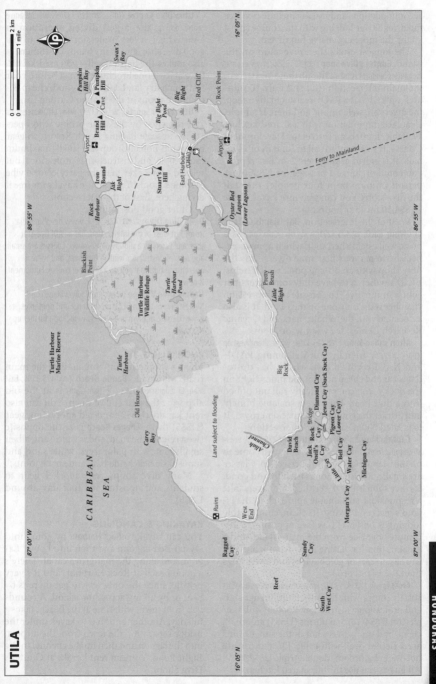

UTILA

0 — 2 km
0 — 1 mile

CARIBBEAN SEA

Turtle Harbour Marine Reserve

Blackish Point

Old House

Turtle Harbour

Turtle Harbour Wildlife Refuge

Turtle Harbour Pond

Land subject to flooding

Ruins

West End

Ragged Cay

Carey Bay

Reef

Sandy Cay

South West Cay

Canal

Rock Harbour

Iron Bound

Jak Bight

Stuart's Hill

Airport

Brand Hill

Pumpkin Hill Bay

Pumpkin Hill

Cave

Swan's Bay

Big Bight Pond

Big Bight

Red Cliff

Rock Point

East Harbour (Utila)

Airport

Reef

Ferry to Mainland

Oyster Bed Lagoon (Lower Lagoon)

Pretty Brush

Little Bight

Big Rock

Bridge

Rock Cay

Jack Cay

Oneil's Cay

Little Cay

Diamond Cay

Jewel Cay (Suck Suck Cay)

Pigeon Cay

Bell Cay (Lower Cay)

Water Cay

Morgan's Cay

Michigan Cay

David Beach

Allah Channel

86° 55' W

87° 00' W

86° 55' W

87° 00' W

16° 05' N

16° 05' N

accommodations and usually include two free fun dives or free lodging with the course (most go for the more expensive fun dives).

The longest-established dive shop on the island, **Gunter's Dive Shop** (☎ 425 3350; www.ecomar inegunters.blogpsot.com) is the furthest away from the main intersection (but still only 10 minutes' walk). It has a PADI-registered dive shop, the divers are welcoming, and there is simple, clean accommodation with a shared kitchen available. It offers an Instructor Development Course. If you want to sail to Roatán or Guanaja, it is worth asking here – at last report, you could organize a passage for US$50 per person (minimum of four people) through the dive store. You can also hire kayaks here (US$4.50 for four hours).

West of the intersection, **Bay Islands College of Diving** (BICD; ☎ 425 3291; www.dive-utila.com) is a busy, well established shop which appeals especially to nervous first-time divers. It is the only shop with an on-site pool, which helps. BICD's policy is to have only four divers per course or fun dive. The on-site recompression chamber is the only one on the island. It is also associated with the Whale Shark and Oceanic Research Center; see www.wsorc.com.

Alton's Dive Shop (☎ 425 3704; www.altondiveshop .com), a very friendly and welcoming PADI- and NAUI-certified dive school, has up-to-date gear and cheap accommodations right on the dock – you can practically roll out of bed into a dive boat. They are a sociable bunch, and attract the younger backpacker crowd. It is located 300m east of the intersection.

Captain Morgan's Dive Centre (☎ 425 3349; www .divingutila.com) is the first dive shop you come to on the island, right on the intersection. Classes are small and instruction is friendly and good. Its dive shop is PADI-certified. Managers take a responsible, sustainable approach to the island's reefs and diving. Its clean, comfortable lodging is on Jewel Cay (see opposite), a 20-minute boat ride from the main island, and a great option for getting away from it all. The cay has no cars or golf buggies and fewer bugs than the island proper.

Cross Creek (☎ 425 3397; www.crosscreekutila.com; East Main St) comes with friendly multilingual staff and professional instruction. Rooms (with fan/air-con US$4/16) and dorms (US$3) are small, clean, and can get very hot in the sun. Cabins are a decent deal, with cable TV and private hot-water bathroom (double/triple US$28/33). All guests can use the big shared kitchen.

Utila Dive Centre (UDC; ☎ 425 3326; www.utiladive centre.com) is the largest diving operation in Utila. This is a very professional outfit with a good dive shop and many happy customers. It also makes the hardest sell – you are likely to have at least one brochure almost before your feet touch dry land. UDC has good, cheap accommodations at the Mango Garden Inn.

Utila Water Sports (☎ 425 3239; www.utilawatersports .com) is owned by the same people who operate the upscale Laguna Beach Resort, so gear here is top-notch. Groups are small (maximum four people) and instruction is professional but relaxed – lower key than the party-central vibe of some schools. You can use kayaks for free if diving here. East of the intersection.

Other good possibilities:

Deep Blue Divers (☎ 425 3211; www.deepblueutila .com) Just west of the intersection, has a PADI five-star shop and caters to a slightly older crowd. Courses are small and relaxed; instructors lead all fun dives, and there is one-on-one tuition if you do a refresher course. Equipment is new.

Utopia Dive Village (www.utopiadivevillage.com) Newest dive outfit on Utila; professional and upmarket. It is well outside of town in an exclusive location further up the coast.

SNORKELING
There's snorkeling on both ends of the main road. Manmade **Bando Beach** (☎ 425 3190; East Main St; admission US$3; ☼ 9am-5pm) is at the old airport at the east end of town. You can also rent kayaks (US$3) and old snorkeling gear (US$5) there. **Chepes Beach** is at the opposite (west) end of the road, and is a pleasant, albeit small, spot, with palm trees, white sand and some basic beachside bars and snack joints.

Many dive shops rent snorkel gear to students and nonstudents (per day around US$5).

KAYAKING & CANOEING
You can kayak to **Rock Harbour** by going into Oyster Bed Lagoon and then into Lower Lagoon and along the mangrove canal. There's a good beach at Rock Harbour, and it's very private, since the only way to get there is by boat or by hiking across the island. A round-trip from town, with time at the beach, takes a full day. Another option is to kayak under the bridge separating the town from the airport, into the lagoon and then up the channel to Big Bight Pond. You can rent kayaks at Gunter's Dive Shop.

Many local fishermen and families have signs in their windows for boat tours. They can take you to Water Cay, to Rock Harbour via the mangrove canal, though the lagoon, etc.

HIKING

For a complete escape from town, walk 3km across the island to the caves of **Pumpkin Hill Bay**. You will get an idea of what the island used to be like before the tourism boom. One of the caves was allegedly a hideout for the pirate Henry Morgan.

THE CAYS

Several cays on Utila's southwest shore make good day trips. **Jewel** and **Pigeon Cays**, connected by a small bridge, are home to a charming village and the best fish burgers on the north coast. Captain Morgan's Dive Centre operates from here, and loans kayaks and snorkel gear to students.

Water Cay, just beyond Pigeon and Jewel Cays, is a beautiful, uninhabited little island covered with palm trees. A caretaker is supposed to keep it clean and collect US$2 per visitor for the upkeep of the island – although there was no sign of him or much litter-collecting when we showed up last. Utila's annual **Sun Jam party** is held here, usually in August, when hundreds of locals and visitors pack the island for a fun night of dancing, drinking and general mayhem. The best snorkeling is off the southeastern corner, but watch for boat traffic.

There are several ways of traveling to the cays – you will quickly spot the signs around town. Bundu Café organizes fairly regular day trips (per person US$8, plus US$2 for the caretaker, minimum four people).

Courses

Utila is not a natural spot for learning Spanish as many of its residents speak English. However, there are a couple of language schools, and opportunities to speak Spanish are increasing with the large number of mainland migrants.

Central American Spanish School (☎ 425 3788; www.ca-spanish.com), west of the intersection, across from Rubi's Inn, offers Spanish classes at all levels. One week one-on-one classes cost US$125 for the first week and US$100 for subsequent weeks. Hourly rates are available (US$6). It has received some glowing feedback from customers and has recently introduced homestay options (including full board and lodging US$100).

Sleeping

Utila has a bunch of good cheap places to stay, and several midrange ones. It doesn't take long to walk around and find something that suits you (you can leave your backpack at Captain Morgan's, near the pier). Many dive shops, including Captain Morgan's Dive Center, Utila Water Sports and Utila Dive Center, have good, cheap (or free) accommodations for students. Only hotels open to walk-ins are listed here.

Note that it can be hard to get a good room during the busy tourist seasons (July to August and mid-December to Easter), and also during the Sun Jam festival (usually in August). Reservations are advisable at these times.

MAIN ROAD

Bayview Hotel (☎ 425 3114; d with fan US$18, with air-con US$35; 🔀) Reasonable rooms all have bathrooms with hot water. White tiles and floral patterns are not the most stylish, nor is this the best value that you will find, but the hotel pier is good for a cold drink and sunbathing. It lies west of the intersection.

Rubi's Inn (☎ 425 3240; s/d with fan US$16/20, r with air-con US$35, honeymoon r US$45; 🔀) Probably the best deal on the island, Rubi's Inn has spotless rooms with polished floors, white bedspreads, and compact, neatly tiled bathrooms (even with attractive shower curtains). The property has a delightful little jetty that juts out onto the waters of Utila harbor. There is a honeymoon suite on the 2nd floor for all you romantics out there. It is no secret, however, and books up fast. It's next to the Reef Cinema.

Margaritaville Beach Hotel (☎ 425 3366; fax 425 3266; West Main St, Sandy Bay; r with fan/air-con US$15/30, cabins with air-con US$50; 🔀) Just under 100 yards from Chepes Beach, Margaritaville is a two-story Caribbean-style house with porches. Rooms are simple – two beds, a fan and a bathroom – while across the street, the cabins are a slight step up – updated furnishings, private porches, and on the bay.

Freddy's Place (☎ 425 3142; East Main St; d with fan/ air-con US$16/35; 🔀) This has four reasonable apartments with two rooms apiece (rented individually) sharing a bathroom and kitchen. The doors are darkly varnished, while hammocks on the outside porch apparently catch 'the best breeze in Utila.' Located east of the intersection over the bridge.

HONDURAS

INLAND

From the pier, go straight across the main road for a number of good budget lodging options.

Tony's Place (☎ 425 3376; s/d US$5.40/7.30) These basic but neat wooden box rooms, stacked on two floors, all have shared bathrooms. They are on the same site as the owner's house, and are a reasonable long-term rent option. Look out for the white-and-green building around the corner from the Mango Inn.

Blueberry Hill (☎ 425 3141; Cola de Mico; s or d US$8) This is a ramshackle collection of houses, on the hill up from the dock. Rooms have a shared kitchen and bathroom; upstairs rooms have a porch so you can watch the crowds go by. There are some cabins to rent too.

Hotel Bavaria (☎ 425 3809; Cola de Mico; s/d US$8/10) Rooms above a family house with lively children. The rooms are impeccably kept, right down to the polished floorboards, all with bathrooms (cold water only). Each has one double and one single bed. It is perched on the hill, just a short way up from the Mango Inn.

Roses Inn (☎ 425 3283; Mamey's La; r with/without bathroom US$12/8) These quieter rooms in a house on stilts about five minutes' walk up the hill from the fire station (west of the intersection) are the cheapest deal, with hot water included. Guests in the clean, no-frill rooms share a kitchen. There is an attractive flower garden at the front. Arrange your stay at Rose's supermarket at the bottom of the hill.

Colibri Hill Resort (☎ 425 3329; www.colibri-resort.com; s/d US$41/43; ❄ ⚑) This upmarket newcomer is a clear cut above anything else on Utila, although sadly it is beyond the average backpacker's budget. Whitewashed rooms complement lovingly shellacked hardwood floorboards while the luscious, rambling gardens include a small pool bar. Upstairs rooms

have superb sweeping views across the bay, and fresh coffee is available in the morning. To get there, turn left from the pier and take a right at the Bayview Hotel.

Eating

There's a good selection of eating options for such a small settlement. Several places to stay also have kitchens where you can cook. You may want to stock up on fruits and vegetables on the mainland – they are scarcer and more expensive on the island.

Mermaids Fast Food (☎ 425 3395; dishes US$2-4.50; ☺ 10am-10pm Mon-Thu, 10am-6pm Fri, 10am-3pm Sat & Sun) Something of a Utila institution, Mermaids has an open front and canteen-style plastic chairs. Its style and prices are fast-food but the nosh is much better than that sounds. Dishes include baked chicken.

Thompson's Bakery (☎ 425 3803; breakfast US$2.50; ☺ 6am-8pm Mon-Sat, 6am-3pm Sun) This honest, hard-working café can break your fast before the day's first dive with filling *baleadas* (usually filled with beans and cream). In the evening, a grill and BBQ are often wheeled out. Its fresh Johnny cakes (a type of doughy biscuit) are famous.

Ultralight Café (☎ 425 3514; West Main St; mains US$3-7; ☺ breakfast, lunch & dinner Sun-Thu, breakfast & lunch Fri) An Israeli restaurant with an interesting history, serving up *shakshuka* (a popular Israeli egg dish), falafel, *sabich* (a pita sandwich) and the best pita bread in Central America. The conch soup is also excellent.

Bundu Café (☎ 425 3557; dishes US$2.50-7; ☺ 8am-4pm Thu-Tue, 6-11pm Fri-Sun) This is still one of the best traveler cafés in Honduras. The large, comfy interior is a fine place to meet people, read or hang out, and there is always something going on – pub quizzes on Fridays, salsa on Saturdays and occasional piano performances on a Sunday. It has a big-portioned,

---

SPLURGE!

Rent your own island! It is not every day you have the chance to step out your front door and let the sands of your own Caribbean island run between your toes. But that's exactly what you can do just off Utila for surprisingly little money. You can choose between two different cays, both of which have cabins and facilities – as well as the essential crystal-clear waters lapping at the edge. If you do it in a group, it can even work out reasonably cheap. **Sandy Cay** is available for US$85 a night, (three-night minimum). It has a butane fridge and solar power and sleeps six. The slightly more luxurious **Little Cay** goes for US$125 a night. It has its own generator. To arrange your own private getaway, contact George Jackson on **Pigeon Cay** (☎ 425 3161) or ask at Captain Morgan's Dive Centre (p420).

good-value menu, catering to the backpacker crowd with bagels, fresh homemade *panini* bread, pancakes, salads, fruit and yogurt, as well as some island-style dishes. It is located east of the intersection (turn right at the pier). Ask here about trips to Water Cay.

La Dolce Vita Pizzeria (☎ 425 3410; dishes US$4-7; ⊗ 6:30am-10pm) Up a lush garden path at the Mango Inn, it does great brick-oven pizzas, seafood pastas and good breakfasts. Many people come just to prop up the adjoining bar.

Driftwood Café (☎ 408 5168; mains US$5-8; ⊗ 7am-10pm) This delightful option is a little way west, offering respite from the pumping tunes that blast out in the center of town. The eating area is beyond the bar, out on a jetty over the water. We tried the snapper battered in beer, which took a while to get to our table – but hey, what's the rush? It was worth waiting for.

Munchies Café (☎ 425 3168; sandwiches US$3.50, main dishes US$5-9; ⊗ 8:30am-10:30pm) A lot of surf, some turf and even some good vegetarian platters are dished out on the attractive veranda of this restaurant. The chef's specials are worth looking out for, and there are good reasonably priced sandwich options for those peckish moments between dives.

Jade Seahorse Restaurant (☎ 425 3270; dishes US$5-11; ⊗ 7:30am-2pm & 5-10pm Thu-Tue) The colorfully chaotic interior – including plastic iguanas poised on columns – is the island's most distinctive restaurant setting. The creativity continues in the cuisine, which includes inventive, well-prepared seafood and pasta dishes.

La Piccola (☎ 425 3746; dishes US$6-8; ⊗ 5-10pm Sat-Thu) This warm, authentically Italian restaurant serves up reasonably priced backpacker specials on candlelit tables with ruby tablecloths, in a simple stone-floor setting. There are discounts if you come in a group of six or more.

Café Mariposa (☎ 425 3979; dishes US$6-9; ⊗ 11:30am-2pm & 5-10pm Fri, Sat, Mon & Tue, 10:30am-2pm Sun) Set up in May 2006, this is in a lovely upstairs setting overlooking the bay. It is at its finest when the jetty below is illuminated at night. Business is yet to pick up but it deserves to. The cuisine takes much of its inspiration from New Orleans (links between the Louisiana town and the Bay Islands are strong). There are occasional live-music performances.

Bush's Supermarket (☎ 425 3147; ⊗ 6:20am-6pm Mon-Sat, 6:20-11:20am Sun) Opens early so you can get your day's supplies before you hop on a dive boat.

Drinking

Past the Mango Inn, the Bar in the Bush is popular, but can get rowdy. It usually is just open on Friday nights. Lone travelers should take care at night, since the pathway to the bar is unlit.

Treetanic (⊗ 7pm-midnight Fri-Wed) Who needs LSD with this imaginatively landscaped bar and garden that goes on forever? Its mad little assortment of arches, shelters, bridges and exotic tropical flora – an extension of the luxury cabins on the same site – are a must-see. The drinks and cocktails are good too.

Tranquila Bar (⊗ 4pm-midnight Sun-Thu, 4pm-3am Fri & Sat) Jutting out on a small jetty, this is a relaxed place to swap dive tales and travel stories. Reggae tunes on the sound system add to the easygoing vibe. It also serves Cajun and Po Boy food (US$5 to US$7) from a hole-in-the-wall just down from the bar.

Coco Loco Bar (⊗ 4pm-midnight, later in high season) A perennial favorite among the younger backpacker crowd, the music is faster and more furious than in the neighboring Tranquila Bar, and the shots seem to flow faster and more furiously too. It is *champa* style, with a jetty out onto the water. Happy hour is from 4pm to 7pm.

Entertainment

Reef Video & Cinema (☎ 425 3754; ⊗ 1-8pm Mon-Fri, 11:30am-6pm Sat) Lends DVDs (US$2.15), and shows different films each night in a cute little upstairs 60-seater cinema (US$2.45). It is east of the intersection.

Shopping

Gunter's Driftwood Gallery (☎ 425 3113; ⊗ hours vary) is a quirky workshop a couple of blocks inland, where the eponymous Gunter carves and displays sculptures (lots of sharks) made from driftwood. Turn left just before Mango Inn; you'll see the sign on your right. It is more likely to be open in the afternoon.

Getting There & Away
AIR
Flights between Utila and La Ceiba cost about US$45 and take about 15 minutes.

Atlantic Airlines (☎ 425 3364; ⊗ 8am-noon & 2-5pm Mon-Sat) has an office on the main road, across from Banco Atlántida.

HONDURAS

BOAT

The *Utila Princess II* runs from La Ceiba to Utila at 9:30am and 4pm. Crossings take one hour. Prepare for a fun but wet ride if you sit up front! The same boat returns from Utila to La Ceiba at 6:20am and 2pm. Tickets are US$16.25 each way; arrive half an hour in advance. There is a US$0.60 docking tax on the return from Utila. Occasional charter boats go to the mainland or to Roatán, but they can be expensive and don't run to a set schedule. Don't depend on them.

Getting Around

Golf carts now zip up and down the main road (keep an eye out for them) and charge a standard US$1 for any distance.

Lance Bodden (☎ 425 3245; ☻ 8am-5pm Mon-Sat) Rents four-wheel ATVs (per day US$60), golf buggies (per day US$50), motorcycles and scooters (per day US$45), and good mountain bikes (per day US$5 to US$8). Straight ahead from the pier.

Delco Bike (☻ 8am-6pm Sun-Fri) Rents out bikes for US$2.75 (with a US$11 returnable deposit). Also hires out scooters (per day US$20). Left of intersection.

GUANAJA

pop 10,000

Easternmost of the three Bay Islands, Guanaja is a small island, roughly 18km long and 6km wide at its widest point.

It is blessed with a great reef, beaches and laid-back fishing villages. A handful of cays around the island harbor shipwrecks and offer some good snorkeling and diving. Although several dive resorts have appeared on the island, diving and tourism on the scale of Roatán and Utila is yet to reach Guanaja.

The island is certainly not a haven for budget travelers – getting around by water taxis is expensive, and lodging is pricier than you will find on either Utila or Roatán. With ferries going there only infrequently, it can be more expensive to get to as well. It does feel a lot more off the beaten track than the other two islands, however, and you could make your budget stretch with a bit of resourcefulness.

Guanaja was badly hit by Hurricane Mitch in 1998, which damaged the island's famous forest of Caribbean pine – Christopher Columbus named the island Isla de Pinos (Isle of Pines) when he landed here in 1502. Reforestation is helping the island to recover. The waters around the island are a designated marine park.

Orientation & Information

There are a few tiny settlements on the main island, including one on Savannah Bight and another on Mangrove Bight. However, the island's principal town, called Bonacca by the locals, is on a small cay just off the island's east coast. Every inch of the cay has been built on: wooden houses with sloping roofs stand on stilts at different heights. There are no cars on the cay and no roads; walkways wind around the houses and narrow canals allow the residents to pull their boats right up to the houses.

Banco BGA changes traveler's checks and gives cash advances on Visa cards.

Sights & Activities

Snorkeling, **diving** and visits to the **cays** and **beaches** are the activities on Guanaja. You can snorkel right off the town cay. There's good snorkeling around South West Cay and several other cays, at Michael Rock Beach on the main island and at many other places.

On the main island are a number of **hiking trails** and a **waterfall**. You can hire a boat to take you across if you're staying in Bonacca. Diving trips can be arranged through the dive resorts on the main island.

Sleeping & Eating

There are places to stay both in Bonacca and on the main island.

Hotel Miller (☎ 453 4327; Bonacca; r US$32; ☒) This is a simple hotel with cable TV, private hot-water bathroom, air-con and an on-site restaurant. It is right in the center of town, on the main street.

Hotel Hillton (☎ 453 4469; d US$50) Right by the airport, run by a colorful American expat, these are reasonable, airy rooms. The owner is a good source of information about the island, and you can hire motorboats here.

End of the World Resort (☎ 419 1405; www.guanaja .com; d with all-inclusive dive package US$800) On the far north side of the island, this is an upscale resort, way out of range of the average backpacker, but it is one of the best around, offering cabins with lovely ocean panoramas, as well as kayaking, snorkeling, fishing and hiking possibilities.

Graham's Place (☎ 453 4498; ☻ 7am-10pm) On a cay, this has a lovely beach setting, a fine restaurant and three rooms. You will need to get a water taxi over from Bonacca, but the pleasant setting and good cuisine makes it

HONDURAS

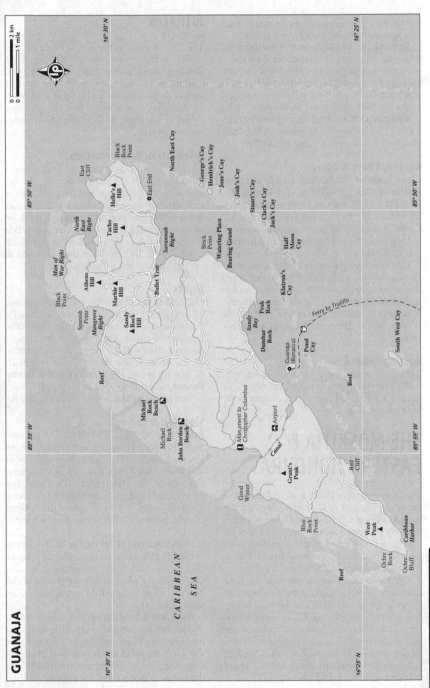

GUANAJA

CARIBBEAN SEA

428 THE MOSKITIA & EASTERN HONDURAS •• Juticalpa

worth the trip. You can see a rainbow of marine species from the dock as you arrive.

Best Stop (☎ 453 4523; Bonacca; ☺ breakfast, lunch & dinner Mon-Fri, dinner 6:30-11pm Sat & Sun) This is indeed the best stop on the island – if you are looking for good hamburgers, sandwiches, and pastries, that is. You will find it just opposite the basketball court on Bonacca.

Mexi-Treats (☎ 453 4170; Bonacca; ☺ breakfast, lunch & dinner) This is the genuine article – a Mexican chef prepares the good-value snacks here.

Getting There & Away

Isleña Regional (☎ 453 4208; www.flyislena.com), **Aerolineas SOSA** (☎ 453 4359) and **Atlantic Airlines** (☎ 453 4211; www.atlanticairlines.com.ni) have 25-minute flights between Guanaja and La Ceiba. A motorboat meets air passengers at a dock near the airport for the five-minute ride to Bonacca.

One scheduled passenger boat goes between Trujillo and Guanaja. Called the *Island Tour,* this aging vessel makes the crossing from the mainland at 3pm on Thursday and Sunday. It returns at 9am on Friday and Tuesday. It is often late; if the weather is rough it won't leave at all.

Getting Around

Transport on the island is by motorboat. Virtually everybody on the island has a boat, so finding a ride is not tough. Ask at your hotel for a trusted boat driver.

THE MOSKITIA & EASTERN HONDURAS

The eastern part of Honduras, including the entire department of Gracias a Dios and the eastern sides of Olancho and Colón, is a vast, sparsely inhabited area of rivers and forests. The largely untamed tropical, easternmost part of Honduras is known as the Moskitia. The area abounds in animal and birdlife.

Only two major roads traverse the area northeast of Tegucigalpa. Both run between Tegucigalpa and Trujillo, and are traveled by bus routes. One goes via Tocoa, Savá, Olanchito, La Unión and Limones; it climbs the mountains west of Juticalpa and can be driven in about 10 or 11 hours. The other, longer, route goes via Juticalpa (three hours). These areas are little visited by tourists.

JUTICALPA
pop 35,619

The largest town in the area is Juticalpa, the capital of the department of Olancho. It's a bustling town, with a dusty approach road leading to the parque central. The central square is also the town's prettiest spot, with an abundance of different tree species from palms to eucalypti and an attractive whitewashed church.

Orientation & Information

There are two bus terminals, both several blocks south of the parque central; the *iglesia* is on the eastern side of the park. Hotels and restaurants are either on the main road between the bus stop and parque central, or north/northwest of the park. The post office is right on the park; Hondutel is one block north. The BGA bank is on the south side of the parque and has a Unibanc ATM.

Sights

The **Casa de la Cultura** (☎ 785 3510; admission free; ☺ 8am-noon & 1-5pm Mon-Fri, 8am-noon Sat) may be worth a visit for history and archaeology buffs. Exhibits are sparse at the moment, but the enthusiastic staff will explain the pre-Columbine origins of the region (some Spanish needed). A new museum, the **Olancho Regional History Museum**, was due to open in mid-2007.

The **annual festival** is held on December 8.

Sleeping & Eating

Hotel Reyes (☎ 785 2232; s/d US$3.25/6.50, with bathroom US$4.30/8.60) This is the sort of place where you get a single naked lightbulb in your room and walls that haven't seen a lick of paint this side of the 21st century. That said, the linen is clean and you cannot complain about the room rates. Some may resent the 9:30pm curfew, however. There's free purified water on tap.

Hotel Honduras (☎ 785 1580; fax 785 1456; s/d with fan US$13.50/20.50, with air-con US$20.50/30; 🖳) Neatly tiled rooms and helpful, welcoming staff make this midrange place comfortably one of the best central options. All 22 rooms have bathrooms and cable TV.

Fresh Juice & Food (☎ 785 2490; dishes US$2.50-5; ☺ 7am-11pm Mon-Sat) This busy little café may not boast the most switched-on service, but the juices are good and it's an ideal breakfast stop. It is right by the entrance to Hotel Honduras, two block west of the parque.

Restaurante El Nuevo Rancho (☎ 785 1202; mains US$4-6; ⏱ 11am-11pm Mon-Sat) This has hearty, good-value meat staples that would satisfy the hardest working ranch hand. It is in the street behind the main church, in a covered patio with wooden tables.

Getting There & Away

You are most likely to need the **Transportes Aurora** (☎ 785 2237) terminal about 1km from the town center on the main entrance road. It has services to Catacamas (US$1.10, 45 minutes, 40km, hourly 8am to 8pm) and Tegucigalpa (US$3.70, hourly from 6:15am to 6:15pm). Give yourself an extra half an hour before departure – queues can be hideous. Make sure you get on the much faster direct service.

Across the street, down by the market, is the dusty chicken-bus terminal. Buses leave there for Limones, La Unión, Mangulile, Tocoa and Trujillo.

Plenty of taxis run between town and both terminals (US$0.80).

Some departures: La Unión (US$2.70, three hours, 95km) buses depart at 11:30am, 1pm (to Mangulile), or take any bus to Limones and transfer (start early to make sure of a connection); Tocoa (US$6.50, eight hours, 235km, 6am); and for Trujillo (US$6.50, nine hours, 278km) catch a bus on the highway at 9:30am.

CATACAMAS

pop 35,200

There's not a whole lot for travelers in Catacamas, 40km northeast of Juticalpa (45 minutes by bus), but it is a useful base for hikes to the surrounding area, including to caves used in prehistoric times near Río Talgua (8km from town). Irregular buses head toward the Cuevas de Talgua. Ask around or take a taxi for around US$6. You can often hitch a ride all or part of the way there too.

You can climb **El Boquerón**, 15km west of town – ask any bus driver to let you off. Ask at your hotel about conditions, as roads sometimes flood.

Hotels are gathered near the parque central. To get there when you get off the bus, take a cab (US$1) or walk: turn left out of the terminal, right on the wide road (500m), then left at the cemetery to reach the parque, which has an ancient, moss-carpeted ceiba tree. The best cheapie is family-run **Hospedaje San Jose** (☎ 799 3222; s/d with shared bathroom from US$2.20/4.40) on the

west corner of the square. Its very basic rooms, some with fold-up beds, are well kept.

Hotel Colina (☎ 799 4488; s/d with cable TV US$9.75/10.50) has dour service, but is otherwise a sweet place with a lengthy courtyard. The rooms have attractive, wood-framed beds.

Eating is limited to a Chinese restaurant and a *comedor* on the parque central. You can also fill up on standard chicken fast food at **Pollolandia** (☎ 799 5623; ⏱ 9am-7pm).

About 10 **Aurora/Discovery** (☎ 799 4154) buses leave for Tegucigalpa each day. It's best to get the faster, direct service (US$4.60). There are three, pricey luxury buses each day (US$10, 6:30am, 11:45am and 3:15pm). Frequent services go to nearby Juticalpa (US$1.10). Other buses traverse the dirt road to the small town of Dulce Nombre de Culmí.

LA MOSKITIA

The Moskitia, that vast part of Honduras you see on maps, with very few roads, is unlike anything else you will experience in the country. It is one of Central America's last frontiers of untamed wilderness. Huge expanses of land are virtually untouched jungle, where people and animals are living much as they would have lived two centuries ago. It is sometimes referred to as Central America's Amazon, and the description is apt, both in that its natural beauty is just as awe-inspiring – and also that it is under threat.

Manatees, tapirs and jaguars all still thrive here – they have learnt to be circumspect around man, and they may not be easy to spot. Crocodiles can be seen in the waters, while birdlife is raucous. Toucans, macaws, parrots, egrets and herons are among the many species that keep ornithologists coming back again and again.

The different human cultures here are fascinating too. There are five different groups, with isolated pockets of Pech and Tawahka in the interior, as well as Moskito, Garífuna and Ladino populations.

A visit to the region is not for the fainthearted. Conditions are rustic at best, and you will find little air-conditioned comfort. A bit of Spanish will come in handy too. Expect your traveling expenses to go up significantly here. Its isolation means prices are noticeably higher. But the intrepid few that make the effort are often thrilled by what they find and the memories they take back. How this unspoiled paradise is developed and protected is crucial. Environmentalists say that La Moski-tia offers one last chance to get it right. And gliding down the river in a dugout canoe, past mud houses backed by vine-heavy trees, you can't help but hope they – we – do.

Dangers & Annoyances

This is wild country and needs to be treated with respect. Crucially, never venture into the rain forest without a guide. Trails are faint and overgrown, and hikers can quickly become hopelessly lost. Travel by night can also be dangerous. Don't be too ambitious – try to leave yourself time in daylight in case problems arise.

Avoid crossing the bigger lagoons late in the day – afternoon winds can create swampingly large waves.

Malaria occurs here: bring insect repellent, a mosquito net and antimalarial pills. A water purification kit (a filter or iodine tablets) is also a good idea.

Finally, the Moskitia is known to be used by drug-runners. The chances of it affecting you are slim, but note that smuggling is often done at certain times of year (the rainy season in particular) when the chances of detection are smaller. Ask around to minimize your chances of being caught in the crossfire.

Tours

Several travel companies undertake tours into the Moskitia region, providing an easier (and not necessarily much more expensive) way to get a taste of the Moskitia. All of the following ones have been recommended: Basecamp in Copán Ruinas; Omega Tours, Jungle River Tours and La Moskitia Ecoaventuras in La Ceiba; and Mesoamerica Travel in San Pedro Sula; see the relevant towns for more information on these tour companies.

When planning your trip, **La Ruta Moskitia** (☎ 443 1276; www.larutamoskitia.com) is an excellent resource. A nonprofit tourism initiative started by Rare Conservation, it can advise how to get there independently – and ensures that money gets to the guides, guesthouse owners and boatmen. It also has recommended package tours.

Laguna de Ibans

The small traditional coastal communities around Laguna de Ibans are likely to be your first overnight stop if you come the overland route. The quiet Miskito village of **Rais Ta** has

wooden houses on stilts and narrow dirt paths beneath a high leafy canopy. A new **butterfly farm** was in the works at the time of research. There are a few very simple accommodation options. **Raista Eco Lodge** (r with shared bathroom per person US$10) has sturdy, rustic wooden rooms with basic latrine toilets. Large, filling meals (US$2 to US$4) are prepared here.

Belén is practically an extension of the same settlement. It has good lodging at **Pawanka Beach Cabins** (per person US$10; meals US$4) – although there's only two cabins (with real flush toilets).

Colectivo boats headed to Palacios pass Rais Ta and Belén at around 3am to 3:30am (US$8, two hours). There is an airport between the two towns – arrange flights with the SAMI office in Rais Ta. You can also arrange transport to Las Marías, for the Río Plátano Biosphere Reserve, from here; the trip takes five to six hours (round-trip US$190). An early-morning colectivo boat takes passengers from Rais Ta to Palacios in time to catch the first speedboat to Iriona.

For Río Plátano, a colectivo pickup truck passes every hour (US$2.75, 45 minutes); another passes in the other direction at the same frequency, making stops in Cocobila, Ibans and Plaplaya.

Reserva de la Biósfera del Río Plátano

The Río Plátano Biosphere Reserve is a magnificent nature reserve, declared a World Heritage site in 1980. A vast unspoiled, untamed wilderness, it is home to extraordinary animal life, including a number of endangered species. The best time of year to visit is from November to July, and the best time for seeing birds is during February and March, when many migratory birds are here.

One of the best places to organize tours is in **Las Marías**, a one-phone town at the heart of the reserve, with around 100 Miskito and Pech families. There is no running water or electricity. There are several basic lodgings there, which will also cook you simple meals. Clean, airy **Hospedaje Doña Justa** (center of town; r with shared bathroom per person US$5) with a large flower garden, and the sprawling **Hospedaje Doña Rutilia** (r with shared bathroom per person US$6), on the river, are good options.

A head guide assigns guides, according to your requirements, for a fee of US$4. Trips vary from one-day excursions to a nearby petroglyph to amazing, but arduous, three-day trips through primary rain forest (Pico

EXPLORE MORE AROUND THE MOSKITIA

For intrepid eyes, the vast expanse of La Moskitia conceals fascinating insights into indigenous cultures and a finely balanced jungle ecosystem.

■ One of the most isolated and fragile of Honduras' indigenous peoples is the Tawahka, found deep in La Moskitia. To visit these communities you need to venture a long way up Río Patuca, to the towns of **Krausirpe** and **Krautara**, using Wampusirpi (see below) as a base. Krautara is smaller and more isolated, and remains 100% Tawahka.

■ If you get the chance, take in **Plaplaya**, a lovely traditional Garífuna village a short boat ride from Rais Ta (see opposite), where giant leatherback sea turtles nest and are released by volunteers each year.

■ One of the most rewarding trips is a three-day hike up **Pico Dama** into the heart of the Reserva de la Biósfera del Río Plátano. Go to Las Marías to arrange it; see opposite.

Dama), which require more guides. Guides cost from around US$11 a day, and you will also need to cover expenses. Bring camping equipment. Get an early start for your best chance to see the wildlife.

An *expreso* from Rais Ta to Las Marías has a hefty fixed price of US$190 (five to six hours). See p432 for how to get to Rais Ta. Hook up with other travelers to spread the costs. The fare is for a round trip, with two nights at Las Marías included. The boatman waits in Las Marías, so after the second night it'll cost you an extra US$8 per night.

The super intrepid can also access the biosphere by a multiday raft ride down the river from Dulce Nombre de Culmí. Contact Omega Tours (see p395) for more information.

Palacios

Many travelers will have to pass through Palacios, a tense, rather lawless place known as a drug-courier corridor. People tend to move on from here swiftly, but if you do get stuck, **Hotel Río Tinto** (☎ 966 6465; r US$8) by the old airstrip is about the best place in town. A boat is the most common way out of town, with services to Belén and a morning speedboat to Iriona.

Brus Laguna
pop 4300
Beside the lagoon of the same name at the mouth of the Río Patuca, Brus Laguna is an accessible entry point to La Moskitia, as flights come here. You can head to Rais Ta or even straight to Las Marías from here. The most comfortable place to stay is surprisingly well-appointed **Hotel La Estancia** (☎ 433 8043; Main St; s/d with shared bathroom US$9/12). **Aerolineas Sosa** (www

.aerolineassosa.com) has flights from La Ceiba to Brus Laguna (one way US$89, one hour) on Monday, Wednesday and Friday, returning from Brus Laguna the same days.

Wampusirpi

This appealingly rustic place is a good base for exploring the Tawahka region upriver (see above). Locals, mainly Moskito people, survive on small plots of rice, beans, bananas and yucca, and by fishing the Patuca River. Houses are mostly on stilts as this area is prone to flooding. There are basic unmarked accommodations if you ask around, and you can do the same to arrange somewhere to eat.

SAMI (☎ Brus Laguna 433 8031, Puerto Lempira 433 6016) has air service to Wampusirpi.

Puerto Lempira
pop 5375
Puerto Lempira, the largest town in the Moskitia, is situated on the inland side of the Laguna de Caratasca. It has good airlines, which is the main reason for visiting, although the town does have a few modern conveniences such as restaurants and internet.

Puerto Lempira has several sleeping options. The best is **Hotel Yu Baiwan** (☎ 433 6348; s/d with fan US$16/19, with air-con US$19/24; 🖳), which has friendly service, fresh linen and cable TV.

Aerolineas Sosa (☎ 433 6432; www.aerolineassosa .com; 🕒 8:30am-5:30pm Mon-Fri, to noon Sat & Sun) flies here. Its office faces the airstrip. **SAMI/Air Honduras** (☎ 433 6016) and **Atlantic Airlines** (☎ 433 6016; 🕒 airport 6am-5pm) share counter space at the airport. You can also buy tickets for either at an ice-cream shop (open 8am to 6pm) a block and a half from the pier.

Kaukira

On the north side of Laguna de Caratasca, this medium-sized town has beach access (and great **fishing**) but is mostly known for its bird-watching opportunities – red and blue macaws can sometimes be seen flying around town. **Ralston Haylock** (☎ community phone 433 6081) can arrange excursions of just about any kind and length, and keeps a simple lodge for overnight trips. He's a fount of local knowledge, and also speaks English.

From Puerto Lempira, colectivo boats leave around 10am to 11am (US$4, 1½ hours). They return every morning between 5am and 6am, and sometimes do an afternoon run – check in advance.

Getting There & Away

AIR

All flights to the Moskitia depart from La Ceiba. Scheduled flights go to Brus Laguna and Puerto Lempira. These change regularly, so check beforehand.

Aerolineas Sosa (☎ in La Ceiba 443 1894, in Puerto Lempira 433 6432; in Brus Laguna 433 8042; www .aerolineassosa.com; Av San Isidro btwn 8a & 9a Calles, La Ceiba; ☀ 7am-5pm Mon-Fri)

Atlantic Airlines (☎ in La Ceiba 440 2343, in Puerto Lempira 433 6016; www.atlanticairlines.com.ni; 11a Calle near Av República, La Ceiba; ☀ 8am-noon & 1-5pm Mon-Fri, 8am-noon Sat)

SAMI (☎ in La Ceiba 442 2565, in Brus Laguna 433 8031)

OVERLAND

Going overland via the north coast is an increasingly popular and accessible entry point to the Moskitia. You will need to start while the roosters are still dozing to be able to do it in a day. From La Ceiba, take an early Trujillo bus (5am) to Tocoa. From there, get the next

paila (pickup) to Batalla, a small Garífuna town (US$21.50, four to five hours). They leave hourly from 7am to noon every day. Get the 7am to reach Belén and Rais Ta before dark – these villages are a good jumping-off point for your Moskitia adventure (see p430). Coming from Trujillo, you can catch the same trucks at the Corocito turnoff (again, with an eye-rubbingly early start – any bus going from Trujillo to La Ceiba will drop you off here).

From Batalla colectivo boats make many stops – tell the driver you want to go to Rais Ta or Belén (US$8, one to two hours). If you catch the 7am pickup in Tocoa, you should arrive by early afternoon.

Occasionally storms wash out the roads to Batalla. In that case, you can go via Iriona. The bus leaves Tocoa between 6:30am and 7:30am (the schedule varies so check first). Again, if you are coming from Trujillo, stop at Corocito (taking the 5:45am bus) where the bus passes through. From Iriona you can get the next speedboat to Belén (US$19, two hours).

To return, take the 3am to 4am boat in Belén, Rais Ta, Cocobila and Ibans daily to Batalla (US$8, one to two hours), for a 6am truck to Tocoa or to Palacios (US$8, one to two hours) and get a 6am speedboat to Iriona, where a bus goes to Tocoa.

When planning your trip, check www.larutamoskitia.com for latest on travel conditions in the area.

Getting Around

Different seasons present different challenges in terms of getting around the Moskitia. The rainy reason (November to January) is the most difficult.

GETTING TO PUERTO CABEZAS, NICARAGUA

From Puerto Lempira, trucks leave once a day for the town of **Leimus** along the Río Coco (US$11, four to five hours, 7:30am). You can pick up the truck outside its owners' house – three blocks west and two blocks south of the pier – or on parque central, near Banco Atlántida. Look for a large truck with a canvas covering. In Leimus, you pass Honduran immigration on one side of the river, and Nicaraguan immigration on the other. A new road means you can board a bus right there for **Puerto Cabezas** (four hours).

Before the new highway was built, you had to take a boat or 4WD downriver to **Waspán** to clear Nicaraguan immigration and catch a bus to Puerto Cabezas. That remains an alternative if there are no buses from Leimus or the immigration office there is closed.

It costs US$7 to enter Nicaragua, US$3 to enter Honduras. Trucks return from Leimus to Puerto Lempira twice daily, around 7am and 4pm.

AIR

SAMI (☎ in Brus Laguna 433 8031, in Puerto Lempira 433 6016) has irregular flights between the main towns, averaging from US$30 to US$60.

BOAT

Most transportation in Moskitia is by boat. Upriver, the most common boat is a *pipantes*, a flat-bottomed boat made from a single tree trunk that's propelled by a pole or paddle. A *cayuco* is a wood-planked boat with an outboard motor that is commonly used on longer trips, either as an *expreso* (private taxi) or a cheaper set-route colectivo. Trips include Río Plátano to Brus Laguna (US$11, 1½ hours) or Batalla to Rais Ta (US$8, one to two hours).

PICKUPS

Pickup trucks ply the single dirt road along the Laguna de Ibans from the town of Ibans west through Cocobila, Rais Ta and Belén, and east to the town of Río Plátano.

SOUTHERN HONDURAS

Honduras touches the Pacific with a 124km coastline on the Golfo de Fonseca. Bordered by the gulf on the seaward side and by hills on the land side, the strip of land here is part of the hot coastal plain that extends down the Pacific side of Central America through several countries. It's a fertile agricultural and fishing region; much of Tegucigalpa's fish, shrimp, rice, sugarcane and hot-weather fruits (like watermelon) come from this area. Honduras' Pacific port is at San Lorenzo.

Southern Honduras is much traveled; it is where the Interamericana crosses Honduras, carrying all the north- and southbound traffic of Central America, and also where the highway branches north from the Interamericana toward the rest of Honduras.

TEGUCIGALPA TO THE NICARAGUAN BORDER

Between Tegucigalpa and the border post of Las Manos (the quickest route to Nicaragua), there are several interesting stops. Notice the scars of clear-cutting in this area, a legacy of indiscriminate logging. Many Hondurans fear they are headed down the same path as El Salvador, the most deforested country in Central America.

About 40km east of the capital, at Zamorano, there's a turnoff for **San Antonio de Oriente**, an attractive Spanish colonial mining village about 5km north of the highway. This is the village immortalized by Honduran primitivist painter José Antonio Velásquez.

Further east is a turnoff south to **Yuscarán**, 66km from Tegucigalpa. Capital of the department of El Paraíso, it is a picture-postcard colonial mining town. Its **annual fair** is on December 8.

A large town 92km east of Tegucigalpa and 19km from El Paraíso, **Danlí** (population 126,000) is the biggest town on this route and the center of a sugarcane- and tobacco-producing region. There are also several **cigar factories** where you can buy good hand-rolled cigars. The annual festival at Danlí, the **Festival del Maíz** in the last weekend in August, is a big event and attracts people from far and wide. The **Laguna de San Julian**, 18km north of Danlí, is a manmade lake popular for outings.

In Danlí, the central **Hotel La Esperanza** (☎ 763 2123; s/d US$7.60/12.10, with bathroom US$15.20/24.30), is easily the best budget option in town, with rooms that stretch alongside a long, green patio. It is cleaned with zealous fervor making the cheaper shared bathroom option a good one. All rooms have cable TVs. In dire straits or cases of extreme inertia, **Hotel Las Vegas** (☎ 763 2145; s/d with bathroom US$9/12) is across from the bus terminal with barely acceptable, sporadically cleaned rooms. Just off the central park, the cavernous **Rancho Mexicano** (☎ 763 4528; ☼ 11am-10pm) is good for a bite.

In El Paraíso, the **Quinta Av Hotel-Restaurante** (☎ 793 4298; s/d/tr US$7.60/10.80/13.50) is on 5a Ave and Calle Real. It is a bit dusty but fine for a night before crossing the border. The señora at the helm is a good laugh. There is also a little restaurant, mostly offering staple beef and chicken dishes. The bus to and from Danlí passes in front – if you're not making a connection, get off early to save yourself an eight-block walk from the terminal.

Getting There & Away

Only 122km from Tegucigalpa is the border crossing at **Las Manos** (☼ 7am-5pm). You can make it in a day if you get an early start.

There are two direct buses from Tegucigalpa to the border; otherwise, take a bus to El Paraíso or Danlí and transfer. All buses leave from the **Discua Litena bus terminal** (☎ 230 0470) at Mercado Jacaleapa in Tegucigalpa; you can take a colectivo from the post a block east of Parque La Merced. Actual taxis should cost you US$2.

There are several routes, so be sure you're on one that passes the Danlí bus terminal.

The routes: Danlí (direct US$2.50, 1½ hours, many departures from 6am to 5:45pm); El Paraíso (direct US$2.80, two hours); Las Manos (USS$3.25, three hours, two direct departures at 6am and 11:40am; or connect in Danlí or El Paraíso).

The last bus from El Paraíso to the border is at 4pm; last bus from Las Manos to El Paraíso at 5pm. The first bus departs at 6:30am, and from the border to El Paraíso the first leaves at 7am. Once you cross, catch a bus to Ocotal and transfer to Managua.

TEGUCIGALPA TO THE PACIFIC

Highway CA 5 heads south about 95km from Tegucigalpa until it meets the Interamericana at **Jícaro Galán**, winding down from the pine-covered hills around the capital to the hot coastal plain. From the crossroads at Jícaro Galán, it's 40km west to the border with El Salvador at **El Amatillo**, passing through the town of **Nacaome** 6km west of Jícaro Galán, or it's 115km east to the Nicaraguan border at **El Espino**, passing through **Choluteca** 50km from Jícaro Galán.

If you are traveling along the Interamericana, crossing only this part of Honduras in transit between El Salvador and Nicaragua, you can easily make the crossing in a day; from border to border it's only 150km (three hours by bus). If, however, you want to stop off, there are a few possibilities. The border stations sometimes close at 5pm (although they are nominally open 24 hours), so if you can't make it by that time, you'll have to spend the night.

GOLFO DE FONSECA

The shores of Honduras, El Salvador and Nicaragua all touch the Golfo de Fonseca; Honduras has the middle and largest share, with 124km of coastline and jurisdiction over nearly all of the 30-plus islands in the gulf. In September 1992 the International Court of Justice eased previous disputes by ruling that sovereignty in the gulf must be shared by the three nations, barring a 3-mile (5km) maritime belt around the coast. Of the islands in the gulf, sovereignty was disputed by Honduras and El Salvador in three cases. The court found in favor of Honduras regarding the island of El Tigre, but El Salvador prevailed on Meanguera and Meanguerita. Tensions re-

main over the islands and the Honduran press regularly print unabashedly patriotic articles articulating Honduras' ownership rights.

The European discovery of the Golfo de Fonseca was made in 1522 by Andrés Niño, who named the gulf in honor of his benefactor, Bishop Juan Rodríguez de Fonseca. In 1578 the buccaneer Sir Francis Drake occupied the gulf, using El Tigre as a base, as he made raids as far afield as Peru and Baja California. There are still rumors that Drake left a hidden treasure, but it has never been found.

El Salvador has a major town on the gulf (La Unión), but Honduras doesn't; on the Honduran part of the coastline, there are only small settlements, and the highway never meets the sea except on the outskirts of San Lorenzo. The Golfo de Fonseca is an extremely hot region.

San Lorenzo
pop 23,100

The Interamericana touches the Golfo de Fonseca only on the outskirts of San Lorenzo. San Lorenzo is Honduras' Pacific port town. It is a hot, sleepy and largely unattractive place with a few seedy bars and hotels 2km from the highway at the water-edge end of town, just along from a shrimp-packing plant. Connections to Amapala on the island of El Tigre leave from here.

If you get stuck, **Hotel Rivera** (☎ 781 3499; s/d US$21.65/27; 🅿 🔀) is your best option with spacious, air-conditioned rooms off a long courtyard. Free drinking water is available. It is centrally located on the main road that goes through the market.

Buses plying the Interamericana go through San Lorenzo. Most stop on the highway, some come the few blocks into town to the market.

Isla El Tigre
pop 2400

The inactive volcanic island of El Tigre, with a 783m peak, is a ferociously hot place with a kind of untouched charm – there are few cars here and nobody is any rush. Its main town is **Amapala**, a sleepy fishing village founded in 1833. It was once Honduras' Pacific port town, before the port was moved to mainland San Lorenzo. A lot of visitors descend on the island for the **Semana Santa** holidays – otherwise there is a trickle of backpackers,

GETTING TO SAN MIGUEL, EL SALVADOR

The border crossing between Honduras and El Salvador at **El Amatillo** is officially open 24 hours although it is best to get there in daylight hours. It's crowded with trucks but otherwise a relaxed border post; Honduran *campesinos* (farmers) cross here every day to go to market in **Santa Rosa de Lima**, 18km from the border on the El Salvador side. There are basic hotels at the border, on both sides. On the Salvadoran side, there are a few places to stay at Santa Rosa de Lima, but there are more options in **San Miguel** or **La Unión**, each a two-hour bus ride from El Amatillo; the last bus to San Miguel leaves at 6:30pm.

If you are entering Honduras here, buses leave El Amatillo frequently for Tegucigalpa (US$2.40, three hours, 130km) and Choluteca (US$1.70, two hours, 85km).

See p313 for information on crossing the border from El Salvador.

who come for an off-the-beaten-track trip and the island's fine seafood.

There is a **tourist office** (8am-noon & 2-5pm Mon-Fri, 8am-noon Sat) on the dock with a complete list of all the accommodations options and a map of the island's many beaches. Check out the back of a two-lempira note for a view of Amapala.

ACTIVITIES

You can hike up **El Vijía**, about 100m up, where there's a good view of the gulf and its islands. El Tigre also has several beaches of varying quality: **Playa Grande** is the biggest and most popular. There are views right over to El Salvador from the black-sand **Playa Negra** to the north of the island. Rays can be a painful danger at low tide – ask people whether it is safe before you go for a dip.

SLEEPING & EATING

Accommodations are more expensive than on the mainland.

Hotel Internacional (795 8539; s/d US$8.10/10.80) A bare basic option, the first building you get to right at the end of the Amapala pier. It is poorly kept and the showers – well, you may rather stay dirty.

Hotel Veleros (795 8040; Playa El Mora; r/tr US$16.25/21.60) Has clean, comfortable rooms (cold-water bathroom only). Right next door is the well-known Veleros beachfront restaurant, with good seafood dishes starting from US$2.50. Maritza Grande, the owner, is well versed on tourist activities on the island, and can sort out alternative lodging if her place is full. It is on Playa El Mora (also known as Playa el Burro), a US$2 taxi ride from Amapala.

Mirador de Amapala (232 0632; s/d US$35/40.50;) Has a swimming pool, rooms with fridges and neat white-tiled bathrooms as well as a seafood restaurant (open 6am to 10pm). The owner has a somewhat dodgy plan to create a fake beach at the front. It is a US$1.60 taxi from the pier, or you could walk it in 20 minutes.

GETTING THERE & AROUND

Small colectivo boats (US$0.80, 20 minutes) and a car ferry depart from Coyolito, 30km from the Interamericana. You have to wait until the boat fills up with 10 passengers. Otherwise you can pay US$7.60 for a private boat trip. Buses go to Coyolito from San Lorenzo (US$0.80, one hour, 30km, every 40 minutes until 5pm) from the terminal behind San Lorenzo's pre-fabricated market or from a dusty turnoff 2km north of town. Note that there are no overnight facilities at Coyolito.

To get around town, minibuses leave from the parque central, generally doing semicircle circuits half-way around the island and returning the same way. A few buses go all the way around.

CHOLUTECA

pop 78,300

Choluteca, capital of the department of the same name, is the largest town in southern Honduras. The town is built near Río Choluteca, the same river that runs through Tegucigalpa. The first thing you will notice is the heat, which has even long-term residents mopping sweat from their brow before morning tea. There is an old, somewhat neglected, historical quarter.

There's not much to do in Choluteca; it's principally a commercial center for the agricultural region and a stopping-off point between the borders. The **annual festival day** is December 8.

HONDURAS

GETTING TO NICARAGUA

Getting to Chinandega or León, Nicaragua

The border crossing at **Guasaule** is open 24 hours, but it's best to arrive between 8am and 5pm. Buses operate every half hour between Guasaule and Choluteca (*directo* US$1.20, 45 minutes; *ordinario* US$1, one hour) for the 44km trip. On the Nicaraguan side, buses go to both **Chinandega** and **León**. The last bus from the border to Choluteca is at 5pm.

If you're coming from El Salvador, microbuses go directly to the Guasaule crossing from **El Amatillo** (US$5, two hours, departs when full).

See p488 for information on crossing the border from Nicaragua.

Getting to Estelí or Managua, Nicaragua

The border station at **El Espino** is open 7:30am to 5pm daily though hours may vary. From Choluteca, take any bus to the town of **San Marcos** and catch a colectivo (US$0.80) the last 7km (they often charge more coming the other way). Nicaraguan immigration officials were charging travelers US$7 for the privilege of crossing the border when we passed through.

On the Nicaraguan side, buses run to the town of **Somoto** (20km), where you can connect to **Estelí** (last bus at 5:20pm) or to **Managua** (US$3.50, 4½ hours, direct buses until 3pm). If you need a visa for either country, be sure you already have it before you reach the border.

If it's getting late in the day, stay over in Choluteca or San Marcos and cross the following day. The choice of accommodations is better here than on the Nicaraguan side near the border. There is nowhere to stay at El Espino.

Coming into Honduras, six buses leave the **Mi Esperanza terminal** (☎ 788 3705) in San Marcos for Tegucigalpa (US$3.15, four hours, 191km) each day at 6am, 7:45am, 10am, 12:30pm, 2pm and 4pm. Buses to Choluteca (US$0.90, 1½ hours, 58km) operate until 4pm; from there you can connect to **El Amatillo** on the Salvadoran border.

See p479 for information on crossing the border from Nicaragua.

Orientation & Information

The streets in Choluteca follow a standard grid, with calles running east-west, and avenidas north-south. The city is divided into four zones: NO (*noroeste*, northwest), NE (*noreste*, northeast), SO (*suroeste*, southwest) and SE (*sureste*, southeast). The parque central is in the middle.

The bus terminal is in the southeast zone, on Blvd Carranza and 3a Av SE. The Mi Esperanza bus terminal is 1½ blocks north. The old market (Mercado Viejo San Antonio) is nine long blocks west and two blocks north – best to take a cab (US$0.80).

The **post office** (cnr 2a Calle NO & 3a Av NO) is three blocks east of the old market. The state phone company, Hondutel, is next door.

Sleeping

Choluteca has several good-value hotels near the bus terminal and in the city center.

Hotel Santa Rosa (☎ 782 0355; s/d with bathroom & fan US$4.90/7.60, with TV US$6/9.70, with air-con & TV US$10.30/14.60; ✹) This cheap and friendly hotel stretches right back away from the main street along an extensive, well-tended courtyard lined with hammocks. Rooms are tidy, although mattresses are soft. There is a water dispenser. On the west side of the market.

Hotel Mi Esperanza (☎ 782 0885; 2a Calle NO; s/d with fan & TV US$5.40/8.65, with air-con & TV US$8.65/13.50; P ✹) Half a block west of the market, this has basic, clean rooms with worn red-and-cream tiles. The rooms are arranged around a large courtyard and each has a private bathroom. There is a good *comedor* next door. Service can be abrupt.

Hotel Pacífico (☎ 782 0838; 4a Av NE, s/d with bathroom & fan US$7.10/10.80, with air-con US$11.50/16.70; ✹) Particularly convenient for the buses, this is four blocks north and one block east of the terminal. You even get pictures in some rooms, but they can't disguise that this is basic – showers are essentially taps on the wall. That said, it is well kept and completely adequate for a night. There's a courtyard with hammocks, and cable TV in the tiny lounge area.

Hotel Pacífico Anexo (s/d with bathroom & fan US$7.10/10.80, with air-con US$11.50/16.70; ✹) Across the street from Hotel Pacífico, it has the same prices. A little *comedor* serves breakfast, lunch and dinner.

Eating

Comedor Mi Esperanza (dishes US$2; ⏰ 6am-8:30pm)
This exceptionally good-value café, often frequented by local workers, serves breakfast, lunch and dinner. The tablecloths could do with a wipe though.

Ilo Rico (☎ 782 0308; Calle Vicente Williams; dishes US$3-5; ⏰ 8am-10pm Mon-Thu, 8am-2am Fri & Sat, 10am-10pm Sun) This well-known local no-frills restaurant and bar with plastic chairs can get raucous on weekend nights. The menu tries nothing new, just relying on simple typical Honduran dishes with one or two salad options for vegetarians.

Getting There & Away

Several companies share a bus terminal on Blvd Carranza, at the corner of 3a Av NE. Some buses swing by the market after leaving the station.

El Amatillo/Salvadoran border (US$1.70, two to 2½ hours, 85km, buses every 25 minutes from 3:30am to 5:50pm) Last bus from border to Choluteca at 5:30pm.

El Espino/Nicaraguan border Take bus to San Marcos and catch colectivo: US$0.80.

Guasaule/Nicaraguan border (*directo* minibuses US$1.20, 45 minutes; *ordinario buses* US$1, one hour, 44km, departures every 30 minutes 6am to 5:30pm) Last bus from border to Choluteca at 5pm.

San Marcos de Colón, near Nicaraguan border (US$0.90, 1½ hours, 58km, buses every 30 minutes from 6am to 5pm) From there take colectivo to border at El Espino (US$0.80, 15 minutes, 7km) Last bus from San Marcos to Choluteca at 4pm.

Tegucigalpa (US$2.50, four hours, 133km, buses every 30 minutes from 4:15am to 6:15pm)

Mi Esperanza has its own **bus terminal** (☎ 782 0841; 3a Av NE), 1½ blocks north of the other station. It runs the Tegucigalpa–Choluteca–San Marcos de Colón route and the buses are usually more direct and comfortable. Destinations include the following:

San Marcos de Colón, near Nicaraguan border (US$0.90, one to 1½ hours, 58km, six buses daily at 7am, 10am, 12:30pm, 2pm, 5pm and 7pm)

Tegucigalpa (normal US$2.50, three hours, 133km, 12 daily buses daily leaving each hour from 6am to 5pm)

SAN MARCOS DE COLÓN

If it is getting late and you are heading for the El Espino border, stop off for the night at the pretty town of San Marcos de Colón. It is surprisingly tranquil for somewhere so close

to a border and is very well kept – some would even say manicured. **Hotel Colonial** (☎ 788 3832; s/d US$10.80/12.20), two blocks south of the parque central, is excellent value, with cool, comfortable rooms including etched wooden headboards, private bathrooms and cable TV. **Restaurante Bonanza** (⏰ 8am-9:30pm) is a large, open restaurant that prepares tender fajitas and *pinchos* (kabab) dishes.

HONDURAS DIRECTORY

ACCOMMODATIONS

Economical accommodations are available just about everywhere in Honduras. The cheapest places have a shared cold-water bathroom, but can range from the truly awful to not-so-bad. A fair number of innocent-looking hotels are in fact used by the hourly crowd, so look at a room or two and get a sense of the place before staying there. Prices range from US$3.50 to US$15 for a budget room.

A room with a private cold-water bathroom is a step up, and hot water a step beyond that. You'll usually pay more for two beds than for one – save money and sleep with a friend. The same goes for air-con, only more so. Electricity costs are high, so it's an expensive luxury – sometimes doubling the price of the room. Most budget travelers will stick with fans.

Camping is not a vacation activity followed by many Hondurans, and organized campsites such as those in the USA or Europe do not exist. That said, camping is allowed in several national parks and reserves and is mentioned in the text wherever it is relevant. Water and toilets or latrines are sometimes available, and occasionally even kitchens, but generally you should bring your own gear.

If you are in one of the more touristy areas and are thinking about improving your Spanish, consider a homestay with a local family, which you can organize through a language school. Starting from around US$70 a week, often including full board, these are often a very economical and culturally rewarding option.

ACTIVITIES

Honduras' national parks are great places for hiking. Several of the parks offer trails that are well-maintained, visitors centers for information and orientation, and even guides. Guides are sometimes necessary, but the majority do not speak English. Having a guide will often allow you to learn more about the environment you're in and to see more wildlife. The north coast and the Bay Islands have great beaches and several excellent parks, plus, of course, some of the best snorkeling and diving in the world.

Bird-Watching

Bird-watching is becoming a popular activity in Honduras, where you can spot hundreds of species. It's difficult to name the most impressive birds, as there are so many: quetzals, toucans, scarlet macaws (Honduras' national bird) and the brilliant green and green-and-yellow parrots are all contenders. National parks and wildlife refuges have been established to protect many environments good for seeing birds – for example, cloud forests, tropical rain forests and coastal wetlands. Quetzals are seen in many of the cloud forest national parks, including Cusuco (p366), Celaque (p381) and La Tigra (p351).

Migratory birds are present along the north coast during the northern winter months from November to February. Good places for birders to see them are in the lagoons, national parks and wildlife refuges, and at Lancetilla Botanical Gardens (p390) near Tela. Each December 14 and 15, the Audubon Society does a 24-hour bird count at Lancetilla and other nearby places. Contact the office of **Fundación Prolansate** (☎ 448 2042; www.prolansate-ecoturismo.com; Bo Independencia, opposite Villas Telamar, Tela; ☑ 7am-noon & 1:30-5:30pm Mon-Sat, 8:30-noon Sun) if you'd like to participate.

The Lago de Yojoa (p359) is another excellent place for bird-watching – more than half of Honduras' species have been counted here so far.

In some places you can go on bird-watching tours. A couple of companies in Copán Ruinas offer birding tours (p369) in the local area and further afield, including La Moskitia.

Diving & Snorkeling

The Bay Islands reef is magnificent, and you can learn to dive here for less money than anywhere else in the Caribbean. Dozens of dive shops offer all levels of courses, from beginner to instructor. Snorkeling gear can be rented or bought, or you can bring your own – all three islands have great snorkeling right from shore. The Cayos Cochinos (Hog Islands) also have turquoise seas and kaleidoscopic marine life.

Horseback Riding

Horseback riding is a popular activity at Copán Ruinas (p367). Horseback tours are also conducted into Parque Nacional Pico Bonito (p394) near La Ceiba and at West End (p414) on Roatán Island.

Kayaking, Canoeing & Small-Boat Tours

Small-boat tours are a good way to visit a number of national parks, wildlife refuges and nature reserves along the north coast, including Punta Sal and the Laguna de los Micos (p391) near Tela, Cuero y Salado near La Ceiba (p400) and the Laguna de Guaimoreto (p405) near Trujillo. Kayaking tours of the Refugio de Vida Punta Izopo (p391) near Tela let you slip silently among the canals of the mangrove forests, where you'll see plenty of wildlife.

The Moskitia region, though more remote, is accessible by airplane and bus and offers many more possibilities for canoe and boat trips on rivers and lagoons, especially via the Río Patuca.

White-Water Rafting

White-water rafting is popular on the Río Cangrejal near La Ceiba; several companies in La Ceiba offer rafting tours on this river (see p395).

BOOKS

Topics such as the Copán archaeological site, the banana industry and the Contra war have been well studied, while others, like non-Maya indigenous communities and environmental issues, have not.

Gangs are currently a hot topic and have received extensive newspaper and magazine coverage.

Honduras: A Country Guide by Tom Barry and Kent Norsworthy (1991) and *Honduras:*

A Country Study (1990) by the US Federal Research Division are oldish but have concise historical information.

The United States, Honduras, and the Crisis in Central America by Donald E Schultz and Deborah Sundloff Schulz (1994) discusses the role of the US in Central America during the region's tumultuous civil wars.

Don't be Afraid, Gringo (1987) is the intriguing first-hand story of peasant Elvia Alvarado's reluctant rise as a labor leader, and of the Honduran labor movement, flaws and all.

Bitter Fruit by Stephen C Schlesinger is mostly about the United Fruit Company in Guatemala, but provides insight on the banana giant's impact on Honduras as well. *The Banana Men: American Mercenaries and Entrepreneurs in Central America, 1880–1930* (1995) and *The Banana Wars: United States Intervention in the Caribbean, 1898–1934* (2002), both by Lester D Langley, are incisive accounts of the banana companies' political and economic influence in Central America and the Caribbean.

Los Barcos (The Ships; 1992), and *El Humano y La Diosa* (The Human and the Goddess; 1996) and *The Big Banana* (1999) are all by Roberto Quesada, one of Honduras' best known living novelists. *Gringos in Honduras: The Good, the Bad, and the Ugly* (1995) and *Velasquez: The Man and His Art,* are two of many books by Guillermo Yuscarán, aka William Lewis, an American writer and painter living in Honduras. *Around the Edge* (1991) by English journalist Peter Ford relates Ford's journey along the Caribbean coast from Belize to Panama, especially in La Moskitia.

Love Paul Theroux or hate him, his *The Mosquito Coast* is a vivid fictional account of life in the jungle and the characters it attracts. O Henry also wrote an evocative novel *Cabbages and Kings* loosely based on Trujillo.

BUSINESS HOURS

Businesses are open during the following hours.

Banks 8:30am to 4:30pm Monday to Friday and 8:30 to 11:30am Saturday
Restaurants 7am to 9pm daily
Shops 9am to 6pm Monday to Saturday and 9am to 1pm or 5pm Sunday

Any exceptions to these hours are noted in specific listings.

CLIMATE

The mountainous interior is much cooler than the coastal lowlands. Tegucigalpa, at 975m, has a temperate climate, with maximum/minimum temperatures varying from 25/14°C in January to 30/18°C in May. The coastal lowlands are much warmer and more humid year-round; the Pacific coastal plain near the Golfo de Fonseca is hot indeed. December and January are the coolest months.

The rainfall also varies in different parts of the country. The rainy season runs from around May to October. On the Pacific side and in the interior, this means a relatively dry season from around November to April. However, the amount of rain, and when it falls, varies considerably from year to year.

On the Caribbean coast, it rains year round, but the wettest months are from September to January or February. During this time floods can occur on the north coast, impeding travel and occasionally causing severe damage (400 people died in floods in November 1993).

Hurricane season is June to November. For climate charts see p723.

DANGERS & ANNOYANCES

Most travelers enjoy their time in Honduras and their trips pass without unpleasant incidents. That said, Honduras does have a crime problem, as many developing countries do. The country's ingrained gun culture may unsettle visitors, but the chances of a firearms assault are slim – petty theft is a far more likely risk. You should be cautious – but not paranoid – in the cities, especially San Pedro Sula and Tegucigalpa, which both have gang problems (again, travelers are rarely targeted). Walking in the center in the daytime is usually fine – although don't flash your belongings about. Spring for a cab at night if you are downtown.

In general, small towns are much safer than the big cities. Watch yourself on the north coast, especially on the beach. Avoid leaving items unattended and do not walk on the beach alone or at night. Although still rare, thefts, muggings and even rapes have occurred on the beaches here.

Malaria-carrying mosquitoes and biting sand flies on the north coast, the Bay Islands and the Moskitia are an annoyance and, along with unpurified water, can be the greatest threat to your well-being. Also watch out for jellyfish and stingrays, which are present on both the Caribbean and Pacific Coasts.

HONDURAS

If you go hiking through wild places, beware of poisonous snakes, especially the fer-de-lance (known locally as *barba amarilla*); the coral snake is also present. Crocodiles and caimans live in the waterways of the Moskitia, as do the peaceful manatee and much other wildlife. Honduras also has scorpions (not lethal), black widow spiders, wasps and other stinging insects. You probably will never see a dangerous animal, but be aware that they exist.

DISABLED TRAVELERS

Honduras has few facilities for disabled travelers, other than in upmarket hotels and resorts. Wheelchair-bound visitors will find it difficult to negotiate Tegucigalpa and San Pedro Sula because of street congestion and generally poor road or sidewalk surfaces. Even smaller towns are difficult to negotiate as roads surfaces are often unpaved or made up of cobblestones. Public transport is often crowded, dirty and inefficient, and rarely geared to less able travelers. Toilets for the disabled are virtually nonexistent, other than in four- or five-star hotels.

EMBASSIES & CONSULATES
Embassies & Consulates in Honduras

Diplomatic representation in Tegucigalpa:

Belize (☎ 238 4616; fax 238 4617; Centro Comercial Hotel Honduras Maya, Av República de Chile; ☺ 9am-noon & 2-5pm Mon-Fri)

Canada (☎ 232 4551; fax 239 7767; Edif Financiero Banexpo, Local 3, Blvd San Juan Bosco; ☺ 8am-4:30pm Mon-Thu, 8am-1:30pm Fri)

El Salvador (☎ 239 7017, 239 7909; Diagonal Aguán 2952; ☺ 8am-3:30pm Mon-Fri)

France (☎ 236 6800; fax 236 8051; 3a Calle at Av Juan Lindo; ☺ 8am-12:30pm Mon-Fri)

Germany (☎ 232 3161; fax 232 9018; Edif Paysen 3rd fl, Blvd Morazáni)

Israel (☎ 232 0776; fax 231 1874; inside Conversa Language School; Paseo República de Argentina 257; ☺ 8am-5:30pm)

Japan (☎ 236 6828; fax 236 6100; Calzada República de Paraguay btwn 4a & 5a Calles; ☺ 8:30am-noon Mon-Fri)

Netherlands (☎ 239 0525; fax 239 0526; 3a Av 2315; ☺ 9am-noon Mon-Fri)

Spain (☎ 236 6589; fax 236 8682; embesphn@hondutel .hn; Calle Santander 801; ☺ 9am-1pm Mon-Fri)

USA (☎ 236 9320; fax 238 4357; www.usmission.hn; Av La Paz; ☺ walk-ins 8-11:30am Mon-Fri, phone service 8am-5pm Mon-Fri) Near 3a Av.

For some other embassies and consulates, see Map pp342–3.

Honduran Embassies & Consulates Abroad

Canada (☎ 613-233 8900; fax 613-232 0193; www .embassyhonduras.ca; 151 Slater St, Suite 805, Ottawa, Ontario K1P 5H3)

France (☎ 01 47 55 86 45; fax 01 47 55 86 48; 8 Rue Crevaux, 75116 Paris)

Germany (☎ 30-3974 9710; fax 30-3974 9712; www.embahonduras.de; Cuxhavener Str 14, Berlin, D-10555)

UK (☎ 020-7486 4880; fax 020-7486 4550; hondurasuk@lineone.net; 115 Gloucester Pl, London W1H 3PJ)

USA (☎ 202-966 7702; fax 202-966 9751; www.hondu rasemb.org; 3007 Tilden Street NW, Suite 4M, Washington DC 20008)

FESTIVALS & EVENTS

Just about every city, town and village in Honduras has a patron saint and celebrates an annual festival or fair in the days around their saint's day. Some are big events, attracting crowds from far and wide. These are mentioned in the various town sections, where relevant.

Feria de Suyapa The patron saint of Honduras is celebrated in Suyapa, near Tegucigalpa, from around February 2 to 11. February 3 is the saint's day. The services and festivities bring pilgrims and celebrants from all over Central America.

Carnaval at La Ceiba Celebrated during the third week in May, the third Saturday is the biggest day, with parades, costumes, music and celebrations in the streets.

San Pedro Sula Held in the last week of June, this is another popular celebration.

Feria Centroamericana de Turismo y Artesanía (Fecatai) Every year, from December 6 to 16, this all–Central American international tourism and crafts fair is held in Tegucigalpa.

Artisans' & Cultural Fair An annual all-Honduras artisans' and cultural fair held in the town of Copán Ruinas from December 15 to 21.

The fairs at Tela (June 13), Trujillo (June 24), Danlí (last weekend in August) and Copán Ruinas (March 15 to 20) are also good, and there are many others.

Several Garífuna music and dance troupes give presentations throughout the country, including the excellent Ballet Folklórico Garífuna. April 12, the anniversary of the arrival of the Garífuna people in Honduras in 1797, is a joyful occasion celebrated in all Garífuna communities.

FOOD & DRINK

Honduras does not have the wealth of local cuisine that Mexico or Guatemala has, but a few dishes are distinctive. Garífuna communities are famous for coconut bread and *casabe* (a crispy flat bread common throughout the Caribbean) – both are quite tasty. Seafood, especially fish, crab and lobster, is ubiquitous on the north coast, while fried chicken is a street-food staple nationwide. Honduras has several beers on offer – Port Royal is a favorite among travelers, then there is Salva Vida, Imperial (popular in Olancho) and the lighter Barena. They are all produced by the same brewery, Cerveceria Hondureña (owned by the SAB Miller multinational). All are cheap but nothing to write home about. For excellent, home-brewed beers, visit D&D Brewery in Lago de Yojoa (p359).

It is normally expected that you tip 10% apart from basic eateries; some restaurants will automatically add a tip to the bill.

GAY & LESBIAN TRAVELERS

Honduras is very much 'in the closet,' and open displays of affection between gay or lesbian couples are often frowned upon. Discreet homosexual behavior was tolerated more before the advent of HIV/AIDS in Honduras around 1985. Since then anti-gay incidents have increased, along with stricter legislation. Organizations serving the gay, lesbian and transsexual/transgender communities include **Grupo Prisma** (☎ 232 8342; prisma@sdnhon.org.hn), **Colectiva Violeta** (☎ 237 6398; alfredo@optinet.hn) and **Comunidad Gay San Pedrana** (☎ 550 6868).

HOLIDAYS

New Year's Day January 1
Day of the Americas April 14
Semana Santa (Holy Week) Thursday, Friday and Saturday before Easter Sunday.
Labor Day May 1
Independence Day September 15
Francisco Morazán Day October 3
Día de la Raza (Columbus Day) October 12
Army Day October 21
Christmas Day December 25

INTERNET ACCESS

Every city and most towns and villages usually have at least one internet café. Connections tend to be reasonable, and cost US$0.50 to US$1.10 per hour. Access on the Bay Islands has improved thanks to satellite connection, but is still the country's most expensive at around US$8 per hour.

INTERNET RESOURCES

A quick search on any decent internet search engine will bring you a host of hits on Honduras. Try the following links that we have dug up for you. They will inevitably lead you to other interesting sites.
http://lanic.utexas.edu/la/ca/honduras Extensive list of links to article and websites on everything from politics to sports to tourism.
www.hondurasnews.com Translations of the latest big news issues to hit Honduras.
www.hondurastips.honduras.com The website of the free tourist magazine *Honduras Tips*.
www.letsgohonduras.com Honduras' ministry of tourism website.
www.lonelyplanet.com/worldguide The source of updated Lonely Planet coverage.
www.marrder.com/htw The official site of *Honduras This Week*, Honduras' only English-language newspaper.
www.sidewalkmystic.com Private website with practical info on travel in Honduras.
www.travel-to-honduras.com Links to various services, including volunteer organizations.

LANGUAGE

Spanish is spoken throughout the mainland, although it is a second language for some indigenous communities in the Moskitia and Garífuna towns on the north coast. On the Bay Islands, Spanish is gaining ground on English and Garífuna, especially in Roatán.

LEGAL MATTERS

Police officers in Honduras aren't immune to corruption. If you plan to rent a car, for example, be aware that transit police are not above looking for infractions to get a little money for gas. Tourist police are fairly new to Honduras – you should be seeing more of them, especially in places like Tela and La Ceiba – and they are generally trustworthy. While travelers should not hesitate to contact the nearest police officer or station in emergencies, look for tourist police for less urgent matters.

MAPS

Good maps are hard to find in Honduras. Tourist offices and visitors centers are the best places for them. Bookstores occasionally carry maps.

HONDURAS

The Instituto Geográfico Nacional in Tegucigalpa (p340) publishes high-quality maps of the various departments (states), both political and topographic.

It sells a few city and municipal maps as well.

MEDIA

Honduras Tips is a bilingual (English and Spanish) magazine-directory indispensable for travelers. It gives lots of information on things to see and do and places to stay and eat, with maps and photos. The magazine is published twice a year and is available for free in many hotels, travel agencies, tourist information offices and other places frequented by travelers.

Honduras This Week is a useful English-language newspaper published every Saturday in Tegucigalpa. It can be found in major hotels and in English-language bookshops in Tegucigalpa, San Pedro Sula, La Ceiba, Roatán and Utila. You can read the newspaper online at www.marrder.com/htw. Honduras has five national newspapers: *El Heraldo* (www.elheraldo.hn) and *La Tribuna* (www.latribunahon.com) are published in Tegucigalpa, *La Prensa* (www.laprensahn.com), *El Tiempo* (www.tiempo.hn) and *El Nuevo Día* in San Pedro Sula, all prone to varying degrees of sensationalism.

MONEY

The unit of currency in Honduras is the lempira. Notes are of one, two, five, 10, 20, 50, 100 and 500 lempiras. There are 100 centavos in a lempira; coins are of one, two, five, 10, 20 and 50 centavos. Centavos are virtually worthless, except for occasional use on urban bus routes.

ATMs

There are cash machines in all cities and towns throughout the country. ATMs operated by BAC/Credomatic, Banco Atlántida and Unibanc are the most reliable, and most likely to accept out-of-country debit cards. Always be alert when withdrawing cash; whenever possible, take out money during the day, and at a machine that's in a lockable cabin (to get in, you typically have to swipe your ATM card at the door) or inside the bank itself.

ATMs typically spit out 500-lempira bills, which can be a hassle to break – get in the habit of using big bills at hotels and larger

restaurants, and saving the small bills for taxis, small eateries, street stands, markets and so forth.

Bargaining

Crafts are fairly rare in Honduras, so you won't find many opportunities to bargain while shopping. Prices for many services are fixed, so there shouldn't be any need to bargain. In large cities, for example, both colectivo and private taxis have a single fixed price for rides around town.

Ask at your hotel what taxis should cost; if you get in knowing what the price should be, most drivers won't argue. In La Moskitia, prices are fixed (and high); bargaining isn't too fruitful.

Black Market

There is no real black market as such in Honduras, and the advantages gained from changing money with street dealers have more to do with convenience than any gain. Moneychangers are commonly found at both Tegucigalpa and San Pedro Sula airports, as well as in the city center of both places, and also at all border crossings.

Cash

Banks will exchange US dollars and occasionally euros. Bring your passport and go in the morning. Your hotel may let you pay in US dollars (worth doing to avoid the bank queues), or exchange them for you, as may some places in the more heavily touristed areas.

Credit Cards

Visa and MasterCard are widely accepted, including at major supermarkets, retail stores, hotels and car rental agencies. Expect a 6% to 12% surcharge.

Cash advances on Visa cards are available at most banks, including BAC/Credomatic, Banco Atlántida and Banco de Occidente. BAC/Credomatic can usually process advances on MasterCard too. There's typically no transaction charge on the Honduran end for Visa or MasterCard cash advances, but of course the interest rates charged tend to be astronomical.

Exchange Rates

The US dollar and (to a lesser extent) the euro are the only foreign currencies that are easily exchanged in Honduras; away from the borders you will even find it difficult to change the currencies of Guatemala, El Salvador or Nicaragua.

The table below shows currency exchange rates at the time this book went to press.

Country	Unit	Lempiras (L)
Australia	A$1	16.10
Canada	C$1	17.80
euro zone	€1	25.70
Japan	¥100	15.40
New Zealand	NZ$1	14.70
UK	UK£1	38.00
USA	US$1	18.80

Traveler's Checks

American Express traveler's checks can be changed in all major towns; Banco Atlántida and BAC/Credomatic are the best banks to use. They will need your passport, and may charge a commission. Go to banks in the morning, as queues tend to be long.

POST

Post offices in most Honduran towns typically are open Monday to Friday 8am to 5pm (often with a couple of hours off for lunch between noon and 2pm) and on Saturday from 8am to noon. Postcards/letters cost US$0.80/1.30 to the US, US$1.30/1.80 to Europe and US$1.80/2.15 to Australia. Delivery takes 10 to 14 days, longer for Australia. Despite the apparently long delivery times for postal items, Honducor, the Honduran postal service, is considered relatively reliable. In fact, travelers from Nicaragua or Guatemala often hang on to their postcards and mail them from Honduras.

For more secure delivery try FedEx, DHL, Express Mail Service (EMS), or Urgent Express; all have offices in Tegucigalpa, San Pedro Sula and other major cities.

RESPONSIBLE TRAVEL

Travelers should not buy anything made of coral – the reefs are widely protected and the items, like coral necklaces or bracelets, probably come from illegal harvests. On the Bay Islands, particularly Utila, fresh water, energy and landfill space are in short supply. Have short showers, and refill your water bottles, rather than buying new ones. If you go diving, make sure you go with a dive outfit that is fully signed up to protecting the environment.

Be very aware of the cultural differences in indigenous communities. Tread sensitively – taking lots of photos in an indigenous area can rouse suspicion.

STUDYING

Spanish courses are popular in Copán Ruinas, La Ceiba, Tela and the Bay Islands. As well as open-water and advanced open-water certifications, shops on the Bay Islands offer most or all upper-level courses and specialties, including nitrox, divemaster and instructor.

TELEPHONE

Many internet cafés offer clear, inexpensive phone service using high-speed internet connections. Calls to the US typically cost US$0.10 per minute, occasionally with rates as low as US$0.05. Expect to pay a bit more to call Europe: per minute US$0.25 to US$0.50.

Hondutel has call centers at its offices throughout the country. Rates to the US are competitive at just US$0.10 per minute. Calls to the rest of the world are higher. Call centers are usually open from 7am until around 9pm every day.

Some Hondutel offices and internet cafés with phone service have fax services. Prices vary widely, but are usually per page, as opposed to per minute. You can receive faxes as well, with a minimal per-page fee. Fax service typically has more limited hours, usually 8am to 4pm Monday to Friday.

Honduran carriers Aló and Telefónica use GSM 850 and 1900 protocols, which are used by North American carriers Cingular, T-Mobile, Fido and others, but will be incompatible with GSM 900/1800 phones common in Europe, Australia, New Zealand and many Asian countries.

Honduras' country code is ☎ 504. There are no area codes beyond the country code; when dialing Honduras from abroad simply dial the international access code plus the Honduran country code plus the local number. For domestic long-distance calls within Honduras, there is no need to dial the area code.

To reach a domestic long-distance operator dial ☎ 191; for local directory assistance dial ☎ 192; for directory assistance for government telephone numbers dial ☎ 193; for an international operator dial ☎ 197. A direct connection to an operator in the USA is available by dialing ☎ 800 0121 for Sprint, ☎ 800

HONDURAS

0122 for MCI WorldCom and ☎ 800 0123 for AT&T.

Hondutel offices sell 'Telecards' which have a code on the back. Simply follow the instructions on the back to make a call from any pay phone.

TOILETS

Public toilets are few and far between in Honduras – stop at your hotel or at restaurants. Western-style flush toilets are the norm in most places although toilet paper goes in the wastepaper basket, not down the hatch. The exception to the rule is La Moskitia, where running water is rare and latrines are typical.

TOURIST INFORMATION

The national tourist office is the **Instituto Hondureño de Turismo** (IHT; ☎ 220 1600, toll free 800 222 8687; www.letsgohonduras.com) in Tegucigalpa. IHT also maintains a **US office** (☎ toll free 800 460 9608, PO Box 140458, Coral Gables, FL 33114). Around the country, tourist information offices are run by the municipal government and public agencies (listed in the Information section of each destination).

VISAS & DOCUMENTS

Citizens of most western European countries, Australia, Canada, Japan, and New Zealand normally receive 90-day tourist cards when entering the country; US citizens get 30 days. This applies to the countries signed up to the CA-4 border agreement – Guatemala, Nicaragua, Honduras and El Salvador. You do not receive a stamp on your passport when passing between these countries.

Upon arrival you will fill out a short immigration form, the yellow portion of which will be stapled into your passport. Do not lose it!

This form will be collected when you depart, and it will be stamped if you seek an extension of your stay. Once inside Honduras you can either apply for a 30-day extension or take a trip to Belize or Costa Rica.

To extend your stay, take your passport to any immigration office and ask for a *prórroga*; you'll have to fill out a form and pay around US$20. Most cities and towns in Honduras have an immigration office *(migración)* where you can do this.

VOLUNTEERING

A number of organizations offer volunteer opportunities in Honduras, on projects in many parts of the country and ranging from building homes to teaching English to involving school children in environmental programs. The website www.travel-to-honduras.com has a long list of groups that run volunteer programs in Honduras, from large operations like Casa Alianza, Houses for Humanity and i-to-i, to smaller ones like the Cofradía Bilingual School and the Utila Iguana Conservation Project.

WOMEN TRAVELERS

Honduras is basically a good country for women travelers. As elsewhere, you'll probably attract less attention if you dress modestly. On the Bay Islands, where lots of beach-going foreign tourists tend to congregate, standards of modesty in dress are much more relaxed, though topless bathing is most definitely frowned upon.

Cases of rape against foreign tourists have been reported in a few places along the north coast. As peaceful and idyllic as the coast looks – and usually is – be wary of going to isolated stretches of beach alone, and don't walk on the beach at night.

Nicaragua

HIGHLIGHTS

- **Isla de Ometepe** Scramble to the summits of the two volcanoes that join to make this majestic island (p503)
- **Corn Islands** Snack on coconuts and swim crystal-clear waters – this unspoiled place is so Caribbean it's almost a joke (p516)
- **Granada & León** Savor the delights of these cultured colonial towns, easily reached from Managua (p488) and (p480)
- **Río San Juan** Board a riverboat to explore this picturesque watercourse, home to abundant birdlife and an unexpected fortress (p511)
- **Matagalpa & Estelí** Discover the hard-working highlands in these earthy, open cities, coffee and cowboy country respectively (p469) and (p474)
- **Off the beaten track** Bargain with local fishermen to take you boating in the intriguing Miskito area of Laguna de Perlas (p515)

FAST FACTS

- **Area** 129,494 sq km (approximately Greece/New York State)
- **ATMs** Widespread in major towns
- **Budget** US$15-25 per day
- **Capital** Managua
- **Costs** Hostel in León US$4-6, bottle of beer US$0.70, 3hr bus ride US$2.50, lunch US$1.50
- **Country Code** ☎ 505
- **Electricity** 110V AC, 60Hz (same as USA)
- **Famous for** Sandinistas, volcanoes
- **Head of State** President Daniel Ortega Saavedra
- **Languages** Spanish, English
- **Money** US$1 = C$18.50 (córdobas)
- **Phrases** Nicas (Nicaraguan guys and gals), *vos* (you), *tuanis* (right on)
- **Population** 5,142,100
- **Time** GMT minus 6 hours , no daylight saving
- **Visas** Nearly all need only a valid passport

TRAVEL HINTS

Figure out your cash situation for popular spots such as the Corn Islands (no ATM) and Ometepe (Visa only). US dollars are accepted everywhere. Exchange córdobas before leaving.

OVERLAND ROUTES

Nicaragua's border with Honduras can be crossed at Las Manos–El Espino (p479) and Guasaule (p488). Costa Rica can be reached via Sapoá (p502) or by boat via San Carlos (p509).

To the new generation of travelers, Nicaragua represents booming beach breaks, volcano hiking, thrilling island paradises, and laid-back colonial towns, so it seems that the message – 'the civil war finished decades ago people!' – has finally gotten across to an audience who had it pegged as a trouble spot. In fact, it's now the safest country in Central America, and a surprisingly easy place to travel around.

Yet the iconic images of idealistic young people giving their lives for a dream of liberty have never quite disappeared, and Nicaragua remains a land where people, whatever their beliefs, tend to go beyond cheap chatter. A place of poets and artists, of opinions both well-informed and cheerily imparted. Despite the landscape being extra well-endowed with natural beauty, it is the Nicaraguans themselves who remain their country's chief asset.

Nicaragua boasts both a Pacific and a Caribbean coast, and these two sides of the country differ in myriad ways. In the west of the country you can zip between colonial cities on good paved roads, while in the east is an enormous wilderness that, a couple of golden Caribbean paradises apart, won't be touristy any time this century.

CURRENT EVENTS

After 16 years in opposition, the leftist FSLN (Sandinista) party returned to political power in January 2007, ending a long neoliberal period that had, significant advances in the tourism sector notwithstanding, failed to kickstart the country's economy. However, the left had been far from united behind President Daniel Ortega, a father of the revolution but these days considered by many on both sides of the political fence to be a power-hungry crackpot.

The early days of his current presidency were a flurry of activity, with Nicaragua's energy crisis seemingly solved via a deal with Venezuela's Hugo Chávez, Ortega pledging to maintain good relations with the USA (then jeopardizing that by announcing a meaningless goodwill treaty with Iran), and afterwards taking some rather antiparliamentary legislative steps. One thing is certain; life with Ortega won't be dull.

HISTORY
Early History

Fascinatingly, the earliest traces of human habitation in Nicaragua are some 6000-year-old footprints found near the banks of Lago de Managua, within the area occupied by the present-day capital.

At the site, you can see the squelches made as these early Nicaraguans headed lakewards, perhaps migrating.

Nicaragua was home to several indigenous groups, including the ancestors of today's Rama who live on the Caribbean coast, and the Chorotegas and Nicaraos, on the Pacific side. The latter spoke a form of Nahuatl, the language of the Aztecs. Many Nicaraguan places retain their Nahuatl names.

European Arrival

The indigenous inhabitants' first contact with Europeans was in 1502, when Columbus sailed down Nicaragua's Caribbean coast.

The next exploratory mission, led by Gil González de Ávila, came north from the Spanish settlement at Panama, arriving in 1522. It found a chieftain, Cacique Nicarao, governing the southern shores of Lago de Nicaragua and the tribe of the same name. The Spaniards thus named the region Nicaragua.

Two years later the Spanish were back to colonize, led this time by Francisco Fernández de Córdoba, who founded the cities of Granada and León in 1524. Both were established near indigenous settlements whose inhabitants were subjugated and put to work. Attempts at founding a similar city near Managua were resisted; the indigenous settlement was destroyed as punishment.

Colonial Settlement

The gold that had initially attracted the Spaniards soon gave out, but Granada and León remained. Granada, on Lago de Nicaragua, became a comparatively rich colonial city, its wealth due not only to surrounding agriculture but also to its importance as a trading center. The navigable Río San Juan, flowing out of the lake, gave Granada a direct shipping connection to the Caribbean and thus Europe. With its wealthy business class, Granada eventually became the center for the Conservative Party, favoring traditional values of monarchy and ecclesiastical authority.

Originally founded on Lago de Managua, León was destroyed by earthquake in 1610 and a new city established some 30km northwest. It was poorer than Granada, but the Spanish made it the capital of the colonial province.

León in time became the center for radical clerics and intellectuals, who formed the Liberal Party and supported the unification of Central America and reforms based on those of the French and American revolutions.

The difference in wealth between the two cities, and the political supremacy of León, led to conflicts that raged into the 1850s, at times erupting into outright civil war. The continual fighting between them stopped only when the capital was moved to the neutral location of Managua in 1857.

While the Spanish were settling the Pacific lowlands, the English were the dominant influence on the Caribbean side of Nicaragua. English, French and Dutch pirates plying the Caribbean established settlements and attacked the east coast in the 17th century, at times even penetrating to Granada via the Río San Juan.

Early Independence

Along with the rest of Central America, Nicaragua gained independence from Spain in 1821, was briefly part of Mexico, was then incorporated into the new Central American Federation, and finally achieved complete independence in 1838. The cities of León and Granada continued to feud.

After independence, the Liberals and Conservatives weren't the only groups vying for power. With the Spanish out of the picture, Britain and the USA both became interested in Nicaragua and its strategically important passage from Lago de Nicaragua to the Caribbean. Both countries wanted to build an interoceanic canal through Central America, and Nicaragua looked the likeliest spot.

In 1848 the British seized the Caribbean port of San Juan del Norte, at the mouth of the Río San Juan, and renamed it Greytown. Meanwhile, the California gold rush had added fire to the quest for an Atlantic–Pacific passage, and prospectors were transported to America's west coast via the Río San Juan and a Pacific steamer service.

The Late 19th Century

In 1857 the Liberals, disgraced after inviting William Walker (see below) into the country, lost power to the Conservatives and were unable to regain it for the next 36 years. In the same year, the capital was transferred to Managua, then little more than a village between the two cities, in an attempt to quell the rivalry between Granada and León.

In 1860 the British signed a treaty ceding the Caribbean region to the now-independent governments of Honduras and Nicaragua. The Nicaraguan section remained an autonomous region until the 1890s.

Zelaya's Coup & US Intervention

In 1893 a Liberal general named José Santos Zelaya deposed the Conservative president and became dictator. Zelaya soon antagonized the US by seeking a canal deal with Germany and Japan. Encouraged by Washington, which

---

DOING THINGS THE WILLIAM WALKER WAY

Latin America's turbulent history is littered with colorful characters, but there were few messiah complexes bigger than that of William Walker, an American adventurer who directed and starred in *Conquistador 2*, more than three centuries after Cortéz took the New World by storm with the original hit. He started his one-man mission in 1853, leading a small party to attack Mexico, where he declared himself president of 'independent' Sonora before being ignominiously driven out.

In 1855 the Liberals of León asked Walker to help them seize power from Granada's Conservatives. Walker entered Nicaragua with 56 followers, attacked Granada and prevailed. Instead of ceding it to his employers, he soon had himself elected president of Nicaragua (in 'free and fair elections' no doubt), and the US recognized his government. He then reinstituted slavery, declared English the country's official language, mortgaged the entire nation to fund personal borrowing, and invaded Costa Rica, announcing his intention to control the whole of Central America. This was a step too far, and those nations united to drive him out. Walker fled Granada, leaving the city alight, and was forced to return to the USA.

Not easily put off, he landed with a small army at Greytown six months later, only to be arrested and deported by the US Navy. He tried again in 1860; this time the British Navy captured him and turned him over to the Hondurans, who ended his adventures with a volley of rifle fire in 1860. His grave is in Trujillo's Old Cemetery (see p403).

NICARAGUA

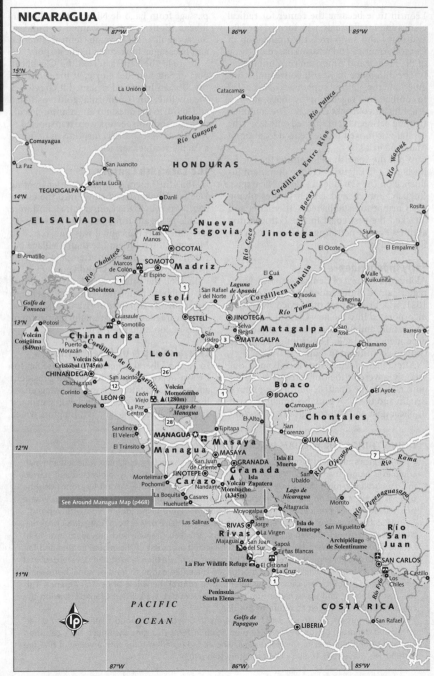

NICARAGUA

See Around Managua Map (p468)

sought to monopolize a transisthmian canal in Panama, the Conservatives rebelled in 1909. After Zelaya ordered the execution of two US mercenaries accused of aiding the Conservatives, the American government forced his resignation. In 1912 the US responded to another rebellion, this time against the corrupt Conservative administration, by sending 2500 marines to Nicaragua.

For most of the next two decades the US dominated politics in Nicaragua, installing presidents it favored and ousting those it didn't (sound familiar?), using its marines as persuasion. In 1914 the Bryan-Chamorro Treaty was signed, granting the US exclusive canal rights in Nicaragua; America actually had no intention of building such a canal, but wanted to ensure that no one else did.

In 1925 a new cycle of violence began with a Conservative coup. The marines were withdrawn, but as political turmoil ensued, they returned the following year.

Sandino & the Somoza Era

The Conservative regime was opposed by a group of Liberal rebels including Augusto C Sandino, who eventually became leader of a long-term rebel campaign resisting US involvement. When the marines headed home in 1933, the enemy became the new US-trained Guardia Nacional, whose aim was to put down resistance by Sandino's guerrillas. This military force was led by Anastasio Somoza García.

In February 1934 Somoza engineered the assassination of Sandino by inviting him to dinner for a peace conference. Sandino headed down from the mountains for the meal, which went well until the national guardsmen that were his lift back to the airport gunned him down. Somoza, with his main enemy out of the way, then set his sights on supreme power. Overthrowing Liberal president Sacasa a couple of years later, he established himself as president in 1937, founding a family dynasty that was to rule for four decades.

After creating a new constitution to grant himself more power, Somoza García ruled Nicaragua as an internationally notorious dictator for the next 20 years, sometimes as president, at other times behind a puppet president. He amassed huge personal wealth by corrupt means (the Somoza landholdings attained were the size of El Salvador). Of course, the majority of Nicaraguans remained entrenched in poverty.

Somoza supported the USA (the CIA used Nicaragua as a launchpad for both the 1954 overthrow of Guatemalan leader Colon Jacobo Arbenz Guzmán and the 1961 invasion of Cuba) and was in turn supported by the US government.

After his assassination in León in 1956 (p483), Somoza was succeeded by his elder son, Luis Somoza Debayle, and the Somoza family, with the help of the Guardia Nacional, continued to rule Nicaragua. In 1967 Luis died, and his younger brother, Anastasio Somoza Debayle, assumed control.

Rising Opposition

In 1961 Carlos Fonseca Amador, a prominent figure in the student movement that had opposed the Somoza regime in the 1950s, joined forces with Colonel Santos López (an old fighting partner of Sandino's), and other activists to form the Frente Sandinista de Liberación Nacional (Sandinista National Liberation Front), or FSLN.

On December 23, 1972, at around midnight, an earthquake devastated Managua, leveling over 250 city blocks, killing over 6000 people and leaving 300,000 homeless. As international aid poured in, the money was diverted to Anastasio Somoza and his associates, while the people who needed it suffered and died. This obvious abuse dramatically increased opposition to Somoza among all classes of society. Wealthy businesspeople also turned against Somoza as they saw their own ventures being eclipsed by the Somoza family's corrupt empire.

By 1974 opposition was widespread. Two groups were widely recognized – the FSLN (Sandinistas), led by Carlos Fonseca, and the Unión Democrática de Liberación, led by Pedro Joaquín Chamorro, popular owner and editor of the Managua newspaper La Prensa, which had long printed articles critical of the Somoza regime.

In December 1974 the FSLN kidnapped several leading members of the Somoza regime, gaining ransoms and the freeing of political prisoners in exchange for the release of the hostages. The Somoza government responded with a campaign of systematic killings over the following 2½ years. Fonseca was killed in a skirmish in 1976.

Revolution & the FSLN

The last straw for the Nicaraguan public was the assassination in January 1978 of Chamorro. Violence erupted and a general strike was declared. Business interests united with moderate factions in the Frente Amplio Opositor (FAO; Broad Opposition Front) and unsuccessfully attempted to negotiate an end to the Somoza dictatorship.

In August 1978 the FSLN occupied the Palacio Nacional and took over 2000 hostages, demanding freedom for 60 imprisoned Sandinistas. The government acceded, and the hostages were released. Nevertheless, the revolt spread, with spontaneous uprisings in many major towns. The Guardia Nacional responded swiftly and ruthlessly, shelling those cities and exterminating thousands.

The FAO, having exhausted its negotiating efforts, threw in its lot with the Sandinistas, whom they now perceived as the only viable means to oust the dictatorship. This broad alliance formed a revolutionary government provisionally based in San José, Costa Rica, which gained recognition from some Latin American and European governments and military support in the form of arms shipments. Thus the FSLN was well prepared to launch its final offensive in June 1979. The revolutionary forces took city after city, with the support of thousands of civilians. On July 17, as the Sandinistas were preparing to enter Managua, Somoza resigned the presidency and fled the country. (He was assassinated by Sandinista agents a year later in Asunción, Paraguay.) The Sandinistas marched victorious into Managua on July 19, 1979.

They inherited a shambles. Poverty, homelessness, illiteracy and staggeringly inadequate health care were just a few of the widespread problems. An estimated 50,000 people had been killed in the revolutionary struggle, and perhaps 150,000 more left homeless.

The FSLN and prominent anti-Somoza moderates (including Violeta Barrios de Chamorro, widow of the martyred Pedro Joaquín Chamorro) set up a five-member junta to administer the country. The constitution was suspended, the national congress dissolved and the Guardia Nacional replaced by the Sandinista People's Army.

However, the alliance between moderates and the FSLN didn't last long. In April 1980 Chamorro and the one other moderate resigned from the ruling junta when it became clear that the FSLN intended to dominate the Council of State, which was being set up to serve as the nation's interim legislature. The junta thus was reduced from five members to three, with revolutionary commander Daniel Ortega Saavedra appointed coordinator.

Trying to salvage what it could of its influence over the country, the US (under President Jimmy Carter) authorized US$75 million in emergency aid to the Sandinista-led government. However, by late 1980 it was becoming concerned about the increasing numbers of Soviet and Cuban advisors in Nicaragua and allegations that the Sandinistas were beginning to provide arms to leftist rebels in El Salvador.

The Contra War

After Ronald Reagan became US president in January 1981, relations between Nicaragua and the US took a turn for the worse. Reagan suspended all aid to Nicaragua and began funding the counterrevolutionary military groups known as Contras, operating out of Honduras and eventually out of Costa Rica as well. Most of the original Contras were ex-soldiers of Somoza's Guardia Nacional, but as time passed, their ranks filled with disaffected local people.

The Contra war escalated throughout the 1980s. As US money flowed to the Contras, their numbers grew to over 15,000 fighters. Honduras was heavily militarized, with large-scale US-Honduran maneuvers threatening an invasion of Nicaragua. The Sandinistas responded by instituting conscription and building an army that eventually numbered 95,000. Soviet and Cuban military and economic aid poured in, reaching US$700 million in 1987. A CIA scheme to mine Nicaragua's harbors was revealed in 1984 and resulted in a judgment against the US by the International Court of Justice.

Elections in November 1984 were boycotted by leading non-Sandinistas, who complained of sweeping FSLN control of the nation's media. (In fact, the Chamorro family's *La Prensa* acknowledged receiving CIA funding for publishing anti-Sandinista views, while still operating freely. This publishing freedom was finally curtailed as the Contra war escalated, a state of emergency was declared and censorship was implemented.) Daniel Ortega was elected president with 63% of the vote, and the FSLN won 61 of the 96 seats in the new National Assembly.

In May 1985 the USA initiated a trade embargo of Nicaragua and pressured other countries to do the same. The embargo lasted for the next five years and helped to strangle Nicaragua's economy.

After the US Congress rejected further military aid for the Contras in 1985, the Reagan administration secretly continued funding them through a scheme in which the CIA illegally sold weapons to Iran and diverted the proceeds to the Contras. When the details leaked out, the infamous 'Iran-Contra Affair' blew up.

After many failed peace initiatives, the Costa Rican president, Oscar Arías Sánchez, finally came up with an accord that was signed in August 1987 by the leaders of Costa Rica, El Salvador, Nicaragua, Guatemala and Honduras. Though a great stride forward (Arías won the Nobel Prize), it proved difficult to implement, as participating nations failed to follow through on their commitments, while the US took measures that seemed intentionally aimed at undermining the peace process.

The 1990 Election

By the late 1980s the Nicaraguan economy was again desperate. Civil war, the US trade embargo, and the inefficiencies of a Soviet-style centralized economy had produced hyperinflation, falling production and rising unemployment. As it became clear that the US Congress was preparing to grant the Contras further aid, Daniel Ortega called elections that he expected would give the Sandinistas a popular mandate to govern.

The FSLN, however, underestimated the disillusionment and fatigue of the Nicaraguan people. Economic problems and the daily grind had eclipsed the dramatic accomplishments of the Sandinistas' early years: redistributing Somoza lands to small farming cooperatives, reducing illiteracy from 50% to 13%, eliminating polio through a massive immunization program and reducing the rate of infant mortality by a third.

The Unión Nacional Opositora (UNO), a broad coalition of 14 political parties opposing the Sandinista government, was formed in 1989. UNO presidential candidate Violeta Barrios de Chamorro had the backing and financing of the US, which had promised to lift the embargo and give hundreds of millions of dollars in economic aid to Nicaragua if UNO won. With such bribes in place, the UNO handily took the elections of February 25, 1990, gaining 55% of the presidential votes and 51 of the 110 seats in the National Assembly, compared with the FSLN's 39. Ortega had plenty of grounds for complaint, but, to his credit, in the end he went quietly, perhaps avoiding further conflict.

Politics in the '90s

Chamorro took office in April 1990. The Contras stopped fighting at the end of June with a symbolic and heavily publicized turning-in of their weapons. The US trade embargo was lifted, and US and other foreign aid began to pour in.

She faced a tricky balancing act in trying to reunify the country and satisfy all interests. The promised economic recovery was slow in coming; growth was sluggish, and unemployment remained stubbornly high. Nevertheless, in 1996, when Nicaragua went to the polls again, the people rejected the FSLN's Ortega and opted for former Managua mayor Arnoldo Alemán of the PLC, a center-right liberal alliance.

Alemán's achievements included investing heavily in infrastructure and reducing the size of the army by a factor of 10, but his administration was plagued by scandal, as corruption soared and Alemán amassed a personal fortune from the state's coffers. Meanwhile, however, the Sandinistas had their own image problems, as the ever-present Ortega was accused by his stepdaughter of sexual abuse. In a gesture of mutual self-preservation, Ortega and Alemán struck a sordid little deal, popularly known as *el pacto* (the pact), aimed at nullifying the threat of the opposition, pulling the teeth of anticorruption watchdogs and guaranteeing Alemán immunity from further investigation.

Sandinista diehards felt betrayed by Ortega's underhanded dealings, but many still believed in their party, and Ortega remained an important figure.

Currents in the New Millennium

With scandals gripping the country, the 2001 elections were heavily monitored. Enrique Bolaños, vice-president under Alemán, ran on a platform reminding Nicaraguans of the hardships endured under the Sandinistas. Ortega, reinvented himself and declared his party of 'peace and love,' complete with pink posters and flower-covered banners.

Voters turned out in record numbers (96%) and elected the 73-year-old Bolaños by a small margin. After 11 years of trying to make a comeback, it was Ortega's third defeat, although he again had a point when he complained of US intervention – the George W Bush government had promised 'dire consequences' for Nicaragua if Ortega were elected. They had also invited Bolaños to hand out US-donated food and pressured a third candidate to leave the race.

Bolaños took office pledging to clean up the country's corrupt government, a policy which was odds with his party. Although he managed to have Alemán stripped of his immunity, wily Arnoldo (sentenced to 20 years in prison), has, at press time, still not been finally convicted and is under house arrest pending an appeal, confidently predicting his own return to the presidency in 2011. Worse for Bolaños, in 2003 he himself was implicated in the ongoing corruption investigation.

The combination of his own party's distrust, and the general failure of the much-vaunted 'neoliberal' reforms he had proposed (although he had significant successes in the tourism sector) saw Bolaños became something of a lame-duck president and the stage was set for a return to the left in the November 2006 elections. Ortega, however, had become something of an embarrassment to large sections of his former support base, and many set their hopes on popular Herty Lewites, a former Sandinista who rapidly became an acceptable candidate for a broad spectrum of Nicaraguan society. However, when he died of a heart attack just four months before the election, the race was left open for Ortega to finally reclaim what he regarded as his birthright. He did so, with only 38% of the popular vote. Taking office in January 2007, he proclaimed a new era of leftist Latin American unity, leaving the USA and some international investors a little jumpy.

THE CULTURE
The National Psyche

Nicaraguans are a proud people and vocal about their views. Opinions differ over whether the Sandinista years were a failure or a success, but one thing they established was the unhindered exchange of information – in the press and on the streets. Nicas (Nicaraguans) love to debate, and if you spend time chatting you'll learn more about the current political scene than you ever would reading a paper (or guidebook!). Nicaraguans rightly have a lot of respect for their artistic, literary and cultural history, and are never afraid to cheerily big-up local achievements.

While there are plenty of regional attitudes – on the Caribbean coast many feel little affinity with the rest of the country, and the Granada/ León rivalry goes back centuries – Nicaraguans get on surprisingly well with each other given their turbulent recent history. One thing they all seem to have in common is an almost comical disdain for their southern neighbor Costa Rica.

Lifestyle

It's not easy to generalize about Nicaraguan lifestyle. Observing the well-dressed crowds in Managua's trendy shopping malls, you might assume they are a westernized, urban, wealthy elite. Some are, but probing a little more you'll find that a good number are impoverished single parents from the country on a once-a-year trip to buy their children toys that they can barely afford.

Some 50% of Nicaraguans live below the poverty line, and huge numbers move to Nicaragua's capital of Managua, Costa Rica, or the US in order to get work. This has put a great strain on the traditional family structure; it's common for young parents to leave their children to be brought up by relatives while they send money home for their upbringing and education.

While traditional conservative values are still strong in some areas, these were shattered by the revolution in other parts of the country. The Sandinista ideal considered women as absolute equals in all aspects of society, and Nicaragua is still well ahead of the game in this respect. Predictably, attitudes to homosexuality differ according to where and whom you ask.

People

Nicaragua has the lowest population density in Central America, around 33 per sq km. Mestizos, of mixed Spanish and indigenous ancestry, form the majority, with 69% of the population; Spanish and other whites comprise 17%, blacks 9% and indigenous people 5%.

The great majority of the population lives in the Pacific lowland belt. The Caribbean region is sparsely populated; it makes up half the country's land area but has only 12% of its population. This zone includes the Sumos and Ramas, and the Miskitos, all of whom have their own language. English is also spoken on this coast.

Nicaragua is a nation of young people: 72% of the population is under 30 years old, and 40% is under 15. The population is 54% urban.

ARTS

Nicaragua is a bright star in the firmament of Latin American literature, and poetry is the country's most important and beloved art. Rubén 'Darío' (1867–1916), a poet who lived in León, is one of the most renowned authors in the Spanish language, and his writings have inspired literary movements and trends throughout the Latin world.

Three outstanding writers emerged soon after Darío, and their works are still popular: Azarías Pallais (1884–1954), Salomón de la Selva (1893–1959) and Alfonso Cortés (1893–1969). In the 1930s the experimental 'Vanguardia' movement came on the scene, led by José Coronel Urtecho, Pablo Antonio Cuadra, Joaquín Cuadra Pasos and Manolo Cuadra. Most importantly, the work of all these poets is widely read and quoted by the populace. A number of leading personalities in the Sandinista leadership, including Sergio Ramírez, Rosario Murillo and Ernesto Cardenal, made literary contributions as well as political ones.

Cardenal, in fact, was responsible for a whole new style of Nicaraguan art when he

---

FEVER PITCH

When you hear someone talk about 'El Presidente,' they may not be referring to the country's leader, but to former Montreal Expos pitcher Denis Martínez, a Nicaraguan legend in the national sport, *beisbol*, which pushes soccer into a distant second place. Ever since US marines introduced it in the early 20th century, Nicaraguans have been fanatical about it, and the Nicaraguans playing in the US and Mexican leagues are closely followed. There's a local league too; Managua attracts crowds of 20,000 or more to see its Bóer club play against the three other major league teams: Masaya, León and Chinandega (teams vary depending on who can raise the annual registration fee). Check www.lnpb.net for fixtures.

harnessed the talents of the local population of the Solentiname archipelago. The result, a distinctive, colorful, primitivist style of painting, is famous worldwide.

The Caribbean coast, with its distinct culture, has its own art forms, too. In Bluefields, the calypso-influenced *palo de mayo* (maypole), is a widely popular musical genre.

RELIGION

Catholicism is the dominant religion in Nicaragua, claiming some 73% of the population, but large bites of the theological cake have been taken in recent years by evangelical Protestant sects, who claim almost one in six of the population these days. The importance of religious issues is high – a recent ban on abortion (even to save the mother's life) was ratified by most of parliament, including Daniel Ortega, an avowed atheist who has now found God (some say for votes).

ENVIRONMENT
The Land

Nicaragua, comprising 129,494 sq km, is the largest country in Central America. It is bordered on the north by Honduras, the south by Costa Rica, the east by the Caribbean Sea and the west by the Pacific Ocean.

The country has three distinct geographical regions.

PACIFIC LOWLANDS

The western coastal region is a broad, hot, fertile lowland plain broken by 11 major volcanoes. Some of the tallest are San Cristóbal (1745m), northeast of Chinandega; Concepción (1610m), on Isla de Ometepe in Lago de Nicaragua; and Mombacho (1345m), near Granada.

The fertile volcanic soil and the hot climate, with its distinct rainy and dry seasons, make this the most productive agricultural area in the country. It holds the country's major population centers.

Also in the area are Lago de Nicaragua, the largest lake in Central America, studded with over 400 islands, and the smaller Lago de Managua.

NORTH-CENTRAL MOUNTAINS

The north-central region, with its high mountains and valleys, is cooler than the Pacific lowlands and also very fertile. About 25% of the country's agriculture is concentrated here,

including most coffee production. The highest point in the country, Pico Mogotón (2438m), is near the Honduran border, in the region around Ocotal.

CARIBBEAN COAST

The Caribbean ('Atlantic') region occupies about half of Nicaragua's area. The 541km coastline is broken by many large lagoons and deltas. Twenty-three rivers flow from the central mountains into the Caribbean, including the Río Coco (685km), Nicaragua's longest river, and the Río San Juan (199km), which flows from Lago de Nicaragua. These define much of the borders with Honduras and Costa Rica respectively. The Caribbean region gets an immense amount of rainfall. It is sparsely populated and covered by tropical rain forest. The largest towns are Bluefields and Bilwi (Puerto Cabezas), both coastal ports. Several small islands, including the much-visited Corn Islands, lie off the Caribbean coast, surrounded by coral reefs.

Wildlife

Boasting the highest percentage of forest of any Central American country, combined with the lowest population density, Nicaragua is one of the most biologically diverse regions in the Americas.

ANIMALS

Three species of sea turtle make their annual nesting grounds along the extensive undeveloped beaches of Nicaragua's Pacific coast and on islands off the Caribbean coast. Other reptiles and amphibians found in Nicaragua include green iguanas, black iguanas, and numerous species of lizards and caymans.

The country has a wealth of birdlife, from tropical species resident in a variety of forest environments to waterbirds on the lakes and rivers, and migrants passing between North and South America. Urracas (white-throated magpie jays) are found throughout the country, but scissor-tailed flycatchers, scarlet macaws and the colorful national bird, the guarda barranco (blue-crowned motmot), may be more difficult to spot.

Mantled howler monkeys are easy to see and hear in the private reserve of Selva Negra north of Matagalpa and around the volcanoes of Ometepe, but Nicaragua also hosts Geoffrey's spider monkeys and white-faced capuchin monkeys.

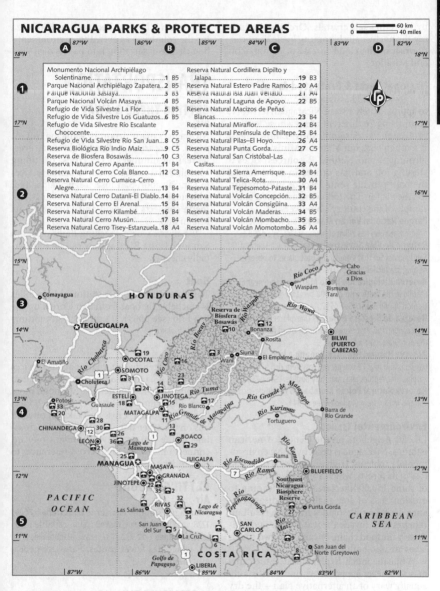

NICARAGUA PARKS & PROTECTED AREAS

Monumento Nacional Archipiélago Solentiname.....................1 B5	Reserva Natural Cordillera Dipilto y Jalapa..........................19 B3
Parque Nacional Archipiélago Zapatera..2 B5	Reserva Natural Estero Padre Ramos...20 A4
Parque Nacional Saslaya...........5 B3	Reserva Natural Isla Juan Venado......21 A4
Parque Nacional Volcán Masaya...........4 B5	Reserva Natural Laguna de Apoyo......22 B5
Refugio de Vida Silvestre La Flor.........5 B5	Reserva Natural Macizos de Peñas
Refugio de Vida Silvestre Los Guatuzos..6 B5	Blancas..........................23 B4
Refugio de Vida Silvestre Río Escalante Chococente.....................7 B5	Reserva Natural Miraflor............24 B4
	Reserva Natural Península de Chiltepe.25 B4
Refugio de Vida Silvestre Río San Juan..8 C5	Reserva Natural Pilas–El Hoyo.........26 A4
Reserva Biológica Río Indio Maíz........9 C5	Reserva Natural Punta Gorda.........27 C5
Reserva de Biosfera Bosawás............10 C3	Reserva Natural San Cristóbal-Las
Reserva Natural Cerro Apante..........11 B4	Casitas..........................28 A4
Reserva Natural Cerro Cola Blanco....12 C3	Reserva Natural Sierra Amerrisque......29 B4
Reserva Natural Cerro Cumaica-Cerro Alegre.........................13 B4	Reserva Natural Telica-Rota..........30 A4
	Reserva Natural Tepesomoto-Pataste..31 B4
Reserva Natural Cerro Datanlí-El Diablo..14 B4	Reserva Natural Volcán Concepción...32 B5
Reserva Natural Cerro El Arenal.......15 B4	Reserva Natural Volcán Consigüina....33 A4
Reserva Natural Cerro Kilambé.........16 B4	Reserva Natural Volcán Maderas......34 B5
Reserva Natural Cerro Musún..........17 B4	Reserva Natural Volcán Mombacho....35 B5
Reserva Natural Cerro Tisey-Estanzuela..18 A4	Reserva Natural Volcán Momotombo..36 B4

Among the more curious aquatic species are the sharks of Lago de Nicaragua. A member of the bull shark family, Carcharhinus leucas is the world's only known shark species that can pass between saltwater and freshwater. These were once in great abundance in the lake; today, owing to massive overfishing, they are rarely seen.

PLANTS

Nicaragua's plant life is at least as diverse as its animal life. The various ecosystems, ranging from dry tropical forest to cloud forest to rainforest, provide fertile territory for botanical exploration. Tree varieties include tamarind, kapok, frangipani and *palo de sal,* which adapts to its high-salinity coastal environment by excreting salt crystals. Orchids, including the nocturnally blooming *huele de noche*, flourish in the cloud forests of Mombacho and Miraflor.

National Parks & Protected Areas

The government has assigned protected status to approximately 18% of Nicaraguan territory, comprising 76 different areas whose level of protection varies significantly. Enforcement is a tough task, but Marena (Ministry of Environment and Natural Resources) does a sterling job and has offices in most towns that can provide some level of information for the visitor. The following are just a small sample of the country's biodiversity:

Parque Nacional Volcán Masaya This active volcano near Masaya also has 20km of hiking trails. (See p498.)

Refugio de Vida Silvestre La Flor A beach south of San Juan del Sur that's one of the best places to observe nesting sea turtles. (See p503.)

Reserva Biológica Río Indio Maíz A reserve near El Castillo in the south with 264,000 hectares of virgin tropical humid forest. (See p512.)

Reserva de Biosfera Bosawás Unexplored and rather inaccessible, this vast expanse of virgin cloud forest lies in the northeast. (See p480.)

Reserva Natural Isla Juan Venado A long, narrow barrier island near León with an ecosystem rich in amphibians, reptiles and migratory birdlife. (See p486.)

Reserva Natural Volcán Mombacho A wildlife-rich volcano not far from Granada. (See p494.)

Environmental Issues

Like its neighbors on the Central American isthmus, Nicaragua is beset by grave environmental problems. High on the list is the rapid loss of its forests, which are cleared at the rate of some 150,000 hectares a year, leading to erosion, loss of soil quality and disappearance of species. Pesticides from the resultant ranches then invade the water table and ultimately the food chain. Nicaragua's two major lakes are also both heavily polluted.

While the much-hyped interoceanic canal may well never happen, environmentalists are equally wary of an alternative plan – the dry canal, which would be a high-speed railroad to transport shipping containers from ocean to ocean.

Nevertheless, there is some hope. Strict new laws have improved protection of endangered species and environments, and drastically ramped-up punishments for offenders. The Nicaraguan government is well aware that ecotourism is likely to become a real bonanza for the country – as ever, the environment's best chance of salvation is to pay its own way.

TRANSPORTATION

GETTING THERE & AWAY
Air

Nicaragua's main airport is Managua (MGA; p466). There are daily direct flights to an ever-increasing number of US cities, including Miami, Dallas and Houston, as well as services to San Salvador, San José, Tegucigalpa, and, with stops, other Latin American destinations. Iberia connects to Spain and Europe via its Miami hub.

It's always worth checking flight prices to San José, Costa Rica, as they can be substantially cheaper.

Boat

The Costa Rican border station at Los Chiles is reachable by boat from San Carlos up the Río Frío (see p509). It's an easy, straightforward crossing.

Bus

There are extensive international bus services from Managua to the other Central American nations. See p466 for details. Although more time-consuming, it's cheaper to take a local bus to the border, cross and take an onward bus on the other side. All of the border crossings in the country have abundant onward connections. See p445 for cross-references to the border crossings.

GETTING AROUND
Air

Nicaragua's major carrier is **La Costeña** (☎ 263 1228; jcaballero@lacostena.com.ni). Also reliable is **Atlantic Airlines** (☎ 222 3037; www.atlanticairlines.com.ni), which has fewer routes. Fares are generally identical.

DEPARTURE TAX

Anyone flying out of the country must pay a US$25 international departure tax, usually included in your ticket price. Domestic departure tax is US$2. To leave the country overland, it costs US$2, and to enter by air or land costs US$5.

Boat

Boats are the only form of transport in some parts of Nicaragua, particularly on the Caribbean side of the country, where rivers are the main highways. There are several scheduled routes on Lago de Nicaragua, including one from Granada to Ometepe and on to San Carlos. From San Carlos, public boats travel down the Río San Juan to El Castillo and San Juan del Norte, and also across to the Solentiname archipelago.

Bus

Buses travel to destinations all over the western half of the country and to some points east as well (the Caribbean coast generally lacks accessible roads). Intercity buses – most of which are former US school buses – are reliable, frequent, cheap and crowded. There are also express minibuses between major cities. Bus services usually start very early in the morning and finish in the late afternoon. See p467 for specific routes and fares to and from the capital.

Car & Motorcycle

The roads in western Nicaragua are generally good between major towns. Get off the beaten track a little, and the quality deteriorates sharply. There are no particularly unusual traffic regulations, and Managua driving is the only experience likely to get your pulse racing.

Renting a car is common, and is neither complicated nor expensive. Be sure to confirm kilometer allowances, though. Oftentimes rentals include unlimited kilometers and cost, on average, US$25 to US$35 per day for a small economy car. There are several car-rental agencies in Managua; see p467 for details.

Hitchhiking

Hitchhiking is a common and accepted practice in Nicaragua. It's polite to offer a little money when you're given a ride.

Taxi

Shared taxis operate in all the major towns. They're not metered, so be sure to negotiate the fare before getting in. Most towns have a set fare, usually US$0.50 per person or so; more in Managua. You can also often negotiate quite a fair price to use taxis to travel between cities.

MANAGUA

pop 910,000 (Managua city)

Nicaragua's lakeside capital and largest city literally had its heart ripped out in 1972 by a quake that destroyed its old center, leaving Managua as a sprawling series of widespread suburbs, with shopping malls rather than central plazas as centers of community life.

But it's only heartless in a geographical sense. While it lacks the colonial charms of León or Granada, it's a pulsating, occasionally chaotic medley of rich and poor, traditional and westernized, and can be truly fascinating. Plus, its spread-out nature (best glimpsed while speeding around corners, chatty cab-driver gesticulating with both hands) means that there's plenty of drooping tropical greenery and little crowding. There are also a couple of standout sights, and plenty of big-city amenities.

Managua spreads across the southern shore of Lago de Managua, known to indigenous inhabitants as Xolotlán. Other lakes fill the craters of old volcanoes within and near the city.

More than one in five Nicaraguans lives in or around the capital, which is the national center for commerce, manufacturing, higher education and government. Only 50m above sea level, it is always hot and humid: daytime temperatures hover around 32°C year-round.

HISTORY

At the time of the Spanish conquest, Managua was an indigenous lakeshore settlement whose inhabitants practiced agriculture, hunting and fishing. These early Managuans put up a vigorous resistance to the Spanish, who responded by destroying their city. Managua subsequently remained a village until the mid-19th century.

The city rose out of obscurity in 1857 after conflicts between liberal León and conservative Granada repeatedly erupted into civil war. Lying midway between the two, Managua was chosen as a compromise capital; the Nicaraguan equivalent of Ottawa, Canberra or Brasilia.

Since then, a series of natural disasters has thrashed the city. The colonial center was destroyed by earthquake in March 1931, and burned down five years later. It was completely rebuilt, only to be razed again by an even more devastating earthquake in 1972.

MANAGUA

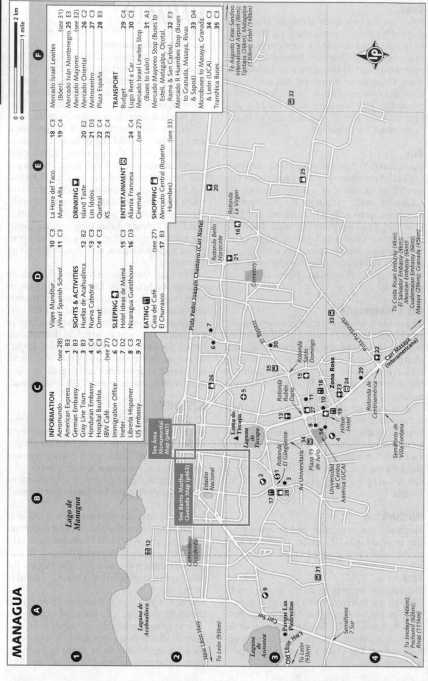

INFORMATION
Aeromundo....................................(see 28)
American Express.............................1 B3
German Embassy..............................2 B3
Gray Line Tours...............................3 B3
Honduran Embassy...........................4 C4
Hospital Bautista..............................5 C3
IBW Café......................................(see 27)
Immigration Office...........................6 C2
Inter..7 D2
Librería Hispamer............................8 C3
US Embassy....................................9 A3

SIGHTS & ACTIVITIES
Viajes Munditur...............................10 C3
¡Viva! Spanish School.......................11 C3
Huellas de Acahualinca.....................12 B2
Nueva Catedral................................13 D3
Ormat...14 C3

SLEEPING
Hotel Ideas de Mamá........................15 C3
Nicaragua Guesthouse.......................16 D3

EATING
Casa del Café................................(see 27)
El Churrasco...................................17 B3
La Hora del Taco.............................18 C3
Marea Alta.....................................19 C4

DRINKING
Island Taste....................................20 E2
Los Idolos......................................21 D3
Quetzal...22 C4
XS...23 C4

ENTERTAINMENT
Alianza Francesa..............................24 C4
Cinemark.....................................(see 27)

SHOPPING
Mercado Central (Roberto Huembes)....(see 33)
Mercado Israel Lewites (8cer)...........(see 31)
Mercado Iván Montenegro..................25 E3
Mercado Mayoreo..........................(see 32)
Mercado Oriental..............................26 C2
Metrocentro....................................27 C3
Plaza España...................................28 B3

TRANSPORT
Budget..29 C4
Lugo Rent a Car...............................30 C3
Mercado Israel Lewites Stop
(Buses to León).............................31 A3
Mercado Mayoreo Stop (Buses to
Estelí, Matagalpa, Ocotal,
Rama & San Carlos)........................32 F3
Mercado R Huembes Stop (Buses
to Granada, Masaya, Rivas
& Sapoá)......................................33 D4
Microbuses to Masaya, Granada
& León (UCA)...............................34 C3
TransNica Buses...............................35 C3

GETTING INTO TOWN

From the Airport

Augusto César Sandino international airport is 11km east of Managua, right on the Interamericana. Taxis at the airport charge up to US$15 for the ride into town, while street taxis charge US$3 to US$5, a little more for two or three passengers. To pay the normal fare, just cross the road outside the airport and hail any moving cab. Buses also run along this road to Mercado Roberto Huembes (US$0.15), from which buses depart for all parts of town. In the reverse direction, from Mercado Huembes catch one of the frequent buses heading for Tipitapa and get off at the airport. Many of Managua's accommodations offer transfers to and from the airport, usually costing US$10 to US$20.

From the Bus Stations

The Tica Bus station is in **Barrio Martha Quezada**. Across the street is Transportes El Sol, while King Quality buses arrive nearby. From any of these locations, it's a few blocks to most of Managua's budget accommodations. TransNica buses arrive near Metrocentro, in the commercial center of town.

Long-distance buses arrive at the city's major markets. Buses from southern destinations and the Costa Rican border arrive at the Mercado Roberto Huembes; buses from León and the border with Honduras go to Mercado Israel Lewites (Bóer); and buses from Matagalpa, Estelí and other northern destinations, including the Honduran border, arrive at Mercado Mayoreo, as do services from San Carlos and Rama. From the stations it's best to take a taxi into town (US$0.70 to US$2).

When geologists found the downtown area riddled with faults, the decision was made to leave the site behind. The new Managua is decentralized, with markets, shopping centers and residential districts built on the outskirts, with no real center.

ORIENTATION

Managua's spread-out collection of barrios sits on the southern shore of Lago de Managua (Xolotlán). The former center on the lakeshore is now largely derelict, having been left vacant after the 1972 quake, but has several visitor attractions. South of here, the Tiscapa hill and crater lake is the city's main landmark. To its west is the pyramidal Crowne Plaza hotel and the Barrio Martha Quezada, home of much of the city's budget accommodation, while to the south is a thriving commercial zone running along the Interamericana (Interamerican Hwy, also known as the Pan-Americana or Pan-American Hwy), here called Carr Masaya.

Managua's central market, Mercado Roberto Huembes, lies 2km east of Metrocentro; other major markets (and adjacent bus stations) are at the western (Bóer), northern (Oriental, confusingly) and eastern (Mayoreo) ends of town.

Like other Nicaraguan cities and towns, Managua has few street signs, and only the major roads are named. Large buildings, *rotondas* (traffic circles) and traffic lights serve as de facto points of reference, and locations are described in terms of their direction and distance, usually in blocks, from these points.

In addition, a special system is used for the cardinal points, whereby *al lago* (to the lake) means 'north' while *a la montaña* (to the mountains) means 'south.' *Arriba* (up) is 'east' and *abajo* (down) is 'west,' both derived from the sun's movement. Thus: '*del Ticabus, una cuadra al lago y dos arriba*' ('from the Tica bus station, one block toward the lake and two blocks up').

INFORMATION

Bookstores

Librería Hispamer (Map p458; ☎ 278 1210) A block west of Metrocentro, and near the UCA, this excellent bookstore offers the nation's best selection of Nicaraguan and Latin American literature and history, as well as a treasure-trove of Spanish-language titles. It also has local news and arts periodicals. There are other branches, but this is the biggest and best.

Cultural Centers

Centro Cultural Managua (Map p461; ☎ 222 5291) One block south of Plaza de la República in the Área Monumental, Managua's cultural center (once a smart hotel) has changing art exhibits, concerts and dances. Handicrafts fairs are held the first Saturday of each month.

Emergency

Ambulance (Cruz Roja or Red Cross; ☎ 128)
Fire (☎ 115)
Police (☎ 249 5714, for emergency 118)

Immigration

Immigration office (Migración; Map p458; ☎ 244 3989; www.migracion.gob.ni; 🕒 8am-11:30am, 1-3pm Mon-Fri) Stays can be extended for up to three months for US$25 per month. The office is 200m north of the Tenderí traffic signal near the Ciudad Jardín area. There's a US$1.50-per-day fine for overstaying your allotted period.

Internet Access

There are numerous internet cafés throughout Managua. Convenient ones:

Cyber @ Center (Map p463; Av Monumental; per hr US$1)

IBW Café (Map p458; per hr US$1.60; 🕒 8:30am-8pm) In Metrocentro, this space-age internet café has air-con and finger-snap quick access.

Plaza Inter (Map p463; per hr US$2; 🕒 10am-10pm) On ground floor, offers plush seats and high-speed connections.

Medical Services

Pharmacies, found all over Managua, are usually open until 10pm.

Hospital Bautista (Map p458; ☎ 249 7070, 249 7277) About 1km east of Crowne Plaza hotel, this is Managua's best hospital. Some staff speak English.

Money

There are numerous ATMs in Managua. Many are Visa/Plus only, but those operated by Banpro and Banco de América Central (BAC) also take MasterCard/Cirrus and Amex. Handy locations include the airport, Plaza Inter, and Metrocentro, as well as Esso service stations on the eastern edge of Barrio Martha Quezada and elsewhere.

Finding a bank in Managua to change US dollars is no problem; if they're closed, street-corner 'coyotes' will also change dollars at more or less the official rate; they're often found at Plaza España (Map p458). Merchants throughout the country gladly accept US dollars.

Any major bank in Managua will change traveler's checks, as will (for Amex checks) **American Express** (Map p458; ☎ 266 4050; Viajes Atlántida office; 🕒 8:30am-5pm Mon-Fri, to noon Sat), one block east of Rotonda El Güegüense. You can change euros at the airport and at a slowly growing number of banks.

Post

Palacio de Correos (Map p461; ☎ 124; 🕒 8am-5pm Mon-Fri, to 1pm Sat) Two blocks west of Plaza de la República is the main post office. An Express Mail office is also here.

Telephone

Enitel is adjacent to the post office. Handier are the numerous internet cafés from which cheap international calls can be made.

Tourist Information

Intur (Nicaraguan Institute of Tourism; www.visitanicaragua.com); airport office (☎ 263 3176; 🕒 8am-9pm Mon-Fri, to 5pm Sat & Sun); main office (Map p463; ☎ 254 5191; 🕒 8am-12:30pm & 1:30-5pm Mon-Fri) Has helpful maps, listings and brochures. The airport office, open longer hours, gives advice by phone. The main office is one block south and one west of Hotel Crowne Plaza. Intur's Managua map is also useful, but you might find the ones given out in some hotels more useful.

Travel Agencies

Aeromundo (Map p458; ☎ 266 8725; aeromundo@ibw.com.ni) In Plaza España, offers airline ticketing, auto reservations and visa processing.

Viajes Munditur (Map p458; ☎ 267 0047; www.viajesmunditur.com; Carr Masaya Km 4.5) Opposite the Hilton Hotel, and just south of Metrocentro, these guys can book flights and all the rest.

DANGERS & ANNOYANCES

Managua's not as dangerous as it looks, but crime has risen in the last few years, and it's the place in Nicaragua where you are most likely to have problems. Except in the upmarket areas, always take a taxi after dark, and to the Área Monumental even during daylight hours. Barrio Martha Quezada has its share of incidents, mostly on its northern edge and between it and Plaza Inter; take a southerly route if heading in that direction.

Managua is spread out and gets pretty hot, so drink plenty of water and remember that a dollar and a bit will buy you a cab fare to nearly anywhere in town.

SIGHTS

Área Monumental

What was once the heart of Nicaragua's capital is an eerie, evocative zone of monuments and ruined buildings (Map p458) that have largely been untouched since an earthquake leveled the area in 1972. Bits are being rehabilitated, but funds are still too short (and the likelihood of another quake too high) to comprehensively restore the area. It's an intriguing spot to visit, but take care when walking around here, and use taxis if you don't feel safe.

Dotted with mango trees and flamboyanes, **Plaza de la República** marks the center of the zone. On the eastern side rests the tomb of Sandinista commander Carlos Fonseca, while a tackily impressive fountain dances to Strauss waltzes at 6pm (water pressure allowing). The area's most emotive ruin is the still-impressive old **cathedral**. Built in 1929, the imposing shell of the neoclassical edifice is still beautiful, and houses frescoes and sculpted angels, but is closed to the public. Every visiting head of state gets brought here, in the hope that they'll write out a check for the restoration on the spot.

Across from the cathedral is the **Museo Nacional** (Map p461; ☎ 222 3845; admission US$2; ☼ 8am-5pm Mon-Fri, 9am-4pm Sat & Sun). Set around two leafy courtyards, the museum is well presented, and includes an excellent selection of pre-Hispanic ceramics, a geological overview, and some fine contemporary Nicaraguan art. Another display exhibits a range of elaborate animal-headed grinding stones, reflecting the traditional importance of maize in indigenous society. It's worth visiting, and a tranquil break from city life. Admission includes an optional guided tour.

Opposite the Palacio Nacional is the shiny new **Casa Presidencial**, the offices of Nicaragua's chief executive. Directly south of the plaza is the old Grand Hotel, now the **Centro Cultural Managua** (see p459). On the lake side of the Plaza de la República, the **Monumento a Rubén Darío** pays homage to Nicaragua's foremost poet, whose likeness adorns the 100-córdoba note. Toward the lake is the oblong **Teatro Rubén Darío** (see p466). The theater faces the **Malecón**, a promenade looking over the heavily polluted (don't swim) Lago de Managua. It's a popular spot on Sundays, when kiosks serve beer and snacks.

Near here is the newly inaugurated open-air theater overlooking the **Plaza de la Fé Juan Pablo II**, scene of notable public ceremonies and independence celebrations.

The unabashedly political **Estatua al Soldado** stands on the west side of Av Bolívar, diagonally across from the Centro Cultural. 'Workers and *campesinos* onward till the end,' reads the inscription below a bronze giant, who holds a pickax and an assault rifle bear-

ing the Sandinista colors. As if in response, **Parque de la Paz** three blocks east proclaims an end to conflict. It was here that the weapons from the 1980s conflict were gathered to be destroyed and buried, and it is still possible to glimpse twisted gun barrels sticking out of the concrete that encircles a burned-out tank. Behind the monument, a handful of abandoned buildings occupied by squatters reinforces the general air of neglect.

Huellas de Acahualinca

These ancient **footprints** (Map p458; ☎ 266 5774; admission US$2, photography fee US$1.35; ☼ 8am-5pm Mon-Fri, 9am-4pm Sat) are Managua's most fascinating attraction, and highly recommended for the glimpse of a long-vanished human past that it affords. Buried 4m deep under compacted volcanic material, the tracks were discovered by quarrying workmen in 1874. There are 12 sets of human footprints (men, women and children) that have been dated to some 6000 to 7000 years ago; they pace in one direction, toward the lake. The lack of returning footprints has led to theories that the tracks represent a migration rather than a routine fishing or foraging trip, but the slow, steady pace probably rules out flight. A further excavated area shows the prints continuing nearby. There are also tracks of deer and *mapache* (a type of raccoon) present. The small museum has ceramics and human remains of a similar age – the footprints indicate that these people weren't dissimilar in size to today's Nicaraguans. The entry fee includes an optional guided tour in Spanish or English that's worth taking.

The neighborhood around here is a little sketchy, and you are well advised to take a taxi to the door.

Loma de Tiscapa

It's well worth climbing this **hill** (Map p458; admission free; 8am-8pm) that rises behind the Crowne Plaza hotel. It's a short stroll up the road, and perfectly safe, as the path is guarded. There are great views down over the Tiscapa crater lake below, as well as over the rest of the city. Here too is the lugubrious silhouette of Sandino, visible from all around town. The hilltop was once the site of Somoza's presidential palace and it was here that Sandino was executed.

A couple of beat-up tanks gifted to the dictator by Mussolini are on display. What looks like a wrecked car park was once a notoriously brutal prison. There's also a canopy tour here (see below).

Nueva Catedral

South of Tiscapa along the road to the Rotonda Rubén Darío is another Managua landmark, the new **cathedral** (Map p458; 278 4232), a curious building studded with dozens of domes that help provide structural support during earthquakes and represent the 63 churches in the Managua diocese. Inside the monumental entrance is a strikingly colorful postmodern interior with a nice shrine on the northwest side.

ACTIVITIES

Atop the Loma de Tiscapa hill, some enterprising locals have set up **Canopy Tiscapa** (840 1277, 893 5017; US$11.50), a short but spectacular three-platform, 1400m jaunt around the crater lake, a lot of fun for the views.

COURSES

¡Viva! Spanish School (Map p458; 270 2339; www.vivaspanishschool.com) This school offers intensive Spanish courses for US$125 a week (US$185

for a couple) and can arrange flexible homestays. It's two blocks south of the FNI building, just east of Metrocentro.

TOURS

Gray Line Tours (Map p458; 268 2412; www.graylinenicaragua.com) Just south of Rotonda El Güegüense, this operator offers half-day tours of the capital with English-speaking guides for US$35 per person (minimum two), which includes entrance fees.

FESTIVALS & EVENTS

The **Festival de Santo Domingo** (August 1–10) is Managua's main fiesta and features a carnival, sporting events, a horse parade, cockfights and more. A procession with music and dancers takes the statue of the saint to its shrine, culminating in fireworks.

May Day (May 1), the **anniversary of the 1979 Sandinista revolution** (July 19) and **Independence Day** (September 15) are also celebrated with gusto in Managua.

SLEEPING

Barrio Martha Quezada, a compact residential district west of the Crowne Plaza hotel, has many cheap guesthouses and places to eat. Budget travelers have always tended to congregate here, not least for its proximity to the Tica international bus station. Like in the U2 song, the streets have no name, so directions following are given in relation to the Tica Bus terminal.

Barrio Martha Quezada

Don't believe touts at the Tica Bus station who will lead you to some dive, insisting that it is, in fact, one of the places listed here! These places are all on Map p463.

Guest House Santos (222 3713; r per person US$5) Just northwest of the Tica Bus station, the rooms here are neither particularly clean nor well maintained. Nevertheless, it's a popular backpacker social spot – a good place to meet other travelers – and has rooms that are OK for the price, with bathroom and fan.

Hospedaje El Ensueño (228 1078; s/d US$6/8) A guidebook cliché is 'better than it looks from outside'; well, this is worse than it looks from outside. The bright and breezy exterior gives no hint of the gloomy rooms, some of which have shared bathroom. Nonetheless, it's good value, and sold by its cute enclosed balcony on the street.

BARRIO MARTHA QUEZADA

INFORMATION	
ATM	(see 34)
Cyber@Center	1 B3
Esso (ATM)	2 D3
French Embassy	3 A2
Intur	4 D3
Italian Embassy	5 A2
Panamanian Embassy	6 A2

SLEEPING	
Casa Azul	7 C3
Casa Gabrinma	8 C3
Casa Vanegas	9 C3
Comidas Sara	10 C3
Guest House Santos	11 B3
Hospedaje El Dorado	12 B3
Hospedaje El Ensueño	13 B3

Hospedaje El Molinito	14 C3
Hospedaje Meza	15 C3
Hotel Jardín de Italia	16 C3
Hotel Los Cisneros	17 B3
Mansión Teodolinda	18 C3
Posada de Ruth	19 C3

EATING	
Bar Los Chepes	20 B3
Buffete #2	21 C3
Cafetín Mirna	22 B3
Cafetín Tonalli	23 C3
Comida a la Vista	24 B3
Comidas Sara 2	25 B3
Doña Pilar	26 C3
La Cazuela	27 B3
Licuados Ananda	28 A2

DRINKING	
Bar Goussen	29 C3
Bar La Curva	30 D3
Fresh Hill	31 D3
Shannon Bar	32 C3

ENTERTAINMENT	
Cinema Plaza Inter	(see 34)
La Casa de los Mejía	
Godoy	33 D3

SHOPPING	
Plaza Inter	34 D3

TRANSPORT	
King Quality	35 C3
Tica Bus Station	36 C3
Transportes El Sol	37 C3

Hospedaje El Molinito (☎ 222 2013; r per person US$6) Very handy for Tica buses, this is a place you can't help liking. The friendly owner has your best interests at heart; the simple rooms are comfortable, and have OK bathrooms, fans, and cable TV (except the singles). Overflow rooms have external bathroom. It's secure – would you climb that razorwire?

Comidas Sara (☎ 865 8933; r per person US$10; P ✕) Right next to Tica Bus, this cheerfully chaotic spot guarantees a warm welcome. Three attractive rooms with air-con sharing OK bathrooms; and there are improvements underway all the time. You'll feel more part of the family than a guest, and they'll wake you up to make sure you get that early bus.

Casa Gabrinma (☎ 222 6650; r per person US$10) Just southeast of Tica Bus, this Catalan-owned spot is welcoming and has decent rooms, which have up to eight beds (ask for a group price). There's more space in the bathrooms than in the rooms themselves, but there's a narrow garden area to stretch out in, as well as an inviting front lounge area with books available for browsing.

Casa Vanegas (☎ 222 4043; casavanegas@cablenet .com.ni; s/d with bathroom US$10/12; ✕ 💻) At the east end of the Tica Bus block, this excellent choice has spotless rooms with cable TV, a small patio, drinks, snacks, and a spacious lounge with internet access (per hour US$1). It's run by a welcoming family and has laundry service. A top option.

Posada de Ruth (☎ 222 4051; s/d with fan US$10/12, with air-con US$20/22; ✕ 💻) Across from Shannon Bar, this cheerful and hospitable choice offers bright, renovated rooms in a family house with speedy on-site internet as a well-earned bonus.

Other options:

Hospedaje Meza (☎ 222 2046; s/d US$4/8) A place to save your córdobas for beer. Rather cheerless rooms, despite the murals, and those pallet beds look familiar – which prison movie was it? Actually, some rooms are better than others.

Casa Azul (☎ 813 4003; r per person US$6) A flop east from Tica Bus, it's grungy with dark rooms but otherwise OK with laid-back management.

Hospedaje El Dorado (☎ 222 6012; r per person US$6; P) Has smallish, dark rooms but you'll enjoy the welcome and the rocking chairs.

NICARAGUA

For a few córdobas more, you'll find more spacious and comfortable accommodations.

Hotel Jardín de Italia (☎ 222 7967; www.jardin deitalia.com; s/d with fan US$15/30, with air-con US$25/40; P ⊠ ⏟) With an efficient, well-run feel and a peaceful, sunny hammocked patio, this makes a sound choice for a tranquil stay. Rooms are comfy, tidy and homey, and have decent bathrooms. The matrimoniales are particularly good, with a big beast of a double bed. The air-con rooms are the same as the fanned ones; it just costs more if you turn the unit on.

Hotel Los Cisneros (☎ 222 7373; www.hotelloscis neros.com; s/d with fan US$25/35, with air-con US$35/50; P ⊠ ⏟) Something of a retreat from any Managua cares, this excellent, warmly welcoming option is run by a cheerful local family. The rooms are apartments, with comfortable beds, kitchen, bathroom, an airy lounge room with rocking chairs, and an outside hammock. All this surrounds a peaceable courtyard full of plants and shaded by mango trees.

Mansión Teodolinda (☎ 228 1050; www.teodo linda.com; Crowne Plaza 2c al sur, 2c abajo; s/d US$75/86; P ⊠ ⏟ ⏴) A significant step up in quality, this endearing boutique hotel has numerous lovely touches, a pretty pool and an excellent restaurant, and is close to some appealing nightlife options.

Bus travelers en route can stay at the **Tica Bus station** (☎ 222 6094; s/d with fan US$12/20, with air-con US$25/33; ⊠) itself, which has smart, renovated rooms within the spick-and-span terminal. Internet access was being planned at time of research.

Elsewhere in Managua

Nicaragua Guesthouse (Map p458; ☎ 249 8963; oscar 3701@tmx.com.ni; r US$13, r with air-con US$25; ⊠) In a tranquil leafy barrio in the eastern part of the city, and a short hop from the airport, this peaceful spot makes an excellent choice. Rooms are comfortable, with fan and bathroom, and the owner is very solicitous. You've also got the lively nightlife of Bello Horizonte just down the road. It's two blocks south and 2½ blocks west of Rotonda de la Virgen.

Hotel Ideas de Mamá (Map p458; ☎ 278 2908; www .hotelideasdemama.com; Rotonda Santo Domingo 5c sur, 2½c abajo; r with shared bathroom per person US$12, s/d with air-con US$35/45; ⊠ ⏟) This is a lovely choice, with clean fan-cooled rooms with shared bathroom, and very attractive air-con choices with cable TV. Both rates include breakfast, the

latter also gives you free internet and transport around town.

EATING
Barrio Martha Quezada

This area (Map p463) boasts a number of good cheap eateries frequented by budget travelers.

Cafetín Mirna (Map p463; breakfast dishes US$1-1.50; ⏱ 6:30am-3pm Mon-Fri, to 11am Sat & Sun) Avocado colored, reliable, welcoming, and run by a local family, this is a top option for breakfast. From traditional *gallo pinto* (a common meal of blended rice and beans) to fluffy pancakes, eggs, fresh juices, and weak but tasty coffee, there's something for all. There's also a lunch buffet weekdays.

Comidas Sara (Map p463; dishes US$1.70-4; ⏱ 4pm-late) There are two places of this name (one is listed under Sleeping), run by sisters, who are daughters of the friendly matriarch Sara herself, who still keeps a grandmotherly eye on things. They are famous for their chicken and mango curry, and also do a great Spanish omelet as well as other traveler-friendly fare. We daren't choose which of the tiny places we like more – we'll leave that up to you.

Bar Los Chepes (Map p463; dishes US$2-3; ⏱ 3-11pm) This unassuming unsigned spot is little more than a few outdoor tables and a friendly boss. It's a fine place to sit with a cold beer of an evening, but it also serves large plates of food – stewed meat or pieces of fish – for a couple of dollars. The quantity is definitely better than the quality, but it's a good deal nonetheless.

There are a number of lunchtime buffets.

Buffete #2 (Map p463; lunch US$2-4; ⏱ 11:30am-3pm Mon-Sat) Why are the streets eerily quiet at lunchtime? Because everyone is here, enjoying food of excellent quality for a pittance, at this unsigned restaurant (the owners are still thinking up a name) a little northeast of Tica Bus. It's so good that they've had to build a second comedor in what was the mechanics' workshop opposite.

Doña Pilar (Map p463; dishes US$2-4; ⏱ 6-9pm Mon-Sat) Get mouthwatering *típico* (regional) fare at this popular evening *fritanga* (sidewalk BBQ). Chicken or enchiladas are served with *gallo pinto*, chopped pickled cabbage and plantain chips. On Sunday, Doña Pilar prepares a big tub of *baho* (plantain and beef stew), which is a tasty local favorite (noon to 2pm only).

La Cazuela (Map p463; dishes US$2-12; ⏱ 8am-10pm) An enduringly popular choice, this place has a large menu suitable for every budget. It specializes in seafood, which is OK but not what you can find on the coast. You're sure to find something that appeals, however, and the overall quality is high. You are what you eat, so think twice (or not…) about the brain and testicle soup.

Licuados Ananda (Map p463; mains US$1.20-3, lunch buffet US$2.20; 🕑 7am-9pm Mon-Sat) This outdoor vegetarian restaurant overlooks lush gardens near the Montoya statue west of Martha Quezada. As well as a fabulous array of *licuados* (sweet fruit juice blends), it has a decent if unarousing lunch buffet (11am to 3pm) and other snacks.

For other food options try:

Comida a la Vista (Map p463; lunch US$2-5; 🕑 11:30am-3pm Mon-Sat) Another excellent noontide choice, but get there early for maximum choice; has vegetarian options.

Cafetín Tonalli (Map p463; dishes US$2-6; 🕑 7am-3pm Mon-Sat) Yogurt, herbal tea and inviting lunches, in the lovely garden at the back of this pleasant café. There's also an attached bakery, run by a women's co-op.

Elsewhere in Managua

All the usual overpriced, mediocre fast-food franchises can be found at Plaza Inter and Metrocentro. The latter also houses **Casa del Café** (Map p458; ☎ 271 9535; light meals US$2.50-5; 🖳), which, in spite of its location in the mall, is a pleasant place to sip cappuccino or nibble on decadent brownies. It's got wi-fi access.

La Hora del Taco (Map p458; Hilton Hotel 1c arriba; dishes US$1.70-6; 🕑 noon-midnight) In the trendy back streets southeast of Metrocentro, this upbeat orange spot has an airy upstairs lounge and dining area and some seriously good, stylishly presented Mexican food at fairly córdoba-stretching prices.

Marea Alta (Map p458; ☎ 276 2459; Hilton Hotel 1c abajo; mains US$6-15) Bad news first: it's set in a group of tasteless neon-signed bar-restaurants behind the Hilton Hotel, and the waiters wear sailor suits. But the seafood is truly excellent; with delicate fish *carpaccios* a suitable warm-up for mixed platters of grilled prawns, squid, and fish or tasty steamed black clams. Service (aye-aye sir) is excellent and most seating is outside on the covered terrace.

El Churrasco (Map p458; Rotonda El Güegüense; steaks US$11-17) Blow the budget on a meaty meal here. Despite being located on a busy rotonda (traffic circle), there's little traffic noise, and the atmosphere is boosted by unobtrusive live

music. There's polite service, and a wide range of steaks as well as a decent (for Nicaragua) choice of overpriced wines.

DRINKING & NIGHTLIFE

Managua is far and away the country's nightlife capital. There are three particularly interesting zones: the Zona Rosa around Carr Masaya where there are several *discotecas*, the area around the Intur office, and Bello Horizonte, where there's a cluster of boisterous bars. There's no real gay or lesbian scene here.

Shannon Bar (Map p463; 🕑 4pm-2am) There's bottled Guinness, darts and quiet corners at this low-key Irish pub in Barrio Martha Quezada. It's a popular meeting point for travelers and locals.

Bar La Curva (Map p463; Av Bolívar) Featuring live music at 10pm weekends, this open-air bar, with its mellow globe lights and tropical ambience, oozes a laid-back vibe. It's just south of the Crowne Plaza. There are several other choices around here, including Fresh Hill (Map p463) tucked off the road in a garden setting.

Los Ídolos (Map p458; ☎ 249 0517; Rotonda Bello Horizonte; med pizzas US$4-7) The centerpiece of the boisterous Bello Horizonte scene, this cracking bar is always lively with folk downing pizzas and crates of beer. The jukebox competes for attention against the mariachi hordes: smiling assassins who will make or break your night.

Two blocks east of the Tica Bus station, Bar Goussen (Map p463) is a buzzy local bar and a great spot for a couple of cold ones. And that's not just lazy journalistic cliché – the beer (US$0.65) comes out of the fridge at Arctic temperatures. Sit at a table or perch at the long green bar and chat to the sociable barrio locals.

Live Music

La Casa de los Mejía Godoy (Map p463; ☎ 222 6110; www.losmejiagodoy.org; Costado Oeste de Plaza Inter; cover US$4-10) Revolutionary-era singers Carlos and Luis Enrique Mejía Godoy and other artists perform their famous Nicaraguan folk songs at their new venue opposite the Crowne Plaza hotel. It's an appealing, thatched space with friendly staff. There's live music from Thursday to Saturday; for the bigger-name concerts, it's wise to drop in the day before to buy your ticket.

Bar La Cavanga (Map p461; ☎ 228 1098; Centro Cultural Managua; cover US$4; ☺ from 9:30pm Thu-Sat) Right in the middle of what was once central Managua but was devastated by the 1972 earthquake, this '50s-era gem stages live folk and jazz shows. It's a lot of fun, and very atmospheric, but it's definitely a place to take a taxi to.

Discotecas

Quetzal (Map p458; ☎ 277 0890) Near Rotonda de Centroamérica, Quetzal has been going strong for years, with one of the city's largest and liveliest dance floors. Salsa, merengue and *cumbia* (Colombian dance tunes) are in heavy rotation at this cavernous club.

XS (Map p458; ☎ 277 3806; Carr Masaya Km 4.5; ☺ Wed-Sat) This happy shiny modern club, one of several in this zone, draws plenty of beautiful young Managuans with its curious blend of danceable music.

Island Taste (Map p458; ☎ 240 0010) On weekends the Caribbean crowd packs the floor to *soca* (defined by fast beats and calypso-like undertones) and reggae grooves at this spot on Km 6.5 of the Carr Norte.

ENTERTAINMENT
Theater & Cinemas

Alianza Francesa (Map p458) One block north of the Mexican embassy, with indie films screened once or twice weekly. Check www.clickmanagua.com (actividades/cine alternativa) for show times.

Cinema Plaza Inter (Map p463; ☎ 225 5090; top fl, Plaza Inter; tickets US$2.80)

Cinemark (Map p458; ☎ 271 9037; Metrocentro; tickets US$2.80)

Teatro Rubén Darío (Map p461; ☎ 222 7426; www.tnrubendario.gob.ni) This theater hosts high-quality plays, concerts, and exhibitions by national and visiting artists.

Sport

Estadio Nacional (Map p463; tickets around US$1.50-5) Managua's Bóer baseball team faces its first-division rivals from October to April at this stadium, just northwest of Barrio Martha Quezada. Weekend games start at 4pm, weekday games at 6pm. Check www.lnbp.net for schedules.

Estadio Cranshaw (Map p463; tickets around US$1.50-3.50) Professional soccer is played at this stadium, adjacent to the Estadio Nacional, from September to April. Games are at 3pm Sunday.

SHOPPING

Almost anything can be found in the huge, chaotic Mercado Central (Map p458), commonly known as Mercado Roberto Huembes. A large section is devoted to *artesanías* (handicrafts) from around the country. Scores of vendors display hammocks from Tipitapa and pottery from San Juan del Oriente, as well as woodwork, leather bags and rocking chairs. Take bus 119 from Plaza España and watch your valuables. The other major markets, well located around town, stock mostly food and household items.

GETTING THERE & AWAY
Air

The airport is small and manageable, with a modern international section and a quainter domestic terminal alongside. In the international section there's an all-card ATM, car hire, and a post office with internet access. See p459 for transport details.

La Costeña (☎ 263 2142) and **Atlantic Airlines** (☎ 233 2791) both have offices in the airport. Often you can show up and book a flight out for the same afternoon, but it's wise to call ahead and make a reservation (no credit card needed). Always book your return flight when you arrive at your destination.

The two airlines charge the same fares; La Costeña has more departures. One-way fares are 60% to 65% of the return fare. The following prices are samples of round-trip fares on common routes.

Bluefields US$127; six Monday to Saturday, four Sunday

Corn Islands US$164; four daily

Puerto Cabezas US$149; four Monday to Saturday, three Sunday

San Carlos US$116; twice daily Monday to Friday, daily weekends

Bus
INTERNATIONAL

International buses are run by **Tica Bus** (Map p463; ☎ 222 6094; www.ticabus.com), **King Quality** (Map p463; ☎ 222 3065; www.kingqualityca.com), **Trans-Nica** (Map p458; ☎ 270 3133; www.transnica.com) and **Transportes El Sol** (Map p463; ☎ 222 7785), all with daily departures to other Central American destinations.

Principal international bus departures:

San José, Costa Rica Tica Bus (US$12.50; 9hr; 6am, 7am, noon; US$17 *ejecutivo* around noon); King Quality (US$19; 9hr; 1:30pm); TransNica (US$12.50; 9hr; 5:30am, 7am, 10am; US$25 *ejecutivo*; 8hr; noon)

Panama City Tica Bus (6am & 7am) Services to San José connect with onward service to Panama City (US$37.50 total), a further 18 hour journey.

Tegucigalpa, Honduras King Quality (US$28; 8hr; 5:30am, 10:30am); Tica Bus (US$20; 7-8hr; 5am, 2pm) Tica Bus' morning service continues to San Pedro Sula (US$28)

San Salvador, El Salvador Tica Bus (US$25; 11hr, 5am; US$30 *ejecutivo* around noon); Transportes El Sol (US$27; 11 hr; 6am); King Quality (US$33; 10hr; 3:30am, 5:30am, 10:30am)

Guatemala City King Quality (US$60; 17 hours; 2:30am, 3:30am) Also, Tica Bus' 5am service to San Salvador continues on next day to Guatemala City (US$36; another 5hr).

DOMESTIC

Intercity buses depart from the city's major markets (see Map p458). Buses heading for southwestern destinations and the Costa Rican border depart from Mercado Roberto Huembes; for León and the border with Honduras from **Mercado Israel Lewites (Bóer)** (☎ 265 2152); and for Matagalpa, Estelí and other northern destinations, including the Honduran border, as well as Rama, for the Caribbean coast, and San Carlos, from **Mercado Mayoreo** (☎ 233 4235).

On the routes to Granada, León, Rivas and a few other large towns, there are additional services in microbuses (minivans). These are quicker and more comfortable. Microbuses for León, Masaya, and Granada depart from opposite the UCA university, others from their corresponding bus stations.

Particularly at Mercado Roberto Huembes, aggressive touts will accost you and find you a seat on a bus to your destination in exchange for a few córdobas. In any case, you're better off simply talking to the bus conductors who are constantly bawling out their destination.

Main destinations include the following.

Estelí (US$2.25; 2¼hr; almost half-hourly 3:30am-6pm; US$3 express services; 2hr; 5:45am to 5:45pm; Mercado Mayoreo)

Granada ordinarios (US$0.65; 1hr; every 15min 5am-10pm; Mercado R Huembes); microbuses (US$1; 45min; every 20min 5:40am-8pm; UCA)

León expresos (US$1; 1¼hr; every 30min); ordinarios (US$0.80; 2¼hr; every 20min 6:30am to 5pm via old highway; Mercado Bóer); microbuses (US$1.25; 1¼hr; depart when full; UCA)

Masaya microbuses (US$0.70; 30min; every 20min; UCA); ordinarios (US$0.35; 40min; every 25min; Mercado R Huembes)

Matagalpa (US$3 express; 2hr; hourly; US$2.15 regular, 2½ hr, every 30min 5:30am-6pm; Mercado Mayoreo)

Ocotal (US$3.70; 3½hr; roughly hourly 5:10am-5:15pm; Mercado Mayoreo)

Rama (US$8.30; 5-6hr; 6 daily; Mercado Mayoreo)

Rivas ordinarios (US$1.10; 2½hr; every 25mins 4am to 6:30pm); expresos (US$2.20; 1½ hr,; 10 daily); microbuses (US$1.55; 1½hr; every 30min 5am to 6:45pm) All depart from Mercado R Huembes.

San Carlos (US$8.30; 8-10hr; 6 daily; Mercado Mayoreo)

San Juan del Sur (US$3.30; 2½hr; 2 daily; Mercado R Huembes) Otherwise change in Rivas or jump off a Sapoá-bound bus at the San Juan junction and wait for a connection.

Sapoá (Costa Rican border) (US$3.30; 2hr; half-hourly 6am to 5pm; Mercado R Huembes)

GETTING AROUND
Bus

Local buses are frequent and crowded; watch your pockets. Buses do not generally stop en route – look for the nearest bus shelter. The fare is US$0.25.

Useful routes include the following.

109 Plaza de la República to Mercado Roberto Huembes, stopping en route at Plaza Inter.

110 Mercado Bóer to Mercado Mayoreo, via the UCA, Metrocentro, Rotonda de Centroamérica, Mercado R Huembes and Mercado Iván Montenegro.

116 Montoya statue, Plaza Inter, Mercado Oriental, Rotonda Bello Horizonte.

118 From Parque Las Piedrecitas, heads down Carr Sur, then east, passing by the Mercado Israel Lewites (Bóer), Rotonda El Güegüense (Plaza España), Plaza Inter and Mercado Oriental on its way to Mercado Mayoreo.

119 From Lindavista to Mercado R Huembes, with stops at Rotonda El Güegüense and the UCA.

Car

The usual multinationals compete with a few local operators. It's significantly more expensive to hire a car at the airport. Most operators will deliver cars to where you are staying in Managua. Lower-priced operators include:

Budget (Map p458; ☎ 266 6226; www.budget.com.ni; Montoya 1c abajo) Competitive rates and good service.

Dollar Rent a Car (Map p463; ☎ 266 3620; www .dollar.com.ni) Weekly rates start at US$160/119 in high/low season. Office in Hotel Crowne Plaza.

Lugo Rent-a-Car (Map p458; ☎ 266 5240; www .lugorentacar.com.ni; Casa del Obrero 5c sur, 3 abajo) High-season rates from US$20.

Taxi

Finding a cab in Managua is never a problem; drivers honk as they pass to signal their availability. Drivers pick up additional passengers along the way, so you can hail a taxi even if it's occupied. Around the bus stations and at night do not get into a cab that has more than one person in it.

Taxis are not metered and fares should be agreed on before you get in; locals always vigorously prenegotiate the fare. The standard rate for a short ride is about US$1 to US$1.50 (20 to 30 córdobas) per person; longer journeys right across town should not exceed US$2.50 per person. Fares go up a little after dark.

AROUND MANAGUA

LAGUNAS DE XILOÁ & APOYEQUE

Half a dozen *lagunas*, or volcanic crater lakes, lie near Managua's city limits. Of these, the best for swimming is **Laguna de Xiloá**, on the

Península de Chiltepe, about 20km northwest of Managua off the road to León. Xiloá is also suitable for diving; its clear waters provide the habitat for at least 15 endemic aquatic species. Though crowded on weekends, the *laguna* remains quite peaceful during the week. There are a few food kiosks, though you can still see the damage from Hurricane Mitch. You pay US$1 per person to enter the area. To get here, take bus 110 from Managua's UCA bus station (p467) to Ciudad Sandino, where you can catch an onward bus to the lagoons.

A contrast to developed Xiloá is picturesque **Laguna de Apoyeque**, set deep within a steep 500m-high volcanic crater; small alligators bask beside its sulfurous waters. It's a strenuous 40-minute scramble-hike from Xiloá.

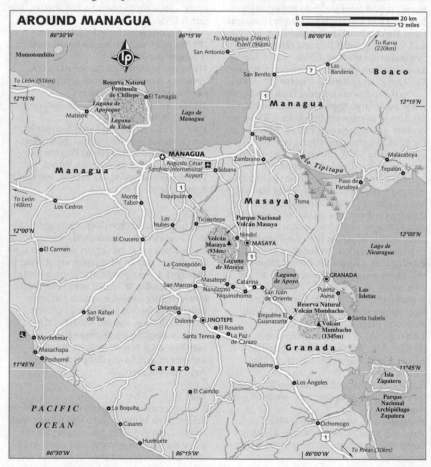

AROUND MANAGUA

TIPITAPA

This rural town 21km east of Managua is mostly visited for its *aguas termales* (hot springs). The **complex** (entry US$0.55) consists of three pools of varying temperatures (the hot one, is), gardens and sauna. There's also a restaurant here doing fish plates (US$2.80). It makes a relaxing day trip from the city. Buses depart regularly from Managua's Mercado R Huembes.

POCHOMIL & PACIFIC BEACHES

A famous Nicaraguan vacation spot, **Pochomil** is a gorgeous swimming beach on the Pacific coast 62km from Managua. The promenade is stocked with bars, restaurants, and a few hotels which, the place having been eclipsed by San Juan del Sur in recent years, are usually fairly empty (Easter apart). The restaurant owners fight (sometimes literally) for your custom. The beach is wide, sandy and good for swimming or sunning; the sunsets are fabulous.

Dozens of thatched-roof restaurants prepare fresh seafood, each charging roughly the same. Red snapper costs US$6 and lobster is US$8.

If you want to stay, **Hotel Altamar** (☎ 269 9204; r with fan/air-con US$15/25; P ⊠) is a bright, cheery place with hammocks and a variety of mediocre rooms that accommodate up to three people. The restaurant, with lovely views, has moderate prices and tasty seafood.

The fishing village of **Masachapa** is just 2km north of Pochomil. While the beach here isn't as inviting, it feels more real and is significantly cheaper. **Hospedaje Bar Flipper** (☎ 269 7509; r US$6), where the road branches off toward Pochomil, has concrete boxes with adequate beds, fans and basic bathrooms.

There's great surfing in these parts; the best breaks are north of Montelimar (where the resort complex has a Visa ATM) at **Playa Los Cardones**. Here, overpriced but enticing **Los Cardones Surf Lodge** (☎ 618 7314; www.loscardones.com; s/d/tr incl all meals US$82/113/138; P) rents boards (US$15 per day), gives surf lessons (US$10 per hour) and offers day use of their facilities (US$10 per person, redeemable in beer or food). It also offers accommodations in ecofriendly (powerless) cabañas. There's plenty for nonsurfers, including turtle-watching and horse riding.

Buses from Managua's Mercado Bóer go to Masachapa and Pochomil (US$1.10, 1½ hours) every 40 minutes from 7am to 5:30pm. For Los Cardones, get a San Cayetano–bound bus from the same station. Jump off at California and walk, hitch, or organize a lift the last 15km.

NORTHERN NICARAGUA

Cooler than the coastal lowlands, the mountainous region just south of Honduras is cowboy country, with luminous cloud formations and crisp, chilly nights. The departments of Matagalpa, Estelí, Jinotega and Madriz compose this highland region, rich with coffee, tobacco and livestock.

Estelí is the principal town between Managua and the Honduran border, and the Miraflor Nature Reserve lies just northeast of it. South of Estelí, a turnoff at Sébaco (Route 3) leads to the pleasant mountain towns of Matagalpa and Jinotega, and several private reserves and coffee plantations that make for intriguing visits.

Torn apart by Hurricane Mitch in 1998, the area has since bounced back. Fair-trade coffee buyers, as well as various investments in education and infrastructure by foreign aid groups and governments has given the region a sound basis for the future.

MATAGALPA
pop 80,230

The coffee capital of Matagalpa (682m) is blessed with a refreshing climate that comes as delicious relief after the sweaty lowlands. Surrounded by lovely green mountains, it's a bustling, unkempt but prosperous town spread unevenly over hilly terrain. Though tiny here, the Río Grande de Matagalpa is the nation's second-longest river, flowing all the way to the Caribbean.

Spanish conquistadors found several indigenous communities coexisting here, including the Molagüina, whose tongue-twisting Nahuatl name for the town, Matlatlcallipan (House of Nets), became Matagalpa.

Matagalpa makes a good destination with its down-to-earth ways, friendly people, proximity to cloud-forest reserves, and selection of great places to stay.

Orientation

Bordered on its western edge by the river, Matagalpa's central zone lies between two principal plazas, Parque Morazán on the north side and Parque Rubén Darío to the south. The municipal cathedral faces Morazán; budget accommodations are concentrated around Darío. Ten blocks west of the latter you'll find the market and bus station. The main street,

NICARAGUA

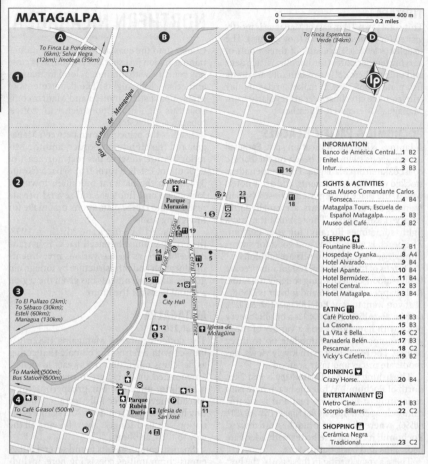

MATAGALPA

0 ——————————— 400 m
0 ——————————— 0.2 miles

To Finca La Ponderosa
(6km); Selva Negra
(12km); Jinotega (35km)

To Finca Esperanza
Verde (34km)

Río Grande de Matagalpa

Cathedral

Parque
Morazán

Av José Benito Escobar

Av Central Don Bartolomé Martínez

City Hall

To El Pullazo (2km);
To Sébaco (30km);
Estelí (60km);
Managua (130km)

Iglesia de
Molagüina

To Market (500m);
Bus Station (500m)

To Café Girasol (500m)

Parque
Rubén
Darío

Iglesia de
San José

INFORMATION	
Banco de América Central...**1**	B2
Enitel...................................**2**	C2
Intur....................................**3**	B3

SIGHTS & ACTIVITIES	
Casa Museo Comandante Carlos	
Fonseca.............................**4**	B4
Matagalpa Tours, Escuela de	
Español Matagalpa..........**5**	B3
Museo del Café.................**6**	B2

SLEEPING	
Fountaine Blue...................**7**	B1
Hospedaje Oyanka............**8**	A4
Hotel Alvarado.................**9**	B4
Hotel Apante..................**10**	B4
Hotel Bermúdez..............**11**	B4
Hotel Central..................**12**	B3
Hotel Matagalpa..............**13**	B4

EATING	
Café Picoteo..................**14**	B3
La Casona......................**15**	B3
La Vita é Bella................**16**	C2
Panadería Belén.............**17**	B3
Pescamar......................**18**	C2
Vicky's Cafetín...............**19**	B2

DRINKING	
Crazy Horse...................**20**	B4

ENTERTAINMENT	
Metro Cine....................**21**	B3
Scorpio Billares..............**22**	C2

SHOPPING	
Cerámica Negra	
Tradicional...................**23**	C2

Av José Benito Escobar, runs between the two parques, while roughly parallel Av Central Don Bartolomé Martínez, named after local *indigena* who became president, also runs from Parque Morazán. Confusingly, locals tend to refer to the former as Av Central, and the latter as Av de los Bancos.

Information

There are numerous cybercafés dotted through the center. One, Cyber Molaguiña, is famous for its coffee and juices, but was closed and due to change location at research time.

Banco de América Central (BAC) With Visa/Plus/MC/Cirrus/Amex ATM, a block east of Parque Morazán.

Enitel A block east of the cathedral; public phones are prevalent.

Intur (☎ 612 7060; ⏰ 9am-5pm) Just off the main drag, it's run by friendly staff who can suggest activities in the area, including visits to nearby *fincas* (farms). Closed for lunch.

Post office One block or so south of Parque Morazán.

Sights

Matagalpa's **cathedral** is one of several 19th-century churches that grace the city. Its interior is fairly unadorned, apart from the ornate plasterwork in the vaults of the central nave. Just down from here, the **Museo del Café** (Av Escobar; admission free; ⏰ 9am-12:30pm & 2-6pm) has a bit of everything Matagalpan – local history, archaeology, culture – and does indeed include some information about coffee, with cups of the local brew to try. The friendly staff can also organize tours in the surrounding area and are generous with providing you with information.

Matagalpa is known throughout Nicaragua as the birthplace of Carlos Fonseca, a martyr of the Sandinista revolution. His home has been converted to a museum, the **Casa Museo Comandante Carlos Fonseca**, but at the time of research it wasn't open to the public.

Activities & Tours

There's heaps to do in the surrounding area (see p472). You can learn more from Intur or the Museo del Café. A charitable setup that accepts volunteers, Café Girasol, two blocks southwest of the main bus station right by the main river bridge, sells detailed leaflets for a number of **self-guided walks** in the Matagalpa area (US$1.40). They vary in difficulty and length, from four to eight hours.

Matagalpa Tours (☎ 772 0108, 647 4680; www.matagalpatours.com; ☾ Mon-Fri & Sat morning, always contactable by cell phone) is a well-run, English-speaking setup that offers a wide range of excursions in Matagalpa and the surrounding hills. These range from day hikes in the Cerro Apante dry forest or Cerro El Arenal wet forest to tours of abandoned gold mines, coffee plantations, and even El Castillo del Cacao, a local operation producing organic chocolate in a range of sinful flavors. Excursions are cheaper the more people go. For two, think US$15 each for a couple of hours, US$25 for a half-day and US$50 for a whole day.

Courses

Escuela de Español Matagalpa (☎ 772 0108, 654 4824; www.matagalpa.info) Run out of the same office as Matagalpa Tours, this has a flexible program of classes for different abilities and requirements. Packages including homestay or hotel accommodations and excursions cost from US$160 for a 15-hour week.

Festivals & Events

Don't bother with a lovey-dovey candlelit dinner on February 14 when you could be here for the boisterous partying to celebrate the anniversary of Matagalpa achieving city status. The city's **annual festival** is held during the week of September 24, in honor of its patron saint, La Virgen de la Merced (Our Lady of Mercy). The **Festival de Polkas, Mazurcas y Jamaquellos** livens up the closing weekend celebration with traditional dances from Nicaragua's five northern departments.

Sleeping

The least expensive places are near Parque Rubén Darío.

Hotel Bermúdez (☎ 612 5660; s/d US$2.20/4.40) This offers a motherly welcome and rooms that are clean and decent, if a little run-down. Most have their own cold-water bathroom; all are different, with those at the front quite a bit lighter. The mattresses also vary substantially in quality.

Hotel Matagalpa (☎ 772 3834; r with/without bathroom US$6/4) One block east of the park, the friendly and secure Matagalpa is a favorite among travelers. In spite of thin walls, the fan-cooled rooms offer decent value for the money. You'll need healthy lungs to summon the boss down the long front corridor.

Hospedaje Oyanka (☎ 772 0057; s/d US$3.80/6.60) This clean and cheap flophouse is located behind a little café halfway between the bus station and Parque Rubén Darío. The rooms are OK for the price and share clean bathrooms. Turn left out of the bus station and follow this road; it bends to the right and the place is just ahead on your right.

Hotel Apante (☎ 772 6890; Av Escobar; s/d US$5/8, with bathroom US$7/10, with cable TV & air-con US$12/15; ✷) Bang on Parque Rubén Darío and with plenty of bang for your buck; with a wide choice of value-packed rooms, this place is tops. If you've been traveling a while, you'll weep at how good the showers are. Some rooms have views over the hills but these also suffer from disco noise at weekends. The doorbell is around the corner to your left.

Hotel Alvarado (☎ 772 2830; Av Escobar; s/d US$7.20/13.90) This appealing and courteous central pad has spacious, clean and attractive rooms with bathroom, cable TV, and fans. There's also a small common balcony that's a nice place to sit and watch the street. If there's nobody about, ask in the pharmacy below.

Hotel Central (☎ 772 3140; Av Escobar; s/d US$10/13.90) It's tough to beat this great place on the main street. The modern rooms are very comfortable with cable TV, good bathroom and fan. There are numerous appealing decorative touches, and the place is spotless, friendly and professional.

Fountaine Blue (☎ 772 2733; d with/without bathroom US$21/15) Another heartwarmingly good Matagalpa sleep-spot, with modern, comfortable rooms with big beds and cable TV. The owner is exceptionally benevolent, and a simple but apparently bottomless breakfast is included

---

DAY TRIPPING AROUND MATAGALPA

Fincas & Ecolodges

There are several *fincas* (farms) to visit in the Matagalpa area, giving you the chance to check out the coffee plantations, as well as explore the forested hills. Most famous is **Selva Negra** (☎ 612 5713; www.selvanegra.com; dm/d/cottages US$10/30/50-150; ℗), founded in the 1880s by German immigrants who came at the invitation of the Nicaraguan government to grow coffee. Over half the estate is protected rain forest, covered by a network of trails – be warned, the higher ones are very tough, steep scrambles – where you can see howler monkeys, ocelots, and quetzals. You can stay here – the Bavarian-style cottages are the most appealing option – or just visit, in which case you pay US$1.35, redeemable at the café-restaurant. Selva Negra is a slow 12km north of Matagalpa; take any Jinotega bus and get off at the signed turnoff, marked by an old military tank. From there it's a pleasant 2km walk.

Six kilometers north of Matagalpa is the peaceful **Finca La Ponderosa** (☎ 772 2951), an organic coffee farm. The friendly family that run it will show you round, taking you through the labor-intensive coffee-making process. There are forest trails, a swimming hole under a waterfall, horseback rides, plus food and accommodations available. This is one of several properties on the agricultural tourism Coffee Route – you can book and get more details at Intur or the Museo del Café in Matagalpa.

Thirty-five kilometers east of Matagalpa on the edge of the cloud forest, **Finca Esperanza Verde** (☎ 772 5003; www.fincaesperanzaverde.org; camping per person US$6; s/d US$30/45; ℗) is a delightfully remote and relaxing ecolodge with accommodations high on both comfort and romance. You can hike three short forest trails here; day visitors pay US$1.10. From Matagalpa's northern bus station, get off the Pancasan-bound bus at Yucul; it's an hour's uphill walk from here.

---

in the rates. Just across the bridge that leads to the Jinotega highway.

Eating

Vicky's Cafetín (breakfast US$1.50) Just down from Parque Morazán, Vicky's serves breakfast, snacks and sweet treats under a breezy pavilion. *Raspados* – crushed tropical fruit over shaved ice – are a popular dessert.

Panadería Belén (snacks US$0.60-2.50; ☾ 8am-6pm) The Belén is a decent little café and bakery that comes into its own at weekends, when it serves deliciously greasy *nacatamales* (banana leaf–wrapped bundles of cornmeal, pork, vegetables and herbs).

Café Picoteo (☎ 772 6000; dishes US$2-3; ☾ 10am-10pm) This place is a cozy local hangout serving espresso and cappuccino, as well as a variety of snacks – pizzas, tacos and burgers. Behind the café is a popular local bar; a good place for a beer but it comes with very laid-back service.

La Casona (☎ 772 3901; Av Escobar; mains US$2-4, lunch US$2.40) Both bar and restaurant, this spot has an ample buffet lunch, and a pleasant rear patio down the stairs. The food isn't remarkable – roast chicken is the main choice, but it's a popular spot, and gets particularly convivial

on Friday and Saturday nights, when there's live music out the back.

El Pullazo (☎ 772 3935; Carr Managua Km 125; dishes US$4; ☾ 11am-11pm) On the road south, about 2km from the center, this place is in a slow building process – you'll likely see the wires in the ceiling for some time to come. No matter, there are just three dishes: chargrilled chicken or pork, and beef; the eponymous *pullazo* (marinated beef fillet), served with *güirila* (green corn tortilla); and *gallo pinto*. It's delicious, and remarkably good value for the high quality involved. Cab fare to here is US$1.50 to US$2.50. There's a *discoteca* just up the road if you want to make a night of it.

Pescamar (☎ 772 3548; dishes US$4-6; ☾ noon-9pm) Sizable servings of fish and seafood in a spacious restaurant northeast of the center. The prawn salad is particularly good if you're a mayonnaise fan. The service, however, is almost comically grumpy.

La Vita é Bella (☎ 772 5476; pasta dishes from US$4; ☾ 1-10pm Tue-Sun) Difficult to find but worth the search, this hidden gem, located on a narrow lane, serves up tasty Italian and vegetarian specialties in an intimate setting. Closed for holidays at time of research, but locals assure it's as good as ever.

Drinking & Entertainment

La Casona is a good spot for a few drinks. One block east of Parque Morazán, Scorpio Billares is the place to impress the local teens with your pool skills. There are heaps of tables, paid for by time.

Crazy Horse (11am-1am) Half a block west of Parque Rubén Darío, this easygoing bar is fairly upmarket for a Nicaraguan drinking spot. With wagon wheels and saddles imparting a cowboy theme and plenty of tequila and cocktails lubricating the throats as the evening gets on, it does the job just fine.

Metro Cinema (Av Martíne; tickets US$1.20) The town's cinema screens Hollywood hits thrice daily for a pittance.

Shopping

Matagalpa is known for its fine black pottery, and some pieces are small enough to easily stow in a backpack. Workshops are scattered throughout town, including one in the center of Parque Rubén Darío.

Cerámica Negra Tradicional, two blocks east of the cathedral, displays the work of Doña Ernestina Rodríguez, including jewelry and tiny tea sets.

Getting There & Away

The main **bus station** (772 4659) is about 1km west of Parque Darío. It's known as Cotran Sur; another minor bus station at the other end of town serves local destinations.

Estelí (US$1.40; 1¾hr; every 30min 5:15am to 5:45pm)
Jinotega (US$1.35; 1¼-2hr; every 30min 5am to 6pm) Journey time depends on how the bus copes with the hill.
León (US$2.75; 2½hr; 6am) Alternatively take any Estelí-bound bus and transfer at San Isidro.
Managua (US$3 express, 2hr, hourly 5:20am to 5:20pm; US$2.15 regular, 2½hr, every 30min 3.35am to 6pm)
Masaya (US$2.55; 3hr; 2pm & 3:30pm)

JINOTEGA

pop 41,130

Aptly nicknamed City of Mists, Jinotega is a quiet town set in a fertile kilometer-high valley in a mountainous coffee-growing region. Murals on the plaza testify to the heavy fighting that took place here and in the surrounding areas during the war years; the town was also massively flooded in the wake of Hurricane Mitch in 1998. The regular mists add a beauty to the town but also can make it cold.

The steep drive up from Matagalpa is one of the most scenic in the country and rea-

son enough for a visit to Jinotega. Colorful roadside stands along the potholed road sell flowers and big bundles of carrots, beets and cabbages.

There's an **Intur office** (782 4552; jinotega@intur .gob.ni) at the southeast corner of Parque Central, while opposite the Hotel Rosa is a **municipal tourist office** (www.jinotega.com) that offers tours and can arrange guides.

Sights

Though unremarkable from the outside, the **church** has a fine white interior bristling with saints; it's an impressive collection of religious art. The most famous statue is the Cristo Negro, a black Christ reminiscent of the more renowned one at Esquipulas in Guatemala.

Across the plaza from the church, a pair of fading **murals** on the walls of the old Somoza jail (now a youth center) serve as reminders of the revolutionary years. A monument to Sandinista leader Carlos Fonseca rests amid the tall trees of Jinotega's charming central plaza.

Sleeping

Hotel Rosa (782 2472; r per person US$1.60-2.80) Run by a gloriously feisty old matriarch, this appealing but very dilapidated old building is about the cheapest spot in town. The rooms, which share bathroom facilities, are dark and musty. The more expensive ones have better beds, but none of them is really honeymoon quality. It's one block east of the park.

Hotel Central (782 2063; Calle Central; r with shared bathroom per person US$3.30, s/d with bathroom US$9.50/12.20) Right by the Esso station (the standard local landmark) in the heart of town, this is a friendly spot with various choices of room. The swish en suite pads have TV, hot water and a fan, and are fairly bright. The cheaper rooms are gradually being made over.

Hotel Bosawás (829 0884; r per person US$5) This welcoming place is a real budget gem and offers excellent value for your córdoba. The rooms are bright and inviting, with polished floorboards. The whole joint, including the shared bathrooms, is absolutely spotless. There's also a good family room with bathroom and cable TV (US$17). The hotel is three blocks north of the church.

Hotel Sollentuna Hem (782 2324; s with/without bathroom US$11/8, d/tr with bathroom US$16/20; P) It's

NICARAGUA

another favorite among travelers; two blocks east, 4½ blocks north of the central plaza. This pleasant hotel (named after a barrio of Stockholm) has hospitable management, and dark but clean rooms which range from cozy singles to roomier doubles with decent beds, cable TV, bathroom and hot water.

Eating & Drinking

There are a few street-food stalls around the park, and *fritangas* fire up around town in the evenings. For more elaborate meals, head to La Colmena, just off Calle Central.

Soda El Tico (☎ 782 2059; buffet lunch US$2; 🕑 7:30am-10pm; 🗶) This gleaming spot wipes all the buffet competitors off the map. Some days it seems that the whole town comes here for lunch. There's a little patio, work from local artists on the walls, and a good choice of steaming plates. It even serves beer. Get there before 1:30pm. There's a simpler branch near the southern bus station.

Cafetín Trebol (dishes US$1-2.20) This unassuming little café on the central park has a small menu consisting mostly of tacos, fried chicken and hamburgers, but it also serves decent breakfasts and refreshing *raspados*.

Sopas Coyote's Bar (dishes US$1-3) Just off Calle Central, round the corner from Soda El Tico, this friendly little spot serves a decent *comida corriente* (mixed plate) and is also a fine spot for a bit of liquid refreshment.

Getting There & Away

There are two bus stations. Northbound buses depart from the main market beside the highway east of town. The **bus station** (☎ 632 4530) for Matagalpa, Estelí and Managua buses sits near the town's southern entrance.

Estelí (US$2.20; 1¾hr; 5 daily)

Managua (express US$3.90; 3½ hr; 10 daily; *ordinario* US$2.80, every 30min) Both via Matagalpa.

Matagalpa (US$1.35; 1½hr; every 30min 5am-6pm)

ESTELÍ

pop 90,290

A place of amazing sunsets and bristling with cowboy hats, Estelí is the center of an agriculturally rich highland valley and is capital of the department of the same name. Tobacco, grains, sesame and other crops, as well as livestock and cheese, are produced in the surrounding area. Unpretentious, nontouristy and very Nicaraguan, Estelí makes a great place to visit.

Partly because of its strategic location on the road to Honduras, Estelí saw heavy fighting during the revolution – it was bombarded in April 1979 and severely damaged – and afterward the town has remained one of the Sandinistas' strongest support bases.

Many *internacionalistas* (volunteers from all over the world who contributed to rebuilding the country) arrived here during the Sandinista years, contributing their efforts to the farming collectives established in the region.

Orientation

The Interamericana Hwy runs north–south along the eastern side of the town; both bus stations are on the highway.

Atypically, Estelí utilizes a street numbering system, and every block is clearly signed. The intersection of Av Central and Calle Transversal is the center of the system. Calles (streets) ascend in number north and south of Calle Transversal; avenidas (avenues) ascend east and west of Av Central. Streets and avenues are suffixed 'NE' (northeast), 'SO' (southwest) etc, according to which quadrant of town they belong to.

Information

Banco America Central (BAC; cnr Calle Transversal & Av 1 SO) All-card-friendly ATM.

Compucenter (Calle Transversal; per hr US$0.60) One of dozens of internet places; also has cheap international phone calls.

Enitel Two blocks east of post office.

Intur (☎ 713 6799; esteli@intur.gob.ni; Calle 2a NE) Friendly tourist office with a range of brochures as well as books to browse.

Post office (cnr Calle Transversal & Av Central)

UCA Miraflor (☎ 713 2971; Av 5a NE; 🕑 8am-1pm, 2-5:30pm) This is the place to go if you're planning a jaunt into the Miraflor reserve. Just north of Calle 9a NE, it's inside the large yard on your right as you enter.

Sights

Galería de Héroes y Mártires (☎ 713 3753; emayorga70@ yahoo.com; Av 1a NE; entry by donation; 🕑 9am-5pm Mon-Sat) is an emotive place to visit, a gallery dedicated to the memory of the town's fallen revolutionaries. The photos of the young men and women who gave their lives are displayed around the single room, and there are various articles and reminiscences dotted among the photos (many translated). The small cabinet of clothes is heart-wrenching. The gallery is

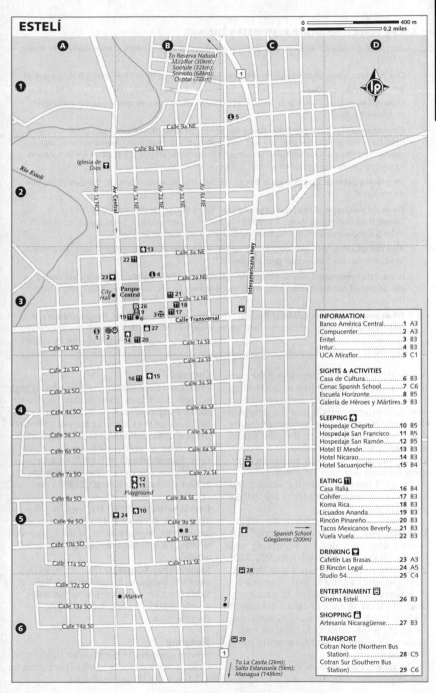

ESTELÍ

INFORMATION
Banco América Central...........1 A3
Compucenter.....................2 A3
Enitel..........................3 B3
Intur...........................4 B3
UCA Miraflor....................5 C1

SIGHTS & ACTIVITIES
Casa de Cultura.................6 B3
Cenac Spanish School............7 C6
Escuela Horizonte...............8 B5
Galería de Héroes y Mártires.9 B3

SLEEPING
Hospedaje Chepito..............10 B5
Hospedaje San Francisco.......11 B5
Hospedaje San Ramón...........12 B5
Hotel El Mesón................13 B3
Hotel Nicarao................14 B3
Hotel Sacuanjoche.............15 B4

EATING
Casa Italia...................16 B4
Cohifer......................17 B3
Koma Rica....................18 B3
Licuados Ananda..............19 B3
Rincón Pinareño..............20 B3
Tacos Mexicanos Beverly.21 B3
Vuela Vuela..................22 B3

DRINKING
Cafetín Las Brasas...........23 A3
El Rincón Legal..............24 A5
Studio 54....................25 C4

ENTERTAINMENT
Cinema Estelí................26 B3

SHOPPING
Artesanía Nicaragüense.......27 B3

TRANSPORT
Cotran Norte (Northern Bus
   Station)...................28 C5
Cotran Sur (Southern Bus
   Station)...................29 C6

NICARAGUA

LOCAL VOICES: A MOTHER REMEMBERS THE WAR

Guillerma Meta Montenegro is the director of the Gallery of Heroes and Martyrs in Estelí (p474).

■ **Did you lose a son or daughter in the Revolution?** My two sons. They died within a week of each other. April 1979.

■ **How old were they?** Seventeen and 14. Well, 14 when he went to the mountain. He turned 15 before he died.

■ **How have things changed since those days?** For the poor, the last 16 years (1990–2006) have been worse than the war. The war was bloody, but at least what food there was, was shared. The liberals have withheld resources from rural Nicaragua. It's difficult for us mothers to see hard-won liberties taken away.

■ **So you are pleased that Ortega is back?** The Sandinistas are the party of the poor. Who else do we have?

■ **What do you hope of the new government?** Three things. Health, education and work. People died to bring us these. And places to live – but no handouts. Small subsidies or loans to help people buy land, but no handouts. That's what sank us last time.

■ **And the USA?** I accept that they didn't want this government to be elected; now they have to accept that the Nicaraguan people wanted it.

■ **Is tourism important?** Very important. In this museum, for example, the worms are eating the photos of our martyrs because we have no money for picture frames. Tourism can help that.

■ **What about American tourists?** (Laughs) They are more than welcome. The people are not responsible for the sins of their leaders. Where would we Nicaraguans be were that the case?!

As told to Andy Symington

run by mothers of the martyrs, and they are the ones who make a visit here so compelling. They are more than willing to share their own stories, providing insight into the struggles that many Nicaraguans experienced (see the boxed text, above). Entry to the gallery is by donation; please be as generous as you can – already many of the photos have been eaten away for want of money for framing.

The 1823 **cathedral** is worth a wander, and murals surrounding the parque central are also interesting.

One of Estelí's most refreshing attractions, **Salto Estanzuela** is a pretty 36m waterfall that forms a deep pool ideal for swimming, and lies outside the city. The road to the falls starts about 1km south of town, just past the hospital, and heads southwest to the community of Estanzuela. This road can be cautiously reached by car or taxi, or take a 6:30am or 1:30pm truck from the market, returning about 1½ hours later. Otherwise, it makes a fine walk, about an hour from town. Bring food and water.

The mountains surrounding the town are very impressive.

Courses

Estelí has a large selection of Spanish language schools, a holdover from its days as a haven for *internacionalistas*. As well as those listed below, ask at the Galería de Héroes y Mártires to see if these mothers of fallen revolutionaries have recommended giving classes.

Cenac Spanish School (☎ 713 2025; www.ibw .com.ni/~cenac; Interamericana Hwy) Homestay plus 20 hours of intensive Spanish costs US$140. It's near Calle 13a.

Escuela Horizonte (☎ 713 4117; www.ibw.com .ni/u/horizont; Av 2 btwn Calles 9 & 10 SE) Gets students involved in the community. Classes cost US$165 per week, for 20 hours of instruction with homestay and scheduled activities.

Spanish School Güegüense (☎ 713 7580; sacuanjo chespanishschool@yahoo.fr; Barrio Primero de Mayo s/n) Six blocks east and one block south of the Shell station, this offers field trips and homestays. Profits go to charitable causes.

Sleeping

Several inexpensive guesthouses lie along Av Central, several blocks south of the center, in a characterful shopping district.

Hospedaje San Ramón (☎ 714 0970; Av Central btwn Calles 7a & 8a SE; s/d US$2.20/3.30) The San Ramón has dark and very basic (four walls, door, bed) rooms behind a shop. Friendly owners, but that's about it. Nonpartners should get two singles unless you want to become partners by accident.

Hospedaje Chepito (☎ 713 3784; Av Central btwn Calles 8a & 9a SE; s/d US$2.40/3.50) A friendly place with nine adequate rooms with a bit of ventilation, and a simple courtyard. It's still not one to show your parents photos of, though.

Hospedaje San Francisco (☎ 713 3787; Av Central btwn Calles 7a & 8a SE; s/d US$2.40/3.90) On the same block as the San Ramón, accommodations here range from narrow, airless rooms to ones with tiny vents over the door and extravagant wallpaper.

Hospedaje Sacuanjoche (☎ 713 2482; Av 1a btwn Calles 2a & 3a SE; s/d US$4/8) This tranquil place has seen better days but has rooms that are cozy and well kept, all with small bathrooms. It's a fine budget choice. Breakfast, served in the aging front dining room, is available for US$1.20.

Hotel Nicarao (☎ 713 2490; Av Central; s/d US$10/12, with bathroom US$15/20) Popular with travelers and also central, this family-run affair is set back from the street around a leafy garden. It makes a fine spot to lounge around or meet other travelers, but it's not quite the value it once was. There's an internet café at the front of the building.

Hotel El Mesón (☎ 713 2655; cnr Av 1a & Calle 3a NE; s/d with fan US$13.50/21; P) This spot has reasonable rooms, with warm showers and cable TV, set around a leafy courtyard. It's pretty good value, although the slightest noise seems to echo through the compound like a gunshot. Ask for a blanket, as it can get chilly at night.

Eating

Licuados Ananda (Calle Transversal; juices US$0.45; 8am-7pm Mon-Sat, 9am-5pm Sun) Set in a garden around an empty swimming pool, this guru-inspired setup has excellent juices and snacks such as veggie burgers (US$0.90). It's east of Av Central.

Koma Rica (Calle 1a NE; dishes US$1-3) This is a popular spot for lunch but really comes into its own in the early evening, when the streetside *fritanga* fires up, and salivating locals queue for the delicious empanadas and brochettes sizzling in the night air.

Tacos Mexicanos Beverly (☎ 713 0009; Av 2a NE; dishes US$2-5; 5:30-11:30pm Tue-Sun) Just southeast of the cathedral, this cheery spot is a fine spot for generous servings of tacos, burritos, döner kebabs, and more. There's an open-air patio and kitschy Mexican decor.

Rincon Pinareño (Av 1a SE; dishes US$2-6; 8:30am-9pm) This popular local place serves excellent, juicy Cuban sandwiches, among other dishes, and also has a selection of cigars. The nicest place to sit is the upstairs terrace.

Vuela Vuela (☎ 713 3830; cnr Calle 3a & Av 1a NE; mains US$7-11) It's worth a splashout at this, Estelí's best restaurant, not least because it runs as a charitable concern for children from broken homes. There's a short but quality menu served in an attractive setting. Meat is what stands out, and the steaks are superbly tender, with tasty sauces. The attached hotel, Los Arcos, is also recommendable (doubles US$45).

La Casita (7:30am-6:30pm Tue-Sat, 9am-6pm Sun) Two kilometers south of town along the Interamericana Hwy, La Casita sits on the lush grounds of Finca Las Nubes. In addition to the best coffee in town, the menu includes fresh baked breads, cheeses, juices and homemade yogurts. A US$0.60 taxi ride will get you there, and it's well worth the trip. Be sure to take a walk around the grounds when you go and greet the geese.

Casa Italia (Av 1a SE near Calle 3a SE; mains US$3-6; noon-9:30pm Tue-Sat, 5-9:30pm Sun) This curious little gardened place has a welcoming boss and is recommended for its very tasty, authentic pasta and pizza dishes. Kick off your meal with a plate of antipasti.

Cohifer (☎ 713 3414; Av 2a NE; mains US$4-7) With an appealing terrace dining area screened from the street by plants, this is a fine hangout for a drink, or to enjoy the wide range of Nicaraguan dishes. The house specialty, *lomo de costilla*, is a steak platter (served on a sizzling grill) that could feed two.

Drinking & Entertainment

Cafetín Las Brasas (Calle 2a NO) Delightfully dark and seedy, Las Brasas, just off Parque Central, serves food but earns its stripes as a drinking den. Try the back if the front doesn't appeal. It's a lively and local evening hangout.

El Rincón Legal (Av 1a NO; 6pm-late) North of Calle 9a, this is an excellent Sandinista bar, with all the posters, murals and slogans you'd expect. There's occasionally live music.

Studio 54 (Interamericana Hwy) The city's most popular *discoteca* is one of several on the Interamericana; this has plenty of space, a pool table, and a lively dance floor.

Cinema Estelí (Calle 1a NE; admission US$2.20) On the south of Parque Central, this quaint single-screener shows a Hollywood hit nightly.

Shopping

Artesanía Nicaragüense (Calle Transversal) Diagonally opposite the Casa de Cultura, this has a good selection of pottery, embroidery and crafted leather items (starting at US$5).

For leather goods and cowboy attire, also check out the shops along Av 1a NO and Av Central.

Getting There & Away

Near each other in the south of town on the Interamericana, Estelí's two bus terminals, Cotran Norte and **Cotran Sur** (☎ 713 6162) serve destinations to the north and south respectively.

Buses from Cotran Norte:

Jinotega (US$2; 3hr; 5 daily 6am-4pm)

León (US$2.25; 2½hr; 3 daily) Alternatively, take the Matagalpa bus and change at San Isidro.

Ocotal (US$1; 2hr; hourly 6am-6pm) For border crossing at Las Manos.

Somoto (US$1.30; 1½hr; every 30min 5:30am-6pm) For border crossing at El Espino.

From Cotran Sur:

León (US$2.70; 2hr; 1 express daily 6:45am) Other services from Cotran Norte.

Managua (US$2.25; 2¼hr; almost half-hourly 3:30am to 6pm; some express services, US$3, 2hr)

Matagalpa (US$1.40; 1¾hr; every 30min 5:20am to 4:50pm)

RESERVA NATURAL MIRAFLOR

Enticing Miraflor, some 30km northeast of Estelí, is an expanse of private land that is community managed and has been declared a nature reserve. It's predominantly farmland, covering three climatic zones from dry to wet, stretching from 800m to 1450m.

Miraflor is a great place to get away from it all, immerse yourself in the lifestyle of traditional coffee-growing communities, and do some low-key walking, bird-watching or horse riding. There are also several volunteer projects that you can get involved with. There is no central town; *fincas* are scattered widely across the area, and around several small community hubs.

As there's no tourist information available once you're there, it's highly advisable to visit the reserve office in Estelí before you head out. UCA Miraflor (see p474) promotes sustainable agriculture among the resident communities, who grow coffee, vegetables and flowers and raise livestock. They have also developed an ecotourism structure, which it is hoped will provide alternative livelihoods.

Sights & Activities

This isn't the place for epic hiking, but there are several interesting walks in the area, which appeal more for the chance to chat to local farmers than for the likelihood of spotting rare fauna, although birds are in great supply. There are also plenty of swimming holes and waterfalls (blessed relief from the sometimes intense heat). You can see coffee being produced, or visit an orchid farm. Taking a guide is the best way to find your way around. Locals sometimes charge US$0.25 to US$1 for crossing their land.

Guides (official charge is US$17 per day for up to five people) can be arranged at UCA Miraflor in Estelí or by some of the accommodations places. They can take you around on foot or horseback (horses US$4 to US$7 per person per day); be firm about what you want to see, whether it be birds, forest, coffee plantations or archaeological sights. You can read descriptions of various possible routes on the website www.miraflor-uca.com.

Sleeping & Eating

There are several accommodations in Miraflor, mostly staying with local coffee-growing families. Some need to be booked and paid for with UCA Miraflor in Estelí in advance (they'll give you a voucher), while other places also accept walk-ins. All the accommodations are very basic, with bucket showers and shared rooms in rough huts. Official UCA prices are US$13 per person, where you'll usually be sharing the house with the family, or US$17 for 'cabañas,' which are usually separate. Rates include simple but delicious traditional local meals. Camping is available at many places for US$1.10 per day.

Some of the many places:

Finca Fuente de Vida A half-hour walk from La Rampla, has hammocks and offers horses and guides. Vegetarian food available.

Posada la Soñada (Corina Picado) Coffee-country cabins with fireplace, tasty food, and a warm welcome.

NICARAGUA

Marlon Villareyna Switched-on to travelers, with horses and guiding available and a friendly laid-back atmosphere. In Sontule.

Getting There & Away

There are bus services from Estelí's Cotran Norte to various parts of the reserve (around US$0.80 for all destinations). The daily bus to Sontule, in the northwest of the region, is at 2:15pm (two hours), returning at 8:10am. For El Coyolito (one hour), in the lower southwestern zone, buses leave at 5:45am and 12:45pm, returning at 8:20am and 3:45pm. Buses for Yali run through the eastern side of the area, passing La Rampla and Puertas Azules, leaving at 6am (this one leaves from Cotran Sur, though), noon and 3:30pm, and taking about two hours. It passes back through La Rampla at about 7am, 11:30am and 4:15pm.

OCOTAL

pop 34,190

Most travelers spend about seven minutes here on their way to Honduras, and Ocotal is in some ways all the better for that. Sitting at the base of the Sierra de Dipilto, Nicaragua's highest mountain range, it's a place of gruff courtesy where nothing is done in too much of a hurry and the blokes are more Marlboro man than metrosexual. For a slice of authentic northern Nicaragua, you could do a lot worse than stop off here for a day or two.

The lovely plaza is a small botanic garden, with many local and imported plants and trees carefully labeled. On the east side of it, the church has one old and one modern tower, while three blocks west, a rather kitsch monument to St Francis offers a vantage point over the town and hills.

The bus station is beside the highway at the south end of town. Banpro, a block west

and two blocks north of the plaza, has an ATM catering to Visa/Plus and Cirrus/MasterCard users.

Ocotal's major fiesta is the **Festival de La Virgen de la Asunción** in mid-August, when its ranching gentry show off their horsemanship through the streets.

Sleeping & Eating

Hospedaje Segovia (☎ 732 2617; r per person US$1.90) Two blocks north of the NW corner of the park, this is on a busy shopping street and is just about decent, although your back won't thank you for making it sleep on these beds.

Hospedaje Francis (☎ 732 0554; r per person US$2.75) This quiet, clean and simple option with shared bathrooms is pretty much the best of Ocotal's cheap lodgings. Rooms are dark and a bit poky, but fine for this price. It's secure and family-run. Head two blocks south from the SW corner of the square, and half a block west.

Hospedaje Llamarada del Bosque (☎ 732 3469; Parque Central; small s/d US$5.50/11, larger s/d US$8.30/16.60; P) Bestowing a smiling welcome on visitors, this newly opened spot makes a fine place to lay your head. The rooms have new beds, fans, TV, and a good hot-water bathroom. It's spotless, and there's a small garden – mind you, who needs it with the botanic fantasy of a main square just opposite?

Llamarada del Bosque (☎ 732 2643; lunch US$1.60) At the southwest corner of the central park, this friendly eatery offers several delicious stews in its lunch buffet, and has patio seating as well as the front *comedor* (basic and cheap eatery).

La Yunta (☎ 732 2180; dishes US$2.60-7) One block west and three blocks south of the park, cowboyish La Yunta serves Nicaraguan dishes on a pleasant outdoor patio. There's also cold beer in iced glasses and the raised dance floor gets busy on weekend evenings.

GETTING TO TEGUCIGALPA, HONDURAS

Of the two routes in this area north to Honduras, the shorter one goes through Ocotal and on to the border crossing at Las Manos. From there, it's 132km (2½ hours by bus) to **Tegucigalpa** (p340). Las Manos is a major crossing, open 24 hours, although there's only bus service from 6am to 6pm.

The alternative route goes through the town of Somoto, crossing the border at El Espino, and passes through the Honduran village of San Marcos de Colón on its way to **Choluteca** (p435). Going this way, you could reach the Salvadoran border in three hours (plus waiting time for connection). El Espino is open from 6am to about 10pm daily.

See p436 or p436 for information on crossing the border from Honduras.

DIY ADVENTURES IN THE RAAN

The North Atlantic Autonomous Region (RAAN) is the vast northeastern province of Nicaragua and fertile ground for exploration. While some parts are most easily accessed from the Caribbean side (see boxed text, p520) you can also head into the region from the Matagalpa and Jinotega areas. The great jewel of the region is the **Reserva de Biosfera Bosawás**, a protected area that forms part of the Mesoamerican Biological Corridor. Access is tough, and travel is easiest done by river. **Wiwilí**, on the Río Coco, is one possible point – it's a mountain town 90km north of Jinotega and from there you can arrange boats and guides – essential in this region, which still has landmines and antisocial characters left over from the Contra War. Another road leads from Jinotega to El Cuá, inside the reserve area. From here you can head on San José de Bocay, where you'll find a ranger station, walking opportunities, and, perhaps, a guide to the semimythical caves of **Belén de Tunowalan**, 50km northeast.

Getting There & Away

All buses depart from the **bus station** (☎ 732 3304), 1km south of Parque Central. Border-bound buses also stop to pick up passengers by the Shell station at the north end of town. A taxi anywhere in town costs US$0.35 (7 córdobas).

Estelí (US$1.40; 2hr; roughly hourly 4:45am-6pm).
Managua expresses also stop here (US$1.70, 1¼hr).

Las Manos (Honduran border) (US$0.75; 1hr; hourly 5am to 4:40pm)

Managua (US$3.70; 3½hr; roughly hourly 4am to 3:30pm)

Somoto (US$0.75; 1½hr; hourly from 5:45am to 6:30pm)

SOMOTO
pop 18,130

This sleepy spot is just 20km from the Honduran border at El Espino, and is a quiet, appealing mountain town that is renowned for baking some of the country's best *rosquillas* (ring-shaped cheese and corn biscuits). The Spaniards founded the spot in the 16th century, and the charming colonial church on the plaza is one of the nation's oldest, dating from 1671.

Reached from a turnoff from the El Espino road some 15km north of town, El Cañon de Somoto, also known as Namancambre, is a spectacular 2.5km-long gorge that remained a well-guarded *campesino* secret until its recent 'discovery.' It's a difficult scramble along its bottom, best accomplished with a guide, organized via **Marena** (☎ 722 2431), a block and a half south of the church in Somoto.

There are many places to stay in Somoto, but it's tough to beat **Hotel Panamericano** (☎ 722 2355; r per person with/without bathroom US$10/3), on the plaza. It has very basic cells with shared hot-water bathrooms or pretty decent en suite rooms with TV. Look at a few, as they are all different.

The hotel can set you up with a canyon guide.

Somoto's bus station is located on the Interamericana Hwy, a short walk from the center of town. Buses depart hourly for the border (US$0.35, 40 minutes) until 4:15pm, and every 40 minutes for Estelí (US$1, two hours) with the last bus at 4pm. Buses bound for Managua (US$3.30, 4½ hours) depart roughly hourly; there are some express services that cost slightly more and shave half an hour off the journey.

LEÓN & NORTHWESTERN NICARAGUA

The most volcanic region in Central America, northwestern Nicaragua is dominated by the Cordillera de los Maribios, a chain of 10 volcanoes, some active, paralleling the Pacific coast from the northwestern shores of Lago de Managua to the Gulf of Fonseca. Momotombo (1280m), the southernmost volcano, towers over Lago de Managua; Cosigüina, the cordillera's northern endpoint, forms a peninsula that juts into the gulf. These volcanoes rise out of hot, agriculturally rich lowlands, where maize, sugarcane, rice and cotton are grown. The region was devastated in 1998 by Hurricane Mitch, but has recovered strongly.

LEÓN
pop 139,430

Long Nicaragua's capital and still principal totem of its artistic, religious, and revolutionary history, proud León is one of Nicaragua's two legendary colonial jewels. A faded romance pervades its eave-shaded streets, where, as the evening approaches, friends and family pull rocking chairs to the street to chew the fat or watch the languorous town life drift by. León's favorite son is Rubén Darío, the famed national poet, who is buried here in the city's centerpiece, the noble 18th-century cathedral, the largest in Central America. Although León's charms are subtler than those you might experience in Granada, for many this is the quintessential city of Nicaragua – real and down-to-earth, but deeply connected to the past.

History

León was originally founded in 1524 by Francisco Fernández de Córdoba at the site of the indigenous village of Imabite, near the foot of Volcán Momotombo (p487). In 1610 the volcanic activity triggered an earthquake that destroyed the old city. It was rebuilt near the existing indigenous capital, Subtiava, where it remains.

León was the nation's capital from the colonial period until Managua took over the role in 1857; this, combined with its role as the ecclesiastical center for both Nicaragua and Costa Rica, means that it preserves a legacy of many fine churches and colonial buildings. The Universidad Autónoma de Nicaragua, Nicaragua's first university, was founded here in 1912.

Traditionally León has been the most politically progressive of Nicaraguan cities. During the revolution, virtually the entire town fought against Somoza. Dramatic

LEÓN

INFORMATION
Alf@nett...................1 A3
Banco América Central....2 B3
Clean Express.............3 B2
Cyberlink................4 B3
Enitel....................5 B3
Intur.....................6 B2
Oficina de Información
Turística...............7 B3

SIGHTS & ACTIVITIES
Big Foot Adventure.........(see 23)
Casa del Obrero.................8 A2
Cathedral......................9 B3
Colegio de San Ramón........10 B3
Colegio La Asunción.........11 B3
Fundación Ortíz.............12 A3
Galería de Héroes y Mártires.13 B3
Iglesia de El Calvario.....14 C3
Iglesia de La Merced........15 B3
Iglesia de La Recolección...16 B3
Iglesia de San Juan.........17 C2
Metropolitana Spanish
School....................18 C3
Museo Rubén Darío...........19 A3

Palacio Episcopal...............20 B3
Quetzaltrekkers.................21 C2
Servitour León..................22 B3
Va Pues Tours................(see 34)

SLEEPING
Big Foot Hostel.................23 B2
Casa Ivana......................24 A3
El Albergue.....................25 C2
El Garaje.......................26 B3
Hostal La Clínica...............27 B3
Hotel América...................28 C3
Hotel Colonial..................29 B3
La Casona Colonial..............30 B2
Lazybones.......................31 B2
Vía Vía.........................32 C2

EATING
Casa Vieja......................33 A2
CocinArte.......................34 A3
Delicias Tropicales.............35 A3
El Buen Gusto...................36 B3
El Sesteo.......................37 B3
Panadería El Leoncito...........38 C3
Puerto Cafe Benjamín Linder.39 B2
Taquezal........................40 B3

DRINKING
Don Señor's.....................41 B3
La Passarela....................42 B2
Las Ruinas......................43 B3

ENTERTAINMENT
Plaza Siglo Nuevo...............44 B3
Teatro Municipal................45 B3

TRANSPORT
Bus Station.....................46 D1

NICARAGUA

murals around town serve as reminders of that period, though many are fading. The city remains a strong Sandinista heartland.

Orientation

Av Central and Calle Central Rubén Darío intersect at the northeast corner of Parque Central, forming northeast, northwest, southeast and southwest quadrants. Calles ascend numerically as they go north or south of Calle Central; avenidas ascend east or west of Av Central. However, the Leonese rarely use this system when giving directions; instead, they prefer the old reliable '2½ blocks east of the Shell station.' The bus station is on the northeastern outskirts of town. The old indigenous town of Subtiava is a western suburb.

Information

INTERNET ACCESS

There are dozens of places to get online (per hour US$0.60 to US$1), including:

Alf@nett (Calle Central) Opposite Museo Rubén Darío; good connection.

CyberLink (cnr 1a Calle NO & 2a Av NO)

LAUNDRY

Most budget hotels have laundry service or a washtub.

Clean Express (cnr 4a Calle NE & Av Central; 7:30am-7:30pm) Has self-service machines and will do pricey service washes (US$4 to US$6).

MEDICAL SERVICES

Hospital San Vicente (311 6990) Beyond the bus station, this is the largest hospital in the region, set in a noble old building.

MONEY

Banco América Central (BAC; 1a Calle NE) Has an all-card ATM giving US dollars or córdobas, and changes traveler's checks.

POST

Post office (1a Av NE) Opposite the Iglesia de La Recolección.

TELEPHONE

Enitel Publitel phones are found outside this office just off the northwest corner of Parque Central. Nearly all internet places offer cheap international phone calls.

TOURIST INFORMATION

Intur (311 3682; 2a Av NO; 8am-12:30pm & 2-5pm Mon-Fri) Helpful staff, and knowledgeable about the area.

Oficina de Información Turística (311 3528; Av Central; 8:30am-noon & 2-6pm Mon-Fri, 9am-5pm Sat & Sun) Just north of the cathedral, this enthusiastic office gives out good information, maps and brochures.

Sights

CHURCHES & PLAZAS

León's **cathedral** is the largest in Central America. Construction began in 1747 and went on for over 100 years. According to local legend, the city's leaders feared their original grandiose design for the structure would be turned down by Spanish imperial authorities, so they submitted a more modest but bogus set of plans.

The fairly sober façade – more triumph-of-the-will neoclassicism than fluttering cherubs – fronts an interior that is a pantheon of Nicaraguan culture. It's a high-vaulted, light and unornamented space. The tomb of Rubén Darío, León's favorite son, is on one side of the altar, guarded by a sorrowful lion. Nearby rest the tombs of Alfonso Cortés (1893–1969) and Salomón de la Selva (1893–1959), also important literary figures. Also buried here is Miguel de Larreynaga, the pioneer of the Central American independence movement whose bespectacled face adorns the 10 córdoba note.

Around the church, you'll find the Stations of the Cross by Antonio Sarría, considered masterpieces of colonial art. They are looking a bit worn these days; indeed a restoration project for the whole building wouldn't go amiss. This would be a major investment; readers?

On the south side of the cathedral you'll find the **Colegio La Asunción** (1a Calle SO), the first theological college in Nicaragua; the attractive **Palacio Episcopal** (Bishop's Palace; 1a Calle SE); and the **Colegio de San Ramón** (1a Calle SE), where Larreynaga was educated.

Three blocks north of the cathedral, the 18th-century **Iglesia de La Recolección** (1a Av NE) has a magnificent yellow baroque façade, with carved vines wound around stone pillars, and symbols in bas-relief medallions depicting the Passion. The **Iglesia de El Calvario** (Calle Central), another 18th-century building, stands at the east end of Calle Central. Its facade, between a pair of red-brick bell towers, displays biblical scenes; enter the building to admire its slender wood columns and ceiling decorated with harvest motifs. Other colonial churches worth visiting include **Iglesia de La Merced** (1a Calle NE) and **Iglesia de San Juan** (3a Av SE).

JUSTICE FROM A WAITER'S HANDS

A key moment in revolutionary history is represented by the image of a pistol and a letter in a mural just off the park. The letter, signed by the poet and journalist Rigoberto López Pérez, declares his intention to assassinate Anastasio Somoza García, patriarch of the Somozas' four-decade dynasty. The house where he carried out his plan, the **Casa del Obrero**, is on 2a Av NO. On September 21, 1956, López Pérez, dressed as a waiter to gain entry to a party for dignitaries, fired the fatal shots; Somoza was flown to a military hospital in Panama, where he later died. López Pérez was killed on the scene and became a national hero. The plaque outside the house says his act marked the 'beginning of the end' of the Somoza dictatorship.

About 1km west of the central plaza is the church of **San Juan Bautista de Subtiava** (13 Av SO), the oldest intact church in León. Built in the first decade of the 18th century and restored (with Spanish support) in the 1990s, it features a typical arched timber roof upon which is affixed an extraordinary sun icon, said to have been a device to attract the indigenous community to worship. The exquisite filigreed altar demonstrates fine woodworking skills. The church stands near the center of the indigenous village of Subtiava, which occupied the area long before the Spaniards arrived.

MUSEUMS & MONUMENTS

Rubén Darío, born on January 18, 1867, is esteemed worldwide as one of Latin America's greatest poets. As the poet most committed to the introduction of 19th-century modernism, he had a major influence on the literature of his time and is a national hero of immense status. The house where he grew up, three blocks west of the plaza, is now the **Museo Rubén Darío** (Calle Central; admission free; 9am-noon & 2-5pm Tue-Sat, 9am-noon Sun), with a selection of his possessions and writings that succeeds in bringing the man to life.

Nearby, **Fundación Ortiz** (3a Av SO; admission free; 11am-6:30pm Tue-Sun) is an artistic treasure-trove set in two attractive colonial buildings on opposite sides of the street. There's an impressive selection of European masters and a quite stunning assembly of Latin American art, including pre-Columbian ceramics and contemporary Nicaraguan painting. Look out for the work of the excellent Armando Morales, whose shadowy figures seem to echo the topography and vulnerability of the nation. This is Nicaragua's finest art gallery by a huge margin.

Another worthwhile visit is to the moving **Galería de Héroes y Mártires** (1a Calle NO; 8am-5pm Mon-Sat), just west of 1a Av NO. Run by mothers of FSLN veterans and fallen heroes, the gallery has photos of over 300 young men and women from the León area who died fighting the Somoza dictatorship and the US-backed Contras. Do chat to one of the mothers; they are more than happy to share their experiences and opinions.

Courses

The **Metropolitana Spanish School** (311 1235; www .metropolitana-ss.com; Iglesia el Calvario ½ c abajo) offers classes, activities and homestay (US$115/195 for a 20-hour week without/with homestay).

Tours

There are many operators offering excursions to León Viejo, surf trips, tours of the Flor de Caña distillery at Chichigalpa, hiking up volcanoes, and even 'surfing' down them again…

Big Foot Adventure (www.bigfootadventure.com) At Big Foot hostel; runs daily volcano boarding trips (US$23) to Cerro Negro, protective suits supplied.

Quetzaltrekkers (311 6695; www.quetzaltrekkers .com; 2a Calle NE) This volunteer-run set-up offers recommended volcano hikes (US$17 to US$56) to several different spots. All profits go to help León street kids. Bookings also at Vía Vía hostel.

Servitour León (311 1927) Runs a range of trips, including excursions to León Viejo (US$25, minimum two). It also hires (expensive) bikes. Half a block north of the cathedral.

Va Pues Tours (315 4099; www.vapues.com) In the CocinArte restaurant; comprehensive range of tours, including party nights. Can also arrange Spanish classes.

Festivals & Events

León is famous for its fiestas:

La Gritería Chiquita (August 14) is held prior to the Day of the Assumption of Mary. This celebration began in 1947 after an erupting Cerro Negro was stopped after a priest vowed to initiate a preliminary *gritería* (shouting), similar to December's but changing the response to *¡La asunción de María!* ('The ascension of Mary!').

Día de la Virgen de Merced (September 24) is León's saint's day, solemnly observed with religious processions through the streets of the city. The preceding day is more festive: revelers don a bull-shaped armature lined with fireworks, called the *toro encohetado*, then charge at panic-stricken onlookers as the rockets fly.

Día de la Purísima Concepción (December 7) is a warm-up for the Día de la Concepción de María (December 8), celebrated throughout Nicaragua. It is the occasion for the *gritería*, in which groups wander around calling on any house that displays an altar and shouting, *¿Quién causa tanta alegría?* ('Who causes so much joy?') to receive the response, *¡La concepción de María!* ('The conception of Mary!'). The household then offers the callers traditional treats such as honey-dipped plantain slices and seasonal fruits.

Sleeping

Vía Vía (☎ 311 6142; www.viaviacafé.com; 2a Av NE; dm/s/d US$3.30/8/12) An original León backpacker spot and a likable choice, this is set around a lush garden courtyard. The dormitory is comfortable enough, with mostly single beds, but it's right by the bar, and very noisy. However, the laid-back atmosphere here is great, the management friendly and socially aware, the restaurant serves tasty Nicabelgian cuisine (slowly), and the convivial bar has a pool table and events.

Casa Ivana (☎ 311 4423; 2a Calle SO; s/d US$5.50/7) Centrally located beside the Teatro Municipal, Casa Ivana is a typical Leonese home. The rooms are neat and simple, but the owners are very grudging hosts.

Hostal La Clínica (☎ 311 2031; 1a Av SO; dm US$3.90, d with/without bathroom US$8.90/7.80) Popular with a good mix of travelers and overseen by a much-loved old *abuela*, this family-run spot has squawking parrots and small, colorful rooms with rather uncomfortable beds.

Big Foot Hostel (2a Av NE; www.bigfootadventure.com; dm/d US$4/10) This popular place is right opposite Vía Vía, so you can easily pick and choose; the vibe in each will appeal to different folk. This has better dorm accommodations and a very relaxing courtyard-café space. There's a good kitchen you can use, and cracking service-with-a-smile. However, don't expect to fit more than one (big) foot at a time in the so-called swimming pool.

El Albergue (☎ 894 1787; Petronic ½ cuadra abajo; dm/d US$4/12) A very relaxed Nicaraguan-run hostel offering a tranquil, no-frills atmosphere. The spacious rooms have comfy beds and colorful sheets; the dorm beds are narrow, with foam mattresses. There's use of a simple kitchen,

a bar, and plenty of rocking chairs to chill out. Tours available and discounts offered to volunteers.

El Garaje (☎ 311 4195; pgamboa_7@hotmail.com; 1a Av SO; s/d US$8/10, with bathroom US$10/12) For peace and quiet and an intimate atmosphere, this curiously appealing conversion of the friendly owner's garage does the trick. There are just three rooms – two share a bathroom between them, and small areas to sit. It's spotlessly clean, very secure and extremely helpful – a real home from home. Breakfast included. 11pm curfew.

Lazybones (☎ 311 3472; www.lazybonesleon.com; 2a Av NO; dm US$6, r with/without bathroom US$22/15; 🖳 🖳) This newly opened backpacker palace is quite a treat on the eyes, set around a lengthy courtyard with murals and hammocks. The rooms are excellent, with firm beds, and the dorms are appealing and comfortable. There's a lovely pool and café area out the back, internet, pool table, and more facilities, as well as relaxed management.

Hotel América (☎ 311 5533; rgalloa@yahoo.com; 1a Calle SE; s/d with bathroom US$10/16) This fading but characterful mansion seems a fitting place from which to appreciate León's timeworn colonial glories. It's got very genial owners, spacious (almost too big), clean rooms with fan, and rocking chairs.

La Casona Colonial (☎ 311 3178; Parque San Juan ½c abajo; s/d US$15/20) Gently relaxing, this lovely, character-filled place makes a highly appealing choice. The dark, fan-cooled rooms have noble old furnishings, including beds you have to clamber up on to. There are also gardens, books, soft chairs, sympathetic management, and total peace and quiet.

Hotel Colonial (☎ 311 2279; 1a Av NO) Two and a half blocks north of the plaza, the Colonial is a charming old hotel that was closed for a complete makeover at time of research.

Eating

Near Mercado Central, **El Buen Gusto** (☎ 311 6617; ⏰ 10am-10pm) offers home-cooked *comida corriente* for under US$1. **Panadería El Leoncito** (☎ 311 1270), just east, has a good selection of fresh-baked breads and pastries.

Delicias Tropicales (1a Calle NO; juices US$0.50) This simple family-run spot does great fresh juices and daily Nica specials such as *gallo pinto* at tables in a secluded patio space.

Puerto Café Benjamín Linder (☎ 311 0548; 1a Av & 2a Calle NO; light meals US$1.50-3; ⏰ 10am-11pm Mon-

Sat) This breezy nonprofit café has a beautiful olden-times interior and a large mural depicting the life of Ben Linder, an American volunteer in Nicaragua who contributed much to the region before dying at the hands of Contras in 1987. It's a fine place for salads, toasted sandwiches, coffee or *comida corriente*.

CocinArte (☎ 315 4099; meals US$2-4; ❤ 11am-10pm) This place wins rave reports from travelers for its delicious vegetarian food and fresh juices. It's opposite Iglesia El Laborío.

Casa Vieja (☎ 311 3701; 3a Av NO; meals US$3-6) Romantic, peaceful and cordial, this attractive spot has a stylish colonial feel and attracts an eclectic mix of people for coffee and snacks, or big, value-packed salads, and tasty *churrasco*.

El Sesteo (Calle Central; dishes US$3-7; ❤ 11am-10pm) A León institution, this is a pricy but pleasant café on the plaza by the cathedral, fabulous for people-watching over a drink or well-prepared regional favorites such as *chancho con yuca* (fried pork, yucca and pickled cabbage).

Taquezal (☎ 311 7282; 2a Av SO; dishes US$4-7) This huge, handsome, upmarket but relaxed restaurant-bar has loads of tables of smart Leonese both young and old, drawn by the pleasant ambience and traditional cuisine. It merges seamlessly into a lively, late-opening bar as the plates get cleared away.

In Subtiava, one block south and 1½ blocks west of Iglesia San Juan Bautista, Los Pescaditos is a popular, moderately priced seafood restaurant whose basic décor gives few hints of its excellent quality.

Drinking & Discotecas

Don Señor's (☎ 311 1212; 1a Calle NO; disco cover US$1.10) One block north of the plaza, this place is more than just a hot nightspot – it's three. There's a disco upstairs, a relaxed bar with tables overlooking the street downstairs, and a restaurant-pub called El Alamo around the corner which has a great upstairs terrace.

Las Ruinas (Calle Central) An essential León experience, this cavernous ruined building offers fried chicken by day and a brilliantly local, divey atmosphere by night. There are heaps of tables and a big dance floor where young Leonese strut their stuff.

La Passarella (cnr Av Central & 2a Calle NE) With a thatched lean-to for upstairs seating, and a large garden with banana palms, this is a great spot for a beer and chat. There's a pool table and jukebox – it also does a daily meal (US$1.20) and decent *variados* (US$3 to US$4).

Entertainment

Teatro Municipal (2a Calle SO) The impressively preserved Teatro Municipal is León's premier venue for music, dance and theater, and most touring ensembles perform here.

Plaza Siglo Nuevo (1a Calle NE; tickets US$2.20) León's cinema shows mostly American films.

Getting There & Around

León's chaotic **bus station** (☎ 311 3909; 6a Calle NE) is 1km northeast of the center. You can take a microbus to Managua (US$1.25, 1¼ hours) or Chinandega (US$1, 45 minutes). These depart continuously from the left side of the main platform, as they fill up.

Chinandega (US$0.70; 1½hr; every 15min 4:30am-6pm)
Estelí (US$2.25; 2½hr; 5:20am & 12:45pm) Alternatively, take bus to San Isidro (more than hourly) and change there.
Managua (Mercado Bóer) expresos (US$1; 1¼hr; every 30min); ordinarios (US$0.80; 2¼hr; every 20min 5am-6:30pm via old hwy)
Matagalpa (US$2.75; 2½hr; 5am & 3pm) Alternatively take bus to San Isidro (more than hourly) and change there.

Local buses and pickup trucks (US$0.10) leave from the Mercado Central for Subtiava, the bus terminal, and the Managua highway. Taxis around town are inexpensive (US$0.35 for a one-person ride).

AROUND LEÓN
Poneloya & Las Peñitas Beaches

Long, inviting beaches lie just 20km west of León. **Poneloya** and its southern extension, **Las Peñitas**, are separated by a rock formation that offers a fine vantage point. Swimming is good – safest at the southern end of Las Peñitas – but be very wary of the currents, which have claimed many lives over the years, and of submerged rocks. Crowds descend here on weekends and holidays, but during the week these darkish sand beaches are practically deserted, apart from the glorious coasting pelicans. You can easily visit as a day trip from León, but the relaxed atmosphere will likely entice you to stay.

SLEEPING & EATING

There are several places along Las Peñitas beach. A landmark here is the excellent **Hotel Suyapa Beach** (☎ 317 0217; www.suyapabeach.com; r with/without air-con US$25/21; ❷ ❸), with recently remodeled rooms with great mattresses and views, a swimming pool, and also a decent beachside restaurant (dishes US$5 to US$17), which offers a few special dishes that require advance ordering.

A couple of hundred meters south of here, **Oasis** (☎ 839 5344; www.oasislaspenitas.com; dm/s/d US$6/12/15) has sullen staff but offers budget beachside lodging, hammocks, and simple meals. It also rent surfboards (US$8 per day) and body boards (US$5 per day). The rooms are spacious with OK bathrooms.

Between the two, low-key **Mi Casita** (☎ 849 6467; seafood US$7-8, r US$15) has rooms that are too dark for this price, but offers very tasty, well-priced seafood, cold beer, and smiley service.

Barca de Oro (☎ 317 0275; www.barcadeoro.com; d with/without bathroom US$15/10, with air-con US$25; P ⚇) is at the end of the road. It's on the rivermouth rather than the ocean, but it's a great place with clean, attractive rooms, popular with backpackers. The bouncy, ecologically minded boss can organize turtle-watching, trips to Juan Venado, and volunteer opportunities for looking after the turtles. There are also kayaks and well-priced meals at its outdoor restaurant.

Poneloya, 2km north, has four places to stay. **Hotel Lacayo** (☎ 887 6747; r per person US$2.80) is very run-down and basic but has character and is right on the beach. The currents are very dangerous just here. **Hotel La Posada** (☎ 317 1378; r with fan/air-con US$10/15; ⚇) is right opposite. The rooms are significantly better, although no bargain. Both these places, and other spots, offer relatively inexpensive seafood meals and cheaper *comida corriente*.

GETTING THERE & AWAY
Buses leave hourly from El Mercadito in Subtiava, one block north and one block west of Iglesia de San Juan Bautista. They stop first in Poneloya, then head down to Las Peñitas (US$0.55, 45 minutes). Day-trippers take note: the last bus returns at 6:40pm. The return bus may take you all the way into León center. A taxi from León should cost around US$8 to US$10.

Reserva Natural Isla Juan Venado
This reserve, south of Las Peñitas, is a long, narrow barrier island extending 22km to Salinas Grandes. The narrow island encloses a network of mangrove-lined estuaries, forming an ecosystem that sustains a variety of migratory birds, reptiles and amphibians, as well as vast squadrons of mosquitoes. It is a nesting area for olive ridley and leatherback turtles between July and January. Hotels in Las Peñitas can organize tours, but you can arrange them yourself at the visitors center there, where rangers will put you in touch with local guides, who can show you the island by boat for US$30 to US$50.

Playa El Velero
Another 40km down the coast, and most easily accessed via the workaday port of Puerto Sandino, is the long sandy crescent of **El Velero** beach. If you're looking for hammocks, beach bars and budget accommodations, it will disappoint; if the beach itself is your goal (and the surf can be great here) you could visit for the day or stay at the depressing **centro turístico** (☎ 312 2270; cabañas with bathroom & air-con US$41; ⚇ Wed-Sun; ⚇) with overpriced cabins and a sporadically open restaurant-bar. Demand a discount. From León, take a Puerto Sandino bus and get off at the gas station, from which sporadic pickup trucks run hourly to El Velero (US$0.50). It'll cost you a couple of coins to enter the beach complex.

CHARGE IT! – NICARAGUA'S TOP SURF SPOTS

- **Las Salinas/Playa Popoyo** has guaranteed large left and right point breaks and several surf camps; respect the locals. Get a bus from Rivas (p499) to Las Salinas.

- Several excellent breaks can be found in the **Playa Los Cardones** area (p469), including a right rivermouth at Quizala.

- There are several waves within a few kilometers of **Playa El Velero** (above), both left and right beach and reef breaks.

- **Playa Madera** (p502) has slowish medium waves; it can get crowded but is easy to reach and reliable.

- There's a loud hollow beach break at **Playa Aserradores** (opposite) and others are nearby.

EXPLORE MORE AROUND LEÓN

The area northwest of León offers fertile ground for exploration, with surfing, rum and volcanoes to tempt you.

■ In the heart of the volcano corridor, **San Jacinto** is base camp for assaults on three volcanoes: Telica, Rota and Santa Clara. Nearby, **Los Hervideros de San Jacinto** are a network of hot springs and boiling mud pools. Local kids will show you around for a few córdobas. To get there take any Estelí- or San Isidro–bound bus and exit at San Jacinto – about 25km from León.

■ Up the main highway from León, you reach **Chichigalpa**, home of the Flor de Caña distillery and the Ingenio San Antonio, the largest sugar mill in Central America.

■ About 15km further is **Chinandega**, where cotton and sugarcane are the principal crops. **Intur** (☎ 341 1935; chinandega@intur.gob.ni; ⏰ 8:30am-12:30pm & 2-5:30pm Mon-Fri) has an office three blocks east of Parque Central, and there's plenty of budget accommodations in town. Chinandega is the jumping-off point for some great beaches. **Playa Aserradores** is one – with a good choice of places to eat and stay, but keen travelers can push on further up the coast to some superb, just-about-unspoiled beaches and fishing communities.

■ Beyond stretches the remote **Cosigüina peninsula**, dominated by the volcano of the same name. Now only 850m, it was once a mighty 3km high, until it erupted with awesome violence in 1835. It's a hot three-hour climb to the top, where you gaze down over a huge crater lake and out over the Salvadoran and Honduran gulf islands to the north. You can sleep over at the El Rosario ranger station, near one of the trailheads. Speak to Intur in Chinandega for a guided trip.

León Viejo

At the foot of Volcán Momotombo are the remains of the original colonial provincial capital, **León Viejo** (admission US$2, photography US$1.40; ⏰ 8am-5pm). Founded in 1524, Old León was abandoned less than a century later and soon destroyed by earthquake and subsequently completely buried under layers of ash from Momotombo.

It was not until 1967 that its location was finally discovered on the shore of Lago de Managua. Excavations have revealed a large plaza, a cathedral, church, and monastery, as well as private dwellings.

The headless remains of Francisco Fernández de Córdoba, founder of both León and Granada, were found buried alongside those of the jealous first governor, Pedrarias Dávila, who had him beheaded. The skeleton of the bishop Antonio de Valdivieso, assassinated in 1550 for his defense of indigenous rights, has also been identified here.

The indigenous community (which numbered many thousands) was treated abominably; a statue commemorates those killed by dogs set loose in a horrific public spectacle.

While the ruins and discoveries are archaeologically fascinating, many visitors are disappointed. All that remains of most buildings is a foundation wall about 0.3m (1 ft) high. The highlight, though, is the fabulous volcano view from what was once the city's fortress. Entry to the site includes a guided tour in Spanish, which basically repeats what is written (in English also) on the information panels.

You can take a tour here from León, or, cheaper, get a cab (US$15 to US$20 for a round-trip with an hour at the site). If coming by vehicle, the turnoff is 3km east of La Paz Centro on the León–Managua highway (Rte 28). From there it's a 15km drive along a partially cobblestoned road. Frequent León–Managua buses pass through La Paz Centro, from which buses leave hourly for Puerto Momotombo.

Volcán Momotombo

Baptism of volcanoes is an ancient custom dating back to the beginning of the [Spanish] conquest. All of Nicaragua's craters were thus sanctified, except Momotombo, whence no priest sent to plant the cross was ever seen to return

Ephraim Squier

NICARAGUA

The perfect cone of Momotombo is a symbol of Nicaragua and rises 1280m over the northwest shore of Lago de Managua. Momotombito, its Mini-Me, pokes from the water nearby. The subject of notable poems by Rubén Darío and Victor Hugo, the volcano, whose name means 'great boiling peak,' has erupted 14 times since the 16th century, when the Spanish began keeping track.

A geothermal plant on the volcano's south slopes supplies some 10% of Nicaragua's electrical power. Permits from the power company **Ormat** (☎ 270 5622; Centro Finarca, off Carr Masaya, Managua) are required to enter the area; otherwise **Ecotours Nicaragua** (☎ 222 2752; turismo@cablenet.com.ni) offer trips that climb partway by truck and continue on foot for two hours over a lava-strewn landscape to the crater. Fees are US$70 per person, with a minimum of two. The trip leaves Managua at 8am, returning at 7:30pm. The Ormat office is a block west of Sandy's, a well-known landmark.

GRANADA & THE MASAYA REGION

This geographically rich area boasts a number of Nicaragua's most vaunted attractions, including the spellbinding colonial town of Granada and the handicraft center of Masaya. The area is also rich in biodiversity. Wildlife abounds on the flanks of Volcán Mombacho, and Parque Nacional Volcán Masaya is one of the country's most visibly active craters. Lush tropical forest surrounds the banks of the crystalline Laguna de Apoyo, and Las Isletas on Lago de Nicaragua make for another fine swim setting.

Just west of Granada, the Pueblos Blancos (White Villages) of Catarina, San Juan de Oriente and Niquinohomo stand amid a highland coffee-growing region rich in pre-Columbian traditions. These charming towns are an excellent place to observe some of Nicaragua's most beautiful craftwork in the making.

GRANADA
pop 79,420

The goose that laid Nicaraguan tourism's golden egg is beguiling Granada, whose restored colonial glories render it a high point of many travelers' time in Central America. The carved colonial portals, elegant churches, and fine plaza, as well as its location on Lago de Nicaragua, have enchanted visitors for centuries since the city was founded in 1524.

With the sun-dappled colors of its adobe buildings making the streets an absolute joy to stroll, and Nicaragua's best selection of places to stay and eat, Granada is the sort of place where you can while away a lot of time, and its proximity to sprinkled islets on Lago de Nicaragua and to two major volcanoes only increases your options.

Tourism is having a significant impact here, both positive and negative. Expats buying up colonial homes are driving prices out of reach of locals, who are forced further out, leaving the picturesque center a little lifeless. Try to be conscious of spreading your money around here, patronizing local- and not just foreign-owned businesses.

History

Nicknamed 'the Great Sultan' in reference to its Moorish namesake across the Atlantic, Granada is Nicaragua's oldest colonial city. Founded in 1524 by Francisco Fernández de Córdoba, it stands at the foot of Volcán Mombacho on the northwestern shore of Lago de Nicaragua. With access to the Caribbean Sea via the lake and the Río San Juan, Granada soon became a rich and important trade center and remained so into the 19th century. This same Caribbean passage made Granada an easy target for English and French buccaneers, who sacked the city three times between its founding and 1685. Captain Henry Morgan, incredibly, made his way back to Jamaica with half a million pounds in 1665.

Conservative Granada was ever-locked in bitter rivalry with liberal León, which erupted into full-blown civil war in the 1850s. To

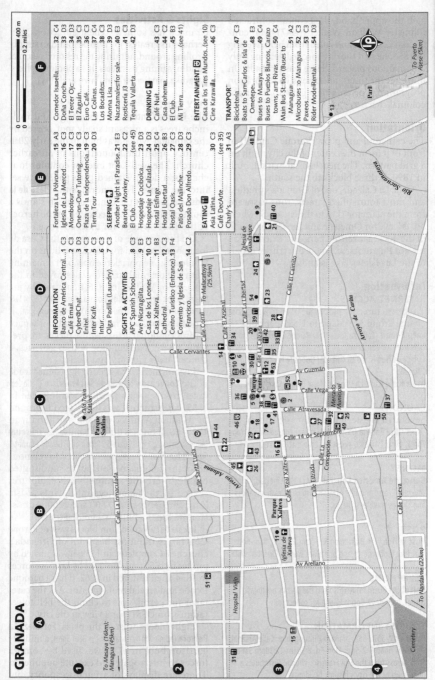

gain the upper hand, the Leonese contracted filibuster William Walker (p447), who conquered Granada and ruled from here. Fleeing in 1856, he had the city torched, leaving only the infamous placard, 'Here was Granada.' In more recent times, an expensive restoration program has given a new glow to its bright colonial charms.

Orientation

The cathedral and plaza (Parque Central) in front of it form the center of the city, built on a grid pattern. The neoclassical market, built in 1890, is three blocks to the south.

Calle La Calzada, one of Granada's prettiest and most touristified streets, runs eastward from the plaza for 1km to the city dock, where boats leave for Ometepe and San Carlos. South of the dock, a lakefront park area extends 3km toward Puerto Asese, where day cruises depart to the Las Isletas lake islands.

Information

INTERNET ACCESS

There are internet places all over town. Most charge around US$0.60 to US$1 per hour.

Café E-mail (Calle Xalteva) Near Parque Central; cheap calls from air-con booth.

Cyber@Chat (Calle La Calzada) Opposite Hospedaje La Calzada.

Inter Kafé (Calle La Libertad) Near Parque Central and fast.

LAUNDRY

Several of the sleeping options do laundry, as does **Olga Padilla** (☎ 552 6532; Calle Consulado; ☼ 7am-7pm), two blocks west of the cathedral.

MONEY

Banco de América Central (BAC; Calle Libertad) One of several all-card-friendly ATMs; it also gives cash advances and cashes traveler's checks.

POST

Post office (☼ 8am-noon & 1-5pm Mon-Fri, 8am-noon Sat) Two blocks north and one block west of Cine Karawala.

TELEPHONE

Enitel (Av Guzmán) Across from the plaza's northeast corner, includes a Sprint phone for collect calls.

TOURIST INFORMATION

Intur (☎ 552 6858; granada@intur.gob.ni; Calle Arsenal; ☼ 8am-noon & 2-5pm Mon-Fri, 8:30am-12:30pm Sat & Sun) Across from the San Francisco church. Distributes a good map of the city's historic buildings.

Sights & Activities

Granada has some excellent attractions, but perhaps its greatest joy is to be found in simply strolling around, admiring the restored colonial buildings lining its streets. It's a photographers' paradise, particularly at dawn and dusk.

CITY CENTER

The **Parque Central** with its mango and malinche trees is a pleasant shady spot, bossed by the **cathedral**, which was built in the early 20th century upon the foundations of an earlier church. The well-kept interior contains four chapels; a dozen stained-glass panels are set into the dome. To its north is the **Plaza de la Independencia**, at the center of which stands a monumental obelisk dedicated to the heroes of the 1821 struggle for independence.

On the east side of this plaza is the Casa de los Leones, named for the carved lions on the fabulous stone portal, the only part remaining from the original structure, destroyed in the blaze set by Walker in 1856. Renovated by the **Casa de los Tres Mundos Foundation** (☎ 552 4176; www.c3mundos.org.ni; admission US$1.10; ☼ 8am-6pm), it now functions as a residence and workspace for international artists whose pieces are presented here. The building houses galleries, a concert hall, a library and a café.

Just northeast, the striking light-blue façade of the **Convento y Iglesia de San Francisco** (Calle Cervantes) fronts a complex that was initiated in 1585. The structure was burned to the ground by William Walker in 1856 and rebuilt in 1867–68. It houses the city's must-see **museum** (admission US$2; ☼ 8:30am-5:30pm Mon-Fri, 9am-4pm Sat & Sun). The front section is devoted to religious art of the colonial period, but the undisputed highlight are the sombre basalt sculptures carved by the Chorotega inhabitants of Isla Zapatera between AD 800 and 1200. Admission includes a bilingual guided tour.

Iglesia de La Merced, four blocks west of Parque Central, is the most beautiful of Granada's churches. Completed in 1539, it was sacked by pirates in 1655 and damaged by Leonese forces in 1854, then restored in 1862. It has a baroque façade and an elaborate interior. Ask the caretaker for permission to climb the bell tower (admission US$1) for a view of the city.

Eight blocks west of the plaza, **Fortaleza La Pólvora** (admission by donation; ☼ 8am-5pm), a military garrison built in 1749, was used by Somoza forces to interrogate and execute opponents. There are displays of art and weaponry, but the best feature is the view down over town to Lago de Nicaragua.

LAGO DE NICARAGUA

On the lake, the **Centro Turístico** (admission per person/car US$0.10/0.90) is a 2km stretch of restaurants, picnic areas and playgrounds, all shaded by mango trees. Though people do swim here, the water is polluted. Boats depart for day trips to Las Isletas from restaurants at the southern end of the beach, or from the Puerto Asese dock (see p494).

Courses

Granada is a popular spot for learning Spanish and there are many schools and private teachers.

APC Spanish Schools (☎ 552 4203; www.apc-spanish schools.com; Parque Central) Conversation-based courses in this friendly place on the square by Hotel Alhambra.

Ave Nicaragüita (☎ 552 8538; www.avenicaraguita .com; Calle La Calzada) Based in the old Red Cross building. Offer a wide variety of interesting options, including some where you move around different parts of Nicaragua as you take your course.

Casa Xalteva (☎ 552 2436; www.casaxalteva.com; Calle Xalteva) Not-for-profit setup; your payment funds social programs. Tuition is US$135 per week, homestay US$77.

One-on-One Tutoring (☎ 552 6771; www.1on1 tutoring.net; Calle La Calzada) Flexible and rigorous, with teachers changing over every hour. Homestays with meals cost US$70 per week, classes two hours daily for five days is US$50; four hours is US$95.

Tours

Picturesque horse-drawn carriages hang out in Parque Central; an hour's ride around town costs around US$10 for up to five people and comes with some eloquent commentary in Spanish.

The classic lake circuit heads to Las Isletas (p494). Other popular excursions include Volcán Mombacho and tours of Granada itself.

Operators include the following.

Tierra Tour (☎ 552 8723; www.tierratour.com; Calle La Calzada; 3hr trip US$12-15, 6hr US$22-25) Recommended operator offering wide range of trips: Las Isletas, the Masaya region, hiking on Volcán Mombacho, canopy tours, kayaking and more.

Mombotour (☎ 552 4548; www.mombotour.com; Calle Atravesada) Leads excellent canopy tours down Volcán Mombacho starting at US$35. They also have bird-watching excursions, coffee tours, and kayaking in Lago de Nicaragua.

Festivals & Events

Fiestas de Agosto (third week of August) is Granada celebration of the Assumption of Mary, with fireworks, concerts, bullsports, and horse parades by the lakefront.

Inmaculada Concepción (also known as 'Purísimas' – November 28 to December 7) sees neighborhoods bear elaborate floats through the streets in honor of Granada's patron, the Virgen Concepción de María. People arrive blowing conch shells to drive the demons away.

Sleeping

Granada has a huge choice of inviting accommodations, although it's not so cheap.

Hostal Esfinge (☎ 552 4826; Calle Atravesada; dm US$3.30, s/d US$6.60/10, with bathroom US$10/13.90; **P**) An old-style ambience pervades this gorgeous historic building in the boisterous market zone. It's a good deal; rooms come off a large courtyard space, and guests have access to kitchen, washtub and Ping Pong. It's run with gracious courtesy, and monkey business is not appreciated.

Hospedaje La Calzada (☎ 668 8816; guesthousela calzada@yahoo.com; Calle La Calzada; s/d US$8.30/11, with bathroom US$11/12.90) With a good location, dignified La Calzada is run by a benevolent family and features simple, clean rooms with thin mattresses, and use of a kitchen, Ping-Pong table and washtub.

Hostal Libertad (☎ 552 4017; hospedaje_lalibertad@ yahoo.com; Calle La Libertad; dm/r US$6/20; ✂ 💻) Having the shower in the dorm means sleeping-in is a noisy business, but the comfy courtyard hammocks offer plenty of opportunity to doze later. With breakfast and free internet included, it's a good deal. There are also air-con rooms available in a nearby annex.

Bearded Monkey (☎ 552 4028; www.thebearded monkey.com; Calle 14 de Septiembre; dm/s/d US$6/9/17; 💻) Busy and perennially popular, this is a center of Granada's backpacker social scene. Set around a pleasant garden, which functions as a café-bar, the hostel offers OK dorms and plenty of facilities – free internet, nightly films, and tours, but no kitchen. If they are full, crash on a hammock (US$4), but you won't get much privacy. For sale at time of research.

Hostal Oasis (☎ 552 8006; www.nicaraguahostel.com; Calle Estrada; dm US$7, d with/without bathroom US$28/19; ✂ 💻 🔊) This popular hostel has top-notch facilities, with a petite but pretty swimming pool, free internet access, and a free phone call home (unless you're Danish) each day. The airy dorms are pretty good value, but the private rooms are small and cramped.

NICARAGUA

Hospedaje Cocibolca (☎ 552 7223; carlosgomez 00@hotmail.com; s/d/tr with bathroom US$13/15/21; 💻) Convenient, friendly and traveler-savvy, this is a long-appreciated Granada option. Clean and well-maintained rooms have fan and decent bathroom – go for an upstairs room for breezes and gazing over the rooftops; guests can use the kitchen, and there's internet and a book exchange.

Posada Don Alfredo (☎ 552 4455; alfredpaulbaganz@ hotmail.com; Calle 14 de Septiembre; r US$20-28, with bathroom US$35, with air-con US$40; 🌂) The disordered, homey colonial elegance of this lovely old building has a real appeal for those who prefer to pay for character than facilities. The rooms, which mostly share bathrooms, vary widely, but nearly all are very spacious.

El Club (☎ 552 4245; www.elclub-nicaragua.com; Calle La Libertad; s/d US$40/51; 🌂) For party people, having a pad in the town's best nightclub is the ultimate in decadence. Decorated in great minimalist style, the rooms, which include duplexes that could sleep two couples, are short on natural light but high on style and comfort. Just be aware that at weekends, the fiesta is in full swing until 2am right outside your door.

Patio del Malinche (☎ 552 2235; www.patiodel malinche.com; Calle El Caimito; s/d US$57/67; 🌂 🛏) A welcoming Catalan couple run this noble and lovingly restored colonial home that is one of Granada's most appealing places to stay. The personal attention makes it feel more like a guesthouse than a hotel, but it has excellent facilities too, including wireless internet, and unadorned, comfortable rooms that surround the appealing pool. Delicious, massive breakfasts (included) are a highlight.

Eating

Stop in Parque Central for icy fruit juices and *vigorón* (yucca steamed and topped with *chicharrón* – fried pork rind – and cabbage salad; US$1), a Granada specialty. Around the corner from the Hotel Granada, a family home sells piping-hot *nacatamales* (US$0.55) from Friday to Sunday. Check the website of **Building New Hope** (www.buildingnewhope.org) for the new location of Café Chavalos, a project which takes kids off the streets and teaches them to run a sophisticated restaurant. The organization also welcomes volunteers.

Los Bocaditos (dishes US$1.50-6; 🕙 8am-10pm) This cheery local spot has decent Nicaraguan breakfasts, sandwiches and a fine lunchtime buffet at low prices.

Euro Café (☎ 552 2146; Parque Central; snacks US$2-3; 🕙 7:30am-9pm) At one corner of Parque Central, this has really excellent coffee, an airy patio, salads, hummus, and a sizable collection of books for sale (they'll buy yours if they are decent).

Café DecArte (☎ 552 6461; Calle La Calzada; snacks US$2-4; 🕙 11am-4pm Wed-Mon) Set in a bright and seductive courtyard with tinkling fountain, this is a great spot for gourmet pitta-bread sandwiches, juices, and tasty desserts. So far so good, but in the evening (6pm to 10pm) it transforms itself into a mediocre pasta restaurant – why?

Rostería J3 (cnr Calles Xalteva & Atravesada; roast chicken US$2) Inside a mini-mall, this is an indefatigably cheery place that serves up big plates of roast chicken.

El Tercer Ojo (☎ 552 6541; Calle Arsenal; dishes US$2-6; 🕙 11am-11pm Tue-Sun) Relax in comfort at this popular new-agey hangout by the San Francisco church. With an eclectic range of cuisine, including daily specials, great salads, and many vegetarian choices, there's something for anyone, and it comes at a very fair price.

Tequila Vallarta (☎ 552 8488; Calle La Calzada; mains US$3-7) Great fresh salsa and corn chips are just the garnish to what is an excellent and authentic Mexican restaurant with attentive service and a well-stocked bar. The dishes come out generously proportioned, and the sauces spicy.

Asia Latina (☎ 552 4672; cnr Calle La Libertad & Cervantes; mains US$4-7) Cozy and welcoming, this has restaurant tables and a lounge area and serves very reasonable approximations of mostly Thai food in a soothing ambience.

Las Colinas (Calle Atravesada; mains US$4-8) This legendary local spot has no frills, with its dirt floor and unpretentious fittings. But it draws all sorts for its delicious and low-priced *guapote* drawn straight from the lake. It's easiest reached by taxi.

Charly's (☎ 552 2942; mains US$4-8; 🕙 Wed-Mon) In a village-like barrio that few travelers see, this idiosyncratic German bar-restaurant is worth the trip out here (get a taxi at night). Reasons to come: the draft beer, the tasty Swabian specialties such as *maultaschen*, and the peaceful atmosphere. If you order several days in advance, groups can enjoy delicious marinated game dishes, including *tepezcuintle* (paca, a large forest-dwelling rodent). There are also air-con rooms available (US$30). It's four blocks west of Hospital Viejo.

Doña Conchi (Calle El Caimito; mains US$5-12; ☺ closed Tue) This classy and romantic spot has very appealing seating both indoors and in a lovely garden. The cuisine is fairly sophisticated, with Spanish influences; it's a top venue for dinner with someone you want to impress.

El Zaguán (☎ 552 2522; steaks US$11-13) This place, on the street running at the back of the cathedral, is pricey, but is a strong candidate for having Nicaragua's most sublime steaks. They're not huge, but are grilled over wood and are butter-tender (don't dare order them well done!). The setting is stylishly colonial and service very professional. Opposite is the house where Garibaldi stayed for a few weeks in 1851.

Other worthwhile eat spots include the following:

Comedor Isabella (Calle La Concepción; lunch US$2) Cheap and tasty lunch buffet with plenty of choice near the market.

Monna Lisa (☎ 820 0474; Calle La Calzada; meals US$3-8) Pretty much the best of the pizza options.

Drinking & Discotecas

By the lake are *discotecas*, packed with young locals at weekends. They are fun but volatile, and you should definitely get a cab down here at night.

Café Nuit (Calle La Libertad; ☺ Wed-Mon) Featuring live music nightly (US$0.55 cover charge), Café Nuit is set back from the street in a lush outdoor courtyard, with round tables beneath the palms. There's a cheery mix of Nicas and foreigners who come here, socializing under the stars.

El Club (Calle La Libertad; ☺ 10am-midnight, to 2am Fri & Sat) Hold the back page, it's a stylish club with staff that haven't disappeared up their own backsides! Contemporary but comfortable, the modish front bar gives way to an appealing palmy courtyard where smart food is also served. The place really takes off on Friday and Saturday nights, with decent DJs and plenty of tequila guzzled.

Mi Tierra (cnr Calles Xalteva & Atravesada) Local in character, this upstairs bar bends around a small shopping arcade. It's very typical but also offbeat, with popular Latino and reggaeton hits enjoyed by all, from grumpy grandpas to the local transvestite crew. Fridays are quiet but Saturdays kick off.

Casa Bohemia (Calle Corral) You can chat rather than shout at this mellow spot around the corner from the Bearded Monkey. The low-lit front bar has plenty of stools and a loyal population of Granada volunteers; there's also a pretty courtyard and pool table out the back. Don't confuse with the mediocre hotel bar of the same name.

Entertainment

Casa de los Tres Mundos (☎ 552 4176; www.c3mundos .org.ni; Plaza Independencia) In addition to hosting visiting artists and writers, this venue stages concerts and plays throughout the month. Stop in or visit its website to see what's on.

Bearded Monkey (tickets US$1) This backpacker place screens two decent films every evening.

Cine Karawala (Calle Atravesada) Shows Hollywood (mostly Western) films at weekends.

Getting There & Away
BOAT

Boats leave from the **dock** (ticket office ☎ 552 4605) at the east end of Calle La Calzada, departing for Altagracia on Isla de Ometepe (US$1.50, three hours) on Monday and Thursday at 3pm and on Saturday at 11am. The boats continue on to San Carlos at the south end of Lago de Nicaragua, arriving around 14 hours later (US$3). These return on Tuesday and Friday, departing from San Carlos at 3pm, and from Altagracia at around 1am.

BUS

For Managua (US$1, 45 minutes, every 20 minutes), microbuses depart half a block south of the park from 5am to 7pm, and then pass through the park and west up Calle Libertad (handy for several accommodations) collecting passengers; in Managua they arrive at the UCA stop. Buses depart from the main bus station on the west side of town and go to Managua's Mercado Roberto Huembes (US$0.80, one hour, every 20 minutes until 8pm).

Either mode of transportation will also stop on the highway at the entrance to Masaya; buses for Masaya itself (US$0.30, 30 minutes) leave from a point two blocks west of the market.

From one block south of the market, buses depart for the following destinations:

Carazo towns & Pueblos Blancos (US$0.40-0.80; 45min; every 30min until 6pm)

Peñas Blancas (Costa Rican border) Change in Rivas (p499) to a border-bound service.

Rivas (US$1; 1½hr; 8 daily until 3.10pm)

NICARAGUA

TAXI & TRANSFERS

Taxis to other destinations are relatively cheap if you bargain a little. Sample fares include Masaya (US$5 to US$8), and San Jorge (for Ometepe; US$15 to US$25).

Paxeos (☎ 552 8291; www.paxeos.com; in juice bar on Parque Central) runs an air-con minibus shuttle service to and from Managua airport. It costs US$15 per person; if you are two or more, you can beat this price in a taxi.

Getting Around

The Bearded Monkey hostel rents bikes (US$5 per day) as does Bicicletería (US$9), half a block south of the park, and Tierra Tour.

Rider Mode Rental (☎ 813 2545; Calle La Calzada) rents well-kept motorbikes for US$20 (125cc) to US$30 (250cc) a day.

A taxi ride anywhere in central Granada costs US$0.55 for one, and a little more for each additional person.

AROUND GRANADA
Las Isletas & Isla Zapatera

Just offshore from Granada, Las Isletas are a group of some 350 diminutive islands formed 10,000 years ago by an erupting Volcán Mombacho. Divided by narrow channels, they are memorably scenic and easily reached by motorboat. Many are inhabited (by traditional fishing families and now by Nicaragua's super-wealthy), and some have hotels and restaurants. There's a proliferation of birdlife throughout, with egrets, herons and cranes particularly numerous around sunrise and sunset.

Most tour companies run daily trips to the islets, or you can arrange it yourself at the southern end of the Centro Turístico, or from Puerto Asese, 2km further south. A covered boat holding up to 12 people costs about US$15 per hour. You can arrange to be dropped off on an island and picked up later. At **Puerto Asese** itself, there's a deck restaurant by the harbor from which you can watch birds flitting among lilies or gaze at distant volcanic peaks.

On Isla San Pablo, a half-hour boat ride out, you can visit **El Castillo**, a small fort built in 1784 to guard against British incursions. Its rooftop observation deck affords great views of both Granada and Mombacho.

Hotel Isleta La Ceiba (☎ 266 1694; www.nicaraolake .com.ni; ✗ ✗), on Isla La Ceiba, offers a package including a cabin, three meals, drinks,

water sports and a round-trip boat ride from Puerto Asese for US$55 per person.

Beyond Las Isletas is the much larger Isla Zapatera, centerpiece of the national park of the same name. Two hours away by motorboat from Granada, this island is one of Nicaragua's most important archaeological areas, though the giant pre-Columbian stone statues have been moved to museums. Tombs and rock carvings remain on adjacent Isla El Muerto. The cheapest way to get there is by tour from Granada.

Reserva Natural Volcán Mombacho

Mombacho's jagged peaks – the highest is 1345m – stand guard over Granada. The slopes of the volcano form an island of biodiversity; vegetation and wildlife vary with altitude, and above 800m the volcano becomes a cloud forest where ferns, mosses and bromeliads cling to the trees. Still higher, the landscape transforms to dwarf forest. The moisture-rich environment of the lower slopes is perfect for the cultivation of coffee.

The last recorded major activity was in 1570, when a massive tremor caused the wall of Mombacho's crater to collapse, draining the lagoon it held and washing away an indigenous village of 400 inhabitants. The volcano is still definitely active and sends up a smoke ring now and then to keep people edgy.

The reserve is managed by **Fundación Cocibolca** (☎ 552 5858; www.mombacho.org; admission US$9; ☽ 8am-5pm Thu-Sun), which maintains a biological research station and trains guides. Any Nandaime-bound bus can drop you at the reserve entrance, from where it's a steep 2km hike to an information center, from which park rangers can drive you up in a 4WD 'ecomobile' (departures 8:30am, 10am, 1pm and 3pm) to the biological station. Otherwise, many Granada tour operators run day trips to the reserve for US$20 to US$30 per person.

From the station at 1150m, where there's also a café-restaurant and shop, a 1km self-guided trail traverses the cloud forest. Much tougher and much more interesting is the 4km, four-hour Sendero El Puma, which climbs sharply and runs along the edge of the crater for a while. You need a guide for this walk.

For US$30 per person (prebooking essential), you can stay at the hostel here, sleeping in a clean, communal dorm. The price includes dinner, breakfast, transport to the reserve from Granada, and a spooky guided night walk where you'll spot crawlies galore. The money helps maintain the reserve, and it's a highly recommended experience.

Canopy Tours Mombacho (☎ 267 8256; tour US$30 per person), up the road from the parking lot of the official reserve entrance, offers a canopy tour adventure, involving 16 platforms over the 1700m course. Granada tour operators including the affiliated Mombotour offer return trips from town.

Laguna de Apoyo

Set in a picturesque valley brimming with wildlife, the lovely Apoyo crater lake is another one of Nicaragua's many natural wonders. Dry tropical rain forest along the surrounding slopes contains much biodiversity – turquoise-browed motmot and montezuma oropendola (large, brightly plumed birds famed – by birders – for their bizarre singing) inhabit the region, along with some 60 species of bat, and howler monkeys dwell in the treetops. The pristine waters of the lagoon are great for swimming and diving.

The diversity of the region also extends to humans, and you'll see a mix of rustic houses and opulent mansions. Although the spot is a natural reserve, protection is inadequate, so do your bit by patronizing low-impact businesses in the increasingly touristy development here.

In a bucolic setting on the wooded banks of the lake, the nonprofit **Proyecto Ecológico** (☎ 882 3992; www.gaianicaragua.org) research station offers fairly intensive Spanish courses (US$190 for a 25-hour week, including bed and board). There's a lodge here, but if students prefer they can live with local families in the area.

Lodging for nonstudents is available in the large ranch-style home or in adjacent **cabins** (dm US$7.50, s/d without bathroom US$16/19, d with bathroom US$25). The kitchen (which you can use) prepares tasty set meals. Bicycles and kayaks can be rented, and PADI-approved divers can join expeditions to research the lake's endemic fishes.

There's an increasing number of other places to stay and eat. Two popular sleeping choices are affiliated to hostels in Granada, which offer transportation. The **Monkey Hut** (☎ 887 3546; www.thebeardedmonkey.com; dm/s/d US$10/18/25; P) is a lovely house overlooking the lake. Entrance for the day costs US$6 (waived for overnight guests), and includes use of canoes, inner tubes, assorted sporting equipment and the kitchen. Don't forget to bring your own food.

Shuttles depart from the Bearded Monkey in Granada on Monday, Wednesday and Friday at 10:30am, returning at 6pm (US$1 each way).

Friendly Hospedaje Crater's Edge (☎ 895 3202; www.craters-edge.com; dm US$10, r US$20-37; 🗷) is associated with the Oasis hostel in Granada (minibus at 10am and 4pm daily, US$3 round-trip). There's a variety of breezy, spacious rooms with or without bathroom, and a secure dorm looking out over the lake, where you'll find kayaks, tubes, and a bar. There's also a restaurant.

The lake is most easily accessed by public transport from Masaya. Every half-hour, buses run to the crater rim (US$0.25, 25 minutes), but only three (6:30am, 11:30am, 4:30pm) descend the further 2km to the lake.

Pueblos Blancos

The mountainous coffee-growing region between the Managua–Masaya highway and the Interamericana Hwy is dotted with pretty villages, so named for their typically white-stuccoed homes with brightly painted doors and window frames.

Pottery making is the main activity in **San Juan de Oriente**. You can shop at the Cooperativa Quetzalcóatl or at a number of workshops along the main road. Ask vendors if you can take a peek at the potters at work.

The gorgeous nearby village of **Catarina** is known for its *mirador* (lookout), which offers sweeping views of Laguna de Apoyo, Lago de Nicaragua and the city of Granada. The town offers appealing places to stay, including **Hospedaje Euro** (☎ 558 0045; r per person US$2.80), which is a bargain for such a clean, cheery flophouse.

Augusto Sandino was born and raised in **Niquinohomo**, aptly translated as 'Valley of the Warriors.' His boyhood home, in the house opposite the northwest corner of the main plaza, is now a library, with a small display on the man's life.

Buses to these villages (US$0.70, 30 minutes, every 20 minutes until 5pm) leave regularly from one block south of the market in Granada.

Carazo Towns

Southwest of the Pueblos Blancos, in Carazo department, **San Marcos** and the 'twin cities' of **Jinotepe** and **Diriamba** are set in a citrus- and coffee-cultivation area. The three towns celebrate a distinctive religious and folklore

NICARAGUA

ritual known as 'Toro Guaco,' in which the Nicarao town of Jinotepe and Diriamba, its Chorotega rival before the European conquest, commemorate their relationship. Jinotepe's patron is Santiago (St James), whose day is July 25; Diriamba's is San Sebastián (January 20). These two towns, along with San Marcos, carry out ceremonial visits to each other, livened up with striking costumes and masks displayed in dances, mock battles and plays satirizing their Spanish invaders. The pantomime figure of 'El Güegüense' is a symbol of Nicaraguan identity.

Buses to Diriamba, Jinotepe and San Marcos depart from one block south of the market in Granada (US$0.75, 45 minutes, every hour until 6pm). There are extremely frequent departures from Masaya and Managua as well.

MASAYA
Pop 92,600

This appealing working-class city between Managua and Granada is famous across the country as being Nicaragua's epicenter of *artesanías* and is a great place to buy gifts and souvenirs. The fabulous products crafted in characterful workshops around town are united in the memorable central market.

In 2000, Masaya was an epicenter of another kind, as a series of earthquakes destroyed much of the city's center. Hundreds of old adobe buildings collapsed, and the restoration is very much a work in progress.

Many visit Masaya on day trips, but it makes a highly appealing place to stay, with the welcoming locals and the adjacent volcano enticing one to linger.

Orientation & Information

Masaya is just 29km southeast of Managua, with Granada another 16km down the road. The city sits at the edge of the Masaya crater lake, beyond which rises Volcán Masaya (see p498).

Banco de América Central Has an all-card ATM and will change traveler's checks.

Cyber King (Av Delgadillo; per hr US$0.55) One of several central internet spots.

DHL office (Mercado Viejo) When you realize you've bought more than you can carry.

Enitel For international calls. Facing Parque 17 de Octubre.

Intur (☎ 522 7615; masaya@intur.gob.ni; Banpro ½ al sur; ⌚ 8am-12:30pm & 1:30-5pm Mon-Fri, 8am-12:30pm Sat) Half a block south of Mercado Viejo.

Post office (Mercado Viejo)

Sights
MARKETS & WORKSHOPS

Masaya's famous *artesanías* can be found in many places around town. The most concentrated area is in the original market, the fabulous **Mercado Viejo**, restored to its former glory after destruction in the Revolution. It's quite a sight, girt by an ornate carved basalt wall punctured with numerous carved portals and complete with turrets. Here you will find a variety of stalls selling excellent-quality cotton hammocks, colorful basketry and woven mats, wood carvings, marimbas, carved and painted gourds, paintings, ceramics and pottery, coral jewelry and leatherwork. It's touristy, but competition keeps prices fair. Many vendors speak English, and they're not at all pushy. Thursday nights feature live music here.

Much more local in character, the **Mercado Municipal Ernesto Fernández**, 500m east of the old market, also has some *artesanías* for sale, as well as *comedores* (basic, cheap eateries) and standard market goods. The market has a particularly large selection of leather sandals and stuffed reptiles and amphibians.

Near the Malecón on the lake is **Barrio San Juan**, famous for its hammocks and *tapices* (woven straw canvases portraying rural scenes); it's fun to stroll around the workshops here. Even more so is **Monimbó** (an indigenous suburb), the heart of which is around the Iglesia de San Sebastián about 1km south of the main plaza. Intur can give you a map showing the many workshops scattered throughout this barrio. People will invite you into their homes to show you how the shoes, saddles, baskets, wood carvings and other crafts are made.

CHURCHES & PLAZAS

Many of Masaya's historic churches suffered significant damage in the earthquake of July 2000. Worst hit was the city's symbolic **Iglesia de San Jerónimo**, on the northern side of town between two plazas, though it remains open to visitors as rebuilding goes on. The Spanish government has earmarked funds for the reconstruction of the early-19th-century **Iglesia de La Asunción**, on the main plaza, Parque 17 de Octubre. Other churches worth seeing include **San Miguel**, **San Juan** and **San Sebastián**, the last of which is in the Monimbó section of town.

COYOTEPE

The century-old **fortress** (admission US$0.60; ⌚ 8am-6pm) of Coyotepe stands on a hill north

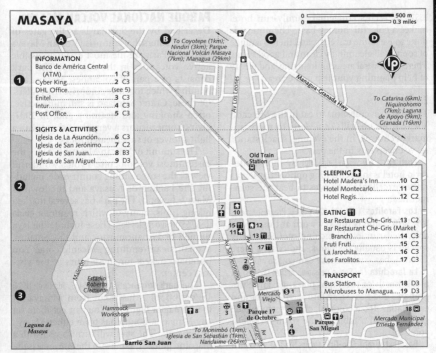

MASAYA

INFORMATION
Banco de América Central
(ATM)..........................1 C3
Cyber King.....................2 C3
DHL Office...................(see 5)
Enitel..........................3 C3
Intur...........................4 C3
Post Office.....................5 C3

SIGHTS & ACTIVITIES
Iglesia de La Asunción.........6 C3
Iglesia de San Jerónimo........7 C2
Iglesia de San Juan............8 B3
Iglesia de San Miguel..........9 D3

To Coyotepe (1km);
Nindiri (3km); Parque
Nacional Volcán Masaya
(7km); Managua (29km)

To Catarina (6km);
Niquinohomo
(7km); Laguna
de Apoyo (9km);
Granada (16km)

Old Train
Station

SLEEPING
Hotel Madera's Inn............10 C2
Hotel Montecarlo.............11 C2
Hotel Regis....................12 C2

EATING
Bar Restaurant Che-Gris.....13 C2
Bar Restaurant Che-Gris (Market
Branch).......................14 C3
Fruti Fruti....................15 C2
La Jarochita...................16 C3
Los Farolitos..................17 C3

TRANSPORT
Bus Station...................18 D3
Microbuses to Managua....19 D3

Estadio
Roberto
Clemente

Laguna de
Masaya

Hammock
Workshops

Mercado
Viejo

Parque 17
de Octubre

Parque
San Miguel

Mercado Municipal
Ernesto Fernández

To Monimbó (1km);
Iglesia de San Sebastián (1km);
Nandaime (26km)

Barrio San Juan

---

of town overlooking the Managua–Granada highway. Here was the last stand of Benjamín Zeledón, the 1912 hero of resistance to US intervention. During the revolution of 1979, Somoza's Guardia Nacional fired mortars on Masaya from here but were eventually overrun during the Sandinistas' final push to victory. From Masaya, get any Managua-bound bus to the bottom of the hill, from where it's a 1km hike to the top. A taxi is the soft option. Even those not fond of exploring old forts will enjoy the panoramic view of the entire region.

Festivals & Events

The **Día de San Jerónimo** (September 30) is so popular it now encompasses nearly three months of partying. Festivities kick off on September 20 when the patron saint, in the form of a bearded campesino called 'Tata Chombó' (also known as the 'Doctor of the Poor'), is taken from his usual perch on the San Jerónimo church altar. September 30 and October 7 are the main procession days, when the saint is borne on a flowery platform down to La Asunción and back home again.

The festival continues each Sunday through November, with fireworks, marimbas and vibrant parades.

Other big festivals include the **Día de San Lázaro**, a week before Palm Sunday, which includes a procession of costumed dogs.

Sleeping

Hotel Regis (☎ 522 2300; Av Sergio Delgadillo; r per person US$4.15) Three and a half blocks north of the main plaza, likable Hotel Regis offers tidy rooms with fan alongside a pleasant courtyard, at the end of which are several spick-and-span bathrooms. The elderly couple who run the place are especially helpful and glad to impart their abundant knowledge of the town.

Hotel Montecarlo (☎ 522 2927; Av Sergio Delgadillo; d US$10) In a converted home across the street from Regis, the clean, comfortable, and welcoming Montecarlo offers a range of rooms that are pretty good value (for two people) with decent shared bathrooms. Survey more than one before choosing.

Hotel Madera's Inn (☎ 522 5825; maderasinn@yahoo .com; Av Sergio Delgadillo; d US$15-20, with breakfast & air-con

US$30;) This congenial, family-run hotel makes a colorful, homey base. The utmost is done to welcome travelers, and there's a range of rooms, all gleamingly clean and good value. There are several areas for lounging, and plenty of help planning your trip in the area.

Eating

There are several spots to eat in the Mercado Viejo, from no-frills *comedores* to more up-market choices. In the evening, snack stands serve cheap eats in the park.

Fruti Fruti (Av Sergio Delgadillo) By the Monte-carlo hotel is this refreshing option that serves rather excellent smoothies to beat the summer heat.

Los Farolitos (☎ 522 0297; Av El Progreso; meals US$1.50-3) Value is the key word at this enjoyable, well-run local lunching spot. The daily special is usually delicious, and costs a mere 25 córdobas – what more can you say?

La Jarochita (Av Sergio Delgadillo; dishes US$2-3) A block north of the main plaza, La Jarochita prepares good Mexican fare such as tacos and enchiladas. It's a colorful, characterful place; grab yourself a table on the small terrace if you can.

Bar Restaurant Che-Gris (mains US$3-6) Around the corner from Hotel Regis, this popular spot has a selection of meat, seafood and vegetarian meals; a *comida corriente* is US$2. Even more appealing is the other location inside the Mercado Viejo, where good service and people-watching tables make it a winner.

Drinking & Nightlife

Masaya has lively nightlife, with popular bars in and around the park, and *discoteca* action at the *malecón* (pier or jetty). On Av Sergio Delgadillo, near the budget hotels, are a couple of cheesy but enjoyable bar-restaurants.

Getting There & Away

Buses arrive and depart from the eastern side of the Mercado Municipal Ernesto Fernández. There are departures for Managua (US$0.45, 45 minutes, every 20 minutes from 4:30am to 5pm) and Granada (US$0.45, 40 minutes, every 25 minutes from 5am to 6pm). Microbuses to Managua (US$0.70, 30 minutes, frequent) run from Parque San Miguel, one block east of the Mercado Viejo. From the main road, there are frequent microbuses and buses to both Managua and Granada. A taxi to Granada should cost no more than US$5 to US$7.

PARQUE NACIONAL VOLCÁN MASAYA

Described by the Spaniards as the gates of hell, the craters that comprise Volcán Masaya National Park are the most easily accessible active volcanoes in the country. The park consists of a pair of volcanoes, Masaya and Nindirí, which together comprise five craters. Of these, Cráter Santiago is still quite active, often smoking and steaming and, in 2001, giving some visitors a very close shave with a light shower of superheated rocks.

The summit of Volcán Masaya (632m), the easternmost volcano, offers you a wonderful view of the surrounding countryside, including the Laguna de Masaya and the town of Masaya beyond. The park has several marked hiking trails, many of which require a **guide** (US$0.55 per group plus tip). These include the lava tunnels of Tzinancanostoc and El Comalito, a small steam-emitting volcanic cone. You purchase tickets for these tours at the visitors center.

The **park entrance** (☎ 522 5415; admission US$4; 9am-4:45pm) is just 6km from Masaya on the Managua highway. You can get there on any Managua-bound bus from either Masaya or Granada. The staff will furnish you with a map and guide; 1.5km from the entrance is the visitors center, museum and butterfly garden. From there it's 5km up to the **Plaza de Oviedo**, a clearing by the rim of the crater named after the 16th-century Spanish monk who, suspecting that the bubbling lava was pure gold, descended to the crater with a plastic bag and a pooper-scooper and came back alive. Here, the smell of sulfur is strong, and it's easy to imagine Lucifer lurking in the depths below.

There's no public transportation, but you may be able to hitch a ride; tour operators in Granada and Masaya (speak with Intur) are another option.

A FIERY PAST

According to legend, pre-Hispanic inhabitants of the area would throw young women into the boiling lava at the bottom of the crater to appease Chaciutique, the goddess of fire, and skeletons of these human sacrifices have been found in nearby lava tunnels. A cross overlooking Cráter Santiago is said to have been placed there in the 16th century by the Spanish, who hoped to exorcise the demons who dwelled within.

SOUTHWESTERN NICARAGUA

Continuing south toward the Costa Rican border, the largest settlement is Rivas, from whose lake port, San Jorge, ferries head to Isla de Ometepe. Further down the Interamericana Hwy at La Virgen is the turnoff for San Juan del Sur, a popular beach resort and the jumping-off point for a string of fabulous Pacific beaches as well as being a major turtle-nesting zone.

This isthmus of land, only 20km wide at one point, is all that separates Lago de Nicaragua, and hence the Caribbean, from the Pacific.

RIVAS

pop 27,650

The crossroad town of Rivas is a departmental capital and center of a flourishing agricultural region where maize, beans, rice, sugarcane and tobacco are grown. Although most travelers only pass by here on their way to Isla de Ometepe and San Juan del Sur, Rivas is worth investigating: it's quite an attractive colonial town, and has a down-to-earth authenticity that can be quite refreshing after the gringo-heavy scene at the nearby beaches.

Ometepe only has a Visa/Plus ATM, so grab your cash here in Rivas if that doesn't do it for you. There are oodles of cybercafés charging around US$0.80 per hour.

BAC Three blocks west and one north of the park; changes traveler's checks, gives no-fee cash advances on credit cards, and has an all-card ATM.

Intur (☎ 563 4914; rivas@intur.gob.ni; ☒ 8am-noon & 2-5pm Mon-Fri) Half a block west of the Texaco station on the Interamericana Hwy.

Sights

Investigate the **church** on Parque Central for its curious artworks, among which is a fresco in the cupola showing a battle at sea, with communism, Protestantism and secularism as burning hulks, and Catholicism as a victorious ship entering the harbor. Also worth visiting is the enthusiastically run **Museo de Antropología** (admission US$1; ☒ 9am-noon & 2-5pm), set in a fabulous historic mansion four blocks northwest of the main plaza. Best on show is the collection of pre-Columbian ceramics and stonework found in the Rivas province.

Sleeping & Eating

Hospedaje Internacional (☎ 563 3652; r per person US$4, with bathroom US$10) There are several cheap places lining the Interamericana near the Texaco station. This is about the best of them, with accommodating staff, and a variety of fan-cooled rooms – those with bathroom and TV are significantly better.

Hospedaje Lidia (☎ 563 3477; r per person US$4.40, with bathroom US$8.80) Opposite Intur, this amiable, family-run operation offers the nicest budget lodging in town, with well-scrubbed rooms and a good attitude. The only gripe is the rather uncomfortable beds. A tasty traditional breakfast is available.

Soda Rayuela (mains US$2-5) A step up in quality from most of the typical eating choices in town, this place has excellent local food and Mexican-influenced dishes such as *tacos el pastor* (pork kebab-style meat served on a tortilla). You'll come across it a block north and one east of Parque Central.

If you're just here to catch a bus, grab a plate of food at the market stalls beside the open lot where the buses pull in.

Getting There & Around

Rivas' **bus terminal** (☎ 453 4333) is adjacent to the market, about 10 blocks west of the Interamericana. Buses also stop at the Texaco station on the highway before leaving town, and Managua–Peñas Blancas express services also pick up and drop off on the highway. You can travel between the two locations by taxi or by cycle cab (from US$0.40).

Intercity buses from Rivas include the following:

Granada (US$1.10; 1½hr; 7 daily) You can also take a Managua bus and change at Nandaime.

Managua (US$1.50; 2½hr; every 25min 4:30am-6pm)

San Juan del Sur (US$0.80; 45min; every 30min 6am-6pm)

Sapoá/Peñas Blancas (Costa Rica) (US$0.50; 45min; every 30min 5am-6pm)

If going to San Jorge for the Ometepe ferry, there's no need to go into Rivas; buses leave every 30 minutes from the Shell station on the highway (US$0.20). Taxis for the trip cost about US$1 per person. Shared taxis are also available to San Juan del Sur for US$3.30 per person.

From Rivas, there are also daily buses north to Las Salinas, a bumpy 1½-hour ride (US$1). The reward: the great surfing at nearby Playa Popoyo.

NICARAGUA

SAN JORGE

This relaxed spot, 6km east of Rivas, is where most travelers head to cross over to Isla de Ometepe. The center of town is 1km from the ferry dock, by which stretches a beach with plenty of places to eat seafood with magnificent views across the lake to Ometepe. There are also several places to stay.

See p508 for details of the boat crossing to Ometepe.

SAN JUAN DEL SUR

pop 9860

Set on a horseshoe-shaped bay framed by picturesque cliffs, San Juan del Sur is Nicaragua's main beach resort, and tourism is rapidly replacing fishing as the town's *raison d'être*. The charms it offers to a burgeoning population of expats and backpackers are easy to identify: surfing, fishing and simply *being* – watching the Pacific sunset from a hammock, rum in hand is a great stress antidote. It's a fun place; travelers looking for a lively party scene or some mellow tanning-time will love it here, but if you're looking for culture or local ambience, you may find the place vacuous and gringofied.

Information

San Juan has no Intur office, but Casa Oro hostel and Big Wave Dave's usually have local newsletters, events guides and maps. There are slowish internet places on every block (about US$1 per hour); most also offer cheap international calls. A useful website with maps and information is www.sanjuandelsurguide.com.

Banco de América Central (BAC) All-card-friendly ATM located in the Hotel Casa Blanca on the beachside strip.

El Gato Negro (☎ 828 5534; www.elgatonegronica .com; ☺ 7am-3pm) This café and bookshop has an excellent selection of English-language books for sale, including a comprehensive selection of tough-to-find tomes on Nicaragua. It's not a book exchange, although the boss might buy books from you if they're interesting and in good condition.

Gaby's Laundromat Opposite Hospedaje Eleonora, this offers laundry service as well as breakfasts and massages.

Hospital Opposite the Texaco station at the entrance to town.

Post office/Enitel phone center (☺ 8am-8pm Mon-Fri, 8am-noon & 1-5pm Sat & Sun) At the southern end of the beachfront drive.

Sights & Activities

Apart from the attractive church on the plaza, the main sight here is the **beach**, a wide and attractive stretch of sand whose southern end is the fishing port. Even better beaches, though, are to be found nearby (p502).

There are numerous operators offering everything from deep-sea fishing to zipline tours; this is just a selection of what's available:

Arena Caliente (☎ 815 3247; www.arenacaliente .com) One-stop shop for all your surfing needs. Board rental, surf lessons, plus transport to the best breaks in the region.

Casa Oro (☎ 568 2415; www.casaeloro.com) Hires surfboards for US$8 to US$10 per day, runs a daily shuttle to Majagual and Maderas (US$5.50 round-trip), and can arrange fishing excursions and horse-riding trips in the hills behind town. It also offers nightly trips in season to see turtles nesting and hatching at Refugio de Vida Silvestre La Flor (see p503) for US$25 per head including park entry fee.

Scuba Shack (www.scubashack-nicaragua.com) On the beachfront, these plungers offer PADI courses, guided dives and equipment hire.

Courses

There are several low-key Spanish schools and private teachers in town offering hourly rates and weekly courses. Check the noticeboards in hotels and cafés around town for contacts.

Nicaspanish Language School (☎ 832 4668; www .nicaspanish.com) A block east of the park, this is a popular choice for Spanish classes.

San Juan del Sur Spanish School (☎ 568 2115; www.sjdsspanish.com) On the beach, this is another well-established choice. As do others, it offers immersion courses and cultural activities.

Sleeping

There's a huge choice of accommodations, and you tend to get less value for money than in the rest of Nicaragua. At Easter and other Nicaraguan holiday times, prices rise significantly from those listed here.

Hospedaje Eleonora (☎ 568 2191; r per person with/without bathroom US$5/3.30) There are several choices on the market street right near where the buses pull in. This clean and blameless choice is one of the cheaper options.

Hotel Beach Fun/Casa 28 (☎ 568 2441; r per person US$5) Breezy and simple, this surfer favorite is a block back from the beach. Surrounding a dirt courtyard, livable rooms are clean enough, but the mattresses waved the white flag long ago. Rooms share a central shower.

Hotel Estrella (☎ 568 2210; r per person US$5) This historic hotel on the beach strip has seen a few changes in San Juan since it opened in the '20s. While it was probably once quite elegant, it's now a pretty basic budget flophouse, with graffiti on the paper-thin walls. However, some rooms have little balconies, there's a nice lounge area, a book exchange, and a beautiful café out front.

Casa Oro (☎ 568 2415; www.casaeloro.com; dm US$5-6, r with/without bathroom US$18/12) Deservedly popular and always heavily booked, this well-run hostel is in an appealing old building which is gradually being restored to its former glories. The cheaper dorms open onto the convivial but noisy courtyard area; it's well worth paying the extra dollar for one of the lovely upstairs rooms, which have more space, more peace and quiet, and their own bathroom. There are also good private rooms available. Facilities include lockers and use of the kitchen. A block west and one south of the bus stop.

Hotel Joxi (☎ 568 2438; r per person US$13; 🐾 💻) Half a block back from the beach, this makes a sound choice, with fairly comfortable aircon rooms with bathroom and cable TV. Try for upstairs, where there's a pleasant balcony area; the downstairs rooms are a little dark and depressing. The restaurant is OK.

Hostal La Marimba (☎ 568 2491; mb100980@hotmail .com; dm/s/d US$6/12/18) Calm and quiet, this has plenty of relaxing appeal in a secure family home with a friendly hound onboard. The dorm room has thin mattresses but is clean and acceptable; guests can use the kitchen and get a front door key. All private rooms have a spotless bathroom.

Hospedaje Elizabeth (☎ 568 2270; r per person US$5, d with bathroom US$15) Opposite the market, this friendly guesthouse has a lively social scene and rooms varying in size and comfort; breezy upstairs rooms facing the ocean are best.

Rebecca's Inn (☎ 675 1048; martha_urcuyo@yahoo.es; d/tr US$15/18; 🅿 🐾) This enticingly tranquil option just west of Parque Central has an owner who rightly prides herself on the cleanliness of the place. The rooms are comfortable, with shared bathroom; try for room 1, with more natural light. There's also a family room with optional air-con (US$20 to US$28).

Hospedaje Nicaragua (☎ 568 2134; r with/without bathroom US$20/15) Half a block north of the bus stop, this is no longer as cheap as it once was, but is still a cheerful, extremely clean spot that won't disappoint. Given the small price differential, you'd be well advised to go for one of the upstairs rooms, which have good

bathroom, a tiny balcony, and are lighter and breezier. Solo travelers might be able to wheedle a few dollars off the room price.

Eating

There's a long row of similar restaurants along the beachfront that offer ocean breezes and fish, seafood and chicken plates for US$4 to US$10. The least expensive place to eat is San Juan's market, with a string of neat little kitchens, all serving hearty local fare.

Cafetín El Faro (snacks US$0.50-1.50; 🕙 7am-9pm) Behind the church, this bakery and café is run by the local youth center and offers an inviting shady spot to kick back and wonder about your friends beavering away back home.

El Gato Negro (☎ 828 5534) What's that smell? It's proper coffee, organically grown, roasted on the bar in front of you, and turned out to perfection by the polished espresso machine. Fabulous. Add to that salads, sandwiches, breakfasts, and a huge selection of books for sale and it's no wonder you'll have to fight for a table.

Big Wave Dave's (dishes US$4-9) This attractively decorated gringo parlor has famous breakfasts (US$2 to US$5) – the all-in-one sandwich will well and truly set you up for the day – as well as drinks specials and hearty portions of American-influenced cuisine, with salads, spicy pastas, and steaks. It's half a block back from El Timón on the beach.

El Timón (☎ 568 2243; dishes US$5-10) Just about the most upmarket of the beach restaurants, this excellent choice has professional service and delicious seafood; the *pulpo al vapor* (steamed octopus with a tasty garlicky sauce) is highly recommended. Remember that the menu prices don't include tip or tax, so it'll be another 25% on top.

El Colibrí (☎ 863 8612; mains US$8-10) It's expensive but you may just deserve it. Airy and romantic, this labor of love is tucked away behind the church away from the beachfront scene. Dishes are served on appealing wooden plates, and daily specials always point the way to satisfaction. All the food is well prepared and presented, and there's plenty of vegetarian choice.

Two other eateries:

Chicken Lady (roast chicken US$2.50; 🕙 4-9pm) Delicious roast chicken sold from a green and yellow house on the west side of Parque Central.

Pizzeria San Juan (☎ 568 2295; pizzas US$4-6; 🕙 5-10pm) This is the best pizza place in town. No contest. It's got a pleasant courtyard out the back too.

NICARAGUA

GETTING TO SAN JOSÉ, COSTA RICA

Just 45 minutes from Rivas, the border between Nicaragua and Costa Rica at **Sapoá** is the only road crossing between the two. It's quite busy, full of trucks and buses, as well as enthusiastic 'helpers.' There's about 1km to cross – pedicabs will whisk you along. There are plenty of moneychangers – go for one with an official badge – and a bank with ATM on the Costa Rican side.

The border station (Nicaragua side) at **Peñas Blancas** is open 24 hours but is best crossed during daylight hours. There's an **Intur office** (☎ 854 0711; ☒ 8am-9pm Mon-Fri, to 5pm Sat & Sun). As well as the normal US$2 fee for leaving Nicaragua, you pay an extra US$1 to the local community.

Entering Costa Rica is free; you technically have to show an onward ticket but this is rarely enforced. If it is, you'll have to buy a San José–Managua bus ticket from one of the bus companies outside.

There are frequent buses on both sides on to San José and Managua. See p589 for information on crossing the border from Costa Rica.

Drinking

Iguana Bar (☒ Fri-Tue) The most consistently lively night-time option, this beachside joint fills up with a cheerful crowd of Nicaraguans and gringos banging back the rum as if prohibition started tomorrow.

Otangani (☒ Thu-Sun) San Juan del Sur's only disco, Otangani has the all the trimmings – colored lights, smoke and extensive lounge space. It's at the northern end of the main strip; be alert walking home.

Two blocks back from the beach from Hotel Estrella, Republika is an enticing little spot with a polished wood ceiling, streetside tables, and friendly staff. As well as the usual, you can suck on a hookah if it takes your fancy.

Getting There & Around

Buses arrive and depart beside the market, two blocks from the beach. *Expresos* to Managua (US$2.80, two hours) depart at 5am, 6am and 7am daily. Buses for Rivas (US$0.60, 45 minutes), with connections to Managua and the border, depart every 30 minutes; services from 3:30am to 7pm. You can also get a taxi to Rivas (US$2 to US$5 depending on your persuasive powers). See opposite for routes to area beaches.

You can rent bikes at Rebecca's, Hotel Nina, Hospedaje Elizabeth and Casa Oro (p500) for US$5 a day.

AROUND SAN JUAN DEL SUR

There are some fabulous beaches both south and north of San Juan del Sur. The majority are still pretty unspoiled, but it's definitely not undiscovered territory any more. However, these stretches of sand haven't succumbed quite yet, and are still mighty appealing places

to pop into for a little bit of pleasant surfing or swimming. There's no public transportation to these beaches.

North of San Juan del Sur

Some 7km north of San Juan del Sur, **Playa Marsella** is a spectacularly beautiful beach with good snorkeling and an OK estuary break. Be sure to watch the currents here. There's little shade, but you can always kick back with a cool drink at the upmarket beach resort complex.

At **Bahía Majagual**, 12km north of San Juan del Sur, there's a sheltered beach that's great for swimming. With a stunning setting, the popular lodge here was closed at time of research, probably pending development into an upmarket resort. This may render the beach private – make inquiries in San Juan before setting out.

The finest surf beach in the area, **Playa Madera** (Los Playones) is a short walk south of here. With sumptuous white sand, and slowish left and right breaks that hollow out as the tide rises, it can get pretty crowded offshore, but is nevertheless one of the country's best surf spots, with something for both experts and beginners. You can stay here at the basic but well-loved **Madera Surf Camp** (camping or hammock per person US$2, r per person US$4). Staff serve simple meals, and it's tough to imagine a more laid-back spot.

South of San Juan del Sur

The first beach to the south is **Playa El Remanso**, where caves and tidal pools can be explored. While you can walk the 7km from San Juan del Sur, the route is notorious for muggings, so you're much better with wheels or a keel.

Further south – half an hour's walk between each – from Remanso are Playas Tamarindo and Hermosa, with smallish but consistent beach breaks.

Beyond Playa Yanqui, with a gated resort community, is **Playa El Coco**, a fabulous beach ringed by postcard-pretty cliffs. Here, on a hill, **Casa Canada** (☎ 877 9590; s/d US$10/15) offers simple rooms, great views, and very tasty food.

Getting To/From the Beaches

There are two daily buses heading to Rivas via all the northern beaches, with departures at 6:45am and 12:45pm (US$1.50). Three daily buses head south to the Remanso turnoff, Playa El Coco, Reserva la Flor, and El Ostional (US$1). Check the timetables, as they vary frequently. There are fixed rates for taxi trips from San Juan to the beaches, which vary from US$10 to US$30.

The nicest way to reach a beach is by boat. A **water taxi** (☎ 877 9255) leaves San Juan daily at 11am to Majagual, stopping at the beaches along the way (US$8 return). Book your ticket at the kiosk opposite Hotel Estrella. You can also take it to the southern beaches if there's enough demand.

Casa Oro run a daily shuttle to Majagual and Madera beaches (US$5.50 return), which gives you plenty of time to enjoy the sand and surf.

Refugio de Vida Silvestre La Flor

Playa La Flor is one of the world's principal nesting areas for olive ridley and leatherback turtles. The ungainly beasts lay their eggs here at night between July and January; most spectacular are the amazing *arribadas,* when thousands of olive ridleys arrive together, packing the beaches. The eggs start hatching a month and a half after laying.

The reserve, which is 20km south of San Juan del Sur along a shocking road, is managed by **Fundación Cocibolca** (☎ 277 1681; admission US$12), who have been aided in their efforts by strong new pro-environmental legislation, which offers the turtles much more substantial protection than before.

The park guards sell soft drinks, but bring your own insect repellent and food – it may be a long night of waiting. You can camp here, but they charge an extortionate US$30 per tent; you might prefer to stay at Playa El Coco, about a half-hour walk north (opposite).

Casa Oro (p500) offers popular daily trips to the reserve from San Juan del Sur, the easy option. Unfortunately, the level of protection of turtle rights on these trips leaves much to be desired. We can't stress strongly enough that appropriate behavior on turtle tours, with the laying mothers and clueless babies extremely vulnerable, is your absolute responsibility. Distance and respect (strictly no camera flashes or flashlights) are vital to their welfare.

ISLA DE OMETEPE

pop 35,000

Ometepe is the sort of place that belongs in fairytales or fantasy novels; an island formed by twin volcanoes rising out of a lake. The ecological jewel that is Ometepe sees plenty of visitors these days but is still very unspoiled, a rough-and-ready sort of place with shocking roads and sleeping places whose charm lies in location and relaxation potential rather than state-of-the-art facilities. The island is a must, whether you plan to lounge on the beach, chat to plantain pickers, or tackle a steep volcano climb.

The two large volcanoes are Concepción, which rises 1610m above the lake in an almost perfect cone, and Maderas (1394m). Lava flows created an isthmus between them, creating the island, whose name means 'between two hills' in Nahuatl. Brooding Concepción is still active: its last major eruption was in 1957.

Ometepe is dotted by small coastal settlements where people live by fishing and farming – plantains, citrus, maize, and other crops all flourish in the volcanic soil. Parts of the island are still covered in primary forest, which harbors abundant wildlife, including howler monkeys and green parrots. The gorgeous blue-tailed birds seen everywhere on the island are called urracas (white-throated magpie jays).

Ometepe is famous for its ancient **stone statues** and **petroglyphs** depicting humans, animals, birds and geometric shapes. These remnants of Chorotega settlement have been found all over the island, but they are most densely clustered along the northern side of Volcán Maderas, between Santa Cruz and La Palma.

Both volcanoes are circled by roads, which connect along the isthmus. Between

NICARAGUA

ISLA DE OMETEPE

Moyogalpa and Altagracia the road is paved; however, the rest of the roads are rough and rocky. Between San Ramón and Balgüe it's abominable.

The island's two major settlements, Altagracia and Moyogalpa, both offer accommodations and restaurants, but to experience the true charms of Ometepe, travel further out: Charco Verde, Playa Santo Domingo, Balgüe and Mérida all offer lovely settings amid the island's rich biodiversity.

The bank in Moyogalpa has a Visa-friendly ATM; this is the only cash machine on the island. Some hotels accept credit cards, and traveler's checks can be exchanged at the bank, but if in doubt, make sure you bring plenty of money – people often stay here much longer than they planned!

ACTIVITIES

Ometepe is great for hiking, exploring and swimming. However, the terrain is rough, signage minimal and trails hard to follow. Even independent travelers are well advised to hire an inexpensive guide (see opposite), particularly for going up the volcanoes.

Both of the volcanoes are climbable. **Maderas** is the more accessible of the two, a tough, muddy scramble through cloud forest to the crater, where there's a greenish lake below, best reached with the help of a rope (your guide will have one). It's about eight hours there and back. There are several routes to the top; the trails leaving from Finca Magdalena, Mérida, San Ramón, and El Porvenir are the most used.

Concepción is a pretty serious 10- to 12-hour hike, the last bit up steep and slippy volcanic scree. Be prepared for intense heat (sun, not lava), and also for chills at the summit. The two main trails leave from points near Altagracia and Moyogalpa.

The downside is that both summits are often wreathed in cloud, but you get some great views on the way up; indeed, many people only ascend to the cloud line – these make excellent half-day hikes offering a chance to enter the deep forest, see monkeys and birds, and admire the vistas. On the Maderas side, there are also several trails to see petroglyphs. The **petroglyphs** near the hotel of El Porvenir are a 45-minute horseback ride from Santo

Domingo; ask hotel staffers for directions. Others are found at El Socorro, Finca Magdalena and El Corozal. On the south side of Maderas, a 35m-high waterfall is located a couple hours' hike above San Ramón.

There are great **beaches** and swimming spots all around the island; check out Punta Jesús María, a nice swimming and picnic spot 5.5km south of Moyogalpa; Playa Venecia, 12km southeast of Moyogalpa; the Isla de Quiste, a beautiful islet not far from Charco Verde; and Punta Tagüizapa, 2km east of Altagracia. The most popular beach, **Playa Santo Domingo**, is on the isthmus connecting the two volcanoes, and has plenty of places to stay and eat.

Many of the sleeping options have horses, bikes or kayaks to hire at reasonable rates.

TOURS

Inexpensive local guides are highly recommended for hikes, for safety (people have perished fairly regularly climbing here), to increase your chances of spotting wildlife, and for enhanced insight into the island's culture. Guides basically live off your tips, so be generous. Any hotel can arrange a guide, as can the following:

Exploring Ometepe (☎ 647 5179; ometepeisland@ hotmail.com) Just up from the dock in Moyogalpa. The best for volcano climbs. Excellent information and professional bilingual guides.

Ometepe Tours (☎ 569 4242) Another good setup, with an office by the ferry terminal in San Jorge and one in Moyogalpa.

MOYOGALPA

pop 3940

Catching the ferry from San Jorge, you'll arrive in Moyogalpa, the larger of the island's two main villages. While it's not a pretty place, it can make a good base, with plenty of accommodations choices and easy access to transport and guides to explore the rest of the island.

The **Sala Arqueológica Ometepe** (admission US$1; ☿ 8am-9pm) is worth a visit. The small museum, 3½ blocks from the dock, displays a decent little collection of pre-Columbian pieces, including funerary urns carved with bat, snake and frog motifs. Entry includes a guided tour.

The Sala offers internet access, as does Arcía, two blocks up from the dock on the right. On the same block, Banco Pro Credit has a Visa/Plus ATM; at time of research,

this was the only cash machine on the island. There's a Publitel phone in front of the Enitel office, two blocks up from the dock and two blocks south.

Sleeping

Hospedaje Central/El Indio Viejo (☎ 569 4262; dm US$2.60, s/d US$7.30/8.40) This popular travelers' haunt three blocks up from the dock and one block south has clean, basic accommodations in a courtyard behind a colorful restaurant. If eating, go for the excellent fish plates rather than the sad sandwiches or cabbage-stuffed 'burritos.'

Hotel Bahía (☎ 569 4116; r per person US$3.30) On the main street opposite the petrol station, the family-run Bahía is secure and offers somewhat dingy rooms at a low price.

Hotelito y Restaurante Ali (☎ 569 4196; r per person US$5, with bathroom US$6) Two blocks up the main road from the ferry terminal, the friendly Aly/Ali has a peaceful central patio with hammocks, trees and lots of plants. It offers a range of clean and comfortable rooms and good food.

Arenas Negras (☎ 833 6167; s/d/tr US$8/10/15) This sound budget choice is just up from the ferry dock, opposite the Hotel Ometepetl. Compact but colorful rooms have an adequate little bathroom and a fan, and there's a café which sees few customers but is a fine place to sit and play cards.

Hotel Ometepetl (☎ 569 4276, ometepetlng@hotmail .com; d with fan/air-con US$15/25; P ⚇ ⚈) While objectively it's hardly a luxury option, the Ometepetl is the Ritz of Moyogalpa. The decent, air-con doubles are OK value, and backed up by helpful service and a pleasant porch and restaurant. There's a pool, but it was dry at last look. There are tempting prices on rooms for groups.

Eating & Drinking

Casa Familiar (fish dishes US$3-4) Of the many lodgings that serve meals (two blocks up from the dock and half a block south), Casa Familiar has a pleasant little *rancho* (thatched-roof café) with exceptionally well-prepared lake fish.

Los Ranchitos (☎ 569 4112; mains US$2-7) Two blocks up from the dock and half a block south, thatched Los Ranchitos is popular for its warmhearted service and big portions of both local dishes and surprisingly tasty pizza. There's also a couple of rooms out the back (US$6 per person).

Yogi's (☎ 827 3549; dishes US$2-4; ✆ 8am-9pm) Named after the owners' handsome black dog, this hospitable place knows how to treat a traveler, with truly excellent sandwiches, burgers, and breakfasts as well as internet access, cheap phone calls, and big-screen movies in the peaceful courtyard space. It's half a block south of Hospedaje Central; just holler out if the front door's shut.

Hotel Bahía (☎ 569 4116) This hotel has a back bar opposite the petrol station in the center of town. It offers highly enjoyable no-frills drinking at plastic tables set out beside the roadside.

Discoteca Cocibolca (cover weekends US$0.80) Opposite Hospedaje Central, this is a quiet bar with surly staff most of the week but turns up the sound and opens up the courtyard area at weekends. Friday is 'ladies' night.'

ALTAGRACIA
pop 2770

Not a great deal goes down in sleepy Altagracia, an attractive town at the other end of the paved road from busier Moyogalpa. It's a handy base for climbing Concepción. There's a dock 2km from town from where ferries run to Granada and San Carlos.

There's not much to see in town except for the fine ancient **stone statues** beside the church near the pretty parque central, and the **Museo de Ometepe** (admission US$1; ✆ 8am-4pm Mon-Sat), which displays an assortment of archaeological, geological and cultural artifacts. Most interesting is a wall painting depicting the legend of Chico Largo, an angular farmer who heads a mythical community underneath the lake.

Sleeping & Eating

Hotel Castillo (☎ 552 8744; hotelcastillo@hotmail.com.ni; r per person US$3, s/d with bathroom US$6/10, with air-con & breakfast US$20/30; ✖ ⬚) A couple of blocks south of the park, the popular Castillo has quiet, airy rooms that are pretty decent for this price and surround a thatched, hammocked courtyard. There's a good bar and restaurant and helpful management.

Hospedaje Kencho (☎ 552 8772; r per person US$3) Shabby but sympathetically run, this has bare quarters with clean shared bathrooms. The restaurant is decent value and a low-key spot for a cool drink and chat.

Hotel Central (☎ 552 8770; r per person US$3.50, with bathroom US$4.50, cabins per person US$7) Near the Castillo, this is a solid all-rounder offering smiley staff and decent cool rooms with good

---

LAGO DE NICARAGUA (COCIBOLCA)

Massive Lago de Nicaragua, also known by its indigenous name, Cocibolca (sweet sea), was the spiritual heart of precolonial Nicaragua and is Central America's largest lake. Among its treasures are the twin volcanoes of Ometepe island, and the Solentiname archipelago, revered by artists both ancient and modern.

The statistics (8624 sq km, 177km long, 58km wide) may not allow you to imagine just how big it is, but ride a boat across it and you'll soon appreciate its dimensions; it can be difficult not to believe you are in mid-ocean.

Though the lake actually drains to the Caribbean, via the Río San Juan, it is separated from the Pacific by only 20km. It's home to many remarkable aquatic species, including freshwater sawfish and tarpon and some 20 varieties of cichlids. It also contains rare freshwater bull sharks, though scientists have concluded that these creatures are not a distinct species but rather migrate up the Río San Juan from the Caribbean. Although they are big – about 3m long – the sharks are rarely seen, and their numbers have greatly decreased, owing to their wholesale butchering during the Somoza years (as many as 20,000 a year were slaughtered for sale to foreign markets). An excellent description of this rare species and its sometimes mythical relationship to local communities can be found in *Savage Shore,* by Edward Marriott (p521).

Pablo Antonio Cuadra's *Cantos de Cífar,* one of the most famous works of contemporary Nicaraguan literature, is another book to describe the lake and its communities.

Evidence of ancient human habitation on the lake's 400 islands is abundant. Over 360 of these are in the group called Las Isletas (p494), just offshore from Granada. Zapatera, the second-largest island in the lake, is just to the south of this group. Solentiname archipelago (p510), near the south end of the lake, has 36 islands, while magnificent Ometepe fulfilled an ancient Nahuatl prophecy of finding twin volcanoes in a freshwater sea.

bathrooms and OK beds. The round cabins are a great deal. It also rents bikes and can arrange guides. Book here for El Porvenir or the attractively upmarket Las Kabañas at Playa Santo Domingo.

There are several hearty *fritangas* and other budget eating options around Parque Central.

CHARCO VERDE & PLAYA VENECIA

On the south side of Concepción and 10km from Moyogalpa, this zone of beautiful beaches and forests of abundant wildlife is a fine place to visit or stay. The **Reserva Charco Verde** (admission US$0.25) has a hiking trail through the woods; you'll likely see monkeys. The lovely Playa Bancón looks across at the swimmable **Isla de Quiste**, a prime camping spot. Ask one of the hotels for boat service across.

There are three places to stay here, run by members of the same family. Bookings are often necessary. The **Hotel Finca Playa Venecia** (☎ 887 0191; fincavenecia@yahoo.es; d/tr with bathroom US$12/15, cabin US$25-35; ℗ ✄) is extremely well run and overlooks the beach. There's a variety of appealing cabins available (you'll pay some US$10 more if you want to use the air-con), simpler rooms with bathroom, and a sociable thatched restaurant. You can arrange all sorts of activities here, and the hotel rents bikes (US$1 per hour) and horses (US$5 per hour with guide).

Right next door, **Hospedaje Chico Largo** (dm US$3.50, r per person US$6; ℗) is a handsome building with a wraparound veranda and honking geese. There are dorm beds, OK rooms and you can also camp on the lawn (US$2 per person).

A hundred meters east of these, **Hotel Charco Verde** (☎ 887 9302; www.charcoverde.com.ni; r per person with bathroom US$7, cabins US$35-45; ℗ ✄) has modern cabins – ask for a lake view – and characterful old rooms – sleep upstairs. Trees surround the grounds, and it's a short walk from there to the lagoon.

A few kilometers beyond here, **Tesoro del Pirata** (☎ 820 2259; dm US$4, r with bathroom & air-con US$30; ℗ ✄) is an away-from-it-all spot on a sheltered beach. It's a cordial place with a thatched restaurant and OK clean rooms that aren't as good value as the dorms. There's a rowboat and kayak available; you can also go out on fishing trips. It's 1km off the paved road some 14km from Moyogalpa.

SANTO DOMINGO

With a fabulous beach and many of the choicest accommodations, the little community of Santo Domingo, on the island's waist between the volcanoes, is where many people head.

Two kilometers west of Santo Domingo, you'll see signs for the **Ojo de Agua** (admission US$1) waterhole. Keep along the muddy road and after 20 minutes you'll reach the picturesque swimming hole, which has a kiosk selling drinks. It's a relaxing place, and good to chat to locals, who lug elaborate picnics down the trail.

Finca Santo Domingo (☎ 552 8787; hotel-santo-domingo@yahoo.com; r with fan US$18-23, with air-con US$25-30; ℗ ✄ 💻) is an immensely appealing option, with rooms where waves will lull you to sleep, and a strandside restaurant-bar that's a great spot. The rooms in the main building are more appealing than the darkish cabins on the other side of the road. There are horses and bikes, as well as a short but cheap zipline tour opposite.

Also here, **Hospedaje Buena Vista** (r with/without bathroom US$10/8) is a great budget choice, with a genial boss and appealing fan-cooled rooms, with plenty of hammocks around to loll about in. There's a cheap spot to eat next door.

There are other places to stay nearby, including a couple of more upmarket options.

SANTA CRUZ & BALGÜE

Beyond Santo Domingo, the road divides at Santa Cruz, with the left fork heading to Balgüe, and the right to Mérida. There's a restaurant at the junction, a cheap and worthy *comedor* just down the Balgüe road, and, down the Mérida road (1km in total) a cracking place to stay. **El Porvenir** (☎ 855 1426 or via Hotel Central in Altagracia; r per person US$7) is set in an outstandingly beautiful location on a hilltop with superb views and no noise, and is perhaps the island's supreme spot for relaxation. The simple rooms have sturdy wooden beds, bathroom, and porch and are set around a lovely flowery garden. There's a restaurant, petroglyphs just below, and walking paths, including one that ascends Maderas.

From the junction, 1km toward Balgüe will bring you to **El Zopilote** (www.ometepezopilote .com; hammocks US$1.25, dm US$2, r per person US$6), a laid-back ecological farm. Facilities are very basic, but it's a welcoming place with great views and a convivial atmosphere. The trail is signposted to the right off the road.

Travelers looking to climb Maderas might also opt to stay beyond Balgüe at **Finca Magdalena** (☎ 880 2041; www.fincamagdalena.com; hammock US$1.25, dm/s US$2/2.50, d US$7-8; P). With gorgeous views over the hillside, the old farmhouse is set on an organic coffee plantation and offers rustic accommodations as well as more modern cabañas (US$30 to US$40) and camping facilities. Tasty, fresh-cooked meals are available and within the grounds are various petroglyphs.

MÉRIDA & SAN RAMÓN

On the other side of Maderas lies the beautiful, wind-swept shoreline of Mérida, a spreadout town with some 1800 inhabitants in it and the surrounding area. Further south, San Ramón is a simple agricultural village, typical of the Maderas side of the island. Beyond here, the road degenerates even further but passes through some friendly and fascinatingly isolated plantain-farming communities before emerging at Balgüe.

There are several appealing places to stay around Mérida and San Ramón. All have (or can arrange) horses or bikes to hire. The northernmost, **Playa Volcán** (☎ 871 8303; www .playavolcan.tk; hammock or camp site US$1, dm US$1.50; P) is signposted from the main road. The accommodations are in very simple huts – you're probably more comfy in a hammock – but it's a friendly place with a communal vibe.

On the main road south of town, **Hacienda Mérida** (☎ 868 8973; www.lasuerte.org; campsite per person US$1.50, dm US$3-4, r per person US$6; 🖳) was a former ranch of the Somoza family. It's now a popular traveler's R&R spot. The rooms are clean, and shared bathrooms are well maintained. The buffet dinners are very toothsome, and you can rent kayaks, climb a steep path up Maderas volcano, or just laze by the water, where there's a jetty just perfect for lounging.

Not far past here, **Hotel Omaja** (☎ 855 7656; dm US$5-10, r with fan/air-con US$25/50; P 🍴) is a very attractive hillside hotel with excellent cabins offering fabulous views. The dorm accommodations are clean and good, and you even get warm showers. The restaurant is also recommended.

Just beyond, **Monkey's Island Hotel** (☎ 844 1529; monkeysislandjacinto@hotmail.com; dm US$2.50, r with bathroom US$8; P 🖳) is run with pride by a hospitable local family. Simple but immensely inviting, it sits on a breezy spur with the beach

below. There are plenty of rocking chairs to lounge in; the concrete-floored rooms with bathroom offer plenty of value, while the simpler shareable rooms are basic but more than adequate. You can also camp here (US$1.50). Delicious no-frills meals (US$1 to US$2.50) are available.

On a hillside in San Ramón is **Estación Biológica de Ometepe** (☎ 883 1107; lasuerte@safari.net; dm US$10, cabañas US$25, ste US$65-80; P 🍴 🖳), a center for research in tropical ecology designed to house international university groups. It's a big grassy compound with a jetty and appealing rooms shaded by wide hammocked verandas. There are very tasty meals. Book ahead.

From the center, you can climb 3km (four hours return) to the fabulous waterfall of **Cascada San Ramón** (admission US$3, guests free); this is also a popular route up Volcán Maderas.

GETTING THERE & AWAY

The fastest and most popular way of reaching the island is via San Jorge near Rivas, from where boats make the 15km crossing to Moyogalpa on Ometepe.

There are two types of boat: car/passenger ferries (1st/2nd class US$3.30/2.20) and fairly basic *lanchas* (small motorboats; US$1.60). The crossing, which takes just over an hour, can be fairly rough, particularly in the afternoon. The ferries are significantly more comfortable – 1st class has a bar and air-conditioned lounge, but the grungy *lancha* crossing can be quite an experience; if you don't fancy sliding around on deck as the tub pitches in the swell, get there early and grab a seat. Your bags may well get wet, so wrap important stuff up in plastic, or stick your whole pack in a potato sack.

You can purchase tickets on board, or (for ferry departures only) at the ticket office. There are 11 daily departures each way.

San Jorge–Moyogalpa ferry (7:45am, noon, 2:30pm, 4:30pm, 5:30pm); lancha (9am, 9:30am, 10:30am, 11:30am, 1:30pm, 3:30pm)

Moyogalpa–San Jorge ferry (6am, 7am, 9am, 12:30pm, 1:30pm, 4pm); lancha (5:30am, 6:30am, 6:45am, 10am, 11:30am)

The boat from Granada to San Carlos, near the Costa Rican border, departs on Monday and Thursday at 2pm. It arrives in Altagracia (US$1.50) about four hours later and takes off for the 10-hour trip to San Carlos (US$2.50) at

7pm. The returning boat departs San Carlos at 2pm Tuesday and Friday, calling at Altagracia between 11pm and 1am. Travelers are urged to buy tickets ahead of departure time at the dockside ticket offices.

GETTING AROUND

The cheapest way to get around the island is by using the rickety buses, which follow schedules in an erratic but dogged manner. There's hourly service from Moyogalpa to Altagracia via the paved road (US$0.60, 45 minutes). This route passes the turnoff to the Maderas side of the island.

From Moyogalpa, there are two daily buses to Balgüe (US$1.25, two hours), leaving at 10:30am and 3:30pm. To Mérida (US$1.40, two to three hours), services leave at 8:15am, 2:30pm and 3:30pm. From Altagracia, buses head to Balgüe at 4:30am, 9:30am, 11:30am, 1:30pm and 5pm, and to Mérida at 10:30am, 4pm and 5:30pm. For Santo Domingo (US$1), you can catch either a Mérida or a Balgüe bus. It's also easy to hike or hitch from the turnoff from the paved road.

There are around 30 taxis on the island, either comfortable minibuses or hardier pickup trucks. They are most easily picked up by the dock in Moyogalpa, and will take you just about anywhere on the island. Expect to pay US$15 to US$20 one-way to Playa Santo Domingo, US$30 to Balgüe or Mérida, and US$8 to Altagracia. If you're just going somewhere for the day, it's sensible to pre-arrange your return ride with the driver at a set time.

To explore on your own, it's possible to rent a no-frills Suzuki jeep in Moyogalpa at Hotel Ometepetl (US$40 for 12 hours). Comercial Arcía, two blocks south of the church, has reasonable bike rentals at US$0.75 an hour. Motorcycle rental is sporadically offered, but the poor condition of the roads means it can cost US$30 to US$35 for a day's rental. Ask at Exploring Ometepe.

SAN CARLOS & AROUND

The steamy riverside town of San Carlos is an important hub for river transport, and launch-pad for a number of highly appealing attractions including the Solentiname archipelago, several wildlife reserves, and the fabulously unlikely Spanish castle at El Castillo.

SAN CARLOS

River ports are always intriguing places and hot swampy San Carlos is no exception. Standing on the southeastern corner of Lago de Nicaragua, it's the place to go to catch a boat down the Río San Juan, over to Costa Rica, or across to the artists' archipelago, Solentiname.

There's not a great deal to do in town except explore what remains of the **old fortress**, built in 1793 by the Spanish to keep invading forces from entering the lake and gaining access to Granada's wealth. The ruins lie just above Parque Central and have a few uninformative wildlife panels. In July and August a plague of insects descends upon the port, and movement about the town becomes highly unpleasant; do as locals do and stay indoors in the evening until about 9pm, when the beasts are tucked up in bed. The town's main **fiesta** is on November 4.

The excellent **Intur office** (☎ 583 0301; riosanjuan@intur.gob.ni; ⏰ 8am-noon & 1:30-5pm Mon-Fri, 8:30am-12:30pm Sat & Sun) is helpful, enthusiastic, and full of suggestions about things to do in the area. There are a few internet places in town, including one on the corner down from Hotel Carelhys (per hour US$0.90).

All sleeping options in San Carlos suffer from frequent power and water cuts. There are a couple of cheap *hospedajes* near the boat dock. Better is friendly **Hospedaje Peña** (☎ 583 0298; r per person US$1.65), a block west of the Intur office, with basic rooms with shared bathroom. A block east of the boat dock, **Hotel San Carlos** (☎ 583 0265; r per person US$5) has a balcony overlooking the water and spacious clean

---

GETTING TO COSTA RICA BY BOAT

From San Carlos you can take a small boat up the Río Frío to the Costa Rican border station at **Los Chiles** (US$6.60, 1½ hours). Boats depart at 10:30am, 1:30pm and 4pm Monday to Saturday, and 12:30pm Sunday (return journeys 1pm and 4pm Monday to Saturday with extra services if demand is high, 4pm Sunday). Before departing, be sure to get your US$2 exit stamp at the San Carlos immigration office a block west of the dock. The office is open from 8am to 5pm daily.

See p583 for information on crossing the border from Costa Rica.

NICARAGUA

rooms. Up a step is gruff **Hotel Carelhys** (☎ 583 0389; r per person US$12), which has breezy rooms with comfy beds and good bathrooms. **Hotel Leyko** (☎ 583 0354; d with/without bathroom US$15/10, with air-con US$40; P ❸) is the best in town, with a variety of clean rooms and cabins, some with air-con.

A gastronomic tour–bar crawl of San Carlos should include:

El Granadino (lunches US$2-3, mains US$5-6) Comfortably the town's best restaurant, with high ceilings, sizzling steaks, fair prices, great service, and a big Sandinista mural. It's half a block east of Intur.

El Mirador (mains US$4-7) Set in an old Spanish bastion southwest of Intur, it has a terrace and real cannons at your disposal.

Kaoma (mains US$2-6.50) Surly service but a great upstairs wooden deck. Lively on weekend nights. It's southwest of Intur, on the waterfront.

Mirasol (mains US$3-6) Weatherbeaten wooden deck with a top location on stilts over the water at the western end of the riverfront. Attractive but uncomfortable furniture, reasonably priced beef, pork, chicken and fish.

Getting There & Away

The airline **La Costeña** (☎ 583 0271), opposite the post office, has flights from Managua (US$116 return, twice daily Monday to Friday, daily Saturday and Sunday) to San Carlos's grass strip, 3km north of town. You should be able to find your way around the airport; ask if you get lost. A taxi into town costs US$0.55. Confirm your return flight in San Carlos as soon as you arrive; it's easy to get stranded as there are only 12 seats on the plane and they are often block-booked by tour companies.

There are six daily direct services between San Carlos and Managua's Mercado Mayoreo terminal (US$8.30, eight hours). The stretch between San Carlos and Juigalpa is Nicaragua's worst major road; it's a very uncomfortable ride. In the wet season, this trip may take several hours longer or not be possible at all.

Boats leave from Granada for San Carlos (1st/2nd class US$6/3, 16 hours, 2pm Monday and Thursday) via Altagracia on Isla de Ometepe and San Miguelito, heading back 3pm Tuesday and Friday.

San Carlos is the western terminal of the San Juan riverway. There are six to seven departures Monday to Friday (two on Saturday and Sunday) to El Castillo (US$3.50, 2½ hours) via Boca de Sábalos (US$3, two hours). The 10:30am departure is a fast boat that does the trip in 1½ hours.

For San Juan del Norte, at the mouth of the river on the Caribbean coast, boats depart at 6am Tuesday, Thursday and Friday (US$14.40, 10 to 14 hours). They stop for bathroom stops and food along the way. Boats return at 4:30am Thursday, Saturday and Sunday.

ARCHIPIÉLAGO DE SOLENTINAME

Isolated Solentiname Archipelago, in the southern part of Lago de Nicaragua, is a traditional haven for artists and a fascinating place to visit. Ernesto Cardenal, the versatile artist-poet-monk who was minister of culture during the Sandinista years, set up a communal society here for craftspeople, poets and painters, inspired by the principles of liberation theology. A distinctive school of colorful primitivist painting arose out of these revolutionary-era workshops and has become world-famous.

Solentiname comprises 36 islands; the largest are Mancarrón, San Fernando (also called Isla Elvis Chavarría) and Venada (Isla Donald Guevara). The first two have the principal facilities for travelers. **Mancarrón** also has the islands' most famous sight, the thatched church that was the spiritual and communal center of Cardenal's community. Near here is an interesting archaeological exhibition – San Fernando also has a worthwhile museum.

There are many **petroglyphs** scattered around the island, which make appealing destinations for hikes – there are also caves to explore on San Fernando. Fishing is good around here, and Zapote has great bird-watching possibilities. Otherwise, the islands are just great for taking it easy.

Hotel Mancarrón (☎ 583 0083; r per person US$8), near the church in Mancarrón, offers plenty of value in spacious rooms with bathroom and fan. The management are helpful and can offer plenty of information on what to see, and there's a good restaurant.

Hospedaje Buen Amigo (r per person US$12) on the island of Mancarrón is a cute place to stay, with comfy and colorful rooms with shared bathroom, and local artists whittling away outside. The price of lodging includes two meals per day.

Albergue Celentiname (☎ 506 377 4299, 583 0083 in San Carlos; r per person US$20, cabin with bathroom per person US$25), situated on a lovely point on San Fernando island, has appealing cabañas in a lovely garden setting. Rates include three meals per day. Guests have access to the fine

---

WETLAND WANDERINGS

Another great spot to visit in this vicinity is the Refugio de Vida Silvestre Los Guatuzos, a fabulous wetland zone that abuts the Costa Rican border and was once a minefield (it's safe now!) – a fact that ironically ensured the region remained inviolate. There are public boats to Río Papaturro on Tuesday, Wednesday and Friday from San Carlos leaving at 7am (US$3.90, four hours), returning Monday, Tuesday and Thursday at 6am. It docks near the **Centro Ecológico Los Guatuzos** (☎ 583 0139; dm US$11), which is a research station offering dorm accommodations for students and travelers. It runs walking and boating tours, and will lend you wellies for exploring on your own. As well as the abundant bird and animal life, there's a cayman reserve and butterfly farm to visit.

It's also reasonably easy to get here from the Solentiname archipelago. Wherever you arrive from, bring plenty of insect repellent!

---

porch, kayaks and a rowboat. Guided fishing trips are offered.

Getting to Solentiname takes a bit of advance planning as boats don't leave every day. Boats leave Macarrón for San Carlos at 4:30am on Tuesday and Friday, and return at noon on the same days (US$1.60, three hours). Otherwise you can charter a boat from San Carlos for the trip (US$100), or take a day trip from San Carlos to the islands (US$14) – these leave from the dock by the El Ranchón restaurant at 9:30am. Some boats heading for Papaturro also stop in the archipelago – check with Intur in San Carlos (p509) for schedules.

RÍO SAN JUAN

The river that makes Nicaraguan hearts stir with pride flows 199km from Lago de Nicaragua to the Caribbean. For much of its length, the river forms the border between Nicaragua and Costa Rica, and has been a frequent source of tensions between the two nations.

A trip on the San Juan is a fabulous experience – it's an avian paradise, and you may well spot caymans sunning themselves on logs. These creatures will likely face eviction should Nicaragua's grand plans of a transithmian canal ever come to fruition.

Boca de Sábalos

The friendly town of Boca de Sábalos is the first major settlement downstream from San Carlos. It's lively and sociable, always with a few people hanging around keen to strike up a conversation. There's a couple of cheap but decent *alojamientos* (basic places to stay) here (ask for Katiana or Clarissa) as well as **Sábalos Lodge** (☎ 583 0046; www.sabaloslodge.com; r US$11, cabins US$30), which has a range of rustic cabañas, forest trails where you'll see monkeys, and kayaks

and bikes available. **Hotel Sábalos** (☎ 894 9377; www.hotelsabalos.com.ni; r per person incl breakfast US$15), with a wooden veranda right on the water, also appeals – it'll cost you a córdoba to get rowed across here from the dock.

El Castillo

About one-third of the way from the lake to the ocean is El Castillo (pop 1200), a fortress built by the Spanish in 1675 at a strategic bend in the river to try to halt the passage of pirates heading for the fabled gold of Granada. It's an utterly memorable spot, with the unlikely castle looking over the lively rapids below.

Bitter battles were fought at El Castillo against flotillas of assailants. In 1762 the British and their Miskito allies attacked the fort, but Spanish forces, led by the daughter of their fallen commander, managed to hold off the invaders. The fort was besieged and briefly held by a British force in 1780 – a young Horatio Nelson was among their numbers – but the ill-equipped expedition succumbed to dysentery and once again had to retreat. The **fort** (admission US$2, camera US$1.35; ⏰ 8am-noon & 1-5pm) offers top views and has decent displays on its turbulent history. Admission includes a well-informed guided tour.

Right opposite the dock, a **tourist office** (⏰ 8-11am & 2-5pm Mon-Sat) gives information in the area and offers a well-organized system of guided excursions in the area (see the boxed text, p512). A couple of doors along, Soda Carolina offers unreliable internet access.

SLEEPING & EATING

Of the three budget places on the main path near the dock, **Hospedaje Universal** (r per person US$3.30) is the better, with small, spare rooms and tiny windows opening onto the river.

EXPLORING THE RÍO SAN JUAN

Helped by an NGO, the Río San Juan area has developed a substantial ecotourism structure. A few kilometers downriver from El Castillo, the **Reserva Biológica Río Indio Maíz** is administered by Marena. From the Bartola lodge, there's a two-hour walking trail into the reserve; a more complex one leads from the Aguas Frescas station further downstream. You can book trips from El Castillo that include a guide and transport for US$55 to US$65 per person; other excursions include night alligator-spotting jaunts (US$40), a trip to see typical *campesino* villages (US$8), and horse rides (US$10), perhaps to the Costa Rican border. There are also several other places to stay along the riverbank, including the Bartola reserve.

If you're really loving those riverboats, you might consider taking one all the way to **San Juan del Norte** on the Caribbean coast, a trip of some 12 hours from San Carlos (see p510). Here there are a couple of gruff hotels (US$5 to US$10 per person) – and, better, homestays for around US$4 per person. You can visit the ruins of old Greytown in a boat and, if you're lucky, find a cargo boat heading for **Bluefields** or, more likely, to nearby Costa Rica. Otherwise, it's back up the ol' river again.

Just off the main footpath beyond here, **Hotel Richardson** (☎ 552 8825; r per person US$10) is a laid-back spot with good beds in cramped rooms with bathroom, murals, and a pleasant patio area, where a relaxed breakfast (included) is served.

Albergue El Castillo (☎ 892 0174; r per person with breakfast US$15) is a large homely wooden building that looms over the center of town. While the price is high considering you have to share a bathroom, the rooms (which offer character but not luxury) open onto a fabulous veranda with great views.

Heading a couple of hundred meters left from the dock, you'll reach the new **Hotel Victoria** (☎ 583 0188; hotelvictoria01@yahoo.es; r per person US$15), a well-run place with wood-lined rooms with new bathrooms and hot water. You might get your towel folded in a heron shape if the staff are in the mood. Breakfast is included in the price, and there's a terrace bar-restaurant.

Be sure to try *camarones* (river shrimps) while in town. These bad bastards are massive, with pincers that could castrate a bull. There are several places to eat along the riverside walkway. **Soda Vanessa** (dishes US$1-6) has a fabulous open *comedor* right on the rapids and offers great food, from low-priced *comida corriente* to exceedingly tastily prepared *camarones*.

Getting There & Around

Pangas (small motorboats) depart San Carlos for El Castillo (US$3.50, 2½ hours) via Boca de Sábalos (two hours) six to seven times daily (but only twice at weekends). Boats return at 5am, 5:20am (fast boat taking 1½ hours), 6am, 7am, 11am and 2pm. The trip takes three hours back to San Carlos; to get the afternoon flight to Managua you'll need to leave at 7am. On Saturdays there are only departures from El Castillo at 5am and 7am, on Sundays only at 6am and 2pm.

CARIBBEAN COAST

Nicaragua's Caribbean coast is a very distinct part of the country, and can feel like another nation. A remote rainy region scored by dozens of rivers and swathed in tropical forest, it comprises more than half the country but much of it is virtually untouched by travelers; a veritable wilderness.

As well as being geographically and climatically distinct, the region also has a very different ethnic makeup. The Miskitos (indigenous people), who give their name to Moskitia (or Mosquitia), or 'the Mosquito Coast,' today number around 70,000 and live both here and in Honduras, while the Sumo and Rama tribes, black Creoles brought from other parts of the Caribbean by the British, and other groups are also present. The races have mingled a good deal over the centuries.

Much of this coastline was never colonized by Spain. In the 18th century, leaders of the Moskitia area requested that it be made a British protectorate, as a defense against the Spanish. It remained British for over a century, with a capital at Bluefields, where the Miskito kings were crowned in the Protestant church.

The British signed the Moskitia over to the Nicaraguan government in 1859. The region retained its autonomy until 1894, when it was brought under direct Nicaraguan government control. The English language and the Protestant religion brought by British missionaries persist as important aspects of the regional culture. Timber, shrimp and lobster are key exports.

The steamy coast gets much more rain than the Pacific and inland regions: anywhere between 330cm and 635cm annually. Even during the March to May 'dry' season, rain is possible any time.

As well as the port of Bluefields, and the fabulous Corn Islands, there are numerous appealing destinations along this coastline, from isolated Miskito fishing communities to golden sand–fringed islets, and remote rivers. If you're a fan of getting off the beaten track, this is the spot for you.

MANAGUA TO THE CARIBBEAN

While many travelers choose to fly to the Caribbean from Managua, it's relatively easy these days to travel by land and water there. From Managua a good paved road leads to the important port town of **El Rama**, from where fast boats zip down to Bluefields. Piece of cake really, and a lovely river trip, plus you could schedule a stop in the delightful colonial town of **Juigalpa** along the way – check out the fine collection of pre-Columbian basalt idols in the museum.

From Managua, six daily express buses head from the Mercado Mayoreo to Rama (US$8.30, five hours) via Juigalpa (2½ hours), the first leaving at 7am. The *panga* dock in Rama is near the bus station, and boats leave every hour or so when full to Bluefields (US$9.50, 1½ hours), a speedy downriver jaunt. Slower boats run on Tuesday, Thursday, Saturday, and sometimes Sunday (US$3, 4½ hours). A slow car ferry does this trip on

Monday, Wednesday and Friday (US$8.35, cars US$22.30, eight hours); the Friday trip continues to Big Corn Island.

Rama isn't as seedy as it was, but it was pretty damn seedy. **Hospedaje García** (r US$7.80) is a block west and south of the bus station. It offers spacious, basic rooms that don't seem to be rented out by the hour. **Restaurante Expreso** (mains US$2-5) is a mighty cheerful open-air restaurant that does steak, seafood, and beer just as they should be.

BLUEFIELDS
pop 38,620

The Caribbean side of Central America is very different to the Pacific side, and Bluefields, with its slow pace, ready smiles, decayed tropical charm, and slightly sketchy underbelly, is quintessential. Named after the Dutch pirate, Blewfeldt, who made a base here in the mid-17th century, the town ranks in these parts as a metropolis, and is definitely worth getting to know, even if you're en route to the Corn Islands. It has a fascinating mix of ethnic groups, a lively nightlife scene, and one of Nicaragua's most humming festivals.

Bluefields was destroyed by Hurricane Juana (Joan) in 1988 but has been rebuilt (including its beautiful bayside Moravian church). The town's economy is based on shrimp, lobster and deepwater fish; the main cargo port is across the bay at Bluff.

Bluefields is not a particularly safe place; if you go out after dark, always take a taxi.

Orientation & Information

Most of Bluefields' commerce, *hospedajes* and restaurants are found in the blocks between Parque Reyes and the Caribbean. The airport is about 3km south of town.

Many of the shops in the center change dollars; look for the sign.

Banpro This has a Visa/Plus/Cirrus/MasterCard/Amex ATM. It's opposite the Moravian church.

CELEBRATING AROUND THE MAYPOLE

Never afraid to kick up its heels on Friday night, Bluefields really pushes the boat out for its annual May fiesta, **Palo de Mayo**. Deriving in part from traditional British maypole celebrations, it's a riotous party that celebrates fertility (and, in many cases, puts it to the test).

Bluefields's 30 neighborhoods each put on a procession, with gaudy floats, sexy dancers, and screechingly loud music. These go on for four weeks leading up to the culmination on May 31. The centerpiece of events is the *palo* itself, a tall maypole hung with fruits and wrapped in ribbons.

NICARAGUA

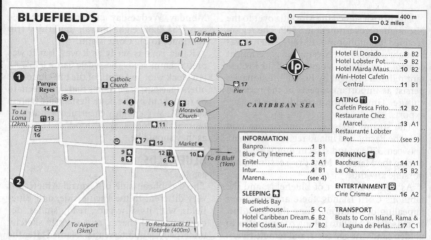

Blue City Internet (per hr US$0.70) Just down from the Intur office, this is one of many central internet spots.

Enitel On the southeast corner of Parque Reyes.

Intur (☎ 822 0221; bluefields@intur.gob.ni; ⏱ 8am-noon & 1:30-5pm) A block west of the Moravian church. There's a Marena (national parks service) office two doors down.

Post office Southeast of the park.

Sights & Activities

The town's most striking building is the **Moravian church**, a lovely building with characteristic stained glass. Although it dated from 1849, what you see now is an exact replica of the original, flattened by vengeful Hurricane Juana (Joan).

Bluefields is the jumping-off point for any number of intriguing and untouristed spots. You could ask at the Marena office about the Cerro Silva and Punta Gorda **natural reserves**, or head on down to the port to try to find a fisherman who'll take you across to the island of **Rama Key**, 15km away with a population of indigenous Rama, who have their own language and distinct social systems.

Sleeping

Many of Bluefields's cheaper lodging options cater to prostitutes and their clients. Vaguely seedy characters also inhabit them; solo female travelers might want to upgrade to somewhere else.

If you're traveling on the morning *lancha* to the Corn Islands, you can theoretically sleep free on board. It's not comfortable, but there's a cheerful scene, with islanders cooking and chatting.

Hotel El Dorado (☎ 822 1435; r US$8.30) This hospitable choice is one of several budget lodgings on this street, but there's more sleeping and less whoring done here than most. The rooms are clean and OK for this price; some are lighter and airier than others.

Mini-Hotel Cafetín Central (☎ 572 2362; s/d with bathroom US$11/25; ⛶) At the rear of a lively café, the Central offers very neat, if cramped, rooms with tiny bathroom, cable TV and phone. The doubles have air-con; couples can also kip down in a single for a couple of dollars more than the solo rate.

Hotel Marda Maus (☎ 822 2429; r US$15) Opposite the market, and 50m into a vaguely dodgy zone, Maus feels secure and is a good standby. Well-kept rooms have bathroom, cable TV and fans.

Hotel Caribbean Dream (☎ 822 0107; r US$20-25; ⛶ 🖳) This professional and reliable option is set in a pretty green house two blocks south of the Moravian church. The rooms are uninteresting but clean, and well-equipped, with good hot-water bathrooms. Somewhat more spacious ones cost US$5 more. Security is good.

Bluefields Bay Guesthouse (☎ 822 2143; kriolb@ hotmail.com; s/d with bathroom US$28/45; ⛶) The nicest accommodations lie a block north of the pier. The guesthouse has spacious, comfy rooms, all with hot water and air-con, and there's a cozy common area with book exchange. Breakfast is included in the excellent bayside restaurant.

Eating

Bluefields is a rewarding place to eat, with tasty coconut milk–based Caribbean dishes and superfresh prawns and lobster for much less than you'd pay elsewhere in Nicaragua. There's very good street food around the intersection half a block east of the post office.

Cafetín Pesca Frito (mains US$4-5) This noble and likeable local spot makes a great place for a drink or a cheap meal. It's got bags of character and is sympathetically run; the generously proportioned dishes range from morning *gallo pinto* to heaped plates of fish and chicken. You can also enjoy cheap lobster (US$6.50).

Restaurante El Flotante (meals US$4-8) South of the Moravian church where the bayside street meets the water, El Flotante has dining on a covered patio with a marvelous view of the bay.

La Loma (mains US$3-6; 🕙 11am-1am) Set on a hill overlooking the city, this pleasant thatched open-air restaurant has a wide range of seafood dishes, with especially good lobster. It becomes one of Bluefields's best nightspots once the washing-up's done.

Restaurante Chez Marcel (☎ 822 2347; most dishes US$6-10; ✖) This attractive air-con restaurant is a step up in quality from most, but fairly reasonably priced. There's a wide range of fish and meat dishes (but no Caribbean specialties); the chef's salad with beef strips and crumbled cheese is a tasty way to start. The service, from bow-tied waiters, is high-quality and scarily speedy.

Drinking & Entertainment

Bluefields has vibrant nightlife, with the beer and rum flowing very liberally. Hot spots change often, but you'll hear the bass pumping from wherever's in fashion from blocks away. Late at night, it's wise to take a taxi.

Bacchus (🕙 Thu-Sun) A very popular central *discoteca* that has a seedy but strangely appealing feel and very loud music.

Excellent La Ola sells ice-creams downstairs, but the top floor is cooler, with local chatter at tables groaning under the weight of rum and beer bottles. There's balcony seating, swift service, and the rattle of rain on the iron roof. Food is available too.

Unsigned Fresh Point is a pleasant bar, 2km north of town, set on the water with a large dance floor and a lush outdoor area of palm trees and picnic tables.

La Loma (left) is perhaps Bluefields's most enjoyable weekend experience, as the open floor space in this place transforms into a vibrant *discoteca*.

New Cine Crismar has nightly sessions at 7pm and 8:30pm. It shows Hollywood releases but seem to be a few months behind the rest of Nicaragua.

Getting There & Away

La Costeña (☎ 822 2500) and **Atlantic Airlines** (☎ 822 1299) fly daily between Managua and Bluefields (US$82/127 one-way/round-trip, six daily Monday to Saturday, four Sunday). There's a Costeña flight from Bluefields to Puerto Cabezas at 12:10pm Monday, Wednesday and Friday. A taxi to the airport costs US$0.55 per person.

It's quite easy these days to get from Managua to Bluefields by road and boat. See p513 for details. In the return direction, *pangas* head up to Rama as they fill, but it's best early in the morning. The slow boats return at 5am Tuesday, Thursday and Saturday, and the ferry at 3am Sunday.

See Laguna de Perlas (p516) and Corn Island (p519) for details on getting to these destinations.

LAGUNA DE PERLAS

The Laguna de Perlas (Pearl Lagoon), formed where the Río Kurinwas meets the sea about 80km north of Bluefields, is about 50km long and very wide in places. Miskitos living in the villages around the lagoon make a living from the abundant fish, shrimp and lobster. One can spend a few relaxing days in this peaceful multiethnic community talking to locals, observing aquatic birdlife and visiting nearby indigenous villages. Within hiking distance is **Awas**, the best swimming beach in the area. **Enitel** (☎ 822 2355; 🕙 8am-noon & 2-5pm Mon-Fri) has a local office. There are a couple of places set up to organize guides for hiking, fishing, or boat trips, including to the Pearl Keys, a group of idyllic Caribbean islets offshore whose ownership is currently under dispute.

Sleeping & Eating

There are several budget choices; **Green Lodge B&B** (☎ 572 0507; r per person US$4) is more than just a pleasant guesthouse – manager Wesley is a knowledgeable source of information on local history and culture. The rooms (which share bathrooms) vary, and there's a peaceful

NICARAGUA

patio with hammocks. Moving up a level, **Casa Blanca** (☎ 572 0508; s/d US$15/20) is a lively household with cheery hosts. Double rooms have screened windows and woodwork crafted in the proprietors' own shop. The kitchen serves creatively seasoned meals. To get there, turn left as you leave the dock and follow the signs.

Getting There & Away

Pangas leave Bluefields for Laguna de Perlas (US$10, one hour) every morning between 7am and 8am and later as they fill. The last boat back leaves between noon and 3pm; show up early to reserve a place, then be patient.

CORN ISLANDS

Once a haven for buccaneers, the world-apart Corn Islands are now low-key vacation spots in an isolated corner of the Caribbean. The two isles – Big and Little Corn – retain all the magic associated with the Caribbean – clear turquoise water, white sandy beaches fringed with coconut palms, excellent fishing, coral reefs and an unhurried, peaceful pace of life – without the crass development of better-known 'paradises.' Little Corn in particular lives up to this, with no cars or many other trappings of urban life.

Big Corn, 70km off the coast of Bluefields, measures about 6 sq km; its diminutive sister to the northeast is only 1.6 sq km (you can walk end to end in an hour). Most people on the islands are of British West Indian descent and speak English. Almost all live on the larger island, making a living from fishing, particularly lobster.

While the security situation on Little Corn is good now that there's a permanent police presence, Big Corn has had its share of problems; several travelers (and locals) have been mugged at knife- or gun-point on this island, which is a staging post for drug deals. Don't stay in rock-bottom accommodations, carry a flashlight, and always get a cab at night. If exploring the island off-road, take a guide.

Big Corn Island
pop 5930

Big Corn has heaps to offer, with a wide range of accommodations, fabulous beaches, diving and hiking opportunities. The main township is Brig Bay, where boats arrive. The airport is a 15-minute walk (if you cut across the runway). There are plenty of lodging options in and

around Brig Bay, but the best beaches are further south at Picnic Center or on the east side of the island at Long Bay. Taxis are US$0.80 per person regardless of distance traveled.

A 10-minute stroll from the dock, **Nautilus** (☎ 575 5077; www.divebigcorn.com) offer all sorts of aquatic activities, including diving (US$55 for two guided dives, US$250 for the PADI Open Water), snorkeling tours (US$15), fishing (US$60), and trips in a glass-bottomed *panga* (US$15). There's also hiking, horse riding and massages available; there's also accommodations and a café-restaurant available.

SLEEPING

Hotel Creole (☎ 848 4862; r per person US$8.30) North of the town dock, the unsigned Creole offers friendly service, with clean and cozy accommodations. Most rooms feature bathroom, and you can relax on the spacious porch.

Yellow Tail (☎ 575 5059; r US$10) Just east of Seva's restaurant, this has just one lovely cabin on offer in a lovely part of the island. The friendly owner rents snorkels and can also take you out on guided trips.

Beach View Hotel (☎ 575 5062; r US$10-35; ☒) A great budget choice, this appealing aquamarine spot is right on the water a 15-minute walk from the dock. The charismatic owner likes travelers who can look after themselves, and offers peaceful rooms with bathroom, some with air-con and stylish décor. Those upstairs are much nicer – a very good deal – and enjoy plenty of breezy terrace space with the sea at your feet.

Nautilus Eco-tours (☎ 575 5077; www.divebigcorn .com; small/regular US$10/15) Right by its diving school and restaurant, the Nautilus offers rooms in this characterful old house. They share a good bathroom, and guests have access to a large, sunny living room and a kitchen. Rooms are US$5 cheaper if you do some diving with the outfit. There's also a two-roomed house available for rental at the northern end of Long Bay (US$50).

Sweet Dream (☎ 575 5195; r with/without bathroom US$20/15, with air-con US$25; ☒) Right by the boat dock, this laid-back and smiley spot wins the 'cleanest spot on the island' award outright; the tiled rooms and hallways positively gleam. The rooms are fine value, the bathrooms modern, and the terrace offers views out over the water. There's also tasty food available.

Silver Sand (☎ 636 5199; r US$15-20; ℗) At a palm-studded point on the north end of lovely

BIG CORN ISLAND

SIGHTS & ACTIVITIES			EATING 🍽		
Nautilus Eco-tours	(see 8)		Fisher's Cave	12	A2
			Nautilus Eco-tours	(see 8)	
SLEEPING 🛏			Picnic Center Hotel	13	A3
Beach View Hotel	1	B1	Seva's	14	D1
Best View	2	B1	Virgil Place/Relax	15	C2
Guest House Ruppie	3	B2			
Hotel Creole	4	B1	**DRINKING** 🍷		
Hotel Morgan	5	B1	Reggae Palace	16	A2
La Princesa de la Isla	6	A2			
Martha's Bed & Breakfast	7	A4	**TRANSPORT**		
Nautilus Eco-tours	8	B1	Airline Offices	17	B2
Silver Sand	9	C2	Boats to Bluefields &		
Sweet Dream	10	A2	Little Corn Island	18	A2
Yellow Tail	11	D1			

Long Bay, rustic cabins sit just a stone's throw from the water's edge. The friendly owners will let you camp for a small fee, or string up a hammock somewhere.

Best View (☎ 575 5082; r US$20-25) This cheerfully painted spot offers excellent rooms with good modern bathrooms. Eschew the darkish one by the front door and upgrade to the 25-buck jobs with views, cable TV, and even a fridge in some cases. The upstairs ones have even better views over the water. All have good modern bathrooms.

La Princesa de la Isla (☎ 854 2403; www.laprincesa delaisla.com; r US$45; **P**) Secluded at Waula Point, La Princesa is a highly characterful choice, with lovingly decorated stone-and-timber rooms with shell showerheads. You are pay-ing for charisma here rather than televisions and minibars; it's better value for two people. The location is fabulous, with good snorkeling right in front, and the sound of the waves to lull you to sleep. You can pre-order excellent home-style Italian meals, served in an intimate lounge or on an open-air terrace.

Martha's Bed & Breakfast (☎ 835 5930; d/tr US$50/ 60; ✂) This is the most appealing of three mid-range choices on one of the most beautiful beaches of the island. Run by a warm-hearted Caribbean family, it offers cozy, caringly decorated rooms looking over the garden or toward the sea. They have cable TV, round-the-clock electricity and good bathrooms. Breakfast is included and served in the beach-side restaurant.

Also check out:

Guest House Ruppie (☎ 575 5162; r US$8.30) In Brig Bay, this low-key and friendly guesthouse offers simple, clean rooms. But on weekends the Reggae Palace nearby won't let you sleep much at weekends.

Hotel Morgan (☎ 575 5502; d with/without bathroom US$35/15; ⌘) Suburban feel with two rooms sharing a bathroom at the north end of Brig Bay, with porch and rocker looking out over the sea. Has a good restaurant.

EATING

Virgil Place/Relax (dishes US$1-3) As well as ice-creams and tasty juices, this spot in the northeast of the island serves cheap *comida corriente*, tacos and fried chicken. It's got tables out front where you can watch the 'busy' road.

Nautilus (☎ 575 5077; mains US$4-7; ⏰ 8am-9pm) A real blessing for the traveler weary of fried chicken, this spot prepares great breakfasts (US$2.50 to US$5), some truly inspired salads (US$3 to US$6), pizzas (US$10), coconut curries, and many other dishes of both local and international flavor. There's sometimes live music here too, and there's a shop selling appealing locally produced handicrafts.

Seva's (breakfast US$2, mains US$4-8) This simple but welcoming spot at the northeast tip of the island has hearty breakfasts and good seafood dishes that depend heavily on availability – try your luck on the day. There's a breezy (well, it was blowing a gale when we visited, anyway) terrace looking over the water.

Fisher's Cave (dishes US$5-10) With a fabulous terrace overlooking the harbor, and enclosed tanks with fish and turtles to gaze at below, this is an appealing choice just by the dock. The food is fairly island standard – seafood, fried fish and chicken, but it's well priced. If you order the day before, you can enjoy a *rondón* (beef, coconut and plantain stew) that feeds three to four (US$15).

Picnic Center Hotel (mains US$5-13) The spacious thatched bar and restaurant of this hotel is a popular spot on the beach at Southwest Bay. Although the lobster dishes are overpriced, the *pescado a la caribeña* is an excellent deal, coming smothered in a creamy coconut sauce. Also a fine spot for a couple of cold beers.

DRINKING

The spot that really gets going on the island is Reggae Palace, a sweaty weekend nightspot in Brig Bay, with a strong local character. Several of the spots mentioned in Eating earlier are also fine places for a drink or three.

Little Corn Island
pop 700

This tiny, enchanting *isleta* is a real unspoiled gem, a rough and ready Caribbean paradise with deserted palm-fringed white-sand beaches interspersed with rocky coves lining the eastern shore and plenty of simple budget lodgings that'll cook you up fresh fish in their own sweet time. Take a deep breath, relax, and… has a week gone by already?

Right by the dock, the recommended **Dive Little Corn** (☎ 823 1154; www.divelittlecorn.com) offers guided dives, PADI courses, and also rents snorkel gear (US$5 per day). It also gives out a very handy map of the island too and staff are happy to help you out with information. Farm Peace & Love can arrange guided horseback circuits of the island – you can book these at the dive shop too.

SLEEPING & EATING

The three cheapest sleeping spots are all in a row on Cocal Beach, a 10-minute walk from the dock; just wander on over and see which of them takes your fancy.

Cool Spot/Grace's (☎ 853 8179; s/d US$5/8, d with bathroom US$10) The central one of the three, this offers decent, colorfully painted huts at a good price. Shared showers are of the bucket variety. There's food available and a relaxed atmosphere.

Sweet Breeze/Elsa's (☎ 623 4060, 857 0023; r per person US$5) A longtime favorite with backpackers, Elsa offers cramped, dark rooms right on the beach; some are nicer than others – try for one with a mosquito net. There's also food available, and electric light until 9pm.

Sunrise Paradise (☎ 657 0806; cabañas with/without bathroom US$15/12) More upmarket than its neighbors, this has clean-swept cabins with reasonable beds on wooden frames and little porches. Abundant windows ensure fine evening breezes; the bathrooms are adequate, and there's a thatched bar-restaurant.

Ensueños (dm US$5, d with/without bathroom US$25/15) On a good beach in the far north of the island, this quirky and charming spot has visionary grotto-like cabañas, offbeat driftwood sculptures, and a relaxed, palmy, feel. All the cabins are different, and there's a communal one with mattresses and hammocks. There's good snorkeling offshore. Food is sometimes available, but you'll need to be very persuasive.

Derek's Place (www.derekslacelittlecorn.com; 2-/4-person hut US$25/40) In a lovely grassy spot near the northeastern tip of the island, this offers immensely appealing raised cabins with palm roof and a swinging hammock by the door. It's very relaxed and rustically stylish. If you're staying here, there are tasty meals available, as well as evening bonfires. There are also bikes available for guests only.

Casa Iguana (www.casaiguana.com; cabañas US$25, casitas US$55, apt US$80; 🖳) At the southern end of the island, this popular spot should be booked ahead by email. Set among trees with the beach just below, it offers simple cabins with shared bathrooms, much nicer *casitas* (bungalows) with bathroom, and an apartment with kitchenette and hot water. Most have a great deck facing toward the sea. It feels overpriced, but is undeniably a lovely spot. Breakfast is available, and convivial two-course dinners (US$9) are served at a communal table; if you want a romantic meal for two, eat elsewhere. Someone from the lodge meets all incoming *pangas,* so you can ask about whether there's a vacancy on the off-chance.

Hotel Los Delfines (☎ 836 2013; hotellosdelfines@ hotmail.com; s/d US$35/40; 🆒 🖳) Turn right from the boat dock and you'll soon come to this comfortable hotel, with large, attractive, air-con rooms with a little porch, hot showers, and cable TV. Management are welcoming, and there's a dive school as well as a good bar-restaurant with great sunset views.

Farm Peace & Love (www.farmpeacelove.com; d/tr/ cottage US$50/60/75; 3-course meal US$15) At the top end of the island, right by the beach, this makes a cracking spot to stay or eat. Book 24 hours in advance (via the dive shop by the dock) for top-quality Italian cooking; reservations are also recommended for the charming rooms with comfortable beds and abundant books, and for the self-contained cottage. If you're staying here, they'll pick you up in a boat from the dock.

Miss Marta's/Sweet Oasis (mains US$5-7) One of several no-frills places offering fresh seafood and chicken dishes, this is a reliable choice with a charismatic owner. There's also a bar where you can chat to locals. Turn right from the dock.

Habana Libre/El Cubano (mains US$7-10) Very near the dock, this is one of the best places to eat on the island. Plates of lobster, prawns, or fish are pricey but well-prepared. There are a couple of intriguing Cuban specialties that need to be ordered in advance.

Getting There & Around

There are three to four daily flights between Managua and Big Corn Island run by **La Costeña** (☎ 575 5131) and **Atlantic Airlines** (☎ 575 5055) in small planes (US$106/164 one-way/ round-trip, one hour). Most of those flights stop in Bluefields, where a ticket to Corn Island runs at US$60 one way.

Two *lanchas* run between Bluefields and Corn Island (US$9, nine hours), leaving at 6am Wednesday and Saturday, returning the following day at 9am. The rough boat crossing leaves many travelers wishing they'd packed seasickness pills or shelled out for the plane. The trip can take significantly longer if the sea is rough. You should book the ticket the day before.

Still uncomfortable, although stabler, the old Greek Islands ferry known as **Ferry 1** (info ☎ 277 0970) leaves Bluefields for Big Corn Island at 6pm Fridays, arriving at 6am Saturday morning (US$8.40). It returns at 6am Sunday, arriving in Bluefields at 10pm.

From Big Corn to Little Corn, a *panga* makes the bumpy journey (US$6, 30 minutes) at 10am and 4:30pm, returning from the small island at 7am and 2pm. Boat service is conveniently coordinated with the daily flights. The crossing can be rough; for less pain, sit in the rear.

BILWI (PUERTO CABEZAS)
pop 39,430

Bilwi, on the northeast coast of Nicaragua, is the capital of the North Atlantic region (RAAN) and still normally known as Puerto Cabezas.

It's still an important Caribbean port, but the main interest here is the local inhabitants. It's a great place to learn about Miskito culture; the **Asociación de Mujeres Indígenas de la Costa Atlántica** (Amica; ☎ 792 2219; asociacionamica@yahoo .es) arranges personalized excursions to traditional fishing communities, including transportation, food and lodging with local families, and opportunities to learn local crafts or do volunteer work. The office is a block and a half south of the stadium. BanPro, a block north of the stadium, has an all-card-friendly ATM. There are several internet places around.

Be a little careful in Bilwi; there's plenty of cocaine smuggling going on, and some fairly shifty characters hanging out on street corners.

NICARAGUA

EXPLORE MORE OF THE CARIBBEAN COAST

The Caribbean coast offers a world of opportunities for no-frills watery adventures:

- Try to persuade a lobster fisherman to take you with him to the **Miskito Keys**, a biological reserve of fabulous islets, coral reefs and stilt houses 50km from Puerto Cabezas. Talk to Marena in town for more info.

- Investigate the **Río Coco**, heart of Miskito country, which runs along the Honduran border. Waspám, the main settlement, is reachable by plane from Managua or bus from Bilwi.

- Head down the Río San Juan to the Caribbean at **San Juan del Norte**, explore the ruins of old **Greytown**, then try to make your way up the coast to Bluefields in a boat.

Sleeping & Eating

Tininiska (☎ 792 2381; dm US$5) Part of a small Miskito museum and craft center a block south of the Moravian church, this place (the name means 'hummingbird') is really appealing, with roomy dorms, and very decent shared bathrooms. It has the best budget accommodations in town, featuring clean single rooms with shared bathroom.

Hotel El Pelícano (☎ 792 2336; s/d US$9/12) Two blocks east of Parque Central, this comfortable spot has simple rooms with fan, and a vibrant porch with sea views and rockers (chairs not musicians). The owner is helpful and hospitable.

Hotel Pérez (☎ 792 2362; r with bathroom US$20; P ✗ ▣) This homey hotel, half a block from the *alcaldía* (town hall), offers secure rooms and plenty of upstairs deck space to stretch out with a book.

Kabu Payaska (☎ 792 2318; dishes US$2-10; ☉ 11am-midnight) The best restaurant is Kabu Payaska (the name means 'sea breeze' in Miskito), about 2km north of town overlooking the area's best beach. The views and relaxed thatched ambience make it worth stopping for a beer, if not a plate of fish or lobster (slow service). Get a cab here at any time.

Getting There & Away

There are four to five daily flights from Managua run by La Costeña and Atlantic Airlines (US$149 return, one hour and 20 minutes). La Costeña also flies thrice weekly to Bluefields and Minas. Tickets are sold at the airport, 2km north of town (taxi US$1).

It's a tough slog in a bus to Managua (US$16, 24 hours) – there are two daily services. The bus station is 2km west of town.

For information on getting here from Honduras, see p432.

NICARAGUA DIRECTORY

ACCOMMODATIONS

Most budget options are in family-operated *hospedajes*. Usual costs are US$3 to US$5 per person for a minimally furnished room, with shared facilities and fans. You'll pay between US$5 and US$10 for your own bathroom. A room for one often costs the same as a room for two. Spending US$8 to US$15 per person will yield substantial upgrades in space and comfort; accommodations in this price category are widely available. Adding air-con usually doubles the price. With a few exceptions, upmarket accommodations are on offer only in Granada and Managua. A growing number of hostels, some quite luxurious, offer dorm-style accommodations for US$3 to US$7 per person.

ACTIVITIES

Nicaragua is becoming an increasingly popular destination for active tourism, with kayaking on Lago de Nicaragua (p491), volcano surfing (p483), and zipline tours (p495) all available and well-subscribed.

Diving & Snorkeling

Reefs full of marine life near Little and Big Corn Islands (p516) offer outstanding

---

BOOK ACCOMMODATIONS ONLINE

For more accommodations reviews and recommendations by Lonely Planet authors, check out the online booking service at www.lonelyplanet.com. You'll find the true, insider lowdown on the best places to stay. Reviews are thorough and independent. Best of all, you can book online.

opportunities for snorkelers and divers (with equipment rental and guided dives available on both islands). There's also diving at Laguna de Apoyo (p495) and San Juan del Sur (p500).

Hiking

There are several enticing opportunities for hiking in forest reserves rich in wildlife, with the biologically varied heights of Volcán Mombacho (p494), or the area around Matagalpa (p472) particularly appealing. Fit walkers will want to bag a couple of the country's many volcanoes: one of the two on Ometepe (p503), for example, or one of the several in the northwest of the country (see the boxed text, p487). Guides are recommended for most hikes; this is also a way to put something back into the local community and to learn far more than you would otherwise have done.

Surfing

Surfing is huge right now in Nicaragua, with prime spots right up and down the Pacific coast, many only reachable by boat. San Juan del Sur (p500) is the jumping-off point for several decent beaches; check the box, p486, for some other great waves. News travels fast on the surf grapevine, and surf camps are springing up left, right, and center: keep your ear to the ground. Even remote spots are becoming more crowded – be considerate to locals anywhere you go.

BOOKS

Books on Nicaragua tend to focus on its political history. There are numerous titles.

A Twilight Struggle: American Power and Nicaragua, 1977–1990, by Robert Kagan, is an insider's view of the debate that raged within various branches of the US government on how to respond to the Nicaraguan revolution.

Culture and Politics in Nicaragua, by Steven White, is a fascinating interview and related material on the link between literature and revolution in Nicaragua.

The Death of Ben Linder, by Joan Kruckewitt, is the compelling story of the US volunteer who died at the hands of Contras while working on a rural development project in the country. His death is framed by the turbulent political events of the time.

Life is Hard: Machismo, Danger, and the Intimacy of Power in Nicaragua, by Roger Lancaster, is a brilliant ethnographic study of the effects of political events on the Nicaraguan family. Lancaster's work explores issues of sexuality, racism and gender identity – topics often overlooked when discussing the revolution.

The Country Under My Skin: A Memoir of Love and War, by Gioconda Belli, is a memoir from one of Nicaragua's most esteemed writers detailing her – at times – harrowing involvement in the revolution.

Savage Shore: Life and Death with Nicaragua's Last Shark Hunters, by Edward Marriott, is a fascinating portrait of Nicaragua's once-prevalent freshwater shark, and its relationship to the communities that feared and revered it.

Poetry lies at the core of Nicaraguan culture and is thus worth getting to know.

Poets of Nicaragua: A Bilingual Anthology, 1918–1979, translated by Stephen White, presents a good overview of Nicaragua's greatest 20th-century poets.

Prosas Profanas, by Rubén Darío – for those whose Spanish is up to it – is a slim volume by the country's celebrated poet.

The Birth of the Sun: Selected Poems, by Pablo Antonio Cuadra, is a judicious selection from the work of Nicaragua's outstanding contemporary writer, in Spanish and English.

BUSINESS HOURS

Business and government hours are 8am to noon and 2pm to 5pm weekdays. Many businesses, including most Intur offices, are also open 8am to noon Saturday. Banks are generally open 8:30am to 5pm.

CLIMATE

Nicaragua has two distinct seasons, the timing of which varies from coast to coast. The Caribbean coast is best visited from mid-January to April, when skies are more likely to be dry and sunny. Hurricane season runs from September to November. The most pleasant time to visit the Pacific or central regions is early in the dry season (December and January), when temperatures are cooler and the foliage still lush. For climate charts see p723.

DANGERS & ANNOYANCES

Although there's less tourist crime in Nicaragua than in other central American countries, it pays to be careful. Increasing violence in Managua make it the least safe of Nicaragua's cities, while the whole Caribbean coast, including the Corn Islands, can be sketchy – it's a big drug-trafficking area and armed robberies of locals and tourists are not unknown.

But you're unlikely to have problems. Get taxis at night, don't make drunken scenes in public, and keep an eye on your things in buses and markets.

While crime is unlikely to affect you, poverty is a fact of life that you'll confront on a daily basis. Nicaragua is a poor country. You'll be approached regularly in some areas by street kids asking for money but they are rarely insistent.

Biting insects are a menace, particularly on the Caribbean coast – take plenty of high-grade repellent.

Strong currents and riptides at Pacific beaches cause dozens of swimmers to drown each year. Lifeguards and rescue facilities are uncommon enough to warrant extreme caution when approaching the waves.

DISABLED TRAVELERS

For those with special needs, travel in Nicaragua should be carefully planned. Where they exist, sidewalks are narrow and uneven. Outside the business-class hotels of Managua, accommodations provide little if any concession to those with limited mobility. Taking a tour (p726) is a common solution.

EMBASSIES & CONSULATES
Embassies & Consulates in Nicaragua

These are all in Managua. Get a full list from the tourist office or phone book.

Costa Rica (☎ 276 1352; infombcr@cablenet.com.ni; Calle Prado Ecuestre 304, Las Colinas)
Denmark (☎ 268 0250; mgaambu@um.dk) From Rotonda El Güegüense, one block west, two blocks north.
El Salvador (☎ 276 0712; Av del Campo 142, Las Colinas)
France (Map p463; ☎ 222 6210; fax 228 1057) One and a half blocks west of El Carmen church.
Germany (Map p458; ☎ 266 3918) From Rotonda El Güegüense, 1½ blocks north.
Guatemala (☎ 279 9609; fax 279 9610; Carr Masaya Km 11.5) There is also a consulate in León.
Honduras (Map p458; ☎ 278 3043; embhonduras@ideay.com.ni; Gimnasio Hércules 1c sur & ½ c arriba)
Italy (Map p463; ☎ 266 6486; italdipl@tmx.com.ni) From the Montoya statue one block north.
Mexico (☎ 278 4919; embamex@cablenet.com.ni; Carr a Masaya Km 4.5) One block east.

Panama (Map p463; ☎ 266 2224; embdpma@yahoo .com; No 93 Colonia Mántica) From the main fire station, head one block west.
USA (Map p458; ☎ 266 6010; chowmj@pd.state.gov; Carr Sur Km 4.5)

Nicaraguan Embassies & Consulates Abroad

See www.cancilleria.gob.ni/embajadas for a full list. See other Central American countries in this book for details of Nicaraguan missions there.

Canada See the USA.
Denmark (☎ 3 555 4870; www.emb-nicaragua.dk; Kastelsvej 7, København) Also serves Finland and Ireland.
France (☎ 1 4405 9042; embanifr@free.fr; 34 Ave Bugeaud, 75116 Paris)
Germany (☎ 30 206 4380; embajada.berlin@embanic.de; Joachim-Karnatzallee 45, Berlin) Also serves Switzerland.
Ireland See Denish embassy.
Italy (☎ 6 841 3471; Via Brescia 16, Roma)
Mexico (☎ 5 540 5625; embanic@prodigy.net.mx; Prado de Norte 470, Mexico DF)
Netherlands (☎ 70 322 5063; embajada@embanic.nl; Laan Copes Van Cetterburch 84, 2585GD Den Haag)
Spain (☎ 915 555 510; embanicesp@embanicespana .e.telefonica.net; Paseo Castellana 127, Madrid)
Sweden (☎ 468 667 1754; embajada.nicaragua@telia .com; Sandhamnasgatan 40-6 TR, Stockholm) Also serves Norway.
UK (☎ 171 938 2373; embaniclondon@btconnect.com; 58 Kensington Church St, London)
USA (☎ 202-939 6531; www.embanic.org; 1627 New Hampshire Ave NW, Washington, DC 20009) Also services Canada.

FESTIVALS & EVENTS

Every town and village throws an annual festival for its patron saint. National holidays and major celebrations include the following:
New Year's Day January 1
Semana Santa (Holy Week) Thursday, Friday and Saturday before Easter Sunday, March or April.
Labor Day May 1
Palo de Mayo Riotous celebrations in Bluefields throughout May.
San Juan Bautista Numerous towns including Estelí and San Juan del Sur on June 24.
Virgen del Carmen San Juan del Sur on July 16.
Liberation Day Commemorated by Sandinistas with parades and speeches on July 19.
Santa Ana Chinandega and Isla de Ometepe on July 26.
Santo Domingo Managua on 1-10 August.
Virgen de la Asunción Granada, Juigalpa and Ocotal on August 15.

Independence Day Two-day national holiday on September 14-15.
Virgen La Merced Matagalpa and León on September 24.
San Jerónimo Masaya on September 30.
Día de los Muertos All Souls' Day, November 2.
La Purísima Immaculate Conception. Huge in León on December 8.
Navidad Christmas, December 25.

FOOD & DRINK
Food
A variety of restaurants can be found around Managua, serving some good, if pricy, international cuisine. Outside the capital city, only León, Granada and San Juan del Sur offer European or specifically vegetarian fare. Vegetarians will find plenty to eat among the buffet-style *comedores* that are popular at noon.

The most typical (and inexpensive) fare can usually be found in street stands and market stalls. Local favorites include: *gallo pinto* (a blend of rice and beans often served with eggs for breakfast); *nacatamales* (banana leaf-wrapped bundles of cornmeal, pork, vegetables and herbs, traditionally served on weekends); *quesillos* (soft cheese and onions folded in a tortilla); and *vigorón* (yucca steamed and topped with *chicharrón* – fried pork rind – and cabbage salad).

In the evenings, *fritangas* open up on street corners, at door fronts, and around the central plazas to grill meat alongside a variety of fried treats. Try a hearty plate of *tajadas* – plantains thinly sliced lengthwise, served as a base for grilled beef or chicken and cabbage salad. A weekend treat is *baho*, a 'stew' of beef, various types of plantains and yucca steamed together for hours in a giant banana leaf-lined pot.

Drinks
Bottled water and *gaseosas* (soft drinks) are found nearly everywhere in Nicaragua. Many restaurants serve fresh *jugos* (juices) and *refrescos*, made from local fruits, herbs and seeds blended with water and sugar and poured over crushed ice.

These can be a delightful treat and an opportunity to sample unusual fruits such as *pithaya*, a purple cactus fruit; tamarindo, from the tamarind tree; and *chía,* a mucilaginous seed usually blended with lemon. *Tiste* is a traditional drink made from cocoa beans and corn.

In spite of the importance of coffee farming instant is what is most commonly served. The major two Nicaraguan beers are delicious Toña and Victoria. Rum is also produced in Nicaragua; the major brand is the tasty Flor de Caña, basis of the *macuá*, a tasty cocktail produced with guava and orange juices that is being promoted as the nation's national drink.

GAY & LESBIAN TRAVELERS
A Nicaraguan statute forbids homosexual activity, but in reality the law is rarely enforced, except in cases involving a minor. Still, gay travelers should generally avoid public displays of affection.

For information on the gay community in Nicaragua, contact **Fundación Xochiquetzal** (☎ 249 0585; xochiquetzal@alfanumeric.com.ni), a gay and lesbian advocacy group. The biggest gay scenes are in Granada and Managua.

INTERNET ACCESS
There are internet cafés absolutely everywhere, charging US$0.40 to US$1.20 per hour. Wireless internet access (wi-fi) is becoming fairly common in larger cities.

INTERNET RESOURCES
IBW Internet Gateway (www.ibw.com.ni, in Spanish) A reasonable portal site.
Intur (www.intur.gob.ni) Good tourist board website.
La Prensa (www.laprensa.com.ni, in Spanish) Nicaragua's leading newspaper.
Lanic (www.lanic.utexas.edu/la/ca/nicaragua) University of Texas' outstanding collection of links relating to the country.
Marena (www.marena.gob.ni) Copious info in Spanish on national parks and reserves.
Nica Times (www.nicatimes.net) Online edition with good articles.
Nicaliving (www.nicaliving.com) Expat network and forum.
Nicaragua Network (www.nicanet.org) Extensive information about current labor and environmental issues, as well as news on the political situation.
Thorn Tree (http://thorntree.lonelyplanet.com) Popular travelers' forum with plenty of advice.
ViaNica (www.vianica.com) Private tour company with a very informative website.

MAPS
Intur produces reasonable country and regional maps with enlarged sections of the most visited zones. **Ineter** (☎ 249 2768), opposite the Immigration office in Managua, has topographic maps covering the whole country.

MEDIA

The leading daily newspapers are the conservative *La Prensa,* owned by the Chamorro family, and *El Nuevo Diario,* run by a breakaway faction of the Sandinistas. Look for the fortnightly *Nica Times,* which has eight pages of good English content covering a copy of the Costa Rican *Tico Times.* Intur also distributes other free English-language tourist magazines.

MONEY

The national currency is the córdoba, though you will often hear prices quoted in US dollars. The córdoba is divided into 100 centavos. Bills are in denominations of 10, 20, 50, 100 and 500 córdobas. Coins are issued in 25, 50-centavo and 1- and 5-córdoba denominations. *Peso* is a slang term for the currency.

The Nicaraguan government devalues the córdoba by 6% annually against the US dollar in order to maintain stable relative prices despite local inflation.

It is often difficult to get change for 500-córdoba notes, so break them into smaller bills when you can. Note that Nicaraguan córdobas cannot readily be changed in any other country. Once you cross the border, they're good only as souvenirs.

In better restaurants, the 15% tax and 10% 'voluntary' tip is often added to the bill. You should tip all guides.

Credit & Debit Cards

Automatic teller machines (ATMs) are the way to go in most of Nicaragua. There are branches of Banpro and Banco América Central (BAC) in all major towns – these take Visa/Plus, MasterCard/Cirrus, Amex, and Diners debit and credit cards. There are many more ATMs that take Visa only. You'll also find ATMs in petrol stations and shopping arcades.

All over Nicaragua, moderately priced hotels and restaurants will accept Visa and MasterCard. However, they will usually add about 5% to the bill for doing so. Most banks will provide cash advances on credit cards.

Traveler's checks are the way of the past. You can exchange them in many banks, but be prepared to queue.

Exchange Rates

The table following shows currency exchange rates at the time this book went to press.

Country	Unit	Córdobas (C$)
Australia	A$1	15.90
Canada	C$1	17.50
euro zone	€1	25.20
Japan	¥100	15.10
New Zealand	NZ$1	14.50
UK	UK£1	37.20
USA	US$1	18.50

POST

Postal services, and increasingly phone and fax services, are handled by Correos de Nicaragua. Airmail letters to the USA/Europe cost US$0.50/0.65 and take at least a week to arrive.

RESPONSIBLE TRAVEL

Traveling sensitively in Nicaragua means being mindful of the environment around you. Try to patronize local businesses and industries, and spend your money where it will go directly to the people working for it.

SHOPPING

Distinctive Nicaraguan handicrafts include cotton hammocks, ceramics, woodwork, textile arts, basketry, carved and painted gourds, and leatherwork.

Masaya, 29km from Managua, is the country's principal *artesanía* center, with two major crafts markets. Its old market building has been restored and is devoted entirely to quality work; the main market for everyday items houses a major crafts section as well. In Managua, the Mercado Central (also known as Mercado Roberto Huembes) contains a substantial *artesanías* department but the selection is not as vast as Masaya's.

Alternatively, you can go to the places where handicrafts are produced, see how they're made and buy them there. San Juan de Oriente, La Paz Centro and Somoto are known for their fine ceramics. The Monimbó neighborhood of Masaya is a center of production for leather goods, woodwork, embroidery and toys.

Art aficionados can purchase canvases created in the unique primitivist style of the islands of Solentiname. The best places to buy the paintings are from the artists who live there.

STUDYING

Nicaragua is a very popular place to learn some Spanish. Granada and Estelí have the biggest choice, while there are also reputable schools in Managua, León, San Juan del Sur, and Laguna de Apoyo. See the individual towns for details.

Most schools charge between US$150 and US$200 per week for 20 hours of instruction (four hours per day, weekdays), including room and board with a local family. Excursions to lakes, volcanoes, beaches and cultural and historic sites, as well as meetings with community organizations, may be included in the package. The weekly price is often lower for students who commit to longer stays.

TELEPHONE

When calling between cities in Nicaragua, dial ☎ 0 before the seven-digit number; there are no area codes. To call Nicaragua from abroad, use the international code (☎ 505) before the number.

The best places to make phone calls are the numerous internet cafés that offer booths or handsets connected to an online phone service. Quality is usually OK, and it can cost as little as US$0.15 a minute to phone the USA, or US$0.30 to phone Europe.

To use a payphone, purchase a phonecard from a *pulpería* (corner store). You can also make calls (or send faxes) from the post office or Enitel.

Cell phones have taken off in a big way in Nicaragua but are still quite expensive. However, you can easily buy a SIM card to fit in your own phone and buy charge vouchers at *pulperías*.

TOURIST INFORMATION

The tourist board **Intur** (www.intur.gob.ni) has a helpful office in nearly every major town, and also at the airport and Costa Rican border. To email a branch, just add the town name to the front of the website address above (eg granada@intur.gob.ni). The environmental ministry **Marena** (☎ 263 2830; www.marena.gob.ni) also has offices everywhere that can provide some information on local national parks and reserves.

TOURS

The following operators provide a wide selection of tours all over the country:
Careli Tours (☎ 278 6919; www.carelitours.com)
Gray Line (☎ 266 6134; www.graylinenicaragua.com)
Tours Nicaragua (☎ 228 7063; www.nvmundo.com/toursnicaragua)

VISAS

Visitors from most countries can enter without a visa, as long as they have a passport valid for at least the next six months. You must pay US$5 to enter the country and will be granted either a 90-day (most) or 30-day stay.

Among those who do require a visa are citizens of India and China. Check the website www.cancilleria.gob.ni for up-to-date details in all cases, as this information is always vulnerable to change.

Stays can be extended for up to three months. See p460 for details of the immigration office in Managua, where you can apply for a visa extension. Alternatively, you could head out of the country to Costa Rica or Honduras for 72 hours and then re-enter.

VOLUNTEERING

Volunteer opportunities in Nicaragua are very common. Check at local hostels, Spanish schools, or at the *alcaldía*, or arrange it with an organization in your home country before setting off. Among the many choices:
Barca de Oro Can arrange turtle-oriented projects (p486).
Building New Hope (☎ 552 7113; www.buildingnewhope.org) Many Granada opportunities. A month minimum commitment (p492).
Café Girasol (☎ 612 6030) Offers and finds placements in Matagalpa (p471).
La Esperanza (☎ 837 3497; www.la-esperanza-granada.org) Educational project in impoverished villages. Two months' minimum.
Quetzaltrekkers Guide hikes and help street kids (p483).
Reserva Miraflor This community-run reserve has several ongoing projects (p478).

WOMEN TRAVELERS

There are no special dangers for women traveling in Nicaragua, but the same advice applies as for the rest of Central America about dress, catcalls, and so on. In fact, with the normal precautions, many women find Nicaragua to be a surprisingly pleasant country in which to travel. The Caribbean coast, however, is definitely a place to be more careful if solo.

WORKING

Because of a combined unemployment and underemployment rate of over 50%, it is difficult for foreigners to find paid work. Teaching English remains an option, but the pay is minimal. Traveler-related businesses may offer you work in bars, restaurants, or hostels on a short-term, low-paid basis.

Costa Rica

HIGHLIGHTS

- **Parque Nacional Tortuguero** Paddle a maze of canals with growling howlers, sloths, crocs, turtles and manatees (p571)
- **Caribbean Coast** Groove to the reggae beat and rugged surf of Puerto Viejo de Talamanca (p565)
- **Montezuma** Wander the luminous sands of Reserva Natural Absoluto Cabo Blanco (p601)
- **Parque Nacional Chirripó** Scale Costa Rica's highest peak (3820m), where the panorama yawns from the Atlantic to Pacific (p616)
- **Monteverde** Stalk two-toed sloths and tarantulas in a night tour of the cloud forest (p575)
- **Off the beaten track** Blaze a trail through the pristine rain forest of Parque Nacional Corcovado, pulsing and chattering with wildlife (p618)

FAST FACTS

- **Area** 51,100 sq km
- **ATMs** Plentiful (except for the Caribbean coast) using Cirrus & Plus systems
- **Budget** US$35 per day
- **Capital** San José
- **Costs** Dorm bed US$10, bottle of beer US$1.50, 3hr bus ride US$4, set lunch US$4
- **Country Code** ☎ 506
- **Electricity** 110V AC, 60Hz (same as the USA)
- **Famous for** rain forests, sloths, surf spots, coffee plantations & canopy tours
- **Head of State** President Oscar Arias Sánchez
- **Languages** Spanish, English on the Caribbean coast
- **Money** US$1 = C$518 (colones)
- **Phrases** Pura vida (literally 'pure life'; thumbs up, a salutation), maje (dude or buddy), Tico (Costa Rican)
- **Population** Four million

- **Time** GMT minus 6 hours; no daylight savings time
- **Traveler's Checks** Cashed at most banks (1-3% commission)
- **Visas** Not required for residents of the USA, Canada, EU, Australia or New Zealand

TRAVEL HINTS

Splurging to hike with a naturalist your first time out will clue you into what to look for on independent hikes, and make them more rewarding. The best bet for cheap eats are sodas, which offer healthy and fresh local fare.

OVERLAND ROUTES

You can enter overland from Nicaragua (Peñas Blancas, Los Chiles) and Panama (Sixaola, Paso Canoas). Check visa requirements in advance.

Mention Costa Rica and people think paradise. The country's Disneylike cast of creatures – ranging from howler monkeys to toucans – are populous and relatively easy to spot. The waves are prime, the beauty is staggering and the sluggish pace seductive. A peaceful oasis in a tumultuous region, this tiny nation draws 1.5 million visitors every year.

What's on tap? The question is what isn't. Active travelers can surf, hike, snorkel and spot wildlife for starters. The incredibly varied topography means you can cruise the cloud forest one day, climb a volcano the next, and finish passed out on a hot sandy beach. Adrenaline junkies have a myriad ways to make mothers worry – among them zipping through canopy lines hundreds of meters long and riding the rough surf of the Pacific. Choice and variety name the game.

Of course, the frenzy to snatch up a piece of Shangri-la has its consequences. Since the boom, tourism is more chic and less cheap. Classic destinations are now crowded destinations and local culture is often lost or cast aside. Lucky for Costa Rica that its do-gooder fans, ranging from ecologists to proud Ticos (Costa Ricans), are vocal and vigilant. Nature here suffers its blows, like everywhere, but at least it is taken seriously.

CURRENT EVENTS

With a huge influx of expats, US retirees and foreign travelers, Costa Rica has become the tropical backyard of gringos. This has ignited a real-estate frenzy alongside a focus on expensive goods and services (SUV dealerships and bagel shops) geared toward this new market. While foreigners bring much-needed investment, they also drive up property prices and displace cash-strapped locals.

It's no wonder Ticos bristle at the thought of being in Uncle Sam's pocket. This fear has been a major impetus behind the current debate to ratify the Central American Free Trade Agreement (Cafta). Its proponents, foremost President Oscar Arias, tout its economic benefits which include increased access to US markets and thousands of new jobs. Critics argue Costa Rica's small farmers and domestic industries will come out the losers, unable to compete with the anticipated flood of cheap US products.

What's interesting is that this economic and cultural alignment with the USA is unique in today's Central America. While most of Latin America has elected leftist, socialist governments in a turning away from the USA, Costa Rica has placed its bets on this strategic alliance, sometimes to the ire of its citizens.

HISTORY
Lost Civilization

Costa Rica's rain forests have been inhabited for 10,000 years. The region long served as an intersection for America's native cultures. About 500 years ago, on the eve of European discovery, as many as 400,000 people lived in today's Costa Rica.

The Central Valley hosted roughly 20 small tribes, organized into chiefdoms, with a *cacique* (chief) leading a hierarchical society that included shaman, warriors, workers and slaves. To the east, the fierce Caribs dominated the Atlantic coastal lowlands. Adept at seafaring, they provided a conduit of trade with the South American mainland. Concentrated tribes of indigenous people in the northwest tended cornfields and were connected to the great Meso-American cultures. Aztec religious practices and Maya jade and craftsmanship are in evidence in the Península de Nicoya, while Costa Rican quetzal feathers and golden trinkets have turned up in Mexico. The three chiefdoms found in the southwest showed the influence of native Andean cultures, including coca leaves, yucca and sweet potatoes.

Heirs of Columbus

On his fourth and final voyage to the New World in 1502, Christopher Columbus was forced to drop anchor near today's Puerto Limón after a hurricane damaged his ship. Waiting for repairs, Columbus ventured into the verdant terrain and exchanged gifts with welcoming natives. He returned from this encounter claiming to have seen 'more gold in two days than in four years in Spain.' Columbus dubbed the stretch of shoreline from Honduras to Panama as Veragua, but his excited descriptions of 'la costa rica' gave the region its lasting name.

Anxious to claim its bounty, Columbus petitioned the Spanish Crown to have himself appointed governor. However, by the time he returned to Seville, his royal patron Queen Isabella was on her deathbed, and King Ferdinand awarded the prize to a rival.

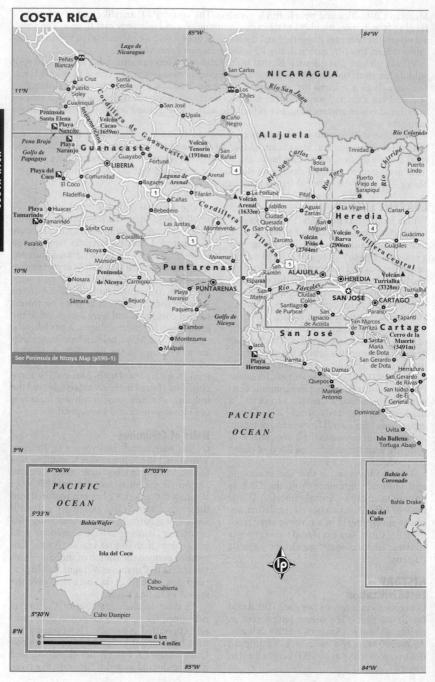

COSTA RICA

Columbus never returned to the 'Rich Coast.' Worn down by ill health and court politics, he died in 1506.

To the disappointment of his conquistador heirs, the region did not abound with gold and the locals were not so affable. The pestilent swamps, volcano-topped mountains and oppressive jungles made Columbus's paradise seem more like hell for new colonies. Balboa's crossing of Panama in 1513 found a western beachhead from which to assault Costa Rica. The Spanish targeted the indigenous groups living near the Golfo de Nicoya. Intercontinental germ warfare caused outbreaks of feverish death on both sides. Scarce in mineral wealth and indigenous laborers, the Spanish eventually came to regard the region as the poorest and most miserable in all the Americas.

It was not until the 1560s that a Spanish colony was established at Cartago. This small community in the interior settled to cultivate the rich volcanic soil of the Central Valley.

Central Valley Sunday

Central America formed a loosely administered colony. Its political-military headquarters was in Guatemala and the closest bishop was in Nicaragua. Lacking strategic significance or exploitable riches, Costa Rica became a minor provincial outpost.

Costa Rica's colonial path diverged from the typical Spanish pattern in that a powerful landholding elite and slave-based economy never gained prominence. Instead of large estates, mining operations and coastal cities, modest-sized villages of small-holders developed in the interior Central Valley. Workers toiled six days a week, while Central Valley Sundays were just for prayer and rest. There were several well-connected families whose lineage went back to the founding of the colony, but anyone could acquire wealth by agricultural processing or trade. In national lore, this relative egalitarianism is touted as 'rural democracy.'

Colonial life centered on agriculture. Costa Ricans grew corn, beans and plantains for subsistence, and produced sugar, cacao and tobacco for sale. However, indigenous raids and pirate attacks kept villagers on nervous guard. When Cartago was leveled in 1723 by Volcán Irazú, new settlements sprouted in Heredia, San José and Alajuela. As the 18th century closed, the population topped 50,000.

As Spanish settlement expanded, the indigenous population plummeted. From 400,000 at the time Columbus first sailed, the number was reduced to 20,000 a century later, and to 8000 a century after that. While disease was the main source of death, the Spanish exploited native labor relentlessly. Outside the valley, several tribes managed to prolong survival under forest cover, staging occasional raids, but were eventually defeated by military campaigns.

A Sovereign Struggle

In 1821 the Americas wriggled free of Spain's imperial grip. The newly liberated colonies pondered their fate: stay together in a United States of Central America or go their separate national ways. The first solution, the Central American Federation (CAF), suffered an imbalance of power and no ability to raise taxes or have defense. Costa Rica formally withdrew in 1938.

An independent Costa Rica took shape under Juan Mora Fernandez, first head of state (1824–33). In 1824 the Nicoya-Guanacaste province seceded from Nicaragua and joined its more easygoing southern neighbor, defining the territorial borders. In 1852 Costa Rica received its first diplomatic emissaries from the USA and Great Britain.

As one empire receded, another rose. In the 19th century, the USA was in an expansive mood and Spanish America looked vulnerable. In 1856 the soldier of fortune William Walker landed in Nicaragua intending to conquer Central America, establish slavery and construct an interoceanic canal. When Walker marched on Costa Rica, he faced a hastily mobilized volunteer army of 9000 civilians. They stopped the Yankee mercenaries at Santa Rosa, chasing them back into Nicaragua. During the fight, a daring drummer boy from Alajuela, Juan Santamaría, was killed while setting fire to Walker's defenses. The battle became a national legend and Santamaría a national hero (and inspiration for an airport). You can see a memorial to this battle in Parque Nacional in San José.

Coffee Rica

In the 19th century, the introduction of the caffeinated red bean transformed the impoverished nation into the wealthiest in the region.

When an export market emerged, the government promoted coffee to farmers by providing free saplings. By the 1840s, local merchants scoped out their own overseas markets, persuading the captain of the HMS *Monarch* to transport several hundred sacks of Costa Rican coffee to London, percolating the beginning of a beautiful friendship.

Children of the 1940s learned to read with a text that stated, 'Coffee is good for me. I drink coffee every morning.' Coffee's quick fix made it popular among working-class consumers in the industrializing north. Enterprising German immigrants improved the technical and financial aspects of the business. By century's end, more than one-third of the Central Valley was dedicated to coffee cultivation, and coffee accounted for more than 90% of all exports.

The coffee industry in Costa Rica developed differently than in the rest of Central America. The coffee economy created a wide network of high-end traders and small-scale growers; in the rest of Central America, a narrow elite controlled large estates, worked by tenant laborers. However, with three-quarters of the coffee barons descended from just two colonial families, the coffee elite's economic interests became a priority in national politics. Today Costa Rica has an estimated 130,000 coffee farms.

The Banana Boom

The coffee trade unintentionally gave rise to Costa Rica's next export boom – bananas. Getting coffee out to world markets necessitated a rail link from the central highlands to the coast and Limón's deep harbor made an ideal port. But inland was dense jungle and infested swamps. The government contracted the task to Minor Keith, nephew of an American railroad tycoon.

The project was a disaster. Malaria and accidents forced a constant replenishing of workers. Tico recruits gave way to US convicts and Chinese indentured servants, who were replaced by freed Jamaican slaves. Keith's two brothers died during the arduous first decade that laid 100km of track. The government defaulted on funding and construction costs soared over budget. To entice Keith to continue, the government turned over 324,000 hectares of land along the route and a 99-year lease to run the railroad. In 1890, the line was finally completed, and running at a loss.

Bananas were first grown along the railroad tracks as a cheap food source for workers. Desperate to recoup his investment, Keith shipped some to New Orleans. Consumers went, well, bananas. *Fincas* (plantations) replaced lowland forests and bananas surpassed coffee as Costa Rica's most lucrative export by the early 20th century. Although Costa Rica became the world's leading banana exporter, the profits shipped out along with the bananas.

Joining with another American importer, Keith founded the infamous United Fruit Company, soon the largest employer in Central America. Known as *el pulpo*, the octopus, to locals, United Fruit owned huge swathes of lush lowlands, much of the transportation and communication infrastructure, and bunches of bureaucrats. The company promoted a wave of migrant laborers from Jamaica, changing the country's ethnic complexion and provoking racial tensions.

In 1913, a banana blight known as 'Panama disease' shut down many Caribbean plantations and the industry relocated to the Pacific. Eventually United Fruit lost its banana monopoly.

Unarmed Democracy

Early Costa Rican politics followed the Central American pattern of violence and dictatorship. In the 19th century, a few favored aristocrats competed to control patronage in the new state. The military, the Church and, most of all, the coffee barons were the main sources of influence. Presidents were more often removed at gunpoint than by the ballot box.

By the late 19th century, the eligible electorate expanded from 2% to 10% of the adult population. Military strongman Tomas Guardia forced higher taxes on the coffee barons to finance social reform. By the early 20th century, Costa Rica had free public education, a guaranteed minimum wage and child protection laws. Denied the right to participate, disenfranchised groups resorted to protest politics. In 1918 female schoolteachers and students staged effective strikes against the despotic displays of President Frederico Tinoco, who soon resigned.

Beginning in 1940, events would lead Costa Rica onto a more democratic path. At this time, President Rafael Calderon defied elite expectations by championing the rights of the working class and the poor. Calderon orchestrated a powerful alliance between workers and the Church. The conservative backlash resulted in civil war after disputed elections. Armed workers battled military forces, and

Nicaraguan and US forces joined in the fray. Peace was restored in under two months at the cost of 2000 deaths.

Coffee grower and utopian democrat, José Figueres Ferrer became head of a temporary junta government. The 1949 constitution granted full citizenship and voting rights to women, Blacks, indigenous groups and Chinese minorities. His copious decrees taxed the wealthy, nationalized banks and built a modern welfare state. Most extraordinarily, Figueres abolished the military, calling it a threat to democracy. These actions became the foundation for Costa Rica's unique and unarmed democracy.

The Contra Conflict

The sovereignty of the small nations of Central America was limited by their northern neighbor, the USA. Yankees, with their big sticks, gunboats and dollar diplomacy, were hostile toward leftist politics. During the 1970s, radical socialists forced the military regimes of Guatemala, El Salvador and Nicaragua onto the defensive. When they toppled the American-backed Somoza dictatorship in Nicaragua in 1970, President Ronald Reagan decided to intervene. The Cold War arrived in the hot tropics.

Under intense US pressure, politically moderate Costa Rica was reluctantly dragged in. The Contras set up camp in Costa Rica, from where they staged guerrilla raids and built a secret jungle airstrip to fly in weapons and supplies. Costa Rican authorities were bribed to keep quiet. Diplomatic relations between Costa Rica and Nicaragua grew nastier and border clashes became bloodier.

The war polarized Costa Rica. Conservatives pushed to re-establish the military and join the anticommunist crusade. On the opposing side, in May 1984, over 20,000 demonstrators marched through San José to give peace a chance. The debate peaked with the 1986 presidential election. The victor was 44-year-old Oscar Arias, an intellectual reformer in the reformist mold of Figueres.

Once in office, Arias affirmed his commitment to a negotiated resolution and reasserted Costa Rican national independence. He vowed to uphold neutrality and kick out the Contras. Soon, the US ambassador quit his post and a public ceremony had Costa Rican schoolchildren planting trees on the secret CIA airfield. Most notably, Arias became the driving force in uniting Central America around a peace plan, which ended the Nicaraguan war. In 1987, he was awarded the Nobel Peace Prize.

Paradise Found

Five hundred years later, the same dense rain forest that conquistadors had cursed revealed a hidden wealth: ecotourism.

An oversupply of coffee caused a crash in prices in the 1970s. The new market unpredictability brought together an unusual alliance of big business and environmentalists. If wealth could not be sustained through the country's exports, then what about imports – of tourists? Costa Rica embarked on a green revolution. By 1995, there were more than 125 government-protected sites. Almost one-third of the entire country is under some form of environmental protection.

Success encouraged private landholders to build reserves as well. It started slowly: Monteverde reserve recorded only 500 tourists in 1975; 20 years later the number surpassed 50,000. Tourism contributed more than US$750 million in 1995, passing coffee and bananas as the main source of foreign currency earnings.

Modern Currents

Costa Rica's clean-living image has proven wildly alluring, but is it really the Switzerland of Central America? Skyrocketing numbers of tourists and the accoutrements that serve them have created great stress on ecological habitats – ironic, since nature is the country's primary attraction. The market is saturated with a host of largely unregulated small hotels and services which struggle for their piece of an increasingly divided pie. Big-business developers pose another, perhaps greater threat. Costa Rica is finding that, with a fine line between economic profits and environmental conservation, sustainable tourism is difficult to execute. Communities also must face the tourism boom's nasty side effects of rampant child prostitution and drug addiction.

With economic change has come social change. Call it the hamburger effect, but the ubiquitous rice and beans has been upgraded to regular doses of American fast food. Homes are changing. Divorce rates have increased and family size has shrunk. More women have entered the workforce though opportunities in the tourism and service sectors.

More Ticos are entering higher education while migrant laborers from Nicaragua work the coffee plantations. Rightly or wrongly, immigrants are often blamed for increases in crime, fueling ongoing animosity between Nicas and Ticos.

As the country becomes more diverse and cosmopolitan it faces inevitable tensions and growing pains. In 2006 Oscar Arias was re-elected president. This time around the tables appear to have turned. After just a year in office, his support of Cafta and strong US relations has drawn sharp criticism from the voting public.

THE CULTURE
The National Psyche

Costa Ricans take pride in defining themselves by what they are not. In comparison with their Central American neighbors, they aren't poor, illiterate or beleaguered by political instability. Their country is an oasis of peace, in a land degraded by warfare. To keep the peace, they will avoid conflict at all costs. Costa Ricans say 'yes' even if they mean 'no' and 'maybe' replaces 'I don't know.' They are well-mannered to a fault, sparing no effort to *quedar bien* (leave a good impression). You will rarely see a Tico engaged in a heated debate or fight. And while the stereotype of Costa Rican friendliness is largely true, it's sometimes hard to distinguish good manners from genuine affection.

Lifestyle

The absence of war, strong exports and stronger tourism has meant that Costa Rica enjoys the highest standard of living in Central America. Primary education is free and compulsory for all school-aged children and though it is overburdened, a nationwide system provides free health care. Even though 23% of the populace lives below the poverty line, beggars are few and you won't see abject poverty in plain view. Families have the requisite 2.4 children and for the large part, Costa Rican youths spend ample time worrying about dating, music, fashion and *fútbol* (soccer).

People

Costa Ricans call themselves Ticos (men; groups of men and women) or Ticas (females). Spanish is the dominant language. Two-thirds of the nation's four-million-plus people live in the *Meseta Central,* a central plain that lies at an altitude between about 1000m and 1500m.

Most inhabitants are mestizo (of mixed Spanish and indigenous blood). Indigenous groups comprise only 1% of the population; and including the Bribrí from the Talamanca in the southeast and the Borucas in the southern Pacific coastal areas.

Less than 3% of the population are Black, concentrated on the Caribbean coast. They speak English, Spanish and a Creole dialect and trace their ancestry to immigrants from Jamaica who built railroads and worked banana plantations in the late 19th century. Chinese (1% of the population) also first arrived to work on the railroads and since then have had regular waves of immigration, particularly from Taiwan.

The great increase of North American and European immigration lead some to feel that Costa Rica represents a 'less authentic' Latin American experience. But it is worth noting some of these very immigrants were instrumental in founding the first national parks.

With a life expectancy of 76 years, Costa Rica enjoys the highest life expectancy in Latin America after Cuba. Over 30% of the population is below the age of 15.

ARTS

There is little indigenous cultural influence in the nation's arts. Cultural activities of any kind are centered primarily on Western-style entertainment. San José has the lion's share of museums, in addition to a lively theater and music scene. International rock, folk and hip hop artists visit the capital and venues around the city host live performances in a variety of musical styles.

RELIGION

More than 75% of Ticos are Catholic (at least in principle) and 14% are evangelical Christians. The Black community on the Caribbean coast is largely Protestant. While a healthy reverence for the Virgin Mary is typical, few are married to the dictates coming from Rome – apparently *pura vida* has its concessions.

ENVIRONMENT
The Land

Smaller than West Virginia and larger than Switzerland, Costa Rica (51,100 sq km) packs in some of the world's most diverse natural landscapes. Wedged between Nicaragua and Panama, its craggy western border is constantly pounded by Pacific surf, while the temperate Caribbean hugs tropical lowlands and swamps to the east. Costa Rica is defined by its diverse climates and topography: mangroves, swamps, sandy beaches, numerous gulfs and peninsulas, tropical dry forests, rain forests, cloud forests, temperate highlands and a variety of offshore islands. It is split in two by a series of volcanic mountain chains that run from Nicaragua in the northwest to Panama in the southeast. The highlands reach up to 3820m above sea level.

Wildlife
ANIMALS

Poison arrow frogs, giant tarantulas and spider monkeys inhabit our imagination of the tropics. In reality, few places live up to our wild expectations – except for Costa Rica. Considered the world nucleus of wildlife diversity, it has over 615 species (per 10,000 sq km). Compare that to the USA's 104 species.

Birding calls naturalists to Costa Rica, where there are over 850 recorded species. Because many species have restricted ranges, completely distinct populations are found region to region. Some 200-plus species of migrating birds come from as far away as Alaska and Australia, so it's not unusual to see your backyard birds feeding alongside trogons and toucans.

WE LOVE IT TO DEATH

Tourism may be the hidden threat to Costa Rica's environment. Some 1.5 million tourists visit every year. Not only are many parks taxed, but tourist infrastructure is strained and the local flavor is leaking out of places. What can you do?

- Ask hotels how they dispose of waste water. Or have a look around – foul odors and pipes that empty into the street all say something.

- Buy at markets instead of supermarkets, support small businesses and use local guides.

- Communicate with locals. Find out what the local issues are and follow through with sensitivity toward them.

For more ideas, see p630.

COSTA RICA

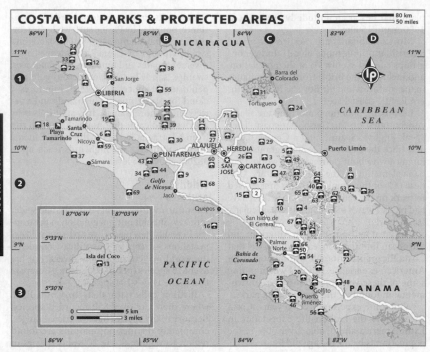

COSTA RICA PARKS & PROTECTED AREAS

Spotting wild monkeys and sloths is a highlight, yet an additional 260 animal species await the patient observer. The most exotic sightings include species such as the four-eyed opossum, the jaguarundi and the elusive tapir. The prime places to spot wildlife are national parks, wildlife refuges and other protected areas (as well as their buffer zones). Early morning is the best time to see animals, as many species stay still during the hotter part of the day. Nocturnal species – such as Baird's tapir, the silky anteater and the kinkajou – require night sightings, preferably with a guide.

Working with a knowledgeable guide increases the probability of seeing wildlife and understanding its behavior. Good local guides can recognize bird calls and animal sounds. They also know where creatures tend to congregate – whether because they like the fruit of a certain tree (as the quetzal in the avocado tree), or because they fish at the mouth of the river (as the American crocodile).

ENDANGERED SPECIES

The number-one threat to most of Costa Rica's endangered species is habitat destruc-

tion, followed by hunting and trapping. Numerous species have declining populations or are danger of extinction.

The legendary resplendent quetzal – topping every naturalist's must-see list – approaches extinction as its home forests are felled. A booming pet trade has extirpated the population of large, squawky scarlet macaws. Endangered sea turtles get a lot of attention in Costa Rica, with a wide variety of programs supporting population growth. Central America's largest land mammal, Baird's tapir, is a target for hunters, as is the placid gigantic West Indian manatee. A host of volunteer programs help visitors participate in preservation.

PLANTS

Floral biodiversity is staggering – over 10,000 species of vascular plants have been described in Costa Rica, and more join the list every year. Orchids alone account for about 1300 species. Use your visit to explore the rich variety of plant communities found in rain forests, mangrove swamps, tropical dry forests and cloud forests.

COSTA RICA

National Parks & Protected Areas

The national-park system began in the 1960s, and today 35 national parks cover 11% of the country. Scores of other protected zones include wetlands and mangroves, in addition to a slew of privately owned and operated reserves. For this reason Costa Rican authorities claim that over 25% of the country is under conservation. There are hundreds of small, privately owned lodges and reserves set up to protect the land, and many are well worth visiting.

While the national-park system appears impressive, much of the protected area is at risk. Logging, hunting and overfishing are classic problems. The government doesn't own all of this land – almost half of the areas are in private ownership – and there is no budget to buy it. Technically, the private lands are protected from development, but many landowners are finding loopholes in the restrictions and selling or developing their properties.

Most national parks can be entered without permits, though a few limit the number they admit on a daily basis and others require advance reservations to sleep within the park's boundaries (Chirripó, Corcovado and La Amistad). The entrance fee to most parks is US$6 to US$8 per day for foreigners, plus an additional US$2 to US$5 for overnight camping where it is permitted. Some of the more isolated parks may charge higher rates.

Environmental Issues

Despite Costa Rica's national-park system, the major problem facing the nation's environment is deforestation. Originally, Costa Rica was almost all forest, but it has mostly been cleared for pasture or agriculture. Illegal logging compounds the problem. About only 5% of the lands outside of parks and reserves remains forested, while only 1% of the dry forests of northwestern Costa Rica are left.

Apart from the direct loss of tropical forests, and the plants and animals that depend on them, deforestation has led directly or indirectly to other severe environmental problems. The greatest issue is soil erosion. Forests protect the soil beneath them from the ravages of tropical rainstorms – after deforestation much of the topsoil is washed away, lowering the productivity of the land and silting up watersheds. Some deforested lands are planted with Costa Rica's main agricultural product, bananas, the production of which entails the use of pesticides and blue plastic bags to protect the fruit. Both the pesticides and the plastic bags end up polluting the environment.

Deforestation and related logging activities also create inroads into formerly inaccessible regions, leading to an influx of humans. One consequence, especially in national parks where wildlife is concentrated, is unrestrained poaching. Because the government has little funding for enforcement, some companies illegally clear-cut without fear of consequences.

National parks in remote areas suffer from a lack of rangers and protection. Others are extremely popular for their world-class scenic and natural beauty, as well as their wildlife.

In the once-idyllic Parque Nacional Manuel Antonio, a tiny park on the Pacific coast, annual visits rocketed from about 36,000 visitors in 1982 to more than 150,000 by 1991. This invasion threatened to ruin the diminutive area by driving away the wildlife, polluting the beaches and replacing wilderness with hotel development.

In response, park visitors have since been 'limited' to 600 per day, and the park is closed on Monday to allow a brief respite from the onslaught. But any visitor to Manuel Antonio can tell you that, yes, the animals are plentiful but conditions (with many visitors feeding the wildlife and wildlife becoming aggressive) can be horrendous.

Costa Rica has a world-famous reputation for its national-park system – but a lack of funds, concentrated visitor use and sometimes fuzzy leadership show troubles in paradise. As the Costa Rican government changes every four years, there is an apparent lack of cohesive, standard-operation plans. Earnings from the patronage of parks contribute significantly to both the national and local economies. The country has a vested interest in land preservation, and its citizens appreciate the income and jobs ecotourism generates. In spite of all this, questions remain as to how ecotourism will co-exist with expanding agricultural enterprises.

TRANSPORTATION

GETTING THERE & AWAY

Entering Costa Rica is usually hassle-free. There are no fees or taxes payable on entering the country, though some foreign nationals will require a visa. Be aware that those who need visas cannot get them at the border. For information on visas, see p631. Travelers officially need a ticket out of Costa Rica before they are allowed to enter, but the rule is rarely enforced.

DEPARTURE TAX

There is a US$26 departure tax on all international outbound flights, payable in cash (US dollars or colones, or a mix of the two). At the Juan Santamaría airport you can pay with credit cards, and Banco de Costa Rica has an ATM (on the Plus system) by the departure-tax station.

Air

Costa Rica is well connected by air to other Central and Latin American countries, as well as the USA. The national airline, Lacsa (part of the Central American Airline consortium Grupo TACA), flies to numerous points in the USA and Latin America, including Cuba. The US Federal Aviation Administration has assessed Costa Rica's aviation authorities to be in compliance with international safety standards. Fares go up during high season (from December through April).

International airport Juan Santamaría is about 17km outside San José, in the city of Alajuela.

Bus & Boat

Costa Rica shares land borders with Nicaragua and Panama. Many travelers, particularly shoestringers, enter the country by bus since an extensive bus system links the Central American capitals and it's vastly cheaper than flying.

If crossing the border by bus, note that international buses may cost slightly more than taking a local bus to the border, then another onwards from the border, but they're worth it. These better-quality buses travel faster and can help you cross efficiently.

The most popular crossing point between Nicaragua and Costa Rica is on the Interamericana at Peñas Blancas. While processing is slow, travelers report that for the most part, it's hassle-free. The crossing at Los Chiles, further east, is infrequently used but reportedly easy to navigate. There is a regular boat service connecting Los Chiles with San Carlos, on the southeast corner of Lake Nicaragua.

For Panama, the main point is on the Interamericana at Paso Canoas. Expect long lines, generally free of complications. On the Caribbean side, the crossing at Sixaola is much more sedate.

See p631 for entry requirements.

GETTING AROUND
Air

Costa Rica's domestic airlines are **NatureAir** (☎ 220 3054; www.natureair.com) and **Sansa** (☎ 221 9414; www.flysansa.com); the latter is linked with Grupo TACA.

NatureAir flies from Tobías Bolaños airport, 8km west of the center of San José in the suburb of Pavas. Sansa operates out of Juan Santamaría airport. Both fly small passenger planes with a baggage allowance of 12kg. Space is limited and demand great in high season, so reserve ahead.

Bicycle

The traffic may be hazardous and the roads narrow, steep and winding, but cyclists do pedal Costa Rica. Mountain bikes and beach cruisers can be rented in towns with a significant tourist presence for US$8 to US$15 per day.

Boat

Ferries cross the Golfo de Nicoya connecting the central Pacific coast with the southern tip of Península de Nicoya. The **Coonatramar ferry** (☎ 661 1069; passenger/car US$2/9) links Puntarenas with Playa Naranjo four times daily. The **Ferry Peninsular** (☎ 641 0515; passenger/car US$2/9) travels between Puntarenas and Vaquero every two hours.

On the Golfo Dulce, a daily passenger ferry links Golfito with Puerto Jiménez on the Península de Osa, and a weekday water taxi travels to and from Playa Zancudo. On the other side of the Península de Osa, water taxis connect Bahía Drake with Sierpe.

On the Caribbean coast, a bus-and-boat service runs several times daily, linking Cariari and Tortuguero (p572). Canal boats travel from Moín to Tortuguero, although no regular service exists. A daily water taxi connects Puerto Viejo de Sarapiquí with Trinidad, Nicaragua on the Río San Juan. Arrange boat transport in any of these towns for Barra del Colorado.

Bus

Buses are the best way of getting around Costa Rica. They are frequent and cheap, with the longest domestic journey out of San José costing less than US$10.

San José is the transportation hub for the country (see p548), but there is no central terminal. Bus offices are scattered around the city: some large bus companies have big terminals that sell tickets in advance, while others have little more than a stop – sometimes unmarked. (One San José bus station consists of a guy with a clipboard sitting on a lawn chair.)

Normally there's room for everyone on the bus, and if there isn't, squeeze in. The exceptions are days before and after a major holiday, especially Easter, when buses are ridiculously full. (Note that there are no buses on the Thursday to Saturday before Easter Sunday.) There are two types of bus: *directo* and *colectivo*. *Directos* charge more and presumably make few stops. However, it goes against the instinct of Costa Rican bus drivers not to pick up every single roadside passenger.

Trips longer than four hours usually include a rest stop (buses do not have bathrooms). Space is limited on board, so periodically check that your stored luggage isn't 'accidentally' given away at intermediate stops. Keep your day pack with important documents on you at all times. Thefts from overhead racks are rampant.

Bus schedules fluctuate, so always confirm the time when you purchase your ticket. If you are catching a bus roadside, arrive early. Departure times are estimated and if the bus comes early, it will leave early.

For information on departures from San José, the master schedule is online at www.visitcostarica.com. Another more thorough but less reliable source is www.costaricabybus.com.

SHUTTLE BUS

Tourist-van shuttles are provided by **Grayling's Fantasy Bus** (☎ 220 2126; www.graylinecostarica.com) and **Interbus** (☎ 283 5573; www.interbusonline.com). Both run overland transport from San José to the most popular destinations and between other destinations (see their websites for information). Fares start at US$19 for trips between San José and Puntarenas, and US$29 for the bumpy ride to Monteverde. These services provide hotel pick-up, air-con and are faster than public buses. Reserve online or through local travel agencies and hotels.

Car & Motorcycle

The roads vary from quite good (the Interamericana) to barely passable (just about everywhere else). Even the good ones can suffer from landslides, sudden flooding and fog. Most roads are single lane and winding, lacking hard shoulders – others are dirt-and-mud affairs that climb mountains and traverse rivers.

Speed limits are 100km per hour or less on primary roads and 60km per hour or less on others. Traffic police use radar and enforce speed limits. The wearing of seat belts is compulsory.

COSTA RICA

Most car-rental agencies can be found in San José and in popular tourist destinations on the Pacific coast (Tamarindo, Jacó, Quepos and Puerto Jiménez). Car rental is not cheap, but it is worth investing in a 4WD. Prices start at US$450 per week for a 4WD, including *kilometraje libre* (unlimited mileage). Required basic insurance costs an additional US$12 to US$20 per day. Above and beyond this, you can purchase full insurance. Alternately, your credit card may insure you for car rentals – check. As most insurance plans do not cover water damage, be extra careful when cruising through those rivers (drive slowly so as not to flood the engine).

To rent a car you need to be 21 years old, have a valid driver's license, a major credit card and a passport. A foreign driver's license is acceptable for up to 90 days. Carefully inspect the car and make sure any previous damage is noted on the rental agreement.

If you plan to drive from North America, you'll need all the usual insurance and ownership papers. In addition, you must buy Costa Rican insurance at the border (about US$20 a month) and pay a US$10 road tax. You are not allowed to sell the car in Costa Rica. If you need to leave the country without the car, you must leave it in a customs warehouse in San José.

Never leave valuables inside your car, even for brief periods. Always use a guarded parking lot at night and remove all luggage.

Motorcycles (even Harleys) can be rented in San José.

Hitchhiking

People who hitchhike will be safer if they travel in pairs and let someone know where they are planning to go. Single women should use greater discretion. Hitchhiking is never entirely safe and Lonely Planet doesn't recommend it.

Hitching in Costa Rica is unusual on main roads with frequent buses. On minor rural roads, it's more common. To get picked up, most locals wave to cars in a friendly manner. Hitchhikers should offer to pay upon arrival: *¿Cuanto le debo?* (How much do I owe you?) Many will wave the offer aside, but it is polite.

Taxi

Taxis serve urban and remote areas. They are useful for remote destinations, such as national parks, where bus services are unavailable. In small villages without clearly marked taxis, ask at the local *pulpería* (corner store) about service. If the taxi doesn't have a meter, set the fare ahead of time.

SAN JOSÉ

pop 343,000 / metropolitan area 1.5 million

Chepe, as it's affectionately called by Ticos, teeters between the cosmopolitan and just plain ol' commercial. On first impressions, the city center, thick with office towers, malls and fried-chicken chains, could be *anywhere* in today's modern world. But wander Barrio Amón and you'll find that colonial stylings still radiate. In the shifting light of dusk Parque España becomes a riot of tropical birdsong. Cool clubs and bars abound and *Josefinos* (inhabitants of San José) are friendly and fast to order up another round of beers.

San José was founded in 1737, but little remains of its colonial era. Booming capitalism has left many disenfranchised and the city struggles to manage a growing crime rate so atypical of the *pura vida* spirit. For travelers, a stopover in San José is regarded as a necessary evil before heading to the 'real' Costa Rica. However, as the home of one-third of all Ticos, Chepe's complexity offers an unadulterated vista on modern-day Costa Rica.

ORIENTATION

The city is in the heart of a wide and fertile valley called the *Meseta Central* (Central Valley). San José's center is arranged in a grid with avenidas running east to west and calles running north to south. Av Central, the nucleus of the city, becomes a pedestrian mall between Calles 6 and 9. It turns into Paseo Colón west of Calle 14.

The center has several loosely defined districts or barrios. The central area is a commercial area with bus stops and cultural sights. Perhaps the most interesting district to visitors is Barrio Amón, northeast of Av 5 and Calle 1, with its concentration of landmark mansions, largely converted into hotels and fine-dining establishments. Just west of the city center is La Sabana, named after the park.

While this book indicates streets and avenues, most locals instead use landmarks to guide themselves. Learn how to decipher Tico directions by turning to the boxed text, p629.

GETTING INTO TOWN

From the Airport

Taxis to downtown San José from Juan Santamaría airport cost between US$15 to US$20, depending on traffic. When leaving the airport terminal, look for the official **Taxi Aeropuerto stand** (☎ 221 6865; www.taxiaeropuerto.com) as you exit baggage claim, and pay in advance. The official airport taxis are orange. The 20-minute ride can take over an hour during rush hour.

The cheapest option is the red **Tuasa bus** (US$0.60; up to 45min), which runs between Alajuela and San José, and passes the airport every few minutes from 5am to 11pm. The stop is on the far side of the parking lot outside the terminal (a short walk, even with luggage.) **Interbus** (☎ 283 5573; www.interbusonline.com) airport shuttle service costs US$5 per person; you can reserve online.

From the Bus Stations

International and domestic buses arrive at various bus terminals west and south of downtown. The area is perfectly walkable provided you aren't hauling a lot of luggage. If arriving at night, take a taxi to your hotel as most bus terminals are in seedy areas; taxis cost US$1 to US$2 within downtown.

A warning – many taxi drivers are commissioned by hotels to bring in customers. In the capital, the hotel scene is so competitive that drivers say just about anything to steer you to the places they represent. They'll tell you the establishment you've chosen is a notorious drug den, it's closed down, or that, sadly, it's overbooked. Don't believe them. Be firm, and if you're still met with resistance, grab another taxi.

INFORMATION
Bookstores

7th Street Books (☎ 256 8251; Calle 7 btwn Avs Central & 1; ☿ 9am-6pm) New and used books in English and other languages as well as magazines and newspapers.

Mora Books (Omni Center, Av 1 btwn Calles 3 & 5) Highly recommended secondhand bookstore has books mainly in English; guidebooks and comics are a specialty.

Emergency

Emergencies (☎ 911)
Fire (☎ 118)
Police (☎ 117)
Traffic police (☎ 222 9330)

Internet Access

Checking email is easy in San José, where cybercafés are more plentiful than lottery peddlers. Rates run US$1 to US$2 per hour. These days most hotels provide free internet to guests.

1@10 Café Internet (☎ 258 4561; www.1en10.com; Calle 3 btwn Avs 5 & 7; per hr US$1) Also a gay and lesbian information center.

CyberCafé searchcostarica.com (☎ 233 3310; Las Arcadas, Av 2 btwn Calles 1 & 3; per hr US$0.75; ☿ 7am-11pm) Also houses a book exchange and a pizza and fresh-juice bar.

Medical Services

Clínica Bíblica (☎ 257 5252; www.clinicabiblica.com; Av 14 btwn Calles Central & 1) The top private clinic in the downtown area; doctors speak English, French and German; an emergency room is open 24 hours.

Hospital Clínica Católica (☎ 246 3000; www.clinicacatolica.com; Guadalupe) A private clinic north of downtown.

Hospital San Juan de Dios (☎ 257 6282; cnr Paseo Colón & Calle 14) The free public hospital is centrally located, but waits are long.

Money

Any bank will change foreign currency into colones, but US dollars are by far the most accepted currency for exchange.

Banco de Costa Rica (☎ 221 8143; www.bancobcr.com; Av 1 btwn Calles 7 & 9; ☿ 8:30am-6pm Mon-Fri)

Banco de San José (☎ 295 9595; www.bancosanjose.fi.cr; Av 2 btwn Calles Central & 1; ☿ 8am-7pm Mon-Fri, 9am-1pm Sat) Has ATMs on the Plus and Cirrus systems.

Banco Nacional de Costa Rica Exchange House (cnr Av Central & Calle 4; ☿ 10:30am-6pm) A good find in the event of a Sunday cash-exchange emergency since it's open seven days. Expect long lines.

Credomatic (☎ 295 9000; inside Banco de San José; Calle Central btwn Avs 3 & 5) Gives cash advances on Visa and MasterCard.

SAN JOSÉ

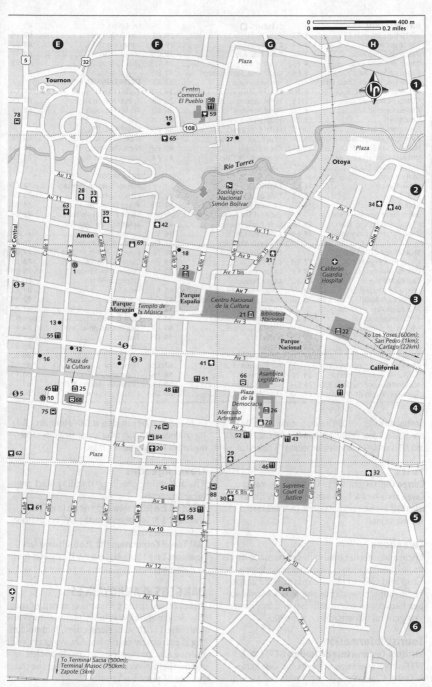

COSTA RICA

Scotiabank (☎ 287 8700; www.scotiabank.com; Av 1 btwn Calles 2 & 4; ⏰ 8:15am-5pm Mon-Fri) Good service and ATMs on the Cirrus system dispensing US dollars too.

Post

Correo Central (Central Post Office; www.correos.go.cr; Calle 2 btwn Avs 1 & 3; ⏰ 8am-5pm Mon-Fri, 7:30am-noon Sat) The most efficient place in Costa Rica to send and receive mail.

Telephone

Local and international calls can be made from most public phones, which are widespread. Chip and Colibrí phonecards are sold at souvenir shops, newsstands and Más X Menos supermarkets. Hotels usually have lobby phones. For general information, see p630.

Tourist Information

Instituto Costarricense de Turismo (ICT) (☎ 223 1733 ext 277; www.tourism-costarica.com; Calle 5 btwn Av Central & 2; ⏰ 9am-5pm with flexible lunch Mon-Fri)

Correo Central (in the post office at Calle 2 btwn Avs 1 & 3) The government tourism office is good for a copy of the master bus schedule and free maps.

Travel Agencies

The following are long-standing and reputable agencies.

OTEC (☎ 256 0633; www.turismojoven.com; Calle 3 btwn Avs 1 & 3) Specializes in youth travel; can also issue student discount cards.

TAM Travel Corporation (☎ 256 0203; www.tam travel.com; Calle 1 btwn Avs Central & 1) Airline ticketing, local travel and more.

DANGERS & ANNOYANCES

Street crime is the principal concern of most travelers in the city. While violent crime is low compared with American cities, pickpocketing is extremely common. Always carry your money and passport in an inside pocket or a money belt. Never leave valuables in the outer pocket of your backpack.

Between January 2004 and April 2005, there were 599 reported tourist assaults in Costa Rica, most of which occurred in San José. If you're held at knife or gunpoint, do not resist or fight back. Stay anonymous by not wearing flashy jewelry or watches and by walking confidently. If lost, go inside a store or café to check a map or get directions. After dark, always travel by taxi – they are cheap and will save you plenty of aggravation. Women walking alone at night are sometimes tailed and mistaken for prostitutes. If bar-hopping, don't go alone.

In a common scam, thieves spill something on a passerby, who is then pick-pocketed by the person who steps in to help 'clean up.' Another trend is for motorists to mug pedestrians and speed off.

Neighborhoods reviewed in this book are generally safe during the day, though be especially careful around the Coca-Cola bus terminal and the red-light district south of the parque central, especially at night. Men should beware of friendly Ticas who turn out to be prostitutes. They may take more than their customers bargained for – namely their wallets. Also, AIDS is on the rise in Central America and prostitution is certainly not regulated.

SIGHTS & ACTIVITIES
Museo Nacional de Costa Rica

Located inside the Bellavista Fortress, the **Museo Nacional** (☎ 257 1433; Calle 17 btwn Avs Central & 2; adult/student US$4/2; ☺ 8:30am-4:30pm Tue-Sun) offers a quick survey of Costa Rican history. You'll find a wide range of pre-Columbian artifacts as well as numerous colonial objects and religious art. The natural-history wing has flora and fauna specimens, minerals and fossils.

Museo de Oro Precolombino/Museo de Numismática

This three-in-one **museum** (☎ 243 4202; www .museosdelbancocentral.org; Plaza de la Cultura basement; admission US$5; ☺ 9:15am-4:30pm Tue-Sun) houses a glittering collection of pre-Columbian gold artifacts, a small exhibit detailing the history of Costa Rican currency and a temporary display space for local art. Security is tight – all visitors must leave bags at the door.

Museo de Arte y Diseño Contemporáneo

Commonly referred to as MADC, the **contemporary art and design museum** (☎ 257 7202; www.madc.ac.cr/; Av 3 btwn Calles 13 & 15; admission US$1; ☺ 10am-5pm Tue-Sat) is housed in the historic

National Liquor Factory building, which dates from 1856. MADC primarily shows the contemporary work of Costa Rican and Central American artists, though there are frequent rotating exhibitions on display here as well.

Museo de Jade

San José's most famous **museum** (☎ 287 6034; Edificio INS, Av 7 btwn Calles 9 & 11, 11th fl; adult/child 10 & under US$2/free; ☺ 8:30am-3:30pm Mon-Fri) is located on the 11th floor of the Instituto Nacional de Seguros (National Insurance Institute). It houses the world's largest collection of American jade (pronounced ha-day). Archaeological exhibits of ceramics and stonework offer insight into Costa Rica's pre-Colombian cultures.

Museo de los Niños & Galería Nacional

This unique **children's museum** (☎ 258 4929; www .museoscr.com; Calle 4, north of Av 9; admission US$2; ☺ 8am-4:30pm Tue-Fri, 9:30am-5pm Sat & Sun) resides in an old penitentiary built in 1909. Science, music and geography displays are plentiful but grown-ups will be captivated by the **Galería Nacional** (admission free), which displays modern art in old, abandoned prison cells.

Museo de Arte Costarricense

This sunny **museum** (☎ 222 7155; www.musarco .go.cr; Parque La Sabana; US$1, free on Sun; ☺ 10am-4pm Tue-Sun) features Costa Rican art from the 19th and 20th centuries. Rotating exhibits feature works by Tico artists past and present. Next to this Spanish colonial-style building you'll find an impressive open-air sculpture garden.

Museo de Formas, Espacios y Sonidos

This **interactive museum** (☎ 222 9462; Av 3 btwn Calles 17 & 23; admission US$1; ☺ 9:30am-3pm Mon-Fri) is geared to small kids or people who like to act like them. Housed in the old San José Atlantic train station, you can clamber on an antique locomotive and traipse through old rail cars. There are also several small exhibits dedicated to the senses of sound, touch and sight.

Teatro Nacional

The **National Theater** (☎ 221 1329; Calles 3 & 5 btw Avs Central & 2; admission US$3; ☺ 9am-5pm Mon-Fri, 9am-12:30pm & 1:30-5:30pm Sat) is the city's most impressive public building. Built in 1897, it features a columned neoclassical facade. It is flanked by statues of Beethoven and Calderón de la Barca, a 17th-century Spanish dramatist. Paintings depicting 19th-century life line the lavish lobby and auditorium. The most famous is *Alegoría al café y el banano*, portraying idyllic coffee and banana harvests, painted by an Italian with no apparent experience in the matter (observe how the laborers hold the banana bunches). Across the street, the theater's **Galería Jaoquín García Monge** (cnr Av 2 & Calle 5) shows worthwhile exhibits by contemporary artists. Admission is free.

Galería Andrómeda

If you're wandering around Barrio Amón, the **Galería Andrómeda** (☎ 223 3529; andromeda@amnet .co.cr; cnr Calle 9 & Av 9) is a free local art space behind the Museo de Jade, worth a peek to see works by emerging local artists.

Spirogyra Jardín de Mariposas

This small **butterfly garden** (☎ 222 2937; adult/student US$6/5; ☼ 8am-4pm), 150m east and 150m south of Centro Comercial El Pueblo, houses over 30 different species of butterflies and five hummingbird species. Morning is the best time to visit. Arrive on foot (about a 20- to 30-minute walk from downtown), by taxi, or bus to El Pueblo where there is a sign.

Parks & Plazas

The shady, cobblestone-lined **Parque Nacional** (Avs 1 & 3 btwn Calles 15 & 19) ranks as one of the best parks in San José. In its center is the dramatic **Monumento Nacional**, which depicts the Central American nations (with Costa Rica in the lead, of course) driving out the American filibuster William Walker.

South of the Asamblea is the stark **Plaza de la Democracia** (Avs Central & 2, Calles 13 & 15) which is unremarkable, except for the crafts market.

Parque España (Avs 3 & 7 btwn Calles 9 & 11) is surrounded by heavy traffic, but manages to become a riot of birdsong every day at sunset when the local avians come here to roost. It is also the most notorious prostitution center in the country. Tragically (or perhaps fittingly), the concrete gazebo in its center is referred to as the **Templo de Música** (Music Temple), and is regarded by many as the symbol of San José.

The heart of the city is the **Plaza de la Cultura** (Avs Central & 2, Calles 3 & 5), an unremarkable park that's nonetheless safe since security guards protecting the Museo de Oro Precolombino (located underground) stroll it. The nearby **parque central** (Avs 2 & 4, Calles Central & 2) is the place to catch a taxi or a local city bus. To the east

is the modern and well-maintained **Catedral Metropolitana**.

Parque La Sabana, at the west end of Paseo Colón, is the most popular retreat from the grit and the grime. La Sabana is home to two museums, a lagoon, a fountain and a variety of sports facilities including the Estadio Nacional, where international and division-one soccer matches are played. During the daytime, it's a great place for a stroll, picnic or a relaxed jog. During the nighttime, it's a great place for getting mugged.

COURSES

The San José area has fine Spanish-language schools. Those listed here are well established or have received reader recommendations. Most also organize volunteer placements, a great way to learn Spanish while giving back to those who need it most.

Prices include five four-hour days of instruction, with/without a week's homestay with a local family and breakfast and dinner.

Academia Latinoamericana de Español (☎ 224 9917; www.alespanish.com; Av 8 btwn Calles 31 & 33, San Pedro; US$290/135) This highly professional institute caters to groups of less than six students, and is staffed with linguists and philologists.

Central America Institute for International Affairs (ICAI; ☎ 233 8571; www.educaturs.com; 25m west from the emergency room entrance of Hospital Calderón Guardia; US$450/300) With over 20 years' experience, this institute offers substantially cheaper rates for longer courses of study.

Centro Lingüístico Conversa (☎ 221 7649, in the USA 800 367 7726; www.conversa.net; Centro Colón, cnr Calle 38 & Paseo Colón, La Sabana; US$500) Students can live on the school's private campus for US$125 to US$220 per week, depending on occupancy.

TOURS

Tired of the dull babble of most city tours? **Urban Addicts** (www.urbanaddicts.com) gives them rooted in psycho-geography. Urbanist Juan Ignacio Salom designed these original jaunts through San José's blue-collar neighborhoods, whose initial guides have been the kids who live there.

SLEEPING
Central San José

Though close to the buses, downtown isn't the most desirable location for travelers. At nighttime the bustle winds down and security can be an issue.

Hotel Musoc (☎ 222 9437; Calle 16 btwn Avs 1 & 3; s/d US$9/15, with bathroom US$12/16) An oasis in the not-so-great Coca-Cola neighborhood, Musoc proves nicer inside than out, where immaculate but airless little singles have stiff mattresses and desks. It's hard to miss your bus here – the back rooms look out over the terminal.

Hotel Nuevo Johnson (☎ 223 7633; www.hotelnuevo johnson.com; Calle 8 btwn Avs Central & 2; r per person US$10) If this is the New Johnson, we'd shudder to see the old. But beyond dark hallways and paneling there's decent-sized rooms with firm beds and clean, hot showers. A game room with a pool table makes it more palatable.

Hotel Nuevo Alameda (☎ 233 3551; www.hotel nuevoalameda.com; cnr Calle 12 & Av Central; r per person US$12; 🗙) A clean but tired option in the city center. Bright rooms have views of Plaza de la Merced but mattresses are bowed and the carpet is downtrodden. It does sport an elevator.

Hotel Príncipe (☎ 222 7983; Av 6 btwn Calles 2 & Central; r US$13) A pleasant surprise with bright, spacious tiled rooms with solid beds and funky retro headboards. The bathrooms are spanking new. The only bummer is the barrio, definitely not fit for princes.

Barrio Amón & Surrounds

Most travelers lodge in this amenable area within easy walking distance of downtown and grocery stores. Hostels listed following offer airport transfers.

Tranquilo Backpackers (☎ 223 3189, 222 2493, 355 5103; www.tranquilobackpackers.com; Calle 7 btwn Avs 9 & 11; dm/s US$8/13; 🖳) Located in an old mansion, relaxed Tranquilo is a reader favorite. Japanese lanterns, bright murals and low hammocks adorn the big common rooms where mounted guitars can satisfy impromptu sing-alongs. The shared rooms are tall and narrow but skylights help you battle the claustrophobia. Perks include a communal kitchen and the universally loved free pancake breakfast.

Costa Rica Backpackers (☎ 221 6191; www.costarica backpackers.com; Av 6 btwn Calles 21 & 23; dm/d US$9/22; 🖳 🐦) This sprawling hostel complex centers around beautiful gardens and a free-form pool. Friendly and ultra-cool, it offers communal kitchens and a TV lounge, showing two movies nightly. The rooms are plain and pillows pancake-thin.

Hostel Pangea (☎ 221 1992; www.hostelpangea.com; cnr Av 13 & Calle 3 bis, Av 11 btwn Calles 3 & 3 bis, Av 7 btwn Calles 3 & 3 bis; dm US$10, d with/without bathroom US$29/25;

🗙 🖳 🐦) A backpacker's dream digs. Start with the rooftop deck, serving great breakfasts, sandwiches and beer. The many shared spaces nurture a social atmosphere – where you can play pool, swim in one, or check internet (wait a sec, that's not social…). The installations are well looked after and the bilingual service is typically outstanding. There are two locations: the older is quieter and has access to the new building's many amenities, which now even includes a mechanical bull.

Casa Ridgway (☎ 233 6168; www.amigosparalapaz .org; casaridgway@yahoo.es; cnr Calle 15 & Av 6 bis; dm/s US$10/12; 🗙) This welcoming guesthouse, on a quiet dead-end street near the Supreme Court building, is run by the adjacent Friends' Peace Center which promotes peace and social justice. Rooms are tidy, the shared showers are hot, the communal kitchen is spotless and the atmosphere is, well, peaceful. The library offers an extensive collection of books on religion, Central American politics and society. It's less ideal for party people – there's no smoking, alcohol or drugs allowed and quiet hours are from 10pm to 6am.

Casa León (☎ 843 8633; casa_leon_sa@hotmail.com; Av 6 btwn Calles 13 & 15; s/d US$10/15/23, s/d with bathroom US$25/33) This small Swiss-run guesthouse is quiet, clean and modern. Perfect for the dorm-weary, its remodeled rooms are well-appointed and there's wi-fi, laundry service and breakfast available at an extra charge.

Pensión de la Cuesta (☎ 256 7946; www.suntours andfun.com/lacuesta; Av 1 btwn Calles 11 & 15; s/d/tr incl breakfast US$14/28/39, child under 12 free) Situated on a little hill behind the Asamblea Legislativa, this 1920s wooden house looks styled by Barbie and Ken. Nine small but appealing rooms with private bathrooms share a homey TV lounge, perfect for relaxing with the owners and guests.

Hotel Aranjuez (☎ 256 1825; www.hotelaranjuez .com; Calle 19 btwn Avs 11 & 13; s/d US$22/25, with bathroom US$28/38; 🖳) Great value, this quiet charmer consists of vintage homes linked by gardens and a lush backyard. The spotless rooms vary in size and price. The hosts serve a sumptuous breakfast of omelets to order (included in the rates) under the mango tree.

Kap's Place (☎ 221 1169; www.kapsplace.com; Calle 19 btwn Avs 11 & 13; s US$22-38, d US$24-48, tr US$36-58, 2-/3-/4-/5-person apt US$90/100/110/120; 🖳) This original guesthouse gushes cheer. Tropical colors and mosaic floors adorn a sprawling space with rooms of every price, shape and size. Cozy is the operative word here and you'll find beds in batik covers, and free tea and coffee. There's also a shared kitchen and free internet. Spanish, English and French are spoken. It also has an annex nearby.

Casa Hilda (☎ 221 0037; c1hilda@racsa.co.cr; Av 11 btwn Calles 3 & 3 bis; s/d incl breakfast US$26/36) This peach-colored inn is home to the friendly Quesada family. While the rooms are simple, domestic warmth abounds. Check out the natural spring in the center of the house – it's been bubbling for 90 years.

Cinco Hormigas Rojas (☎ 257 8581; www.cincohormigasrojas.com; Calle 15 btwn Avs 9 & 11; r US$30-58; ✖) Set amid rampant greenery, this guesthouse is the love child of artist and conservationist Mayra. Chirping birds take you far from the city streets but the patchouli ambience of swirly nude paintings and batiks is not necessarily for all.

Joluva Guesthouse (☎ 223 7961; www.joluva.com; Calle 3 bis btwn Avs 9 & 11; s/d US$36/50; 🖳) This quaint guesthouse has seven small but well-appointed rooms scattered around a number of cozy public areas. The management speaks English and can provide information on the gay scene.

La Sabana

Upmarket and secure, La Sabana is ideal for those settling in for a while. Lodgings are close to San José's best park and a slew of language schools. Modernity, in the form of ubiquitous car dealerships and fast-food joints, may be its only drawback.

Galileo Hostel (☎ 221 8831, 248 2094; www.galileohostel.com; dm US$7, d US$16; 🖳) In a sturdy colonial building, the Galileo is well maintained but lacking flavor. Its rooms are drab and even singles come equipped with bunks. Perks include the communal kitchen, hot showers, TV lounge, and outdoor patio. It's 100m south of the Banco de Costa Rica.

Gaudy's (☎ 258 2937; www.backpacker.co.cr; Av 5 btwn Calles 36 & 38; dm US$7, d with bathroom US$25; 🖳) This big, bright stone-and-cement home has well-appointed dorms, each with its own bath. Ample doubles have impeccable private bathrooms. Though worn at the seams, the house has a pleasant air and free wi-fi. It's 200m north and 150m east of Banco de Costa Rica.

Mi Casa Hostel (☎ 231 4700; www.micasahostel.com; dm US$8-10, r US$25-30; 🖳) La Sabana's best backpacker option is this airy, modern home with polished-wood floors and antique furnishings.

Fusbol, pool and a decked-out kitchen round out the amenities. Dorms are sex-separate and the staff are extremely helpful. Rates include breakfast and internet. To get here, go 50m west and 150m north of the ICE Building.

JC & Friends (☎ 374 8246; www.jcfriendshostel.com; cnr Calle 34 & Av 3; dm US$10, s/d US$16/24, campsite US$7; 🖳) JC is a friendly, can-do personality whose hostel is decked out in whimsical colors and smartened up with a deluxe recreation room and outdoor hammock lounge (complete with artificial 'sand'). Only fans are lacking. Enjoy a free cereal-and-toast breakfast and 2nd-floor volcano views. The Tuasa airport bus (see p539) conveniently stops in front.

EATING

The popular proverb *panza llena, corazon contento* (full stomach, happy heart) sums up what Costa Ricans value most: abundant food, preferably consumed in good company. In San José's multitude of restaurants it's not hard to find something for most tastes and budgets.

Ticos adore the increasingly prevalent American fast-food. Local families save all week and dress up to treat the kids at air-conditioned McDonald's or Pizza Hut come Saturday.

Central San José

Mercado Central (Av Central btwn Calles 6 & 8) One of the cheapest places for a good lunch is at the market where you'll find a variety of restaurants and *sodas* serving *casados* (cheap set meals) tamales, seafood and everything in between.

Vishnu (Av 1 btwn Calles 1 & 3; also Calle Central btwn Avs 6 & 8; US$3-5) Vinyl booths and plastic countertops betray that this vegetarian restaurant is actually a chain, but it's still fresh, bountiful and cheap. Veggie burgers on whole-wheat bread are heaped with fresh coleslaw, and yogurt parfaits make a smooth finish.

Churrería Manolo's (Av Central btwn Calles Central & 2, also Av Central btwn Calles 9 & 11; churros US$0.50, meals US$3-5; ⏰ 24hr) The cream-filled *churros* (doughnut tubes) here draw crowds in search of a sugar fix. They're freshest around 5pm, when the hungry office workers are released from their cubes. The downtown west location serves killer *casados*, with a 2nd-floor balcony overlooking the lively pedestrian mall below.

Restaurant Shakti (☎ 222 4475; cnr Av 8 & Calle 13; dishes US$4-6; ⏰ 7am-7pm Mon-Sat) Fresh whole-grain breads, greens and local root vegetables comprise the wholly healthy fare here. The service is fast and friendly, and even despairing carnivores can sometimes get chicken on the sly.

Café de Correo (Calle 2 near Av 3; dishes US$5-6; 9am-7pm Mon-Fri, 9am-5pm Sat) Located in the Correo Central, this is an excellent spot to sip a hot (or iced) espresso while writing postcards – the drop box is right around the corner. The small selection of pasta dishes will satisfy the ravenous.

Café del Teatro Nacional (Plaza de la Cultura; dishes US$5-6; 9am-5pm Mon-Fri, 9am-12:30pm & 1:30-5:30pm Sat) The most beautiful café in the city is, not surprisingly, located in the most beautiful building in the city. The coffee drinks and small sandwiches here are good enough, though the real reason you're here is to soak up the ambience of the building's stunning frescoes.

Café Parisienne (Plaza de la Cultura; dishes US$5-10; 24hr) The perfect place for people-watching is this overpriced European-style café in the Gran Hotel Costa Rica. Views of the Teatro Nacional aren't bad either. Meals are fairly ordinary but if you grab a cup of coffee the wait staff will leave you alone.

Barrio Amón & Surrounds

Cafe de la Posada (☎ 258 1027; Calle 17 btwn Avs 2 & 4; US$3-6; 11am-7pm Mon-Fri, 11am-5pm Sat & Sun) Atmosphere emanates from this Argentine café, decked in prints and paintings. Tables front a quiet pedestrian walkway where patrons sip superb coffee drinks and eat authentic Argentine *empanadas*. For substance, the 'plate of the day' is a good choice.

Café Saudade (☎ 233 2534; Calle 17 btwn Avs 2 & 4; US$4-12; 10am-6:30pm Mon-Thu, 11am-5pm Fri & Sat, closed Sun) This hidden gem is coveted for its eclectic menu of sushi, hummus, crêpes and salads in addition to standard café fare. Tabletop displays showcase the work of local artists and photographers.

Kafé Ko (☎ 258 7453; cnr Av Central & Calle 21; US$5-10; 11am-midnight Mon-Fri, 5pm-1am Sat) Hip and candlelit Ko serves gourmet Western-style sandwiches, quiche and salads. On week nights it becomes a hotspot for live music – it cooks with live DJs spinning on weekends.

La Cocina de Leña (☎ 223 3704, 255 1360; Centro Comercial El Pueblo; dishes US$5-9; 11am-11pm Sun-Thu, 11am-midnight Fri & Sat) One of the best-known restaurants in town, 'the Wood Stove' prints its menu on brown paper bags. The long list

of national favorites served here includes black-bean soup, tamales and stuffed peppers, and oxtail served with fried plantain. Try the *guaro*, a highly recommended local firewater. Live marimba bands occasionally liven up dinner.

Nuestra Tierra (cnr Av 2 & Calle 15; casados US$7; 24hr) With rustic tables surrounded by hanging bunches of onions and plantains, this popular spot charms the bills out of your wallet. OK, musical trios and tasty, fresh *chorreadas* (pan-grilled corn cakes) make a good match, but some steep prices need wrangling.

Restaurante Tin-Jo (☎ 222 2868; cnr Calle 11 & Av 8; appetizers US$3-5, mains US$6-12; 11:30am-3pm & 5:30-10pm Mon-Thu, 11:30am-3pm & 5:30-11pm Fri & Sat, 11:30am-10pm Sun) Screened rooms with lovely Asian artwork and artifacts set the scene for this relaxed dining experience. Let loose on all things Asian – you won't be disappointed. The menu somehow manages Szechwan, Thai, Indian, Cantonese, Indonesian and Japanese cuisine with aplomb. Reservations are recommended – this place gets packed.

La Sabana & Surrounds

Soda Tapia (cnr Av 2 & Calle 42; casados US$3-4; 6am-midnight) This unpretentious spot is a local favorite – you can't go wrong with any of their featured *casados*, though it's worth saving some room for the sinful sundaes.

Machu Picchu (☎ 222 7384; Calle 32 btwn Av 1 & 3; US$6-11; 11am-3pm & 6-10pm Mon-Sat) This highly recommended Peruvian outpost is hot with the upmarket crowd, and with good reason. Patrons can choose from a variety of *ceviches*, tremendous seafood stews and traditionally prepared meat and fish. Start your engine with a pisco sour, a tart and potent drink.

DRINKING & NIGHTLIFE

The much recommended Centro Comercial El Pueblo or simply 'El Pueblo' is a mall-type complex jam-packed with hip bars and clubs. It gets going at about 9pm and shuts down by 3am. Stringent security keeps any trouble outside, making this one place in Chepe where you can kick back a few and let loose. Bring your ID.

Across the street and about 100m west of Centro Comercial El Pueblo, you'll find **¿Por Que No?** (☎ 233 6622), connected to Hotel Villa Tournón. The bar is a local favorite, especially on Friday when there's live music.

COSTA RICA

Leave the zip-off pants at home and don black for **Luna Roja Café** (☎ 223 2432; Calle 3 btwn Avs 9 & 11), a bastion of the young and trendy. There's a US$2.50 cover most nights, though Wednesday is free.

Next to the Barrio México church, **México Bar** (cnr Av 13 & Calle 16) is a trendy but interesting bar with good *bocas* (appetizers) and mariachis some nights. It's undoubtedly local, with few tourists or expats, and the neighborhood leading to it is a poor one, so go by taxi.

The historic, 77-year-old **Bar Chavelona** (Av 10 btwn Calles 10 & 12; ☼ 24hr) bar is frequented by radio and theater workers, giving the place an old-world bohemian feel. The area south of the town center becomes somewhat deserted at night, so take a taxi.

Gay & Lesbian Venues

San José's thriving gay-and-lesbian scene tends toward the periphery, meaning the best clubs operate in some of the worst areas. Travel by cab at night and, if possible, bring a friend. Clubs charge US$2 to US$5 covers on weekends. For the latest, log on to **Gay Costa Rica** (www.gaycostarica.com), providing info in English and Spanish.

Upmarket gay bar **Bochinche** (☎ 221 0500; Calle 11 btwn Avs 10 & 12) is preferred by young professionals. The rocking **Deja Vú** (☎ 223 3758; Calle 2 btwn Avs 14 & 16) is a massive dance club with open-bar for men on Wednesday and go-go boys on Saturday.

Popular with men, reader-recommended **La Avispa** (☎ 223 5343; Calle 1 btwn Avs 8 & 10) features pool tables and a boisterous dance floor. Known for raucous, over-the-top drag shows, **Los Cucharones** (☎ 233 5797; Av 6 btwn Calles Central & 1) caters to the young working class.

ENTERTAINMENT

Pick up *La Nación* on Thursday for a complete listing (in Spanish) of the coming week's nightlife and cultural events. The *Tico Times* 'Weekend' section (in English) has a calendar of events. Available at the tourist office, *Guía de Ciudad*, published by *El Financiero*, features local happenings. Visit www.entretenimiento .co.cr for more up-to-date movie, bar and club listings all over the San José area.

San José has a booming Spanish theatrical scene. The most revered theater is the **Teatro Nacional** (performance listing ☎ 221 5341), staging plays, dance, symphony and Latin music from March to November. Other major venues include the **Teatro Fanal** (☎ 257 5524; Av 3 btwn Calles 11 & 15), adjacent to the contemporary arts museum, the restored 1920s **Teatro Melico Salazar** (☎ 221 4952; cnr Av 2 & Calle Central), opposite the parque central and the **Auditorio Nacional** (☎ 249 1208), inside Museo de los Niños.

SHOPPING

Assuming you've dressed down and stuck a wad of extra cash in your sock, the gritty **Mercado Central** (Avs Central & 1 btwn Calles 6 & 8) is the best place for hammocks *hecho en* (made in) Nicaragua and '*Pura Vida*' tees (made in China). To really go native, get some export-quality coffee beans sold here for a fraction of the boutique price.

One of the city's best shopping experiences, the **Mercado Artesanal** (Plaza de la Democracia; Avs Central & 2 btwn Calles 13 & 15) has a hundred open-air stalls hawking handcrafted jewelry, elaborate woodwork, Guatemalan sarongs and Cuban cigars.

For a quick education about local indigenous cultures, **Galería Namu** (Av 7 btwn Calles 5 & 7; ☼ 9:30am-6:30pm Mon-Sat, 9:30am-1:30pm Sun) selectively brings together quality artwork and crafts from Costa Rica's small but diverse population. And where else can you pick up a Bribrí dugout canoe?

GETTING THERE & AWAY
Air

The two airports serving San José are **Aeropuerto Juan Santamaría** (☎ 437 2626), near Alajuela, and **Aeropuerto Tobias Bolaños** (☎ 232 2820) in Pavas. The former handles international traffic. Tobias Bolaños is for domestic flights by NatureAir. Airlines with offices in San José include:

Continental (☎ 296 4911; next to Hotel Barceló, La Uruca)

Delta (☎ 256 7909, press 5 for reservations; Paseo Colón) Located 100m east and 50m south of Toyota.

Grupo TACA (☎ 296 0909; cnr Calle 42 & Av 5) Across from the Datsun dealership.

Iberia (☎ 257 8266; Centro Colón, 2nd fl)

Mexicana (☎ 295 6969; Torre Mercedes Benz on Paseo Colón, 3rd fl)

United (☎ 220 4844; Sabana Sur)

Varig (☎ 290 5222) About 150m south of Channel 7, west of Parque La Sabana

To get to Aeropuerto Juan Santamaría, catch the Tuasa bus bound for Alajuela (US$0.60) from Calle 10 on the corner of Av 2. **Interbus**

(☎ 283 5573) charges US$5 and does hotel pick-ups. A street taxi will cost from US$15 to US$20. It's best to reserve a pick-up with **Taxi Aeropuerto** (☎ 221 6865).

Buses to Aeropuerto Tobías Bolaños depart every half hour from Av 1, 150m west of the Coca-Cola terminal. A taxi from downtown costs about US$3.

Bus

The **Coca-Cola bus terminal** (Av 1 btwn Calles 16 & 18), is a well-known local landmark. Scores of buses leave from a four-block radius around it. Several terminals serve specific regions. Just northeast of the Coca-Cola, the **Terminal San Carlos** (cnr Av 9 & Calle 12) serves northern destinations such as Monteverde, La Fortuna and Sarapiquí. The **Gran Terminal del Caribe** (Caribe Terminal; Calle Central, north of Av 13) serves the Caribbean coast. On the south end of town, **Terminal Musoc** (Av 22 btwn Calles Central & 1) caters for San Isidro. Other companies have no more than a bus stop (in this case pay the driver directly); some have a tiny office with a window on the street; some operate out of a terminal.

Buses are crowded on Friday evening and Saturday morning, even more so during Christmas and Easter. Thefts are common around the Coca-Cola terminal, so stay alert. Bus schedules change regularly and prices change with fluctuating fuel costs. Get a master bus schedule at the ICT office (p542) or online at www.visitcostarica.com.

INTERNATIONAL BUSES

Take a copy of your passport when buying tickets to international destinations.

Changuinola/Bocas del Toro, Panama (Panaline; cnr Calle 16 & Av 3) US$15; 8hr; departs 10am

David, Panama (Tracopa; Calle 14 btwn Avs 3 & 5) US$14; 9hr; 7:30am

Guatemala City (Tica Bus; cnr Calle 9 & Av 4) US$39; 60hr; 6am & 7:30am

Managua, Nicaragua US$12; 9hr; Nica Bus (Caribe Terminal) departs at 5:30am & 9am; Transportes Deldu/Sirca Express (Calle 16 btwn Avs 3 & 5) departs 4:30am; Tica Bus (cnr Calle 9 & Av 4) departs 6am & 7:30am; Trans Nica (Calle 22 btwn Avs 3 & 5) departs 4:30am, 5:30am & 9am

Panama City US$25/42 for Tica/Panaline; 15hr; Tica Bus (cnr Calle 9 & Av 4) departs 10pm; Panaline (cnr Calle 16 & Av 3) departs 1pm

San Salvador, El Salvador (Tica Bus; cnr Calle 9 & Av 4) US$42; 48hr; 6am & 7:30am

Tegucigalpa, Honduras (Tica Bus; cnr Calle 9 & Av 4) US$32; 48hr; 6am & 7:30am

DOMESTIC BUSES
To the Central Valley

Alajuela (Tuasa; Av 2 btwn Calles 12 & 14) US$0.60; 40min; departs every 15min from 4:45am to 11pm

Cartago US$0.50; 40min; Sacsa (Calle 5 btwn Avs 18 & 20) departs every 5min; Transtusa (Calle 13 btwn Avs 6 & 8) departs hourly from 8am to 8pm

Heredia (Av 2 btwn Calles 10 & 12) US$0.50; 20min; departs every 20 to 30min from 4:40am to 11pm

Turrialba (Calle 13 btwn Avs 6 & 8) US$2; 1¾hr; departs hourly 8am to 8pm

Volcán Irazú (Av 2 btwn Calles 1 & 3) US$4.50; departs 8am on weekends only

Volcán Poás (Tuasa; Av 2 btwn Calles 12 & 14) US$4, 5hr; departs 8:30am

To the Central Pacific Coast

Dominical (Transportes Morales; Coca-Cola) US$4.50; 6½hr; departs 7am, 8am, 1:30pm & 4pm

Jacó (Transportes Jacó; Coca-Cola) US$2.50; 3hr; 7:30am, 10:30am, 1pm, 3:30pm & 6:30pm

Puntarenas (Empresarios Unidos; cnr Av 12 & Calle 16) US$2.50; 2¼hr; many buses from 6am to 7pm

Quepos/Manuel Antonio (Transportes Morales; Coca-Cola) US$4; 4hr; 6am, 7am, 10am, noon, 2pm, 4pm & 6pm

Uvita, via Dominical (Transportes Morales; Coca-Cola) US$5; 7hr; 6am & 3pm

To Península de Nicoya

Nicoya (Empresas Alfaro; Av 5 btwn Calle 14 & 16) US$5.25-6; 5hr; departs 6am, 6:30am, 8am, 10am, 10:30am, 12:30pm, 1:30pm, 2pm, 3pm, 4pm, 5pm & 6:30pm

Playa del Coco (Pullmitan; Calle 24 btwn Avs 5 & 7) US$5.25; 5hr; 8am, 2pm & 4pm

Playa Nosara (Empresas Alfaro; Calle 16 btwn Avs 3 & 5) US$5; 7hr; 6am

Playa Sámara (Empresas Alfaro; Calle 16 btwn Avs 3 & 5) US$5; 5hr; 12:30am

Playa Tamarindo (Empresas Alfaro; Calle 16 btwn Avs 3 & 5) US$5; 5hr; 11am & 3:30pm

Santa Cruz, via Tempisque bridge US$5.25; 4¼hr; Tralapa (Av 7 btwn Calles 20 & 22) departs 7am, 10am, 10:30am, noon, 1pm & 4pm; Empresas Alfaro (Calle 16 btwn Avs 3 & 5) departs 6:30am, 8am, 10am, 1:30pm, 3pm & 5pm

To Northwestern Costa Rica & Northern Lowlands

Cañas US$3; 3¼hr; Tralapa (Av 7 btwn Calles 20 & 22) departs hourly; Transportes Cañas (Calle 16 btwn Avs 1 & 3) departs 8:30am, 9:50am, 11:50am, 1:40pm, 3pm & 4:45pm

Ciudad Quesada (San Carlos) (Autotransportes San Carlos; San Carlos terminal) US$2.50; 2½hr; departs hourly 5am to 7pm

COSTA RICA

La Fortuna (San Carlos terminal) US$3, 4½hr; departs 6:15am, 8:40am & 11:30am

Liberia US$5; 4hr; Pullmitan (Calle 24 btwn Avs 5 & 7) departs hourly from 6am to 7pm; Tralapa (Av 7 btwn Calles 20 & 22) departs 3:25pm

Los Chiles, the Nicaragua Border Crossing (San Carlos terminal) US$3.75; 5hr; departs 5:30am & 3:30pm

Monteverde/Santa Elena (Trans Monteverde; San Carlos terminal) US$4.50, 4½hr; departs 6:30am & 2:30pm (this bus fills very quickly – book ahead)

Peñas Blancas, the Nicaragua Border Crossing (Transportes Deldú; Calle 16 btwn Avs 3 & 5) US$5.50; 4½hr; departs 4am, 5am, 7am, 7:30am, 10:30am, 1:20pm & 4pm weekdays, every 15min from 3am to 4pm weekends

Puerto Viejo de Sarapiquí (Autotransportes Sarapiquí; Caribe Terminal) US$2.50; 1½hr; 7:30am, 10am, 11:30am, 1:30pm, 2:30pm, 3:30pm, 4:30pm, 5:30pm & 6pm

Tilarán (Autotransportes Tilarán; San Carlos terminal) US$3.50; 4hr; departs 7:30am, 9:30am, 12:45pm, 3:45pm & 6:30pm

To the Caribbean Coast

The following services depart from the Caribe terminal:

Cahuita (Autotransportes Mepe) US$6.50; 3¾hr; departs 6am, 10am, 1:30pm & 3:30pm

Cariari, for transfer to Tortuguero (Empresarios Guapileños) US$2.50; 2¼hr; 6:30am, 9am, 10:30am, 1pm, 3pm, 4:30pm, 6pm & 7pm; for detailed information on transfer to Tortuguero, see p572

Guápiles (Empresarios Guapileños) US$1.75; 1¼hr; departs hourly from 6:30am to 7pm

Puerto Limón (Autotransportes Caribeños) US$3.50; 3hr; departs every 30min from 5:30am to 7pm

Puerto Viejo de Talamanca (Autotransportes Mepe) US$7.75; 4¼hr; 6am, 10am, 1:30pm & 3:30pm

Siquirres (Líneas Nuevo Atlántico) US$2; 1¾hr; departs 6:30am to 7pm

Sixaola, the Panama Border Crossing (Autotransportes Mepe) US$9.50; 5hr; 6am, 10am, 1:30pm & 3:30pm

To Southern Costa Rica & Península de Osa

Ciudad Neily (Tracopa; Calle 14 btwn Avs 3 & 5) US$8.25; 7hr; departs 5am, 7:30am, 11am, 1pm, 4:30pm & 6pm

Golfito (Tracopa; Calle 14 btwn Avs 3 & 5) US$8.25, 8hr; 7am & 3pm

Palmar Norte (Tracopa; Calle 14 btwn Avs 3 & 5) US$5; 5hr; 5am, 7am, 8:30am, 10am, 1pm, 2:30pm & 6pm

Paso Canoas, the Panama Border Crossing (Tracopa; Calle 14 btwn Avs 3 & 5) US$9; 7¼hr; 5am, 7:30am, 11am, 1pm, 4:30pm & 6pm

Puerto Jiménez (Blanco Lobo; Calle 12 btwn Avs 9 & 11) US$6.50; 8hr; 6:30am & 3:30pm

San Isidro de El General Transportes Musoc (cnr Calle Central & Av 22) US$3.25; 3hr; departs hourly from 5:30am to 6:30pm; Tracopa (Av 4 btwn Calle 14 & 16) US$3.75; 3hr; departs hourly from 5am to 6pm

TOURIST BUSES

Grayline's Fantasy Bus (☎ 220 2126; www.grayline costarica.com) and **Interbus** (☎ 283 5573; www.inter busonline.com) shuttle passengers from all over San José to popular tourist destinations. More expensive than standard bus services, they are also much faster.

GETTING AROUND
Bus

Local buses generally run from 5am to 10pm and cost from US$0.25 to US$0.60. Buses into downtown from Parque La Sabana head east on Paseo Colón then jog over to Av 2 at the hospital before heading into the center by various routes. To return, catch a 'Sabana-Cementario' along Calle 11 (between Avs Central and 2). For San Pedro and Los Yoses, take a 'Mall San Pedro' from Av 2 (between Calles 9 and 11) and to get to Escazú, look for the blue buses just east of the **Coca-Cola bus terminal** (Calle 16 btwn Avs 1 & 3).

Taxi

Red taxis can be hailed day or night. *Marías* (meters) are supposedly used, but some drivers will pretend they are broken or forget to turn them on and try to charge you more. Make sure the *maría* is operating when you get in or negotiate the fare up front. Within San José fares are US$0.60 for the first kilometer and US$0.30 for each extra one. Short rides downtown cost about US$1. There's a 20% surcharge after 10pm. Taxi drivers are not usually tipped.

AROUND SAN JOSÉ
Los Yoses & San Pedro

About 2km east of central San José, hoity-toity residential areas **Los Yoses** and **San Pedro** are home to a number of embassies as well as the most prestigious university in the country, la Universidad de Costa Rica (UCR). The area serves as the nightlife hub of under-30 *Josefínos*, with trendy bars, restaurants and nightclubs. Much like a Latin love affair, hot spots sizzle and fizzle quickly.

In San Pedro, the **Scotiabank** (Av Central btwn Calles 5 & 7) changes cash and has a 24-hour ATM on the Cirrus network. The neighborhood abounds with internet cafés; try **Internet Café Costa Rica** (☎ 224 7295; 75m west of old Banco Popular;

per hr US$0.60; 24hr). In Barrio Dent, **Librería Internacional** (☎ 253 9553; 300m west of Taco Bell, behind San Pedro Mall; 9:30am-7:30pm Mon-Sat, 1-5pm Sun) has new books mostly in Spanish (but some in English) as well as travel and wildlife guides.

SIGHTS

San Pedro's principal attraction is partying on Calle La Amargura. If you're not the drinking type, head to the malls and movie theaters for a quick Western culture-fix. The **Museo de Insectos** (☎ 207 5318, 207 5647; admission US$1; 1-5pm Mon-Fri) brings you up close and a bit too personal with a vast assortment of exotic creepy crawlies. At **Boliche Dent** (☎ 234 2777; cnr Av Central & Calle 23, Los Yoses) you can bowl for US$5 per hour.

SLEEPING & EATING

Hostel Bekuo (☎ 234 5486; www.hostelbekuo.com; Av 8 btwn Calles 29 & 41; dm US$9, s/d/tr US$18/26/33; 🖵) This place is a gorgeous take on Japanese minimalist design – think low tables, bean-bag chairs and hanging lanterns. Facilities include a communal kitchen, a recreation room with pool table and a TV lounge. Guests have free internet access (including wireless).

Casa Yoses (☎ 234 5486; www.casayoses.com; Av 8 at Calle 41; dm US$9, s/d/tr US$18/25/33; 🖵) Kick back in this 19th-century mansion tailored to traveling couples and upmarket backpackers. A garden with hammocks, sun chairs and tropical plants invites guests to read a book or nurse a hangover. The three Tico-owners speak English and French.

Hostel Toruma (☎ 234 8186; www.hosteltoruma .com; Av Central btwn Calles 29 & 31; dm US$10, s/d/tr with bathroom & private garden US$30/40/50; 🖵) Snooze soundly in a former president's digs at this cool Spanish-colonial mansion. It's abuzz with amenities like a swimming pool, TV lounge, free internet and a communal kitchen, all extremely well kept. Owned by the folks at Hostal Pangea, you can count on great bilingual service and camaraderie.

Pizzería Il Pomodoro (meals US$3-7) About 100m north of the San Pedro church, this place attracts a loyal following for its tasty Italian food. It's also open on Sunday.

Comida Para Sentir (Calle Central; daily specials US$4-8) This veggie venue, 50m north of the church, serves whole-grain pastas, meatless mains and mean cappuccinos to a packed house.

Spoon (Calle 43 & Av 10; mains US$2-8; 8am-7pm Mon-Fri, 9am-5pm Sat & Sun) Locals hit this place for big breakfasts after a rough night.

Al Muluk (Calle 3 north of Av Central; dishes US$3-7) Pleasant Al Muluk has delectable falafel and a wide variety of Lebanese specialties.

DRINKING & NIGHTLIFE

In San Pedro, Calle 3, north of Av Central, is also known as Calle la Amargura (Sorrow St). However, Calle la Cruda (Hangovers St) would be more apt, as it offers the highest concentration of bars of any street in town. Many pack with customers even during daylight. Terra U, Mosakos, Caccio's and Tavarúa are raucous, beer-soaked places packed with a steady stream of rowdy young patrons. A more relaxed (and slightly grown-up) spot is La Villa, in a distinctive wood house with a candlelit back patio. There's live music some weekends.

For live music, the top choice is the stylish **Jazz Café** (Av Central at Calle la Amargura; cover US$4-6; 6pm-2am), featuring different live bands each night. The recommended **El Retro-visor** (Arte Plaza San Pedro; 6pm-2am) is an Argentinean-owned retro café adorned with '80s pop culture memorabilia, hip amongst trendy UCR students.

ENTERTAINMENT

Multicines San Pedro (☎ 283 5715/6; top level of Mall San Pedro; admission US$4) has 10 screens showing the latest Hollywood flicks. Your other option is **Cine El Semáforo** (☎ 253 9126; www.cine selsemaforo.com; beside train tracks, east of Calle 3; admission US$3; 11am-8pm), a hip little theater showing Spanish and Latin American movie classics every day in Spanish.

GETTING THERE & AWAY

From the Plaza de la Cultura in San José, take any bus marked 'Mall San Pedro.' A taxi ride from downtown will cost US$1.50 to US$2.

CENTRAL VALLEY & HIGHLANDS

First cultivated by indigenous people, then coffee barons and now computer companies, the fertile Central Valley is Costa Rica's quintessential heartland. With San José at its booming core, and the cities of Alajuela, Heredia and Cartago filling its perimeter, *el valle* is the country's main population center. It is also one of the world's largest microchip production centers, tapping a workforce that's young, educated and increasingly bilingual. While

CENTRAL VALLEY & HIGHLANDS

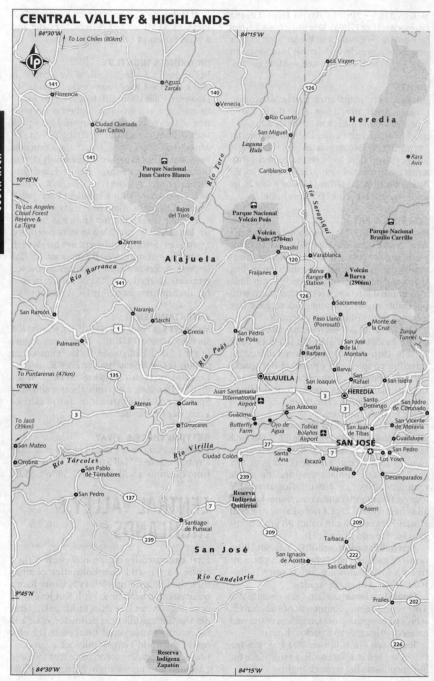

COSTA RICA

84°30'W
84°15'W

To Los Chiles (80km)

To Los Angeles Cloud Forest Reserve & La Tigra

Florencia
141

Aguas Zarcás
140
Venecia

Ciudad Quesada (San Carlos)

141

10°15'N

Parque Nacional Juan Castro Blanco

Heredia

La Virgen
126

Río Cuarto
San Miguel
Laguna Hule
Cariblanco

Rara Avis

Río Toro

Bajos del Toro

Parque Nacional Volcán Poás

Volcán Poás (2704m)
Poasito
120

Parque Nacional Braulio Carrillo

Zarcero

Alajuela

Fraijanes

Varablanca

Barva Ranger Station
126

Volcán Barva (2906m)

Sacramento

Río Barranca

141

Naranjo
Sarchí
1

Grecia

San Pedro de Poás

Paso Llano (Porrosatí)

Santa Barbara

San José de la Montaña

Monte de la Cruz

Zurquí Tunnel

San Ramón

Palmares

Río Poás

Barva

San Rafael
San Isidro

To Puntarenas (47km)
135

10°00'N

Atenas

Garita

Juan Santamaría International Airport

ALAJUELA

San Joaquín
3

HEREDIA
Santo Domingo

San Isidro de Coronado

3

San Antonio

San Vicente de Moravia

To Jacó (39km)
3

Túrrucares

Guácima

Butterfly Farm

Ojo de Agua

Tobías Bolaños Airport

San Juan de Tibas

Guadalupe

San Mateo

Orotina

Río Tárcoles

San Pablo de Túrrubares

Río Virilla

Ciudad Colón

27

Santa Ana

Escazú

SAN JOSÉ
7

Los Yoses
San Pedro

Alajuelita

Desamparados

San Pedro

137

239

Santiago de Puriscal

7

Reserva Indígena Quitirrisí

239
209

Aserri
209

San Ignacio de Acosta

Tárbaca

222

San Gabriel

San José

Río Candelaria

9°45'N

Frailes
202

Reserva Indígena Zapatón

226

84°30'W
84°15'W

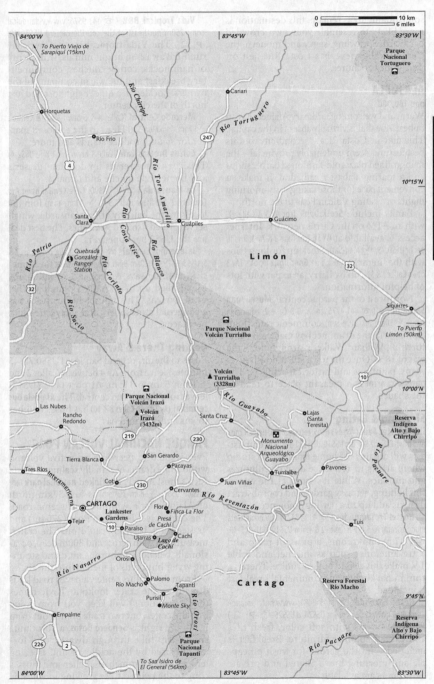

some quaint areas remain, this destination is more likely to resemble your own crowded backyard. Sprawling, savvy and modern, the Central Valley reveals a Costa Rica left off most tour brochures.

ALAJUELA
pop 160,000

Warm and welcoming, ordinary Alajuela has an upbeat vibe that is virtually absent in the capital. This may be Costa Rica's 'second city' but its best features seem undeniably provincial – the mango-lined plaza, old-fashioned barbershops and a soaring alabaster cathedral. It makes a convenient base for those taking early-morning flights or visiting Volcán Poás to the north.

Banks include **Scotiabank** (cnr Av 3 & Calle 2), with an ATM on the Cirrus network. Internet access is available at **BYTE** (cnr Calle 3 & Av 1, 2nd fl; per hr US$0.75; ☺ Mon-Sat). Stock up for long trips with the literary snacks at **Goodlight Books** (Av 3 btwn Calles 1 & 3), run by Larry, an expat with lots of helpful information.

Northwest of the parque central, **Museo Juan Santamaría** (☎ 441 4775; cnr Av 3 & Calle 2; admission free; ☺ 10am-6pm Tue-Sun) commemorates Juan Santamaría, the drummer boy martyred while torching William Walker's stronghold in the war of 1856. Once the town jail, it now houses maps, paintings and historical artifacts. The **parque central** is a pleasant place to read in the shade.

Sleeping & Eating

Hotel Cortéz Azul (☎ 443 6145; cortezazul@latinmail.com; Av 5 btwn Calles 2 & 4; dm US$10, d US$20-30) Art enthusiasts will dig this old home fronted by a studio where artists-in-residence design sculptures and mosaics. While it's worn at the edges, soft lighting, a grassy garden and cool abstract designs add up to a darling ambience.

Hostel Trotamundos (☎ 430 5832; www.hosteltrotamundos.com; Av 5 btwn Calles 2 & 4; dm US$10, d US$25-30; 🖳) Tidy bunkrooms, a pleasant patio and extra amenities such as internet and cable TV make this a solid budget choice. There's a communal kitchen and continental breakfast is included.

Hotel Pacandé (☎ 443 8481; www.hotelpacande.com; Av 5 btwn Calles 2 & 4; s US$20, d US$25-45; P 🖳) Pacandé beams with soft color, fresh tiles and carved colonial furniture. Breakfast is included – hit the garden for fresh pineapple and morning brew. Shared and private bathrooms are available.

Vida Tropical B&B (☎ 443 9576; www.vidatropical.com; 250m northeast of the courthouse; s/d US$30/40; P 🖳) The Vida tropical is an American-run B&B awash in bright murals, with plenty of hammocks, comfy couches, complimentary breakfast and the warm company of the owners. Located in a quiet neighborhood just north of the city center.

Mercado Central (Calles 4 & 6 btwn Avs 1 & Central; ☺ 7am-6pm Mon-Sat) Head to the enclosed market for *sodas*, produce stands and more.

Coffee Dreams Café (Calle 1 btwn Avs 1 & 3; US$2-4) This cozy place serves up decadent desserts and homemade quiche and tamales.

La Mansarda (☎ 441 4390; Calle Central btwn Avs Central & 2, 2nd fl; meals US$3-7; ☺ 11am-1am) Join the locals on the balcony at La Mansarda, which serves grilled fish and *patacones*. The best deal are the US$2 bar appetizers.

Jalepeños Central (☎ 430 4027; Calle 1 btwn Avs 3 & 5; US$3-6; ☺ 11:20am-9pm, closed Sun) For the homesick, nothing says American like eating Tex Mex grilled up by a chatty Colombian chef from Queens. This unpretentious place has a congenial atmosphere and spicy shredded-beef tacos.

Getting There & Away

Buses to the airport and San José (US$0.75, 45 minutes) leave from Av 4 between Calles 2 and 4, from 5am to 11pm. Airport taxis (US$5) leave from the parque central. The **Alajuela bus terminal** (Av 1 btwn Calles 8 & 10) has buses to other towns and Volcán Poás.

PARQUE NACIONAL VOLCÁN POÁS

Ever wanted to peer into an active volcano without the drama of actually scaling it? Costa Rica's most heavily trafficked **national park** (admission US$7; ☺ 8am-3:30pm) is just 37km north of Alajuela by a winding and scenic road. The centerpiece is Volcán Poás (2704m) and its steaming, belching cauldron. The crater, measuring 1.3km across and 300m deep, occasionally belches sulphurous mud and steaming water hundreds of meters into the air.

From the visitors center, a paved road leads directly to the crater lookout. Toxic fumes (and regulations) will keep you from going into the crater, but two trails branch out from it. To the right is **Sendero Botos**, a 30-minute round-trip hike through dwarf cloud forest nurtured by the acidic air and freezing temperatures. Bromeliads, lichen and mosses cling to the twisted trees growing in volcanic soil. Birds abound; look for the magnificent fiery-throated hummingbird, a high-altitude specialty of Costa Rica. The trail ends at **Laguna Botos**, a peculiar cold-water lake that has filled in one of the extinct craters. Going left of the crater is **Sendero Escalonia**, a slightly longer trail through taller forest. It gets significantly less traffic than the other parts of the park.

A veil of clouds envelops the mountain almost daily, appearing at around 10am. Even if it's clear, get to the park as early as possible or you won't see much. The best time to visit is dry season and on the less-crowded weekdays.

From San José, Tuasa buses (US$4, three hours) depart 8:30am daily from Av 2 between Calles 12 and 14, stopping in Alajuela at 9:30am, and returning at 2:30pm. Hours are inexact, it's best to arrive early if departing from Alajuela.

HEREDIA
pop 80,000

Although only 11km from San José, Heredia is worlds away from the grit and grime of the capital. Its cosmopolitan bustle comes courtesy of the multinational high-tech corporations whose Central American headquarters are here. More bohemian stylings radiate from the National University. Heredia's historic center is one of the most attractive in the country, and the city serves as a convenient base for exploring the diverse attractions of the province.

Scotiabank (Av 4 btwn Calles Central & 2) changes money and has a 24-hour ATM on the Cirrus network. The university district is full of copy shops and internet cafés.

Watch the older generation square off in checker tournaments at the **parque central**. It's also the place to soak up Heredia's colonial heritage. Built in 1798, **La Inmaculada Concepción** sits east of the park. This squat and sturdy construction has survived the worst earthquakes in Costa Rica. North of the park, the 1867 guard tower called **El Fortín** is the last remaining turret of a Spanish fortress, and the official symbol of Heredia. You'll find the **Casa de la Cultura** (☎ 262 2505; www.heredianet.co.cr/casacult.htm, in Spanish; cnr Calle Central & Av Central; admission free; ☼ hours vary) at the park's northeast corner. This former residence of President Alfredo González Flores (1913–17) now houses permanent historical exhibits, art shows and events.

Courses

Spanish courses are available at a couple of places.

Centro Panamericano de Idiomas (☎ 265 6306; www.cpi-edu.com; without/with homestay US$275/395) In the Heredia suburb of San Joaquín de Flores.

Intercultura (☎ 260 8480, in the USA ☎ 800 552 2051; www.spanish-intercultura.com; without/with homestay US$260/370) Also arranges volunteer positions.

Sleeping

Hotel El Verano (☎ 237 1616; Calle 4 btwn Avs 6 & 8; s/d US$8/10) Friendly but dilapidated, at least Verano spruces up its paper-thin walls with bright colors. It's in the seedy area by the bus terminal.

Hotel las Flores (☎ 261 1477; Av 12 btwn Calles 12 & 14; s/d US$12/22) Heredia's best value is this large peach building on the city outskirts. It boasts tip-top rooms in earthy tones with tiled floors and modern baths – request one with a balcony.

Hotel Heredia (☎ 238 0880; www.hamerica.net; Calle 6 btwn Avs 3 & 5; s/d/tr US$15/20/30) This conspicuously adorable house was recently renovated from the ground up. The beds here continue to be noodly soft but the rooms are ample and bright, with solar-heated showers and cable TV.

Hotel Rambles (☎ 238 3829; Av 8 btwn Calles 10 & 12; s/d US$16/20) Elegant and airy, this impeccable white stucco colonial hotel is a refreshing upgrade. The rooms are lovely, as is the older hostess, who unfortunately has two-tiered prices for locals and foreigners.

Eating & Drinking

Mercado Municipal (Calle 2 btwn Avs 6 & 8; ☼ 6am-6pm) Compensate for your overpriced hotel by eating cheap at the market where there's fresh produce and *sodas* to spare.

Vishnu Mango Verde (Calle 7 btwn Avs Central & 1; US$3-5; ☼ 9am-6pm Mon-Sat) This is known for fresh veggie fare.

Fresas (cnr Av 1 & Calle 7; mains US$3-8; ☼ 8am-midnight) Popular with students, Fresas serves fresh fruit shakes and salads, and *casados* round out the menu.

La Candelaria (☎ 237 4630; 150m west of road to Aurora; mains US$4-8; ☼ 11:30am-10pm) The best dinner in town is a short taxi hop away at this romantic Portuguese restaurant with a creative menu including trout crêpes, grilled meat and fish. Order the *tiramisu* – it's arguably more stimulating than most dates.

A thriving and thirsty student body means there's no shortage of live music, *fusbol* or the odd happening. La Choza, El Bulevar and **El Rancho de Fofo** (cnr Calle 7 & Av Central) are three popular student spots.

Getting There & Away

There is no central terminal; buses leave from stops near the parque central and the market. Buses to **San José** (US$0.50, 20 minutes) depart from Av 4 between Calles Central and 1, every half-hour. Buses for Barva (US$0.25, 20 minutes) leave from **Cruz Roja** (Red Cross; Calle Central btwn Avs 1 & 3). Buses to San José de la Montaña and Sacramento, with connections to Volcán Barva in Parque Nacional Braulio Carrillo, leave from Av 8 between Calles 2 and 4.

PARQUE NACIONAL BRAULIO CARRILLO

Thick virgin forest, gushing waterfalls, swift rivers and deep canyons – it's hard to believe that you are only 30 minutes north of San José while walking around this underexplored national park. Braulio Carrillo's extraordinary biodiversity is attributed to its range in altitude, from Volcán Barva's misty cloud forest to the lush, humid lowlands reaching toward the Caribbean.

Founded in 1978, the park protects primary forest threatened when the highway between San José and Puerto Limón was built. Driving through it will give you an idea of what Costa Rica looked like prior to the 1950s – rushing rivers and rolling hills steeped in mountain rain forest.

Several rivers traverse the park: the Río Sucio ('Dirty River'), whose yellow waters carry volcanic minerals, and the crystal-clear Río Hondura. They intersect next to the main highway, and it's fascinating to see the contrast of colors. Volcán Barva is located at the southwestern corner of the park.

There have been many reports of thefts from cars and armed robbers on the trails or along the highway. It's best to either hike with a park ranger or arrange for a guide through any of the stations.

For more details, check the website of **Minae** (www.minae.go.cr/accvc/braulio.htm).

Quebrada González Sector

The most popular hiking area is accessed at the northern end of the park at the **Quebrada González ranger station** (☎ 233 4533; admission US$6; ☯ 7am-4pm), 22km past the Zurquí tunnel to the right of the San José–Limón highway. It has a guarded parking lot, toilets and well-marked trails. Hourly buses between San José and Guápiles can drop you off at the entrance, but it's a 2km walk back along the highway to reach the restaurant where returning buses stop. Take precautions, as muggings have been reported along this stretch.

Barva Sector

Climbing Volcán Barva is a good four- to five-hour round-trip along a well-maintained trail. Begin on the western side of the park at the Sacramento entrance, north of Heredia. From there, the trail is signed and fairly obvious. It's a leisurely climb to the summit. Keep your eyes peeled for a quetzal. Near the summit there are several chilly lakes.

It is best to hike in the dry, or less-wet, season between December and April, as paths get muddy and cloud cover can disorientate hikers. Night temperatures can drop below freezing. Camping is allowed but there are no facilities.

From Heredia, three buses a day (6:30am, 11am and 4pm) pass Paso Llano (also called Porrosatí). From there, it's a 5km walk to Sacramento and then another 3km to the **Barva ranger station** (☎ 261 2619; ☯ 7am-4pm high season), which may or may not be manned.

CARTAGO

pop 127,000

Peace rules Cartago, where the quiet of the central plaza is only broken by rogue pigeons and the shouts of the lottery lady. Once the colonial capital, Cartago's grandeur has been somewhat diminished by mother nature's rumblings. Still, it retains great religious significance and a certain conservative charm. For most visitors, Cartago is the spot to catch your breath, a peaceful modern city with attractions nearby.

Considered to be the holiest shrine in Costa Rica, **La Basílica de Nuestra Señora de los Angeles** (Av 2 at Calle 16) is the home of the revered La Negrita (see boxed text, opposite). Leveled by the 1926 earthquake, the church is now rebuilt in Byzantine style. The **parque central** (cnr Av 2 & Calle 2) houses the shell of another church destroyed by the 1910 earthquake, known as **Las Ruinas**. It now has a pleasant garden to visit.

You can check your email 50m east of Las Ruinas at **Internet Alta Velocidad** (Calle 1 btwn Av 1 &

> ### LOCAL LORE: LA NEGRITA
>
> *La Negrita* or 'The Black Virgin' is a statuette of an indigenous Virgin Mary found by a *mulatto* woman named Juana Pereira in Cartago on August 2, 1635. According to lore, Juana twice took the statuette home with her, though on each occasion it reappeared where she had first found it. Astounded by the miracle that transpired, the townspeople built the Basílica de Nuestra Señora de Los Ángeles on the original spot where it was found. In 1824 La Negrita was declared Costa Rica's patron saint.
>
> On two separate occasions, La Negrita was stolen from the basilica, though each time it later reappeared on its altar (once was by future novelist José León Sánchez, who was sentenced to Isla San Lucas for 20 years). These strange occurrences have led people to believe that the statuette has curative properties, and it's common for petitioners to offer *milagrosos* (metal charms) representing the body parts they hope to have healed. Even the spring that flows near the basilica is said to have curative properties, and the statuette has been credited with everything from healing toe fungus to football victories.
>
> Each August 2, on the anniversary of the statuette's discovery, devotees walk a grueling 22km in the summer heat from San José to Cartago, arriving on their knees. It's an incredible sight, and you're more than welcome (*sans* kneepads) to participate.

3; per hr US$1; ☼ 9am-9pm). Several banks change money – try **Banco Nacional** (cnr Av 4 & Calle 5).

The family-run **Mistiko B&B** (☎ 371 3216; dm US$13, s/d with bathroom US$20/35; ☐) offers rooms in a spotless concrete apartment with cable TV, internet, kitchen, sun deck and backyard BBQ. Fruit and coffee are set out in the morning. It is 200m north of Av 6 between Calles 1 and 2. With balconies overlooking the Plaza de la Basílica, the comfortable **Los Ángeles Lodge** (☎ 551 0957; Av 4 btwn Calles 14 & 16; s/d incl breakfast US$25/40; ✺) stands out. Indulge in the steamy showers and big breakfasts made to order.

Stroll Avs 2 and 4 for a range of *sodas* and bakeries. **La Puerta del Sol** (Av 4; mains US$2-8; ☼ 8am-midnight), opposite the basilica, draws a hearty hometown crowd to its cushioned booths and long narrow bar; fare runs from sandwiches to meat and seafood.

Getting There & Away

Most buses arrive along Av 2 and reach the Basílica before returning to the main terminal on Av 4. Destinations:

Finca la Flor de Paraíso (US$1) Take a La Flor/Birrisito/ El Yas bus from in front of Padres Capuchinos church, 150m southeast of Las Ruinas. Get off at the pink church in La Flor; entrance to the *finca* is 100m to the south.

Paraíso & Lankester Gardens (US$0.50) Departs from the corner of Calle 4 and Av 1 hourly from 7am to 10pm. For the gardens, ask the driver to drop you off at the turnoff – from there, walk 750m to the entrance.

Orosi (US$0.75; 40min) Departs hourly from the corner of Calle 4 and Av 1 from 8am to 10pm Monday to Saturday. The bus will stop in front of the Orosi Mirador.

San José (US$0.50; 45min) Departs every 15 minutes from Calle 2 and Av 6, north of the parque central.

Turrialba (US$1; 1½hr) Departs from Av 3 between Calles 8 and 10 (in front of Tribunales de Justicia) every 45 minutes from 6am to 10pm weekdays; 8:30am, 11:30am, 1:30pm, 3pm and 5:45pm weekends.

Volcán Irazú (US$4; 1hr) Departs only on weekends from Padres Capuchinos church, 150m southeast of Las Ruinas. The bus originates in San José at 8am, stops in Cartago at about 8:30am and returns from Irazú at 12:30pm.

AROUND CARTAGO

While Cartago may not be a hotbed of excitement, the surrounding areas provide plenty to do. Visitors can explore botanical gardens, serene mountain towns, organic farms and an active volcano, all within a two-hour radius. See left for transportation.

Lankester Gardens

The University of Costa Rica runs the exceptional **Lankester Gardens** (☎ 552 3247; admission US$3.50; ☼ 8:30am-4:30pm), started by a British orchid enthusiast. Orchids are the big draw, with 800 at their showiest from February to April. A trail through the winding gardens browses tropical forest filled with bromeliads, palms and heliconias. It's 6km east of Cartago.

Finca la Flor de Paraíso

Dirty your hands at the nonprofit organic farm **Finca la Flor** (☎ 534 8003; www.la-flor-de-paraiso .org; two-day visit with lodging & guide US$35, volunteers US$15 daily). Highly recommended volunteer programs offer instruction in sustainable ag-riculture and reforestation. There are hiking trails and Spanish courses (per week US$370 with homestay and meals). Check out the website for details. Advise the *finca* well be-fore your intended arrival. It's 14km west of Cartago on the road to El Yas.

Río Orosi Valley

Resplendent mountain vistas, crumbling churches and lazy hot springs define the ap-peal of this valley of coffee plantations south-east of Cartago.

Beyond Paraíso, head south 8km to the pleasant village of **Orosi**, named after a 16th-century Huetar chief. Built in 1743, the white-washed **Iglesia de San José** is the country's oldest church still in the business of serving wafers and wine. Nearby hot springs include **Los Bal-nearios** (☎ 533 2156; admission US$2; ☼ 7:30am-4pm), on the southwest side of town next to Orosi Lodge, and **Los Patios** (☎ 533 3009; admission US$2; ☼ 8am-4pm, closed Mon), 1.5km south of town. These modest pools of warm water are popular with locals and a few foreigners in the know.

Festive hostel **Montaña Linda** (☎ 533 3640; www.montanalinda.com; dm US$6.50, s/d US$10.50/17, d with bathroom US$25, campsite US$3.50; ☐) offers top-notch budget lodgings, with hot showers and kitchen privileges (US$1) or home-cooked meals (US$1 to US$3). In addition, it has a reader-recommended **Spanish school** (per week with homestay US$155). It's located two blocks south and three blocks west of the bus stop.

Outside of **Purisil**, 8km southeast of Orosi, the private reserve **Monte Sky** (www.intnet.co.cr/mon tesky) offers excellent birding. Ask at Montaña Linda about guided walks (US$10), camp-ing and overnight stays (per person US$25 including meals). Almost 3km further east is the little-known **Parque Nacional Tapantí** (admission US$7; ☼ 6am-4pm) where dense woods, waterfalls and over 200 bird species flourish in the wet-test park in the country. Few trails break the rugged terrain – dry-season visits are recom-mended. There's a visitors center and a basic but adequate **guesthouse** (dm US$5; meals US$3) with a communal kitchen and bathrooms at the ranger station.

Parque Nacional Volcán Irazú

Named Thunderpoint (*ara-tzu*) by the indig-enous, the large and looming Irazú is Costa Rica's tallest (3432m) active volcano. Its last major eruption was on March 19, 1963,

MILKING THE MENNONITE LIFE

Sample tropical farming Mennonite-style with **Mighty Rivers Eco-farm** (☎ 765 1116, 307 9218; www.mightyrivers.net; San Bosco; per person with breakfast US$15, full day-night package per person US$20). Run by a sincere and wel-coming family from upstate New York, this holistic tropical-lowland dairy is wedged between two stunning rivers. The serene atmosphere speaks volumes for the simple life. You can start the day at 4am to help with milking (or not), ride a cart driven by rare Norwegian Fjords horses or hike to wa-terfalls and swimming holes. Meals feature fresh fixings from the farm. It's 30 minutes from Siquirres; the hosts can arrange trans-port from the bus station for a fee.

welcoming the visiting US President John F Kennedy by throwing a blanket of hot vol-canic ash over most of the Central Valley. Since then, activity has dissipated to a few hissing fumaroles and tremors.

There's a small **visitors center** (☎ 551 9398; US$7; ☼ 8am-3:30pm) and basic café, but no ac-commodations or camping facilities. A paved road reaches the summit. From the parking lot, a 1km trail leads to a lookout over the bare landscape of craters and ash. When the clouds clear there are amazing views of the Pacific and Caribbean, but most days you have to employ your imagination. Clear skies are most probable in the early morning from January to April. Temperatures can drop so bring appropriate clothing.

The park is 19km north of Cartago. Most visitors arrive with an organized tour or pri-vate transportation. The only public transport to Irazú departs San José (US$4.50, 1½ hours) on Saturday and Sunday. It stops in Cartago (US$4, one hour), departing about 8:30am. The bus departs Irazú at 12:30pm.

TURRIALBA
pop 80,000

Turrialba is a laid-back town near the head-waters of the Río Reventazón, a favorite of rafters and kayakers. It's also a good base for jaunts to the Monumento Nacional Ar-queológico Guayabo to the north. For river running, reputable local outfitters include **Tico's River Adventures** (☎ 556 1231; www.ticoriver .com), 150m east of the gas station, **Loco's** (☎ 556

6035; riolocos@racsa.co.cr), 500m east of town, and **Exploranatura** (☎ 556 4932; www.costaricacanyoning.com), 250m southwest of the park, which also runs a reader-recommended canyoning course.

Agronomists the world over recognize **Centro Agronómico Tropical de Investigación y Enseñanza** (Catie, Center for Tropical Agronomy Research & Education; ☎ 556 6431; www.catie.ac.cr; admission free; ☼ 7am-4pm) as one of the most important agricultural stations in the tropics. Visitors can reserve for tours of the agricultural projects in advance, or pick up a free map for a self-tour. Walk or take a taxi (US$2); it's 4km east of town.

Sleeping & Eating

Hotel la Roche (☎ 556 7915; Calle 4 btwn Avs 2 & Central; d with/without bathroom US$10/8) You know it's a gem when signs posted say, 'Don't stick your gum here.' Still, it's cheap.

Whittingham's Hotel (☎ 550 8927; Calle 4 btwn Avs 2 & Central; s/d US$8/10) Seasoned budget travelers won't mind the cool, clean and cavernous rooms with private bathrooms, served up with cement walls and lace curtains.

Hotel Interamericano (☎ 556 0142; www.hotelinteramericano.com; hotelint@racsa.co.cr; Av 1; s/d US$11/20, with bathroom US$25/35; ☐) This rambling house is a kayaker favorite, offering bilingual service and immaculate rooms with super-sturdy mattresses. Open spaces are ideal for cozying up with a book or a beer after a hard day's paddle. Heck, there's even labradors to pat. Perks include the white-water shuttle and in-house bar and restaurant.

Café Azul (Av Central btwn Calle 2 & 4; set lunch US$3.50; ☼ 7am-7pm Mon-Sat) With such great coffee growing on the hillsides, it is a relief to find a great little café. Here, the ambience is relaxed, the pastries are fresh and the coffee is strong.

La Feria (☎ 556 0386; dishes US$3-8; ☼ 10am-10pm) Considered solid value by the locals, La Feria is a friendly spot with blaring *telenovelas*, filling *casados* and typical meat and fish dishes. A quick snack of beans and chips costs only US$1.

There are several *sodas*, Chinese restaurants, bakeries and grocery stores in town.

Getting There & Away

The spanking-new bus terminal is on the western edge of town off of Hwy 10. Destinations include:

Monumento Nacional Guayabo (US$0.75; 1hr) Departs 11:15am, 3:10pm & 5:20pm

San José (US$2; 1¾hr) Departs hourly from 5am to 9pm.

Siquirres, with transfer to Puerto Limón (US$1.50; 1¾hr) Departs almost hourly.

MONUMENTO NACIONAL ARQUEOLÓGICO GUAYABO

This is the largest and most important **archaeological site** (☎ 559 1220; admission US$4, ☼ 8am-3:30pm) in Costa Rica, though it pales alongside the Maya sites of northern Central America. Only 19km north of Turrialba, the area was occupied from about 1000 BC to AD 1400, its peak population reached around 10,000. Thought to be an ancient ceremonial center, it featured paved streets, an aqueduct and decorative gold. The still-functioning aqueduct is considered the most impressive find (especially considering some of the plumbing in modern-day coastal towns). Archaeologists are unsure of the site's exact significance and the reason for its abandonment. Visitors can explore its cobbled roads, stone aqueducts, mounds and petroglyphs. Much has yet to be excavated.

There's an information and exhibit center, but many of the best pieces are displayed at the Museo Nacional in San José (p543). **Camping** (US$2) services include latrines and running water.

See left for arrival info for Turrialba.

SOUTHERN CARIBBEAN COAST

You knew it would have something to do with seduction. Around you thick emerald forests rim sandy beaches, coconut stews simmer on gas cookers, and reggae beats drift from open doors. The heat beckons you to retreat to a hammock or float in the salty bay. Traveling the Caribbean coast is like leaving Costa Rica. But it is not just hotter and wetter. The definitive difference is cultural, with over one-third of the population descended from English-speaking Jamaicans and Barbadians.

Afro-Caribbean immigrants arrived in the 19th century to build the railroad and harvest bananas. Marginalized by a succession of governments (Black Costa Ricans were not allowed to even access the Central Valley until after 1948), the Caribbean coast developed to its own beat and it shows. Cultural isolation nurtured a relaxed, Rasta-inflected culture that most visitors can't get enough of.

COSTA RICA

A steady flow of visitors go to the coastal towns where enclaves of North Americans and Europeans are cropping up. A few thousand Bribrí and Cabecar populate the remote Cordillera de Talamanca to the south. To the north, Parque Nacional Tortuguero hosts prolific wildlife and is the seasonal nesting site for endangered marine turtles.

PUERTO LIMÓN
pop 85,000

A ragged port city with a faded colonial air, Puerto Limón has a deservedly rough reputation, but it is not without appeal. The birthplace of the United Fruit Company, Limón is removed from San José's sphere of influence and totally without pretension. After all, busi-

ness around here still means shuffling tons of bananas, not tourists. A wacky plan to expand the port for cruise ships should help bring some investment for much-needed infrastructure. In the meanwhile, most travelers zip through town heading south to Cahuita and Puerto Viejo de Talamanca or north to Tortuguero.

Information & Sights

Upstairs at Terminal Caribeño, **Internet Café** (☎ 798 0128; per hr US$1; ☿ 8am-7pm Mon-Fri, noon-7pm Sat) has fairly fast computers. Take advantage of the banking facilities since they are scarce on the coast. **Scotiabank** (☎ 798 0009; cnr Av 3 & Calle 2; ☿ 8:30am-4:30pm Mon-Fri, 8:30am-3:30pm Sat) exchanges money and traveler's checks, and

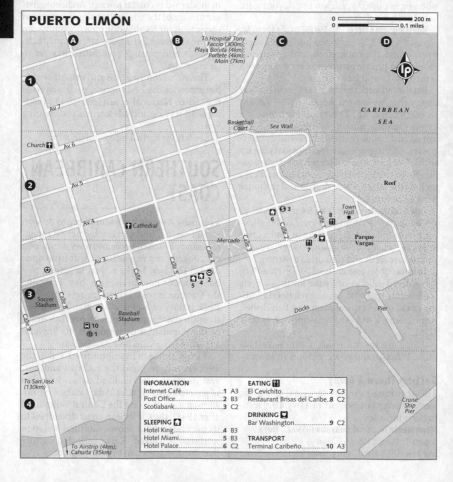

PUERTO LIMÓN

0 .... 200 m
0 .... 0.1 miles

To Hospital Tony
Faccio (300m);
Playa Bonita (4km);
Portete (4km);
Moín (7km)

CARIBBEAN
SEA

Basketball
Court   Sea Wall

Church 🕆   Av 6

Av 7

Av 5

Reef

Av 4

🕆 Cathedral

Town
Hall

Mercado

Parque
Vargas

Av 3

Docks   Pier

Soccer
Stadium

Baseball
Stadium

Av 1

To San José
(130km)

Cruise
Ship
Pier

To Airstrip (4km);
Cahuita (35km)

INFORMATION		EATING 🍴	
Internet Café	1 A3	El Cevichito	7 C3
Post Office	2 B3	Restaurant Brisas del Caribe	8 C2
Scotiabank	3 C2		
		DRINKING 🍸	
SLEEPING 🛏		Bar Washington	9 C2
Hotel King	4 B3		
Hotel Miami	5 B3	TRANSPORT	
Hotel Palace	6 C2	Terminal Caribeño	10 A3

COSTA RICA

has a 24-hour ATM on the Plus and Cirrus systems.

Always abuzz, the dusty **mercado** is the spot to grab a beach blanket or rhinestone push-up bra if you forgot yours. The waterfront **Parque Vargas** has a run-down bandstand shaded by tropical trees and flowers. Local legend has it that sloths live in the tree. Beware those on the ground (downing bottles wrapped in paper bags) if you investigate.

Limón's big claim to fame is that Christopher Columbus landed at **Isla Uvita** (1km to the east) on his fourth and final trans-Atlantic voyage in 1502. As a result, **Día de la Raza** (Columbus Day) is celebrated with aplomb – even Ticos stream in for the frenetic five-day carnival, celebrated around October 12. Book hotels in advance during this time.

The nearest beach with acceptable swimming is **Playa Bonita**, 4km northwest of town.

Dangers & Annoyances

Limón has an unsavory reputation. Take precautions against pickpockets during the day, particularly in the market. People get mugged, so stick to well-lit main streets at night, avoiding the sea wall and Parque Vargas.

Sleeping & Eating

Port town Limón has little touristy about it. As a result, lodging options can be grim, with budget options populated by dock workers and prostitutes. Restaurants tend to specialize in the fried and deep-fried but due to a large Chinese population, Chinese food is plentiful.

Hotel King (☎ 758 1033; Av 2 btwn Calles 4 & 5; r per person US$5, s/d with bathroom US$9/12) The King is valued for its bargain rate and location – a quick dash from the bus station – otherwise it's rather dark and cramped.

Hotel Palace (☎ 798 2604; Calle 2 btwn Avs 2 & 3; d US$12) A whiff of former grandeur adds style points to this now-dilapidated palace with peeling paint and cracked tiles. Potted plants and tidy housekeeping do brighten it up.

Hotel Miami (☎ 758 0490; hmiamilimon@yahoo.com; Av 2 btwn Calles 4 & 5; s/d with fan US$15/20, with air-con & hot water US$20/28; ❄) Fresh and cool, this modern hotel is the best bet for travelers, with strong security and decent-sized rooms with muted colors and industrial-strength fans.

Restaurant Brisas del Caribe (☎ 758 0138; mains US$3-5; ⊙ 7am-11pm Mon-Fri, 10am-11pm Sat & Sun) Outdoor tables and a breezy balcony make

this an easy pick. The offerings are staggering (we counted 88). Somewhere between the *gallo pinto* and chop suey there's Caribbean fare – your best bet.

El Cevichito (Av 2 btwn Calles 1 & 2; meals US$4) A cold bottle of Imperial and a plate of garlic fish are the charms of this no-frills patio filled with locals.

Bar Washington (cnr Calle 1 & Av 2; ⊙ 9am-3am) Sink into an oversized bamboo chair and watch the world go by from this rock 'n' roll bar in the thick of it, on the pedestrian mall.

Getting There & Away

Buses from San José, Moín, Guápiles and Siquirres arrive at the **Terminal Caribeño** (Av 2 btwn Calles 7 & 8) on the west side, walking distance from hotels. These are the principal points served by the station:

Moín, for boats to Tortuguero (US$0.25; 20min) Tracasa departs hourly from 5:30am to 6:30pm.
San José (US$3.50; 3hr) Autotransportes Caribeños departs hourly from 5am to 8pm.

Buses to points south depart from **Autotransportes Mepe** (Av 4 btwn Calles 2 & 4), one block north of the *mercado*.

Bribrí & Sixaola (US$3; 3hr) Departs 5am, 7am, 8am, 10am, noon, 1pm, 4pm and 6pm.
Cahuita (US$1; 1½hr) Departs 5am, 6am, 8am, 10am, 1pm, 2:30pm, 4pm and 6pm.
Manzanillo (US$2; 2½hr) Departs 6am, 10:30am, 3pm and 6pm.
Puerto Viejo de Talamanca (US$1.75; 2½hr) Departs 5am, 8am, 10am, 1pm, 4pm and 6pm.

CAHUITA

Imagine a sandy beach town where howler monkeys wake up the dogs, the electrician makes calls by bicycle and the locals recognize you after two days. Welcome to Cahuita, a cool little Afro-Caribbean beach settlement 43km south of Limón. Diversions include jungle walks and white- and black-sand beaches backed by almond groves. Don't expect to get a head start during lunch hour; the cook will keep you waiting as your fish simmers and stews an hour or more. The lesson here? Relax.

Founded by turtle fisherman William Smith in 1828, Cahuita is a tight-knit and proud community. When the park service proposed visitor's fees, residents protested by physically blocking the entrance to keep it under their control (and succeeded).

COSTA RICA

COSTA RICA

CAHUITA

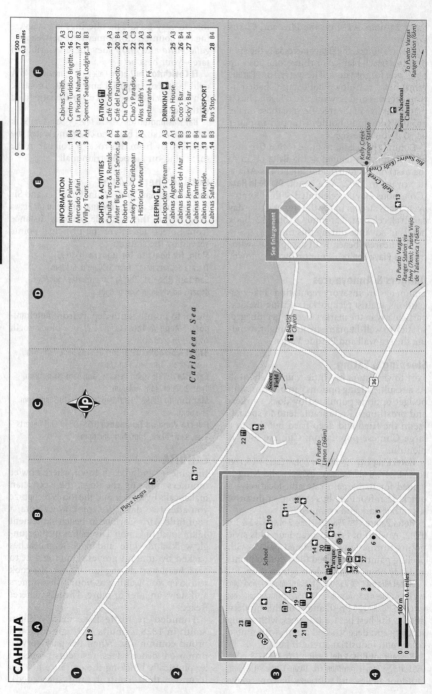

INFORMATION	
Internet Palmer................1	B4
Mercado Safari...............2	A3
Willy's Tours..................3	A4

SIGHTS & ACTIVITIES	
Cahuita Tours & Rentals....4	A3
Mister Big J Tourist Service.5	B4
Roberto Tours.................6	B4
Sankey's Afro-Caribbean	
Historical Museum........7	A3

SLEEPING 🏠	
Backpacker's Dream.........8	A3
Cabinas Algebra..............9	A1
Cabinas Brisas del Mar....10	B3
Cabinas Jenny................11	B3
Cabinas Palmer..............12	B4
Cabinas Riverside...........13	E4
Cabinas Safari................14	B3

Cabinas Smith................15	A3
Centro Turístico Brigitte..16	C3
La Piscina Natural..........17	B2
Spencer Seaside Lodging..18	B3

EATING 🍴	
Café Corleone...............19	A3
Café del Parquecito........20	B4
Cha Cha Chal...............21	B4
Chao's Paradise.............22	C3
Miss Edith's..................23	A3
Restaurante La Fé...........24	B4

DRINKING 🍸	
Beach House..................25	A3
Coco's Bar....................26	B4
Ricky's Bar....................27	B4

TRANSPORT	
Bus Stop......................28	B4

Caribbean Sea

Playa Negra

Baptist Church

Soccer Field

To Puerto Limón (36km)

To Puerto Vargas
Ranger Station via
Hwy (7km); Puerto Viejo
de Talamanca (16km)

Kelly Creek
Ranger Station

Río Suárez (Kelly Creek)

Kelly Creek

Parque Nacional
Cahuita

To Puerto Vargas
Ranger Station (6km)

See Enlargement

School

Parque
Central

Sensimilla might be in the air, but locals don't put up with any funny stuff.

Information

Come with cash as there are no banks here. Get online at **Internet Palmer** (per hr US$2; 9am-8pm) or at numerous hotels. You can exchange money or traveler's checks at **Mercado Safari** (6am-4pm); fees are steep.

For a better understanding of local culture, pick up the book *What Happen?*, a collection of oral histories, available at JC's store and souvenir shops.

Dangers & Annoyances

The biggest security concerns are petty theft and residential burglaries. Keep an eye on your belongings, especially at the beach, and make sure your hotel room is secure.

Sights & Activities

Curiosities abound at home-grown **Sankey's Afro-Caribbean Historical Museum** (755 0183; entry by donation; 7am-noon & 2-7pm Mon-Sat), with a collection of household objects from Black colonial times, but probably the most interesting part is the heartfelt presentation by Sankey himself.

Northwest of town, **Playa Negra** is a long, black-sand beach flying the *bandera azul ecológica*, indicating its cleanliness. This is undoubtedly Cahuita's top spot for swimming. Most importantly, it is far enough from town that it never gets crowded. Your other option is to swim at the park beach.

Playa Negra's excellent beach break is not on the surfer circuit, which means more waves for you. Early-morning surfing is best, especially with a swell from the south or east. Sign up for a lesson (US$25 for two hours) or just rent a board at the **Beach House** (369 4254; cariberen@yahoo.com).

In Playa Negra, the Swiss-run **Centro Turístico Brigitte** (755 0053; www.brigittecahuita.com) has guided horseback riding (US$35 to US$45) on the beach and through the jungle, with well-cared-for horses. It also rents mountain bikes for US$8 a day.

Guides are required for snorkeling since the reef is a protected area. Local guides include **Mister Big J Tourist Service** (755 0328; 8am-7pm), **Roberto's Tours** (755 0117) and **Willie's Tours** (843 4700; www.willies-costarica-tours.com). The going rate is US$15 to US$25 per person, but prices vary according to the size

of your group and the mood of the guide. **Cahuita Tours** (755 0000/0232) offers an all-day trip on a glass-bottom boat, which includes snorkeling and hiking (US$35 per person). These agencies can also provide park guides. **Cabinas Algebra** (755 0057; Playa Negra) runs recommended culturally sensitive trips to the Bribrí indigenous reserves.

Sleeping

The town overflows with accommodation options; most are eerily identical. Cold showers are the norm.

IN TOWN

Backpacker's Dream (755 0174; s/d US$6/10) These cramped clapboard rooms are furnished with a bed and fan, nothing more. Ignore the stairs to nowhere and the discarded planks. The real charm of the cheapest digs in town is its owner José – who might pen a tune mid-sentence if the mood strikes.

Spencer Seaside Lodging (755 0210; spencer@racsa.co.cr; s US$12-15, d US$20-30;) A rambling wooden lodge with hammocks strung beneath the coconut palms. Sure, it's nothing fancy, but it is seaside and relaxed. Rooms on the 2nd floor provide an extra dose of privacy.

Cabinas Riverside (553 0153; s/d US$15/20) Sometimes squeaky clean surfaces and hot water is all you need. This German-run budget option by Kelly Creek delivers just that. Simple rooms have mosquito nets and stone showers.

Cabinas Smith (755 0068; s/d/tr US$15/20/25;) These basic concrete *cabinas* sport well-scrubbed units with metal bunks, nice sheets and private bathrooms. The annex runs slightly cheaper.

Cabinas Palmer (755 0046; kainepalmer@racsa.co.cr; s/d US$15/20) Small and friendly, this hotel offers clean rooms around a cement courtyard, close to the action (and the noise).

Cabinas Safari (755 0405; s/d/tr US$15/20/30) Average rooms come a touch frilly, but you get your own hammock and the charm of host George to boot.

Cabinas Brisas del Mar (755 0011; s/d US$20/25) Run by a gregarious local, these three spotless *cabinas* are set amidst overgrown gardens that face the water. Hammocks are conveniently hung to catch the sea breeze, as the name promises. Fenced and secure.

Cabinas Jenny (755 0256; d US$20-30, extra person US$5) Looming over the foaming surf, these

COSTA RICA

rooms are earthy and cozy, with raw wood details, fresh paint, soft sheets and mosquito nets. The private decks with sling-back lounges are a treat for tired guests. Call ahead to reserve.

PLAYA NEGRA
Northwest of town about 1.5km, Playa Negra is quieter and pleasant, with a limited choice of restaurants and services. If you want to bar-hop, stay in town as walking back at night is not recommended.

Centro Turístico Brigitte (☎ 755 0053; www.brigitte cahuita.com; d US$20; ☐) Simple and spartan cabins have firm mattresses and mosquito nets, but the cozy ambience comes from the café and the quiet surrounds. Also provides bikes and horse tours.

Cabinas Algebra (☎ 755 0057; d $18, d/tr with kitchen US$25/33) This former cocoa plantation is now a German-run guesthouse ideal for families. Cabins are simple and cheerful, and the owners will pick you up if you call in advance. Eating in is not a sacrifice – the kitchen serves flavorful Creole dishes.

La Piscina Natural (☎ 755 0146; d/tr US$30/35) Imagine a wild lawn with hibiscus bushes and almond trees that front the surf. This low-key retreat has spotless rooms with firm beds and stucco walls. With drinks available from the breezy bar, you may never feel the need to trek back into town.

Eating
Café del Parquecito (breakfast US$3-5; ☾ 6:30am-noon) This thatched hut is all about breakfast, featuring strong coffee, scrambled eggs and huge fruit-filled crêpes.

Miss Edith's (☎ 755 0248; mains US$7-12; ☾ 11am-10pm) One expat says, 'If you have two hours to kill, eat here.' The food – picture jerk chicken spiced with chili and cloves, or fragrant fish stews – is scandalously good and served up by Miss Edith herself. The best bet is to make orders in advance.

Restaurant la Fé (meals US$5-10; ☾ 7am-11pm) Though service takes half an eternity (thus the name 'The Faith'), you're rewarded by shrimp in fresh coconut sauce and crispy *patacones*.

Café Corleone (☎ 394 4153; mains US$4-8; ☾ 5pm-10pm Thu-Tue) This Italian-run pizzeria pays homage to the old country with thin-crust spinach pizzas dribbling with mozzarella. There's also homemade pastas, wild mushrooms and other delectable combos on offer.

Cha Cha Cha! (☎ 394 4153; mains US$6-9; ☾ 6pm-10pm Tue-Sun) For candlelit ambience this converted clapboard is your best bet. The menu offers creative world cuisine without missing a beat. The Thai shrimp salad, with rice noodles and cashews, makes a strong showing, as do the cheesecakes. Vegetarians, it's your lucky night.

Chao's Paradise (☎ 755 0421; seafood mains US$6-10; ☾ 11am-close) Along Playa Negra, this open-air place offers spicy Caribbean cuisine. There's also a pool table and live reggae and calypso music some nights.

Drinking
Coco's Bar (☾ 4pm-midnight) Jam to a three-man reggae band or sip rum-somethings at this Rasta bar popular with the local and traveling crowds. Live music plays on Wednesday and weekends.

Ricky's Bar (☎ 755 0228; ☾ 4pm-midnight or so) Opposite Coco's and sharing the same clientele, thatched Ricky's offers outdoor seating and ample space to cut a groove. Live music usually goes down on Saturday nights.

Beach House (☎ 369 4254; caribeeren@yahoo.com) An expat surf haunt renting boards by day and selling beers by night. Get in on the *quesadillas* (US$6) and live calypso from Thursday through Saturday.

Getting There & Away
Buses arrive and depart from the stop at the parque central.
Puerto Limón/San José (US$1/7; 1½/4hr) Autotransportes Mepe departs at 7:30am, 8:30am, 9:30am, 11:30am and 4:30pm, additional bus at 2pm on weekends.
Puerto Viejo de Talamanca/Bribrí/Sixaola (US$1/2/3; 30min/1hr/1½hr) Departs hourly from 7am to 9pm.

PARQUE NACIONAL CAHUITA
Among the country's most visited parks, Cahuita is small but beautiful. Humidity nurtures a dense tropical foliage of coconut palms, mango trees and sea grapes. The forest skirts white sandy beaches on a tranquil bay. Easy to access, it attracts scads of visitors who loll in the mild surf, scan the trails for sloths and monkeys and snorkel the coral reef.

At the east end of Cahuita, **Kelly Creek ranger station** (☎ 755 0461; entry by donation; ☾ 6am-5pm) sits next to **Playa Blanca** stretching 2km east. Signs the first 500m warn not to swim, but beyond this point the waves are gentle. After the rocky Punta Cahuita you'll find Vargas

Beach and **Puerto Vargas ranger station** (☎ 755 0302; admission US$6; ☼ 6am-5pm). An easily navigable 7km **coastal trail** leads through the jungle from Kelly Creek to Puerto Vargas. Beware, Río Perezoso, near the end of the first beach, can be thigh-deep at high tide or dangerous to cross in rainy season.

Camping (US$3) is permitted at Playa Vargas, less than 1km from the Puerto Vargas ranger station. The facilities include cold outdoor showers, drinking water and pit latrines. Don't leave anything unattended. Be especially careful to store food carefully as monkeys will scarf what's left unattended.

Snorkeling conditions vary daily. In general, the drier months in the highlands (from February to April) are best for **snorkeling** on the coast, as less runoff in the rivers means less silting in the sea. To protect the reef from further damage, snorkeling is permitted only with a licensed guide.

For a good day **hike**, take the Cahuita–Puerto Viejo bus at 8am to the Puerto Vargas entrance. Walk 1km to the coast then 7km more back to Cahuita. For birding or guided hikes, contact the travel agencies in Cahuita or ATEC in Puerto Viejo de Talamanca, next section.

PUERTO VIEJO DE TALAMANCA

Party town Puerto Viejo de Talamanca (not to be confused with Puerto Viejo de Sarapiquí in the northern lowlands) shakes up a Caribbean concoction of palm-fringed beaches, slick surfing and stoned grins. The nightlife is young and thumping with great music and restaurants – easily the best on the coast. And yes, it's touristy, with a heavy stream of Tico students, backpackers and expat settlers. But

if you can let go of getting in touch with 'the real Costa Rica' for a moment, you'll have a blast.

'Downtown' Puerto Viejo is little more than one paved road following the coastline. It's stuffed with tourist traps, surf shops and open-air bars, exuding good music and Rasta vibes.

Information

The **Talamanca Association for Ecotourism & Conservation** (ATEC; ☎ 750 0398; www.greencoast.com/atec.htm; ☼ 8am-9pm; ☐) is a grassroots organization offering community tourism and one-stop shopping – books on nature, birding and culture, as well as **internet service** (per hr US$2.45).

Do your banking at **Banco de Costa Rica** (main drag; ☼ 9am-4pm Mon-Fri) with a Plus-system ATM. Visit www.greencoast.com for more information about Puerto Viejo.

Dangers & Annoyances

Crime, in the form of robberies and drug trafficking, is on the up and foreign visitors make easy targets. Locals are frustrated with the lack of police response; part of the problem is that offenders are rarely held on charges. Many responsible hotel owners are looking to combat crime by hiring private security patrols.

Most people visit Puerto Viejo without any problem – just use your smarts. Be very selective when choosing your accommodation. Check hotels for screens and secure locks and be wary of places without any reception person around. Always lock up valuables, and walk around with a copy of your passport only.

After dark, stay away from the beach and the area south of the soccer field (considered

COSTA RICA

GOT DRUGS, WILL TRAVEL

Drugs are plentiful in Costa Rica and tourists take it for granted that *pura vida* means pass the spliff. However, drugs are 100% illegal here. Recently the government put in place a zero-tolerance policy. Those charged with possession can be fined and imprisoned.

Nonetheless, hard drugs are becoming more prevalent. Both the Pacific and Atlantic coasts are used as a *puente* (bridge) with drug runners from further south, much to the chagrin of officials. On beaches such as Jacó, Puerto Viejo and Tamarindo, dealers approach backpackers fresh off the bus. The club scene is full of cocaine, and ecstasy, or what passes for it.

Ticos will tell you that the Colombians, Jamaicans, Panamanians and just about every other nationality are to blame for importing drugs into their country, but the truth is that they share an equal amount of blame. An eight-ball of cocaine yields a much larger profit than a woodcarving of a tree-frog, and many backpackers are happy to shell out US dollars for a dime-bag of dubious quality.

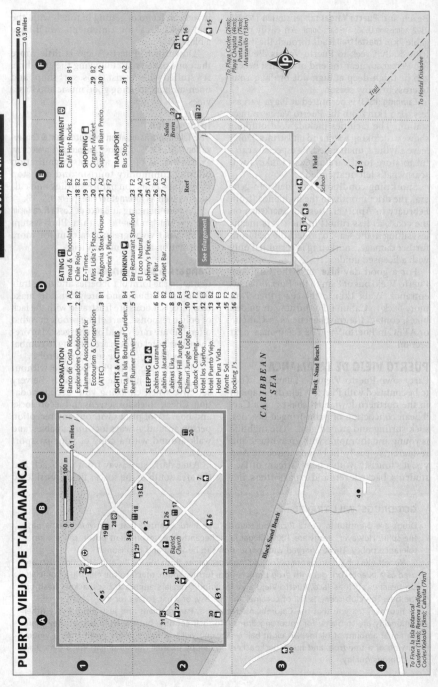

PUERTO VIEJO DE TALAMANCA

COSTA RICA

INFORMATION
Banco de Costa Rica................1 A2
Exploradores Outdoors............2 B2
Talamanca Association for
 Ecotourism & Conservation
 (ATEC)..................................3 B1

SIGHTS & ACTIVITIES
Finca la Isla Botanical Garden...4 B4
Reef Runner Divers...................5 A1

SLEEPING 🛏
Cabinas Guaraná......................6 B2
Cabinas Jacaranda....................7 B2
Cabinas Lika............................8 E3
Cashew Hill Jungle Lodge.........9 E4
Chimuri Jungle Lodge.............10 A3
Cutback Camping....................11 F2
Hotel los Sueños....................12 E3
Hotel Puerto Viejo..................13 B2
Hotel Pura Vida.....................14 E3
Monte Sol.............................15 F2
Rocking J's............................16 F2

EATING 🍴
Bread & Chocolate.................17 B2
Chile Rojo............................18 B2
EZ-Times.............................19 B1
Miss Lidia's Place..................20 C2
Patagonia Steak House..........21 A2
Veronica's Place...................22 F2

DRINKING 🍷
Bar Restaurant Stanford.........23 F2
El Loco Natural.....................24 A2
Johnny's Place......................25 A1
Mi Bar.................................26 B2
Sunset Bar...........................27 A2

ENTERTAINMENT 🎭
Café Hot Rocks....................28 B1

SHOPPING 🛍
Organic Market.....................29 B2
Super del Buen Precio............30 A2

TRANSPORT
Bus Stop.............................31 A2

To Finca la Isla Botanical
Garden (1km); Reserva Indígena
Cocles/Kekoldi (5km); Cahuita (7km)

To Playa Cocles (2km);
Playa Chiquita (4km);
Punta Uva (7km);
Manzanillo (13km)

To Hostal Kiskadee

CARIBBEAN SEA

Black Sand Beach

Black Sand Beach

Reef

Salsa Brava

Baptist Church

School

Field

Trail

500 m
0.3 miles

100 m
0.1 miles

See Enlargement

the red-light district). Muggings regularly occur on the road between Rocking J's and the town center – even to those walking in groups. Take a taxi at night.

Sights & Activities
BOTANICAL GARDEN
West of town, **Finca la Isla Botanical Garden** (☎ 750 0046; www.greencoast.com/garden.htm; self-guided/guided tour US$2/5; ☸ 10am-4pm Fri-Mon) is a working tropical farm and botanical garden ideal for birding and wildlife observation (look for sloths and poison dart frogs).

CYCLING
The forested road to **Manzanillo** (13km) offers a scenic ride. Take the swimsuit and watch for howler monkeys and butterflies on the way.

DIVING & SNORKELING
Costa Rica's only two living reef systems form a naturally protected sanctuary from Cahuita to Manzanillo. They are home to 35 species of coral and over 400 species of fish, not to mention dolphins, sharks and, occasionally, whales. Underwater visibility is best when the sea is calm. If the surfing is bad, snorkeling is good.

Snorkel just south of **Punta Uva**, in front of the Arrecife restaurant, where you will find stunning examples of reindeer coral, sheet coral and lettuce coral. The reef at **Manzanillo** (p569) is also easily accessible. Rent equipment at Aquamor Talamanca Adventure in Manzanillo. Tour companies (right) offer guided trips for about US$45 per person.

Dive outfitters include **Reef Runner Divers** (☎ 750 0480; www.reefrunnerdivers.net; one-/two-tank dive US$55/80; ☸ 7am-8pm) and Aquamor Talamanca Adventure (see p569) in Manzanillo.

SURFING
Locals boast the country's best wave is **Salsa Brava**, a thick and fast moving break. The shallow reef means serious scrapes if you lose it; this is not beginners' territory. Almost as impressive are the waves at **Playa Cocles**, about 2km east of town. Lefts and rights both break close to the steep beach. Conditions are usually best early in the day, before the wind picks up. Waves are best from December to March, and in June and July. **Kurt** (☎ 750 0620) at Puerto Viejo Hotel offers surf reports.

Surf schools charge US$30 to US$35 for two-hour lessons. Recommended are Puerto

Viejo Hotel or **Cut Bak** (☎ 366 9222, 885 9688), along the road south of town.

SWIMMING
Just northwest of town, **Playa Negra** offers the area's safest swimming, as well as excellent body-boarding. Southeast of town the jungle meets the sea and the waves are perfect for swimming and body-surfing.

Riptides and undertows can be dangerous. Inquire at your hotel or with local tour operators about current conditions.

Tours
Talamanca Association for Ecotourism & Conservation (ATEC; ☎ 750 0398; www.greencoast.com/atec.htm; half-/full-day US$17/27; ☸ 8am-9pm; ▯) ATEC arranges tours with local guides to the nearby Reserva Indígena Kekoldi. It also offers rain forest hikes in Punta Uva, tropical farm and jungle walks, visits to Cahuita National Park and the Gandoca-Manzanillo Wildlife Refuge. Tours focus on native culture, natural history and environment.

Exploradores Outdoors (☎ 222 6262; www.exploradoresoutdoors.com) Offers rafting the Río Pacuare (US$95), canopy tours and more.

Sleeping
IN TOWN
Hotel Puerto Viejo (☎ 750 0620; r per person with/without bathroom US$10/8, d with air-con US$25; ▧ ▯) This surfer warehouse offers clean, functional rooms, hot showers and a security box. The new addition is screened and wood-trimmed – a big upgrade. Guests gather in the communal kitchen to talk waves, the specialty subject of surfer-owner Kurt Van Dyke.

Cabinas Lika (☎ 750 0209; r per person US$8) A new cheap-and-clean budget option with private rooms with bathrooms. It's in an unsavory area but is fenced and gated.

Chimuri Jungle Lodge (☎ 750 0119; www.greencoast.com/chimurilodge.htm; dm/d/q US$10/30/46) Four bungalows on the edge of the Kekoldi reserve offer consummate peace and quiet. There's a communal kitchen and a 2km walking trail with birds and wildlife.

Cabinas Jacaranda (☎ 750 0069; www.cabinasjacaranda.com; s/d US$20/28) Mosaic walkways wind through a blooming garden in this hippie fantasy, a nice spot for kicking back. Rooms are decorated with batiks and hand-painted walls. Perks include hot water, weekly yoga (US$10) and a security box – use it.

Hotel los Sueños (☎ 750 0369; www.costaricaguide.info/lossuenos.htm; s/d/tr US$16/20/24) A peaceful Swiss-run spot with rustic, well-kept rooms with fans and mosquito nets. Shared bathrooms have hot showers and guests get kitchen privileges.

Hotel Pura Vida (☎ 750 0002; www.hotel-puravida.com in German; s/d/tr US$20/25/33, with bathroom US$25/30/40) Bright and stylish, Pura Vida pampers with an elegant open-air living-and-dining area, hot water, large spotless rooms and the affection of spoiled hound Duche. The owners are a helpful German-Chilean couple. Breakfasts (extra) are abundant and tasty.

Cabinas Guaraná (☎ 750 0244; www.hotelguarana.com; s/d/tr US$25/35) From tree-house views of the Caribbean to the coconut-grove courtyard, this place spells hideaway. Shady *cabinas* with woven hammocks have high-ceiling rooms with stenciled walls. There's also a communal kitchen.

Cashew Hill Jungle Lodge (☎ 750 0256; www.cashewhilllodge.co.cr; d US$35-55; 💻) Clean living (recycling, composting and water treatment) doesn't come cheap but it's a sure sign of success when all the guests look chipper and rested. Newly renovated rooms have bright walls, colorful tiles and orthopedic mattresses. The extensive grounds are well kept and secure, with a high fence and a few Hyundai-sized English mastiffs. Ask about low-season discounts.

EAST OF TOWN

Cutbak Camping (campsite US$3, hammock US$2) The only recommended campground is this surfer haven in an almond grove, a 15-minute walk from Playa Cocles. Guests have lockers, bathrooms and use of the communal kitchen. The onsite restaurant serves good, cheap grub and surfboards can be rented (US$15) or repaired.

Rocking J's (☎ 750 0665; www.rockingjs.com; hammock US$5, dm/d US$7/20, campsite US$4) The style is ghetto-cool, with basic bunkrooms as well as an immense tent village and hammock hut with 'Refugee Camp' written all over them. However, folks *love* Rocking J's. Maybe it's the homemade ice cream, graffiti-style mosaics or the lively bar, with arguably the best social scene (for foreigners) in town. Lockers and laundry service (US$5) are available, as is a communal kitchen.

Monte Sol (☎ 750 0098; www.montesol.net in German; d US$20-30; 💻) Away from the hubbub, this German-run place says low-key with a welcoming hammock terrace and immaculate cabins with barn-style shuttered windows and mosaic-tile baths.

Eating

Get groceries at **Super el Buen Precio** (🕑 6:30am-8:30pm) or the weekly **Organic Market** (🕑 6am-6pm Sat), with produce and typical regional snacks.

Miss Lidia's Place (mains US$2-6) Locals and travelers alike pack the patio for good home cooking that ranges from *casados* to fish filets. Satisfy your stomach for under US$2 with a BBQ chicken sandwich on homemade bread.

EZ-Times (mains US$3-10; 🕑 10am-2:30am) Grab a veggie burger or portobello pizza on the outdoor terrace and you're good to go. Friday is live music night.

Bread & Chocolate (breakfast US$2-4, lunch US$4-8; 🕑 6:30am-6:30pm Wed-Sat, 6:30am-2:30pm Sun) Run by the amiable Tom, this café is a veritable addiction. Pick your passion – homemade bagels, eggs and biscuits or heaping rustic wheat sandwiches. Whatever's in the oven will make you want to linger for the next meal. Everything is fresh and made on site.

Veronica's Place (meals US$3-5; 🕑 7am-9pm Sun-Thu, 7am-4:30pm Fri) Behind Supermercado El Pueblo, Veronica's Place revamps Caribbean cuisine with an emphasis on veggies and fruits. And where else can you get soy burgers and soy milk?

El Loco Natural (☎ 750 0263; meals US$8-12; 🕑 6-11pm) Tacos, stir-fries and healthy salads are the staples of this upmarket fusion eatery. Twinkling with Christmas lights, a skinny balcony and a killer cocktail list, it's all about atmosphere.

Chile Rojo (☎ 750 0025; mains US$8-12; 🕑 noon-10pm) The smell of Thai curry wafting from this stylish shoebox might stop you in your tracks. Serving excellent Asian and Middle Eastern fare, it is a very popular spot.

Patagonia Steak House (☎ 390 5677; mains US$5-11; 🕑 5pm-11pm) What ambience? It's all about the grill, where steaks sear and chorizo sausages cook. Uncork a vintage Malbec; this Argentine-owned restaurant is a godsend to carnivores.

Drinking & Entertainment

No-frills **Mi Bar** (near Jungle Internet) is basically a row of brightly painted seats topped with equally colorful characters, all fronting a narrow bar. In a big top tent in the town center, **Café Hot Rocks** (☎ 750 0525; meals US$3-8; ❍ 11am-2:30am) shows free flicks most evenings and also hosts live calypso, reggae and rock bands. Booze and bonfires light up Johnny's Place, a Puerto Viejo institution where DJs spin reggae, hip-hop and salsa. Bar Restaurant Stanford does a brisk business with a local crowd shaking to salsa music. Local favorite **Sunset Bar** (☎ 750 0025; ❍ noon-close) is one of the few places in town to perfect your pool. Upmarket **El Loco Natural** (☎ 750 0263; ❍ 6-11pm) hosts jazz and other acts at 8:30pm on Thursday and Saturday.

Getting There & Away
Buses arrive and depart at the main stop in town by the beach. Buses for Manzanillo stop at Playa Cocles, Playa Chiquita and Punta Uva.
Bribrí/Sixaola (US$1/2, 30min/1½hr) At 6:30am, 8:30am, 9:30am, 10:30am; 12:30pm, 1:30pm, 2:30pm, 3:30pm, 5:30pm, 6:30pm and 7:30pm.
Cahuita/Puerto Limón (US$1/2, 30min/1½hr) Every hour on the half-hour from 5:30am to 7:30pm.
Manzanillo (US$1.50, 30min) Departs 7:30am, 11:45am, 4:30pm and 7:30pm.
San José (US$7.50, 5hr) At 7am, 9am, 11am and 4pm.

EAST OF PUERTO VIEJO
The 13km coastal route to Manzanillo slips past sandy beaches and dense canopy, passing through beach villages and the Reserva Indígena Cocles/Kekoldi, and ending up in Refugio Nacional de Vida Silvestre Gandoca-Manzanillo. Take a cruiser; the road is paved, but don't get too distracted spotting wildlife as the potholes are doozies.

Playa Cocles
The big waves and long beach break called Cocles lies 2km east of Puerto Viejo. The riptide claims lives every season; note that green flags mark safe areas.

The American-owned **Echo Books** (desserts US$1-3; ❍ 11am-6pm Fri-Tue; ✉) is a rainy-day godsend, with probably the best collection of English-language books in Costa Rica, handpicked by owner Shawn and spanning Cahill to Theroux. Treat yourself to a homemade chocolate, iced-coconut chai or coffee drink while you browse the stacks. To get here follow the signs from the main road.

For a homey atmosphere, **Cabinas El Tesoro** (☎ 750 0128; www.puertoviejo.net; dm US$9, s/d/tr US$21/28/41; ✉ ▢) has great-value dorms, a cool hammock patio, community kitchen

and nightly movies. Freebies include coffee and internet.

Playa Chiquita
Playa Chiquita's beaches stretch 4km to 6km east of town. The cafés are worth a trip out.

The perfect budget getaway, **Cabinas Slothclub** (☎ 750 0358; d/apt US$20/60) has five basic beachfront cabins set back in the tall grass, with snorkeling on the reef out the front.

In a country of rice and beans, you may find their most memorable incarnation at **Restaurante Elena Brown** (☎ 750 0265; mains US$4-7; ❍ 8am-11pm), ladled up by Elena herself. Foodies can feast on fusion fare at **Jungle Love Garden Café** (☎ 750 0356; mains US$6-8; ❍ lunch). Tokyo tuna with tamarind-ginger sauce (US$8) is the house masterpiece, but there are generous wraps and salads too.

Punta Uva
Punta Uva has lovely, swimmable beaches, each better than the last. Newbie surfers longboard the point and swimmers take to its western side. Budget **Albergue Walaba** (☎ 750 0147; r per person US$12) offers funky rooms and a communal kitchen amidst overgrown jungle. A hippie haven, yes, but a somewhat musty one.

Manzanillo
The road ends in Manzanillo, a happy dead-end with convivial locals and quiet beaches. The town itself is part of **Refugio Nacional de Vida Silvestre Gandoca-Manzanillo**, a pristine remnant of wild Caribbean coastline stretching all the way to Panama.

Gandoca-Manzanillo's stunning coastal trail leads 5.5km through the rain forest and desolate beaches to Punta Mona. Wildlife includes the rare harpy eagle, monkeys and toucans. Accommodations can be found at **Punta Mona** (www.puntamona.org; dm US$30; transportation US$10; ▢), an organic farm and retreat center, 5km south of Manzanillo, which also welcomes volunteers. A note of caution: trail robberies in the depths of the reserve have been reported, so it is advisable to hire a guide, or at least avoid hiking alone.

The coral reef 200m offshore is 10 times the size of the Cahuita reef, with the clearest waters and best diversity of sea life in Costa Rica. The best resource on the area is the Larkin family at **Aquamor Talamanca Adventures** (☎ 759 9012; www .greencoast.com), 100m west of Maxi's. Long-term area residents, they run a PADI dive school,

COSTA RICA

rent snorkeling gear (US$4 per hour) and kayaks, and offer dolphin-observation trips with excellent naturalist guides.

On the way into the village, **Cabinas Manzanillo** (☎ 759 9043; s/d/tr US$15/20/25) offers immaculate rooms with TV and fans in a friendly setting. **Cabinas las Veraneras** (☎ 759 9050; s/d with fan US$16/26) has scrubbed motel rooms and a pleasant *soda*. Free camping is permitted on the beach, but there are no organized facilities.

Local matrons preside over pleasant, informal *sodas* or sell *patis,* spicy meat and plantain turnovers. The big, breezy beachfront shanty **Maxi's** (meals US$7-15) is a Caribbean institution, serving red snapper grilled to perfection and frosty cold ones. The atmosphere is lively – folks stay even when the lights short out, and there's live music some weekends.

Getting There & Away

Buses to Puerto Viejo (stopping at beaches) leave Manzanillo at 5am, 8:15am, 12:45pm and 5:15pm. The first two and last departures continue to Puerto Limón.

SIXAOLA

Falling in love in Sixaola would be tragic, as it's not the kind of place to be any length of time. Still, it has a relaxed border crossing, the fast track to Bocas del Toro, although most foreign tourists chose to travel via Paso Canoas.

Accommodation and restaurants are basic, those in Panama are a better value. The quiet and clean **Hotel Imperio** (☎ 754 2289; d with/without bathroom US$9/7) is right across the street from the police checkpoint.

The bus station is one block north of the border crossing. Buses go to San José (US$10, five hours) at 6am, 8am, 10am and 3pm. Eight buses travel to and from Puerto Limón (US$3, three hours) via Cahuita and Puerto Viejo, departing between 5am and 6pm.

NORTHERN CARIBBEAN COAST

Rural and rain-drenched, this area is a top spot to see jungle wildlife. Most visitors choose Parque Nacional Tortuguero as the departure point for canoe trips but those who want a true backcountry experience should check out the remote outpost of Barra de Colorado.

TORTUGUERO
pop 750

In the rainiest of all rain forests, this remote village is wedged between the silty Atlantic surf and Parque Nacional Tortuguero's teeming green canals. At times, the spongy strip of clapboard houses saturates, flooding the narrow boardwalks. It is impossible to drive here. Big motor canoes rule the waterways and drivers enjoy a certain status relegated to diplomats and royalty in other cultures. Maybe you came here for the wildlife, specifically the turtles, but Tortuguero itself is a unique place to visit, with the bonus of good Creole cooking.

The town does have a seedy side, namely the international drug-running circuit which touches this remote area. Stay alert and careful, and don't go into isolated areas alone.

Information

Tortuguero's goods and services run higher than elsewhere, there's no avoiding it. There is no bank and few businesses accept credit cards, so bring all the cash you will need and stash it creatively.

Opposite the Catholic church, the **Tortuguero Information Center** (per hr US$3; ☺ 8am-7pm) sells Sansa tickets and has internet.

Rain gear and insect repellent are necessary here.

Sights & Activities

PARQUE NACIONAL TORTUGUERO

This misty green coastal park sits on a broad flood plain parted by a jigsaw of canals. Referred to as the 'mini-Amazon,' Parque Nacional Tortuguero's intense biodiversity includes over 400 bird species, 60 known species of frogs, 30 species of freshwater fish, three monkey species as well as the threatened West Indian manatee. Caimans and crocodiles can be seen lounging on river banks while freshwater turtles bask on logs.

Over 50,000 visitors a year come to boat the canals and see the wildlife, particularly to watch turtles lay eggs. This is the most important Caribbean breeding site of the green sea turtle, 40,000 of which arrive every season to nest. Of the eight species of marine turtle in the world, six nest in Costa Rica, and four nest in Tortuguero. The problem of poaching is addressed by the vigilance of various volunteer organizations (see right).

Park headquarters is at **Cuatro Esquinas** (☎ 709 8086; one-/three-day admission US$7/10; ☽ 5:30am-7pm), just north of Tortuguero village.

Sharks and strong currents make the beaches unsuitable for swimming.

Boating & Canoeing

A variety of guided **boat tours** (US$15 plus park-entry fee) depart at 6am daily from the town of Tortuguero and surrounding lodges to see the canals and spot wildlife. Canoe and kayak rental and boat tours are available in the village.

Four aquatic trails wind their way through the Parque Nacional Tortuguero. The **Río Tortuguero** acts as the entrance way to the network of trails. This wide, still river is often covered with water lilies and frequented by aquatic birds such as herons and kingfishers, as well as peacocks.

The **Caño Chiquero** is thick with vegetation, especially artichoke trees and red *guacimo* trees. Black turtles and green iguanas hang out here. Caño Chiqero leads to the narrow **Caño Mora** and **Caño Harold**, popular with Jesus Christ lizards and caimans.

Hiking

Behind Cuatro Esquinas station, **El Gavilan Land Trail** is the park's only public trail. The muddy, 2km loop traverses tropical humid forest and follows a stretch of beach. Green parrots and several species of monkeys are commonly

sighted here. It is well-marked and does not require a guide.

Turtle Watching

Visitors are allowed to check out the turtle rookeries at night from March to October (late July through August is prime time) and observe eggs being laid or hatching. Seeing a 180kg turtle haul itself up onto the beach, dig a nest, lay 120 eggs the size of Ping-Pong balls and scoot back to sea, exhausted, can be awe-inspiring. Obviously, turtle sightings are not guaranteed. A guide must accompany all visitors. Camera flashes and flashlights are prohibited by law, as they disturb the egg-laying process.

If you're unable to visit during the peak green turtle breeding season, the next best time is February to July, when leatherback turtles nest in small numbers (the peak is from mid-April to mid-May). Hawksbill turtles nest sporadically from March to October, and loggerhead turtles are also sometimes seen. The tour fee is US$10, which does not include admission to the park.

Volunteer Opportunities

Caribbean Conservation Corporation (CCC; ☎ in San José 710 0680 ; www.cccturtle.org; admission US$1; ☽ 10am-noon & 2-5:30pm) operates a research station 1km north of the village with a worthwhile visitors center. Volunteers assist scientists with tagging and research of both green and leatherback turtles (March to October). One-week volunteer programs (US$1400 to US$1600) include dorm lodging, meals and transportation from San José.

Volunteers at **Coterc** (☎ 709 8052, in Canada 905-831 8809; www.coterc.org; per day US$65) assist with sea-turtle conservation, bird banding, and animal and plant diversity inventories. Lodging is in a brand-new dorm building, with full access to facilities. Fees include room and board.

CERRO TORTUGUERO

This 119m hill, 6km north of the village, is the highest coastal point north of Limón. The steep, muddy climb rewards with excellent views of the forest, canals and ocean. Look for colorful poison dart frogs.

Tours

A two-hour turtle tour costs around US$10 per person, and half-day hikes or boat excursions cost US$15. Some readers have reported guides uncovering nests or allowing flash photography. If you see unscrupulous behavior, please report it and also write to us at Lonely Planet. Recommended local guides:

Barbara Hartung (☎ 709 8004; www.tinamontours .com) Offers culture tours and hiking, canoe and turtle tours in German, English, French or Spanish.

Castor Hunter Thomas (☎ 709 8050; ask at Soda Doña María)

Chico (☎ 709 8033; ask at Miss Miriam's) Hiking and canoe tours with rave reviews from readers.

Daryl Loth (☎ 833 0827, 392 3201; safari@racsa.co.cr) Canadian naturalist (formerly of Coterc) with boat trips and turtle tours.

Sleeping

Cabinas Meryscar (☎ 711 0971; s with/without bathroom US$7/5) These budget rooms barely squeeze in a bed, and claustrophobics should splurge for those with bath. Beds have fresh sheets but the cement-floor rooms are damp.

Tropical Lodge (☎ 840 2731; r per person US$10) A last resort, with small, low beds and sandy showers, located behind Tienda Bambú and with an attached bar.

Cabinas Tortuguero (☎ 709 8114; s/d US$10/16, with bathroom US$20/26) A cheerful spot a few steps south of the main dock, set amongst pretty gardens hung with hammocks. Rooms are bare but clean with mint walls and hardwood floors.

Cabinas Aracari (☎ 798 6059 in Limón; s/d US$10/15) Pleasing rooms with Spanish tile wrap around overgrown gardens. Set back by the sea, these *cabinas* enjoy a quiet, out-of-the-way location. Bathrooms have hot water.

Miss Miriam's (s/d US$15/20) A top choice with immaculate linoleum rooms (towels folded into swans) and a balcony facing the sea. The restaurant serves excellent Caribbean fare.

Cabinas Princesa (☎ 709 8107; s/d US$15/20) Couples will prefer this ample nouveau-colonial building, south of the soccer field, with a sense of privacy. Three rooms have private baths and fans. The shared balcony offers views of the waves tumbling onto the beach. It's owned by Miss Miriam's hospitable clan.

Hotel Miss Junie (☎ 709 8029; s/d US$22/32) At the northern end of the village, Miss Junie's extensive shady grounds straddle the river and the sea. Screened rooms let a breeze into the comfortable interior and hammocks dot the grounds. Prices include a full breakfast by the illustrious Miss Junie.

Eating

Mundo Natural (☼ 9am-10pm) For an afternoon refresher, Mundo Natural serves fresh juice, homemade ice cream and organic coffee.

Caribbean Flavor (mains US$3-5, lobster US$7) This place facing the soccer field does a bang-up job of cooking up rice and beans, and fresh whole lobsters.

Buddha Cafe (meals US$4-6; ☼ 9am-9pm) This sleek-and-sophisticated café might seem out of place, but that shouldn't stop you from getting a pizza, savory shrimp crêpes or big bowl of fresh greens.

La Casona Restaurant (meals US$4-7; ☼ 11am-10pm) Highly recommended La Casona, on the soccer field, offers a garlic-laden hearts-of-palm lasagna, pastas and Tico fare.

Miss Junie's (☎ 709 8029; dinner US$8-10; ☼ 6-9pm) Order early here to let the seafood simmer and soak in the spicy coconut sauce. For truly memorable Caribbean food, it's an obligatory visit.

Getting There & Away

AIR

NatureAir (☎ 710 0323; one way US$68) and **Sansa** (☎ 709 8015; US$63) have daily flights to and from San José. The airstrip is 4km north of the village.

BUS & BOAT

Tortuguero is accessible by boat from Cariari or Moín. If you are traveling to Parismina, you should be able to get one of the boats to Moín to drop you off on the way.

To/From Moín

While tour boats ply these canals frequently, there is no reliable regular service. It is much easier to boat from Moín to Tortuguero than to return.

In theory, **Viajes Bananeros** (☎ 709 8005; www .tortuguero-costarica.com; US$30) offers a daily transfer to Moín at 10am. Another **water taxi** (☎ 709 8005; each way US$20) departs from Moín at 11am and returns from Tortuguero at 1:30pm.

To/From Cariari

The more common route to and from Tortuguero is through Cariari, from where you can catch buses to San José or Puerto Limón.

If you are coming to Tortuguero through Cariari, you have two options. The most common route to Tortuguero is through La Pavona. **Coopatreca** (☎ 767 7137; US$10; departs 6am,

11:30am & 3pm) leaves for La Pavona from the central bus terminal in Siquirres, behind the police station. **Viajes Bananeros** (☎ 709 8005; US$10; departs 7am & 11am) leaves from the San José bus terminal for Geest.

For return travel, buy tickets on the boat or at an information center in Tortuguero. Once the boat arrives in La Pavona or La Geest, a bus transfers passengers to Cariari. Those traveling on to San José should take a 6am boat to connect with the 11:30am bus from Cariari.

BARRA DEL COLORADO

Deep in the watery heart of nowhere, **Refugio Nacional de Fauna Silvestre Barra del Colorado** is the biggest national wildlife refuge in Costa Rica, with 90,400 hectares. It constitutes a wildlife bonanza – hosting the endangered West Indian manatee, caimans, crocodiles, big cats, Baird's tapirs and more. Anglers go for tarpon from January to June and snook from September to December.

Near the mouth of the Río Colorado, the village is reached only by plane or boat. Regional travel is almost exclusively by boat. Most residents live on the north side (Barra del Norte). The airstrip and **ranger station** (admission US$6) are on the south bank (Barra del Sur).

If traveling on the Río San Juan to the north of Barra, take your passport. The river lies within Nicaraguan territory. Checkpoints along the way may charge a US$10 fee for entry.

Camping is allowed in the refuge, but there are no facilities. Hotels are mostly sport fishing lodges, some accessed by boat. If you are coming for wildlife tours, let your hotel know in advance so that they may make arrangements. If you are not fishing, you can paddle these waterways in a canoe or kayak, available from some of the local lodges.

The cheapest hotel is **Tarponland Lodge** (☎ 710 2141; r per person US$20; 🅿), next to the airstrip. Run-down rooms have screens and private bathroom. Meals are extra. The long-established **Río Colorado Lodge** (☎ 232 4063, in the USA 800-243 9777; www.riocoloradolodge.com; r per person without/with fishing incl meals US$120/400; 🅿 🖧) has breezy rooms in stilted buildings near the mouth of the Río Colorado. You can trade fish tales (or swap them for bus tales) at the happy hour with free rum drinks. It's walking distance from the airport.

Getting There & Away

AIR

The easiest way to get to Barra del Colorado is by plane. Sansa (one way US$63) and Nature-Air (US$68) fly daily from San José.

BOAT

There is no regular boat service to Barra, although you may be able to arrange a boat from Tortuguero (US$50 per boat), Puerto Viejo de Sarapiquí (p583; US$60 per boat) or Moín. During the dry season, buses run from Cariari (opposite) to Puerto Lindo, from where you can try to hop on a lodge boat or a water taxi on Río Colorado to Barra.

NORTH CENTRAL COSTA RICA

The spark of adventure lures travelers to this sector, home of Monteverde's misty cloud forests and the smoking Volcán Arenal. Where else can you see iridescent tarantulas, careen through canopy on zip lines and top the day with a soak in bubbling hot springs? But good old-fashioned exploration (*sans* steel cables or zip-off pants) means a stop in the flat, tropical lowlands of Costa Rica's cattle country in rodeo season, or exploring the world-class wetlands at Refugio Nacional Caño Negro. At the region's northern limit, the Río San Juan forms the border with Nicaragua. In an earlier era it served as an important link with the Caribbean coast. Today, intrepid travelers can boat across the border, or all the way to Barra de Colorado. Now that's adventure.

Most travelers short for time take the popular circuit which shortcuts around Laguna Arenal from Monteverde with a jeep-boat-jeep (actually, van-boat-van) connection to La Fortuna, or vice-versa.

TILARÁN

This ranching boomtown makes a mellow rest stop for travelers. Friendly and western Tilarán showcases its first love – bulls – the last weekend in April with a **rodeo** and on June 13 with a bullfight dedicated to San Antonio. It's near the southwestern end of Laguna de Arenal.

You can check email while waiting for your bus at **Cybercafé Tilarán** (25m west of bus terminal; per hr US$1.25; ⊙ 9am-10pm Mon-Sat), with speedy connections.

Sleeping & Eating

Hotel Tilarán (☎ 695 5043; s/d US$6/12) On the west side of the parque central, this is an excellent budget choice as the rooms with cable TV are well cared for (and quiet if you can get one facing the rear).

Hotel y Restaurant Mary (☎ 695 5479; s/d US$12/16) An amiable and tidy option featuring linens that grandma would love. Wooden chairs on the balcony help you survey the local scene. The downstairs restaurant (mains US$3 to US$6; open 6am to midnight) with a cool tin counter serves Tico and Chino favorites.

Hotel & Restaurante y Cafetería Guadalupe (☎ 695 5943; s/d US$16/28) Upstairs rooms are spacious and quiet, arranged around common areas made for rocking and reading. Locals pack the downstairs cafeteria (mains US$2 to US$6; open 6am to 9pm Monday to Friday, 7am to 5pm Saturday), serving a good fish fillet, nachos or mild fajitas.

Restaurante El Parque (☎ 695 5425; mains US$3-5; 🕒 7am-11pm) Metal tables and Mexican *ranchera* music offer an everyman-type ambience to savor alongside *pinto gallo* and chop suey.

Getting There & Away

Buses depart from the terminal just west of the parque central. The route between Tilarán and San José goes via the Interamericana, not La Fortuna. Sunday afternoon buses to San José are often sold out by Saturday. Some routes:

Cañas (US$0.50; 45min) Departs 5am, 6:40am, 7:30am, 8am, 10am, 11:30am and 3:30pm.

Ciudad Quesada, via La Fortuna (US$2.50; 4hr) At 7am and 12:30pm.

Nuevo Arenal (US$0.75; 1¼hr) Departs 5am, 6am, 8am, 9am, 10am, 11am, 1pm, 2:30pm and 3:30pm.

Puntarenas (US$2.50; 2hr) At 6am and 1pm.

San José (US$3.50; 3hr) Autotransportes Tilarán departs 4:45am, 7am, 9:30am, 2pm and 5pm.

Santa Elena (US$1.75; 3 to 4hr) At 12:30pm.

MONTEVERDE & SANTA ELENA

Snug in the misty greenbelt of two cloud forest reserves, this slim corridor of human habitation consists of the Tico village of Santa Elena and the Quaker settlement of Monteverde. The area, first settled by loggers and farmers who came in the 1930s, later became populated by North American Quakers (a pacifist religious group also known as the 'Friends') in 1951. The emigration forever changed local history.

As pacifists, four Quakers refused to be drafted into the Korean War. They were jailed in Alabama in 1949. The incident ignited an exodus and members of the group came to dairy farm in these greener pastures, eventually conserving them. Tourism grabbed hold when a 1983 *National Geographic* feature described this unique landscape, and subsequently billed the area as *the* place to view one of Central America's most famous birds – the resplendent quetzal. Tourism here hasn't waned since.

Given the popularity of this area, it's important to respect the wildlife (by not feeding it) and others (by hiking quietly) and pack out all trash. Tourism takes its toll on the local population as well. Keep the small-town atmosphere by taking the time to say hello. Infrastructure is wobbly in these places – the electricity, water and phones blink off when you most need them. Blaming or moaning won't fix it any faster. Kick back for a candlelit dinner. It's part of the rustic charm – you'll see.

Orientation

In the cloud forest at 1200m to 1600m, the community of Monteverde is scattered along the several kilometers of road that leads to the reserve. Most of the budget hotels and restaurants are in the village of Santa Elena, while the more expensive lodges are found along the road. The Monteverde reserve is 6km southeast of Santa Elena, and the Santa Elena reserve is 5km north and east.

Information

Chunches (☎ 645 5147) offers all sorts of travel and natural history books, US newspapers, laundry service and coffee and snacks. Find events posted on flyers by the door. The Banco Nacional has an ATM and provides advances on Visa cards.

The town has an official website; www.monteverdeforever.com.

Sights

Donning rubbery rain gear and mud boots (for rent at park offices) is a rite of passage for those visiting these dripping, mossy cloud forests in search of resplendent quetzals, hummingbirds, howler monkeys, sloths, snakes and more. Just remember that wildlife absconds in the mist, so hold back wild expectations. Hiring a guide is often worth the expense.

BOSQUE ETERNO DE LOS NIÑOS

Founded by school children fed up with the childish squandering of our natural resources, **Bosque Eterno de los Niños** (Children's Eternal Forest; ☎ 645 5003; www.acmcr.org; adult/student day use US$7/4, guided night hike US$15/10; ⏱ 7:30am-5:30pm) is an enormous 22,000-hectare reserve providing a home for local wildlife among the primary and secondary forest (and to allow former agricultural land to be slowly reclaimed by the jungle). The night tours here are highly recommended.

SAN GERARDO ECOLODGE & RESEARCH STATION

Administered by the **Monteverde Conservation League** (☎ 645 5003; www.acmcr.org), this research station on the Atlantic slope sits at an elevation of 1200m. There are no crowds, the views of Arenal are gorgeous and wildlife spotting can be very good. The entrance is next to Santa Elena Reserve. Hike 3.5km downhill on a dirt track to the **research station** (adult/student US$7/4; room per adult/student with 3 meals US$45/28) with a number of trails through primary and secondary forest.

RESERVA BIOLÓGICA BOSQUE NUBOSO MONTEVERDE

When Quaker settlers first arrived, they agreed to preserve about a third of their property in order to protect the watershed above Monteverde. Fighting off squatters with the help of the Nature Conservancy and the World Wildlife Fund, they began what is now known as one of the country's most eminent reserves.

Trails in the reserve are clearly marked. The **Sendero Bosque Nuboso** is a pretty 2km (one-way) walk through the cloud forest to the continental divide. From there you can return via the wide **Sendero El Camino**, which branches off to a 25m-high suspension bridge. The circuit takes two to three hours. Half-day **tours** (US$15) in English leave at 7:30am; call ahead to reserve a space or to arrange a night or birding tour.

You can't camp but three basic **shelters** (dm US$5) provide drinking water, showers, propane stoves and cooking utensils. Hikers need to carry a sleeping bag, candles, food and other necessities (such as toilet paper). Make reservations at least one week in advance for the **dorms** (adult/student US$37/33) near the park entrance. The **visitors center** (☎ 645 5122; www.monteverdeinfo.com/monteverde.htm; adult/student US$13/6.50; ⏱ 7am-4pm) has free trail maps, a snack bar and a restaurant.

RESERVA SANTA ELENA

When Monteverde gets crowded, this park provides a great alternative. An exquisitely misty reserve with 12km of trails, Santa Elena is slightly higher in elevation than Monteverde, with some secondary-growth forest. Open spots help for spotting birds and other animals. Monkeys and sloths may even be seen on the road in. Go on your own or book a guided tour (US$15 plus entry fee), leaving from the **information center** (☎ 661 8290; www.monteverdeinfo.com/reserve-santa-elena-monteverde; adult/student US$10/6; ⏱ 7am-4pm) at 7:30am and 11:30am. Call to reserve.

OTHER ATTRACTIONS

The **Monteverde Butterfly Garden** (☎ 645 5512; adult/student US$8/6; ⏱ 9:30am-4pm) offers fantastic naturalist-led tours (in Spanish, English or German) that include a fascinating walk through live insect exhibits (leave the fly-swatter at home). See the greenhouses where butterflies are raised and screened gardens where hundreds flutter about. Mornings are the best time to visit. Visitors can also explore on their own.

Hopping at night, the **Ranario** (Frog Pond; ☎ 645 6320; ranariomv@racsa.co.cr; adult/student US$8/5; ⏱ 9:30am-8:30pm) exhibits over 30 species of frogs, toads and salamanders. For more cold-blooded marvels, the **serpentarium** (☎ 645 6002; www.snaketour.com; adult/student/child US$7/5/3; ⏱ 9am-8pm) has 40 species of snakes.

The roadside **orchid garden** (☎ 645 5510; adult/child US$5/3; ⏱ 8am-5pm) has shady trails winding past more than 400 types of orchids organized into taxonomic groups. Peak blooming period is November to February.

Casem (☎ 645 5190), a women's arts and crafts cooperative, sells crafts and souvenirs with profits benefiting the community. A number of art galleries around town are also worth exploring.

Activities

CANOPY TOURS & HANGING BRIDGES

On the grounds of Cloud Forest Lodge, **Original Canopy Tour** (☎ 291 4465; www.canopytour.com; adult/student/child US$45/35/25; ⏱ 7:30am-2:30pm) has the fabled zip lines that started an ecotourism movement of questionable ecological value.

COSTA RICA

MONTEVERDE & SANTA ELENA

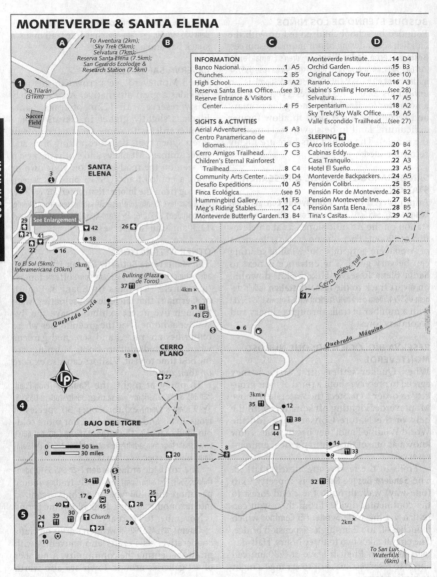

To Aventura (2km);
Sky Trek (5km);
Reserva Santa Elena (7.5km);
San Gerardo Ecolodge &
Research Station (7.5km)

To Tilarán (31km)

Soccer Field

SANTA ELENA

See Enlargement

To El Sol (5km);
Interamericana (30km)

Bullring (Plaza de Toros)

Quebrada Sucia

CERRO PLANO

BAJO DEL TIGRE

Church

Cerro Amigos Trail

Quebrada Máquina

To San Luis Waterfalls (6km)

INFORMATION	
Banco Nacional	1 A5
Chunches	2 B5
High School	3 A2
Reserva Santa Elena Office	(see 3)
Reserve Entrance & Visitors Center	4 F5

SIGHTS & ACTIVITIES	
Aerial Adventures	5 A3
Centro Panamericano de Idiomas	6 C3
Cerro Amigos Trailhead	7 C3
Children's Eternal Rainforest Trailhead	8 C4
Community Arts Center	9 D4
Desafío Expeditions	10 A5
Finca Ecológica	(see 5)
Hummingbird Gallery	11 F5
Meg's Riding Stables	12 C4
Monteverde Butterfly Garden	13 B4

Monteverde Institute	14 D4
Orchid Garden	15 B3
Original Canopy Tour	(see 10)
Ranario	16 A3
Sabine's Smiling Horses	(see 28)
Selvatura	17 A5
Serpentarium	18 A5
Sky Trek/Sky Walk Office	19 A5
Valle Escondido Trailhead	(see 27)

SLEEPING	
Arco Iris Ecolodge	20 B4
Cabinas Eddy	21 A2
Casa Tranquilo	22 A3
Hotel El Sueño	23 A5
Monteverde Backpackers	24 A5
Pensión Colibrí	25 B5
Pensión Flor de Monteverde	26 B2
Pensión Monteverde Inn	27 B4
Pensión Santa Elena	28 B5
Tina's Casitas	29 A2

0   50 km
0   30 miles

It's less elaborate than others, but at least living history here entertains more than most museums.

Aventura (☎ 645 6959; www.aventuramonteverde.com; adult/student US$35/28; ☼ 7am-2:30pm) has 16 platforms, a Tarzan-swing and a 15m rappel. It's 3km north of Santa Elena. Hotel pick-ups are included in the price.

Selvatura (☎ 645 5929; www.selvatura.com; adult/child US$40/30; ☼ 7:30am-4pm) is for those who find statistics sexy. It has 3km of cables, 18 platforms and one Tarzan-swing in primary forest. The office is across from the church in Santa Elena. For grannies there are hanging bridges.

If speed's your poison, then **SkyTrek** (☎ 645 5796; www.skywalk.co.cr; adult/student US$40/32; ☼ 7:30am-

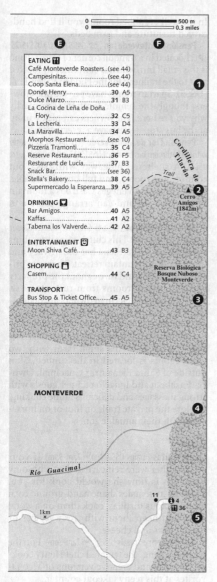

EATING 🍴
Café Monteverde Roasters...(see 44)
Campesinitas........................(see 44)
Coop Santa Elena................(see 44)
Donde Henry........................**30** A5
Dulce Marzo.........................**31** B3
La Cocina de Leña de Doña
  Flory.................................**32** C5
La Lechería.........................**33** D4
La Maravilla.........................**34** A5
Morphos Restaurant............(see 10)
Pizzería Tramonti..................**35** C4
Reserve Restaurant...............**36** F5
Restaurant de Lucía..............**37** B3
Snack Bar............................(see 36)
Stella's Bakery.......................**38** C4
Supermercado la Esperanza...**39** A5

DRINKING 🍸
Bar Amigos............................**40** A5
Kaffas...................................**41** A2
Taberna los Valverde...........**42** A2

ENTERTAINMENT 🎭
Moon Shiva Café....................**43** B3

SHOPPING 🛍
Casem...................................**44** C4

TRANSPORT
Bus Stop & Ticket Office.......**45** A5

5pm) is for you. Steel towers join 11 platforms spread out along a road. You'll be thankful they invested in a real brake system. Hanging bridges provide a less balls-out alternative.

HIKING
Take a free hike up 1842m **Cerro Amigos** on a clear day for great views of Volcán Arenal,

20km away to the northeast. Near the top of the mountain, you'll pass by the TV towers for channels 7 and 13. The trail leaves Monteverde from behind Hotel Belmar (the road behind the gas station), ascending roughly 300m in 3km. From the hotel, take the dirt road going downhill, then the next left.

The strenuous hike to the **San Luis Waterfall** rewards you with views of a gorgeous stream cascading from the cloud forests into a series of swimming holes just begging for a picnic. It's only a few kilometers, but it's steep and the rocky, mud-filled terrain can get very slick. A taxi from town costs about U$12.

HORSEBACK RIDING
A number of trails and scenic panoramas make the area ideal for horse riding. Inquire at Pensión Santa Elena for reader-recommended **Sabine's Smiling Horses** (☎ 645 6894; www.horseback-riding-tour.com; per hr US$15), offering multiday trips and even a five-hour full-moon ride. Also popular is **Meg's Riding Stables** (☎ 645 5560; www.guanacaste.com/sites/stellas/stables.htm).

Riding from Monteverde and Fortuna is offered by most outfitters. Overworked horses made the route controversial in the past, but client pressure has really upped local standards. Of the two routes, the Mirador Trail is steep and unmanageably muddy in rainy season while the Lake Trail is flatter and easier. **Desafío Expeditions** (☎ 645 5874; www.monteverdetours.com) takes the Lake Trail to La Fortuna (US$65).

Courses & Volunteering
The nonprofit **Monteverde Institute** (☎ 645 5053; www.mvinstitute.org) offers courses in tropical biology, conservation, sustainable development, Spanish and women's studies. It also offers internships and places student volunteers.

The **Children's Eternal Forest** (www.acmcr.org) is always looking for help. For information visit the website. To volunteer in the schools, check out opportunities online for the English-language **Monteverde Friends School** (www.mfschool.org) or the **Cloudforest School** (www.cloudforest school.org).

Centro-Panamericano de Idiomas (☎ 265 6306; www.cpi-edu.com; classes without/with homestay US$255/380) offers Spanish courses.

Sleeping
An overflow of hotels means you can find many options in addition to those following

if need be. These offer hot showers, unless otherwise noted.

In Santa Elena

Cabinas Eddy (☎ 645 6635; per person with/without bathroom US$8/5; 🖳) Readers recommend Eddy's for the cheap and clean rooms, helpful staff and the marimba-playing prowess of the owner. English is spoken.

Pensión Santa Elena (☎ 645 6240; www.pensionsantaelena.com; dm US$6, s/d/tr US$10/14/21, with bathroom US$15/20/25, s/d/tr/q cabins US$20/25/30/40; 🖳) Running on pure personality, this backpacker favorite has bare-bones rooms but stellar service. Tireless Texas natives Ran and Shannon man the free-advice booth all day. Help yourself to morning coffee and the occasional donated pineapple.

Casa Tranquilo (☎ 645 6782; www.casatranquilo.net; per person with/without bathroom US$10/7; 🖳) This place is geared toward backpackers with its plain wood-frame rooms with skylights and a chilled-out common space under the tin roof. Hearty buffet breakfasts and internet access are included.

Monteverde Backpackers (☎ 645 5844; www.monteverdebackpackers.com; dm/s/d incl breakfast US$10/15/30; 🖳) The bilingual managers work above and beyond to offer a five-star hostel experience. Breakfast comes out early on request and rooms are cozy, spotless and wood-paneled, all with new mattresses and private bathrooms. A hammock garden is in the works.

Cabinas El Pueblo (☎ 645 6192; www.cabinaselpueblo.com; s/d US$8/10, with bathroom US$15/20; Ⓟ) Owners Marleny and Freddy are eager to please (you'll probably meet them first at the bus stop). They offer adequate cement rooms and homey common areas.

Pensión Colibrí (☎ 645 5682; r per person with bathroom US$10) Down the street and up a quiet lane, the pension feels like it's perched among the trees. Country décor adorns large rooms and mini-balconies overlook the woods.

Hotel El Sueño (☎ 645 6695; d incl breakfast US$20; 🖳) This Tico-run hotel has huge, renovated wooden rooms and a great balcony with sweeping views of the area. Upstairs rooms are airier, though the best ones are in the new addition.

Around Santa Elena

Tina's Casitas (☎ 820 4821; www.tinascasitas.de; r per person US$5, with bathroom US$20) This is a terrific budget spot west of La Esperanza supermarket.

In the well-scrubbed rooms you'll find hand-carved furniture and firm beds.

Pensión Monteverde Inn (☎ 645 5156; s/d US$15/25; Ⓟ) Located in a tranquil corner of Cerro Plano is this small inn, which is conveniently located next to the trailhead for the Hidden Valley Trail (US$5). Spartan rooms have private hot showers, though the remote location is primarily why you're here. The owners can pick you up at the bus stop if you have a reservation.

Pensión Flor de Monteverde (☎ 645 5236; d with/without bathroom incl breakfast US$15/12, other meals extra US$15) A sheltered hideaway with basic but comfortable rooms, and full board available. Owner Eduardo Venegas Castro is a fountain of information and can arrange tours and transportation.

Arco Iris Ecolodge (☎ 645 5067; www.arcoirislodge.com; d US$45-85; Ⓟ) This clutch of pretty cabins overlooking Santa Elena has the privacy and intimacy of a mountain retreat. There are private trails that wind throughout the property and a variety of rooms from rustic to ritzy. The multilingual German owners are delightful. Their excellent meals sometimes feature organic vegetables grown on the grounds.

El Sol (☎ 645 5838; www.elsolnuestro.com; d small/large cabin US$60/80; Ⓟ) This small farm with two guest cabins is located in the sunbelt, 5km outside of Santa Elena near Guacimal. Owners Elisabeth and Ignacio pamper guests with strong massages and delicious home cooking. Explore the private trails on foot or on horseback with their amiable son.

Eating

Campesinitas (mains US$2-4; ☽ 7am-5pm) If your own mother were reincarnated as a bosomy Tica, this is how she would cook for you. Three feisty females shape hand-ground corn into delicious tortillas, cook them on a wood stove and heap them with fresh veggies or meat, beans and cheese.

Donde Henry (meals US$3; ☽ 7am-8pm) For the price of a song, the talented chef Henry cooks up flavorful and creative versions of Tico favorites at this teeny takeout counter.

Stella's Bakery (mains US$2-5; ☽ 6am-6pm) Gourmet sandwiches made to order and a pastry case brimming with fresh pies, sticky buns and cookies – jackpot for hungry trekkers. Eat in the bright vaulted space with oil paintings by the owner's mom, or in the garden yard.

Dulce Marzo (snacks US$2-5; ☽ 8am-7pm) Run by a Californian native with a keen take on caffeine treats, this cool little café is the favorite of locals. Stop by for a brownie and espresso or a heaping flatbread sandwich.

La Maravilla (meals US$2-5; 6am-9pm) The most popular *soda* in Santa Elena is this haunt festooned with the napkin artwork of its worldwide clientele. On the menu? *Casados*, albeit damn good ones.

La Cocina de Leña de Doña Flory (mains US$4-6; 8am-8pm Sun-Fri) An outdoor *soda* run by one of the area's original Quakers. Corn-husk tamales are tops and Sunday means a special stew. The turnoff, by La Colina Lodge, is signposted.

Morpho's Restaurant (mains US$5-10; 7:30am-9:30pm) Typical Costa Rican food gets gourmet flair (and gourmet prices). The sandwiches are especially hearty and fresh salads make a nice change.

Pizzería Tramonti (☎ 645 6120; mains US$5-11; 11:30am-3pm & 5:30-10pm Tue-Sun) Nothing says *te adoro* like thin-crust pizza sizzled to crispness in a wood-fired oven. The pastas and seafood are tasty too.

Restaurant de Lucía (☎ 645 5337; mains US$7-15; 11am-8:30pm) Uncork a bottle of red (it's Chilean owned) and feast on flawless eggplant parmesan or steak with mushrooms. Fare is conventional (no fusion here) but impeccably prepared and the starters always include a basket of warm tortillas with toppings.

Go to the source for homemade ice cream and cheeses at La Lechería (Monteverde Cheese Factory). Visit nearby Café Monteverde roasters for a fresh cup of brew.

Drinking & Entertainment

Nightlife usually means a guided tour of glow-in-the-dark creepy-crawlies. More urbane pursuits include a visit to **Kaffas** (11am-2am), a relaxed lounge with occasional live music. Locals fill Amigos Bar to drink brewskis and shoot pool. An interesting mix filters into Taberna los Valverde late night – but most have to bolster their dance floor (Latin and rock) courage with a shot of tequila. Look for cultural events at the Galeron Cultural, and live music or jam sessions at Bromelia's amphitheatre or **Moon Shiva** (10am-10pm; covers US$3-5) restaurant.

Getting There & Around

All intercity buses stop at the terminal in downtown Santa Elena, and most continue on to the cheese factory in Monteverde. For safety tips see p580. Destinations include:

La Fortuna via Tilarán (US$2; 7hr) Departs at 7am and includes a two-hour wait in Tilarán.

Puntarenas (US$2.50; 3hr) Departs from Banco Nacional at 6am.

Reserva Monteverde (US$0.50; 30min) Departs from Banco Nacional at 6:30am, 7:30am, 9:30am, 11:30am, 1pm and 2:30pm; returns 6:40am, 8am, 10:40am, noon, 2:10pm and 3pm.

Reserva Santa Elena (US$2; 30min) Departs from Banco Nacional at 6:30am, 8:30am, 10:30am, 2:30pm and 3:30pm; returns 11am, 1pm and 4pm.

San José (US$4.50; 4½hr) TransMonteverde departs from La Lechería at 6:30am and 2:30pm, with pick-up at the bus station in Santa Elena.

JEEP-BOAT-JEEP

The fastest route between Monteverde/Santa Elena and La Fortuna is a land/water combo (US$30, three hours), arranged through hotels and tour operators. A taxi from La Fortuna takes you to Laguna de Arenal, meeting a boat that crosses the lake to the other side where a 4WD taxi continues to Monteverde. It's a popular option since it's incredibly scenic, reasonably priced and saves you half a day of rough travel.

LA FORTUNA & VOLCÁN ARENAL
pop 7000

Even without an active volcano popping fireworks overhead, the former farming town of La Fortuna would be a relaxing place to kick back for a few days. The flat grid town is near a playground of cascading waterfalls, steep trails and luxurious hot springs. As rapid development takes its toll, you might find yourself batting off tour-hawkers the minute you step off the bus. Relax, once you get settled in, these pests disperse and you can enjoy nature's many distractions – probably a good thing since it takes time for Volcán Arenal to peek out from the cloud cover.

Orientation & Information

La Fortuna offers few street signs, and most locals give directions using landmarks. The town is centered on a small park adjacent to the taxi stand. The clinic, police station and post office are all within two blocks of the plaza.

Quick internet access is available at **Expediciones** (per hr US$1.55; 9am-10pm Mon-Sat), across from the parque central. The banks in town all change US dollars and Banco de Costa Rica has a Visa Plus ATM. Pay phones are on the main street and in the parque central.

COSTA RICA

COSTA RICA

USE YOUR WITS

On Theft

Talented thieves ride the bus between San José and La Fortuna or Monteverde. When traveling these routes, do not leave your belongings on the shelf above the seats. Keep them on you and stay awake, even if that means drumming up a conversation with your seatmate in Spanglish. When in public spaces, resist the urge to repack your bag. And remember that lodgings that allow visitors *and* lodgers who insist on inviting new friends to visit put other guests at risk for theft or general creepiness.

On Tours

Sometimes the cheapest tours are scams, like the supposed raft trip to Río Pacuare that actually goes to a closer, tamer river, or the tour bus that was supposed to arrive at 8am but never comes. We've heard them all. It's worth going through a reputable agency or hotel to book your tours, even if that means paying more. At least you'll get to go, and if there's quality issues, you can hold someone accountable.

On Faith

Does this mean that all locals are out to scam you? No.

Sights & Activities

VOLCÁN ARENAL

Just 15km west of Fortuna, **Parque Nacional Volcán Arenal** (admission US$6; ☽ 8am-4pm) is home to Arenal – Costa Rica's most active volcano, producing ash columns, explosions and red streamers of molten rock almost daily since 1968. Climbing it is not allowed – hikers have been killed by explosions. Independent travelers can take an 8am bus toward Tilarán (ask to get off at the park) and catch the 2pm bus back to La Fortuna. From the 'Parque Nacional' sign off the main road, a 2km dirt road leads to the park. From the ranger station grab a trail map to choose from trails through old lava flows, tropical rain forest or to the lake.

HOT SPRINGS

For a Vegas feel, try **Baldi Hot Springs** (☎ 479 9651; without/with buffet US$17/27; ☽ 10am-10pm), 5km west of La Fortuna, where pyramids sprout waterslides. If you're rich or simply fulfilling that last living wish, megaresort and spa **Tabacón Hot Springs** (☎ 256 1500; www.tabacon.com; adult/child US$45/20, after 7pm US$19/17; ☽ 10am-10pm), 13km west of La Fortuna, offers hyperbolic decadence. Hot tubs, a water slide, waterfalls and 12 cold and hot pools for swimming and soaking. The brochure's swimsuit models are conspicuously absent.

LA CATARATA DE FORTUNA

A ribbon of cold, clear water called **La Catarata de la Fortuna** (admission US$6; ☽ 8am-5pm) pours

through a sheer canyon thick with bromeliads and ferns. Though it's dangerous to dive beneath the thundering 70m falls, you can take a dip in its perfect swimming holes. Keep an eye on your backpack. Rent a bike or walk. It's 7km from La Fortuna – all uphill – through pastureland and papaya trees.

VENADO CAVERNS

Located on a private farm outside town, these subterranean 2700m limestone caves attract fearless mud-trekkers to see colorless frogs, fish and countless bats. Operators in town book tours for about US$45. Claustrophobics, avoid this one.

Tours

Tours are big business in La Fortuna, with scammers sneaking a piece of the action. Especially here, visitors need to be smart consumers. Ask other travelers for references, shop around and never buy a tour on the street.

Groups can work out discounts in advance with most outfitters. Hotels arranging trips may charge a small commission but provide a place to complain if the service stinks.

Volcán Arenal trips generally include afternoon excursions to the national park or a private overlook, a hot-springs visit, dinner and an evening jaunt to see some lava. Prices run US$25 to US$65 per person. Make sure your tour includes the entry fees. Make appropriate sacrifices to the god of clear skies since there are no refunds if it's cloudy.

Most agencies also arrange Jeep-Boat-Jeep transportation to Monteverde (see p579), which is the easiest and most scenic way to visit the cloud forests. The tour operators listed below are recommended by travelers:

Bobo Adventures (☎ 479 1952; tour US$40) Bobo, 200m west of the park, specializes in caving in the spectacular Venado Caves.

Jacamar Tours (☎ 479 9767; www.arenaltours.com) Offers an incredible variety of naturalist hikes.

Sunset Tours (☎ 479 9800; www.sunsettourcr.com) Gives high-quality tours with bilingual guides.

Sleeping

There's no shortage of sleeping options in La Fortuna; just make sure yours is secure. Some lodgings (not included here) have experienced thefts.

Gringo Pete's (☎ 479 8521; gringopetes2003@yahoo .com; dm US$3, r per person with/without bathroom US$5/4, campsite US$2) A content communal vibe emanates from the purple house, 100m south of the school, and why not? Lodging's cheaper than breakfast. The cavernous shared bunk-rooms offer raw walls under a corrugated tin roof while cozier rooms have wooden bunks, fresh paint and mirrors. There's an ample kitchen and yard but don't expect privacy – the price of popularity.

La Posada Inn (☎ 479 9793; r per person with/without bathroom US$7/5) A frayed but funky house across from the school with Rasta colors and, you got it, relaxed vibes. Rooms with bathroom are a steal – the installations are brand new (even if mattresses clearly aren't).

Sleep Inn Guesthouse (☎ 394 7033; carlossleep inn@hotmail.com; r per person with shared bathroom US$5) Wacky and welcoming Carlos (aka Mr Lava-Lava) and Cándida run a modest guesthouse out of their home, 250m west of MegaSuper, and a hipper one in the center. Mr Lava-Lava, certainly the most hardworking man in (La Fortuna) show business, guarantees lava sightings or you tour again for free.

Hotel Dorothy (☎ 479 8068; noelsamuelsdouglas@hot mail.com; r per person US$6; 🖳) Beaming with Caribbean warmth, this worn but warm hotel, 300m south of town next to the bullring, offers large, bright rooms with clean shared baths and volcano views. The location, a few blocks out of town, guarantees your peace and quiet.

La Roca Virgen (☎ 479 9363; s/d/tr US$8/12/15, with bathroom US$14/18/24) A cozy, gay-friendly guest-house, 400m north and 50m east of the park,

with a singing aesthetic of bright colors, Spanish tiles and wood sculptures. The tidy rooms vary but all have hot showers, and some have TVs and mini-fridges. The owners offer lots of travel information as well as bike rentals and internet.

Arenal Backpackers Resort (☎ 479 7000; www.are nalbackpackers.com; dm US$10, d/tr/q US$50/66/80; campsite US$6; 🖭 🖳 🔡) As glamorous as hostels get, starting with a crystalline swimming pool and covered bar area. Springy mattresses, air-con and scrupulously clean bathrooms guarantee your comfort. Unlimited internet and wi-fi, a shared kitchen and pool table offer you sustenance and entertainment. Guarded and 300m west of the church, it's the most secure hotel in town and offers great service to boot. Will you ever leave?

Hotel las Colinas (☎ 479 9107; www.lascolinasare nal.com; s US$12-15) There's some character to this three-story place in the noisy heart of town, with worn wooden doors, soft vinyl sofas, large windows and saggy beds. Rooms look painstakingly scrubbed and all have private hot-water bathrooms.

Mayol Lodge (☎ 479 9110; s/d US$16/32; 🛋) A collection of cozy, yellow-paneled rooms 200m southeast of the parque central, with sparkling tile bathrooms, thick mattresses and matching bedding. Enjoy the volcano views from the swimming pool.

Eating

Soda El Río (casados US$3) This casual place is the top choice for cheap eats. Pull up a plastic chair to enjoy *casados* topped with fresh shredded cabbage and tomato.

Mi Casa (pastries US$1-2; 🕙 8am-5pm) For a brisk cup of joe, waffles or homemade pastries, try this Euro-style café, 200m east of the parque central.

Chelas (☎ 479 9594; mains US$3-7) This popular, open-air place, next to Valle Cocodrilo, has great *bocas* including *chicharrrones* (stewed pork meat) and *ceviche de pulpo* (octopus cured in lime). The bar stays open until 1am, so you can wash your meal down with a cold Imperial (or four).

La Choza de Laurel (meals US$6; 🕙 7am-11pm) The smoky wood-fire grill seduces famished passersby to join the ranks at open-air picnic tables for charred roast chicken served with homemade tortillas.

Rancho la Cascada (dinner US$4-15; 🕙 7-11am & 6pm-2am) Craving for a cocktail? Slip into this thatched-roofed place on the northeastern corner of the parque central, with fires cackling on chilly nights.

Don Rufino (mains US$7-15; ☺ 11am-10pm) Even if you can't afford to eat at gourmet Don Rufino, 100m east of the parque central, the bar by the street is fun and lively – the spot to slowly sip that Ron Centenario.

Getting There & Away

Buses now depart from a new terminal 100m south of the Iglesia Católica.

Ciudad Quesada (US$1; 1hr) Autotransportes San José-San Carlos departs 5am, 8am, 12:15pm and 3:30pm.

Monteverde (US$2; 6-8hr) At 8am – change at Tilarán at 12:30pm for Monteverde.

Monteverde via Jeep-boat-Jeep See p579.

San José (US$3; 4½hr) Autotransportes San José-San Carlos departs 12:45pm and 2:45pm.

Tilarán (US$1.40; 3½hr) Autotransportes Tilarán departs 8am and 5:30pm.

CIUDAD QUESADA

pop 34,000

Locals know Ciudad Quesada as San Carlos, the destination listed by local buses. For travelers, however, it's more of a stopover. Gritty and congested, this farm town is best known for its *talabaterías* selling top-notch saddles. The city is also home to the **Feria del Ganado** (cattle fair and auction), held every April and accompanied by carnival rides.

Check your email at **Internet Café** (per hr US$1; ☺ 8am-9pm Mon-Sat, 3-7pm Sun), 100m north of parque central. Banco de San José, 200m north of the parque, has an ATM.

You can grab some shut-eye at **Hotel del Norte** (☎ 460 1959; s/d US$6/9, with bathroom US$9/13), 200m north of Banco Nacional, where wafer-thin walls separate clean rooms with TVs (hope you enjoy what your neighbor is watching). The pleasant **Hotel Don Goyo** (☎ 460 1780; s/d US$12/22), 100m south of the parque central, is the most established hotel in town, with private hot showers. The attached restaurant (US$4 to US$10) serves quality Tico favorites and a variety of Western dishes.

Twenty-somethings flank the upper deck of **Restaurant los Geranios** (mains US$2-5), 100m south of the church, to down beers and *casados*. Those who have overdosed on rice and beans can visit *soda* **Restaurant El Parque** (mains US$3-6; ☺ 11am-9pm), 50m north of the parque, specializing in Italian pastas.

Terminal Quesada is 2km from the center, reached by taxis (US$1) and a twice-hourly bus (US$0.20). Cooptrac buses to La Fortuna (US$0.75, 1½ hours) depart at 6am, 10:30am, 1pm, 3:30pm, 5:15pm and 6pm. Chilsaca buses to Los Chiles (US$3, two hours) depart 12 times daily from 5am to 7:15pm. Empresarios Guapileños goes to Puerto Viejo de Sarapiquí (US$1.50, 2½ hours) at 4:40am, 6am, 9:15am, 10am, 3pm and 5:30pm. Autotransportes San Carlos departs for San José (US$2.50, 2½ hours) hourly from 5am to 6pm. Transportes Tilarán goes to Tilarán (US$4, 4½ hours) at 6:30am and 4pm.

LOS CHILES

pop 7000

Sweltering and sleepy, Los Chiles sits three rutted kilometers south of Nicaragua. Originally settled by merchants and fishermen, it recently served as an important supply route for Nicaraguan Contras, with a strong US military presence throughout the 1980s. Today gringo-traffic refers to travelers exploring the scenic water route to Caño Negro or the river route to Nicaragua, a one- to two-hour boat ride. Travelers crossing here must stop in Los Chiles for the necessary paperwork.

The Banco Nacional changes cash. **Viajes y Excursiones Cabo Rey** (☎ 471 1251, 839 7458) provides a boat service to the Caño Negro refuge (US$45 per group) as well as to El Castillo and the Solentiname Islands in Nicaragua. Cabo himself can usually be found by the dock.

Sleeping & Eating

Hotel Río Frío (☎ 471 1127; r per person US$3) Expect worn but clean plank rooms with a shared cold shower. It's where to meet migrant workers.

Cabinas Jabirú (☎ 471 1055; d with/without bathroom US$20/10; ☐) Next to the bus terminal, this popular budget spot has bare rooms and cold water. The friendly owner Manfred Rojas also arranges Caño Negro tours and horseback riding.

Rancho Tulipán (☎ 471 1414; cocas34@hotmail.com; s/d incl breakfast US$25/30; ✱ ☐) Relative luxury here means air-con, private hot-water bathrooms and cable TV, right next to the docks. The on-site restaurant (mains US$3 to US$7, open 7am to 10pm) offers good breakfasts and memorable pan-fried sea bass.

Restaurant El Parque (☎ 471 1373, 471 1090; mains US$3-5; ☺ 6am-9pm) Cheap and crowded, El Parque opens early if you need a coffee fix before setting out on the river.

COSTA RICA

GETTING TO SAN CARLOS, NICARAGUA

Although there's a 14km dirt road between the **Los Chiles–San Carlos** border, using this crossing requires special permission. Most travelers cross by boat, which is easily arranged in Los Chiles proper. First process your paperwork at **migración** (☎ 471 1223; ☼ 8am-5pm), 100m west of the dock.

Regular boats (US$7, 1½ hours) leave Los Chiles at 1pm and 4pm daily, with extra boats at 11am and 2:30pm if demand is high. Boats leave San Carlos for Los Chiles at 1pm and 3:30pm, with extras scheduled as needed. The Nicaragua–Costa Rican border is not known for its reliability, so make sure you confirm these times before setting out. While cruising Río San Juan, keep your fingers and toes in the boat as there are river sharks (we're not kidding).

Nicaragua charges a US$9 entry fee (paid in US dollars). Those making day trips to Lago de Nicaragua or El Castillo probably won't be charged the fee but should bring a passport and a few US dollars, just in case.

See p509 for details on crossing the border from Nicaragua.

Getting There & Away

Twelve buses run daily between Ciudad Quesada and Los Chiles (US$3, two hours), from 5am to 7:15pm. Buses to San José (US$5, five hours) depart at 5:30am and 3:30pm. A bus to Upala (US$2.50, 2½ hours), leaving at 5am and 2pm, passes by the entrance to Caño Negro Refuge. Regular boat transport is limited to shuttles across the Nicaraguan border (US$7) and various day trips throughout the region.

REFUGIO NACIONAL DE VIDA SILVESTRE CAÑO NEGRO

World-renowned, this expanse of swamp marsh is defined by the Río Frío, which breaks its banks every rainy season to pour out an 800-hectare lake. Here anglers search for that elusive 20kg snook and birders search for roseate spoonbills, great potoos, northern jacanas, boat-billed herons and ospreys. January to March is the best time to spot large flocks though illegal poaching and logging are putting the reserve in grave danger.

Most of the year the refuge is only reached by boat from Los Chiles or Puerto Viejo de Sarapiquí. In the dry season you can take a horse trail from the village of Caño Negro.

LA VIRGEN

Steeped in the tangled shores of the wild and scenic Río Sarapiquí, La Virgen prospered in the heyday of the banana trade (no double-entendres here). Today it's a little-known destination for world-class kayaking and rafting. Businesses line the highway. Check email at **Internet Café** (per hr US$1.50; ☼ 8am-9pm Mon-Sat).

The area has numerous budget options. Our pick of the litter is **Rancho Leona** (☎ 761 1019; www.rancholeona.com; dm US$12; ⊠), a shady, riverside spot where you can swap tales of gnarly rapids, detox in the Native American-style sweat lodge and enjoy family-style dinners. Rooms (some private) share hot-water showers and a communal kitchen. **Kayaking trips** (6hr trip per person incl lunch US$75) and guided hikes are arranged on an ad hoc basis.

Down the road is the friendly **Sarapiquí Outdoor Center** (☎ 761 1123; Sarapaqui outdoor@hotmail.com; d US$25, campsite US$5), where impeccable campsites overlook the river, with access to showers and bathrooms. The simple rooms are a bit overpriced. In addition to rafting and kayaking trips, the owners also arrange horseback rides and guided hikes to a nearby waterfall.

All the buses between Ciudad Quesada and Puerto Viejo de Sarapiquí make stops in La Virgen.

PUERTO VIEJO DE SARAPIQUÍ
pop 6000

Banana and coffee booms once made Puerto Viejo the country's most important port. Largely reclaimed by the jungle, today it is redefined as a slightly seedy border town. It isn't to be confused with touristy Puerto Viejo de Talamanca on the Caribbean coast. There are, however, great opportunities here for bird-watching, rafting, boating and jungle exploration.

Banco Popular changes money and has an ATM. **Internet Sarapiqui** (☼ 8am-10pm) is at the west end of town. Stop by **Souvenir Río Sarapiquí** (☎ 766 6727), on the main street, for information on birding, kayaking, white-water rafting and zip lining.

Sights & Activities

ESTACIÓN BIOLÓGICA LA SELVA

The Organization of Tropical Studies (OTS) runs a **biological research station** (☎ 524 0629; www.ots.ac.cr; s/d with shared bathroom US$56/70), 5km southeast of Puerto Viejo. On any given day, the station teems with scientists and students researching in the nearby private reserve. La Selva welcomes drop-ins, though it's best to phone ahead and reserve. Rooms here are basic, with fan and bunk beds (a few have doubles), but rates include all meals and guided hikes. You can day-trip here too (hikes US$26/40 per person for four/eight hours; 8am and 1:30pm daily). A taxi from Puerto Viejo costs US$5.

Sleeping & Eating

Cabinas Restaurant Monteverde (☎ 766 6236; s/d US$4/8) The cheapest digs in town are dark and dingy. An attached restaurant, with low prices, serves Tico fare.

Mi Lindo Sarapiquí (☎ 766 6281; s/d US$12/20; P) Rooms are simple but spacious and clean, and have hot showers and fans. The restaurant (mains US$4-9, open 8am to 10pm) offers some of the freshest seafood in town. Located on the south side of the soccer field.

Trinidad Lodge (☎ 213 0661, 381 0621; s/d US$15/20) Travelers rave about these rustic cabins on a working ranch with hearty home-cooked meals (US$4 to US$8), horse rentals and boat tours. Located on the Río San Juan across from the Nicaraguan border post, it's only accessible only by boat (US$5), departing at 11am from Puerto Viejo de Sarapiquí.

Posada Andrea Cristina B&B (☎ 766 6265; www .andreacristina.com; s/d/tr US$25/45/65) About 1km west of the center, this recommended B&B offers quiet garden cabins in a rain forest with fans and private hot-water bathrooms. Birders can scope the action while enjoying an outdoor breakfast. The owner, Alex Martínez, is an excellent guide and a passionate frontline conservationist.

Soda Judith (mains US$2-4; ☺ 6am-7pm) Early risers can grab brewed coffee, big breakfasts or an *empanada* to start the day at this *soda*, one block off the main road.

Getting There & Away

BOAT

There's regular service to Trinidad Lodge. You can arrange transportation anywhere along the river (seasonal conditions permit-ting) through independent boat captains. Short trips cost about US$10 per hour per person for a group of four, or US$20 per hour for a single person.

Serious voyages to Tortuguero or Barra del Colorado cost about US$350 for a round trip in a private boat. Rumor has it that from Trinidad you can take a public boat to Puerto San Juan on Tuesdays and Fridays, and look for further transportation there (write to us if it works!).

BUS

The bus terminal is across from the park. Empresarios Guapileños goes to Ciudad Quesada/San Carlos via La Virgen (US$1.50, three hours), departing at 5:30am, 9am, 2pm, 3:30pm and 7:30pm; its buses go to Guápiles (US$1.50, one hour) eight times daily from 5:30am to 6:40pm. Autotransportes Sarapiquí goes to San José (US$2.50, two hours), with frequent departures until 5:30pm.

GUANACASTE

Like the prized, gnarled shade tree the region is named after, there is something singular and stubborn about Guanacaste. It could be the cowboy culture, which consumes cattle fairs and saddle soap like the rest of the country craves shopping centers. Call it the backwater blessing – a slow, colonial pace means that locals are laid-back and cordial, and roads still lead to nowhere. Of course, this is all poised to change.

With Liberia's expanding international airport, the city is fast in line to being crowned Costa Rica's second city, a status backed up by its easy accessibility to the Interamericana. And although Guanacaste's cities are seemingly at a standstill, mother nature looms large in the background. Volcanoes, hot springs and horse packing trips take travelers high above the cowboy plains. Rare, dry tropical forests lead into remote Pacific beaches, turtle havens with riotously sweet surf breaks. In the name of adventure, Guanacaste seems on the verge of being tamed.

CAÑAS

pop 25,200

Hot, dusty streets, custom pick-ups and machete cowboys mean you've made it to Cañas. It's typically rural Latin America, where the gait is slow and businesses lock up for lunch. At the crossroads of the Interamericana and the eastern road to Monteverde, Cañas provides visitors with a base for organizing rafting trips on the nearby Río Corobicí or for exploring Parque Nacional Palo Verde.

Wildlife tours take gentle float trips down the Río Corobicí. Book with **Safaris Corobicí** (☎ 669 6091; www.safariscorobici.com), whose office is on the Interamericana, 4.5km north of Cañas.

Accommodations are geared more toward truckers than tourists. At the southeastern end of town, **Cabinas Corobicí** (☎ 669 0241; cnr Av 2 & Calle 5; r per person US$9) maintains comfortable, good-sized rooms. Ask for a standard room at **Hotel El Corral** (☎ 669 1467; s/d US$15/25; ❄), right on the Interamericana. Optional extras include air-con, hot shower and TV. The quieter rooms are in back. With the best chow mien and views in town, **Restaurante El Primero** (US$2-4; ☺ 11am-10pm) sits across from the church.

Getting There & Away

Terminal Cañas sits on the north end of town.

Liberia (US$1.35, 1½hr) Eight departures daily.
Puntarenas (US$2; 2hr) Nine departures daily.
San José (US$3; 3½hr) At 4am, 4:50am, 6am, 9:30am, 12:30pm, 1:40pm and 5pm.
Tilarán (US$0.75; 45min) Eight departures daily.
Upala (US$2; 2hr) Five buses daily.

PARQUE NACIONAL PALO VERDE

Palo Verde has the greatest concentrations of waterfowl and shorebirds in Central America, with over 300 recorded bird species. Visitors can spot large flocks of herons (including rare black-crowned night herons), storks, spoonbills and scarlet macaws. When the dry season begins in December, birds congregate in lakes and marshes, trees lose their leaves and the flocks become easier to see.

Visitors can **camp** (US$2) near the Palo Verde ranger station, with toilets and hot-water showers. Additional dorms at the **ranger station** (☎ 200 0125; dm US$10) have mosquito nets and cold showers. Find good accommodations and information at the **Hacienda Palo Verde Research Station** (☎ 661 4717; www.ots.ac.cr; s/d US$55/100, meals US$10), run by the Organization of Tropical Studies (OTS). It also guides recommended **tours** (half-/full-day US$15/30) and **horseback riding** (US$6 per hr per person) excursions.

Palo Verde is 30km west of Cañas. Buses connecting Cañas and Liberia (see p587) can drop you at the ACT office on the Interamericana, opposite the turnoff to the park. If you call the office in advance, rangers may be able to drive you on the gravel road from here into the **park entrance** (☎ 200 0125; admission US$6).

RESERVA BIOLÓGICA LOMAS BARBUDAL

The 2646-hectare Lomas de Barbudal reserve forms a cohesive unit with Palo Verde, and protects several species of endangered trees such as mahogany and rosewood as well as the common and quite spectacular *corteza amarilla*. In March all the yellow cortezas in the forest burst into bloom on the same day, creating a four-day profusion of color. Endangered birds spotted here include king vultures and scarlet macaws.

THE WATERFALL HUNT

If you're not one to hop on the Interbus and cruise into adventure with the air-con on, we've got one for you. Getting to **Volcán Tenorio** (admission US$6), one of Costa Rica's newest parks, isn't easy. But since there is no public transportation, you're liable to have it to yourself – if you don't run into a tapir.

The hook? A chilly cascade the color of gaudy gemstones, part of the Río Celeste. Refresh yourself then follow through ephiphyte forests and fumaroles to bubbling hot spots and thermal baths (which may be scalding, so your best bet is to hire a guide). Reaching the crater requires overnight camping. No trail is marked.

Take any bus headed to Upala. At Bijagua you can hire a taxi (US$30) – some local's worn-out Cavelier – or arrange in advance with local guide **Alexander Ordónez** (☎ 359 6235 in Spanish; rioceleste2011@yahoo.com) for pick up. Alex offers a wealth of information; his father helped pioneer the area and first discovered the waterfall while tapir hunting (yes, these were the old days). His warm, family-run **Río Celeste Lodge** (campsite US$2, r per person US$5), modest rooms with home cooking and plenty of tales to tell.

COSTA RICA

The **information center** (entry to the park US$6; ◷ 7am-4pm) offers maps, though you have to wade across the Río Cabuyo to access the actual reserve and a small network of hiking trails. There is no camping or public transportation. Buses can leave you at the turnoff to Lomas Barbudal at Pijije (on the Interamericana, 2km northwest of Bagaces). Walk or use a 4WD for the remaining 7km.

LIBERIA
pop 45,100

This sleepy and hot provincial capital has long been a ranching and transportation center but the relatively new international airport is making it the preferred hub for foreign travelers. And why not – visitors find Liberia manageable, dare we say, charming? It's a quick hop from here to the popular Nicoya beaches and a great regional base to explore Rincón de la Vieja and Santa Rosa national parks. Don't expect to get errands done on lunch hour, though. Some things must remain sacred.

The colonial charm of Calle Real, south of the parque central, has transformed it into backpacker central; a wander through other areas reveals a scruffier ambience.

Late July rings in the raucous festivities of **Guanacaste Day** (July 25) at the fair grounds on the west side of town. The cherry-on-top is the *tope* (horse parade) – a mix of rodeo and country fair complete with a cattle auction, dancing, drinking and bull-riding.

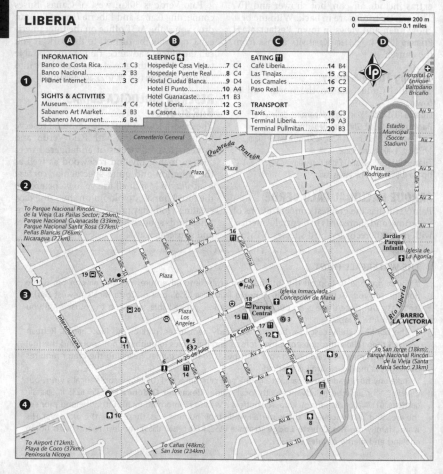

LIBERIA

INFORMATION	
Banco de Costa Rica.............1 C3	
Banco Nacional.....................2 B3	
Pl@net Internet.....................3 C3	
SIGHTS & ACTIVITIES	
Museum..............................4 C4	
Sabanero Art Market............5 B3	
Sabanero Monument............6 B4	
SLEEPING 🏠	
Hospedaje Casa Vieja.........7 C4	
Hospedaje Puente Real.......8 C4	
Hostal Ciudad Blanca..........9 D4	
Hotel El Punto...................10 A4	
Hotel Guanacaste.............11 B3	
Hotel Liberia...................12 C3	
La Casona......................13 C4	
EATING 🍴	
Café Liberia....................14 B4	
Las Tinajas.....................15 C3	
Los Camales...................16 C2	
Paso Real......................17 C3	
TRANSPORT	
Taxis...........................18 C3	
Terminal Liberia..............19 A3	
Terminal Pullmitan...........20 B3	

0 — 200 m
0 — 0.1 miles

Cementerio General

Quebrada Panteón

Plaza

Plaza

Plaza

To Parque Nacional Rincón de la Vieja (Las Pailas Sector; 25km); Parque Nacional Guanacaste (33km); Parque Nacional Santa Rosa (37km); Peñas Blancas (76km); Nicaragua (72km)

Market

Plaza

Plaza Los Angeles

City Hall

Iglesia Inmaculada Concepción de María

Parque Central

Av Central

Av 25 de Julio

Interamericana

Hospital Dr Enrique Baltodano Briceño

Estadio Municipal (Soccer Stadium)

Plaza Rodriguez

Jardin y Parque Infantil

Iglesia de La Agonía

Río Liberia

BARRIO LA VICTORIA

To San Jorge (18km); Parque Nacional Rincón de la Vieja (Santa María Sector; 23km)

To Airport (12km); Playa de Coco (37km); Peninsula Nicoya

To Cañas (48km); San José (234km)

Information

Pl@net Internet (Calle Real btwn Avs Central & 2; per hr US$1; ☻ 8am-10pm) offers travelers speedy machines in spacious, air-con cubes. Both **Banco Nacional** (Av 25 de Julio btwn Calles 6 & 8) and **Banco de Costa Rica** (cnr Calle Central & Av 1) have 24-hour ATMs.

The useful **Sabanero Art Market & Tourist Information Center** (☎ 362 6926; www.elsabanero.8k .com; Calle 8 btwn Avs Central & 1) provides bus schedules, tour information and taxi assistance. A number of area hotels provide good deals on car rentals.

Sleeping

Hotel Liberia (☎ 666 0161; Calle Real btwn Avs Central & 2; s/d US$7/10, with bathroom US$11/20) At the heart of this faded backpacker haven you'll find a courtyard abuzz with travelers. Rooms with worn bunks and crumbling cement walls beg for a remodel, but the staff are attentive and helpful.

Hotel Guanacaste (☎ 666 0085; www.higuanacaste.com; cnr Av 3 & Calle 12; dm/s US$7/15) Convenient to buses but slim on charm, this cement HI-affiliate has small windowless rooms with all the ambience of a truck stop. That said, it's very clean.

Hospedaje Puente Real (☎ 666 1112; Calle Real btwn Av 8 & 10; r per person without/with air-con US$10/14; ☒) This beautiful colonial home with sloping wood ceilings, balcony and original fixtures is a pleasant lodging run mostly by the owner's chatty teenagers. Beds are comfortable and the shared baths are squeaky clean. Breakfast is included.

Hospedaje Casa Vieja (☎ 665 5826; Av 4 btwn Calle Real & Calle 2; r per person without/with air-con US$14/18; ☒) A romantic haven for couples with Victorian furniture, rose-colored tiles and sheer gauzy curtains. There's an attractive patch of lawn out back and a small kitchen for fixing breakfast.

La Casona (☎ 666 2971; marijozuniga@hotmail.com; cnr Calle Real & Av 6; s/d with bathroom US$14/28; ☒) Aside from the indifferent welcome, this pink, wooden house seeks to comfort and cheer, with rockers, bright colors and natural fibers. The TV room is perfect for lounging.

Hotel El Punto (☎ 666 8493; Interamericana btwn Avs 25 de Julio & 2; s/d/tr/q incl breakfast US$21/41/48/53) Once an elementary school, El Punto is now one of the chicest hotels in Liberia. Rooms here include ultra-modern loft apartments with private showers, small kitchens, minimalist accents and MOMA-worthy art.

Hostal Ciudad Blanca (☎ 666 3962; Av 4 btwn Calles 1 & 3; s/d US$30/50; ☒) This completely refurbished colonial mansion offers attractive rooms with cable TV and hot-water bathrooms. The attached restaurant-bar oozes charm – a perfect spot for a nightcap.

Eating

Café Liberia (Calle 8 btwn Avs 25 de Julio & 2; snacks US$1-2; ☻ 10am-8pm Mon-Sat) This hip travelers' haunt serves stiff espresso, strong tea and home-made pastries.

Los Camales (Calle Central btwn 7 & 5; plates US$2-5) This women's collective serves traditional Guanacaste food – great pots of chicken and salsa for the masses.

Las Tinajas (Calle 2 btwn Av Central & 1; meals US$4-7) On the west side of the parque central, this is the spot to watch the town mutts run around while sipping a cold beer.

Paso Real (☎ 666 3455; Av Central btwn Calles Real & 2; mains US$5-10; ☻ 11am-10pm) It's worth shelling out for seafood here with deadly good mussels au gratin and snappy service. It's upstairs from Tienda la Nueva. The coveted balcony offers breezy views of the parque central.

Getting There & Away

AIR

Aeropuerto Internacional Daniel Oduber Quirós (LIR) is 12km east of Liberia. International airlines currently landing here include American Airlines, Continental and Delta. NatureAir and Sansa fly daily between Liberia and San José (with connections all over the country) for about US$80 one way, US$160 round trip. A taxi to Liberia costs US$10.

BUS

From **Terminal Pullmitan** (Av 5 btwn Calles 10 & 12):
La Cruz/Peñas Blancas (US$1.25; 2hr) Departs 5:30am, 8:30am, 9am, 11am, noon, 2pm, 4:45pm and 8pm.
Managua, Nicaragua (US$10; 5hr) Departs 8:30am, 9:30am and 1pm (buy ticket in advance).
Playa del Coco (US$0.75; 1hr) Departs 5:30am, 8am, 9am, 12:30pm, 2pm, 4pm and 6pm.
San José (US$5; 4hr) Departs hourly 6am to 7pm.

From **Terminal Liberia** (Av 7 btwn Calles 12 & 14):
Cañas (US$1; 1½hr) Departs 5:45am, 1:30pm, 4:30pm and 5:10pm.
Nicoya, via Filadelfia & Santa Cruz (US$1.25; 2hr) Alfaro departs hourly from 4am to 8pm.
Playa Hermosa, Playa Panamá (US$0.75; 1¼hr) Tralapa departs 7:30am, 11:30am, 3:30pm, 5:30pm, 7pm.
Playa Tamarindo (US$1.25; 2hr) Departs 5:15am, 7am, 10:15am, 12:15pm, 2:30pm and 6pm.
Puntarenas (US$1.40; 3hr) Departs from 5am to 3:30pm.

COSTA RICA

PARQUE NACIONAL RINCÓN DE LA VIEJA

Active Volcán Rincón de la Vieja (1895m) is the steamy main attraction, but the region bubbles with fumaroles, tepid springs, and steaming, flatulent mud pits. (If this doesn't sound like fun, you never read Dr Seuss). All these can be visited on well-maintained but sometimes steep trails, and if you've never visited Yellowstone National Park, this is a good substitute.

The park is home to 300 bird species as well as morpho butterflies, tapirs, monkeys and pumas. Watch out for ticks, especially in grassy areas – wear closed shoes and trousers. About 700m west of Las Pailas ranger station, the Sendero Cangreja leads 5km to **Catarata la Cangreja**, a waterfall plunging from a high cliff into a blue lagoon ideal for swimming. Hiking the volcano **Rincón de la Vieja** is an adventurous 16km round trip. Take a guide or be extra careful to avoid stumbling into geysers (it's happened).

The park is 25km northeast of Liberia, reached by a poor road. There are two entrances with a park ranger station, each with camping areas. Most visitors enter through the **Las Pailas sector** (☎ 661 8139; admission US$7) on its western flank. (A private road is needed to reach the park and costs US$2 per person.) Going east from the ranger station, a circular trail (about 8km) takes you past boiling mud pools (Las Pailas), sulphurous fumaroles and a miniature volcano. Heading north, trails lead 8km one way to the summit area. There are two waterfalls to the west of the ranger station, the largest dropping from a cliff into a lagoon where you can swim.

The **Santa María ranger station** to the east is the closest to the sulphurous hot springs and also has an observation tower and a nearby waterfall.

Sleeping

Both ranger stations have **camping** (US$2) with water, pit toilets, showers, tables and grills. No fuel is available, so bring wood, charcoal or a camping stove. Mosquito nets or insect repellent are needed in the wet season.

Just 3km from the park's Santa María sector, **Rinconcito Lodge** (☎ 200 0074; www.rinconcito lodge.com; s/d US$18/30, campsite US$3; meals US$4-6) is a recommended budget option. Cabins are attractive and rustic and the scenery whispers pastoral and lovely. The lodge is the best

place around for inexpensive package deals. Regular shuttles provide transportation to and from Liberia.

Getting There & Away

The Las Pailas sector is accessible via a 20km gravel road beginning at a signed turnoff from the Interamericana 5km north of Liberia. To reach the park you must use a private road (US$2 per person). Drivers must have 4WD in the rainy season. There's no public transportation, but hotels in Liberia can arrange transport from Liberia for around US$15 per person each way. Alternately, you can hire a 4WD taxi for about US$25 each way.

The Santa María ranger station is accessible via a rougher road beginning at Barrio la Victoria in Liberia. There is no public bus service. Taxis cost US$45 each way.

PARQUE NACIONAL SANTA ROSA

The park is a wild space of pristine beaches, tropical dry forests and savannahs of thorn trees and swaying *jaragua* grass. For visitors it's sensory delight. The wildlife on Península Santa Elena is both varied and prolific, especially during the dry season. The rainy months of September and October are best for turtle watching. Here you'll find *arribadas* (mass-nesting) of up to 8000 olive ridley sea turtles.

The surfing at Playa Naranjo is world renowned, especially near Witch's Rock and Ollie's Point.

Buses between Liberia and the Nicaragua border of Peñas Blancas stop at the entrance; rangers can help you catch a return bus. You can also arrange private transportation from the hotels in Liberia for about US$15 per person round trip.

Information

The **park entrance** (☎ 666 5051; admission US$6, campsite US$2; ⏰ 8am-4pm) is on the west side of the Interamericana, 35km north of Liberia. From there, it is another 7km walk to the **park headquarters** (☎ 666 5051), where you'll find an information center, campground, museum, research station and nature trail. This is also the administrative center for the Area de Conservación Guanacaste (ACG) and has information about Parque Nacional Rincón de la Vieja and Parque Nacional Guanacaste. Reserve ahead to stay at the **research station** (dm US$20, meals US$3-7), with bunk rooms, cold showers and electricity.

There is a shady developed **campground** (US$2) close to the park headquarters, with a picnic area, toilets and cold-water showers. A 12km trail leads down to the coast to Playa Naranjo. The campsites have pit toilets and showers, but no potable water – bring your own. To drive you need a high-clearance 4WD vehicle for river crossings, inquire with rangers for road conditions.

Sights & Activities

Playa Naranjo, a spectacular beach to the south, has good surfing and is close to the **Witch's Rock** break, famous for its 3m curls (not recommended for beginners). There's a campground with pit toilets, but no potable water. Call ahead regarding road conditions. Although this is a beach break, there are rocks near the river mouth, and be especially careful near the estuary as it's a rich feeding ground for crocodiles during the tide changes. The surfing is equally legendary off Playa Portero Grande at **Ollie's Point**, which boasts the best right-hander in Costa Rica.

The historic Santa Rosa Hacienda unfortunately burnt down in 2001, but has now been completely rebuilt. A small **museum** inside describes the 1856 battle fought here and has displays on Costa Rican life in the 19th century. A few antique artifacts that survived the fire are on display. Another exhibit deals with the ecological significance and wildlife of the park.

Near the museum is a 1km **nature trail**, with signs explaining the varied plant and animal life of Santa Rosa. You will see a fine selection of the park's 240 species of trees and shrubs, and 253 species of bird. Monkeys, snakes, iguanas and other animals are also seen regularly, with bats being the most common: 50 or 60 species have been identified here.

The best turtle beach is **Playa Nancite** in the south, and during September and October you may see as many as 8000 olive ridley turtles on the beach at once. Nancite is restricted, but permission can be obtained from the park service to see this spectacle. Flashlights and flash photography are prohibited, as is fishing and hunting.

PARQUE NACIONAL GUANACASTE

Parque Nacional Guanacaste is an eastern extension of the habitat of Parque Nacional Santa Rosa, with dry tropical rain forest climbing toward the humid cloud forest of Volcán Orosí (1487m) and Volcán Cacao (1659m). The protection of this ancient migratory route between the coast and highlands allows various animals to continue as they have for millennia.

Hiking trails are mostly undeveloped as the area is primarily used for scientific research. For information, contact the **ACG headquarters** (☎ 666 5051) in Parque Nacional Santa Rosa. Day tours from Liberia include a horseback ride to Volcán Cacao.

PEÑAS BLANCAS & LA CRUZ

Peñas Blancas is a busy border herding traffic through to Rivas, Nicaragua. As there is no lodging here, spend the night and change money in the hill town of **La Cruz**, 20km south. Shoestringers and migrant workers grab their Zs at **Cabinas Santa Rita** (☎ 679 9062; s/d US$3/6, with air-con US$13/21; 🅿) , in dark, clean doubles. Overlooking Bahía Salinas, German-run **Hotel Bella Vista** (☎ 679 8060; www.bavarian-construc tions.com/hotelbv; per person with breakfast US$15, dinner extra US$5; 🖥 🅿) offers well-furnished rooms with hot water, cable TV and terraces. Guests can relax at the pool or enjoy *casados* and beer at the attached restaurant.

GETTING TO RIVAS, NICARAGUA

Peñas Blancas–Rivas is a busy border crossing so get there early. The entry fee into Nicaragua is US$7. There is no charge to enter Costa Rica, but leaving Nicaragua costs US$2, payable in US dollars only (banks on either side will change local colones and córdobas for dollars).

The border posts, generally open 6am to 8pm daily, are 1km apart; you can hire a golf cart (US$2) to make the run. Hordes of totally useless touts will offer to 'guide' you through the simple crossing. If you let them carry your luggage, they will charge you whatever they want. From the border, buses to Rivas (US$0.75, 45 minutes) depart every 30 minutes.

Alternatively, taxis on the Nicaraguan side of the border can whisk you to Rivas (US$6), the San Jorge ferry (US$8), San Juan del Sur (US$8) and Granada (US$25).

See p502 for information on crossing the border from Nicaragua.

PENÍNSULA DE NICOYA

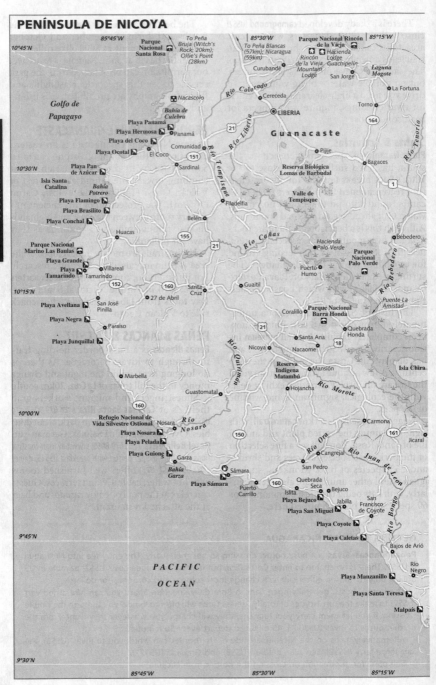

In La Cruz, the Transportes Deldú counter sells tickets and stores bags. Buses to Peñas Blancas (US$1, 45 minutes) go at 5am, 7am, 7:45am, 10:45am, 1:20pm and 4:10pm. Those to Bahía Salinas (US$1, one hour) depart at 7am, noon and 4pm. Transportes Deldú goes to Liberia (US$1, two hours) roughly every two hours between 6:15am and 6:30pm. Buses for San José (US$5, five hours) go at 5:45am, 8am, 10am, 11am, 12:20pm, 2pm and 4:15pm.

PENÍNSULA DE NICOYA

The Nicoya Peninsula is a sun-drenched strip of land with over 130km of stunning coastline backed by dry, tropical rain forest. As looks go, it's a beauty and the most popular tourist destination in the whole country.

Much of the Nicoya Peninsula is home to the *sabanero*, Guanacaste's cowboy. While the coastline experiences a real-estate frenzy of colonizing gringos, the interior is still the heartland of farming and ranching. Some spots do still exist where you need to order your *casado* in Spanish.

In the past, poor access kept development in check. The recently constructed Friendship Bridge and the international airport in Liberia have created fast-track access. The resort mania around Playa Panamá and Playa Tambor is quickly spreading south. With record numbers of foreigners flocking to Nicoya, it's more important than ever for visitors to be conscientious about their impact.

PLAYA DEL COCO

Connected by good roads to San José and just 37km west of Liberia, El Coco is the most accessible of the peninsula's beaches. There's a party atmosphere and plenty of marine activities, but the town itself is scruffy. Some might like its chaotic, unpolished feel, but a burgeoning ambience of condo villages and a littered coastline has beach connoisseurs headed elsewhere.

In mid-July, the **Fiesta de la Virgen del Mar** features a colorful boat procession in the harbor and a horse pageant.

Information

Surf the internet with a tall, cold papaya shake at **Internet Juice Bar** (8am-9pm; per hr US$1), on the road into town. It also rents mountain bikes for US$8 per day.

COSTA RICA

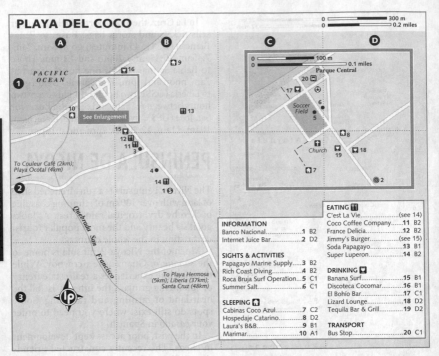

PLAYA DEL COCO

INFORMATION	
Banco Nacional.....................**1** B2	
Internet Juice Bar..................**2** D2	

SIGHTS & ACTIVITIES	
Papagayo Marine Supply......**3** B2	
Rich Coast Diving.................**4** B2	
Roca Bruja Surf Operation....**5** C1	
Summer Salt.........................**6** C1	

SLEEPING	
Cabinas Coco Azul................**7** C2	
Hospedaje Catarino..............**8** D2	
Laura's B&B.........................**9** B1	
Marimar.............................**10** A1	

EATING	
C'est La Vie.....................(see 14)	
Coco Coffee Company........**11** B2	
France Delicia....................**12** B2	
Jimmy's Burger...............(see 15)	
Soda Papagayo..................**13** B1	
Super Luperon...................**14** B2	

DRINKING	
Banana Surf......................**15** B1	
Discoteca Cocomar............**16** B1	
El Bohío Bar......................**17** C1	
Lizard Lounge....................**18** D2	
Tequila Bar & Grill.............**19** D2	

TRANSPORT	
Bus Stop............................**20** C1	

The Banco Nacional exchanges US dollars and traveler's checks and has an ATM.

Activities

A prime site to dive or snorkel, El Coco's diverse marine life includes stingrays, turtles, dolphins and whales. Recommended outfitters include **Rich Coast Diving** (☎ 670 0176; www .richcoastdiving.com) and Swiss-owned **Summer Salt** (☎ 670 0380; www.summer-salt.com; two dives US$70).

If you want to surf, local boat charters access Witch's Rock and Ollie's Point in Parque Nacional Santa Rosa. **Roca Bruja Surf Operation** (☎ 381 9166; www.rocabruja.50g.com) is a licensed operator. An eight-hour tour to both breaks is US$250 for five people.

Sport fishing, sailing and sea kayaking are also popular. **Papagayo Marine Supply** (☎ 670 0354; papagayo@infoweb.co.cr) offers info and supplies for anglers. The preferred beach for swimming and snorkeling is **Playa Ocotal**, 4km away.

Sleeping & Eating

If only the lodgings were half as attractive as the dining options. Budget digs have cold-water showers unless otherwise noted.

Hospedaje Catarino (☎ 670 0156; r per person US$8; 🖳) If you're shooting for cheap this place should do it, but a nearby disco might short-change your shuteye.

Marimar (☎ 670 1212; r per person US$14; 🖳) Near the water, offers ample, unglorified rooms with starchy white sheets.

Cabinas Coco Azul (☎ 670 0431; r US$23) The rooms here are superclean, run by Ray, an affable retiree.

Laura's B&B (☎ 670 0751; www.laurashousecr.com; s/d with fan US$25/35, r with air-con US$35-45; 🗶 🕏) Laura's B&B, 250m east of Lizard Lounge, is inviting, cozy and meticulous. It offers all the perks and a terribly tempting miniature pool surrounded by deck chairs.

Coco Coffee Company (bagels US$2; 🕑 7am-4pm Mon-Sat) Wake up to the cappuccinos and bacon-and-egg sandwiches here, an expat magnet if we ever saw one.

Soda Papagayo (daily special US$3.50; 🕑 7am-4pm) The town's best *casados* are here. Dine at plastic tables under the tin roof.

France Delicia (meals US$3-14; 🕑 10am-7:30pm Mon-Sat) This is a take-out kitchen that whips up quiche, salads and daily specials from scratch.

Super Luperon (🕑 7:30-8pm) Next to Banco Nacional this food warehouse stocks all things edible, its secret weapon is the authentic French-run bakery C'est la Vie. We dare you not to scarf your warm almond croissant or baguette while waiting in line to pay.

Couleur Cafe (☎ 670 1696; Triangulo los Mongos, road to Ocotal; mains US$8-15; 🕑 11am-2:30pm & 6pm-10pm Tue-Sat, 6pm-10pm Sun) This is further evidence of the French invasion – a new Belgian-French-run restaurant and bar in a knockout setting. The tropical garden has thatched tables and bamboo stylings. Start with cocktails and brie pastries or eggplant with goat's cheese. Mains include big salads and roasted duck and Sunday means a huge BBQ. It's definitely worth the taxi out.

On the plaza, El Bohío Bar is a favorite watering hole. A hotspot for liver damage, Banana Surf serves perennial favorites such as Jaegermeister and Red Bull. Tequila Bar & Grill is the spot for margarita pitchers.

Cut the rug at Lizard Lounge or Discoteca Cocomar on the beach, the biggest (and sweatiest) dance-fest around. Finally, hit **Jimmy's Burger** (burgers US$2; 🕑 3pm-3am) trailer for a post-party patty.

Getting There & Away

Taxis between Playa del Coco and Playa Hermosa or Ocotal cost between US$5 and US$7. Buses stop on the parque central, across from the police station.

Filadelfia, for connection to Santa Cruz (US$0.75; 45min) At 11:30am and 4:30pm.

Liberia (US$0.75; 1hr) Departs 5:30am, 7am, 9am, 11am, 1pm, 3pm, 5pm and 6pm.

San José (US$5.25; 5hr) Pullman leaves 4am, 8am, 2pm.

PLAYA TAMARINDO

A little more than 30 years ago Tamarindo was home to 21 families. Then *Endless Summer II* was made and it burgeoned into southern California, without adequate plumbing and roads to support it. The expats who first came to take refuge in a *pura vida* lifestyle (and create tourism) now look at their Frankenstein a bit bewildered.

The question? Sustainability. Alas, the sea turtles are long gone, and in their place are high-rise condos. A constant stream of delivery and construction trucks rip down the strip, covering the boutique eateries, souvenir stands, even the sarong-clad *turistas* from Denver and London, in a thick coat of golden dust.

To be fair, plenty of people do enjoy themselves in Tamarindo. It is one place that absolutely caters to visitors. If you came to Costa Rica to party all night long, hook up with strangers, swim and surf some great (but crowded) waves, welcome to paradise.

Information

Tourist information is available from any of the tour operators in town. A helpful website is www.tamarindobeach.org.

Bookstore **Jaime Peligro** (☎ 820 9004; 🕑 10am-8pm Mon-Sat, noon-5pm Sun) sells new and used books, CDs and DVDs. Internet cafés are plentiful, with **@Internet** (per hr US$4; 🕑 9am-9pm) as good as any. For laundry service, hit **Backwash** (per kg US$1.25; 🕑 Mon-Sat). There's an ATM at **San José Bank** (☎ 653 1617; 🕑 8:30am-3:30pm), which also exchanges US dollars cash and traveler's checks.

For a refreshingly frank vision of modern Tamarindo, pick up a copy of the local 'zine *Flyswatter*.

Dangers & Annoyances

The tourist invasion has left Tamarindo grappling with growing drug and prostitution problems. Vendors openly ply their wares (and their women) on the main road by the

---

CHARGE IT! – COSTA RICA'S TOP FIVE SURF SPOTS

Costa Rica offers some great surfing. We asked Greg Gordon of Costa Rica Surf Report to rank the country's top breaks and he came up with the following. For a daily surf report, log onto www.crsurf.com.

Pavones (p622) Costa Rica's legendary longest left.

Playa Hermosa (p606) Monster waves, day-in, day-out.

Playa Grande (p596) Wilderness waves in a national park.

Salsa Brava (p567) A big bruiser, thanks to the rough reef.

Witch's Rock/Ollie's Point (p589) Wild, out-of-the-way waves in Santa Rosa.

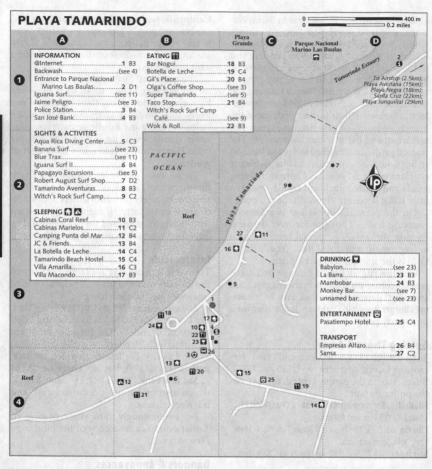

PLAYA TAMARINDO

0	400 m
0	0.2 miles

INFORMATION
@Internet...................................**1** B3
Backwash..............................(see 4)
Entrance to Parque Nacional
  Marino Las Baulas...............**2** D1
Iguana Surf........................(see 11)
Jaime Peligro.......................(see 3)
Police Station..........................**3** B4
San José Bank.........................**4** B3

SIGHTS & ACTIVITIES
Aqua Rica Diving Center..........**5** C3
Banana Surf.......................(see 23)
Blue Trax...........................(see 11)
Iguana Surf II.........................**6** B4
Papagayo Excursions............(see 5)
Robert August Surf Shop.........**7** D2
Tamarindo Aventuras................**8** B3
Witch's Rock Surf Camp.........**9** C2

SLEEPING
Cabinas Coral Reef..................**10** B3
Cabinas Marielos....................**11** C2
Camping Punta del Mar........**12** B4
JC & Friends...........................**13** B4
La Botella de Leche..................**14** C4
Tamarindo Beach Hostel........**15** C4
Villa Amarilla...........................**16** C3
Villa Macondo........................**17** B3

EATING
Bar Nogui.............................**18** B3
Botella de Leche....................**19** C4
Gil's Place.............................**20** B4
Olga's Coffee Shop...............(see 3)
Super Tamarindo..................(see 5)
Taco Stop.............................**21** B4
Witch's Rock Surf Camp
  Café....................................(see 9)
Wok & Roll...........................**22** B3

DRINKING
Babylon...............................(see 23)
La Barra.................................**23** B3
Mambobar.............................**24** B3
Monkey Bar...........................(see 7)
unnamed bar........................(see 23)

ENTERTAINMENT
Pasatiempo Hotel...................**25** C4

TRANSPORT
Empresas Alfaro.....................**26** B4
Sansa....................................**27** C2

Playa Grande

Parque Nacional Marino Las Baulas

Tamarindo Estuary

To Airstrip (2.5km);
Playa Avellana (15km);
Playa Negra (18km);
Santa Cruz (22km);
Playa Junquillal (29km)

PACIFIC OCEAN

Playa Tamarindo

Reef

Reef

---

rotunda, and some bars can get rough at closing time when everyone has had a little too much of everything.

Also, be aware that theft is a problem. Leave your hotel room locked, use a safe and don't leave valuables on the beach.

Activities
SURFING
The most popular wave around Tamarindo is a medium-sized right-hander that breaks directly in front of the Diriá Hotel. The waters here are full of beginner surfers learning the ropes. There is also a good left that's fed by the river mouth, a spot also popular with crocodiles during the rising tide (coincidently the best time to surf). Locals know a few other

spots in the area, but we're certainly not going to ruin their fun – ask around.

More advanced surfers will appreciate the bigger, faster and less-crowded waves at Avellana & Negra (p596) and Junquillal (p596) to the south and Playa Grande (p596) to the north. Note that the best months for surfing coincide with the rainy season.

Surf schools charge US$30 for 1½ to two-hour lessons. Often you can keep the board for a few hours beyond that to do some practice. All outfits can organize excursions to popular breaks, rent equipment and give surf lessons. If you're going to be surfing a lot, it's worth it to buy a board here or in Jacó, then sell it when the trip is over. For surfing outfitters try:

Banana Surf (☎ 653 1270; www.bananasurfclub.com) This Argentinean-run outfit has the fairest prices in town on new and used boards.

Iguana Surf (☎ 653 0148; www.iguanasurf.net) Has two locations. Surf taxi service goes to Playa Grande (US$10 per person) and Playa Negra (US$25 per person).

Robert August Surf Shop (☎ 653 0114; rasurfshop@ yahoo.com) Based in the Best Western Tamarindo Vista Villas, this famous shop is an obligatory stop.

Witch's Rock Surf Camp (☎ 653 0239; www.witchs rocksurfcamp.com) Board rentals, surf camps, lessons and regular excursions to Witch's Rock and Ollie's Point (p588) are available, though pricey.

Tours

Local agencies offer boat trips, scuba diving, snorkeling, scooter rentals, and turtle observation. Many also rent equipment. The most reputable include the following agencies:

Agua Rica Diving Center (☎ 653 0094; www .aguarica.net)

Blue Trax (☎ 653 1705; www.bluetraxcr.com) For mountain biking.

Papagayo Excursions (☎ 653 0254; www.papagayo excursions.com)

Tamarindo Aventuras (☎ 653 0108; www.tamarindo adventures.net) For rentals.

Sleeping

Rates given are for high season but low season runs 25% cheaper.

Camping Punta del Mar (US$3) Hang with the local grunge. The bathrooms are primitive; watch your stuff.

La Botella de Leche (☎ 653 0189; www.botella deleche.com; dm US$8, s/d US$14/28; 🔀) Chaotic in that homey way, this Argentine-run hostel is attentive and attractive. Air-con keeps even the cramped rooms as fresh as a dairy case. The common area is studded with bean-bag chairs and fuzzy (yes, real) pets.

JC & Friends (☎ 374 8246; Calle Real; campsite US$9; dm/s/d US$11/15/30; 🔀 🖳) A great new option one block from the beach in front of Iguana Surf II, the first feature you'll notice is the cool blue pool. In addition, there are comfortable dorms, a pool table and congenial staff. Look for monkeys that visit to pig out on the fruit trees. Internet is free and there's a clean communal kitchen.

Tamarindo Beach Hostel (☎ 653 0944; dm US$12; 🔀 🖳) The flat-screen TV, wrap-around sofa and impeccable large kitchen let you know this is upmarket as hostels go. Just don't be

here when the pipes occasionally back up. The atmosphere is social and air-con ensures a comfortable night's sleep.

Cabinas Coral Reef (☎ 653 0291; s/d US$10/15) This is a decent-enough flophouse with shared bathrooms, dark rooms and just wafer-thin mattresses.

Cabinas Marielos (☎ 653 0141; d without/with air-con US$25/35; 🔀) You can squeeze some personality out of the bougainvillea, otherwise this option is nondescript, overpriced for single travelers, but amenable.

Villa Amarilla (☎ 653 0038; carpen@racsa.co.cr; d with/without bathroom US$45/30, extra person US$10; 🔀) A beachfront inn with a quaint atmosphere. All rooms have hot water, a fridge and safe, and share an outdoor kitchen.

Villas Macondo (☎ 653 0812; www.villasmacondo.com; s/d/tr US$30/35/45, with air-con US$50/55/65; 🔀 🖳) A warm and personal atmosphere makes this spot a nice retreat from the hubbub (although high-rises are coming up next door). Guests enjoy an inviting pool, communal kitchen and spacious, colorful rooms.

Eating

New eateries are always popping up in Tamarindo (and shutting down), so we list the classic favorites here. Get groceries at Super Tamarindo. Visitors are challenged to find cheap eats but the sushi is divine.

Olga's Coffee Shop (dishes US$1-3) Grab a stool at this Russian-owned café and sling back homemade pastries with organic coffee. Be nice, as Olga's not always chipper in the morning.

Taco Stop (dishes US$3-5) A happy Santa Fé ambience permeates this shady shack serving fresh tacos, shrimp and chicken burritos. Shoestringers will revel in the generous portions and low prices.

Gil's Place (dishes US$4-6) You can come to hear a real Queens accent but you might as well try a loaded breakfast burrito or tasty Mexican *tostada*. Gil's is simple, good food.

Witch's Rock Surf Camp Café (dishes US$4-7) Hunker down at this seafront surfer haven for hearty breakfasts and seriously stacked snacks (see the 'nachos as big as your ass'). It's a great spot to grab a cold one and banish your munchies.

Bar Nogui (dishes US$6-11) Upmarket *casados* feature grilled fish, mixed meats and unbelievable shrimp and lobster at this popular beachside restaurant. Come early for dinner or join the bank line out the door.

Wok & Roll (dishes US$9-15) In an open kitchen chef Kandice chops, wraps, woks and steams noodles, sushi and stir-fries before your hungry eyes. The tantalizing pan-Asian menu raises the stakes with original offerings like spicy ginger sesame or green bean noodles. Hands down the best Asian this side of San Francisco.

Drinking & Nightlife
The wild spot in town is Mambobar, where the mood can get downright predatory. The Monkey Bar, inside the Best Western, has a more low-key ladies' night on Friday.

The Pasatiempo Hotel has a great Tuesday night live-music jam. Wednesday night means Latin dancing at La Barra and Thursday night means reggae at Babylon. Any night of the week music pumps *loudly* at the unnamed bar, even if no-one is there.

Getting There & Away
AIR
The airstrip is 3km north of town. Sansa has 14 daily flights to and from San José (one way US$78), while NatureAir (US$80) has five.

BUS
Buses from San José (US$5, six hours) depart from the Empresas Alfaro office next to the police station at 3:30am, 5:45am and 1pm.

Catch the following buses at any point on the main road:
Liberia (US$1; 2hr) Departs 5:30am, 9am, 11:30am, 3pm and 5pm.
Santa Cruz (US$0.75; 1¼hr) At 6am, 9am, 11am, 3:30pm and 4pm.

PARQUE NACIONAL MARINO LAS BAULAS
This seaside reserve just north of Tamarindo village includes Playa Grande. It is a major surf destination and one of the most important nesting sites for the *baula* (leatherback turtle). The world's largest turtle, leatherbacks can top 300kg. Nesting season is October to March, when more than a hundred turtles can be seen laying their eggs during the course of a night.

Visitors must watch the activities from specified areas, accompanied by a guide or ranger, and flash photography or lights are not allowed, as they disturb the laying process.

The **park office** (☎ 653 0470; admission US$16) is by the northern entrance. Reserve a turtle tour in advance. A good way to begin your tour is with a visit to **El Mundo de la Tortuga** (☎ 653 0471; admission US$5; ☼ 4pm-dawn), an informative self-guided exhibit about leatherback turtles, near the northern end of the park. If you're looking for a volunteer project, the park office usually accepts volunteers to help monitor nesting.

PLAYA AVELLANA & PLAYA NEGRA
These popular surfing beaches have some of the best, most consistent waves in the area. One part of Avellana is known as 'Pequeño Hawaii' for its fast, hollow breaks. The beaches are 15km south of Tamarindo by road. The road is dismal and requires a 4WD in the wet season to cross three rivers. The difficult access keeps it refreshingly uncrowded.

Among the upmarket lodges, there are a few cheap options. **Cabinas Gregorios** (☎ 658 8319; per person US$4, campsite US$3) tests shoestringers with 'rooms' meaning open-air stalls with shared bathroom. Bring repellent! **Rancho Iguana Verde** (☎ 658 8310; r per person US$10) has six dark but reasonably clean rooms. All of the *cabinas* have *sodas* that serve basic meals. In Avellana, kick back at **Lola's on the Beach** (meals US$5-10) with pizza and a beer. In Playa Negra to the south, you'll find surfer outpost **Pablo's Picasso** (☎ 658 8158; dm US$9, r per person US$15, deluxe d US$45; ☒). Dorms and standard rooms share cold-water bathrooms. If your stomach's rumbling, take on the restaurant's half-kilo 'burger as big as your head.' Before leaving the area, you'll pass the French-owned **Playa Negra Surf Camp** (☎ 658 8140; playanegrasc@hotmail.com; s/d US$25/30), a great option for self-caterers since there's a fully equipped kitchen. The friendly owner Alan is eager to offer surf tips, and gives lessons for reasonable prices.

There is no public transport here, though surf camps in Tamarindo organize trips.

PLAYA JUNQUILLAL
Junquillal is a 2km-wide, grey-sand wilderness beach that's absolutely stunning and always deserted – probably because the surf is high and the rips are fierce. Ridley turtles nest here from July to November, but in smaller numbers than at the refuges.

You can camp on the beach provided you have your own food and water. Lodging is expensive; among the cheapest is **El Lugarcito** (☎ 658 8436; ellugarcito@racsa.co.cr; d incl breakfast US$50), a hospitable Dutch-run B&B. Intimate and quaint, it's decorated with indigenous pottery and has stone floors and vaulted ceilings.

Buses leave from the beach for Santa Cruz at 5:45am, noon and 4pm.

SANTA CRUZ

pop 16,000

This small cowboy town, 57km southwest of Liberia, holds the dubious title of being the hottest city in Costa Rica. Most travelers' experience here consists of changing buses and buying a mango or two. A **rodeo** and **fiesta** are held during the second week in January and on July 25th for **Día de Guanacaste**. The fun festivities showcase prize bulls, fried food and ear-popping music.

An interesting excursion is to the nearby village of **Guaitil**, 12km away, where you can buy pre-Columbian Chorotega-style pottery from the families who make it. Take a taxi or an infrequent local bus (ask for schedules at Plaza de los Mangos).

Sleeping & Eating

Pensión Isabel (☎ 680 0173; per person US$6) This friendly budget place, 400m south and 50m east of the plaza, offers bare, whitewashed rooms with shared bathroom.

Hotel la Estancia (☎ 680 0476; s/d US$20/32; 🐾) Upmarket by comparison, Estancia, 100m west of the plaza, has comfortable rooms with cable TV and private bathroom set around a motor court.

Hotel la Pampa (☎ 680 4586; d with/without air-con US$37/30; 🐾) Thirty-three simple and clean modern rooms 50m west of the plaza, all with bathroom and cable TV.

La Fábrica de Tortillas (casados US$2.50; 🕐 6am-6:30pm) Feast on *casados* here, aka Coopetortillas, 700m south of the plaza. The corrugated warehouse offers shared wooden tables in view of a wood-stove kitchen.

El Milenio (dishes US$3-6) A Chinese restaurant, 100m west of the plaza, serving colossal portions of fried rice and decent stir-fries with a big-screen TV and blessed air-con.

Getting There & Away

Departing from the terminal on the north side of Plaza de los Mangos:

Liberia (US$1; 1½hr) Every 30min from 5:30am to 7:30pm.

Nicoya (US$0.50; 1hr) Every 30min from 6am to 9:30pm.

San José (US$5.50; 4¼hr) Tralapa has nine buses from 3am to 5pm; Empresas Alfaro departs at 5:30am, 7:30am, 10am, 10:30am, 11:30am, 12:30pm, 3pm and 5pm – buy Alfaro tickets at the office 200m south of the Plaza, the bus leaves on the main road north of town.

Departing from the terminal 400m east of Plaza de los Mangos:

Playa Junquillal (US$2; 1½hr) Departs in the afternoon.

Playa Tamarindo (US$2; 1½hr) Every two to three hours.

NICOYA

pop 28,000

Pleasant Nicoya is a regional hub and capital, although its laid-back character and inland location lend it a dallying air. Situated 23km south of Santa Cruz, it is named after a Chorotega chief who welcomed the first Spaniards in 1523. (A gesture he no doubt regretted.) The attractive **Iglesia de San Blas** on the parque central dates from the mid-17th century.

Banks will exchange US dollars and there's a 24-hour ATM 100m east and 100m north of the parque central. For internet access, head to **Ciber Club** (per hr US$1; 🕐 9am-9pm Mon-Sat, 1-8pm Sun), 50m south of the parque central.

The **Área de Conservación Tempisque** (ACT; ☎ 685 5667; 🕐 8am-4pm Mon-Fri) assists with accommodation and cave exploration at Parque Nacional Barra Honda.

Sleeping & Eating

Hotel Chorotega (☎ 685 5245; Calle Central btwn Avs 4 & 6; r per person US$4) Our budget pick, where a pleasant family keeps clean bare-bones rooms.

Hotel Venecia (☎ 685 5325; Av Central btwn Calles Central & 1; r per person US$4) On the north side of the parque central, Venecia has cramped rooms with tired mattresses, but the reception staff are friendly.

Hotel las Tinajas (☎ 685 5081; 200m east & 100m north of the parque; s/d US$10/14) Has dated but decent rooms across from the Nicoya terminal. Management is cheerful and there's an attached café.

Hotel Jenny (☎ 685 5050; s/d US$16/25; 🐾) Hotel Jenny, 100m south of the parque central, is the best bet, but is often booked out. Spick-and-span rooms feature air-con, cable TV and private bathroom.

Café Daniela (mains US$3) This is the best spot for grub, 100m east of the parque central. It's a bustling and bright café serving tasty *huevos rancheros* or breakfast eggs and pastries. Burgers and *casados* round out the lunch and dinner options.

Guayacan Real (US$2-4) Grab a drink and delicious *bocas* at this consistently packed sports café serving exceptional *ceviche* and *patacones* (fried plantain with bean dip). It's west of the parque central.

Getting There & Away

Leaving from the terminal 100m north and 200m east of the parque, buses for Santa Cruz, Filadelfia and Liberia depart every 30 minutes from 3:50am to 8:30pm. The following leave from the terminal 200m east and 200m south of the parque central:

Liberia (US$1.25; 2½hr) Departs every 30min from 3am to 8pm.

Playa Naranjo, connects with ferry (US$1.75; 3hr) At 5am, 9am, 1pm and 5pm.

Playa Nosara (US$1.50; 4hr) At 5am, 10am, noon, 3pm.

Puntarenas (US$2.75; 2½hr) Departs 7:35am & 4:20pm.

Sámara (US$1; 2hr) At 6am, 7:45am, 10am, noon, 2:30pm, 4:20pm, 3:30pm, 6:30pm and 9:45pm.

San José, via Liberia (US$6; 5hr) Empresas Alfaro departs five times daily.

San José, via Río Tempisque bridge (US$5.25; 4hr) Empresas Alfaro seven buses from 3am to 5:20pm; Tralapa has buses at 3:20am, 5:20am, 6:50am, 10:45am and 1:45pm.

If you need a taxi, call **Taxis Unidos de Nicoya** (☎ 686 6857).

PARQUE NACIONAL BARRA HONDA

Midway between Nicoya and the mouth of the Río Tempisque, this 2295-hectare national park protects a vast underground system of more than 40 caves. The caverns, which are composed of soft limestone, were carved by rainfall and erosion over a period of about 70 million years. The caves have stalagmites, stalactites and a host of beautiful formations with names such as fried eggs, organ, soda straws, popcorn…you get the idea.

The **ranger station** (☎ 659 1551; admission US$6; ☼ 8am-4pm) provides information. The caves are only accessible in the dry season, though hiking is year-round. Carry water and let the rangers know where you are going.

You must explore the caves with a guide from the Asociación de Guías Ecologistas de Barra Honda. Make arrangements with a **national-park office** (☎ in Nicoya 686 6760, in Santa Cruz 680 1920, in Bagaces 671 1455). Guides charge about US$20 for groups of four, and equipment rental is an additional US$15 per person. Note that caves cannot be entered after 1pm.

At the park entrance you can **camp** (US$2), with bathrooms and shower facilities, or stay in dorm-style **cabins** (per person US$12). Reserve accommodations and meals through the ACT office in Nicoya or the rangers.

No bus goes directly to the park, but buses to Santa Ana (1km away) leave Nicoya at 8am,

12:30pm and 3:30pm. The return bus is at 6pm. A taxi from Nicoya costs US$10.

PLAYA NOSARA

An attractive white-sand beach is backed by a pocket of luxuriant vegetation that attracts birds and wildlife. Expensive hotels clutter the shore and the closest cheap accommodations are in the town, 5km inland. **Backpacker's Bunkhouse** (☎ 682 0249; nosarabunkhouse@yahoo.com; r per person US$10, campsite US$6; P ❑) is a recommended base for exploring the area. Open-air rooms share warm-water bathrooms, and there's a small communal kitchen and trail access.

There are a few grocery stores in town as well as a number of small *sodas*, though the best *casados* are at **Rancho Tico** (US$4-6) at the western end of town. Try the catch of the day, which is usually farm-raised tilapia or red snapper.

Both Sansa and NatureAir have three daily flights to and from San José for about US$80 each way.

Empresas Alfaro buses to San José (US$5, five to six hours) depart from the pharmacy by the soccer field at 12:30pm. Traroc departs for Nicoya (US$2.30, two hours) at 5am, 7am, 12:25pm and 3pm. For US$0.25 any of these buses will drop you off at the beach.

REFUGIO NACIONAL DE VIDA SILVESTRE OSTIONAL

The small reserve was created in 1992 to protect the *arribadas* or mass-nesting of the olive ridley sea turtles, which arrive by the thousands from July to November with a peak from August to October.

The refuge includes the coastal village of **Ostional**, 8km northwest of Playa Nosara. In the village, both **Hospedaje Guacamaya** (☎ 682 0430; r per person US$5) and **Cabinas Ostional** (☎ 682 0428; r per person US$10) have decent rooms with shared bathrooms. **Camping** (US$3) is permitted behind the centrally located Soda la Plaza, which has a portable toilet.

During the dry months, buses leave twice daily from Santa Cruz. Hitching from Nosara is reportedly easy.

PLAYA SÁMARA

Sámara's crescent beach is one of the most beloved in Costa Rica – it's safe, tranquil, reasonably developed and easily accessible. Not surprisingly, it's popular with vacationing Ticos, backpackers, wealthy tourists, snorkelers and surfers alike, and is starting to go upmarket.

Jesse's Samara Beach Gym & Surf School (☎ 656 0055; whiteagle@racsa.co.cr), 500m east of the police station on the beach, comes recommended by readers.

Information

You can change money at the **Banco Nacional** (☎ 656 0086; 9am-5pm Mon-Fri) behind the church. Check your email at **Tropical Latitude** (☎ 656 0120; per hr US$2), 100m east of the main road. The amiable American owner can provide you with information on everything there is to do in town.

A good source of information is the website www.samarabeach.com.

Sleeping & Eating

Camping los Coco (☎ 656 0496; US$3) On the eastern edge of the beach with well-maintained facilities.

Cabinas Playa Sámara (☎ 656 0190; per person US$7) You'll find clean lime-green rooms at this place near the soccer field and dismayingly close to a throbbing nightclub.

Cabinas Villa Kunterbunt (☎ 656 0235; www.cabinas-villa-kunterbunt.com; r per person US$10;) Located 3km outside of town on the road to Playa Carillo, this is a great choice if you have your own wheels. Tommy, the German owner, offers colorful cabins alongside a quiet section of beach with a good reef break. Guests can use the communal kitchen.

Bar Restaurant las Olas (☎ 656 0187; d US$25, camping per person US$3) This offers the most unique accommodation in town: one- and two-story thatched huts with private bathrooms. As the name implies, there is a very pleasant bar and restaurant.

Soda Ananas (☎ 656 0491; dishes US$2-5) Near the entrance to town with delicious veggie burgers, fresh salads and fruit smoothies.

Pizza & Pasta a Go-Go (main road; US$4-9) Custom thin-crust pizzas and fresh pastas with all the fixings.

Shake Joe's (☎ 656 0252; dishes US$5-10) Flop on an outdoor couch at Shake Joe's, a hip beachside spot awash with electronica and chilled-out travelers. The French toast starts the day right, though the sunset cocktail ambience is the main attraction.

Getting There & Away
AIR

The Sámara airport is south of town. Sansa flies daily to/from San José (one way US$78).

BUS
Nicoya (US$1; 2hr) Traroc departs at 5:30am, 7am, 8:45am, 11:30am, 1:30pm and 4:30pm from the *pulpería* by the soccer field.
San José (US$5; 5hr) Empresas Alfaro departs from the main drag at 4:30am and 8:30am.

PLAYA NARANJO

This small port on the eastern side of the peninsula has neither a beach nor oranges. It serves only as the terminal for the Puntarenas car ferry. There isn't any reason to hang around, and you probably won't have to as the ferries tend to run reasonably on time.

All transportation is geared to the arrival and departure of the Puntarenas ferry. Buses for Nicoya (US$1.75, three hours) meet incoming ferries. The **Coonatramar ferry** (☎ 661 1069; passenger/car US$2/9; 1½hr) to Puntarenas operates daily at 7:30am, 12:30am, 5pm and 9pm. You must have your ticket before boarding.

The right side of the boat has views of Isla San Lucas, the former site of one of Latin America's most notorious prisons. A famous memoir, *La Isla de los Hombres Solos* (available in English as *God was Looking the Other Way*), by José León Sánchez, tells the a gripping tale of life inside it.

PAQUERA

There isn't much around the Puntarenas–Paquera passenger ferry terminal. Paquera village, 4km away, is reached by a very crowded bus. The town has a bank and a couple of budget lodging options though there isn't much to see.

Most travelers take the bus from the ferry terminal directly to Montezuma (US$2.30, two hours). It's faster to take a taxi, if you can cobble a group together, for about US$7 per person to Montezuma and to Malpaís for about US$10.

The **Ferry Peninsular** (☎ 641 0118/515, 661 8282; passenger/car US$2/9; 1hr) goes to Punta Arenas at 4:30am, 6:30am, 8:30am, 10:30am, 12:30pm, 2:30pm, 4:30pm and 10pm.

MONTEZUMA

The road arrives at Montezuma, plunging steeply and funneling into a circle of shops and cafés. Here clusters of locals converse, hippies hock their handmade jewelry and gypsies wiggle for a spot of change. Charming is a corny word. Let's just say Montezuma is touristy yet still small, and striving to preserve the bohemia that first brought folks here.

It remains largely worthwhile. Lovely white-sand beaches offer great beach-combing and tide-pool studying. Following the coast curving north, beaches become more isolated, more pristine. Low tide offers snorkeling in tide pools, while the rising high-tide offers surf.

Information

Librería Topsy (8am-4pm in high season) has American newspapers and magazines, mails letters and sells books on wildlife and Costa Rica.

There are no banks. Tour operators can exchange US dollars, euros or traveler's checks. Internet is available at **El Sano Banano** (per hr US$2). Web resources include www.nicoyapeninsula .com and www.playamontezuma.net.

Activities

A 40-minute river hike leads to a waterfall with a delicious swimming hole. As you head south past Restaurant la Cascada, take the trail to the right just after the bridge. It starts left of the river, crosses and continues on the right. Do not jump the falls – it's the fast-track to a Darwin award. A smaller set of falls is further upriver.

A number of agencies in town offer snorkeling tours to Isla Tortuga (US$40), guided hikes in Cabo Blanco (US$25) and horseback tours along the beach and to waterfalls (US$25). Local outfitters include **Cocozuma** (642 0911; www.cocozuma.com) and **Montezuma Eco-Tours** (642 0467; www.playamontezuma.net).

Beautiful beaches line the coast, separated by small rocky headlands. Swimming is possible but the riptides are strong. Be careful and consult locals when in doubt. You can rent a bike (US$15) from a tour operator to explore the coastal route headed south.

Sleeping

Montezuma can get crowded (especially weekends) and most hotels don't take reservations. The best time to hunt for rooms is 10am, before the buses come. Getting digs with kitchen privileges will save you breakfasts that average US$4.

Camping is illegal on the beaches. A **campsite** (US$3) with bathrooms and cold showers is only a 10-minute walk north of town.

Pensión Lucy (642 0273; s/d US$6/12, d with bathroom US$16) An outstanding budget option, this sturdy beachside bunkhouse is a work of varnished timber with creative use of linoleum. The rooms are simple but immaculate.

Hotel Jenny (r per person US$6) A rambling house with cramped rooms with mushy beds and cold water out of a spigot. At least the location behind the soccer field promises a quiet night.

Luna Llena (642 0390; dm US$9, d US$15-20) On the hillside and decked in bright blues and mosaic designs, this friendly German-run hotel is terrific value. Rooms share clean kitchens and hot-water bathrooms. Ocean views are lovely and you might spot armadillos and monkeys rustling about.

Hotel Lys (642 0642; www.hotellyysmontezuma .net; d US$15, campsite US$6) If you missed the '60s, check out this basic bohemian hotel with small rooms and dark shared bathrooms, amped up with cool colors and Cubist-inspired art. It is run by a group of Italians who allow long-term guests to pay their way by cooking and painting. The community vibe is best appreciated with a beer on the seafront terrace.

Pensión Tucán (642 0284; d with/without bathroom US$20/14) A rickety two-story place attentively managed by the crotchety Doña Marta, though rooms are spotless, as are the communal showers.

Mochila Inn (642 0030; dm US$9, d/tr cabin US$25/30) On a forested hillside north of town, this hostel is relaxed and friendly. A rustic bunkhouse has lockers and decks, and there are also secluded wooden cabins. Get intimate with nature in the outdoor showers.

Hotel la Aurora (642 0051; www.playamontezuma .net/aurora.htm; d US$25-50, extra person US$5;) This canary-yellow modern hotel has tile rooms that are airy and clean. Guests have kitchen privileges and laundry service (US$3).

Hotel los Mangos (642 0076; www.hotellosmangos .com; d with shared bathroom US$33, d/tr bungalow US$30/65;) Resembling a lake house but plopped in the tropics amidst lush, manicured grounds. Groups will dig the ultra-private thatched bungalows. But the real reason to stay here? The pool and Jacuzzi stay open all night.

Eating

Soda Naranjo (casados US$3) This is the best place for cheap eats in town, where you can get a heaping and delicious fresh fish *casado*.

Bakery Café (meals US$4-10; 6am-6pm) Scrumptious baked goods and inventive vegetarian cuisine.

El Sano Banano (642 0638; dishes from US$6; 6am-6pm) El Sano Banano offers yogurt, juices and fruit salads, as well as vegetarian and seafood meals. It also shows films nightly (US$5 minimum consumption).

Tairona (meals US$4-6; 🕑 5pm-10pm) Argentine-run, this place serves outstanding caprese salads, fresh pasta and bubbly thin-crust mozzarella pizzas. Try the focaccia with smoked fish and herbs.

Playa de las Artistas (meals US$8-20; 🕑 10am-10:30pm) One worthy splurge is this outrageously romantic restaurant, with worn wooden tables set in the sand, lit by flickering candelabras. The illegible handwritten menu changes nightly, but includes delicacies such as smoked cheeses with honey and chilies or Mediterranean-style whole fish cooked to perfection. Service is excellent, as are the fruit-infused cocktails.

Drinking & Nightlife

Chico's Bar is the center of town nightlife and the place to listen to music and ogle strangers. Check in at Luz de Mono for live music; there's house music on Thursday and reggae on Saturday. Otherwise, take in the 7:30pm movie at El Sano Banano (see opposite).

Getting There & Away

BOAT

Jet boats to Jacó (US$30, one hour) depart at about 9:30am. Make reservations at a tour agency.

BUS

Buses depart in front of Café Iguana; buy your ticket on board.

Cabo Blanco (US$1; 30min) Departs 8:15am, 10:15am, 2:15pm and 6:15pm.

Paquera (US$2; 1½hr) At 5:30am, 8am, 10am, noon, 2pm, 4pm and 6pm.

San José (US$10; 9½hr) At 4:45am.

Santa Teresa (US$1.20; 45min) At 10:30am and 2:30am.

TAXI

A 4WD taxi can carry five people. Services include Cóbano (US$6), Cabo Blanco (US$12), Tambor (US$25), Malpaís (US$30) and Paquera (US$30).

MALPAÍS & SANTA TERESA

Situated on little more than a dirt road, these villages are sudden boomtowns for tourists hunting the next great destination. Make no mistake. Unlike other 'surf towns,' these are all about surfing. While a funky crop of new establishments make it more palatable, there is little more to do here than ride the wild

rollers. Nightlife means board waxing, beer in hand. But if it's your scene, you will adore it. A useful website is www.malpais.net.

Surf Shop Malpaís (☎ 640 0173) rents and fixes boards and also provides lessons.

Five-hundred meters south of Malpaís, **Malpaís Surf Camp & Resort** (☎ 640 0061; www.malpais surfcamp.com; dm US$12, d/q US$20/45, campsite US$7.50; 🏊) has dorm beds in an open-air *rancho*; bring the repellent.

Heading into Santa Teresa, **Tranquilo Backpackers** (☎ 640 0589; www.tranquilobackpackers.com; dm US$10, d/tr US$30/45, d with bathroom US$35, loft apt US$60; 🖳) offers hip and functional dorm digs. Surfers enjoy the self-serve pancakes. Amenities include shared kitchen, shared hot-water bathrooms, and free internet, bike rental and surfboards. It's 400m north.

Asian-inspired guesthouse **Casa Zen** (☎ 640 0523; www.casazencr.com; dm US$12, d with shared bathroom US$22-30) emanates good vibes – it should, there's plenty of Buddhas to belly-rub. Rooms are smart and spare and shared baths are kept squeaky clean. A hopping onsite fusion restaurant (US$3 to US$7) cooks up everything from burgers to fresh Thai curries with aplomb. There's yoga and free movies are screened most nights. It's 500m north.

Israeli-owned café **Zula** (mains US$4-5; 🕑 9am-10pm) serves scrumptious falafel and pita plates heaped with fresh salad and fries to a barefoot crowd hypnotized by surf videos.

The villages are reached by two daily buses from Cóbano departing at 10:30am and 2pm.

Buses depart from the new blue shopping complex at the crossroads. Transportes Cóbano goes direct to San José (US$10, 5½ hours) at 4:30am. Buses to Cóbano depart at 6:45am and 11am.

RESERVA NATURAL ABSOLUTA CABO BLANCO

On the southwestern tip of Península de Nicoya, this is Costa Rica's oldest protected wilderness area, established by pioneering conservationists. Encompassing evergreen forests, pristine white-sand beaches and offshore islands, the reserve is 11km south of Montezuma by dirt road.

The park was originally established by a Danish-Swedish couple – the late Karen Morgenson and Olof Wessberg – who settled in Montezuma in the 1950s, and were among the first conservationists in Costa Rica. In 1960 the couple was distraught when they discovered

COSTA RICA

that sections of Cabo Blanco had been clear-cut. At the time, the Costa Rican government was primarily focused on the agricultural development of the country, and not on conservation. However, Karen and Olof were instrumental in convincing the government to establish a national-park system, which eventually led to the creation of the Cabo Blanco reserve in 1963. Although the couple continued to fight for increased conservation of ecologically rich areas, Olof was tragically murdered in 1975 during a campaign in the Osa Peninsula. Karen continued the cause until her death 1994.

Cabo Blanco is called an 'absolute' nature reserve because prior to the late 1980s, visitors were not permitted. Even though the name has remained, a limited number of trails have been opened to visitors, though the reserve remains closed on Monday and Tuesday to minimize environmental impact.

A **ranger station** (☎ 642 0093; admission US$8; ⏱ 8am-4pm Wed-Sun) offers trail maps. Camping is not permitted. From the ranger station, the **Swedish Trail** and the **Danish Trail** lead 4.5km down to a wilderness beach at the tip of the peninsula. Note that both trails intersect at various points, and it's possible to follow one down and return on the other. Be advised that the trail can get very muddy (especially in the rainy season), and fairly steep in certain parts – plan for about two hours in each direction. From the beach at the end of the trails, it's possible to follow another trail to a second beach, though you should first check with park rangers as this trail is impassable at high tide.

Buses depart from the park entrance for Montezuma at 7am, 9am, 1pm and 4pm. A 4WD taxi from Montezuma to the park costs about US$12, prearrange for the return trip.

EXPLORE MORE OF THE PENINSULA

If you've got the time, we've got the fix:

■ Rent a 4WD and map your way from **Playa Carrillo** (near Sámara) to **Malpaís** via the famous Monkey Trail.

■ Grab a mountain bike to explore the isolated beaches between Malpaís and **Cabuya** – see p601.

■ Watch the leatherbacks in **Playa Grande** (p596), or the thousands of olive ridley turtles arriving at full moon on **Ostional** (p598).

CENTRAL PACIFIC COAST

Once defined by fishing villages and African palm-oil plantations, the central Pacific coast is now a favored haven for vacationers seeking big fish and bigger surf. Good roads from San José paved the way for quickie vacations for *capitalinos* and foreigners alike. Here wildlife isn't crocodiles and scarlet macaws (although they're here too), as much as its raging parties and a candy-counter assortment of illegal substances and girls for hire.

Nonetheless, the savvy traveler will find great hikes and surf to suit all tastes and spots where we haven't marred what mother nature gave us – yet.

The coast has marked dry and wet (April to December) seasons. Dry (high) season rates are given throughout.

PUNTARENAS
pop 107,000

The 'Pearl of the Pacific' is a battered port city at the tip of a sandy peninsula (8km long but only 100m to 600m wide). Lively and hot, the provincial capital served as a major coffee port during the 19th century. During dry season, Tico vacationers pack the beaches. Otherwise, it's the home of rowdy dockworkers and sailors alongside elderly ladies who scrub their sidewalks and keep the bougainvilleas blooming. Most travelers come here just to catch the ferry to the Nicoya peninsula. The water is polluted but swimmers can use the south side of the point.

Information
Check email at **caf@PuntaArenas** (plaza; per hr US$1; ⏱ 9:30am-8pm Mon-Sat, noon-7pm Sun). In front of the bus terminal, **Banco Popular** (cnr Calle 2 & Paseo de los Turistas) has an ATM.

Sleeping
Hotels have cold water only unless otherwise stated.

Hotel Cabezas (☎ 661 1045; Av 1 btwn Calles 2 & 4; s/d US$7/14, with bathroom US$10/20) Scrubbed and freshly painted, the Cabezas offers sound sleep in crisp white sheets and melon-bright rooms – quiet hours (after 10pm) are respected.

Gran Hotel Chorotega (☎ 661 0998; cnr Av 3 & Calle 1; s/d US$14/20, with bathroom US$22/30) Sparkling and tidy, this is modern in that boxy way,

COSTA RICA

PUNTARENAS

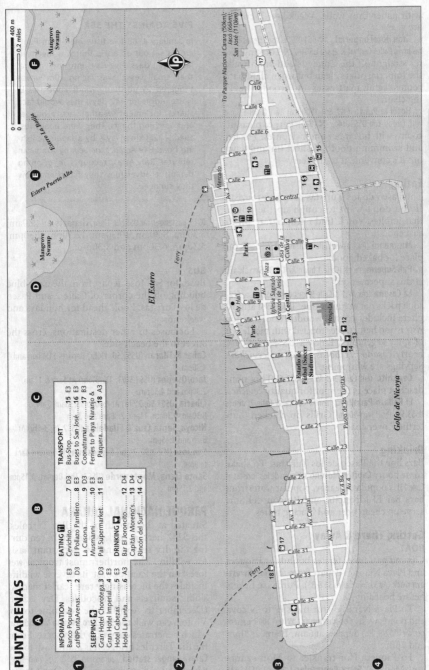

INFORMATION
Banco Popular............................**1** E3
caf@PuntaArenas.......................**2** D3

SLEEPING 🛏
Gran Hotel Chorotega.................**3** D3
Gran Hotel Imperial.....................**4** E3
Hotel Cabezas............................**5** E3
Hotel La Punta............................**6** A3

EATING 🍴
Cevichito....................................**7** D3
El Pollazo Parrillero....................**8** E3
La Casona..................................**9** D3
Musmanni...................................**10** E3
Palí Supermarket.........................**11** E3

DRINKING 🍸
Bar El Joroncito..........................**12** D4
Capitán Moreno's........................**13** D4
Rincón del Surf...........................**14** C4

TRANSPORT
Bus Stop....................................**15** E3
Buses to San José.......................**16** E3
Coonatramar..............................**17** B3
Ferries to Playa Naranjo &
Paquera....................................**18** A3

To Parque Nacional Carara (50km);
Jacó (66km);
San José (110km)

Mangrove Swamp

Estero La Bocita

Estero Puerto Alto

Mangrove Swamp

El Estero

Golfo de Nicoya

Ferry

Calle 10
Calle 8
Calle 6
Calle 4
Calle 2
Calle Central
Calle 1
Calle 3
Calle 5
Calle 7
Calle 9
Calle 11
Calle 13
Calle 15
Calle 17
Calle 19
Calle 21
Calle 23
Calle 25
Calle 27
Calle 29
Calle 31
Calle 33
Calle 35
Calle 37

Mercado
Park
City Hall
Casa de la Cultura
Plaza
Iglesia Sagrado Corazón de Jesús
Hospital
Estadio de Fútbol (Soccer Stadium)
Paseo de los Turistas

Av Central
Av 1
Av 2
Av 3
Av 4
Av 4 Bis

400 m
0.2 miles

with paper-thin walls. Weekday discounts are given.

Gran Hotel Imperial (☎ 661 0579; Paseo de los Turistas btwn Calles Central & 2; s/d US$16/27) Looking like it's straight off the Coney Island boardwalk, the Imperial offers clean but worn clapboard rooms, aging mattresses and wooden rocking chairs.

Hotel la Punta (☎ 661 1900; cnr Av 1 & Calle 35; d with fan/air-con US$30/40; 🆒 🏊) Large, pleasant rooms with hot water and balconies. The bar and swimming pool fall short on ambience but it's convenient to the ferry.

Eating

The Paseo de los Turistas caters to tourists. If you don't want to cough up the dough that implies, you'll find cheaper fare on its east end.

Musmanni (Av 1 btwn Calle Central & 1) This is the place for baked goods.

Palí Supermarket (Calle 1 btwn Av 1 & 3) Stock up at this supermarket.

La Casona (cnr Av 1 & Calle 9; casados US$2) La Casona packs out at lunchtime. The cool atmosphere includes carved wooden doors, onion *ristras* and hefty tables topped with pickle jars of spicy vegetables. Enjoy a US$2 breakfast, hearty *casados* or *bocas* (tacos or *ceviches*). Servings are whopping.

Cevichito (cnr Calle 3 & Av 2; US$2-5) This nondescript place is the spot for quality *ceviches*.

El Pollazo Parrillero (cnr Av Central & Calle 2; dishes US$3.50; ⏰ 11am-10pm) Grills up chicken 'butterflied' over coals.

Drinking

Bars line the Paseo de los Turistas. To shake some booty **Capitán Moreno's** (Paseo de los Turistas at Calle 13) is popular. Nearby, popular waterfront bars Bar El Joroncito and Rincón del Surf serve up cheap beer and blaring tunes.

Getting There & Away

BOAT

Car and passenger ferries bound for Paquera and Playa Naranjo depart from the **northwestern dock** (Av 3 btwn Calles 31 & 33). Purchase tickets before boarding.

To Playa Naranjo (for transfer to Nicoya and points west) **Coonatramar** (☎ 661 1069; passenger/car US$2/9; 2hr) departs at 6am, 10am, 2:20pm and 7pm.

To Paquera (for transfer to Montezuma and Malpaís) **Ferry Peninsular** (☎ 641 0118, 641

0515; passenger/car US$2/9; 1½hr) departs at 4:30am, 6:30am, 8:30am, 10:30am, 12:30pm, 2:30pm, 4:30pm, 6:30pm and 8:30pm.

BUS

Buses for San José depart from the navy-blue building on the corner of Calle 2 and Paseo de los Turistas. Book ahead for holidays and weekends.

For buses to other destinations, cross the street to the beach side.

Cañas & Tilarán (US$2.50, 1½hr) Departs 11:45am and 4:30pm.

Jacó/Quepos (US$1.50/3; 1½/3½hr) At 5am & 11am, 2:30pm and 4:30pm.

Liberia (US$1.50; 2½hr) At 4:40am, 5:30am, 7am, 8:30am, 9:30am, 11am, 2:30pm and 3pm.

Nicoya, Santa Cruz & Filadelfia (US$2.75; 3-5hr) At 6am and 3:45pm

San José (US$2.50; 2½hr) Departs every hour from 4am to 9pm.

Santa Elena, Monteverde (US$2; 3hr) Departs 1:15pm and 2:15pm

PARQUE NACIONAL CARARA

Situated at the mouth of the Río Tárcoles, this 5242-hectare park is a green haven during the dry season and an important oasis for wildlife. The northernmost tropical wet forest on the Pacific coast, its diverse wildlife includes the increasingly rare scarlet macaw, sloths, squirrels and crocodiles. Dry season (December to April) is the best time to go. Visitors can walk the **Sendero Laguna Meándrica**, which penetrates deep into the reserve. From the Río Tárcoles bridge, it is 3km south to the **Carara ranger station** (admission US$8; ⏰ 7am-4pm) where you can get information. Don't travel alone or carry valuables as occasional muggings are reported.

At the mouth of Río Tárcoles, Carara is 50km southeast of Puntarenas. You can get off at Carara from any bus bound for Jacó or Quepos, though avoid weekends when buses are jam-packed.

JACÓ

Jacó (pronounced ha-*ko*) plays party central to *capitalinos* itching for a quick hit of sea and surf. Ten years ago it had it all – warm water, great year-round surf and world-class fishing; now, in addition, there's rampant prostitution and a little drug problem. Yet, this surf town continues to be a magnet for all kinds – backpackers, Tico tourists and

that slimy old gringo looking to score a gal. Rapid growth might mean all the trimmings of a tourist trap, but the atmosphere can be congenial, the surfing addictive and the fun contagious.

Nearby Playa Hermosa, 5km south, hosts an annual **surfing tournament**. Note that riptides are common. The cleanest and safest city beaches are on the fringes. Avoid the estuaries.

Information

Banco de San José (Av Pastor Díaz at Calle Cocal) has a Cirrus ATM on the 2nd floor of the Il Galeone shopping center. Internet center **Mexican Joe's** (Av Pastor Díaz btwn Calles las Olas & Bohío; per hr US$0.75) has air-con.

COSTA RICA

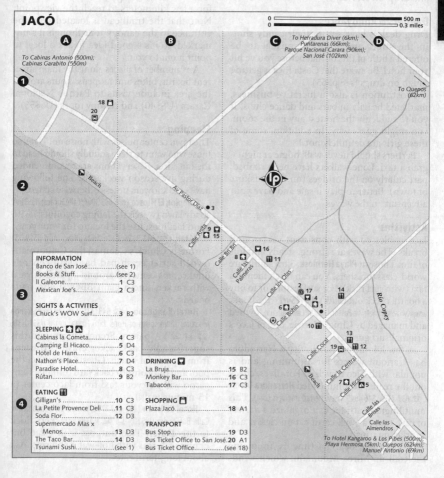

BOARDING SCHOOL

If you didn't bring a surfboard from home and want to get in plenty of water time, it may be worth your while investing in a board and selling it before you leave. The best place to do this is Jacó or Playa Tamarindo.

Since board materials have gotten all fancy, and the old standby went bankrupt, new toughlite ones (that last three times longer) now run around US$900. Oh, did you want to still eat too? That's the rub. Your other alternative is to go used. Those of a decent quality will run about half that price. Make sure the board is in no way noodly but solid and stiff (not patched together).

Budding longboarders beware – buses don't allow boards 2.4m (8 ft) and up. You'll have to downsize.

Books & Stuff (Av Pastor Díaz btwn Calles las Olas & Bohío) sells foreign newspapers. **Aquamatic Coin Laundry** (☑ 7:30am-12:30pm & 1-5pm) offers do-it-yourself and drop-off service.

Dangers & Annoyances
Drug dealers have set up their candy shop in the street and it's not unusual to be offered a little of this or that before you've hit your hotel. Be aware that Costa Rica is getting tough on drugs (see p565).

Prostitution is also a lucrative business, marketed heavily in bars and dance clubs. If you're suddenly the hottest guy in the room, you might guess why. In addition, some of these girls are definitely not 18.

Partiers should never walk home at night – grab a taxi. Lone walkers have been robbed, particularly on the bridges (on the outskirts of town). Better to play it safe and have your adventure in the waves.

Activities
Jacó is blessed with consistent year-round breaks. The waves are strong, steady and lots of fun. Those at **Playa Hermosa**, 5km south, are world-class thrashers. You can reach them via taxi (with surf rack). For surf lessons or to buy a board, check out **Chuck's WOW Surf** (☎ 643 3844; www.wowsurf.net; Av Pastor Díaz at Calle Ancha), owned and managed by Chuck Herwig, one of Jacó's original surf gurus.

A few kilometers north, Playa Herradura has tranquil waters for swimming and is popular with Tico travelers. For dives, check out the reader-recommended **Herradura Divers** (☎ 637 7123, 846 4649; www.herraduradivers.com). This multilingual outfitter can organize a variety of dive tours as well certification classes and snorkeling trips.

A popular local pastime is following the trail up Miros Mountain, which winds through primary and secondary rain forest, and offers spectacular views of Jacó and Playa Hermosa. The trail actually leads as far as the Central Valley, though you only need to hike for a few kilometers to reach the viewpoint. Note that the trailhead is located near the entrance to the canopy tour though it's unmarked, so it's a good idea to ask a local to point it out to you.

Any number of places along the main street rent boards, bikes and mopeds. Tours around the area include visits to Parque Nacional Carara (US$40) and canopy tours (US$55).

Sleeping
The town center pulses with noise until late, so those who want to sleep soundly should head to the outskirts. Reservations are recommended during dry-season weekends. The following have cold showers unless otherwise stated.

Camping El Hicaco (☎ 643 3004; Calle Hicaco; US$3) A shady lawn (watch the falling coconuts!) with good facilities; use the lockup for your gear.

Rútan (☎ 643 3328; Calle Anita alley; dm/d US$9/15) Formerly Chuck's Cabinas, this Californian-owned surfer crash-pad has clean concrete bunkrooms centered around a patch of yard with rockers and a giant BBQ. It also rents boards.

Hotel Kangaroo (☎ 643 3351; www.hotel-kangaroo.com; 300m south of Hotel Jacó Fiesta; dm/d US$10/30; ⊠ 🖳 🖳) A pair of French surfers run this superfriendly backpacker crash-pad, steps from a peaceful beach. Guests groove on the pool and impromptu backyard dinners. Kangaroo will pay your taxi from Jacó center (a 15-minute walk).

Hotel de Haan (☎ 643 1795; www.hoteldehaan.com; Calle Bohío; dm US$10; 🖳 🖳) Backpackers flock to this Dutch-Tico outpost with clean but cramped dorms with hot-water showers. Ask about long-term rates.

Nathon's Place (☎ 355 4359; Calle Hicaco; dm/d US$10/25; 🐾 💻) While the rooms have the charm of a cell, the gregarious Texas owners make up for it. Perks include hot-water bathrooms, air-con and free bike rentals.

Cabinas Antonio (☎ 643 3043; cnr Av Pastor Díaz & Boulevard; d US$15; 🐾) Uninspired but clean cabins come with private showers and cable TV, close to a quiet beach.

Cabinas Garabito (☎ 643 3321; d US$20) The plain cabins at this place are well kept but nothing special – the real plus is the friendly Tico owners.

Cabinas La Cometa (☎ 643 3615; Av Pastor Díaz, south of Calle Bohío; d with/without bathroom US$32/20) Snoozy and sweet, this peaceful hotel has ample tidy rooms with red-tile floors and soft ambient lighting. Private bathrooms have hot water and there's a spotless shared kitchen.

Paradise Hotel (☎ 643 2563; www.paradisehotel jaco.com; Av Pastor Diaz; d US$35; 🐾 🐾) Recently renovated, the Paradise has well-maintained rooms equipped with full amenities. Guests can catch ultraviolet rays by the swimming pool or shoot pool in the comfy lounge.

Eating

Los Pibes (South Av Pastor Díaz; meals US$2) Don't miss this place for cheap and tasty pizza, straight from Argentina. It serves authentic *empanadas* (US$1) too.

La Petite Provence Deli (Centro Pacifica, North Av Pastor Díaz; sandwich US$3.50) This is the best take-out in town where chef Jean Marie bakes baguettes and tarts. The fresh sandwiches are tops.

Soda Flor (Av Pastor Díaz btwn Calles Cocal & La Central; casados US$3) In the center, this is a perennial favorite for heaping *casados*.

Gilligan's (Av Pastor Díaz, north of Calle Cocal; breakfast US$3-5, mains US$8-12) Gilligan's serves up deluxe pancake breakfasts and hearty meatloaf.

The Taco Bar (US$6-8) Mexico meets Japan meets LA, a sleek outdoor *palapa* bar with huge smoothies, salads, fresh sashimi and, um, tacos.

Tsunami Sushi (Av Pastor Díaz, north of Calle Cocal; sushi & rolls US$3-11) This is a sexy restaurant if we ever saw one, serving an exquisite assortment of sushi, sashimi and rolls.

Drinking

Jacó may be a cultural wasteland, but it sure knows how to have a good time. That said, a good portion of the nightlife revolves around prostitution.

The sleek bar at **Tabacon** (Calle Bohio) has the most respectable nightlife around. There's live calypso and reggae, a slew of pool tables, and – drum roll – Men's night on Wednesday (yes, guys you drink free). We love equal opportunity.

A relaxed watering hole, **La Bruja** (south of Calle Anita) is an old standby that locals like. But if

---

LOCAL VOICES: SURFER EXPATS

French surfers Stefan and Nico came to Jacó four years ago and opened a hostel. They now split their days between mopping the floor and riding the mighty rollers. Stefan did most of the talking:

What brought you here? Just luck. We wanted a different world, a different everything.

What advice do you have for travelers? Do not make plans because they are meant to change. People plan two nights in this place, two nights in that. They are stuck in a schedule. Just come.

What's Costa Rica like? Very slow and really, really friendly. The country is perfect.

What's your favorite local spot? Hermosa is a nice beach break, pretty huge and steep.

How far are you from the beach? Eighty-five meters and 23 centimeters.

A lot of travelers have a fantasy to move somewhere and start a hostel. What are some of the unexpected difficulties? Plumbing. If it rains too much, *everything* overflows. Or there is no power, no water, no internet...

Tico lifestyle, *Nico says.*

Pura vida! says Stefan.

So? One day with, one day without. You just have to get used to it, *Nico says.*

And be relaxed. Don't wait for people to do things your way, *Stefan says.*

Any other advice? Just shake it up.

As told to Carolyn McCarthy

you want to get in the thick of it, hit meat-market **Monkey Bar** (Calle Las Palmeras), but don't say we didn't warn you.

Getting There & Away
BOAT
Jet boats to Montezuma (US$35, one hour) leave several times daily. Reserve with a tour operator in town.

BUS
Buses for San José (US$2.50, three hours) stop at the Plaza Jacó mall, north of the center. Buy tickets well in advance at **Transportes Jacó** (☎ 7am-noon & 1-5pm). Buses depart at 5am, 7:30am, 11am, 3pm and 5pm.

Other buses stop in front of the Más X Menos supermarket. (Stand here for destinations north; wait across the street for destinations south.) Buses to Puntarenas (US$1.50, 1½ hours) depart at 6am, 9am, noon and 4:30pm.

Buses to Quepos (US$2, 1½ hours) depart at 6am, noon, 4:30pm and 6pm. These are approximate departure times since buses originate in Puntarenas or Quepos. Get to the stop early!

QUEPOS
pop 13,300
Quepos feels like the accidental destination, a port with neither the Ritz of resorts in Manuel Antonio nor the grinding fervor of Jacó's fiestas. A major sport fishing center and gateway to Parque Nacional Manuel Antonio, it attracts plenty of backpackers as well as the fussier 'dry-socks' crowd, but manages to stay unperturbed. Crickets and frogs bleat under the African palms, while the polluted coastline is largely ignored. Locals keep about their business, whether it's waiting in bank lines during the day or filling the bars and soccer bleachers at night.

Banco de San José and Coopealianza both have 24-hour ATMs on the Cirrus and Plus systems. Check email at **Internet Quepos.com** (per hr US$2; ☎ 8am-8pm Mon-Sat).

Activities & Tours
Sport fishers come here to nab the big one. If you're one of them, try **Costa Mar Dream Catcher** (☎ 777 0725; www.costamarsportfishing.com), next to Cafe Milagró. Sailfish season peaks from December to April. Readers recommend **Manuel Antonio Divers** (☎ 777 3483; www.manuelantoniodivers

.com) for diving. Adventure outfitter **Iguana Tours** (☎ 777 1262; www.iguanatours.com) offers rafting, sea kayaking, horseback rides, mangrove tours and dolphin-watching excursions.

The beaches are polluted and not recommended for swimming.

Sleeping
All hotels have cold-water showers unless otherwise stated.

Wide-Mouth Frog Backpackers (☎ 777 2798; dm US$7, d with/without bathroom US$30/20; ☒ ☐ ☑) This is a welcoming bunkhouse with spacious dorms with lockers and a basic outdoor kitchen. Rooms wrap around a pool area enclosed in leafy gardens. Shared bathrooms have bright checkered tiles and stalls. The hostel recycles and its British-Kiwi owners are fine hosts.

Cabinas Mary (☎ 777 0128; s/d US$10/16) South of the soccer field, these freshly painted units have private bathrooms looking a bit dated. Beds are narrow and threadbare.

Hostal Vista Serena (☎ 777 5162; www.vistaserena.com; dm/d US$12/50; ☐) Perched on a hillside, this hostel offers spectacular sunsets from a hammock-strewn terrace, with a trail leading to a remote beach. Dorms decked out in white tiles are spotless and have hot-water bathrooms. The owners are fully bilingual and great hosts. It's on the road between Quepos and Manuel Antonio; ask the driver to drop you off.

Hotel Mar y Luna (☎ 777 0394; s/d US$12/16) The Tico owner Alvaro runs a smooth operation as all room are well-maintained, supercheap and have private bathrooms with a hot shower.

Hotel El Parque (☎ 777 0063; s/d US$12/16) A throwback to yesterday with garish turquoise paint and scratched dressers. Still, it's friendly and central.

Hotel Hellen (☎ 777 0504; d US$30) Nothing remarkable, but the waddling duck statues and gingham frills remind you that it's family run and well-looked after.

Hotel Ceciliano (☎ 777 0192; d with/without bathroom US$24/16) The doubles with hot showers prove comfortable and the outdoor garden and living area is an agreeable retreat. It may change ownership.

Cabinas Alicia (☎ 777 0419; www.cabinasalicia.com; d US$25; ☒) The Alicia is a canary-yellow complex with large rooms with sparkling surfaces. Guests have the option of fan or air-con and hot water.

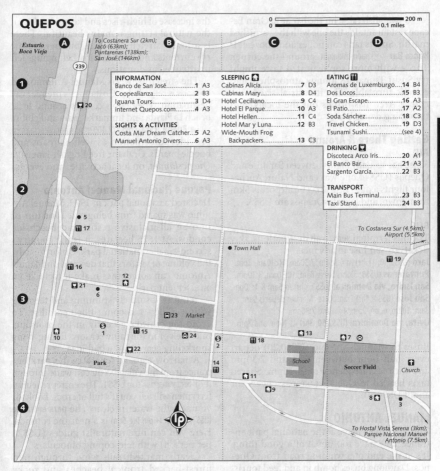

QUEPOS

INFORMATION
Banco de San José..............1	A3
Coopealianza.....................2	B3
Iguana Tours.....................3	D4
internet Quepos.com.........4	A3

SIGHTS & ACTIVITIES
Costa Mar Dream Catcher...5	A2
Manuel Antonio Divers.......6	A3

SLEEPING
Cabinas Alicia....................7	D3
Cabinas Mary.....................8	D4
Hotel Ceciliano..................9	C4
Hotel El Parque................10	A3
Hotel Hellen....................11	C4
Hotel Mar y Luna.............12	B3
Wide-Mouth Frog	
Backpackers.................13	C3

EATING
Aromas de Luxemburgo....14	B4
Dos Locos.......................15	B3
El Gran Escape................16	A3
El Patio.........................17	A2
Soda Sánchez..................18	C3
Travel Chicken................19	D3
Tsunami Sushi.................(see 4)	

DRINKING
Discoteca Arco Iris...........20	A1
El Banco Bar....................21	A3
Sargento García...............22	B3

TRANSPORT
Main Bus Terminal............23	B3
Taxi Stand.....................24	B3

COSTA RICA

Eating

Soda Sánchez (meals US$2-3; 6am-10pm) Fresh, friendly and always packed. No wonder – it's cheap and clean, with great service and the occasional seafood specialty.

Travel Chicken (US$2-4) Grab a drumstick for the road (we've seen stranger things) at this roadside venue where locals line up.

Aromas de Luxemburgo (snacks US$2-4; 7am-6pm Mon-Sat, 3-6pm Sun;) This air-conditioned Euro-style café serves organic teas, crêpes and desserts at sleek metal tables or a bright patio.

Dos Locos (dishes US$4-14; 7am-11pm Mon-Sat, 11am-10pm Sun) Mariachis and expats frequent this festive eatery serving Mexican fare and the tenderest steaks in town.

Tsunami Sushi (8 pieces US$5-15; dinner) If you're itching to splurge, the sashimi at Tsunami Sushi is practically a religious experience. Don't miss creative combinations such as the crunch roll in this ultra-chic setting.

El Patio (breakfast US$3-4, dinner mains US$8-15; 6am-10pm) This popular bistro sexes up Latin cuisine (who knew it needed it?) with options such as roasted tomato gazpacho, and shrimp in tamarind coconut sauce. A stone fountain and birds of paradise make it very romantic, but daytime it's ideal for a cup of joe and dessert.

Drinking

The town's funky favorite is Sargento García, with twinkling lights and MIA flags. Lounge nights are Tuesday and Thursday.

To swap fish tales, hit the bar at El Gran Escape restaurant. It's the one with the varnished marlin. Sports fans can holler and booze at **El Banco Bar** (noon-midnight) around the corner. Those with more sophisticated taste might try Sushi Tsunami's loungy atmosphere and eclectic turntable. The industrial-sized Discoteca Arco Iris brings out the locals with thumping dance beats.

Getting There & Around

AIR

Sansa has six daily flights between San José and Quepos (US$44 one way) and NatureAir has four flights a day (US$50). The airport is 5km from town, and taxis to Quepos are US$3.

BUS

The bus terminal serves all destinations. Buy tickets to San José in advance.
Jacó (US$1.50; 1½hr) At 4:30am, 7:30am, 10:30am, 3pm.
Puntarenas (US$3; 3½hr) Leave 8am, 10:30am, 3:30pm.
San Isidro, via Dominical (US$2; 4hr) At 5am & 1:30pm.
San José (US$4; 4hr) Transportes Morales departs 5am, 8am, 10am, noon, 2pm, 4pm and 7:30pm.
Uvita, via Dominical (US$2.50; 3hr) At 10am and 7pm.

Buses to Manuel Antonio (US$0.20) depart every half-hour between 6am and 7:30pm and with less frequency until 10pm. Shared taxis headed to Quepos take passengers for about US$0.50.

MANUEL ANTONIO

This adorable village at the national park entrance may have too much of a good thing. It's at the end of a winding road from Quepos. Day-long buses bomb in and feed tourist hordes into its souvenir fly-trap. Yet, despite

---

BOMBS AWAY!

On the Quepos–Manuel Antonio road, you'll find **El Avión** (777 3378), a bar constructed from the body of a 1954 Fairchild C-123. Affectionately referred to as 'Ollie's Folly,' the plane had been purchased by the USA in the '80s for the Nicaraguan Contras, but stayed grounded due to the Iran-Contra scandal. It's found a permanent home on the side of the main road, and serves up meals (not of the airplane variety) and live music. It's a great spot for a beer, guacamole and a Pacific sunset.

---

the increase of high-rises and keepsake clutter, the natural setting remains beautiful. There is a lovely stretch of beach, but beware the rip currents and consider any belongings left unattended as donations.

The stretch between Manuel Antonio and Quepos is regarded as Costa Rica's premier gay destination. The action centers around local beach **La Playita** and upmarket bars and clubs.

La Buena Nota (777 1002; buennota@racsa.co.cr) provides information as well as maps and boogie boards. Grab the free English-language *Queposlandia*, on local activities and events.

Parque Nacional Manuel Antonio

Declared a national park in 1972, Manuel Antonio was spared from being razed and turned into an all-inclusive resort and beachside condos. At 1625 hectares, it is the country's second-smallest national park. Unfortunately, the volume of visitors that descend on Manuel Antonio can sometimes make it feel like an amusement park.

Yet, it is absolutely stunning and teeming with wildlife – a coconut-filled paradise. To avoid the crowds, go early in the morning, midweek or in the rainy season. Taking along snorkeling gear is not a bad idea.

A narrow estuary separates the park entrance from the village. You can wade through it or ferry across for US$1. The entrepreneurial ferrymen will tell you it's full of crocs. Look for yourself, the water is clear. The **park entrance** (US$7; 7am-4pm Tue-Sun) is a near the rotunda. Here you can hire naturalist guides (US$20 per person) with telescoping binoculars.

Clearly marked trails wind through rain forest-backed tropical beaches and rocky headlands. With an early start you can see all the sights in a day. Most visitors who spend the day hiking will see monkeys and sometimes sloths, agoutis, armadillos, coatis and lizards. From the park entrance, it's a 30-minute walk to **Playa Espadilla Sur** where there are mangroves and the isthmus widens into a rocky, forested peninsula. A trail leads around the peninsula to **Punta Catedral**, with great views of the Pacific and rocky islets inhabited by brown boobies and pelicans.

You can continue around the peninsula to **Playa Manuel Antonio**, or you can cut across the isthmus on a direct trail to this beach. A nearby **visitors center** has drinking water, toilets and beach showers. Beyond Playa Manuel Antonio, the trail divides. The steep lower trail

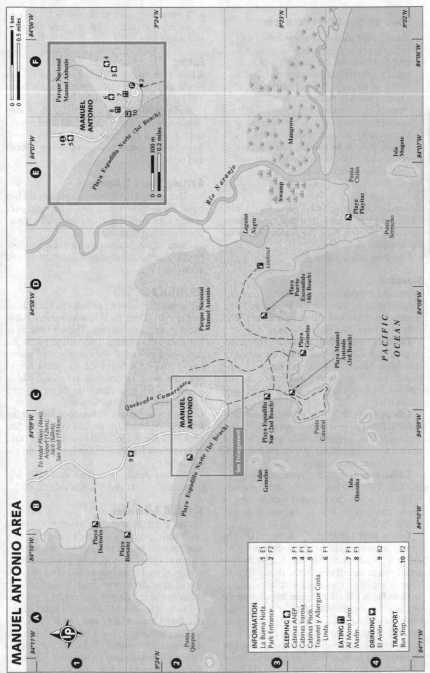

MANUEL ANTONIO AREA

COSTA RICA

INFORMATION	
La Buena Nota................1 E1	
Park Entrance.................2 F2	

SLEEPING
Cabinas ANEP.....................3 F1
Cabinas Irarosa..................4 F1
Cabinas Piscis....................5 E1
Travotel y Albergue Costa
Linda...............................6 F1

EATING
Al Mono Loco....................7 F1
Marlin..............................8 F1

DRINKING
El Avión............................9 B2

TRANSPORT
Bus Stop..........................10 F2

LOVE 'EM BUT DON'T FEED 'EM

Sharing your banana with a monkey isn't the innocent act you might imagine. It is prohibited and has the side effect of making wild animals aggressive and susceptible to human illnesses. This has gotten out of hand in Manuel Antonio, where critters move in on unattended bags and snatch sandwiches from picnickers. It's not a pretty picture. Since the park is understaffed, it's unlikely you will be fined or even scolded, but consider the stinky karma that will plague your next 17 lives.

descends to the quiet Playa Puerto Escondido. The upper trail climbs to a stunning **lookout** on a bluff. Rangers limit the number of hikers on this trail.

Camping is not allowed.

Sleeping

With most options overpriced, consider lodging in Quepos or on the road into town (especially if you want to go upmarket). The following have cold-water showers.

Travotel y Albergue Costa Linda (☎ 777 0304; r per person US$10) A German-run establishment with tiny lime-colored rooms and shared bathrooms. Avoid top-floor rooms that cook. The café is a good spot to grab a cheap burger and yucca fries.

Cabinas Piscis (☎ 777 0046; s/d US$15/25, with bathroom US$35/45) The best budget option in town, these sparkling, ample rooms come in tropical shades with wire rockers. A convenient kiosk sells ice cream and smokes.

Cabinas Irarosa (☎ 777 5085; d with/without bathroom US$35/25) This modest motel (with immodest prices) offers clean rooms with linoleum floors and droopy beds. However, it smells a little dank.

Cabinas ANEP (☎ 777 0565; 7-person r US$29) On sprawling and attractive grounds these bare dorm-style cabins offer seven slim beds. Perfect if you're traveling with the Brady Bunch. There's a grilling area and soccer field.

Hotel Plinio (☎ 777 0055; www.hotelplinio.com; d without/with air-con US$65/75; ❄ 🏊) On the road into Manuel Antonio and nestled on a forested slope, these lodge rooms are styled with cathedral ceilings, polished-wood decks, hot showers and hammocks. The grounds boast 10km of forest trails leading to a 17m-high lookout tower (open to the public). The recommended restaurant serves great German and Asian fare.

Eating

Al Mono Loco (meals US$4-10) Just north of the rotunda, this friendly place serves *casados*, pasta and burgers under a thatched roof.

Marlin (breakfast US$2-5, fish dishes US$6-8; 🕑 7am-10pm) Early risers come here for filling breakfasts. Fresh fish is your best bet for dinner. Enjoy two-for-one rum drinks between 4:30pm and 6pm.

Getting There & Away

See Quepos (p610) for details on air and bus travel. Buses leave from near the national park entrance and will stop along the road to Quepos if you flag them down.

Buses depart Manuel Antonio for San José (US$4, four hours) at 6am, 9:30am, noon and also 5pm.

DOMINICAL

With monster waves, mellow vibes and kind bud aplenty, Dominical inhales surfers, backpackers and do-nothings. There's little to it, but that's the charm. The village roads are dusty and potholed. Its complicated access has spared it the hyper-development fate of other Pacific coast beaches. Yet gringo-radar, attuned to its 'potential,' has its glassy-eyed fans rapidly spreading the word.

Check your email at **Dominical Internet** (per hr US$4.50; 🕑 9:30am-7pm Mon-Sat) above the San Clemente Bar & Grill and have laundry done at **Lavandería las Olas** (🕑 7am-9pm), inside the minisuper.

The free publication *Domincal Days* features local events and a handy tide chart.

Sights & Activities

Waves, currents and riptides are very strong and many people have drowned here. Dominical's lifeguards are among the country's best trained and funded by private citizen groups. Two hours before and after low tide are the most dangerous times. Enter the water between the red flags (which mark riptides).

For surf lessons (US$50) and tours, check out **Green Iguana Surf Camp** (☎ 815 3733; www.greeniguanasurfcamp.com), on a side street leading to the beach. Surf shop El Tubo next to Tortilla Flats does rentals and repairs. San Clemente Bar & Grill rents bicycles and surfboards.

On the coastal hills 3km north of Dominical, **Hacienda Barú** (☎ 787 0003; www.haciendabaru .com; admission US$6) is a 330-hectare private nature reserve with stunning biodiversity. You can hike the trails and visit the birding tower on your own, take a guided tour or sample the zip line. A taxi from Dominical costs about US$5.

Dominical is emerging as a base for day trips to Parque Nacional Corcovado and Parque Nacional Marino Ballena. **Southern Expeditions** (☎ 787 0100; www.dominical.biz/expeditions/; trips from US$55), at the entrance to the village, organizes trips. It also visits the Guaymí indigenous reserve near Boruca.

Volunteers on organic farm **Finca Ipe** (www .fincaipe.com; daily US$15), 13km from Dominical, learn about organic tropical farming and medicinal plants. Fees include room and board.

Sleeping

All hotels have cold-water showers unless noted otherwise.

Antorchas Camping (☎ 787 0307; campsite US$5, s/d US$15/28) Pop your tent (or rent one for US$1) next to lockers, showers and a communal kitchen (US$3). There's free morning coffee. The private rooms are slouchy but livable.

San Clemente Cabinas (☎ 787 0026; dm/d US$10/30, d with fan US$40; 🏊) While they're a twinge musty, these rooms are good value, in a lime-green cement structure. The adjoining Dominical Backpackers is not recommended since units are unlocked and unattended.

Sundancer Cabinas (☎ 787 0189; d US$20-30; 🏊) These small motel units are plain but well-kept, with sturdy mattresses and hot showers. The quiet location allows you to sleep soundly.

Tortilla Flats (☎ 787 0033; q without/with air-con US$30/40; 🏊) Make friends quickly so you can take advantage of the cheap group rate at this popular budget option. Rooms have hot-water bathrooms and a patio hammock.

Posada del Sol (☎ 787 0085; d US$36) The rooms here are well-decorated and have spotless, private bathrooms with hot water and a patio hammock that'll satisfy all your swinging needs.

Roca Verde (☎ 787 0036; www.rocaverde.net; r US$85; 🏊 🍴) A stylish American hotel overlooking the beach, located 1km south of the village. With hardwood details and tile mosaics, each room accommodates four guests. Air-con and hot water are included.

Eating & Drinking

Start your day here with a gargantuan sandwich of bacon, egg and avocado at **Tortilla Flats** (mains from US$3). The self-serve coffee is a lifesaver. Afternoons it becomes the spot for that post-surf margarita. **Soda Sirasa** (casados US$2), across from the soccer field, has the best cheap eats in town.

Decorated with broken surfboards, the **San Clemente Bar & Grill** (dishes US$4-8) serves whopping portions of Tex Mex food in a cool and cavernous setting. The best spot for cheesy pizzas and a dose of local nightlife is Thrusters Bar, also featuring a pool table. **Maracatu** (mains US$4-8; 🕚 11am-late) dishes up great vegetarian fare and has regular live reggae and salsa after 9pm. Wednesday is ladies night.

Getting There & Away

Buses all arrive and depart at the end of the road next to Cabinas Coco.

Ciudad Cortés (US$2.50; 2hr) Departs 4:15am and 10am.

Quepos (US$2; 4hr) At 7:30am, 8am, 10:30am, 1:45pm, 4pm & 5pm.

San Isidro (US$1; 1hr) Departs 6:45am, 7:15am, 2:30pm and 3:30pm

Uvita (US$0.75; 1hr) At 4:30am, 10:30am, noon & 6:15pm.

UVITA

A loose straggle of farms with back roads swallowed in tall grass, this hamlet 17km south of Dominical shows what coastal Costa Rica was like before the tourist boom. The highway section is known as Uvita, and the beach area is called Playa Uvita. While nightlife may be limited to stargazing, Uvita boasts fantastic stretches of flat sand that comprise Parque Nacional Marino Ballena.

A few kilometers before you get to Uvita, a signed turnoff to the left leads 3.5km to **Reserva Biológica Oro Verde** (☎ 743 8072, 843 8833). This private reserve is on the farm of the friendly Duarte family. Roughly two-thirds of their 150-hectare property is rain forest and they offer guided hikes (US$15 per person), horseback tours (US$25) and birding walks (US$30).

On the way into town, **Banco Coopealianza** (☎ 743 8231) exchanges US dollars. The helpful **Ballena Tours** (☎ 743 8019; www.ballenatourcr.com; Playa Uvita) arranges bilingual snorkeling and whale-watching tours.

Top hostel **Hotel Toucan** (☎ 743 8140; www.tucan hotel.com; dm/d US$8/25, campsite US$4; 🖥), 100m east of the highway, exudes a sociable, chilled-out ambience fostered by its Tennessee owners Tra and Penny. They offer taxi service to the beach (and maybe the bar). Spotless rooms connect at an enormous hangar with communal kitchen, library, wi-fi and a happening café. Bikes and surfboards are for rent.

Local hotels are friendly, family-run enterprises. The rural **Cabinas María Jesús** (☎ 743 8121; s/d US$20/24; 🏊), 200m before bus the stop, has air-con cabins set amidst the cows and sugarcane.

About 200m from the park entrance, **Cabinas Punta Uvita** (☎ 771 2311; r per person with/without bathroom US$8/6, campsite US$3) offers small linoleum cabins. Up the road, friendly **Cabinas Hegalva** (☎ 743 8016; r per person US$10, campsite US$2) offers very clean but basic rooms with private bathroom.

Next door, the farmlike **Cabinas Dagmar** (☎ 743 8181; cabinasdagmar@hotmail.com; r per person US$10, campsite US$2) has raked campsites separated by sorrel hedges and tidy mint-green rooms. Even the cats, chicken and dogs seem pampered.

By the beach, **Soda El Ranchito** (mains US$3-5) serves the freshest fish and burgers. For bohemian evenings in a thatched café, don't miss the German-run **Mistura** (🕐 until 10pm), 1.5km from the highway on the Toucan road, with candlelit ambience and cool vintage rock. Full moon means howling time with live drumming. The venue's private waterfall and swimming hole (US$0.50) is a popular daytime excursion.

Daily buses to San José (US$5, seven hours) via Dominical and Quepos depart at 5am, 6am and 2pm. Buses to San Isidro de El General (US$1.50, 1½ hours) via Dominical depart at 6am and 2pm. Buses to Ciudad Cortés originate in Dominical and stop in Uvita for pickups at about 4:45am and 10:30am.

PARQUE NACIONAL MARINO BALLENA

This pristine marine park protects coral and rock reefs in more than 5300 hectares of ocean and 110 hectares of land around Isla Ballena, south of Uvita. Although the park gets few human visitors, these beautiful beaches are frequented by nesting seabirds, bottle-nosed dolphins and a variety of lizards. From May to November (peaking in September and October) both olive ridley and hawksbill turtles bury their eggs in the sand nightly. The star attraction are the pods of humpback whales that pass through from August to October and December to April.

The **ranger station** (☎ 743 8236; admission US$3) is in Playa Bahía, the seaside extension of Uvita. Snorkelers can hit Punta Uvita at low tide. Local agencies arrange boat tours for snorkeling (US$45) or whale-watching (US$65).

SOUTHERN COSTA RICA & PENÍNSULA DE OSA

Few used to bother with this other, less convenient Costa Rica, but those who stumbled off the beaten path uncovered podunk charm and a muddy land of contrasts. The mist-shrouded Cordillera de Talamanca is marked with clear, turbulent rivers plunging to the lowlands. Pristine beaches are lapped by rain forest. *National Geographic* penned the Osa peninsula 'the most biologically intense place on earth.' It is certainly one of the few where nature takes *its* course and not ours.

Heading south from San José, the Interamericana reaches its 3491m-high point at the Cerro de la Muerte, the so-called mountain of death, fitted with spine-tingling turns (though it was called this before the road was built). San Isidro de El General is the gateway to Parque Nacional Chirripó, with the country's highest peaks. Southeast of San Isidro, farm towns and banana and palm-oil plantations fill the landscape. Most visitors blast through on their way to the magnificent wilderness of Parque Nacional Corcovado.

SAN ISIDRO DE EL GENERAL
pop 40,000

Called 'Pérez' by locals, this city's Latin vibe manifests in its chaotic center. The busy grid is packed with bric-a-brac shops selling platform shoes and plastic accessories, ice-cream parlors and fruit stands, all coated in a fine film of tailpipe dust. The main town on the southern Interamericana, it serves as a transportation hub and the commercial center for coffee *fincas*, cattle ranches and plant nurseries on the steep surrounding slopes. There isn't much to see in San Isidro, but locals are hospitable and it is a convenient gateway for Parque Nacional Chirripó and the Pacific coast.

In early February, the **agricultural fair** displays prize cattle and on May 15, livestock are hauled into town to be blessed in honor of San Isidro, patron saint of farmers.

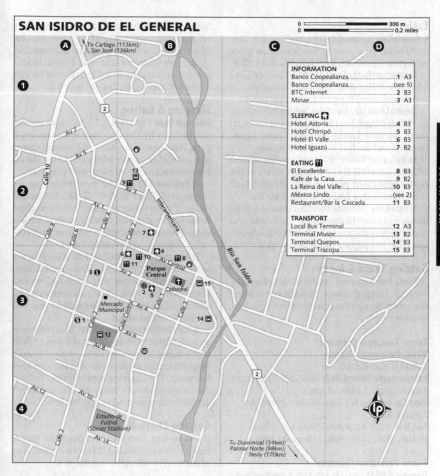

SAN ISIDRO DE EL GENERAL

0 —————— 300 m
0 —————— 0.2 miles

INFORMATION
Banco Coopealianza.............................**1** A3
Banco Coopealianza.........................(see 5)
BTC Internet.......................................**2** B3
Minae..**3** A3

SLEEPING 🛏
Hotel Astoria......................................**4** B3
Hotel Chirripó....................................**5** B3
Hotel El Valle.....................................**6** B3
Hotel Iguazú......................................**7** B2

EATING 🍴
El Excellente.......................................**8** B3
Kafe de la Casa...................................**9** B2
La Reina del Valle.............................**10** B3
México Lindo..................................(see 2)
Restaurant/Bar la Cascada...............**11** B3

TRANSPORT
Local Bus Terminal...........................**12** A3
Terminal Musoc................................**13** B2
Terminal Quepos..............................**14** B3
Terminal Tracopa.............................**15** B3

Information

BTC Internet (Av 2 btwn Calles Central & 1; per hr US$1; ⏱ 8:30am-8pm Mon-Sat, 10am-4pm Sun) has speedy connections. **Banco Coopealianza** (Hotel Chirripó Av 2 btwn Calles Central & 1; Av 6 Av 6, btwn Calles 2 & 4) has 24-hour ATMs on the Cirrus network.

If you're hiking Chirripó, make reservations for the mountaintop hostel at **Minae** (☎ 771 3155; Calle 2 btwn Avs 4 & 6; ⏱ 8am-noon & 1-4pm Mon-Fri), the park service office.

Sleeping

The following places all have cold showers unless otherwise stated.

Hotel Astoria (☎ 771 0914; Av Central btwn Calles Central & 1; r per person US$4, d with bathroom & TV US$20) With all the charm of a state psychiatric ward,

the Astoria wins guests with its cleanliness and rock-bottom price.

Hotel Chirripó (☎ 771 0529; Av 2 btwn Calles Central & 1; s/d US$7/12, with bathroom US$12/20) Dated but clean, these stark rooms have worn wooden dressers and a shower spout that barely clears the wall.

Hotel El Valle (☎ 771 0246; fax 771 0220; Calle 2 btwn Avs Central & 2; s/d US$11/15; 🅿) Quiet and spacious, rooms have decent mattresses and large windows. Some bathrooms are better kept than others – have a look.

Hotel Iguazú (☎ 771 2571; cnr Av 1 & Calle Central; s/d/tr US$12/20/28) The best option by far are these fresh white rooms with wooden trim, closets and matching furniture. The hotel is immaculate and boasts hot water, TV and fans.

COSTA RICA

Eating

Kafe de la Casa (Av 3 btwn Calles 2 & 4; meals US$4-6; ☺ 7am-8pm) Follow your nose to this bohemian place with great breakfasts, light lunches and coffee.

Restaurant/Bar La Cascada (☎ 771 6479; cnr Calle 2 & Av 2; dishes US$3.50-9) A trendy bar caters to local youth with beer, burgers and music videos.

México Lindo (Av 2 btwn Calles Central & 1; dishes US$3-5; ☺ 10am-8:30pm) Tucked inside a commercial plaza, México Lindo dishes up tasty tacos, burritos and nachos in a cheery setting.

La Reina del Valle (☎ 771 4860; cnr Calle Central & Av Central; dishes US$3-5) Get the best views of the newly renovated plaza at this tile-and-teak restaurant with a 2nd-floor open-air bar.

El Excelente (Av Central btwn Calles Central & 1; dishes US$4-6; ☺ 11:30am-10:30pm Thu-Tue) This clean and cool Chinese restaurant offers typical dishes spiced in hot pepper sauce, if you like.

Getting There & Away

A local bus terminal on Av 6 serves nearby villages. Long-distance buses leave around the Interamericana and are frequently packed, so arrive early.

From Tracopa Terminal

David, Panama At 10:30am.

Golfito At 10am and 6pm.

Palmar Norte/Ciudad Neily (US$2.75/5; 3/6hr) Depart 4:45am, 7:30am 12:30pm and 3pm.

Paso Canoas (5hr) At 8:30am, 10:30am, 2:30pm, 4pm, 7:30pm & 9pm.

San José (US$3; 3hr) Departs 7:30am, 8am, 9:30am, 10:30am, 11am, 1:30am, 4pm, 5:45pm and 7:30pm.

From Terminal Quepos

Dominical (US$1; 2½hr) At 7am, 8am, 1:30pm and 4pm.

Palmar Norte/Puerto Jiménez (US$2.75/5; 3/6hr) 6:30am and 3pm.

Quepos (US$3; 3hr) At 7am and 1:30pm.

Uvita (US$1.25; 1½hr) At 8:30am and 4pm.

From Other Bus Stops

San Gerardo de Rivas, for Parque Nacional Chirripó (US$1; 2½hr) Departs from the parque central at 5am and from the main terminal on Av 6 at 2pm.

San José (US$3; 3hr) Departs from Terminal Musoc on Interamericana between Calles 2 and 4 every hour from 5:30am to 5:30pm.

SAN GERARDO DE RIVAS

Fresh mountain air and a gushing river make this mountain village a pleasant stop on the way to climbing Chirripó. Buses from San Isidro leaves hikers at the **ranger station** at the village entrance to make hiking reservations. About 2km north are **hot springs** (admission US$3; ☺ 7am-6pm) where you can soak to your heart's content. At the cement bridge, take the turnoff to the left and follow the signs uphill.

Sleeping & Eating

Albergue Urán (☎ 388 2333, 771 1669; www.hotelelur an .com; dm US$9) By the entrance to the national park, Albergue Urán has bright, clean rooms and an affable owner who guests rave about. It's convenient for an early-morning start.

El Pelicano (☎ 382 3000; www.hotelelpelicano.net; r per person US$10, d/tr US$30/60; ☐ ♨) Before the ranger station is this gorgeous retreat run by a wood sculptor and his family. Spotless, simple lodge rooms sprout off a balcony with fine valley views. You'll want to linger.

El Descanso (☎ 369 0067; campsite US$4, r per person with/without bathroom US$15/10) This quiet homestead offers spacious, well-furnished rooms, some with a view. The accommodating Elizondo family also rents mountain gear and cooks dinner to order.

Hotel y Restaurant La Roca Dura (☎ 771 1866; campsite US$5, d/tr US$16/30) Right on the soccer field is this funky lodge with rustic charm. Murals brighten up the stone rooms and showers have hot water. The camping area (summer only) is a wooded garden by the river. The restaurant serves fresh trout and veggie burgers.

Getting There & Away

Buses to San Isidro depart from the soccer field at 7am and 4pm (US$1, two hours). Any of the hotels can call a taxi for you.

PARQUE NACIONAL CHIRRIPÓ

At 3820m Cerro Chirripó is Costa Rica's highest peak and the centerpiece of a gorgeous national park set in the rugged Cordillera de Talamanca. Lush cloud forest, high alpine lakes and bare *paramó* define the landscape. A well-marked hiking trail leads to the top where trekkers can sleep over in a mountain hostel. It's a two-day climb.

Get ready for mud. The steep 16km ascent goes through constantly changing scenery with abundant vegetation. Wildlife includes the harpy eagle and resplendent quetzal (visible March to May). Start early and allow six to eight hours to reach the hostel. Take plenty of water and all provisions. The grind to the hostel is the hardest part. From there, the terrain flattens and it's a two-hour hike to the summit.

Crestones Base Lodge (dm US$10) houses up to 60 people in dorm-style bunks. A solar panel provides light from 6pm to 8pm and sporadic heat for showers. The lodge rents sleeping bags (US$1.60), blankets (US$0.80), cooking equipment and gas. Spaces fill up quickly, so reserve in advance with Minae (☎ 771 3155) in San Isidro (see p615) or the **Chirripó ranger station** (Sinac; ☎ 200 5348; ☼ 6:30am-4:30pm) in San Gerardo de Rivas. All hikers must register at the ranger station and pay the park entry fee (US$15 for two days, plus US$10 for each additional day). Decent trail maps are for sale. You can also make arrangements here to hire a porter (US$22 for 14kg) or to store your luggage while you hike.

It's possible to camp in the designated area near Cerro Urán. For serious trekkers there's a guided three-day loop offered by hotels in San Gerardo.

From San Gerardo de Rivas there is free transportation to the trailhead at 5am from opposite the ranger station, in front of Cabinas El Bosque. Also, several hotels offer early-morning trailhead transportation for their guests.

PALMAR NORTE & PALMAR SUR
pop 6100

This hot and dusty banana-belt town is split into two by the Río Grande de Térraba. For travelers it is the northern gateway to Parque Nacional Corcovado. Facilities such as banks, buses and hotels center in Palmar Norte, while Palmar Sur has the airport.

Lack of allure aside, Palmar is the place to admire **granite spheres** left by pre-Columbian cultures. Some exceed 2m in diameter. They are scattered all over town, including at the airstrip; the most impressive sit in front of the peach-colored school (*el colegio*) on the Interamericana.

Banks include the Banco Coopealianza on the Interamericana, with an ATM. An internet café next door charges US$2 an hour.

Sleeping & Eating

Few linger in Palmar, but those who miss a connection can find the best-value places on the Interamericana.

Cabinas & Restaurante Wah Lok (☎ 786 6262; s/d US$6/8) This roadside motel offers clean rooms and Chinese food at the restaurant.

Brunka Lodge (☎ 786 7944; brunkalodge@costarricen se.cr; s/d/tr US$15/20/25, with air-con US$25/35/40; ▣ ▨) More inviting is Brunka Lodge, with bright and scrubbed bungalows with hot-water bathrooms and cable TV. Rooms are clustered around a swimming pool and there's a popular open-air restaurant.

Bar/Restaurante El Puente (dishes US$3-5) Off the main road into town serving palatable Tico favorites.

Supermercado Térraba (Transportes Térraba bus stop) Self-caterers can stock up here before heading to Osa peninsula.

Getting There & Away

AIR

Sansa has two daily flights to and from San José (US$72 one way), while NatureAir has one (US$80). Taxis from the airport go to Palmar Norte (US$3).

BUS

Tracopa buses to San José and San Isidro stop on the east side of the Interamericana. Others leave from Panadería Palenquito or Supermercado Térraba, a block apart on main street.

Ciudad Cortés Transportes Térraba departs from 6:30am to 6:30pm, six times daily.

Dominical At 8am.

Neily Transportes Térraba departs 5am, 6am, 7am, 9:30am, noon, 1pm, 2:20pm and 4:50pm.

Puerto Jiménez Departs from in front of Banco Coopealianza at 8am, 11am and 5pm (times are approximate).

San Isidro (US$3.50; 3hr) Departs 8:30am, 11:30am, 2:30pm and 4:30pm.

San José (US$6.50; 5hr) At 5:25am, 6:15am, 7:45am, 10am, 1pm, 3pm and 4:45pm.

Sierpe (US$0.60; 1hr) Departs 4:30am, 7am, 9:30am, 11:30am, 2:30pm and 5:30pm.

Uvita (US$1.25; 1½hr) At 12:30pm.

SIERPE

This sleepy village on the Río Sierpe sees bursts of activity as packs of travelers pass through to Bahía Drake by boat. Boats depart from the dock in front of Hotel Oleaje Sereno daily at 10:30am (US$20, 1½ hours). **Hotel Margarita** (☎ 786 7574; d US$10-12), west side of the soccer field, offers bare, basic lodgings. The rooms with private bathrooms and fans provide a comfortable upgrade.

Buses to Palmar Norte (US$0.50, 30 minutes) depart from in front of the Pulpería Fenix at 5:30am, 8:30am, 10:30am, 12:30pm, 3:30pm and 6pm.

BAHÍA DRAKE

This scenic village sits between the great green tangle of Parque Nacional Corcovado and the shimmering Drake Bay. It is not only next to Corcovado, but feels like the park's extra appendage, as sightings of macaws, monkeys and other wildlife form part of everyday routine. Traditionally this has been a remote and expensive destination but with the improvement of transportation and hotels, shoestringers can definitely still enjoy it.

Most hotels offer guided tours to the park, snorkeling trips to Isla del Caño and dolphin- and whale-watching trips at varying prices. The highly recommended **Corcovado Expeditions** (☎ 833 2384; www.corcovadoexpeditions.net) does it all at a highly professional level with bilingual guides. It also offers internet (US$3 per hour), rents kayaks (US$10) and leads mountain-bike tours. Join the Bug Lady for **The Night Tour** (www.thenighttour.com; US$35; ☼ 7:45-10pm), a highly recommended after-hours jungle hike featuring night-vision scopes.

Excellent volunteer opportunities can be found at **Fundación Corcovado** (☎ 297 3013; www .fundacioncorcovado.org), a nonprofit institute working with the community and park system for environmental education and preservation. It also provides insurance and housing (two-week minimum commitment).

Sleeping & Eating

While upmarket resorts dominate the village, budget offerings are expanding and improving. Most include meals in the price.

B&B Bambú Sol (r US$7) This no-frills place offers screened singles with fan in a muggy spot that truly requires it.

El Mirador Lodge (☎ 214 2711, 387 9138; www.mira dor.co.cr; per person with 3 meals US$40; per person in rancho US$10) With a harpy eagle's view of Drake Bay, El Mirador feels like a total retreat and the hospitality is outstanding. On a wooded hillside, screened wooden cabins are flanked by decks and hammocks. The family is building a *rancho* (basic refuge), where campers can bring a sleeping bag and cook independently, near the organic garden. Just before the village, take a marked left up a short, steep hill to the hotel.

Cabinas Manolo (s/tr US$15/30) The friendly Cabinas Manolo offers simple, brightly painted rooms with shared cold-water bathrooms. Meals are not included but the laundry service is free.

Getting There & Away

Boat transfers between Sierpe and Bahía Drake are exhilarating and scenic. Arrange a transfer with your hotel or take the collective water taxi (US$15, 1½ hours), which departs at 10am from the dock in front of Hotel Oleaje Sereno in Sierpe.

NatureAir and Sansa each have a daily flight between San José and Bahía Drake.

Bus service connects Drake to La Palma (US$3, two hours), leaving at 4am. From La Palma frequent buses go to nearby Puerto Jiménez. This service is sometimes suspended because of road conditions. Confirm times and availability with your hotel.

PARQUE NACIONAL CORCOVADO

This unspoiled national park is the last great tract of original moist tropical forest of Pacific Central America. Remote and wild, it covers the southwest corner of the Península de Osa. Costa Rica's largest population of scarlet macaws call it home, as do countless plant and animal species, including jaguars, coatis, toucans and snakes. The fantastic biodiversity, long the focus of tropical ecologists, is attracting a growing stream of adventurers who pour in from Puerto Jiménez and Bahía Drake.

Information

Information and maps are available at the **Área de Conservación Osa office** (☎ 735 5036, 735 5580; park fee per person per day US$10; ☼ 8am-4pm) in Puerto Jiménez.

Hiking

Paths are primitive and the hiking is hot, humid and insect-ridden, but the challenge of the trek and the interaction with wildlife at Corcovado are thrilling. The main routes across Parque Nacional Corcovado are well marked, making this journey easy enough to complete independently, although guides will provide a much more thorough understanding of the environment. Dry season (January to April) is the best for hiking. Trails lead to all four ranger stations – three border the park boundaries, and Sirena station, the headquarters, is in the middle of the park.

The most popular route traverses the park from Los Patos to Sirena, then exits the park at La Leona (or vice versa). This allows hikers to begin and end their journey in or near Puerto Jiménez, which offers easy access to both La Leona and Los Patos. From Carate, it's a

PENÍNSULA DE OSA & GOLFO DULCE

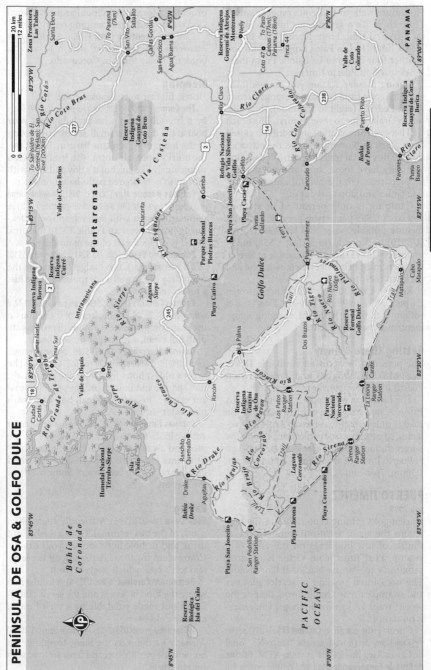

COSTA RICA

90-minute walk to La Leona ranger station. From there it's a seven-hour hike to Sirena on a coastal trail. From Sirena, hike inland for six hours to Los Patos ranger station and another four hours to La Palma. From there buses travel to Puerto Jiménez.

During the dry season, you can continue along the coast from Sirena to the ranger station at San Pedrillo (eight to 10 hours), then hike out to Drake (five to seven hours). The beach trail between Sirena and San Pedrillo is closed from April to November when the estuaries flood. The coastal trails often involve wading and may have loose sand and no shade – be prepared. Ask the helpful rangers about tide tables and don't get cut off.

Camping is only permitted in stations and costs US$5 per person per day. Facilities include potable water and latrines. Dorms (US$10) and meals (breakfast US$8, lunch or dinner US$11) are only available at Sirena. Campers must bring all of their own food and pack out their trash.

Reserve 15 to 30 days in advance through the park office in Puerto Jiménez. Don't travel without a compass, flashlight, camping equipment and insect repellent.

Getting there & Away

The park can be accessed via Bahía Drake (see p618), La Palma or Carate (reached from Puerto Jiménez, opposite).

The La Palma route takes visitors into Los Patos. A taxi may take you partway but the road is only sometimes passable to 4WD vehicles, so be prepared to hike the 14km to the ranger station. Return buses from La Palma go to Puerto Jiménez at 8:30am, 10am, 11:30am, 1:30pm, 7pm and 8:30pm.

PUERTO JIMÉNEZ

pop 7000

Once a gold-mining center, Puerto Jiménez retains the air of a flat-out frontier post. A shuffle of low buildings on the edge of a swamp, Port Jim's main virtue is its close proximity to Parque Nacional Corcovado. The occasional rustling of scarlet macaws and swamp caimans remind you, despite the tourist traps and souvenir shops, wilderness is not far off.

Check your email at **Cafenet El Sol** (US$3 per hr; 7am-10pm) ,with wi-fi access. Banco Nacional de Costa Rica has a Plus-system ATM. **Oficina de Area de Conservación Osa** (☎ 735 5036; Mon-Fri)

provides information about Parque Nacional Corcovado and takes camping reservations.

Call **Osa Aventura** (☎ 735 5670, 830 9832; www .osaaventura.com; Puerto Jimenez) well in advance to book multiday tours in Corcovado.

Sleeping

Hotels fill fast so try booking ahead.

The Corner (☎ 735 5328; dm/r per person US$5/7) Run by a friendly expat who probably met your boat at the dock, this small, secure hostel, west of the main drag, screams bargain. Of course, the quirky open-air dorm with iron bars feels suspiciously like jail, but it's tidy and airy, with mosquito nets. Shared baths have hot water.

Cabinas Bosque Mar (☎ 735 5681; www.bosquema rosa.com; per person US$10, d & tr with air-con US$30;) A popular bargain with superclean rooms featuring hot showers and cable TV in this pink motel one block east of the main drag.

Cabinas Oro Verde (☎ 735 5241; r per person US$10) With helpful staff, this budget lodging on the main drag offers well-kept rooms that are just a bit frayed.

Cabinas Carolina (☎ 735 5696; r per person US$10-12, d with air-con US$35;) In the heart of the action on the main drag, these enormous tile rooms are drab but clean, with spigot shower heads.

Cabinas Marcelina (☎ 755 5286; cabmarce@hotmail .com; s US$18, d without/with air-con US$30/40;) The town's oldest hotel feels a lot like grandma's: tiles sparkle and flower gardens provide pleasant respite. Rooms are small but fresh, with hot-water showers.

Cabinas Jiménez (☎ 735 5090; www.cabinasjimenez .com; s/d US$25/40, with air-con US$35/50;) By the pier and away from the hubbub, these softly lit rooms are spare and classic, with wood details and woven bed covers. Some overlook the lagoon.

Eating

Soda Deya (meals US$3-6) A friendly spot, 200m south of the bus terminal. Grab a slushy fruit drink and dribble hot sauce on your *casado*. Convenient for those departing on the jeep-taxi to Carate, which stops in front.

Restaurant Carolina (dishes US$3-8) A tourist hub where the food is decent and the service indifferent but made palatable by a varied menu and ice-cold beers.

Il Giardino (meals US$10-12; 10am-2pm & 5-10pm) A shady garden sets the scene to splurge on homemade pasta, pizza and fresh seafood with Italian wines.

Juanita's (5am-2am) Juanita's, east of the main drag, serves Mexican fare but it's far better known as the place to hob-nob at the low-lit cocktail hour. Happy hour is between 4pm and 6pm.

Getting There & Away

AIR
To and from San José, **Sansa** (735 5017; one way US$78) has three flights daily and **NatureAir** (735 5062, 735 5722; at Osa Tropical; US$87) has four flights daily.

BOAT
The **passenger ferry** (US$2) leaves at 6am for Golfito. **Taboga Aquatic Tours** (735 5265) runs water taxis to Zancudo for US$35.

BUS
Buses leave from the terminal. The following all pass La Palma (23km away) for the eastern entry into Corcovado. Buy tickets to San José in advance.
La Palma (US$1.50; 1½hr) At 5am & 5:30am – connect to Bahía Drake in La Palma at 11am.
Neily (US$3; 3hr) Departs 5:30am and 2pm.
San Isidro (US$4.25; 4hr) At 1pm.
San José, via San Isidro (US$6.50; 9hr) At 5am, 11am.

SHARED TAXI
Colectivo Transportation (837 3120, 832 8680; Soda Deya), 200m south of the bus terminal, runs a collective jeep-taxi service to Matapalo (US$3) and Carate (US$6) on the southern tip of the national park. Departures are from the Soda Deya at 6am and 1:30pm, returning at 8:30am and 4pm.

AROUND PUERTO JIMÉNEZ
A popular mountain tent lodge run by former gold-miners, **Río Nuevo Lodge** (735 5411, 365 8982; www.rionuevolodge.com; s/d US$65/100) is 2km west of Río Nuevo. Rough it in comfortable, furnished tents on covered platforms, with access to shared cold-water facilities and some solar-power electricity. The included meals are served family style in a thatched *rancho*. Rates include transportation from Puerto Jiménez.

In the Guayamí Indigenous Reserve, **Aguas Ricas Lodge** (messages 214 0769, in San Jose, 775 0433 in reserve; albergueaguarica@costarricense.cr; campsite US$5, r per person US$10, meals US$5), 8km from La Palma, offers guests a unique opportunity to learn about the culture with a warm and personable Guayamí family. Horseback tours go to Corcovado. English lessons may be exchanged for room and board. Contact Mariano Marquinez in the reserve or Klaus, who speaks English, in San José to arrange a visit.

GOLFITO
pop 14,000
Formerly a bustling banana port, Golfito is now being slowly reclaimed by the jungle behind it. Ticos enthusiastically duty-free shop here but for backpackers it's a mere springboard to the Osa Peninsula or Pavones. Bars and businesses, including a seedy red-light district, flank the south side of town.

Covering the steep surrounding slopes, **Refugio Nacional de Vida Silvestre Golfito** is home to exotic plant species and animals. Access it behind the north end of the landing strip. Entry is free and trails lead to waterfalls and scenic overlooks of the gulf. Hikers should not go alone.

Check your email at air-con **Golfito On-line** (per hr US$1.20) below Hotel Golfito. **Banco Coopealianza** on the north end has a 24-hour ATM on the Cirrus network.

Sleeping & Eating
Tico shoppers descend on the duty-free area on weekends, particularly in December, when cheaper hotels fill up.

Cabinas El Tucán (775 0553; r per person without/with air-con US$6/12;) This family-run places offers spacious rooms clustered around a shady courtyard and a welcoming atmosphere.

Cabinas Marisquera (775 0442; s/d US$10/30;) In a rambling house, Cabinas Marisquera has very clean renovated doubles with air-con and TV, luxurious next to the concrete singles.

Hotel Golfito (775 0047; s/d US$12/20;) Big, yellow and offering plain rooms that are dated but well scrubbed.

Cheap *sodas* are everywhere.

Restaurante Buenos Días (775 1124; meals US$4-6; 6am-10pm) One great eating option is this bustling restaurant, opposite the Muellecito, where you can get a stack of hotcakes, scrambled eggs or a cheeseburger served in a shiny booth.

Getting There & Around

AIR
The airport is 4km north of the town center. Sansa flies five times a day to/from San José (US$78 one way).

COSTA RICA

BOAT

Ferries to Puerto Jiménez (US$2, 1½ hours) depart at 11:30am and 1:30pm daily from the Muellecito. The water taxi to Zancudo (US$4, 45 minutes) departs at noon, Monday to Saturday, from the dock at Samoa del Sur. It returns at 7:30am the next day (except Sunday).

BUS

Buses (US$0.25) and collective taxis (US$0.75) travel up and down the main road. Tracopa buses to San José (US$8.50, seven hours) via San Isidro leave at 5am and 1:30pm from the terminal by the loading dock. Buses to Neily (US$1, 1½ hours) leave hourly from the main road, as do buses to Pavones (US$1.20, three hours), leaving at 10am and 3pm.

AROUND GOLFITO
Zancudo

With mangroves on one side and a picture-perfect swimming beach on the other, Zancudo makes a great lazy getaway. Only 15km south of Golfito, this one-road, one-horse town packs out with Ticos in the holiday season.

Cabinas Tío Froylan (☎ 776 0128; r per person US$7) has whitewashed rooms with private bathrooms and fan; there is an attached disco. About a 15-minute walk from the dock, **Bar/ Cabinas Sussy** (☎ 776 0107; s/d US$5/10) has clean rooms with a restaurant and a popular pool bar. Set back from the road, **Macondo** (☎ 776 0157; d/tr US$35/45; 🌐 ⚷) has groomed grounds, spacious rooms and a sparkling pool. The **Italian restaurant** (dishes US$5-10) serves homemade pastas, fresh pastries and espresso.

Boat taxis to and from Puerto Jiménez (US$15) and Golfito (US$12.50) are arranged through **Zancudo Boat Tours** (☎ 776 0012; www .loscocos.com) at Cabinas Los Cocos.

A bus to Neily leaves from the *pulpería* near the dock at 5:30am (US$1.50, three hours). The bus for Golfito leaves at 5am for the three-hour trip, with a ferry transfer at the Río Coto Colorado. Service is erratic during the wet season, so inquire before setting out.

Pavones

Narrow gravel lanes and breezy palm-frocked beaches welcome you to Pavones, an end-of-the-road destination a skip away from Panama. The world-class surf, bands of scarlet macaws, and rogue children on evening bike patrol make it feel something like paradise. In light of a budding expat community, the word is out.

Pavones is legendary amongst surfers for its wicked long left-hander, lasting up to three minutes. When big, the wave schools surfers on the sharp rocks at the end of the bay. The surf can also flatten out for weeks at a time – contact a local business before going. Conditions are best with a southern swell, usually between April and October. **Sea Kings** (☎ 393 6982; www .surfpavones.com) rents surfboards and bodyboards and offers lessons (US$50 per hour).

The town has two areas. Buses arrive first at Pavones, then head further south to Punta Banco where the road ends and jungle stretches to Panama. Punta Banco has volunteer programs caring for turtles (p631). Transportation between the two areas is scant, but it is a pleasant long walk.

The only public phone is at **Doña Dora's** (☎ 770 8221) by the soccer field.

SLEEPING & EATING

Listings are in order of appearance in the town. Punto Banco is a 20-minute walk south of town, reached also by the Golfito bus. Showers are cold.

Hotel Maureen (☎ 880 1561, 732 1655; per person US$10) A large rambler with friendly management and large, dark rooms featuring bunk beds or twins.

Cabinas Carol (☎ 827 3394; r per person US$10; **P**) Rooms are spare and simple, with some mosquito nets and shared outdoor baths in tile and bamboo. The best features are the shady hammock-strewn garden and the outdoor kitchen. It's 50m east of the soccer field.

Rancho Burica (www.ranchoburica.com; r per person US$8-22) Backpacker heaven, this Dutch-run complex of beachfront cabins offers sun, surf and friendly service. Room size and features vary but all have sparkling bathrooms and mosquito nets. Group dinners are assembled nightly and the grounds, dotted with lounges and hammocks, were made for repose. Reservations are not accepted: 'just show up like everyone else.' It's in Punto Banco where the road ends.

The Yoga Farm (www.yogafarmcostarica.org; r per person US$20) If your idea of vacation is chowing organic carrots and practicing your warrior pose, this retreat and conservation center is for you. Simple clean rooms have wooden bunks and shared bathrooms. Rates include three vegetarian meals, prepared with the garden harvest. It's a 15-minute walk from Rancho Burica – take the road uphill to the left, enter the first gate on the left and keep walking uphill.

Café de la Suerte (meals US$6; ☼ 8am-5pm Mon-Sat) This Israeli café, opposite the soccer field, dishes up scrumptious breakfasts of eggs with avocado and fruit salad or heaping muesli bowls. Fresh smoothies and daily specials fill the blackboard.

La Plaza (meals US$3-6) Locals and surfers pack this open-air spot to down cold frosty ones with *casados* or grilled fish.

GETTING THERE & AWAY
Buses to Golfito (US$1.20, three hours) leave at 5:30am from the end of the road at Rancho Burica in Punta Banco and at 12:30pm from the Esquina del Mar Cantina.

NEILY
This steamy agricultural center serves as a transportation hub 17km from Panama. Dubbed 'Villa Neily' by locals, it's a more pleasant spot to overnight than Paso Canoas. Banco Coopealianza, southwest of the mercado, has a 24-hour Cirrus ATM.

Motel-style **Cabinas Heileen** (☎ 783 3080; s/d US$10/14) is tidy and secure, with old-fashioned rooms, locked gates and barred windows. Also straight out of the '50s, superhospitable **Cabinas Helga** (☎ 783 3146; s/d US$16/21) offers immaculate rooms and tight security. Rooms have cable TV. Aspiring Roman villa **Hotel Andrea** (☎ 783 3784; s/d/tr US$19/20/24, s/d/tr/q with air-con US$23/24/26/28; ⊠) sparkles with white-tiled units featuring hot showers and cable TV. The attached restaurant serves quality breakfasts and Tico staples.

One block east of the park, **Restaurant la Moderna** (meals US$2-6) runs the gamut from hot dogs to pepper steaks. It's also the only restaurant in this book with a swing set inside!

Sansa has a daily flight between San José and Coto 47 (US$78/156 one way/round trip), the airport located 7km southwest of Neily. Buses leave from the main terminal on the east side of town:

Dominical Departs 6am and 2:30pm.

Golfito (US$0.50; 1½hr) Departs 13 times daily from 6am to 7:30pm

Palmar departs 4:45am, 9:15am, noon, 12:30pm, 2:30pm, 4:30pm and 5:45pm

Paso Canoas (30min) Departs 19 times daily from 6am to 6pm.

Puerto Jiménez At 7am and 2pm.

San Isidro (US$5; 5hr) Tracopa departs 7am, 10am, 1pm and 3pm.

San José (US$8.50; 7hr) Tracopa departs 4:30am, 5am, 8:30am, 11:30am and 3:30pm.

PASO CANOAS
This small border town is the main port of entry between Costa Rica and Panama. Hotels are often full of Tico bargain hunters looking for duty-free specials, especially on weekends and holidays.

Báncredito (☼ 8am-4:30pm Mon-Fri) near Costa Rican *migración* changes traveler's checks and there is an ATM on the Visa Plus system near the border. Money changers have acceptable rates for converting US dollars into colones. The **Instituto Panameño de Turismo** (☎ 727 6524; ☼ 6am-11pm) has information on travel to Panama.

Good-value **Hotel Real Victoria** (☎ 732 2586; r per person US$6; ℗ ⊠ ⊠) has clean, cool rooms lacking windows. The pleasant **Cabinas Romy** (☎ 732 2873; s/d US$8/12) has spotless pastel rooms set around a courtyard. This bright yellow building is the best-value option in Paso Canoas, but a few other decent options are found along this strip. There is no shortage of cheap *sodas*.

Tracopa (☎ 732 2201) is north of the border post, on the east side of the main road. Sunday afternoon buses fill up, so buy tickets in advance. Buses for San José (US$12.50, nine hours) leave at 4am, 7:30am, 9am and 3pm. Buses for Neily (US$0.50, 30 minutes) leave from in front of the post office every hour from 6am to 6pm. Taxis to Neily cost about US$6.

GETTING TO DAVID, PANAMA

On the Carr Interamericana, the 24-hour **Paso Canoas–David** border crossing is crowded and confusing, especially during holiday periods when shoppers pass through.

Costa Rican *migración* is on the eastern side of the highway, north of the Tracopa bus terminal. After securing an exit visa, walk 400m east to the Panamanian immigration post, in a yellow building, to purchase a tourist card (US$5 for US citizens) to enter Panama. You might be asked for an onward ticket and evidence of financial solvency (present a credit card). From here dozens of minivans go to David, 1½ hours away (US$2 per person).

See p669 for information on crossing the border from Panama.

COSTA RICA DIRECTORY

ACCOMMODATIONS

The hotel situation in Costa Rica ranges from luxurious and sparkling all-inclusive resorts to dingy, overpriced quarters. The sheer number of hotels means that it's rare to arrive in a town and find nowhere to sleep.

In tourist towns, you'll find plenty of *cabinas*, a loose term for cheap to midrange lodging. High-season (December to April) prices are provided throughout this book, though many lodges lower their prices during the low season. Some beach towns will also charge high-season prices in June and July, when travelers from the northern hemisphere arrive in droves. During Semana Santa (Easter Week) and the week between Christmas and New Year, hotels raise their rates beyond what's listed in this book. During this time, advance reservations are completely necessary. During school-vacation weekends in January and February it's advisable to book in advance.

There are numerous independently run hostels around the country, which are considerably cheaper than the Hostelling International (HI) ones. San José has several places, as does Manuel Antonio, Puerto Viejo de Talamanca, Monteverde and Tamarindo. The least expensive private rooms in budget hotels are often as cheap as hostels.

Most destinations have at least one campground, which usually includes toilets and cold showers, and are crowded, noisy affairs. Campsites are available at many national parks as well; take insect repellent, food and supplies. Camping prices in this book are listed per person, per night.

If you're traveling in from another part of Central America, note that prices in Costa Rica are much higher than in the rest of the region. Sleeping options are listed in order of budget, unless otherwise specified.

ACTIVITIES
Bungee Jumping

No vacation appears to be complete without a head-first, screaming plunge off a bridge. **Tropical Bungee** (☎ 248 2212; www.bungee.co.cr; 1st/2nd jump US$60/30), in San José, has been organizing jumps off the Río Colorado bridge since 1992.

Canopy Tours

There's nothing quite like sailing through the rain forest at high speeds in Tarzan-fashion. Operators sell it as a great way to see nature, though all you see are blurry broccoli-sized trees as you whiz by at full throttle. This is a damn fine adrenaline rush and it seems that nearly every town in Costa Rica has one.

Zip-line adventures are not without risk. Travelers have been injured, and in a couple of cases killed. Go with well-recommended tour operators. Minimal gear is a secure harness with two straps that attach to the cable (one is a safety strap), a hard hat and gloves.

Diving & Snorkeling

Costa Rica's water is body temperature and packed with marine life. As a general rule, water visibility is not good during the rainy months, when rivers swell and their outflow clouds the ocean. At this time, boats to locations offshore offer better viewing opportunities.

Hiking

For long-distance hiking and trekking, it's best to travel in the dry season. One of the best trips is the multiday hike across Parque Nacional Corcovado (p618). Parque Nacional Santa Rosa (p588) offers extensive trails in tropical dry forest and Chirripó (p616) is the best choice for mountain trekking. Assaults and robberies have been reported in some national parks, namely Carara, Braulio Carrillo, Gandoca-Manzanillo and on the road between La Palma and Los Patos near Corcovado. For maximum safety, go in a group or with a guide.

TO TAKE OR NOT TO TAKE HIKING BOOTS

With its ample supply of mud, streams and army ants, hiking through Costa Rica's parks can be quite an adventure – particularly for your shoes. If you come during the rainy season, or to the rainiest destinations, boots are required. A US$6 pair of rubber boots (found at any Costa Rican shoe or farm supply store) can save you from that nasty fatal viper bite *and* keeps you in style with the local *campesinos*. If traveling in dry season, you can risk using an old pair of running shoes (and something else for when those are drying out, which will be often).

Horseback Riding

Whether on mountain trails or the beach, horseback riding is a popular offering. Rates vary from US$25 for an hour or two, to US$100 for a full day. Overnight trips can also be arranged.

Not all outfitters are created equally. Some overwork and mistreat horses so ask to see the condition of the horses before setting out. Travelers should continue to recommend good outfitters (and give us the heads up on bad ones) by writing in to Lonely Planet.

White-Water Rafting & Kayaking

The months between June and October are considered the wildest months for rafting, but some rivers offer good runs all year. Bring sunblock, a spare change of clothes, a waterproof bag for your camera and river sandals. The regulation of outfitters is poor, so make sure that your guide is well-versed in safety and has had emergency medical training.

River kayaking can be organized in conjunction with rafting trips if you are experienced; sea kayaking is popular year-round.

Surfing

Most international airlines accept surfboards (properly packed in a padded board bag) as checked luggage. Domestic airlines accept surfboards (for an extra charge), but the board must be under 2.1m (6.9 ft) in length. If the plane is full, there's a chance your board won't make it on because of weight restrictions. It's also possible to buy a board (new or used) in Costa Rica, and then sell it before you leave. Outfitters in many of the popular surf towns rent short and long boards, fix dings, give classes and organize excursions.

Wildlife-Watching

Costa Rica is the easiest country in Central America to spot wildlife; it will often find you. Birding is world class and most visitors regularly see monkeys, sloths, leaf-cutter ants, morpho butterflies, poison arrow frogs, turtles, crocodiles and iguanas, to name but a few. There are ample whale- and dolphin-watching opportunities on both coasts.

The national parks are good places for observation, as are the many private reserves. Early morning and late afternoon are the best times to watch for wildlife, and a pair of binoculars will improve your observations tremendously.

Have realistic expectations, this isn't a zoo. Thick rain forest vegetation can make it hard to see wildlife. Walk slowly and quietly, listen as well as look. Hiring a guide vastly improves your chances.

BOOKS

English-language guidebooks can be found in San José bookstores (p539) and in tourist centers. To try out the local lingo pick up Lonely Planet's *Costa Rica Spanish Phrasebook*.

For a broad and well-written review of Costa Rican history, culture and economy, read *The Ticos: Culture and Social Change in Costa Rica,* by Mavis, Richard and Karen Biesanz.

Costa Rica: A Traveler's Literary Companion, edited by Barbara Ras, compiles 26 short stories by modern Costa Rican writers. Wildlife enthusiasts check out the following guides:

Butterflies of Costa Rica and Their Natural History by Philip J DeVries – everything you ever wanted to know about butterflies.

Costa Rica: The Ecotravelers' Wildlife Guide by Les Beletsky – a thorough introduction to Central American wildlife that is never boring.

A Guide to the Birds of Costa Rica by F Gary Stiles and Alexander F Skutch – the source for everything avian.

Neotropical Rainforest Mammals: A Field Guide by Louise H Emmons – a color-illustrated field guide to the more than 200 mammal species.

Tropical Nature by Adrian Forsyth – a well-written introduction to the rain forest that will undoubtedly get you excited about your journey.

BUSINESS HOURS

Government offices open 8am to 4pm Monday to Friday, closing between 11:30am and 1pm for lunch. Stores operate from 8am to 7pm Monday to Saturday, with two-hour lunch breaks common in small towns. Banks open Monday through Friday from 8am to 4pm, and some have Saturday hours.

CLIMATE

For a small country, Costa Rica's got an awful lot of weather going on. The highlands are cold, the cloud forest is misty and cool, San José and the Central Valley get an 'eternal spring' and both the Pacific and Caribbean coasts are pretty much sweltering year-round. (Get ready for some bad-hair days when you're here.)

For climate charts see p723.

COSTA RICA

CUSTOMS

All travelers over the age of 18 are allowed to enter the country with 5L of wine or spirits and 500g of processed tobacco (400 cigarettes or 50 cigars). Camera gear and binoculars, and camping, snorkeling and other sporting equipment, are readily allowed into the country. Officially, you are limited to six rolls of film, but this is rarely enforced.

DANGERS & ANNOYANCES

The biggest danger that most travelers face is theft, primarily from pickpockets who ply their trade at bus stations, on buses and in crowded areas. Theft is ridiculously commonplace. Don't wear nice jewelry or hang your camera around your neck. Keep your passport and money in the hotel safe and carry a photocopy. Never leave belongings in the overhead compartment on a bus or unattended on a beach.

Of greater concern is the growing rate of armed robberies in San José as well as tourist-heavy areas. In downtown San José, avoid walking around at night – take taxis instead. In the countryside, don't walk around isolated areas at night by yourself. It is always safest to travel in groups. If you are robbed, police reports (for insurance claims) should be filed with the **Organismo de Investigación Judicial** (OIJ; ☎ 222 1365; Av 6 btwn Calles 17 & 19, San José) in the Corte Suprema de Justicia (Supreme Court).

Both coasts have dangerous riptides – strong currents that pull the swimmer out to sea. Additionally, few beaches have lifeguards but some areas flag swimming areas (green) or danger spots (red). River-rafting expeditions may be risky during periods of heavy rain when flash floods can capsize rafts. Use reputable tour operators.

If you are caught in an earthquake, the best shelter in a building is in a doorframe or under a sturdy table. In the open, don't stand near anything that could collapse on you.

The **general emergency number** (☎ 911) is available in the central provinces and is expanding. **Police** (☎ 117) and **fire brigade** (☎ 118) are reachable throughout the country. The main tourist office in San José (p542) publishes a helpful brochure with an up-to-date list of emergency numbers around the country.

DISABLED TRAVELERS

Although Costa Rica has laws on equal-opportunity for disabled people, the law applies only to new or newly remodeled businesses and is loosely enforced. Buses don't have provisions for wheelchairs and few hotels, restaurants or parks have features specifically suited to wheelchair use. One exceptions is Parque Nacional Volcán Poás (p554).

Outfitter **Vaya con Silla de Ruedas** (☎ 454 2810; www.gowithwheelchairs.com) offers specialty trips for the wheelchair-bound traveler.

EMBASSIES & CONSULATES
Embassies & Consulates in Costa Rica

Mornings are the best time to go. Australia and New Zealand do not have consular representation in Costa Rica – the closest embassies are in Mexico City. All of the following are in San José. For visa information see p631.

Canada (☎ 242 4400; Oficentro Ejecutivo, 3rd fl, behind La Contraloría, Sabana Sur)

El Salvador (☎ 257 7855; 500m north & 25m west of Toyota dealership on Paseo Colón)

France (☎ 253 5010; road to Curridabat, 200m south & 50m west of Indoor Club)

Germany (☎ 232 5533; 200m north and 75m east of ex-president Oscar Arias' residence, Rohrmoser)

Guatemala (☎ 283 2557; Carr a Curridabat, 500m south and 30m east of Pops)

Honduras (☎ 291 5143; 250m east, 200m north then another 100m east from Universidad Las Veritas)

Israel (☎ 221 6011; Edificio Centro Colón, 11th fl, Paseo Colón)

Italy (☎ 234 2326; Calle 33, btwn Avs 8 & 10, 50m west of Restaurant Río, Los Yoses)

Mexico (☎ 280 5690; 250m south of the Subaru dealership, Los Yoses)

Netherlands (☎ 296 1490; Oficentro Ejecutivo La Sabana, Edificio 3, 3rd fl, behind La Contraloría, Sabana Sur)

Nicaragua (☎ 283 8222; Av Central 2540 btwn Calles 25 & 27, Barrio La California)

Panama (☎ 281 2442; 200m south and 25m east from the antiguo higuerón, San Pedro)

Spain (☎ 222 1933; Calle 32 btwn Paseo Colón & Av 2)

UK (☎ 258 2025; Edificio Centro Colón, 11th fl, Paseo Colón btwn Calles 38 & 40)

USA (☎ 220 3939; Carr a Pavas opposite Centro Commercial del Oeste)

Costa Rican Embassies & Consulates Abroad

For a full list of embassies in Spanish, log on to the **Foreign Ministry website** (www.rree.go.cr) and click on 'Viajando al Exterior.'

The following are the principal Costa Rican embassies and consulates abroad:

Australia (☎ 02-9261 1177; 11th fl, 30 Clarence St, Sydney, NSW 2000)
Canada (☎ 613-562 2855; 325 Dailhouise St, Ottawa, Ontario K1N 7G2)
France (☎ 01 45 78 9696; 78 av Emile Zola, Paris 75015)
Germany (☎ 030-2639 8990; Dessauerstrasse 28-29 D-10963, Berlin)
Israel (☎ 02-2566 6197; Rehov Diskin 13, No 1, Jerusalem 92473)
Italy (☎ 06-84 242 853; Viali Liegi 2, Int 8 Rome)
Japan (☎ 03-3486 1812; Kowa Bldg No 38, fl 12-24, Nishi-Azabu 4, Chome Minato-Ku, Tokyo, 106-0031)
Netherlands (☎ 070-354 0780; Laan Copes Van Cattenburg 46, The Hague 2585 GB)
Spain (☎ 91 345 9622; Paseo de la Castellana 164, No 17A, Madrid 28046)
UK (☎ 020-7706 8844; Flat 1, 14 Lancaster Gate, London W2 3LH)
USA (☎ 202-234 2945; www.costarica-embassy.org; 2112 S St NW, Washington, DC 20008)

FESTIVALS & EVENTS
The following events are listed from January to December:

Las Fiestas de Palmares (mid-January) Ten days of beer drinking, horse shows and other carnival events in the tiny town of Palmares.

Fiesta de los Diablitos (December 31-January 2 in Reserva Indígena Boruca; February 5-8 in Curré) During the fiesta men wear carved-wooden devil masks and burlap masks to re-enact the fight between the Indians and the Spanish. In this version, the Spanish lose.

Día de San José (St Joseph's Day; March 19th) Honors the capital's patron saint.

Fiesta de La Virgen del Mar (Festival of the Virgin of the Sea; Mid-July) Held in Puntarenas (p602) and Playa del Coco (p591), it involves colorful regattas and boat parades.

Día de Guanacaste (July 25) Celebrates the annexation of Guanacaste from Nicaragua. There's a rodeo in Santa Cruz (p597) on this day.

Virgen de Los Angeles (August 2) The patron saint is celebrated with a particularly important religious procession from San José to Cartago (p556).

El Día de la Raza (Columbus Day; October 12) Puerto Limón (p560) celebrates with gusto the explorer's landing at nearby Isla Uvita. The four-day carnival is full of colorful street parades and dancing, music, singing, drinking.

Día de los Muertos (All Souls' Day; November 2nd) Families visit graveyards and have religious parades in honor of the deceased.

Las Fiestas de Zapote (December 25 – January 1) A week-long celebration of all things Costa Rican (namely rodeos, cowboys, carnival rides, fried food and a whole lot of drinking) in Zapote, southeast of San José.

FOOD & DRINK
Costa Rican food, for the most part, is basic and fairly bland. The best food is on the Caribbean coast where coconut and chili peppers spice stews. Rice and beans (or beans and rice) are gussied up with *curtido*, pickled hot peppers and vegetables; Tabasco sauce; and *salsa lizano*, the Tico version of Worcestershire sauce.

Breakfast largely consists of *gallo pinto*, a stir-fry of rice and beans, served with eggs, cheese or *natilla* (sour cream). These are generally cheap (US$2) and filling. Restaurants offer a set meal at lunch and dinner called a *casado*. It usually includes meat, beans, rice and cabbage salad. Veggie *casados* can be made on request.

Sodas are cheap lunch counters serving *casados* as well as sandwiches or burgers. Other cheapies include the countless fried and rotisserie chicken stands. (Ticos *love* fried chicken.) Reasonably priced Chinese restaurants and pizza parlors are found in most towns. Better restaurants add a 13% tax plus 10% service to the bill.

Costa Rican specialties include:
agua dulce – sugarcane water
arreglados – puff pastries stuffed with beef, chicken or cheese
cajeta – a thick caramel fudge
chan – the black seeds of the chan plant, soaked and served in *agua dulce* or with tamarind juice; served primarily in the Guanacaste region
chorreada – a pan-fried cornmeal cake served with sour cream
gallos – tortilla sandwiches containing meat, beans or cheese
mazamorra – a pudding made from cornstarch
palmitos – hearts of palm, usually served in a salad
pejibaye – a rather starchy-tasting palm fruit also eaten as a salad
queque seco – pound cake
rondón – thick seafood based soup blended with coconut milk, found on the Caribbean side
tortillas – either Mexican-style corn pancakes or Spanish omelets

GAY & LESBIAN TRAVELERS
The situation facing gay and lesbian travelers is better than in most Central American countries. Homosexual acts between two consenting adults (aged 18 and over) are legal, but most Costa Ricans are tolerant only at a 'Don't ask, don't tell' level. Outside of gay spots, public displays of affection are not recommended.

COSTA RICA

San José offers is a good selection of night-clubs ranging from cruising joints to pounding dance clubs to more intimate places (see p548). The Pacific resort town of Manuel Antonio (p610) is a popular gay vacation center.

The monthly newspaper *Gayness* and the magazine *Gente 10* (in Spanish) are both available at gay bars in San José. Other resources include:

Agua Buena Human Rights Association (☎ 280 3548; www.aguabuena.org in Spanish) This noteworthy nonprofit organization has campaigned steadily for fairness in medical treatment for people living with HIV/AIDS in Costa Rica.

Gay Costa Rica (www.gaycostarica.com in Spanish) Provides up-to-the-minute information on nightlife, travel and many links.

INTERNET ACCESS

Finding cheap and speedy internet access at cybercafés or hotels is easy. Rates run US$1 to US$2 per hour in San José and up to US$5 per hour in more remote places. Wi-fi spots are up-and-coming (the few around are listed in this chapter).

INTERNET RESOURCES

Costa Rica Guide (www.costa-rica-guide.com) Nicely organized website with detailed maps and regional travel information.

Costa Rica Link (www.1costaricalink.com) Provides a great deal of information on transport, hotels, activities and more.

Guías Costa Rica (www.guiascostarica.com) Has informative links.

Lanic (http://lanic.utexas.edu/la/ca/cr) An exceptional collection of links to sites of many Costa Rican organizations (mostly in Spanish).

Tico Times (www.ticotimes.net) The online edition of Costa Rica's English-language weekly.

LANGUAGE

Spanish is the official language but English is widely understood and spoken exclusively along much of the Caribbean coast. Some Costa Rican slang:

¡adiós! – hello; used as a salutation in remote rural areas; also means 'farewell'

buena nota – OK, excellent; literally 'good grade'

chunche – thing; can refer to almost anything

cien metros – one city block; literally 100m

listo pa' la foto – drunk; literally, ready for the picture

pulpería – corner grocery store

pura vida – super, right on; literally 'pure life,' an expression of approval or greeting

sabanero – Costa Rican cowboy from the province of Guanacaste

salado – too bad, tough luck

tuanis – cool

una roja – a red one, literally a 1000-colón note; '*Me costó dos rojas*' means 'It cost me two red ones.'

¿upe? – anybody home? pronounced oo-pay; used in the countryside at people's homes instead of knocking

LEGAL MATTERS

If you get into legal trouble and are jailed, your embassy can offer only limited assistance. Embassy officials will not bail you out and you are subject to Costa Rican laws, not those of your own country.

In many beach towns, police tend to turn a blind eye on marijuana use. However, penalties in Costa Rica for possession of even small amounts of illegal drugs are much stricter than in the USA or Europe. Defendants often spend many months in jail before they are brought to trial and, if convicted, can expect sentences of several years in jail.

Drivers should carry their passport and a valid driver's license. In the event of an accident, leave the vehicles in place until the police arrive and make a report. This is essential for all insurance claims. If the accident results in injury or death, you may be prevented from leaving the country until all legalities are handled.

Prostitution is legal for women over 18. Prostitutes carry cards showing how recently they have had a medical check-up, though these are quite unreliable. Sex with a minor under the age of 18 is illegal in Costa Rica and penalties are severe.

MAPS

Detailed maps are hard to come by. An excellent option is the waterproof 1:330,000 *Costa Rica* sheet produced by **International Travel Map** (ITMB; www.itmb.com; 530 W Broadway, Vancouver, BC, V5Z 1E, Canada) with a San José inset.

Available in San José bookstores, **Fundación Neotropica** (www.neotropica.org) has published a 1:500,000 map showing national parks and other protected areas.

The Instituto Costarricense de Turismo (ICT; see p542) publishes a free 1:700,000 Costa Rica map with a 1:12,500 Central San José map on the reverse.

Online, **Maptak** (www.maptak.com) has maps of Costa Rica's seven provinces and their capitals.

COSTA RICA

WHAT'S THAT ADDRESS?

Though some larger cities have streets that have been dutifully named, signage is rare and finding a Tico who knows what street they are standing on is even rarer. Everybody uses landmarks when providing directions; an address may be given as 200m south and 150m east of a church. (A city block is *cien metros* – literally 100m – so '250 metros al sur' means 2½ blocks south, regardless of the distance.) Churches, parks, office buildings, fast-food joints and car dealerships are the most common landmarks used – but these are often meaningless to the foreign traveler who will have no idea where the Subaru dealership is to begin with. Better yet, Ticos frequently refer to landmarks that no longer exist. In San Pedro, outside of San José, locals still use the sight of an old fig tree *(el antiguo higuerón)* to provide directions.

Confused? Get used to it…

MEDIA

The **Tico Times** (www.ticotimes.net) is the weekly English-language newspaper and hits the streets every Friday. The most widely distributed paper is **La Nación** (www.nacion.co.cr), which has conservative coverage of national and international news. For a liberal perspective, pick up **La Prensa Libre** (www.prensalibre.co.cr), the afternoon daily.

Cable and satellite TV are widely available. There are more than 100 local radio stations. Radio 107.5 FM is a popular English-language station, playing current hits and providing a regular BBC news feed.

MONEY

The Costa Rican currency is the colón (plural colones), normally written as ¢. Bills come in 500, 1000, 5000 and 10,000 colones; coins come in denominations of 5, 10, 20, 25, 50 and 100 colones. US dollars are increasingly common, used to pay for tours, park fees, hotel rooms and large-ticket items. Meals, bus fares and the like should all be paid with colones.

ATMs

It's increasingly easy to find ATMs (*cajeros automáticos* in Spanish). The Visa Plus network is the standard, but machines on the Cirrus network, which accept most foreign ATM cards, can be found in San José and in larger towns. Some ATM machines will dispense US dollars. Note that some machines (eg at Banco Nacional) will only accept cards held by their own customers.

Bargaining

A high standard of living along with a steady stream of international tourist traffic means that haggling is fast dying out here. Beach communities, especially, have fixed prices on hotels that cannot be negotiated. (Expect some business owners to be offended if you try). Some smaller hotels in the interior still accept the practice.

Negotiating prices at outdoor markets is acceptable and some bargaining is accepted when hiring long-distance taxis.

Credit Cards

Holders of credit and debit cards can buy colones and sometimes US dollars in some banks. Better hotels and restaurants, car-rental agencies and some travel agencies take plastic. Visa is the most widely accepted, MasterCard less so and American Express (Amex) rarely. Some hotels might charge a 7% fee, in addition to government and service taxes.

Exchange Rates

The table shows currency exchange rates at the time this book went to press.

Country	Unit	Colones (C$)
Australia	A$1	450
Canada	C$1	490
Euro Zone	€1	720
Japan	¥100	430
New Zealand	NZ$1	410
UK	UK£1	1060
USA	US$1	520

Exchanging Money

All banks will exchange US dollars, and some will exchange euros; other currencies are more difficult. State-run institutions (Banco Nacional, Banco de Costa Rica and Banco Popular) may have long lines but they don't charge commissions on cash exchanges. Make sure your dollar bills are in good condition or they may be refused.

Hotels and travel agencies efficiently change money but many charge hefty commissions. Changing money on the streets is not recommended, except possibly at land borders. Street changers don't give better rates, and scammers abound.

Carry your passport when exchanging currency. The airport has two ATM machines to get dollars or colones as soon as you arrive.

Traveler's Checks

Most banks and exchange houses will cash traveler's checks at a commission of between 1% to 3%.

POST

Airmail letters abroad cost about US$0.35 for the first 20g. Parcels can be shipped at the rate of US$7 per kilo.

RESPONSIBLE TRAVEL

The ubiquitous buzzword 'ecotourism' boils down to marketing claims that are almost never substantiated. Real responsible travel depends on the behavior of your service provider as well as your own. Ecotourism providers accredited by outside institutions can be found at the **ICT sustainable tourism accreditation service** (www.turismo-sostentible.co.cr/EN/home .shtml) as well as planeta.com. Otherwise, businesses may be evaluated in terms of disposal of wastewater, recycling, energy efficiency, contributions to the local community and living wages for employees.

Visitors should follow the cardinal rules of never littering, never feeding the wildlife, staying on marked trails and not buying endangered products (turtleshell, feathers, skins, coral, shells and exotic hardwoods). An active approach means using mass transportation instead of driving or taking a taxi (if alone), volunteering (opposite), informing yourself on the local issues and promoting goodwill by respecting local cultures and engaging with locals. For more information, see p533.

SHOPPING

Coffee is the most popular souvenir, and deservedly so. Boozers can fill up on Ron Centenario, the coffee liqueur Café Rica and also *guaro*, the local firewater.

Uniquely Costa Rican, colorfully painted replicas of traditional oxcarts *(carretas)* are produced in Sarchí. Ceramics and tropical hardwood items are also popular. Check to see if wood products are made of endangered hardwoods. Avoid purchasing animal products, including turtleshell, animal skulls and anything made with feathers, coral and shells.

STUDYING

There is no shortage of language academies ready and willing to teach you Spanish around Costa Rica. Many operate in San José, the Central Valley as well as popular beach towns such as Jacó, Tamarindo and Puerto Viejo de Talamanca.

TELEPHONE

Public phones are found all over Costa Rica and Chip or Colibrí phonecards are available in 1000, 2000 and 3000 colón denominations. Chip cards are inserted into the phone and scanned. Colibrí cards (the most common) require dialing a toll-free number (☎ 199) and entering an access code. Instructions are provided in English or Spanish. These are the preferred card of travelers since they can be used from any phone. Purchase cards in supermarkets, pharmacies and *pulperías*.

The cheapest international calls are direct-dialed using a phonecard. Costs of calls from Costa Rica per minute are approximately US$0.55 to North America and US$0.80 to Europe and Australia. Dial '00' followed by the country code and number.

To call Costa Rica from abroad, use the international code (☎ 506) before the seven-digit number.

TOILETS

Public restrooms are rare. Restaurants and cafés usually loan their facilities at a small charge – between US$0.25 to US$0.50. Bus terminals and other major public buildings have lavatories, also at a charge.

If you're particularly fond of using toilet paper, carry it with you at all times as it is not always available. Just don't flush it down! Costa Rican plumbing is poor and has very low pressure with few exceptions. Dispose of toilet paper in the rubbish bin inside every bathroom.

TOURIST INFORMATION

The government-run tourism board, the Instituto Costarricense de Turismo (ICT) has two offices in the capital (see p542). Travel advice may be overly positive – it's their job to paint it pretty. Staff speak English.

The ICT is a good resource for free maps, a master bus schedule and information on road conditions in the hinterlands. Consult the ICT's flashy English-language website (www .visitcostarica.com) for information, or call the **ICT's toll-free number** (in the USA ☎ 800 343 6332) for brochures and information.

TOURS

Some well-established companies:

Birding Costa Rica (☎ 229 5922; www.birdscostarica .com) Custom birding trips.

Ecole Travel (☎ 223 2240; www.ecoletravel.com) Offers a variety of tours.

Euphoria Expeditions (☎ 849 1271; www.euforia expeditions.com) Specializes in cultural travel and expedition-style adventure trips.

Swiss Travel Service (☎ 282 4898; www.swisstravelcr .com) Tour agency.

VISAS & DOCUMENTS

Passport-carrying nationals of the following countries are allowed 90 days' stay with no visa: most western European countries, Argentina, Canada, Israel, Japan, Panama and the USA.

Citizens of Australia, Iceland, Ireland, Mexico, Russia, New Zealand, South Africa and Venezuela are allowed to stay for 30 days with no visa. Others require a visa from a Costa Rican embassy or consulate. A list of some embassies is on p626. For the latest info, check the websites of the **ICT** (www.visitcostarica.com) or the **Costa Rican embassy** (www.costarica-embassy.org) in Washington DC.

Onward Ticket

Travelers officially need a ticket out of Costa Rica before they are allowed to enter, but rules are enforced erratically. Overland travelers can meet this requirement by purchasing a round-trip ticket from Tica Bus, with offices in Managua and Panama City.

Visa Extensions

Extending your stay beyond the authorized 30 or 90 days is a time-consuming hassle. It is far easier to leave the country for 72 hours and re-enter. Otherwise go to the office of **migración** (Immigration; ☎ 220 0355; ☷ 8am-4pm) in San José, opposite Channel 6 about 4km north of Parque La Sabana. Requirements for stay extensions change so allow several working days.

VOLUNTEERING

In addition to these listings there are volunteer opportunities within the chapter.

Amistad Institute (☎ 269 0000; www.amistadinsti tute.net) Joint volunteer programs and Spanish instruction; participants practice language skills in local community organizations, schools and parks.

Asociación de Voluntarios para el Servicio en las Areas Protegidas de Costa Rica (ASVO; ☎ 233 4989; www.asvocr.com) Has 30-day work programs in the national parks; volunteers pay US$14 per day for meal costs. A 15-day commitment is required.

Habitat for Humanity (☎ 447 2330; www.habitat costarica.org) Has community building projects around the country. Constructions volunteers pay a US$100 registration fee, US$15 per day for accommodations, and must commit for one week.

International Student Volunteers (☎ in the USA 714-779 7392; www.isvonline.com) This excellent organization offers four-week programs with two weeks of volunteer work in local conservation or community development programs, and two weeks of fun and travel.

Volunteer Latin America (☎ 020-7193 9163; www .volunteerlatinamerica.com) Offers diverse opportunities, from working in an orphanage to gardening and trail maintenance to doing research on animal species. Some programs require special skills and/or minimum time commitments.

DOING TIME FOR THE TURTLES

Want to give back before heading back? Since 1998, **Pretoma** or **Programa Restauracíon de Tortugas Marinas** (Marine Turtle Restoration Program) has collaborated with locals to monitor the nesting activity and the operation of hatcheries in order to guarantee the efficient protection of nesting sea turtles and the production of hatchlings. Members of the community are hired as field assistants and environmental education activities are held with local kids. The project also involves tagging, measuring and protecting nesting turtles, which has resulted in a drastic reduction in poaching levels

Pretoma has projects in Playa San Miguel, Playa Caletas (7km south of San Miguel) and Punta Banco near the border with Panama. For more information on volunteering, visit the website at www.tortugamarina.org or contact the organization at tortugas@tortugamarina.org.

World Teach (☎ in the USA 800 483 2240; www.world teach.org) Volunteers receive a stipend of US$75 per month teaching English in public elementary schools. One-year commitment; lodging and transportation are included.

WOMEN TRAVELERS

A whispered *mi amor* or appreciative hiss will remind you you're south of the border, but even solo female travelers have few problems here. Be aware the norms are different.

Scant clothing is OK for the dance floor and the beach, but keep your top on (this isn't the Riviera) and cover up in town (especially the highlands). Shorts make you stick out.

Overall, men are usually gentlemen. But Costa Rican men do consider foreign women to have looser morals than Ticas and some may try to prove that theory. The best way to deal with this is obtaining a black belt in karate. Alternatively, try what Ticas do – ignore it. After passing this 'test' you usually get some respect.

Use normal caution: avoid walking alone in isolated places or through city streets late at night and skip the hitchhiking. Do not take unlicensed 'pirate' cabs (licensed cabs are red and have medallions) as reports of assaults by unlicensed drivers against women have been reported.

Most pharmacies sell birth-control pills without prescription. Tampons are scarce outside of major cities.

WORKING

Getting a bona fide job necessitates obtaining a work permit, a time-consuming and difficult process. The most likely source of paid employment is as an English teacher at one of the language institutes, or waiting tables or tending bar in a resort town. Naturalists or river guides may be able to find work with private lodges or adventure-travel operators. Don't expect to make more than survival wages from these jobs.

Panama

HIGHLIGHTS

- **Bocas del Toro** Soak up the Caribbean charm of laid-back Isla Colón before exploring the untouched beaches and forests of the surrounding islands (p681)
- **Boquete** Fuel yourself with mountain-grown coffee before hiking through the cloud forests in search of the elusive quetzal (p674)
- **Panama City** Spend the day admiring the faded glory of the old city, then party till sunrise on Calle Uruguay (p648)
- **Panama Canal** Marvel as hulking freighter ships are raised and lowered through sets of enormous locks (p664)
- **Comarca de Kuna Yala** Explore the tiny palm-covered islands of the Archipiélago de San Blás, home to one of Central America's most independent groups, the Kuna (p700)
- **Off the beaten track** Head to the virgin jungles and isolated rivers of the Western hemisphere's wildest frontier at Darién Province (p703)

FAST FACTS

- **Area** 78,200 sq km (slightly smaller than South Carolina)
- **ATMs** Widely available
- **Budget** US$20-30 per day
- **Capital** Panama City
- **Costs** Hostel in Bocas US$7, bottle of beer US$1, 3hr bus ride US$6, set lunch US$3
- **Country Code** ☎ 507
- **Electricity** 120V, 60Hz
- **Famous for** Panama Canal, panama hats, Manuel Noriega
- **Head of State** President Martin Torrijos
- **Languages** Spanish, Kuna & 14 others
- **Money** The Balboa – aka the US dollar
- **Phrases** *Panameños* (Panamanians), *chévere* (cool), *chau* (bye), *discúlpeme* (excuse me)
- **Population** 3.19 million

- **Time** GMT minus 5 hours
- **Traveler's Checks** Only accepted in US dollars; Amex checks accepted at most banks
- **Visas** Not necessary for most nationalities

TRAVEL HINTS

Take a light sweater and a poncho if you plan to hike and camp in the Chiriquí highlands. Get malaria tablets (anything but chloroquine) if you're heading to the Darién.

OVERLAND ROUTES

The principal Costa Rican crossing is on the Pan-American Hwy at Paso Canoas. Guabito on the Caribbean side and Río Sereno in the highlands are less chaotic border posts. For more information, see p669.

Unfettered by tourist crowds, Panama's natural gifts shine. Although most backpackers to Central America set their sights on tourist-soaked Costa Rica and Guatemala, it's hard to shake the feeling in Panama that you're in on a secret the rest of the traveling world has yet to discover. Although the 'gringo trail' has already swung south to the Caribbean archipelago of Bocas del Toro, the careless overdevelopment plaguing most Costa Rican beach towns is still refreshingly absent here. In fact, Panama's highlights are still very much off-the-beaten-path destinations, though it's likely that this will change in the years to come.

Panamanians have been eagerly anticipating the tourist boom, though the unexpected delay has allowed the country to plan ahead. With its high standard of living and recent growth in foreign investment, Panama will likely adopt a low-volume, high-profit model of tourism in the near future. In the meantime however, Panama remains accessible to backpackers on a budget, and there's no shortage of beaches, mountains and rain forests to explore. Panama is also home to one of Central America's most independent indigenous groups, the Kuna, as well as one of the last true frontiers in the Americas, the infamous Darién.

CURRENT AFFAIRS

On December 31, 1999, the US relinquished control of the Panama Canal and closed its military bases. Over 4000 Panamanians employed by the US military lost their jobs immediately, and the US took with them an economic impact of up to US$350 million. Despite the desire to cast off this last vestige of American colonialism, polls taken before the withdrawal showed that a majority of Panamanians wanted the USA to undertake a phased pull out because of the economic consequences.

Although there was both international and national skepticism regarding Panama's ability to run the canal, Panama has defied expectations, racking up impressive safety records and decreasing transit time for ships passing through the canal. However, the canal has not been without its problems. Forests within the Panama Canal's 'protected' watershed, which are vital to prevent silt build-up, have been cleared, and the lethal garbage left by the USA still needs to be dealt with. Target practice by US planes has left an estimated 105,000 unexploded bombs scattered throughout 7800 acres of rain forest.

However, the canal remains the lifeline of the country's economy, and there are hopes that it will bring greater wealth in the future. In October 2006, Panamanian voters overwhelmingly endorsed President Martín Torrijos' ambitious US$5 billion project to expand the canal by widening and deepening existing navigation channels in addition to creating a third set of locks. By enabling increased canal traffic and the passage of larger vessels, the Panamanian government is betting on a much needed boost into the country's economy.

Skeptics, though, note that plans for the expansion have been several years in the making. But with foreign investment at an all time high and tourism increasing in leaps and bounds, it's likely that Panama's economic growth and political stability will continue for years to come.

HISTORY
Lost Panama

The coastlines and rain forests of Panama have been inhabited by humans for at least 11,000 years, and it's estimated that several dozen indigenous groups including the Kuna, the Ngöbe-Buglé, the Emberá, the Wounaan, the Bokatá, the Bribri and the Naso were living on the isthmus prior to the Spanish arrival. However, the historical tragedy of Panama is that despite its rich cultural history, there are virtually no physical remains of these great civilizations.

Unlike the massive pyramid complexes found throughout Latin America, the ancient towns and cities of Panama have vanished into the jungles. However, tales of lost cities still survive in the oral histories of Panama's indigenous communities, and there is hope among Panamanian archaeologists that a great discovery lies ahead.

What is known about pre-Columbian Panama is that early inhabitants were part of an extensive trading zone that extended as far south as Peru and as far north as Mexico. Archaeologists have uncovered exquisite gold ornaments and unusual life-size stone statues of human figures as well as distinctive types of pottery and *metates* (stone platforms that were used for grinding corn). Panama's first peoples also lived beside both oceans, and fished in mangrove swamps, estuaries and coral reefs. Given the tremendous impact that fishing has had on the lives of Isthmians, it seems only fitting that the country's name is derived from an indigenous word meaning 'abundance of fish.'

New World Order

In 1501 the discovery of Panama by Spanish explorer Rodrigo de Bastidas marked the beginning of the age of conquest and colonization in the isthmus. However, it was his first mate Vasco Núñez de Balboa who was to be immortalized in the history books following his discovery of the Pacific Ocean 12 years later.

On his fourth and final voyage to the New World in 1502, Christopher Columbus went ashore in present-day Costa Rica, and returned from the encounter claiming to have seen 'more gold in two days than in four years in Spain.' Although his attempts to establish a colony at the mouth of the Río Belén failed in 1503 due to fierce local resistance, Columbus petitioned the Spanish Crown to have himself appointed as governor of Veragua, the stretch of shoreline from Honduras to Panama. However, with his primary benefactor, Queen Isabella, on her deathbed, the prize was awarded to Columbus' rival by King Ferdinand. In 1506 Columbus died in Spain a very rich man, though his colonial dreams were never realized.

Following Columbus' death, King Ferdinand appointed Diego de Nicuesa to settle the newly claimed land. In 1510 Nicuesa

followed Columbus's lead and tried to establish a Spanish colony at Río Belén. However, local resistance once again beat back Spanish occupation, and Nicuesa was forced to flee. Leading a small fleet with 280 starving men aboard, the weary explorer looked upon a protected bay 23km east of what is now Portobelo and exclaimed: *¡Paremos aqui, en nombre de Dios!* ('Let us stop here, in the name of God!'). Thus was named the town of Nombre de Dios, one of the first Spanish settlements in the New World.

Much to the disappointment of Columbus' conquistador heirs, Panama was not rich in gold. Add to the mix tropical diseases, inhospitable terrain and less than welcoming natives, and it's easy to see why Nombre de Dios failed several times during its early years as a Spanish colony. Later, in 1513, Balboa heard rumors about a large sea and a wealthy, gold-producing civilization across the mountains of the isthmus – almost certainly referring to the Inca Empire of Peru. Driven by ambition and greed, Balboa scaled the continental divide and on September 26, 1513, became the first European to set eyes on the Pacific Ocean. Keeping up with the European fashion of the day, Balboa immediately proceeded to claim the ocean and all the lands it touched for the king of Spain.

The Empire Expands

In 1519 a cruel and very vindictive Spaniard named Pedro Arias de Ávila (or Pedrarias, as many of his contemporaries called him)

BANANAS ARE OUR BUSINESS

Panama's banana industry dates from 1890, when three American brothers arrived in Bocas del Toro and founded the Snyder Brothers Banana Company. In the years that followed, the brothers planted banana trees all along the shores of the Laguna de Chiriquí. In 1899, however, the United Fruit Company planted itself in Bocas town, and took complete control of the Snyders' young company. In the century that followed, United Fruit established vast plantations that stretched across the entire peninsula. It also constructed elaborate networks of roads, bridges and canals, as well as entire towns and cities to house its workers.

Today United Fruit is part of the multinational Chiquita Brands International. Chiquita's workers in Bocas del Toro province grow and export three-quarters of a million tons of bananas annually. They also comprise the largest workforce in the province and the most diverse workforce in the country; on the payroll are West Indians, Latinos, Chinese and indigenous workers.

Unlike the oil-palm harvesting typical of Costa Rica, plantation fieldwork is unspecialized and requires a large, unskilled workforce. As a result, the main complaint from workers is that the industry does not pay adequate salaries. Though work is generally available year round, it is laborious as the banana pods are heavy and extremely unwieldy, and it can get brutally hot underneath the tropical sun.

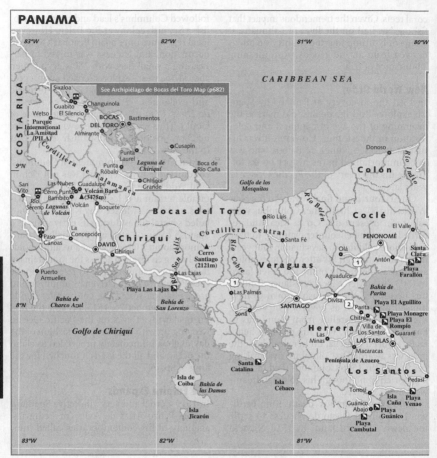

PANAMA

founded the city of Panamá on the Pacific side, near where Panama City stands today. The governor is best remembered for such benevolent acts as ordering the beheading of Balboa in 1517 on a trumped-up charge of treason, as well as ordering murderous attacks against the indigenous population, whom he roasted alive or fed to dogs when the opportunity permitted. Spanish swords and the introduction of European diseases soon decimated the indigenous population.

Despite his less than admirable humanitarian record, Pedrarias established Panamá as an important Spanish settlement, a commercial center and a base for further explorations, including the conquest of Peru. From Panamá, vast riches including Peruvian gold

and Oriental spices were transported across the isthmus by foot to the town of Venta de Cruces, and then by boat to Nombre de Dios via the Río Chagres. Vestiges of this famous trade route, which was known as the Sendero Las Cruces (Las Cruces Trail), can still be found throughout Panama.

As the Spaniards grew fat and soft on the wealth of plundered civilizations, the world began to notice the prospering colony, especially the English privateers lurking in coastal waters. In 1573 Sir Francis Drake destroyed Nombre de Dios, and set sail for England with a galleon laden with Spanish gold.

Hoping to stave off further ransacking and pillaging, the Spanish built large stone fortresses; one at San Lorenzo and another

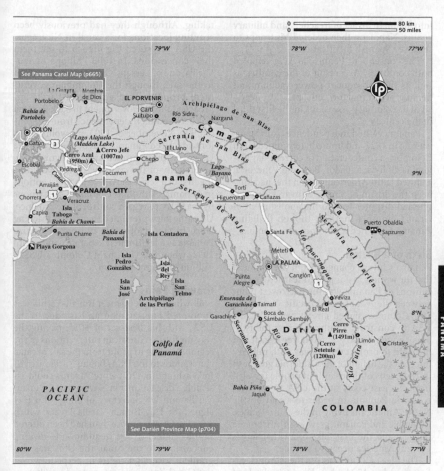

at Portobelo. However, these fortifications weren't enough to stop Welsh buccaneer Sir Henry Morgan from overpowering Fuerte San Lorenzo and sailing up the Río Chagres in 1671. After crossing the length of the isthmus, Morgan destroyed the city of Panamá, burning it to the ground, and he made off with its treasure and arrived back on the Caribbean coast with 200 mules loaded with Spanish loot.

The Spanish rebuilt the city of Panamá a few years later on a cape several kilometers west of its original site. The ruins of the old settlement, now known as Panamá Viejo, as well as the colonial city of Casco Viejo, are both located within the city limits of present-day metropolis of Panama City.

Of course, British privateering didn't cease with the destruction of Panamá. The final nail in the coffin was hammered in when Admiral Edward Vernon destroyed the fortress of Portobelo in 1739. Humiliated by their defeat and robbed of one of their greatest defenses, the Spanish abandoned the Panamanian crossing in favor of sailing the long way around Cape Horn to the west coast of South America.

The Empire Ends

On October 27, 1807, the Treaty of Fontainebleau, which defined the occupation of Portugal, was signed between Spain and France. Under the guise of reinforcing the Franco-Spanish army occupying Portugal, Napoleon moved tens of thousands of troops into Spain. In an act of treachery and military genius, Napoleon then ordered his troops to seize key Spanish fortifications.

The consequent Peninsular War crippled both countries. As a result of the conflict, as well as the subsequent power vacuum and decades of internal turmoil, Spain lost nearly all of its colonial possessions in the first third of the century.

Panama gained independence from Spanish rule in 1821 and immediately joined Gran Colombia, a confederation of current-day Colombia, Bolivia, Ecuador, Peru and Venezuela, a united Latin American nation that had long been the dream of Simón Bolívar. However, internal disputes lead to the abolishment of Gran Colombia in 1831, though fledgling Panama remained a province of Colombia.

Birth of a Nation

Panama's future changed from the moment that the world's major powers learned that the isthmus of Panama was the narrowest point between the Atlantic and Pacific Oceans. In 1846 Colombia signed a treaty permitting the USA to construct a railway across the isthmus, though it also granted it free transit and the right to protect the railway with military force. At the height of the California gold rush in 1849, tens of thousands of people traveled from the east coast of the USA to the west coast via Panama in order to avoid hostile Native Americans living in the central states. Colombia and Panama grew wealthy from the railway, and the first talks of a canal across Central America began to surface.

The idea of a canal across the isthmus was first raised in 1524 when King Charles V of Spain ordered that a survey be undertaken to determine the feasibility of constructing such a waterway. Later, Emperor Napoleon III of France also considered the idea. Finally, in 1878, French builder Ferdinand de Lesseps, basking in the warm glory of the recently constructed Suez canal, was contracted by Colombia to build the canal, bringing his crew to Panama in 1881. Much like Napoleon, Lesseps severely underestimated the task, and over 22,000 workers died from yellow fever and malaria in less than a decade. In 1889 insurmountable construction problems and financial mismanagement drove the company bankrupt.

The USA saw the French failure as a lucrative business opportunity that was ripe for the taking. Although they had previously been scouting locations for a canal in Nicaragua, the USA pressured the French to sell them their concessions. In 1903 Philippe Bunau-Varilla, one of Lesseps' chief engineers, agreed to the sale, though the Colombian government promptly refused. Bunau-Varilla approached the US government to back Panama if it declared its independence from Colombia. On November 3, 1903, a revolutionary junta declared Panama independent, and the US government immediately recognized the sovereignty of the country – what would be the first of a series of American interventions in Panama. Although Colombia sent troops by sea to try to regain control of the province, US battleships prevented them from reaching land. In fact, Colombia did not recognize Panama as a legitimately separate nation until 1921, when the USA paid Colombia US$25 million in 'compensation.'

Growing Pains

Following independence, Bunau-Varilla was appointed Panamanian ambassador to the USA, with his first act of office paving the way for future American interventions in the region. Hoping to profit from the sale of canal concessions to the USA, Bunau-Varilla arrived in Washington, DC before Panama could assemble a delegation. On November 18, Bunau-Varilla and US Secretary of State John Hay signed the Hay-Bunau-Varilla Treaty, which gave the USA far more than had been offered in the original treaty. In addition to owning concessions to the canal, the USA was also granted 'sovereign rights in perpetuity over the Canal Zone,' an area extending 8km on either side of the canal, and a broad right of intervention in Panamanian affairs.

Despite opposition from the tardy Panamanian delegation as well as lingering questions about its legality, the treaty was ratified, ushering in an era of friction between the USA and Panama. Construction began again on the canal in 1904 and despite disease, landslides and harsh weather, the world's greatest engineering marvel was finally completed in only a decade. The first ship sailed through the canal on August 15, 1914.

In the years following the completion of the canal, the US military repeatedly intervened in the country's political affairs. In response to growing Panamanian disenchantment with frequent US interventions, the Hay-Bunau-

Varilla Treaty was replaced in 1936 by the Hull-Alfaro Treaty. The USA relinquished its rights to use its troops outside the Canal Zone and to seize land for canal purposes, and the annual sum paid to Panama for use of the Canal Zone was raised. However, this was not enough to stem the growing wave of Panamanian opposition to US occupation. Anti-US sentiments reached boiling point in 1964 during a student protest that left 27 Panamanians dead and 500 injured. Today, the event is commemorated as Día de Los Mártires, or National Martyrs Day.

As US influence waned, the Panamanian army grew more powerful. In 1968 the Guardia Nacional deposed the elected president and took control of the government. Soon after, the constitution was suspended, the national assembly was dissolved, the press censored and the Guardia's General Omar Torrijos Herrera emerged as the new leader. Despite plunging the country into debt as a result of a massive public works program, Torrijos was successful in pressuring US president Jimmy Carter into ceding control of the canal to Panama. While the resultant Torrijos-Carter Treaty was less than popular in the USA, it guaranteed full Panamanian control of the canal as of December 31, 1999, as well as a complete withdrawal of US military forces.

The Rise of Noriega

Still basking in the glory of the recently signed treaty, Panama was unprepared for the sudden death of Torrijos in a plane crash in 1981. Rumors of foul play swept across the country, and in 1983 Colonel Manuel Antonio Noriega seized the Guardia Nacional, promoted himself to general and made himself the de facto ruler of Panama. Noriega, a former head of Panama's secret police, a former CIA operative and a graduate of the School of the Americas, quickly began to consolidate his power. He enlarged the Guardia Nacional, significantly expanded its authority and renamed it the Panama Defense Forces. He also created a paramilitary 'Dignity Battalion' in every city, town and village, its members armed and ready to inform on any of their neighbors showing less than complete loyalty to the Noriega regime.

Things went from bad to worse in early 1987 when Noriega was publicly accused of involvement in drug trafficking with Colom-

bian drug cartels, murdering his opponents and rigging elections. Many Panamanians demanded Noriega's dismissal, protesting with general strikes and street demonstrations that resulted in violent clashes with the Panama Defense Forces. In February 1988, Panamanian President Eric Arturo Delvalle attempted to dismiss Noriega, but the stalwart general held on to the reins of power, deposed Delvalle and forced him to flee Panama. Noriega subsequently appointed a substitute president who was more sympathetic to his cause.

Noriega's regime became an international embarrassment. In March 1988, the USA imposed economic sanctions against Panama, ending a preferential trade agreement, freezing Panamanian assets in US banks and refusing to pay canal fees. A few days after the sanctions were imposed, an unsuccessful military coup prompted Noriega to step up violent repression of his critics. After Noriega's candidate failed to win the presidential election in May 1989, the general declared the election null and void. Meanwhile, Guillermo Endara, the winning candidate, and his two vice-presidential running mates, were badly beaten by some of Noriega's thugs, and the entire bloody scene was captured by a TV crew and broadcasted internationally. A second failed coup in October 1989 was followed by even more repressive measures.

On December 15, 1989, Noriega's legislature declared him president, and his first official act of office was to declare war on the USA. The following day, an unarmed US marine dressed in civilian clothes was killed by Panamanian soldiers while leaving a restaurant in Panama City.

The Fall of Noriega

The US reaction was swift and unrelenting. In the first hour of December 20, 1989, Panama City was attacked by aircraft, tanks and 26,000 US troops. The invasion, intended to bring Noriega to justice and create a democracy better suited to US interests, left more than 2000 civilians dead, tens of thousands homeless and destroyed entire tracts of Panama City.

On Christmas Day, Noriega claimed asylum in the Vatican embassy. US forces surrounded the embassy and pressured the Vatican to release him. They memorably used that psychological tactic loved by disgruntled teenagers, namely bombarding the embassy with blaring rock music (Van Halen and

Metallica were among the selections). The embassy was also surrounded by mobs of angry Panamanians calling for Noriega to be ousted.

After 10 days of psychological warfare, the chief of the Vatican embassy persuaded Noriega to give himself up by threatening to cancel his asylum. Noriega surrendered to US forces on January 3, and was flown to Miami where he was convicted of conspiracy to manufacture and distribute cocaine. Although he was sentenced in 1992 to 40 years in a Florida prison, he was scheduled to be released on good behavior in September 2007.

Modern Woes

After Noriega's forced removal, Guillermo Endara, the legitimate winner of the 1989 election, was sworn in as president, and Panama attempted to put itself back together. The country's image and economy were in shambles, and its capital had suffered damage not only from the invasion itself, but from the widespread looting that followed. Unfortunately, Endara proved to be an ineffective leader whose policies cut jobs and cost his administration the popularity it initially enjoyed. By the time he was voted out of office in 1994, he was suffering from single-digit approval ratings.

In the 1994 elections, the fairest in recent Panamanian history, Ernesto Pérez Balladares came into office. Under his direction, the Panamanian government implemented a program of privatization that focused on infrastructure improvements, health care and education. Although Pérez Balladares allocated unprecedented levels of funding to Panama's development, he was viewed as corrupt. In the spring of 1999, voters rejected his attempt to change constitutional limits barring a president from serving two consecutive terms.

In 1999 Mireya Moscoso, the widow of popular former president Arnulfo Arias, and Panama's first female leader and head of the conservative Arnulfista Party (PA), took office. Moscoso had ambitious plans for the country, and promised to improve education, health care and housing for the two-thirds of Panamanians below the poverty line. She also promised to generate much-needed jobs and to reduce the staggering unemployment rate.

As Panama celebrated its centenary in 2003, unemployment rose to 18% while underemployment reached 30%. Moscoso also angered many with her wasteful spending – as parts of the country went without food, she paid US$10 million to bring the Miss Universe pageant to Panama. Moscoso was also accused of looking the other way during Colombian military incursions into the Darién, implying indifference to the terrorism occurring inside the country's borders. When she left office in 2004, Moscoso left behind a legacy of gross incompetence.

Panama is currently under the leadership of Martín Torrijos, a member of the Revolutionary Democratic Party (PRD) and the son of former leader Omar Torrijos. Although there is still much debate regarding the successes and failures of his administration, he has already implemented a number of much-needed fiscal reforms, including an overhaul of the nation's social security system. Furthermore, his proposal to expand the Panama Canal was overwhelmingly approved in a national referendum on October 22, 2006.

THE CULTURE
The National Psyche

At the crossroads of the Americas, the narrow isthmus of Panama bridges not only two continents but two vastly different paradigms of Panamanian culture and society. While one sphere of Panama clings to the traditions of the past, the other looks to the modernizing influences of a growing economy.

In some ways, these opposing forces are only natural given the many years that Panama has been the object of another country's meddling. From the US-backed independence of 1903 to the strong-armed removal of Noriega in 1989, with half-a-dozen other interventions in between, the USA left a strong legacy in the country. Nearly every Panamanian has a relative or at least an acquaintance living in the USA. Parts of the country seem swept up in mall-fervor, with architectural inspiration straight out of North America.

Others, however, are not so ready to embrace gringo culture. Indigenous groups such as the Emberá and Kuna are struggling to keep their traditions alive, as more and more of their youth are lured into the Westernized lifestyle of the city.

Given the clash between old and new, it's surprising the country isn't suffering from a serious case of cognitive dissonance. Somehow, the exceptionally tolerant Panamanian character weathers many contradictions – the old and the new, the grave disparity between rich and poor, and the gorgeous natural environment and its rapid destruction.

Lifestyle

In spite of the skyscrapers and gleaming restaurants lining the wealthier districts of Panama City, nearly a third of the country's population lives in poverty. Furthermore, almost a quarter of a million Panamanians struggle just to satisfy their basic dietary needs. Those hardest hit by poverty tend to be in the least populated provinces: Darién, Bocas del Toro, Veraguas, Los Santos and Colón. There are also a substantial number of very poor people living in the slums of Panama City, where an estimated 20% of the urban population lives. Countrywide, 9% of the population lives in *barriados* (squatter) settlements.

For *campesinos* (farmers), life is hard. A subsistence farmer in the interior might earn as little as a few hundred dollars a year, far below the national average of US$7400 annually per capita. The dwelling might consist of a simple cinderblock building, with a roof and four walls and perhaps a porch. Families have few possessions, and every member assists with working the land or contributing to the household.

The middle and upper class largely reside in Panama City environs, enjoying a level of comfort similar to their economic brethren in Europe and the USA. They live in large homes or apartments, have a maid, a car or two, and for the lucky few a second home on the beach or in the mountains. Cell phones are de rigueur. Vacations are often enjoyed outside of the country in Europe or the USA. Most middle-class adults can speak some English, and their children usually attend English-speaking schools.

In the Emberá villages of the Darién, traditional subsistence life continues as it has for hundreds of years. The majority of these people lack clean water and basic sanitation.

People

Of Panama's three million souls, 57% live in urban areas. The majority of the population (65%) is mestizo, which is generally a mix of indigenous and Spanish descent. Many non-black immigrants are also thrown into this category, including a sizable Chinese population: some estimate that as much as 10% of the population is of Chinese ancestry. There are also a number of other sizable groups. About 14% of Panamanians are of African descent, 10% of Spanish descent, 5% of mixed African and Spanish descent, and 6% are indigenous.

Black Panamanians are mostly descendants of English-speaking West Indians such as Jamaicans and Trinidadians, who were brought to Panama as laborers. Of the several dozen native tribes that inhabited Panama when the Spanish arrived, only seven remain. Most famous is the Kuna tribe, which lives along the Caribbean coast between Colón Province and Colombia. The Emberá and Wounaan inhabit the jungle of the eastern Panamá province and the Darién, while the Ngöbe-Buglé can be found in Chiriquí, Veraguas and Bocas del Toro. The Teribe and Bokotá inhabit Bocas province, while the Bribri are found both in

PANAMA

PANAMA HATS

A panama hat or simply a panama is a traditional brimmed hat made from a panama-hat palm (*Carludovica palmata*). Although originally from Ecuador, the hat became popular in Panama during the construction of the canal when thousands of hats were imported for use by the workers. After USA president Theodore Roosevelt donned a panama during his historic visit to the canal, the hats became the height of fashion.

Unlike the better-known panamas from Ecuador, which are woven from crown to brim in one piece, this kind is made by a braiding process using a half-inch braid of palm fiber, usually of alternating or mixed white and black. The finished braid is wound around a wooden form and sewn together at the edges, producing a round-crowned, black-striped hat. It's a common sight in the rural parts of Panama, and it's not unusual for political contenders to don hats periodically to appear as 'one of the people.'

There's no one place to buy panama hats, though the highest quality panamas typically come from the interior. Prices range from US$10 to US$150.

Costa Rica and in Panama along the Talamanca reserve.

Despite modernizing influences, each of Panama's indigenous groups maintains its own language and culture. The Ngöbe-Buglé is Panama's largest tribe, and numbers about 125,000. The Kuna, who govern their ancestral territory as the autonomous region of the Comarca de Kuna Yala, are the most politically organized, and regularly send representatives to the national legislature.

ARTS

Panama's music scene reflects its ethnic mix. A slow spin on the radio dial or a hard look at Panamanian nightclubs will reveal salsa, Latin and American jazz, traditional music from the central provinces, reggae, reggaeton and Latin, British and American rock 'n' roll. The country's most renowned salsa singer, Harvard-educated Rubén Blades, has had several international hits and appeared in several movies – he even ran for president in 1994, finishing third. The jazz composer and pianist Danilo Pérez is widely acclaimed by critics, while Los Rabanes is the most well-known rock group in the country. Heavy on the accordion, Panamanian folk music (called *típico*), is well represented by Victorio Vergara and Samy and Sandra Sandoval.

Several of Panama's best novelists wrote around the mid-20th century. *El Ahogado* (The Drowned Man), a 1937 novel by Tristán Solarte (pen name for Guillermo Sánchez Borbón, a well-known poet, novelist and journalist), ingeniously blends elements of the detective, gothic and psychological genres, with a famous local myth. *El Desván* (In the Garret), a 1954 novel by Ramón H Jurado, explores the emotional limits of the human condition. *Gamboa Road Gang,* by Joaquín Beleño, is the best work of fiction about the political and social events surrounding the Panama Canal.

Trained in France, Roberto Lewis (1874–1949) became the first prominent figure on Panama's art scene. He painted portraits of the nation's leaders and allegorical images to decorate public buildings; among his most notable works are those in the Palacio de las Garzas in Panama City. In 1913 Lewis became the director of Panama's first art academy, where he and his successor, Humberto Ivaldi (1909–47), educated a generation of artists. Among the school's students were

Juan Manuel Cedeño and Isaac Benítez, as well as the painters who would come to the fore in the 1950s and '60s, including Alfredo Sinclair, Guillermo Trujillo, Eudoro Silvera and others.

SPORT

Owing to the legacy of US military occupation, baseball is the national pastime in Panama. Although there are no professional teams in Panama, the amateur leagues host games in stadiums throughout the country. Panamanians have their favorite teams, but are usually more interested in their favorite players in the US major leagues. Mariano Rivera, the record-setting Panamanian pitcher for the New York Yankees, is a household name. The batting champ Rod Carew is another (former) Panamanian star – inducted into the Hall of Fame in 1991. Roberto Kelly, who played for the Yankees for many years, is also fondly remembered.

Boxing is another popular spectator sport, and it's been a source of pride to Panamanians ever since Roberto Durán, a Panama City native and international boxing legend, won the world championship lightweight title in 1972. He subsequently went on to further great deeds, becoming the world champion in each of the welterweight (1980), light middleweight (1983) and super middleweight (1989) categories.

RELIGION

The many religions of Panama can best be observed by walking the streets of the capital. Among the scores of Catholic churches you'll find breezy Anglican churches filled with worshippers from the West Indies, as well as synagogues, mosques, a shiny Greek Orthodox church, an impressive Hindu temple and a surreal Baha'i house of worship (the headquarters for Latin America).

Freedom of religion is constitutionally guaranteed in Panama, although the preeminence of Roman Catholicism is officially recognized, with 77% of the country filling its ranks. Schoolchildren in Panama are given the opportunity to study theology, although it's not compulsory. Protestant denominations account for 12%, Muslims 4.4% and Baha'i 1.2%. Additionally, the country has several thousand Jews, many of whom are recent immigrants from Israel, as well as nearly 25,000 Buddhists and 10,000 Hindus.

The various indigenous groups in Panama also have their own belief systems, although these are fading quickly due to the influence of Christian missionaries. As in other parts of Latin America, the evangelical movement is spreading like wildfire.

Although Catholicism holds the majority, only about 20% of Catholics attend church regularly. The religious orders aren't particularly strong in Panama either – only about 25% of Catholic clergy are Panamanian, while the rest are foreign missionaries.

ENVIRONMENT
The Land
Panama is both the narrowest and the southernmost country in Central America. The long S-shaped isthmus borders Costa Rica in the west and Colombia in the east. Its northern Caribbean coastline measures 1160km, compared to a 1690km Pacific coastline in the south, and its total land area is 78,056km. By comparison, Panama is slightly bigger than Ireland or Austria, and roughly the same size as South Carolina.

Panama is just 50km wide at its leanest point, an impressive statistic given that it separates two great oceans. The Panama Canal, which is about 80km long, effectively divides the country into eastern and western regions. Panama is also home to two great mountain ranges, which run along Panama's spine in both the east and the west. The highest point in the country, Volcán Barú, is located in Chiriquí Province, and is also the country's only volcano.

Like all of the Central American countries, Panama has large, flat coastal lowlands, covered in places by huge banana plantations. There are about 480 rivers in Panama and 1518 islands near its shores. The two main island groups are the San Blás and Bocas del Toro Archipelagos on the Caribbean side, but most of the islands are on the Pacific side. Even the Panama Canal has islands, including Isla Barro Colorado, which has a world-famous tropical rain forest research station.

Wildlife
Panama's position as a narrow land bridge between two huge continents has given it a remarkable variety of plant and animal life. Species migrating between the continents have gathered in Panama, which means that it's possible to see South American armadillos, anteaters and sloths alongside North American tapirs, jaguars and deer. With its wide variety of native and migratory species, Panama is one of the world's best places for bird-watchers.

Panama has more than 940 recorded bird species and more than 10,000 plant species, in addition to 125 animal species found nowhere else in the world. The country also has 105 rare and endangered species, including scarlet macaws, harpy eagles (the national bird of Panama), golden frogs, jaguars and various species of sea turtle. Panama has some of the best places to see the quezal.

Lovers of sea turtles and primates are also drawn to the country. Five species of sea turtle can be seen here, while among the primates

---

STRIKING A DELICATE BALANCE

As little as 50 years ago, over 70% of Panama's total land mass was covered by forest. This sobering statistic gives a quick indication of the country's gravest environmental problem, deforestation. Today, trees continue to be felled at a frightening pace, with the Darién serving as the ecological ground zero.

Unfortunately, much of the population of Panama seems unconcerned with the rain forest's ongoing destruction. For much of the population, hunting and logging have been a way of life for generations, and many communities maintain the belief that their economic welfare depends on these practices. Furthermore, Panama's national parks are staffed by a handful of rangers, though their areas of coverage are colossal; in the Parque Nacional Darién there are never more than 20 rangers assigned to protect 576,000 hectares, an area larger than some countries.

The destruction of the rain forest wipes out native fauna as well as migratory animals, and causes regional water shortages, pollution and erosion. It also threatens the traditional cultures of the Emberá and the Wounaan, who still rely on the rain forest for survival.

The home page of **Ancon** (Asociación Nacional para la Conservación de la Naturaleza; Map pp648-9; ☎ 314 0060; www.ancon.org in Spanish), a private conservation group that has lobbied strongly for the preservation of Panama's forests, has more information.

PANAMA PARKS & PROTECTED AREAS

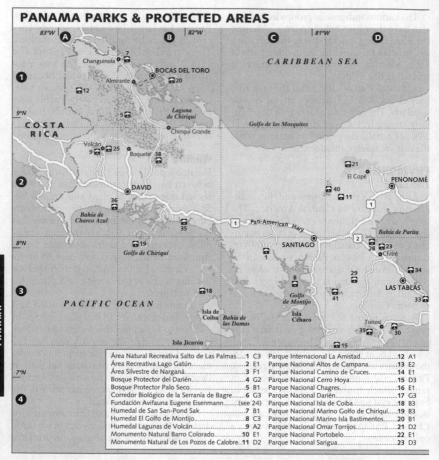

Área Natural Recreativa Salto de Las Palmas....**1** C3		Parque Internacional La Amistad...................**12** A1
Área Recreativa Lago Gatún..............................**2** E1		Parque Nacional Altos de Campana..................**13** E2
Área Silvestre de Narganá...............................**3** F1		Parque Nacional Camino de Cruces..................**14** E1
Bosque Protector del Darién.............................**4** G2		Parque Nacional Cerro Hoya.............................**15** D3
Bosque Protector Palo Seco.............................**5** B1		Parque Nacional Chagres..................................**16** E1
Corredor Biológico de la Serranía de Bagre......**6** G3		Parque Nacional Darién....................................**17** G3
Fundación Avifauna Eugene Eisenmann.......(see **24**)		Parque Nacional Isla de Coiba..........................**18** B3
Humedal de San San-Pond Sak.........................**7** B1		Parque Nacional Marino Golfo de Chiriquí........**19** B3
Humedal El Golfo de Montijo.............................**8** C3		Parque Nacional Marino Isla Bastimentos........**20** B1
Humedal Lagunas de Volcán..............................**9** A2		Parque Nacional Omar Torrijos.........................**21** D2
Monumento Natural Barro Colorado.............**10** E1		Parque Nacional Portobelo................................**22** E1
Monumento Natural de Los Pozos de Calobre..**11** D2		Parque Nacional Sarigua..................................**23** D3

are capuchins, tamarins and squirrel, spider and howler monkeys.

Tropical rain forest is the dominant vegetation in the canal area, along the Caribbean coast and in most of the eastern half of the country. The Parque Nacional Darién protects much of Panama's largest tropical rainforest region. Other vegetation zones include grasslands on the Pacific coast, mountain forest in the highlands, cloud forest on the highest peaks and mangrove forest on both coasts.

National Parks & Reserves

Panama has 11 national parks and more than two dozen officially protected areas. About one-quarter of Panama is set aside

for conservation, while about 45% of land remains covered by forest. Panama also has more land set aside for habitat protection than any other Central America country, and Panama's forests contain the greatest number of species of all New World countries north of Colombia.

In many of the national parks and protected areas, you'll find mestizo and indigenous villages scattered about. In the most successful scenarios, the communities help protect and maintain the park and its wildlife. However, in regions such as the Darién, trees are being felled at an alarming rate. A 2003 study showed that in the previous 10 years 80,000 hectares of rain forest was hacked down in Darién Province alone.

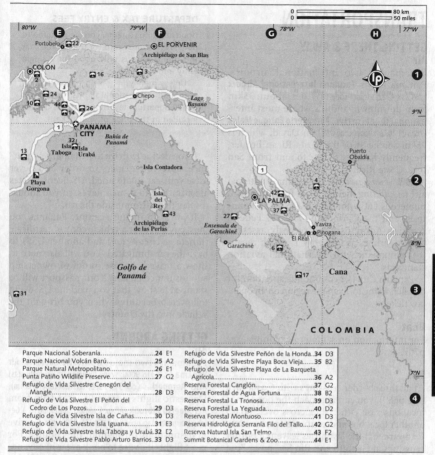

Water pollution is most evident around Panama City and Colón, where 90% of Panamanians live. Most of the sewage from these cities is untreated and discharged directly into coastal waters and canals. Mangroves, which are important for maintaining the balance of delicate marine ecosystems, are being destroyed at an unsustainable pace. Coral reefs throughout the Caribbean are also endangered. Given the destruction to the environment, it shouldn't come as a surprise that there are over 100 animal species threatened with extinction in Panama.

The country's national environmental authority is **ANAM** (Autoridad Nacional del Ambiente; Map pp652-3; ☎ 315 0855; Panama City; ⏰ 8am-4pm), which manages the national-park system. To enter a national park, visitors must pay US$3 (US$10 if it is a marine park) at either the ANAM headquarters in Panama City, a regional ANAM office or at an ANAM ranger station within a national park. Permits to camp or stay at an ANAM ranger station (US$5 to US$10) can be obtained at the same places as well.

The chief private environmental group, however, is the **Asociación Nacional para la Conservación de la Naturaleza** (National Association for the Conservation of Nature; Ancon; Map pp648-9; ☎ 314 0060; www.ancon.org in Spanish). Ancon has played a major role in the creation of national parks and on many occasions has spurred ANAM into action. Ancon also provides nature guides and access to its lodges through its subsidiary, Ancon Expeditions (p658).

TRANSPORTATION

GETTING THERE & AWAY
Air

Panama has two international airports. Panama City's **Tocumen International Airport** (☎ 238 4322; airport code PTY) lies about 35km from downtown, and it's where most international flights arrive. **Aeropuerto Enrique Malek** (☎ 721 1072; airport code DAV), in David, which is 75km southeast of the Costa Rican border, frequently handles flights to and from San José, Costa Rica.

COPA (www.copaair.com) is Panama's national airline, offering flights to and from the USA, numerous Latin and South American countries, and the Caribbean. The US Federal Aviation Administration recently assessed COPA Airlines as Category 1, which means it is compliant with international aviation standards.

Panama City is a common destination for travelers flying to/from the region on an open-jaw ticket.

Boat

For information on sailing to Colombia, see p707.

Bus

At all three border crossings with Costa Rica (see p669); you can approach the border via local buses on either side, cross over, board another local bus and continue on your way. Be aware that the last buses leave the border crossings at Guabito and Río Sereno at 7pm and 5pm, respectively; the last bus leaves Paso Canoas for Panama City at 10pm.

Two companies, **Panaline** (☎ 227 8648) and **Tica Bus** (☎ 262 2084), operate direct buses daily between San José in Costa Rica, and Panama City, departing from the Albrook bus terminal (Map pp652–3). It's recommended that you make reservations a few days in advance.

Car & Motorcycle

You can drive your own car from North America to Panama, but the costs of insurance, fuel, border permits, food and accommodations will be much higher than the cost of an airline ticket. As a result, most people opt to fly down and rent cars when they arrive in Panama City.

DEPARTURE TAX & ENTRY FEES

Upon entering Panama, you are required to purchase a tourist card for US$5. Note that this tourist card is only good for a single entry into Panama.

Unless merely in transit, passengers on outbound international flights must pay a US$20 departure tax, though this is usually included in the price of your ticket.

If you decide to drive to Panama, get insurance, have your papers in order and never leave your car unattended. US license plates are attractive to some thieves, so you should display these from inside the car.

If you are bringing a car into Panama, you must pay US$5 for a vehicle control certificate (*tarjeta de circulación*) and another US$1 to have the car fumigated. You will also need to show a driver's license, proof of ownership and insurance papers. Your passport will be stamped to show that you paid the US$6 and followed procedures when you brought the vehicle into the country.

GETTING AROUND
Air

Panama has two major domestic carriers: **Air Panama** (☎ 316 9000; www.flyairpanama.com/tickets) and **Aeroperlas** (☎ 315 7500; www.aeroperlas.com). Domestic flights depart Panama City from **Aeropuerto Albrook** (Albrook airport, also Marcos A Gelabert airport; Map pp648-9; ☎ 315 0403) and arrive in destinations throughout the country. For most flights it's wise to book as far in advance as possible – this is particularly true of flights to Comarca de Kuna Yala.

Even if you're on a tight budget, one-way domestic flights are never more than US$75, and you can sometimes turn a one- or two-day bus/boat journey into a 45-minute flight.

Bicycle

You can bicycle through Panama easily enough, but using a bicycle to travel within larger Panamanian cities – particularly Panama City – is not wise. The roads tend to be narrow, there are no bike lanes, bus drivers and motorists drive aggressively and it rains a lot, reducing motorists' visibility and your tires' ability to grip the road.

Outside the cities, roads tend to be in fine shape, although parts of the Pan-American

Hwy are narrow, leaving little room to move aside should a car pass by. Lodging is rarely more than a day's bike ride away.

Boat

Boats are the chief means of transportation in several areas of Panama, particularly in Darién Province, the Archipiélago de las Perlas, and the San Blás and Bocas del Toro island chains. While at least one eccentric soul has swum the entire length of the Panama Canal, most people find that a boat simplifies the transit enormously.

The backpacker mecca of Bocas del Toro on Isla Colón is accessible from Changuinola by speedy and inexpensive water taxis – see p692 for details.

Colombian and Kuna merchant boats carry cargo and passengers along the San Blás coast between Colón and Puerto Obaldía, stopping at up to 48 of the islands to load and unload passengers and cargo. However, these boats are occasionally used to traffic narcotics, and they're often dangerously overloaded. Hiring a local boatman is a wiser option – see Comarca de Kuna Yala, p707, for more details.

Since there aren't many roads in eastern Darién Province, boat travel is often the most feasible way to get from one town to another, especially during the rainy season. The boat of choice here is a *piragua* (long canoe), carved from the trunk of a giant ceiba tree. *Piraguas'* shallow hulls allow them to ride the many rivers of eastern Panama. Many such boats – including the ones travelers usually hire – are motorized. See the Darién Province (p706) for more details.

Bus

You can take a bus to just about any community in Panama that is reachable by road. Some of the buses are huge, new Mercedes Benzes equipped with air-con, movie screens and reclining seats. These top-of-the-line buses generally cruise long stretches of highway.

More frequently used – and often seen on the Carretera Interamericana – are Toyota Coaster buses that can seat 28 people. These are affectionately called *chivas,* and although they're not as comfortable as the Mercedes Benzes, they're certainly not expensive. They are an excellent way to visit towns in the interior and along the Interamericana.

Panama does have its share of school buses – colorfully painted machines nicknamed

diablos rojos (red devils) – but these operate only in urban areas. In Panama City, they're a cheap (US$0.25) and easy way to get around, though not always the fastest.

Car & Motorcycle

Due to the low cost and ready availability of buses and taxis, it isn't necessary to rent a vehicle in Panama unless you intend to go to places far off the beaten track. Should you choose to rent, however, you'll find car-rental agencies in Panama City, David and Chitré. Several agencies also have offices at Tocumen International Airport in the capital. To rent a vehicle in Panama, you must be 25 years of age or older and present a passport and driver's license, though some places will rent vehicles to 21-year-olds if you ask politely, pay higher insurance costs, and supply them with a major credit card.

Prices for rentals in Panama run from US$45 per day for a tiny car to US$100 per day for a 4WD vehicle (*cuatro por cuatro*). When you rent, carefully inspect the car for minor dents and scratches, missing radio antennae, hubcaps and the spare tire. These damages *must* be noted on your rental agreement; otherwise you may be charged for them when you return the car.

There have been many reports of theft from rental cars so don't leave valuable or luggage unattended. Many hotels provide parking areas for cars.

Hitchhiking

Hitchhiking is not as widespread in Panama as elsewhere in Central America. Most Panamanians travel by bus, and travelers would do best to follow suit. The exception is holiday weekends, when buses are full to overflowing, and hitchhiking may be the only way out of a place. If you get a ride, offer to pay for it when you arrive – '*¿Cuánto le debo?*' ('How much do I owe you?') is the standard way of doing this.

Hitchhiking is never entirely safe in any country, but it's not uncommon in rural areas of the country.

Taxi

Panamanian taxis don't have meters, but there are some set fares. Taxis are cheap, and most of the time plentiful. However, they can be difficult to hail late at night and just before and during holidays. During these times, it's best to call for a radio taxi. Listings for reliable radio taxis can be found in the Yellow Pages of phone directories throughout Panama, under the heading Taxis.

There is one group of taxis that does charge more than others, and you'd do best to avoid them if possible. These 'sedan' taxis generally mill about the front doors of hotels, restaurants and malls, and ask every exiting individual if he or she would like a cab. Sedan drivers charge at least twice the normal price, so try to avoid them and hail a normal taxi instead.

Train

For details on the scenic train trip between Panama City and Colón, see p663.

PANAMA CITY

pop 446,000

Undoubtedly the most cosmopolitan capital in Central America, Panama City is both a gateway to the country's natural riches and a vibrant destination in its own right. As a thriving center for international banking and trade, Panama City sports a skyline of shimmering glass-and-steel towers that's reminiscent of Miami. Not surprisingly, the city residents often joke that Panama City is the 'Miami of the South,' except that more English is spoken.

Although there's no shortage of sophisticated dining and chic dance clubs, visitors

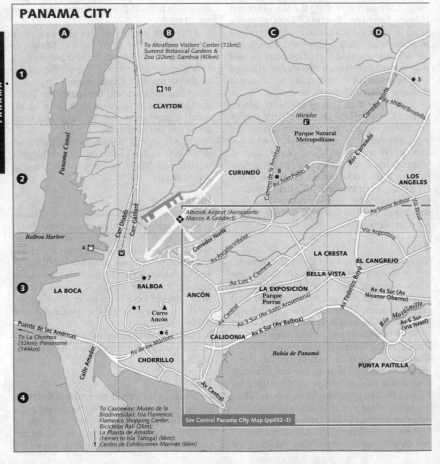

PANAMA CITY

To Miraflores Visitors' Center (12km); Summit Botanical Gardens & Zoo (22km); Gamboa (40km)

CLAYTON

Panama Canal

Mirador

Parque Natural Metropolitano

Corredor Norte

Av Miguel Brostella

CURUNDÚ

Camino de la Amistad

Av Juan Pablo II

Río Curundú

LOS ANGELES

Av Simón Bolívar

Carr Diablo

Carr Gaillard

Albrook Airport (Aeropuerto Marcos A Gelabert)

Corredor Norte

Av Ascanio Villalaz

Vía Argentina

Balboa Harbor

Av Luis F Clement

LA CRESTA

EL CANGREJO

BELLA VISTA

BALBOA

ANCÓN

LA EXPOSICIÓN

Parque Porras

Av 4a Sur (Av Nicanor Obarrio)

Av Federico Boyd

Río Matasnillo

LA BOCA

Cerro Ancón

Av Central

Av 3 Sur (Av Justo Arosemena)

Av 6 Sur (Via Israel)

Puente de las Américas

To La Chorrera (32km); Penonomé (144km)

Av de los Mártires

CALIDONIA

Av 6 Sur (Av Balboa)

Calle Amador

CHORRILLO

Bahía de Panamá

PUNTA PAITILLA

Av Central

To Causeway; Museo de la Biodiversidad; Isla Flamenco; Flamenco Shopping Center; Bicicletas Rali (2km); La Playita de Amador (Ferries to Isla Taboga) (6km); Centro de Exhibiciones Marinas (6km)

See Central Panama City Map (pp652-3)

PANAMA

to Panama City are often awestruck by the colonial district of Casco Viejo, a dilapidated neighborhood with cobblesones, old churches and scenic plazas that is reminiscent of old Havana. Abandoned by the city's elite in favor of more stylish neighborhoods, Casco Viejo lay crumbling on the edge of the sea for decades. Following an ambitious reclamation of the old city in recent years, Casco Viejo is priming itself to charm and enchant visitors once more.

Whether you measure the pulse of the city by the beat of the salsa clubs along Calle Uruguay, or by the staccato of the street vendors' voices in Casco Viejo, the chances are you'll slip into the rhythm of this Latin playground.

HISTORY

Panama City was founded in 1519 by the Spanish governor Pedro Arias de Ávila (Pedrarias) not long after Balboa first saw the Pacific. Although the Spanish settlement quickly became an important center of government and church authorities, the city was ransacked and destroyed in 1671 by the Welsh pirate Sir Henry Morgan, leaving only the stone ruins of Panamá Viejo.

Three years later, the city was re-established about 8km to the southwest in the area now known as Casco Viejo. Although the city's peninsular location meant that it was well defended, the destruction of the Caribbean port at Portobelo in 1746 dealt a heavy blow to the Spanish overland trade route. Panama

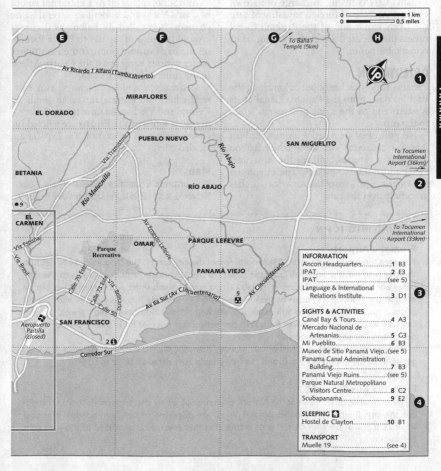

INFORMATION	
Ancon Headquarters	1 B3
IPAT	2 E3
IPAT	(see 5)
Language & International Relations Institute	3 D1

SIGHTS & ACTIVITIES	
Canal Bay & Tours	4 A3
Mercado Nacional de Artesanías	5 G3
Mi Pueblito	6 B3
Museo de Sitio Panamá Viejo	(see 5)
Panama Canal Administration Building	7 B3
Panamá Viejo Ruins	(see 5)
Parque Natural Metropolitano Visitors Centre	8 C2
Scubapanama	9 E2

SLEEPING	
Hostel de Clayton	10 B1

TRANSPORT	
Muelle 19	(see 4)

PANAMA

City subsequently declined in importance, though it returned to prominence in the 1850s when the Panama Railroad was completed, and gold seekers on the way to California flooded across the isthmus by train.

After Panama declared its independence from Colombia on November 3, 1903, Panama City was firmly established as the capital of the new nation. Since the Panama Canal was completed in 1914, the city has emerged as a center for international business and trade.

Today, Panama City is by far the wealthiest city in Central America, and residents are wholly optimistic about the future – and with good reason. Following the handover of the Canal in 1999 and the subsequent closure of American military bases in the country, Panama City is finally in charge of its own destiny. A spate of foreign investment and the likely expansion of the Panama Canal means that the capital is likely to continue its remarkable boom.

ORIENTATION

Panama City stretches about 20km along the Pacific coast, from the Panama Canal at its western end to the ruins of Panamá Viejo to the east.

Near the canal are Albrook airport, the Fort Amador causeway and the wealthy Balboa and Ancón suburbs built for the American canal and military workers. The Puente de las Américas (Bridge of the Americas) arches gracefully over the canal.

The colonial part of the city, Casco Viejo (also called San Felipe and Casco Antiguo), juts into the sea on the southwestern side of town. From here, two major roads head east through the city.

The main drag is Av Central, which runs past the cathedral in Casco Viejo to Parque Santa Ana and Plaza Cinco de Mayo; between these two plazas, the avenue is a pedestrian-only shopping street. At a fork further east, the avenue becomes Av Central España; the section that traverses El Cangrejo business and financial district is called Vía España. The other part of the fork becomes Av 1 Norte (José D Espinar), Av Simón Bolívar and finally Vía Transístmica as it heads out of town and across the isthmus toward Colón.

Av 6 Sur branches off Av Central not far out of Casco Viejo and undergoes several name changes. It is called Av Balboa as it curves around the edge of the bay to Punta Paitilla, on the bay's eastern point; it then continues under various names past the Centro Atlapa to the ruins of Panamá Viejo.

Generally, *avenidas* (avenues) run east-west, while *calles* (streets) run north-south. Av Central and Vía España form the boundary – *avenidas* south of Vía España are labeled *sur* (south) while *calles* east of Vía España are labeled *este*.

Maps

The **Instituto Geográfico Nacional** (Tommy Guardia; Map pp652-3; ☎ 236 2444; ◷ 8am-4pm Mon-Fri), just off

---

GETTING INTO TOWN

From the Airports

Tocumen International Airport is 35km northeast of the city center. The cheapest way to get into the **city** is to exit the terminal, cross the street (to the bus shelter) and catch a bus to the city. Buses are marked 'España-Tocumen' (US$0.25, two hours). Much faster and costlier, taxis can be hired at the Transportes Turísticos desk at the airport exit. Beside it is a taxi stand, with posted prices. Unlicensed taxi drivers will assail you, offering rides at ridiculously high prices, but you can take a *colectivo* (shared taxi) for US$10 per person (for three or more passengers) or US$12 per person (for two passengers).

Albrook airport north of Cerro Ancón handles domestic flights. However, the easiest way to get to/from the airport is by taxi, and the ride should cost between US$2 to US$4.

From the Bus Terminal

All long-distance buses arrive at the Albrook bus terminal, where there are connections throughout the city. Routes (Vía España, Panamá Viejo) are displayed in the front window and cost US$0.25. If you arrive after dark, it is recommended that you take a taxi (US$2 to US$4) to your destination.

Av Simón Bolívar opposite the Universidad de Panamá, has an excellent map collection for sale.

INFORMATION
Bookshops
Exedra Books (Map pp652-3; ☎ 264 4252; cnr Vías España & Brasil; ⏲ 9:30am-9:30pm Mon-Sat, 11am-8:30pm Sun) Easily one of Central America's best bookstores.

Earl S Tupper Tropical Sciences Library/ Smithsonian Tropical Research Institute (STRI; Map pp652-3; ☎ 212 8000; ⏲ 10am-4:30pm Mon-Fri) Stocks books on wildlife and the environment.

Emergency
Ambulance (☎ 228 2187, 229 1133)
Fire (☎ 103)
Police (☎ 104)

Immigration
Immigration office (Migración y Naturalización; Map pp652-3; ☎ 225 1373; cnr Av Cuba & Calle 29 Este; ⏲ 8am-3pm Mon-Fri) In La Exposición.

Internet Access
Internet cafés are plentiful in Panama City, especially in the El Cangrejo district.
Evolution Planet (Map pp652-3; Av 1a A Norte; per hr US$1; ⏲ 9am-4am)
La Red (Map pp652-3; per hr US$1; ⏲ 10am-midnight) In Casco Antiguo, facing Parque Santa Ana.

Libraries
Earl S Tupper Tropical Sciences Library (Map pp652-3; ☎ 212 8113) A world-class resource for information on tropical biology and conservation.

Medical Services
Medicine in Panama, especially in Panama City, is of a high standard.
Centro Medico Paitilla (Map pp652-3; ☎ 265 8800, 265 8883; Calle 53 Este & Av Balboa) Has well-trained physicians who speak both Spanish and English.

Money
There are plenty of 24-hour ATMs throughout the city.
Banco Nacional de Panamá This counter at Tocumen International Airport is one of the few places in Panama City that exchanges foreign currency.
Panacambios (Map pp652-3; ☎ 223 1800; ground fl, Plaza Regency Bldg, Vía España; ⏲ 8am-5pm Mon-Fri) Buys and sells international currencies.

Post
Many hotels sell stamps and some will mail guests' letters.
Main post office (Map pp652-3; Av Balboa btwn Calles 30 & 31; ⏲ 7am-5:45pm Mon-Fri, 7am-4:45pm Sat) Holds post restante items for 30 days.

Telephone
Tarjetas (phonecards) in denominations of US$3, US$5 and US$10 can be purchased at pharmacies for local and regional calls, which can be made from any card phone.

Tourist Information
All the IPAT offices give out free maps. The usefulness of a given office depends on the individual employees; note that few IPAT employees speak English. In addition to the listings here there are also IPAT offices at Tocumen International Airport, Albrook airport and a counter at Panamá Viejo.
ANAM (Autoridad Nacional del Ambiente; Map pp652-3; ☎ 315 0855; ⏲ 8am-4pm) ANAM can occasionally provide maps and information on national parks. However, they are not organized to provide much assistance to tourists. Located inside Building 804 of the Albrook district – best reached by taxi.
IPAT (Map pp648-9; www.panamainfo.com; ☎ 226 7000; fax 226 3483; Centro Atlapa, Vía Israel; ⏲ 8:30am-4:30pm Mon-Fri) The entrance is at the rear of the large building.
IPAT branch (Map pp652-3) The pedestrian mall north of Casco Antiguo near Av Balboa.
IPAT kiosk (Map pp652-3; Vía España) Near Calle Ricardo Arias.

DANGERS & ANNOYANCES
Casco Viejo is currently the focus of an ambitious urban renewal program, though it's still a work in progress. Generally speaking, the tip of the peninsula southeast of the Iglesia de la Merced is safe for tourists, especially since the area is heavily patrolled by police officers on bicycles. But exercise caution, stay where it's well lit and where there are plenty of people around, and take taxis at night.

Moving from the tip of the peninsula, you will enter high-density slums where many tourists have been the target of criminals. Other high-crime areas include Curundú, El Chorrillo, Santa Ana, San Miguelito and Río Abajo.

When walking the city streets, be aware that drivers do not yield to pedestrians. Also, be on the lookout for missing storm and sewer covers as well as high curbs.

PANAMA

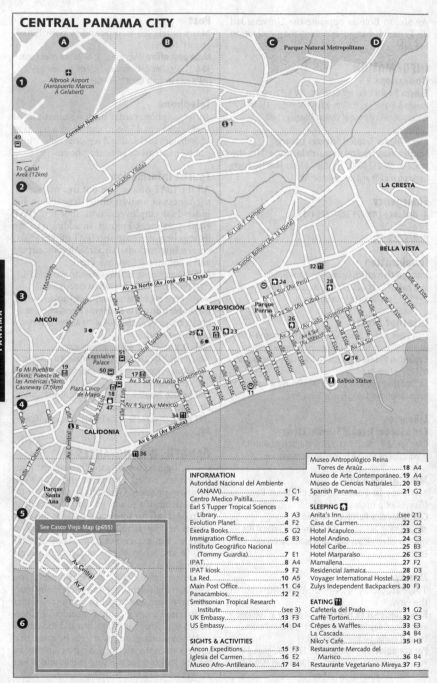

CENTRAL PANAMA CITY

INFORMATION

Autoridad Nacional del Ambiente (ANAM)	1	C1
Centro Medico Paitilla	2	F4
Earl S Tupper Tropical Sciences Library	3	A3
Evolution Planet	4	F2
Exedra Books	5	G2
Immigration Office	6	B3
Instituto Geográfico Nacional (Tommy Guardia)	7	E1
IPAT	8	A4
IPAT kiosk	9	F2
La Red	10	A5
Main Post Office	11	C4
Panacambios	12	F2
Smithsonian Tropical Research Institute	(see 3)	
UK Embassy	13	F3
US Embassy	14	D4

SIGHTS & ACTIVITIES

Ancon Expeditions	15	F3
Iglesia del Carmen	16	E2
Museo Afro-Antilleano	17	B4
Museo Antropológico Reina Torres de Araúz	18	A4
Museo de Arte Contemporáneo	19	A4
Museo de Ciencias Naturales	20	B3
Spanish Panama	21	G2

SLEEPING

Anita's Inn	(see 21)	
Casa de Carmen	22	G2
Hotel Acapulco	23	C3
Hotel Andino	24	C3
Hotel Caribe	25	C3
Hotel Marparaíso	26	C3
Mamallena	27	F2
Residencial Jamaica	28	D3
Voyager International Hostel	29	F2
Zulys Independent Backpackers	30	F3

EATING

Cafetería del Prado	31	G2
Caffé Tortoni	32	C3
Crêpes & Waffles	33	E3
La Cascada	34	B4
Niko's Café	35	H3
Restaurante Mercado del Marisco	36	B4
Restaurante Vegetariano Mireya	37	F3

See Casco Viejo Map (p655)

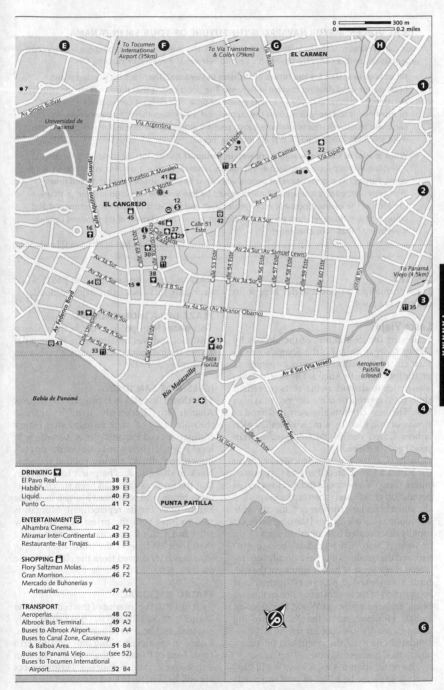

PANAMA

LOCAL VOICES: MAYOR NAVARRO & THE FUTURE OF TOURISM IN PANAMA

Juan Carlos Navarro is the founding director of Ancon, the country's most prominent conservation organization, and is currently serving his second term as the mayor of Panama City.

■ **What is your vision for the future of tourism in Panama?** There is a lot of interest and pressure for us to develop tourism in Panama. The good side is that tourism is an opportunity to generate income and jobs in a short period of time. The difficult part is that sustainable tourism needs to take into account the culture and the environment. As an example, you can build massive hotels to promote beach tourism almost anywhere in the world, but if you want to create long-term value, there must be more.

■ **What model of tourism would work well in Panama?** It is important to develop Panama as a destination for people who seek extraordinary landscapes. But, I am also interested in developing Panama as a destination for people who want to learn about our culture and history. In my opinion, quality tourism in Panama would be low-volume and high-income so that we can receive the greatest possible economic impact and the least possible environmental and cultural shock. However, how do you achieve this model in a climate of tremendous capital investment? That's our challenge!

As told to Matthew D Firestone

SIGHTS

For information on possible day trips from the city, see p664.

Casco Viejo

Following the destruction of the old city by Henry Morgan in 1671, the Spanish moved their city 8km southwest to a rocky peninsula on the foot of Cerro Ancón. The new location was easier to defend as the reefs prevented ships from approaching the city except at high tide. The new city was also easy to defend as it was surrounded by a massive wall, which is how Casco Viejo (Old Compound; Map p655) got its name.

In 1904, at the time construction began on the Panama Canal, all of Panama City existed where Casco Viejo stands today. However, as population growth and urban expansion pushed the urban boundaries further east, the city's elite abandoned Casco Viejo, and the neighborhood rapidly deteriorated into an urban slum.

Today, Casco Viejo is gradually being gentrified, and the buildings that have already been restored give a sense of how magnificent the area must have looked in past years. International recognition of these efforts resulted in the area being declared a Unesco World Heritage Site in 2003. However, part of the allure of strolling along Casco Viejo's cobbled streets is the dilapidated charm of the crumbling buildings, abandoned houses and boarded-up ruins.

The restoration of Casco Viejo is still happening, so please be aware of your surroundings, and exercise caution (see p651) while exploring this fascinating neighborhood.

PLAZA DE LA INDEPENDENCIA

This **plaza** (Map p655) is the heart of Casco Antiguo, and was the site where Panama declared its independence from Colombia on November 3, 1903.

IGLESIA DE SAN JOSÉ

This **church** (Map p655; Av A) protects the famous Altar de Oro (Golden Altar), which was about the only thing of value salvaged after Henry Morgan sacked Panamá Viejo. According to local legend, when word came of the pirate's impending attack, a priest painted the altar black to disguise it. The priest told Morgan that the famous altar had been stolen by another pirate, and convinced Morgan to donate handsomely for its replacement. Morgan is said to have told the priest, 'I don't know why, but I think you are more of a pirate than I am.' Whatever the truth, the baroque altar was later moved from the old city to the present site.

TEATRO NACIONAL

Built in 1907, the interior of this ornate **theater** (Map p655; ☎ 262 3525; Av B) has been completely restored, and boasts red and gold decorations, a once-magnificent ceiling mural by Roberto Lewis (one of Panama's finest painters) and an impressive crystal chandelier. Performances are still held here; to find out about them, or just to have a look at the theater, go around to the office door at the side of the building.

PLAZA DE FRANCIA

At the tip of the point is this **plaza** (Map p655), which displays large stone tablets and statues dictating the story (in Spanish) of the French role in the construction of the canal. The plaza is dedicated to the memory of the 22,000 workers, most of them from France, Guadeloupe and Martinique, who died trying to create a canal. Most were killed by yellow fever and malaria, and among the busts is a monument to the Cuban doctor Carlos J Finlay, who discovered how mosquitoes transmit yellow fever. His work led to the eradication of the disease in Panama.

PASEO LAS BÓVEDAS

This **esplanade** (Map p655) runs along the top of the sea wall built by the Spanish to protect the city. From here, you can see the Bridge of the Americas arching over the waterway and the ships lining up to enter the canal.

PALACIO DE LAS GARZAS

The **presidential palace** (Map p655; Av Alfaro) is named after the great white herons that reside here. The president of Panama lives on the upper floor.

CLUB DE CLASES Y TROPAS

This abandoned **ruin** (Map p655; Calle 1a Oeste) was once the favorite hang-out of General Noriega, though it was virtually destroyed

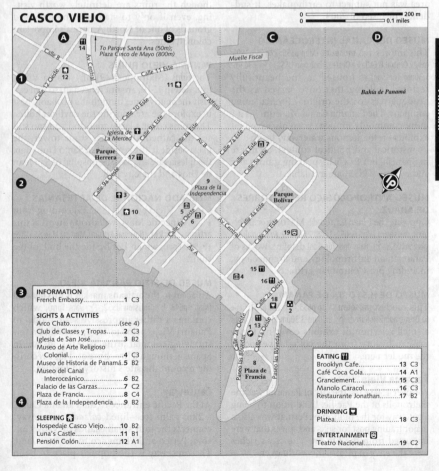

CASCO VIEJO

0 — 200 m
0 — 0.1 miles

Muelle Fiscal

Bahía de Panamá

To Parque Santa Ana (50m); Plaza Cinco de Mayo (800m)

Iglesia de La Merced

Parque Herrera

Plaza de la Independencia

Parque Bolívar

Plaza de Francia

PANAMA

INFORMATION
French Embassy.........................1 C3

SIGHTS & ACTIVITIES
Arco Chato...........................(see 4)
Club de Clases y Tropas.........2 C3
Iglesia de San José................3 B2
Museo de Arte Religioso
  Colonial..............................4 C3
Museo de Historia de Panamá.5 B2
Museo del Canal
  Interoceánico.....................6 B2
Palacio de las Garzas.............7 C2
Plaza de Francia.....................8 C4
Plaza de la Independencia....9 B2

SLEEPING
Hospedaje Casco Viejo........10 B2
Luna's Castle.......................11 B1
Pensión Colón.....................12 A1

EATING
Brooklyn Cafe.....................13 C3
Café Coca Cola....................14 A1
Granclement.......................15 C3
Manolo Caracol...................16 C3
Restaurante Jonathan.........17 B2

DRINKING
Platea.................................18 C3

ENTERTAINMENT
Teatro Nacional...................19 C2

during the 1989 invasion. Some fresh paint was selectively applied in early 2000, when scenes from the movie *The Tailor of Panama* were filmed here.

MUSEO DE ARTE RELIGIOSO COLONIAL

Housed beside the ruins of the Iglesia y Convento de Santo Domingo, this **art museum** (Map p655; ☎ 228 2897; cnr Av A & Calle 3 Este; admission US$1; ☻ 8am-4pm Tue-Sat) has a collection of colonial-era religious artifacts, some dating from the 16th century. Just inside the doorway of the ruins is the **Arco Chato**, a long arch that has stood here, unsupported, for centuries. It reportedly played a part in the selection of Panama over Nicaragua as the site for the canal: its survival was taken as proof that the area was not subject to earthquakes. It suddenly collapsed in 2003.

MUSEO DEL CANAL INTEROCEÁNICO

This impressive **museum** (Map p655; ☎ 211 1995; cnr Av Central & Calle 6a Oeste; admission US$2; ☻ 9:30am-5:30pm Tue-Sun) is housed in the beautifully restored building that once served as the headquarters for the original French canal company. The Panama Canal Museum (as it's more commonly known) presents excellent exhibits on the famous waterway, framed in its historical and political context. Signs are in Spanish, but English-speaking guides and audio tours (US$5) are available.

MUSEO ANTROPOLÓGICO REINA TORRES DE ARAÚZ

Opposite the Plaza Cinco de Mayo, this excellent **museum** (Map pp652-3; ☎ 212 3079; Av Central; admission US$2; ☻ 10am-4pm Tue-Sun) displays works of Panamanian anthropology and archaeology, including pre-Columbian artifacts.

MUSEO DE HISTORIA DE PANAMÁ

This modest **museum** (Map p655; ☎ 228 6231; Calle 6a Oeste; admission free; ☻ 8:30am-3:30pm Mon-Fri) has a small selection of exhibits covering Panamanian history from the colonial period to the modern era.

Panamá Viejo

For over 150 years, the city of Panamá was the metropolis of the Pacific. In addition to being a gateway for the bullion of Peru, it was also a major trading post for silks and spices that were imported from the Orient. The city's riches were the envy of pirates the world over.

When Panamá fell to Henry Morgan in 1671, the city contained a magnificent cathedral, several beautiful churches, thousands of colonial homes and hundreds of warehouses stocked with foreign goods. However, after the plundering had ceased, Panamá Viejo was reduced to mere beams and stone blocks.

Although the ruins were left intact as recently as 1950, the expansion of the capital resulted in the transformation of Panamá into a squatter camp. Although the government declared the ruins a protected site in 1976 (Unesco followed suit in 1997), most of the old city had already been dismantled and overrun.

Today much of Panama Viejo lies buried under a poor residential neighborhood, though the ruins are definitely worth visiting, even if only to stand on the hallowed grounds of one of North America's important colonial cities.

PANAMÁ VIEJO RUINS

The **ruins** (Map pp648-9) of Panamá Viejo, founded in 1519, are not fenced in, so you can visit them anytime, though it's probably best to explore the area during the daylight hours. The ruins cover a large area, and you can still see the cathedral with its stone tower, the plaza beside it, the convent of Santo Domingo, the Iglesia de San José, the hospital of San Juan de Dios and the city hall.

MERCADO NACIONAL DE ARTESANÍAS

Panamá Viejo buses (US$0.25) coming from Plaza Cinco de Mayo will drop you off at this **artisans market** (National Artisans Market; Map pp648-9; ☻ 9am-6pm), which lies beside the bulk of the ruins.

MUSEO DE SITIO PANAMÁ VIEJO

Adjacent to the artisans market is this **museum** (Map pp648-9; admission US$2; ☻ 9am-5pm), which contains a rather impressive scale model of Panamá Viejo prior to 1671, as well as a few surviving colonial artifacts. All signs are in Spanish, though a brochure and tape recording recount the site's history in English.

Causeway

At the Pacific entrance to the Panama Canal, a 2km palm tree–lined *calzada* (causeway) connects the four small islands of Naos, Culebra, Perico and Flamenco to the mainland. The causeway is the popular place to be in the early morning and late afternoon when residents head here to walk, jog, skate, cycle or simply escape the noise and pollution of the city. The causeway also offers sweeping views of the skyline and the old city, and you can see flocks of brown pelicans diving into the sea here most times of the year.

At the causeway entrance, **Bicicletas Rali** (8am-6pm Sat & Sun) operates a booth where you can rent a bicycle for US$3 per hour or in-line skates for US$1 per hour.

The interesting **Centro de Exhibiciones Marines** (212 8000 ext 2366; admission US$1; 1-5pm Tue-Fri, 10am-5pm Sat & Sun), operated by the Smithsonian Tropical Research Institute (STRI), includes an informative marine museum with signs in English and Spanish, two small aquariums and a nature trail through a patch of dry forest containing sloths and iguanas.

Isla Flamenco is home to an enormous shopping center that is chock full of open-air restaurants as well as number of high-class bars and clubs.

The easiest way to reach the causeway is by taxi (US$4 to US$6).

Parque Natural Metropolitano

Up on a hill, north of downtown, this 265-hectare national park (Map pp648–9) protects a wild area of tropical forest within the city limits. It has two main walking trails, the **Nature Trail** and the **Tití Monkey Trail**, which join to form one long loop. The 150m-high **mirador** (lookout) offers views of Panama City, the bay and the canal all the way to the Miraflores Locks.

Mammals in the park include *tití* monkeys, anteaters, sloths and white-tailed deer; reptiles include iguanas, turtles and tortoises. More than 250 bird species have been spotted here.

The park was the site of an important battle during the US invasion to oust Noriega. Also of historical significance are the concrete structures just past the park entrance, which were used during WWII as a testing and assembly plant for aircraft engines.

The park is bordered on the west and north by Camino de la Amistad; Av Juan Pablo II runs right through the park. For a self-guided tour, pick up a pamphlet in Spanish and English at the **visitors center** (Map pp648-9; 232 5516; admission US$1; 8am-5pm Mon-Fri, 8am-1pm Sat), about 40m north of the park entrance. Rangers offer one-hour tours to groups of five or more (per person US$6), but you need to call in advance.

Museums

The strength of Panama City's museums lies not in a single institution or two, but in their tremendous variety. In addition to those listed in Casco Viejo, Panama City is home to several other interesting museums.

Note that at the time of writing, construction on the **Museo de la Biodiversidad** (Museum of Biodiversity; www.biomuseopanama.org), designed by world-renowned architect Frank Gehry, was nearing completion. It's by the Causeway.

Museo Afro-Antilleano (Map pp652-3; 262 5348; cnr Av Justo Arosemena & Calle 24 Este; admission US$1; 8:30am-3:30pm Tue-Sat) has exhibits on the history of Panama's West Indian community.

Near Av de los Mártires in the Ancón district, **Museo de Arte Contemporáneo** (Map pp652-3; 262 8012; admission free; 9am-4pm Mon-Fri, 9am-noon Sat & 9am-3pm Sun) hosts permanent and changing contemporary art exhibits by prominent Latin-American artists.

Museo de Ciencias Naturales (Map pp652-3; 225 0645; Av Cuba btwn Calles 29 Este & 30 Este; admission US$1; 9am-3:45pm Tue-Sat) features works on the

PANAMA

EL DONALDO

As an old city with European airs and a nightlife to rival Miami, Panama City has it all, not to mention the fact it's less than an hour away from mountains, beaches and rain forests. Not surprisingly, some seriously swish high-rise apartments are going up by the dozen.

In 2005 the American Association of Retired Persons (AARP) ranked Panama as the No 4 place in the world to retire, dubbing Panama City the 'Dubai of the Western hemisphere,' due in part to the Panamanian government's generous pension program. The real-estate boom is so lucrative that 'the Donald' himself is getting in on the action. Invigorated by the success of his absurd reality-TV show, Donald Trump has already begun constructing the Trump Ocean Club, a US$220 million project that will boast a 65-story condominium tower, an international casino and also a private beach club. Just how the Donald can be stopped is anyone's guess.

natural sciences, flora, fauna, geology and paleontology of Panama.

The **Panama Canal Administration Building** (Map pp648-9; ☎ 225 0345; Balboa Heights; admission free; ⏰ 7:30am-4:15pm Mon-Fri) has an impressive display of murals in its rotunda room, which depict the story of the canal's construction.

Mi Pueblito

At the foot of Cerro Ancón, on the western side of town, **Mi Pueblito** (My Little Village; Map pp648-9; Av de Los Mártires; admission US$1; ⏰ 9am-9pm Tue-Sun) features life-size replicas of rural villages found on the Península de Azuero, in Bocas del Toro and in the Darién. It also features extensive shops that sell handicrafts from throughout the country, as well as a handful of decent restaurants. Folk dances accompanied by live music are staged on Friday and Saturday at around 6pm – they're touristy but still worth a look.

Baha'i House of Worship

On the outskirts of Panama City, 11km from the city center on the Transisthmian Hwy, the white-domed **Baha'i temple** (☎ 231 1137; ⏰ 10am-6pm) looms like a giant egg atop the crest of a hill. The inside is surprisingly beautiful, with a fresh breeze always present. The Baha'i House of Worship serves all of Latin America.

Information about the faith is available in English and Spanish at the temple; readings from the Baha'i writings (also in English and Spanish) are held Sunday mornings at 10am. Any bus to Colón can let you off on the highway, but it's a long walk up the hill. A taxi from Panama City costs around US$10.

COURSES

Language & International Relations Institute
(Ileri; Map pp648-9; ☎ /fax 260 4424; isls.com/panama /schools/ileri.html; Camino de la Amistad) Located in the El Dorado neighborhood, Ileri offers four hours of one-on-one Spanish instruction per day, five days a week. Costs start at US$300 for the first week (with lodging, meals, trips and activities), and then go down with each subsequent week. The weekly rate without lodging starts at US$200.

Spanish Panama (Map pp652-3; ☎ 213 3121; www .spanishpanama.com; Av 2a B Norte) This immensely popular language school gets rave reviews from travelers. It has a similar structure to Ileri: four hours of one-on-one classes daily and homestays with meals for US$375 per week (long-term discounts are available). It also offers a 'backpacker special,' which includes classes with dorm stay for US$275 per week.

TOURS

Ancon Expeditions (Map pp652-3; ☎ 269 9415; www .anconexpeditions.com; El Dorado Bldg, Calle 49 Este near Av 3 Sur) Highly recommended by travelers the world over, Ancon was created by Panama's top conservation organization, and employs some of the country's finest nature guides. Ancon offers a number of unique trips including forays into the Darién jungle (see p706) and overnight stays at private lodges.

Scubapanama (Map pp648-9; ☎ 261 3841; www .scubapanama.com) Located in the El Carmen area of Panama City, Scubapanama is the country's oldest and most respected dive operator, and offers a variety of dive trips throughout Panama.

VOLUNTEERING

SOS Children's Villages (☎ in Austria 43 368 6678; www .sos-childrensvillages.org) is a nongovernmental organization that is active in the field of children's needs, concerns and rights. Its activities focus on neglected and abandoned children and orphans, as well as disadvantaged families. A variety of volunteer placements are available, though it's essential that you contact SOS in advance.

For more on volunteering see also p717.

FESTIVALS & EVENTS

Although not as famous as the celebrations in Rio de Janeiro or New Orleans, **Carnaval** in Panama City is celebrated with the same level of merriment and wild abandon during the days preceding Ash Wednesday. From Saturday until the following Tuesday, work is put away, and masks, costumes and confetti are brought forth. For a period of 96 hours, almost anything goes.

For a list of events, check out the arts section in the Sunday edition of *La Prensa* as well as the back pages of the *Panama News*.

SLEEPING

In comparison to other major cities in Central America (especially San José), the backpacker scene in Panama City is still in its infancy. Don't expect to find upmarket backpacker hotels complete with swimming pools, hot showers and rooftop bars. However, there are still a number of cheap and comfortable spots worth checking out.

Casco Viejo

In the past, accommodations in Casco Viejo (Map p655) were best avoided, unless you were looking to rent by the hour. Today this rapidly changing neighborhood is home to a handful of recommended places; bedding down in Casco Viejo is a great away to soak up its old-world charm.

Pensión Colón (☎ 228 8506; cnr Calles 12 Oeste & B; s/d US$9/10, with bathroom US$10/11) Originally built to house Panama Canal workers, this handsome hotel has an impressive lobby complete with the original ornate Spanish tile work. Unfortunately, the place has seen many years of neglect, so it's best to check out a few rooms first, though a sagging mattress and a leaky sink are offset by incredible views from the balcony.

Hospedaje Casco Viejo (☎ 211 2027; www.hospedaje cascoviejo.com; Calles 8a Este; dm US$7; s with/without bathroom US$12/10; 🖳) A welcome addition to the Casco Viejo scene, this warm and inviting colonial mansion turned *hospedaje* (guesthouse) is arguably the best deal in town. Whether you bed down in the dorm or splurge on a private bathroom, it's hard to beat these prices, especially since guests can take advantage of the communal kitchen, free wi-fi and the open-air courtyard.

Luna's Castle (☎ 262 1540; www.lunascastle.com; Calle 9; dm US$9, d incl breakfast US$22; 🗙 🖳) From the same crazy, twisted minds that brought you Mondo Taitu and Hostel Heike in Bocas del Toro, Luna's Castle is, bar-none, the best backpacker spot in Panama City. Housed in a creaky, colonial mansion near the water's edge, it masterfully blends historic Spanish colonial architecture with funky, laidback backpacker vibes. In the evenings, the attached 9th Avenue Bar is the best joint in the city for anyone smitten with an incurable case of wanderlust.

La Exposición & Bella Vista

The neighborhoods of La Exposición and Bella Vista (Map pp652–3) are home to a number of fairly standard budget and mid-range hotels.

Residencial Jamaica (☎ 225 9870; Av Cuba & Calle 38 Este; d US$20; 🗙) This coral pink palace offers secure, clean rooms in a mellow corner location. The light-filled rooms are a good deal at this price, especially since they come with air-con, cable TV and private hot-water bathrooms.

Hotel Acapulco (☎ 225 3832; Calle 30 Este; s/d US$20/22; 🗙) A discernible step up from the standard hotel fare in this part of town, the Acapulco combines professionalism with a certain no-nonsense style. This is reflected in the spotless rooms complete with air-con, private hot-water bathroom, cable TV and balconies with French doors.

Hotel Andino (☎ 225 1162; Calle 35; s/d US$22/25; 🗙) Rooms at the Hotel Andino lack charm (almost to the point of dowdiness), but they're clean, big and breezy and equipped like a start-up apartment. If you don't feel like leaving the hotel at all, there's a bar and restaurant here, making it a convenient choice if you just have to crash overnight between bus departures.

Hotel Marparaíso (☎ 227 6767; Calle 34 Este; s/d US$22/28; 🗙 🖳) Travelers in the know choose Hotel Marparaíso simply because staff pick you up at the airport for free, which saves you some serious cash. The rooms themselves are fairly unremarkable, though at least you can take a hot shower, watch some satellite TV and blast the air-con while recuperating from a long flight.

Hotel Caribe (☎ 225 0404; cnr Calle 28 Este & Av Perú; s/d US$28/34; 🗙 🖳) Psychedelic and slightly retro (by default rather than design), this 250-room hotel has an intrigue that grows on you. Lurid orange and brown dominate the color scheme and the lighting is terrible, but there's something surreal about the rooftop pool overlooking the city.

El Cangrejo

The modern banking district, El Cangrejo (Map pp652–3) is new and shiny. Most of the hotels here are pricey affairs, though there are a handful of recommended hostels and budget hotels.

Zulys Independent Backpackers (☎ 6605 4742; www .geocities.com/zulys_independent_backpacker; Calle Ricardo Arias 8; s-/d-bed dm US$6.90/11; 🗙 🖳) The cheapest dorm bed in the city can be yours at this relaxed spot, which was designed with the backpacker in mind. It's still working out the kinks, but the warm atmosphere is likely to make Zulys a popular stop on the gringo trail.

Voyager International Hostel (☎ 260 5913; www .geocities.com/voyagerih/english.html; Calle Maria Icaza; dm/d US$8/17; 🗙 🖳) Panama City's first hostel still boasts incredible wraparound views of the city, though its reputation amongst backpackers has plummeted in recent years. Ragged dorms, poor facilities and surly staff are reason enough to look elsewhere.

Mamallena (☎ 6538 9745; www.mamallena.com; Calle Maria Icaza; dm US$10; 🗙 🖳) Literally next door

PANAMA

to Voyager, Mamallena is one of the newest hostels in Panama City, and offers clean and comfortable air-conditioned dorm rooms and basic shared facilities. The atmosphere is as sterile as a hospital waiting room, which means the quality of your time at Mamallena depends on the company.

Anita's Inn (☎ 213 3121; www.hostelspanama.com; Av 2a B Norte; dm US$10, s from US$15; ✖ 🖳) Affiliated with Spanish Panama (p658), this cozy guesthouse is conveniently located in the same building as the language school. Even if you're not brushing up on your Spanish, the communal atmosphere, comfortable rooms and relaxing location make Anita's an excellent choice.

Casa de Carmen (☎ 263 4366; serviturisa@cableonda .net; Calle 1a de Carmen 32 near Vía Brasil; dm/d US$14/30; ✖ 🖳) Although slightly more expensive than other budget accommodations, repeat customers agree that Casa de Carmen is Panama City's loveliest budget accommodation. Located in a festive colonial house, it features a variety of individually decorated rooms, each painted a different shade, with matching furniture. Guests can also relax in the lush backyard patio, or hit up the friendly owners for their wealth of knowledge about the city. Reservations recommended.

Clayton

The former US-occupied neighborhood of Clayton is adjacent to the Miraflores Locks of the Panama Canal. You're a taxicab away from downtown, but staying out here is a welcome respite from the noise and congestion of Panama City.

Hostel de Clayton (Map pp648-9; ☎ 317 1634; www .hosteldeclayton.com; Calle Guanabana edificio 605B; dm US$11.50, tw with/without bathroom US$15/13.50; ✖ 🖳) Reminiscent of an army barracks (well, it was one!), this unique hostel is located on the site of the former US Army base of Clayton, though today it's one of the city's up-and-coming residential areas. The rooms and amenities are perfectly suited to the budget traveler, though the real reason you're staying here is to explore the area's quiet, suburban setting and attractive gardens.

EATING

Panama City has hundreds of places to eat, from the gritty working-class hole in the wall to the garden bistro, with everything in between.

Casco Viejo

Casco Viejo (Map p655) is unique in that it's home to some of the city's most exclusive eateries, as well as its cheapest dives.

Café Coca Cola (cnr Av Central & Plaza Santa Ana; set meals under US$2; ✖ 7:30am-11:30pm) A neighborhood institution, Café Coca Cola is an old-school diner, complete with chess-playing *señores* and no-nonsense staff. The set meals are excellent.

Restaurante Jonathan (Av Central; meals under US$2; ✖ 7:30am-11:30pm) A hearty plate of chicken and lentils, or a heavy helping of pork fried rice – you'd be hard-pressed to spend more than a couple of dollars at this local cafeteria-style haunt.

Brooklyn Cafe (Calle 1a Oeste; coffee & pastry US$2-3; ✖ 7:30am-7pm) Owned by a Panamanian who fondly recalls her time in the States, this NYC-style café is the perfect spot to linger over a frothy cappuccino and buttery muffin.

Granclement (Av Central; gelato US$2.50-3.50) Nothing beats the tropical heat like a cool scoop of mango gelato, and there's no better gourmet spot in the city than this French-owned parlor.

Manolo Caracol (Av Central; set lunch US$10) It's arguably the finest restaurant in the city. Stop by this legendary spot for the affordable set lunch where you indulge in a five-course tapas feast that changes daily.

La Exposición & Bella Vista

Unfortunately, the neighborhoods of La Exposición and Bella Vista (Map pp652-3) lack quality eateries.

Caffé Tortoni (Av Central España btwn Calles 37 & 43 Este; dishes US$2-4; ✖) This small eatery is popular with lunching locals who come for the air-conditioning, though the traditional Panamanian dishes on offer are perfect for filling the gut and not breaking the bank.

Restaurante Mercado del Marisco (cnr Av Balboa & Calle 15 Este; dishes US$5-12; ✖ 10am-5pm) This casual spot above the fish market serves some of the freshest catch in town, and there's usually an extensive variety of shrimp, lobster and squid on offer.

La Cascada (cnr Av Balboa & Calle 25 Este; dishes US$3-6) La Cascada has a large garden dining patio and a bilingual menu larger than Noriega's dossier, though you can stick to your budget and still feast on anything from roasted chicken to the catch of the day.

El Cangrejo

El Cangrejo (Map pp652–3) is restaurant-rich.

Restaurante Vegetariano Mireya (cnr Calle Ricardo Arias & Av 3a Sur; most items under US$1.25; 6am-10pm Mon-Sat) Mireya is a budget traveler's delight, especially if you're tempted by tasty vegetarian offerings including eggplant parmesan, soy burgers and freshly squeezed juices.

Niko's Café (Calle 51 Este; meals US$1-3; 24hr) This Panama City staple is famous among locals, and serves everything from authentic Greek gyros to the local *sancocho* (a spicy meat-and-vegetable stew).

Cafetería del Prado (Vía Argentina; dishes US$2-6; 24hr) If you've been hitting the clubs on Calle Uruguay, this is the perfect spot to go for pancakes at five in the morning.

Crêpes & Waffles (Av 5a B Sur; crepes US$3-6) Crêpe and waffle lovers rejoice at this popular spot – favorite items include spinach, ricotta and tomato crepes, though carnivores can opt for the *lomito á la pimienta* (strips of roast beef with pepper sauce).

DRINKING & NIGHTLIFE

Bars and clubs open and close with alarming frequency in Panama City, though generally speaking, nightlife is stylish, sophisticated and fairly pricey (US$5 to US$30 for cover charge and US$3 to US$10 for drinks). With that said, the well-to-do denizens of Panama City love a good scene, so it's worth scrubbing up, donning some nice threads and parting with some dough. You might regret blowing your budget in the morning, but that's the price you pay to party with the beautiful people.

Big areas for nightlife are Casco Viejo, Marbella and the causeway. Bars in Casco Viejo are generally subdued and cater to an older crowd, though there's nothing quite like sipping a perfectly crafted cocktail in a crumbling colonial mansion.

The district of Marbella is home to the always fashionable Calle Uruguay, a strip of trendy bars and clubs that's reminiscent of Miami's South Beach. Although you have to pay to play here, there's nothing quite like a night in Panama City's playground of the rich and sexy.

At the Isla Flamenco shopping center on the causeway you'll find a number of nightlife spots, ranging from packed dance clubs to more low-key watering holes. However, the vibe here is not unlike what you might find in Las Vegas, so shop around and pick the theme that you like, be it a pirate bar or an Egyptian club.

Pick up a copy of *La Prensa* with the weekend listings, available Thursday and Friday; look for the '*De Noche*' section.

Although Panama City is far from being a liberal, or even tolerant, city when it comes to gay rights, there are some excellent gay clubs here. For more information on the gay scene, check out www.farraurbana.com (in Spanish).

Although half the fun of partying it up in Panama City is finding a hidden gem, here's a few of our favorite spots to get you started.

Platea (Map p655; Calle 1a Oeste) With exposed brick walls and a small, intimate stage, this jazz club near Av A wouldn't be out of place in Greenwich Village – minus the Spanish of course.

Habibi's (Map pp652–3; Calle Uruguay) The upstairs lounge at this pricey Middle Eastern restaurant is decked out to look like a sheikh's tent – if the spirit inspires, smoke from the hookah, sip a mojito and space out to the electronic music.

El Pavo Real (Map pp652–3; Av 3B Sur) This British pub attracts a more sedate expat crowd with its pool tables, live music on weekends and, of course, completely authentic fish and chips.

Punto G (Map pp652–3; Calle D) Guests at this stylish gay club are served by bare-chested bartenders (complete with cowboy hats and spandex), and the occasional transvestite show makes for an interlude between serious dancing.

Liquid (Map pp652–3; Plaza Florida, Calle 53 Este) With lots of polished metal and tubular lighting, this sleek club pounds heavy beats to a sharply dressed crowd looking to have a good time.

ENTERTAINMENT

If you're not looking to get blotto, there are numerous ways to spend a moonlit (or maybe rainy) evening in the city. A good place to start is the arts section in the Sunday edition of *La Prensa*, or the back pages of the *Panama News*.

Panamanians have a love affair with Hollywood, and there is no shortage of air-conditioned cinemas in and around the city. One of the best places in the city for a little escapism is the **MultiCentro** (Av Balboa), where you can catch the latest Hollywood releases in English, with Spanish subtitles, for less than US$4. If you're

PANAMA

more independently minded, the **Alhambra Cinema** (Map pp652-3; Vía España; admission US$2) screens art-house films.

Panamanians love to gamble, and there are flashy casinos scattered around the city. Even if you're not a big card player, it's hard to pass up US$5 blackjack, especially when the drinks are free – a good spot is the **Miramar Inter-Continental** (Map pp652-3; Av Balboa).

A good place to see traditional Panamanian folk dancing is the **Restaurante-Bar Tinajas** (Map pp652-3; ☎ 263 7890; Av 3a A Sur near Av Frederico Boyd; ☽ closed Sun) Sure, it's touristy, but nicely done just the same. Shows are staged here on Tuesday, Thursday, and Friday and Saturday nights at 9pm; there's a US$5 entertainment fee, as well as a US$5.50 minimum per person for drinks and food. Make a reservation before dining.

If you're looking for a little culture in your life, the **Teatro Nacional** (Map p655; ☎ 262 3525; Av B) offers dance, music and live performances, though just sitting in this historic theater is enjoyable enough.

SHOPPING

Merchandise from around the world is sold very cheaply in Panama. Clothes, radios, shoes and textiles (including fabrics the Kuna purchase to make clothes) spill onto the pedestrian walkway along Av Central.

Authentic handicrafts can be found at the following:

Flory Saltzman Molas (Map pp652-3; Calle 49 B Oeste near Vía España) Flory Saltzman has a large selection and perhaps the best quality *molas* (colorful hand-stitched appliqué textiles made by the Kuna) you'll find outside the islands.

Gran Morrison (Map pp652-3; Vía España near Calle 51 Este) This ubiquitous department store sells a small variety of Panamanian handicrafts.

Mercado de Buhonerías y Artesanías (Map pp652-3) Behind the Museo Antropológico Reina Torres de Araúz.

Mercado Nacional de Artesanías (Map pp648-9) Beside the ruins of Panamá Viejo.

Mi Pueblito (Map pp648-9; Av de los Mártires) Good-quality items available at the many shops inside the replicated villages at the foot of Cerro Ancón.

Tupper Center of the Smithsonian Tropical Research Institute (STRI; Map pp652-3) At STRI's bookstore near Av de los Mártires, opposite the Legislative Palace in the Ancón district, you'll find a nice selection of *tagua* nut carvings (from the egg-sized *tagua* nut).

GETTING THERE & AWAY

Air

International flights arrive at **Tocumen International Airport** (☎ 238 4160), 35km northeast of the city center.

Panama's airlines are **Air Panama** (☎ 316 9000; www.flyairpanama.com/tickets) and **Aeroperlas** (Map pp652-3; ☎ 315 7500; www.aeroperlas.com).

Domestic flights depart from **Albrook airport** (☎ 315 0403), aka Aeropuerto Marcos A Gelabert, in the former Albrook Air Force Station near the canal.

For information on getting to town from the airports see p650.

All flights within Panama last under one hour and prices vary according to season and availability. Both Aeroperlas and Air Panama fly to the following destinations: Bocas del Toro and David (one-way US$60), El Porvenir and Río Sidra for San Blás (US$35), Isla Contadora (US$30), La Palma for Darién (US$40). In addition, Aeroperlas has one flight per week to Puerto Obaldía for Darién (US$40).

Boat

For information on getting to Isla Taboga, see p669. For information on sailing to Colombia, see p707.

Bus

The new Albrook Bus Terminal (Map pp652-3), near Albrook airport, is a convenient one-stop location for most buses leaving Panama City. The terminal includes a food court, banks, shops, a sports bar, storage room, bathrooms and showers. There is a mall lies next door, complete with supermarket and a cinema.

Local buses from the city's major routes stop at the terminal, and in back of the station there are direct buses to and from Tocumen International Airport.

To get to the station from the city, take any of the frequent buses (US$0.25) that pass in front of the Legislative Palace or along Vía España (look for the 'via Albrook' sign in the front window).

Major bus routes are as follows: Changuinola (US$25, 10 hours, at 8pm daily); Colón (US$2.50, two hours, every 20 minutes, departures 5am to 11pm); David (US$12.50; seven to eight hours, 13 per day; *expresos* US$15, five to six hours, two per day at 10:45pm and midnight), El Valle (US$4; 2½ hours, frequent;

departures 7am to 7pm), Soná (US$7, six hours, six buses daily from 8:30am to 6pm) and Yaviza (US$15; seven to 10 hours, eight per day, departures 5am to 3:45pm). Panaline buses to San José, Costa Rica depart at noon, while Tica Bus departs at 11am. Both cost US$25.

Buses departing for the Canal Zone (Miraflores and Pedro Miguel Locks, Paraíso, Gamboa and other locales) depart from the bus stop on Av Roosevelt across from the Legislative Palace.

Car
Many of the car-rental agencies have offices throughout the city. A number of them lie clustered around Calle 49 B Oeste in the El Cangrejo area.

Daily rates run from US$30 to US$50 per day for the most economical cars, with insurance and unlimited kilometers.

Rental car companies in Panama City:
Avis (☎ 264 0722, airport 238 4056)
Barriga (☎ 269 0221, airport 238 4495)
Budget (☎ 263 8777, airport 238 4069)
Central (☎ 223 5745, airport 238 4936)
Dollar (☎ 270 0355, airport 238 4032)
Hertz (☎ 264 1111, airport 238 4081)
National (☎ 265 2222, airport 238 4144)
Thrifty (☎ 264 1402, airport 238 4955)

Train
The **Panama Railway Company** (☎ 317 6070; info@panarail.com; Carr Gaillard) operates a glass-domed luxury passenger train from Panama City to Colón (one-way/round-trip US$22/38, one hour), leaving at 7:15am and returning at 5:15pm daily. It's a lovely ride that follows the canal, and at times the train is surrounded by nothing but thick vine-strewn jungle. If you want to pretend that you're a luxury traveler for an hour or two, this is definitely the way to do it.

A taxi to the station, located in the town of Corazal, from Panama City centre costs about US$3.

GETTING AROUND
Bicycle
The best spot to rent bicycles in Panama City is at **Bicicletas Rali** (☎ 220 3844; ☽ 8am-6pm Sat & Sun), which operates a booth at the causeway entrance.

You can rent a bicycle for US$2.50 per hour or in-line skates for US$1 per hour.

Bus
Panama City has a good network of local buses (nicknamed *diablos rojos* or 'red devils'), which run daily from around 5am to 11pm. A ride costs US$0.25, and we promise you've never seen anything quite like these tricked-out street rockets. Buses run along the three major west-to-east routes: Av Central-Vía España, Av Balboa-Vía Israel, and Av Simón Bolívar-Vía Transístmica. The Av Central-Vía España streets are one-way going west for much of the route; eastbound buses use Av Perú and Av 4 Sur; these buses will take you into the banking district of El Cangrejo. Buses also run along Av Ricardo J Alfaro (known as Tumba Muerto). There are plenty of bus stops along the street, but you can usually hail one from anywhere. Many of these buses stop at Albrook Bus Terminal, near Albrook airport.

The Plaza Cinco de Mayo area has three major bus stops. On the corner of Av Central and Av Justo Arosemena, buses depart for the Tocumen International Airport (US$0.75, one hour, departs every 15 minutes) and Panama Viejo. Buses for the Albrook domestic airport (US$0.25) depart in front of the Legislative Palace. Buses depart from the station on Av Roosevelt, opposite the Legislative Palace, for the Balboa and Ancón area (including the causeway) and other destinations. A ride usually costs no more than US$1.

Taxi
Taxis are plentiful. They are not metered, but there is a list of standard fares that drivers are supposed to charge, measured by zones.

The fare for one zone is a minimum of US$1; the maximum fare within the city is US$4. An average ride, crossing a couple of zones, would cost US$1.25 to US$2, plus US$0.25 for each additional passenger. Always agree on a fare before you get into the cab. A taxi from downtown to the airport should cost no more than US$12 for one person, US$15 for two or more. Taxis can also be rented for US$8 an hour.

Watch out for unmarked large-model US cars serving hotels as cabs. Their prices are up to four times that of regular street taxis. You can phone for a taxi:
America (☎ 223 7694)
America Libre (☎ 223 7342)
Latino (☎ 224 0677)
Metro (☎ 264 6788)
Taxi Unico Cooperativa (☎ 221 3191)

AROUND PANAMA CITY

Panamá Province, which encompasses the area around Panama City, has a rich history of pirates, plunder, pearls and the world's most daring engineering marvel. Even before Henry Morgan's successful raid of Panamá, pirates such as Sir Francis Drake used Isla Taboga as a hideout and as a springboard for attacks on the mainland. Further off the coast, an even better hideout was the remote Islas de Perlas, which were named by Balboa upon learning of the abundance of pearls in the archipelago. Today Panamá Province is famous more for the canal than for anything else, though there are other fine attractions.

Panamá Province contains the largest population of Panama's nine provinces – 1,349,000 people according to the 2000 census – and its attractions serve as popular day trips or mini-breaks for Panama City's weekend warriors.

PANAMA CANAL

The canal is truly one of the world's greatest engineering marvels. Stretching for 80km from Panama City on the Pacific side to Colón on the Atlantic side, the canal cuts right through the Continental Divide. Nearly 14,000 vessels pass through the canal each year, and ships worldwide are built with the dimensions of the Panama Canal's locks in mind: 305m long and 33.5m wide.

Ships pay according to their weight, with the average fee around US$30,000. The highest amount, around US$200,000, was paid in 2001 by the 90,000-ton French cruise ship *Infinity*; the lowest amount was US$0.36, paid in 1928 by Richard Halliburton, who swam through.

The canal has three sets of double locks: Miraflores and Pedro Miguel Locks on the Pacific side and Gatún Locks on the Atlantic side. Between the locks, ships pass through a huge artificial lake, Lago Gatún, created by the Gatún Dam across the Río Chagres (when created they were the largest dam and largest artificial lake on Earth), and the Gaillard Cut, a 14km cut through the rock and shale of the isthmian mountains. With the passage of each ship, a staggering 52 million gallons of fresh water is released into the ocean.

In a referendum that took place in October 2006, Panamanian voters overwhelmingly endorsed an ambitious project to expand the Panama Canal. The US$5 billion plan, which calls for the largest expansion of the canal since it opened in 1914, will widen and deepen existing navigation channels as well as enable the construction of another set of locks.

At present, the canal can only handle ships carrying up to 4000 containers, though the new locks and larger channels will allow the passage of ships carrying up to 10,000 containers. Although supporters say that the cost of the upgrades will be met from increased tolls (supplemented by a $2.3 billion loan), opponents claim that when the work is finished in 2014/15, the canal will still be unable to meet world shipping needs.

For more information on the history of the canal, see p638.

Sights

MIRAFLORES LOCKS

The easiest and best way to visit the canal is to go to the **Miraflores Visitors' Center** (☎ 276 8325; www.pancanal.com; admission to viewing deck/full access US$5/8; ⏱ 9am-5pm), located just outside Panama City. The recently inaugurated visitors' center features a large, four-floor museum, several viewing platforms and an excellent restaurant that overlooks the locks. A tip: the best time to view big liners passing through is from 9am to 11am and from 3pm to 5pm.

To get there, take any Paraíso or Gamboa bus from the bus stop on Av Roosevelt across from the Legislative Palace in Panama City. These buses, passing along the canal-side highway to Gamboa, will let you off at the 'Miraflores Locks' sign on the highway, 12km from the city center. It's about a 15-minute walk to the locks from the sign. Or, you can take a taxi. Even with a 30-minute wait, expect to pay no more than US$15 for the round-trip – agree on the price beforehand.

OTHER LOCKS

Further north, beyond the Miraflores Locks, are the **Pedro Miguel Locks**. You will pass them if you're taking the highway to Gamboa. The only facilities here are a parking lot, from where you can see the locks.

On the Atlantic side, the **Gatún Locks** have a viewing stand for visitors. You can also drive across the locks themselves; you will pass over them if you cross the canal to visit Fuerte San Lorenzo. For more details on these locks, see p697.

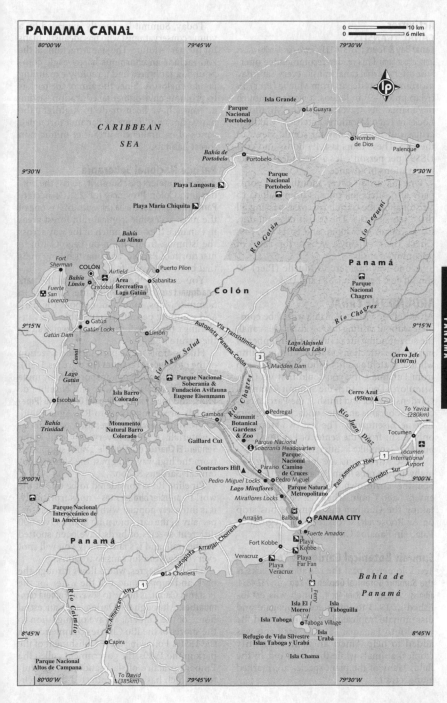

PANAMA CANAL

0   10 km
0   6 miles

80°00'W   79°45'W   79°30'W

Isla Grande

Parque Nacional Portobelo

La Guayra

Nombre de Dios

Palenque

CARIBBEAN SEA

Bahía de Portobelo

Portobelo

Parque Nacional Portobelo

9°30'N   9°30'N

Playa Langosta

Río Gatún

Río Pequení

Playa María Chiquita

Bahía Las Minas

Panamá

Fort Sherman

COLÓN

Bahía Limón

Airfield

Area Recreativa Lago Gatún

Puerto Pilon

Cristóbal

Sabanitas

Colón

Parque Nacional Chagres

Fuerte San Lorenzo

Río Chagres

9°15'N   9°15'N

Gatún

Gatún Locks

Limón

Gatún Dam

Vía Transístmica

Autopista Panama-Colón

Lago Alajuela (Madden Lake)

Cerro Jefe (1007m)

Canal

Río Agua Salud

3

Madden Dam

Escobal

Lago Gatún

Isla Barro Colorado

Parque Nacional Soberanía & Fundación Avifauna Eugene Eisenmann

Río Chagres

Cerro Azul (950m)

To Yaviza (280km)

Bahía Trinidad

Monumento Natural Barro Colorado

Gamboa

Summit Botanical Gardens & Zoo

Pedregal

Río Juan Díaz

Tocumen

Gaillard Cut

Parque Nacional Soberanía Headquarters

Contractors Hill

Parque Nacional Camino de Cruces

Paraíso

Pan-American Hwy

Tocumen International Airport

Pedro Miguel Locks

Lago Miraflores

Pedro Miguel

Parque Natural Metropolitano

Corredor Sur

9°00'N   9°00'N

Parque Nacional Interoceánico de las Américas

Miraflores Locks

Balboa

PANAMA CITY

Panamá

Arraiján

Fuerte Amador

Fort Kobbe

Playa Kobbe

Autopista Arraiján-Chorrera

Veracruz

Playa Far Fan

Playa Veracruz

Bahía de Panamá

Río Caimito

La Chorrera

Ferry

Isla El Morro

Isla Taboguilla

8°45'N   8°45'N

Pan-American Hwy

1

Isla Taboga

Taboga Village

Isla Urabá

Capira

Refugio de Vida Silvestre Islas Taboga y Urabá

Parque Nacional Altos de Campana

Isla Chama

To David (385km)

80°00'W   79°45'W   79°30'W

PANAMA

Activities

CANAL TRANSITS

Canal Bay & Tours (☎ 314 1339; www.canalandbaytours
.com/about.htm) This reader-recommended operator offers partial canal transits every Saturday
morning. Boats depart from Muelle (Pier) 19
(Map pp648–9) in Balboa, a western suburb
of Panama City, travel through the Miraflores
Locks to Lago Miraflores and back, and then
cruise out into the bay for scenic views of
the city. These tours last 4½ hours and cost
US$99 per person – it's a good idea to make
reservations in advance.

One Saturday every month, the company also offers full transits from Balboa to
Cristóbal on the Caribbean coast, passing all
three sets of locks. The transit takes all day,
from 7:30am to 5:30pm, and costs US$149.
Check the company's website for dates of
upcoming transits.

A one-way taxi fare to Muelle (Pier) 19
should cost between US$3 and US$6.

AROUND THE CANAL

Although no visit to Panama would be complete without visiting the world-famous canal,
the surrounding area is home to a number of
impressive attractions, especially if you're into
wildlife-watching and birding. On a day trip
from Panama City, you could first visit the
Miraflores Locks, then the Summit Botanical
Gardens & Zoo, and finish at the Parque Nacional Soberanía and the Fundación Avifauna
Eugene Eisenmann. The last two stops are
only 25km from the center of Panama City,
but they seem like a different world.

These attractions are located along the
highway that runs from Panama City to Gamboa, the small town where the Río Chagres
enters Lago Gatún. They can be reached by
taking the Gamboa bus from the bus stop
on Av Roosevelt, across from the Legislative
Palace in Panama City.

Summit Botanical Gardens & Zoo

Ten kilometers past the Miraflores Locks is
the **Summit Botanical Gardens & Zoo** (☎ 232 4854;
admission US$1; ⏰ 8am-4pm), which was estab-
lished in 1923 to introduce, propagate and
disseminate tropical plants from around the
world into Panama. Later, a small zoo was
added to help American soldiers identify
tropical animals while they were out in the
field. Many of the plant species are marked
along a trail.

Today, Summit is expertly managed by a
young conservationist who has idealistic plans
for the park's future. The star attractions at the
zoo include an enormous harpy-eagle compound, a tapir area and a rapidly expanding
jaguar enclosure. Since the aim of the park is
to promote environmental education, strong
attempts have been made to highlight the
native flora and fauna of Panama through a
series of natural enclosures that mimic rain
forest habitats.

Parque Nacional Soberanía

A few kilometers past Summit, across the border into Colón Province, the 22,104-hectare
Parque Nacional Soberanía (admission US$3) is one of
the most accessible tropical rain forest areas
in Panama. It extends much of the way across
the isthmus, from Limón on Lago Gatún to
just north of Paraíso, and boasts hiking trails
that brim with wildlife.

You can pay the entrance fee at the **park
headquarters** (☎ 276 6370) at the turn-off to
Summit. Maps, information about the park
and camping permits are available here, including a brochure for self-guided walks along
the nature trail.

Hiking trails in the park include a section
of the old **Sendero Las Cruces** (Las Cruces Trail),
used by the Spanish to transport gold by mule
train between Panama City and Nombre de
Dios, and the 17km **Camino del Oleoducto (Pipeline Rd)**, providing access to Río Agua Salud,
where you can walk upriver for a swim under
a waterfall. A shorter, very easy trail is the
Sendero El Charco (the Puddle Trail), signposted
from the highway, 3km past the Summit Botanical Gardens & Zoo.

Pipeline Rd is considered to be one of the
world's **premier birding sites** – not surprisingly,
it is intensely popular with bird-watchers, especially in the early morning hours. Over 500
different species of birds have been spotted
on the trail, and it's fairly likely you will spot
everything from toucans to trogons.

The Río Chagres, which flows through the
park and supplies most of the water for the
Panama Canal, is home to several **Emberá communities**. Although the Darién is the ancestral
home of the Emberá, a wave of migration to
the shores of the Río Chagres commenced in
the 1950s. Following the establishment of the
park in the 1980s, the government culled the
Emberá practice of slash-and-burn agriculture, which has severely affected their liveli-

---

EXPLORE MORE OF THE CANAL ZONE

Tired of the tourist crowds? Looking for a bit of an adventure? Here's a list of LP-author-tested excursions to spice up your travels:

- Stare in awe at the **Gaillard Cut** from Contractors Hill. Hire a taxi and visit this remote 111m-high hill on the western side of the canal where you can see the extent of the Gaillard Cut.

- Explore the rain forest at the **Monumento Natural Barro Colorado**. Arrange a tour with **Ancon Expeditions** (Map pp652-3; ☎ 269 9415; www.anconexpeditions.com; El Dorado Bldg, Calle 49 Este near Av 3 Sur, Panama City) to this vast rain forest reserve, which borders the canal.

- Watch ships queue for the canal from **Playa Kobbe**. Get on a bus heading west from the Albrook terminal and jump off at this popular beach, located just across from the canal.

- Beach-hop along the Pacific in the **San Carlos area**. Grab a bus heading west from the Albrook terminal and get off at any of the beaches from Playa Gorgona to Playa Farallón.

---

hood. Today, several Emberá communities, most notably Parara Puru, are turning to tourism for survival. Although intrepid travelers can seek out local guides, tours of riverside communities are offered through **Aventuras Panama** (☎ 266 0044; www.aventuraspanama.com).

Fundación Avifauna Eugene Eisenmann

At the time of writing, the finishing touches were being applied to the **Fundación Avifauna Eugene Eisenmann** (☎ 264 6266; www.avifauna.org .pa), an ambitious project with the mission to protect Panama's bird fauna and rain forest habitat. The first wave of this project is the construction of a visitors' center, hiking trails and a canopy tower near the entrance to Pipeline Rd (1.6km from the gate). Successive phases will aim to promote sustainable tourism in the area by using revenues to protect the surrounding environment. As there are currently no facilities for birders accessing Pipeline Rd, this project is likely to receive a lot of publicity following its launch.

ISLA BARRO COLORADO

This lush island in the middle of Lago Gatún was formed by the damming of the Río Chagres and the creation of the lake. In 1923, Isla Barro Colorado (BCI) became one of the first biological reserves in the New World. Since that time, the island has become one of the most intensively studied areas in the tropics. Home to 1316 recorded plant species, 381 bird species and 102 mammal species, the island also contains a 59km network of marked and protected trails. It is managed by the Smithsonian Tropical Research Institute (STRI), which administers a world-renowned research facility here.

Although the 1500-hectare island was once restricted to scientists, a limited number of guided tourists are now allowed. The trip includes an STRI boat ride down an attractive part of the canal, from **Gamboa** across the lake to the island. Tour reservations are essential; book as far in advance as possible. Reservations can be made through the Panama City visitor services office of **STRI** (Map pp652-3; ☎ 212 8026; www.stri.org; Tupper Bldg, Av Roosevelt, Ancón district; foreign adult/student US$70/40, Panamanian adult/student US$25/12; ⏰ 8:30am-4:30pm Mon-Fri).

The boat to BCI leaves the Gamboa pier at 7:15am on Tuesday, Wednesday and Friday, and at 8am on Saturday and Sunday. There are no visits on Mondays, Thursdays and on certain holidays. The entire trip lasts four to six hours, depending on the size of the group and on the weather. A buffet lunch (with vegetarian options) is included.

ISLA TABOGA

A tropical island with only one road and no traffic, Isla Taboga is a pleasant place to escape the hustle and bustle of Panama City. Although it is only 20km offshore, the 'Island of Flowers' is covered with sweet-smelling blossoms at certain times of the year. First settled by the Spanish in 1515, the quaint village of Taboga is also home to the second-oldest church in the Western hemisphere. However, the main appeal of the island is its string of sandy beaches lapped by warm waters, which can quickly rejuvenate even the most hardened urbanite.

Isla Taboga is currently in the midst of an image makeover. Ferries for the island now depart from the most exclusive of berths – the causeway – p656. Also, rumors abound that the now defunct Hotel Taboga will be knocked down to make way for a upmarket resort. In the meantime, Taboga is still a laid-back day trip from Panama City, for a little fun in the sun.

History

Taboga is part of a chain of islands that were inhabited by indigenous peoples who resided in thatch huts and lived off the bounty of the sea. In 1515, Spanish soldiers announced their arrival on Taboga by killing or enslaving the islanders and establishing a small colony. However, peace did not reign, especially since a number of pirates, including Henry Morgan and Francis Drake, frequented the island, and used it as a base from which to attack Spanish ships and towns. As late as 1819 Taboga was still sought after for its strategic location, a fact made abundantly clear when the pirate Captain Illingsworth and his crew of Chileans sacked the island. However, aside from a few live rounds fired at Taboga by the US Navy during a WWII session of target practice, recent years have been peaceful.

Orientation & Information

Ferries from the causeway in Panama City tie up at a pier near the north end of the island. As you exit the pier, you'll see the entrance to the abandoned Hotel Taboga to your right. To your left, you'll see a narrow street that is the island's main road. From this point, the street meanders for 5.2km before ending at the old US military installation atop the island's highest hill, Cerro El Vigia.

For more information on the island, check the excellent English-language site, www .taboga.panamanow.com.

Sights & Activities

There are fine **beaches** in Taboga, all free, in either direction from the ferry dock. Many visitors head straight for the Hotel Taboga, to the right as you walk off the ferry dock; the hotel faces onto the island's most popular beach, arcing between Taboga and tiny Isla El Morro.

On weekends, when the most people visit Taboga, you can find fishermen at the pier who will take you around the island, allowing you to see it from all sides and reach some good **snorkeling** spots. Caves on the island's western side are rumored to hold golden treasure left there by pirates. During the week, when the small boats aren't taking people around, you can still snorkel around Isla El Morro, which doesn't have coral but attracts some large fish.

Walk left from the pier along the island's only road for about 75m until you reach the fork. If you take the high road, after a few more paces you will come to a modest **church**, in front of which is a simple square. This unassuming church was founded in 1550 and is the second-oldest church in the western hemisphere; inside is a handsome altar and lovely artwork. Further down the road is a beautiful public garden, which bears the statue of the island's patroness, **Nuestra Señora del Carmen**.

For a fine view, you can walk up the hill on the east side of the island, **Cerro de la Cruz**, to the cross on the top. Another trail leads to a viewpoint atop **Cerro El Vigia**, on the western side of the island.

A wildlife refuge, the **Refugio de Vida Silvestre Isla Taboga y Urabá**, covers about a third of the island, as well as the island of Urabá just off Taboga's southeastern coast. This refuge is home to one of the largest breeding colonies of brown pelicans in the world. May is the height of nesting season, but pelicans can be seen from January to June.

On your way to and from the island, keep an eye on the ocean. On rare occasions during August, September and October, migrating humpback and sei whales can be seen leaping from the water near Taboga in spectacular displays.

Festivals & Events

Taboga's **annual festival** takes place on July 16, the day of its patron saint, Nuestra Señora del Carmen. The statue of the saint is carried upon the shoulders of followers to the shore, placed on a boat and ferried around the island. Upon her return, she is carried around the island while crowds follow.

Sleeping & Eating

Most people choose to visit Isla Taboga as a day trip from Panama City, though there are a few affordable places to stay on this island.

Kool Hostel (☎ 690 2545; luisveron@hotmail.com; dm US$10, house US$25) Perched on a hill overlooking the bay, this clean and comfortable family-run hostel is a good place to bed down if you want to extend your time on the island. Rooms are fairly standard and lacking in personality. There are shared bathrooms with hot water, as well as a communal kitchen. Guests can rent bikes, snorkel gear and fishing tackle. To reach the hostel, turn left as you exit the dock and walk for a few minutes until you see a sign leading up the hill.

Vereda Tropical Hotel (☎ 250 2154; veredatropical hotel@hotmail.com; d from US$45; 🔀) Also perched on a hill overlooking the bay, this charming inn has colorful rooms with high ceilings, comfortable beds and shutters or balconies facing either the village or the sea. Vereda Tropical is located about 100m past the path leading up to Kool Hostel.

Aquario (mains US$4-7; ☽ 7am-10pm) This simple eatery along the main road in the center of town is a good spot for traditional Panamanian food – peel a few more bucks out of your wallet and sample the catch of the day.

Getting There & Away

The scenic boat trip out to Isla Taboga is part of the island's attraction. **Barcos Calypso** (☎ 314 1730; round-trip US$10) has departures from Panama City at 8:30am and 3pm on Monday, Wednesday and Friday, 8:30am on Tuesday and Thursday and 8:30am, 10:30am and 4pm on Saturday and Sunday. Ferries depart Isla Taboga at 9:30am and 4pm Monday, Wednesday and Friday, 4:30pm on Tuesday and Thursday and 9am, 3pm and 5pm on Saturday and Sunday.

Ferries depart from La Playita de Amador, which is located behind the Centro de Exhibiciones Marinas on the causeway. The easiest way to reach the dock is by taxi (US$4 to US$6).

ARCHIPIÉLAGO DE LAS PERLAS

In January 1979, after the followers of the Ayatollah Ruholla Khomeini had forced Shah Mohammed Reza Pahlavi to pack up his hundreds of millions of dollars and flee Iran, the shah looked the world over and moved to Isla Contadora, one of the islands in the Archipiélago de las Perlas, or Pearl Islands, any one of which is fit for a king – or a shah.

Named for the large pearls that were once found in its waters, the Pearl Islands are comprised of 90 named islands and over 100 unnamed islets, each surrounded by white-sand beaches and turquoise waters. Isla Contadora is the best-known island of the group, especially since the island is home to the palatial mansions of the rich and powerful. The Pearl Islands were also the site of the popular US TV show *Survivor*, which filmed its 2003 season on an unnamed island in the chain.

Orientation & Information

With few exceptions, tourists visit only four of Las Perlas: Isla Contadora, which is the most accessible, developed and visited island; Isla San José, the site of an pricey resort; Isla Casaya and neighboring Isla Casayeta, which are frequented by pearl shoppers. Less than a dozen of the Pearl Islands are inhabited, and there are ample opportunities here for independent exploration, especially if you have a sense of adventure and the help of a local guide.

PANAMA

GETTING TO COSTA RICA

The most heavily trafficked Panama-Costa Rica border crossing is at **Paso Canoas** (☽ 24hr), 53km west of David on the Pan-American Hwy. Allow at least one to two hours to get through the formalities on both sides. Buses depart frequently for the border from David (US$1.50, 1½ hours, every 30 minutes from 4:30am to 9:30pm). On the Costa Rican side of the border, you can catch regular buses to San José or other parts of the country. See p623 for information on crossing the border from Costa Rica.

The less-traveled post northern border post at **Guabito–Sixaola** (☽ 8am-noon & 2-6pm), north of Changuinola, is straightforward, and most travelers find it hassle free. Buses from Changuinola depart frequently for the border (US$0.50, 30 minutes) every half-hour from 6am to 7pm. On the Costa Rican side, you can catch regular buses on to Puerto Limón and San José, as well as regional destinations. See p570 for more information on this crossing from Costa Rica.

The least trafficked crossing into Costa Rica is the border post at **Río Sereno** (☽ 9am-5pm Mon-Sat, 9am-3pm Sun), 47km west of Volcán. Buses to the border depart from David and travel via La Concepción, Volcán and Santa Clara (US$4, three hours, every 30 minutes). On the Costa Rican side of the border, you can take a 15-minute bus or taxi ride to San Vito, where you can catch buses to regional destinations.

Note that you can be asked for an onward ticket when entering Costa Rica. If you do not possess one, it is acceptable to buy a return bus ticket back to Panama. Also note that Costa Rica is one hour behind Panama – opening and closing times in this box are given in Panama time.

Sights & Activities

Isla Contadora is home to no less than 12 beaches, all of which are covered with tan sand, and virtually abandoned except during major holidays. Five **beaches** are particularly lovely: Playa Larga, Playa de las Suecas, Playa Cacique, Playa Ejecutiva and Playa Galeón. Although spread around three sides of the island, all can be visited in as little as 20 minutes in a rented 4WD.

Snorkeling around Contadora can be fantastic. There are five coral fields near the island where you can expect to see schools of angelfish, damselfish, moray eels, parrotfish, puffer fish, butterfly fish, white-tip reef sharks and a whole lot more. In the waters off Playa Larga, you can often spot sea turtles and manta rays.

Sleeping & Eating

Budget accommodations in the Pearl Islands are limited to Isla Contadora.

Cabañas de Contadora (☎ 265 5691; d from US$30) Located in a lush, upscale residential neighborhood, these bare-bones cabinas are the most affordable option on the island, especially since they're equipped with hot plates, fridges and microwaves. To get to the Cabañas, take the road up the hill as you leave the airport runway. When the road forks, take the left fork and follow it for the next 200m. When the road ends, take the road to the left, and you'll soon reach the cabins on your left.

Casa del Sol (☎ 250 4212; www.panama-isla-contadora .com; s/d with breakfast US$40/50) Located in a pleasant residential neighborhood full of hummingbirds, the Casa del Sol has just one guestroom, though it's cheerfully decorated and has a hot-water bathroom. The German owners are an excellent source of information on the Pearl Islands, and they can take you to unoccupied islands aboard their boat. Advanced reservations are necessary – call ahead to arrange for a pickup from the airstrip.

Punta Galeón (mains US$8-15; ☒ noon-3pm & 6-10pm Mon-Sat) Restaurants are a pricey affair in Contadora, though this popular dinner spot in the Hotel Punta Galeón Resort is a good deal, especially if you can get a table on the beach.

Getting There & Away

Air Panama (☎ 316 9000; www.flyairpanama.com/tickets) and **Aeroperlas** (☎ 315 7500; www.aeroperlas.com) fly direct from Panama City to Isla Contadora (round-trip US$60, 20 minutes). Each airline has two daily departures on weekdays and four daily departures on weekends.

CHIRIQUÍ PROVINCE

Chiricanos claim to have it all, and there's an element of truth in what they say: Panama's tallest mountains, longest rivers and most fertile valleys are in Chiriquí. The province is also home to spectacular highland rain forests as well as the country's most productive agricultural and cattle-ranching regions. Not surprisingly, many Chiricanos often dream about creating an independent República de Chiriquí.

Bordering Costa Rica to the west, Chiriquí is often the first province in Panama encountered by overland travelers. It also serves as a suitable introduction to the not-so-subtle beauty Panama has to offer. Although the mist-covered mountains near Boquete are slowly being colonized by waves of North American and European retirees, the town serves as a good base for exploring the flanks of towering Volcán Barú, Panama's only volcano and its highest point (3475m). The region is also home to the Parque Internacional La Amistad, a bi-national park that is shared by Costa Rica and Panama. The park offers excellent hiking through lush rain forests, largely unfettered by tourist crowds.

DAVID

pop 124,000

Although it feels more like a country town, David is Panama's second-largest city, the capital of Chiriquí Province and a major agricultural center. However, David is rapidly growing in terms of wealth and importance as a result of the powerful wave of foreign capital flowing into Chiriquí. With tens of thousands of North American and European retirees likely to settle in the region in the years to come, David's economy is expected to boom.

For most travelers, David serves as an important transportation hub for anyone heading to/from Costa Rica, the Chiriquí highlands, Golfo de Chiriquí, Panama City and Bocas del Toro. Although the city has few attractions in its own right, David is a pleasant enough place to stay, and there's no shortage of interesting things to see and do in the surrounding area.

Orientation

David is halfway between San José in Costa Rica and Panama City – about seven hours

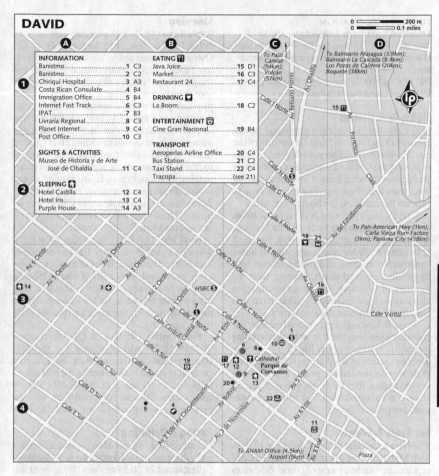

DAVID

0 ————— 200 m
0 ————— 0.1 miles

INFORMATION		
Banistmo	1	C3
Banistmo	2	C2
Chiriquí Hospital	3	A3
Costa Rican Consulate	4	B4
Immigration Office	5	B4
Internet Fast Track	6	C3
IPAT	7	B3
Livraría Regional	8	C3
Planet Internet	9	C4
Post Office	10	C3

SIGHTS & ACTIVITIES		
Museo de Historia y de Arte José de Obaldía	11	C4

SLEEPING		
Hotel Castilla	12	C4
Hotel Iris	13	C4
Purple House	14	A3

EATING		
Java Juice	15	D1
Market	16	C3
Restaurant 24	17	C4

DRINKING		
La Boom	18	C2

ENTERTAINMENT		
Cine Gran Nacional	19	B4

TRANSPORT		
Aeroperlas Airline Office	20	C4
Bus Station	21	C4
Taxi Stand	22	C4
Tracopa	(see 21)	

To Paso Canoas (54km); Volcán (57km)

To Balneario Majagua (3.9km); Balneario La Cascada (8.4km); Los Pozos de Caldera (20km); Boquete (38km)

To Pan-American Hwy (1km); Carta Vieja Rum Factory (3km); Panama City (438km)

Parque de Cervantes

To ANAM Office (4.5km); Airport (5km)

Plaza

PANAMA

by road from either place. The Pan-American Hwy does not enter the town, but skirts around its northern and western sides. The city's heart is its fine central plaza, the Parque de Cervantes, about 1.5km southwest of the highway.

Information
BOOKSTORES
Livraría Regional (Av Bolivar) Modest bookstore with a handful of titles in English including coffee-table books on Panama.

CONSULATES
Costa Rican consulate (☎ /fax 774 1923; cosurica@ chiriqui.com; cnr Calle B Sur & Av 1 Este; ☒ 8am-3pm Mon-Fri)

INTERNET ACCESS
Internet Fast Track (Av 2 Este; per hr US$1; ☒ 24hr)
Planet Internet (Calle Central; per hr US$1; ☒ 9am-midnight)

MEDICAL SERVICES
Chiriquí Hospital (☎ 777 8814; Calle Central & Av 3 Oeste) One of the best hospitals in the country.

MONEY
Banistmo (Calle C Norte) Branches near the park and on Av Obaldía north of the bus station.
HSBC (Av Central)

POST
Post office (Calle C Norte; ☒ 7am-6pm Mon-Fri, 7am-4:30pm Sat)

TOURIST INFORMATION

Autoridad Nacional de Ambiente (ANAM; ☎ 775 7840; fax 774 6671; ◷ 8am-4pm Mon-Fri) Provides tourist information and gives permits to camp in the national parks. It's near the airport.

IPAT (☎ 775 2839; Av Central; ◷ 8:30am-4:30pm Mon-Fri) Provides information on Chiriquí Province.

Sights & Activities

Despite its size and role as a provincial capital, most of David's attractions lie outside of the city. However, David serves as a great base for exploring the Chiriquí lowlands, and it's likely you'll pass through here a few times during your travels in Panama. For tips on how to explore the area, see the boxed text, below.

David's sole attraction is the modest **Museo de Historia y de Arte José de Obaldía** (Av 8 Este btwn Calles Central & A Norte; admission US$1; ◷ 8:30am-noon & 12:45-4:30pm Mon-Sat), a two-story colonial home constructed in 1880, and still furnished with its original art and decor. Named after the founder of Chiriquí Province, the museum also houses local archaeological artifacts and old photos of the canal constructions.

If you're looking to get your adrenaline fix, consider spending the day **white-water rafting** on the Río Chiriquí or the Río Chiriquí Viejo. Tour operators in Boquete pass by David on their way to the launch point, and with advanced notice, they'll be happy to pick you up at your accommodation. For more information, see p676.

Festivals & Events

The **Feria de San José de David**, held for 10 days each March, is a big international fair. La Concepción, half an hour west of David, celebrates it's **saint's day** on February 2.

Sleeping

Purple House (☎ 774-4059; www.purplehousehostel.com; cnr Calle C Sur & Av 6 Oeste; dm US$8.80, r US$18-23; ❄ 💻) Owned and managed by a warm and welcoming Peace Corp veteran named Andrea, the Purple House (yes, it's all purple!) is a popular spot to link up with other backpackers. Andrea provides guests with a communal kitchen, an outdoor patio, cable TV, DVD rentals and free internet access. She is an incredible source of information on the surrounding area. Located in a commercial area, the Purple House is close to lots of restaurants, supermarkets and pharmacies. If enough people are staying at the hostel, the owner can arrange transport to Isla Bocas Brava (four people about US$50; see opposite). There's limited availability in October – call or email first. Wi-fi is available.

Hotel Iris (☎ 775 2251; Calle A Norte; r from US$12; ❄) The faded three-story Iris has definitely seen better days, though any of its worn rooms are a good deal, especially if you're looking for a bit of privacy. It's conveniently located across from the park, so it's easy enough to flop down here for the night and get out early in the morning.

Hotel Castilla (☎ 774 5260; Calle A Norte; d from US$30-40; ❄ 💻) Although rooms at the Castilla are more expensive than the Iris, this centrally located hotel is one of the best values in David. Every room at the Castilla is fairly cheap, cheerful and equipped with air-con, private hot-water bathrooms and cable TV.

Eating & Drinking

If you're looking for cheap produce, don't miss the bustling **market** (cnr Avs Bolívar & Obaldía).

Restaurant 24 (Av 2 Este; mains US$2-3; ◷ till late) Popular with locals for its grilled meats and

---

EXPLORE MORE OF THE CHIRIQUÍ LOWLANDS

The Chiriquí lowlands offer some good options for getting off the Gringo Trail:

■ Rest those tired bones in the **Los Pozos de Caldera hot springs**. Take a bus to the town of Caldera, hike along the dirt road for 45 minutes and soak up the health-giving properties of the spring.

■ Learn to appreciate rum before you down a tumbler or two. Contact **Mr Garcia** (☎ 772 7073) to arrange a private tour of the nearby **Carta Vieja rum factory**.

■ Swim with Chiricanos at **Balneario Majagua** and **Balneario La Cascada** by hopping on a Boquete-bound bus and jumping off at either of these local swimming spots.

■ Beat the David heat; grab some friends and take a taxi to the lovely dark-sand beach of nearby **Playa Barqueta**.

inexpensive lunch specials – this is the perfect spot to get your fill without breaking the budget.

Java Juice (Av Francisco Clark; mains US$2.50-4; ☺ 11am-11pm Mon-Sat, 4-10pm Sun) Ice coffee, fresh-fruit smoothies, healthy salads and juicy grilled burgers are the fare at this charming outdoor café northeast of the bus terminal.

La Boom (Av Obaldía near Av 1 Este) David's largest bar and disco features a sleek dance floor that packs in young crowds on Friday and Saturday nights.

Entertainment

Cine Gran Nacional (Av 1 Este btwn Calles Central & A Sur) David's small cinema screens mostly American new releases.

Getting There & Away

AIR

David's airport, the Aeropuerto Enrique Malek, is about 5km from town. There are no buses to the airport; take a taxi (US$2).

Air Panama (☎ 721 0841; www.flyairpanama.com /tickets) and **Aeroperlas** (☎ 721 1195; www.aeroperlas .com) fly direct from Panama City to David (US$60, 45 minutes). Air Panama has two daily flights from Monday to Saturday and one flight on Sunday while Aeroperlas has two flights daily. Aeroperlas also has one daily flight from Monday to Friday to Bocas del Toro via Changuinola (US$35, 35 minutes).

BUS

The David **bus station** (Av del Estudiante) is about 600m northeast of the central plaza.

Buses run to these destinations: Boquete (US$1.50, one hour, every 30 minutes from 6am to 9:30pm), Caldera (US$1.50, 45 minutes, hourly from 8:15am to 7:30pm), Cerro Punta (US$3, 2¼ hours, every 20 minutes from 5am to 8pm), Changuinola (US$12.50, 4½hr; hourly from 5am to 6:30pm), Horconcitos (US$1.50, 45 minutes, 11am and 5pm), Panama City (US$12.60, seven to eight hours, every 45 minutes from 6:45am to 8pm; express US$15, six hours, 10:45pm and midnight), Paso Canoas (US$1.50; 1½ hours, every 10 minutes from 4:30am to 9:30pm) and Río Sereno (US$4, 2½ hours, every 30 minutes from 5am to 5pm).

Tracopa (☎ 775 0585) operates direct buses between David and San José, Costa Rica (US$12.50, eight hours). Buses depart at 8:30am daily from the David bus station and

return at 7:30am. Bus tickets can be purchased up to two days in advance.

GOLFO DE CHIRIQUÍ

The undisputed gem of the Chiriquí lowlands is the Golfo de Chiriquí, which is home to the **Parque Nacional Marino Golfo de Chiriquí**, a national marine park with an area of 14,740 hectares protecting 25 islands, 19 coral reefs and abundant wildlife. The marine park also protects the 3000-hectare **Isla Boca Brava**, a lovely little island that is criss-crossed by hiking trails and home to monkeys, nesting sea turtles and 280 recorded bird species. Whether you want to lie on the beach, snorkel clear waters or go wildlife-watching underneath the rain forest canopy, there's something for everyone in this off-the-beaten-path destination.

A great place (and the only place) to stay on Boca Brava is at the **Restaurante y Cabañas Boca Brava** (☎ 676 3244; hammock per person US$3, r US$10, cabin US$18-35), comprising four spacious cabins with private bathrooms and four rustic rooms with shared bathrooms. Owners Frank and Yadira Köhler speak English, German and Spanish. Reservations are not accepted, but they'll always find you a place to stay, if you're willing to sleep in a hammock. The breezy restaurant-bar (meals US$4) features a large selection of seafood (such as red snapper).

Frank and Yadira can arrange any number of fine excursions around the islands: snorkeling, whale-watching or just lounging on a gorgeous uninhabited island (depending on the tour and the number of participants prices range from US$12 to US$70). From the restaurant, you're just a stone's throw from the boundary of the national marine park.

Getting There & Away

To reach the island, take a bus to the Horconcitos turn-off, which is 39km east of David. You can also take any bus heading from David to Panama City that goes past the turn-off, as long as you tell the driver to drop you at the Horconcitos turnoff.

From the turnoff, take a pickup-truck taxi 13km to the fishing village of Boca Chica (US$15, one hour). If you see no taxis at the turn-off, walk into Horconcitos and call either **Jovené** (☎ 653 1549) or **Roberto** (☎ 628 0651); both are taxi drivers in the area. At the Boca Chica dock, hire a water taxi (US$1 per person) to take you the 200m to the island.

If there are enough interested people, the Purple House in David (p672) can sometimes arrange all of your transportation.

PUNTA BURICA

This lush peninsula jutting into the Pacific is a lovely spot for absorbing the beauty of both the rain forest and the coastline. Four years in the making, **Mono Feliz** (☎ 595 0388; mono_feliz@hotmail.com; cabin 1st night/extra nights per person US$20/15; camping per person US$5; 🖳)) offers visitors a chance to enjoy this untouched natural beauty. Wildlife is a key feature here, and the Mono Feliz (happy monkey) certainly has its share of its namesake.

Facilities include three stand-alone cabins – two in the garden and one on the beach. It also has a large pool (fed by cool spring water, and you may be surrounded by monkeys at times), fresh-water showers and an outdoor kitchen for guest use. Those who'd rather not cook can pay US$20 per day extra for three home-cooked meals, ranging from fresh seasonal fish to conch or lobster when available (individual meals available: breakfast/lunch/dinner US$6/8/10). Beds have mosquito nets. Camping on the beach is also available (bring your own gear), and you have access to the pool and bathrooms.

The friendly American and Canadian owners (Allegra and John or 'Juancho' as he's known to locals) offer a range of activities including nature walks (an excursion to **Isla Burica** at low tide is a highlight), fishing, birdwatching, surfing (several boards available) and horseback riding. Remedial massage and yoga is available for guests in need of deeper relaxation. All activities except horseback riding (US$5) are free. The owners speak English, French and Spanish.

Getting There & Away

Owing to its isolation, reaching Mono Feliz requires a bit of work. You'll first need to go to the small coastal town of Puerto Armuelles. Departures from David to Puerto Armuelles leave every 15 minutes (US$2.75, 2½ hours). Be sure to arrive in Puerto Armuelles no later than noon.

The bus drops you off in the *mercado municipal,* and from there take a truck to Bella Vista. It's approximately a one-hour walk down the hill from here to Mono Feliz. You can also exit at El Medio, the last stop before the trucks go inland to Bella Vista.

From El Medio it's an hour's walk along the beach. Mono Feliz is directly in front of Isla Burica.

PLAYA LAS LAJAS

Playa Las Lajas, 51km east of David and 26km south of the Pan-American Hwy, is one of several long, palm-lined beaches along this stretch of the Pacific coast. Playa Las Lajas gathers crowds on the weekends, but often lies empty during the week, when you can have serious stretches of sand all to yourself.

Several new accommodations are currently in the works; meanwhile you can stay at **Las Lajas Beach Cabins** (☎ 720 2430, 618 7723; dm/d US$6.50/35, cabins US$25). The cabins consist of nine small rustic *cabañas* right on the beach, a clam's toss from the surf, while the bathrooms are communal in a nearby concrete structure. There is also an additional concrete structure 50m back from the beach with six private rooms and two dorms.

Back where the road dead-ends at the beach sits **La Estrella del Pacifico** (dishes from US$3), the only restaurant in the area. Simple fish dishes are especially good when the catch is fresh, and you can count on great ocean views anytime.

To reach Las Lajas, take any bus from David (US$2, 1½ hours) that travels by the Las Lajas turn-off on the Interamericana. At the turnoff, take a taxi (US$5) to where the road reaches the sea. Turn right and proceed 1.5km until you arrive at the cabins.

BOQUETE

pop 5000

The mountain-valley town of Boquete, with the sparkling Río Caldera running through it, is known throughout Panama for its cool, fresh climate and pristine natural setting. Flowers, coffee, vegetables and citrus fruits flourish in Boquete's rich soil, and the friendliness of the locals seems to rub off on everyone who passes through.

Boquete is one of the country's top destinations for outdoor lovers. You can hike, climb, raft, visit coffee plantations, soak in hot springs, study Spanish or go on a canopy tour. And of course, there's nothing quite like starting your day with a glass of freshly squeezed OJ, or perking up with a cup of locally grown coffee. It can get chilly here at night.

Although Boquete very much intended to remain as a small town, something happened

PANAMA

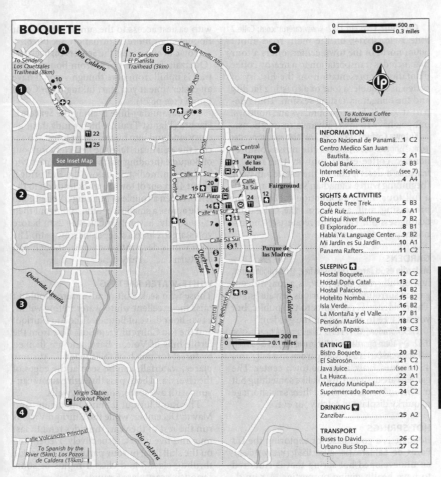

BOQUETE

INFORMATION
Banco Nacional de Panamá....**1**	C2
Centro Medico San Juan Bautista..........................**2**	A1
Global Bank...........................**3**	B3
Internet Kelnix.................(see 7)	
IPAT....................................**4**	A4

SIGHTS & ACTIVITIES
Boquete Tree Trek...............**5**	B3
Café Ruíz............................**6**	A1
Chiriquí River Rafting..........**7**	B2
El Explorador.......................**8**	B1
Habla Ya Language Center...**9**	B2
Mi Jardín es Su Jardín.........**10**	A1
Panama Rafters...................**11**	C2

SLEEPING
Hostal Boquete...................**12**	C2
Hostal Doña Catal..............**13**	C2
Hostal Palacios..................**14**	B2
Hotelito Nomba..................**15**	B2
Isla Verde...........................**16**	B2
La Montaña y el Valle.........**17**	B1
Pensión Marilós..................**18**	C3
Pensión Topas....................**19**	C3

EATING
Bistro Boquete...................**20**	B2
El Sabrosón........................**21**	C2
Java Juice.......................(see 11)	
La Huaca...........................**22**	A1
Mercado Municipal.............**23**	C2
Supermercado Romero.......**24**	C2

DRINKING
Zanzibar............................**25**	A2

TRANSPORT
Buses to David...................**26**	C2
Urbano Bus Stop................**27**	C2

that was completely beyond anyone's control – baby boomers overseas started getting old. When *Modern Maturity* magazine of the American Association for Retired Persons chose Boquete in 2001 as one of the four top places in the world to retire, a flock of foreign retirees started snatching up mountain plots in town. Today gated communities dot the hillsides, and the face of Boquete is slowly being transformed.

Orientation

Boquete's central area is only a few square blocks. The main road, Av Central, comes north from David, passes along the western side of the plaza and continues up the hill past the church.

Information

Banco Nacional de Panama (Av Central) Has 24hr ATM.
Centro Medico San Juan Bautista (☎ 720 1881)
Global Bank (Av Central)
Internet Kelnix (Av Central; per hr US$1)
IPAT (⏲ 9:30am-6pm) It's about 1.5km south of town, sitting atop a bluff overlooking Boquete. You can pick up maps here and obtain information on area attractions. On the 2nd floor is an exhibit detailing the history of the region (Spanish only).
Post office (⏲ 7am-6pm Mon-Fri, 7am-5pm Sat)

Sights
COFFEE PLANTATIONS
No trip to Boquete is complete without learning the secrets of a perfectly blended cup of joe.

PANAMA

Café Ruíz (☎ 720 1392; www.caféruiz.com; Calle 2 Norte; 3hr tour US$14), on the main road about 600m north of the town center, offers a tour that includes transportation to a nearby coffee plantation, a presentation on the history of coffee in Boquete, a tour of a roasting facility and the obligatory tasting session. Tours depart at 9am daily except Sundays and holidays, but you have to make advance reservations.

Kotowa Coffee Estate (☎ 720 1430; www.myroaster .com; 2½hr tour US$19) offers the most comprehensive coffee-estate tour in the area. It features a description of the estate's history (beginning with a Canadian's arrival in 1918), a full tour of the production facilities and processing mill, and again, the obligatory tasting session. The estate requests 24 hours' notice prior to your visit.

GARDENS
Mi Jardín es Su Jardín (admission free; ☼ daylight hours), just uphill from Café Ruíz, is a magnificent garden surrounding a luxurious private estate. The residence is off-limits to the public, but you are free to stroll about the garden.

El Explorador (☎ 775 2643; Calle Jarmillo Alto; admission US$2; ☼ 10am-6pm daily mid-Dec to mid-Apr, Sat & Sun only mid-Apr to mid-Dec) is a private garden in a hilly area 45 minutes' walk from the town center. The gardens are designed to look like something out of *Alice in Wonderland,* and there's no shortage of quirky displays to catch your eye.

HOT SPRINGS
Boquete is a good base for exploring the **Los Pozos de Caldera** (admission US$1; ☼ dawn-dusk), an undeveloped hot spring that is rumored to have health-giving properties. A round-trip taxicab from the town center to the hot springs should cost about US$6.

Activities
HIKING
With its breathtaking vistas of mist-covered hills and nearby forests, Boquete is one of the most idyllic regions for hiking and walking. Several good paved roads lead out of town into the surrounding hills, passing coffee plantations, fields and farms, gardens and virgin forest.

Although saunterers will be content with picturesque strolls along the river, the more ambitious can climb **Volcán Barú** (3475m), Panama's highest point and only volcano. There are several entrances to the park, but the trail with easiest access to the summit starts near Boquete. For more information, see p678.

You can also access the **Sendero Los Quetzales** (Quetzals Trail; see p679) from Boquete; the trail is uphill from here though – you'll have an easier time if you start hiking from Cerro Punta (see p679).

A pleasant day-hike is along the **Sendero El Pianista** (Pianist Trail), which winds through dairy land and into humid cloud forest. To access the trail head, take the first right fork out of Boquete (heading north) and cross over two bridges. Immediately before the 3rd bridge, about 4km out of town, a track leads off to the left between a couple of buildings. You need to wade across a small river after 200m, but then it's a steady, leisurely incline for 2km before you start to climb a steeper, narrow path. The path winds deep into the forest, though you can turn back at any time.

WHITE-WATER RAFTING
Those who seek a bit of adventure shouldn't miss the excellent white-water rafting within a two-hour drive of Boquete. The Río Chiriquí and the Río Chiriquí Viejo both flow from the fertile hills of Volcán Barú, and are flanked by forest for much of their lengths. At some places, waterfalls can be seen at the edges of the rivers, and both pass through narrow canyons with awesome, sheer rock walls.

The Río Chiriquí is most often run from May to December, while the Chiriquí Viejo is run the rest of the year; the rides tend to last four and five hours, respectively. Depending on the skill level of your party, you can tackle thrilling class 3 and class 4 rapids or some seriously scary class 5 rapids.

The country's two best white-water rafting outfits are **Chiriquí River Rafting** (☎ 720 1505; www .panama-rafting.com) and **Panama Rafters** (☎ 720 2712; www.panamarafters.com), both of which are located in downtown Boquete. Both companies have bilingual employees, so you can get all the information you need in either English or Spanish. All-day trips are offered for US$75 to US$100, depending on the run and the size of the party.

CANOPY TOURS
Although canopy tours are about as prevalent as rice and beans in Costa Rica, they're still quite new to the Panama tourist scene. For the uninitiated, a canopy tour consists of a series of platforms anchored into the forest canopy

and connected by zip lines. Although they were originally used by biologists to study the rain-forest canopy, today they function primarily as a way for gringos to get their ecokicks.

If you're game to strap yourself into a harness and zip along the tree line, the **Boquete Tree Trek** (☎ 720 1635; www.aventurist.com; 3hr tour US$60) is located in secondary forest, and consists of 14 platforms, 13 zip lines, a rappel and a Tarzanswing. The company stresses fun instead of ecology, and these lines pick up some serious speed, so you might want to consider going a little heavy on the hand-brake.

Courses

Spanish by the River (☎ /fax 720 3456; www.spanish bythesea.com) is the sister school to the popular Spanish school (p686) in Bocas del Toro. Rates for group/private lessons are US$70/130 for two hours a day, five days a week, though cheaper rates are available for more comprehensive packages and longer stays. The school also offers a popular traveler's survival-Spanish course (US$40) that includes six hours of instruction. Homestays can be arranged (per night with breakfast US$12) or you can rent one of their simple dorms/rooms (per night US$7.50/12). The school is located 5km south of town near the turn-off to Palmira.

The reader-recommended **Habla Ya Language Center** (☎ 720 1294; www.hablayapanama.com; Central Av) offers both group and private lessons. Five hours of group/private lessons starts at US$50/75, though significant discounts are given for lengthier programs – 25 hours of group/private lessons costs only US$200/300. The language school is also well-connected to local businesses, so students can take advantage of discounts on everything from accommodations to tours.

Festivals & Events

The town's annual festival is the **Feria de las Flores y del Café** (Flower and Coffee Fair), held for 10 days each January. Another popular event is the **Feria de Las Orquídeas** (Orchid Fair), held every April.

Sleeping
CAMPING

Nights are chilly here, and temperatures can drop to near freezing – pack some warm clothes if you plan to camp. You can also camp in nearby Parque Nacional Volcán Barú (p679).

La Montaña y el Valle (☎ /fax 720 2211; information@ coffeeestateinn.com; campsite 1-/2-people US$7/10, extra person US$3) This working coffee estate, 2.5km from town, has camping on a weather-permitting basis (usually January through March). There are three tent sites, and facilities include hot showers, flush toilets, electricity and a covered cooking area. You must call ahead to let the owners know you're coming.

HOTELS

Because of the cool climate, all the places to stay in Boquete have hot showers.

Hotelito Nomba (☎ 720 1076; dm/r per person US$6.60/8.80) The self-proclaimed chill-out hostel is bare-bones and fairly sterile, though it's certainly cheap. The management is laid-back, and a good time can be had here if you meet the right people.

Hostal Palacios (☎ 720 1653; dm/r per person US$6.60/8.80) This long-standing budget guesthouse has a friendly and vibrant atmosphere, thanks in part to the energetic owner, Pancho. Although the rooms have definitely seen better days, this place is well-suited to backpackers, especially since there is a shared kitchen, room to pitch a tent and a fireplace out the back where you can stay warm while chatting up other travelers.

Pensión Marilós (☎ 720 1380; marilos66@hotmail .com; cnr Av A Este & Calle 6 Sur; s/d US$7/11, with bathroom US$10/14) This cozy, family-run spot is a good choice for travelers looking for a little bit of peace and quiet. Rooms are warmly decorated with assorted knick-knacks, and the pleasant owner, Frank Glavas, can help you make the most of your time in Boquete.

Pensión Topas (☎ /fax 720 1005; schoeb@chiriqui.com; Av Belisario Porras; s/d from US$10/15) Built around a small organic garden, this German-run pensión features a variety of rooms to suit all budgets. Cheaper rooms share an outdoor solar-heated bathroom, while the more expensive rooms have bathrooms with steamy showers.

Hostal Doña Catal (☎ 720 1260; d with/without bathroom US$15/10) On the central plaza, the faded blue Hostal Doña Cata is suffering from a bit of wear and tear, though the price is right, especially if you splurge for the upstairs rooms. For a few bucks more you can enjoy a private bathroom and a balcony overlooking the park.

Hostal Boquete (☎ 720 2573; s/d US$15/20) Overlooking the Río Caldera, this quaint country inn is excellent value. Rooms are basic, but they have lovely terraces overlooking the river, and it's likely you'll sleep well at night to the sounds of the flowing water.

Isla Verde (☎ 720 2533; islaverde@cwpanama.net; Av B Oeste; small/large cabins US$50/65) These centrally located cabins offer some of the loveliest accommodations in Boquete. Set in a beautiful, lush, landscaped garden are six modern, comfortable two-story cabins with tall ceilings, kitchens and roomy bathrooms.

Eating & Drinking

Café Ruiz (Calle 2 Norte; coffee US$1-2) The outdoor patio at Ruiz makes a good spot to sip locally produced coffee and watch the mist move across the mountains. It offers tours to coffee plantations (p675).

El Sabrosón (Av Central; mains US$2-3) This much-loved local institution cooks up cheap and filling Panamanian cuisine served caféteria style.

Java Juice (Av Central; sandwiches US$3-4; ☻ 9am-10pm) The sister-store to the café in David, Java Juice is your spot for veggie burgers, fresh salads, juices, iced cappuccinos and tasty milkshakes.

Bistro Boquete (Av Central; mains US$3-7; ☻ 11am-10pm) This handsome yet casual bistro in the center of town serves a range of eclectic cuisine ranging from curry chicken salad to chili-rubbed filet mignon.

La Huaca (Av Central; pizzas US$5-7) North of the plaza, La Huaca is set in a beautifully restored colonial-style building with river and mountain views – it's locally famous for its tasty stone-baked pizzas.

Zanzibar (Av Central; drinks US$1-2) Nightlife in Boquete is about as common as a bad cup of coffee, though this low-key jazz bar has the cure for 'what ails ya'.

If you're self-catering, the area's produce is some of the best in Panama. Check out the *mercado municipal* on the northeastern corner of the plaza as well as **Supermercado Romero** (Av A Este).

Getting There & Around

Buses to Boquete depart David's main bus terminal regularly (US$1.50, one hour, every 30 minutes from 6am to 9:30pm). Buses to David depart from the northern side of Boquete's plaza (every 30 minutes from 5am to 6:30pm). A taxi between David and Boquete costs around US$12.

Boquete's small size lends itself to easy exploration, and walking is a great way to see the area. The local *(urbano)* buses winding through the hills cost US$0.50. They depart from the main road one block north of the plaza. Taxis charge US$1 to US$2 to get to most places around town.

PARQUE NACIONAL VOLCÁN BARÚ

This 14,300-hectare national park is home to Volcán Barú, which is Panama's only volcano as well as the dominant geographical feature of Chiriquí. Volcán Barú is no longer active (there is in fact no record of its most recent eruption), and it has not one but seven craters. Its summit, which tops out at 3475m, is the highest point in Panama; on a clear day it affords views of both the Pacific and Caribbean coasts.

The national park is also home to the Sendero Los Quetzales, one of the most scenic treks in the entire country. As its name implies, the trail is one of the best places in Central America to spot the rare resplendent quetzal, especially during the dry season (November to April). However, even if the Maya bird of paradise fails to show, the park is home to over 250 bird species as well as pumas, tapirs and the *conejo pintado* (a spotted raccoon-like animal).

Information

Admission to the park (US$3) is paid at either of the trailheads leading to the summit or at the ranger station on the Cerro Punto side of the Sendero Los Quetzales.

The best time to visit is during the dry season, especially early in the morning when wildlife is most active.

Overnight temperatures can drop below freezing, and it may be windy and cold during the day, particularly in the morning – dress accordingly.

Sights & Activities
VOLCÁN BARÚ

There are entrances to the park, with summit access, on the eastern and western sides of the volcano. The eastern access to the summit, from Boquete, is the easiest, but it involves a strenuous uphill hike along a 14km dirt/mud road that goes from the park entrance – about 8km northwest of the center of Boquete – to the summit. If you drive or take a taxi as far up as you can and then walk the rest of the way, it takes about five or six hours to reach the summit from the park gate; walking from town would take another two or three hours each way. It's best to camp on the mountain for at least one night; and you should be prepared for the cold. Camping will also allow you to be at the top during the morning, when the views are best.

The other park entrance is just outside the town of Volcán, on the road to Cerro Punta. The rugged road into the park – which soon becomes too rough for anything but a 4WD vehicle – goes only a short way off the main road, to the foot of the volcano. The view of the summit and nearby peaks from this entrance is impressive, and there's a lovely loop trail that winds through secondary and virgin forest. The climb from this side is steep and technical.

Sendero Los Quetzales

The park's most accessible trail is the scenic Sendero Los Quetzales (Quetzal Trail) near Cerro Punta. One of the most beautiful in Panama, this trail runs for 8km between Cerro Punta and Boquete, crossing back and forth over the Río Caldera. The trail can be done in either direction, but is easiest from west to east: the town of Cerro Punta is almost 1000m higher than Boquete, so hiking east is more downhill. A guide is not necessary as the trail is very well maintained and easily visible.

The trail itself takes about four to five hours walking west to east, though getting to and from the trailhead will take another couple of hours of walking on either side. A 4WD taxi can take you to the start of the trail on the Cerro Punta side for about US$12; taxi drivers know the area as **Respingo**. The trail is 5km uphill from the main road and 2km from the last paved road. When you exit the trail, it's another 8km along the road to Boquete, though you may be able to catch a taxi along the road.

In total, the hike is about 23km, so plan accordingly if you intend to walk the length of the trail.

After arriving in Boquete, you can stay overnight or take a bus to David and then Cerro Punta; note that the last Cerro Punta bus leaves David at 6pm. You can also leave your luggage at one of the hotels in David (the Purple House will store luggage, as will others) and save yourself the hassle of backtracking. Take only the bare essentials with you on the walk (and a little cash for a good meal and/or lodging in Boquete).

Sleeping

Camping (US$5) is available in the park and on the trail to the summit from the Boquete side, along the Sendero Los Quetzales or at the ranger station at the entrance to the Sendero Los Quetzales on the Cerro Punta side. You can also stay in bunk beds at the **ranger station** (dm US$5); bring your own food and bedding. If you plan to stay in the station, let them know you're coming by calling **ANAM** (☎ 775 7840) in David.

Getting There & Away

See Volcán Barú (opposite) and Sendero Los Quetzales (left) for information.

CERRO PUNTA

At an altitude of 1800m, this small town is surrounded by beautiful, rich agricultural lands, and offers spectacular views across a fertile valley to the peaks of Parque Internacional La Amistad. Although the scenery is inspiring enough, the main reason travelers pass through here is to access the Sendero Los Quetzales or the Parque Internacional La Amistad.

If you find yourself crashing here for the night, the **Hotel Cerro Punta** (☎ /fax 771 2020; hotelcer@hotmail.com; s/d US$20/30) is located on the main room in town, and has 10 well-maintained rooms with picture windows and private hot-water bathrooms. Whether you stay here or not, drop by the restaurant for a smoothie, a slice of pie or pancakes with compote – the local strawberries are the best you'll ever taste.

Buses run from David to Cerro Punta (US$3, 2¼ hours, every 20 minutes, from 5:30am to 8pm). If you're coming from Costa Rica, you can catch this bus at the turn-off from the Interamericana at Concepción.

PARQUE INTERNACIONAL LA AMISTAD

This 407,000-hectare national park was established jointly by Panama and Costa Rica – hence its name, La Amistad (Friendship). In Panama, the 207,000 hectares of the park covers portions of Chiriquí and Bocas del Toro Provinces, and is home to members of three indigenous groups: the Teribe, the Bribri and the Ngöbe-Buglé.

The bi-national park also contains large swaths of virgin rain forest that remain home to a recorded 90 mammal species (including jaguars and pumas) and more than 300 bird species (including resplendent quetzals and harpy eagles). Although most of the park's area is high up in the Talamanca Mountains and remains inaccessible, there is no shortage of hiking and camping opportunities available for intrepid travelers.

Information

Admission to the **park** (admission US$3, parking US$1, camping US$5; 8am-4pm) is paid at either of the two Panamanian entrances: one at Las Nubes, near Cerro Punta on the Chiriquí side and one at Wetso, near Changuinola on the Bocas del Toro side.

Permits to camp in the park are available at the ranger station.

If you plan to spend much time at Las Nubes, be sure to bring a jacket. This side of the park, at 2280m above sea level, has a cool climate. Temperatures are usually around 24°C (75°F) in the daytime and drop to about 3°C (38°F) at night.

Sights & Activities

LAS NUBES

Three main trails originate at Las Nubes ranger station. The **Sendero La Cascada** (Waterfall Trail) is a 3.4km round-trip hike that takes in three *miradors* (lookout points) as well as a 45m-high waterfall with a lovely bathing pool. The **Sendero El Retoño** (Rebirth Trail) loops 2.1km through secondary forest, crosses a number of rustic bridges and winds through bamboo groves. The **Vereda La Montaña** (Mountain Lane) is a more strenuous 8km round-trip hike that ascends Cerro Picacho.

The Las Nubes entrance is about 7km from Cerro Punta; a sign on the main road in Cerro Punta marks the turnoff. The road starts out good and paved, but by the time you reach the park, it's a rutted track suitable only for 4WD vehicles. A taxi will bring you from Cerro Punta for US$4 for up to two people, then US$2 per extra person.

WETSO

To get near the park you first have to catch a bus from Changuinola to the hamlet of El Silencio. From there you take a 45-minute boat ride up the Río Teribe. In El Silencio there's often a colectivo boat, which will cost about

US$5 per person; if you have to hire the boat yourself it will cost US$15 to US$25. If you go to the **ANAM office** (758 8967) in Changuinola and tell the people there that you want to go to Wetso, ANAM can radio ahead and make sure there is someone at the river's edge.

Once on the river, you'll pass hills blanketed with rain forest and intermittent waterfalls; the backdrop is always the glorious Talamanca range. After about 45 minutes on the river, you'll see a sign on the right bank that announces your arrival at Wetso, which is actually a protected area but still some way from the park. There's a 3.5km loop trail at Wetso that cuts through secondary and virgin rain forest, with excellent bird-watching. You can also take a dip in the river (the water is too swift for crocodiles), but be careful not to wade out very far or the current will carry you downstream.

Sleeping

Ranger station (dm US$5) The station at Las Nubes has a dorm with bunk beds. Due to the popularity of these beds among school groups from Canada and the USA, reservations are advised. To reserve a spot, call **ANAM** (775 3163, 775 7840) in David. Guests have access to the kitchen; stock up on provisions in Cerro Punta. You'll also need to bring your own bedding.

Guest lodge (lodgings per person US$12, meals US$3-4) There's a rustic lodge in Wetso that is run by and benefits the Teribe (Naso) indigenous people. They can prepare meals for you, and lead you on guided tours through the jungle. It's a five-hour hike from Wetso to the Parque Internacional La Amistad. For reservations, contact ANAM or call **Odesen** (Organización para el Desarrollo Sostenible Ecoturístico Naso; Organization for the Sustainable Development of Naso Ecotourism; 620 0192).

Getting There & Away

See Las Nubes (left) and Wetso (left) for transportation information.

FINCA LA SUIZA

If you travel along the paved road that crosses the Cordillera Central from the Pan-American Hwy to Chiriquí Grande, providing access to Bocas del Toro, you will pass a wonderful place for hiking, with excellent accommodations options.

About 41km from the Pan-American Hwy is the lodge **Finca La Suiza** (615 3774, in David 774 4030;

afinis@chiriqui.com; s/d with bathroom US$31/40; (closed Jun, Sep & Oct), a highly recommended accommodation that boasts some of the best mountain views in Panama. The lodge has three clean, comfortable rooms with private hot-water bathrooms and large windows. On a clear day, you can see the islands in the Golfo de Chiriquí. The enthusiastic and warm German owners – Herbert Brüllman and Monika Kohler – will provide breakfast for about US$3.50 and dinner for US$9. English, Spanish and German are spoken. Be sure to make reservations, as it's a long way to the next available lodging in Chiriquí Grande or David.

Also on the property are several kilometers of well-marked hiking trails, which pass through primary tropical rain and cloud forest. The scenery features towering trees, hundreds of bird species and views of the Fortuna Park Forest Reserve, the Chiriquí mountains and the Pacific islands. Entrance to the trails costs guests US$8 for the duration of their stay; nonguests pay US$8 per day.

To get to Finca La Suiza, take any Changuinola-bound bus from David (hourly starting at 5am) and ask the driver to drop you off. Coming from the Pan-American Hwy, the lodge is to the right just after the Accel gas station (the only gas station on this road). Coming from the north, the lodge is on the left 1.3km after a toll plaza for trucks. While hiking, you can leave luggage with the caretaker near the entrance gate.

BOCAS DEL TORO

Located just 32km from the Costa Rican border, the Archipiélago de Bocas del Toro consists of six densely forested islands, scores of uninhabited islets and Parque Nacional Marino Isla Bastimentos, the country's oldest marine park. Although Bocas is Panama's principle tourist draw card, there's still a fair measure of authenticity left to the islands. Low-key development has maintained the charm of small-town Caribbean life, while the absence of mega-hotels has preserved the idyllic beauty of the archipelago.

The laid-back Caribbean vibe of Bocas is enhanced by the archipelago's spectacular natural setting. The islands are covered in dense jungles of vine tangles and forest palms that open up to pristine beaches fringed by reeds and mangroves. Beneath the water, an extensive coral reef ecosystem supports countless species of tropical fish while simultaneously providing some seriously gnarly surf breaks.

Unfortunately the secret is out, and although locals have thus far welcomed the increase in tourism, bulldozers have already started clearing land for condos and resorts. It's difficult to predict the future of the islands, but one thing is certain – see Bocas now, as the unspoiled beauty of the islands won't last forever.

ISLA COLÓN

The archipelago's largest and most developed island is home to the provincial capital of **Bocas del Toro**, a colorful town of wooden houses built by the United Fruit Company in the early 20th century. Today, Bocas is a slow-paced community of West Indians, Latinos and resident gringos, and the town's relaxed, friendly atmosphere seems to rub off on everyone who visits. Bocas also serves as a convenient base for exploring the marine national park, as *taxis marinos* (water taxis) ply the waters and can whisk you away to remote beaches and snorkeling sites for a few dollars.

Relaxed as it is, Isla Colón is in the middle of a major development boom. Since the mid-1990s, foreign investors have been buying up land like crazy, and there are constantly new hotels, restaurants and condos springing up around the island. Fortunately, there's still a heavy dose of local flavor left on Isla Colón, and the lack of beachside Pizza Huts is testament to the fact that development is still years behind similar destinations in nearby Costa Rica.

Orientation

Bocas town is laid out in a grid pattern with most of the hotels and restaurants on Calle 3. The only airport in the archipelago is on Av E, four blocks from Calle 3.

Note that the town, the archipelago and the province all share the name Bocas del Toro. Isla Colón and Bocas del Toro town are also referred to as Bocas Isla. It rains a lot in Bocas – even in the dry season, there can be long periods of constant showers.

Information

For more information on the islands, see the useful English website www.bocas.com. For a rundown on the good, the bad and the ugly, check out the island's monthly bilingual publication, *The Bocas Breeze*.

PANAMA

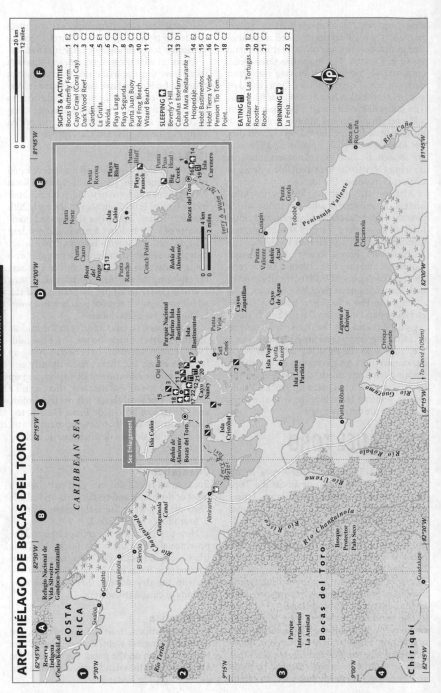

ARCHIPIÉLAGO DE BOCAS DEL TORO

SIGHTS & ACTIVITIES	
Bocas Butterfly Farm.........1	E2
Cayo Crawl (Coral Cay).....2	C2
Dark Wood Reef................3	C2
Garden.............................4	C2
La Gruta............................5	E1
Nivida..............................6	C2
Playa Larga.......................7	C2
Playa Segunda...................8	C2
Punta Juan Buoy...............9	C2
Red Frog Beach.................10	C2
Wizard Beach...................11	C2

SLEEPING 🏠	
Beverly's Hill....................12	C2
Cabañas Estefany..............13	D1
Doña Mara Restaurante y	
Hospedaje....................14	E2
Hotel Bastimentos............15	E2
Hotel Tierra Verde............16	E2
Pension Tío Tom...............17	C2
Point.................................18	C2

EATING 🍴	
Restaurante Las Tortugas..19	E2
Rooster............................20	C2
Roots................................21	C2

DRINKING 🍷	
La Feria............................22	C2

ANAM (Map p684; ☎ 757 9442; Calle 1) Not really set up as a tourist information office, though they can answer questions about the national park or other protected areas. If you want to camp out in any of the protected areas, you must first get a permit from this or any other ANAM office.

Banco Nacional de Panamá (Map p684; cnr Calle 4 & Av E; ☿ 8am-2pm Mon-Fri, 8am-noon Sat) Exchanges traveler's checks and has a 24-hour ATM.

Bocas Internet Café (Map p684; Calle 3; per hr US$2; ☿ 8am-10pm)

Bravo Center (Map p684; Calle 3; per hr US$2; ☿ 10am-7pm) Internet access is available here.

Cable & Wireless (Map p684; Calle 1) International calls can be made here.

Hospital (Map p684; ☎ 757 9201; Av G; ☿ 24hr) The island's only hospital has a 24-hour emergency room.

IPAT (Map p684; ☎ 757 9642; ipatbocas@cwp.net.pa; ☿ 8:30am-3:30pm Mon-Fri) In Centro de Facilidades Turísticas e Interpretación (Cefati) on the eastern waterfront. A color map in English and Spanish is available. The center also houses an interesting display on the natural and anthropological history of the area.

Post office (Map p684; Governmental Bldg, Calle 3)

Dangers & Annoyances
The surf can be quite dangerous on some of the island's beaches, and there are frequently strong riptides – use caution when going out into the waves. If you get caught in a rip, swim parallel to the shore and don't panic.

Unlike in most other places in Panama, tap water is not safe to drink in Bocas del Toro. Bottled water is readily available and costs about US$1.50 for a 1.5L bottle. Gallon jugs for US$2 are better value if you can find them.

Bocas del Toro is a conservative place, and local law prevents men (and women too) from walking down the streets topless. Even if you are on your way to the beach, wear a shirt or you will be sent back to your hotel if you are spotted by the police.

Sights
BOCA DEL DRAGO
Located on the western side of Isla Colón, this sleepy beach (Map p682) is famed for its huge numbers of starfish, particularly around the bend. The calm and relaxed vibe at Boca del Drago is perfect for beach bums. The swimming and snorkeling here is good, especially when the sea is calm and the water is clear. Although not as stunning as the wilderness

beaches on Isla Bastimentos, the lack of surge means that this is the safest spot in the archipelago for nonsurfers.

To reach Boca del Drago, you can take the big maroon shuttle bus (US$2.50, 25 minutes), which leaves Parque Simón Bolívar at 10am, noon and 3pm (there is also an 8:45am departure on weekends). If you miss the bus, water taxis will also drop you off at the beach for US$25 round-trip. Finally, if you're feeling particularly fit, you can cycle the 15km cross-island road; it's all paved but extremely hilly.

OTHER BEACHES
There is a string of beaches on the eastern side of Isla Colón that can be reached by a road that skirts up the coast from town. There's no public transportation to the beaches, but a 4WD taxi will take you to any of them and pick you up at an appointed time for a negotiable price – expect to pay US$16 for a round-trip taxi to Playa Bluff.

Playa El Istmito (Map p684), which is also called Playa La Cabaña, is the closest beach to town. It's on Sand Fly Bay and the *chitras* (sand flies) that live here have an itchy bite. This is not the most attractive beach, and unless you're walking, it's worth heading further north.

Further up the coast is **Playa Punch** (Map p682), which is dangerous for swimming but good for surfing.

After you round Punta Bluff, the road takes you along **Playa Bluff** (Map p682), a secluded wilderness beach that is pounded by intense waves. Although you wouldn't want to get into the water here without a board, the soft, yellow sand and palm-fringed shores are pristine and well worth the trip. Playa Bluff stretches for 5km all the way to Punta Rocosa, and serves as a nesting area for sea turtles from May to September.

LA GRUTA
If sun, sand and surf aren't your persuasion, then consider taking a trip to **La Gruta** (the cavern; Map p682) where you can wade through waist-high water while trying not to disturb the thousands of sleeping bats overhead, The entrance to the cave, which is marked by a statue of the Virgin Mary, is located 8km from Bocas town along the road to Boca del Drago. A taxi should cost about US$10 for a round-trip.

BOCAS DEL TORO (ISLA COLÓN)

INFORMATION		SIGHTS & ACTIVITIES		SLEEPING	
ANAM.....................1 D3		Bocas Water Sports.............9 D4		Casa Amarilla.................15 C2	
Banco Nacional Panama......2 D3		Cap 'n Dons...............(see 21)		Casa Max.....................16 D2	
Bravo Center.................3 D4		Empresa Lau................10 D3		Hostal de Hansi 17 D3	
Cable & Wireless.............4 D3		J&J Tours....................11 D4		Hostel Heike.................18 D3	
Hospital.....................5 B2		Spanish by the Sea...........12 D4		Hotel Dos Palmas...........19 C4	
Bocas Internet Café...........6 D3		Starfleet Eco-Adventures.....13 D3		Hotel La Veranda...........20 C2	
IPAT........................7 D3		Tropix Surf..................14 D3		Hotel Las Brisas.............21 D3	
Post Office...................8 D3				Hotel Las Olas................22 C4	
				Mondo Taitu.................23 D2	

EATING
Alberto's Pizzeria..............**24** D3
Café Europeo..................**25** D3
El Chitré.......................**26** D3
Isla Supermarket Colon.......(see 6)
La Casbah......................**27** D2
Lemongrass Bistro...........(see 13)
Lilli's Cafe.....................**28** D3
Om Café......................**29** D3
Posada Los Delfines..........**30** C2
Super Gourmet................**31** D4

DRINKING
Bar El Encanto.................**32** D4
Barco Hundido................**33** D3
Blowfish Sushi Bar............**34** D3
Cafe D'Artiste.................(see 7)
La Iguana.....................**35** D3
Mondo Taitu Bar...........(see 23)

TRANSPORT
Bocas Marine & Tours.......**36** D4

BOCAS BUTTERFLY FARM

Assuming you're not burned out from looking at all the butterfly gardens in Costa Rica, this adorable **farm** (Map p682; ☎ 6483 5741; admission US$5; ☑ 10pm-4am) makes for a great afternoon trip. Water taxis can whisk you away from Bocas town to the entrance of the farm on nearby Isla Carenero for only US$1.

Activities
DIVING & SNORKELING

With nearly 40 rivers unloading silt into the seas around Bocas del Toro, the archipelago's waters are notorious for their poor visibility. If it has rained a lot in recent days, visibility may be limited to only 3m; at best visibility is about 15m. Although experienced divers

accustomed to crystal-clear Caribbean diving may be disappointed with Bocas, the islands still have much to offer.

The emerald green waters of the archipelago are home to the usual assortment of tropical species, and with a little luck you might see barracuda, stingrays, dolphins and nurse sharks. Better sites nearby include **Dark Wood Reef**, northwest of Bastimentos; **Hospital Point**, a 50-foot (16m) wall off Cayo Nancy; and the base of the **Punta Juan buoy** north of Isla Cristóbal; see Map p682.

Diving trips are offered by **Starfleet Eco-Adventures** (Map p684; ☎ 757 9630; www.explorepanama .com/starfleet.htm; Calle 1) and **Bocas Water Sports** (Map p684; ☎ /fax 757 9541; www.bocaswatersports.com; Calle 3). Most diving trips cost about US$35 for a one-tank, one-site dive, US$50 for two tanks and two sites. PADI open-water and advanced-diver courses are also available. Starfleet offers instruction in English, and enjoys a sterling reputation among locals and travelers.

Both dive shops also offer snorkeling on their boat tours, see below.

BOAT TOURS

The most popular tours in the area are all-day snorkeling trips, which are perfect for nondivers who want a taste of the area's rich marine life. A typical tour costs US$15 per person, and goes to **Dolphin Bay**, **Cayo Crawl**, **Red Frog Beach** and **Hospital Point**. A trip to the distant **Cayos Zapatillas** costs US$20 (plus an additional US$10 for admission to the marine park), and includes lunch, a laze on the beach and a jungle walkabout on **Cayo Zapatilla Sur**.

Many 'tours' are really little more than boat transportation to a pretty spot. If you have your own snorkel gear (or if you rent it), you can also get the local boatmen to take you around the area in their small, motorized canoes. They know several good snorkeling spots, and this option can be cheaper than the dive companies' trips, depending on the size of your group. Agree on a price before you go.

In addition to the dive operators listed earlier, a recommended tour operator is **J&J Tours** (Map p684; ☎ 757 9915; transparentetour@hotmail.com; Calle 3).

SURFING

Although everyone (and their grandmother) seems to have picked up surfing in nearby Puerto Viejo (p567), Bocas del Toro is still emerging as an international surf destination. However, the archipelago offers an excellent mix of beginner beach breaks, ripping reefs breaks and some seriously suicidal breaks.

For surfing information on nearby Isla Bastimentos and Isla Carenero, see p690 and p691 respectively.

Beginner surfers looking for a bit of reef experience should check out **Playa Punch**, which offers a good mix of lefts and rights. Although it can get heavy when big, Punch generally offers some of the kindest waves around.

Just past Punch on route to Playa Bluff is a popular reef break known as **Dumps**. This left break can get up to 3m, and should only be ridden by experienced surfers as wiping out on the reef here is a dangerous affair. There is also an inner break known as **Inner Dumps**,

which also breaks left, but is more forgiving than its outer brother.

Be careful walking out on the reefs as they are sharp and full of urchins – wear booties. If you wipe out and get cut up, be sure to properly disinfect your wounds. Although salt water heals, sea water doesn't, especially in the Caribbean where the water temperature means that the ocean is full of live bacteria.

The island's most notorious surf spot is **Playa Bluff**, which throws out powerful barreling waves that break in shallow water along the beach, and have a reputation for snapping boards (and occasionally bones). Though waves close quickly, the tubes here are truly awesome, especially when the swells are strong.

You can rent fairly thrashed surfboards for US$10 to US$15 per day from **Tropix Surf** (Map p684; ☎ 757 9727; Calle 3; 🕑 9am-7pm). The guys at **Mondo Taitu** (☎ /fax 757 9425; Av I) in Isla Colón (p686) also rent boards for negotiable prices. If heading out to Isla Bastimentos or Isla Carenero, arrange your board in advance as there are no surf shops on either island.

KAYAKING

You will need to be wary of boat traffic and the occasional swell, but sea kayak is a great way to travel between islands. **Cap 'n Dons** (Map p684; ☎ 757 9248; Calle 3; 🕑 9am-7pm) rents kayaks for US$10 per day, as well as paddle boats, sailboats and a big water trampoline.

CYCLING

Whether you're heading to Boca del Drago on the paved road or taking the dirt path to Playa Bluff, a bike can seriously increase your mobility. Note that the bike ride to Boca del Drago is taxing, especially when the sun is beaming. If you're unsure of your fitness level, head to Bluff instead; be aware that the road floods after heavy rains. You can rent a bike for US$8 per day and support a local Kuna by heading to **Empresa Lau** (Map p684; Calle 3; 🕑 9am-7pm), located next to Hostel Heike.

HIKING

If you're looking to seriously get off the beaten path, there is a network of undeveloped hiking trails that fans out across the island. One of the most popular hikes starts at the end of the coastal road in Mimbi Timbi and carries on along the coast to Boca del Drago. You will need about six hours of daylight to complete the hike, and you must carry in all your fresh water. The trail winds past caves, caverns and plenty of vine-encrusted jungle. A bike will help speed things up a bit, though you will be carrying it part of the way, especially if it's been raining recently.

FISHING
The best budget option for aspiring anglers is to go surf casting with the local boat-taxi drivers. The hand lines are a bit tricky at first, though you'll soon get the hang of it. It's best to go early in the morning when the fish are biting; prices are negotiable.

Courses
Spanish by the Sea (☎ /fax 757 9518; www.spanishbythe sea.com; Calle 4) is a reader-recommended language school that offers affordable Spanish classes in a relaxed setting. Rates for group/private lessons are US$70/130 for two hours a day five days a week, though cheaper rates are available for more comprehensive packages and longer stays. The school also offers a popular traveler's survival-Spanish course (US$40) that includes six hours of instruction.

Homestays can be arranged (per night with breakfast US$12) or you can rent one of its simple dorms/rooms (per night US$7.50/12). Spanish by the Sea also organizes parties, dance classes and open lectures. English, Spanish, French, German and Dutch are spoken.

Festivals & Events
Bocas celebrates all of Panama's holidays, with a few enjoyable local ones besides. Annual events celebrated on Bocas and Bastimentos include the following:

May Day (May 1) While the rest of Panama is celebrating Labor Day, the Palo de Mayo (a Maypole dance) is performed by local girls.

Día de la Virgen del Carmen (third Sunday in July) Bocatoreños make a pilgrimage to La Gruta, the cave in the middle of the Isla Colón, for a mass in honor of the Virgen del Carmen.

Feria del Mar (September 28-October 2) The Fair of the Sea is held on Playa El Istmito, a few kilometers north of Bocas.

Fundación de la Provincia de Bocas del Toro (November 16) Celebrating the foundation of the province in 1904, this is a day of parades and other events; it's a big affair, attracting people from all over the province, and the Panamanian president also attends.

Día de Bastimentos (November 23) Bastimentos Day is celebrated on the island with a huge parade and drumming exhibitions.

Sleeping
The town of Bocas has become a major tourist draw. Both expats and locals run hotels, and a few Bocas residents rent rooms in their houses. Reservations are a good idea between December and April and during national holidays and local festivals.

Other accommodations centers are Isla Bastimentos (p690) and Isla Carenero (p691).

Mondo Taitu (Map p684; ☎ /fax 757 9425; Av H; dm/s/d US$7/8/16) This legendary backpacker joint is reason enough to cancel your travel plans and post up in Bocas for weeks on end. Owned and managed by three fun-loving Americans, Mondo is a wacky tree house–like building that is famous locally for its wild events. On Tuesdays and Fridays, the bar at Mondo hosts a variety of festivities ranging from Sake Bomb parties to '80s Night; you can kick back here any time with a beer in one hand and a hookah in the other. All of the usual backpackers amenities are on offer including a communal kitchen, lounge area, laundry facilities, free bikes and surfboards.

Hostel Heike (Map p684; ☎ 757 9708; Calle 3; dm US$8) The sister hostel to Mondo Taitu, Heike proudly serves as the ying to Mondo's yang. Awash with colorfully painted murals and natural woods, Heike is the perfect spot for chilling out and soaking up the Caribbean ambiance. The upstairs balcony overlooks the town's park, and is a perfect spot to indulge in a cold beer and a good book. Like Mondo, the amenities at Heike are perfectly suited to backpackers.

Cabañas Estefany (Map p682; ☎ 618 3155; d US$15; 2-/8-person cabin US$30/55) On Boca del Drago, this cute clutch of cabins is one of the only accommodations on Isla Colón located on a beach. In addition to basic rooms with shared bathrooms, Cabañas Estefany has small two-person cabins with a bathroom and kitchen, and larger cabins for up to eight people. The cabins are often booked with researchers from the US, so it's recommended that you call ahead.

Hotel Las Brisas (Map p684; ☎ 757 9248; brisasbocas@ cwp.net.pa; Calle 3; d US$17-40; 🛇) On the northern end of Calle 3, Hotel Las Brisas is built over the water, and offers a variety of rooms to meet your budget. The cheaper rooms are definitely starting to show their age, though a few extra dollars can get you nicer furnishings, better views and even air-con.

Hotel La Veranda (Map p684; ☎ 757 9211; www .explorepanama.com/veranda.htm; Av G; US$16-35; 🛇) This charming renovated vintage home features furnishings and fixtures in early 20th-century Caribbean style. Individually decorated rooms are priced according to their size, views and amenities.

Hostal de Hansi (Map p684; ☎ 757 9932; Calle 3; s US$10-16, d US$22) Run by a cheery German woman, this quite intimate spot features well-designed rooms with colorful wooden planks, set amid a tropical garden. Cheaper singles have shared facilities while the more expensive rooms (and doubles) have bathrooms.

Hotel Dos Palmas (Map p684; ☎ 757 9906; Av Sur; d/tr US$22/28) Proudly touting the hotel as '100% Bocatoreño,' the friendly owners of Dos Palmas offer basic wooden rooms with old-fashioned furnishings. The entire hotel sits above the water, and boasts exceptional views of the bay.

Casa Max (Map p684; ☎ 757 9120; casa1max@hotmail.com; Av H; s/d/tr US$20/25/30) This Dutch-owned spot offers a handful of brightly painted wooden rooms with high ceilings, and some come complete with dreamy balconies. The free breakfast of fresh fruit and hot coffee sweetens the deal.

Casa Amarilla (Map p684; ☎ 757 9938; Calle 5; d US$35; ❌ 🖥) Run by a lovely retired couple from Denver, Colorado, this quaint yellow house is one of the best deals on the island. For only a few more dollars more than other hotels, you can rack in the amenities, which include cable TV, private safe, hot showers and free wireless internet.

Hotel Las Olas (Map p684; ☎ 757 9930; Calle 6; s/d US$37/42; ❌ 🖥) Rapidly becoming one of the most popular hotels on the island, this Israeli-owned spot has polished wooden rooms that are worth every dollar. Hotel Las Olas is also built over the water, and features an intimate bar and restaurant with sweeping views. Wireless internet is available.

Eating

Although Bocas town is a small place, there's no shortage of great restaurants serving up an impressive offering of international cuisine. Most places may be slightly out of the shoestring price range, but it's worth splurging – your stomach will thank you. All are on Map p684.

A number of food carts ply their wares around town – local favorites include the 'Chicken Lady,' the 'Batido Lady,' the 'Chicken Sandwich Guy' and the infamous 'Meat-on-a-stick Guy.'

Isla Supermarket Colon (Calle 3) If you're self-catering, this is the largest supermarket on the island.

Super Gourmet (Calle 3) This boutique place has everything from Japanese *panko* bread crumbs to California wines.

Café Europeo (Av D; pastries US$0.75-1.50) Sample the island's best baked goods at this tasty bakery; be warned that the huge, fluffy cinnamon rolls are highly addictive.

Posada Los Delfines (Calle 5; breakfast special US$2.50) The cheapest breakfast on the island is yours to be had at this hotel restaurant – go on and order your eggs anyway you want.

El Chitré (Calle 3; plates US$2-3) Adored by locals and travelers alike, this no-frills cafeteria-style hole-in-the-wall is the best spot in town for cheap but tasty grub.

Lilli's Cafe (Calle 1; plates US$3-6) Whether you feast on an omelet packed with fresh veggies or a club sandwich made with homemade bread, be sure to go heavy on the homemade 'Killin' Me Man' pepper sauce.

Alberto's Pizzeria (Calle 5; pizzas $4-6) Nothing fills the gut like a big and cheesy pepperoni pizza – stop by this Italian-run spot and Alberto will make sure you're taken care of.

Om Café (Av E; dishes US$4-6) There are only a handful of tables on offer at this handsome outdoor Indian restaurant, though they're all traditional family recipes that are guaranteed to make your palette water and your brow sweat.

Lemongrass Bistro (Calle 1; lunch US$6-8) Although it's a bit pricey in the evening, don't miss the lunch specials at this popular Asian fusion restaurant, which gets rave reviews from the local gringo community.

La Casbah (Av H; dinner US$7-12) Even backpackers need a good meal sometimes, and there's no better place than at this Mediterranean-inspired restaurant – one bite of the steak with blue-cheese sauce and you'll stop caring about your budget.

Drinking

All these are on Map p684.

La Iguana (Calle 1) A great place to kick off your crazy Bocas night is at this popular surfer bar that serves up two-for-one cocktails from 6:30pm to 7:30pm. This is a great spot for a frothy piña colada, though you can't go wrong with an ice-cold Balboa lager.

Café D'Artiste (Calle 1; coffee $1.50) This eclectic café is a great place for a freshly brewed cup

PANAMA

of Panama's finest grains; don't leave without perusing the art and curios that are available for purchase.

Mondo Taitu Bar (Av H) Head to backpacker central; always guaranteed to be a good time. On Tuesday and Friday, the party-loving owners entertain their guests with a variety of themed events, though the creative cocktail list and hookahs (US$5) make Mondo a good choice any night. If you're feeling brave (and cheap), order a tequila suicide – a snort of salt, a squeeze of lime in the eye and a shot of the worst tequila they can find (at least it's free!).

Bar El Encanto (Calle 3) All the rage among the island's youth if you're looking for a little local flair. Most nights are heavy on the reggaeton, but there is the occasional live performance here.

Blowfish Sushi Bar (Calle 1) At the time of research the owners had just finished installing a fireman's pole on the bar. So now there's raw fish, and pole-dancing.

Barco Hundido (Calle 1) Most nights in Bocas end at this open-air thatched-roof bar that's affectionately known as the Wreck Deck – the name comes from the sunken banana boat that rests in the clear Caribbean waters in the front. A short boardwalk extends from the bar over the vessel to an island seating area that's perfect for star-gazing. The fun-loving American owner also arranges private parties on his *Barco Loco* (Crazy Boat), which is arguably the most unique sea-going vessel you've ever seen.

Getting There & Away
AIR
Bocas del Toro has a fine airport that's the pride of the town. **Aeroperlas** (☎ 757 9341) and **Air Panama** (☎ 757 9841) offer daily flights connecting Bocas with Panama City (US$74, one hour, one to two per day). Aeroperlas also has flights from David to Bocas (US$35, 50 minutes, one daily Monday to Friday) stopping first in Changuinola. Air Panama has flights from San José, Costa Rica to Bocas (US$100, 1½ hours, one per day on Monday, Wednesday and Friday).

BOAT
If you don't fly into Bocas, you'll have to take a water taxi from Changuinola. **Bocas Marine & Tours** (Map p684; Calle 3) has regular boat services to Changuinola (one way US$5, 45 minutes,

eight daily); the first departs at 7am, the last at 5:20pm. The boat ride to Changuinola travels through the old canals formerly used by the banana plantations – it's a scenic trip that's well worth taking. Changuinola is connected by bus to David and to the Costa Rican border at Guabito-Sixaola.

Getting Around
WATER TAXIS
To reach nearby islands, you can hire boatmen operating motorized boats and canoes along the waterfront. As a general rule, you should always sort out the rate beforehand, and clarify if it is one-way or a round-trip. Although rates vary, you will get a better deal if you speak Spanish, are part of a group and arrange for a pick-up. Although most fishermen will perceive you as a rich gringo (and comparatively, you are), don't get angry – most boatmen are just trying to feed their families.

Round-trip rates are generally as follows: US$4 to the near side of Isla Bastimentos, US$2 to Isla Carenero and US$10 to Red Frog Beach. You should always pay on the return leg – this guarantees a pick up – but most boatmen will want some money upfront so that they can buy petrol.

BIKES
You can rent bicycles from **Empresa Lau** (Map p684; Calle 3; ☉ 9am-7pm), located next to Hostel Heike, for US$8 per day, as well as mopeds for US$20 per day.

ISLA BASTIMENTOS
Although it's a mere 10-minute boat ride from the town of Bocas del Toro, Isla Bastimentos is a different world. The northern coast of the island is home to palm-fringed wilderness beaches that serve as nesting grounds for sea turtles, while most of the southern coast consists of mangrove islands and coral reefs that fall within the boundaries of the Parque Nacional Marino Isla Bastimentos. The main settlement on Bastimentos is the historic West Indian town of Old Bank, which has its origins in the banana industry. The island is also home to the Ngöbe-Buglé village of Quebrada Sal, which is separated from Old Bank by a huge swath of jungle.

Unfortunately, the face of Bastimentos is changing rapidly as construction has already begun on the controversial Red Frog Beach

Club. Although the development project is outside the confines of the Parque Nacional Marino Isla Bastimentos, it will completely transform the face of the island, and set a precedent for future development projects in Bocas del Toro.

Orientation

The small village of Old Bank has no roads, just a wide, concrete footpath lined on both sides with colorfully painted wooden houses. From the town, there is a path leading across the island to Wizard Beach and Red Frog Beach, though the route can turn into a virtual swamp following the rains.

On the southeastern side of the island is the remote Ngöbe-Buglé village of Quebrada Sal. Tropical forest covers the interior of the island; you can explore it, but go only with a guide, as it's very easy to get lost.

Sights

OLD BANK

Located on the western tip of the island, Old Bank or simply Bastimentos Town is a small enclave of 1500 residents of West Indian descent. Until the 1990s, most of the adults in Old Bank traveled to Almirante daily to tend the banana fields, though today residents have taken to fishing, farming small plots or just hanging out.

Although Old Bank is very poor and devoid of any real sights, it has a much more pronounced Caribbean vibe than Bocas town,

and it's a relaxing place to stroll around and soak up the atmosphere. It's also the best place in Bocas del Toro to hear Guari-Guari, a fascinating Spanish-English Creole that's native to the island.

BEACHES

Bastimentos has some amazing beaches, though be careful swimming as the surf can really pick up on the north coast of the island.

The most beautiful beach on the island is **Wizard Beach** (also known as Playa Primera), which is awash in powder-yellow sand and backed by thick vine-strewn jungle. Although Wizard Beach is connected to Old Bank via a wilderness path, the mere 30 minute walk can turn into an all-day trek through the muck if it's been raining heavily.

Assuming the weather is cooperating, you can continue walking along the coast to **Playa Segunda** (Second Beach) and **Red Frog Beach**. Like Wizard, both beaches are stunning and virtually abandoned, though it's likely that this will change as development on the island continues (see below). If the weather isn't cooperating, you can access Red Frog Beach by water taxi via a small marina on the south side of the island; entrance to the beach is US$2. While you are on Red Frog beach, keep an eye out for the *rana rojo* (strawberry poison-dart frog) as they might not be on the island for too much longer.

The path continues past Red Frog Beach to **Playa Larga** (Long Beach), where sea turtles

PANAMA

THE DEAD FROG BEACH CLUB

On Isla Bastimentos the construction of a massive residential development project called the Red Frog Beach Club (RFBC) is well underway. Although the RFBC has launched a flashy public-relations campaign espousing its involvement in rural development, locals, resident expats and concerned tourists are furious about the environmental impact that the club will have on the island. The principle concerns are that the presence of the RFBC will limit local access to Red Frog Beach, have an adverse impact on nesting sea turtles and irreversibly damage terrestrial and marine ecosystems.

Despite increasing local and foreign opposition to the RFBC, it is unlikely that the project will be halted. Experts ranging from conservation biologists to sea-turtle specialists continue to petition ANAM, Panama's environmental authority, though it is feared that the RFBC's principal investors have some clout with the decision makers. However, frequent setbacks have slowed progress, and the opposition hopes that this extra time will enable them to influence the RFBC's agenda. It is almost certain that Isla Bastimentos will be the home of an exclusive residential community in the years to come – although there is hope that the developers will take it upon themselves to make their community more ecofriendly.

For more information on the Red Frog Beach Club, visit its website at www.redfrogbeach club.com.

nest from April to August. Playa Larga and much of the eastern side of the island fall under the protection of Parque Nacional Marino Isla Bastimentos.

PARQUE NACIONAL MARINO ISLA BASTIMENTOS

Established in 1988, this was Panama's first **marine park** (admission US$10). Protecting various areas of the Bocas del Toro Archipelago including parts of Isla Bastimentos and the Cayos Zapatillas, the marine park is an important nature reserve for countless species of Caribbean wildlife.

You can get current park information from the IPAT or ANAM offices in Bocas del Toro (p683). The dive operators and boatmen in Bocas are also good sources of information about the park and its attractions. If you want to camp out anywhere in the park, you are required to first obtain a permit from ANAM.

QUEBRADA SAL

On the southeastern edge of Bastimentos at the end of a long canal cut through the mangrove forest is the Ngöbe-Buglé village of Quebrada Sal (Salt Creek). The community consists of 60-odd thatch and bamboo houses, an elementary school, a handicrafts store, a general store and a soccer field. Water taxis can drop you off at the entrance, and you will need to pay the US$1 entry fee and sign the visitor's log.

The Quebrada Sal is slowly modernizing along with the rest of the archipelago. The villagers are friendly and open to visitors, especially if you can speak Spanish. If you have the time, it's worth hiring a local guide to walk with you along the cross-island trail that leads to Playa Larga (about one hour each way).

Activities

DIVING & SNORKELING

For more information on diving and snorkeling, see p684. If you're staying on the island, diving trips are offered by **Dutch Pirate** (☎ 6567 1812; www.thedutchpirate.com). There is a small booking office in Old Bank, though it's best to phone ahead to make a reservation.

SURFING

If you're looking for a solid beach break, both **Wizard Beach** and **Red Frog Beach** offer fairly constant sets of lefts and rights that are perfect for beginner and intermediate surfers. When the

swells are in, Wizard occasionally throws out some huge barrels, though they tend to close up pretty quickly.

SPELUNKING & HIKING

Nivida is the name of a cavern recently discovered by one of Bastimentos's residents. The cave is one of the island's most fascinating natural wonders and half the fun of the place is getting to it. To reach Nivida, go to Roots (see opposite) to arrange a trip with Oscar (prices negotiable), a very reliable local guide. You'll then travel by small motorboat up a channel through lush vegetation full of wildlife. A short walk through the jungle leads to a massive cavern complete with swarms of nectar bats and a very swimmable subterranean lake.

Oscar can also arrange a challenging cross-island hike to **Laguna de Bastimentos**, a jungle lake completely surrounded by dense vegetation. This swath of rain forest is the terra firma section of the Parque Nacional Marino Isla Bastimentos.

Sleeping

If you're packing the proper gear and prepared to self-cater, the abandoned beaches of the island are perfectly suitable for wilderness camping.

Although the majority of the action is on Isla Colón, accommodations on Bastimentos are perfect for travelers seeking rustic digs and a laid-back atmosphere.

Hotel Bastimentos (☎ 757 9053; dm/d US$5/10) On a hill off the main path, this rough-and-ready budget hotel has bright and airy rooms with great balconies overlooking the shoreline. More in touch with backpacker needs than other hotels on the island, Hotel Bastimentos offers a common room with a bar, TV, dartboard and views, and a well-equipped communal kitchen.

Beverly's Hill (☎ 757 9923; s/d US$10/15) Rooms in clean cabins set amid a lush garden make Beverly's excellent value. The friendly hosts, Beverly and Wulf, will make you feel welcome the moment you arrive. You can sleep well at night knowing that the on-site composting and water filtration system makes this one of the most environmentally friendly hotels on the island.

Pension Tío Tom (☎ /fax 757 9831; tomina@cwp .net.pa; d with/without bathroom $20/10) This plank-and-thatch building has been offering cheap, clean and unfussy rooms for years. Insanely popular and justifiably so, it epitomizes the type of rustic backpacker place that blazed the gringo trail through Central America. The five rooms at Tío Tom are built right over the water, which is part of the attraction – plank windows open to a sea view. The friendly German owners rent snorkel gear (per day US$5), offer tours and can cook up some seriously gourmet dinners for pennies.

Point (☎ 757 9704; cabin US$40) At the northern tip of Bastimentos lie two cabins overlooking the sea, with crashing waves just a few meters from the doorsteps. Each of the cabins boasts handsomely designed rooms with wooden accents, ecologically designed septic systems, and private hot-water bathrooms. Guests also have free use of the kayaks, and you can surf right off the tip of the island (bring your own board).

Eating & Drinking

Although you're just a short boat ride away from Isla Colón, there are a handful of interesting spots on the island that are worth checking out.

Rooster (mains US$2-4) This inexpensive, low-key spot is also known as Pete's Place, and specializes in dishes that are hearty, healthy and heavy on the island's fresh produce.

Roots (mains US$3-5) This universally loved restaurant over the water is a Bocas institution, and is famous for its masterfully prepared dishes of local meats and seafood that are perfectly accented with fresh coconut milk. Yummm.

La Feria (drinks US$1) This blue, barn-like structure is the seat of the island's nightlife – during the evening hours, just follow the sound of reggae.

Getting There & Away

To get to Isla Bastimentos from Bocas del Toro, just walk down to the waterfront and ask a boatman to take you over. The ride will cost about US$2 to get to the near side of the island or US$4 to the far side.

ISLA CARENERO

A few hundred meters from Isla Colón is the oft-forgotten island of Isla Carenero. The island takes its name from 'careening,' which in nautical talk means to lean a ship on one side for cleaning or repairing. It was on Careening Cay in October 1502 that ships

> ### EXPLORE MORE OF BOCAS DEL TORO
>
> Hire a boatman and go check out the following.
>
> - Don some snorkeling gear and explore the 20m wall at **Hospital Point** near Isla Solarte.
> - Clean your binoculars and then keep your eyes peeled for red-billed tropic birds and white-crowned pigeons in **Swan Cay** near Isla de los Pájaros.
> - Apply some sunscreen and set out for the pristine white-sand beaches and virgin forests of the **Cayos Zapatillas**.
> - Break out your camera and get lost in the mangrove-dotted channels of **Cayo Crawl** near Isla Bastimentos.

under the command of Christopher Columbus were careened and cleaned while the admiral recovered from a bellyache.

Today, the wave of development that transformed Isla Colón is also making headway on Isla Carenero. Although the majority of the accommodations on Isla Carenero are borderline resorts, staying on the island is a great alternative to Isla Colón, especially if you're looking for a bit of peace and quiet.

Orientation

Water taxis dock at the small marina on the tip of the island. From here, there is a path that leads to the island's fledgling town, and continues across the island.

Activities
SURFING

If you've got some serious surfing experience under your belt, then you're going to want to build up the courage to tackle **Silverbacks**, an enormous barreling right that breaks over a reef and can reach heights of over 5m. On a good day Silverbacks is a truly world-class break that wouldn't look out of place on Hawaii's North Shore. Silverbacks breaks off the coast, so you're going to need to hire a water taxi (round-trip US$3) to get out there.

Sleeping & Eating

Doña Mara Restaurante y Hospedaje (☎ 757 9551; d US$55) On the far side of the island is this Panamanian-run spot, which consists of six guestrooms located on a secluded beach.

Although it's a bit pricey for what you're getting, the remote location makes up for the sterility of the rooms.

Hotel Tierra Verde (☎ 757 9042; www.hotelier raverde.com; s/d/tr US$45/$50/55) Offering excellent value for money, this lovely three-story building sits just back from the beach in a shady area full of soaring palm trees. The handful of spacious rooms features beautiful wood details, picture windows and steamy hot-water showers.

Restaurante Las Tortugas (mains US$4-6) This low-key restaurant boasts fine views of Bocas town, and the local seafood on offer is about as cheap as it gets.

GETTING THERE & AWAY

Isla Carenero is a quick and easy US$1 boat ride from Bocas town.

CHANGUINOLA

pop 50,000

Headquarters of the Chiriquí Land Company, the very same people that bring you Chiquita bananas, Changuinola is a hot and rather dusty town surrounded by a sea of banana plantations. Although there is little reason to spend any more time in Changuinola than you have to, overland travelers en route from Costa Rica to Isla Colón will have to stop here.

In addition to serving as a transit point for the Bocas del Toro archipelago, Changuinola also serves as the access point for the Wetso entrance to the Parque Internacional La Amistad. The **ANAM** (☎ 758 8967) office near the center of town has information on the park.

Sleeping & Eating

Hotel Carol (☎ 758 8731; Av 17 de Abril; d with bathroom US$12-16) Although rooms here could inspire a horror film, this budget hotel will do in a pinch. It's conveniently located across from the cemetery (room with a view), and it's a pretty good deal considering that the rooms have private bathrooms, some with hot water.

Restaurant/Bar Chiquita Banana (meals US$2-4) On the main road opposite the bus station, this local favorite serves Panamanian fare, but surprisingly no bananas. (Indeed, bananas are hard to find in town as they are marked for export.)

Getting There & Away

For information on getting to Costa Rica, see p669.

BOAT

Water taxis connecting Changuinola to Bocas town (US$4, 45 minutes, eight daily) leave from Finca 60, which is 5km south of town. Colectivos run regularly from the bus station in town to Finca 60 for US$0.40.

BUSES

Buses depart from the station in the center of town for these destinations: El Silencio (Parque Internacional Amistad) (US$0.50, 30 minutes, every 20 minutes from 5am to 8:30pm), Guabito-Sixaola (US$0.50, 30 minutes, every half hour from 6am to 7pm), Panama City (US$24, 10 hours, at 7am daily), David US$12.50, 4½ hours, every half hour from 5am to 6pm), San José in Costa Rica (US$8, six hours, at 10am daily).

TAXI

You can take a shared taxi from Changuinola to the Costa Rican border at Guabito (per person US$3, 15 minutes).

THE INTERIOR

Between Chiriquí and Panama City, the regions of Veraguas, Península de Azuero and Coclé – all part of the interior – have long been overshadowed by the flash of the capital, the tranquility of the Chiriquí highlands and the Caribbean lure of Bocas del Toro. You may be one of the few tourists around, but if it's Panama's heart and soul you seek, this may be the best place to look. Here, some of Panama's friendliest citizens welcome visitors to their colonial towns and hillside villages. Founded by the Spanish four centuries ago, many settlements are not much bigger now than they were then, and the majority still retain their original, well-preserved colonial churches.

Due to the relative isolation of the region, some of Panama's oldest traditions live on here, and old-world festivals straight out of Spain occur throughout the year. Today the region has an economy primarily based on agriculture, though the interior is known throughout Panama for its exquisite handicrafts. The region is also home to Santa Catalina, which is regarded as one of the best surf destinations in Central America, as well as the scenic mountain towns of Santa Fé and El Valle.

SANTA FÉ

Lacking the tourist infrastructure of Boquete, this tiny mountain is a perfect destination for independent-minded hikers and birders looking to escape the crowds.

The **Orquideario** (☎ 954 0910; orquiberta@hotmail.com; admission by donation), owned by friendly Bertha Castrellón, has one of the country's most impressive collections of orchids (over 265 species). To get here, take the right branch where the Santiago-Santa Fé road forks, then take the second right and look for the sign at that reads '*Orquideario y Cultivos…*'. As this is a home, please be respectful and visit at a reasonable hour (9am to 5pm). Bertha is also Santa Fé's top birding guide, and is a wealth of knowledge.

If you're looking to cool off in a lovely mountain stream, the refreshing **Salto de Bermejo** is only a 10-minute walk from Bertha's – proceed along the same road and take the first right down to the river.

If you take one of the roads heading west from town, you will reach the **Hacia Alto de Piedra**, a vast wilderness area that is ripe for exploration. However, it's best to go with a local guide as this forest quickly becomes a jungle as you clear the ridge.

An excellent spot to bed down for the night is the centrally located **Hostal La Qhia** (☎ 954 0903; hostal_laqhia@yahoo.es; dm US$8, r US$15-20), which is a Belgian-Argentinean–owned oasis of lovely gardens and comfortable beds.

Frequent buses travel from Santiago to Santa Fé (US$2, 1½ hours, every 30 minutes), from 5am to 6pm. From Santiago you can catch frequent buses to David (US$6, three hours) and Panama City (US$6, three hours).

SANTA CATALINA

Although lagging behind Costa Rica in terms of tourist development, Santa Catalina is regarded as one of the best surf destinations in Central America. On a bad day, you can choose from any number of beach breaks on Playa Santa Catalina. On a good day, the rights and lefts here are easily comparable to Oahu's Sunset Beach. Generally speaking, the surf is at its best from December to April.

If you want to really explore the area, many of the local fishermen make excellent guides, and they know the best snorkeling and spearfishing spots as well as some empty surf breaks – look for them on the beach and ask around.

There is no shortage of prime beach real-estate for pitching a tent, though theft is most

definitely a problem. If there's an international surf competition taking place in town, this may in fact be your only option.

Sleeping & Eating

If you want to be on the beach, follow the road out of town – there are a number of signed turn-offs advertising accommodations.

Cabañas Rolo (☎ 998 8600; per person US$7) If you want to bed down in the center of town, this is a good option – basic but adequate. It's owned by a friendly local named Rolo. He cooks meals by request (typically US$3), rents surfboards (per day US$10), and can help you find local guides for tours around the area.

Casablanca Surf Resort (☎ /fax 226 3786; per person US$5-35; ❄) An excellent choice, this has a number of housing options in a parklike setting bordering the beach. Despite the lavish name, surfers on a budget are the main clientele at Casablanca.

Pizzeria Jamming (pizza US$3-5; ☯ 6:30-11pm Tue-Sun) A much-loved Santa Catalina institution, located on the road to the beach-facing hotels. This pizzeria offers delicious thin-crust pizzas made from fresh ingredients, and the open-air rancho is Santa Catalina's liveliest gathering spot.

Getting There & Away

To reach Santa Catalina from Panama City, first take a bus to Soná (US$7, six hours, six buses daily 8:30am to 6pm). From Soná, three buses serve Santa Catalina daily, leaving at 5am, noon and 4pm (US$3, one hour). Unless the driver is pushed for time, he will take you to any one of the hotels listed for an additional US$1. If you miss the bus, you can hire a taxi from Soná to Santa Catalina for about US$25.

From Santa Catalina, three buses serve Soná daily – they leave at 7am, 8am and 2pm. In Santa Catalina, the bus stops near the Restaurant La Fonda – a conch-shell's throw from Cabañas Rolo. If you're staying at one of the other hotels, it's a 1km walk on mostly flat terrain. There are no taxis in town.

CHITRÉ

pop 40,000

Capital of Herrera Province, cowboy-esque Chitré is a good place to experience the rural charm of the interior. Although there's not too much in town aside from the friendly locals and hearty cuisine, Chitré serves as a good base for exploring the Península de Azuero.

Sights & Activities

Chitré is centered on its understated **cathedral**, which is striking for its elegant simplicity and fine balance of gold and wood. The town is also home to the modest **Museo de Herrera** (☎ 996 0077; Paseo Enrique Geenzier at Av Julio Arjona; admission US$1; ☉ 8am-noon & 1-4pm Tue-Sat, 8-11am Sun), a small but worthwhile anthropology and natural history museum. It contains many well-preserved pieces of pottery dating from 5000 BC until the time of the Spanish conquest, as well as photographs depicting Azuero residents, authentic folkloric costumes and also religious artifacts of the region.

Ten kilometers north of downtown Chitré, **Parque Nacional Sarigua** (admission US$3) is a sad monument to the effects of environmental devastation. The park's land is the end product of slash-and-burn agriculture, which created a tropical desert. It's morbidly fascinating as an example of environmental apocalypse. The admission is payable at the ANAM station at the entrance. Buses do not go here; a round-trip taxi ride from Chitré will cost you about US$20.

Playa El Agallito, 7km from Chitré, is not so much a beach as it is a mudflat, where migratory birds arrive by the thousands. These shorebirds are studied by Francisco Delgado and local volunteers at the **Humboldt Ecological Station**. You're welcome to stop by the station, where there are displays on the outside wall. If Francisco isn't around, you can try reaching him at the **restaurant-bar** (☎ 996 1820) beside the beach or at **home** (☎ 996 1725).

Sleeping & Eating

There's no shortage of cheap hotels in town.

Hotel El Prado (☎ 996 4620; Av Herrera; s US$10-15, d US$15-20; ✘) Just to the south of Calle Manuel Maria Correa, this is one of the best. It's a clean, well-kept hotel with a 2nd-floor restaurant, sitting area and open balcony overlooking the street.

Restaurante y Refresquería Aire Libre (dishes US$1.50-3) If you're looking to sample traditional country cuisine, then look no further than this pleasant open-air café facing the western end of the plaza.

Getting There & Away

Chitré is a center for regional bus transportation. Buses arrive and depart from the Terminal de Transportes de Herrera, 1km from downtown. To get to the station, take a taxi (US$2) or catch a 'Terminal' bus (US$0.25) at the intersection of Calle Aminta Burgos de Amado and Av Herrera.

To get to David or Panama City from Chitré, first take a bus to Divisa (US$1, 30 minutes, hourly) and then catch a *directo* (direct bus) to either city. Buses leave from the Delta station that is at the intersection of the Interamericana and Carretera Nacional Hwys. You likely won't have to wait more than 30 minutes. The bus fare to both destinations will set you back US$8, and the trip will take approximately six hours to both David and Panama City.

EL VALLE

pop 6000

This picturesque town (officially El Valle de Antón) is nestled in the crater of a giant extinct volcano that blew off its top three million years ago. Like Santa Fé, El Valle is a superb place for independent exploration, with many forested trails leading into the hills around the valley.

Sights & Activities

In addition to outdoor pursuits, El Valle's main attraction is its Sunday **handicrafts market**, where local indigenous groups – mostly Ngöbe-Buglé but also some Emberá and Wounaan – sell excellent-quality fiber baskets and hats, woodwork, ceramics, soapstone carvings, flowers and plants (including orchids) as well as a variety of fresh produce. It's held in the marketplace in the center of town, starting at 8am and running until early afternoon.

The one-room **Museo de El Valle** (admission US$0.25; ☉ 10am-2pm Sun), in the church at the center of town, features exhibits on the geologic and human history of the valley.

El Nispero (admission US$2; ☉ 7am-5pm) is a large, beautiful garden of exotic plants, located about 1km north of the town center. El Valle's famous golden frogs can be seen in grottos at El Nispero.

El Valle's famous *arboles cuadrados* or **square trees**, an unusual native species, are located in a thicket along a hiking trail behind the Hotel Campestre, east and north of the town center.

Pozos Termales (thermal baths; admission US$1; ☉ 8am-5pm), on the west side of town (follow the signs), is a pleasant place to soak away the afternoon. The forested complex is rustic, with two concrete swimming pools and an area (a bucket, to be precise) for applying healing mud to one's skin.

The hills around El Valle are excellent for walking and horseback riding (Residencial El Valle, below, hires out both bikes and horses). The trails are well-defined since they're frequently used by locals. **Piedra El Sapo** (Toad Stone), west of town near **La India Dormida** (a mountain ridge that resembles a sleeping Indian girl), is said to have some of the most beautiful trails. Nearby, in the neighborhood of La Pintada, are some unusual ancient **petroglyphs** depicting humans, animals and other shapes.

Chorro El Macho (admission US$2; ☯ 8am-4pm) is one of the valley's most beautiful spots. The short hike to this 60m waterfall takes you through a lush rain forest that is protected as an ecological refuge. The waterfall is 2km northwest of town, reachable by the bus to La Mesa (US$0.35). A lovely swimming pool made of rocks and surrounded by rain forest lies just below the falls – bring along your swimsuit.

Sleeping & Eating

Cabañas Potosí (☎ 983 6507; fax 264 3713; campsite US$10, d cabins US$30) A good option that lies about 1.5km west of the town center, on peaceful, park-like grounds with views of the surrounding mountains. The four cabins have two beds apiece with private hot-water bathrooms, and there is also a small campsite here (two-person tents are provided).

Residencial El Valle (☎ 983 6536; residencialelvalle@ hotmail.com; s/d US$20/25) Conveniently located along the main road in town, this spot offers friendly service and excellent rooms with private hot-water bathrooms. You can also rent bicycles (per hour US$2) or horses (per hour US$3.50) here.

Pinocchio's (pizzas US$3-7; ☯ 3-9pm Fri, 11am-9pm Sat, 11am-4pm Sun) A weekend tradition in El Valle is a hot, cheesy slice of pizza at this spot in the western part of town.

Getting There & Away

Buses leave Panama City for El Valle (US$4, 2½ hours, hourly from 7am to 7pm).

The center of town is small, but many of El Valle's attractions are a distance from there. Taxis within town cost no more than US$2. Buses to La Mesa (US$0.35) pass by Chorro El Macho, and run along El Valle's main street.

> **EXPLORE MORE OF THE INTERIOR**
>
> Fiestas are part of the draw of this region.
>
> ■ Four days before Ash Wednesday, **Carnaval** (February/March) in Las Tablas is considered to be Panama's most authentic.
>
> ■ Forty days after Easter, from Thursday to Sunday, the famous **Fiesta de Corpus Christi** (May/June) celebration in Villa de Los Santos features medieval dances and traditional costumes.
>
> ■ This lively **Festival de la Mejorana, Festival de la Virgen de las Mercedes** (September 24 to 27) festival in the tiny village of Guararé is highlighted by folkloric dance and music.
>
> ■ One of the region's biggest festivals, the **Founding of District of Chitré 1848** (October 19) is celebrated with parades of people wearing historical costumes.

COLÓN PROVINCE

The mere mention of Colón sends shivers down the spines of hardened travelers and Panamanians alike, though there is much more to the province than its notorious provincial capital. Extending for over 200km along the Caribbean coast from Veraguas Province in the west to the Comarca de Kuna Yala in the east, Colón Province is mostly undeveloped and virtually inaccessible. However, the province is home to the Spanish colonial city of Portobelo, which at one time was the most prominent port on the Caribbean, as well as the famed tropical getaway of Isla Grande.

Colón definitely deserves its bad rep, and while the city itself is probably best avoided, there are many nearby attractions worth checking out, especially the Gatún Locks and the old Spanish fort of San Lorenzo. And of course, it's worth mentioning that the luxury train connecting Panama City to Colón is arguably one of the world's greatest rail journeys.

COLÓN

pop 45,000

Simply put, Panama's most notorious city is a sprawling slum of decaying colonial grandeur and desperate human existence. Prior to 1869

PANAMA

the Panama Railroad connecting Panama City and Colón was the only rapid transit across the continental western hemisphere. However, once the US transcontinental railroad was established, and the transisthmian trade route suddenly diminished in importance, Colón became an economically depressed city almost overnight. Although the city was temporarily reinvigorated during the construction of the Panama Canal, the city's economy collapsed following the canal's completion, with thousands of laborers suddenly rendered unemployed.

In 1948 a huge free trade zone known as the Zona Libre (Free Zone) was created in an attempt to revive the city. Unfortunately, none of the US$10 billion in annual commercial turnover seems to get beyond the compound's walls. Today, the Zona Libre is an island of materialism in a sea of unemployment, poverty and crime.

History

Colón was founded in 1850 as the Caribbean terminus of the Panama Railroad, though it faded into obscurity less than 20 years later. At the peak of its economic depression in 1881, the French arrived in Colón to start construction of an interoceanic canal, though the city was burnt to the ground four years later by a Colombian hoping to spark a revolution. In the years to follow, Colón entered a second golden age as the city was entirely rebuilt in the French Colonial architectural style that was popular at the time. Rivaling Panama City in beauty and wealth, life in the top of the Canal Zone was pleasurable and highly profitable.

Following the collapse of Colón's economy in 1914, the city spiraled into the depths of depravity. Today, most of the colonial city is still intact, though the buildings are on the verge of collapse, with countless squatters still living inside them.

Orientation & Information

The city is reached via two major roads on the southern side of town. The roads become Av Amador Guerrero and Av Bolivar at the entrance to the town, and run straight up the grid-patterned city, ending near Colon's northern waterfront.

Perpendicular to these avenues are numbered streets. Calle 16 is the first of these you'll cross as you enter the town while Calle 1 is at the northern end of town. The Zone Libre occupies the southeastern corner of the city while the city's cruise-ship port, Colón 2000, is located just north of the Free Zone.

Given Colón's high rate of crime, the safest place to withdraw money is the BNP ATM in the Colón 2000 cruise port.

Dangers & Annoyances

Despite Colón's new cruise port on the eastern side of the city, Colón is still a dangerous slum. Crime is a serious problem, and you need to exercise caution when walking around, even during the day; always travel by taxi at night.

Sights

For some great sights just outside of Colón, see opposite.

ZONA LIBRE

The Free Zone is a huge fortress-like area of giant international stores selling items duty free. It's the world's second-largest duty-free port after Hong Kong. However, most of these stores only deal in bulk merchandise; they aren't set up to sell to individual tourists, and simple window-shopping is not very interesting. Many travelers leave disappointed. If you do buy something, the store usually sends it to the Tocumen International Airport in Panama City, where you can retrieve your purchase before departing the country. You can enter the Zona Libre by presenting your passport at the security office.

PANAMA CANAL YACHT CLUB

This **yacht club** (Calle 16; ☎ 441 5882) in Cristóbal is a safe haven for 'yachties' heading through the canal. It has a restaurant, bar, showers and a bulletin board with notices from people offering or seeking positions as crew. This is the place to inquire about work as a line handler. Don't expect to show up and get work; it can often take several weeks. Still, seeing the canal from the inside is the best way to experience it.

COLÓN 2000

In December of 2000, the self-proclaimed 'Caribbean cruise port of shopping and entertainment' opened on the east side of Colón. Actually it's a rather modest affair, though it does have a good selection of restaurants and souvenir shops.

Sleeping & Eating

There's no shortage of hotels in Colón, though most are in seedy areas and have serious security issues. The hotels listed below are mentioned because they have 24-hour security guards.

Hotel Carlton (☎ 441 0111; Calle 10; s/d US$20/30; ✱) The closest hotel to the Zona Libre features well-appointed rooms complete with queen-size beds, air-con, cable TV and private hot-water showers. There's also an on-site bar-restaurant, which saves you the trouble of having to leave the hotel at night.

Hotel Washington (☎ 441 7133; Calle 2; s/d US$50/60; ✱ ▨) The Washington bills itself as the grand dame of Colón's hotels – and indeed it once was grand – though today its fading colonial elegance is in desperate need of a makeover. Still, the hotel's popularity makes it a safe bet, and the amenity-laden rooms are sweetened by the on-site bar, restaurant, casino and swimming pool.

Getting There & Away

BUS

From Panama City, regular bus service to Colón (US$2.50, two hours, every 30 minutes) departs from the Albrook Bus Terminal from 5am to 9pm.

Colón's Terminal de Buses is at the intersection of Calle Terminal and Av Bolívar. The terminal serves towns throughout Colón Province, including La Guayra (US$2.50, 1½ hours, hourly), from where you can catch the boat to Isla Grande, and Portobelo (US$1.50, one hour, hourly).

The same buses can be boarded at Sabanitas, the turnoff for Portobelo, thus avoiding a trip into Colón.

TRAIN

The **Panama Railway Company** (☎ 317 6070; info@panarail.com; Carr Gaillard) operates a glass-domed luxury passenger train along the canal and through jungle to/from Panama City (US$22/38 one-way/round-trip, one hour), leaving Colón at 5:15pm daily. The Colón train station is in the city but is best accessed by taxi.

Getting Around

While in Colón, it's a good idea to not walk much. Fortunately, taxis congregate at the bus station, train station and the Zone Libre, and fares across the city are usually around US$1.

AROUND COLÓN

Many of these sights are on the Panama Canal map (Map p665).

Gatún Locks

The **Gatún Locks** (admission free; ✆ 8am-4pm), just 10km south of Colón, raise southbound ships 29.5m from Caribbean waters to the level of Lago Gatún. From there, ships travel 37km to the Pedro Miguel Locks, which lower southbound ships 9.3m to Lago Miraflores, a small body of water that separates the two sets of Pacific locks. The ships are lowered to sea level at the Miraflores Locks.

The Gatún Locks are the largest of the three sets, and their size is truly mind-boggling. In his superlative book *The Path Between the Seas*, David McCullough notes that if stood on its end, a single lock would have been the tallest structure on Earth at the time it was built, taller by several meters than even the Eiffel Tower. Each chamber could have accommodated the *Titanic* with plenty of room to spare.

From a well-placed viewing stand opposite the control tower, you can watch the locks in action. The whole process takes about two hours; it's probably the most interesting stage of the Canal transit, and the English brochure does a good job of describing what you're watching.

Buses to the Gatún Locks leave the bus terminal in Colón hourly (US$1.25, 20 minutes). A taxi ride from Colón to the locks and back should cost no more than US$15 per party – agree on a price before leaving.

Fuerte San Lorenzo

On a promontory to the west of the canal, Fuerte (Fort) San Lorenzo is perched at the mouth of the Río Chagres. It was via this river that the Welsh pirate Henry Morgan gained access to the interior in 1671, enabling him to sack the first Panama City, today the ruins of Panamá Viejo.

This Spanish fortress is built of blocks of cut coral with rows of old cannons jutting out. Among the many Spanish cannons, you might spot a British one – evidence of the time when British pirates overcame the fort. Much of the fort is well preserved, including the moat, the cannons and the arched rooms.

There is unfortunately no public transportation to Fuerte San Lorenzo from Colón. However, a round-trip taxi ride from Colón should cost around US$30.

PORTOBELO

pop 4100

Today it is little more than a sleepy fishing village on the shores of the Caribbean, but Portobelo was once the greatest Spanish port in Central America. Gold from Peru and treasures from the Orient entered Panama City and were carried overland by mule to the fortresses at Portobelo. During the annual trade fair, galleons laden with goods from Spain arrived to trade for gold and other products from the New World. Unfortunately, Portobelo met the same fate as Panamá Viejo when it was destroyed by the British in 1746.

Visitors to Portobelo can explore the extensive ruins of the Spanish stone fortresses that once graced the city. In addition to its historical attractions, Portobelo has also established itself as a popular Caribbean scuba-diving destination.

History

Portobelo, the 'beautiful port,' was named by Columbus in 1502, when he stopped here on his fourth New World voyage. For the next 200 years, Portobelo served as the principal Spanish Caribbean port in Central America.

Aiming to disrupt the Spanish treasure route, Portobelo was destroyed in 1739 by an attack led by the British admiral Edward Vernon. Discouraged by the loss of the city, the Spanish abandoned the overland Panama route, and instead started sailing the long way around Cape Horn to and from the western coast of South America.

Portobelo was rebuilt in 1751, though it never attained its former prominence, and in time became a virtual ruin. Later, much of the outermost fortress was dismantled to build the Panama Canal, and many of the larger stones were used in the construction of the Gatún Locks. There are still considerable parts of the town and fortresses left, and today Portobelo is protected as a national park and historic site.

Orientation

Portobelo, located 43km from Colón, consists of about 15 blocks of homes and businesses that line a paved, two-lane road. This road intersects with the Panama City-Colón road at the town of Sabanitas, 33km to the west.

East of Portobelo, the road forks after 9km. The left branch extends 11km to the village of La Guayra, where you can hire boats to take you to Isla Grande.

Sights

The remnants of **Fuerte San Jerónimo** and **Fuerte Santiago** can still be seen near town, and the ruins of **Fuerte San Fernando** occupy a grassy flat across the bay. The ruins of Santiago, 500m west of Portobelo's center, include officers' quarters, an artillery shed, a sentry box, a barracks and batteries. You can climb up a hill behind the fort for a fine view overlooking the ruins and bay. At the center of Portobelo, Fuerte San Jerónimo is a more complete fort than Santiago.

The restored **Real Aduana de Portobelo** (Customs House; admission US$0.50), also known as the *contaduría* (counting house), has interesting exhibits of Portobelo's history as well as a three-dimensional model of the area.

Another notable feature of Portobelo is its large **colonial church**, which was built in 1776. It contains a life-size statue of the Black Christ, which is believed to have miraculous powers. On October 21 each year, the **Festival of the Black Christ** attracts hundreds of pilgrims, many dressed in the same royal purple color as the statue's clothes. The statue is paraded through the streets starting at 6pm, and street festivities follow.

On the way to Portobelo, the black-sand **Playa María Chiquita** and the white-sand **Playa Langosta** are two attractive beaches.

Activities

Although the clarity of the water here is not spectacular, Portobelo enjoys a good diving reputation due to two unique sites off the coast, namely a 33m (110ft) cargo ship and a C-45 twin-engine plane.

There are two dive operators in Portobelo, both located along the Sabanitas-Portobelo road 2km west of town. A 1-/2-tank dive will cost US$60/80 whereas an open water/advanced course will cost US$200/275. If you're planning to dive with either, it's best to phone ahead. **Twin Oceans Dive Center** (☎ 448 2067; www.twinoceans.com) is in the Coco Plum Hotel, while **Scubaportobelo** (☎ 261 3841; www.scubapanama.com) offers dorm-bed accommodation (per night US$10).

Sleeping & Eating

Several local families in town advertise spare rooms for about US$5 to US$10 per night – ask around for details.

Hospedaje La Aduana (☎ 448 2925; d with fan/aircon US$15/20; 🏠) Conveniently located in the center of town, this bare-bones budget hotel offers a handful of spartan rooms. If possible, ask to see a few as the better ones have a private bathroom.

Coco Plum Hotel (☎ 264 1338; s/d with bathroom US$35/45; ✿) This newly constructed lodge is located 2km west of town along the Sabanitas-Portobelo road, and is home to the Twin Oceans Dive Center. Although the rooms are simple, they all feature air-con, cable TV and private hot-water bathrooms, and the on-site restaurant is perfect for getting your energy back after a long day diving.

Restaurante La Torre (dishes US$3-6) One of the few restaurants in town, this centrally located spot serves some of the best seafood in town (conch in coconut sauce) and juicy cheese-burgers.

Getting There & Away

Buses to Portobelo (US$1.50, one hour, hourly) depart from Colón's Terminal de Buses from 6:30am to 6pm. If you're coming by bus from Panama City, take the bus heading for Colón and get off at Sabanitas, 10km before Colón, about a 1½-hour ride from Panama City. Next, catch the bus coming from Colón to Portobelo when it passes through Sabanitas, thus avoiding a trip into Colón.

ISLA GRANDE

Palm trees and white-sand beaches form the backdrop to this lovely island 15km northeast of Portobelo. A popular getaway for Panama City folk, Isla Grande is an ideal setting for snorkeling, scuba diving or simply soaking up the island's relaxed vibe. About 300 people of African descent live on the island, most of whom eke out a living from fishing and coconuts – you'll get a taste of both when you sample the fine island cuisine.

Activities

Some lovely **beaches** on the northern side of the island can be reached by boat (hire a water taxi at the dock in front of Cabañas Super Jackson) or on foot (there's a water's-edge trail that loops around the 5km long, 1.5km wide island, as well as a slippery cross-island trail).

If you're looking for a good **surf** break, take a water taxi out to La Guayra where you can find a good reef break that peaks right and left.

The trail across the island leads to **Bananas Village Resort** (☎ 263 9766; www.bananasresort.com),

where US$25 will get you use of their facilities for the day, including access to the beach, snorkeling equipment and kayaks.

Some fine snorkeling and dive sites are within a 10-minute boat ride of the island. **Isla Grande Dive Center** (☎ 223 5943), located 50m west of Cabañas Super Jackson, offers a variety of dives around the island and in the San Blás archipelago.

For US$30, one of the boatmen in front of Cabañas Super Jackson will take you on a half-day adventure – the possibilities are quite appealing. The mangroves east of Isla Grande are fun to explore, or you could go snorkeling off the coast of the nearby islets.

Festivals & Events

The **Festival of San Juan Bautista** is celebrated here on June 24, with swimming and canoe races. The **Virgen del Carmen** is honored on July 16, with a land and sea procession, baptisms and masses.

Carnaval is also celebrated here in rare form. Women wear traditional *pollera* dresses while men wear ragged pants tied at the waist with old sea rope – everyone dances the conga. Along with the dancing, there are also satirical songs about current events and a lot of joking in the Caribbean calypso tradition.

Sleeping & Eating

Cabañas Super Jackson (☎ 448 2311; d with fan/air-con US$20/35; ✿) Closest to the main pier, this Isla Grande landmark offers a handful of cheap and cheerful rooms with private bathrooms. There are definitely more comfortable spots on the island, but it's hard to beat the price, the convenience factor and the humorous name.

Cabañas Cholita (☎ 448 2962; fax 232 4561; d/tr US$40/50; ✿) Just east of the Super Jackson, Cabañas Cholita offers 14 oceanside rooms complete with private cold-water bathrooms and tranquil views. The on-site restaurant has delicious cinnamon French toast for breakfast (US$3) and spicy Caribbean fare (US$5 to US$7) for lunch and dinner.

Hotel Isla Grande (☎ 267 3643; d US$45-60; ✿) About 200m west of Super Jackson, the Hotel Grande features double rooms with private hot-water bathrooms and ocean views. Although the Isla Grande has definitely seen better years, you're paying for the privilege of accessing the hotel's private beach, though the barb wire is slightly off-putting.

PANAMA

Sister Moon Hotel (☎ 226 9861; d from US$50) A 10-minute walk east of Super Jackson brings you to this lovely clutch of cabins perched on a hillside at the end of the island. Surrounded by swaying palms and crashing waves, each cabin boasts fabulous views from its porch (and hammock). The hotel also has an excellent bar-restaurant that's built right over the water, and features the island's incredible seafood (US$5 to US$8).

Getting There & Away

Buses from Colón go to La Guayra (US$2.50, 1½ hours, hourly). A five-minute boat ride from there to Isla Grande costs US$2. Parking costs US$1 per day.

COMARCA DE KUNA YALA

The Comarca de Kuna Yala is a narrow, 226km-long strip on the Caribbean coast that includes the Archipiélago de San Blás, which stretches from the Golfo de San Blás to the edge of the Colombian border. Many of the nearly 400 islands of San Blás are real *Fantasy Island*-type settings: uninhabited islands covered by coconut trees and ringed by white-sand beaches with the turquoise Caribbean lapping at their shores. The ones that aren't uninhabited contrast sharply with those that are: acre-sized cays are packed with bamboo huts and people, allowing barely enough room to maneuver among the detritus-lined pathways.

The islands are home to the Kuna, who run San Blás as a *comarca* – an autonomous region – with minimal interference from the national government. They have their own system of governance, consultation and decision making, while maintaining their own economic system, language, customs and culture. Given that the Kuna have been in contact with Europeans ever since Columbus sailed along here in 1502, this has been no small achievement. Their success is the result of remarkable tenacity, and their zealous efforts to preserve a traditional way of life. Today, they have one of the greatest degrees of political autonomy of any indigenous group in Latin America.

HISTORY

The Kuna have lived in Eastern Panama for at least two centuries, though scholars fiercely debate their origins. Language similarities with people who once lived several hundred kilometers to the west would indicate that the Kuna migrated eastward. However, oral tradition has it that the Kuna migrated to San Blás from Colombia after the 16th century, following a series of devastating encounters with other tribes armed with poison-dart blowguns.

No matter where the Kuna came from, however, scholars agree that life on the islands is relatively new for the Kuna. Historians at the end of the 18th century wrote that the only people who used the San Blás islands at the time were pirates, Spaniards and the odd explorer.

Today, there are an estimated 70,000 Kuna; 32,000 live on the district's islands, 8000 live on tribal land along the coast and 30,000 live outside the district. So communal are the island Kuna that they inhabit only 40 of the 400 cays – the rest are mostly left to coconut trees, sea turtles and iguanas. On the inhabited islands, so many traditional bamboo-sided, thatched-roof houses are clustered together that there's scarcely room to walk between them.

Historically, the Kuna subsisted on freshly caught seafood including fish, lobster, shrimp, Caribbean king crab and octopus. This was accompanied by food crops, including rice, yams, yucca, bananas and pineapples, which were grown in plots on the mainland, a short distance away. Today, this traditional diet is supplemented by food products obtained by bartering coconuts with passing Colombian ships.

ORIENTATION

The only practical way of visiting the Comarca region is to fly here; the inaccessibility of the place has helped preserve traditional Kuna culture. At the northwest end of the province, El Porvenir is the gateway to the San Blás islands, and one of the most popular destinations for visitors. From here, boat transportation can be arranged to other islands in the archipelago, several of which have basic hotels. If you're planning on staying at any of the far-flung islands, you can also fly into Río Sidra.

INFORMATION

Although a trip to the Archipiélago de San Blás may not fit in the budget, these culturally rich Caribbean islands are a good place for a splurge if you can swing it. Prices vary, but if you stick to the cheaper hotels, you can survive on about US$35 per day; this includes meals, lodging and daily boating excursions.

Owing to the limited number of flights to the area, you should book as far in advance as possible. It's also recommended that you reserve your hotels in advance, especially since package deals are pretty much the norm in the Comarca. You're also going to want to hit an ATM before you touch down on the islands.

The Kuna are very particular about what foreigners do on their islands (see p702). As a result, they require that tourists register and pay a visitation fee between US$3 and US$5 on the main islands. On smaller, privately owned islands, visitors must seek out the owner, receive permission and pay a fee (around US$2).

Visitors must also pay for any photo they take of the Kuna. If you want to take someone's photo, ask their permission first and be prepared to pay US$1 per subject (some Kuna expect to be paid US$1 per photo). You may not be expected to pay for a photo taken of an artisan from whom you buy crafts from, but it depends on the subject. Some islands may charge you US$50 just for possessing a video camera.

ACTIVITIES

Most hotels offer complete packages, where a fixed price gets you a room, three meals a day and boat rides to neighboring islands for swimming, snorkeling and lounging on the beach. Before swimming off the shores of a heavily populated island, take a look at the number of outhouses built over the ocean – they may change your mind. Snorkeling is good in places, although many of the coral reefs in the region are badly damaged. You can often rent snorkeling equipment from your

hotel, but serious snorkelers should bring their own gear. If you seek community life, you can also arrange visits to more populated islands such as Cartí Suitupo, Nusatupo and Río Sidra.

Independent travelers often complain that they feel trapped inside their hotels, but striking off on your own and exploring the Comarca is definitely possible, albeit tricky, as you will need to negotiate boat rides between islands and find places to stay and eat. If you speak a fair bit of Spanish (or better yet a smattering of Kuna), it can be done. Another option is to grab a spot on a chartered boat to Colombia (see p707).

Plenty of adventurous travelers succeed in hiring a boat and a guide to take them to the far-flung reaches of the Comarca, though this takes a bit of time and cash. Costs, however, can be kept to a minimum if you're prepared to camp on small islands or stay with local families. Although it can be tough going at times, this is perhaps the best way to truly experience the lifestyle and culture of the Kuna.

SLEEPING & EATING

In a protectionist move to preserve local culture, the Kuna Congress passed a law several years ago that prohibits outsiders from owning property in the Comarca. One direct consequence of the law was that a handful of foreigners living on the islands were kicked out without compensation. However, the law has kept foreign investment out of the region, and the few hotels in the Comarca are 100% owned by local families.

Since there are no restaurants on the islands; each hotel provides all the meals for its guests. The meals are usually based on seafood, with lobster and fish the specialties. Quality varies, as some of the fishing stocks have been

---

THE TRADITIONAL DRESS OF THE KUNA

The distinctive dress of the Kuna is immediately recognizable no matter where you are in the country. Most Kuna women continue to dress as their ancestors did. Their faces are adorned with a black line painted from the forehead to the tip of the nose, with a gold ring worn through the septum. Colorful fabric is wrapped around the waist as a skirt, topped by a short-sleeved blouse covered in brilliantly colored *molas* (traditional Kuna textiles). The women wrap their legs, from ankle to knee, in long strands of tiny beads, forming colorful geometric patterns. A printed headscarf and many necklaces, rings and bracelets complete the wardrobe. In sharp contrast to the elaborate women's wear, the Kuna men have adopted Western dress, which in these warm islands often means shorts and a sleeveless shirt.

RESPONSIBLE TRAVEL IN THE COMARCA DE KUNA YALA

If you're thinking about whether or not to visit the Comarca de Kuna Yala, please consider the impact that you might have on the Kuna community. On the one hand, revenue from tourism can play a vital role in the development of the region, particularly if you are buying locally produced crafts or paying for the services of a Kuna guide. On the other hand, the San Blás archipelago is not a human zoo; unfortunately indigenous tourism is often an exploitative force. If you decide to visit, please remember that Western interests have already caused an irreversible amount of damage to the region – be aware of your surroundings, and be sensitive to the plight of the Kuna.

It's worth noting that the Kuna sometimes appear unfriendly to tourists, and understandably so, given that most visitors view them as oddities who must be photographed. Cruise ships visit several islands, and when the ships arrive, the number of people on an already congested island can triple. Nonetheless, nearly two-thirds of the populace (the tourists) are trying like crazy to photograph the other third (the Kuna). It's a pretty ugly scene that's repeated again and again.

Furthermore, the behavior of many tourists is appalling to the Kuna. For example, Kuna women dress conservatively, and always keep their cleavage, bellies, and most of their legs covered. Yet many foreign women arrive in Kuna villages in bikini tops and short skirts, an act that is nearly always interpreted by the Kuna as a sign of disrespect. Likewise, Kuna men never go shirtless, and travelers who do so risk offending local sensibilities.

As a result of repeated violations, the Kuna ask that travelers pay fees for photographs taken of them as well as visitation fees for each island. Travelers who consider these policies intolerable should leave their cameras tucked away and see what a little personal interaction can bring.

Unfortunately, tourism is developing too rapidly in the region, and according to Kuna elders, the invasion of foreigners poses a major threat to the preservation of Kuna culture. In response, the Kuna Congress has started to debate the extent to which foreigners should be granted access to their Comarca. In the years to follow, it is likely that the Kuna Congress will ban photography in certain areas while prohibiting tourist traffic in others. As an informed and conscientious traveler, please do your best to always inquire locally about proper conduct in the Comarca.

depleted through over-fishing; there is always a healthy stock of fresh coconuts on hand.

If you want to camp on a relatively uninhabited island, US$5 a night per couple will usually do the trick. However, there's a risk of encountering unwanted visitors in the night. The Kuna do not allow the Panamanian coast guard or US antidrug vessels to operate in the archipelago, so the uninhabited islands are occasionally used by Colombian narcotraffickers running cocaine up the coast. If you're thinking about camping, you may want to check into one of the hotels for a day or two to get oriented, and then start inquiring locally for up-to-date information.

Note that the hotels following are arranged by island (west to east) instead of by price.

Hotel San Blás (☎ 290 6528; Nalunega; r per person incl meals & boat tours US$35) Near El Porvenir, the Hotel San Blás is the most popular and accessible hotel in Kuna Yala. The ocean-side hotel consists of rustic Kuna-style palm cabins with sand floors as well as modern rooms with hard floors – if you like the simple life, this is a good place to enjoy it.

Kuna Niskua Lodge (☎ 225 5200; Wichub-Walá; r per person incl meals & boat tours US$35) A five minute boat ride from El Porvenir brings you to this attractive bamboo-and-thatch hotel, located near the island's interior. Although the rooms are lacking the ocean views found at other spots, the Kuna Niskua is artfully strung up with ample hammocks, and the island's rural charm is infectious.

Ikuptupu Hotel (☎ 220 9082; Ikuptupu; r per person incl meals & boat tours US$35) On the tiny artificial island of Ikuptupu, just a few hundred meters from Wichub-Walá, this hotel was a former research facility used by the Smithsonian Tropical Research Institute from 1974 to 1998. Although this is not the best choice if you want to mingle with Kuna, if you are in the mood for a break, you can't beat the isolation and setting.

Hotel Kuna Yala (☎ 315 7520; Nusatupo; r US$40) Accessible by the airstrip in Río Sidra, this bare-bones hotel sacrifices comfort for location, though it's a worthwhile trade when you set out for the pristine Isla Aguja (Needle Island). Although the rooms leave something to be desired, the kitchen here will stuff you until you roll out of your chair.

Robinson's Cabins (☎ 299 9058; Kuanidup; huts per person & boat tours US$17.50) Also accessible by the airstrip in Río Sidra, Robinson's is set on an uninhabited island surrounded by a fine sandy beach. The accommodations consist of rustic bamboo huts. There's fine snorkeling off the island, and the friendly Robinsons can also take you to other islands in the area.

SHOPPING

Molas are the most famous of Panamanian traditional handicrafts. Made of brightly colored squares of cotton fabric sewn together, the finished product reveals landscape scenes, birds, sea turtles or fish – often surrounded by a mazelike pattern. Craftsmanship varies considerably between *molas*. The simplest are peddled for a few dollars; more elaborate designs are works of art and can cost several hundred dollars. You can find *molas* on the islands (or rather, the *mola*-sellers will find you).

GETTING THERE & AWAY

Both **Air Panama** (☎ 316 9000; www.flyairpanama.com /tickets in Spanish) and **Aeroperlas** (☎ 315 7500; www .aeroperlas.com) fly to the San Blás Archipelago. Air Panama has one flight per day to El Porvenir (San Blás) and Río Sidra (both one-way US$35), while Aeroperlas flies to both places three times per week. Book as far in advance as possible as demand far exceeds supply. Note that planes may stop at other islands in the archipelago, loading and unloading passengers or cargo before continuing on. Flights depart from Albrook airport.

You can get around the islands by boat (see p707).

DARIÉN PROVINCE

The Darién is one of the wildest and most ravaged areas in the Americas. It is the largest province in Panama, and the country's most sparsely inhabited province, with fewer than three people per square kilometer. Home to Panama's most spectacular national park and to its worst scenes of habitat destruction, it is two worlds, divided into north and south.

Although the northern Darién has suffered serious environmental damage in previous decades, southern Darién is an adventurer's

dream. Home to the 576,000-hectare Parque Nacional Darién, a Unesco World Heritage site, southern Darién is where the primeval meets the present – where the scenery appears much as it did over a million years ago. Even today, the local Emberá and Wounaan population still maintain many of their traditional practices, and remain as the guardians of generations-old knowledge of the rain forest.

The Darién offers spectacular opportunities for rugged exploration by trail or by river – it's best approached by travelers with youthful hearts, intrepid spirits and a yearning for something truly wild. If you're afraid of growing old in a concrete jungle, spend some time in this verdant one.

HISTORY

Living within the boundaries of the Darién are the Chocóes, as they are commonly called, who emigrated from the Chocó region of Colombia thousands of years ago. Anthropologists place the Chocóes in two linguistic groups – the Emberá and the Wounaan – though with the exception of language, the groups' cultural features are virtually identical. However, both groups prefer to be thought of as two separate peoples.

Before the introduction of the gun, the Emberá and Wounaan were expert users of the *boroquera* (blowgun), and they envenomed their darts with lethal toxins from poisonous frogs and bullet ants. Many scholars believe that it was these people who forced the Kuna out of the Darién and into the Caribbean coastal area they now inhabit.

Until it left Panama in the late 1990s, the US Air Force turned to the Emberá and Wounaan for help, but for an entirely different reason: jungle survival. Because both groups have the ability to not only survive but to thrive in the tropical wilderness, quite a few of them were added to the corps of instructors that trained US astronauts and air force pilots at Fort Sherman, near Colón.

Today, the majority of the 8000 Emberá and Wounaan in Panama live deep in the rain forests of the Darién, particularly along the Sambú, Jaqué, Chico, Tuquesa, Membrillo, Tuira, Yape and Tucutí rivers. Along with subsistence agriculture, hunting, fishing and poultry raising, both *indígena* groups also work on nearby commercial rice and maize plantations.

PANAMA

DARIÉN PROVINCE

PANAMA

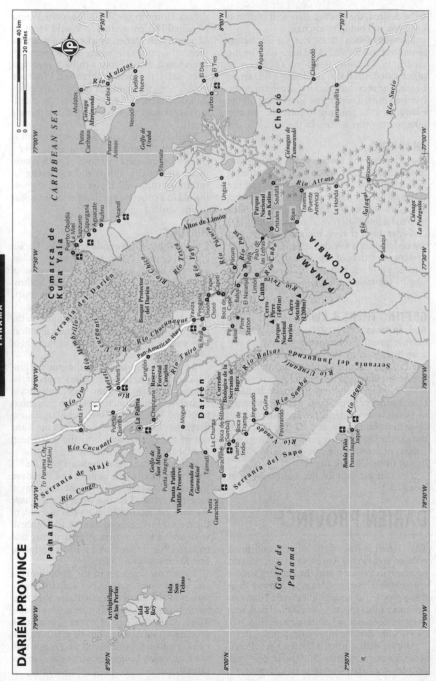

ORIENTATION & INFORMATION

The Pan-American Hwy does not go all the way through Panama but terminates in the middle of the jungle near a town called Yaviza in the vast wilderness region of the Darién, before starting again 150km further on in Colombia. This transportation break between Central and South America is known as the **Darién Gap**. It's literally the end of the road.

Despite occasional announcements by international authorities eager to improve transportation and trade between the continents, it is unlikely that the Pan-American Hwy will be pushed through the Darién Gap any time soon. Panamanians are concerned that a road could help Colombia's civil war spill over into Panama. A road could also increase illegal immigration and drug traffic, and help spread foot-and-mouth disease in cattle, which is presently limited to South America. A paved road would also make logging easier, perhaps leading to deforestation of the largest forested area in the country.

Any printed information on the Darién can become rapidly outdated. Travelers should always seek up-to-date information on local dangers. The best source of this information is a guide who leads frequent trips to the area.

Local ANAM offices in towns such as El Real or La Palma can provide some information on the park and help you find guides. Travelers should also check in with the police in these towns before heading out into the jungle.

Panama City's **Instituto Geográfico Nacional** (Tommy Guardia; Map pp652-3; ☎ 236 2444; ☼ 8am-4pm Mon-Fri) usually sells topographical maps for some regions of the Darién.

The website www.outbackofbeyond.com describes Patricia and Loren Upton's adventures through the Darién Gap. It also sells the guidebook *Through the Darién Gap* for US$13. However, you should view any printed information as being dangerously out of date.

Keep your baggage to a minimum on any trek through the jungle. You will need insect repellent, sun block, a hat and rain gear. Food can only be found in the few towns, including Metetí, La Palma and Yaviza; otherwise bring your own. Food is not available at the ranger stations. Bring drinking water or a means of purifying water.

Remember to plan your trip for the dry season (mid-December through mid-April), or you'll be slogging through thick mud and swatting moth-size mosquitoes.

DANGERS & ANNOYANCES

Parts of the Darién Province are extremely dangerous. The greatest hazards are the result of the difficult environment. The Darién is hot and humid. Trails, when they exist at all, are often poorly defined and are never marked. The many large rivers that form the backbone of the Darién transportation network create their own hazards. Any help at all, much less medical help, is very far away. If you get lost out here, you are done for.

Dengue and malaria are serious risks in the area. Take a prophylaxis – not chloroquinine – and cover up as much as possible. Areas of the Parque Nacional Darién are prime territory for the deadly fer-de-lance snake. The chance of getting a snakebite is remote, but you should be careful; wear boots around the camp and in the forest.

In addition to the natural dangers, the human threat to travelers must not be underestimated. Illegal immigrants heading north – including Colombians fleeing the conflict in their country – make their way through the jungle. Roaming bandits prey on jungle travelers. As an outsider, you may be viewed with suspicion, and some villages do not greet tourists with open arms. Narcotraffickers also utilize jungle routes, and they don't appreciate bumping into travelers trekking through the woods. Police presence in the area south of Boca de Cupe is limited.

Parts of the Darién have also become areas of activity for guerrillas from neighboring Colombia, although they usually come to rest and hide, not to attack. Colombian paramilitary forces often cross the border to hunt guerrillas. There are real dangers in the Darién: missionaries and travelers alike have been kidnapped and killed in Southern Darién.

The US State department has strongly advised against crossing an imaginary line drawn from Puerto Obaldía in the north to Bahía Piña in the south, with Yaviza in the center. Unfortunately, this includes the Parque Nacional Darién, though Cana and Pirre Station, both excellent places to view wildlife, are considered safe to visit. Particularly treacherous are the areas between Boca de Cupe and Colombia, the traditional path through the Darién Gap, which includes the towns of Púcuro, Paya, Limón, Balsal and Palo de las Letras. The areas north and east of this are also considered dangerous, including the mountains Altos de Limón, the Río Tuquesa and the trail from Puerto Obaldía. Note, however, that the Boca de Cupe trail leading to Cana, the focus of the Darien Explorer Trek (see below), was safe at the time of writing. Check with local authorities to assess the situation before visiting the Darién.

Despite these warnings, there are parts of the Darién that can be visited in relative safety; these are covered later in this section. Even then, however, travelers should always hire a guide – either locally or through a reputable tour company. A knowledgeable guide will ensure up-to-date information on no-go areas, and that you don't get lost. Hiring one also supports ecotourism in the local economy, and provides safety through numbers.

TOURS
The Darién is the only major part of Panama where a guide is necessary. If you speak Spanish, you can hire guides locally who can show you the way and cook for you. The cost is reasonable: about US$10 to US$20 per day, plus food. Otherwise, go with a reputable tour operator, who will take care of all arrangements, provide all the food and relieve you of the necessity of speaking Spanish or one of the native languages.

Ancon Expeditions (Map pp652-3; ☎ 269 9415; www.anconexpeditions.com; El Dorado Bldg, Calle 49 Este near Av 3 Sur) in Panama City has by far the most extensive trips to the Darién, and is highly recommended for the quality and professionalism of its tours. Offerings include the following:

Darién Explorer Trek A two-week trip that includes Punta Patiño on the Pacific coast, El Real, the Pirre Station and Cana. The cost is US$2450 per person, and the trip leaves on fixed departure dates with a minimum of four people. The highlight is a two-day trek along the Boca de Cupe trail to Cana.

Ultimate Darién Experience A five-day trip to Ancon's field station in Cana, an outstanding place for bird-watching. The cost is US$1300 per person, and the trip leaves on fixed departure dates in the high season (December to April) with a minimum of four people. An eight-day version is also available.

Coastal Darién Explorer A three-day trip to Ancon's lodge in Punta Patiño on the Pacific coast. The cost is US$575 per person (minimum four people), and the trip is available on request (subject to availability).

Realm of the Harpy Eagle A four-day trip to Ancon's lodge in Punta Patiño and a visit to a Mogue Emberá village on the Pacific coast. The cost is US$695 per person (minimum four people), and the trip is available on request (subject to availability).

VOLUNTEERING
An excellent organization that takes volunteers from time to time is the **Fundación Pro-Niños de Darién** (☎ 254 4333; www.darien.org.pa). This nonprofit organization was started in 1990, and works on a variety of projects throughout the Darién. The foundation aims to improve the lives of *niños* (children) through educational and nutritional programs. The organization also works to help residents develop sustainable agriculture.

SHOPPING
The Emberá and Wounaan are excellent woodcarvers and basket weavers. Traditionally the men carved boas, frogs and birds from the dark *cocobolo* hardwood. More recently they have taken to carving tiny figurines (typically of iguanas, turtles, crocodiles and birds) from the ivory-colored *tagua* nut. The women, however, continue to weave traditional baskets with intricate designs. Crafts are typically available in towns throughout the Darién, though you'll get better prices (and support the artisans) if you buy directly from villages.

GETTING THERE & AWAY
Panama City to Yaviza is a 266km journey along the Interamericana that passes through Chepo, El Llano, Cañita, Ipetí, Tortí, Higueronal and smaller, unmapped communities in Panamá Province before crossing into the Darién. All these towns are served by buses running between Panama City and Yaviza. There are eight buses daily to Yaviza between 5am and 3:45pm (US$15, seven to 10 hours). Be sure to tell the bus driver your destination.

Travelers can also fly into the region. **Aeroperlas** (☎ 315 7500; www.aeroperlas.com) has three flights per week and **Air Panama** (☎ 316 9000; www.flyairpanama.com/tickets) has one flight per week to La Palma (US$40, one hour). From La Palma, Aeroperlas offers three flights per week to El Real (US$35, 15 minutes).

GETTING AROUND
In the jungles of the Darién, rivers are sometimes the only means of getting from one point to another, with dugout canoes providing the transport. In La Palma you can hire a motorized boat for US$120 to US$200 per day, which can take you to Río Sambú. From either of these rivers you'll have to negotiate with indigenous villages (in Mogué or La Chunga).

SAILING TO CARTAGENA, COLOMBIA

Want to be the envy of your friends and a disappointment to your concerned parents? One of the best ways is to explore the **Archipiélago de San Blás** by grabbing a spot on a chartered sail boat to Colombia. Although there's no shortage of merchant ships plying the waters between Colón and Cartagena, Colombia, sailing with a reputable captain pretty much guarantees that you won't be a stowaway on a ship full of narcotics. Adventure travel is one thing, but getting caught in the crossfire between narcotraffickers and border guards is another.

The best place to enquire about scheduled departures is at any of the youth hostels in Panama City (p658). At these spots, there are usually postings on the notice boards advertising specific boats and their fearless captains. If you're worried about your budget, don't be – a five-day sailing including food, drinks and activities should cost about US$275. Of course, you will need to be responsible for your travel back to Panama; a flight back from Cartagena costs less than US$200. And in case your parents are worried sick, you can honestly tell them that the walled-city of Cartagena is easily the safest (and most beautiful) city in Colombia. Buen Viaje!

---

to take you further upriver in *cayucos* (dugout canoes). Hiring boats in Río Jaqué is possible but strongly not advised owing to the dangers of guerilla activity. A shorter (and cheaper) boat trip goes from Puerto Quimba to La Palma.

LA PALMA
pop 4200

Located at the mouth of the Río Tuira, La Palma is the provincial capital and the most populous town in the Darién. However, despite its lofty position as capital of the largest province in Panama, La Palma is literally a one-street town.

Most travelers pass through La Palma for one of two reasons: they're here to catch a plane to somewhere else or they're here to take a boat ride to somewhere else. The two most popular boating destinations are the Ancon nature reserve and lodge at Reserva Natural Punta Patiño and the Emberá villages along the banks of the Río Sambú.

Every facility of possible interest to the traveler is located on the town's only street, which is about 300m from the airstrip. La Palma is home to the only bank in the Darién, the Banco Nacional de Panamá, as well as a hospital, a port and a police station – if you intend to go anywhere near the Colombian border, you should talk to the police here first

If you have to spend the night in La Palma, the **Hotel Biaquira Bagara** (☎ /fax 299 6224; r with/without bathroom US$20/15) is run by the friendly Ramady family, who live in a home beneath the rooms they rent. All of the rooms have private cold-water bathrooms with a tub, which is a godsend after a week or two in the jungle.

Air Panama (☎ 316 9000; www.flyairpanama.com /tickets) and **Aeroperlas** (☎ 315 7500; www.aeroperlas .com) fly direct from Panama City to La Palma (US$40, one hour). Air Panama has one flight per week while Aeroperlas has three flights per week.

If you're looking to hire a boat and a guide, you can usually find someone near the dock who owns a vessel and is willing to go on an adventure with you for the right price (US$120 to US$200 per day, gas included).

RESERVA NATURAL PUNTA PATIÑO

Twenty-five kilometers south of La Palma is Punta Patiño, which is home to a 26,315-hectare **wildlife reserve** that is owned by the government conservation group Ancon. The only way to reach the reserve, short of hacking your way through many kilometers of jungle, is by boat; the scenic ride is definitely part of the Punta Patiño experience. The reserve itself protects species-rich primary forest, and visitors are treated to guided night and morning nature hikes.

If you prefer, you can arrive at the reserve without booking a guided tour through Ancon Expeditions, but you must notify it in advance of your arrival so that it can reserve a cabin for you. If you visit without Ancon Expeditions' help, lodging and three daily meals will cost you US$90 per person per day. You can hire boats in La Palma to reach Punta Patiño; expect to pay your boatman about US$120 to US$150 per day.

Ancon Expeditions (Map pp652-3; ☎ 269 9415; www .anconexpeditions.com; El Dorado Bldg, Calle 49 Este near Av 3 Sur, Panama City) offers a package tour to Punta Patiño that includes the round-trip airfare

PANAMA

THE STYLIZED TRADITIONS OF THE EMBERÁ & WOUNAAN

Unlike the Kuna, the Emberá and Wounaan have gradually replaced their traditional attire with Western wear. Except for a few older individuals, the men have set aside their loincloths in favor of short pants, and now prefer short-sleeved shirts to going around bare-chested. The women, who traditionally wore only a skirt, increasingly don bras, and some have taken to wearing shirts as well. However, many women still wear traditional jewelry, especially wide silver bracelets and elaborate necklaces made of silver coins. Many Emberá and Wounaan also continue to stain their bodies purplish black with juice from the *jagua* fruit. The dye from this fruit is believed to have health-giving properties, and it has the added bonus of warding off insects.

---

between Panama City and La Palma, a boat ride up the Río Mogué to the Emberá village, a visit to Punta Alegre, hikes in the reserve, guide service and all meals. The three-day, two-night adventure costs about US$600 per person (party of two) and substantially less per person for larger parties.

RÍO SAMBÚ

The mouth of the wide, brown Río Sambú is 1½ hours by fast boat south of Punta Patiño. Traveling it is a heart-of-darkness experience: you pass through spectacular jungle inhabited by megafauna including jaguars and pumas while gliding past traditional Emberá and Wounaan villages.

Be forewarned: a trip far up the Río Sambú is not everyone's cup of tea. But the Sambú offers you true adventure, something that may not even be possible anywhere in the Tropics 50 years from now. Even if you travel deep into the Amazon, you'd be hard-pressed to find such wilderness these days.

Boats and boatmen can be hired in La Palma, though once you reach the Río Sambú, you will need to hire a separate dugout canoe and a guide to get further upriver. You will need to do this because the boat you'll hire in La Palma to reach the Sambú will sit too low in the water to navigate the upper portions of the river; to get any further upriver, you must negotiate the use of a shallow dugout in one of the Emberá villages. During the rainy season, the river is navigable by dugout all the way to Pavarandó, the most inland of the eight Emberá communities on the Sambú.

At night, you can make camp where you please if you have a tent. However, unless you've brought an individual tent for your boatman, he will prefer an alternative – making a deal to sleep on the floor of an Emberá family's home. If you can speak Spanish, finding a family to move in with for the night isn't

difficult, and even getting a hot meal is easy. Expect to pay about US$10 per person for shelter and US$5 for food.

EL REAL
pop 1300

El Real dates from the days of the early conquistadors, when they constructed a fort beside the Río Tuira to prevent pirates from sailing upriver and attacking Santa María. Gold from mines in the valley of Cana, to the south, was brought to Santa María, and stored until there was a quantity sufficient to warrant assembling an armada and moving the bullion to Panama City. Today, El Real is one of the largest towns in the Darién, though it's still very much a backwater settlement.

For travelers heading to the Pirre Station, El Real serves as a transit point since flights arrive here from La Palma. Prior to visiting Pirre, you must also stop by the ANAM office in town and pay your entry fee. The best way to locate this office is to ask someone to point you toward it, as none of the wide paths in town have names.

From La Palma, **Aeroperlas** (☎ 315 7500; www .aeroperlas.com) offers three flights per week to El Real (US$35, 15 minutes). For information on getting to Pirre, see opposite.

RANCHO FRÍO (PIRRE STATION)

Pirre is an ANAM ranger station just inside the Parque Nacional Darién, 13km south of El Real as the lemon-spectacled tanager flies. The area around Pirre is the most accessible section of the national park, and the station's strength is that two good hiking trails originate from it. One trail leads to Pirre Mountain ridge, which takes most hikers two days to reach – a tent is a necessity, and you will have to be completely self-sufficient. The other trail winds through jungle to a series of cascades about an hour's hike away. Neither trail should be attempted without a ranger or a local guide as they are not well marked and if you get lost out here, you're finished.

At Pirre Station are **barracks** (cots per person US$10) with a front room with fold-out cots for visitors, a dining area that consists of two tables and four benches beside a very rustic kitchen, a *palapa* (open-sided shelter) with a few chairs, and one outhouse. Bathing is done in a nearby creek, and there is no electricity at the station.

If you plan on eating, you must bring your own food. The rangers will cook your food for you (US$5 a day is most appreciated), but you must provide bottled water or bring a water-purification system or tablets.

Beware: most of Parque Nacional Darién is prime fer-de-lance territory, and these very deadly snakes have been found near the station. Always wear boots and long trousers when you're walking in camp at night or entering the forest at any time.

Getting There & Away
Pirre Station can only be reached by hiking or by a combination of hiking and boating. The hike from El Real takes three hours. You can also take a one-hour canoe ride from El Real to the village of Piji Baisal and then hike for one hour from Piji Baisal to Pirre Station.

If you prefer to hike, take the 'road' connecting El Real and Pirre Station, which is basically a dirt path covered with 2m-high lemongrass. Hiking this barely discernible road takes about three hours and pretty much requires a guide. The ANAM station in El Real can help you find a local guide (expect to pay about US$20).

The alternative is to hire a boatman to take you up the Río Pirre to Piji Baisal. Expect to pay about US$40, plus the cost of gasoline. From Piji Baisal, it's a one-hour hike to the station. Again, you'll need a guide to lead you to the station, as no signs mark the way.

CANA
Nestled in foothills on the eastern slope of Pirre Ridge, the Cana valley is the most isolated place in the Republic of Panama. It's also the heart of the Parque Nacional Darién, and is regarded as one of the finest bird-watching spots in the world. In addition to four species of macaw, Cana is known for its harpy eagles, black-tipped cotingas, dusky-backed jacamars, rufous-cheeked hummingbirds and golden-headed quetzals.

Cana is home to the **ANAM/Ancon field station**, a wooden structure that was built by gold workers during the 1970s, and enlarged in mid-1998 by the wildlife conservation group Ancon. Today, it is the star-attraction in Ancon Expeditions' portfolio of tour offerings. The building itself offers rustic dorms, shared bathrooms and candle-lit evenings. When you consider the awesome hiking and the bird-watching possibilities in the area, the station is simply outstanding.

Ancon Expeditions (Map pp652-3; ☎ 269 9415; www .anconexpeditions.com; El Dorado Bldg, Calle 49 Este near Av 3 Sur, Panama City) offers an excellent five-day, four-night package that includes private charter flights between Panama City and Cana, an

GETTING TO COLOMBIA
The Carr Pan-Americana (Pan-American Hwy) stops at the town of **Yaviza**, and reappears 150km further on, far beyond the Colombian border. Although a trickle of travelers have walked through the infamous **Darién Gap**, the presence of Colombian guerillas, paramilitary, smugglers and bandits make this a potentially suicidal trip.

The border can also be crossed at a rugged point on the Caribbean coast between **Puerto Obaldía** on the Panamanian side, where you can obtain your exit stamp, and the town of **Capurganá** on the Colombian side, where you can obtain your entry stamp. **Aeroperlas** (☎ 315 7500; www.aeroperlas.com) has one flight per week from Panama City to Puerto Obaldía (US$40, one hour). From Puerto Obaldía, you can either walk or boat to the Colombian village of Sapzurro. On foot this takes about 2½ hours, but the track is indistinct in places, and the presence of bandits and smugglers in the area makes boating the better option. From Sapzurro, it's a two-hour walk to Capurganá. Be advised that there is a fair amount of risk crossing here, and you should get solid information about the security situation before attempting it.

For information on sailing to Colombia, which is by far the safest of the available options, see p707.

English-speaking guide, all meals and accommodations (including tent camping along the Pirre Mountain Trail, with all provisions carried by porters). For rates, see p706.

YAVIZA
pop 3300

Yaviza is the end of the road – literally. Here, the Interamericana stops abruptly without so much as a sign announcing that you've reached the famous Darién Gap. From here, a narrow stretch of dirt road is lined with a few odd buildings and people who appear to have nothing but time on their hands.

If you have a pressing need to spend the night in Yaviza, the **Hotel 3 Americas** (r from US$8) has some tired-looking rooms with a mess of a communal bathroom.

There are eight buses daily between Panama City and Yaviza (US$15, seven to 10 hours). From here, foolish travelers can hike along the Darién Gap if they so choose, though you'd best sort out your personal affairs first (see p709). If you do make it to Colombia – and we can't emphasize enough how seriously dangerous and inadvisable this route is – send us a postcard.

PANAMA DIRECTORY

ACCOMMODATIONS

Prices cited in this book for accommodations are low-season rates, and they include Panama's 10% tax on hotel rooms. High-season rates are generally about 15% higher.

There is usually no shortage of places to stay in Panama, except during holidays or special events outside Panama City, when advance reservations may be necessary.

Budget lodgings typically range from US$5 per person to US$20 for a double room. Hotels in the midrange category usually charge about US$20 to US$40 for a double room.

ACTIVITIES
Bird-Watching

Go birding in Panama, and you'll see more variety than anywhere else in Central America. More than 940 species of bird – native, migratory and endemic – have been identified here. This diversity of species is due to Panama's location relative to two continents and its narrow girth. Birds migrating between North and South America tend to be funneled into a small area.

The famous resplendent quetzal, the Maya bird of paradise and the symbol of Central America, is most abundant in western Panama. It inhabits areas around **Parque Nacional Volcán Barú** (p678), where it is commonly sighted throughout the year.

The **Camino del Oleoducto** (Pipeline Rd; p666) trail near Panama City is a favorite with birders; more than 500 species were sighted there in a single day during a Christmas bird count.

The ANAM/Ancon field station in **Cana** (p709) is often regarded as one of the top birding destinations in the world, and is the best place in Panama to spot the national bird, the harpy eagle.

Diving & Snorkeling

Panama has numerous islands with good snorkeling and diving sights. On the Caribbean coast, **Bocas del Toro** (p681) and the **San Blás Archipelago** (p700) are prime spots. Dive shops on Bocas del Toro rent snorkeling and diving gear, and offer PADI-certified classes, while snorkeling in San Blás is more of the do-it-yourself variety. There is also good diving and snorkeling around **Portobelo** (p698) as well as a couple of reputable dive shops in town.

On the Pacific coast, there is good snorkeling in the **Golfo de Chiriquí** (p673) and in the **Archipiélago de las Perlas** (p670). Although coral reefs in the Pacific are not as vibrant as their Caribbean counterparts, you're bound to see some big fish here as well as the occasional pelagic creature.

You can rent equipment at the destinations listed above, but avid snorkelers should bring their own. **Scubapanama** (Map pp648-9; ☎ 261 3841; www.scubapanama.com), based in Panama City, offers diving trips throughout the country.

Fishing

With 1518 islands, 2988km of coast and 480 rivers, there's no problem finding a fishing spot in Panama. Possibilities include deep-sea fishing, fishing for bass in **Lago Gatún** on the Panama Canal, trout fishing in the rivers running down **Volcán Barú** (p678) and surf casting on any of Panama's Pacific and Caribbean beaches.

Hiking

Hiking opportunities abound in Panama. In the Chiriquí highlands, the **Sendero Los Quetzales** (p679) winds through Parque Nacional Volcán Barú, and is regarded as the country's top hike. **Parque Internacional La Amistad** also has some fine, short trails, starting near its Cerro Punta (p679) entrance.

From Boquete, you can hike to the top of **Volcán Barú** (p676), Panama's highest point and only volcano. The little town of **El Valle** (p694), which is nestled in a picturesque valley, is a fine place for casual walkers.

Near Panama City on the shores of the canal, **Parque Nacional Soberanía** (p666) contains a section of the old Sendero Las Cruces used by the Spanish to cross between the coasts. **Parque Natural Metropolitano** (p657), on the outskirts of Panama City, also has some good walks leading to a panorama of the city.

You can also go trekking through lush rain forests in the **Parque Nacional Darién** (p703), though this is best arranged through a reputable guide owing to the guerilla activity in the region.

See p712 for some advice on hiking.

Surfing

The country's top surfing destination is the Caribbean archipelago of **Bocas del Toro** (p685), which attracts strong winter swells and surfers from around the world. Although it remains an off-the-beaten-path destination, **Santa Catalina** (p693) on the Pacific Coast has some of the most challenging breaks in Central America. There is also uncrowded surfing on the laid-back island Caribbean island of **Isla Grande** (p699).

White-Water Rafting

White-water rafting trips are available on the Ríos Chiriquí and Chiriquí Vieja in Chiriquí Province, and are best arranged in the mountain town of **Boquete** (p676).

BOOKS

Excellent books dealing with facets of Panamanian history include the following:

The Sack of Panamá: Sir Henry Morgan's Adventures on the Spanish Main, by Peter Earle, is a vivid account of the Welsh pirate's looting and destruction of Panama City in 1671.

The Path Between the Seas: The Creation of the Panama Canal, by David McCullough, is a readable and exciting account of the building of the Panama Canal. It's 700 pages long and reads like a suspense novel.

How Wall Street Created a Nation: J.P. Morgan, Teddy Roosevelt and the Panama Canal, by Ovidio Diaz Espino, probes deeply into the dark alliances and backroom deals that culminated in the Canal's construction.

On a more recent note, *Inside Panama,* by Tom Barry and John Lindsay-Poland, is a look at the political, economic and human-rights scenes in Panama, with special emphasis on Panamanian society since the 1960s and on US-Panama relations from that time through to the mid-1990s.

BUSINESS HOURS

Opening hours for travel agents, tour operators and other businesses are normally 8am to noon and 1:30pm to 5pm weekdays, and 8am to noon on Saturdays. Government offices, including post offices, are open 8am to 4pm on weekdays and don't close for lunch. Most banks are open 8:30am to 1pm or 3pm on weekdays; some have Saturday hours as well. Shops and pharmacies are generally open from around 9am or 10am until 6pm or 7pm Monday to Saturday.

Grocery stores keep longer hours, opening around 8am and closing around 8pm or 9pm. A handful of grocery stores in Panama City stay open 24 hours.

Restaurants usually open for lunch from noon to 3pm and dinner from 6pm to 10pm. Those that offer breakfast open from 7am to 10am. On Sundays, many restaurants are closed. In Panama City and David, restaurants open later on Fridays and Saturdays, until about 11pm or midnight. Most bars are open from around noon to 10pm, later on Friday and Saturday nights (typically 2am). Nightclubs in Panama City open around 10pm or 11pm and close at 3am or 4am.

CLIMATE

Panama's tourist season is during the dry season from mid-December to mid-April. The weather can be hot and steamy in the lowlands during the rainy season, when the humidity makes the heat oppressive. But it won't rain nonstop; rain in Panama, as elsewhere in the tropics, tends to come in sudden short downpours that freshen the air, and is followed by sunshine. It's more comfortable to do long, strenuous hiking in the dry season.

DANGERS & ANNOYANCES

Crime is a problem in certain parts of Panama City. The city's better districts, however, are safer than in many other capitals: witness

PANAMA

the all-night restaurants and activity on the streets at night. On the other hand, it is not safe to walk around at night on the outskirts of Casco Viejo – be careful in the side streets of this district even in the daytime. In general, stay where it's well lit and there are plenty of people around.

Colón has some upscale residential areas, but most of the city is a sad slum widely known for street crime. If you walk around, even in the middle of the day, well-meaning residents will inform you that you are in danger.

Parts of the Darién Province, which borders Colombia, are extremely dangerous. Not only is it easy to get hopelessly lost, but parts of the province are used by guerillas from Colombia, the paramilitary chasing the guerillas, and even plain old thieves pretending to be guerillas. Particularly treacherous is the area between Boca de Cupe and Colombia, which is the traditional path through the Darién Gap. Dengue and malaria (chloroquine-resistant) are serious hazards in this area.

Plying the waters of the Archipiélago de San Blás are numerous Colombian boats that run back and forth between the Zona Libre in Colón and Cartagena, Colombia. It has been well documented that some of these boats carry cocaine on their northbound voyages. If you decide to ride on one of these slow cargo boats, be forewarned that your crew may be trafficking drugs.

Most other areas of Panama are quite safe. Police corruption is no longer a big problem in Panama, but it's not unheard of for a police officer to stop a motorist and levy a fine to be paid on the spot. Your only option may be to bargain the fine down.

You should be adequately prepared for hiking trips. Always carry plenty of water, even on short journeys, and always bring adequate clothing; jungles *do* cool down at night, particularly at higher elevations. Hikers have been known to get lost in rain forests – even seemingly user-friendly ones such as Parque Nacional Volcán Barú. A Panamanian hiker who entered that park in 1995 was never seen again; it's assumed that he got lost, died of hypothermia and was fed upon by various creatures.

Never walk in unmarked rain forest; if there's no trail going in, you can assume that there won't be one when you decide to turn around and come back out. Always let someone know where you are going, in order to narrow the search area if need be.

DISABLED TRAVELERS

The **Instituto Panameño de Habilitación Especial** (IPHE; Panamanian Institute for Special Rehabilitation; ☎ 261 0500; Camino Real, Betania, Panama City; ⏲ 7am-4pm) was created by the government to assist all disabled people in Panama, including foreign tourists. However, the law does not require – and Panamanian businesses do not provide – discounts for foreign tourists with disabilities.

Panama is not wheelchair friendly; with the exception of wheelchair ramps outside a few upscale hotels, parking spaces for the disabled and perhaps a few dozen oversized bathroom stalls, accommodation for people with physical disabilities does not exist in Panama. Even at the best hotels, you won't find railings in showers or beside toilets.

If you have a disability and want to communicate with another disabled person who might have been to Panama recently, consider becoming a member of **Travelin' Talk Network** (TTN; ☎ in the USA 303-232-2979; www.travelintalk .net; membership per year US$20). This organization offers a worldwide directory of members with various disabilities who communicate among themselves about travel.

EMBASSIES & CONSULATES
Panamanian Embassies & Consulates
Panama has embassies and consulates in the following countries:

Canada (☎ 613-236 7177; fax 613-236 5775; 130 Albert St, Suite 300, Ottawa, Ontario K1P 5G4)

Colombia (☎ 257 5067, 257 5068; fax 257 5068; Calle 92, No 7-70, Bogotá)

France (☎ 01 47 83 23 32, 01 45 66 42 44; fax 01 45 67 99 43; 145 Av de Suffren, 75015 Paris)

Germany (☎ 228-36 1036; fax 228-36 3558; Lutzowstrasse 1, 53173 Bonn)

Mexico (☎ 5-250 4229; fax 5-250 4045; Schiller 326, 8th fl, Colonia Chapultepec-Morales, CP 11570, Mexico DF)

UK (☎ 171-493 4646; fax 171-493 4499; 48 Park St, London W1Y 3PD)

USA (☎ 202-483-1407; fax 202-483-8413; 2862 McGill Tce NW, Washington, DC 20008)

Embassies & Consulates in Panama
More than 50 countries have embassies or consulates in Panama City. For contact details see the Panama White Pages, listed under 'Embajada de [country]' or 'Consulados.' With the exception of the USA and France, you'll find most embassies in the Marbella district of Panama City.

Ireland, Australia and New Zealand have no representation in Panama.

Canada (☎ 264 9731; fax 263 8083; World Trade Center, Calle 53 Este, Marbella)

Colombia (☎ 264 9266; World Trade Center, Calle 53 Este, Marbella)

Costa Rica David (☎ /fax 774 1923; Calle C Sur btwn Avs 1 & 2 Este); Panama City (☎ 264 2980; fax 264 4057; Av Samuel Lewis)

France (Map p655; ☎ 228 7824; Plaza de Francia, Paseo las Bóvedas, Casco Viejo)

Germany (☎ 263 7733; World Trade Center, Calle 53 Este, Marbella)

Holland (☎ 264 7257; Calle 50, Marbella)

UK (Map pp652-3; ☎ 269 0866; Swiss Tower Calle 53 Este, Marbella)

USA (Map pp652-3; ☎ 207 7000; Avs Balboa & Calle 37 Este, La Exposición)

FESTIVALS & EVENTS

Panama has a range of colorful festivals that encompass everything from traditional folkloric fests to indigenous celebrations. For the lion's share of the country's revelry, head to the interior, where some of Panama's most famous events take place. For more details see p695.

The following events are the country's better known celebrations:

Carnaval (February/March) On the four days preceding Ash Wednesday, costumes, music, dancing and general merriment prevail in Panama City and in the Península de Azuero towns of Las Tablas, Chitré, Villa de Los Santos and Parita.

Semana Santa (March/April) On Holy Week (the week before Easter), the country hosts many special events, including the re-enactment of the crucifixion and resurrection of Christ; on Good Friday, religious processions are held across the country.

Corpus Christi (May/June) Held 40 days after Easter, this religious holiday features colorful celebrations in Villa de Los Santos. Masked and costumed dancers representing angels, devils, imps and other mythological figures enact dances, acrobatics and dramas.

Festival of the Black Christ On October 21, thousands of visitors come to honor the black Christ in Portobelo.

FOOD & DRINK
Food

The national dish of Panama is *sancocho*, a fairly spicy chicken-and-vegetable stew. *Ropa vieja* (literally 'old clothes'), a spicy shredded beef combination served over rice, is another common and tasty dish. Rice – grown on dry land – is the staple of Panama and is seemingly served with everything.

As elsewhere in the Americas, meat figures prominently in the Panamanian diet. In addition to staples such as *bistec* (steak) and *carne asado* (roast meat), you'll encounter specialties such as *carimañola*, which is a roll made from ground and boiled yuca that is filled with chopped meat and then deep fried. Far more common – in restaurants, snack bars and just about anywhere food is sold – are empanadas, which are corn turnovers filled with ground meat and fried. If you get them fresh, they're a fine treat. Another favorite is the tamale, which is cornmeal with a few spices and chicken or pork, all wrapped in banana leaves and boiled.

Gallo pinto, which means 'spotted rooster,' is traditionally served at breakfast, and consists of a soupy mixture of rice and black beans, often with a pig's tail thrown in for flavor. This dish, lightly spiced with herbs, is filling and tasty, and it sometimes comes with *natilla* (a cross between sour cream and custard) or *huevos fritos/revueltos* (fried/scrambled eggs).

Another item you might see at breakfast is a side of *tortillas de maíz*. Unlike those found in Mexico and Guatemala, Panamanian tortillas are much thicker, and are essentially deep-fried cornmeal cakes. They go quite nicely with eggs or roast meat. *Hojaldras* are also served at breakfasts and available at snack bars. Not unlike a donut, this deep-fried mass of dough is served hot, and you then cover it with sugar.

At lunch *(almuerzo)*, many Panamanians opt for simple *comida corriente* (also called *casado*), the meal of the working class. This is an inexpensive set meal containing various items. Beef, chicken or fish is served alongside *arroz* (rice), *frijoles* (black beans), *plátano* (fried plantain), chopped *repollo* (cabbage) and maybe an egg or an avocado.

Seafood is also abundant in Panama. On the Caribbean coast and islands, everyday foods include shrimp, Caribbean king crab, octopus, lobster and fish such as corvina. In areas along the Caribbean coast, you'll also find a West Indian influence to the dishes. Seafood is often mixed with coconut milk; coconut rice and coconut bread are also Caribbean treats.

In Panama City you'll often see men pushing carts and selling *raspados*, cones filled with shaved ice topped with fruit syrup and sweetened condensed milk. This is no gourmet dish, but it's a favorite among Panamanians, particularly the under-10 crowd.

PANAMA

Drinks

Fresh fruit drinks, sweetened with heaped tablespoons of sugar and mixed with water or milk, are called *chichas,* and are extremely popular.

These drinks originated in Chiriquí Province, and are now commonly found throughout Panama. Also be on the lookout for *chicheme,* a nonalcoholic drink found in Panama and nowhere else. This delicious concoction consists of milk, sweet corn, cinnamon and vanilla.

Coffee is traditionally served very strong and offered with cream or condensed milk. Café Durán is the most popular of the local brands, and is quite good. Cappuccinos and espressos are increasing in popularity, and are commonly available in major cities and tourist destinations. Tea (including herbal tea) is available in the cities but difficult to find in towns. Milk is pasteurized and safe to drink. The usual brands of soft drinks are available.

The national alcoholic drink is made of *seco,* milk and ice. *Seco,* like rum, is distilled from sugarcane, but it doesn't taste anything like the rum you know. This is the drink of campesinos (farmers). Order a *seco con leche* in a martini lounge in Panama City and you'll likely receive some odd looks, but don't leave the country without trying to get a taste of real Panama, .

By far the most popular alcoholic beverage in Panama is *cerveza* (beer), and the most popular local brands are Soberana, Panamá, Balboa, Cristal and Atlas. None of these are very flavorful, but when served ice-cold on a hot day, they do the trick. A large Atlas at a typical cantina can cost as little as US$0.50; the same beer can cost you US$2.50 at a decent restaurant.

There's a drink that the campesinos in the central provinces particularly like: *vino de palma,* which is sap extracted from the trunk of an odd variety of palm tree called *palma de corozo.* The sap from the palm tree can be drunk immediately (it's delicious and sweet) or fermented (which goes down like firewater).

GAY & LESBIAN TRAVELERS

Other than the gay float during Carnaval in the capital, there are few open expressions of homosexuality in Panama. As in other Latin American countries, gay men and lesbians remain closeted or else suffer a great deal of discrimination.

Panama City has a few gay and lesbian clubs (not openly advertised, however). Outside Panama City, gay bars are hard to come by. In most instances, gays and lesbians just blend in with the straight crowd at the hipper places and avoid cantinas and other conventional lairs of homophobia. There are several Panamanian websites for gays and lesbians that focus on upcoming events and parties, new club openings and political issues in Panama City.

HOLIDAYS

New Year's Day (January 1)
Martyrs' Day (January 9)
Carnaval (February to March)
Semana Santa (March to April) Holy Week
Labor Day (May 1)
Founding of Old Panama (August 15)
All Souls' Day (November 2)
Independence from Colombia (November 3)
First Call for Independence (November 10)
Independence from Spain (November 28)
Mothers' Day (December 8)
Christmas Day (December 25)

INTERNET ACCESS

Internet cafés are widely available throughout the country. Most charge around US$1 to US$2 per hour.

INTERNET RESOURCES

IPAT (www.ipat.gob.pa) Panama's tourist website in Spanish. Also has a sister site in English; (www.visit panama.com).
Lanic (http://lanic.utexas.edu/la/ca/panama) Has an outstanding collection of links from the University of Texas Latin American Information Center.
Panama info (www.panamainfo.com) Also in English.

MAPS

The **Instituto Geográfico Nacional** (Tommy Guardia; Map pp652-3; ☎ 236 2444; ☯ 8am-4pm Mon-Fri), in Panama City, sells topographical maps of selected cities and regions. Various free tourist publications distributed in Panama also have maps.

MEDIA
Newspapers & Magazines

La Prensa (www.prensa.com in Spanish) is the most widely circulated daily newspaper in Panama.

Other major Spanish-language dailies include *La Estrella de Panamá, El Panamá América, El Universal* and *Crítica*.

The **Panama News** (www.thepanamanews.com) is published in English every two weeks. It is distributed free in Panama City. *The Visitor*, written in English and Spanish and targeted towards tourists, is another free publication. The *Miami Herald International Edition* is available in some upscale hotels.

Radio & TV

There are three commercial TV stations in Panama (channels two, four and 13) and two devoted to public broadcasting (five and 11). Many hotels have cable TV with Spanish and English channels.

Panama has over 90, mostly commercial, radio stations. The more popular:

Classical 105.7
Latin jazz 88.9
Latin rock 106.7
Reggae 88.1
Salsa 97.1 and 102.1
Traditional Panamanian 94.5
US rock 93.9 and 98.9

MONEY

Panama uses the US dollar as its currency. The official name for it here is the balboa, but it's exactly the same bill, and in practice people use the terms *'dólar'* and 'balboa' interchangeably. Panamanian coins are of the same value, size and metal as US coins; both are used. Coins include one, five, 10, 25 and 50 *centavos* (or *centésimos*); 100 *centavos* equal one balboa. Be aware that most businesses won't break US$50 and US$100 bills and those that do may require you to present your passport. For exchange rates at the time of research, see right.

ATMs

Throughout Panama, ATMs are readily available except in the most isolated places. Look for the red *'sistema clave'* signs to find an ATM. They accept cards on most networks (Plus, Cirrus, MasterCard, Visa and Amex).

Credit Cards

Although accepted at travel agencies, upscale hotels and many restaurants, credit cards can be problematic almost everywhere else. In short, carry enough cash to get you to the next bank or ATM.

Exchange Rates

The table shows currency exchange rates at the time this book went to press.

Country	Unit	US dollars (US$)
Australia	A$1	0.85
Canada	C$1	0.95
Euro Zone	€1	1.40
Japan	¥100	0.80
New Zealand	NZ$1	0.80
UK	UK£1	2.05

Taxes

A tax of 10% is added to the price of hotel rooms – when you inquire about a hotel, ask whether the quoted price includes the tax. Hotel prices given in this book include the 10% tax. A 5% sales tax is levied on nonfood products.

Tipping

The standard tipping rate in Panama is around 10% of the bill; in small cafés and more casual places, tipping is not necessary. Taxi drivers do not expect tips.

Traveler's Checks

Although they can be cashed at a few banks, traveler's checks are rarely accepted by businesses, and traveler's checks in currencies other than US dollars are not accepted anywhere in Panama. Some banks will only accept American Express traveler's checks. The banks that do accept traveler's checks typically charge an exchange fee equal to 1% of the amount of the check.

POST

Airmail to the USA takes five to 10 days and costs US$0.35 (postcards US$0.25); to Europe and Australia it takes 10 days and costs US$0.45 (postcards US$0.40). Panama has neither vending machines for stamps nor drop-off boxes for mail. You may be able to buy stamps and send mail from an upscale hotel to avoid going to the post office and standing in line.

Most post offices are open from 7am to 6pm on weekdays and from 7am to 4:30pm on Saturdays. General delivery mail can be addressed to '(name), Entrega General, (town and province), República de Panamá.' Be sure the sender calls the country 'República de Panamá' rather than simply 'Panamá,' or the mail may be sent back.

RESPONSIBLE TRAVEL

Traveling sensitively in Panama means being mindful of the environment around you. Try to patronize local businesses and industries, and spend your money where it will go directly to the people working for it.

For information on responsible tourism in the Comarca de Kuna Yala, see p702.

Don't support businesses that keep caged animals – it's an offense to keep a parrot, toucan or macaw in a cage; if it bothers you report the crime to **Ancon** (Map pp648-9; ☎ 314 0060). And – hopefully this goes without saying – don't eat endangered species. If you see *tortuga* (sea turtle), *huevos de tortuga* (turtle eggs), *cazón* (shark), *conejo pintado* (paca), *ñeque* (agouti) or *enado* (deer) on the menu, take your business elsewhere.

SHOPPING

A remarkable variety of imported goods, including cameras, electronic equipment and clothing, is sold in Panama, both in Colón's tax-free Zona Libre (p696) and in Panama City (p662).

The favorite handicraft souvenir from Panama is the *mola,* a colorful, intricate, multi-layered appliqué textile sewn by Kuna women of the Archipiélago de San Blás (p703). Small, simple souvenir *molas* can be bought for as little as US$5, but the best ones are sold on the islands and can fetch several hundred dollars.

It's possible to purchase high-quality replicas of *huacas* – golden objects made on the isthmus centuries before the Spanish conquest and placed with Indians at the time of burial. These range in price from US$5 to more than US$1000.

Other handicrafts that can be purchased include wood carvings (from the *cocobolo* tree), *tagua* carvings (from the egg-sized *tagua* nut) and baskets – these are all made by the Wounaan and Emberá tribes.

STUDYING

Panama is home to several Spanish-language schools, which are located in Panama City (p658), Boquete (p677) and Bocas del Toro (p686).

TELEPHONE

Panama's country code is ☎ 507. To phone Panama from abroad, use the country code before the seven-digit Panamanian telephone number. There are no local area codes in Panama.

Telephone calls to anywhere within Panama can be made from pay phones. Local calls cost US$0.10 for the first three minutes, then US$0.05 per minute. You can buy Telechip phonecards at pharmacies, corner shops and Cable & Wireless offices (the national phone company) in denominations of US$3, US$5, US$10, and US$20. You then plug this into the phone and dial the local number. Some public phones accept both cards and coins, but many accept only cards. Note that calling cell phones (which typically begin with a '6') is much pricier (US$0.35 for the first minute, then US$0.10 per minute thereafter).

TOURIST INFORMATION

The **Instituto Panameño de Turismo** (IPAT, Panamanian Institute of Tourism; Map pp648-9; ☎ 226 7000; www.ipat .gob.pa; Centro Atlapa, Vía Israel, San Francisco, Panama City) is the national tourism agency. In addition to this head office, IPAT runs offices in Bocas del Toro, Boquete, Colón, David, Paso Canoas, Penonomé, Portobelo, Santiago, Villa de Los Santos, Las Tablas, El Valle and Pedasí. There are smaller information counters at the ruins of Panamá Viejo, in Casco Viejo, and in both the Tocumen International Airport and the Albrook domestic airport.

IPAT has a few useful maps and brochures, but often has a problem keeping enough in stock for distribution to tourists. Most offices are staffed with people who speak only Spanish, and the helpfulness of any particular office depends on the person at the counter. Some employees really try to help, but others are just passing the time. As a general rule, you will get more useful information if you have specific questions.

Panama provides tourist information in the USA (☎ 800-231-0568), and IPAT literature and other information is sometimes available at Panamanian consulates and embassies.

TOURS

In Panama, the standard for nature guides and tours is set by **Ancon Expeditions** (Map pp652-3; ☎ 269 9414/9415; www.anconexpeditions.com; El Dorado Bldg, Calle 49 A Este, Panama City). Created by Panama's top private conservation organization, Ancon Expeditions employs most of the country's best nature guides, offers a variety of exciting tours, and provides an impeccable level of service. All of Ancon Expeditions' guides are avid birders, speak flawless English and are extremely enthusiastic about their work.

VISAS

A valid passport is required to enter Panama, though additional requirements vary by country. Note that as of January 2007, US citizens can no longer enter Panama with just a driver's license and a birth certificate.

Citizens of the UK, Germany, the Netherlands, Switzerland, Spain, Finland, Austria, as well as a few South and Central American countries, need only a passport. Most other nationals, including US, Canadian, Australian and New Zealand citizens, may enter with a US$5 tourist card, available from consulates, embassies and also from airlines, the Tica Bus company, at the airport or at some border posts upon entry.

Visas must be obtained before entering the country by nationals of many other countries not listed above. Visas are issued at Panamanian embassies and consulates and cost around US$20, depending on the nationality of the applicant.

If you are heading to Colombia, Venezuela or some other South American country, you may need an onward ticket before you'll be allowed entry, or even allowed to board the plane out.

A quick check with the appropriate embassy – easy to do by telephone in Panama City – will tell you whether the country you're heading to has a requirement to have an onward ticket.

You are required by law to carry either your passport or a copy with you at all times, and police officers reserve the right to see your identification at any time.

Visa Extensions

Visas and tourist cards are both good for 90 days. To extend your stay, you'll have to go to an office of Migración y Naturalización (Immigration) – it's advisable to go to the one in Panama City (p651). You must bring your passport and photocopies of the page with your personal information and of the stamp of your most recent entry to Panama. You also must bring two passport-size photos, an onward air or bus ticket, a letter to the director stating your reasons for wishing to extend your visit, and a letter from a Panamanian citizen who accepts responsibility for you during your stay.

You will have to fill out a *próloga de turista* form and pay US$15. You will then be issued a plastic photo ID card.

If you have extended your time, you will also need to obtain a *permiso de salida* (permit to leave the country). For this, bring your passport and a *paz y salvo* form to the immigration office. *Paz y salvos* are issued at Ministerios de Hacienda y Tesoro, found in towns with immigration offices, which simply require that you bring in your passport, fill out a form and pay US$1.

VOLUNTEERING

The **National Association for the Conservation of Nature** (Ancon; ☎ 314 0061; www.ancon.org in Spanish) offers opportunities for volunteering on projects in national parks and other beautiful natural areas. Volunteers might get involved in protecting nesting turtles near Bocas del Toro, do environmental-education work in the Darién or assist park rangers. It's possible to volunteer for any length of time from a week to several months; you won't get paid, but Ancon will supply your basic necessities, such as food and shelter.

For other volunteer opportunities in Panama, see p658 (Panama City) and p706 (Darién Province).

WOMEN TRAVELERS

Female travelers find Panama safe and pleasant to visit. Some Panamanian men may make flirtatious comments or stare at single women, both local and foreign, but comments are rarely blatantly rude; the usual thing is a smiling 'mi amor' (my love) or an appreciative hiss or a honk of the horn.

The best way to deal with this is to do what Panamanian women do – ignore the comments and don't look at the man making them.

Panamanians are generally fairly conservative in dress. Women travelers are advised to avoid skimpy or see-through clothing. And although Emberá women in the Darién go topless, it would be insulting for travelers to follow suit.

Women traveling solo will get more attention than those traveling in pairs or groups. Although assault and rape of foreign travelers is rare, avoid placing yourself in risky scenarios. Don't walk alone in isolated places, don't hitchhike and always pay particular attention to your surroundings.

PANAMA

WORKING

It's difficult for foreigners to find work in Panama as the government doesn't want them to take jobs away from Panamanians. Basically, the only foreigners legally employed in Panama work for their own businesses, possess skills not found in Panama or work for companies that have special agreements with the Panamanian government.

Small boats transiting the Panama Canal sometimes take on backpackers as deckhands (line handlers) in exchange for free passage, room and food. Inquiries can be made at the Panama Canal Yacht Club in Colón; some boat owners post notices in pensións. The official rate for line handling is US$55 per day, but anyone who pays this fee hires experienced locals. Competing with the locals for this work could get you and the boat captain in trouble.

Restaurants that hire foreign staff are often shut down for immigration violations.

Central America Directory

CONTENTS

This chapter provides general information on Central America. Country-specific details are included in the Directory at the back of each country chapter. Also, each country title page displays 'key facts' information, such as travel tips and popular border crossings.

ACCOMMODATIONS

Central America's sleeping options range from thin-wall sand-floor shacks to luxury beach resorts. This book focuses on the cheap guys: bunk-bed hostels, *casas de huéspedes* (guesthouses) with fan-cooled rooms and shared bathrooms, lean-to cabañas (bungalows) on a beach, or simply trees to hang a hammock from. A few worthy splurges – of US$50 or more – are noted here and there.

Unless otherwise noted, prices listed in the book reflect high-season rates (roughly July and August, Christmas to Easter) and include applicable national taxes. Prices do change; use the prices in this book as a gauge, not law. Showing the price listed in the book is a far less successful tactic to getting a lower rate than simply asking for a discount. Do ask. When business is slow or if you're planning on staying several nights, it's often possible to get a cheaper rate. Be prepared to take 'no' for an answer.

Generally Nicaragua, Honduras and Guatemala are the cheapest countries, Mexico and Belize (and many beach destinations), the most expensive. Variables are whether you have a private bathroom, cold water and can handle a fan over air-con (air-con can double the cost in many places!). Generally, hostels are usually around US$6 to US$8 per person, and OK hotels (with shared bathroom and fan) are about US$10 to US$15 per double in the bulk of Central America – if your math skills are in practice, you'll see two people can often stay in a hotel for less than in a dorm.

Reservations – by email, phone or fax – are not possible at many places, much less needed. Key exceptions are tourist areas during peak season, particularly during Semana Santa (Easter Week) when locals are traveling around the region too.

Camping

Organized campgrounds aren't commonly found in the region. If you plan on camping, bring your own gear. And bug repellent. Facilities at campgrounds can vary: some have fire pits, latrines and water. Others have *nada*. Nothing.

Some hostels set aside areas for campers. Some national parks and reserves (particularly in Costa Rica) have basic facilities, but they can be hit-and-miss – sometimes packed and noisy. Prices range from US$3 to US$10 per person. In some places it's feasible to ask to camp on private land.

Guesthouses & Hotels

The most popular places to stay are the cheap guesthouses and hotels. Many are small (10 or so rooms) and family run, and (depending on the family) can be fun, attractive and offer cheap deals that practically plead for another night. That said, you can also expect a night or two on a dumpy bed with smeared mosquito remains on the walls and a smelly leaky-faucet shower (thankfully) down the hall.

Most rooms have a fan and shared bathroom. Many do not provide a towel or soap. Rooms with air-con and TV (generally US$20 and up) start at double the price of a room with fan. Generally breakfast is not included in the overnight rate.

'Hot water' can be lukewarm and working only at certain hours of the day. Beware of the electric shower: a cold-water showerhead juiced by an electric heating element. Don't touch it, or anything metal, while in the shower or you may get a shock.

Used toilet paper should be placed in the receptacle provided.

We've tried our best to avoid including places used by the 'hourly' crowd or prostitutes. If you stumble on some we've included, please let us know.

Hammocks & Bungalows

Sleeping in a hammock can make for a breezier night than on a bed in a stuffy room. Many beach towns have hammock rooms or areas; it's generally the same price as a dorm for a space (and a hammock). Beach cabañas (or *cabinas*) provide memorable stays on the beach or in the jungle. Many of these are simple thatched-roof huts with a dirt or sand floor; others are electrified deals, with fans and fine décor.

Homestays

Nothing offers more insight into local culture than staying with a local family. Towns with Spanish-language school scenes, such as Antigua or Quetzaltenango in Guatemala, or Granada in Nicaragua, can arrange homestays for their students. Many can even arrange for you to stay with a family for a week or longer, even if you're not studying. Homestays can be arranged in many other towns as well. A week's stay ranges from US$50 to US$70 per person, including most meals. See Studying in the Directory for individual countries, or Courses listed under individual towns for more information. See p18 for a suggested itinerary that takes in many opportunities for homestays.

Hostels

Hostels are found throughout Central America – generally charging US$3 to US$10 for a bunk, usually US$8 or so – though your Hostelling International (HI) membership isn't particularly useful here, as many hostels are independently run. Mexico and Costa Rica are exceptions, with many HI-affiliated hostels.

ACTIVITIES

Coastal fun is Central America's most popular draw for tourists: the Pacific is booming on surfers' itineraries, while the Caribbean has the best diving and most of the white-sand beaches. Mountains and volcanoes run through most of the region, offering many compelling (and often tough) hiking and cycling options.

See the Directories for each country for specific details on activities available throughout the region. Also see p11 for a list of our favorite activities and p16 for an activity-based itinerary.

Canopy Tours

These zip-line trips sliding over jungle and mountains may not be the most natural of Central American activities, but you can at least tickle your inner Tarzan. You'll find opportunities all over Costa Rica, including US$45 trips in Monteverde (p575). Outside La Ceiba in Honduras there's a choice; either p395, or an hour-long zip nearby (p399) costs US$36 – about the same cost to go down Volcán Mombacho outside Granada, Nicaragua (p495).

Cycling

Many shops rent bicycles for local exploring. Some places offer guided cycling trips – such as to Maya villages from San Cristóbal de Las Casas, Mexico (p69) and coffee plantations or ridge rides from Antigua, Guatemala (p108). Cycling is also a fine way to explore local villages in other countries, though it is best to bring your own bike for these trips (along with proof that you own the bike).

See p741 for a quick rundown on the joys and pitfalls of cycling your way around the region.

Diving & Snorkeling

Some of Latin America's (and the world's) finest diving and snorkeling spots are found

---

SAFETY GUIDELINES FOR DIVING

Before embarking on a scuba-diving, skin-diving or snorkeling trip, carefully consider the following points to ensure a safe and enjoyable experience. Also see p411 for tips on not harming coral during a reef dive.

- Possess a current diving certification card from a recognized scuba-diving instructional agency (if scuba diving).
- Be sure you are healthy and feel comfortable diving.
- Obtain reliable information about physical and environmental conditions at the dive site (eg from a reputable local dive operator).
- Be aware of local laws, regulations and etiquette relating to marine life and the environment.
- Dive only at sites within your realm of experience; if available, engage the services of a competent, professionally trained dive instructor or dive master.
- Be aware that underwater conditions vary significantly from one region, or even site, to another. Seasonal changes can significantly alter any site and dive conditions. These differences influence the way divers dress for a dive and what diving techniques they use.

---

along the barrier reefs off Central America's Caribbean shores. Sites up and down the coast – from Mexico to Panama – offer rich marine life, sunken ships and deep holes. Some of the most famous dive spots can be found at Bay Islands, Honduras (p408); Cozumel, Mexico (p51); the reefs off Belize's northern cayes (p230); and the more low-key Corn Islands, Nicaragua (p516).

Honduras' Bay Islands are famous for good-value dives and scuba courses; taking the four-day Professional Association of Diving Instructors (PADI) open-water diving certification course here costs about US$250, about US$100 cheaper than in Mexico.

Region-wide, snorkeling day trips out to a couple of reef spots can be taken for US$10 to US$30 or so, and dives start at around US$25 or US$35 in Honduras, or US$70 in Mexico. Most dive shops will rent diving equipment – always check it carefully before going under. Be sure to bring evidence of your certification if you plan to dive.

It's possible to dive in the Pacific too, though conditions are generally murkier. The best time for diving in the Pacific is October to February. San Juan del Sur (p500) in Nicaragua has a dive shop. The crater lakes in Laguna de Apoyo, Nicaragua (see p495) are another good option.

Mexico offers other-worldly dives in cenotes (limestone sinkholes filled with rain water). Check some options reachable from Tulum (p54).

For safety considerations, see above.

Also check out Lonely Planet's detailed diving guides to Cozumel, the Bay Islands and Belize.

Hiking

Central America's stunning natural environment, volcanoes and abundant wildlife makes for great hiking. The terrain ranges from cloud and rain forests to lowland jungles, river trails and palm-lined beaches.

Jungle trekking can be strenuous, and hikers should be prepared. If you want to camp, bring your own gear as its availability is limited here.

Popular hikes in the region range from volcanoes around Antigua in Guatemala (p107) or El Imposible in El Salvador (p304), to prehistoric rock carvings on Nicaragua's Isla de Ometepe (p504), a wilderness beach at Costa Rica's Península de Nicoya (p601) or coffee-scented hills around Panama's only volcano, Volcán Barú, in the Chiriquí highlands (p678).

The ultimate would be the 60km hike to Guatemala's El Mirador (p204), a sprawling, largely unexcavated Maya city reached by an intense hike into the El Petén jungle a couple days each way. Less demanding, but no shorter, is the hike through modern Maya villages from Nebaj (p134) to Todos Santos, also in Guatemala.

Surfing

Surfing's popularity is on the rise in Central America, with many places renting boards

---

TOP SURFING SPOTS

Here's our pick of the best on offer.
Guatemala Sipacate (p157)
El Salvador Punta Roca, at La Libertad (p291)
Nicaragua Las Salina (west of Rivas; p486)
Costa Rica Experts-only Salsa Brava, at Puerto Vieja de Talamanca (p567) or Pavones' three-minute left (p622)
Panama Waves at Santa Catalina (p693) and Bocas del Toro's (p685)

For more top surfing spots in the region, see the boxed texts, p292 (El Salvador), p486 (Nicaragua), and p593 (Costa Rica).

---

to tackle 'perfect' breaks. Costa Rica has the most developed scene, but low-key spots in El Salvador and Nicaragua are, to some, the best places. If you've never surfed, you can find surf lessons for as cheap as US$10, such as at El Salvador's Playa El Tunco (p293). Madera Surf Camp, near San Juan del Sur in Nicaragua (p500), has US$2 hammock spots facing one of the country's most popular waves. Costa Rica's increasingly popular Malpaís (p601) is a big surf camp on the Península de Nicoya, with lessons and US$10 bunks.

White-Water Rafting

Some of the best white-water rafting in the tropics can be found in Central America, and rafting is fast becoming popular all over Latin America. Guatemala and Honduras are developing a rafting industry, and a number of rivers there offer anything from frothing Class IV white water to easy Class II floats. Costa Rica leads the pack in river adventure sports, with many tour operators to choose from. See those countries' Directory for more details on rafting opportunities.

Wildlife-Watching

The unexpected appearance of a toucan, howler monkey, sloth, crocodile, iguana, dolphin or puma rushing past makes for the greatest rush on your trip, and the wildlife-viewing and birding opportunities in every part of Central America are world class. A system of national parks, wildlife refuges, biosphere reserves and other protected areas throughout the region facilitates independent bird and wildlife viewing. Even private areas such as gardens around hotels in the country-side can yield a sample of birds, insects, reptiles and even monkeys.

Early morning and late afternoon are the best times to watch for wildlife activity anywhere.

Leading the rest in terms of wildlife density is Costa Rica, with remarkable places such as the pristine Parque Nacional Corcovado (p618) and many others.

The elusive quetzal – and hordes of other implausibly colorful birds – can be seen at many places; a couple of spots include Honduras' Lago de Yojoa (p359) and Panama's Volcán Barú in the Chiriquí highlands (p678). Belize's Crooked Tree Wildlife Sanctuary (p238) is another hot spot for birders. Morning bird tours at Tikal, Guatemala (p199) add to the experience of seeing the ruins.

Howler monkeys (named for their frightening tiger-like roar) can be seen in treetops around the region, such as on an unforgettable walk through the Yaxchilán Maya ruins (p62) on the Mexico–Guatemala border. The black howler lives only in Belize, and can be seen at the Bermudian Landing Community Baboon Sanctuary (p237).

The best places to see sea turtles are Parque Nacional Tortuguero (p571) in Costa Rica or Refugio de vida Silvestre La Flor (p503) in Nicaragua. Coral reefs are an excellent place to see sea turtles, stingrays, sharks and tons of smaller, more colorful creatures. See p720 for some of Central America's top dive sites.

See p12 for some of the best places to see wildlife. Also see *Where to Watch Birds in Central America, Mexico & the Caribbean,* by Nigel Wheatley, and Lonely Planet's *Watching Wildlife Central America* and *Watching Wildlife Costa Rica* guides.

BOOKS

Suggested reads can be found at relevant sections throughout this guide; see each country Directory for country-specific suggestions. The following books will help with pretrip preparation (and dreaming). Also see p22.

Lonely Planet

Along with country-specific guidebooks to the region, Lonely Planet publishes an in-depth guide to the land of the Maya: *Belize, Guatemala & Yucatán.* If you're heading south from Central America, pick up a copy of *South America,* and there are also several Caribbean titles.

Other useful titles from LP include *Healthy Travel Central & South America*, a guide to minimizing common health risks on the road, and *Read This First: Central & South America*, a know-before-you-go book that covers trip-planning essentials. *Travel Photography: A Guide to Taking Better Pictures* provides some excellent advice on getting the most out of your travel photos.

Also consider reading Lonely Planet's *Latin American Spanish Phrasebook*, and *Travel With Children*.

Travel Literature

The number of books on Central America (travelogues and political essays) swelled during the turbulent '80s and into the early '90s, but have waned in the years since. Many good ones are now, unfortunately, no longer in stock.

Travelers' Tales Central America: True Stories, edited by Larry Habegger, is a collection of glories and failures of trips in the region.

John L Stephens' widely available classic *Incidents of Travel in Central America, Chiapas and Yucatan,* in two volumes, date from the 1840s. These volumes provided the world with the first glimpses of the Maya cities and still provide a good, popular overview.

Ronald Wright's *Time Among the Maya* is a story of travels through the whole Maya region – Guatemala, Mexico, Belize and Honduras – delving into the glorious past and exploited present of the Maya people. Though written in the troubled 1980s, it's still one of the best on-the-road reads of the area.

So Far from God: A Journey to Central America, by Patrick Marnham, was the winner of the 1985 Thomas Cook Travel Book Award. It follows the author's leisurely meander from Texas down to Mexico City and on into Central America. Glen David Short's *An Odd Odyssey: California to Colombia by Bus and Boat* is a much more recent version of a half-year trip through Mexico and Central America.

Dig around for Lonely Planet's out-of-print *Green Dreams: Travels in Central America*, by Stephen Benz, an interesting account of years of trips to Latin America.

BUSINESS HOURS

Much of Central America takes lunch off: that includes some tourist offices, banks and even a restaurant or two. Though opening hours

---

STANDARD HOURS

In this guidebook, for the sake of brevity only variations on standard business hours are included in reviews; otherwise standard hours are assumed. Restaurants are expected to be open roughly 8am to midnight, bars 8am to 2am or so, shops 10am to 8pm, and tourist information offices 8am to 5pm Monday to Friday or Saturday.

---

can vary regionwide (see country Directories for details), generally banks stick it out and don't break for siesta; some are open Saturday mornings as well. Sunday is a real shut-down day in much of the region.

Government offices tend to work shorter hours (8am to 4pm or 5pm) weekdays only, with a couple of hours off at midday. Other businesses are open similar hours (closed for siesta from 12:30pm to 2pm or so), but often have Saturday hours too.

CLIMATE

Central America is within the tropics, but there's a lot of variation in climate within this small region. The land rises from sea level to over 4000m, dividing the region into three primary temperature zones according to altitude, but there is little variation in temperature throughout the year.

In the lowlands (sea level to about 1000m) daytime temperatures range from 29°C to 32°C (84°F to 90°F), night-time temperatures from 21°C to 23°C (70°F to 74°F).

The temperate zone (from around 1000m to 2000m) has a pleasant climate, with daytime temperatures ranging from 23°C to 26°C (74°F to 79°F) and night-time temperatures from about 15°C to 21°C (59°F to 70°F).

The cold zone (above 2000m) has similar daytime temperatures to the temperate zone but is colder at night, around 10°C to 12°C (50°F to 54°F). The very few areas over 4000m are characterized by an alpine climate.

The rainy season, which runs from around April to mid-December in most of Central America, is called *invierno* (winter). The rest of the year constitutes the dry season and is called *verano* (summer). Country Directories explain regional variations. The Caribbean side of Central America gets much more rainfall than the Pacific side – often more than twice as much.

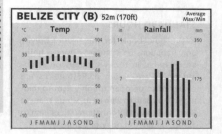

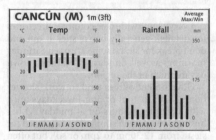

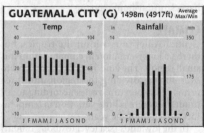

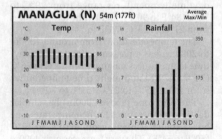

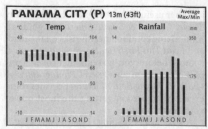

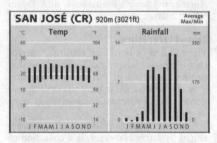

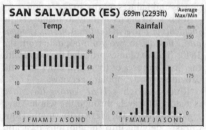

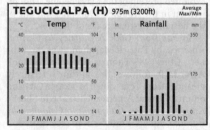

CUSTOMS

All visitors leaving and entering a Central American country go through customs. Be prepared for quick bag checks at airports and land borders too. Most are just a quick gaze-and-poke, more of a formality than a search. But not always. Do not have any illegal drugs (or drug paraphernalia) on you. And it's wise to always be polite with officials and dress conservatively.

DANGERS & ANNOYANCES

Travel in Central America poses a number of potential dangers that require caution, but don't be put off. Most areas are quite safe, and with sensible precautions you are unlikely to have any problems. For most travelers, the worst thing to happen is paying US$1 more than expected to a cab driver, a few (dozen) mosquito or sand fly bites, and the inevitable bout or two of diarrhea. Specific warnings are listed in country Directories and for applicable cities or towns throughout the guide.

The protracted civil wars in El Salvador, Nicaragua and Guatemala are over, but these dangers have been replaced by an alarming rise in the general crime rate and gang activity. Much doesn't involve foreign visitors, but there have been occasions of grab-and-run theft, assault, rape, car jacking and the occasional murder. Capital cities tend to have the highest rates of crime.

El Salvador's murder rate is rising. Towns such as Colón in Panama, are best avoided completely. Many sexual assaults occur on isolated beaches. Parts of Nicaragua's sparse north still have uncovered land mines from the 1980s conflict. Areas in Panama's Darién Province, which borders Colombia, are extremely dangerous because of guerrilla activity.

Avoid night buses anywhere (with the possible exception of Mexico), as highway robberies often happen at night.

The UK's **Foreign & Commonwealth Office** (FCO; www.fco.gov.uk/travel) lists excellent overviews on all countries on their website. Up-to-date 'travel warnings' are available from the **US Department of State** (www.travel.state.gov).

Will you run into trouble? No-one can say. Tens of thousands of foreign visitors enjoy the incomparable beauties of the region and the friendliness of its people every year, the huge majority without untoward incidents of any kind. But then there are the unlucky few or those who don't take precautions.

Ask, ask, ask for updates – from other travelers, tourist offices, police, guesthouse owners and Lonely Planet's **Thorn Tree** (http://thorntree.lonelyplanet.com).

Discrimination

In some Latin American countries, such as Mexico and Guatemala, the lighter one's skin tone, the higher the social status is perceived to be. In areas not inhabited by Afro-Caribbean cultures (which include the Garífuna villages in Belize, Honduras' Bay Islands and Panama's Bocas del Toro Archipelago), African-descendent travelers may encounter some discrimination (eg being refused entry into a nightclub, a stare, a flip remark).

It's sad to say it, but it can help to let locals know you're a foreign tourist (either by speaking English or saying so), thus presumably wealthy.

Asian travelers are less likely to face discrimination in Central America.

Drugs

Marijuana and cocaine are available in many places but illegal everywhere in the region, and penalties are severe. Avoid any conversation with someone who offers you drugs. If you are in an area where drug trafficking is prevalent, ignore it and do not show any interest whatsoever. Be aware that drugs are sometimes used to set up travelers for blackmail and bribery.

Roll-your-own cigarettes or cigarette papers may arouse suspicion.

Natural Hazards

Central America is prone to a wide variety of natural disasters, including earthquakes, hurricanes, floods and volcanic eruptions. General information about natural-disaster preparedness is available from the **US Federal Emergency Management Agency** (FEMA; www.fema.gov).

Police & Military

Corruption is a very serious problem among Latin American police, who are generally poorly paid and poorly supervised. In many countries, they are not reluctant to plant drugs on unsuspecting travelers or enforce minor regulations to the letter in the hope of extracting *coimas* (bribes).

If you are stopped by 'plainclothes policemen,' never get into a vehicle with them. Don't give them any documents or show them any money, and don't take them to your hotel. If the police appear to be the real thing, insist on going to a bona fide police station on foot.

The military often has considerable influence, even under civilian governments. Don't approach military installations, which may display warnings such as 'No stopping or photographs – the sentry will shoot.' Military checkpoints are frequent in places such as Chiapas and El Salvador. Most involve routine passport checks.

Robbery & Theft

No matter where you are, getting your gear stolen is a possibility, particularly in larger cities and transit points such as bus stations. Most theft is of the pickpocket or grab-and-run variety. As economic woes build up in Central America, these types of crimes will likely continue if not increase, and foreign tourists are often singled out as they are presumed to be 'wealthy' and carrying valuables.

Be wary of food, drinks, sweets or cigarettes from strangers on buses, trains or in bars, as they could be laced with sedatives.

To protect yourself, take these common-sense precautions:

- Wear a money belt to keep a bigger stash of money or passport out of sight. Have small amounts of cash in your pockets; use pants with zip pockets.
- Any purse or bag in plain sight can be slashed or grabbed. Often two thieves work together, one cutting the strap, the other grabbing as you walk along the street.
- Be wary of anyone pointing out a spilled substance (mustard, dog feces) on your clothes. It's a classic ploy used by pick-pocket teams: one helps to clean the victim, the other robs them.
- Avoid taking night buses.
- Take taxis after dark, particularly in big cities. Don't wander alone down empty city streets or in isolated areas.
- When possible, keep most of your cash, traveler's checks and valuables (such as airline tickets or jewelry) sealed in a signed envelope in a hotel safe.
- Make sure your room lock works. And consider locking your (locked) backpack to something immovable in your room – such as bathroom pipes.
- Lock your room every time you leave it – even just for a quick bathroom visit down the hall.
- If you're staying in a room that has a dodgy lock (or none), such as a beach cabaña, try to keep your valuables in left luggage.
- Don't camp overnight on beaches or in the countryside unless you can be sure it's safe.
- Ask around for advice – guesthouse owners, tourist offices, other travelers.
- If you're being robbed, fork over whatever they want. Many thieves are armed. It's not worth resisting.

Go to the police after a robbery if you'll need a police statement to present to your insurance company. Otherwise, there's little point. In Spanish-speaking areas, say 'Yo quisiera poner una acta de un robo' (I'd like to report a robbery). You may have to write up the report yourself, then present it for an official stamp and signature.

Swimming Safety

Hundreds of people drown each year at Central America's beaches – about 150 to 200 drownings are recorded annually at Costa Rican beaches alone. Of these, 80% are caused by riptides – strong currents that pull the swimmer out to sea. They can occur even in waist-deep water. The best advice of all: ask about conditions before entering the water. If it's dangerous, don't tempt the ocean; show off on the dance floor instead.

DISABLED TRAVELERS

Latin America generally is not well equipped for disabled travelers, and services (such as phones, toilets, or anything in Braille) are rare to the point of nonexistence. Expensive international hotels are more likely to cater to guests with disabilities than cheap hotels; air travel or pre-arranged transportation will be more feasible than most local buses; off-the-beaten-track destinations will be less accessible than well-developed ones. Careful planning and communication is a must, though information isn't always easy to come by.

In the USA, **Mobility International** (☎ 541-343-1284; www.miusa.org; 132 E Broadway, Ste 343, Eugene, OR 97401) advises disabled travelers on mobility issues and offers educational programs. In the UK, there's the **Royal Association for Disability & Rehabilitation** (Radar; ☎ 020-7250 3222; www.radar .org.uk; 12 City Forum, 250 City Rd, London EC1V 8AF). In Australia and New Zealand, try the **National Information Communication Awareness Network** (Nican; ☎ 02-6241 1220; www.nican.com.au; 48 Brookes St, Unit 5, Mitchell ACT 2911, Australia).

Emerging Horizons (www.emerginghori zons.com) is a good magazine geared to disabled travelers.

Other websites for tips and links include the following:

www.access-able.com Includes links for hotels catering to disabled travelers.

www.disabilitytravel.com Lots of tips, escorted trips in Costa Rica (look under Exotic Tours).

www.sath.org General tips for travelers with a range of different disabilities.

www.travelintalk.net Disabled travelers' group exchanges tips from road.

DISCOUNT CARDS

A Hostelling International (HI) membership card isn't terribly useful in Central America, except in Mexico and Costa Rica, where some hostels offer minimal discounts to cardholders. Those going on to South America, however, may want to invest in the membership as they're more commonly accepted there (see www.iyhf.org for information).

Carriers of the International Student Identity Card (ISIC) can get very good discounts on travel insurance, as well as discounted air tickets. Check www.istc.org for more information.

EMBASSIES & CONSULATES
For embassy and consulate addresses and phone numbers, see individual country Directories. General embassy information can be found at www.embassyworld.com.

As a visitor in a Central American country, it's important to realize what your own country's embassy can and can't do. Generally speaking, it won't be much help in emergencies when you're even remotely at fault. Remember that you are bound by the laws of the country you are in.

Your embassy will not be sympathetic if you end up in jail after committing a crime locally, even if such actions are legal in your own country.

In genuine emergencies you may get some assistance but only if other channels have been exhausted. For example, if you have all your money and documents stolen, it might assist in getting a new passport but a loan for onward travel is out of the question.

FESTIVALS & EVENTS
National holidays (días feriados) are taken seriously in Central America, and banks, public offices and many stores close. The big national holidays are dictated by the Roman Catholic Church calendar. Christmas and Semana Santa (Holy Week), the week leading up to Easter, are the most important. Panama hosts some of the most famous Carnaval celebrations (February), and Mexico's Día de los Muertos (Day of the Dead), on November 2, is another huge celebration.

During events such as these, hotels are usually booked well in advance, especially in beach areas and in towns that have particularly elaborate celebrations, such as Antigua, Guatemala. Bus services may be limited or nonexistent on the Thursday afternoon and Friday leading into Easter, and many businesses are closed for the entire week preceding the holiday. In general, public transportation tends to be tight on all holidays and the days immediately preceding or following them, so book tickets in advance.

See the country Directories for a more detailed listing of festivals, and see p12 for a list of some of the best.

GAY & LESBIAN TRAVELERS
On the whole, Central America is a pitifully unwelcoming place for gay men, and although lesbians have it a bit better, homosexuality is generally shunned in much of the region. In Nicaragua there is a statute criminalizing homosexual behavior, and although enforcement is inconsistent, harassment of gays does occur.

The absence of such laws does not prevent official and police harassment elsewhere, however; Guatemala and Panama are noted for being particularly homophobic, and in El Salvador a series of violent acts against gay men, lesbians and transgender people in recent years has drawn the attention of human-rights groups.

Misinformation about homosexuality in general, and AIDS in particular, has made Latin America that much more inhospitable for gay people.

In general, public displays of affection will not be tolerated, and gay men (and possibly women) could find themselves the target of verbal or physical abuse. Discretion is definitely the rule, especially in the countryside of Central America. Lesbians are generally less maligned than gay men, and women traveling together should encounter few, if any, problems.

Venues
There is usually at least one gay bar in big cities, which makes meeting people easier. Here's a rundown of some of the more in-the-open gay and lesbian scenes in Central America:

Mexico Cancún's bars and May festival; Playa del Carmen's clubs.

Guatemala Drag shows in Quetzaltenango; bars in Guatemala City.

El Salvador Gay scene around San Salvador's Blvd de los Héroes; mountain town San Vicente is gay friendly.

Costa Rica San José's thriving scene; beach hang-out at Manuel Antonio.

Panama Gay float at Carnaval parade in Panama City.

Gay & Lesbian Travelers sections in country Directories offer more information.

Internet Resources

As well as websites listed in the country Directories, good gay/lesbian websites include:

www.thegully.com Online politically charged gay-zine with some Central America coverage.

www.gay.com Travel page with articles and info on Mexico, Guatemala, Panama and Costa Rica.

www.damron.com Publishes annual gay/lesbian guides, plus has database of gay sites on their site.

www.iglhrc Site for International Gay & Lesbian Human Rights Commission.

Additional information on gay and lesbian travel in Latin America can be found through the **International Gay & Lesbian Travel Association** (IGLTA; www.iglta.com). Its website has information on group tours, and links to gay/lesbian-friendly hotels in Costa Rica and Mexico.

INSURANCE

A travel insurance policy covering theft, loss, accidents and illness is highly recommended. Some policies compensate travelers for misrouted or lost luggage. Also check that the coverage includes worst-case scenarios: ambulances, evacuations or an emergency flight home. Some policies specifically exclude 'dangerous activities,' which can include scuba diving, motorcycling or even trekking. Read the small print.

There are a wide variety of policies available; rates start at around US$90 to US$125 for the first month. **World Nomads** (www.worldnomads.com) offers good-deal policies, and policies handled by STA Travel and other student-travel organizations usually offer good value too. If a policy offers lower and higher medical-expense options, the low-expenses policy should be OK for Central America – medical costs are not nearly as high here as elsewhere.

If you have baggage insurance and need to make a claim, the insurance company may demand a receipt as proof that you bought the stuff in the first place. You must usually inform the insurance company by airmail and report the loss or theft to local police within 24 hours. Make a list of stolen items and their value. At the police station, you complete a *denuncia* (statement), a copy of which is given to you for your claim. The *denuncia* usually has to be made on *papel sellado* (stamped paper), which you can buy for pennies at a stationery.

For information on vehicle insurance, see p739. For information on health insurance, see p744.

INTERNET ACCESS

Internet cafés are available nearly everywhere except in the smallest towns. Rates are often under US$1 per hour, rising to US$8 per hour on touristy islands. A wi-fi boom is being felt in bigger cities – we list some places, often cafés, where you can bring your laptop for free access. See city and town Information sections for internet access points.

INTERNET RESOURCES

Honestly, Lonely Planet's discussion board **Thorn Tree** (http://thorntree.lonelyplanet.com) is the best way to get and share tips with fellow travelers before, during and after a trip. Check the Central America or Mexico pages. Lonely Planet's website also has brief country summaries.

Suggested websites appear in relevant sections throughout the book. Some general websites with information on Central America include the following:

CIA World Fact Book (www.odci.gov/cia/publications/factbook) Frequently updated background info on every country.

Latin American Network Information Center (http://lanic.utexas.edu/subject/countries.html) University of Texas site with oodles of Latin American links.

Latin World (www.latinworld.com) Loads of links, by country.

Planeta (www.planeta.com) Ecotourism online journal with articles and links on Central America, plus a free 93-page e-book on responsible travel.

Revue (www.revuemag.com) Free online English-language Guatemala mag with excellent Central America coverage.

South American Explorers (www.saexplorers.org) Handy if you're heading on to South America.

UK Foreign & Commonwealth Office (FCO; www.fco.gov.uk) British government site with travel advisories etc.

US State Department (www.state.gov/travel_warnings.html) Rather alarmist travel advisories and tips.

WHERE IT'S @

The cute little *arroba* (@) can be vexing to find on Latin American keyboards. Either cut and paste it from another email address or hold down the 'Alt' key and hit the '6' key, then the '4' key on the number pad (*not* at the top of the keyboard, and be sure 'Num Lock' is on). Or try 'Alt-Gr' (to the right of the space bar), then '2.' If that doesn't work, ask someone '¿Cómo se hace arroba?' – or send a postcard instead.

LEGAL MATTERS

Police officers in these countries are sometimes (if not often) part of the problem rather than the solution. The less you have to do with the law, the better.

Whatever you do, don't get involved in any way with illegal drugs: don't buy or sell, use or carry, or associate with people who do – even if the locals seem to do so freely. As a foreigner, you are at a disadvantage, and may be set up by others for bribes or arrest. Drug laws in all of these countries are strict, and though enforcement may be uneven, penalties are severe.

MAPS

The best map of the region is the fold-up color 1:1,100,000 *Traveller's Reference Map of Central America* (US$10), produced by **International Travel Maps & Books** (ITMB; www.itmb.com) in Canada. ITMB also publishes separate maps covering each of the Central American countries and various regions of Mexico, as well as several maps of South America.

Other websites that deal with map sales include **Maplink** (www.maplink.com) and London-based **Stanfords** (www.stanfords.co.uk).

MONEY

Regular travelers go with a combination of cash and credit/bank cards, and possibly some traveler's checks. By far the most accepted currency is the US dollar, and two countries (El Salvador and Panama) use it as their own. Note that you'll want to use up local currencies, as they are often not accepted outside the region – or even outside the country!

For sample costs and average daily budgets, see Fast Facts on the title page of each country. For general tips on saving money, see p20.

ATMs

Bring an ATM (or debit) card. ATMs are available in most cities and large towns, and are almost always the most convenient, reliable, secure and economical way of getting cash.

The rate of exchange from ATMs is usually as good as, if not better than, any bank or legal moneychanger. Many ATMs are connected to the MasterCard/Cirrus or Visa/Plus network. If you rely on ATMs, bring two cards in case one is lost or stolen and keep an emergency phone number for your bank in a separate place. Some banks that issue ATM cards charge a fee for international transactions; check the policy before leaving home.

EMERGENCY BUCKS

It's worth always having a small amount of US dollars handy – enough to get a room, a meal, and a taxi, at least. This can be particularly useful when crossing the border – and perhaps overnighting in a border town that doesn't have an ATM. Central American currencies don't always fly in the next country and it can be hard finding anyone willing to change leftover quetzals – but generally it's possible to use US dollars. If you are arriving on a Sunday, when *casas de cambio* (currency exchange office) may be closed, you can be out of luck too.

Bargaining

The art of bargaining can be acquired through practice, and you'll get some in Central America's markets, particularly for souvenirs and craft goods. Most accommodation prices are fixed, but for long-term stays (or during low season) it's worth asking for a discount. Indoor shops (such as groceries) generally have fixed prices. You may need to negotiate a price with a taxi driver, but fares for buses are standardized. Always approach bargaining with patience and humor, and you'll often end up with a price agreeable to both you and the seller.

Black Market

The 'black market' (*mercado negro*) or *mercado paralelo* (parallel market) is generally limited to moneychangers at borders, who are known to slip in torn bills or short-change on occasion. On the plus side, they accept local currencies that banks elsewhere sometimes don't take. Consider only changing a small amount – and count your bills before handing over your money. Such unofficial exchange rates for the US dollar can be higher than official bank rates, which may be artificially high for political reasons.

Cash

It's a good idea to always have a small wad of US dollars tucked away because it can be exchanged practically anywhere. It's particularly useful when you've just crossed a border or when an ATM or exchange service for traveler's checks isn't available. Plan ahead before you head to remote areas; take more than enough cash.

Getting change for bigger notes in local currency is a daily concern. Notes worth even US$2 to US$5 can sometimes be difficult to change.

Credit Cards

A credit card can be handy in emergencies and it enables you to obtain cash or enjoy an unexpected luxury somewhere along the way. It can also be useful if you're asked to demonstrate 'sufficient funds' when entering a country.

American Express, Visa and MasterCard are the most widely accepted credit cards in Central America. Depending on the country, credit cards can often be used to withdraw cash at ATMs. Some credit-card websites have ATM locators that show which towns have this service.

Some travelers rely on cash advances to reduce the need for traveler's checks, but this isn't always possible (particularly in smaller towns). Always inquire about transaction charges for cash advances; in some countries you may be charged a fee in addition to that charged by the card company back home. Some card companies also charge a fee (usually around 2%) for international transactions.

The amount you actually pay your credit-card company will depend on the exchange rate. Consider pre-arranging monthly payments to your account if you're planning to be on the road for some time.

Keep your cards separate from your cash as well as emergency phone numbers for the companies. Hold onto your receipts so you can later double-check payments.

Exchanging Money

Change traveler's checks or foreign cash at a bank or a *casa de cambio* (currency exchange office). Rates are usually similar, but in general *casas de cambio* are quicker, less bureaucratic and open longer or have weekend hours. Street moneychangers, who may or may not be legal, will only handle cash. Sometimes you can also change money unofficially at hotels or in shops that sell imported goods (electronics dealers are an obvious choice). Big cities tend to offer better exchange rates. Some money-changing services are listed in Information sections in this guide. Compare exchange rates and commission fees before you commit.

Don't accept torn notes, as most locals won't when you try to use them.

International Transfers

If you're in a pinch, **Western Union** (www.westernunion.com) has offices in all Central American countries, and can arrange transfers. Generally it's cheapest to arrange through an agent, but it can also send money by phone or the internet. Fees vary from a US$10 set fee to 8% of the balance.

Bank money transfers are possible, but take longer and can run into complications. Ask for a cable transfer (not a mail draft); you'll need to provide a local bank's branch information.

Tipping

Diners are generally expected to tip about 10% at restaurants. Some restaurants add a service charge of 10% to 20% to the bill; ask (*¿La cuenta incluye el servicio?*).

A small tip for taxi drivers or for the cleaning staff at your hotel is not necessary, but is appreciated.

Traveler's Checks

Fewer people are carrying them, but traveler's checks from companies such as American Express, Visa, Thomas Cook and Citibank, which offer replacement in case of loss or theft, remain the safest way to carry money. Don't use those issued by smaller banks. To facilitate replacement in case of theft, keep a record of check numbers and the original bill of sale in a safe place.

In some countries, traveler's checks are more difficult to cash, however, and banks and *casas de cambio* charge high commissions. Note if there's a fixed transaction fee (regardless of the value of the checks) or a percentage fee (usually 1% to 3%); if the fee is fixed, consider cashing larger amounts.

PASSPORT

You need one. Make sure yours is valid for six months beyond the projected end of your trip and has plenty of blank pages for stamp-happy officials. Keep a photocopy of the passport and visa separate from the real thing. It's not a bad idea to carry the copy when walking around town, leaving the passport at your hotel.

PHOTOGRAPHY

Most internet cafés allow you to burn your digital-camera shots onto a blank CD.

If you're still in the 35mm world, film is widely available throughout the region. If you want slide or black-and-white film, you're best advised to bring your own. Developing your film in Central America saves anxieties over putting film through airport X-rays (which shouldn't affect your film), but it is relatively expensive, and sometimes not terrific quality. Avoid mailing unprocessed film back, as that goes through more powerful X-rays.

Generally remember those beach or ruin shots get bleached out in midday sun. Try to photograph when natural light is at its softest, in the early morning or late afternoon. Film speeds are more than just packaging gimmicks. ISO 100 is best for outdoor shots on bright days; ISO 200 is a good all-around speed for varying conditions; ISO 400 is best for night or dim-light situations. An ultraviolet (UV) filter or polarizing filter can help avoid washed-out results. For more tips, get Lonely Planet's *Travel Photography: A Guide to Taking Better Pictures*.

Always ask before photographing individuals, particularly indigenous people. In some places, indigenous people may take offence at being photographed; elsewhere they may ask for a small payment. Indigenous people may also take offence if you photograph images of saints in their local church.

Taking photographs of military installations or security-sensitive places, such as military checkpoints in Chiapas and El Salvador, is very unwise (and probably illegal).

Note that some tourist sites charge an additional fee for tourists with cameras. Others charge fees only for use of video cameras.

POST

The quality of the postal service in the region varies and can be a very uncertain business. Letters airmailed to Europe and North America typically take 14 days, sometimes longer. Generally, important mail and parcels should be sent by registered or certified service, and if you want something to arrive within a reasonable amount of time, be sure to specify airmail *(correo aéreo* or *por avión)*. Sending parcels can be awkward, as often a customs officer must inspect the contents before a postal clerk can accept them. Note that the place for posting overseas parcels is sometimes different from the main post office. UPS, FedEx, DHL and other shipping and private courier services are available in some countries, providing an efficient but expensive alternative.

The simplest way of receiving mail is to have letters sent to you poste restante, (general delivery; known in Latin America as *lista de correos)*, to all of Central America except Guatemala. Address as follows:

Jane SMITH (last name in capitals)
Lista de Correos
Cozumel
Quintana Roo 77609 (post code)
MEXICO

A post-office box is known as an *apartado* (abbreviated to 'Ap' or 'Apto') or a *casilla de correos* ('Casilla' or 'CC').

Note that mail theft can happen. This is primarily a problem with mail sent from the USA to points in Central America, presumably because many Central Americans live and work in the USA and send money home to their families. Postcards make it through more easily.

See Post in the country Directories for country-specific information.

STUDYING

One of Central America's greatest attractions is the language schools. As part of a trip to Central America, studying Spanish (or an indigenous language such as Quiché) is a terrific way to absorb local culture, give a sense of purpose in a secondary town most travelers blaze through, and actually learn something. Schools often work to help the disadvantaged in their communities. Many schools are excellent, and prices throughout the region are cheaper than in Mexico. Outside Mexico it's generally possible to study for four hours a day with a private experienced teacher and stay and eat with a local family for around US$220 per week.

Antigua, Guatemala (p108) is by far the most celebrated language-school haven, with several dozen schools catering to the buzzing travelers' scene.

Quetzaltenango, Guatemala (p140) – big enough to maintain interest for weeks, but far from the main travel circuit – and Estelí, Nicaragua (p476), are a couple of Central America's best places to get serious. It's certainly feasible to study-hop your way around the region – if you don't know Spanish yet, you can before you get to Panama!

It may be possible to show up at a school on Monday morning to start that week. It's preferable, though, to plan ahead by phone or email. Many schools require some sort of one-time registration fee; ask if they'll waive it – often they will. Levels of teaching experience (and engagement) vary wildly. If you're not happy, say so. Most schools are accommodating and will switch teachers.

You can also book courses in the region with an outside organization such as **AmeriSpan** (www.amerispan.com). These courses are generally excellent but cost about twice the price as one booked locally. **ICAD** (www.icadscr.com) combine responsible travel with their year-long immersion courses in Costa Rica. It's about US$1700 for the year, plus US$400 to US$600 monthly expenses.

Do try to stay with a family – it can offer a fascinating glimpse into local life not seen from the hostel. You'll witness such phenomena as the 'Latin bed' (the whole family sleeping in one room – don't worry, you'll get a private room) and the fluid family count, as new cousins suddenly pop up for a few days then leave as unexpectedly.

See individual country Directories for more study information.

TELEPHONE

Prepaid phone cards, available for national telecommunications systems in each country, allow local and long-distance (and international in some countries, such as Costa Rica and Mexico) calls, with 'units' of time displayed on public pay phones. These are bought from newsstands and shops at pre-set denominations.

Local, long-distance and international phone and fax services are available at centralized telephone offices in every city and town. Avoid credit-card phones in Mexico, and the black 'press button' phones in Guatemala, which charge extortionate rates.

Often a far cheaper alternative is using on-line phone services from internet cafés, where international rates start at US$0.15 per minute to the USA, US$0.25 to Europe.

Note that it is not possible to make collect (reverse-charge) calls to a number of countries from Central America – collect calls will only be accepted in countries having reciprocal agreements with the country from which you are calling; check with the telephone office. You can usually place them to the USA. It is sometimes cheaper to make a collect or credit-card call to Europe or North America than to pay for the call where you are. Often

the best way is to make a quick international call and have the other party call you back (some telephone offices allow this).

Direct lines abroad, accessed via special numbers and billed to an account at home, have made international calls much simpler. There are different access numbers for each telephone company in each country – get a list from your phone company before you leave home.

Cell (mobile) phones are in wide use around Central America's bigger towns and cities, but using one can be quite expensive. Prepaid SIM cards are available. Central America doesn't subscribe to a consistent system. El Salvador, Guatemala and Honduras use the GSM 1900/850 (like the USA); Belize, Mexico and Nicaragua the GSM 1900; Costa Rica GSM 1800 and Panama GSM 850 (like the UK's GSM 1800/850 system). It's sometimes possible to rent cell phones; cheapies cost about US$25.

See also individual country Directories for country-specific details.

TOILETS

The toilets of Central America are fine, it's just the plumbing that has issues. Nowhere in the region should you deposit toilet paper or anything else in the toilet unless a sign specifies that it's OK to do so. Wastebaskets are generally provided for that purpose.

Some public toilets have attendants who charge a small fee (US$0.10 or so) and provide paper. It's a good idea to keep a spare roll of toilet paper handy.

TOURIST INFORMATION

Travelers will find a tourist office in the capital city of each country; some countries have them in outlying towns as well. If you're a student, look for student travel agencies in the capital cities of Costa Rica and Panama, and Cancún, Mexico.

Check www.visitcentroamerica.com (in Spanish only), with standard tourist-board coverage of all countries.

South American Explorers (www.saexplorers.org) is a helpful membership-based organization with information for travel in Latin American, particularly South America. It has traveler clubhouses in Lima, Cuzco, Quito and Buenos Aires; its **US office** (☎ 607-277-0488; 126 Indian Creek Rd, Ithaca, NY 14850) publishes the quarterly magazine, *South American Explorer*.

VISAS & DOCUMENTS
Visas
Presently citizens of the USA, EU, Canada, Australia, New Zealand and many other nations can arrive in all Central American countries (including Mexico) without arranging a visa beforehand. Check ahead from your country before planning your trip, as this may change.

Many countries charge an entry or tourist fee upon arrival – from US$5 to US$20. Check country Directory sections for country-specific visa information, as well as the Transportation sections in country chapters for departure tax fees.

Note that if you need a visa for a certain country and arrive at a land border without one, you will probably have to return to the nearest town that has a consulate and obtain a visa. Airlines will not normally let you board a plane for a country for which you don't have the necessary visa. Also, a visa in itself may not guarantee entry: in rare cases, you may still be turned back at the border if you don't have 'sufficient funds' or an onward or return ticket.

Sufficient Funds & Onward Tickets
Checking passports is a routine procedure upon arriving a country, but some officials may ask verbally or on the application form, about your financial resources. If you lack 'sufficient funds' for your proposed visit, officials may limit the length of your stay. (US$500 per month of your planned stay is generally considered sufficient; traveler's checks, and sometimes a credit card, should qualify toward the total amount.)

Several Central American countries require you to have a ticket out of the country (see p737).

Visa Extensions
Once you are inside a country, you can always apply for an extension at the country's immigration office. Usually there is a limit to how many extensions you can receive; if you leave the country and re-enter, your time starts over again. See individual country's Directory sections for more on this.

VOLUNTEERING
Considering that well over half the population of countries such as Nicaragua and Guatemala live in poverty, volunteering can both

---

> ### VIVA EL CA-4!
> Guatemala, Honduras, El Salvador and Nicaragua's 'CA-4 Border Control' agreement allows free travel for up to 90 days between this subregion for citizens of the four countries and many foreign nationalities (including residents of the USA, Canada, the UK and Australia). On paper, at least, you should only have to pay a tourist fee once to enter these four countries. The catch is that many border patrols try to sneak in a few dollars (for 'paperwork') when crossing borders. It's not true. If they ask, politely remind them of the 'CA-4.'

---

make a trip more meaningful and help out the region you visit. On offer are programs to teach those who can't afford classes, help build homes, work to preserve the environment, or help out at hill town medical clinics. Many who volunteer end up staying on longer than expected and find it to be the best part of a bigger trip. Volunteers – sometimes working alone, seven days a week – usually work hard. Note that studying Spanish at schools that pool profits to help communities is another way of contributing (see p731).

You can find volunteering organizations once in Central America (cheaper), or arrange programs with international organizations before your trip. Be aware that some organizations seek a minimum-period commitment, and may prefer that you organize your visit before turning up at the doorstep.

For more information on volunteering, get a copy of Lonely Planet's *Volunteer*.

International Organizations
Many international organizations will help you peg a program to match job/school requirements, and get college credit for it. Nearly all programs cost money – usually a bit more than you'd pay on a trip. Some volunteers find sponsors – at school or privately – to fund a program. Spanish is not mandatory for all. Often programs begin with a few weeks of Spanish classes, as part of the on-location transition. A sample three-month program to Guatemala, for example, including four weeks of Spanish study, runs at about US$2500 (not including the airfare). Costa Rica has the most opportunities (such as in Monteverde), and Guatemala and Mexico have many too.

VOLUNTEERING HIGHLIGHTS

These stand out as easy and rewarding options that can be arranged by local organizations, often during your trip.

- Teach English to Maya children outside Quetzaltenango, Guatemala (p141)
- Help monitor sea turtle nests in Costa Rica (p631).
- Learn organic farming by volunteering (at US$15 per day, including room and board) at a sustainable agriculture ranch in Costa Rica (p613)
- Provide English courses at Cumaro, El Salvador (p315)
- Work with wildlife-related conservation projects in El Petén, Guatemala (p189)

Travel agencies such as **STA Travel** (www.sta travel.com) can arrange volunteering projects. A couple of other organizations that offer a variety of programs to Latin America include the following. Prices don't include transportation to the region unless otherwise noted.

AmeriSpan (in the USA ☎ 800-879 6640, 215-751 1100; in the UK ☎ 020-8123 6086; www.amerispan .com) Sends volunteers to Costa Rica, Guatemala and the Yucatán on varied programs – building homes, teaching children, working with animals. Guatemala's programs are the cheapest – from US$900 for six weeks (including two weeks' Spanish study and homestay).

Amigos de las Américas (www.amigoslink.org) Youth-oriented summer programs – costing about US$3850 (including flight to/from USA) – ranging from national-park work to community development in Honduras, Costa Rica and Mexico.

Habitat for Humanity (www.habitat.org) Generally is more about funding than on-field programs, though it listed several options in Costa Rica at research time.

Idealist.org (www.idealist.org) Hundreds of links for volunteering opportunities around the world.

i-to-i (www.i-to-i.com) Has UK, US and Ireland offices; four- to 24-week volunteer and study programs to Guatemala, Honduras, Costa Rica and Mexico, with no language requirement. Prices range from US$1000 to US$3000, including a homestay and most meals.

International Volunteer Programs Association (www.volunteerinternational.org) Lists many programs in Latin America, most from US$900 for a couple weeks.

ResponsibleTravel (www.responsibletravel.com) UK-based ecofriendly tour operator with many volunteer trips.

Transition Abroad (www.transitionabroad.com) Heaps of volunteer links; look under Central America – working at Nicaragua's Miraflor Nature Preserve for US$30 per week sounds like a winner.

Organizations in Central America

There are many smaller, privately run volunteer organizations in Central America, and it's not difficult to find short-term (one or two weeks) or longer programs once you're on the road. This will save you the higher costs of pre-arranging a program, but it isn't always easy to find them. We've tried to help by listing volunteer programs as we found them. Start by looking at the individual country Directories for more volunteering options.

WOMEN TRAVELERS

Women traveling solo through Central America typically find that popular perceptions over-estimate the dangers faced. Take all the normal precautions you would elsewhere in new territory or big cities. The biggest adjustment is getting used to a very vocal male population who hoot, hiss and whistle. Ignore this behavior and most of the time you will be simply left alone. Certain bars and soccer games tend to be testosterone territory and your incursion will invite attention.

Dress according to local norms to avoid unwanted attention (often this means wearing long skirts or pants instead of shorts). Match locals' formality in dress because disheveled clothing can be a sign of disrespect. Being gracious and behaving somewhat formal will win you allies. Talk to locals to find out which areas to avoid. Locals, particularly families, will often go out of their way to help a single female traveler.

Though there's no need to be paranoid, women travelers should be aware that sexual assault, rape and mugging incidents do occur. The greatest risk is in remote or dark areas, on lone stretches of beach, or sometimes to women trekking. Always keep enough money for a taxi ride to your accommodation – it's not wise to be walking after dark.

In general, Central American police are not likely to be very helpful in rape cases. The tourist police may be more sympathetic, but it's possibly better to contact your embassy and see a doctor.

JourneyWoman (www.journeywoman.com) is a useful online source for female travelers with lots of tips and advice.

WORKING

According to law you must have a permit to work in any of the countries covered in this guide. In practice you may get paid under the table or through some bureaucratic loophole, if you can find suitable work. Many travelers work short-term jobs – through that aforementioned loophole – in restaurants, hostels or bars geared to international travelers for survival wages. Before taking such a job, consider volunteering instead (see p733), as many of these jobs could just as well be performed by locals.

Teaching English is another option. Consult the classified advertisements in local newspapers (both English- and Spanish-language papers), browse the bulletin boards in spots where foreigners gather and ask around. Big cities offer the best possibilities for schools or private tutoring. Generally it doesn't involve big money, but often you could trade classes for room and board. If you do teach, teach well. Even small fees can be big sacrifices for locals trying to learn a language to better their chances in school or work. It's not as easy as it looks. Many schools will require Teaching English as a Foreign Language (TEFL) teaching certificates.

Some international organizations help place individuals in various work jobs, including organizations such as CIEE and i-to-i (see p733).

Transitions Abroad (www.transitionsabroad .com) is an excellent bimonthly magazine highlighting work and study abroad options. The website has many useful links.

Transportation

CONTENTS

GETTING THERE & AWAY

Most visitors reach Central America by air or overland from Mexico. Fights, tours and rail tickets can be booked online at www.lonely planet.com/travel_services.

AIR

All Central American countries have international airports. The major ones are Cancún, Mexico (airport code CUN); Guatemala City, Guatemala (GUA); Belize City, Belize (BZE); San Salvador, El Salvador (SAL); San Pedro Sula (SAP) and Tegucigalpa (TGU), Honduras; Managua, Nicaragua (MGA); San José, Costa Rica (SJO); and Panama City, Panama (PAC). A limited number of international flights also reach Flores, Guatemala (FRS); Roatán, Honduras (RTB); and David,

---

THINGS CHANGE...

The information in this chapter is particularly vulnerable to change. Check directly with the airline or a travel agent to make sure you understand how a fare (and ticket you may buy) works and be aware of the security requirements for international travel. Shop carefully. The details in this chapter should be regarded as pointers and are not a substitute for your own careful, up-to-date research.

Panama (DAV). Other than South American flights, nearly all go via US gateways (particularly Houston, Miami or New York's JFK) or Mexico City.

Airlines

Central America's national airlines have frequent connections to North and South America. Four of the national airlines have combined forces as San Salvador–based **Grupo TACA** (code TA; www.taca.com), comprising TACA (El Salvador), Aviateca (Guatemala), Lacsa (Costa Rica), and Nica (Nicaragua). The website also lists office addresses worldwide. In the USA you can reach them toll free at ☎ 800 400-8222 and in Canada ☎ 800 722-8222; in the UK call ☎ 8702-410 340, in Australia ☎ 02-8248 0020.

Panama's **COPA** (code CM; www.copaair.com) connects Panama with Los Angeles, Mexico City, Miami, New York and many South American cities.

Following are other airlines with frequent service to Central America.

Aeroméxico (code AM; www.aeromexico.com) To Cancún from many US cities and Madrid.

American Airlines (AA; www.americanairlines.com) All of Central America from Dallas and Miami.

Avianca (AV; www.avianca.com) Flights between Panama City and Bogotá, Columbia.

British Airways (BA; www.britishairways.com) Flights to Belize City, Guatemala City, San José and Panama City via Miami.

Continental Airlines (CO; www.continental.com) All of Central America from Newark and Houston.

Delta Airlines (DL; www.delta.com) Flights to Central America from Atlanta and Los Angeles.

Jet Blue (B6; www.jetblue.com) Connects Boston and New York with Cancún.

Lloyd Aéreo Boliviano (LB; www.labairlines.com.bo) To Panama City from Havana, Miami and Santa Cruz, Bolivia.

Mexicana (MX; www.mexicana.com) To Cancún, Guatemala City, San Salvador, San José and Panama City and Tuxtla Gutierrez, Mexico, via Mexico City.

United Airlines (UA; www.united.com) Reaches several Central American cities.

US Airways (US; www.usairways.com) Goes to Guatemala City, San José, Cancún from Charlotte, Las Vegas, Phoenix and Philadelphia.

Tickets

Central America's slender isthmus shape makes 'open jaw' tickets – flying into one place (say Cancún or Guatemala City) and out another (Panama City) – an attractive option, and the good news is that it's often not much more expensive than a round-trip ticket. If you're flexible on where you start and end, shop around – discount fares come and go.

You might think going to a hub city – such as San Salvador on TACA – would save money, but sometimes it's *more* expensive; we found some tickets through San Salvador to Belize City from Los Angeles, for example, to be cheaper than return tickets to San Salvador. The reason – in the confusing world of airline ticket pricing – is airlines trying to compete with more direct options. Again, shop around.

Typically Panama City is more expensive to reach from the US gateways than Guatemala City, but otherwise no Central American city is consistently cheaper than another.

High-season rates (generally July and August, Christmas to New Year's, and around Semana Santa) can be US$100 to US$250 more expensive.

Student travel agencies such as **STA Travel** (www.statravel.com) offer student discounts for those under 26.

If you're flying from Europe or Australia, chances are you can get a free stopover in a US gateway city such as Los Angeles or Miami.

See Air in individual country Transportation sections for the departure taxes

collected when leaving from Central American airports.

AIR PASSES & RTW TICKETS

Air passes that include flights into Central America have faded out in recent years; TACA and COPA's Copass no longer exist.

Round-the-world (RTW) ticket options are an option if coming from the USA or Europe, but lack of flight connections between Australasia and Central America have all but put Latin America off RTW ticket options from that part of the world.

COURIER FLIGHTS

Sadly, the salad days of dirt-cheap courier flights have wilted after September 11, 2001. Get more information from the following:
www.courier.org US$45 per year subscription.
www.couriertravel.org US$40 one-time fee; New York–Cancún flight.

From Australia & New Zealand

No direct flights to Central America from Australia or New Zealand exist. (Sydney and Auckland do have services via Argentina and Chile.) The cheapest option to Central America is through the USA, usually Los Angeles or Miami. It is often considerably cheaper to get two individual tickets – one to the USA, another to Central America.

Two of the best travel agents specializing in cheap airfares are **STA Travel** (☎ 1300 733-035, 03-9207-5900; www.statravel.com.au) and **Flight**

ONWARD-TICKET REQUIREMENTS

If you're planning on flying into one country and back from another, note that increasingly immigration officials require travelers show proof of onward or continuing travel. We talked with the embassies, and heard, for example, from Panama's 'yes, it's necessary,' which quickly softened to 'well, we don't want to say it's OK in case you have problems.' The restriction is there mainly to ensure nonresidents don't stay long-term in the country without permission.

Showing 'continuing travel' from another country (say a flight home from another country) and explaining how you'll get there is almost always enough. Overwhelmingly most travelers are never asked; as one travel agent summed up, 'It's rarely a problem, but it's up to the mood of the person checking your passport and whether their supervisor is watching or not.'

It's a good idea to ask the airlines – as they can be fined for bringing in a passenger without proper documentation. Also it may be worth showing a print-out of a 'bus reservation' out of the country, emailed from a local travel agency listed throughout the book.

This requirement also pops up at land borders on occasion. Crossing into Costa Rica, for instance, it's sometimes necessary to purchase a bus ticket at the border leaving Costa Rica – even if you don't plan to use it. If you enter by private car, no onward ticket is required obviously, but proper documentation for the car is needed.

If you're continuing on to South America, check beforehand for similar restrictions in those countries.

Centre (☎ 133 133; www.flightcentre.com.au). Both have many offices nationwide.

For discount tickets in New Zealand, try **STA Travel** (☎ 0800 474 400; www.statravel.co.nz) or **Flight Centre** (☎ 0800 243 544; www.flightcentre.co.nz). Both have offices in Auckland and other cities.

For online fares try www.travel.com.au or www.zuji.com from Australia, and www.goholidays.co.nz or www.zuji.co.nz from New Zealand.

From Continental Europe

The best deals are often found at 'student' travel agencies (nonstudents are welcome too) in Amsterdam, Brussels, Paris, Berlin and Frankfurt, and sometimes Athens. Alternatively you can try booking via a London agent.

In Paris, student/discount travel agencies include **Nouvelles Frontières** (☎ 08 25 00 07 47; www.nouvelles-frontieres.fr), with nationwide offices, including services in Belgium. Another is **Havas Voyages** (☎ 01 48 51 86 19; www.havasvoyages.fr).

In the Netherlands, the official student agency **NBBS Reizen** (☎ 0900-10 20 300; www.nbbs.nl) is good.

STA Travel (www.statravel.com) has offices throughout Germany and in Austria, Denmark, Finland, Sweden and Switzerland.

From South America

Grupo TACA and COPA airlines connect Central American cities to and from Venezuela, Colombia, Ecuador, Peru, Chile and Argentina. Some US airlines, such as American Airlines, have a few connections too.

If you're planning to visit Central America and South America on a trip, note that TACA (and other airlines) often allow a free stop-over (in San José for TACA), meaning you can visit Central America for no extra charge. Brazilian discount airline **Gol** (www.voegol.com.br) may offer Central American services at some point.

Panama City is generally the cheapest link to and from South America with Colombia, Ecuador and Venezuela, unsurprisingly, offering the least-expensive deals.

Note that many South American countries require onward air tickets upon arrival (see p737).

Helpful travel agencies and services in South America include the following:

South American Explorers Lima (☎ 01-445-3306; www.saexplorers.org; Calle Piura 135, Miraflores) Quito (☎ 02-222-5228; quitoclub@saexplorers.org; Apt 17-21-431, Eloy Alfaro)

Trotamundos (☎ 1-599-6413; www.trotamundos.com.co; Diagonal 35 No 5-73; ☎ 1-341-8986; Carrera 6, No 14-43, Bogotá, Colombia)

CLIMATE CHANGE & TRAVEL

Climate change is a serious threat to the ecosystems that humans rely upon, and air travel is the fastest-growing contributor to the problem. Lonely Planet regards travel, overall, as a global benefit, but believes we all have a responsibility to limit our personal impact on global warming.

Flying & Climate Change

Pretty much every form of motor travel generates CO_2 (the main cause of human-induced climate change) but planes are far and away the worst offenders, not just because of the sheer distances they allow us to travel, but because they release greenhouse gases high into the atmosphere. The statistics are frightening: two people taking a return flight between Europe and the US will contribute as much to climate change as an average household's gas and electricity consumption over a whole year.

Carbon Offset Schemes

Climatecare.org and other websites use 'carbon calculators' that allow jetsetters to offset the greenhouse gases they are responsible for with contributions to energy-saving projects and other climate-friendly initiatives in the developing world – including projects in India, Honduras, Kazakhstan and Uganda.

Lonely Planet, together with Rough Guides and other concerned partners in the travel industry, supports the carbon offset scheme run by climatecare.org. Lonely Planet offsets all of its staff and author travel.

For more information check out our website: lonelyplanet.com.

From the UK

No flights link the UK directly with Central America. British Airways has weekly flights direct to Mexico City, which run at about £150 to £180 less than Central American fares. Otherwise it's possible to reach any Central American country in a day via the USA (where it's necessary to clear customs, even if you're only making a connection). It's possible to get free stopovers in US cities such as Houston or New York on Continental Airlines, or Atlanta, Cincinnati, Los Angeles or San Francisco on Delta Airlines. British Airways and Iberia often go via Miami.

Book way ahead if you're planning to go from mid-December through January, or July through mid-September.

If planning on globe-trotting, ask about discounted one-way tickets through Central and South America. Check the weekend editions of national newspapers for airfare listings.

For student discounts, **STA Travel** (☎ 0871-230 0040; www.statravel.co.uk) has offices throughout the UK.

An excellent travel agency geared toward trips in the region is **Journey Latin America** (☎ 020-874 7108; www.journeylatinamerica.co.uk), with offices in London and Manchester.

South American Experience (☎ 0870-499 0683; www.southamericanexperience.co.uk) has discounted fares to Belize City, Guatemala City and San José, plus plenty of region-wide information on its website.

Bucket shops selling discounted fares abound in London and in the UK. Check for travel agents that arc bonded by organizations (such as ATOL, ABTA or AITO) that give some protection to ticket buyers if the company goes broke.

From the USA & Canada

Most flights from the USA and Canada go through Dallas/Fort Worth, Houston, Los Angeles or Miami. Other major gateways are Atlanta, Chicago, Newark, New York, San Francisco, Charlotte, Toronto and Washington, DC.

Tickets bought here usually have restrictions, including a two-week advance-purchase requirement. Often prices rise if you stay over three or four months.

Travel agencies known as 'consolidators' have some of the best deals; they buy tickets in bulk, then sell at discounts.

A couple of excellent Latin American-focused agencies are worth contacting, even if you're not in their immediate area: the Colorado-based **Exito Travel** (☎ 800 655-4053, 925-952 9322; www.exitotravel.com) and San Francisco-based **Americas Travel** (☎ 888-703-9955, 415-703 9955; www.americastravel.net).

The USA's largest student travel agency is **STA Travel** (☎ 800 781-4040; www.statravel.com), with nationwide offices and cheaper prices for students. Booking tours and tickets, the **Adventure Travel Company** (in USA or Canada ☎ 888-238-2887; www.atcadventure.com) has offices in the USA and Canada.

A few online ticket services include www.cheaptickets.com, www.expedia.com and www.travelocity.com. You can try bidding for a cheaper one at www.priceline.com or www.skyauction.com.

LAND

For details on border crossings between Central American nations and also country-specific requirements, see Transportation sections and the border crossing boxed texts in each country chapter. For general advice on crossing borders, see p741.

From Mexico

BUS & BOAT

It's possible to bus from the USA or Canada into Mexico and directly into Central America. The three most convenient land borders between Mexico and Central America are at the Chetumal–Corozal (Belize) border in Quintana Roo (Yucatán Peninsula; see p56); Ciudad Cuauhtémoc–La Mesilla (Guatemala) in Chiapas (see p69); and Ciudad Hidalgo–Ciudad Tecún Umán (Guatemala; see p153) in Chiapas state (about 38km to the south of Tapachula).

Another popular border crossing is by boat across the Río Usumacinta at the Frontera Corozal–Bethel (Guatemala) border, south of Palenque (see p249).

CAR & MOTORCYCLE

Most people driving to Central America do so from the USA (or Canada). Buying a car in the region (including Mexico) is very complicated. If you drive, you will *not* save money, but it can make for a great trip. But there are a lot of fees, paperwork, red tape, tolls and parking worries involved. You'll need to be prepared to stop for passport checks at

TRANSPORTATION

DEPARTURE TAXES

Air taxes in countries vary. Costa Rica and Panama have the smallest taxes (5%), while Guatemala and El Salvador have a 20% tax jacking up airfares. These taxes are generally included in fares quoted by travel agents (but not when booking online), both abroad and in Central America. Departure taxes are covered in the Transportation sections of individual country chapters.

---

military checkpoints. Also, highway robberies aren't unknown. Avoid driving at night.

Note that you'll need liability insurance that covers Mexico and Central America – your policy back home isn't recognized here. It's available at many border towns. Texas-based **Sanborn's Insurance** (☎ 800-222-0158; www .sanbornsinsurance.com) sells separate coverage (only) for Mexico and Central America. A two-week liability/full coverage policy in Mexico is US$125/183; in Central America, sadly, coverage doesn't include Belize or Nicaragua. Monthly rates for liability/full coverage are US$186/386. It's possible to get a policy by phone or online – so you can get Mexico coverage on the road in Central America for your return through Mexico.

A few other pretrip considerations:
- You need a valid driver's license from your home country.
- Unleaded petrol is now available throughout Central America.
- Be sure that the shock absorbers and suspension are in good shape for the bumpy roads.
- A spare fuel filter, and other spare parts, could be invaluable.
- Check with a national tourist board or consulate on any changes of bringing a car into Mexico, or Central America, before showing up in your vehicle.

From South America

There are no road connections between South America and Central America (via Panama), and guerrilla activity in Colombia (plus the difficulty of travel) have essentially made the trip over the Darién Gap on foot an impossibility.

In the past travelers have made the trip, with the help of local guides.

SEA

Unless you're a filthy-rich yachtie or on a cruise ship, options for boat travel heading to/from the region are very limited and very expensive. The most plausible way is going on a chartered sailboat from the San Blás Archipelago, Panama, to Cartagena, Colombia – a US$275 (or so), five-day trip (with a few days spent on the islands and two days' transit to/from Colombia). Note that smuggling is common on the Colón–Cartagena cargo route. See p707 for more on this.

In Cartagena, check with the hostel **Casa Viena** (☎ 05-664 6242; www.casaviena.com; Calle San Andrés 30-53, Getsemaní) for schedule info. The manager there told us they hadn't heard of any travelers making the trip by cargo since around 2001, and that two cargo boats had actually sunk in recent years.

GETTING AROUND

Like buses? Buses are the cheapest and most accessible way to get around Central America, particularly along the Pan-American Hwy (sometimes called the Pan-Americana or Interamericana – we've alternated usage based on local parlance), which runs through all the countries but Belize.

Because of the region's skinny stature, a flight can save several hours of backtracking. Islands and some borders are served by various types of boat. See p14 for suggested itineraries.

AIR

Many flights connect the region by some international carriers as well as the national airlines; see p736 for listings. Some smaller domestic airlines provide service too; see country chapters for more information. Occasionally it will be necessary to change planes in the carrier's hub city (a Managua–Panama City flight may change planes up north in San Salvador).

Prices are an obstacle. Despite relatively short distances, individual one-way and round-trip tickets within Central America (either bought abroad or in the region) can be very expensive. Note that if you fly to Central America on TACA, they sometimes sell regional flights – generally to or from San José – at a discount. Not infrequently, one-way tickets run just a few dollars less than a round-trip ticket.

Flights can sometimes be overbooked; reconfirm yours before arriving at the airport. See Onward-Ticket Requirements (p737) for potential problems with entering one country and flying out of another.

Air Passes

Air passes are 'de-evolving,' to quote one travel agent. They didn't offer much better deals than you'd get buying an individual ticket or two anyway. Ask a local agent about passes, as things may change.

Sample Fares

What you're about to see borders on sacrilege. Airfares can vary wildly – depending on the length of stay, time of year and special promotions – so treat these high-season fares as a rough gauge only in identifying potential routes.

Note that San Salvador and San José are the most popular hubs – promotional flights between them are sometimes as low as US$139 return. Occasionally a promotional return flight may be even cheaper than a one-way fare.

Here are some sample fares:

Origin	Destination	One-way	Round-trip
Cancún	Flores	US$199	US$279
Guatemala City	Panama City	US$259	US$429
Guatemala City	San José	US$199	US$299
Managua	Guatemala City	US$264	US$229(!)
Managua	Panama City	US$259	US$414

Worthwhile domestic flights include Managua to Corn Islands (about US$164 return), which saves a two-day bus/boat trip each way (about US$50 return).

BICYCLE

Long-distance cycling can be dangerous, as few drivers are accustomed to sharing narrow streets in cities or (often) shoulderless two-lane highways with bicycles. That said, cycling is on an upswing – with mountain rides and coffee plantation tours (including guide and bike) available all over Central America.

You can rent bicycles in several cities and travelers hang-outs, such as San Cristóbal de Las Casas (Mexico), Flores (Guatemala), Granada (Nicaragua) and Panama City. There are many mountain-bike tours available (notably in cooler locales such as Guatemala's highlands and San Cristóbal de Las Casas). Consider

TRANSPORTATION

HINTS FOR BORDER CROSSINGS

Going from one of Central America's seven countries (or Mexico) into another can be a frenetic, confusing, even scam-ridden experience. But with a little planning it's usually a breeze (make that a slo-o-ow breeze). Some considerations:

- Before you leave one country for another, read that country's entry requirements in the Visas section in the Directory at the back of each country chapter.

- Don't leave a country without getting your passport stamped at that country's immigration office. Occasionally no one will flag you down to do this; be on the lookout for it.

- Often you'll be changing buses at the border, perhaps walking a few hundred meters across, or catching a colectivo (jitney taxi or minibus taxi) to the nearest bus station. Not all of the borders are open 24 hours, but bus schedules tend to match opening hours.

- Many travel agents offer organized trips across the borders; many travelers prefer the ease of having someone there (a driver for example) to help if things get sticky.

- Moneychangers linger around nearly all borders; rates can be fair but some changers do try to shortchange; count carefully. If you're carrying only a local currency, try to change at least some before moving on, as it's possible no one will accept it once you're across.

- Note that, technically, there's a border agreement between Guatemala, Honduras, El Salvador and Nicaragua, allowing travel up to 90 days in the four-country region – and you shouldn't have to pay to cross into another country; see p733

Also see Overland Routes boxed texts at the beginning of country chapters for border information. Border crossing details appear in boxed texts in relevant sections of the book.

TRANSPORTATION

the seasons if you're planning to cycle much. The dry season (roughly December to April) should spare you from soakings.

If you're planning to bike across borders, it's a good idea to keep a document of your ownership handy for immigration officials.

Though dated, the best guide to cycling the region is *Latin America by Bike: A Complete Touring Guide* (1993), by Walter Sienko. Richard Ballantine's *Richard's New Bicycle Book* helps understand the parts. Ian Benford and Peter Hodkinson's *Cycle Central America* covers southern Mexico, Belize, Guatemala and Honduras.

BOAT

Aside from domestic water-related activities (such as white-water rafting or boating to volcanic islands), a few water journeys connect countries. Travelers between Palenque, Mexico, and Flores, Guatemala, cross the Río Usumacinta near Frontera Corozal, Mexico, and Bethel, Guatemala. Another interesting crossing is between Punta Gorda, Belize, and Puerto Barrios (and sometimes Lívingston), Guatemala. There's a rather off-track river border crossing between San Carlos, Nicaragua, and Los Chiles, Costa Rica.

Key domestic water journeys include the ride down the Río Escondidas to Bluefields, Nicaragua, and then out to the Corn Islands in the Caribbean. Guatemala's Río Dulce is another famous ride. Other Caribbean islands that are reached by boat include Honduras' Bay Islands, Belize's Caye Caulker and Mexico's Cozumel and Isla Mujeres.

The Panama Canal is one of the world's most important waterways, connecting the Caribbean and the Pacific.

BUS

Half the stories of the trip will be of how you got around by bus. Bus service is well developed throughout the region, though not always comfortable. While some buses are air-conditioned with reservable reclining seats, you're sure to bounce a time or 20 in one of the famed 'chicken buses.' These are often colorfully repainted former US school buses with a liberal 'bring on what you want' policy (ie chickens).

Avoid night buses throughout the region (with the possible exception of Mexico), as these have been popular targets for highway robbers.

First-class and some 2nd-class buses depart on scheduled times from *terminal de autobuses* (long-distance bus stations); others leave from parking-lot bus terminals once they are full (these stop to collect more passengers all along the way – thus, you're likely to get a lift from the highway if need be). Be aware that many cities have more than one bus station. Bus companies can have their own terminals as well.

Bus frequency can vary. In bigger cities and on more popular routes, smoke-spewing giants troll the streets every few minutes, while in remote places, if you oversleep you'll be staying another night.

Luggage may be stored in a lower compartment or piled on the roof of the bus. Keep an eye on your luggage on bus trips if you can, particularly on the easily accessible racks in a packed bus. Always keep your valuables tucked away on your person. Watch out for pickpockets on crowded buses and in bus stations.

In some places, travel agents run shuttle services (mostly vans with air-con) to popular destinations. They're more comfortable and more expensive (and carry a lot less street cred). An example: Antigua to Panajachel in Guatemala is about US$8 by shuttle; or you can take three chicken buses and do the route for about a dollar.

Getting There & Away sections following towns and cities list most bus routes and fares; also see the Transportation sections in individual country chapters.

Colectivos & Minibuses

Around Central America, and usually connecting hub towns with smaller ones on short-haul trips, are an array of minibuses of various conditions and nomenclature (called *rapidito* in Honduras, *chiva* in Panama, and colectivo in Costa Rica and Mexico). These are cheaper transport options than 1st-class buses, when available, and go frequently – the catch is the frequent stops and that the driver knows no word for 'full.'

Sample Bus Durations

Seeing most of Central America by bus is not difficult, but you'll need time. Here are the durations of some sample bus journeys. Remember that bus connections and border-crossing formalities can add extra time to the trip.

Origin	Destination	Duration
San Cristóbal de Las Casas (M)	Antigua (G)	11 hours
Cancún (M)	Belize City (B)	9-10 hours
Flores (G)	Guatemala City (G)	8-10 hours
Guatemala City (G)	Copán Ruinas (H)	5 hours
San Salvador (ES)	Tegucigalpa (H)	8 hours
Tegucigalpa (H)	Managua (N)	9 hours
Managua (N)	San José (CR)	8-10 hours
San José (CR)	Panama City (P)	15-18 hours

CAR & MOTORCYCLE
Driver's License

If you're planning to drive anywhere, check before you leave to see if your country's driver's license is honored in all the countries you plan to hit the road in. It's possible you may need an International Driving Permit (IDP), which is issued by automobile associations worldwide.

Be prepared for police checkpoints – always stop and have your papers handy.

Car Hire

Central America is relatively easy to explore by private vehicle, and would be more popular if it weren't for the cost (rental and petrol) and hassle. Rentals range from about US$20 per day in Nicaragua to US$80 per day in Belize. However, rentals are usually not allowed to leave the country – though Budget, for example, allows it if you rent from Nicaragua or Guatemala (only). But renting can make for a memorable splurge day or two, and get you into areas you might otherwise miss (such as isolated beaches south of Tulum in Mexico and around Costa Rica's Península de Nicoya).

In many cases it's cheaper to arrange (even same-day) rentals with major car-rental agencies on their websites; during research in Tulum we saved 50% on the quoted local fare by going to an internet café next door and booking a car online!

4WD vehicles are more expensive (generally US$80 to US$100 per week), and petrol is about US$1 or US$1.50 per liter.

Insurance is required – and your coverage back home isn't recognized here. Make sure you have at least collision damage insurance coverage.

To rent a car, you'll need a passport and driver's license. Some agencies rent to those 21 and over, while others to only those 25 and over. All of Central America drives on the right-hand side of the road.

Scooters and bigger motorcycles are available in some places, the latter usually costing about the same price as a compact car.

For more information and general advice on driving in Central America, including liability insurance, see p739.

HITCHHIKING

Hitching (*tomando un jalón*; taking a hitch) is never entirely safe in any country in the world, and Lonely Planet does not recommend it. However, it is common in parts of Central America. Side roads – or wherever the last bus just went by – may tempt you to try. If you do, try to be in groups; solo women should never hitch. If you get a ride, offer to pay petrol money, even if the driver may turn it down.

TRAIN

The only train trip in the region is a very scenic, glass-domed luxury ride from Panama City to Colón, Panama, along the Panama Canal (see p663).

Health Dr David Goldberg

CONTENTS

Travelers to Central America need to be concerned about food-borne as well as mosquito-borne infections. Most of these illnesses are not life threatening, but they can certainly ruin your trip. Besides getting the proper vaccinations, it's important that you bring along a good insect repellent and exercise great care in what you eat and drink.

BEFORE YOU GO

Bring medications in their original containers, clearly labeled. A signed, dated letter from your physician describing all medical conditions and medications (including generic names) is a good idea. If carrying syringes or needles, take a physician's letter documenting their medical necessity.

INSURANCE

If your health insurance does not cover you for medical expenses abroad, consider supplemental insurance. Check www.lonely planet.com for more information. US travelers can find a list of recommended doctors abroad and emergency evacuation details on the **US State Department website** (www.travel.state .gov). Find out in advance if your insurance plan will make payments directly to providers or reimburse you later for overseas health expenditures. If the latter, be sure to collect receipts.

MEDICAL CHECKLIST

- acetaminophen/paracetamol (Tylenol) or aspirin
- adhesive or paper tape
- antibacterial ointment (eg Bactroban) for cuts and abrasions
- antibiotics
- antidiarrheal drugs (eg loperamide)
- antihistamines (for hay fever and allergic reactions)
- anti-inflammatory drugs (eg ibuprofen)
- bandages, gauze and gauze rolls
- DEET-containing insect repellent for the skin
- iodine tablets (for water purification)
- oral rehydration salts
- permethrin-containing insect spray for clothing, tents and bed nets
- pocketknife
- scissors, safety pins and tweezers
- steroid cream or cortisone (for poison ivy and other allergic rashes)
- sunblock
- syringes and sterile needles
- thermometer

RECOMMENDED VACCINATIONS

Since most vaccines don't produce immunity until at least two weeks after they're given, visit a physician four to eight weeks before departure. Ask your doctor to provide you with an international certificate of vaccination (otherwise known as the yellow booklet), which will list all the vaccinations you've received. This is mandatory for countries that require proof of yellow fever vaccination upon entry, but it's a good idea to carry it wherever you travel.

The only required vaccine is yellow fever, and that's only if you're arriving from a yellow fever–infected country in Africa or South America. However, a number of vaccines are recommended. Note that some of these are not approved for use by children and pregnant women – check with your physician.

RECOMMENDED VACCINATIONS

Vaccine	Recommended for	Dosage	Side effects
chickenpox	travelers who've never had chickenpox	2 doses 1 month apart	fever, mild case of chickenpox
hepatitis A	all travelers	1 dose before trip; booster 6-12 months later	soreness at injection site, headaches, body aches
hepatitis B	long-term travelers in close contact with the local population	3 doses over 6-month period	soreness at injection site, low-grade fever
measles	travelers born after 1956 who've had only 1 measles vaccination	1 dose	fever, rash, joint pains, allergic reactions
rabies	travelers who may have contact with animals and may not have access to medical care	3 doses over 3- to 4-week period	soreness at injection site, headaches, body aches
tetanus-diphtheria	all travelers who haven't had a booster within 10 yrs	1 dose lasts 10 years	soreness at injection site
typhoid fever	all travelers	4 capsules by mouth; 1 taken every other day	abdominal pain, nausea, rash
yellow fever	required for travelers arriving from a yellow fever-infected area in Africa or the Americas	1 dose lasts 10 years	headaches, body aches; severe reactions are rare

ONLINE RESOURCES

The **World Health Organization** (www.who.int/ith/) publishes a superb book called *International Travel and Health,* which is revised annually and is available on its website at no cost. Its website lists updated risks and worldwide vaccination certificate requirements . Another website of general interest is **MD Travel Health** (www.mdtravelhealth.com), which provides complete travel health recommendations for every country, updated daily, also at no cost.

It's usually a good idea to consult your government's travel health website before departure, if one is available.

Australia www.smarttraveller.gov.au/
Canada www.hc-sc.gc.ca/index_e.html
UK www.doh.gov.uk
USA www.cdc.gov/travel/

FURTHER READING

For further information, see *Healthy Travel Central & South America,* also from Lonely Planet. If you're traveling with children, Lonely Planet's *Travel with Children* may be useful. The *ABC of Healthy Travel,* by E Walker et al, and *Medicine for the Outdoors,* by Paul S Auerbach, are other valuable travel-health resources.

IN TRANSIT

DEEP VEIN THROMBOSIS (DVT)

Blood clots may form in the legs during plane flights, chiefly because of prolonged immobility. The longer the flight, the greater the risk. Though most blood clots are reabsorbed uneventfully, some may break off and travel through the blood vessels to the lungs, where they could cause life-threatening complications.

The chief symptom of deep vein thrombosis is swelling or pain in the foot, ankle or calf, usually but not always on just one side. When a blood clot travels to the lungs, it may cause chest pain and difficulty in breathing. Travelers with any of these symptoms should immediately seek medical attention.

HEALTH

To prevent the development of deep vein thrombosis on long flights, you should walk about the cabin, perform isometric compressions of the leg muscles (ie contract the leg muscles while sitting), drink plenty of fluids and avoid alcohol and tobacco.

JET LAG & MOTION SICKNESS

Jet lag is common when crossing more than five time zones, and is characterized by insomnia, fatigue, malaise or nausea. To avoid jet lag, try drinking plenty of fluids (nonalcoholic) and eating light meals. Upon arrival, get exposure to natural sunlight and readjust your schedule (for meals, sleep etc) as soon as possible.

Antihistamines such as dimenhydrinate (Dramamine) and meclizine (Antivert, Bonine) are usually the first choice for treating motion sickness. Their main side effect is drowsiness. A herbal alternative is ginger, which works like a charm for some people.

IN CENTRAL AMERICA

AVAILABILITY & COST OF HEALTH CARE

Good medical care is available in most of the region's capital cities, but options are limited elsewhere. In general, private hospitals are more reliable than public facilities, which may experience significant shortages of equipment and supplies.

Many doctors and hospitals expect payment in cash, regardless of whether you have travel health insurance. If you develop a life-threatening medical problem, you'll probably want to be evacuated to a country with state-of-the-art medical care. Since this may cost tens of thousands of dollars, be sure you have insurance to cover this before you depart.

Many pharmacies are well supplied, but important medications may not be consistently available. Be sure to bring along adequate supplies of all prescription drugs.

INFECTIOUS DISEASES
Cholera

Cholera is an intestinal infection acquired through ingestion of contaminated food or water. The main symptom is profuse, watery diarrhea, which may be so severe that it causes life-threatening dehydration. The key treatment is drinking oral rehydration solution. Antibiotics are also given, usually tetracycline

or doxycycline, though quinolone antibiotics such as ciprofloxacin and levofloxacin are also effective.

Cholera outbreaks occur periodically in parts of Central America, but the disease is rare among travelers. A cholera vaccine is no longer required, and is in fact no longer available in some countries, including the United States, because the old vaccine was relatively ineffective and caused side effects. There are new vaccines that are safer and more effective, but they're not available in many countries and are only recommended for those at particularly high risk.

Dengue Fever

Dengue fever is a viral infection found throughout Central America. Dengue is transmitted by aedes mosquitoes, which bite predominantly during the daytime and are usually found close to human habitations, often indoors. They breed primarily in artificial water containers, such as jars, barrels, cans, cisterns, metal drums, plastic containers and discarded tires. As a result, dengue is especially common in densely populated, urban environments.

Dengue usually causes flu-like symptoms, including fever, muscle aches, joint pains, headaches, nausea and vomiting, often followed by a rash. The body aches may be quite uncomfortable, but most cases resolve themselves uneventfully in a few days. Severe cases usually occur in children under the age of 15 who are experiencing their second dengue infection.

There is no treatment for dengue except to take analgesics such as acetaminophen/paracetamol (Tylenol) and to drink plenty of fluids. Severe cases may require hospitalization for intravenous fluids and supportive care. There is no vaccine. The cornerstone of prevention is to avoid being bitten by a mosquito (see p749 for prevention advice).

Hemorrhagic Conjunctivitis

Outbreaks of hemorrhagic conjunctivitis (pink-eye) have recently been reported from several Central American countries, including El Salvador, Guatemala, and Nicaragua. The chief symptoms are redness, discomfort, and swelling around the eyes, usually associated with a discharge. Hemorrhagic conjunctivitis may be spread by the hands (after an infected person has rubbed his or her eyes) or by inanimate objects, such as towels. It doesn't usually cause any long-term eye problems, but it's highly contagious and extremely uncomfortable. You can reduce your risk by washing your hands frequently and having good personal hygiene.

Hepatitis A

Hepatitis A occurs throughout Central America. It's a viral infection of the liver that is usually acquired by ingestion of contaminated water, food or ice, though it may also be acquired by direct contact with infected persons. The illness occurs all over the world, but the incidence is higher in developing nations. Symptoms may include fever, malaise, jaundice, nausea, vomiting and abdominal pain. Most cases resolve themselves uneventfully, though hepatitis A occasionally causes severe liver damage. There is no treatment.

The vaccine for hepatitis A is extremely safe and highly effective. If you get a booster six to 12 months later, it lasts for at least 10 years. You really should get it before you go to Central America or any other developing region. Because the safety of the hepatitis A vaccine has not been established for pregnant women or children under the age of two, they should instead be given a gamma-globulin injection.

Hepatitis B

Like hepatitis A, hepatitis B is a liver infection that occurs worldwide but is more common in developing nations. Unlike hepatitis A, the disease is usually acquired by sexual contact or by exposure to infected blood, generally through blood transfusions or contaminated needles. The vaccine is recommended only for long-term travelers (on the road more than six months) who expect to live in rural areas or have close physical contact with the local population. Additionally, the vaccine is recommended for anyone who anticipates sexual contact with the local inhabitants or a possible need for medical, dental or other treatments while abroad, especially if a need for transfusions or injections is expected.

Hepatitis B vaccine is safe and highly effective. However, a total of three injections are necessary to establish full immunity. Several countries added hepatitis B vaccine to the list of routine childhood immunizations in the 1980s, so many young adults are already protected.

Malaria

Malaria occurs in every country in Central America. It's transmitted by mosquito bites, usually between dusk and dawn. The main symptom is high spiking fevers, which may be accompanied by chills, sweats, headache, body aches, weakness, vomiting or diarrhea. Severe cases may involve the central nervous system and lead to seizures, confusion, coma and death.

Taking malaria pills is recommended for rural areas in certain parts of Central America (to find out which areas, you can go to the **US Centers for Disease Control website** (www.cdc .gov/travel/regionalmalaria/camerica.htm). Transmission is greatest during the rainy season (June through November). Except in Panama, the first-choice malaria pill is chloroquine, taken once weekly in a dosage of 500mg, starting one to two weeks before arriving in Central America and continuing through the trip and for four weeks after departure. Chloroquine is safe, inexpensive and highly effective. Side effects are typically mild and may include nausea, abdominal discomfort, headache, dizziness, blurred vision or itching. Severe reactions are uncommon. In Panama, either mefloquine (Lariam), atovaquone/proguanil (Malarone) or doxycycline should be taken.

Protecting yourself against mosquito bites (p749) is just as important as taking malaria pills, since no pills are 100% effective.

If you may not have access to medical care while traveling, you should bring along additional pills for emergency self-treatment, which you should undergo if you can't reach a doctor and you develop symptoms that suggest malaria, such as high spiking fevers. One option is to take four tablets of Malarone once daily for three days. If you self-treat for malaria, it may also be appropriate to start a broad-spectrum antibiotic to cover typhoid fever and other bacterial infections. The drug of choice is usually a quinolone antibiotic such as ciprofloxacin (Cipro) or levofloxacin (Levaquin). If you start self-medication, you should try to see a doctor at the earliest possible opportunity.

If you develop a fever after returning home, see a physician, as malaria symptoms may not occur for months.

Rabies

Rabies is a viral infection of the brain and spinal cord that is almost always fatal. The

HEALTH

rabies virus is carried in the saliva of infected animals and is typically transmitted through an animal bite, though contamination of any break in the skin with infected saliva may result in rabies. Rabies occurs in all Central American countries. Most cases are related to bites from dogs or bats.

The rabies vaccine is safe but a full series requires three injections and is quite expensive. Those at high risk for rabies, such as animal handlers and spelunkers (cave explorers), should certainly get the vaccine. In addition, those at lower risk for animal bites should consider asking for the vaccine if they might be traveling to remote areas and might not have access to appropriate medical care if needed. The treatment for a possibly rabid bite consists of the rabies vaccine with rabies immune globulin. It's effective but must be given promptly. Most travelers don't need rabies vaccine.

All animal bites and scratches must be promptly and thoroughly cleansed with large amounts of soap and water, and local health authorities should be contacted to help determine whether or not further treatment is necessary (see opposite for more information).

Typhoid Fever

Typhoid fever is common throughout Central America. The infection is acquired by ingestion of food or water contaminated by a species of salmonella known as salmonella typhi. Fever occurs in virtually all cases. Other symptoms may include headache, malaise, muscle aches, dizziness, loss of appetite, nausea and abdominal pain. Either diarrhea or constipation may occur. Possible complications include intestinal perforation, intestinal bleeding, confusion, delirium and (rarely) coma.

Unless you expect to take all your meals in major hotels and restaurants, a typhoid vaccine is a good idea. It's usually given orally, but is also available as an injection. Neither vaccine is approved for use in children under the age of two.

The drug of choice for typhoid fever is usually a quinolone antibiotic such as ciprofloxacin (Cipro) or levofloxacin (Levaquin), which many travelers carry for treatment of travelers' diarrhea. However, if you self-treat for typhoid fever, you may also need to self-treat for malaria, since the symptoms of the two diseases may be indistinguishable.

Yellow Fever

Yellow fever no longer occurs in Central America, but many Central American countries, including Belize, El Salvador, Guatemala, Honduras and Nicaragua, require you to have a yellow-fever vaccine before entry if you're arriving from a country in Africa or South America where yellow fever is known to occur. If you're not arriving from a country with yellow fever, the vaccine is neither required nor recommended. The vaccine is given only in approved yellow-fever vaccination centers, which provide validated international certificates of vaccination ('yellow booklets'). The vaccine should be given at least 10 days before departure and remains effective for approximately 10 years. It is not recommended for pregnant women or children less than nine months old. Reactions to the vaccine are generally mild and may include headaches, muscle aches, low-grade fevers, or discomfort at the injection site. Severe, life-threatening reactions have been described but are extremely rare.

Other Infections
BRUCELLOSIS

Brucellosis is an infection of domestic and wild animals that may be transmitted to humans by direct animal contact or by consumption of unpasteurized dairy products from infected animals. Brucellosis occurs in the northern part of Central America. Symptoms may include fever, malaise, depression, loss of appetite, headache, muscle aches and back pain, and may linger for months if not treated. Complications may include arthritis, hepatitis, meningitis and endocarditis (heart valve infection).

CHAGAS' DISEASE

Chagas' disease is a parasitic infection that is transmitted by triatomine insects (reduviid bugs), which inhabit crevices in the walls and roofs of substandard housing in South and Central America. The triatomine insect lays its feces on human skin as it bites, usually at night. A person becomes infected when he or she unknowingly rubs the feces into the bite wound or any other open sore. Chagas' disease is extremely rare in travelers. However, if you sleep in a poorly constructed house, especially one made of mud, adobe or thatch, you should be sure to protect yourself with a bed net and a good insecticide.

HISTOPLASMOSIS

Histoplasmosis is caused by a soil-based fungus that is acquired by inhalation, often when the soil has been disrupted. Initial symptoms may include fever, chills, dry cough, chest pain and headache, sometimes leading to pneumonia.

HIV/AIDS

HIV/AIDS has been reported in all Central American countries. Be sure to use condoms for all sexual encounters. Avoid needles, including those used for tattoos and body-piercing.

LEISHMANIASIS

Leishmaniasis occurs in the mountains and jungles of all Central American countries. The infection is transmitted by sand flies, which are about one-third the size of mosquitoes. Leishmaniasis may be limited to the skin, causing slowly growing ulcers over exposed parts of the body, or (less commonly) disseminate to the bone marrow, liver and spleen. The disease may be particularly severe in those with HIV. There is no vaccine for leishmaniasis. To protect yourself from sand flies, follow the same precautions as for mosquitoes (see following), except that netting must be made of a finer mesh (at least 18 holes to the linear inch).

LEPTOSPIROSIS

Leptospirosis is acquired by exposure to water contaminated by the urine of infected animals. Outbreaks often occur at times of flooding, when sewage overflow may contaminate water sources. The initial symptoms, which resemble a mild flu, usually subside uneventfully in a few days, with or without treatment, but a minority of cases are complicated by jaundice or meningitis. There is no vaccine. You can minimize your risk by staying out of bodies of fresh water that may be contaminated by animal urine. If you're visiting an area where an outbreak is in progress, you can take 200mg of doxycycline once weekly as a preventative measure. If you actually develop leptospirosis, the treatment is 100mg of doxycycline twice daily.

TRAVELERS' DIARRHEA

To prevent diarrhea, avoid tap water unless it has been boiled, filtered or chemically disinfected (with iodine tablets); only eat fresh fruits or vegetables if cooked or peeled; be wary of dairy products that might contain unpasteurized milk; and be highly selective when eating food from street vendors.

If you develop diarrhea, be sure to drink plenty of fluids, preferably an oral rehydration solution containing lots of salt and sugar. A few loose stools don't require treatment, but if you start having more than four or five stools a day, you should start taking an antibiotic (usually a quinolone drug) and an antidiarrheal agent (such as loperamide). If diarrhea is bloody or persists for more than 72 hours or is accompanied by fever, shaking chills or severe abdominal pain, you should seek medical attention.

ENVIRONMENTAL HAZARDS
Animal Bites

Do not attempt to pet, handle or feed any animal, with the exception of domestic animals known to be free of any infectious disease. Most animal injuries are directly related to a person's attempt to touch or feed the animal.

Any bite or scratch by a mammal, including bats, should be promptly and thoroughly cleansed with large amounts of soap and water, followed by application of an antiseptic such as iodine or alcohol. The local health authorities should be contacted immediately for possible post-exposure rabies treatment, whether or not you've been immunized against rabies. It may also be advisable to start an antibiotic, since wounds caused by animal bites and scratches frequently become infected.

One of the newer quinolones, such as levofloxacin (Levaquin), which many travelers carry in case of diarrhea, would be an appropriate choice.

Mosquito Bites

The best solution is prevention. To prevent mosquito bites, wear long sleeves, long pants, hats and shoes (rather than sandals). Bring along a good insect repellent, preferably one containing DEET, which should be applied to exposed skin and clothing but not to eyes, mouth, cuts, wounds or irritated skin. Products containing lower concentrations of DEET are as effective, but for shorter periods of time. In general, adults and children over 12 should use preparations containing 25% to 35% DEET, which usually lasts about six

HEALTH

hours. Children between two and 12 years of age should use preparations containing no more than 10% DEET, applied sparingly, which will usually last about three hours. Neurological toxicity has been reported from DEET, especially in children, but appears to be extremely uncommon and generally related to overuse. DEET-containing compounds should not be used on children under the age of two.

Insect repellents containing certain botanical products, including oil of eucalyptus and soybean oil, are effective but last only 1½ to two hours. DEET-containing repellents are preferable for areas where there is a high risk of malaria or yellow fever. Products based on citronella are not effective.

For additional protection, you can apply permethrin to clothing, shoes, tents and bed nets. Permethrin treatments are safe and remain effective for at least two weeks, even when items are laundered. Permethrin should not be applied directly to skin.

Don't sleep in buildings with the window open unless there is a screen. If sleeping outdoors or in an accommodation that allows entry of mosquitoes, use a bed net, preferably treated with the permethrin, with edges tucked in under the mattress.

The mesh size should be less than 1.5mm. If the sleeping area is not otherwise protected, use a mosquito coil, which will fill the room with insecticide through the night. Repellent-impregnated wristbands are not effective.

Snake Bites
Snakes are a hazard in some areas of Central America. The chief concern is the fer-de-lance, a heavy-bodied snake up to 2m in length. In the event of a venomous snake bite, place the victim at rest, keep the bitten area immobilized and move the victim immediately to the nearest medical facility. Avoid tourniquets, which are no longer recommended.

Scorpion Bites
Scorpions are a problem in some regions. If stung, you should immediately apply ice or cold packs, immobilize the affected body part and go to the nearest emergency room. To prevent scorpion stings, be sure to inspect and shake out clothing, shoes and sleeping bags before use, and wear gloves and protective clothing when working around piles of wood or leaves.

Sun
To protect yourself from excessive sun exposure, you should stay out of the midday sun, wear sunglasses and a wide-brimmed sun hat, and apply sunscreen with SPF 15 or higher, with both UVA and UVB protection. Sunscreen should be generously applied to all exposed parts of the body approximately 30 minutes before sun exposure and should be reapplied after swimming or vigorous activity. Travelers should also drink plenty of fluids and avoid strenuous exercise when the temperature is high.

Water
Tap water in Central America is generally not safe to drink. Vigorous boiling for one minute is the most effective means of water purification. At altitudes greater than 2000m (6500 feet), boil for three minutes.

Another option is to disinfect water with iodine pills. Instructions are usually enclosed and should be carefully followed. Or you can add 2% tincture of iodine to one quart or liter of water (five drops to clear water, 10 drops to cloudy water) and let it stand for 30 minutes. If the water is cold, longer times may be required. The taste of iodinated water may be improved by adding vitamin C (ascorbic acid). Iodinated water should not be consumed for more than a few weeks. Pregnant women, those with a history of thyroid disease and those allergic to iodine should not drink iodinated water.

A number of water filters are on the market. Those with smaller pores (reverse osmosis filters) provide the broadest protection, but they are relatively large and are readily plugged by debris. Those that have somewhat larger pores (microstrainer filters) are ineffective against viruses, although they do remove other organisms. Manufacturers' instructions must be carefully followed.

CHILDREN & PREGNANT WOMEN
In general, it's safe for children and pregnant women to go to Central America. However, because some of the vaccines listed, p744 are not approved for use in children and pregnant women, these travelers should be particularly careful not to drink tap water or consume any questionable food or beverage. Also, when traveling with children, make sure they're up to date on all routine immunizations. It's sometimes appropriate to give children some

of their vaccines a little early before visiting a developing nation. You should discuss this with your pediatrician. Lastly, if pregnant, you should bear in mind that should a complication such as premature labor develop while abroad, the quality of medical care may not be comparable to that in your home country.

Since the yellow fever vaccine is not recommended for pregnant women or children less than nine months old, these travelers, if arriving from a country with yellow fever, should obtain a waiver letter, preferably written on letterhead stationary and bearing the

stamp used by official immunization centers to validate the international certificate of vaccination.

TRADITIONAL MEDICINE

Common traditional remedies include the following:

Problem	Treatment
jet lag	melatonin
motion sickness	ginger
mosquito bite prevention	oil of eucalyptus, soybean oil

HEALTH

Language

CONTENTS

Spanish is the most commonly spoken language in Central America. While English is the official language of Belize, both Spanish and a local Creole are also widely spoken. British and US influences have left other English-speaking pockets in the region, most notably among the descendants of West Indian settlers on the Caribbean coast, but also in Panama, particularly in the Canal Zone. Maya is the most common of a number of indigenous languages and dialects spoken throughout the region.

Every visitor to Central America will benefit from learning some Spanish, and it's easy to pick up the basics. A language course taken before departure can lead to a far more relaxed and rewarding travel experience. You can also enrich your stay by enrolling in a language course in Central America. Don't hesitate to practice your new skills – in general, Latin Americans meet attempts to communicate in their language, however halting, with enthusiasm and appreciation. Even if classes are impractical, learning a few basic phrases and pleasantries is a must.

CENTRAL AMERICAN SPANISH

The Spanish of the Americas comes in a bewildering array of varieties, depending on the areas in which you travel. Consonants may be glossed over, vowels squashed into each other, and syllables – even whole words – dropped entirely. Slang and regional vocabulary, much of it derived from indigenous languages, can further add to the mix. For example, in Guatemala and Honduras a soft drink is called a *refresco*, but a *gaseosa* in El Salvador and Nicaragua, and a *soda* in Panama. Frequent travel among the small Central American republics is common, however, so people are generally familiar with these variations; you should have few problems being understood. (For examples of local slang words, see the Fast Facts section of the individual country chapter introductions.)

Throughout Latin America, the Spanish language is referred to as *castellano* more often than *español*. The letters c and z are never lisped in Latin America; attempts to do so could well provoke amusement.

Another notable difference is that the plural of the familiar *tú* (you) is *ustedes* rather than *vosotros*; the latter term will sound quaint and archaic in the Americas. In many parts of El Salvador, Honduras and Costa Rica, the term *vos* is used instead of *tú*, and as a result the conjugation of some verbs can vary slightly. To avoid complication, we haven't used the *vos* form in the following list of words and phrases. It's a variant that only affects the familiar form of speech, so no offence will be taken when you use *tú* and you'll still be understood everywhere without problem.

For a more in-depth guide to the Spanish of Central and South America, pick up a copy of Lonely Planet's *Latin American Spanish Phrasebook*. Lonely Planet also offers the *Costa Rica Spanish Phrasebook* for those interested in the linguistic particulars of that destination. Another useful resource worth looking for is the compact *University of Chicago Spanish-English, English-Spanish Dictionary*.

PRONUNCIATION

Spanish spelling is phonetically consistent, meaning that there's a clear and consistent relationship between what you see in writing and how it's pronounced.

Vowels

a	as in 'father'
e	as in 'met'
i	as in 'marine'
o	as in 'or' (without the 'r' sound)
u	as in 'rule'; the 'u' is not pronounced after **q** and in the letter combinations **gue** and **gui**, unless it's marked with a diaeresis (eg *argüir*), in which case it's pronounced as English 'w'
y	at the end of a word or when it stands alone, it's pronounced as the Spanish **i** (eg *ley*); between vowels within a word it's as the 'y' in 'yonder'

Consonants

As a rule, Spanish consonants resemble their English counterparts. The exceptions are listed below. Note that while the consonants **ch**, **ll** and **ñ** are generally considered distinct letters, **ch** and **ll** are now often listed alphabetically under **c** and **l** respectively. The letter **ñ** is still treated as a separate letter and comes after **n** in dictionaries.

b	similar to English 'b,' but softer; referred to as 'b larga'
c	as in 'celery' before **e** and **i**; otherwise as English 'k'
ch	as in 'church'
d	as in 'dog,' but between vowels and after **l** or **n**, the sound is closer to the 'th' in 'this'
g	as the 'ch' in the Scottish *loch* before **e** and **i** (written as 'kh' in our guides to pronunciation); elsewhere, **g** is pronounced as in 'go'
h	invariably silent. If your name begins with this letter, listen carefully if you're waiting for public officials to call you.
j	as the 'ch' in the Scottish *loch* ('kh' in our guides to pronunciation)
ll	as the 'y' in 'yellow'
ñ	as the 'ni' in 'onion'
r	a short **r** except at the beginning of a word, and after **l**, **n** or **s**, when it's often rolled
rr	very strongly rolled
v	similar to English 'b,' but softer; referred to as 'b corta'
x	as in 'taxi' except for a very few words, when it's pronounced as **j**
z	as the 's' in 'sun'

Word Stress

In general, words ending in vowels or the letters **n** or **s** have stress on the next-to-last syllable, while those with other endings have stress on the last syllable.

Written accents denote stress, and override the rules above, eg *sótano* (basement), *América* and *porción* (portion).

GENDER & PLURALS

In Spanish, nouns are either masculine or feminine, and there are rules to help determine gender – with exceptions, of course! Feminine nouns generally end with -**a**, -**ción**, -**sión** or -**dad**. Other endings typically signify a masculine noun. Endings for adjectives also change to agree with the gender of the noun they modify (masculine/feminine -**o**/-**a**). Where both masculine and feminine forms are included in this language guide, they are separated by a slash, with the masculine form first, eg *perdido/a*.

If a noun or adjective ends in a vowel, the plural is formed by adding **s** to the end. If it ends in a consonant, the plural is formed by adding **es** to the end.

ACCOMMODATIONS

I'm looking for ...

Estoy buscando ...	e·stoy boos·*kan*·do ...

Where is ...?

¿Dónde hay ...?	*don*·de ai ...

a campground

un terreno de cámping	oon te·*re*·no de *kam*·peen

a guesthouse

una pensión/	*oo*·na pen·*syon*/
casa de huéspedes/	*ka*·sa de we·spe·*des*/
hospedaje	os·pe·*da*·khe

a hotel

un hotel	oon o·*tel*

a youth hostel

un albergue juvenil	oon al·*ber*·ge khoo·ve·*neel*

I'd like a ... room.

Quisiera una habitación ...	kee·*sye*·ra oo·na a·bee·ta·*syon* ...

double

doble	*do*·ble

single

individual	een·dee·vee·*dwal*

twin

con dos camas	kon dos *ka*·mas

How much is it per night/person/week?

¿Cuánto cuesta por noche/	*kwan*·to kwes·ta por *no*·che/
persona/semana?	per·*so*·na/se·*ma*·na

LANGUAGE

MAKING A RESERVATION

(for phone or written requests)

To ...	A ...
From ...	De ...
Date	Fecha
I'd like to book ...	Quisiera reservar ... (see under 'Accommodations' for bed and room options)
in the name of ...	en nombre de ...
for the nights of ...	para las noches del ...
credit card ...	tarjeta de crédito ...
number	número
expiry date	fecha de vencimiento
Please confirm ...	Puede confirmar ...
availability	la disponibilidad
price	el precio

Does it include breakfast?

¿Incluye el desayuno?	een-kloo-ye el de-sa-yoo-no

May I see the room?

¿Puedo ver la habitación?	pwe-do ver la a-bee-ta-syon

I don't like it.

No me gusta.	no me goos-ta

It's fine. I'll take it.

OK. La alquilo.	o-kay la al-kee-lo

I'm leaving now.

Me voy ahora.	me voy a-o-ra

private/shared	baño privado/	ba-nyo pree-va-do/
bathroom	compartido	kom-par-tee-do
too expensive	demasiado caro	de-ma-sya-do ka-ro
cheaper	más económico	mas e-ko-no-mee-ko
discount	descuento	des-kwen-to

CONVERSATION & ESSENTIALS

In their public behavior, Latin Americans are very conscious of civilities. You should never approach a stranger for information without extending a greeting, such as *buenos días* or *buenas tardes*, and you should use only the polite form of address, especially with the police and public officials.

Central America is generally more formal than many of the South American countries. The polite form *usted* (you) is used in all cases in this guide; where options are given, the form is indicated by the abbreviations 'pol' and 'inf.'

Hello.	Hola.	o-la
Good morning.	Buenos días.	bwe-nos dee-as

Good afternoon.	Buenas tardes.	bwe-nas tar-des
Good evening/ night.	Buenas noches.	bwe-nas no-ches

The three most common greetings are often abbreviated to simply *buenos* (for *buenos días*) and *buenas* (for *buenas tardes* and *buenas noches*).

Goodbye.	Adiós.	a-dyos
See you soon.	Hasta luego.	as-ta lwe-go
Yes.	Sí.	see
No.	No.	no
Please.	Por favor.	por fa-vor
Thank you.	Gracias.	gra-syas
Many thanks.	Muchas gracias.	moo-chas gra-syas
You're welcome.	De nada.	de na-da
Pardon me.	Perdón.	per-don
Excuse me.	Permiso.	per-mee-so
(used when asking permission)		
Forgive me.	Disculpe.	dees-kool-pe
(used when apologizing)		

How are things?		
¿Qué tal?	ke tal	
What's your name?		
¿Cómo se llama?	ko-mo se ya-ma (pol)	
¿Cómo te llamas?	ko-mo te ya-mas (inf)	
My name is ...		
Me llamo ...	me ya-mo ...	
It's a pleasure to meet you.		
Mucho gusto.	moo-cho goos-to	
The pleasure is mine.		
El gusto es mío.	el goos-to es mee-o	
Where are you from?		
¿De dónde es/eres?	de don-de es/e-res (pol/inf)	
I'm from ...		
Soy de ...	soy de ...	
Where are you staying?		
¿Dónde está alojado?	don-de es-ta a-lo-kha-do (pol)	
¿Dónde estás alojado?	don-de es-tas a-lo-kha-do (inf)	
May I take a photo?		
¿Puedo sacar una foto?	pwe-do sa-kar oo-na fo-to	

DIRECTIONS

How do I get to ...?	
¿Cómo puedo llegar a ...?	ko-mo pwe-do lye-gar a ...
Is it far?	
¿Está lejos?	es-ta le-khos
Go straight ahead.	
Siga/Vaya derecho.	see-ga/va-ya de-re-cho
Turn left.	
Voltée a la izquierda.	vol-te-e a la ees-kyer-da
Turn right.	
Voltée a la derecha.	vol-te-e a la de-re-cha

SIGNS

Entrada	Entrance
Salida	Exit
Información	Information
Abierto	Open
Cerrado	Closed
Prohibido	Prohibited
Comisaria	Police Station
Servicios/Baños	Toilets
Hombres/Varones	Men
Señoras/Damas	Women

I'm lost.
Estoy perdido/a.   es·*toy* per·*dee*·do/a
Can you show me (on the map)?
¿Me lo podría indicar   me lo po·*dree*·a een·dee·*kar*
(en el mapa)?   (en el *ma*·pa)

north	*norte*	*nor*·te
south	*sur*	soor
east	*este/oriente*	*es*·te/o·*ryen*·te
west	*oeste/occidente*	o·*es*·te/ok·see·*den*·te
here	*aquí*	a·*kee*
there	*allí*	a·*yee*
avenue	*avenida*	a·ve·*nee*·da
block	*cuadra*	*kwa*·dra
street	*calle/paseo*	*ka*·lye/pa·*se*·o

HEALTH

I'm sick.
Estoy enfermo/a.   es·*toy* en·*fer*·mo/a
I need a doctor.
Necesito un médico.   ne·se·*see*·to oon *me*·dee·ko
Where's the hospital?
¿Dónde está el hospital?   *don*·de es·*ta* el os·pee·*tal*
I'm pregnant.
Estoy embarazada.   es·*toy* em·ba·ra·*sa*·da
I've been vaccinated.
Estoy vacunado/a.   es·*toy* va·koo·*na*·do/a

I'm allergic to ...
Soy alérgico/a ...   soy a·*ler*·khee·ko/a a ...
  antibiotics
  a los antibióticos   los an·tee·*byo*·tee·kos
  penicillin
  a la penicilina   la pe·nee·see·*lee*·na
  peauts
  al maní   al ma·*nee*

I'm ...	*Soy ...*	soy ...
asthmatic	*asmático/a*	as·*ma*·tee·ko/a
diabetic	*diabético/a*	dya·*be*·tee·ko/a
epileptic	*epiléptico/a*	e·pee·*lep*·tee·ko/a

EMERGENCIES

Help!	*¡Socorro!*	so·*ko*·ro
Fire!	*¡Incendio!*	een·*sen*·dyo
Go away!	*¡Déjeme!*	*de*·khe·me
Get lost!	*¡Váyase!*	*va*·ya·se

It's an emergency.
Es una emergencia.   es oo·na e·mer·*khen*·sya
Could you help me, please?
¿Me puede ayudar,   me *pwe*·de a·yoo·*dar*
por favor?   por fa·*vor*
I'm lost.
Estoy perdido/a.   es·*toy* per·*dee*·do/a
I've been robbed.
Me robaron.   me ro·*ba*·ron
Where are the toilets?
¿Dónde están los baños?   *don*·de es·*tan* los *ba*·nyos

Call ...!
¡Llame a ...!   *ya*·me a
  an ambulance
  una ambulancia   oo·na am·boo·*lan*·sya
  a doctor
  un médico   oon *me*·dee·ko
  the police
  la policía   la po·lee·*see*·a

I have ...	*Tengo ...*	*ten*·go ...
diarrhea	*diarrea*	dya·*re*·a
nausea	*náusea*	*now*·se·a
a headache	*un dolor de*	oon do·*lor* de
	cabeza	ka·*be*·sa

LANGUAGE DIFFICULTIES

Do you speak (English)?
¿Habla/Hablas (inglés)?   a·bla/a·blas (een·*gles*) (pol/inf)
Does anyone here speak English?
¿Hay alguien que hable   ai al·*gyen* ke a·ble
inglés?   een·*gles*
I (don't) understand.
Yo (no) entiendo.   yo (no) en·*tyen*·do
How do you say ...?
¿Cómo se dice ...?   *ko*·mo se *dee*·se ...
What does ... mean?
¿Qué quiere decir ...?   ke *kye*·re de·*seer* ...

Could you please ...?
¿Puede ..., por favor?   *pwe*·de ... por fa·*vor*
  repeat that
  repetirlo   re·pe·*teer*·lo
  speak more slowly
  hablar más despacio   a·*blar* mas des·*pa*·syo
  write it down
  escribirlo   es·kree·*beer*·lo

NUMBERS

1	uno	oo·no
2	dos	dos
3	tres	tres
4	cuatro	kwa·tro
5	cinco	seen·ko
6	seis	says
7	siete	sye·te
8	ocho	o·cho
9	nueve	nwe·ve
10	diez	dyes
11	once	on·se
12	doce	do·se
13	trece	tre·se
14	catorce	ka·tor·se
15	quince	keen·se
16	dieciséis	dye·see·says
17	diecisiete	dye·see·sye·te
18	dieciocho	dye·see·o·cho
19	diecinueve	dye·see·nwe·ve
20	veinte	vayn·te
21	veintiuno	vayn·tee·oo·no
30	treinta	trayn·ta
31	treinta y uno	trayn·ta ee oo·no
40	cuarenta	kwa·ren·ta
50	cincuenta	seen·kwen·ta
60	sesenta	se·sen·ta
70	setenta	se·ten·ta
80	ochenta	o·chen·ta
90	noventa	no·ven·ta
100	cien	syen
101	ciento uno	syen·to oo·no
200	doscientos	do·syen·tos
1000	mil	meel
5000	cinco mil	seen·ko meel
10,000	diez mil	dyes meel
50,000	cincuenta mil	seen·kwen·ta meel
100,000	cien mil	syen meel

SHOPPING & SERVICES

I'd like to buy ...
Quisiera comprar ...   kee·sye·ra kom·prar
I'm just looking.
Sólo estoy mirando.   so·lo es·toy mee·ran·do
May I look at it?
¿Puedo mirarlo/la?   pwe·do mee·rar·lo/la
How much is it?
¿Cuánto cuesta?   kwan·to kwes·ta
That's too expensive for me.
Es demasiado caro   es de·ma·sya·do ka·ro
  para mí.   pa·ra mee
Could you lower the price?
¿Podría bajar un poco   po·dree·a ba·khar oon po·ko
  el precio?   el pre·syo

I don't like it.
No me gusta.   no me goos·ta
I'll take it.
Lo llevo.   lo ye·vo

Do you accept ...?
¿Aceptan ...?   a·sep·tan
  American dollars
  dólares americanos   do·la·res a·me·ree·ka·nos
  credit cards
  tarjetas de crédito   tar·khe·tas de kre·dee·to
  traveler's checks
  cheques de viajero   che·kes de vya·khe·ro

less	menos	me·nos
more	más	mas
large	grande	gran·de
small	pequeño/a	pe·ke·nyo/a

I'm looking for the ...	Estoy buscando ...	es·toy boos·kan·do
ATM	el cajero automático	el ka·khe·ro ow·to·ma·tee·ko
bank	el banco	el ban·ko
bookstore	la librería	la lee·bre·ree·a
embassy	la embajada	la em·ba·kha·da
exchange house	la casa de cambio	la ka·sa de kam·byo
general store	la tienda	la tyen·da
laundry	la lavandería	la la·van·de·ree·a
market	el mercado	el mer·ka·do
pharmacy/ chemist	la farmacia/ la botica	la far·ma·sya/ la bo·tee·ka
post office	el correo	el ko·re·o
supermarket	el supermercado	el soo·per·mer·ka·do
tourist office	la oficina de turismo	la o·fee·see·na de too·rees·mo

What time does it open/close?
¿A qué hora abre/cierra?
a ke o·ra a·bre/sye·ra
I want to change some money/traveler's checks.
Quiero cambiar dinero/cheques de viajero.
kye·ro kam·byar dee·ne·ro/che·kes de vya·khe·ro
What is the exchange rate?
¿Cuál es el tipo de cambio?
kwal es el tee·po de kam·byo
I want to call ...
Quiero llamar a ...
kye·ro lya·mar a ...

airmail	correo aéreo	ko·re·o a·e·re·o
black market	mercado (negro/ paralelo)	mer·ka·do ne·gro/ pa·ra·le·lo

letter	carta	kar·ta
registered mail	certificado	ser·tee·fee·ka·do
stamps	estampillas	es·tam·pee·lyas

TIME & DATES

What time is it?	¿Qué hora es?	ke o·ra es
It's one o'clock.	Es la una.	es la oo·na
It's seven o'clock.	Son las siete.	son las sye·te
midnight	medianoche	me·dya·no·che
noon	mediodía	me·dyo·dee·a
half past two	dos y media	dos ee me·dya
now	ahora	a·o·ra
today	hoy	oy
tonight	esta noche	es·ta no·che
tomorrow	mañana	ma·nya·na
yesterday	ayer	a·yer
Monday	lunes	loo·nes
Tuesday	martes	mar·tes
Wednesday	miércoles	myer·ko·les
Thursday	jueves	khwe·ves
Friday	viernes	vyer·nes
Saturday	sábado	sa·ba·do
Sunday	domingo	do·meen·go
January	enero	e·ne·ro
February	febrero	fe·bre·ro
March	marzo	mar·so
April	abril	a·breel
May	mayo	ma·yo
June	junio	khoo·nyo
July	julio	khoo·lyo
August	agosto	a·gos·to
September	septiembre	sep·tyem·bre
October	octubre	ok·too·bre
November	noviembre	no·vyem·bre
December	diciembre	dee·syem·bre

TRANSPORTATION
Public Transportation

What time does ... leave/arrive?	¿A qué hora sale/llega ...?	a ke o·ra sa·le/ye·ga ...
the bus	el autobús	el ow·to·boos
the plane	el avión	el a·vyon
the ship	el barco/buque	el bar·ko/boo·ke
the train	el tren	el tren
airport	el aeropuerto	el a·e·ro·pwer·to
train station	la estación de ferrocarril	la es·ta·syon de fe·ro·ka·reel
bus station	la estación de autobuses	la es·ta·syon de ow·to·boo·ses
bus stop	la parada de autobuses	la pa·ra·da de ow·to·boo·ses

| luggage check room | guardería/ equipaje | gwar·de·ree·a/ e·kee·pa·khe |
| ticket office | la boletería | la bo·le·te·ree·a |

I'd like a ticket to ...
Quisiera un boleto a ...   kee·sye·ra oon bo·le·to a ...
What's the fare to ...?
¿Cuánto cuesta hasta ...?   kwan·to kwes·ta a·sta ...

1st class	primera clase	pree·me·ra kla·se
2nd class	segunda clase	se·goon·da kla·se
single/one-way	ida	ee·da
return/round-trip	ida y vuelta	ee·da ee vwel·ta
taxi	taxi	tak·see

Private Transportation

I'd like to hire a ...	Quisiera alquilar ...	kee·sye·ra al·kee·lar ...
bicycle	una bicicleta	oo·na bee·see·kle·ta
car	un auto	oon ow·to
4WD	un todo terreno	oon to·do te·re·no
motorcycle	una moto	oo·na mo·to
pickup (truck)	camioneta	ka·myo·ne·ta
truck	camión	ka·myon
hitchhike	hacer dedo/ pedir un ride	a·ser de·do/ pe·deer oon ride

ROAD SIGNS

Acceso	Entrance
Aparcamiento	Parking
Ceda el Paso	Give Way
Despacio	Slow
Dirección Única	One-way
Mantenga Su Derecha	Keep to the Right
No Adelantar/ No Rebase	No Passing
Peaje	Toll
Peligro	Danger
Prohibido Aparcar/ No Estacionar	No Parking
Prohibido el Paso	No Entry
Pare/Stop	Stop
Salida de Autopista	Freeway Exit

Is this the road to (...)?
¿Se va a (...) por esta carretera?   se va a (...) por es·ta ka·re·te·ra
Where's a petrol station?
¿Dónde hay una gasolinera/un grifo?   don·de ai oo·na ga·so·lee·ne·ra/oon gree·fo

LANGUAGE

CROSSING THE BORDER

birth certificate	*certificado de nacimiento*
border (frontier)	*la frontera*
car registration	*registración*
car-owner's title	*título de propiedad*
customs	*aduana*
driver's license	*licencia de manejar*
identification	*identificación*
immigration	*inmigración*
insurance	*seguro*
passport	*pasaporte*
temporary vehicle	*permiso de importación*
import permit	*temporal de vehículo*
tourist card	*tarjeta de turista*
visa	*visado*

Please fill it up.
Lleno, por favor.   ye·no por fa·*vor*
I'd like (20) liters.
Quiero (veinte) litros.   kye·ro (vayn·te) lee·tros

diesel	*diesel*	dee·sel
leaded (regular)	*gasolina con*	ga·so·*lee*·na kon
	plomo	*plo*·mo
petrol (gas)	*gasolina*	ga·so·*lee*·na
unleaded	*gasolina sin*	ga·so·*lee*·na seen
	plomo	*plo*·mo

(How long) Can I park here?
¿(Por cuánto tiempo)   (por kwan·to tyem·po)
Puedo aparcar aquí?   pwe·do a·par·kar a·*kee*
Where do I pay?
¿Dónde se paga?   don·de se *pa*·ga
I need a mechanic.
Necesito un   ne·se·*see*·to oon
mecánico.   me·*ka*·nee·ko
The car has broken down (in ...).
El carro se ha averiado   el *ka*·ro se a a·ve·*rya*·do
(en ...).   (en ...)
The motorcycle won't start.
No arranca la moto.   no a·*ran*·ka la *mo*·to

Also available from Lonely Planet:
Latin American Spanish Phrasebook

I have a flat tyre.
Tengo un pinchazo.   ten·go oon peen·*cha*·so
I've run out of petrol.
Me quedé sin gasolina.   me ke·*de* seen ga·so·*lee*·na
I've had an accident.
Tuve un accidente.   *too*·ve oon ak·see·*den*·te

TRAVEL WITH CHILDREN

I need ...
Necesito ...   ne·se·*see*·to ...
Do you have ...?
¿Hay ...?   ai ...
  a car baby seat
  un asiento de seguridad   oon a·*syen*·to de se·goo·ree·*da*
  para bebés   pa·ra be·*bes*
  a child-minding service
  un servicio de cuidado   oon ser·*vee*·syo de kwee·*da*·do
  de niños   de *nee*·nyos
  a children's menu
  una carta infantil   oo·na *kar*·ta een·fan·*teel*
  a creche
  una guardería   oo·na gwar·de·*ree*·a
  (disposable) diapers/nappies
  pañales (de usar y   pa·*nya*·les (de oo·*sar* ee
  tirar)   tee·*rar*)
  an (English-speaking) babysitter
  una niñera   oo·na nee·*nye*·ra
  (de habla inglesa)   (de *a*·bla een·*gle*·sa)
  formula (milk)
  leche en polvo   *le*·che en *pol*·vo
  a highchair
  una trona   oo·na *tro*·na
  a potty
  una pelela   oo·na pe·*le*·la
  a pusher/stroller
  un cochecito   oon ko·che·*see*·to

Do you mind if I breast-feed here?
¿Le molesta que dé   le mo·*les*·ta ke de
de pecho aquí?   de *pe*·cho a·*kee*
Are children allowed?
¿Se admiten niños?   se ad·*mee*·ten *nee*·nyos

Glossary

See the Language chapter, p752, for other useful words and phrases.

aguardiente – clear, potent liquor made from sugarcane; also referred to as *caña*

aguas de frutas – fruit flavoured water drink

almuerzo – lunch; sometimes used to mean an inexpensive set lunch

apartado – post-office box

artesanía – handicraft

Av – abbreviation for *avenida* (avenue)

ayuntamiento – municipal government

bahía – bay

bajareque – traditional wall construction, where a core of stones is held in place by poles of bamboo or other wood then covered with stucco or mud

balboa – national currency of Panama

balneario – public beach or swimming area

barrio – district; neighborhood

bistec – grilled or fried beef steak

Black Caribs – see *Garífuna*

bocas – appetizers, often served with drinks in a bar

caballeros – literally 'horsemen,' but corresponds to the English 'gentlemen'; look for the term on bathroom doors

cabaña – cabin or bungalow

cabina – see *cabaña*; also a loose term for cheap lodging in Costa Rica (in some cases it refers to cabins or bungalows, in others it refers merely to an economical hotel room)

cafetería – literally 'coffee shop'; any informal restaurant with waiter service (not a self–service establishment as implied by the English 'cafeteria')

cafetín – small *cafetería*

cajero automático – automated teller machine (ATM)

calle – street

callejón – alley; small, narrow or very short street

calzada – causeway

camión – truck; bus

camioneta – pickup truck

campesino – farmer

caña – see *aguardiente*

Carr – abbreviation for *carretera* (highway)

Carretera Interamericana – Interamerican Hwy, or Interamericana (also referred to as the Pan-American Hwy, or Pan-Americana); the nearly continuous highway running from Alaska to Chile (it breaks at the Darién Gap in Panama)

casa de cambio – currency exchange office

casa de huéspedes – guesthouse

casado – cheap set meal, usually served at lunchtime

cascada – waterfall

caseta teléfonica – telephone call station

catedral – cathedral

cay – small island of sand or coral fragments

caye – see *cay*

cayo – see *cay*

cayuco – dugout canoe

cenote – large, natural limestone cave used for water storage or ceremonial purposes

cerro – hill

cerveza – beer

ceviche – seafood marinated in lemon or lime juice, garlic and seasonings

Chac – Maya rain god; his likeness appears on many ruins

chacmool – Maya sacrificial stone sculpture

chamarra – thick, heavy woolen blanket (Guatemala)

chapín – citizen of Guatemala; Guatemalan

chicha – fruit juice mixed with sugar and water (Panama)

chicken bus – former US school bus used for public transportation

cine – movie theater

ciudad – city

cocina – literally 'kitchen'; small, basic restaurant, or cookshop, usually found in or near municipal markets

cofradía – religious brotherhood, particularly in highland Guatemala

colectivo – shared taxi or minibus that picks up and drops off passengers along its route

colón – national currency of Costa Rica

comedor – basic and cheap eatery, usually with a limited menu

comida a la vista – meal served buffet- or cafeteria-style

comida corrida – meal of the day; set meal of several courses, usually offered at lunchtime

comida corriente – mixed plate of different foods typical of the local region

conquistador – any of the Spanish explorer-conquerors of Latin America

Contras – counterrevolutionary military groups fighting against the Sandinista government in Nicaragua throughout the 1980s

cordillera – mountain range

córdoba – national currency of Nicaragua

correo aéreo – airmail

corte – piece of material 7m to 10m long that is used as a wraparound skirt

costa – coast

criollo – Creole; born in Latin America of Spanish parentage; on the Caribbean coast it refers to someone of mixed African and European descent; see also *mestizo* and *ladino*

cuadra – city block

cueva – cave

damas – ladies; the usual sign on bathroom doors

edificio – building

empanada – Chilean-style turnover stuffed with meat or cheese and raisins

entrada – entrance

expreso – express bus

faja – waist sash that binds garments and holds what would otherwise be put in pockets

finca – farm; plantation; ranch

fritanga – sidewalk barbecue, widely seen in Nicaragua

fuerte – fort

gallo pinto – common meal of blended rice and beans

Garífuna – descendants of West African slaves and Carib Indians, brought to the Caribbean coast of Central America in the late 18th century from the island of St Vincent; also referred to as *Black Caribs*

Garinagu – see *Garífuna*

gaseosa – soft drink

gibnut – small, brown-spotted rodent similar to a guinea pig; also called *paca*

golfo – gulf

gringo/a – mildly pejorative term used in Latin America to describe male/female foreigners, particularly those from North America; often applied to any visitor of European heritage

gruta – cave

guacamole – a salad of mashed or chopped avocados, onions and tomatoes

guaro – local firewater made with sugarcane (Costa Rica)

hacienda – agricultural estate or plantation; treasury, as in Departamento de Hacienda (Treasury Department)

hospedaje – guesthouse

huipil – long, woven, white sleeveless tunic with intricate, colorful embroidery (Maya regions)

iglesia – church

indígena – indigenous

Interamericana – see *Carretera Interamericana*

internacionalistas – volunteers from all over the world who contributed to rebuilding Nicaragua when the Sandinistas assumed power

invierno – winter; Central America's wet season, which extends roughly from April through mid-December

isla – island

IVA – *impuesto al valor agregado;* value-added tax

junco – type of basket weaving

ladino – person of mixed indigenous and European parentage, often used to describe a *mestizo* who speaks Spanish; see also *mestizo* and *criollo*

lago – lake

laguna – lagoon; lake

lancha – small motorboat

lempira – national currency of Honduras

leng – colloquial Mayan term for coins (Guatemalan highlands)

licuado – fresh fruit drink, blended with milk or water

lista de correos – poste restante (general delivery) mail

malecón – waterfront promenade

mar – sea

marimba – xylophone-like instrument

menú del día – fixed-price meal of several courses

mercado – market

Mesoamerica – a geographical region extending from central Mexico to northwestern Costa Rica

mestizo – person of mixed ancestry, usually Spanish and indigenous; see also *criollo* and *ladino*

metate – flat stone on which corn is ground

migración – immigration; immigration office

milpa – cornfield

mirador – lookout

mola – colorful hand-stitched appliqué textile made by Kuna Indians

muelle – pier

municipalidad – town hall

museo – museum

Navidad – Christmas

oficina de correos – post office

ordinario – slow bus

paca – see *gibnut*

PADI – Professional Association of Diving Instructors

palacio de gobierno – building housing the executive offices of a state or regional government

palacio municipal – city hall; seat of the corporation or municipal government

palapa – thatched, palm leaf-roofed shelter with open sides

Pan–Americana – see *Carretera Interamericana*

pan de coco – coconut bread

panadería – bakery

panga – small motorboat

parada – bus stop

parque – park; sometimes also used to describe a plaza

parque nacional – national park

peña – folkloric club; evening of music, song and dance

pensión – guesthouse

petén – island

plato del día – plate (or meal) of the day
plato típico – mixed plate of various foods typical or characteristic of a place or region
playa – beach
pollera – Spanish-influenced 'national dress' of Panamanian women, worn for festive occasions
pozo – spring
propina – tip; gratuity
pueblo – small town or village
puente – bridge
puerta – gate; door
puerto – port; harbor
pulpería – corner store; minimart
punta – point; traditional Garífuna dance involving much hip movement
pupusa – cornmeal mass stuffed with cheese or refried beans, or a mixture of both (El Salvador)

quebrada – ravine; brook
quetzal – national currency of Guatemala, named for the tropical bird

rancho – thatched-roof restaurant
refresco – soda, or soft drink; drink made with local fruits (Costa Rica)
río – river
ropa vieja – literally 'old clothes'; spicy shredded beef and rice dish (Panama)
rosticería – restaurant selling roast meats
Ruta Maya – Maya Route, describing travels to the Mayan sites of Mexico, Guatemala and Belize (chiefly), but also El Salvador and Honduras

sacbé – ceremonial limestone avenue or path between Maya cities
salida – exit
sancocho – spicy meat-and-vegetable stew, the 'national dish' of Panama
santo – saint

Semana Santa – Holy Week, the week preceding Easter
sendero – path or trail
sierra – mountain range; saw
soda – place that serves a counter lunch; soda or soft drink (Panama)
sorbetería – ice-cream parlor
stela, stelae – standing stone monument of the ancient Maya, usually carved
supermercado – supermarket, from a corner store to a large, Western-style supermarket

taller – shop; workshop
tamale – boiled or steamed cornmeal filled with chicken or pork, usually wrapped in a banana leaf
tapado – rich Garífuna stew made from fish, shrimp, shellfish, coconut milk and plantain, spiced with coriander
templo – temple; church
terminal de autobus – bus terminal
Tico/a – male/female inhabitant of Costa Rica
tienda – small shop
típica – see *típico*
típico – typical or characteristic of a region, particularly used to describe food; also a form of Panamanian folkloric music
traje – traditional handmade clothing
turicentro – literally 'tourist center'; outdoor recreation center with swimming facilities, restaurants and camping (El Salvador)

vegetariano/a – male/female vegetarian
venado – deer; venison
verano – summer; Central America's dry season, roughly from mid-December to April
viajero/a – male/female traveler
volcán – volcano

Zapatistas – members of the left–wing group Ejército Zapatista de Liberación Nacional (EZLN), fighting for indigenous rights in Chiapas, Mexico

Behind the Scenes

THIS BOOK

This 6th edition of *Central America on a Shoestring* was written by a very capable team of authors led by Robert Reid (aka Señor Shoestring). Robert wrote the chapter on Mexico's Yucatán & Chiapas in addition to the book's front and back sections. The authors of the other destination chapters were Jolyon Attwooll (Honduras), Matthew D Firestone (Panama), Carolyn McCarthy (El Salvador and Costa Rica), Andy Symington (Nicaragua) and Lucas Vidgen (Guatemala and Belize). Dr David Goldberg wrote the Health chapter. Robert also coordinated the previous edition and wrote the text along with Gary Chandler Prado, Carolina A Miranda, Regis St Louis and Lucas Vidgen. The author team is indebted to the work of all authors from the previous five editions of this book, including David Zingarelli, who coordinated the 4th edition, and Nancy Keller, who coordinated the 3rd edition.

This guidebook was commissioned in Lonely Planet's Oakland office, and produced by the following:

Commissioning Editors Greg Benchwick, David Zingarelli, Catherine Craddock
Coordinating Editor Evan Jones
Coordinating Cartographer Andrew Smith
Coordinating Layout Designer Pablo Gastar
Managing Editor Geoff Howard
Managing Cartographer Alison Lyall, Amanda Sierp
Assisting Editors Sally O'Brien, Maryanne Netto, Rowan McKinnon, Sasha Baskett, Stephanie Ong, Phillip Tang, Averil Robertson, Louise Clarke
Assisting Cartographers Sally Gerdan, Anneka Imkamp, Anita Banh
Cover Designers Christopher Ong, Wendy Wright
Project Managers Fabrice Rocher, Sarah Sloane
Language Content Coordinator Quentin Frayne

Thanks to David Burnett, Sally Darmody, James Hardy, Marina Kosmatos, Adriana Mammarella, Adam McCrow, Wayne Murphy, Raphael Richards, Celia Wood

---

LONELY PLANET: TRAVEL WIDELY, TREAD LIGHTLY, GIVE SUSTAINABLY

The Lonely Planet Story

The story begins with a classic travel adventure: Tony and Maureen Wheeler's 1972 journey across Europe and Asia to Australia. There was no useful information about the overland trail then, so Tony and Maureen published the first Lonely Planet guidebook to meet a growing need.

From a kitchen table, Lonely Planet has grown to become the largest independent travel publisher in the world, with offices in Melbourne (Australia), Oakland (USA) and London (UK). Today Lonely Planet guidebooks cover the globe. There is an ever-growing list of books and information in a variety of media. Some things haven't changed. The main aim is still to make it possible for adventurous individuals to get out there – to explore and better understand the world.

The Lonely Planet Foundation

The Lonely Planet Foundation proudly supports nimble nonprofit institutions working for change in the world. Each year the foundation donates 5% of Lonely Planet company profits to projects selected by staff and authors. Our partners range from Kabissa, which provides small nonprofit groups across Africa with access to technology, to the Foundation for Developing Cambodian Orphans, which supports girls at risk of falling victim to sex traffickers.

Our nonprofit partners are linked by a grass-roots approach to the areas of health, education or sustainable tourism. Many projects we support – such as one with BaAka (Pygmy) children in the forested areas of Central African Republic – choose to focus on women and children as one of the most effective ways to support the whole community.

Sometimes foundation assistance is as simple as helping to preserve a local ruin such as the Minaret of Jam in Afghanistan; this incredible monument now draws intrepid tourists to the area and its restoration has greatly improved options for local people.

Just as travel is often about learning to see with new eyes, so many of the groups we work with aim to change the way people see themselves and the future for their children and communities.

THANKS

ROBERT REID

Huge thanks to Greg Benchwick for keeping an eye on Central America from the Oakland office – and for the job! And all the authors on the book – not one complaint about the moustache counts, that's magical. Thanks especially go to many people around Mexico, particularly the 12-year-old taxi driver at Chinkultic ruins for nearly (but not) running over the cyclist, and Dana, Cesar and Romeo in San Cristóbal de Las Casas. Thanks at home to Mai for letting me do this type of work. And lastly a big thanks to the Academy.

JOLYON ATTWOOLL

I can only mention a few of the many people who made a positive contribution to this Honduras update. In San Pedro Sula, Juan Carlos, Angela and Olli provided a great introduction and send-off. In Roatán, Will Welbourn was especially helpful, and thanks also to David Valerio. Joy Lee was a mine of information in Trujillo; in Tegus, *gracias* to Patrick Ahern, Anette from *Honduras This Week* and her friend David for taking me under his wing. Same too to Hans and Iris in Gracias, and Howard and Gerardo in Copán. José Luis' emails were invaluable. Big thanks too to Liza Prado and Gary Chandler, whose footsteps and hard work I followed.

And, of course, thanks to Greg Benchwick and the team, especially Carolyn for a memorable alternative Christmas in Perquín and Robert Reid for his patience.

MATTHEW D FIRESTONE

As always, my warmest thanks go to my family. To my always supportive mother and father, thank you for teaching me how to live life to its fullest, even though I have a hard time keeping up with your Vegas lifestyle! To my incredibly successful sister, thank you for abandoning your New York stylings for a taste of life on the road with your wanderlust-ridden brother. Second, I'd like to give a big shout out to the entire Lonely Planet team. I'd especially like to thank Greg, who saw potential in me from the beginning, Robert for coaching the entire CAM team and Carolyn for sharing her gorgeous mountain retreat (sans Chagas). Finally, I'd like to thank all of the Panamanians great and small, who welcomed me to their beautiful country with open arms and minds.

CAROLYN MCCARTHY

Thanks to the Ticos and Salvadorans who were truly excellent to me. The Peace Corps volunteers of El Salvador were incredibly generous with tips and information – thank you. Rachel, Judi and Ralph kept me sane, surfed and well accompanied on the Nicoya Peninsula. Anyone willing to tag along on these foolish quests deserves hearty praise, as well as a real vacation afterwards. Thanks to Jol for the mince pies and Matt for his good influence during write up. I am indebted to Greg for sending me on this assignment and the staff at Lonely Planet for their skillful wrap-up.

ANDY SYMINGTON

As ever, it's a pleasure to cooperate on a project like this with the consistently excellent Lonely Planet staff and authors. Profuse thanks are also due to many people around Nicaragua, including personal friends, helpful Intur staff, enthusiastic volunteers, bartenders, kids and cabdrivers for offering excellent advice, information, chat and support on the road. I'd also like to thank my family and close friends for their support and last but by no means least, thanks to several excellent fellow travellers for sharing a Toña or two along the way…

LUCAS VIDGEN

In Belize, thanks to Lucky Walker for driving me around way more than necessary and filling me in on all the details. The gang at Monkey Bay also deserves a mention, for info and hospitality, as does Austin Rodriguez for taking time out to provide an interview. In Guatemala, the whole project would have been much trickier without Tom Lingenfelter, Pedro Rodríguez, Eduardo Tatzan and the patience of Nora López.

On the home front, thanks to Brian Benson and Ana Marie Madison for keeping it all together while I was away, and América and Sofia Celeste for being there when I got back. Big ups also to the hundreds of travelers that I bumped into on the road and who wrote in with snippets of info – you guys make the job a whole lot easier and we really do read every letter and email. Keep 'em coming.

OUR READERS

Many thanks to the travelers who used the last edition and wrote to us with helpful hints, useful advice and interesting anecdotes:

A Eelco Aartsen, Basandeelco Aartsensommeijer, Zoe Abrams, Pablo Aguila, Kristoffer Alfthan, Jorge Alvar Villegas, Christine Amon, Phil Amos, Lourdes Andino, Patrik Aqvist, Juan Carlos Arias Ruiz, Marina Auburn **B** Anders Backstrom, Colby Balch, Jo Baldwin, Melissa Banton, Chris Baumgartner, Tony Bellette, Pepijn Ten Berge, Tanja Berger, Wallace Blocker, Kati Boege, Saskia Boesjes, Johannes Bolle, Antje Bomsdorf, Anna Bosch, Dan Bosley, Jonathan Boyd, Jose Bravo, Caitlin Brazill, Barry Buchanan, Nicole

Buergin, Jared Bundra, Fred Burgess, Rosie Burn, Jessica Burnham, Sonia Burns, Caio Buzzolini **C** Andrew Cameron, Rolando Campollo, Traci Carl, Mike Carswell, Emmanuelle Cathelineau, Daniella Cervantes, Reva Chandrasekaran, Cydney Chartier, Chuang Chin-Ping, Katrin Christl, Carina Cisneros, Lori Clarke, Gregory Cohen, Dawn Collier, Sharon Collins, Keith Connolly, James Conway, Julian Cook, Eleanor Cornwall, Xana Coronado, Bettina Costa, Benoit & Corinne Couvreur, Ian Cummins, Cole Curtis, Scott Cutler **D** Susan Daloia, Katherine Davis, Donald Day, Nele De Meyer, Otto De Voogd, Irena Delave, Kerry Deichmann-Ramirez, Ingrid Downie, Donna Doyle, Paul Dressler, Chris & Sally Drysdale, Wolfgang Dörfler **E** Daniel Egli, Monique Eller, Tom Evans, Reidar Evensen, Andres Eves, Carl Ewald **F** C Fabre, Sandra Fehlmann, Anat & Gil Feldman, Juan-Pablo Fernández, Sabrina Ferretti, Richard Finch, Hanne Finholt, Petra Fleck, Lizzie Flew, Kelly Folliard, Jens Forsmark, Isabelle Et Catherine Fortier Et Brodeur, Christopher Fowler, Dirk Franz, Johanna Fuchs **G** Vikky Gallagher, Allene (Ali) Gaskell, Magdalena Geigenberger, Earl Gerheim, Michael Girling, Michael Glasgow, Claus Goettfert, Natalie Goharriz, Luz M Gonzalez, Ana Mercedes Gonzalez, Stevfe Goosens, Melanie Grosser, Seb Grothaus **H** Mike Haaijer, Terry Halpin, Erik Halvorson, Jesselyn Hamilton, Jody Hanson, Kelly Harland, Lynne Harrington, Sigrid Havemann, Robert Hawk, Katharina Heermann, Alexx Henke, Anne Hezemans, Martina Hoesli, Claudia Hoess, Sebastian Hoffmann, Sophia Hoffmann, Paul Holt, Yvonne Hoorman, Duncan Hornby, Nicola Howard, Denise Hughes **I** Martin Ineichen, Shamim Islam, Guy Israeli **J** Jeff Jacobson, Angela Jenkins, Thomas Jensen, Andrew Jessep, Ayan Jobse, Michael Judd, Andrea Julian **K** Natalie Kaelin, Molly Kavanaugh, Lisa Kandes, Erin Kennedy, Anouk Kesselring, Anuschka Knettig, Jetske Kodde, Nora Koim, Zoltan Konder, Bart Konings, Mary Ann Koops, Jennifer Kuhlman **L** Tanita Lafleur, Amy Laging, Ryan Lai, Daniel Lambert, Charly Lance, Rachel Latham, Cynthia Legros, Merel Lelivelt, Rebecca Logan, Carley Lovorn, Francesco Lugli, Ola Lönnqvist, Sally Lynch **M** Sarah Macdonald, Colin Maier, Frank Maiolo, Swaroop Manjunath, Paul Mantia, Vincent Marchal, Yossi Margoninsky, Philippe Marois, Allegra Marshall, Lisa Martinez, Anna Maruyama, Marcel Matte, Ted McCarthy, Claire McKenzie, Gene McPherson, Kelly McDonough, Christine McNeill, Meredith Meacham, Charles Meador, Stephen Metz, Thomas Ming, Amit Morali, Aitor Moreno, Ernest Motta, Marco Mwaniki **N** Frank Nasser, Andrew Needham, Rebecca Newbold, Vincent Nicolier, Tony Noble, D Novack, Laura Novoa **O** Jeremy Omer, Catherine Orland, Douglas Ortiz **P** Sarah Lynne Palomo, Paco Panconcelli, Angela Paone, Andrew Parker, Jean-Lionel Payeur, Katherine Payne, Julio Cesar Rivera Pena, Ingeli Penninga, Mariana Pereira, Bill Phelan, Therese Picado, Leo Piet, Gabi Preisach, Patti Pride **Q** Jose Quintanilla **R** Bruce Radtke, Rebekah Ramsay, Matthew Rapley, Jerome Rattier, Ziv Raviv, Bill Reckling, Bev Redmond, Danny Redo, Dorien Regeer, Ronald Reinds, Elise Remling, Silvia Rey, Andy Richmond, Carlos Rivas, Mary Robinson, Peter Robinson, Ian Rose, Matthew Rowe, Jonah Rubin, Jon Russell, James Russell, Zac Ryan, Shannon Ryan **S** Ana Saldana, Barbara Sanders, Michelle Sargent, Marcel Schapers, Uwe Scheibner, Karen Scheuerer, Greg Schlotthauer, Milena Schmidt, Michael Schwebel, Jennifer Schwinn, Jani Schwob, Mark Scott, Aimee Serafini, Nadav Shlezinger, Arnon Shomer, Pasquale Siciliani, Barbara Sigmund, Lorna Sinclair, Jeffrey Smith, Corrine Spencer, Eva Lotta Stein, Kilian Stephan, Jack Stephens, Craig Stephens, Jim Stephenson, Ian C Story, Martin Straub, David Strevens, Geri Sutts **T** Yiftach Talmon, Lee-Anne Taylor, Texas Tea, Jennifer Tee, Pepijn Ten Berge, Jeff Thompson, Philip Trageser, Elliot Trester, Christina Trotter, Julie Turcotte **U** Stefan Usee **V** Gonzalo Vaccalluzzo, Janus & Denice Valentin Helt, Jasper Van Den Hout, Marja Van Deurse, Pieter Van Der Vlugt, Ian Veitch, Augustin Verlinde, Sam Vermeire, Monika Vetsch, Stefan Vettiger **W** Sebastian Wellers, Peter Walker, Daniel Wall, Matthew Warden, Douglas Webster, Gesa Wedig, JJ Weizel, JJ Wentworth, Matt Williamson, Paul Wilson, Shane Wilson, Dietmar Wuelfing **Y** Hector Yague Davila **Z** Natasja Zak, Bernd Ziermann, Jessica Zukerman

ACKNOWLEDGMENTS

Many thanks to the following for the use of their content:

Globe on back cover ©Mountain High Maps 1993 Digital Wisdom, Inc.

SEND US YOUR FEEDBACK

We love to hear from travellers – your comments keep us on our toes and help make our books better. Our well-travelled team reads every word on what you loved or loathed about this book. Although we cannot reply individually to postal submissions, we always guarantee that your feedback goes straight to the appropriate authors, in time for the next edition. Each person who sends us information is thanked in the next edition – and the most useful submissions are rewarded with a free book.

To send us your updates – and find out about Lonely Planet events, newsletters and travel news – visit our award-winning website: **www.lonelyplanet.com/feedback.**

Note: we may edit, reproduce and incorporate your comments in Lonely Planet products such as guidebooks, websites and digital products, so let us know if you don't want your comments reproduced or your name acknowledged. To see our privacy policy visit www.lonelyplanet.com/privacy.

Index

INDEX

000 Map pages
000 Location of colour photographs

INDEX

INDEX

INDEX

INDEX

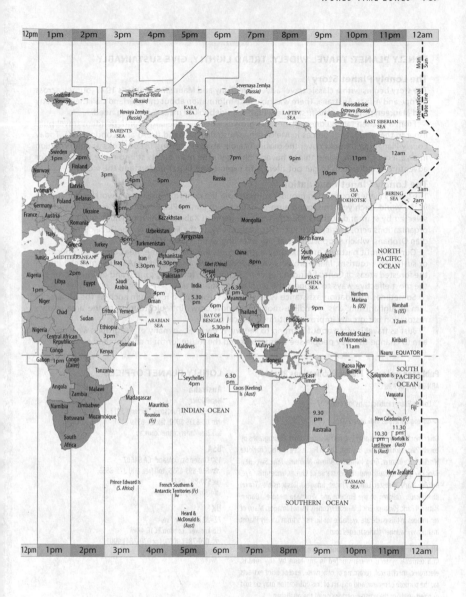

12pm	1pm	2pm	3pm	4pm	5pm	6pm	7pm	8pm	9pm	10pm	11pm	12am

Svalbard (Norway)

Zemlya Frantsa-Iosifa (Russia)

Severnaya Zemlya (Russia)

KARA SEA

Novaya Zemlya (Russia)

LAPTEV SEA

Novosibirskie Ostrovo (Russia)

EAST SIBERIAN SEA

International Date Line

Mon / Sun

BARENTS SEA

Sweden 1pm

2pm

Finland

3pm

4pm

5pm

Russia

7pm

9pm

11pm

12am

10pm

SEA OF OKHOTSK

BERING SEA

3am

2am

Norway

Denmark

Germany

France

Poland

Belarus

Latvia

Austria

Ukraine

Italy

Romania

Greece

Turkey

Tunisia

MEDITERRANEAN SEA

2pm

Algeria

Libya

Egypt

Niger

Chad

Sudan

Nigeria

Central African Republic

Congo

Gabon

Congo (Zaire)

1pm

Kenya

Angola

Zambia

Tanzania

Malawi

Namibia

Zimbabwe

Botswana

Mozambique

South Africa

Syria

Iraq

Saudi Arabia

Yemen

Eritrea

Ethiopia

3pm

Somalia

Iran 3.30pm

Oman

ARABIAN SEA

Afghanistan 4.30pm

Turkmenistan

Uzbekistan

Kazakhstan

Kyrgyzstan

Pakistan

5pm

Tibet (China)

Nepal 5.45 pm

India 5.30 pm

Mongolia

China 8pm

North Korea

South Korea

Japan

9pm

Taiwan

EAST CHINA SEA

NORTH PACIFIC OCEAN

Northern Mariana Is (US)

Marshall Is (US)

12am

Myanmar 6.30 pm

BAY OF BENGAL

Thailand

6pm

Vietnam

Philippines

Palau

Federated States of Micronesia 11am

Kiribati

Nauru EQUATOR

Sri Lanka 5.30pm

Maldives

Malaysia

Indonesia

East Timor

Papua New Guinea

Solomon Is

SOUTH PACIFIC OCEAN

Seychelles 4pm

Cocos (Keeling) Is (Aust)

6.30 pm

Vanuatu

Madagascar

Mauritius

Reunion (Fr)

INDIAN OCEAN

Australia

9.30 pm

New Caledonia (Fr)

Fiji

11.30 pm

Norfolk Is (Aust)

10.30 pm

Lord Howe Is (Aust)

Prince Edward Is (S. Africa)

French Southern & Antarctic Territories (Fr)

Heard & McDonald Is (Aust)

SOUTHERN OCEAN

TASMAN SEA

New Zealand

12pm	1pm	2pm	3pm	4pm	5pm	6pm	7pm	8pm	9pm	10pm	11pm	12am

LONELY PLANET: TRAVEL WIDELY, TREAD LIGHTLY, GIVE SUSTAINABLY

The Lonely Planet Story

The story begins with a classic travel adventure: Tony and Maureen Wheeler's 1972 journey across Europe and Asia to Australia. There was no useful information about the overland trail then, so Tony and Maureen published the first Lonely Planet guidebook to meet a growing need.

From a kitchen table, Lonely Planet has grown to become the largest independent travel publisher in the world, with offices in Melbourne (Australia), Oakland (USA) and London (UK). Today Lonely Planet guidebooks cover the globe. There is an ever-growing list of books and information in a variety of media. Some things haven't changed. The main aim is still to make it possible for adventurous individuals to get out there – to explore and better understand the world.

The Lonely Planet Foundation

The Lonely Planet Foundation proudly supports nimble nonprofit institutions working for change in the world. Each year the foundation donates 5% of Lonely Planet company profits to projects selected by staff and authors. Our partners range from Kabissa, which provides small nonprofit organizations across Africa with access to technology, to the Foundation for Developing Cambodian Orphans, which supports girls at risk of falling victim to sex traffickers.

Our nonprofit partners are linked by a grass-roots approach to the areas of health, education or sustainable tourism. Many projects we support – such as one with BaAka (Pygmy) children in the forested areas of Central African Republic – choose to focus on women and children as one of the most effective ways to support the whole community.

Sometimes foundation assistance is as simple as restoring a local ruin such as the Minaret of Jam in Afghanistan; this incredible monument now draws intrepid tourists to the area and its restoration has greatly improved options for local people.

Just as travel is often about learning to see with new eyes, so many of the groups we work with aim to change the way people see themselves and the future for their children and communities.

Published by Lonely Planet Publications Pty Ltd

ABN 36 005 607 983

© Lonely Planet Publications Pty Ltd 2007

© photographers as indicated 2007

Cover montage by Christopher Ong and Wendy Wright. Photographs by Lonely Planet Images: Tom Boyden, Simon Foale, Lee Foster, Charlotte Hindle, Luke Hunter, Greg Johnston, Alfredo Maiquez, Jane Sweeney. Back cover photograph: underwater statue of Christ, Ambergris Caye, Belize, Mark Webster/Lonely Planet Images. Responsible Travel photograph: children of the Emberá and Wounaan peoples, Darién National Park, Panama, Eric L Wheater/Lonely Planet Images. Many of the images in this guide are available for licensing from Lonely Planet Images: www.lonelyplanetimages.com.

Printed through Colorcraft Ltd, Hong Kong. Printed in China

LONELY PLANET OFFICES

Australia
Head Office
Locked Bag 1, Footscray, Victoria 3011
☎ 03-8379 8000, fax 03-8379 8111
talk2us@lonelyplanet.com.au

USA
150 Linden St, Oakland, CA 94607
☎ 510-893-8555, toll free 800 275-8555
fax 510-893-8572
info@lonelyplanet.com

UK
72–82 Rosebery Ave,
Clerkenwell, London EC1R 4RW
☎ 020-7841 9000, fax 020-7841 9001
go@lonelyplanet.co.uk